THE PERSON
A NEW INTRODUCTION TO
PERSONALITY PSYCHOLOGY

Fourth Edition

DAN P. MCADAMS

Northwestern University

JOHN WILEY & SONS, INC.

Publisher   *Jay O'Callaghan*
Executive Editor   *Ryan Flahive*
Assistant Editor   *Jessica Bartelt*
Marketing Manager   *Jeff Rucker*
Production Manager   *Sarah Wolfman-Robichaud*
Managing Editor   *Shoshanna Turek*
Layout Editor   *Wendy Stokes Hodge*
Cover Design   *Benjamin Reece*
Photo Credits   *Left: Mel Curtis/Getty Images; Right: © Tanya Constantine/Getty Images*

This book was set in Minion by Leyh Publishing, LLC and printed and bound by R.R. Donnelly-Crawfordsville. The cover was printed by Pheonix Color.

This book is printed on acid free paper. ∞

ISBN 0-471-71699-5

Printed in the United States of America
10 9 8 7 6 5 4 3 2 1

TO THE MEMORY OF MY TWO TEACHERS:

George W. Goethals
(1920–1995)

David C. McClelland
(1917–1998)

Brief Contents

Contents

Preface

Personality psychology is not what it used to be. In the beginning, Freudians fought with Jungians, behaviorists lashed out against humanists, and everybody picked their favorite grand theory of personality and defended it to the death. Once upon a time, personality research was viewed to be trivial—mainly about dubious labels that we apply to people in order to predict what they will do, labels that turn out not to predict very well at all. But things have changed, and dramatically so. In the last twenty years, personality psychology has emerged as a vital and fascinating field of study, filled with new theoretical insights and important findings that speak to what it means to be *a person* in today's world. With strong connections to social psychology, clinical psychology, life-span developmental studies, and cognitive neuroscience, personality psychology is today, first and foremost, the scientific study of the person. There is nothing more interesting to persons than persons. And there is nothing more important.

This textbook breaks the mold. Today's undergraduate textbooks in personality psychology follow two different formats, both of which were developed in the 1960s. One type of book devotes a chapter apiece to each of the grand theories of personality developed in the first half of the twentieth century. Freud usually gets the first chapter, then Jung, and on and on. Textbooks on theories of personality are interesting from an historical point of view, but they have little to say about the scientific field of personality psychology as it exists today. The second type of text focuses on research topics and issues. While these books try to reflect the scientific work that personality psychologists actually do, they offer no vision or organization regarding what that work is fundamentally about. *I believe it is time for a new kind of textbook in the field of personality psychology*—one that reflects the dramatic developments that the field has seen in the past twenty years and offers an integrative vision for what personality psychology is all about. And it needs to be a vision that students can appreciate. It needs to connect to their lives and their deep concerns.

The fourth edition of *The Person* presents a unifying vision of what personality psychology is and should be for the twenty-first century. It is a vision that reintegrates the classic theories with contemporary research and links it all to a central question that almost every student is interested in. That question is this: *What do we know when we know a person?* I believe that the best and brightest ideas in personality psychology all connect to this question. In order to "know" a person—both from the standpoint of science and the standpoint of everyday life—we must first have some sense of what all persons have in common by virtue of *human nature* and how social context and *culture* shape every person's life. Once we have an understanding of human nature and cultural context, then we can proceed to consider human individuality on three successive levels. Level 1 is the level of *dispositional traits*: What are the person's general tendencies? (Is he friendly? Is she competitive? Does he tend to take risks?) Level 2 is the level of specific features and concerns, or what I call *characteristic adaptations*: What does she desire? What does he believe? How does she cope? What is he mainly concerned about these days? Level 3 is the level of the *life story*: What does her life mean? What gives his life a sense of unity and purpose? *Put simply, dispositional traits sketch an outline of the person; characteristic adaptations fill in the details; and integrative life stories tell you what a life means in the overall.* Put another way, traits describe what people *do* in general; characteristic adaptations tell what people *want* and how they go about trying to get what they want (and avoid what they do not want); and life stories speak to what kinds of lives people are trying to *make*.

Personality is a patterning of dispositional traits, characteristic adaptations, and integrative life stories set in culture and shaped by human nature (Hooker & McAdams, 2003; McAdams, 1994, 1995, 1996a; Sheldon, 2004). When you think of personality this way, it becomes surprisingly easy to bring together the best research being done in personality psychology today and the best theoretical ideas in the classic theories from yesterday. Just as important, students can readily see what is so unique and powerful about personality psychology, compared to other branches of psychology, and they can organize their understanding of the field in terms of these three levels of human individuality. You can see how to build a scientifically credible account of the individual person by beginning with human nature and social context and then moving from basic traits, to more specific adaptations, to broad and culturally-shaped life stories. Finally, this organizational scheme gives me, the author, an advantage that other textbook authors rarely have. Many textbooks in personality psychology are but glorified *lists* of terms and ideas. My organizational frame helps me to do something that, I hope, you find more interesting. In each chapter, I endeavor to make an argument of some kind, to get across a point, *to tell a larger story* that puts the many different ideas in personality psychology into a meaningful structure.

Accordingly, I have organized the fourth edition of *The Person* according to the vision I have described. Part I of the text (chapters 1–3) lays the groundwork by considering how evolution has shaped human nature and how social context shapes individual lives. Part II (chapters 4–6) surveys dispositional traits in personality psychology, focusing on their measurement, their biological underpinnings, their consistency over time, and the substantial evidence for their efficacy in predicting broad trends in human behavior. Part III (chapters 7–9) examines the many different kinds of characteristic adaptations that fill in the details of human individuality, from motives and goals to social-cognitive variables to developmental stages and tasks. Finally, Part IV (chapters 10–12) explores the role of stories in human lives, how people construct stories to make sense of their lives, how stories provide identity and purpose for modern life, and how personality psychologists have struggled, going back to the time of Freud, with the problems inherent in the *interpretation* of the stories people tell about their lives.

What about the great theories? What about Freud? The behaviorists? They are still here, but I have reorganized theories and research to fit the integrated vision I have sketched above. This actually turns out to be very easy to do, for different theories address different aspects of human nature, cultural context, and human individuality. For instance, Bowlby's attachment theory comes out of an evolutionary understanding of human nature and fits comfortably into chapter 2. The traditions of behaviorism and social learning theories are mainly about social context and how persons are shaped by their environments, as chapter 3 makes clear. The trait theories of Allport, Eysenck, Cattell, and the proponents of the Big Five framework are the stuff of chapters 4 and 5, while chapter 6 examines traits across the lifespan and asks fundamental questions about the origins of traits, their remarkable stability over time, and the extent to which they can change over the life course.

Chapter 7 brings together many different theories on motivation from the writings of Freud, Maslow, Rogers, Murray, and contemporary self-determination theory (Deci & Ryan, 1991). This is where we also find the work of David McClelland and many contemporary researchers who show us how motives, goals, and strivings help fill in the details of human personality. George Kelly offered one of the first cognitive theories of personality, which is nicely integrated with more modern cognitive theories and research in chapter 8, where we examine *social-cognitive* adaptations. The influential stage theories of self-development, such as those proposed by Erikson and Loevinger, provide the backdrop for chapter 9's examination of *developmental* adaptations. Finally, chapters 10–12 consider some classic and modern approaches to personality and the study of lives that put life stories at the center of human meaning. Chapter 10 considers the foundational ideas of Jerome Bruner, the increasingly influential theory of life scripts developed by Silvan Tomkins, and my own life-story theory of identity. Freud, Jung, and Adler all had a great deal to say about interpreting the stories people tell about their lives, and I examine their ideas in detail in chapter 11, along with more contemporary interpretive approaches that come from postmodern and feminist understandings of human lives. The scientific examination of life stories represents an exciting new research agenda in personality psychology, but its roots are ancient. Psychologists are coming back to a very old idea—that certain kinds of truth about life and about people are best conveyed in stories (Bruner, 1990).

You can see that this new edition of *The Person* is more than just an update with a fancy new cover. Still, people who have used the first three editions will surely recognize a great deal of what is contained herein. I hope I have kept all the good stuff. I have built on the distinctive strengths of the first three editions. As before, the person remains at the center. As before, I have incorporated many examples from classic and contemporary literature, mythology, biography, and the media to illustrate points and concepts. I have even drawn on a few personal anecdotes. As before, I have tried to bring in the most recent research findings so that the student can understand what is happening today in the scientific study of persons. I have also worked to streamline the presentation and to adopt a more conversational style. In my classes, I have the luxury of conversing with my students; they hear me, and I hear them. When I write the textbook, though, I do not have that luxury. But I try to make up for it by imagining what you, the reader, might be thinking and what you might say to me if we were lucky enough to be talking together about persons and personality psychology.

When you teach personality psychology for over twenty years and you talk about it almost every day with colleagues, friends, and captive family members, you run up a pretty long list of people who manage to have an impact on how you understand your intellectual obsession. Consequently, I cannot begin to provide a complete and accurate list of the people I would like to thank for their direct and indirect input into this textbook. The undergraduate and graduate students who have worked with me and taken my courses have had a great and positive influence on this book, even when they didn't like the class. I would like to thank them and their parents for giving me the opportunity to teach them and for enabling me to participate, in a small way, in their own development. My colleagues at Northwestern University have also exerted a strong influence. In this regard, I would especially like to thank Phil Bowman, Sonny Cytrynbaum, Alexandra Freund, Gunhild

Hagestad, Bart Hirsch, Dan Lewis, Andrew Ortony, Penelope Peterson, Bill Pinsof, Peter Zeldow, and the regular members of our once-a-month personality lunch: Mike Bailey, Emily Durbin, Win Hill, Jen Pals, Bill Revelle, Tony Tang, and Rick Zinbarg. Some of my most treasured colleagues are members of the Society for Personology, and among those who have had the greatest positive impact on my thinking about personality are Jim Anderson, Irv Alexander, Bert Cohler, Ed de St. Aubin, Gary Gregg, Ravenna Helson, Bert Hermans, Oliver John, Ruthellen Josselson, Jane Loevinger, Mac Runyan, Jefferson Singer, Brewster Smith, Avril Thorne, and Paul Wink.

Finally, let me thank my wife, Rebecca Pallmeyer. In that she is the core of who I am and in that this book is, for better or worse, an extension of me, Rebecca turns out to be the most important and the most positive force behind the making of this text.

—Dan P. McAdams
Northwestern University

The Background: Persons, Human Nature, and Culture

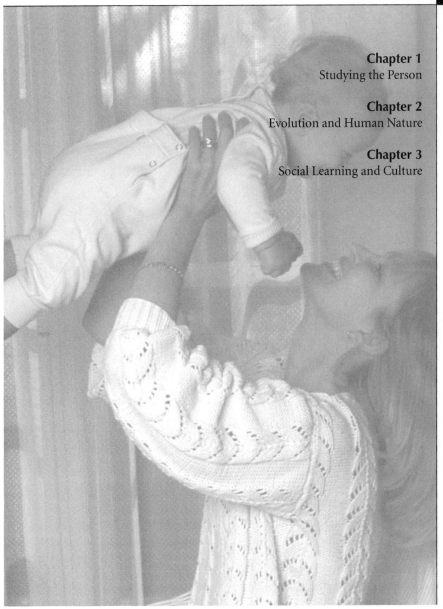

CHAPTER 1

Studying the Person

If you are reading this book, then you are (most likely) a person! Personality psychology is the *scientific study of the whole person.* Therefore, personality psychology and this book are fundamentally about you.

When you began to study psychology, you may have expected that all of the courses you might take—indeed the entire field of psychology itself—would be about you, or at least about people like you. After all, what is psychology about if not people? But if you have taken an introductory psychology class, you probably now know that psychology is about many things: perception and attention, cognition and memory, neurons and brain circuitry, abnormal behavior, social behavior, therapy, the behavior of birds, chimps, and the white rat, and on and on. Although many fields in psychology examine particular parts or views of the person, only one field purports to study the person as a whole. In personality psychology we try to put it all together. We try to understand the individual human being as a complex whole. Welcome to personality psychology! I am happy we have finally found each other.

The ultimate goal of personality psychology is to construct a scientifically credible account of human individuality. Such an account must situate a person in a biological and cultural context while specifying how that person is similar to and different from other persons. Personality psychologists often study **individual differences** in people. They develop ways to classify, categorize, and organize the diversity of human individuality, and they look for the biological and environmental forces and factors that explain those differences. How do personality psychologists do this? How do they endeavor to give a scientific account of an individual human life?

In truth, it turns out that personality psychologists proceed in a manner that is similar to what we all do when we try to understand ourselves and one another. In that each of us expends a good deal of energy talking and thinking about particular persons, each of us is something of an amateur personality psychologist. Personality psychology formalizes and systematizes the general human effort to know persons. But we all already have a great deal of experience with knowing persons. What do we know when we know a person? And how do we talk about what we know?

WHAT DO WE KNOW WHEN WE KNOW A PERSON?

Imagine for a moment that you are new on campus. You have transferred to the university after attending a college in your hometown for 2 years. Or maybe you have come back to school after working in your parents' business for 10 years. Or maybe you are a freshman. The point is that you are new, and you know hardly anybody in this new setting. You want to meet people, and you want to make some new friends. You are also eager to pursue some of your professional interests, which include writing and journalism. So you attend a planning meeting for the student newspaper. You would like to work as a reporter for the paper. It is a good meeting, and you learn a great deal about the newspaper and the staff. You listen to stories about how much fun it is to work on the paper and about how difficult it can be to balance work on the newspaper with the other things you need to do in college, such as attend classes. Afterward, one of the senior reporters asks you to join her and a few editors for coffee at her apartment. You say yes. You don't want to miss any opportunities to become more involved.

The evening goes very well. At the party, you have many opportunities to observe the young woman who invited you in the first place. Let us call her Amanda. Amanda seems very different from the rest of this friendly crowd. Everybody else is lounging around the apartment, freely talking, eating, drinking, and generally having a very good time. But at the beginning of the evening, Amanda seems tense. You expect that since she invited people to her apartment, she would feel right at home, that she would be welcoming and comfortable. Instead she stays out of the boisterous conversations of the group; she never tells any stories, even after one of the editors asks her what she thinks about a professor they both know. She hardly smiles at all. Her friends do not seem to be bothered by this, as if she acts this way often. Nonetheless, you think it is strange, and stranger still when you spot her a little later typing on her computer in the bedroom. It looks as if she is sending an e-mail message. Returning to the living room, you make a mild joke about Amanda preferring the Internet to the company of real people. "No," the paper's sports editor maintains, "Amanda likes everybody. She is just a little moody and unpredictable. I wouldn't worry about her."

The rest of the evening proves him right, at least with respect to his claim that Amanda is unpredictable. When she returns from her computer, Amanda warms up appreciably. She is hardly the life of the party, but now she smiles more and seems much more attentive to what is going on. Later, she seeks you out and asks you about your past, your tastes in music, courses you might take, why you moved from sunny California to this colder clime, whether or not you read your daily horoscope, whether or not you have met some of the more annoying people on campus—the usual sorts of things people talk about when they are just getting to know each other. She tells you about herself. Over the course of a half-hour conversation, you learn the following things about Amanda:

1. Amanda once shared this apartment with two roommates, but both moved out because they did not like Amanda's boyfriend, who visited frequently. Amanda doesn't like him anymore, either. They broke up last month.

2. Amanda stepped down from an editorial position on the paper last year in order to devote more time to her classes. Had she not, she might have been editor-in-chief this year, but she might have also flunked out of school. She is happier now that she is a reporter again, but she misses the power that came with her previous position.

3. The apartment is filled with books on psychology, philosophy, and religion. Amanda's major, however, is political science. She eventually wants to go to law school, that is, if her grades improve. She doesn't seem to know much about law or politics, however.

4. Amanda used to do yoga. She works out at the gym almost everyday. She loves junk food, and she eats a great deal of it over the course of the evening. She is tall and slim. She claims she has never dieted.

5. Despite all the books on religion, Amanda maintains she is an atheist. Her father, who died two years ago, was a Baptist minister. After squandering years of his youth on alcohol and drugs, her father experienced a religious conversion in young adulthood. He always said that the day he was "saved" was the happiest day of his life. Shortly after that experience, he married the woman who was to become Amanda's mother. But the two divorced three years before he died. "I loved him and I hated him," she says.

6. Amanda doesn't like the popular music that you like. She prefers jazz and bands popular in the 1970s.

Around 11:00 P.M., the party winds down, and people begin to leave. Amanda and you have agreed to get together tomorrow for lunch, to talk more about the newspaper and life on campus. You are struck by how much she seems to have changed over the course of the evening. Amanda was nervous and sullen at the beginning. Now she is kissing people good-bye! She seems to linger a bit longer than you expect with her goodbye to the sports editor. You hadn't noticed anything special between them before, but now you begin to wonder.

SKETCHING AN OUTLINE: DISPOSITIONAL TRAITS

How well do you know Amanda now? After an evening with her friends and coworkers and after spending some time talking with her alone, you have surely begun to form some impressions about this woman. How would you describe her?

One of the first things you might say about Amanda is that she is a little moody and unpredictable. Of course, you have seen her in only one setting. It is difficult to generalize with any confidence. But you were surprised by how sullen and tense she was at the beginning of the evening and how much more comfortable she seemed by the end. Throughout the evening, however, Amanda was kind and considerate toward everybody. The sports editor remarked that Amanda likes everybody, and it seemed to you that everybody likes Amanda as well. She was certainly friendly to you during the second half of the evening. She asked a lot of questions about your life; she listened very intently; she seemed genuinely interested in you; she invited you for lunch tomorrow. What does this all mean? You might say that, in very general terms, Amanda seems to be moody but very warm and caring. There is a gentleness about her that is evident in her speech and actions. She is not a domineering person.

In suggesting that Amanda is relatively moody, warm, and nondomineering, you have begun to sketch a personality portrait. You have begun to organize what you think you might now know about Amanda into some general statements concerning her characteristic patterns of behavior, thought, and feeling. Of course, you are doing this with skimpy behavioral evidence that is not sufficient to give you complete confidence in your initial attributions. In other words, it may turn out that you do not know what you are talking about! You may be completely wrong about her. After all, you have observed her behavior on only one occasion. Maybe she is rarely moody; maybe she dominates many other social situations. Maybe she is warm and friendly with strangers, like you, but as you get to know her better she becomes distant and cool. Maybe she was having an especially good day, or an especially bad one. You just don't know much yet. But you have to start somewhere. And where I think you are likely to start is with traits.

Personality **traits** are those *general, internal, and comparative dispositions* that we attribute to people in our initial efforts to sort individuals into meaningful behavioral categories and to *account for consistencies we perceive or expect in behavior from one situation to the next and over time.* You do not know Amanda well yet, but based on what you have observed you might begin to suppose that, in general, she tends to be relatively more moody, warm, and caring than many, if not most, other people, and relatively less domineering. These kinds of trait attributions might guide you in your future interactions with Amanda in that they might give you some clues about what to expect from her.

Personality psychologists have identified many different methods for quantifying individual differences in dispositional traits. The most common procedure is to administer self-report questionnaires, such as the one presented in Table 1.1. The theory behind this method is that most people probably have a fairly good idea of what their basic traits are. People know, for example, how friendly they are compared to other individuals. They have a pretty good read on how conscientious, moody, dominant, open-minded, or gullible they may be. Therefore, it makes good sense to present them with simple questions or items

TABLE 1.1	A TRAIT QUESTIONNAIRE

For each of the following 20 questions, answer either yes (if it is generally true for you) or no (if it is generally not true for you).

1. Do you often long for excitement?

2. Are you usually carefree?

3. Do you stop and think things over before doing anything?

4. Would you do almost anything for a dare?

5. Do you often do things on the spur of the moment?

6. Generally, do you prefer reading to meeting people?

7. Do you prefer to have few but special friends?

8. When people shout at you, do you shout back?

9. Do other people think of you as very lively?

10. Are you mostly quiet when you are with people?

11. If there is something you want to know about, would you rather look it up in a book than talk to someone about it?

12. Do you like the kind of work that you need to pay close attention to?

13. Do you hate being with a crowd of people who play jokes on one another?

14. Do you like doing things in which you have to act quickly?

15. Are you slow and unhurried in the way you move?

16. Do you like talking to people so much that you never miss a chance to talk to a stranger?

17. Would you be unhappy if you could not see lots of people most of the time?

18. Do you find it hard to enjoy yourself at a lively party?

19. Would you say that you are fairly self-confident?

20. Do you like playing pranks on others?

To arrive at your score, give one point for each of the following items answered yes: #1, 2, 4, 5, 8, 9, 14, 16, 17, 19, 20. Then, give yourself one point for each of the following items answered no: #3, 6, 7, 10, 11, 12, 13, 15, 18. Add up all the points to arrive at a total score. Your total score should be between 0 and 20, inclusive.

As you may have guessed by now, this scale measures the trait of extraversion. The higher your score, the higher your extraversion (and, therefore, the lower your introversion). Therefore, high scores suggest a tendency toward extraversion and low scores suggest a tendency toward introversion. Most people score somewhere in the middle.

SOURCE: Wilson (1978), p. 219. Properly standardized self-scoring scales may be found in Eysenck and Wilson (1976) and in Eysenck and Eysenck (1964).

similar to those in Table 1.1 and ask them to respond honestly. You should answer each of the 20 items in Table 1.1 to see how you score on the trait measured therein. What do you think the scale measures?

Personality psychologists make good use of the concept of trait in their efforts to sketch an overall outline of a person's individuality. Some of the most influential theories in the history of personality psychology, such as those proposed by Hans Eysenck (1952) and Raymond B. Cattell (1943), have been built around the concept of the personality trait. One of the singular contributions of personality psychology is the construction and validation of scientifically useful measures of individual differences in personality traits (Jackson & Paunonen, 1980; Wiggins, 1973). Good trait measures are useful in predicting behavior over time and across situations (Epstein, 1979). They have also been employed in efforts to discern the biological bases of human behavior (Zuckerman, 1995).

How many dispositional traits might there be? Many years ago, two psychologists went to the English-language dictionary and counted more than 18,000 words that referred to psychological states, traits, and evaluations (Allport & Odbert, 1936). Of those, about 4,500 seemed to refer to relatively stable and enduring dispositional traits. Since then, psychological research has winnowed the list down considerably. Today a growing number of personality psychologists argue that the many different dispositional traits that might be invoked to outline human individuality can be grouped into about five categories (Costa & McCrae, 1985; Goldberg, 1990; John & Srivastava, 1999; Wiggins & Trapnell, 1997). The **Big Five** trait categories are listed in Table 1.2, using their most common names: openness to experience (*O*), conscientiousness (*C*), extraversion (*E*), agreeableness (*A*), and neuroticism (*N*). The five superordinate trait categories are easy to remember because their first letters spell the word OCEAN. The Big Five traits provide a comprehensive description of basic dimensions of variability in human psychological qualities that are implicated in consequential social behavior—a vast ocean of concepts for describing general psychological differences between persons. The Big Five traits sketch the outline of the person. But if you want to fill in some of the details, you have to go beyond dispositional traits.

TABLE 1.2	**THE BIG FIVE: ADJECTIVE ITEMS THAT DESCRIBE EACH OF FIVE BASIC DISPOSITIONAL TRAITS**

Extraversion *(E)*
   Sociable–Retiring
   Fun loving–Sober
   Affectionate–Reserved
   Friendly–Aloof
   Spontaneous–Inhibited
   Talkative–Quiet

Neuroticism *(N)*
   Worrying–Calm
   Nervous–At ease
   High-strung–Relaxed
   Insecure–Secure
   Self-pitying–Self-satisfied
   Vulnerable–Hardy

Openness to Experience *(O)*
   Original–Conventional
   Imaginative–Down to earth
   Creative–Uncreative
   Broad interests–Narrow interests
   Complex–Simple
   Curious–Incurious

Agreeableness *(A)*
   Good natured–Irritable
   Soft hearted–Ruthless
   Courteous–Rude
   Forgiving–Vengeful
   Sympathetic–Callous
   Agreeable–Disagreeable

Conscientiousness *(C)*
   Conscientious–Negligent
   Careful–Careless
   Reliable–Undependable
   Well-organized–Disorganized
   Self-disciplined–Weak-willed
   Persevering–Quitting

SOURCE: Modified from McCrae and Costa (1987), p. 85.

FILLING IN THE DETAILS: CHARACTERISTIC ADAPTATIONS

In your evening with Amanda, you learned a number of things and developed a number of ideas about her that do not fit neatly into the categories of personality traits. For example, you learned that she likes junk food and jazz, that she works out at the gym regularly, that she wants to be a lawyer but doesn't know much about law, that she wanted to be editor-in-chief of the newspaper but dropped out of the running when her grades began to suffer, that she is very interested in popular psychology and mysticism, that she is an atheist, that she may be having a romantic relationship with the sports editor, that she recently broke off a romantic relationship, that she once stole off to her bedroom to type an e-mail message while hosting a party (you saw her do it). All of this material helps to fill in the details of Amanda's individuality. As you spend more time with Amanda, you will gather many more details.

As you move beyond dispositional traits in your assessment of Amanda's individuality, you look for ways to organize the details. Personality psychologists offer a number of ways to do this. There is a vast domain in personality research that includes concepts for thinking and talking about the details of human individuality. In Amanda's case, we might talk about her relatively strong *need* for power, as expressed in her desire to be editor-in-chief of the student newspaper, and the ways in which that need conflicts with other needs and demands in her life. We might consider her pattern of *interests* and *values.* We might suspect that she has substituted mysticism and New Age psychology for her childhood Baptist faith. Her spirituality focuses on her own inner development rather than on the external world. Self-improvement is important to her, as reflected in her reading interests and in her commitment to physical fitness. While she is a warm and caring person, she values the inner life over external and societal concerns, despite the fact that she wants to be a lawyer and that she enjoys wielding influence over others. Not surprising for a young, unmarried woman in contemporary American society, Amanda is concerned about romantic relationships. She has experienced disappointment in love. How does she view the prospects of love and intimacy? Because her parents divorced, does she worry that she will be unable to sustain a long-term romantic relationship?

Trait attributions are useful because they tell us about trends in behavior over time and across different situations, settings, and contexts. In talking about the details of Amanda's individuality, however, we have moved beyond general trait attributions to consider aspects of her personality that are *contextualized in time, place, and/or role.* The particulars of her personality include attributions that are situated in time: *As a child* she was a Baptist, but *now* she is an atheist; *at this time* in her life, she is concerned about romantic relationships; she wants to be a lawyer *in the future.* In addition, some aspects of her personality are couched in terms of particular places or situations: *At parties,* she is slow to warm up; *one-on-one,* she can be very intimate. Finally, we can identify aspects of her individuality that come out only within particular social roles: *As a student,* she works very hard and virtually always succeeds when she has enough time; *as a citizen,* she is unaware of political happenings and has little knowledge of current events.

Borrowing a term from McCrae and Costa (1996), I will use the expression *characteristic adaptations* for these aspects of personality that are contextualized in time, place, and/or role. **Characteristic adaptations** are *contextualized facets of human individuality that speak to motivational, cognitive, and developmental concerns in personality.* As we will see in chapters 8 through 10, characteristic adaptations address many of the most important questions in personality psychology: What do people want? How do people seek what they desire and avoid what they fear? How do people develop plans, goals, and programs for their lives? How do people think about and cope with the challenges of social life? What psychological and social tasks await people at particular stages or times in their lives?

Many of the greatest theories in the history of personality psychology have addressed questions regarding characteristic adaptations. We can group these theories into three major categories. First, there are theories of *human motivation*, which essentially speak to the question of what people fundamentally want or desire in life. Sigmund Freud (1900/1953) suggested that humans are motivated by deep urges regarding sexuality and aggression. By contrast, Carl Rogers (1951) and other humanistic psychologists (e.g., Deci & Ryan, 1991; Maslow, 1968) placed prime importance on needs for self-actualization and other growth-promoting human tendencies. Henry Murray (1938) enumerated a list of more than 20 basic psychological needs or motives, and David McClelland (1985) devoted his long career to studying three of them—the needs for achievement, power, and affiliation/intimacy. Second, there are theories of *cognition and personality,* which underscore the role of cognitive factors—values, beliefs, expectancies, schemas, plans, personality constructs, cognitive styles—in human individuality. Historically, the most famous of these theories is probably George Kelly's (1955) personal construct theory, but many contemporary approaches to personality also emphasize cognitive or social-cognitive factors and processes (e.g., Cantor & Kihlstrom, 1987; Mischel & Shoda, 1995). A third set of theories is more explicitly *developmental*, focusing on the evolution of the self and its relationships with others from birth to old age. Erik Erikson's (1963) theory of psychosocial development and Jane Loevinger's (1976) theory of ego development are among the most influential and far-reaching developmental theories of personality ever created.

Table 1.3 outlines some of the most important ideas and theories that fall under the general rubric of characteristic adaptations. Theories of human motivation, for example, specify such characteristic adaptations as human needs, motives, goals, and strivings. Social-cognitive theories of personality speak to adaptations such as personal constructs, beliefs, values, schemas, and personal ideologies. Developmental theories address questions of stages, pathways, and developmental tasks in human individuality. The different ideas and approaches in Table 1.3 cover a large territory. Different entries in the table emphasize very different aspects of human individuality. But what they all have in common is that they help to address many of the details that must be filled in after a general dispositional outline is sketched. As you move from dispositional traits to characteristic adaptations in the study of persons, you move from a focus on personality structure to one that emphasizes personality dynamics, process, and change (Cantor & Zirkel, 1990; Cervone, Shadel, & Jencius, 2001). In examining the details, you begin to explore aspects of human individuality that may be more fluid and malleable than what you would typically see if you were to stick exclusively to the trait outline with which you began.

CONSTRUCTING A STORY: INTEGRATIVE LIFE NARRATIVES

Now that you have begun to outline Amanda's individuality with dispositional traits and you have filled in some of the details by entertaining characteristic adaptations that speak to motivational, social-cognitive, and developmental concerns, what more is there to do? Is anything missing? What seems to be missing is any mention of what Amanda's life *means.* More specifically, what does her life *in the overall* mean *to her?* In what sense does Amanda organize her life into a unified and purposeful whole? These sorts of questions about persons are questions of *identity* (Erikson, 1959; McAdams, 1985a). Identity is the problem of

| TABLE 1.3 | A SELECTION OF CHARACTERISTIC ADAPTATIONS AND THEIR CORRESPONDING THEORIES |

Motivational theories and concepts: drives, needs, motives, goals, strivings, personal projects, current concerns

Sigmund Freud (1900)	Unconscious drives/needs for sexuality and aggression
Henry Murray (1938)	More than 20 psychogenic needs, such as needs for achievement, power, and affiliation/intimacy
Carl Rogers (1951)	Fundamental need for self-actualization motivates healthy, growth-inducing behavior
Abraham Maslow (1968)	A hierarchy of needs, running from physiological and safety needs to esteem and actualization needs
Deci & Ryan (1991)	Three basic growth needs: autonomy, competence, relatedness

Social-cognitive theories and concepts: personal constructs, beliefs, values, expectancies, schemas, cognitive styles

George Kelly (1955)	Psychology of personal constructs: basic categories for construing subjective experience
Cantor & Kihlstrom (1987)	Social intelligence: schemas and skills

Self-developmental theories and concepts: stages, pathways, developmental tasks

Erik Erikson (1963)	Eight stages of psychosocial development
Jane Loevinger (1976)	Stages of ego development

unity and purpose in life, a problem—or better, a challenge—that many persons, especially those living in modern societies, first encounter as they move from adolescence into young adulthood. Amanda is a young adult. What is her identity? What provides her life with an overall sense of unity, purpose, and meaning?

The question of identity points to a third way to think about human individuality. Beyond traits and adaptations, many people seek an integrative framework for their own lives that gives them a sense that the various pieces of who they are come together into some kind of sensible whole. Of particular interest is the desire on the part of many people to integrate their lives *in time*. Who am I today? How am I different from and similar to who I was in the past and who I may be in the future? What connects my past as I remember it, my present situation as I understand it to be now, and my future as I currently anticipate it? The challenge of modern identity is to come up with a way of understanding and talking about the self such that (a) despite the many different parts of me I am whole and coherent, and (b) despite the many changes that attend the passage of time, the self of my past led up to or set the stage for the self of the present, which in turn will lead up to or set the stage for the self of the future. According to a number of theorists, this kind of integration of the self into an identity is accomplished through the construction and revision of a "life story" (Bruner, 1990; Hermans, Kempen, & van Loon, 1992; McAdams, 1985a, 1996a, 2001a; Singer & Salovey, 1993; Tomkins, 1979). The third level of personality is the level of identity as a life story.

A **life story** is *an internalized and evolving narrative of the self that integrates the recon-structed past, perceived present, and anticipated future in order to provide a life with a sense of unity and purpose.* Beginning in late adolescence, many people in modern societies begin to think about their lives in terms of a unifying and purpose-giving story. Over time and through the adult years, they work on various aspects of the story, rewriting and revising as their views of their lives change with time and circumstances (McAdams, 1993, 1996b). The story is the identity, and thus as identity changes, so changes the story. Let us then entertain these further ideas about Amanda's individuality: Amanda's identity is an inner story, a narration of the self that she continues to author and revise over time to make sense, for herself and others, of her own life in time. It is a story, or perhaps a collection of stories, that Amanda continues to fashion to specify who she is and how she will eventually fit into the world of adults. Incorporating beginning, middle, and anticipated ending, Amanda's story tells how she came to be, where she has been and where she may be going, and who she will become. Amanda continues to revise the story through the adult years as she and her changing social world negotiate niches, places, opportunities, and positions within which she can live meaningfully.

What is Amanda's story about? You do not know Amanda very well yet, but perhaps you can take a few hints from your initial meeting. Amanda told you a kind of life story, implicit and indirect, about her father. Once upon a time, he was a drunken and dissolute youth. Then he found Christianity, which turned his life around. He married and became a Baptist minister. Eventually, his marriage ended in failure. Amanda told you that she both loved and hated her father. She told you she is an atheist. It is clear that she has rejected cer-tain parts of her father's narrative—there are important ways in which her life story will depart from his, she seems to suggest. What have been the high points, the low points, and the turning points in her own life, as she sees it now? Who are her heroes? Who are the vil-lains? What does she anticipate for the future chapters of her life story? What does she make of her own history? How has the past given birth to the present? If you get to know her really well, you may learn the answers to these questions, and you may even participate with her, perhaps as a good friend, in the further construction of her own identity. Indeed, she could even have an impact on how *you* create a story in your own life. In the sharing of stories about themselves, people come to know one another in especially intimate terms. Similarly, the personality psychologist who seeks to know a person in his or her full indi-viduality will eventually need to delve into the private mythology—the storehouse of nar-ratives, characters, plots, settings, and images—that the person invokes to make sense of who he or she is, was, and will be in the future.

How might personality psychologists *interpret* the stories people live by? Some approaches to interpreting people's life stories suggest that people actively and more-or-less consciously make meaning out of their own lives in terms of narratives that are preva-lent in their own cultures (Bruner, 1990; McAdams, 1985a). They pick and choose among different stories that their cultures have to offer in order to create narrative identities that provide their lives with some measure of unity and purpose. Other approaches to under-standing the stories people tell about their lives suggest that these stories are shaped by forces over which individuals have little control, that life narratives are fragmentary and often false, and that individuals do not and typically cannot know what the real meanings of their lives are. More than 100 years ago, Sigmund Freud introduced to the world a way of interpreting people's lives and the stories they tell about them that emphasized the dark and unconscious forces within. From the perspective of Freud and the psychoanalytic tra-dition he launched, interpretation is always a matter of delving deep beneath the surface narrative. If lives are like texts, their meanings are hidden between the lines, cleverly disguised by authors who do not consciously know what they are doing—multiple and conflicting meanings, stories contradicting stories, plots and counterplots that mislead you in your search to know the truth about who you are. A similar idea runs through certain contemporary approaches to understanding life stories, such as those that are tagged with the label *postmodern* (Gergen, 1991). But whereas Freud looked deep within the person, postmodern approaches look to the confusing swirl of narratives in culture and society. People are storytellers who make themselves anew with each new conversation they have, each new story they tell and perform. No story ever really takes hold though, for life moves too quickly in today's society, there are too many things to do and to be.

Like dispositional traits and characteristic adaptations, self-defining life stories are important aspects of personality, of human individuality. As outlined in Table 1.4, a full account of an individual human life must consider that life from at least three different standpoints. What do we know when we know a person? If we know that person well, we should have some sense of (a) where he or she stands on a series of dispositional traits that speak to general tendencies in behavior across situations and over time; (b) how he or she is confronting and adapting to motivational, cognitive, and developmental tasks and concerns that are contextualized in place, time, and/or role; and (c) what kind of identity he or she is articulating in life through the construction of stories about the self. Individuality is conveyed, therefore, through the patterning of traits, adaptations, and stories.

TABLE 1.4	THREE LEVELS OF PERSONALITY

Level	Definition	Examples
Dispositional traits	Broad dimensions of personality that describe assumedly internal, global, and stable individual differences in behavior, thought, and feeling. Traits account for consistency in individual functioning across different situations and over time.	Dominance Tendency toward depression Punctuality
Characteristic adaptations	More particular facets of personality that describe personal adaptations to motivational, cognitive, and developmental challenges and tasks. Characteristic adaptations are usually contextualized in time, place, situation, or social role.	Goals, motives, and life plans Religious values and beliefs Cognitive schemas Psychosocial stages Developmental tasks
Life stories	Internalized and evolving narratives of the self that people construct to integrate the past, present, and future and provide life with some sense of unity, purpose, and meaning. Life stories address the problems of identity and integration in personality—problems especially characteristic of modern adulthood.	Earliest memory Reconstruction of childhood Anticipations of future self "Rags to riches" stories

SCIENCE AND THE PERSON

Up to this point, I have suggested that in some ways personality psychologists are just like almost everybody else. In that we are all persons, each of us is interested in knowing persons, even if the persons we wish to know are ourselves. Had you or I met Amanda in the example I have been describing, we might have eventually come to some conclusions regarding her traits, adaptations, and stories as we came to learn and to know more about her. Personality psychologists aim to describe and understand persons, too. But they aim to do so in a *scientific* way. It is time to consider the science in all of this. What is science? And how might we study the person in a scientific manner?

In science, we try to make the confusion of everyday experience more understandable. Through science, we formulate statements about reality and then assess their truth value through rigorous and replicable tests. We do this in order to create an orderly and predictable model of the universe and how it functions. Our motivations for doing this are many. They include the desire to control our environments in order to stave off threats and dangers posed by the natural world (disease, natural catastrophe) or by other humans whom we fear (enemies in times of war, people we do not like). Our motivations for conducting scientific evaluation also include the wish to improve our lives and the lives of generations to come by understanding more about the world and by making things (telephones, x-ray machines, jet planes, computers) that promise to enhance our lives in the world. Most basic, however, is the simple desire to understand—the fundamental motive of curiosity. Science depends on the human desire to know for the sake of knowing. Therefore, while the personality psychologist may study the person for a wide variety of reasons—to provide a diagnosis in the clinic, to help select a job candidate, to design an appropriate treatment strategy—the fundamental goal is to understand the person for the sake of understanding.

Science generally proceeds according to three steps: (1) unsystematic observation, (2) building theories, and (3) evaluating propositions. These three steps refer both to what the individual scientist does when exploring a new problem or issue and to what particular fields of science do or have done—fields such as organic chemistry, economics, botany, and personality psychology—as they evolve from "primitive" to more "mature" sciences. Because it is relatively new, personality psychology is still a fairly primitive science. Nonetheless, all three steps in the scientific process are clearly evident in what personality psychologists do today. Let me then describe each of these steps in some detail.

STEP 1: UNSYSTEMATIC OBSERVATION

The first step in developing a scientific understanding of anything is to look at, listen to, feel, smell, and/or taste the thing we want to understand. We may do this with the help of special instruments, such as telescopes and stethoscopes, or we may rely solely on our unassisted five senses (most often seeing and hearing). But however we do it, we must carefully *observe* the phenomenon of interest over a long period of time. Early observation is relatively unsystematic. We explore the phenomenon with few expectations about what we will see (or hear). We look for patterns, regularities in the phenomenon, so that we can arrive at a tentative first ordering or classification of what we are observing. The process requires a playful and almost naive approach to reality on the part of the scientist. The great physicist, Sir Isaac Newton (1642–1727), captured the attitude perfectly in this passage written shortly before his death:

> I do not know what I may appear to the world, but to myself I seem to have been only like a boy playing on the sea shore, and diverting myself in now and then finding a smoother pebble or a prettier shell than ordinary, whilst the great ocean of truth lay all undiscovered before me. (Judson, 1980, p. 114)

Let us not be fooled into thinking, however, that the scientist's curiosity is slaked by collecting innocent sense impressions about the world. The right image of the scientist in Step 1 of the scientific process is that of a *creative observer* who perceives order or pattern where it has not been perceived before. Discussing the physical sciences, Hanson (1972) states that the keen observer is "not the man [or woman] who sees and reports what all normal observers see and report, but the man [or woman] who sees in familiar objects what no one else has seen before" (p. 30). Thus, unsystematic observation is not a passive and casual sort of thing but rather an active attempt to *discern* and then *describe* organization, pattern, design, or structure in a phenomenon that initially seems to be unorganized and without design. This highly descriptive, exploratory phase of the scientific enterprise is crucial, for it provides the scientist and the scientific community with a set of articulately described patterns in the concrete world that can be synthesized into a more general or abstract theory about how that world works.

It may be surprising to learn that science as described in Step 1 is an inherently *subjective* endeavor. We tend to believe science to be a rational, objective, and dispassionate sort of thing. Whereas this view has a good deal of merit with respect to certain aspects of science (especially Step 3, as described later), it is misleading when it comes to Step 1. The

creative observer of reality who sees things in a way different from anybody else is not necessarily "objective" in his or her point of view. Rather, the creative observer interacts in a highly subjective way with the phenomenon of study, in some cases altering the phenomenon by virtue of observing it (Hanson, 1972; Zukav, 1979). The scientist in Step 1, operating in the **context of discovery** (Reichenbach, 1938), seeks to discover new ways of seeing reality, formulating in a highly subjective manner new categories, new terminologies, and new distinctions to describe the careful observations that he or she undertakes. As the scientist begins to organize observations into categories, he or she moves from the *concrete* and *particular* events that are discerned to the more *abstract* and *general* representation of those events, a process that philosophers call **induction.** The ultimate result of induction is the creation of the abstract and general theory of Step 2, which is ultimately grounded in the subjective observations of Step 1 (Glaser & Strauss, 1967).

There are numerous examples in psychology of highly subjective observations of human behavior resulting in new insights and theories. Jean Piaget (1970), the Swiss developmental psychologist, based many aspects of his theory of cognitive development on the careful observations he made of his own three children in their first few years of life. Many of the most influential ideas in the personality theory of Sigmund Freud are results of Freud's highly subjective observations of the dream reports, spontaneous utterances, and behavioral symptoms displayed by his neurotic patients, his colleagues,

A researcher interviews a young man as part of a psychology study. Psychological data can be obtained in many ways—through interviews, questionnaires, experiments, naturalistic observation, psychophysiological and brain studies, and many other approaches.

and (maybe most of all) himself. Both Piaget and Freud organized many of their initial observations within **case studies.** A case study is an in-depth investigation of a single individual, sometimes conducted over a substantial period of time. The case-study method gives the personality psychologist a good deal of information about one human being. Though case studies can be used in a number of different ways, personality psychologists have traditionally used them as ways to organize complex observations about a single person so as to build a theory about some (or all) persons in general (Barenbaum & Winter, 2003; McAdams & West, 1997). In later chapters we will encounter examples of case studies in personality psychology that serve as bridges between the unsystematic observation of single individuals in Step 1 and the building of more general theories in Step 2.

STEP 2: BUILDING THEORIES

The second step of the scientific enterprise involves making a theory. Scientists organize the various observations collected in Step 1 into a more-or-less coherent system that explains the phenomenon of interest. Precisely how scientists do this, however, is one of the great mysteries of science. Though theories arise out of observations, they are not always arrived at in a completely logical or systematic manner. Some highly creative scientists stress the seemingly irrational and unconscious manner in which a theoretical insight may have come to them.

In a famous story, Friedrich Kekule, a German chemist of the 19th century, described how a series of discoveries concerning the structure of organic molecules came to him in hypnagogic reveries, or waking dreams. In Kekule's day, chemists had discerned a number of different chemical compounds containing carbon, hydrogen, oxygen, and a few other elements, but they had found it especially difficult to link these observations together via an abstract theory specifying the rules of their structure. Kekule had dwelt on the compounds' behavior so intensely that, on occasion, the atoms would appear to dance before him in hallucinations. One summer evening, he fell into a reverie and (he later wrote) "Lo! The atoms were gamboling before my eyes. ... I saw how, frequently, two atoms united to form a pair; how a larger one embraced two smaller ones; how still larger ones kept hold of three or even four of the smaller; whilst the whole kept whirling in a giddy dance. I saw how the larger ones formed a chain" (Judson, 1980, p. 115). Another time, when Kekule was nodding in his chair before the fire, the atoms danced again, "all twining and twisting in snakelike motion. But look! What was that? One of the snakes had seized hold of its own tail, and the form whirled mockingly before my eyes" (Judson, 1980, p. 115). The chains and rings that Kekule imagined came to comprise the fundamental models or pictures of organic molecules that underlie basic theories of organic chemistry even today.

I do not want to suggest that scientific theories are always, or even often, formulated through dreams and reverie, but they are sometimes developed in strange ways. The strangeness of development is not necessarily a reflection of how good the theory is. This is an important point in personality psychology because (as we will see in the chapters to follow) the many theories of personality that have been offered have been created in a wide variety of ways, some stranger than others. There is no consensus in the scientific community about the *best* way of proceeding in Step 2 of the scientific process—the step in which the scientist builds a theory.

There is much agreement, however, on what a theory is and what it should do. A **theory** is *a set of interrelated statements proposed to explain certain observations of reality.* A

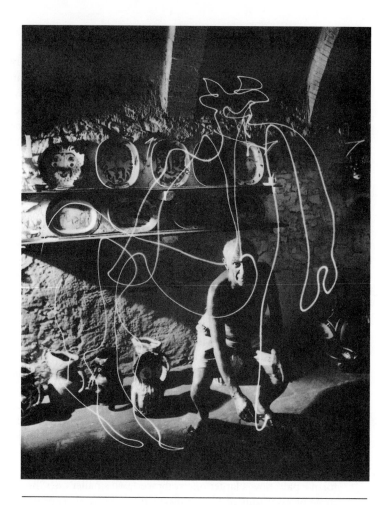

The creative observer, like Pablo Picasso, discovers new ways of looking at reality. In the first step of the scientific process, the scientist observes reality, sometimes with the aid of tools and technology, in order to discover patterns and organization.

theory is always a tentative and somewhat speculative abstraction. A theory is generally accepted by a scientific community to the extent that it is consistent with observations of the phenomena it purports to explain. Theories are subject to change whenever new, inconsistent observations become available.

A theory provides at least four different tools that the scientist can use to increase understanding (Millon, 1973): (a) an abstract *model* or picture that serves as an easily envisioned representation for the structure of the theory, (b) a conceptual *terminology* or set of names for key ideas and major classes of observations in the theory, (c) a set of *correspondence rules* that describe the specific relationships to be expected between the various components, and (d) *hypotheses,* or testable predictions that are logically derived from the correspondence rules. In other words, a theory provides a particular picture of reality, well-defined terms that name the major components of that picture, specified relationships among the components, and specific predictions about how those relationships can be tested in empirical research.

The four aspects of theory are used by scientists to explain a set of observations in a clear and precise manner. Many psychologists in general and personality psychologists in particular lament that their theories do not explain as much as they would like. Nonetheless, virtually all agree that theories are at the heart of science. Furthermore, they agree that some theories are "better" than others, though they disagree wildly as to exactly *which* ones are better. What makes one theory better? What are the criteria of a good theory? Below are seven standards by which a scientific theory may be judged (from Epstein, 1973; Gergen, 1982).

1. Comprehensiveness. The wider the scope of a theory's explanatory abilities, the better. All other things being equal, a theory that explains more is preferred to one that explains less.

2. Parsimony. Science is a simplifying and economizing game. Theories attempt to explain the maximum number of observations with the minimum number of explanatory concepts. Thus, a simpler and more straightforward explanation is generally preferred to a more complex one.

3. Coherence. A theory should be logical and internally consistent. The various statements that make it up should hang together in a sensible manner.

4. Testability. From the theory, a scientist should be able to derive hypotheses that can be readily evaluated (tested) through empirical research.

5. Empirical validity. Empirical tests of hypotheses derived from the theory should support the theory's major claims. In other words, the results of hypothesis-testing research should be in accord with what the theory says.

6. Usefulness. Theories that are able, in some way, to solve humanly significant problems are generally preferred to those that seem less relevant, all other things being equal.

7. Generativity. A good theory should generate new research and new theorizing. It should give birth to a wide variety of creative activity on the part of scientists and laypersons alike. In the social sciences, a generative theory may serve "to challenge guiding assumptions of the culture, to raise fundamental questions regarding contemporary social life, to foster reconsideration of that which is 'taken for granted,' and thereby to generate fresh alternatives for social action" (Gergen, 1982, p. 109).

STEP 3: EVALUATING PROPOSITIONS

Science distinguishes itself from all other modes of understanding the world by virtue of its insistence on evaluating propositions in an empirical fashion. The theories of Step 2 that derive from the observations of Step 1 must be empirically *tested* in Step 3 as the scientist moves from the context of discovery to the **context of justification** (Reichenbach, 1938). In Step 3, the scientist attempts to evaluate or "justify" the truth of a given statement proposed by a given theory. The scientist seeks to subject a portion of a theory to a rigorous and objective test. This is where the image of the scientist as a no-nonsense, hard-headed, cool, and dispassionate examiner of the real world has its origin and its validity. The context of justification is no place for flights of fancy and wild speculation; it is no place for exploring phenomena in an unsystematic and subjective manner. Rather, the scientist carefully determines the truth and utility of theoretical propositions that were formulated in the more freewheeling Steps 1 and 2 of the scientific process.

However, although Steps 1 and 2 are *more* freewheeling than Step 3, they are not so free-wheeling that virtually anything goes. Indeed, the scientist's *anticipation* of Step 3—his or her knowledge that theories must ultimately be subjected to empirical testing—influences the way in which the scientist explores the phenomenon of interest (Step 1) and the kinds of theories he or she eventually produces (Step 2). In other words, the anticipation of Step 3 in the scientific process feeds back to influence what the scientist does in Steps 1 and 2. Therefore, scientists who are proposing theories are urged by the logic of scientific inquiry to put forth theories that present *testable hypotheses.* In the words of the philosopher of science, Karl Popper (1959), a theory should be stated in such a way as to render its propositions *falsifiable.* The theory *should specify what observations it would take to disprove its major propositions,* or such observations should at least be deducible from the theory's propositions.

Popper's standard of falsifiability is a real bugaboo for the more speculative and philosophical among us because it puts fairly substantial constraints on the kinds of theoretical statements we can make. For instance, a personality theory that proposes that all human beings are basically good is not, in and of itself, falsifiable, because any instance of bad behavior can be dismissed as merely superficial behavior that masks the *fundamental* goodness of people. We can design no set of observations that would enable us to prove the statement false, to prove that people are *not* good. Therefore, as a scientific proposition, the statement that all people are good (or that all people are bad, or neutral, or even intelligent) flunks the basic test of falsifiability. There are many statements like this, and some are included as basic assumptions in certain personality theories existing today. Nonetheless, personality theories also contain a number of propositions that *are* falsifiable, such as Alfred Adler's (1927) claim (chapters 6 and 11) that firstborn children tend to be more conservative than other children, or Erik Erikson's (1963) proposition (chapter 9) that healthy psychosocial development involves the establishment of identity *before* one establishes intimacy with others. Statements such as these can be tested using standard personality research methods. Let us now consider in general terms how this is done. In later chapters, we will examine many specific examples of evaluating theoretical propositions through personality research.

Setting Up an Empirical Study

Imagine that we wish to evaluate Alfred Adler's proposition, embedded within his more general personality theory (chapter 11), that firstborn children tend to be more conservative than later-born children. How might we begin? Well, chances are that we have already begun! By stating a testable hypothesis derived from Adler's theory, we are showing that we have some familiarity with Adler's theory. *Scientific hypotheses should be grounded in theories.* Immersing oneself, therefore, in the theoretical and empirical literature that bears on a given proposition is an essential early task of hypothesis-testing research. Thus, our initial responsibility in carrying out this empirical study is to go back to Adler's writings to review exactly what his theory suggests. In doing this, we come to realize that we cannot possibly submit all of Adler's ideas to empirical testing at once. Rather, we can test one hypothesis at a time. We would continue our background reading to include various other theories of birth order and theories about conservatism. We would eventually move to the empirical literature, much of it found in scientific journals, on both birth order and conservatism to see (a) how these ideas have been examined empirically by others (what methods scientists have employed) and (b) what empirical findings or results have been obtained. Our background reading would supply us with invaluable ideas concerning how to think about our present study and how to design it to test the hypothesis in a fair and precise way.

Having reviewed the literature on the relationship between birth order and conservatism, we should next choose an appropriate sample of persons to examine. All hypothesis-testing research in personality psychology must confront the problem of sampling. No sample is perfect. One researcher may choose to investigate Adler's hypothesis in a sample of 100 sophomores attending the University of Illinois in the summer of 2003. Another researcher may prefer to look at a sample of 60 girls attending a preschool in Alabama. Another more ambitious researcher may select a nationwide sample of middle-aged men and women, the data for which exist in a national archive that was established 30 years ago.

It is very easy to criticize another person's research in terms of the sample he or she employs, claiming, for instance, that the sample does not represent all people, that the sample is *biased* in some way. The problem is that *all* samples are biased in some way, though some certainly are more so than others. In general, we should strive to obtain a sample for our study that is appropriate for the proposition to be evaluated. Therefore, if we are testing a hypothesis about, say, clinically depressed adults, a random sample of college students will not do. If we are testing a hypothesis about changes in normal personality development that occur around age 40, then we need a sample of midlife men and women who have little history of serious psychiatric disturbance. To confirm or disconfirm a given hypothesis, different researchers employing different kinds of samples should, over time, produce similar results. Thus, no single study, no matter how representative or large the sample, establishes "truth" in science.

With the choice of an appropriate sample of participants within which to study our hypothesis, the next step is to operationalize the variables that we have chosen to investigate. A variable is *any quality that can assume two or more values.* In our example of testing Adler's hypothesis, both birth order and conservatism are variables because both can be given at least two different values or levels. For instance, a participant in our study can be a firstborn, a second-born, and so on. He or she can also be "extremely conservative," "mildly conservative," "not very conservative," and so on.

To operationalize a variable is *to decide how to measure it*—that is, to specify the "operation" through which it is to be assessed. In our example, birth order is relatively easy to measure. We would merely ask participants to indicate what their birth order is. Conservatism is a trickier variable. We might wish to administer an established paper-and-pencil test of political values to assess conservatism. Or we might wish to interview participants to determine the extent of their conservative orientation. Or we might wish to observe "conservative behavior" in a standard laboratory task. In light of our earlier discussion of Level 1 personality traits, we might consider conservatism to be one piece of the larger trait cluster of openness to experience. For example, Sulloway (1996) has reviewed historical records of famous scientists and politicians to argue that firstborns often show much lower levels of openness to experience compared with later-borns. According to Sulloway, later-borns are "born to rebel" against the conservative authority represented by their parents and their older siblings. Therefore, we might administer to the participants of our hypothetical study a standard questionnaire measuring openness to experience. But whatever measure we used, we would aim to translate our observations about conservatism, or openness to experience, into *numbers* in order to assess our hypothesis. In other words, the operationalization of most variables in personality research requires us to quantify the data. Personality psychologists have devised a number of different procedures for quantifying variables. We will have numerous opportunities to see these methods in action when we examine particular research efforts in subsequent chapters.

As they operationalize variables in order to evaluate theoretical propositions, personality psychologists tend to design studies according to one of two very simple, basic research designs, or combinations of the two. These two general formats for hypothesis-testing research are the **correlational** and the **experimental** design.

The Correlational Design

Empirical studies that assess the extent to which two different variables relate to each other are termed *correlational* ("co-related") studies. In a correlational study, the scientist asks a very simple question: When one variable changes in value, what happens to the other variable?

If an increase in the value of one variable tends to be associated with an increase in value of the other variable, the variables show a *positive correlation* to each other. An example of a positive correlation would be the relationship between the two variables of height and weight in a random sample of 200 American adults. In general, as height goes up, weight goes up, though of course there are exceptions. A positive correlation between height and weight in this sample says that taller people, on the average, tend to be heavier than shorter people. Thus, having information about one of the variables for a given subject gives you a reliable hint about the value of the other variable for that subject: If you know that John is tall, you might guess—with a fair chance of being correct—that he is relatively heavy (compared with a short person).

A *negative correlation* is indicated when an increase in one variable is generally associated with a *decrease* in the other variable. An example here might be the relationship between the variables of age and thumb sucking in a random sample of 500 American children between the ages 12 weeks and 12 years. In general, as age goes up, thumb sucking goes down: Older children suck their thumbs less frequently on average than younger children.

When two variables are not related to each other in any systematic manner, we say that there is little or no correlation between them. An example of this third possibility might be the relationship between the variables of weight and intelligence in a random sample of 1,000 American adults. In general, heavier adults are neither consistently more intelligent nor consistently less intelligent than lighter adults. Therefore, weight and intelligence are uncorrelated with each other: Merely knowing an adult's weight will give you no reliable hint concerning his or her intelligence.

A numerical way of expressing the degree of correlation between two variables is the *correlation coefficient.* Readily calculated with a hand calculator or computer, correlation coefficients range from +1.0 (a perfect positive correlation) through 0.0 (no correlation between the two variables) to −1.0 (a perfect negative correlation). Figure 1.1 illustrates the distribution of scores on two variables that would produce five different values for correlation coefficients. In personality research, correlations generally fall within a "moderate" range. For instance, a moderately strong positive correlation between two personality variables might be +.50 ($r = .50$); a moderately strong negative correlation between two personality variables might be −.50 ($r = −.50$).

Like most statistics used by personality psychologists, individual correlation coefficients are often evaluated in terms of their statistical significance. Statistical significance is a measure of the extent to which a given result can be attributed to chance. As a general convention, personality psychologists maintain that a given effect, relationship, or difference is statistically significant when the probability of obtaining that effect, relationship, or difference by chance is *less than 5%*. We say, in this case, that the finding is "significant at the .05 level,"

FIGURE 1.1	SCATTER DIAGRAMS SHOWING VARIOUS DEGREES OF CORRELATION BETWEEN TWO VARIABLES

A. Perfect Positive (*r* = +1.00)

B. Perfect Negative (*r* = −1.00)

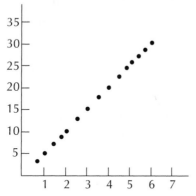

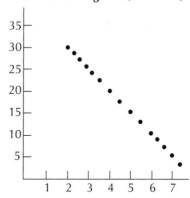

C. Moderate Positive (*r* = +0.67)

D. Moderate Negative (*r* = −0.67)

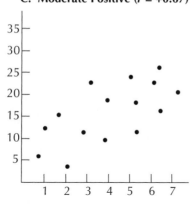

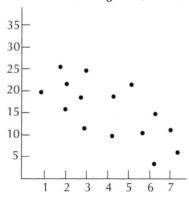

E. Unrelated (*r* = 0.00)

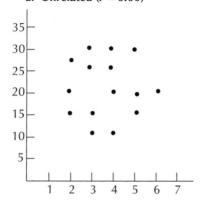

meaning that there is less than a 5% likelihood that the particular finding we have obtained is due to chance (or, saying it another way, there is more than a 95% likelihood that the finding is *not* due to chance). With respect to correlation coefficients, statistical significance is determined by the absolute value of the correlation coefficient and the number of participants from which the correlation was obtained. Thus a relatively strong negative correlation of –.57 would be statistically significant in a sample of 100 people, but the same –.57 would not be strong enough to reach statistical significance in a sample of only 10 people.

Although a correlational study shows which different variables naturally relate to each other, *correlation does not imply causation.* Just because variables A and B are correlated in a statistically significant manner, we cannot legitimately conclude that A causes B or that B causes A. Thus, a statistically significant correlation coefficient of +.45 between two variables—say, number of silk blouses owned and the size of one's office in a sample of 50 female business executives does not mean that owning silk blouses causes one to occupy large offices or that large offices cause one to own silk blouses. We might instead speculate that a third variable, such as executive status, is probably at work here, causally responsible for the other two variables. Female executives with higher status probably, because of their status, occupy larger offices and enjoy greater purchasing power (with which to buy silk blouses) than do lower status executives.

The Experimental Design

It is generally believed that personality psychologists *can* determine cause-and-effect relationships between different variables *in an experiment.* In an experiment, a scientist *manipulates or alters one variable of interest in order to observe its impact on another variable of interest.* The first variable—the one that is manipulated or altered—is termed the *independent variable.* The second variable is the *dependent variable.* The dependent variable is understood as the individual's response to the experimental alteration or manipulation of the independent variable. Thus, the dependent variable is a function of the independent variable: It is "dependent" on the independent variable. In cause-and-effect terms, experimentally controlled variations in the independent variable are seen as *causing* variations in the dependent variable.

If an experiment is to give valid information concerning cause and effect, the experimenter must be sure that the independent variable is the *only* variable that is systematically altered. Therefore, the experimenter designs the study to hold all variables constant except one—the independent variable—so that he or she can conclude that variations in the participant's responses (the dependent variable) are functions of variations in the independent variable, and *only* in the independent variable. Other extraneous variables threaten to confound the results; therefore, they must be controlled, to the greatest extent possible. This is why experiments are usually conducted in highly controlled environments, such as laboratory rooms. In these kinds of settings, the experimenter is able to control the kinds of stimuli to which the participants are exposed and to observe carefully the participants' responses.

Let me illustrate the basic principles of the experiment with a very simple example. Imagine that you wished to design an experiment testing the hypothesis that a person smiles more when interacting with another person who smiles than when interacting with a person who does not smile. You obtain a sample of 100 college students to participate in your study. Each person is asked to come to a laboratory room to engage in a one-on-one interview, which is to be videotaped. Participants are randomly assigned to one of two different groups: the experimental group and the control group. This means that 50 of your

100 participants are chosen by chance (such as by flipping a coin or pulling names out of a hat) to participate in each of the two *conditions,* or groups. For the experimental group, the interviewer talks with the participant for about 20 minutes, emitting smiles at regular intervals determined ahead of time by the experimenter. Participants in the control group experience the same interview except for one critical difference: The interviewer does not smile. *It is essential that the conditions of the experimental and control groups, therefore, be identical with the exception of one variable:* the interviewer's smiling. Thus, the independent variable in this experiment is whether or not the interviewer smiles. The dependent variable is the amount of smiling emitted by the person being interviewed, which could be assessed by observing the videotapes. The hypothesis would receive experimental support if the participants in the experimental group smile more than do participants in the control group, at a level reaching statistical significance. A statistically significant difference between the two groups in this experiment would suggest that variations in the experimentally manipulated independent variable were responsible for, or *caused,* variations in the dependent variable. In other words, the level of smiling of the interviewer was responsible for determining the level of smiling of the interviewee.

Because of the experiment's ability to tease out cause and effect through the careful manipulation and control of variables under standardized conditions, some psychologists consider the experiment superior to the correlational design as a basic method for doing hypothesis-testing research. For instance, one researcher terms the experiment "the basic method of science" (Mischel, 1986, p. 15), while others characterize it as the "preferred" (Byrne & Kelley, 1981) or the "most prestigious" (Singer, 1984) method. By contrast, other personality psychologists are highly critical of laboratory experimentation, arguing that experiments tend to be contrived, artificial, and trivial (Carlson, 1971, 1984; Gergen, 1982). Indeed, many empirical questions in personality psychology defy experimental investigation because the independent variables of concern cannot be systematically varied for individual participants—variables such as sex, age, ethnic origin, birth order, and body size. In some cases in which independent variables can be systematically varied, such an experimental manipulation is unfeasible or unethical. For instance, a scientist wishing to study the effects of child abuse on personality development in humans cannot legally or ethically subject half of the children in a sample to abuse (the experimental group) and half to nonabusive conditions (the control group) and then observe the effects of the manipulation. Rather, child abuse must be studied in the real world through some modification of a general correlational design.

The study of the person is a broad and rich enough endeavor to encompass *both* experimental and correlational approaches to hypothesis-testing research (Duke, 1986). Therefore, the chapters in this book contain numerous examples of good personality research studies that are purely correlational in nature, some that are purely experimental, and some that are combinations of the two. Both correlational and experimental methods are alive and well, and both are extremely valuable in studying the person. When it comes to personality psychology, it is probably misleading to consider either of the two methods *the* basic method of science.

The three basic steps of scientific inquiry—unsystematic observation, building theories, and evaluating propositions—bring us full circle. We begin in Step 1 with observation; we move to abstractions in Step 2, in which our observations are organized within a theory; and then we move back to observation in Step 3—this time, a more systematic form of observation—as we attempt to test hypotheses empirically. The results of our experiments and correlational studies in Step 3 feed back to modify our theory. Therefore, the observations of Step

3 function in much the same way as their less systematic sisters of Step 1: They influence the making and remaking of theory. *Science progresses through a continuous dialogue between observation and theory.* Observations ultimately give rise to theories. Theories give rise to new observations designed to evaluate the theories' propositions. These new observations feed back to influence the theories from which they were derived, occasionally even giving birth to radically new theories. And so on. An underlying assumption of the whole procedure is that over the long course of observation followed by theory followed by observation, science formulates better and better ways of understanding the world, moving closer and closer, over a period of many years, to truth.

PERSONALITY PSYCHOLOGY

The scientific focus on human individuality distinguishes personality psychology from all other branches of psychology and from the social sciences more generally. It takes a fair amount of hubris to place the individual human person at the center of all inquiry, to maintain that the person in his or her very individuality is important enough and cohesive enough to warrant special status as *the* main unit of analysis. Modern personality psychology is the heir to what psychological historian Daniel Robinson has called "Renaissance Humanism," the 16th-century worldview that celebrated "the dignity of man, the theme insisting that the world was made for man" (1981, p. 171). Robinson points out that modern science, in its dispassionate objectivity and urge towards reductionism, has generally rejected Renaissance Humanism. But personality psychology has moved against the tide. For the personality psychologist, scientific investigation *is* made for man and for woman. In focusing unswervingly on the individual, personality psychology has come to occupy a unique and extraordinarily critical place in the world of science.

THE PAST AND THE PRESENT

Personality psychology was born within psychology departments in American universities in the 1930s. Although personality theorists such as Freud, Jung, and Adler had been writing for more than 30 years by then, it was during the 1930s that a number of separate lines of inquiry came together to generate a new academic discipline. The first issue of the journal *Character and Personality* (now the *Journal of Personality*) was published in 1932. The journal aimed to join German studies of character with British and American studies of individual differences in persons, incorporating case studies, correlational surveys, experiments, and theoretical discussions. In 1937, Gordon Allport published the first major textbook on personality: *Personality: A Psychological Interpretation.* Although textbooks on mental hygiene, abnormal psychology, and character and personality had already been published, Allport's was the first to articulate a grand vision for the field of personality and to place it within the context of historical and contemporary scholarship in the arts and sciences. Allport viewed personality psychology as the study of the individual person. He defined the personality as "the dynamic organization within the individual of those psychophysical systems that determine his unique adjustment to his environment" (Allport, 1937, p. 48).

From the beginning, personality psychology was a *dissident* field within the large scene of American psychology (Hall & Lindzey, 1957). In the 1930s, American psychology tended to focus minutely on such things as habits, reflexes, stimuli, and discrete responses—the basic molecular elements of organism behavior. By contrast, personality was holistic, taking on the *whole person* as a primary unit of study, suggesting that unity, coherence, and wholeness are properties of human lives. In the 1930s, American psychology obsessed over the vicissitudes of animal learning, focusing on the relation between external stimuli and publicly observed responses in rats and pigeons. By contrast, personality concerned itself with the problems of human *motivation,* understood in terms of unobservable urges and promptings from within. This orientation is evident even in textbooks written before Allport's. Writes Garnett (1928), "It is surely in the springs of human action, if anywhere, that the key to personality is to be found" (p. 14). In the 1930s, American psychology searched for universal laws applicable to all organisms. American psychology was a thoroughly **nomothetic** enterprise at this time, meaning that it aimed to discover and test general principles or laws of behavior. By contrast, personality emphasized how people were *different* from one another, as well as how they were alike. Allport went so far as to suggest that the scientist should examine each individual personality as a unique entity. He argued for an **idiographic** approach to personality, which, in contrast to the nomothetic approach, would ignore general laws to discern the specific and individual patternings of particular lives. While Allport's insistence on the idiographic has always been controversial, even within the field of personality psychology (e.g., Holt, 1962), personality psychologists have traditionally been much more interested than most other psychologists in the complexities of the single case.

The history of modern personality psychology can be divided into three periods (McAdams, 1997a). The period from approximately 1930 to 1950 was marked by the establishment of the field and the development of a number of general systems. In the 1930s and 1940s, personality psychologists proposed comprehensive conceptual systems for understanding the person. Some of these grand theories of personality are still very influential today and are discussed in subsequent chapters of this text. Among the more influential personality theories proposed during this time were Allport's (1937) psychology of the individual (see Feature 1.A), Murray's (1938) personological system (chapters 7 and 11), the trait theories (chapters 4 and 5) offered by Cattell (1947) and Eysenck (1952), Rogers's (1942) humanistic theory (chapter 7), Kelly's (1955) cognitive theory of personal constructs (chapter 8), Erikson's (1950) psychosocial theory of personality development (chapter 9), and various derivatives of American behaviorism and social learning theory (chapter 3).

By the 1930s, furthermore, Sigmund Freud (chapters 7 and 11), Carl Jung (chapter 11), and Alfred Adler (chapter 12) had all developed comprehensive theories of personality derived from clinical observations and rooted in the European psychoanalytic tradition. These psychoanalytic theories became incorporated within personality psychology proper and began to have a significant influence on how personality psychologists thought about and empirically studied human individuality. Beginning with Hall and Lindzey (1957), personality textbooks organized the field according to these grand systems, variously dividing the systems into psychoanalytic and psychosocial theories (e.g., Freud, Jung, Adler, Horney, Fromm, Sullivan, Erikson), temperament and trait models (e.g., Sheldon, Cattell, Eysenck, Guilford, and sometimes Allport), approaches emphasizing needs and motives (e.g., McDougall, Lewin, Murray, McClelland), humanistic self theories (e.g., Rogers, Maslow, and sometimes Allport), organismic theories (e.g., Goldstein, Angyal, Murphy), cognitive theories (e.g., Kelly), learning theories (e.g., Hull, Skinner, Miller and Dollard), and cognitive/social-learning theories (e.g., Rotter, Bandura, Mischel). No other branch of psychology ever had more competing theories.

The period from 1950 to 1970 marked a second historical phase. With the tremendous expansion of higher education after World War II, psychology departments grew and became more specialized, spawning professional specializations in such personality-related areas as clinical, counseling, and industrial/organizational psychology. In the United States, increased federal funding supported personality research in laboratories and field settings. Personality psychologists focused their research efforts on the examination and elaboration of particular personality *constructs*—such as extraversion (Eysenck, 1952), anxiety (Taylor, 1953), the need for achievement (McClelland, 1961), and a host of other traits, needs, motives, and so on that could be reliably and validly *measured* and whose impact on behavior could be directly *observed*. Overall, personality psychology turned away from the grand theories of the 1930s and 1940s and came to focus instead on problems and controversies concerning personality measurement. What constitutes a valid measure of a personality construct (Cronbach & Meehl, 1955; Loevinger, 1957)? Are objective measurements of personality superior to clinical intuitions (Meehl, 1954; Sawyer, 1966)? Do personality scales measure what they say they measure, or do they simply assess a person's *style* of responding to tests (Block, 1965; Edwards, 1957; Jackson & Messick, 1958)?

In the late 1960s and early 1970s, psychologists delivered a series of devastating critiques of personality psychology that threw the field into a crisis. Carlson (1971) chastised personality psychologists for ignoring the grand theories of the early years and straying away from their implicit mandate to study real lives and whole persons in depth. Fiske (1974) wondered whether perhaps personality psychology had gone about as far as it could go, limited as it is by its reliance on imprecise verbal reports from people. Shweder (1975) questioned the need for any form of psychology based on individual differences. Most influential, however, was Mischel's (1968, 1973) critique, in which he argued against explanations of human behavior based on internal personality traits and in favor of explanations that focused on the situational and cognitive/social-learning determinants of behavior. As we will see in chapter 4, Mischel's critique launched a protracted debate in the field of personality psychology over the efficacy of trait-based versus situation-based approaches to predicting and understanding social behavior. The trait versus situation debate preoccupied the field of personality psychology through the 1970s and into the early 1980s.

A third phase in the brief history of modern personality psychology, therefore, began around 1970 and continues in the present day. The phase began with critique and pervasive doubt concerning the legitimacy and worth of personality studies, but it evolved by the mid-1980s into a broad sense of renewal and revitalization (Buss & Cantor, 1989; Hogan, Johnson, & Briggs, 1997; Maddi, 1984; McAdams, 1990, 1994; Pervin, 1990; West, 1983). As the trait versus situation controversy has died down, contemporary research in personality has become more sensitive to the complex interactions of internal personality variables and external situational factors in the prediction of behavior (Kenrick & Funder, 1988). Trait models for personality have regained their status and influence in psychology as a whole, especially with the emergence of the Big Five factor model for personality traits (McCrae & Costa, 1990; Wiggins, 1996). Having resolved or put aside a number of measurement controversies, personality psychologists have refined new research methodologies for the scientific study of persons (Craik, 1986). Recently, there has been a renewed interest in integrative personality theory (Mischel & Shoda, 1995; Tomkins, 1987; Westen, 1995) and a renewed commitment to studying whole persons in their full biographical complexity (Franz & Stewart, 1994; McAdams & Ochberg, 1988; Nasby & Read, 1997).

The contemporary renaissance in personality studies affirms what I have always felt deeply about this particular field of study: Personality psychology is the centerpiece of psychology as a whole. It is with reference to individual persons that many of the most important theories, findings, and applications in psychology must be oriented. Personality psychology addresses the most general and most fundamental questions in the field: What is human nature? What is a person? How do we understand persons? It is the most fundamental and the most fascinating field in psychology, in my view, because it reflects directly upon each of us, upon the self. While other branches of psychology offer many important insights into human behavior and experience, it is only personality psychology that focuses unswervingly on the individual person—on your particular individuality as a person. Indeed, I would go further, to suggest that personality psychology should be one centerpiece of any constellation of studies and programs promising to educate a person in the broadest sense. One of the goals of a liberal arts education is the conscientious examination of the self and its place in the world, the concerted reflection upon one's own life in culture, history, and the cosmos. It is in personality psychology—if anywhere in psychology—that such an examination may begin, for personality psychology itself begins with just such an examination.

Personality psychology draws on fields as diverse as brain physiology, evolutionary biology, cognitive science, sociology, cultural anthropology, and even literary studies in the study of whole persons. Consequently, personality psychology lies at the crossroads of many disciplines. Within psychology proper, personality psychology shares some affinities with developmental, social, abnormal, and clinical/counseling psychology. Yet important differences may also be identified.

Although personality psychologists are concerned with the development of human beings from birth to death, they differ from most *developmental* psychologists by focusing their inquiries on the adult years. Further, whereas developmental psychology concerns itself with meaningful change and transition over time, personality psychologists tend to focus on those aspects of the person that show some degree of continuity or stability over time. Yet these distinctions are fuzzy and matters of relative emphasis. For example, many personality psychologists are interested in personality change, so their inquiries sometimes overlap with those made by developmental psychologists.

Personality psychology has many ties to *social* psychology. Personality and social psychologists publish in some of the same journals; they belong to some of the same societies; and they tend to share many intellectual interests. Still, there is a fundamental difference between the cores of the two disciplines: *Social psychologists focus on human sociality, while personality psychologists focus on human individuality.* Having said this, I must blur the distinction, for human sociality must always take into consideration the role of human individuals, and human individuality must always be seen in social context. Therefore, in examining social behavior, social psychologists are quite likely to consider carefully the role of the self, as many contemporary textbooks in social psychology will show; similarly, in examining human individuality, personality psychologists must also consider social contexts, as we will see in this book. Still, the general fact remains that personality and social psychologists do exhibit differences in matters of emphasis. To put things in simple behavioral terms, personality psychologists tend to be somewhat more interested in how different people react differently to the same situation, whereas social psychologists emphasize how people in general react differently to different situations. But you can always find exceptions to this tendency, as personality psychologists often examine the efficacy of situations as well, and social psychologists are quite likely to consider individual differences, too.

There is a strong clinical tradition in personality psychology, going back to Freud and the origins of psychoanalysis at the turn of the 20th century. The fields of *abnormal*

FEATURE 1.A

GORDON ALLPORT AND THE ORIGINS OF PERSONALITY PSYCHOLOGY

Gordon W. Allport (1897–1967) may not have invented personality psychology, but more than anybody else he was responsible for establishing personality as a vigorous field of scientific inquiry in university settings. Allport's greatest contribution is probably the textbook he published in 1937: *Personality: A Psychological Interpretation*. In what is generally considered to be the first authoritative text on personality, Allport presented an integrated agenda for the field of personality psychology, and he foresaw many of the issues and controversies that have defined the field ever since.

Allport was born in 1897 in a small town in Indiana, one of four sons of a physician and his wife. He grew up in Cleveland, Ohio, attended Harvard University for his undergraduate and doctoral work, and studied extensively in Europe. He appears to have been influenced greatly by such German psychologists as William Stern and Edward Spranger (Nicholson, 2002). From 1930 to 1967, Allport taught at Harvard, where he helped establish the interdisciplinary Department of Social Relations. In his early years there, he articulated a vision for personality psychology that was to serve as a humanistic alternative to behaviorism and an optimistic antidote to Freud's unflattering view of the human condition. In his autobiography, Allport (1968) stated that he wished to create a field of study centered on an image of man "that would allow us to test in full whatever democratic and humane potential he might possess" (p. 394). In the middle of the Great Depression in Europe and the United States and on the eve of World War II, Allport wrote *Personality* in the spirit of social reform and the hope for a better world. Allport's text was cosmopolitan, erudite, and steeped in old-world European scholarship. But it was also profoundly American in its unabashed optimism and egalitarian tone.

In *Personality*, Allport presented an eclectic array of concepts and hypotheses, loosely tied to one dominant theme: The person is a unique whole. The

Gordon Allport was a pioneer in personality psychology. In the 1930s, he wrote the first authoritative text in the field, and he laid out many of the issues that personality psychologists still study and struggle with today.

person's wholeness is best captured in Allport's concept of the **proprium.** According to Allport (1955), "the proprium includes all aspects of personality that make for inward unity" (p. 40). The uniqueness of individuals is expressed through personality traits. For Allport, the trait was the major structural unit of personality. He defined a trait as a "neuropsychic structure having the capacity to render many stimuli functionally equivalent and to initiate and guide equivalent (meaningfully consistent) forms of adaptive and expressive behavior" (Allport,

(CONTINUES)

FEATURE 1.A (CONTINUED)

1961, p. 347). Allport held that traits are real, causal entities that correspond to as yet unknown neurophysiological structures. They are not mere descriptive categories of functionally equivalent behaviors. Rejecting the distinction between motive and trait, Allport insisted that traits have motivational features, serving to energize, direct, and select behavior. While traits may account for consistency in behavior across situations and over time, Allport knew that human behavior is often inconsistent and strongly shaped by situational factors (Zuroff, 1986). A single person, furthermore, may be characterized by contradictory traits. Therefore, "the ever changing nature of traits and their close dependence upon the fluid conditions of the environment forbid a conception that is over-rigid or over-simple" (Allport, 1937, p. 312).

Allport's brand of trait psychology tended toward the literary in content and style. While he encouraged nomothetic research on common traits, he tended to distrust statistical analyses of group data because, he argued, they tend to blot out the uniqueness of the single person. While large-scale trait studies could be useful for deducing general laws of behavior, Allport believed that these should be supplemented by the idiographic, in-depth examination of the unique and common traits manifested in the single case (Barenbaum, 1997). The best example of this approach is Allport's *Letters*

from Jenny (1965), in which he analyzed a series of personal letters written by one woman over a long period of time in order to delineate the key traits in her personality. Furthermore, in *Letters from Jenny* Allport confronted the problems and possibilities of doing personality studies through the in-depth analysis of the single case. Allport championed idiographic case-study research throughout his career, as well as the use of personal documents such as letters, journals, and autobiographies in personality research (Allport, 1942; Allport, Bruner, & Jandorf, 1941). It was only through the analysis of the single case, he believed, that a psychologist might convey the full individuality of the person.

Beyond his seminal writings on personality, the self, traits, and case studies, Allport made major contributions in a wide range of areas, including the psychology of expressive movements (Allport & Vernon, 1933), the psychology of rumor (Allport & Postman, 1947), the psychology of religion (Allport, 1950), research on attitudes and values (Allport & Vernon, 1933), and the nature of prejudice (Allport, 1954). Through the awesome breadth of his work and his humanistic vision for a science of individuality, Gordon Allport personified the potential and the possibilities of personality psychology. His work and his career have inspired generations of psychologists who have chosen as their intellectual mission the scientific study of the whole person.

---

psychology and *clinical/counseling* psychology consider problems in human life such as psychopathology, mental illness, and behavioral dysfunctions. Many clinicians concern themselves with personality disorders of various kinds. Furthermore, some theories of personality prescribe specific techniques for changing abnormal behavior and enhancing mental health (e.g., psychoanalytic therapy, Rogerian counseling). Nonetheless, personality psychology proper tends to focus more on relatively normal functioning and the wide varieties of individuality that may be expressed among more-or-less well-adjusted people. As the scientific study of the whole person, personality psychology is *not* centrally concerned with psychotherapy and other treatment aspects of clinical practice. However, there is no more important background for effective psychotherapy than a strong understanding of theory and research in personality psychology. And I hope that you will also conclude that such an understanding can enhance your own life, as well.

ORGANIZATION OF THIS BOOK

The Person: A New Introduction to Personality Psychology is organized into four parts. The first part (chapters 1 through 3) considers basic questions in the field and the fundamental *contexts* of human individuality. Before we can examine the three levels of personality that I have identified in this chapter, we need to understand how human lives are situated in time and space. The ultimate context in this regard is human evolution. In chapter 2, we will consider how human nature has been shaped by evolution. Recent years have witnessed an upsurge of interest in "evolutionary personality psychology." While some have argued for the emergence of new "sociobiological" and "evolutionary" theories of personality, I submit that *any* reasonable scientific effort to understand persons must consider the role of evolution as the macrocontext of human individuality. The conception of human evolution, as originally expressed by Charles Darwin (1859), is too important to be left out of any personality theory, in my view, but it is also too general to function as a personality theory itself. Human evolution is best viewed, then, as a fundamental context for human behavior and experience, and understanding human life from an evolutionary point of view is a necessary first step in studying the person, but only a first step.

A second fundamental context is culture. Chapter 3 brings together the many seminal ideas from behaviorism, social learning theory, theories of socialization, theories of human ecology and environments, and cross-cultural psychology that must be considered when examining the exquisite way in which human lives are socially and culturally contextualized. The theories of behaviorism that so dominated American psychology in the middle of the 20th century—theories offered by Clark Hull (1943) and B. F. Skinner (1938)—were never theories of personality. But their cornerstone ideas concerning learning and environments are fundamental for a scientific understanding of human individuality. Behaviorism addresses how organisms learn by interacting with their environments. For human beings, those environments range from immediate physical and social situations to the larger contexts of family, neighborhood, class, and culture.

The remaining three parts of this book follow the tripartite scheme for conceptualizing persons that I have introduced in this chapter. The second part (chapters 4 through 6) focuses on Level 1 in the study of persons—dispositional personality traits. Chapter 4 examines fundamental issues in trait psychology, including defining and measuring traits, the concepts of reliability and validity in trait assessment, and the interactions between traits and situations in the prediction of behavior. Chapter 5 focuses on particular traits that personality psychologists have studied, organized according to the Big Five classification scheme. We will look at how these traits are defined, what they mean, how they influence social behavior, and how they may begrounded in human physiology and the activity of the brain. Chapter 6 considers continuity and change in traits across the human lifespan and addresses these intriguing questions: To what extent are traits a product of genetics? Do traits have their origins in temperament differences apparent in infancy? Can traits change in adulthood?

The book's third part (chapters 7 through 9) focuses on Level 2 in the study of persons—characteristic adaptations. Motivational adaptations are the subject of chapter 7, in which we will examine the most important ideas and research findings about human individuality as manifested in needs, goals, motives, strivings, and other expressions of human desire. Here we find the seminal contributions of Sigmund Freud on unconscious sexual and aggressive drives, Henry Murray and David McClelland on psychogenic needs and social motives, humanistic theories of motivation (such as that offered by Carl Rogers), and the more recent contributions of self-determination theory and the study of personal striv-ings, tasks, and projects. Chapter 8 moves to cognitive adaptations, featuring George Kelly's personal construct psychology and the increasingly influential social–cognitive approaches to personality that address concepts such as social intelligence, cognitive schemas, and the cognitive regulation of behavior. Chapter 9 considers characteristic adaptations that are contextualized in time, as in developmental stages and tasks. The chapter is organized around two highly influential theories of self-development—Jane Loevinger's theory of ego development and Erik Erikson's theory of psychosocial stages. The former theory focuses on the *structure* of the self while the latter mainly considers the *content* of social life.

The book's fourth part (chapters 10 through 12) focuses on Level 3 in the study of persons—life stories. Chapter 10 introduces the concept of a life story and describes recent theory and research on how people construct narratives to make sense of their lives. Silvan Tomkins's script theory, an increasingly influential theory in personality psychology today, is featured in chapter 10. Chapter 11 asks a fundamental question about peoples' lives and the stories they construct to make sense of them: How should psychologists interpret life stories? Here Sigmund Freud, Carl Jung, and more recent psychoanalytic theorists (e.g., Heinz Kohut) offer intriguing and controversial ideas regarding the interpretation of dreams, fantasies, memories, and life stories writ large. Their emphasis on the unconscious meanings and the intrapsychic mysteries of human personality contrasts sharply with cur-rent postmodern approaches to personality, which emphasize the social construction of lives. Yet both psychoanalytic and postmodern approaches agree that the stories people tell about their lives are not what they seem. Finally, chapter 12 considers how personality psy-chologists themselves construct stories to make sense of the stories people tell and live. In considering psychobiography, case studies, and conceptualizations of the human life course, chapter 12 brings us back to the issue with which this book begins: How can we account for the individual life as a whole?

What do we know when we know a person? How can we understand the individual human life? I believe that a scientific understanding of the individual life begins with (1) a solid grounding in the evolutionary and cultural contexts of human behavior and proceeds to a systematic consideration of (2) dispositional personality traits; (3) characteristic moti-vational, social-cognitive, and developmental adaptations; and (4) integrative life stories. I believe that thinking of human individuality in this way brings into a meaningful synthesis the best that personality psychology has to offer. And I also strongly believe that thinking about *who you are* in these terms can help you develop a better and more fulfilling under-standing of your own life and your place in the world.

Summary

1. Personality psychology is the scientific study of the whole person.
2. What do we know when we know a person? Observation of everyday social interactions shows that people tend to make at least three different kinds of attributions about persons in their efforts to know them. They account for a person's individuality in terms of (1) dispositional traits,

(2) characteristic adaptations, and (3) integrative life stories. These three types of attributions about persons correspond to three levels of personality. A full understanding of the individual human life begins with a solid grounding in the evolutionary and cultural contexts of human behavior and experience, and it proceeds to a systematic con-sideration of traits, adaptations, and life stories.

3. At Level 1, personality traits are general, internal, and comparative dispositions that account for consistencies perceived or expected in behavior from one situation to the next and over time. Typically assessed via self-report questionnaires, traits sketch an outline of human individuality.

4. At Level 2, characteristic adaptations are contextualized facets of human individuality that speak to motivational, cognitive, and developmental concerns in personality. Contextualized in time, place, or social role, characteristic adaptations fill in the details of human individuality. Some of the most influential theories in the history of personality psychology have addressed fundamental questions regarding motivational, social–cognitive, and developmental adaptations in life.

5. At Level 3, a life story is an internalized and evolving narrative of the self that integrates the reconstructed past, perceived present, and anticipated future in order to provide a life with a sense of unity and purpose. Throughout the history of personality psychology, scholars and scientists have debated the merits and limitations of different approaches for interpreting the stories people tell about their lives. If traits sketch an outline and adaptations fill in the details of human individuality, life stories speak to what a human life means in the overall.

6. As the scientific study of the whole person, personality psychology follows a three-step sequence of inquiry that is common to most sciences: (1) unsystematic observation, (2) building theories, and (3) evaluating propositions.

7. In the third step, scientists derive hypotheses from theories and test their adequacy in research. One general design of hypothesis-testing research is the correlational design, in which the psychologist determines the extent to which two or more variables co-relate. A second general design is the experiment, in which the psychologist manipulates the independent variable to assess its impact on the dependent variable.

8. Personality psychology was born in university psychology departments in the 1930s. The first authoritative text for the field was Gordon Allport's (1937) *Personality: A Psychological Interpretation*. Allport identified an important distinction in personality research between the nomothetic approach, which aims to discover and test general principles of behavior across many individuals, and the idiographic approach, which focuses on the specific and individual patterning of the single human life.

9. The history of modern personality psychology can be divided into three periods: (1) 1930–1950, the period of developing general systems and grand theories of personality; (2) 1950–1970, the period of refining measurement techniques and elaborating personality constructs; and (3) 1970–today, a period that began with a crisis concerning the legitimacy of personality studies and developed into the present sense of renewal and invigoration in the field of personality psychology.

10. Personality psychology is related to many other branches of psychology and sits at the crossroads of many different disciplines in the social sciences. It is distinguished from other fields, however, by its focus on human individuality, its tendency to examine relatively enduring rather than fleeting and momentary characteristics of persons, its interest in individual differences as manifested in adulthood, and its focus on relatively normal, healthy psychological functioning.

CHAPTER

2

Evolution and Human Nature

Every person is unique. No two persons have the same life, the same experience of the world, or the same personality. And yet we all have very much in common. What binds us all together—whether we live in southern California, rural India, or Bucharest—is that we are all human beings. Now, this may not sound like much, or it may sound like a cliché. But unless we develop some sense of what we all have in common by virtue of our common membership in the same species, we can never fully appreciate, nor even understand, our diversity and our individuality. Therefore, *the study of persons must begin with human nature.* What are human beings fundamentally like?

Throughout history, philosophers and poets have speculated on human nature. By virtue of original sin, we are all fundamentally bad, though redeemable, the Christian church has traditionally taught. The book of Genesis tells the story of Adam's and Eve's original sin, passed down from one human generation to the next. Indeed, all the world's great religions—Hinduism, Buddhism, Judaism, Christianity, and Islam—suggest that the natural state of man and woman is fundamentally flawed in some manner, and that human beings are in need of a deliverance from that original state (James, 1902/1958). Eighteenth century French philosopher Jean-Jacques Rousseau and 19th century romantic poets such as Shelly and Keats offered a more optimistic view, describing human nature as fundamentally innocent and good. We are noble and pure at birth, Rousseau suggested, though society may corrupt us thereafter. Others, such as the 17th-century British philosopher John Locke, have suggested that human nature is basically a blank slate (*tabula rasa,* in Latin). At birth, people are ready to be shaped into any form that their environments can produce.

Contemporary scientific understandings of human nature, however, focus on human *evolution.* The argument is simple, and yet awesome in its elegance and profundity. Like all living organisms, human beings have evolved to survive and reproduce. Those features of human adaptation that have indeed promoted survival and reproduction are, ipso facto, what human nature is fundamentally about. Evolution and human nature, then, provide the most fundamental context for understanding human individuality. No matter how different we all are from each other, what we all have in common is that we are the products of human evolution. If this were not the case, we would not be here to read about it.

ON HUMAN NATURE: OUR EVOLUTIONARY HERITAGE

PRINCIPLES OF EVOLUTION

A fundamental property of living things is that they propagate. All animals and plants produce similar versions of themselves, in one way or another, making for the continuity of life from one generation to the next. The origins of life on earth reside in the first instances of physical reproduction: Once upon a time, a physico-chemical phenomenon reproduced itself through some means, providing the jump start required for the evolution of life to begin. In his book *How the Mind Works,* cognitive scientist Steven Pinker (1997) tells us the story of how evolutionary scientists believe that life on earth began:

> In the beginning was a replicator. This molecule or crystal was a product not of natural selection but of the laws of physics and chemistry. … Replicators were wont to multiply, and a single one multiplying unchecked would fill the universe with its great, great, … great grandcopies. But replicators use up materials to make their copies and energy to power the replication. The world is finite, so the replicators will compete for its resources. Because no copying process is one hundred percent perfect, errors will crop up, and not

all of the daughters will be exact duplicates. Most of the copying errors will be changes for the worse, causing a less efficient uptake of energy and materials or a slower rate or lower probability of replication. But by dumb luck a few errors will be changes for the better, and the replicators bearing them will proliferate over the generations. Their descendants will accumulate any subsequent errors that are changes for the better, including ones that assemble protective covers and supports, manipulators, catalysts for chemical reactions, and other features of what we call bodies. The resulting replicator with its apparently well-engineered body is what we call an organism. (pp. 157–158)

Pinker's imagined scenario for the beginning of life on earth contains the essence of Charles Darwin's (1859) insight about the evolution of life, updated with a contemporary understanding of genetics. Individual organisms are the product of a long chain of evolutionary events whereby replicating systems essentially compete for limited resources, with some systems proving more successful in the long run than others. The more "successful" systems are those that produce more viable copies of themselves for the next "generation." In order to do so, a system must meet the demands posed by the environment wherein it resides. The demands are many, including limited resources and challenges posed by other replicators (that is, other organisms). As time passes, the designs of organisms change, as some designs prove more promoting of replications in certain environments than do others. As environments change, designs of organisms change, not in direct response to environmental changes but simply because some designs of organisms will prove to be more successful in promoting replication than others. Over evolutionary time, as Tooby and Cosmides (1992) describe it, evolution "appears as a succession of designs, each a modification of the one preceding it. Generation by generation, step-by-step, the designs of all of the diverse organisms alive today—from the redwoods and manta rays to humans and yeast—were permuted out of the original, very simple, single-celled ancestor through an immensely long sequence of successive modifications" (p. 52). As Darwin argued, all existing living forms have evolved over time in response to their interactions with environments. Facing limited environmental resources for survival and replication, organisms compete with one another, and ultimately the "fittest" designs win out.

The key to evolution over time is **natural selection,** a process whereby nature gradually selects those characteristics of organisms that promote survival and reproductive success. Darwin observed that organisms within a species manifest wide variation in physical and behavioral characteristics. Certain characteristics may promote the survival of the organism within the environment. Those organisms possessing the advantageous characteristic should live longer and produce more offspring than those organisms not possessing the characteristic. The offspring of those possessing the advantageous characteristic likewise should be more likely to possess the same advantageous characteristic, enabling them in turn to live longer and produce more offspring similarly equipped. In this way, nature selects, and causes to persist, the most adaptive characteristics in a species.

Although Darwin did not understand the precise mechanism for biological transmission of characteristics from parent to offspring, he did recognize that such transmission occurs. Today, we know that *genes* are responsible for the inheritance of characteristics. Genes are segments of chromosomes found in every cell in the body and are composed of deoxyribonucleic acid (DNA), a long threadlike molecule that is particularly well suited for passing on hereditary information.

Because sexual reproduction involves a mixing of parents' genes, an individual organism receives half of his or her genes from the biological mother and half from the biological father, thus inheriting characteristics from both. Through sexual reproduction, then, genes are passed down from one generation to the next. But in the transmission of genes, strange things occasionally occur. Genes may be transformed, generally by accident. Most changes make little or no difference in the organism's life, and what difference they do make may render the organism less fit. Sometimes, however, genetic mutations can make for accidental advantages (what Pinker called "dumb luck"), as when a transformation in the genes gives rise to a characteristic in the organism that promotes survival and success.

The movers and shakers in evolution are the genes, which ultimately produce the designs of the organisms that compete for resources in the environment. In a literal sense, it is the genes, not the organisms themselves, that are replicated. To take a simple example, my own biological children are not literal replications of me (fortunately, for the world), but rather my children contain the replications of my and my wife's (even more fortunately) genes. Through evolution, organisms have been designed to function such that the genes that lie behind those designs are replicated in subsequent generations. The evolutionary imperative, then, is to replicate the genes. Now, if a gene were a person, which of course it isn't (it is simply a DNA structure), then we could say that it is a very "selfish" person. In *The Selfish Gene,* Richard Dawkins (1976) made famous the idea that genes aim for one thing only—self-replication. Genes don't really "care" about anything else. They just "want" to be replicated. Of course, genes don't have the powers of "caring" for or "wanting" anything. It is persons who care for and want. Therefore, to say that the gene is selfish is not to say that persons, who (like all other living organisms) are designed by genes, are themselves selfish, or even that persons themselves want to replicate their own genes. The idea of a selfish gene is rather more metaphorical, and Dawkins's point is instead a more subtle and profound one: *Persons are designed to engage in behaviors that ultimately make for the replication of the genes that determine their design.* Pinker (1997) captures the point well:

> Many people think that the theory of the selfish gene says that "animals try to spread their genes." This misstates the facts and it misstates the theory. Animals, including most people, know nothing about genetics and care even less. People love their children not because they want to spread their genes (consciously or unconsciously) but because they can't help it. That love makes them try to keep their children warm, fed, and safe. What is selfish is not the real motives of the person but the metaphorical motives of the genes that built the person. Genes "try" to spread *themselves* by wiring animals' brains so that animals love their kin and try to keep them warm, fed, and safe. (pp. 400–401)

There are at least two very different ways that persons can promote the likelihood of replicating in the next generation those genes that are responsible for their very design and, indeed, existence. The first and more obvious way is to generate and promote one's own biological offspring. A woman who bears and raises to maturity six children passes down twice as many of "her" genes to the next generation as a woman who bears and raises to maturity three children, all other things being equal. The second and less obvious way is to promote the reproduction and well being of those individuals *who share the same genes.* A woman who bears and raises no children but whose one biological sister bears and raises to maturity six children participates (perhaps unwittingly) in a scenario in which *more* of "her" genes are passed down to the next generation, through her biological sister's children, than is the case for a comparable woman who herself bears and raises to maturity two of her own children but whose one and only sister bears none. In that the first woman shares about half of her genes with her sister (as is the case with all biological siblings), six of her sister's children are genetically equivalent, in a simple quantitative sense, to three of her own. Speaking solely in terms of evolution's cold calculus with respect to the selfish gene, more of the first woman's genes (the equivalent of three offspring) were replicated, even though she produced no offspring herself, compared with the second woman, who bore two of her own children but whose sister bore none. What this contrived example suggests to us is that organisms can participate in the business of replicating the genes that designed them in both direct (through one's offspring) and indirect (through the offspring of kin) ways. With respect to the indirect method, anything that an organism does to enhance the reproductive success of those to whom it is biologically related promotes the likelihood that its "own" genes will be passed down to the next generation, in that many of its "own" genes exist "in" its kin.

Because the scientific community in Darwin's day had not yet discovered the role of genes in reproduction and inheritance, Darwin did not have a clear understanding of the different ways, direct and indirect, that organisms promote self-replication. Therefore, evolutionary understandings of behavior were hamstrung by the common appearance of altruism and self-sacrificial acts in the animal kingdom. Darwin could not provide a satisfactory answer to the question of why any organism would ever do anything that compromised its own survival, and even reproductive success, to assist another organism. It was not until William Hamilton (1964) elaborated the concept of **inclusive fitness** that a solution to the riddle began to appear. An organism's inclusive fitness is its overall (total, inclusive) ability to maximize the replication of the genes that designed it. Part of that total includes the results of the organism's own reproductive success, but part also includes the reproductive success of close relatives, with whom the organism shares genes. Not only, then, should some organisms be predisposed (by virtue of their genetic makeup) to assist their kin, but they might also be predisposed to sacrifice themselves, under certain circumstances, for the good of their kin. It makes good evolutionary sense that a parent might even give up his or her life if such an action appears necessary to assure the survival of his or her offspring, or even the offspring of kin. For human beings and many other social species, certain kinds of caring and altruistic tendencies should be selected by nature, for they may have functioned to enhance the inclusive fitness of those organisms that exhibited such tendencies.

THE ENVIRONMENT OF EVOLUTIONARY ADAPTEDNESS

Current scientific estimates propose that life on earth emerged roughly 3.5 billion years ago. About 3 billion years later (500 million years ago), life evolved beyond simple cells, producing multicellular organisms. Mammals, of which we are one, emerged roughly 200 million years ago. Dinosaurs became extinct about 60 million years ago, and shortly thereafter (that is, 5 million years later) primates, of which we are also one, made their first appearance on the earth. Human beings finally entered the picture 2 to 4 million years ago, emerging most probably in the heart of Africa as a particular kind of primate, which is a particular kind of mammal. Humans gradually migrated in all directions, eventually populating most ecosystems on the planet. The period in which human beings emerged and evolved to their current form, therefore, spans at least the past 2 million years, which corresponds roughly with what geologists call the Pleistocene Epoch of earth history (running from 1.6 million years ago up to 10,000 years ago, marking the end of the last ice age). Human beings evolved to adapt to the challenges of life in the Pleistocene.

Evolutionary psychologists call the Pleistocene world within which human beings lived and evolved the **environment of evolutionary adaptedness (EEA).** What was human life like in the EEA? The consensus among paleoanthropologists and others who study the evolutionary origins of human life is that our Pleistocene ancestors lived as foragers, gathering fruits and vegetables and hunting prey to supply their bodies with the calories and nutrients required for life. In the EEA, it was generally necessary to move from one hunting and gathering region to another, pursuing prey and seeking out the best geographic areas for gathering food. *Humans lived in groups.* Indeed, participation in the daily functioning of small cooperative groups may have been a principal survival strategy of early humans (Brewer & Caporael, 1990). Group life brought with it numerous advantages in the EEA. Humans could better defend themselves against predators and other threats by living together in collectives, looking out for one another in times of danger, and consolidating resources, skills, and strength to meet the many challenges they were likely to face, including threats from other groups of humans (deWaal, 1996). Human children could be nurtured and raised to maturity in the group, with parents relying on other group members to assist them in their efforts to care for, protect, and educate their own progeny, under the expectation, most likely, that those assisted now would in turn assist later. Hunters could work in groups, too, and once they accomplished the big kill, the meat could be shared and distributed within the group. This kind of cooperative activity would appear to benefit the group as a whole, but in addition it might also enhance the inclusive fitness of the individual hunter, for cooperating in the hunt should help to establish the kinds of social relationships and coalitions that benefit the individual's own survival and, ultimately, reproductive success. Pinker (1997) writes:

> The hunter with a dead animal larger than he can eat and about to become a putrefying mass is faced with a unique opportunity. Hunting is largely a matter of luck. In the absence of refrigeration, a good place to store meat for leaner times is in the bodies of other hunters who will return the favor when fortunes reverse. This eases the way for the male coalitions and extensive reciprocity that are ubiquitous in foraging societies. (p. 196)

Most of the human activities necessary for survival and reproductive success in the EEA were set within the parameters of the particular group of human beings into which an individual was born. Human beings are by nature social animals because social life proved to be the most propitious strategy for survival and reproductive success in the EEA. Humans have been designed by natural selection *to want to be* together in groups, to seek out one another in bonds of attachment, friendship, partnership, and various other alliances. Like most primates and certain other social species (e.g., dogs, elephants, and dolphins), humans deeply desire and enjoy the company of others. Those few individuals who do not seem to share this social sense (e.g., hermits, autistic children) stand out as oddities, often eliciting from others reactions of fear, pity, or bafflement.

Group life in the EEA was no picnic. While human beings evolved to be social animals, social life entailed competition and conflict as much as cooperation and care. As deWaal (1996) points out, the "greatest disadvantage [of group life] is that one is continuously surrounded by individuals searching for the same food and attracted to the same mates. Groups are breeding grounds for strife and competition, which ironically also pose the strongest threat to their existence" (p. 170). Certain forms of aggression often pay off handsomely in some group contexts, as the biggest, strongest, and most brutal sometimes get their way and capture the lion's share of the resources (e.g., food, shelter, mates) required for survival and reproductive success. Among human groups, dominance can also be established through cleverness, guile, and deceit. Human groups tend to be organized in hierarchical ways. Some individuals dominate others, and one's position in an elaborate dominance pecking order may be closely linked to the resources for survival and reproductive success to which one has access (Buss, 1995). In addition, groups would appear to compete, sometimes ferociously, with each other. Intertribe warfare is not a recent invention. The fossil record indicates that rival groups of humans fought each other often and with great brutality throughout the Pleistocene. As far as we can tell, there was no ancient time when all human beings lived together in peace.

Over evolutionary time, human beings adapted to the challenges of the EEA by honing a set of characteristics that, when taken together, set them apart from all other species on the planet. Humans stood upright, on two feet, freeing their fingers and opposable thumbs for a wide variety of complex and finely tuned motor tasks. They manufactured and depended upon a great many tools. They lived longer than other apes and bore helpless infants who required many years of care before reaching their sexual maturity. Kin negotiated mating relations, such that groups would often exchange sexually mature daughters to build new families and to discourage intercourse between biological brothers and sisters. Sexual intercourse was not limited to particular times of the month for females (as it is in many mammals) but could occur at any time. Males tended to compete for the opportunity to engage in intercourse with females. Males tended to invest in their children, forming more-or-less stable pair bonds with their children's mother(s) and assisting in the defense and training of their young. They toted their children around, protected them against animals and other humans, gave them food. Females cooperated in the care of children and in gathering fruits and vegetables for the clan. Males cooperated in the defense of the group and in hunting, for meat was often a significant staple of the human diet. Humans transported food over long distances, cooked it with fire and processed it extensively, stored it, and shared it. They exchanged goods and favors over extended periods of time, building coalitions and partnerships, cementing friendships, establishing shared understandings and consensual expectations about reciprocity and fair play. They communicated with one another through language and used language, as well as other symbol systems, to disseminate information, pass on traditions, accumulate knowledge and adaptive wisdom, and create culture.

In the environment of evolutionary adaptedness, human beings lived mainly in nomadic groups and survived through hunting, fishing, and gathering edible plants.

Different human groups developed different cultures. But the cultures may have shared many commonalities, reflecting shared adaptive challenges in the EEA. If indeed such commonalities existed, one might expect to see vestiges of them today in behavioral patterns and social customs that appear to be cross-culturally universal. Anthropological surveys have listed a large number of such universals. These include athletic sports, bodily adornment, cooperative labor, courtship, dancing, education systems, etiquette, family feasting, folklore, food taboos, funeral rites, games, gift giving, incest taboos, inheritance rites, law, marriage, medicine, penal sanctions, personal names, property rights, puberty customs, religious rituals, soul concepts, tool making, weaving, and attempts at weather control. E. O. Wilson (1978) argues that each of these universal patterns can be traced back to hunting-and-gathering societies, in which they promoted individual survival and reproduction: "most and perhaps all of the … prevailing characteristics of modern societies can be identified as … modifications of the biologically meaningful institutions of hunter-gatherer bands and early tribal states" (p. 92). Given that these patterns proved adaptive for thousands, perhaps millions, of years, each has become part of human nature, coded in human genes.

As just one example of a cross-cultural human universal, consider religion. E. O. Wilson (1978) states: "The predisposition to religious belief is the most complex and powerful force in the human mind and in all probability an ineradicable part of human nature" (p. 169). The power of religion today lies in the tremendous advantage it bestowed upon our evolutionary ancestors. Religion played a vital role in enabling hunters and gatherers to live together in bands and tribes. The shared beliefs and feelings of kinship engendered by religion may have helped persuade individuals to subordinate their immediate self-interests to the interests of the group (Irons, 2001). Such subordination promoted cooperative behavior in the acquisition of resources and defense against dangers, which increased the inclusive fitness of tribe members, as they were better able to reproduce and care for their kin. In addition, religious beliefs and practices may have been byproducts of other adaptive mechanisms that enabled humans in the EEA to comprehend their world and solve interpersonal problems (Kirkpatrick, 1999).

THE ADAPTED MIND

When we think about evolution, we find it easier to consider the gross ways in which physical bodies might gradually change over time in response to selective pressures from the environment. If, for example, having a long neck helps an organism survive and ultimately reproduce more efficiently because it enables that organism, say a giraffe, to obtain food that is elevated above the ground, then subsequent generations may eventually and overall have longer necks. The reason is that those individuals who, by dumb luck, had longer necks to begin with would be more successful in reproduction, on the average, and would thus pass on that adaptive characteristic to subsequent generations. Eventually the characteristic would become a universal feature of the organism's design, as we see with giraffes, because it proved to be so beneficial to inclusive fitness. In the case of human beings, we can see an analogous process producing a retooling of the human skeleton and posture over evolutionary time such that human beings were ultimately able to walk efficiently on two feet and to engage in the kinds of fine motor tasks that helped them develop tools. The refinement of the human skeleton is surely no small evolutionary feat. But the grander legacy of human evolution is surely the way in which the human *brain* has evolved, producing complex behavioral patterns and mental programs that have no parallel in the animal kingdom. Let us think of the human *mind* as what the brain mainly *does*—our thinking, planning, wanting, feeling, and so on (Pinker, 1997). The evolution of the human mind may be more subtle and more difficult to discern than the evolution of the giraffe's neck, but it is far and away more spectacular, and it is first and foremost what makes human beings distinctively human.

Human beings survived and reproduced with felicity in the EEA not because they were bigger, stronger, more brutal, or more caring than their competitors, but because they were smarter. All animals must play with the cards they are dealt by evolution, and for humans the strongest suit has always been the human mind. By outwitting the competition, by

Religious rituals can be found in all cultures, suggesting that human beings have been designed by natural selection to engage in religious practices.

teaming up to defend the group, by dividing labor among group members, by developing rational strategies for attack and defense, by refining these strategies through learning and feedback, by communicating these refinements to others and to the next generation via language, by imagining scenarios that have never happened but might and then developing plans to bring those scenarios into reality—through all of this mental activity and much more, human beings have carved out for themselves what Pinker (1997) calls a **cognitive niche** in the evolutionary landscape. Our primary mode of adapting to the challenges of the EEA was and continues to be the use of the human mind's extraordinary cognitive powers.

The human mind evolved to adapt to many different threats, challenges, and opportunities. Although the overall goal of adaptation is reproductive success, the EEA presented human beings with a dizzying array of more particular tasks that had to be accomplished if the overall goal was to be achieved. As a result, the adaptive mind may be organized into many different functional modules, each with a specialized design that makes it an expert in one arena of interaction with the world (Kenrick, Keefe, Bryan, Barr, & Brown, 1995; Pinker, 1997; Tooby & Cosmides, 1992). Rather than viewing the mind, therefore, as a general-purpose information-processing machine, contemporary evolutionary psychologists follow the philosophical writings of Fodor (1983) and others who have argued that the mind is more like a collection of rather more specialized subsystems or modules, each designed to address a particular adaptive task that humans faced in the EEA. The many different modules working in coordination gives the mind its flexibility and adaptive power. To convey this idea, Buss (1997) analogizes the human mind to a carpenter's tool kit:

> A carpenter's flexibility comes not from having a single, domain-general, "all-purpose tool" that is used to cut, screw, twist, wrench, plane, balance, and hammer, but rather from having many, more specialized tools, each designed to perform a particular function. It is the numerousness and specificity of the tools in the entire tool kit that give the carpenter greater flexibility, not a highly "plastic" single tool. (p. 325)

Therefore, the human mind contains evolved cognitive, emotional, and motivational mechanisms that are specially targeted to solve those problems in adaptation that have confronted human beings since the time of the Pleistocene. What are those problems? Simply put, there are problems of survival and problems of reproduction. Darwin (1859) identified many of the survival problems under the heading of "hostile forces of nature." These include food shortages, harsh climate, disease, parasites, predators, and natural hazards. Reproductive problems are typically more social in quality and, therefore, more centrally implicated in personality. Buss (1991a) lists eight classes of reproductive problems:

1. *Successful intrasexual competition:* The individual must win out over competitors in gaining access to desirable members of the opposite sex so that sexual reproduction can occur.

2. *Mate selection:* The individual must select those mates who have the greatest reproductive value to maximize the opportunity for passing his or her genes down to the next generation.

3. *Successful conception:* The individual must engage in the necessary social and sexual behaviors to fertilize a mate or become fertilized by the mate.

4. *Mate retention:* The individual must retain the mate, preventing the encroachment of intrasexual competitors as well as preventing the mate's defection or desertion. This problem is more acute among species and individuals who pursue "long-term

mating strategies" and does not apply to what Buss (1991a, p. 465) calls "brief, opportunistic copulation."

5. *Reciprocal dyadic alliance formation:* The individual must develop a relationship with the mate characterized by a certain degree of cooperation and reciprocity.

6. *Coalition building and maintenance:* The individual must cooperate with others whose interests are aligned with his or her own, building coalitions that compete successfully with rival groups.

7. *Parental care and socialization:* The individual must engage in actions that ensure the survival and reproductive success of his or her own offspring.

8. *Extraparental kin investment:* The individual must sacrifice his or her own self-interests to promote the survival and reproductive success of nondescendant genetic relatives. The reproductive success of genetic relatives is important because they share with the individual some of the same genes.

How do human beings deal with these problems? Drawing upon evolved internal mechanisms, we formulate goal-directed *tactics* and *strategies* that aim ultimately to assure our survival and reproductive success. We must remember, however, that the aims of survival and reproductive success are not typically conscious, or even unconscious, "goals" or "intentions" in human behavior and experience. In general terms, evolution has designed the human mind so that it will generate strategies and tactics to produce goal-directed behaviors that, on the average, tended to promote inclusive fitness in the EEA. To take the obvious example, sexual activity will, on average, produce more babies than will no sexual activity. But people do not usually engage in sexual activity for the express purpose of conceiving children, although of course they sometimes do. Most typically, people are motivated to engage in sexual activity because sexual activity is so pleasurable. Evolution has shaped sexual activity to be extraordinarily pleasurable so that people will engage in it often, assuring that offspring will eventually be produced. It is a brilliant strategy! Rather than leaving it up to people to decide whether they want children or not, the selfish genes have conspired to assure that human beings, prior to the advent of modern contraception, will indeed produce children, whether they intend to or not, by offering them an activity that is so pleasurable and compelling as to be almost irresistible.

The *distal* (evolutionary) reason for human sexual activity is to replicate the genes, but the *proximate* (individual) motivation for engaging in sexual activity is that it feels good. The distinction between distal and proximate is crucial for understanding the significance of human evolution for personality psychology (Archer, 1988; Wright, 1994). To explain behavior in terms of proximate causes is to appeal to the immediate environmental, physiological, and cognitive mechanisms that determine a person's behavior. By contrast, distal explanations consider the significance of behavioral patterns in the ultimate terms of evolution and inclusive fitness. Some proximate causes may be derivatives of distal influences, but the influence of the distal on the proximate is typically very subtle and indirect, and it is typically best expressed in broad terms, such as those applying to human nature in the overall rather than in the particular behaviors of any one individual person.

The distinction between proximate and distal is especially important in considering the different strategies and tactics that women and men may develop for sexual reproduction itself. In most ways, male and female humans faced pretty much the same selection pressures in the EEA. From an evolutionary standpoint, therefore, we would not expect to find strong sex differences in most areas of human behavior and experience. However, evolutionary theory would lead us to predict sex differences in any domain in which women and men faced dramatically different selection pressures and adaptive challenges. In the EEA, that was surely true of reproduction. The indisputable biological facts in this regard are that women, not men, become pregnant, that pregnancy requires a nine-month gestation period, and that at the end of that period women give birth to human infants and provide them with nourishment through breast-feeding. Seen in an evolutionary perspective, these facts suggest that men and women should, on average, operate according to somewhat different strategies and express somewhat different goals when it comes to activities related to sexual reproduction, such as human mating.

MATING

In terms of evolution, men and women mate for the prime reason of producing offspring, who will carry their genes into the next generation. The tactics and strategies whereby men and women seek to accomplish this end, however, differ markedly as a function of gender. For the male, it is to his advantage (technically, to the advantage of his genes) to impregnate as many females as possible, since this is the major way he can be assured of passing down his own genes. Theoretically, it is possible for a male to sire hundreds of offspring. (You may recall that, in a celebrated biography, the former professional basketball player Wilt Chamberlain claimed to have had sexual relations with 20,000 different women.) Hence, males may be biologically more inclined than females toward sexual promiscuity. The female, on the other hand, must invest a great deal of time and energy in each birth and can have only a very limited number of offspring. It is to her advantage (technically, to the advantage of her genes) to be "choosy" when it comes to sexual intercourse, securing a single mate for assistance in protecting and raising her offspring, thereby maximizing the likelihood of passing her own genes to the next generation.

My characterization of sex differences in mating as they apply to human evolution is exaggerated to make a point. But the point is actually rather subtle, and it needs to be qualified in a number of ways. First, an evolutionary explanation for sex differences in human mating strategies may not necessarily contradict or work against cultural and environmental explanations of the same phenomena, which tend to be couched in more proximate rather than distal terms. Proximate factors that discourage female promiscuity, for example, range from the cultural double standard with which most Americans are familiar (young women are supposed to be careful, while young men may "play around") to the oppressive laws and brutal practices (e.g., female circumcision in some African societies) that have been devised to keep women from seeking sexual gratification outside the marriage bond. Societal norms, values, laws, sanctions, and various other cultural practices shape sexuality in profound ways.

Second, natural selection often operates on the emotional and motivational mechanisms behind behavior, rather than behavior per se. Behavioral strategies are manifestations of human *desire*. According to the evolutionary view, men typically *want* to engage in sexual relations with many partners to a greater extent than women typically want to engage in sexual relations with many partners; men can readily wrap their minds around the idea of having intercourse with a great many lovers over time and in many different situations; their *fantasies* go in the direction of promiscuity, even if their behavior often does not.

A third qualification is this: Evolutionary explanations for differences in mating strategies, just like cultural explanations, are not *moral* justifications or rationalizations for sex differences in sexual behavior. To seek a scientific explanation for any behavior pattern is *not* to seek a justification, ethical or legal, for that pattern. If the distal reason for male promiscuity is that such a strategy enhanced inclusive fitness of males in the EEA, we are still left to decide whether such a pattern of behavior today is good, is bad, should be promoted, should be sanctioned, or whatever. It is very dangerous, if not downright wrong, to look to the EEA for moral guidance in today's world.

Fourth, we should consider more carefully the evolutionary logic of sex differences in mating strategies. When it comes to reproduction, most mammals, including humans, show dramatic sex differences with respect to *speed*. Males are fast; females are slow (Bailey, Gaulin, Agyei, & Gladue, 1994). What this means is that any male's single reproductive venture is relatively short-lived, consisting simply of copulation. By contrast, any female's single reproductive venture must include, at minimum, copulation, gestation, and lactation. That all takes a long time. During that long period it does her no good, in terms of inclusive fitness, to have intercourse with another man. She is already pregnant and must patiently wait as the slow process of bringing a viable offspring into the world (and then providing some care for it afterward) unfolds. Theoretically, her faster male counterpart can engage in numerous reproductive ventures (copulations) in the meantime, each offering the possibility of replicating his genes and thus enhancing his inclusive fitness. Of course, there is a limited supply of females to go around, there being roughly a 1:1 sex ratio. The male's reproductive efforts, therefore, are limited by the supply of available females and by the competitive efforts of his male peers to gain access to those females. Put another way, the fast sex (male) is constrained by the limited supply of reproductive opportunities afforded by the slow sex (female). Thus, the fast sex must compete for access to the slow sex, and the slow sex enjoys the relative luxury of picking and choosing among a host of eager mates. According to this logic, the fast sex should be predisposed toward maximizing quantity of offspring. In that sexual activity is the vehicle for accomplishing this, the fast sex should indeed be more promiscuous, *or at least desire to be so.*

That males in fact *are* more promiscuous has been documented repeatedly. In most societies, men in general have sexual relations with more partners than do women, a difference that is most striking when comparing homosexual men to lesbian women (Bailey et al., 1994; Cunningham, 1981). In addition, men appear to be much less discriminating in their choice of sexual partners. In one study, Kenrick (1989) asked college men to consider what personal qualities were required in a prospective sexual partner. Except on the dimension of physical attractiveness, women tended to be much choosier than men with respect to what attributes they insisted their partner should possess before they would consider sexual relations. In many cases, men reported that they were willing to have sexual relations with a woman who, by virtue of her low intelligence or obnoxious personality, they would not even consider dating! In other words, men held up stricter criteria for a casual date than they did for sex.

Cross-culturally, the widespread practice of polygyny—in which one man mates with more than one woman—also supports the evolutionary hypothesis concerning sex differences in mating strategies. In a polygynous arrangement, men are able to mate with many different women (increasing their fitness) while many different women are assured of a mate and (because the practice is culturally sanctioned) an attendant social system supportive of their offspring (increasing their fitness, as well). By contrast, the cultural arrangement of polyandry, whereby one woman mates with many different men, is extremely rare. E. O. Wilson (1978) describes the stark differences:

> [As a species, human beings are] moderately polygynous, with males initiating most of
> the changes in sexual partnership. About three-fourths of all human societies permit

the taking of multiple wives, and most of them encourage the practice by law and custom. In contrast, marriage to multiple husbands is sanctioned in less than one percent of societies. The remaining monogamous societies usually fit that category in a legal sense only, with concubinage and other extramarital stratagems being added to allow *de facto* polygyny. (pp. 125–126)

If men and women have evolved to adopt markedly different reproductive tactics and strategies, then we might expect that these differences would create a good deal of conflict between the sexes, leading to anger and upset. From an evolutionary point of view, we might expect that men should become especially angry and upset about women's refusal to engage them in sexual relations (sexually withholding behaviors). By contrast, women should experience anger and upset as a result of men's excessive insistence on sexual relations (sexually aggressive behaviors). Buss (1989b) presented college students and newlyweds with a long list of behaviors that are likely to evoke anger and upset and asked them to endorse those behaviors that their respective dating partners or spouses had committed during the previous year. The study's results support the evolutionary prediction about sexually withholding behaviors (men report that women do this more) but not the one about sexually aggressive behaviors (women do not report higher levels than do men). As is evident in Table 2.1, the respondents in the study endorsed a wide variety of partner behaviors eliciting anger and upset, most of which do not seem to be associated with sexual relations per se. Compared with men's reports, women tended to complain most about condescending, neglecting, and insulting behaviors on the part of their male partners. By contrast, men reported higher levels of moodiness and self-absorption on the part of their female partners.

Beyond sex differences in evolved reproductive strategies, men and women also look for different qualities in a prospective sexual partner. Evolutionary theory suggests that the choosy female should prefer to mate with a male of high social status and significant material resources, since he is most likely to promote her inclusive fitness. By contrast, the male should prefer to mate with the most fertile young women available, since they are most likely to bear offspring to carry his genes. As a result, the argument goes, older men (who have more necessary resources) tend to marry younger women (who have many years of childbearing ahead of them).

The data from a number of studies are consistent with these predictions (e.g., Kenrick et al., 1995; Sprecher, Sullivan, & Hatfield, 1994). For example, Buss and Barnes (1986) examined mate selection preferences among 92 married couples and 100 unmarried college students. They found that in choosing a sexual mate, men placed major emphasis on a woman's physical beauty (generally associated with youth), while women placed major emphasis on a man's earning potential. One might argue, however, that the inequality in earning potential for most men and women in contemporary American society renders mate selection one of the few viable means for securing adequate material resources for some women. Women's pragmatic approach to choosing a mate, therefore, may have as much to do with present cultural constraints and norms as it does with a biological mandate to maximize inclusive fitness. However, it is interesting to note that the differences Buss and Barnes found in the United States have also been found in a number of other cultures as well. In a study of 37 different cultures, Buss (1989a) found that men tend to prefer younger, physically attractive mates while women place greater value on slightly older mates possessing ambition, an industrious nature, and good financial prospects.

A central tenet of Darwinian theory is that organisms compete with each other for limited reproductive resources. Darwin was intrigued by the existence in the animal kingdom

TABLE 2.1	WHAT UPSETS MEN AND WOMEN IN ROMANTIC RELATIONSHIPS?

	SEX OF TARGET OF COMPLAINT		
Upset Elicitor	**Male**	**Female**	**p**
Condescending	14%	8%	.000
Neglecting–rejecting–unreliable	16%	11%	.000
Inconsiderate	23%	9%	.000
Abuses alcohol–emotionally constricted	16%	13%	.033
Insulting of appearance	4%	2%	.021
Physically self-absorbed	7%	14%	.000
Moody	19%	30%	.000
Sexually withholding	6%	14%	.000
Possessive–jealous–dependent	17%	19%	ns
Abusive	5%	6%	ns
Unfaithful	6%	7%	ns
Sexualizes others	12%	15%	ns
Disheveled	7%	5%	ns
Sexually aggressive	3%	2%	ns
Self-centered	21%	18%	ns
Total	12%	11%	ns

NOTE: N = 528. Values in table are percentages of individuals endorsing the upset elicitor. For example, 14% for condescending for target of male means that 14% of the individuals in the study indicated that their male partner had treated them in a condescending manner in the past year, which upset them. The "p" refers to probability of the difference being due to chance. Any p value lower than .05 is considered statistically significant. "Ns" means the difference between males and females is not statistically significant. Adapted from "Conflict Between the Sexes: Strategic Interference and the Evocation of Anger and Upset," by D. M. Buss, 1989, *Journal of Personality and Social Psychology, 56*, p. 740.

of characteristics that seem to impair survival but nonetheless promote reproductive success by giving an organism a competitive edge. The elaborate plumage, heavy horns, and conspicuous displays of many species seem costly in the currency of survival. However, these characteristics increase success in mating and so evolve despite their cost. When it comes to humans, evolutionary theory predicts that men and women will compete for reproductive resources in contrasting ways. Given the evolutionary premium placed on feminine youth and beauty, women should strive to enhance their physical appearance in competing with one another to attract men. Given the evolutionary premium placed on masculine dominance and status, men should compete to attract women through displays of social dominance, employing tactics such as boasting of their accomplishments and future earning potential.

In order to test these hypotheses, Buss (1988) conducted a series of studies to identify the most common tactics of mate attraction employed by college men and women and by newlyweds. As predicted, women tended to use tactics aimed at enhancing their physical attractiveness, endorsing such behaviors as "wear makeup," "wear stylish clothes," "keep clean and groomed," and "wear jewelry." By contrast, men tended to use such tactics as "display resources" and "brag about resources." Men were more likely than women to display expensive possessions and to boast about accomplishments. However, the research is also noteworthy for the strong agreement that was found between men and women with respect to those behavioral tactics viewed to be most successful in obtaining reproductive resources. The acts frequently performed and considered most highly effective for *both sexes* involved displaying sympathy, kindness, good manners, helpfulness, and humor. In a related vein, Jensen-Campbell, Graziano, and West (1995) found that women find men who exhibit prosocial tendencies (being kind, considerate, altruistic) to be especially attractive and desirable. Despite the sex differences obtained, therefore, men and women still show remarkable similarity in the tactics and strategies they employ to attract mates.

In conclusion, evolutionary theory suggests that overall sex differences should evolve only in those domains in which men and women faced dramatically different selection pressures in the EEA. The one domain in which such differential selection most likely occurred, therefore, is sexual reproduction. Men and women may have evolved different strategies and tactics for attracting and keeping sexual mates, differences that may be grounded in different patterns of desire. One writer has characterized these differences as resulting from an evolutionary arms race between the sexes (Wright, 1994). Men and women have built up two different arsenals in the age-old battle between the sexes. Both have at their disposal powerful weapons, accumulated and perfected over thousands of years of selection, for seducing, attracting, repelling, distracting, deceiving, maintaining, and exploiting their mates. Many popular songs tell it well: Romantic love is not for the faint of heart.

While selection pressures may have functioned as the distal origins of sex differences in human mating patterns, a wide variety of proximate causes for such differences can be observed in cultural norms and rules, religious and political values, and different patterns of socialization. Furthermore, while clear sex differences in mating strategies have been observed, research also indicates that men and women have much in common when it comes to mating. Both sexes, for example, value honesty, compassion, and sincerity in their mates, and both work hard to induce their mates to be faithful. Inclusive fitness, for both females and males, depends on the maturation of *viable* progeny. If a male sires 10 offspring and *none* survive (say, for lack of resources), then the evolutionary scoreboard records a big, fat zero for his inclusive fitness. Human males and females establish long-term pair bonds in all societies. Males and females have a common vested interest today, as they did even in the EEA, in assuring that the carriers of their genes—the next generation—survive, flourish, and ultimately reproduce themselves. Even in mating, then, we are all as much alike as we are different.

GETTING ALONG AND GETTING AHEAD

Whether gathering food, competing for mates, raising offspring, or fighting enemies, human beings evolved to live in groups. For the most part, human life is social life. The demands of social life have shaped human nature. Personality psychologist Robert Hogan has developed a broad theory of personality that blends an evolutionary understanding of the person with perspectives from Freud and sociological role theories. Hogan calls his approach **socioanalytic theory** (Hogan, 1982, 1987; Hogan, Jones, & Cheek, 1985; Jones, Couch, & Scott, 1997). Socioanalytic theory asserts that human beings are biologically predisposed to live in social groups that are variously organized into status hierarchies. Group living provided our evolutionary ancestors with advantages in cooperative ventures, such as defense against predators. At the same time, having high status in one's group conferred decided advantages on

SOME WOMEN (AND MEN) ARE CHOOSIER THAN OTHERS: SOCIOSEXUALITY

Natural selection presents us with a stark question: How are we to maximize the possibility of passing our genes down to the next generation? The biology of sexual reproduction dictates two divergent answers: For men, it is best to impregnate as many females as possible, under the assumption that at least some of the resultant offspring will survive to maturity so that they, too, will reproduce and keep the genes moving down the line. For women, it is best to choose carefully, to select a mate who will provide reliable care and assistance and thus maximize the chance that the very limited number of offspring any particular woman can produce will indeed reach maturity and eventually reproduce themselves. The divergent challenges natural selection poses for men and women may help explain general sex differences in mating strategies, for women do indeed seem to be choosier than men. But we all realize that there is wide variation among both women and men with respect to sexual attitudes and behaviors. Why, for example, are some women choosier than others? And why aren't all men trying to seduce nearly every woman they meet?

In a series of provocative articles, Jeffry Simpson and Steven Gangestad argue that, in terms of inclusive fitness and human evolution, it is to some women's advantage to be especially *non*choosy. Similarly, some men may be naturally selected to adopt a more discriminating approach to sexual relations (Gangestad, 1989; Gangestad & Simpson, 1990; Gangestad, Simpson, DiGeronimo, & Biek, 1992; Simpson & Gangestad, 1991, 1992; Simpson, Gangestad, & Biek, 1993). Simpson and Gangestad attempt to provide an evolutionary explanation for differences in **sociosexuality.** On one end of the continuum, individuals exhibiting a *restricted* sociosexuality insist on commitment and closeness in a relationship prior to engaging in sex with a romantic partner. Like the prototypical choosy female, both men and women with restricted sociosexuality require emotional closeness before

they feel comfortable with sexual relations. They have few sexual partners, but their sexual relationships tend to endure for a long time. On the other end of the spectrum, individuals exhibiting an *unrestricted* sociosexuality tend to feel relatively comfortable engaging in sex without commitment or closeness. Like the prototypical dominant male, both women and men with unrestricted sociosexuality have several different sexual partners, and each sexual relationship is likely to endure for a relatively short period of time.

To assess individual differences in sociosexuality, Simpson and Gangestad have developed a questionnaire that asks respondents (usually college students) to report frequency of sexual relations in the past six months, number of lifetime sexual partners, number of partners in the past year, number of partners desired, number of different partners foreseen for the next five years, number of "one night stands," frequency of sexual thoughts, and frequency of fantasies about having sex with people who are currently not their partners (Simpson & Gangestad, 1991). The research shows that college students scoring toward the unrestricted end of the scale tend (a) to engage in sex at an earlier point in their relationships, (b) to engage in sex with more than one partner during a given period in time, (c) to prefer especially attractive, socially prestigious partners, and (d) to be involved in relationships characterized by less investment, commitment, love, and dependency (Simpson & Gangestad, 1991).

Simpson and Gangestad argue that natural selection may have favored both restricted and unrestricted sociosexuality for both certain males and certain females. While it is easy to see the advantages of unrestricted sociosexuality for some dominant males, it is certainly true that every male cannot be a Don Juan. For one thing, there are not enough available women to go around, and in the starkly nonegalitarian world that Darwin has described,

(CONTINUES)

FEATURE 2.A (CONTINUED)

dominant males will usually attract the most mates, leaving many nondominant males with fewer options. The competitive powers of such nondominant males may be enhanced, however, by exhibiting traits of reliability and willingness to invest in relationships. Therefore, "males in evolutionary history who invested heavily in a mate's offspring should have desired long-term partners who demonstrated sexual exclusivity to the relationship, as revealed by resolute faithfulness and commitment" (Simpson & Gangestad, 1992, p. 34). Restricted sociosexuality can prove adaptive for some men in making them especially appealing to certain women who are most strongly concerned about relational investment.

For many females, the advantage of restricted sociosexuality is very clear. The choosy female enhances her inclusive fitness by selecting the most reliable mate. She may indeed end up "settling down" with a mate whose sociosexual orientation is similarly restricted, as suggested in the previous paragraph. But men have more to offer women than relational investment, Simpson and Gangestad point out. Men can also offer "good genes." For women, relatively unrestricted sociosexuality may have the advantage of enabling them to mate with the most attractive and most dominant men. While some of these attractive men may not prove to be reliable mates in the long run, they still offer the prize of a genetic endowment tending toward dominance and attractiveness. If the distal (evolutionary) goal is to pass one's own genes to succeeding generations, then the unrestricted female who mates with attractive and dominant men enjoys the potential advantage of seeing those traits of attractiveness and dominance replicated in her own offspring. Should these offspring survive to maturity, they themselves may be blessed with an advantage in the mating marketplace. This should be especially apparent in male offspring, or what Simpson and Gangestad refer to as "sexy sons." If a woman's son grows up to be especially attractive and dominant, then he is relatively well positioned

to mate with many different women, potentially passing his own (and his mother's) genes down to the next generation.

If the above reasoning is correct, then the woman exhibiting unrestricted sociosexuality should maximize her genetic fitness in the production of sons, for the "sexy son" may potentially sire a greater number of offspring than the most fertile (and attractive) daughter could ever produce. One would predict, therefore, that natural selection should have arranged things such that unrestricted women should give birth to more sons than should women with a restricted sociosexual orientation. Gangestad and Simpson provide some very limited but tantalizing support for this startling hypothesis, drawing upon data on sexual attitudes and behavior of Americans collected by Alfred Kinsey in the late 1940s and 50s (Gangestad, 1989; Gangestad & Simpson, 1990). Using reported number of premarital sexual partners as a rough index of sociosexuality in women, Simpson and Gangestad found a very modest but statistically significant correlation between number of premarital partners and the tendency to bear male children. Those women who scored in the top 5% of sociosexuality (greatest number of premarital sexual partners) had close to 60% boys, compared with 50% for those women at the bottom of the distribution (fewest number of premarital sexual partners).

Simpson and Gangestad conclude that "both unrestricted and restricted female strategies may, in our evolutionary past have been potentially viable: a restricted strategy enhancing parental investment; an unrestricted strategy enhancing the reproductive abilities of surviving male offspring" (Gangestad & Simpson, 1990, p. 81). Their work suggests that human nature allows for evolutionarily grounded individual differences in reproductive strategies. These differences may be associated with particular personality traits (such as dominance, nurturance, and reliability) that prove especially adaptive in certain kinds of environmental situations and under certain kinds of selection pressures.

the person who had it, providing first choice of food, romantic partners, living space, and whatever other desirable commodities and privileges the group afforded, ultimately promoting reproductive success. Therefore, human beings are mandated by human nature to seek attention and status, to seek to be liked and to be powerful. As Hogan puts it, "getting along and getting ahead are the two great problems in life that each person must solve" (Hogan et al., 1985, p. 178).

These two great problems are always addressed and resolved, argues Hogan, in the context of ritualized social interaction. As sociologists such as George Herbert Mead (1934) and Erving Goffman (1959) maintained, social behavior is an elaborate game, governed by rules and conventions, scripted into roles and routines, and mastered by the most skillful game players among us. Hogan suggests that this was just as true in the EEA as it is today. This is also true of the most informal aspects of living (morning coffee) and the most formal (a presidential inauguration), of the most trivial social interactions (passing strangers in the hallway) and the most personally meaningful (proposing marriage). Like actors on a stage, persons must play roles and follow scripts so that their "performances" in society can be affirmed and rewarded by their "audiences," who are also fellow "actors and actresses." Those human beings who adapt most successfully in a given society—those who are highly popular and powerful—know how and when to play the most effective roles and to engage in the most appropriate social rituals in the society. They are able to present themselves in ways that make positive and significant impressions on others. This is not to trivialize social behavior, nor to suggest that it is natural for people to be insincere. Rather, role playing and impression management are unconscious, central, genetic tendencies for all human beings. Hogan writes:

> Self-presentation and impression management are not trivial party games. They are fundamental processes, rooted in our history as group-living animals. They are archaic, powerful, compulsive tendencies that are closely tied to our chances for survival and reproductive success. (Hogan et al., 1985, p. 181)

Furthermore, role playing and impression management are the major mechanisms through which we define who we are as social beings. The distal, evolutionary goal of life is to produce viable progeny so that the individual's genes can be passed down to the next generation. To achieve this goal, however, the person must first find a part to play, a social identity that specifies a recognized niche in the community. Once such an identity is found, the person must employ role playing and impression management to sustain that identity.

Hogan argues that the expected audience for a person's self-presentational behaviors changes. In childhood, family members (especially parents) are the most important audience. Our ways of displaying the self to them come to comprise our **character structure.** In adulthood, the audience broadens to include colleagues, friends, peers, one's children, and even society at large. The characteristic ways in which we display ourselves to this larger audience become our **role structure.** But the earlier character structure does not go away. Rather, it lingers on as a set of unconscious rules for social interaction, Hogan asserts. Identity conflicts in adulthood may turn on the discordance between unconscious character structure and conscious role structure, as when the blue-collar, working-class boy rises into the professional white-collar echelons of adult society. He may find it difficult to feel comfortable with an elite role structure that so contradicts the street-wise, tough-guy posture that carried him through his childhood years.

In sum, evolution has shaped the human mind to adapt to group life in the EEA. Although you (most likely) did not grow up in a nomadic community of hunters and

Robert Hogan developed the socioanalytic theory of personality. According to Hogan, "getting along" and "getting ahead" are the two prime challenges of social life for humans today, as they were in the environment of evolutionary adaptedness.

gatherers, human natures owes its defining properties to the hundreds of thousands of years wherein your ancestors lived as such. In the EEA as today, getting along and getting ahead were the dominant imperatives for social life. Failures in these two domains could lead to dire consequences for survival and reproduction. As in the EEA, we first learn how to get along and get ahead in the family. According to socioanalytic theory, these early experiences produce an unconscious character structure that influences personality development and expression for the rest of life. Outside the family, we learn about getting along and getting ahead in peer groups and in the larger social community, resulting in the development of a role structure. Therefore, we are designed by human nature to apprehend social life on at least two levels—personal character and social role. While our character structures may tell us one thing in a given situation, our role structures may demand another. Many of the most challenging dilemmas in social life, whether you are talking about the EEA or yesterday, stem from our efforts to get along and to get ahead in families, peer groups, and the wider social world.

HURTING, HELPING, AND LOVING: THREE FACES OF HUMAN NATURE

When I wonder about human nature, I find that my thoughts follow the front pages and feature stories of the newspaper. When headlines scream of war and murder, I am likely to ponder the dark side of it all. Will we eventually kill ourselves off? Will the aggressive forces within win out over human reason and goodness? But just when it all seems pretty bleak, I may happen upon a story of remarkable bravery or kindness. A doctor gives up a lucrative career to fight AIDS in an African village. A mother sacrifices her own life to save her child. Stories of hurting, helping, and loving are among the most compelling narratives in contemporary life, as I suspect they were even in the EEA. These stories describe three different faces of human nature, which sustain three topics of perennial interest for personality psychology—human aggression, altruism, and attachment. What might an understanding of human evolution teach us about each of these?

AGGRESSION

The oldest epic story bequeathed to us by the ancient Greeks is a story of war. From the 8th century B.C.E., Homer begins *The Iliad* with the rage of Achilles:

> *Rage—Goddess, sing the rage of Peleus' son Achilles,*
>
> *murderous, doomed, that cost the Achaeans countless losses,*
>
> *hurling down to the House of Death so many sturdy souls,*
>
> *great fighters' souls, but made their bodies carrion,*
>
> *feasts for the dogs and birds,*
>
> *and the will of Zeus was moving toward its end.*
>
> *Begin, Muse, when the two first broke and clashed,*

Agamemnon lord of men and brilliant Achilles.

What god drove them to fight with such a fury?

(Fagles, trans., 1990, p. 77)

Homer wonders what drove the doomed protagonists of the Trojan War to fight with such a fury. It was the gods, he concludes. But today we might speculate about the many proximal insults, frustrations, and deprivations that drive men to do battle in war. And we might speculate about the distal legacy of human evolution, the adaptive function of brutal aggressiveness in the EEA. Given the virtual universality of warfare across human cultures and over recorded time, and given the fossil evidence to suggest that organized group killings were probably a rather common social phenomenon in the EEA, it is difficult to avoid the conclusion that going to war is something that human beings, in particular male human beings, have been selected by nature to do, an outgrowth of human evolution. This is not to suggest that warfare is good or inevitable, only that human beings seem naturally inclined to engage in this sort of activity, with typically deadly results. In terms of evolutionary theory, E. O. Wilson (1978) has speculated that war has typically resulted from the rupture of the intricate and powerful fabric of the territorial taboos observed in social groups. An outgrowth of human sociality, territoriality is reinforced by the feeling of kinship and affinity that one has toward relatives, fellow citizens, and/or those with whom one shares ideological beliefs. A major force behind many warlike campaigns is ethnocentrism—the tendency of human beings to ally themselves with their own groups and to distrust deeply those groups that are not one's own. In warfare, states, tribes, and other social groups marshal forces and organize aggressive actions to defend or expand their respective geographic, cultural, ethnic, or ideological turfs.

Human warfare is the deadliest and most dramatic expression of human aggression. The myriad incidents of human violence and cruelty that you have read about, seen on television, and witnessed in your own life are all manifestations of aggression. As I write this, the United States is actively involved in two wars (one in Iraq and one in Afghanistan), each of which brings daily death and destruction. Outside the carnage of combat, American soldiers and intelligence officers have been implicated in sadistic attacks on Iraqi inmates in the Baghdad prison at Abu Grahib. Last week, terrorists killed more than 300 Russian children and teachers in a grade school in Chechnya. Tens of thousands have lost their lives this year in ethnic genocide in the Sudan. And just this morning the newspapers report that North Korea may have recently tested a nuclear bomb. We are, by nature, a *moderately aggressive* species, writes E. O. Wilson (1978), a claim that strikes me as a slight understatement. An instinctual predisposition to aggression, encoded indirectly in the human genome, has likely proven adaptive over the long course of human evolution, enabling the more aggressive to survive longer and reproduce with more success. However, human aggression is extremely flexible and malleable, Wilson maintains, and is subject to the limits and opportunities provided by society, learning, and context.

Across the animal kingdom, intraspecies aggression is often ritualistic, involving only threats rather than real attacks. When fights do break out, the combatants often seem to be instinctively guided by inhibitory mechanisms that stop the fighting short of death and serious injury. For example, a dog who is the loser in a fight may present its unprotected neck to the mouth of the victorious dog or roll over on its back to expose its vulnerable underside (Lorenz, 1969). Such an appeasement gesture signals that the fight is over and that the victor emerges dominant. Some observers have argued that this kind of ritualistic

Human aggression can be displayed in a wide range of behaviors, from domestic violence to sports. In warfare, aggression is organized to achieve various political, economic, or ideological ends.

fighting and mock aggression serves to establish stable dominance hierarchies in certain advanced animal societies. Dominance hierarchies, in turn, may promote the more efficient use of resources and space in a given group's habitat (Wynne-Edwards, 1963/1978). By establishing and affirming the status of dominant and submissive members of the group, instinctive ritualistic aggression may serve to decrease actual intraspecies violence.

While this view of benign aggression in the animal kingdom has some merit, more recent studies of hyenas, lions, monkeys, chimpanzees, and certain other species paint a much more menacing picture of intraspecies violence. Lethal fighting, cannibalism, and group warfare are observable in a number of nonhuman species. One of the most gruesome examples is *competitive infanticide,* documented in the Indian monkeys, Hanuman langurs (Konner, 1983). Langur social groups consist of a hierarchy of related females with their offspring and a small number of males attached to the group, often for a year or more. From time to time, new males appear on the scene, drive out the old males, and take over. Within a few days they may kill all infants under the age of 6 months and then reimpregnate the infants' mothers. One can explain such brutality in terms of inclusive fitness. By killing off the owners of competing genes (the children sired by their predecessors) and by producing new offspring to replace them, the new langur males are maximizing the chances of passing on their own genes.

Infanticide is by no means unknown to human societies (see Bakan, 1971), but one is hard pressed to find human examples as grotesque as the langur monkeys. Nonetheless, graphic examples of horrific human violence abound. Konner (1983) suggests that singling out the most violent of human societies—such as the Yanomamo culture of highland Venezuela, the Plains Indians of the United States, the Zulu of southern Africa, the Germans of the Third Reich—is the easy way out in proving the argument that human beings are innately aggressive. More instructive and interesting, he maintains, is to examine the *least violent* societies. A case example is the Semai of Malaysia, a very simple society described as a paragon of peacefulness and tranquility. Dentan (1968) reports that before the 1950s, the Semai knew virtually nothing of war, murder, or violence. Almost all forms of instrumental and hostile aggression were nonexistent in Semai society. This all changed for a time in the early 1950s, when the British recruited troops among the Semai to fight a communist insurgency in the region. Initially lured into the military by high wages and pretty clothes, gentle Semai men proved to be amazing fighters:

> Many people who knew the Semai insisted that such an unwarlike people could never make good soldiers. Interestingly enough, they were wrong. Communist terrorists had killed the kinsmen of some of the Semai counterinsurgency troops. Taken out of their nonviolent society and ordered to kill, they seem to have been swept up in a sort of insanity which they call "blood drunkenness." A typical veteran's story runs like this. "We killed, killed, killed. The Malays would stop and go through people's pockets and take their watches or money. We only thought of killing. Wah, truly we were drunk with blood." One man even told how he drank the blood of a man he had killed. (Konner, 1983, p. 205)

Though one case study cannot prove any generalization, the case of the Semai is provocative and capable of bolstering a number of divergent views of human nature. Those who see human nature through a glass darkly are likely to interpret the aggressive behavior of the Semai as a dramatic triumph of instinctual potential over environmental learning. Even this most peaceful group of men—trained from birth to eschew all violence—was capable of surprising acts of brutality in war. On the other hand, those who prefer to explain human aggression in the proximal terms of learning and cultural influences can argue that the inexperienced Semai were merely *conforming,* with shocking gusto, to the norms of warfare imposed upon them by an alien culture. That the Semai eventually returned to a peaceful way of life after the war, many seemingly baffled by their unorthodox behavior in battle, may be a tribute to the power of culture to control aggression. But it still leaves us wondering how a people so trained to live in peace could suddenly transform themselves into bloodthirsty warriors.

ALTRUISM

If natural selection pulled human nature in the direction of aggression, how do we reconcile the many examples that we can summon forth in which humans exhibit compassion and care, engage in acts of stupendous altruism, and sometimes even sacrifice their own lives for the sake of others? One possible answer is that human aggression and human altruism are really two sides of the same evolutionary coin. Both spring from the fundamental feature of human life in the EEA: *We evolved to live in groups.* Group life is all about competition and cooperation—getting ahead, but also getting along. Like many primate groups, human societies are structured hierarchically (deWaal, 1996). Members of the group jockey for position and status, and those who fight their way to the top command considerable power over their less aggressive and less effective peers. DeWaal (1996) writes: "The desire to dictate the behavior of others is such a timeless and universal attribute of our species that it must rank with the sex drive, maternal instinct, and the will to survive in terms of the likelihood of its being part of our biological heritage" (p. 98). Aggression can be a powerful tool in the quest for social dominance, especially among males. But dominance hierarchies also create the kind of stability and order necessary for the establishment of cooperation, sharing, and social support in the group. "Without agreement on rank and a certain respect for authority there can be no great sensitivity to social rules," writes deWaal (1996, p. 92). "Despite its grounding in competition, the hierarchy is essentially a tool of cooperation and social integration" (p. 123).

Human beings have evolved to be both aggressive and altruistic because both proved adaptive for group life in the EEA (deWaal, 1996; McAndrew, 2002; E. O. Wilson, 1978). Indeed, group life would be unthinkable without both: To the extent that dominance hierarchies are established in and through the aggressive activities of competing individuals, a tendency toward aggression indirectly supports cooperation, caring, and altruistic behavior by ultimately working to establish the social stability and structure that communal human activities require. Of course, aggression can also rip society apart, so natural mechanisms must evolve and cultural norms must be established to keep antisocial aggression more-or-less under control. Because we are by nature an exquisitely social species, human beings have evolved to be "moral animals," writes Wright (1994). "Universally, human communities are moral communities; a morally neutral existence is as impossible for us as a completely solitary existence," writes deWaal (1996, p. 10).

Although human beings can be highly aggressive, they can also display remarkable instances of cooperation, helping, and altruism. Here, members of a Pakistani Muslim relief society provide aid for victims of the south Asian tsunami, in January 2005.

The origins of human morality can be traced back to three conditions of group life in the Pleistocene (deWaal, 1996). First is the condition of *group value:* Individual human beings depended on the group for finding food and defense against enemies and predators. Second is *mutual aid:* Individuals cooperated with one another in group activities and engaged in reciprocal exchange within the group. Third is *internal conflict:* Individual members had disparate interests and competed with one another for resources, status, and so on. Given these three conditions, argues deWaal (1996), intragroup conflict needed to be resolved by balancing individual and collective interests. Such conflict resolution can be accomplished at the dyadic level and at higher levels of social structure. At the *dyadic level,* individuals engage in one-on-one interaction, such as direct reciprocation of aid and reconciliation following fights. At *higher levels,* community concern and care about good relationships between individuals are expressed in mediated reconciliation, peaceful arbitration of disputes, appreciation of altruistic behavior in the group, and group encouragement of individual contributions to the quality of the social environment overall.

What features of human nature have enabled human beings to live effectively in groups and to establish the rudiments of human morality? DeWaal (1996) argues for the existence of biologically ingrained tendencies toward sympathy, reciprocity, rule-making, and peacemaking (Table 2.2). Like many primate species, human beings are naturally inclined to bond with one another and share emotional experiences. In addition, we are blessed with the cognitive ability to imagine another person's subjective experience, a form of empathy that strongly promotes altruistic behavior (Hoffman, 1981). The concepts of giving, trading, and revenge come readily to the human mind, deWaal maintains, suggesting that human beings have evolved to be especially sensitive to the issue of fairness in social life. Indeed, when norms of fairness are broken, we may naturally feel a strong desire for moralistic aggression, revealing the deep and intricate connections between helping and hurting. At the same time, primate and human groups operate according to principles and practices aimed to minimize the kinds of conflicts that seriously disrupt group harmony. Social animals require stable group structures if they, the social animals themselves, are to survive and pass their genes down to the next generation.

Because biologically related animals share some of the same genes, certain species are predisposed to engage in helping behavior *that benefits their relatives* (parents, children, siblings, and grandchildren, for the most part). Through **kin selection,** parents may sacrifice their own interests to benefit their children and thereby increase the likelihood of passing down their own genes, through their offspring, to subsequent generations. Siblings are inclined to help each other; to promote the survival and reproductive success of a sibling is to increase the chances of passing down the genes siblings have in common. In general, the

TABLE 2.2	THE ORIGINS OF HUMAN MORALITY AND ALTRUISM

Sympathy-related tendencies
    Emotional bonding between humans
    Learned adjustment to and special treatment of the disabled and injured
    Cognitive empathy: ability to see the world from another's point of view

Norm-related characteristics
    Tendency to develop prescriptive social rules
    Tendency to internalize the rules and anticipate rewards and punishments

Reciprocity
    A concept of giving, trading, and revenge
    Moralistic aggression against violators of reciprocity rules

Getting along
    Peacemaking and avoidance of conflict
    Accommodation of conflicting interests through negotiation
    Community concern and desire to maintain good relationships

SOURCE: From *Good Natured: The Origins of Right and Wrong in Humans and Other Animals,* by F. deWaal, 1996, Cambridge, MA: Harvard University Press.

closer the blood relationship, the greater the likelihood of altruism. Thus, we are biologically more strongly predisposed to help our children, brothers, or sisters than our cousins, uncles, or aunts. In general, altruism based on kin selection is most likely to occur (a) among closely related rather than distantly related individuals, (b) among individuals who live in close-knit and geographically limited societies wherein they are likely to share kinship ties, and (c) among species capable of recognizing relatives and distinguishing them from nonrelatives.

Even biologically unrelated members of the same species may be motivated to help each other if the helping is likely to result in selective advantages for both (Trivers, 1971). Individuals of certain species, therefore, may be instinctually predisposed to make implicit bargains with each other because such bargains ultimately increase their own reproductive success. For instance, rhesus monkeys, baboons, and anthropoid apes are known to form coalitions based on mutual assistance, while chimpanzees, gibbons, African wild dogs, and wolves beg for food from each other reciprocally (Wilson, 1978). Such **reciprocal altruism** is more likely to occur when the situation involves (a) low risk for the helper, (b) high benefit for the recipient, and (c) high likelihood that the situation will be reversed in the future.

From an evolutionary standpoint, therefore, altruistic behavior is most likely to occur either (a) among closely related individuals (kin selection) or (b) when the cost–benefit ratio for the helper is ultimately favorable (reciprocal altruism). Both forms exist among humans, E. O. Wilson (1978) argues, but the second is far more important for the survival and success of human societies, because it is endlessly flexible and capable of producing strong emotional bonds between completely unrelated peoples. Human beings help each other in a variety of ways for many reasons, but the motivation for much of the helpful behavior, maintains Wilson, is the implicit expectation that the helper will someday be rewarded. This implicit expectation motivates us to surrender our own self-interests, on occasion, for the good of others. Writes E. O. Wilson (1978), "lives of the most towering heroism are paid out in the [conscious or unconscious] expectation of great reward, not the least of which is a belief in personal immortality" (p. 154).

ATTACHMENT

It is universally true that human infants fall in love with their mothers and other caregivers in the first year of life. In all known human cultures, babies bond to their caregivers by the time they reach their first birthday. The extraordinarily rare exceptions to this rule may be seen in profoundly disabled children (e.g., severe brain damage) and sometimes in children who suffer from the rare psychological disorder of autism. That a bond of love should and will develop between the infant and the caregiver in the first year of human life is as notable a feature of human nature as is the tendency for human beings to be born with two eyes, or to walk on two legs as children, or to develop language, or to desire sexual experiences once they pass through puberty. As with human vision, upright posture, language, and sexual desire, the bond of love that ties children to their caregivers evolved to become part of human nature during the Pleistocene epoch and before, functioning to solve adaptational problems that faced our group-living, hunting-and-gathering forebears. How does this bond work? How does it develop? And what problems does it solve?

One of the most influential theories in psychology today is *attachment theory,* developed by John Bowlby and Mary Ainsworth. In his classic three-volume set entitled *Attachment and Loss* (1969, 1973, 1980) and in his last book entitled *A Secure Base* (1988), John Bowlby articulated a grand theory of the dynamics of affectional bonds in human life. The theory couches the sublime experience of human love in the no-nonsense language of natural selection and shows how attachments between human beings have proven exquisitely adaptive over the long course of human evolution. Mary Ainsworth pioneered the assessment and understanding of individual differences in attachment bonds, showing how the quality of early caregiver–infant interaction may have long-term effects on personality (Ainsworth, 1967, 1969, 1989; Ainsworth, Blehar, Waters, & Wall, 1978; Ainsworth & Bowlby, 1991). In recent years, attachment theory has generated a great deal of developmental research focused on infancy and childhood. The theory has also been extended in creative ways into the arenas of adult attachment histories (Main, Kaplan, & Cassidy, 1985) and attachment styles in romantic love (Hazan & Shaver, 1987, 1990).

Along with John Bowlby, Mary Ainsworth pioneered research and theory on caregiver-infant attachment. Ainsworth developed the "strange situation" procedure to measure individual differences in attachment security.

Attachment in Infancy

Virtually no other human experience feels so "natural" as the love we feel for our babies. The **attachment** bond between caregiver (mother, father, or other who cares for the baby) and infant develops through a number of well-defined stages in the first years of the child's life. It begins with the newborn's vague and nondiscriminant orientation to social stimuli, develops through a phase of heightened sociality in which 2 to 7-month-olds smile and show various attachment behaviors toward people, and ends as an affectional partnership between the child and a select few clearly discriminated and preferred caregivers (Ainsworth et al., 1978; Bowlby, 1969). Although many cultural differences can be observed, the caregiver–infant attachment bond appears to develop in approximately the same manner in virtually all known human societies (Bowlby, 1969; Konner, 1983). The attachment experience may feel so natural because it is indeed an integral part of human nature.

In behavioral terms, attachment refers to seeking and maintaining proximity to another individual. Caregivers and infants seek to be physically close to each other and to engage in tender physical contact. Ethologists have regularly observed attachment behavior in nonhuman primates, such as apes and rhesus monkeys. These behavioral patterns are generally considered to have a strong instinctual base. For instance, newborn rhesus monkeys, in the first few weeks of life, are in constant contact with their mothers, spending virtually all daytime hours gripping mother with their hands, feet, and mouth, and being held by her at nighttime. As they get older, the monkeys begin to venture away from mother, making tentative initial forays of a few feet and then checking back with mother as if to see if all is still well. During most of the first year of life, the rhesus monkey uses its mother as a secure base from which to explore the world and as a source of comfort during times of fear and anxiety.

Bowlby (1969, 1973, 1980) argues that the caregiver–infant attachment bond is a *complex, instinctually guided behavioral system that has functioned throughout human evolution to protect the infant from predators.* In the hunting-and-gathering way of life of our ancestors, attachment improved an organism's inclusive fitness by increasing the likelihood that his or her genes would survive and be passed down. By ensuring that mothers and infants would seek contact and physical closeness with each other, the attachment system made it easier for older and stronger caregivers to protect their dependent and defenseless human infants from threats to their survival and ultimate reproductive success.

Bowlby conceives of attachment as a goal-directed system designed to ensure the overall end of caregiver–infant proximity. The system comprises a number of subsystems, called **attachment behaviors,** including sucking, clinging, following, vocalizing, and smiling. Infants emit attachment behaviors that beckon caregivers to seek or maintain physical closeness or contact. Although each attachment behavior follows its own independent

The development of a caregiver-infant attachment bond is a beautiful feature of human nature. Attachment evolved to promote the survival and protection of human infants in the environment of evolutionary adaptedness.

developmental course in the first few months of human life, attachment behaviors become organized and integrated during the second half of the first year. Thus, newborn infants will cry and cling, but they do not show true smiles in response to social stimuli until about 2 months of age, and they are not able to follow mother until they are able to crawl, months after the first smile. Crying, clinging, smiling, following, and other discrete attachment behaviors, however, begin to work together after 6 or 7 months to achieve mother–infant proximity. During this time, infants begin to show clear preferences for mothers, fathers, and other *attachment objects* in their environments, engaging in a variety of behavioral combinations to promote proximity with attachment objects. These behavioral combinations are subtle and flexible instinctual strategies for relating to others, markedly influenced by learning and experience but deeply ingrained in human biology.

With respect to emotional development, the attachment system organizes the earliest experiences of human love and fear (Bowlby, 1969, 1973; Sroufe & Waters, 1977). Toward the end of the first year of life, infants begin to experience *stranger anxiety and separation anxiety,* two benchmarks of normal psychological development. At this time, infants begin to express caution and fear in the face of novel events and objects and when confronted with strangers. Stranger fear makes evolutionary sense, Bowlby suggests, for unfamiliar objects and persons have been associated with threat and dangers throughout evolution. The presence of the attachment object, however, can go a long way to relieve the fear that infants experience when faced with strangers and novelty. The felt security experienced in the attachment bond makes new and strange things seem less threatening and dangerous, as indeed they usually are, and have usually been throughout our evolutionary past, when human infants are in the presence of their caregivers.

When separated from their main caregivers, even for a short period of time, 8-month and older infants may show considerable distress, manifested in extreme wariness or crying. Brief separations from the caregiver are relatively harmless inevitabilities of everyday life, but long separations may be problematic. Feelings of abandonment are the most emotionally painful experiences human beings can know, Bowlby suggests. The pain is deeply rooted in the evolutionary fact that parental abandonment of the infant usually means death. This is why parental threats of abandonment are especially frightening to children and, when issued repeatedly, especially detrimental to healthy personality development. This is also why the experience of prolonged separation from one's attachment object may initiate a process of "mourning," through which the infant or child adjusts, over the period of weeks and months, to the perceived loss of the caregiver. In mourning, the infant will move through stages of angry *protest, despair* and *sadness*, and finally *detachment* (Bowlby, 1973). Detachment marks a defensive severance of the attachment bond. As a tragic example of detachment, observations of infants who have been removed from their caregivers for long periods of time, as during times of war, show that many infants will appear not to recognize their caregivers when they are eventually reunited (Bowlby, 1973). In these cases, the attachment has been emotionally undone.

Over the normal course of the first 2 to 3 years of life, the child builds up a set of expectations about the nature of relationships with other people. The expectations come to comprise a **working model.** Writes Bowlby (1973), "in the working model of the world that anybody builds, a key feature is his notion of who his attachment figures are, where they may be found, and how they may be expected to respond" (p. 203). The working model serves as an internalized template of love (Shaver & Rubenstein, 1980). When the attachment bond is *secure,* the infant may experience a basic trust in his or her surroundings, which provides the self-confidence to explore the world with enthusiasm and aplomb (Erikson, 1963; Sroufe & Waters, 1977). In the best attachment relationships, the human infant, like the rhesus monkey discussed earlier, uses the attachment object as a *secure base* from which to explore the world. When the attachment bond is generally *insecure,* however, the infant may come to consider the world a threatening and dangerous place. Out of this early pessimism about life, the child formulates a working model of the attachment object that underscores uncertainty and rejection. A working model of an inconsistent and rejecting attachment object may lead to subsequent deficits in self-esteem and a lasting vulnerability to loneliness (Bowlby, 1980; Shaver & Rubenstein, 1980).

Virtually all babies become attached to a caregiver in the first year of life. Yet there are significant individual differences in the *quality* of that attachment relationship, and these differences can be measured. By the time the infant is 1 year old, individual differences in attachment quality are apparent. The most popular laboratory method for assessing these individual differences in 1-year-olds is the **Strange Situation** method, developed by Ainsworth and her colleagues (Ainsworth et al., 1978). The Strange Situation involves a series of short laboratory episodes through which the infant, the caregiver (usually mother, sometimes father), and a "stranger" (usually a woman who is working with the experimenter) interact in a comfortable setting and the behaviors of the infant are observed

(Table 2.3). The infant and caregiver arrive and get comfortable; the stranger enters; the caregiver leaves for a short period of time; the caregiver returns, and the stranger leaves; the caregiver exits again, leaving the infant alone; the stranger reenters; and the caregiver finally returns again. Researchers analyze the behavior of the infant in all of the episodes of the Strange Situation, paying special attention to the two "reunion episodes" in which the caregiver returns after a brief separation.

Behavioral observations in the Strange Situation yield three different general patterns of attachment in what have been termed **A-babies, B-babies,** and **C-babies.** Between one-half and two-thirds of mother–baby pairs show *secure attachment.* The infants in these pairs are termed B-babies. Like most of the babies studied, securely attached infants find the brief separation from the caregiver and the entrance of strangers to be at least mildly upsetting. This is a normal manifestation of mistrust shown by virtually all infants, regardless of their attachment classifications, after about 8 months of age or so, at which time separation anxiety and stranger anxiety naturally emerge. However, when the caregiver is present, B-babies explore their environments with great ease and comfort, using the caregiver as a secure base. When the caregiver leaves, they show much less exploration, but when the caregiver returns again in the reunion episodes, they greet the caregiver with great enthusiasm and resume their exploration of the environment.

A-babies and C-babies show patterns of *insecure attachment.* The pattern for A-babies is termed *avoidant.* A-babies are most noted for their tendency to avoid the caregiver in the reunion episodes, as if to say, "Hey! You abandoned me; I'll do the same to you for a while." The pattern of insecure attachment for C-babies is termed *resistant.* C-babies show a mixture of approach and avoidance behavior in the reunion episodes of the Strange Situation. When the caregiver returns after the brief separations, the C-baby may approach the caregiver in a friendly manner but then angrily resist being picked up. C-babies are noted for

TABLE 2.3	EPISODES IN THE "STRANGE SITUATION" PROCEDURE FOR ASSESSING INDIVIDUAL DIFFERENCES IN ATTACHMENT	

Episode	Who Is Involved	What Happens
1	Caregiver, Infant	After being introduced to the room and the many toys it contains, the caregiver (mother or father) sits and looks at a magazine while the infant explores the room and its contents.
2	Stranger, Caregiver, Infant	A woman whom the infant has never seen before enters, greets caregiver, and sits silently for 1 minute. Then the woman engages caregiver in a conversation. Finally she initiates interaction with the infant.
3	Stranger, Infant	Caregiver quietly leaves room. If infant becomes too distressed, the episode is terminated.
4	Caregiver, Infant	Caregiver returns and stranger leaves. This is the first "reunion episode." Caregiver seeks to interest the infant in the toys.
5	Infant	After the infant appears to be comfortable again, caregiver leaves.
6	Stranger, Infant	The stranger enters again. She initiates interaction with the infant. If the infant prefers to play alone, the stranger retreats to a chair and reads a magazine.
7	Caregiver, Infant	Caregiver returns and stranger leaves. This is the second "reunion episode.

NOTE: Each of the episodes is approximately 3 minutes in length. All of the proceedings are observed by researchers behind a one-way mirror. Usually, the episodes are videotaped as well and later analyzed in various ways.

their angry reactions to the caregiver, though they occasionally show passive reactions as well, similar to the standard patterns shown by A-babies.

After about 20 months of age, the Strange Situation is no longer an effective measure for attachment security. Therefore, developmental psychologists have created a number of alternative attachment measures for older children and adolescents, such as rating scales designed to assess individual differences in the level of security people feel in their closest interpersonal relationships. Individual differences in attachment quality appear to be somewhat stable in the first few years of life. In other words, securely attached infants at age 1 tend on average to remain securely attached for the next few years, although changes have also been observed; insecurely attached infants tend to remain insecurely attached, although again there are many exceptions. A recent review of 22 longitudinal studies of attachment patterns indicates that while individuals do show considerable change in attachment security over the course of the first two decades of life, individual differences still show modest levels of stability from age 1 to the late-adolescent years (Fraley, 2002).

Developmental psychologists have undertaken investigations to determine what factors produce patterns of secure and insecure attachment in the first year of life. The quality of the early interaction between caregivers and infants may play an important role. In this regard, Main (1981) has shown that mothers of securely attached infants tend to hold their babies more carefully and tenderly and for longer periods of time during early infancy than do mothers of insecurely attached babies. Studies have shown that maternal sensitivity is also a consistent predictor of attachment (Ainsworth et al., 1978; Egeland & Farber, 1984; NICHD Early Child Care Research Network, 2001; Sroufe, 1985). A mother who is especially sensitive to her baby is "alert to perceive her baby's signals, interprets them accurately, and responds appropriately and promptly" (Ainsworth et al., 1978, p. 142). Observations of mothers and babies at home and in the laboratory during the infant's first 3 months suggest that mothers of infants who are later classified as securely attached respond more frequently to crying, show more affection when holding the baby, are more likely to acknowledge the baby with a smile or conversation when entering the baby's room, and are better at feeding the baby because of their attention to the baby's signals, compared with mothers of babies later deemed insecurely attached. One study of mothers and 12-month-old infants observed twice at home for two hours by two researchers shows a strong relation between secure attachment and maternal sensitivity (Pederson et al., 1990). Mothers of more secure infants were more frequently characterized as noticing their babies' signals and using the signals to guide their behavior; they also were more knowledgeable about their infants and appeared to enjoy them more than mothers of less secure infants.

Social class does not appear to be directly related to attachment classification (Spieker & Booth, 1988). Children from poor and working-class families are no less likely to establish secure attachments than middle-class and upper-class children, as long as cases of known abuse or neglect are eliminated from the samples. However, the stresses of poverty and unemployment may increase the likelihood of abuse and neglect, and therefore negative effects of disadvantaged social class may manifest themselves indirectly. Research suggests that children of abusive parents are indeed at risk for insecure attachment (Egeland & Sroufe, 1981). For example, Lyons-Ruth, Connell, Zoll, and Stahl (1987) found that maltreated infants were more avoidant of their mothers in the Strange Situation than nonmaltreated infants. Other studies suggest that chronic child abuse may promote the development of a "disorganized" attachment pattern—the **D-baby** (Carlson, Cicchetti, Barnett, & Braunwald, 1989). D-babies appear confused and disoriented in the presence of mother. Within this seriously disturbed pattern of attachment, the child appears to do little exploring in the mother's presence, and the mother appears unable to calm the child during periods of distress. It is as if the infant perceives her to be as threatening as, or even more threatening than, the rest of the environment. In a review of research on attachment and behavioral problems in children, Lyons-Ruth (1996) found that infants with disorganized attachment patterns (D-babies) tend to show heightened levels of aggression when they reach grade school, compared with children whose attachment classifications in infancy were A, B, or C.

A large body of research supports the general hypothesis that secure attachment in infancy leads to greater levels of mastery and competence in the preschool years and into elementary school (Schneider, Atkinson, & Rardif, 2001). A representative study in this regard was conducted by Hazen and Durrett (1982). Children aged 30 to 34 months who had been assessed at 12 months for security of attachment were observed exploring with their mothers in a large laboratory playhouse. The researchers measured how much exploration the children showed according to the number of different movements the child made from one area of the playhouse to another, and they measured the extent to which the exploration was "active" (child leads mother) as opposed to "passive" (mother leads child). The results showed that children who 2 years before had been classified as securely attached (B-babies) explored more and engaged in a greater ratio of active to passive exploration compared with children who had been classified as insecurely attached (A- and C-babies).

Other studies examining the relation between quality of attachment in the first year and indices of mastery and independence at ages 2 and 3 have found that secure attachment is positively associated with (a) higher quality of exploration (Main, 1983), (b) higher levels of pretend play (Slade, 1987), (c) greater competence in problem-solving tasks (Matas, Arend, & Sroufe, 1978), and (d) more rapid and smooth adjustments to strangers (Lutkenhaus, Grossmann, & Grossmann, 1985). Following children into elementary school, research has shown that 5-year-olds who were securely attached as infants show more persistence and resourcefulness in challenging tasks than children who in infancy were rated less securely attached (Arend, Gove, & Sroufe, 1979; Sroufe, 1983). LaFreniere and Sroufe (1985) related attachment history to a broad array of assessments of peer competence in the preschool classroom. In this study, the researchers observed 40 children aged 4 and 5 years as they interacted with one another in class. They obtained the following five measurements of competence: (a) teacher ratings of social competence, (b) peer ratings of popularity, (c) observations of the quality of children's social participation, (d) the amount of attention each child received from other children based on analysis of whom the children looked at while playing, and (e) ratings of social dominance. As Figure 2.1 shows, preschool children who were securely attached as infants scored higher on all five measures of social competence than their peers who as infants were classified as insecurely attached.

Adult Attachments

Attachment theory describes an affectional relationship between two persons through which one person provides support, protection, and a secure base for the other. The most obvious example of attachment, therefore, is the bond of love between the mature caregiver and the relatively defenseless infant. However, the dynamics of attachment may be played out in many other relationships, as well, throughout the human lifespan (Ainsworth, 1989; Bowlby, 1980). In recent years, psychologists have extended attachment theory into adulthood. To date their inquiries have focused on two ways in which attachments are influential in the adult years. First, they have examined adults' working models

---

FIGURE 2.1   PEER COMPETENCE AND ATTACHMENT HISTORY

Five-year-olds with histories of secure attachment show higher levels of peer competence in school compared with children who have histories of insecure attachment.

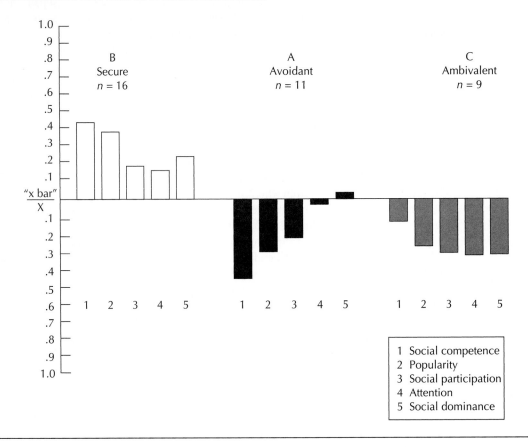

SOURCE: From "Profiles of peer competence in the preschool: Interrelations between measures, influence of social ecology, and relation to attachment history," by P.J. LaFreniere and L.A. Sroufe, *Developmental Psychology, 21,* p. 63.

of their own childhood attachments, asking adults to tell the stories of their earliest relationships (Main, 1991). Second, they have entertained the possibility that romantic love in young adulthood and beyond may be understood in terms of secure and insecure attachment qualities (Hazan & Shaver, 1987).

Mary Main and her colleagues (George, Kaplan, & Main, 1985; Main, 1991; Main, Kaplan, & Cassidy, 1985) have developed an **Adult Attachment Interview** in which men and women respond to open-ended questions about their recollections of their own childhood attachment bonds with their parents or other caregivers. The adult is asked to choose five adjectives that best describe the relationship with each parent during childhood and then to provide an account of a particular episode from childhood illustrating each adjective. Later the adult is asked to describe what he or she did when upset as a child, to which parent he or she felt closer, whether he or she ever felt rejected as a child, why the parents may have acted the way they did, how the relationships with the parents have changed over time, and how the early experiences may have affected the adult's current functioning.

Based on the interview, Main classifies each adult into one of four categories: *secure/autonomous, dismissing* of attachments, *preoccupied* by past attachments, and *unresolved* with respect to traumatic attachment-related events. Her research suggests that mothers with secure/autonomous attachments from childhood tend to raise securely attached infants themselves. Dismissing parents tend to have avoidant children (A-babies); preoccupied parents tend to have resistant children (C-babies); and mothers with unresolved attachments from childhood stemming from traumatic events such as abuse tend to have children with disorganized attachments (D-babies). In a prospective study, researchers administered the Adult Attachment Interview to pregnant women expecting their first child and then conducted the Strange Situation with their babies at age 1 year (Fonagy, Steele, & Steele, 1991). In keeping with Main's results, adult attachments of pregnant women in the interviews tended to match the subsequent attachment classifications of their infants at age 1. (See Table 2.4.)

Main (1991) describes the Adult Attachment Interviews typically produced by secure/autonomous parents with securely attached children. Such parents "focused easily on the questions; showed few departures from usual forms of narrative or discourse; easily marked the principles or rationales behind their responses; and struck judges as both collaborative and truthful" (p. 142). An essential characteristic of their interviews appears to be the ease with which they are able to provide a *coherent* account of their childhood. Whether describing positive or negative experiences from childhood, secure/autonomous adults are able to fashion a story from childhood that is consistent and convincing.

By sharp contrast, dismissing and preoccupied parents tend to be "relatively incoherent in their interview transcripts, exhibiting logical and factual contradictions; inability to stay with the interview topic; contradictions between general descriptors of their relationships with their parents and actual autobiographical episodes offered; apparent inability to access early memories; anomalous changes in wording or intrusions into topics; slips of the tongue; metaphor or rhetoric inappropriate to the discourse context; and inability to focus upon the interviews" (Main, 1991, p. 143). In particular, dismissing parents of avoidant infants are usually distinguished for their insistence that they cannot remember much from their earlier years. Often they will idealize their parents in vague terms but be unable to provide behavioral proof for their claims. Preoccupied parents of resistant infants tend to provide lengthy but rambling responses about childhood that often contradict themselves.

Finally, unresolved parents of infants displaying disorganized attachment tend to provide moderately coherent narratives of childhood, but they slip into magical and bizarre thought patterns when considering attachment-related events such as loss. "In these statements, the adult may indicate beliefs in 'magical' causality surrounding a death or other

TABLE 2.4	CORRESPONDING ATTACHMENT TYPES FROM ADULT INTERVIEWS AND OBSERVATIONS OF INFANTS
Adult Attachment Interview	**Infant Attachment Type**
Secure/autonomous	Secure (B-baby)
Dismissing	Avoidant (A-baby)
Preoccupied	Resistant (C-baby)
Unresolved	Disorganized (D-baby)

trauma, or subtly indicate a belief that a deceased attachment figure is simultaneously dead and alive" (Main, 1991, p. 145). Overall, these accounts lack *plausibility*. Just beneath the surface of a seemingly sensible narrative lie primitive and irrational thought processes linked with unresolved trauma from childhood.

A research review examined 33 studies that employed the Adult Attachment Interview, sampling more than 2,000 adults, including mothers, fathers, and teenagers, from a number of different countries (vanlJzendoorn & Bakermans-Kranenburg, 1996). Each participant in each study was classified into one of Main's first three adult attachment types and then rated independently with respect to the extent to which he or she showed any characteristics of the fourth type (unresolved). The distribution for the first three types read as follows: 58% secure/autonomous, 24% dismissing, and 18% preoccupied. In addition, 19% of the participants showed some evidence of being unresolved with respect to loss or trauma in their lives. No significant sex differences in the distribution of scores were observed. Mothers from low socioeconomic status were more likely to show dismissing attachment representations and to express unresolved trauma or loss compared with mothers from higher social classes. Secure/autonomous women and secure/autonomous men were more often married to each other than would be expected by chance, as was also the case for those showing evidence of unresolved loss and trauma. In addition, those men and women who suffered from psychopathology and mental illness of various kinds were significantly more likely to be classified in the insecure categories (dismissing, preoccupied, and unresolved) compared with nonclinical adults.

Research employing the Adult Attachment Interview suggests that working models of attachment laid down in childhood may continue to influence adult behavior in the realm of caregiving. Cindy Hazan and Philip Shaver have extended this line of thought in a different direction by suggesting that working attachment models may also influence the ways in which adults engage each other in romantic love (Hazan & Shaver, 1987, 1990). Borrowing Ainsworth's original division among B-babies, A-babies, and C-babies, Hazan and Shaver have identified three corresponding **attachment styles** in adult love. (See Table 2.5.) Adults with a secure attachment style say they find it relatively easy to get close to others and are comfortable depending on others and having others depend on them. They don't worry too much about others' getting too close. They describe their most important love experiences as happy, friendly, and trusting. They emphasize being able to accept and

---

TABLE 2.5	**ATTACHMENT STYLES**

Which of the following paragraphs best describes your feelings about being emotionally close to other people? Place a checkmark in front of the one paragraph that best describes you.

_____ I find it relatively easy to get close to others and am comfortable depending on them and having them depend on me. I don't often worry about being abandoned or about someone getting too close to me. *[Secure]*

_____ I am somewhat uncomfortable being close to others; I find it difficult to trust them completely, difficult to allow myself to depend on them. I am nervous when anyone gets too close, and often, love partners want me to be more intimate than I feel comfortable being. *[Avoidant]*

_____ I find that others are reluctant to get as close as I would like. I often worry that my partner doesn't really love me or won't want to stay with me. I want to merge completely with another person, and this desire sometimes scares people away. *[Ambivalent]*

SOURCE: From "Romantic Love Conceptualized as an Attachment Process," by C. Hazan and P. Shaver, *Journal of Personality and Social Psychology, 52,* p. 515.

support their partners despite their partners' faults. Adults with avoidant attachment styles (akin to Ainsworth's A-babies) report that they are somewhat uncomfortable being close to others and find it difficult to trust others completely. They are characterized by a "fear of intimacy," by emotional highs and lows, and by excessive jealousy. Adults with anxious/ambivalent styles (akin to Ainsworth's resistant C-babies) say they want to merge with others but that this desire sometimes scares other people away. They worry that their partners do not love them and will eventually abandon them. They experience love as involving obsession, desire for reciprocation and union, emotional highs and lows, and extreme sexual attraction and jealousy.

Employing a set of simple self-report questions concerning a person's general view of romantic love, Hazan and Shaver (1987) report that approximately 60% of their adult respondents are classified as securely attached, with the remainder falling within avoidant or anxious/ambivalent (resistant) categories. The breakdown is roughly comparable to the ratios of secure and insecure attachments obtained in research on infants. In addition, studies suggest a person's overall attachment style is predictive of love-related behavior. For example, Simpson (1990) found that secure attachment style was associated with greater relationship interdependence, commitment, trust, and satisfaction among dating college students. Mikulincer and Nachson (1991) found that students with secure and ambivalent styles exhibit greater levels of self-disclosure than avoidant students. Kobak and Hazan (1991) found that spouses with secure working models—that is, expectations that partners are psychologically available and ready to be relied upon—deal with their emotional conflicts in more constructive ways and report better marital adjustment.

Simpson, Rholes, and Phillips (1996) videotaped dating couples as they tried to resolve a major problem in their relationship. They found that participants who were classified as ambivalent with respect to attachment style tended to perceive their dating partners in especially negative terms after discussing the major relational problem. Ambivalent men and women found the activity of discussing problems in their relationships to be especially stressful, and they reacted to the stress by lowering their estimation of their partners' worth. In a related study, Simpson, Rholes, and Neligan (1992) videotaped dating couples as they sat in a waiting room before participating in an activity known to provoke anxiety in most people. The researchers coded behaviors such as physical contact, supportive comments, and efforts to seek and give emotional support. They found that those men and women classified as avoidant in attachment tended to express significantly less helping and support behavior with their partners compared with those who had secure attachment styles. In times of anxiety, people with secure attachment styles are more active and effective in providing their romantic partners with a secure base of comfort, encouragement, and support, compared with people who have avoidant styles of attachment.

For both infants and adults, the provision of support is a key function of secure attachment. Securely attached infants experience more secure support in their environments, and adults with secure attachment styles should be especially effective in supporting others when they are in danger and in seeking and finding support for themselves in times of personal stress. Mikulincer, Florian, and Weller (1993) examined reactions to the stress of war by analyzing relations between attachment style and the ways in which Israeli citizens reacted to the Iraqi missile attack in the 1991 Persian Gulf War. A total of 140 Israeli students were interviewed two weeks after the war and classified according to their attachment styles (secure, avoidant, ambivalent) and residence area (dangerous versus less dangerous area). Among students living in dangerous areas during the war (areas directly threatened by missile attack), those with secure attachment styles tended to engage in more support-seeking behavior as a way of coping with trauma, compared with avoidant and ambivalent students. In addition, ambivalent students in high-danger zones reported the highest levels of distress following the war while avoidant students reported the highest levels of hostility and physical symptoms in response to the war.

Research also suggests that attachment styles are predictive of the vicissitudes of everyday social behavior. Tidwell, Reis, and Shaver (1996) asked 125 college students to keep behavioral diaries for a week. In the diaries, the students recorded their social interactions with friends, teachers, family members, acquaintances, romantic partners, and so on. The findings indicated that compared with ambivalent and secure individuals, students with avoidant attachment styles reported lower levels of intimacy, enjoyment, and positive emotions and higher levels of negative emotions in daily interactions, especially interactions with the opposite sex. Avoidant persons tend to structure their interactions in ways that minimize emotional closeness. Compared with avoidant and secure individuals, students with ambivalent attachment styles tended to report a wider variety of emotional experiences in their daily social interactions, reporting many emotional highs and lows in their interactions with others. Overall, then, avoidant individuals experience low levels of joy and happiness in the presence of others and, perhaps as a result, tend to keep people at a distance. Ambivalent individuals experience a rich mixture of both positive and negative interpersonal events, perhaps contributing to their mixed or conflicted working models for attachment. Secure individuals report the highest levels of positive and lowest levels of negative interactions with other people in daily social life. In a similar study, Davilla and Sargent (2003) found that students with insecure attachment styles tend to perceive greater levels of interpersonal loss in daily events compared to students with secure attachments.

Outside the realm of interpersonal relationships, attachment styles appear to be implicated in the ways in which people understand themselves as individuals and how they make sense of their lives in the past, present, and anticipated future. Individuals with secure attachment styles tend to construct a more complex and coherent image of themselves compared with avoidant and ambivalent persons, and secure and avoidant people have generally more positive views of themselves and their lives compared with ambivalent individuals (Mikulincer, 1995). People with secure attachment styles describe themselves as more curious and exploratory, compared with avoidant and ambivalent individuals, and they hold more positive attitudes about being open-minded and curious (Mikulincer, 1997). Both ambivalent and avoidant attachment styles are associated with low levels of self-esteem and with higher levels of depression (Roberts, Gotlib, & Kassel, 1996).

The crucial link between caregiver–infant attachment and adult attachment styles is the concept of inner working models. Hazan and Shaver propose that adult styles are the legacies of internalized models of relating that are laid down in infancy. Modest support for this idea comes from a study by Feeney and Noller (1990) showing that college students with secure attachment styles report relatively positive perceptions of early family relationships. By contrast, avoidant students tend to report childhood separations from their mothers, and anxious/ambivalent students describe fathers who are especially nonsupportive. In another study, researchers found that young adults with a secure attachment style produced highly detailed and well-constructed representations of their parents, emphasizing parental kindness and care, whereas those with insecure attachment styles provided sketchier accounts that emphasized ways in which their parents were punitive and unavailable (Levy, Blatt, & Shaver, 1998). For the most part, however, the precise linkage between infant attachment and adult love remains a mystery. Indeed, there are certain ways in which romantic love is *not* like attachment. Ideally, lovers are relative equals who share themselves with each other in an intimate and egalitarian manner. By contrast, attachment suggests a relation of relative nonequals—the infant attached to the stronger, wiser, more mature attachment object (McAdams, 1992a). Still, there is little doubt that lovers often function as attachment objects for each other, providing secure bases for each other's explorations in the world. The relationship between infant attachment and adult love, therefore, remains an exciting realm for future research.

SUMMARY

1. The scientific study of the person begins with a consideration of human nature, which has been forged over millions of years through human evolution. Evolution is the ultimate context for understanding the person because it provides the most systematic and encompassing scientific framework to account for how the human organism was designed and what all human beings have in common. An evolutionary approach to personality helps to specify the distal and ultimate determinants of human behavior in the overall, which may be combined with an understanding of the more proximal and immediate determinants of any particular person's behavior in order to provide a full account of human individuality.

2. Over the course of evolution, organisms are designed through natural selection to engage in behaviors that ultimately make for the replication of the genes that determine their design. An organism's inclusive fitness refers to its overall or total ability to promote the replication of its own genes from one generation to the next. Inclusive fitness is enhanced through any mechanisms or systems that make it more likely than otherwise that the person's genes, or those genes that he or she shares with biological relatives, will be passed down successfully to the next generation through progeny.

3. Human beings have evolved over a 2 to 4 million year span as hunters and gatherers living in small, migratory groups. During the long period of time during which human beings inhabited this environment of evolutionary adaptedness (EEA), they came to occupy a cognitive niche in the general evolutionary landscape. The greatest adaptive advantages for humans came mainly from their powers of computation—that is, from the power of the human mind. Endowed with considerable cognitive advantages relative to other animals, human beings used tools, developed cooperative partnerships, and eventually created complex societies to adapt to the challenges of the EEA. The human mind evolved to adapt to many different evolutionary challenges, resulting in the mind's evolution toward a loose confederation of subsystems or modules, each designed to solve an evolutionarily significant problem.

4. Over the course of evolution, human beings have faced challenges relating to survival and reproduction. Reproductive challenges include finding and keeping a sexual mate and caring for the progeny that result from sexual reproduction. Evolutionary theory can be invoked to provide distal explanations for the significant sex differences that are typically observed in the realms of human mating and reproduction. Overall, human males may have evolved to adopt mating strategies and goals that maximize the quantity of offspring they produce, pushing them in the direction of promiscuity. By contrast, human females may have evolved to adopt mating strategies and goals that maximize the quality of offspring, given that females must invest a great deal more energy and time in gestation, lactation, and eventually infant care in order to assure that the relatively few progeny they may produce will live long enough to reproduce themselves. As a result, evolutionary theory would predict that females should be relatively choosier when it comes to mating and less inclined toward multiple sexual partners.

5. As described in Hogan's socioanalytic theory of personality, human beings have evolved to live in groups wherein the prime social goals are getting along and getting ahead. Through role

playing, impression management, and effective participation in the elaborate social rituals that define cultural life, human beings seek acceptance and status in groups. Heightened acceptance and status enhance inclusive fitness.

6. Human beings are, by nature, a moderately aggressive species. Evolutionary theory provides distal explanations for the tendency of human beings to engage in many forms of instrumental and hostile aggression, including the deadliest and most organized form of aggression—human warfare. But evolutionary theory, like other explanations that invoke more proximate causes for aggression (e.g., culture, learning), cannot provide a justification for human aggressiveness; nor can it be used to articulate a moral perspective about aggression.

7. Human beings are also, by nature, an exquisitely altruistic species. Altruism and aggression are natural outgrowths of the basic feature of human life in the EEA: Humans evolved to live in groups. Human groups are hierarchical, and hierarchy is at least an indirect result of differential effectiveness in aggressive and dominant behaviors on the part of group members. Dominance hierarchies provide the stability necessary for cooperative and altruistic behavior to occur. Human beings have evolved mental systems to develop emotional attachments, empathy, internalized social rules, concepts of giving and trading, peacemaking, negotiation, community concern, and other prosocial tendencies, most shared in one form or another with other primates but developed in more complex ways in the case of humans. These evolved adaptations aim to keep aggression in check and to undergird social cooperation, which itself enhances the inclusive fitness of those who cooperate. Undergirding altruistic behavior in human beings are the mechanisms of kin selection and reciprocal altruism, both of which enhance the individual's inclusive fitness.

8. One of the most notable features of human nature is caregiver–infant attachment. Attachment theory, articulated by John Bowlby and Mary Ainsworth, suggests that the bond of love that develops between caregiver and infant is a complex, instinctually grounded behavioral system that has functioned throughout human evolution to assure mother–infant proximity and thereby to protect the infant from predators and other dangers. As the attachment relationship develops in the first few years of life, the infant builds up a set of expectations concerning human relationships, which come to comprise an internalized working model.

9. Utilizing the Strange Situation procedure, researchers have identified four different types of attachment bonds in infants: secure (B-babies), avoidant (A-babies), resistant (C-babies), and disorganized (D-babies). Secure attachment is the most common form observed; the other three are variations on insecure attachment. The consequences of secure attachment include positive indices of independence, mastery, and peer popularity in preschool and elementary school.

10. Attachments among adults have been studied in two ways. Through the Adult Attachment Interview, men and women recount stories of early attachment relationships with parents, which are subsequently analyzed to assess the kind of working models that adults may hold: secure/autonomous, dismissing, preoccupied, and unresolved. In a second research approach, psychologists have examined attachment styles in romantic love, identifying three different styles that roughly correspond to the secure, avoidant, and resistant categories obtained with infants. College students with secure attachment styles exhibit more commitment and self-disclosure in their romantic relationships, offer and obtain more social support during periods of stress, experience more positive affect in daily social interactions, and construct a sense of self that is especially positive, complex, and coherent.

CHAPTER 3

Social Learning and Culture

Shortly after World War II, the famous psychologist B. F. Skinner wrote a novel in which he imagined a utopian society built on the principles of *behaviorism*. In *Walden Two,* Skinner (1948/1962) depicted a community of about 1,000 people who lived "together without quarreling, in a social climate of trust rather than suspicion, of love rather than jealousy, of cooperation rather than competition" (Skinner, 1979, p. 346). From birth onward, the citizens of Skinner's mythical society were enrolled in an elaborate educational program that systematically reinforced positive behaviors. Infants and children were trained to restrain negative emotions, practice self-control, and care for themselves and for each other by eschewing jealousy, rivalry, fighting, and pride. The training was accomplished without punishment but instead through **positive reinforcement.** By rewarding socially desirable behavior, the educational system at Walden Two gently and gradually instilled behaviors compatible with a good life for all its citizens.

Skinner's novel put into story form a strong impulse that has run through American psychology from its very beginning. We are created equal, Americans want to believe. Given the right kind of *environment,* anybody can rise to the top, or at least to a position of individual respectability. If a person's behavior is bad or problematic, we can fix it, we can improve, we can change others and ourselves by changing the environments in which we live. For much of the 20th century, mainstream American psychology tended to downplay inherent or biologically ingrained differences between people and emphasized instead the power of social environments to shape human behavior. Espoused most passionately by Skinner, the

behaviorist tradition exemplifies how American psychologists have tended to understand the role of social context and learning in the development of personality. How did you become the person you are? What explains why you do what you do? In Walden Two and in the real world where you and I live, Skinner argued, human behavior and persons' lives are primarily the products of *social learning in culture*.

If human nature is the first fundamental context for understanding human individuality, then the social environment and all it entails—family, neighborhood, community, culture, and history—is the second. Beginning with Skinner's behaviorist view, we turn our attention in this chapter to the role of social learning and culture in the making of persons. We will begin with the particular mechanisms of learning that are spelled out in the behaviorist tradition. We will then consider influential theories of social learning as they bear upon human personality. Next, we will consider the multilayered social ecology of everyday human behavior, how it is that our actions, thoughts, and feelings are always situated in a multitude of overlapping contexts. Moving from the smallest to the most encompassing contexts, we will

B. F. Skinner (1904–1990) was the most influential spokesperson for behaviorism in the 20th century. Skinner championed an approach that emphasized observable behavior over thoughts and feelings, that focused on the ways that environments shape behavior, and that prioritized the study of learning through rewards and punishments.

consider social situations, social class and gender, and finally culture and history as determinants of human behavior and shapers of persons' lives. Our central theme in this chapter is the social environment. Our focus is on those factors and forces that we tend to see as outside our bodies, in the social worlds we inhabit, in the interpersonal and cultural landscape across which we move over time and situations. Our goal is to appreciate the tremendous power of the environment in determining who we are and the intricate ways in which virtually every aspect of our lives is *situated in a complex social and cultural context.*

BEHAVIORISM AND SOCIAL-LEARNING THEORY

AMERICAN ENVIRONMENTALISM: THE BEHAVIORIST TRADITION

Behaviorism is a brand of psychology that explores the ways in which observable behavior is learned and shaped by the environment. B. F. Skinner (1904–1990) was arguably behaviorism's most ardent enthusiast and eloquent spokesman. John B. Watson launched the behaviorist movement in the United States in 1913 with the publication of "Psychology as the Behaviorist Views It." Behaviorism was *the* dominant force in American academic psychology from about 1920 through the 1950s, and its principles are still influential today. Through the 1950s, a number of very different behaviorist theories were developed, such as Clark Hull's (1943) biological-drive theory and Edwin Tolman's (1948) cognitively oriented "purposive behaviorism."

John Watson, the founder of behaviorism, was not a humble man. In a famous claim, he once bragged that he could take virtually any human infant at random and raise him or her to become any kind of adult you might imagine. Just let me create the right kind of environment, Watson maintained, and I can make any kind of human being you want:

> Give me a dozen healthy infants, well-formed, and my own specified world to bring them up in and I'll guarantee to take any one at random and train him to become any type of specialist I might select—doctor, lawyer, artist, merchant, chief and, yes, even beggerman and thief, regardless of his talents, penchants, tendencies, abilities, vocations, and race of his ancestors. There is no such thing as an inheritance of capacity, talent, temperament, mental constitution, and behavioral characteristics. (Watson, 1924, p. 104)

Though overstated, Watson was asserting a position about human life that goes back at least as far as the British philosopher John Locke, who in 1690 set forth the doctrine of the *tabula rasa,* or "blank slate." For the newborn, Locke believed, the mind is like a blank slate, or clean piece of paper. Nothing is written on the slate; it is completely clean and empty. Over time, experience "writes" upon the slate, giving the mind its characteristic content. Locke rejected the notion of innate ideas and argued instead that the *environment* shapes the person. If the human mind is originally a blank slate, then all humans are born psychologically equal. From this view, individual differences in personality are a function of different environmental exposures. Personality is made (by the environment), not inborn. As Skinner (1971) put it, "a person does not act upon the world, the world acts upon him" (p. 211). Therefore, if the environment shapes the person, then a just and happy society should produce just and happy citizens.

How does the environment shape behavior? Through learning, answered the behaviorists. Each of us is who we are because of what we have learned. According to the behaviorists, our environments teach us to be who we are; we are what we learn to be. But why do we learn to be anything at all? What *motivates* us to learn? The behaviorist answer was that we learn in order to obtain pleasure and avoid pain.

That the ultimate determinants of behavior reside in pleasure and pain is an idea at least as old as the teachings of Aristotle, but it found its earliest flowering in the ancient school of thought called Epicureanism. Epicurus (341–270 B.C.E.) was a Greek philosopher who preached that freedom from pain and the pursuit of gentle pleasures and peace of mind were the hallmarks of the Good Life. Not only do optimal pleasure and minimal pain make men and women happy, they also serve as the foundations for ethical action, according to

Epicurus. In an ethical or moral sense, the world is constructed so that, in general, what is good is what eventually brings pleasure and peace of mind; what is ethically or morally bad is what ultimately brings displeasure or pain. Through the ages, this doctrine has been adapted to play a central role in many different philosophical systems, including that of Locke.

In the 18th and 19th centuries, the philosophy of **utilitarianism** put forth the idea that the "good" society should make for the greatest happiness or pleasure for the greatest number of people. Utilitarians such as Jeremy Bentham (1748–1832) and John Stuart Mill (1806–1873) argued that this could be accomplished if societies were structured in a more egalitarian fashion. Thus, the utilitarians advocated equality for all, women's suffrage, abolition of discrimination on the basis of religion and race, and redistribution of society's wealth (Russell, 1945). They tended to distrust the authority of king and church and to glorify democratic education as the answer to many of life's problems. In ethics, the utilitarians were pragmatic and nondogmatic, insisting that principles need to be flexible to accommodate changing ethical circumstances. Behaviorism, in all its different forms, was steeped in a utilitarian ideology. Like its philosophical forerunner, behaviorism was egalitarian, pragmatic, and supremely optimistic about the possibility of changing the person's life for the better through education—that is, through learning or training in social contexts. Ultimately, learning is shaped by pleasure and pain. And learning should, in turn, make for the greatest amount of pleasure and the least amount of pain.

According to Mill and other utilitarians, a great deal of learning occurs through the *association* of actions with either positive (pleasurable) or negative (painful) events. The doctrine of **associationism** purports that various objects and ideas that are contiguous in time or space come to be connected, or associated, with each other into meaningful units. Simple forms of learning proceed via associations.

Classical conditioning represents one such form of simple learning. In Pavlov's well-known examples of classical conditioning, a hungry dog *learns* to salivate in response to a neutral stimulus (a tone) because that neutral stimulus has become associated with a stimulus (meat) that typically elicits salivation naturally. In the terminology of classical conditioning, the meat is an *unconditioned stimulus* that naturally gives rise to salivation, which is the *unconditioned response.* When, in a number of experimental trials, the dog hears the neutral stimulus of the tone immediately *preceding* the presentation of meat, the dog learns to salivate *(conditioned response)* to the tone, now called a *conditioned stimulus,* even when no meat is present. The tone (conditioned stimulus) and meat (unconditioned stimulus) therefore become associated with each other because of their contiguity in time. Figure 3.1 illustrates the process.

Watson believed that classical conditioning was a cornerstone of human learning. In the legendary case study of Little Albert, Watson and Raynor (1920) showed how an 11-month-old infant could be conditioned to fear white rats by being repeatedly exposed to a white rat (a presumably neutral conditioned stimulus) and a loud, frightening noise (unconditioned stimulus) at about the same time. The loud noise naturally gave rise to an unconditioned fear response (Albert would cry and avoid the stimulus), but the previously neutral stimulus of the rat also came to elicit fear (conditioned response) by virtue of its repeated association with the unconditioned stimulus. Although the results of this study are murky, there is some evidence that little Albert's fear of rats may have naturally expanded over time to include other white, furry objects, an example of what behaviorists have called **stimulus generalization.**

Classical conditioning may be implicated in the development of certain neurotic symptoms, especially phobias, and in the ontogeny of more complex attitudes and behavior systems. In some cases, such complex associations are achieved through **higher-order**

FIGURE 3.1	**CLASSICAL CONDITIONING**

A neutral stimulus becomes conditioned through its association with an unconditioned stimulus, and as a result, the conditioned stimulus eventually produces the same kind of response produced by the unconditioned stimulus. In the case of Pavlov's dog, the tone elicits salivation because the tone is consistently paired with meat.

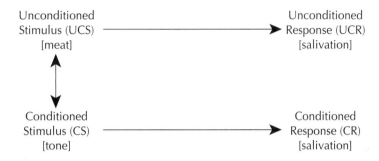

conditioning. In higher-order conditioning, conditioned stimuli, which have obtained their eliciting power through associations with unconditioned stimuli, come to be associated with other neutral stimuli, which themselves become conditioned stimuli by virtue of the association. Therefore, a young man may develop an aversion to a particular brand of women's cologne because that was the cologne his mother wore the summer he broke up with his girlfriend. In other words, the aversion is a higher-order conditioned response to the conditioned stimulus of the previously neutral cologne, now associated with "mother that summer," which is itself a conditioned stimulus by virtue of its association with the aversive unconditioned stimulus of the end of a love affair. Higher-order conditioning could also produce emotionally positive associations, as might be the case if the young man's sister wore the cologne on the day he found out that he had been named his high school's outstanding student.

Traditionally, classical conditioning has been viewed as an extremely simple, low-level form of learning whereby two stimuli become associated because they appear together at the same time. Recent thinking about the phenomenon, however, suggests a more complicated and high-level process. Rescorla (1988) argues that contiguity in time and place is not what makes conditioning work. Instead, classical conditioning enables the organism to form an accurate representation of the world. In the standard Pavlovian example, the tone becomes associated with the bell not because the two arrive on the scene at about the same time but rather because one stimulus (the tone) *provides information* about another (the meat). Rescorla summarizes his cognitive interpretation of classical conditioning by saying:

> Pavlovian conditioning is not a stupid process by which the organism willy-nilly forms associations between any two stimuli that happen to co-occur. Rather, the organism is better seen as an information seeker using logical and perceptual relations among events, along with its own preconceptions, to form a sophisticated representation of the world. (1988, p. 154)

Since the time of Pavlov's dog, psychologists have garnered research support for the importance of classical conditioning in the development of some aspects of personality. For example, there is evidence that people acquire some particular feelings and attitudes about certain objects and groups of people through classical conditioning (Petty & Cacioppo, 1981; Zimbardo & Leippe, 1991). For example, one experiment indicated that when research participants were shown words supposedly representing names of groups of people they had not heard of before, they tended to express liking for those group names that were paired with positive words (e.g., "happy") and dislike for those group names paired with negative words (e.g., "dumb") (Lohr & Staats, 1973). Classical conditioning would also appear to be involved in the development of certain phobias, which are intense fear responses to particular stimuli (Comer, 1995). Behaviorally oriented therapists sometimes apply principles of classical conditioning to help phobic patients deal with their fears. If phobias are learned responses, the logic goes, they can be unlearned through the same kinds of processes that established them in the first place.

A second form of learning is **instrumental conditioning,** termed by Skinner **operant conditioning.** (The basic principles of operant conditioning are outlined in Table 3.1.) In operant conditioning, behavior is modified by its consequences. Positive consequences for a behavior increase the likelihood of its recurrence, thus reinforcing the association between the behavior and the various stimuli in the environment present at the time the behavior occurred. Negative consequences decrease the likelihood the behavior will recur, thus weakening stimulus–response connections.

Skinner conducted the best-known experiments in operant conditioning. In these laboratory studies, he employed the basic principles of reinforcement and punishment to teach animals, such as rats and pigeons, to perform complex behaviors. Typically, the animal was

TABLE 3.1	KEY CONCEPTS OF OPERANT CONDITIONING	
Concept	**Definition**	**Example**
Positive reinforcer	Any stimulus that, because of its presentation after a response, strengthens (increases the probability of) the response. In effect, the organism is rewarded for the response.	A first grade teacher's praise for a child's obedient behavior leads to increased obedience in the future.
Negative reinforcer	Any stimulus that, because of its removal after a response, strengthens (increases the probability of) the response. In effect, the organism experiences relief (a kind of reward) after the response.	Criticism from one's mother-in-law about smoking cigarettes ceases when the individual quits smoking. Removal of criticism is reinforcing, serving as a reward for giving up cigarettes.
Positive punishment	Any stimulus that, because of its presentation after a response, weakens (decreases the probability of) the response. Positive punishments are aversive or painful stimuli that reduce the behavior they follow.	A speeding motorist on his way to the Indianapolis 500 is pulled aside by a state patrolman and given a $100 citation. The traffic ticket serves as a punishment, which leads to less speeding by the motorist in the future.
Negative punishment	Any stimulus that, because of its removal after a response, weakens (decreases the probability of) the response. Negative punishments remove pleasurable stimuli.	A teenager who repeatedly breaks curfew is "grounded" by her parents for a week. A positive reinforcer (going out with her friends) is therefore removed. In subsequent weeks the teenager comes home at the correct time.
Extinction	A previously reinforced behavior is no longer reinforced; eventually the behavior decreases and drops to baseline levels.	A child no longer says "please" and "thank you" at the dinner table because the parents no longer reinforce the behavior with smiles and compliments. *(CONTINUES)*

placed in a tightly controlled laboratory setting and allowed to do whatever it pleased. When, in its random activity, the animal happened to behave approximately as the experimenter wanted it to, the animal was rewarded—often with a small amount of food. The experimenter thus selectively reinforced the desired behavior, and over time the animal exhibited the reinforced behavior with increasing frequency. The process of reinforcing closer and closer approximations to a desired behavior in an attempt to elicit that behavior is called *shaping*. Shaping was a central practice in the educational regimen of *Walden Two*.

Operant conditioning is more than merely a matter of increasing certain behaviors through reinforcement and decreasing others through punishment or lack of reinforcement. Organisms must also learn when and where to perform or refrain from certain behaviors. Quiet activity, therefore, may be reinforced in the classroom but not on the playground. The school child may learn to discriminate between these two environmental settings and to perform the appropriate behaviors for each. Thus, the classroom desks and the teacher may serve as *discriminant stimuli* for the child: When these stimuli are present in the environment, certain behaviors (reading, writing, being quiet) are likely to be reinforced, while others (running and playing ball) are likely not to be reinforced and may even be punished. Certain response patterns, however, may be reinforced in a great variety of environmental settings. In this case, *generalization* occurs. For example, the child may be rewarded for telling the truth at home, in school, *and* on the playground. Ideally, he or she would learn that such behavior is virtually always appropriate and that it should therefore be shown in the presence of a great variety of stimuli.

TABLE 3.1	KEY CONCEPTS OF OPERANT CONDITIONING *(CONTINUED)*	
Concept	**Definition**	**Example**
Shaping	Getting the organism to emit a complex response by reinforcing successive approximations to the behaviors that make up the complex response. A complex, final response may be shaped by rewarding the organism for the simple component responses that make it up.	A Little League coach teaches a child to hit a ball by praising a number of simple behaviors of batting. Early on, the child is reinforced for standing in the appropriate way, then for level swinging of the bat. Then the child is praised when bat actually strikes ball. Finally, praise is delivered only when the child shows the entire proper batting stance and swing and hits the ball solidly.
Continuous reinforcement	Delivering reinforcement after every instance of a particular response. Behavior submitted to a continuous reinforcement schedule is learned rapidly.	Every time a man tells his girlfriend he loves her, she kisses him.
Partial reinforcement	Not reinforcing every instance of the behavior, but rather delivering reinforcement intermittently according to a particular schedule. Interval reinforcement schedules administer reinforcement after a particular period of time. Ratio reinforcement schedules administer reinforcement after a particular number of responses. Behavior submitted to partial reinforcement schedules, either interval or ratio, is more resistant to extinction than behavior that is reinforced continually.	*Interval schedule:* A factory worker receives a paycheck once every two weeks. *Ratio schedule:* A vacuum cleaner salesman receives a bonus after he sells 25 vacuum cleaners.

Concepts of reinforcement and punishment are both intuitively obvious and paradoxical. Most people know that behavior can be shaped through the judicious use of rewards and punishments. Indeed, parents employ basic principles of operant conditioning routinely in daily child care and discipline. However, they employ them wrongly in many cases, Skinner would argue. For instance, many parents rely much too heavily on punishment. Because punishing a response merely alerts the person to what should *not* be done while providing no example of a constructive alternative, punishment is generally a rather weak form of behavioral control, Skinner maintains. Overt punishment played virtually no role in the educational program in *Walden Two.*

Parents also routinely *under*estimate the power of **partial reinforcement.** In partial reinforcement a particular response is reinforced intermittently, whereas in **continuous reinforcement** the response is reinforced every time it occurs. When behavior is no longer reinforced, *extinction* might eventually occur: The behavior decreases in frequency and eventually dies out. However, behavior that has been partially reinforced is much more difficult to extinguish than continuously reinforced behavior. Therefore, a parent who only occasionally rewards a child's temper tantrums may unwittingly be establishing a partial reinforcement schedule for the tantrums, making it difficult to eliminate this undesirable behavior. Particularly thorny problems can arise when the same undesirable behavior—such as a temper tantrum, physical aggression, or immature dependence—is occasionally reinforced, occasionally punished, and occasionally ignored.

Reinforcement comes in many different forms. Although experiments with animals routinely employ such basic reinforcers as food and drink, human beings are typically subject to a multitude of positive consequences that subtly shape behavior. Some of the most powerful reinforcers are called **conditioned generalized reinforcers**—reinforcers that acquire their power because of their association with a variety of other reinforcers. The best example of a conditioned generalized reinforcer is money, which enables one to purchase a great variety of other reinforcers. Many human reinforcers, moreover, are highly social in nature. Arnold Buss (1986) divides social reinforcers into two general classes: *stimulation rewards* and *affective rewards*. Stimulation rewards include receiving attention from others; affective rewards include receiving respect, praise, and affection. Affective rewards constitute an *emotional* response from others; stimulation rewards merely indicate that others are responding in some way to the self.

Although American psychology is no longer dominated by the behaviorist perspective, the radical science of behavior launched by John Watson and dramatized by B.F. Skinner in *Walden Two* has left a powerful legacy. Some of the strongest features of behaviorism have been incorporated into the mainstream of American psychology, such as its pragmatic and functional spirit and its emphasis on empirical rigor and quantification. Behaviorism has also had a major impact on clinical practice and has led to a wide variety of practical techniques for changing problematic behaviors, loosely grouped under the rubric of "behavior modification" or "behavior therapy." With respect to personality theory, behaviorism has spawned a number of influential approaches that fall under the name of **social-learning theories.** These theories retain some of behaviorism's emphasis on environmentalism and learning, while adopting a broader view of human behavior that incorporates important *cognitive* variables that cannot be directly observed.

EXPECTANCIES AND VALUES

One of the first psychologists to introduce cognition into behaviorist accounts of human personality was Julian Rotter. Rotter's eclectic viewpoint broadened the traditional boundaries of behaviorism to account for certain aspects of learning that appeared to be unique to human beings. Rotter (1954, 1972) viewed the person as actively constructing his or her own reality, rather than merely passively responding to it. Most human learning, furthermore, occurs in a social context, as people learn to anticipate what others will do and then act on those anticipations.

A key concept in Rotter's social-learning theory is **expectancy,** a subjectively held probability that a particular reinforcement will occur as the outcome of a specific behavior. Over time and across different situations, each of us learns to expect that we will probably be reinforced for certain behaviors in certain situations but not in others. For instance, a college student may expect that working hard in her psychology class will earn her a high grade. On the other hand, she may also expect that working hard at improving her relationship with her boyfriend is not likely to earn her much satisfaction. In this case, the woman holds very different subjective expectancies as to the probability that "hard work" will pay off in two very different situations. Over time, furthermore, people develop *generalized expectancies* about the nature of reinforcement in the world at large. In chapter 8, we will examine some of the empirical research that has come out of Rotter's view of generalized expectancies, under the topic of "locus of control."

A second key concept is **reinforcement value.** Reinforcement value refers to the subjective attractiveness of a particular reinforcement. For the college student, the reinforcement value of improving her relationship may be much higher than the reinforcement value of obtaining a high grade in her psychology course. Therefore, she may work hard at mending the relationship and may neglect her psychology course, even though her expectancies dictate that she will be more "successful" if she acts in an opposite manner. To predict how a person will behave, the psychologist must take into account that person's particular combination of expectancy and reinforcement value for a particular goal-directed action in a given situation. In Rotter's terminology, behavioral potential *(BP)*, that is, the likelihood that a particular person will perform a given behavior, equals the combination of the expectancy *(E)* and the reinforcement value *(RV)* that the behavior holds for that person: $BP = E + RV$. People are most likely to act to obtain goals for which (a) they expect to be reinforced (high E) and (b) the expected reinforcements are highly valued (high RV). They are least likely to act to obtain goals for which (a) they do not expect to be reinforced (low E) and (b) the reinforcements they might obtain are not especially valued (low RV).

Walter Mischel (1973, 1979) extended Rotter's conception by incorporating **cognitive/social learning/person variables.** These are characteristic strategies or styles of approaching situations, and are thought to grow out of the individual's previous experiences with both situations and rewards. In addition to expectancies and values, Mischel described other cognitive/social learning variables such as competencies, encoding strategies, and self-regulating systems and plans. *Competencies* refer to what a person knows and can do. Each person approaches a situation with his or her own set of skills or competencies. One person may be particularly adept at showing empathy for other people; another person is extremely skillful in analyzing social problems in a cool and dispassionate manner; and a third person has a gift for making small talk. Each skill is likely to influence what each person in fact does in a particular situation.

Encoding strategies deal with the manner in which people interpret information. Each person sees a particular situation from a different point of view. Imagine, for a moment, that two weeks into the semester a professor explodes at his students, chastising them all in class for their poor performance on a written assignment. He tells them that he has been too easy on them for the first two weeks and that the class is now going to be a lot tougher.

For one student, this professor's "no more Mr. Nice Guy" lecture is interpreted as a legitimate threat that may motivate the student to work harder (or perhaps to drop the course and find a more mild-mannered professor). Another student may interpret the outburst as a carefully orchestrated bluff designed to scare students: underneath it all, the professor didn't really mean what he said. A third student may conclude that the professor did mean it at the time, but that he was simply having a bad day and, therefore, there is no need to worry. People clearly behave according to their own characteristic ways of interpreting, or "encoding," information—a theme we return to in some detail in chapter 8.

Self-regulatory systems and plans refer to the ways we regulate and guide our own behavior through self-imposed goals and standards. Monisha's plans to attend law school and eventually work for a large law firm in New York City clearly influence the way she approaches situations. Such a plan dictates that she spend a good deal of her time studying to obtain high grades, that she take certain courses as an undergraduate that best prepare her for law school, and that she discuss with her fiancé, who thinks he might like to be a psychology professor, how the two of them hope ultimately to merge their careers and their lives. Plans provide our lives with guidelines and agendas. They specify how we might achieve important goals, and they help us determine what is worth doing and what is not worth doing at particular times and in particular situations.

BANDURA'S SOCIAL LEARNING THEORY

The most wide-ranging and influential social-learning theorist today is probably Albert Bandura. As a graduate student at the University of Iowa, Bandura came under the influence of the prominent behaviorist Kenneth Spence. He received training as a clinical psychologist at Wichita Guidance Center in Kansas and then assumed a faculty position at Stanford University, where he still teaches today. Bandura provides an especially inclusive social-learning perspective, which greatly expands the domain of learning to encompass observational learning and cognitive processes and which pays close attention to the complex and recursive ways in which person variables, environmental variables, and behavior itself influence one another.

Observational Learning

The traditional principles of learning that are derived from behaviorism—such as the laws of reinforcement and punishment—have more to do with *performance* than with *learning* per se. Rewards and punishments directly shape what people will *do,* Bandura argues, but they may not always be implicated in what people *learn.* Behaviorist theories cannot explain why people learn in the absence of reinforcement and/or the satisfaction of biological needs. Taking issue with the legacy of Epicurus, Bandura contends that certain learning occurs *outside* the bounds of pleasure and pain. We do not need to be rewarded in order to learn. Rather, human beings learn a great deal simply by watching other people behave, reading about what other people do, and generally *observing* the world. This deceptively simple process is called **observational learning.** People routinely learn by observing, and they often perform (behave) by imitating what they see.

Albert Bandura developed a highly influential social-learning theory that widened behaviorism's purview to include the role of observation and cognitive processes in learning and performance.

Figure 3.2 presents Bandura's (1971, 1977) conceptual scheme for observational learning and imitation. Bandura views the process as four sequential component steps through which a person observes another person's behavior (the model) and eventually imitates what the model does. Step 1 specifies the *attentional processes* involved in observing the model. Certain features of the model may increase the likelihood that the person will notice or pay attention to what the model is doing. For instance, a highly distinctive model, or one who is especially attractive, familiar, or even strange, may capture the observer's attention better than a less distinctive model. Conversely, attentional processes can also refer to characteristics of the observer. A person must have the capacity to observe the model. (A blind person cannot imitate what he or she cannot see, but can rely on other sensory modalities in observational learning.) A person must also be motivated to observe. It may not matter how distinctive or attractive a particular model is, for if the observer is too tired to notice the model, no observational learning will occur.

The second step in observational learning is *retention processes.* The person must be able to encode, remember, and make sense of what he or she observes if learning is to

---

FIGURE 3.2	**FOUR STEPS OF OBSERVATIONAL LEARNING**

The person must proceed through attentional, retention, motor reproduction, and motivational processes in order for observational learning to produce successful imitation.

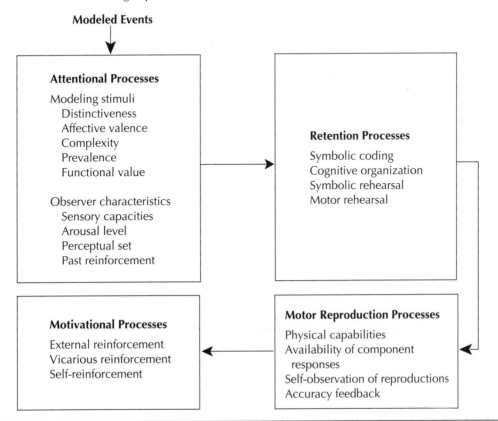

SOURCE: From *Social Learning Theory* (p. 23), by A. Bandura, 1977, Englewood Cliffs, NJ: Prentice-Hall.

occur. However much you present addition and subtraction flashcards to a newborn infant, the infant will not learn basic arithmetic, because newborns cannot encode this kind of symbolic information.

Bandura's third step—*motor reproduction processes*—concerns the capabilities of performing what is observed and the availability of such performance in the observer's repertoire of behavior. My brother and I spent hours—years, in fact—of our youth carefully observing Ernie Banks hit baseballs for the Chicago Cubs. In his glorious career, Ernie hit 512 home runs, and I think we saw most of them on TV. My brother and I obsessively and repeatedly attended to the model (Bandura's Step 1), and both of us can remember Banks' beautiful swing with perfect clarity (Step 2). Yet between the two of us, we hit only two home runs in our many years of playing Little League.

Finally, Step 4 in Bandura's scheme is *motivational processes*. An observer must *want* to imitate behavior if imitation is to occur. It is at this point in Bandura's scheme that rewards and punishments play their strongest roles. Assuming the person has attended to the model's behavior, has encoded the behavior, and is capable of reproducing the behavior, the person is now most likely to imitate the model if reinforced for doing so. Reinforcement in this case might come directly from the external environment, from the individual observer him- or herself (what is called "self-reinforcement"), or by seeing or imagining someone else being reinforced for the behavior ("vicarious reinforcement").

Observational learning is everywhere in your life. Try to imagine some important aspect of the way you characteristically behave that has not been influenced in some way or another by your observations of other people. It is difficult to do so. Researchers have displayed the power of observational learning through studies of language development, impulse control, friendship, competition and cooperation, persuasion, and altruism. An especially influential line of research has examined the relation between observation of violence and aggressive behavior (e.g., Anderson & Bushman, 2002; Anderson, Carnagey, & Eubanks, 2003; Bandura, Ross, & Ross, 1961; Berkowitz & Powers, 1979; Eron, 1982, 1987; Geen, 1997; Huesmann & Miller, 1994). Researchers have paid special attention to violence in the media, especially violent television shows, movies, and song lyrics. The take-home message from these studies is twofold: First, people can learn to act in an aggressive manner by imitating aggressive models of many kinds; second, the more a person observes violence, the greater the likelihood that he or she will become an especially aggressive person, displaying high levels of cruel and destructive behavior towards others. At the same time, there is also evidence to suggest that people who hold aggressive tendencies in the first place tend to expose themselves to more violent media displays. In the case of television violence, therefore, individuals who are more aggressive to begin with tend to watch more television violence, which in turn increases their characteristic aggressiveness, and so on. In other words, media violence and aggression may be related to each other in a reciprocal or circular manner. Each serves as the cause and effect of the other.

Bandura's views on observational learning underscore the profoundly social quality of human learning and performance. Observational learning occurs within a particular interpersonal context. Observer and model are involved in a complex personal relationship, the nature of which can profoundly influence how learning occurs and the extent to which imitation will be shown. Empirical literature on imitation in children, for instance, shows that a number of characteristics of the model and of the relationship between the model and the child may promote or hinder imitation. In general, children are more likely to imitate models of their own sex (Bandura, Ross, & Ross, 1961), models who are perceived as powerful (Bandura, Ross, & Ross, 1963), and models whose behavior is observed to be reinforced by others (Bandura, 1965; Parke & Walters, 1967).

Self-Efficacy

A central concept in Bandura's social-learning theory is **self-efficacy** (Bandura, 1989). Self-efficacy is a person's belief that he or she can successfully carry out "courses of action required to deal with prospective situations containing many ambiguous, unpredictable, and often stressful elements" (Bandura & Schunk, 1981, p. 587). In other words, self-efficacy is our belief in our own behavioral competence in a particular situation. High self-efficacy is reflected in a strong belief that I can perform a particular behavior; low self-efficacy is reflected in the belief that I cannot perform the behavior (Table 3.2)

Self-efficacy should be distinguished from outcome expectancies, which refer to a person's beliefs about what the outcome of a particular action is likely to be in a given situation. A positive outcome expectancy means that I believe that a behavior will produce a desired result; a negative outcome expectancy means that I suspect the behavior will not produce a desired result. It is theoretically possible, therefore, that I might have a high self-efficacy expectation in a given situation but a low outcome expectancy: For example, I might be certain that I can explain logically and forcefully to my good friend why I think that he should not divorce his wife (high self-efficacy), but I might also be sure that any explanation of this sort will nonetheless do very little good (low outcome expectancy).

Research has suggested that self-efficacy judgments help determine whether we undertake particular goal-directed activities, the amount of effort we put into them, and the length of time we persist in striving for goals in particular situations. Manning and Wright (1983) conducted a representative empirical study of the relation between self-efficacy judgments and behavior. These researchers studied 52 pregnant women who were attending childbirth classes designed to teach them how to master the pain of labor and delivery without medication. The women completed self-efficacy questionnaires before and during labor. The questionnaires asked them to assess how well they thought they would be able to handle the pain of childbirth without medication. Outcome expectancy was also assessed before and during labor through a questionnaire that asked the women to rate the extent to which they believed that the pain-control techniques they learned in their childbirth classes were generally effective in enabling a woman to go through labor and delivery without medication. After their babies were born, the women were interviewed to assess the timing and amount of medication used in labor and delivery. The results of the study showed that women who manifested high self-efficacy judgments were ultimately able to cope with pain better during labor and delivery and to resist the use of medication, compared with women scoring low in self-efficacy.

TABLE 3.2	FOUR SOURCES OF SELF-EFFICACY

Performance Accomplishments. Past experiences of success and failure in attempts to accomplish goals are the most important regulators of self-efficacy.

Vicarious Experience. Witnessing other people's successes and failures provides one with a basis of comparison by which to estimate one's own personal competence in similar situations.

Verbal Persuasion. Being told by others that one can or cannot master a task may also increase or decrease self-efficacy, though the effect of such persuasion is usually weak.

Emotional Arousal. A person's feelings of self-efficacy are influenced by the degree and quality of emotional arousal he or she feels in a given performance situation. The degree of anxiety felt provides important information about the perceived degree of difficulty, stress, and persistence that a task represents. Very high levels of anxiety signal to the person that he or she is not feeling very masterful.

The development of self-efficacy is a key mechanism whereby people are able to exercise control over threatening events. Bandura conceives of "threat" as a "relational property concerning the match between perceived coping capabilities and potentially hurtful aspects of the environment" (Ozer & Bandura, 1990, p. 473). A person experiences a situation as threatening when he or she perceives that the personal resources at hand are not adequate to meet the strong demands of the environment. In these situations, the person feels highly anxious and is likely to experience a flood of negative thoughts about the extreme hazards of the situation and his or her personal inadequacies in dealing with the hazards. Heightened self-efficacy reduces anxiety and moves the person's thinking processes in the direction of effective interactions with the environment. In this way, self-efficacy exerts "empowering effects" (Ozer & Bandura, 1990).

Research on self-efficacy has highlighted its clinical applications and possible health benefits. Bandura and his colleagues have designed intervention strategies for promoting self-efficacy among people facing various kinds of environmental threats. For example, Ozer and Bandura (1990) documented increases in self-efficacy among women who participated in a program in which they mastered the physical skills to defend themselves successfully against unarmed sexual assaults. The "mastery modeling" program enhanced self-efficacy, decreased perceived vulnerability to assault, and reduced the incidence of intrusive negative thinking and anxiety arousal in encounters with men.

Another group of researchers focusing on self-efficacy implemented a program to reduce anxiety about snakes among 20 individuals whose snake phobias were so severe that they were unable to engage in camping, biking, gardening, swimming in lakes, or traveling to rustic areas (Wiedenfeld et al., 1990). In this study, increases in self-efficacy were associated with enhanced functioning of the body's immunological system, as measured by the concentration of lymphocytes and "helper" and "suppressor" T cells in the blood. When the subjects participated in the "guided mastery" program, which involved gradual mastery of progressively more threatening forms of interactions with snakes, they initially experienced

Bandura's theory of social learning has alerted psychologists, policy makers, and parents to the ways in which violence in the media may increase aggression among viewers. Here a young boy imitates the shooting of a gun, as portrayed in a popular TV show.

a great deal of anxiety. But this stress activated in the process of gaining coping mastery, and thus increasing self-efficacy, proved to be immuno-enhancing rather than immuno-suppressing. In other words, whereas stress often weakens the body's powers to fight off illness and disease, stress experienced *in the process of building up mastery and self-efficacy* may actually strengthen the body's immune system. Put simply, heightened immune system functioning, and thus better health, is associated with high levels of self-efficacy, but the benefits of self-efficacy training begin to show up even before self-efficacy has had a chance to improve. The sometimes stressful process of *building up* one's self-efficacy in the face of threat may enhance the body's defenses. This kind of stress—stress in the service of promoting self-efficacy—is a good kind of stress to have.

The Social Ecology of Human Behavior

The behaviorists and social-learning theorists have traditionally accounted for human behavior in terms of the environment's influence upon the person. We learn to behave as we do though interaction with the world around us. The world "teaches" us to act in particular ways. Through classical conditioning, operant conditioning, and observational learning, we accumulate a repertoire of behaviors that more or less reflect the learning history we have each experienced. Whether we are learning to act in destructive and aggressive ways or in accord with society's most exalted standards of socialization, we are learning what to do, how to do it, when to do it, why we do it, and who we are according to the ways in which our environments are set up—according to the rewards and punishments we experience, the contingencies of reinforcement we encounter in different situations, the associations we form as a result of our perceptions of environmental stimuli, the models we imitate, the lessons we learn from our parents, teachers, peers, and so on. The behaviorists and the social-learning theorists underscore the extent to which each of us is a reflection of our environment—how our behavior and indeed our very lives sit within and are defined by the environment around us.

But what is the nature of that environment? What are those environmental contexts that influence our behavior and shape who we are? At first glance, these questions seem simple. We might say that at any given moment our "environment" is the situation that we find ourselves in. As I am writing this paragraph, I am sitting in my office at home, on the third floor of an old house in a suburb of Chicago. The air conditioning is on, but I am still hot. The temperature outside is about 95 degrees Fahrenheit. My older daughter is downstairs, and I can hear her practicing the oboe in her room. These things are all part of my current situation. As you read this chapter, you may be sitting in your dormitory room or in the library. You may be studying with a friend. It may be late at night, and you may be facing an examination in the morning. These factors may all be part of your current situation.

But as we think more about our respective situations—mine and yours—we soon realize that each of us is currently acting within and with respect to a number of different situations or contexts that define our respective environments. For me, it is July 30, 2003, and I have promised my publisher that I will finish revising this textbook by the end of the summer—that is, in about two months. Quite frankly, I don't think I am going to make it. This is all part of my current situation, as is the fact that I am 49 years old, married with two children, a white male, was raised in the Baptist church, and went to college at Valparaiso University in the early 1970s. I don't know you, but I am sure that you can spell out similar information about your life—about what is going on in your life now, where you came from, and vital statistics depicting your own demographic profile. All of this is, in a sense, part of the context within which you are currently situated. All of this defines your environment.

When we study the "environment" in the biological sciences, we learn to think about the complex "ecology" of the natural world. Making up that ecology are a number of interrelated environmental systems that define the natural world at a given place and time. In a similar way, we can think about the environments that situate human behavior in terms of a **social ecology** (Bronfenbrenner, 1979; Moen, Elder, & Luscher, 1995). The social ecology consists of the many different environmental contexts that influence a person's behavior and shape his or her life. The social ecology includes those immediate and close-in contexts such as the particular social situation within which one finds oneself at a given point in time. Personality psychologists who have been strongly influenced by behaviorism and

How Should Parents Raise Their Children?

Because all of us have been children and many of us will have children, we tend to formulate our own pet theories about how parents should raise them—how to enforce rules and carry out discipline, how and when to show affection, how to deal with conflicts between children, and what mistakes not to make. As generally optimistic Americans in the great empiricist tradition of John Locke, we tend to hold highly environmentalistic views of child development: We sincerely believe that what we do to, and for, our children really matters, that patterns of child rearing actually make a difference in the child's ultimate adjustment to the world. Like the behaviorists and social-learning theorists, we believe that parents create environments for their children within which crucial learning takes place and personalities are formed. Therefore, we read with great interest the many child-training manuals written by child psychologists, pediatricians, and others whose expertise we consider to be even greater than our own.

Over the past 60 years, child psychologists and other researchers have amassed a huge volume of literature on patterns of child rearing and their effects on personality development. It is impossible to summarize this body of study with any hope of being accurate, comprehensive, and detailed—even textbooks in developmental psychology only skim the surface. Nonetheless, there are three extremely general conclusions that we *can* draw from this body with some degree of assurance.

The first conclusion is that we really don't know much. Many of the rules, norms, tips, and guidelines offered by popular books on child training have virtually no basis in scientific research (Kagan, 1984). This does not mean that these books and manuals are necessarily bad or useless. Rather, it means that many of the conclusions stated with such assurance by experts in child care are based on common sense, intuition, informed speculation, or ideology. In the absence of scientific knowledge,

this is probably the best we can do—but readers should adopt an open-minded and critical approach to reading and evaluating child-rearing advice, perhaps comparing many different views and integrating what they read with what they feel and think, based on their own personal experience.

A second general conclusion is that most of the informed advice offered by experts in child rearing—whether or not such advice is based on scientific evidence—reflects a *cultural ideal* about what it means to be a good (healthy, happy) child and a good (healthy, happy) adult. This cultural ideal in the United States and in a number of other Western industrialized nations emphasizes individualism, freedom, and the autonomous self. To be healthy, happy, and well-adjusted, we believe, the child and the adult should be self-sufficient and able to cope with challenges on their own. Thus, we idealize such personality traits as "competence," "mastery," and "independence," and we seek to nurture such characteristics in our children.

Keeping in mind, therefore, our very limited scientific understanding of child rearing and our cultural bias toward individualism, we can draw a third general conclusion about child rearing and personality. A broad and coherent collection of literature on family patterns points to four basic styles of parenting: the authoritative–reciprocal, authoritarian, indulgent–permissive, and neglecting styles. The four types can be organized according to the two basic dimensions of "demanding/undemanding" and "accepting/rejecting" (Maccoby & Martin, 1983). Figure 3.A.1 illustrates the four types and the two dimensions. *A consistent body of research favors the authoritative–reciprocal pattern as the style most likely to promote competence and mastery in children.*

The *authoritative–reciprocal* pattern of child rearing is one in which "children are required to be responsible to parental demands, and parents accept a reciprocal responsibility to be as responsive as

(CONTINUES)

possible to their children's reasonable demands and points of view" (Maccoby & Martin, 1983, p. 46). In the authoritative–reciprocal pattern, parents establish clear standards for appropriate behavior in the family, but they are open to and accepting of the points of views of the children. Thus, parents are both highly controlling and highly responsive in their relations with their children. A number of studies have shown that the authoritative–reciprocal pattern of child-rearing is positively associated, though at generally moderate statistical levels, with children's independence and autonomy in both cognitive and social realms, with ability to control aggression, with social responsibility, and with self-esteem (Maccoby & Martin, 1983; Steinberg, Darling, & Fletcher, 1995).

The *authoritarian* pattern of child rearing, on the other hand, is high on demands but low on responsiveness. Authoritarian parents may be autocratic and rigid. Strict rules are enforced as if they were divine edicts; the reasons behind rules are rarely explained and virtually never discussed. These parents strongly value obedience and discourage spontaneous give-and-take between children and their elders. Research has shown that children of authoritarian parents tend to lack social competence with their peers; they are somewhat withdrawn and lacking in spontaneity; they

tend to show relatively low levels of self-esteem. Some studies also suggest that authoritarian styles may retard the development of an internalized conscience in children. Children of authoritarian parents are more likely to make moral decisions based on what external authorities tell them to do; other children may rely more on internalized standards.

The *indulgent–permissive* parenting style is the opposite of the authoritarian style. In this case, parents fail to set high standards for behavior but tend to be highly responsive to the demands of children. Indulgent parents take a tolerant and accepting attitude toward the child's impulses, including sexual and aggressive impulses. They use little punishment and avoid, whenever possible, asserting authority or imposing control and restrictions, making few demands for mature behavior. Children raised in these highly egalitarian and freewheeling families tend to be relatively impulsive, aggressive, and lacking in independence or the ability to take responsibility for their behaviors. While certain benefits of highly permissive parenting have also been identified, the indulgent–permissive pattern appears "on the whole to have more negative than positive effects" (Maccoby & Martin, 1983, pp. 45–46).

Finally, the most seriously flawed parenting style is the *neglecting* and uninvolved pattern shown by

FIGURE 3.A.1   **A TWO DIMENSIONAL CLASSIFICATION OF PARENTING PATTERNS**

	Accepting (responsive, child-centered)	Rejecting (unresponsive, parent-centered)
Demanding (controlling)	Authoritative—reciprocal	Authoritarian
Undemanding (low in control attempts)	Indulgent—permissive	Neglecting

SOURCE: From "Socialization in the Context of the Family: Parent–Child Interaction" (p. 39), by E. E. Maccoby & J. A. Martin, 1983. In P.H. Mussen (Ed.), *Handbook of Child Psychology* (4th ed., Vol. 4, pp. 1–102). New York: John Wiley & Sons.

(CONTINUES)

parents who are unresponsive to their children and who place few demands on them. The neglecting pattern comes in different forms, ranging from passive neglect and emotional indifference to active child abuse. Children growing up in these families may show a variety of negative characteristics—from low self-esteem to poor impulse control to high levels of aggression (Baumrind, 1971; Block, 1971; Egeland & Sroufe, 1981; Martin, 1981)

social-learning theories are especially interested in the immediate situational factors that shape behavior at a given time and in a given place. Social situations make up the **microcontexts** of social ecology—the immediate environmental influences for behavior.

Beyond these immediate situations, however, are larger and more distal contexts for behavior, such as our families, neighborhoods, schools, and churches. Take the family, for instance. A family can be a context for behavior in at least two different ways. In the first sense, a person is likely to act in different ways when he or she is in the presence of his or her family than at other times. Psychologists who study family systems speak of how each member of the family regularly assumes a particular role in that family and displays behavior that is consistent for that role (e.g., Minuchin, 1974). In my family of origin, I am typically a kind of authority figure who is supposed to know all the answers and provide guidance for my brother, sister, and mother. (In other contexts, however, I am much less likely to assume this role.) In a second sense, a family is a context in that patterns of behavior and values learned in the family may sometimes generalize to other parts of a person's life. The fact that I am currently writing this chapter rather than spending the afternoon at the beach is perhaps partly due to how I learned to be a conscientious student and hard worker growing up in my family. As such, the legacy of my family is part of my current environment. You can develop similar ideas for your own life with respect to your family, the neighborhood you grew up in, and perhaps the schools and churches of which you have been a member in the past.

The most encompassing and distal contexts for behavior are what we will call **macrocontexts,** and these include social class, gender, race, culture, and the historical context within which we live. At any given time, a person's life is situated within a hierarchy of contexts, ranging from the microcontext of the immediate social situation to the macrocontexts of class, culture, and history. A full understanding of behavior and of the person who displays any given behavior requires our situating that behavior and that person's life in a number of overlapping contexts, ranging from the micro to the macro. Therefore, defining the environment for our behavior is a very ambitious task, for that environment is many different things at many different levels, all operating at the same time. Let us, then, briefly consider some aspects of the social ecology of human behavior, beginning with immediate social "situations" and moving toward the macrocontexts of class, gender, culture, and history.

MICROCONTEXTS: THE SOCIAL SITUATION

What is a situation? Rudolph Moos (1973, 1974, 1976) provides a useful starting point for considering this surprisingly difficult question. Moos formulated a six-part taxonomy of human environments, identifying the various features that can be taken into consideration in conceptualizing a particular situation. The six categories of human environments identified by Moos are (a) dimensions of the physical ecology, (b) behavior settings or episodes, (c) organizational structure, (d) characteristics of persons in the situation, (e) organizational climate, and (f) functional and reinforcement properties. Table 3.3 summarizes the scheme and provides examples.

Barbara Krahe (1992) offers an alternative outline that arranges situational characteristics into a nested hierarchy. At the lowest level of the hierarchy are the *situational stimuli*—single objects or acts inherent in a situation that are meaningful in their own right. For example, in the situation "taking an examination at the end of the term," situational stimuli would include a specific array of tables and chairs, pens and paper, fellow students sitting in the room, and so on. At the second level, we may view *situational events* or episodes. In the examination example, these might include "being told to begin the exam" and "answering the essay questions at the end of the exam." At the third level, events combine into an overall picture, or *total situation*. What is characteristic of the total situation is its unique occurrence in time and space. The examination might be the first one a student takes in her college career, or, say, the only examination she has ever taken in a psychology course. At the fourth level, situations are defined in generalized terms, such as "exams in general." While each exam may be unique, most may share certain features defining the essence of "examness." Finally, at the fifth and most encompassing level, we may talk about *life situations*. According to Krahe (1992) these are "the totality of social and physical factors which affect the person and are affected by his or her actions at a certain stage of development" (p. 196). The life situation pertaining to our example of the college examination might be defined as "being an undergraduate in her first year at college," encompassing all the particular circumstances associated with this point in life.

You might think that since situations are "out there" in the environment, we might easily classify them in terms of objective properties that are outside the self—properties such as air temperature, room size, and number of people present. When psychologists have asked people to classify social situations, however, they have found that people do not typically focus on these kinds of objective external qualities. Instead, people tend to perceive situations in terms of their own subjective criteria, classifying environments in terms of what those environments can make possible for them. People tend to perceive situations in *psychological* rather than physical terms (Krahe, 1992). As such, situations reside as much in the minds of the observers as in the external environment itself. Writes Ball

---

TABLE 3.3	**SIX GENERAL CATEGORIES OF HUMAN ENVIRONMENTS**

Category	Examples
Ecological	Climate, geography, type of building one lives in, physical characteristics of the setting
Behavior settings	Church, football game, kitchen, classroom
Organizational structure	Population density in an organization, site of organization, degree of hierarchic structure, student–teacher ratio in a school
Characteristics of inhabitants	Age, sex, abilities, status, talents, and so on of people in the environment
Organizational climate	Social morale, nature and intensity of personal relations
Functional properties	Reinforcement consequences for particular behaviors in the situation, such as whether aggressive acts are rewarded or encouraged

SOURCE: From "Conceptualizations of Human Environments," by R. H. Moos, 1973, *American Psychologist,* 28, 652–665.

(1972), "the definition of the situation may be conceived as the *sum of all recognized information, from the point of view of the actor, which is relevant to his locating himself and others, so that he can engage in self-determined lines of action and interaction*" (p. 63).

People often characterize particular situations in terms of their psychological *affordances*—what opportunities for behavior and experience the situations afford or offer for the participant (Dworkin & Goldfinger, 1985). For example, Magnusson (1971) asked persons to evaluate 36 heterogeneous situations and found that the key dimensions upon which the situations could be ordered included how rewarding the situation was, the extent to which the situation induced negative feelings, how passive a person might be in the situation, the amount of social interaction afforded in the situation, and level of activity. Forgas (1978) identified four dimensions that organize 15 different kinds of interpersonal environments: the amount of anxiety the situation elicits, the extent to which a person feels involved in the situation, overall goodness versus badness of the situation, and the extent to which the situation involves accomplishing tasks versus socioemotional interaction. Other studies have arrived at different schemes. There are a dauntingly large number of dimensions upon which immediate situations can be compared and contrasted and little agreement about which dimensions are the most important.

In their efforts to analyze the many different kinds of social contexts that influence behavior, personality psychologists sometimes focus on situational prototypes, which are typical kinds of situations in which people often find themselves and within which people typically follow a standard set of expectations for behavior. A family dinner at a restaurant is one example of a situational prototype in middle-class American society.

If situations are best defined in terms of people's subjective psychological affordances, then it becomes extremely difficult to separate what's "really" in the situation from what's "really" in the person. Furthermore, if a person's personality shapes his or her perceptions, then it would seem to be equally difficult to separate internal personality variables from external situations, for personality characteristics may determine how a person interprets the environment. In support of this idea, Forgas (1983) found that introverted people tended to organize information about situations in terms of a self-confidence dimension. Extraverts, by contrast, categorized situations in terms of how pleasant the situations were and how strongly they afforded interpersonal involvement. Put simply, introverts and extroverts are usually in different situations (in terms of their subjective perceptions), even when it appears from the outside that they are in the same situations.

Whether introvert or extravert, however, the average person appears to possess a "vast and varied expertise about situations" that can be tapped and translated into behavioral guidelines (Cantor, Mischel, & Schwartz, 1982, p. 70). According to one approach to the understanding of situations, people may routinely formulate elaborate personal taxonomies specifying **situational prototypes** (Cantor et al., 1982; Schutte, Kenrick, & Sadalla, 1985). A situational prototype is an abstract set of features about a given class of situations. It serves as a working model for the person, telling him or her what to expect and how to behave in situations of a particular type. A situational prototype may include information about the physical setting, the physical features of the people involved, and common behaviors exhibited by the people in the situation.

For example, the situation of "party" may suggest a large number of features typically associated with parties. Perhaps the prototypical party generally occurs in the evening and involves a large number of people congregating in a circumscribed space, informal dress, eating and drinking, lively conversation, laughing, music and dancing, and lots of noise. Of course, parties vary, and each party contains its own constellation of defining features. Nonetheless, we extract from our experience a core of "partyness" that represents for each of us the "best example" or "ideal case" for defining the situation we call "party." Subsequently, each party we encounter may be evaluated in terms of this implicit categorization. A large dance party at a sorority house may, therefore, appear to us to be a highly prototypical party, embodying many of the features that parties tend to have in common. On the other hand, a poetry-reading party at the home of a college English professor may seem less prototypical, farther away from what we typically think of when we think of the party situation.

MACROCONTEXTS: SOCIAL STRUCTURE

There are no perfectly egalitarian human societies on earth. In all societies and in virtually all human groups, power and resources are unevenly distributed. We can debate why this is so and whether or not it has always been so, but it is surely true today that some people have more access to those resources most valued in society than do others. In American society, those resources include especially money and education, each of which can directly or indirectly confer prestige, status, and power. The unequal distribution of resources creates complex relationships among members of society and exerts pervasive influences on how people develop over time, what they strive for, and how they understand themselves and the world. The term **social structure,** therefore, refers to those conditions of society that differentiate people along the lines of power and resources. Social structure provides an encompassing macrocontext for human behavior (Pettigrew, 1997). The impact of this macrocontext on personality is evident when we look at the relation between personality and social class.

In a classic review of social stratification research in different countries, Inkeles (1960) found that people in higher socioeconomic classes (those with higher-paying, professional jobs and with higher levels of education) showed different patterns of attitudes and behavior than people from lower classes. For example, Inkeles found that individuals in higher classes tended to report higher job satisfaction compared with individuals in lower social classes. Social class was also associated with attitudes about one's job and about human nature. Individuals from higher social classes tended to express greater concern that their job be interesting and fulfilling rather than merely a source of steady income, and they tended to believe in the possibility of changing human nature for the better. By contrast, lower-class individuals valued security first and foremost in their work and tended to be much more fatalistic and pessimistic about human nature.

Over the past 35 years, Melvin Kohn and his colleagues have undertaken a series of influential studies examining social structure and personality (Kohn, 1969; Kohn, Naoi, Schoenbach, Schooler, & Slomczynski, 1990; Kohn & Schooler, 1969, 1973). Kohn argues that the impact of social class on personality can be seen both in the demands of the workplace and the dynamics of the family. Professional, higher-status occupations place significant cognitive demands upon workers. Teachers, doctors, lawyers, and other white-collar professionals are challenged to exercise initiative and independent judgment in their work to a greater extent than are blue-collar factory employees and other workers in lower-status jobs. Higher-status employees, therefore, enjoy and cultivate greater levels of *self-direction* at work. By contrast, lower-status employees find fewer cognitive challenges in their work, are given fewer opportunities to exercise initiative, and must typically instead obey the orders of their superiors. Consequently, lower-status employees are socialized to value *obedience to authority*. Kohn et al. (1990) found that American, Japanese, and Polish men from higher social classes all had a more self-directed orientation, encompassing higher internal control and higher trust, compared with men of lower social classes. Higher social class was also associated with lower conformity, lower anxiety, and greater intellectual flexibility.

What is especially fascinating about the distinction between higher-class self-direction and lower-class obedience to authority is that it tends to generalize to the family realm as well. Kohn (1969) showed that in both the United States and Italy, middle-class parents more often stressed intent and self-direction while lower- and working-class parents more often stressed obedience to authority in the family. Children whose parents enjoy professional, high-status jobs, therefore, tend to be socialized in such a way as to encourage self-direction, which itself becomes a valuable asset for those children when they grow up and pursue professional positions themselves. By contrast, children whose parents work in lower-status occupations tend to be socialized toward obedience to authority. While such a socialization pattern fits the demands of lower-class work and family life, it may not prepare these children well for their later efforts to move up into higher-status occupations. Developmental psychologist Jerome Kagan emphasizes how lower- and working-class families value security first and foremost and seek to instill in their children those qualities that have historically reinforced stability and stasis in the occupational world. Kagan (1984) writes:

> Parents who have not attended college, who see themselves and their children as part of the working class, and who live with chronic financial insecurity, often attribute their personal *angst* to economic stress, which they view as being not completely under their control. These families award a high priority to job security; and a central goal in socializing their child is to ensure that he or she will develop the qualities that guarantee a secure job. Two key qualities are acceptance by peers and the ability to resist being exploited by those with more power. (p. 249)

In contrast, middle-class families are likely to be better educated and better off financially. The parents are likely to have professional positions, and the children are likely to be socialized within a much different macrosystem of values, beliefs, and world views:

> College-educated parents, especially those with professional vocations, regard freedom of choice, intellectual challenge, and the status of one's work as more important than job security. They believe that anxiety over peer rejection or disapproval obstructs the attainment of these goals, and they try to inoculate their youngsters against the anxiety that accompanies peer rejection, while emphasizing autonomous choice and competition. (Kagan, 1984, p. 249)

Studies carried out in the United States and in England have shown that middle-class adolescents and adults use more complex and less stereotyped language than do lower-class people, even when their intelligence test scores are similar (Hess & Shipman, 1965). Bernstein (1970) has argued that lower-class parents adopt a restricted linguistic code in communicating with their children, which means that they limit their verbal exchanges to direct expressions of concrete statements and commands. Middle-class parents, on the other hand, tend to use an elaborated linguistic code consisting of complex syntax, conditional statements, and the expression of abstract ideas. Critical of this characterization, Labov (1972) argues that middle-class psychologists are not sensitive to the nuance and range of meaning in lower-class speech. Both Bernstein and Labov would agree, however, that language reflects context, and that differences in verbal behavior between lower- and middle-class people reflect different systems for making meaning in the world and thus different contexts within which behavior can be understood.

While psychologists have long been interested in the relation between social class and personality dispositions, they have only recently begun to examine in depth the effects of *extreme poverty* on the development of personality and well-being. Children in extremely poor families—in both "developed' and "third world" countries—confront widespread environmental disadvantages, many of which are difficult to fathom from the standpoint of the comfortable middle class (Evans, 2004). Compared to more economically advantaged children, poor children are exposed to more family turmoil, violence, separation from their families, instability, and chaotic households. They experience less social support from their parents, are read to less frequently, have less access to books and computers, and watch substantially more TV. Low-income parents are less involved in their children's school activities. In addition, the air and water that poor children consume are more polluted, their homes are noisier and more crowded, their neighborhoods are more dangerous and deteriorated, their day-care centers are inferior, and they benefit from fewer municipal services. Poverty is a macrocontext of awesome and tragic proportions. Its effects on personality are likely to be both broad and subtle.

GENDER AS A MACROCONTEXT

If social structure refers to those conditions of society that differentiate people along the line of resources and power, then one of the great structural divides in human life is *gender*. Gender encompasses all those social and personal characteristics, constructions, and roles typically associated with one or another of the two biological sexes in human life. As a product of social learning, we come to expect that women and men will differ from each other in a number of important ways. In the extreme, we may form *gender role stereotypes,* which are relatively inflexible ideas about how males and females do and should act. For example, we may expect that, overall, men should be relatively more assertive and aggressive than women, while women should be more nurturing, affectionate, and gentle (Spence, 1985). Social psychologists have documented the pervasiveness of gender role stereotypes in American society, as well as in other societies, and have shown how such stereotyping is at the root of sexism and prejudice.

Like social class, gender has profound implications for power and prestige. In many if not most societies (including contemporary American society), men generally have more access to social and economic power than do women. Men control more public resources, make more decisions about the society as a whole, and enjoy more freedom and autonomy. While moves toward equality have accelerated in the past 30 years, American men (especially white men) still occupy most of the highest positions of societal power and prestige. For example, they vastly outnumber women at the levels of top corporate executives and government leaders, and they still make considerably more money than do women, even when their professional positions are roughly comparable. Within the family, men typically occupy the most dominant roles; in many American families women and children are expected to defer to the man of the house when it comes to major life decisions, especially those involving how the money should be spent. On a more brutal and insidious level, men harass, rape, and kill women to a much greater extent than the other way around. While such behavior may spring as much from frustration and rage as it does from social dominance, physical aggression constitutes yet another mechanism through which males can exert power and control over females.

Gender role stereotypes typically reinforce the power differential between men and women. Stereotypically masculine attributions such as "dominant," "assertive," and "controlling" reinforce the idea that men have the power in society, whereas stereotypically feminine attributions of "submissive," "nurturing," and "gentle" suggest that women occupy subservient positions. From an early age, children learn that such characteristics are differentially applicable to human beings as a function of biological sex. Little girls may be rewarded for cooperative and friendly play, while little boys may receive reinforcement for rambunctious outbursts (instrumental conditioning). Both little girls and boys see that women occupy the primary care-giving roles in society, while men tend to be both the breadwinners and the action heroes (observational learning). Gender socialization is pervasive in contemporary American society—in ways both obvious and subtle, well-meaning and invidious. Through rewards, punishments, and observational learning, males and females become intimately familiar with society's expectations as to gender-appropriate behavior (Brody, 1999). Of course, not everybody follows the stereotypical path. But virtually everybody is aware of the expectations, even as those expectations continue to change and as many men and women work hard to change them.

Alice Eagly and Wendy Wood (1991, 1999) argue that socialization into gender roles accounts for most of the general sex differences that are observed in human social behavior. Reviews of the empirical literature indicate, for example, that the sexes typically differ in a variety of social behaviors, including aggression, helping, nonverbal behavior, and interactions in groups (Eagly, 1987). From an early age onward, males tend to be more aggressive than females (Eagly & Steffen, 1986; Maccoby & Jacklin, 1974), a difference that becomes especially apparent by the teenage years, when boys exhibit markedly higher levels of antisocial activity, including violent crime. On the flip side of the coin, men also exhibit higher levels of altruistic, helping behavior in short-term interactions with strangers (e.g., when a stranger is in distress; Eagly & Crowley, 1986). Women, however, show considerably higher levels of daily helping behavior, as in acts of caring for and tending to the needs of others, primarily in close or long-term relationships. In a fascinating study of heroism and gender, Becker and Eagly (2004) showed that men are overrepresented among winners of the Carnegie medal for outstanding bravery in life-threatening situations but that women tend to show equal or higher levels of heroism under less dangerous conditions as expressed in living kidney donations and volunteering for organizations such as the Peace Corps and Doctors for the World.

Compared with men, women tend to be more sensitive to nonverbal cues in social interaction. In social situations, women smile and laugh more than do men, use their faces and bodies more expressively, show more involvement with others' behavior, touch other people more, and approach them more closely (Hall, 1984; Stier & Hall, 1984). Women also report greater empathy for others' emotional experiences (Eisenberg & Lennon, 1983). These sex differences are generally consistent with the widespread belief in our society that women are more socially skilled, emotionally sensitive, and expressive than men, as well as more concerned with personal relationships. In group discussions, women, more than men, act friendly and agree with other group members (Anderson & Blanchard, 1982). In contrast, men, more than women, contribute behaviors that are strictly oriented to accomplishing the task that the group was assigned. In leadership roles, women adopt a more democratic and participatory style than men; men tend to lead in a more authoritarian manner (Eagly & Johnson, 1990).

Although the sex differences that have been documented for social behavior are not always large in magnitude, they tend to be consistent with society's expectations about gender roles. On a most general level, these expectations can be summarized in terms of the constructs of **agency** and **communion** (Bakan, 1966). Agency refers to the tendency of an individual to assert the self in a powerful and expansive manner and is associated with such characteristics as being aggressive, independent, masterful, and instrumentally competent. Communion refers to the tendency of an individual to merge with other individuals and is associated with such characteristics as being friendly, unselfish, concerned with others, and emotionally expressive. In a nutshell, gender roles suggest that men should be slightly more agentic and women slightly more communal. Empirical research into social behavior provides modest support for these expectations. In other words, men and women do seem to behave in accord with gender role expectations, though the tendencies are moderate. Eagly and Wood (1991) maintain that sex differences in agentic and communal qualities are mainly the result of social learning over the life span. Socialization practices and cultural norms reflect the uneven distribution of women and men into different societal roles. Of particular importance in this regard is the traditional assignment of women to the roles of child rearing and domestic work as well as the tendency for men and women to carry out different types of paid employment in a largely sex-segregated economy.

Now, there are at least two very different ways to interpret the empirical literature on sex differences in social behavior and their relation to gender roles and gender socialization. The more upbeat and innocent interpretation is to say that gender roles reflect those differences between men and women that have arisen through a beneficent blending of nature and choice. One variation on this line of argument purports that because women are biologically fit to bear children and because men tend on the average to be somewhat larger and stronger than women, women and men have gravitated toward different but equally valuable (and valued) roles in society. Separate but equal, in a sense. A second, less sanguine

Gender is a powerful macrocontext for human behavior. Women and men often engage in activities that fit neatly with society's expectations and stereotypes for sex-role behavior.

interpretation emphasizes *hegemony,* or the expression of power by one group over another. According to this second line of thinking, gender roles are the result of unequal power between the sexes. In patriarchal societies, men have assumed the most dominant roles. In both conscious and unconscious ways and through both overt and covert means, men's power has worked to subjugate women into those roles that afford less status, impact, and freedom. Why, then, are women somewhat more communal than men? According to arguments that emphasize power and hegemony, women have assumed more communal orientations and developed interpersonal skills as *strategies for survival and success in subservient roles.* It is incumbent upon girls and women to hone their skills in interpersonal relations as a way of exerting what little power they are able to summon forth in a patriarchal society. By contrast, men do not need to be as interpersonally sensitive and communally oriented because they can generally achieve their ends through direct, agentic means.

Whatever interpretation you wish to make of why it is that men and women show differences in social behavior and how those differences relate to gender roles and gender role stereotypes, you are likely to conclude, as you should, that gender is a pervasive macrocontext for human behavior. One of the first things, if not *the* first thing, we learn about a person is whether that person is male or female. That knowledge shapes our expectations as to how that person should behave, who that person is, and how we should interact with that person. Gender roles inform our approaches to a vast array of social situations, everything from what we do on a first date to how we act as a leader of a group. Even when we act in defiance of gender roles, we are acknowledging our understanding that such roles exist, even as we hope to transcend them. Therefore, while gender roles may not control our lives and do not necessarily leave us powerless to engage in role-incongruent behavior, they are nonetheless formidable forces to confront across the human life span. Put another way, gender is a ubiquitous category for human experience. It is fair to say that personality is itself gendered. A human life is, to a certain extent, a gendered construction. And each of us lives in a gendered world.

CULTURE

The most encompassing and far-reaching macrocontext for human behavior is **culture.** Social scientists have formulated many different definitions of culture. Robert LeVine (1982) views culture as a tradition of rules embraced by a particular society of people. According to LeVine, culture is

> an organized body of rules concerning the ways in which individuals in a population should communicate with one another, think about themselves and their environments, and behave toward one another and toward objects in their environments. The rules are not universally or constantly obeyed, but they are recognized by all and they ordinarily operate to limit the range of variation in patterns of communication, belief, value, and social behavior in the population. (LeVine, 1982, p. 4)

When we think of culture as an organized body of rules that binds people together in a society, we may assume that culture exists *outside* the person as a coherent and encompassing whole. In the 1930s and 1940s, social scientists who examined the relations between culture and personality tended to exhibit just this emphasis (LeVine, 2001). Their work was based on the assumption that people's lives corresponded in a coherent manner to the rules of their culture. Therefore, particular cultures might produce distinctive character types or "modal personalities" (e.g., Benedict, 1934). In more recent times, however, anthropologists and other social scientists who examine the intersection of culture and individual lives have come to emphasize the inconsistencies and diversities in any given culture and the inevitable mismatches and incongruencies that follow from the relations between culture and individual lives. For example, Geertz (1973) argues that culture should not be seen as a tightly constructed, rule-governed system. Culture consists of many different elements, some in conflict with each other (Gjerde, 2004; Holland, 1997). Furthermore, people do not match up neatly to the cultures wherein they reside. Instead, each person makes use of the cultural resources that are available to him or her. Each culture provides "a tool kit of habits, skills, styles, perspectives, norms, roles, and values out of which each individual can construct a potentially unique strategy of action" (Triandis, 1997, p. 443). People act and think selectively and strategically within culture. "As constructors of experience, people are capable of selecting among various imperatives, claiming, elaborating, and personalizing some of the available collective resources so that they are both individually and jointly held, while ignoring, resisting, contesting, and rearranging others" (Markus, Kitayama, & Heiman, 1998, p. 859).

In a fundamental sense, culture is as much inside the person as it is in the world surrounding the person. Culture provides a way of knowing and construing the self, the world, and others (Bruner, 1990). Cushman (1990) writes that culture "is not indigenous clothing that covers the universal human; it infuses individuals, fundamentally shaping and forming them and how they conceive of themselves and the world, how they see others, and how they engage in structures of mutual obligation" (p. 31). The idea of culture as the *meanings that infuse human lives* is central to the conception of culture offered by Shweder and Sullivan (1993), who write that a culture is "that subset of possible or available meanings, which by virtue of enculturation—informal or formal, implicit or explicit, unintended or intended—has become so active in giving shape to the psychological processes of individuals in a society that those meanings have become, for those individuals, indistinguishable from experience itself" (p. 29). As a complex macrocontext for human behavior, culture offers up a rich mix of meanings, practices, and discourses that shape individual lives (Holland, 1997). But individuals do not passively submit to culture. Instead, each of us appropriates certain cultural meanings and ignores others, and each of us is likely to do battle with those aspects of culture that we find disagreeable or even repugnant. Culture infuses us with meanings, but as active agents in the world, we each participate in culture and leave our mark on those meanings, making for a dynamic and evolving interplay between culture and self (Holland, 1997).

Individualism and Collectivism

A major theme in the literature on cross-cultural psychology is that while some cultures emphasize the autonomy of individual selves, other cultures provide meanings organized around the interdependence of selves within communities. On a cultural level, **individualism** is a meaning system that exalts the autonomy of the individual over and against the interdependence of the group. People in individualist cultural contexts typically give priority to their own personal goals, even when the goals are in conflict with the goals of family, work group, or country (Greenfield, Keller, Fuligni, & Maynard, 2003; Triandis, 1997; Triandis & Suh, 2002). By contrast, cultural **collectivism** is a meaning system that gives priority to the in-group or collective over and against the individual. People in collectivist cultural contexts typically put the interests and values of their groups (e.g., family, community, nation) ahead of their own personal agendas (Triandis, 1997). On self-report scales designed to measure collectivism, people living in collectivist societies tend to endorse such items as, "I stick with my group even through difficulties" and "I am prepared to do things for my group at any time, even though I have to sacrifice my own self-interests" (Kashima et al., 1995).

Among those societies that appear to express the most individualist cultural meanings are the United States, Canada, Australia, and the democracies of northern and western Europe (e.g., Great Britain, Germany). The emphasis on competition, autonomy, individualism, and the self is generally considered to be a hallmark of industrial and postindustrial Western culture. The emphasis is complexly determined and has historical roots in Western religion, philosophy, economy, and government (Bellah, Madsen, Sullivan, Swidler, & Tipton, 1985, 1991; Bloom, 1987). This pervasive ideological context for behavior suggests that we as Westerners tend to see people as potentially self-sufficient agents endowed with fundamental and even inalienable individual rights—such as the rights to "life, liberty, and the pursuit of happiness," the right of free speech, and the right of assembly. We view society as comprising autonomous agents who freely choose to behave as they do. This position contrasts starkly with the view of persons espoused in, say, a traditional Hindu village in India. Miller (1984) has shown that children in American society tend to explain everyday social events in terms of the personal dispositions of individual persons. Hindu children, on the other hand, tend to explain everyday events in terms of the pressures of the environment and the influences of society on persons.

The emphasis on collectivism is especially strong in many traditional societies and in Asia, the Pacific Islands, and Africa (Triandis, 1997). Collectivist values are at the heart of Eastern Asian religious and cultural traditions, as evidenced in Buddhism and Confucianism. The Buddha taught self-renunciation as a goal of human life, through which the person transcends the limits of the individual self and finds connection to others and the cosmos. Confucius codified a social doctrine of familial and community obligations. In the Confucian tradition, social order takes precedence over individual expression. A person needs to know his or her proper place in the hierarchical order of things. Special emphasis is placed on the vertical (across generations) relationships between parents and children. Sons and daughters are obligated to serve their parents and show them considerable deference (filial piety); the same obligations are to be expressed toward the authority of the state.

Markus, Kitayama, and Heiman (1998) write that the idea of assuming one's proper place within a social hierarchy is so pervasive in some Asian cultures that it shapes language. The earliest language learning by children in Western Samoa contains a set of important assumptions about authority—who can speak when and who can express certain ideas. Children are taught to look for the hidden meanings behind words so that they do not need to ask their parents and teachers the many questions that might ultimately lead them to challenge authority. In Japan, it is said that before asking a question, it is essential—Confucian style—to ask oneself, "Does this question need to be asked?" and if yes, "Am I the right person to ask it?" (Markus, Kitayama, & Heiman, 1998, p. 876). In talking about personality and social life, the Japanese often invoke the concept of *amae* (Doi, 1962). *Amae* roughly translates as "depending on or presuming another's benevolence." While dependency may seem to be an immature, childhood characteristic from an individualistic standpoint, the Japanese conceive of the entire life span in terms of *amae*. Both Japanese children and adults view themselves as being linked to others in a social hierarchy through bonds of benevolent interdependency.

The distinction between individualism and collectivism should not be drawn too sharply but should instead be seen as a matter of degree. Any given culture is not completely individualist or collectivist as a whole. Instead, every culture has both individualist and collectivist meanings. For example, in American society people speak easily about the development of an autonomous self (individualism) as well as their obligations and commitments to families and other groups (collectivism) (Holland, 1997). Therefore, cultures tend to differ from one another in terms of their *relative emphasis* on individualism and collectivism. These relative differences can be further spelled out in terms of four defining attributes of individualism and collectivism—goals, relationships, determinants of social behavior, and construals of the self (Triandis & Gelfand, 1998).

The first attribute concerns goals. From an individualist standpoint, personal goals are more important than the goals of the in-group (e.g., family, community, state), whereas from a collectivist standpoint the in-group goals are more important. It is important to note that a collectivist perspective connects the person to a *particular* in-group rather than, say, to all humankind in general. From a collectivist standpoint, one is loyal to one's own group, and such loyalty may put one in strong opposition to other groups. A second attribute concerns relationships. From an individualist standpoint, rational exchange is the norm in relationships; separate and autonomous selves come together to "trade" resources (e.g., money, help, love), and social life resembles, in many ways, a marketplace. From a collectivist standpoint, people relate to one another more from the standpoint of communal obligations and bonds of loyalty. A third attribute concerns the determinants of social behavior. From an individualist standpoint, the person's own attitudes take precedent over group norms in motivating and guiding behavior. Individualist cultures emphasize the ideas of "standing up for what you think is right" and "being true to your own convictions." By contrast, the collectivist meaning system elevates social norms above the opinions or attitudes of individuals. People are encouraged to act in accord with the standards of the in-group. Finally, individualist and collectivist cultures suggest rather different construals of the self. The individualist self is defined over and against others as an autonomous and independent agent. The collectivist self, by contrast, is viewed as highly interdependent and embedded within the community.

The differences between construals of an *independent* self, so characteristic of individualist cultures, and the contrasting construals of an *interdependent* self, more common in collectivist cultures, have been described in detail by Markus and Kitayama (1991). As spelled out in Table 3.4, Markus and Kitayama propose that in Western, especially North American middle-class cultures, there is a strong belief in the independence of the self from others. The self is defined in terms of internal attributes such as motives, abilities, talents, or "personalities," and a major cultural task is to discover, actualize, or confirm these personal attributes of the self. The independent way of being is widely elaborated in a variety of cultural practices, such as conversational styles that emphasize individual choice and self-fulfillment over and against conformity to social norms, and in such cultural institutions as the merit pay system. By contrast, many non-Western, especially Asian, cultures (and to an important extent some non-European groups in the United States) do not value such a strict separation or independence of the self. These cultures, instead, believe in the fundamental connectedness or interdependence among those within an in-group. The self is made in reference to the relationships of which it is part. The major cultural task is to fit in, adjust to the relationship, while constraining, taming, or otherwise conditioning internal desires or wishes so as to facilitate the paramount goal of interpersonal harmony and unity. The interdependent way of being is elaborated in such cultural practices as conversational styles emphasizing sympathy and kindness to others and in such cultural institutions as the seniority system.

Markus and Kitayama's distinction between independent and interdependent self construals neatly parallels the distinction between individualist and collectivist cultures, and

TABLE 3.4	KEY DIFFERENCES BETWEEN INDEPENDENT AND INTERDEPENDENT CONSTRUALS OF SELF	
Feature	**Independent**	**Interdependent**
Definition	Separate from social context	Connected with social context
Structure	Bounded, unitary, stable	Flexible, variable
Characteristics	Internal, private (abilities, thoughts, relationships)	External, public (statuses, roles, feelings)
Tasks	Be unique	Belong, fit in
	Express self	Occupy one's proper place
	Realize internal attributes	Engage in appropriate action
	Promote own goals	Promote others' goals
	Be direct: "Say what's on your mind"	Be indirect: "Read other's mind"
Role of others	Self-evaluation: others are important for social comparison, reflected appraisals	Self-definition: relationships with others in specific contexts define the self
Basis of self-esteem	Ability to express self, validate internal attributes	Ability to adjust, restrain self, maintain harmony with social context

SOURCE: From "Culture and the Self: Implications for Cognition, Emotion, and Motivation," by H. R. Markus & S. Kitayama, 1991, *Psychological Review, 98*, p. 230.

both distinctions share conceptual space with a contrast we considered earlier when we discussed gender—the distinction between *agency* and *communion* (Bakan, 1966). With respect to gender, we suggested that some of the sex differences in psychological processes that have been identified in the empirical literature paint a portrait of men as somewhat more agentic (power oriented, striving for autonomy) than women, and women as somewhat more communal (intimacy oriented, striving for connection) than men. An important study by Kashima et al. (1995), however, warns against equating cultural and gender differences. The authors examined self-construals in five cultures—Australia, United States, Hawaii, Japan, and Korea. Their findings showed that differences among these cultures were indeed captured by measures of individualism and collectivism. But the same measures did not capture differences between men and women. Instead, gender differences showed up on measures of the extent to which people feel emotionally related to others (a concept that is not related to collectivism), with women scoring higher on these measures than men. Both men and women in individualist cultures (e.g., the United States, Australia), therefore, tended to view their actions and attitudes as expressing their own self-strivings, whereas both men and women in collectivist cultures (e.g., Hawaii, Japan, Korea) tended to view their actions and attitudes as expressing their connections to family and social group. With respect to gender, women in both individualist and collectivist cultures reported greater levels of empathy and emotional connection to other people than did men in both individualist and collectivist cultures. In simple terms, the data suggest that "women are not like Asians" (Kashima et al., 1995, p. 932), and men are not like Americans. The individualist/collectivist distinction applies more to cultural differences than gender differences. Put another way, saying that Asians espouse a more collectivist viewpoint than Americans, overall, does not mean that Asians are more emotionally connected to other people than are Americans. If Kashima's findings are valid, it would appear that emotional connection to others is more tied up with gender than it is with culture.

Modernity

Another cultural concept that is related to the distinction between individualism and collectivism is **modernity.** Modernity refers most generally to the economic, political, and cultural systems spawned in the 19th and 20th centuries by the Industrial Revolution; the expansion of capitalism and the proliferation of markets and trade; the increasing domination of science and technology; and the rising power of nationalist states, especially democracies, beginning in Western Europe and America and eventually spreading to parts of Asia (e.g., Japan) as well. Although there remain substantial cultural differences among those societies that have been impacted by modernity, modern societies still tend to share certain features and outlooks. For example, modernity is often perceived as encouraging a rationalistic and scientifically minded approach to the world (Gergen, 1991). Modernity is associated with growing skepticism toward religion and other traditional sources of authority (such as the monarchy) and the spreading belief that progress and human betterment reside in the advances of science, technology, and economic and political development (Harvey, 1990). The cultures that prevail in modern societies tend to value reason, objectivity, rational discourse, and developmental progress in accord with scientific laws and other consensually validated systems of knowledge and belief. As societies become more modern, values and attitudes of people change. In a study of six developing countries, Inkeles and Smith (1974) found that the move toward modern industrialization was accompanied by an increase in all of the following aspects of personality and social life: (a) openness to new experiences, (b) assertion of independence from traditional authorities, (c) belief in scientific efficacy rather than fatalism, (d) ambitious occupational and educational goals for one's self and children, (e) concern for punctuality and planning, (f) interest and participation in local politics, and (g) interest in national and international news.

Cultural modernity tends to promote individualism. The value systems that promote and are promoted by science, democracy, and free trade tend to celebrate the virtues of self-initiative, self-expression, and independence. But modernity and individualism are not the same concepts. For example, modern societies vary considerably with respect to their emphasis on individualism, with some modern societies, such as Japan and South Korea, tending toward collectivism rather than individualism. Still, it is probably fair to say that as traditionally collectivist societies become more modern they move somewhat in the direction of cultural individualism. Modernity appears to bring with it certain characteristic problems and opportunities in the development of the self (Baumeister, 1986; Giddens, 1991; Langbaum, 1982; McAdams, 1996a; Taylor, 1989). In modern societies, people tend to view the self as a *project* that they "work on," develop, improve, and strive to perfect. In contemporary American society, for example, there is no shortage of advice and instruction on how to improve the self—lessons can be gleaned from television talk shows, popular self-help books, therapists, counselors, advisors, and virtually anybody else who feels the need or qualifications to instruct another person on how to "make the most" of life, to "live up to one's potential," to reach self-fulfillment or self-actualization. Self-making is a veritable industry in many modern societies, and people invest a tremendous amount of psychic energy and real cash into their own projects of self-construction.

The modern view of the self tends to emphasize the extent to which the self is complex and multilayered. Even before Sigmund Freud proclaimed the power of the unconscious,

FEATURE 3.B

RACE AND PERSONALITY IN THE UNITED STATES

Ever since Europeans imported African men and women to the New World as slaves, race has served to divide Americans into different economic and cultural camps. Slavery was abolished in the United States more than 140 years ago, but African Americans and European Americans continue to inhabit somewhat separate cultural worlds. African Americans are still disproportionately represented in the lower economic classes. Therefore, race and class cannot be readily separated from each other. Nonetheless, many sociologists and other scholars insist that a person's racial background, regardless of social class, exerts a marked influence on that person's development and relationships with others. In a provocative and rueful analysis of psychological research comparing African Americans and white Americans, Jones (1983) remarks:

> Over the past few decades, psychological analysis of race has identified an unending stream of dysfunctions, maladaptations, deficient social organization, poor intellectual performance, inadequate motivation, restricted ego domains, doubts, stresses, and fears. One wonders, on the basis of this extensive literature, how black Americans have managed to survive. The genetic versions of these negativistic analyses are based on the assumption that deficient genes explain the poor adaptation to American society; the environmental versions instead point the finger at poverty and racist oppression. While the environmentalists often accuse the geneticists of racism, black psychologists cannot help noticing that neither position recognizes a single attribute, capacity, or contribution of black people that could be considered positive, desirable, or worth preserving. An essential goal of black psychology, then, is to go beyond the reactive conception of black Americans' history to develop a cultural-evolutionary perspective

that recognizes African origins, and more recent developments in the United States (and other countries), and the effects of prolonged oppression. The new perspective should include what is distinctively good and useful in the Afro- or African-American experience. (p. 142)

Jones indicts American social scientists for failing to understand the macrocontext of black culture. Cole (1976) identifies three principal components of black culture: (a) an "American mainstream" component shared with white Americans and espousing such values as individualism and materialism; (b) a "minority sense" component shared with other disadvantaged minorities in American society, reinforcing the sense that being black is likely to make one the subject of discrimination; and (c) a unique "blackness" component that incorporates certain African and African-American values, mannerisms, and styles. The blackness component includes what Cole terms "soul"—a sense of people facing hardship together as a spirited and vital community—and "style," which refers to characteristic ways of talking, walking, dressing, and thinking.

Many black scholars draw sharp contrasts between European-American philosophical orientations (which provide a foundation for the American white culture) and African philosophical orientations (which are more instrumental in the black culture) (e.g., Akbar, 1991; Dixon, 1976; White & Parham, 1990). The differences suggest that black heritage is highly social rather than individualistic, oriented toward the present rather than the future, and focused on subjective emotional experience over and against objective rationality. These are *cultural* rather than personal differences. They represent contrasts in the implicit philosophical contexts behind behavior rather than differences in behavior per se. Again, we see that different contexts imbue a person's behavior with different meanings.

(CONTINUES)

FEATURE 3.B *(CONTINUED)*

Social psychologist Philip Bowman (1989, 1990) is one of a small but growing number of researchers who are working to understand the complex influences of racial macrocontexts on the development of personality. Bowman underscores both the *risks* and the *resiliency* inherent in African-American family life today. According to Bowman, African-American families exhibit at least four distinctive qualities that serve as *adaptive cultural resources*. First, compared to the European-American majority, African-American families tend to incorporate extended kin networks. The many aunts, uncles, grandparents, and other relatives living close to one another create a community of support that is especially significant for the rearing of children. Second, family roles are likely to be especially flexible in the African-American community. For example, black men and women tend to assume both agentic and communal roles in the family, rather than specializing along sex-stereotypic lines (Boyd-Franklin, 1989). Third is the powerful role of religion and spirituality among African Americans. Blacks in the United States have traditionally attended church more often and reported more significant religious involvements than whites. The church has traditionally been an extraordinarily integrative and sustaining force in the black community, functioning as a source of spiritual guidance, agency for social service, and catalyst for societal change. Finally, black racial consciousness can be viewed as an adaptive cultural resource. To the extent that African-American children identify proudly with a distinctive cultural heritage, they can eventually draw on that heritage for shaping their own identities and leading productive and fulfilling lives.

Adopting the frameworks of cross-cultural psychology (e.g., Triandis, 1997), Bowman argues that different cultural groups often have a great deal in common. For example, blacks in the United States tend to want the same kinds of successes and fulfillments for themselves and their children that whites want. They tend to hold very similar values with respect to social and political issues. These commonalities comprise what anthropologists call *etic* dimensions across cultures, or ways in which different cultures share similar means and goals. Nonetheless, every culture also has its own *emic* dimensions, or those characteristics that serve to distinguish it from other cultures. A sensitive and productive approach to understanding the macrocontext of race in the United States must, therefore, focus both on those etic aspects of culture that most all Americans share and those emic features—especially adaptive cultural resources—that are unique to particular cultural groups.

19th-century Europeans were keenly aware of and fascinated by the distinction between the public and private selves. The advent of industrialization in Europe moved men and some women off the family farm to factories—new public spaces where work was to be done. The public experience of modern work came to be separated from the private experience of family life. A person could develop a public self that was very different from the private self. Furthermore, each of the many selves that a person might develop would itself possess significant depth and complexity. Modernity ushered in the idea that there is a great deal about the self that is hidden, buried, or even disguised. The exploration of the deep, inner regions of the self has become an especially appealing psychological adventure in the modern world (Gay, 1984; Taylor, 1989). For many modern people, such an inner voyage promises to reveal some form of personal truth or moral conviction. Modernity teaches us that it is especially important to be "true to one's self."

From the modern perspective, not only does the self possess significant depth and complexity, but the self is also changing constantly over time. Modern men and women routinely use developmental ideas and metaphors to make sense of their lives (Bellah et al., 1985). As the advances of modern medicine have significantly lengthened the expected life span, modern men and women increasingly expect to live a long and full life, growing, changing, and moving through passages and stages on life's journey. Over time, therefore, modern people expect to "make progress," to move ahead, to develop to higher or better stages and levels. Yet amidst the constant change and growth, modern adults also seek to create some kind of coherence in the self. How can a deep and constantly changing self—a self that I work on day in and day out—come together to provide my life with a sense of unity, purpose, and coherence? This is perhaps the most challenging question for the making of the self in modern societies. It is a problem that we will return to in chapter 10 of this book when we consider how modern adults work on their selves by formulating life stories in order to create an *identity*.

HISTORY

The role of macrocontexts in human behavior usually becomes apparent to us when we notice differences. For example, should we encounter people from a culture very different from our own, we may begin to think about how our own culture's values and norms have shaped us to be the people we are. When we witness the great inequalities in economic resources that characterize modern societies today, we cannot help but be struck by the social-structural dimension of class and how it is that different people in the same nation grow up under radically different material circumstances. In noticing cultural and social-structural differences in a given society, we may begin to imagine how our own lives and our very personalities might be rather different if we had grown up in a different set of macrocontexts—if I were black instead of white, for example, rich instead of poor, male instead of female, and so on. But there is a different kind of macrocontext that infuses our lives but that we may rarely think about because we are rarely confronted with differences regarding it. This is the macrocontext of history. Given that everybody reading this book is alive and functioning at the very same historical moment, we are not likely to think about how all of our lives are profoundly shaped by the simple fact that we all live today—here and now at the beginning of the 21st century. Things would be very different, would they not, if this were the year 1901, 1776, or 200 B.C.E.?

The historical context for human behavior situates our lives in time. As people get older, they tend to have a greater sense of the role of history in the shaping of lives. Your grandparents may have told you stories about the good (or not-so-good) old days when they were children, how the world was very different then, before computers, before the existence of hundreds of television channels, when the Soviet Union was the great enemy of "the free world," when Americans fought the Japanese in a ferocious war. (My children still ask me what it was like to live during the Civil War.) It is perhaps in our interactions with people from other generations, as well as in our history classes, that we become most cognizant of how life was once very different than it is today, and how it is likely to be very different in the future. The sociologist Karl Mannheim (1928/1952) argued that different generations of people develop along different paths because of their different historical experiences. For Mannheim, a **generation** consists of those people who are born at the same point in historical time and thereby develop a shared understanding of the world, common beliefs and aims, and a shared generational style. Mannheim maintained that social and historical events occurring during a person's late adolescence and young adulthood are especially likely to shape his or her personality for the future (see also Rogler, 2002).

Abigail Stewart and Joseph Healy (1989) have developed a theory to account for the ways in which history and social events are incorporated into personality. The theory is summarized in Table 3.5. Following Mannheim, Stewart and Healy argue that the influence of history is strongly contingent on a person's age or place in the life course. A major historical event, such as a world war, will have one kind of impact on a 10-year-old child and quite a different impact on a midlife adult. According to Stewart and Healy, historical events occurring during a person's *childhood* are likely to shape his or her fundamental expectations about how the world works. At a very basic level, for example, a child whose family suffers the poverty that comes from a severe economic downturn (e.g., the Great Depression of the late 1920s and early 1930s) may come to assume implicitly that scarcity is the norm in life and that the world is a place where there will never be enough for everybody. Historical events experienced in *late adolescence and early adulthood,* by contrast, may shape life opportunities and choices, especially in the area of occupational identity. One of the outgrowths of the Watergate scandals of the early 1970s, for example, was the rise in prestige of investigative journalism in the United States. The newspaper reporters who exposed the scandals surrounding President Richard Nixon at that time helped to glorify the profession of journalism, which enhanced the appeal of journalism as a vocation for adolescents and young adults like myself. Many college students in my generation were quite taken with the idea of becoming investigative reporters.

In the *early middle-adult years,* Stewart and Healy argue, historical events are less likely to shape fundamental values and vocational identity since adults in their 30s and early 40s have likely consolidated a viewpoint of the world and their place in it. But events can still have a significant impact on what people actually do—that is, on behavior. The eruption of a major war may dramatically change the lifestyle of a 35-year-old homemaker, who may now seek paid employment because of the labor shortage that has resulted from young men being drafted into military service. In a fundamental sense, she may not be changing her values or her identity, but her daily actions are now very different than they were before the war. Finally, events occurring during a person's *later years* (midlife and beyond) may offer new opportunities and stimulate revisions in a person's identity. Adults whose children have now grown up and established their own families may feel freed up to explore new possibilities in lifestyle, occupation, and even personal ideology. Major historical events or social movements may, therefore, feed into this new readiness for change. The women's movement of the 1960s and 1970s afforded new opportunities for women across the life course (Duncan & Agronick, 1995). For mature women who had already brought up their children, the women's movement provided them with new modes of expression and new ways to think about their selves.

TABLE 3.5	LINKS BETWEEN INDIVIDUAL DEVELOPMENT AND SOCIAL/HISTORICAL EVENTS
Age When Event is Experienced	**Focus of Impact of Event**
Childhood and early adolescence	Fundamental values and expectations (e.g., family values, assumptive frameworks)
Late adolescence/early adulthood	Opportunities and life choices; identity (e.g., vocational identity)
Early-middle –adulthood	Behavior (e.g., labor force participation)
Midlife and later	New opportunities and choices; revision of identity

SOURCE: Adapted from "Linking Individual Development and Social Changes," by A. J. Stewart & M. J. Healy, Jr., 1989, *American Psychologist,* 44, p. 32; and "The Intersection of Life Stage and Social Events: Personality and Life Outcomes," by L. E. Duncan & G. S. Agronick, 1995, *Journal of Personality and Social Psychology,* 69, p. 559.

Historical time is perhaps the most complex and subtle macrocontext for human behavior. It is clear that history has an impact on people's lives. But the impact depends, in part, on the particular timing of a life, as Stewart and Healy's theory shows. Therefore, historical time (history) and personal time (biography) interact in very complex ways (Elder, 1995; Mills, 1959). The impact of history, furthermore, is filtered through the macrocontexts of race, class, gender, and culture. For example, many African Americans who lived through the Great Depression of the late 1920s and 1930s report that the economic hardships they experienced were not much worse than what they were used to all along (Angelou, 1970). The economic downturn hit middle- and upper-class whites especially hard because they had much more to lose and were not used to the economic privations that most blacks had known from birth onward. To take another example, wars have traditionally affected men and women in very different ways: Men traditionally fight the wars; women work to keep the home front strong. Moreover, different cultural groups articulate different interpretations of the same historical events. The antiwar protests that rocked American college campuses in the late 1960s shaped the consciousness of many politically liberal and radical young people. The same movement, however, also galvanized politically conservative forces and set the stage for a shift toward political conservatism in the United States in the 1980s and 1990s.

Beyond all of these complications, it is also true that the impact of any historical event or movement is in large part mediated by a person's own, idiosyncratic interpretation of that event. For example, Duncan and Agronick (1995) found that the women's movement of the 1960s and early 1970s certainly had an impact on the lives of many women who were college-aged at the time. But the impact depended on just how "meaningful" a woman considered this historical movement to be. Those women who saw the women's movement to be especially meaningful and important for their own lives ultimately attained higher education levels, work status, and income levels; were employed in upwardly mobile careers by midlife; and reported significant increases in self-confidence and assertiveness in the years following college. For those women in the same generation who did *not* see the women's movement as especially meaningful, however, these trends did not occur.

We will return to the issue of historical time and the timing of lives in chapter 6 when we consider the extent to which personality dispositions are either stable or changing over the human life course. Our take-home message at this point is that historical time is an especially complex and encompassing macrocontext for human behavior. Human lives are time-structured and historically contingent. Like social class, gender, race, and culture, historical time situates a human life within a set of complex and overlapping environments. The social ecology of human behavior incorporates those many contexts within which we learn to be who we are. From the microcontexts of social situations to the macrocontexts of culture and history, personality is always situated in context. You cannot take the person out of that

Historical events may exert subtle and long-term effects on personality. One theory suggests that dramatic historical events and broad social movements witnessed in childhood and early adolescence may influence fundamental values and expectations about life, those experienced in late adolescence and young adulthood may influence identity and life choices, and those experienced later in life may have impacts on behavior and on identity revision.

context; you cannot talk meaningfully about "personality" without examining the context in which personality is embedded. Human individuality is a thoroughly contextualized phenomenon. Only when we understand the worlds in which we live, therefore, can we fully appreciate the ways in which each of us is a singular human being.

SUMMARY

1. A dominant movement in American psychology in the first half of the 20th century, behaviorism focused on how environments shape the observable behavior of organisms. Although behaviorism's presence has faded considerably in recent decades, its fundamental emphases have lived on in social-learning theories of personality and in the widespread recognition that individual lives must be understood in terms of the environmental contexts within which they are situated.

2. According to the behaviorist view, behavior is learned in the environment. Two fundamental forms of learning are classical and instrumental (operant) conditioning. In classical conditioning, an organism forms associations between different stimuli that are contiguous in time. In instrumental conditioning, learning occurs through rewards and punishments, as behavior is shaped by its consequences. From an operant standpoint, personality characteristics are shaped primarily by reward-and-punishment learning that occurs in particular social situations over time. The determinants of any particular behavior, therefore, can be found both in the current situation and in similar situations in the past in which the person has learned similar responses.

3. Behaviorism spawned a number of different social-learning theories that have been and continue to be influential in the field of personality psychology. Social-learning theories incorporate cognitive variables, such as expectancies and values, competencies, encoding strategies, and self-regulatory systems and plans. These variables help to specify how a person will approach and respond to a given situation.

4. Especially influential has been Albert Bandura's social-learning theory. Bandura emphasizes the roles of observational learning and self-efficacy in human behavior. While reinforcement and need satisfaction may be instrumental in behavioral performance, Bandura shows that learning does not necessarily require reinforcement and may proceed instead through simple observation and imitation. As people observe and learn new responses over time, and as they obtain experience in the performance of those responses, they develop beliefs about their abilities to carry out particular behaviors in particular situations, producing characteristic levels of self-efficacy. The development of self-efficacy is a key mechanism whereby people are able to exercise control over threatening events in the environment.

5. Social learning is a pervasive phenomenon in human life. Psychologists have documented the power of social learning in many different areas of human functioning. An especially provocative area in this regard is the study of aggression. Research documents the powerful role of observation in the formation and performance of aggressive responses.

6. People learn and perform behaviors within a social ecology. The social ecology consists of the many different environmental contexts that influence a person's behavior and shape his or her life. The social ecology ranges from the microcontexts of the immediate social situation, to larger contexts of family, neighborhood, and community. At the largest, most distal, and encompassing levels are the macrocontexts of social class, gender, race, culture, and history. At the level of microcontext, psychologists have sought to define the different kinds of situations that people encounter in daily life. Research suggests that situations are best characterized in terms of their subjective psychological affordances, or what people perceive as the opportunities for behavior and expression in a

particular situation. People form situational prototypes or scripts for certain sorts of stock situations, such as prototypes for "party," "classroom," and "sporting event."

7. Social structure defines an important macrocontext for human behavior. Research documents significant relations between social class variables on the one hand and aspects of personality and social life on the other. Individuals in lower socioeconomic strata report lower job satisfaction, greater concerns for security and stability, and more fatalistic and pessimistic views of human nature, compared with individuals in the middle and upper classes. Professional, high-status occupations place significant cognitive demands on workers and encourage them to take initiative and cultivate self-direction at work. By contrast, lower-status employees find fewer cognitive challenges and opportunities for initiative in their work and are strongly urged to follow the demands of supervisors. Research has shown that in both work and family life, higher social class is associated with greater self-direction and internal control while lower social class is associated with an emphasis on obedience to authority and conformity.

8. Like social class, gender constitutes a powerful macrocontext, in part because it tends to differentiate individuals on the basis of social power and resources. In many if not most societies, men control more public resources, make more decisions about the society as a whole, and enjoy more freedom and autonomy than do women. Gender role stereotypes reinforce this power differential, as men are expected to be dominant and assertive while women are expected to be caring and nurturant. Socialization into gender roles may account for many of the sex differences that have been observed in human social behavior. Among the most well-established findings are that men tend to be more aggressive than women, to be somewhat more directive in leadership and group behavior, and to be more instrumental in public acts of helping; by contrast, women

report higher levels of empathy and interpersonal intimacy, show better skills in encoding and decoding nonverbal interpersonal behavior, and express higher levels of friendliness and care in leadership and group roles. On the most general level, gender-congruent behaviors tend to fall along the dimensions of agency (masculine) and communion (feminine). Whatever the source of these differences between men and women, it is quite clear that social environments and social life for human beings are highly gendered.

9. The most encompassing and far-reaching context for human behavior is culture. Among other things, culture is a system of rules and norms that binds people together in a given society or group, providing a toolkit of habits, skills, styles, perspectives, roles, and values out of which the person can construct a life. Culture infuses human lives with meanings. Two major dimensions upon which different cultures can be organized are individualism and collectivism. Individualist cultures give priority to personal goals, individual attitudes and opinions, exchange relationships, and the efficacy of the autonomous and independent self. By contrast, collectivist cultures give priority to the goals and norms of the in-group or community, communal relationships, and the development of an interdependent construal of the self. While some societies tend to exhibit individualist cultures (e.g., North America) and others exhibit collectivist cultures (e.g., Asia), differences in individualism/collectivism are a matter of relative degree, with all societies having concepts and ideas that pertain to both individual agency and collective harmony. A related cultural concept is modernity, which refers to the economic, political, and cultural systems established by the advent of the Industrial Revolution and the proliferation of democracy and capitalism in the 19th and 20th centuries. Modern cultures tend to be individualist (though there are exceptions), and they tend to articulate a view of the self as a complex and

evolving project that a person develops, expands, improves, and generally "works on" over time.

10. History situates lives in time. People from different generations have different historical experiences, which influence the development of personality. One theory links individual development with historical events by proposing that the timing of an event in terms of a person's life course partly determines the way in which that event will influence the person. Historical events (such as wars, economic downturns, social movements, and so on) experienced when a person is a child help to shape the person's basic values and assumptions about how the world works. Events that occur in late adolescence and young adulthood, by contrast, may impact one's developing vocational identity as well as important life choices. Events that occur in early- to mid-adulthood may not have a profound influence on values and identity but are still likely to affect what a person does—that is, behavior. Finally, historical events experienced at midlife and after hold the potential to offer new opportunities for identity change and the revision of one's sense of self. The impact of any historical event on a person's life is largely determined by how that person actively makes sense of the event.

Sketching the Outline: Dispositional Traits and the Prediction of Behavior

CHAPTER 4

Personality Traits: Fundamental Concepts and Issues

Trait talk. We do it all the time. Let me tell you about my wife's family. My brother-in-law, Dwight, is impulsive and very friendly. He strikes up conversations with strangers in the grocery line. His twin sister, Sara, is more serious, more deliberate, and very conscientious. Her husband, Jack, is also very conscientious; more than most adults I know, the two of them are very concerned about doing the right things with their lives, about making a positive contribution to society. But Jack is also very competitive, as, I must confess, am I. He wins in anything that involves hand-eye coordination, but I can run faster. My wife's oldest brother, Tom, is very analytical and has a sharp sense of humor. My wife's oldest sister, Barb, is extremely well organized, is very sensitive and caring, and rarely judges others harshly. Her husband, Bill, is the great optimist in the family. He can put a positive spin on anything. When my kids complain about how rough life is for them, I tell them to be like Uncle Bill. Lois is the youngest sister. She has many of the traits of her siblings and relatives, but she seems to have them all in moderation. She is harder for me to characterize in a word or two. My wife, well, she is perfect. And she is the only one who will still be speaking to me after reading this paragraph.

Actually, I think they will all still speak to me. They probably won't be angry with my trait talk because (a) I have focused on mainly positive-to-neutral traits (I haven't said anything about who is neurotic, domineering, nerdy, or shallow) and (b) they all know, as do you, that people talk this way about other people, and about themselves, all the time, and that it is not necessarily a bad thing to do (although it can be). They know, as do you, that the currency of everyday trait talk is the generalization. Personality generalizations may be true or useful in a relative sense, but they do not apply to every instance of a person's behavior. Therefore, you would not be surprised if I told you that while Bill is the supreme optimist, he does occasionally fall into a dark mood. You would not discount my trait portrayal if I told you that Barb's desk at work is messy sometimes, even though she is very well organized, or that I rarely compete with my wife, even though I am very competitive. You and I both know that trait attributions are relative, approximate, and very general. Imagine if they weren't! Imagine if people displayed their characteristic trait profiles every moment of every day. Imagine if Dwight talked to *everybody* in the grocery line—*every* time! Imagine if the most conscientious man you ever knew was perfectly dutiful, hard working, and righteous in every situation he ever encountered—at home, at work, on vacation, when talking with his mother, when arguing with his wife, when choosing a dessert at a restaurant, when surfing the Internet, in bed, at 5:00 P.M. on January 4, 2004, at 5:10 P.M. that same day, and 20 years before that. Imagine how predictable people would be, how boring life would be.

It is difficult for you and me to imagine life like that because we know that that is not how people are. People are not robots who do the same thing over and over again. Nobody, no matter how strong a given trait, is perfectly consistent; no single trait can characterize any person; life offers too many different situations for people to do the same thing in each one. This is all so obvious that I am almost embarrassed to bring it to your attention at the outset of this chapter. But I feel compelled to do so in order to make clear that just because trait talk is relatively imprecise and general, there is no getting around it in everyday discourse. *And there is no getting around it in personality psychology.* Just as we find ourselves using trait attributions in conversations about people every day (knowing, as we do, that these attributions are not even close to perfect in their predictive power and in their truth value), so, too, do personality psychologists invoke traits to account for human individuality. In everyday talk and in the scientific study of human individuality, we use general descriptors to characterize individual differences between people. We say that somebody is relatively friendly, soft-spoken, spiteful, fastidious, thoughtful, slovenly, arrogant, humble, dominant, considerate, or honest. Trait talk is irresistible. Despite its important limitations, trait talk is a useful and natural way to account for human individuality.

Now, it is important to note at the outset of this chapter that trait talk, like many things, can be used for good or ill. Characterizing somebody in terms of a few well-chosen and carefully considered trait adjectives can provide a compact and efficient portrayal of that person in general terms, a portrayal that may be useful for describing the person to others, for remembering what the person is generally like, and for making better-than-chance predictions about how that person might behave in the future and what to expect from that person when you meet again. But trait talk is also fraught with dangers. Traits can become "labels" or "stereotypes" that objectify people—that is, labels that turn people into objects in the minds of others. A trait description can oversimplify and gloss over the many important details of a personality, to the detriment of the person being described. Trait talk can be the lazy way out—used by people who want to size up others quickly but have little interest or motivation to get to know a person better. Most odious of all is the use of trait attributions in the service of oppression and prejudice. Stereotyping of strangers and out-groups is one of those pervasive human tendencies that has contributed as much as any other to human suffering. One group may consider members of another group to be especially stupid, lazy, arrogant, sinful, barbaric, rapacious, deceitful, or virtually any negative trait you can name. In its mildest forms, we hear trait talk of this sort in ethnic jokes and other common forms of group stereotyping. But this sort of talk may be no joking matter. Trait talk that stereotypes out-groups and strangers can be used to fuel hatred and justify discrimination, warfare, slavery, and even genocide.

In this chapter and the two that follow, I examine how personality psychologists have sought to explore and refine trait talk in the service of behavioral science and human understanding. Now that we have considered the fundamental contexts of human nature (chapter 2) and culture (chapter 3) for the study of human individuality, it is time to focus on the first and most general level of individual differences between people—the level of *dispositional traits*. Over the past 60 years, personality psychologists have learned a great deal about traits. They have developed important conceptualizations of trait ideas. They have built and validated good measures of individual differences in traits. They have linked traits to trends in behavior and have examined the interactions of traits and situational variables in the prediction of behavior. They have studied the stability and change in personality traits over the life course. They have studied the extent to which traits are products of genetic differences between people and products of environmental effects. They have begun to explore the psychophysiology of traits. And they have considered in detail the many controversies surrounding trait talk—as both a form of everyday conversation and a manner of scientific discourse.

Just as trait talk is an unavoidable aspect of everyday conversation, so are traits indispensable units for understanding personality (A. Buss, 1986; Johnson, 1997). It is virtually impossible to account for human individuality without resorting to traits in some way or another. As I suggested in chapter 1, traits provide an initial outline or sketch of a person's individuality. Good and accurate trait talk, of the sort developed by personality psychologists, provides a kind of dispositional signature for a person. From a good and accurate trait description, we get a sense of which general characteristics or dispositions differentiate that person from others. Trait talk, however, can take us only so far. Eventually, we will want to know things about a person that go beyond general dispositions. We will eventually want to fill in details that cannot be captured in trait talk. These other forms of discourse about human individuality will be the topic of chapters 7 through 12 in this book. For now, though, we need to see just how far we can go with traits. It turns out to be pretty far indeed.

THE IDEA OF TRAIT

WHAT IS A TRAIT?

The concept of a personality trait is rooted in common sense and everyday observation. As we watch, and try to make sense of, the behavior of other people, we notice consistencies within a given person and differences between different persons. For example, we notice that Rachel smiles at people and talks with them in a friendly manner in many different situations—in class, at the gym, eating lunch, studying in the library. Maria, on the other hand, seems rarely to smile or exchange friendly words with others. Whereas Rachel appears consistently warm and outgoing, Maria seems cool and detached. Of course, Rachel has her cool moments, and Maria may really warm up to people in certain situations, but Rachel seems *generally* friendlier than Maria.

Personality psychologists consider a number of aspects of personality traits such as "friendliness." First, they generally conceive of traits as *internal* dispositions that are relatively *stable* over time and across situations. If we are to conclude that my sister-in-law Sara has a strong trait of conscientiousness, we must find evidence that she is consistently conscientious in a variety of situations (in her work for the organization Habitat for Humanity, in her volunteer activities, and in her family life) and over time (as an adolescent, a young adult, and at midlife).

Second, traits are typically conceived in *bipolar* terms. Friendliness can be understood as a continuum ranging from one extreme of "high friendliness" to the other extreme of "high unfriendliness" (synonymous with "low friendliness"). Traits, therefore, are often couched in the language of opposites: friendliness *versus* unfriendliness, extraversion *versus* introversion, dominance *versus* submissiveness. People are seen as situated along any particular trait continuum in a relatively normal distribution, with many people residing toward the middle of the continuum (such as "moderately friendly" or "moderately unfriendly") and fewer lying at the extremes.

Third, different traits are generally seen as *additive* and *independent.* My sister-in-law Barb is very high in agreeableness, is highly organized, is relatively nonjudgmental, and is low on a trait of tendency toward risk taking. The four traits thus combine as four independent "ingredients" in Barb's personality. Mix them together in the proper amounts and you have a recipe for predicting consistency in her behavior and for describing how she is different from other people who have different recipes—that is, different trait profiles.

Finally, personality traits usually refer to *broad* individual differences in *socioemotional* functioning. Writes Conley (1985a), "personality traits constitute very generalized behavior patterns in response to emotional tendencies" (p. 94). Personality traits, therefore, may be distinguished from other variables that appear to be less socioemotional and more cognitive in nature, such as values, attitudes, worldviews, and schemas (Conley, 1985a; McClelland, 1951). Indeed, the distinction between socioemotional personality traits on the one hand and cognitive variables on the other goes back at least as far as the philosopher Immanuel Kant (1724–1804), who distinguished between "temperament" (traits) and "character" (schemas) (Conley, 1985a). In a similar vein, concepts that fall directly under the umbrella of "intelligence" are not usually considered to be part of personality per se, though not all personality psychologists agree with that distinction (e.g., Revelle, 1995). For the purposes of this chapter and this book, we will consider the general trait of intelligence to be outside the personality domain, sticking with the common view that personality traits are concerned mainly with socioemotional functioning.

Overall, then, personality traits refer to individual differences between people in characteristic thoughts, feelings, and behaviors (McCrae & Costa, 1995). Psychologists use trait concepts to account for consistencies in behavior from one situation to the next; for example, Rachel is consistently friendly from one situation to the next (though, of course, not always friendly), and Maria is consistently less friendly. Traits are typically viewed to reside within the person in some sense, as relatively general, global, and stable dispositions. These dispositions are typically conceived in bipolar terms, suggesting that people are more-or-less normally distributed on any given linear trait continuum from one extreme to the other. Most people, therefore, fall within the middle range of any given trait. People can be compared and contrasted with respect to their traits. Traits, therefore, are almost always viewed as comparative dimensions, and one's position on a trait continuum is always relative to the positions of others. From the standpoint of traits, each person may be characterized by his or her standing on a series of relatively independent dimensions, which add up to a trait profile. Personality traits, in contrast to traits of intelligence, typically refer to consistencies in thought, feeling, and behavior associated with social interaction and the socioemotional aspects of life.

The characterization of personality traits that I have provided for you is probably consistent with the general impressions you had about the term *(personality trait)* before you read this chapter, even if you have never given the topic much thought. It is perhaps surprising to learn, therefore, that psychologists have fought many long and nasty intellectual battles over what the concept of trait means and just how useful it might be. At least four different positions have been staked out over the years. (These positions are summarized in Table 4.1.) The first position is that traits literally exist in the central nervous system as what Gordon Allport (1961) called "neuropsychic structures" (p. 347). These hypothesized patternings of psychophysiology—say, particular brain circuitry or neurotransmitter pathways—exert a causal influence on behavior, accounting for consistencies over time and across situations. The second position keeps its options open when it comes to psychophysiological substrata but maintains, nonetheless, that traits exist as dispositions that exert a significant impact on behavior. Therefore, both of these positions view traits as causal mechanisms in human functioning. Traits—be they neuropsychic structures or behavioral dispositions—are instrumental in causing behavior to occur and, therefore, in accounting for consistency in behavior across situations and over time.

By contrast, the third and fourth positions argue that traits do not really cause behavior but exist instead as convenient categories for describing the behaviors that people show. The third position was staked out by Buss and Craik (1983, 1984) in their **act-frequency** approach to personality. According to this view, traits are merely language categories for the organization of discrete behavioral acts. As such, traits do not influence behavior per se. Rather, traits *are the behaviors.* The trait of extraversion, for example, consists of the acts that make it up—such acts as "I danced in front of a crowd" and "I entered into a conversation with a group I didn't know." Acts may be grouped together into trait families, with some acts more prototypical or representative of a given category than others.

TABLE 4.1	FOUR POSITIONS OF THE NATURE OF TRAITS	
Traits Are	**Description**	**Theorists**
Neurophysiological substrates	Traits are biological patternings in the central nervous system that cause behavior to occur and account for the consistencies in socioemotional functioning from one situation to the next and over time.	Allport (1937) Eysenck (1967) Gray (1982) Cloninger (1987) Zuckerman (1991)
Behavioral dispositions	Traits are tendencies to act, think, or feel in consistent ways that interact with external influences, such as cultural norms and situational variables, to influence a person's functioning. Trait attributions can be used both to describe behavior summaries and to suggest causal or generative mechanisms for behavior.	Cattell (1957) Wiggins (1973) Hogan (1986) McCrae & Costa (1990)
Act frequencies	Traits are descriptive summary categories for behavioral acts. Acts that have the same functional properties may be grouped together into families, with some acts being more prototypical or representative of the general family features than others.	Buss & Craik (1983)
Linguistic categories	Traits are convenient fictions devised by people to categorize and make sense of the diversity of human behavior and experience. Traits do not exist outside the mind of the observer, and therefore they can have no causal influence. Through social interaction and discourse, people construct meanings for trait terms.	Mischel (1968) Shweder (1975) Hampson (1988) Harre & Gillett (1994)

Finally, a fourth position asserts that traits do not exist in any objective sense, even in the sense of act categories. Instead, traits are merely convenient fictions that people (and personality psychologists) invent in their efforts to understand social life (Shweder, 1975). You and I use trait terms such as "friendly" and "conscientious" to simplify and organize reality, but these terms are just words. They have no meaning beyond our shared social construction. Therefore, it makes no sense, from this fourth position, to explain behavior in terms of traits. To say, for example, that Rachel smiles a lot because she is a relatively friendly person is akin to saying that Rachel is friendly because she is friendly. The label explains nothing. Furthermore, the causes of Rachel's smiling are not likely to be found within the person but rather in the environment in which the person resides. Psychologists who dismiss traits as convenient fictions usually look to the environmental situation for the causes of behavioral consistencies (e.g., Mischel, 1968).

Strong arguments can be made for all four positions on traits. Each position highlights an important aspect of the idea of trait. The first position suggests that traits have a biological reality; the second points to the dispositional nature of traits; the third suggests that traits connect to functionally similar behaviors; and the fourth points out that trait labels are useful in everyday social cognition. At the same time, the four positions contradict one another in many ways. The contradiction is sharpest between the first and fourth positions: Logic tells us that traits cannot be neuropsychic structures that cause the behavior of actors (first position) if, at the same time, they are merely convenient fictions in the minds of observers (fourth position). We cannot resolve the inconsistencies among the different views. As we will see later in this chapter, different understandings of what traits are or should be have been at the heart of important controversies in the field of personality psychology.

Nonetheless, when it comes to the nature of traits, many personality psychologists today seem to have adopted a fuzzy but reasonable compromise view that is probably closest to the second position I have outlined. Most contemporary personality psychologists seem to view traits as dispositions (second position) that have some causal influence on behaviors, though the influences are complex and exist in interaction with situational factors. They tend to see traits as more than mere descriptive summaries of act categories, but they acknowledge that traits line up with certain predictable behavioral acts (third position). Further, personality psychologists are generally open to the possibility that dispositional traits may have neuro-physiological concomitants (first position), but they are also cognizant of the fact that dispositions are language categories with socially determined meanings (consistent with the fourth position). The meaning of a trait is partially determined by its cultural context. Friendliness, therefore, may express itself and be understood somewhat differently from one culture to another. Different cultures may have different rules or conventions for being friendly. A certain kind of smile or a certain way of touching another might be considered friendly behavior in one cultural setting and rude or boorish in another.

A BRIEF HISTORY OF TRAITS

Characterizations of personality traits can be found even in ancient texts (Winter, 1996). In the book of Genesis, Rebekah gives birth to twins whose contrasting natures seem apparent even as they struggle in the womb. Esau, the "hairy" one, grows to be an active and adventurous man who is skilled at the hunt. His brother Jacob is "smooth" in appearance, and he prefers the quiet domestic life, spending more time in the tents. His mother's favorite, Jacob eventually proves more cunning than Esau as he swindles away his brother's birthright and tricks his father, Isaac, into giving him a blessing that Isaac meant to confer upon Esau. In the ancient story, the traits of guile and shrewdness win out over brute strength.

In the fourth century B.C.E., Theophrastus generated one of the first trait taxonomies in Western civilization. A botanist by trade and a pupil of Aristotle, Theophrastus devised a series of semihumorous character sketches depicting different types of people that one might encounter in Athenian social life. Each sketch personifies a trait (Anderson, 1970), producing a recognizable but exaggerated caricature. In each sketch, the hypothetical character possesses one and only one trait in his life, influencing virtually everything he does. Here is how Theophrastus described a type of person that is still with us today, "The Penurious Man":

> Penuriousness is economy carried beyond all measure. A Penurious Man is one who goes to a debtor to ask for his half-obol of interest before the end of the month. At a dinner where expenses are shared, he counts the number of cups each person drinks, and he makes a smaller libation to Artemis than anyone. When his servant breaks a pot or a plate, he deducts the value from his food. If his wife drops a copper, he moves furniture, beds, chests and hunts in the curtains. If he has something to sell he puts such a price on it that the buyer has no profit. He forbids anyone to pick a fig in his garden, to walk on his land, to pick up an olive or a date. Every day he goes to see that the boundary marks of his property have not been moved. ... He forbids his wife to lend anything—neither salt nor lamp-wick nor cinnamon nor marjoram nor meal nor garlands nor cakes for sacrifices. "All these trifles," he says, "mount up in a year." (from Allport, 1961, p. 43)

The most famous ancient system for personality traits is attributed to the Greek physician Galen (A.D. 130–200). Galen developed the theory of the four humors, a "humor" being a bodily fluid associated with a particular behavioral trait. The four key bodily fluids were blood, black bile, yellow bile, and phlegm. Blood was associated with the *sanguine* personality. A person whose blood was the dominant bodily humor was bold, confident, and robust in temperament. Black bile connected to the *melancholic* type. Too much black bile in the system produced a depressed and anxious person, pessimistic and brooding. Yellow bile corresponded to the *choleric* person, who was restless, irritable, and wont to explode in anger. Finally, the *phlegmatic* person, unfortunate enough to be housed in a body with too much phlegm, was aloof, apathetic, cold, and sluggish, and probably no more fun to be around than the melancholic person. Although the sanguine trait seems the best, Galen maintained that a balanced and ideal temperament resulted from a harmonious mixture of the four humors. The optimal mix of traits produced a person who "in his soul … is in the middle of boldness and timidity, of negligence and impertinence, of compassion and envy. He is cheerful, affectionate, charitable, and prudent" (Stelmack & Stalikas, 1991, p. 259)

By the time of the Middle Ages, scholars dismissed the idea that bodily fluids were directly implicated in personality traits. But the behavioral descriptions associated with the four humors lived on and are still referenced today. In the 18th century, Immanuel Kant recast the four temperament types along the dimensions of activity and feelings: cholerics had strong activity and phlegmatics weak activity; sanguines had strong feelings and melancholics weak feelings. In the late 19th century, Wilhelm Wundt argued that the four temperaments sprang from emotional strength and emotional variability. And in the mid-20th century, Hans Eysenck recast the four types along the lines of two superordinate traits: extraversion and neuroticism, as we will shortly see. Eysenck also argued for the biological bases of these traits, though he looked to brain structures and functioning, rather than bodily humors, to find the deep origins of individual differences in dispositional traits.

The ancient belief that bodily forms and differences are associated with personality traits was most famously revived by Ernst Kretschmer (1921) and William Sheldon (1940) who developed a theory of *constitutional psychology.* Few social scientists ascribe to constitutional psychology today (many of its assumptions have been discredited), but in the early part of the 20th century Kretschmer and Sheldon attracted considerable interest. The body's constitution was associated with particular personality characteristics, Kretschmer and Sheldon argued. Sheldon conducted many studies in which he correlated men's body types, rated from photos of nude men, with personality ratings of these men made by observers who studied the men's behavior. His findings clustered into three body types and three corresponding trait profiles. The person whose body is round and soft, with an overdevelopment of fat and underdevelopment of muscle and bone, is an *endomorph.* According to Sheldon, endomorphs tend to be easygoing, affable, very desiring of social approval, and oriented toward relaxation and comfort. The person whose body is thin

These images from a 14th-century manuscript illustrate the four personality temperaments identified in ancient times. Moving clockwise from the upper left, you see illustrations depicting the phlegmatic, sanguine, melancholic, and choleric types. Courtesy of Historical Collections & Services, Claude Moore Health Sciences Library, University of Virginia.

and bony, with an underdevelopment of fat and muscle, is an *ectomorph*. The ectomorph body type is associated with the traits of restraint, privacy, introversion, and self-consciousness. Finally, the *mesomorph* is relatively muscular, exhibiting a physique that is neither round nor skinny and suggestive of physical vigor and stamina. Personality descriptors that correspond to mesomorphy are aggressive, dominant, adventurous, courageous, and sometimes callous toward the feelings of others. Note that each of these body types and corresponding trait profiles refers solely to men. Constitutional psychology never focused much attention on women (Hall & Lindzey, 1957).

The first scientific studies of traits were conducted in the late 19th century. Francis Galton (1884) was one of the first scientifically minded psychologists to focus empirical attention on individual differences. Galton also proposed that important individual differences in personality could be gleaned from language. All languages are full of adjectives for describing differences among people, Galton reasoned, and an examination of these words might provide clues to the nature of traits. Researchers began to collect data on personality traits based on people's ratings of their own characteristics (self-ratings) and ratings made by observers (peer ratings). Advances in statistics, including the invention of the correlation coefficient and the development of factor analysis, paved the way for quantitative studies of personality traits in large groups of people. By the time World War II began, the stage was set for the development of a number of modern trait theories, each articulating a particular research agenda.

Gordon Allport

In his groundbreaking book, *Personality: A Psychological Interpretation,* Gordon Allport (1937) both established personality psychology as a legitimate intellectual discipline (as I described in chapter 1) and introduced one of the first modern trait theories. "In everyday life, no one, not even a psychologist, doubts that underlying the conduct of a mature person there are characteristic dispositions or traits," Allport (1937, p. 339) proclaimed. Traits are the major structural units of personality, and as such, they account for the consistency and coherence of human behavior. Allport defined a trait as "a neuropsychic structure having the capacity to render many stimuli functionally equivalent and to initiate and guide equivalent (meaningfully consistent) forms of adaptive and expressive behavior" (Allport, 1961, p. 347). You should note two important things about this definition. First, Allport insisted that trait labels were more than mere semantic conveniences. Traits really exist—they exist as unobservable neuropsychic structures. As real physiological entities, traits are among the more important causal factors in human behavior. We therefore may infer the existence of traits from observing behavior. Second, by rendering different stimuli "functionally equivalent," traits account for consistency in human behavior. Behavior is more-or-less lawful and predictable because of the action of traits. The existence of a particular trait in a person's life may be ascertained from at least three kinds of evidence: frequency, range of situations, and intensity. A particularly strong trait of "stubbornness," for instance, might be revealed in the person who is frequently stubborn over time and in many situations and who, when behaving stubbornly, does so with prodigious intensity.

Allport was especially interested in characterizing persons' traits such that the individual's uniqueness could come through. To this end, he distinguished between two senses of the term *trait*. The more typical sense, and the one I have employed in this chapter, is what Allport called a **common trait.** Common traits are dimensions of human functioning upon which many different people are likely to differ. Therefore, we can compare many different people on such common traits as friendliness and conscientiousness. A second sense of trait, however, comes across in Allport's conceptualization of the **personal disposition.** A personal disposition is a trait that is especially characteristic of a given individual and is therefore instrumental for depicting that individual person's uniqueness. The distinction is a little confusing because the same trait—say, friendliness—can be viewed either as a common trait or as a personal disposition, depending on the point of reference. If the point of reference is a research study comparing many different people with one another (what Allport called a nomothetic inquiry; see chapter 1), then the researcher can compare and contrast different people's corresponding scores on a scale measuring the common trait of friendliness. But in the intensive study of a single individual (Allport's idiographic approach; see chapter 1), the trait of friendliness—or any trait, for that matter—might be especially important or salient for characterizing that particular person's characteristic approach to the world. In such a case, the trait may be viewed as a personal disposition for that person—one of a handful of traits that must be invoked when considering that particular individual.

Personal dispositions themselves can be broken down into different varieties. A *cardinal disposition* is a very general and pervasive trait for a given person, so general and pervasive that it seems directly or indirectly involved in a wide range of the person's activities. Many people may have no cardinal dispositions at all; at most, a person would have one or two cardinal dispositions. For example, we might say that "generosity" is a cardinal trait in the life of the late Mother Teresa, because this trait seemed to be so powerfully salient in her life. A cardinal disposition serves as a defining feature of a person's personality profile. More common are *central dispositions,* which refer to a wide range of dispositions that may be characteristic for a given person and called into play on a relatively regular basis. People typically have between 5 and 10 central dispositions, Allport suggested. In a famous case study, Allport (1965) analyzed the letters written to her son's friends by a woman named Jenny to derive a set of personality descriptors for the letter writer. Allport concluded that Jenny's personality could be well described by invoking eight central dispositions, including "quarrelsome-suspicious," "aesthetic-artistic," and "self-centered." Finally, *secondary dispositions* are more limited in scope and less critical to the description of overall personality. A person is likely to have a great many secondary dispositions. Each secondary disposition is exhibited under a relatively limited set of conditions. Thus, secondary dispositions differ from central (and cardinal) dispositions in that they are narrower, more contingent on particular situational cues, and less central to defining the overall character of a person's individuality.

Allport anticipated most of the controversies that were to surround trait psychology in subsequent years. For example, Allport discussed, but ultimately rejected, the idea that traits are merely semantic categories in the minds of observers, as opposed to causal agents in the behavior of the actor. Allport discussed the problem of cross-situational consistency in traits. He acknowledged that people's behavior is highly variable from one situation to the next and that traits must be understood against the backdrop of this variability. One can still observe relative consistencies in responding indicative of traits, Allport maintained, if one examines a person's trait-related behavior in a wide variety of situations and over time. Finally, Allport recognized the limitations in the descriptive and explanatory power of common trait profiles. Comparing people's scores on common traits is useful, Allport maintained, but unless one examines personal dispositions, one will never get a sense of what makes a particular person especially unique. Allport's insistence that personality psychologists examine the uniqueness of the individual case rendered him forever ambivalent about the idea of common, comparative traits of personality. He preferred to talk about unique personal dispositions. But most trait research and all other trait theories that followed Allport focused almost exclusively on common traits, examining dispositional dimensions upon which many different people can be said to differ in consistent and important ways.

Raymond B. Cattell

Beginning in the 1940s, Raymond B. Cattell advocated a brand of trait psychology that emphasized rigorous quantification and statistical analysis in research, with the ultimate goal of improving scientists' ability to predict behavior. For Cattell, personality itself was defined in terms of behavioral prediction. He defined personality as "that which permits a prediction of what a person will do in a given situation" (1950, p. 2). Among the many variables that might be employed to predict behavior, Cattell considered traits to be especially important. While Cattell acknowledged the existence of traits that might be unique to certain individuals (what Allport called personal dispositions and what Cattell simply labeled as *unique traits*), he focused his research attention on what Allport called common traits—traits that express individual differences among many different people.

How might a researcher obtain information on people's traits? Cattell distinguished among three different sources for data on traits, as shown in Table 4.2. **L-data** (life-data) consist primarily of information pertaining to a person's real-life behavior. Included in L-data might be public records, such as college transcripts and letters of recommendation; personal accounts, such as diaries or journals; and trait ratings of a person made by others. **Q-data** (questionnaire data) include self-ratings on personality traits and self-report scores on various personality questionnaires of the kinds I will describe later in this chapter. **T-data** (test data) involve observations of an individual in a well-controlled assessment situation, as in behavioral records from laboratory experiments. These different sources of data—public ratings, self-reports, and test behavior—provide very different readings on a person's dispositions. By combining data from all three sources, the researcher can get a more accurate reading on personality traits and enhance behavioral prediction.

Raymond B. Cattell (1905–1998) pioneered the use of advanced statistical procedures and rigorous methodologies in the study of personality traits. Cattell developed an elaborate theory of traits and a popular trait inventory (The 16PF) aimed ultimately at specifying the key variables needed to improve the prediction of behavior.

In an extraordinarily ambitious program of research that Cattell followed for almost 50 years, he employed the statistical approach of **factor analysis** to derive a complex classification scheme for traits. In factor analysis, the researcher examines the ways in which responses to different questions and measures cluster together. Factor analysis enables the researcher to reduce a large number of items or variables to a smaller set of underlying dimensions, called "factors." Cattell's studies produced a large number of what he called **surface traits,** which were related elements of behavior that, when empirically measured and intercorrelated, tended to cluster together. As their name suggests, surface traits are readily observable in behavior. Further factor analysis, however, indicated that the many surface traits that might be observed could be reduced to a smaller number of underlying **source traits.** Therefore, three or four readily observable surface traits—say, friendliness, outgoingness, spontaneity, and cheerfulness—might ultimately stem from the workings of a single, underlying source trait—say, sociability. By subsuming many surface traits under a smaller number of source traits, Cattell formulated one of the first hierarchical models for trait organization. Traits could be further subdivided into three functional categories: *dynamic*

TABLE 4.2	CATTELL'S THREE-PART CLASSIFICATION OF PERSONALITY DATA	
Type of Data	**Description**	**Examples**
L-data	Information derived from observers' ratings and evaluation of individuals leading more or less natural lives and evaluation of individuals in natural settings	Teacher ratings of children in nursery school; parent ratings of children's temperament; peer ratings of personality; psychologists' ratings of family interaction
Q-data	Information derived from self-observations and evaluation of one's own behavior, feelings, and personality characteristics	Various self-report scales and standard personality inventories: the Adjective Check List, the MMPI, trait measures of extraversion, neuroticism, and openness to experience
T-data	Information derived from observations of behavior under structured and controlled conditions, as in the laboratory	Experiments in which observations are made of aggressive, altruistic, or conforming behavior under a variety of controlled conditions

traits, which set the individual into action to accomplish a goal; *ability traits,* which concern the effectiveness with which the individual reaches a goal; and *temperament traits,* which concern such stylistic aspects of response as speed, energy, and emotional reactivity.

Cattell's analyses convinced him that human individuality could be well described in terms of 16 source traits, one of which was intelligence. Individual differences on these source traits can be measured on Cattell's **Sixteen Personality Factor Questionnaire,** or **16PF** for short. The 16PF presents the respondent with 187 questions, each of which asks for a choice among alternatives. For example, one question asks whether in a typical social occasion you would rather "come forward" or "stay quietly in the background." The responses are tallied into 16 separate scores, one for each of the source traits. Cattell gave some of his source traits unusual names to limit their associations with common language. For example, the source trait of "affectia-sizia" measures such characteristics as being warmhearted and outgoing. Table 4.3 lists by letter rather than name 15 of the 16 factors on the 16PF, excluding intelligence. For each source trait, the table provides simple descriptions of high and low scorers and examples of famous people from history who might have scored in one direction or another on the trait.

For Cattell, the proof of a trait measure's value was its ability to predict behavior. To enhance behavioral prediction, Cattell combined scores on different traits into a **specification equation,** which differentially weighted each trait according to its relevance for a given behavioral situation. For example, Cattell (1990) contended that he could predict well a salesperson's annual earnings from the following source trait equation: Earnings = .21 outgoingness + .10 emotional stability + .10 dominance + .21 easygoingness + .10 conscientiousness − .10 suspiciousness − .31 imaginativeness + .21 shrewdness. To increase predictive power for some behavioral outcomes in some situations, the specification equation could also include nontrait variables pertaining to transient *states* (such as fatigue and temporary moods) and particular *roles* demanded by the situation. Therefore, to predict behavior with any degree of precision, Cattell believed, the personality psychologist should obtain precise measures on a host of internal and external variables: personality traits, temporary states and roles, and situational factors.

Hans Eysenck

A contemporary of Cattell's, Hans Eysenck was another pioneer in the history of traits whose voluminous writings and influential conceptualizations have had a major impact on personality psychology. Like Cattell, Eysenck employed the statistical procedure of factor analysis to reduce the many possible traits that could be measured in questionnaires to a reasonable number of basic dimensions. Eysenck and Cattell parted company, however, over a rather esoteric but ultimately consequential controversy in the world of statistics—that is, the question of how to "rotate" factors in a factor analysis. To put it very simply, Eysenck,

TABLE 4.3	THE FIFTEEN SOURCE TRAITS OF PERSONALITY ASSESSED BY THE 16PF			
	TRAIT DESCRIPTIONS		**FAMOUS INDIVIDUALS**	
Trait	**High**	**Low**	**High**	**Low**
A	Outgoing Warmhearted	Reserved Detached	Falstaff	Greta Garbo
C	Unemotional Calm	Emotional Changeable	Washington	Hamlet
E	Assertive Dominant	Humble Cooperative	Genghis Khan	Jesus
F	Cheerful Lively	Sober Taciturn	Groucho Marx	Clint Eastwood
G	Conscientious Persistent	Expedient Undisciplined	Mother Teresa	Casanova
H	Venturesome Socially bold	Shy Retiring	Columbus	Sylvia Plath
I	Tough-minded Self-reliant	Tender-minded Sensitive	James Bond	Robert Burns
L	Suspicious Skeptical	Trusting Accepting	De Gaulle	Pollyanna
M	Imaginative Bohemian	Practical Conventional	Van Gogh	Henry Ford
N	Shrewd Discreet	Forthright Straightforward	Machiavelli	Joan of Arc
O	Guilt-prone Worrying	Resilient Self-assured	Dostoevsky	Stalin
Q1	Radical Experimental	Conservative Traditional	Karl Marx	Queen Victoria
Q2	Self-sufficient Resourceful	Group-dependent Affiliative	Copernicus	Marilyn Monroe
Q3	Controlled Compulsive	Undisciplined Lax	Margaret Thatcher	Mick Jagger
Q4	Tense Driven	Relaxed Tranquil	Macbeth	Buddha

NOTE: Dimension B (Intelligence) is omitted.

SOURCE: Adapted from *Personality Traits* (p. 22), by G. Matthews & I. Deary, 1998, Cambridge, England: Cambridge University Press.

along with another contemporary stalwart in trait psychology named J. P. Guilford (1959), believed that the resultant trait factors obtained from factor analysis should be statistically independent of one another—that is, the factors should be arranged (rotated) so that they are uncorrelated or *orthogonal* (at right angles) to one another. Cattell insisted that this was not necessary, preferring statistical solutions that resulted in correlated factors, or what is called *oblique* factors. Because of this difference, as well as disagreements over the preferred level of generality for basic traits, Eysenck and Cattell differed dramatically with respect to the number of basic traits they believed exist. For Cattell, it was 16 source traits; for Eysenck, it all boiled down to 3.

Eysenck's big three supertraits (sometimes called types) are extraversion–introversion, neuroticism, and psychoticism. The first two factors deal with personality characteristics within a relatively normal range of functioning, whereas psychoticism taps into dimensions of functioning that are typically associated with psychotic and psychopathic behavior, such as delusional thinking, excessive cruelty, and antisocial behavior. Eysenck's first two factors, extraversion–introversion and neuroticism, recapture the ancient typology of humors, as shown in Figure 4.1. As we can see, persons may be classified in a two-dimensional space created by the intersection of these two traits in a way reminiscent of the ancient types. The extraverted and highly neurotic (emotionally unstable) person is outgoing, easily irritated, restless, and excitable—the choleric type. The extraverted and emotionally stable (low neuroticism) person is outgoing, stable, and cheerful, like the sanguine type. The melancholic type is introverted and highly neurotic, resulting in characteristics of moodiness, depression, and anxiety. Finally, the phlegmatic person is introverted and low in neuroticism (emotionally stable), producing such descriptors as quiet, steady, and stoic.

As we will see later, Eysenck's first two dimensions of extraversion–introversion and neuroticism have received a tremendous amount of research attention. Studies provide impressive evidence that individual differences in these two large traits are significantly associated with many behaviors that theory predicts they should be associated with. In addition, longitudinal studies show that individual differences in extraversion– introversion and neuroticism are highly stable over long periods of time, especially in adulthood. Studies with twins suggest that individual differences in these two traits are at least moderately (if not substantially) determined by genetic differences among people. The last fact suggests that extraversion–introversion and neuroticism may be linked to identifiable biological substrates, in particular patternings in the central nervous system. Eysenck (1967) proposed just such a linkage. He theorized that individual differences in extraversion–introversion are linked to the activity of the brain's reticular activating system, which itself is implicated in the modulation of arousal. He proposed further that individual differences in neuroticism might arise from differences in the workings of the brain's limbic system, which has been hypothesized to be implicated in emotionality. Eysenck's bold hypotheses linking brains and traits have generated 30 years of provocative research on these questions, as we will see in chapter 5.

Hans J. Eysenck (1916–1997) argued for a three-factor model of personality traits. Eysenck's factor-analytic studies and his careful experiments convinced him that personality traits can be grouped into three broad dimensions: extraversion/introversion, neuroticism, and psychoticism.

The Big Five

How many traits are there? More than 2,000 years ago, Theophrastus described more than 20 different character types, while Galen's ancient typology listed four. In modern times, Cattell's factor analytic procedures

FIGURE 4.1	THE FOUR ANCIENT PERSONALITY TYPES

The ancient types may be recast as combinations on the traits for extraversion, introversion, neuroticism, and stability.

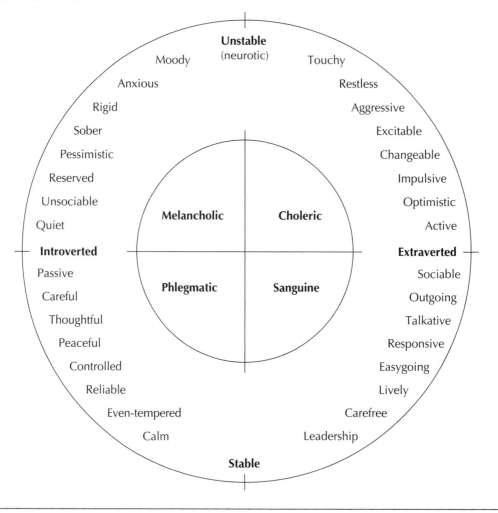

SOURCE: From *Eysenck on Extraversion* (p. 18), by H. J. Eysenck, 1973, New York: John Wiley & Sons.

convinced him that 16 source traits account for much of human individuality, while Eysenck, using similar procedures, arrived at a set of three. In the 19th century, Francis Galton suggested that researchers might look to language to determine what the basic dimensions of individual differences might be. All languages contain many descriptors for traitlike terms. Take English, for example—words like affable, belligerent, callous, dutiful, energetic, friendly, gregarious, hospitable, irritable, jolly, knowledgeable, lazy, magnanimous, neurotic, obnoxious, playful, quarrelsome, righteous, sorrowful, tenacious, unctuous, vivacious, wacky, xenophobic, yielding, and zealous.

I just pulled those adjectives, *a* to *z*, off the top of my head, with some help from the dictionary for the letters *k* and *y*. But, in 1936, Gordon Allport decided to be much more systematic. Following Galton's suggestion and earlier work done in Germany by Klages (1926) and Baumgarten (1933), Allport and Odbert (1936) plowed through an unabridged English dictionary, containing 550,000 entries, to compile a list of all English words referring to individual differences in psychological functioning. They came up with about 18,000 words referring to psychological states, traits, and evaluations. Of these, about 4,500 reflected, in their judgment, relatively stable and enduring personality traits.

Raymond B. Cattell picked up where Allport left off. Cattell (1943) reduced Allport's list of 4,500 to 171 by grouping similar descriptors and eliminating rare and metaphorical usages. He then asked people to rate other people on these 171 traitlike terms. On the basis of correlations among these ratings, Cattell developed a set of 35–40 clusters of related terms and used them for the construction of self-report and peer-report rating scales. At a time when factor analysis was just being invented and long before computers made such a complicated statistical procedure relatively simple to do, Cattell and his colleagues embarked upon the Herculean task of factor analyzing by hand data from hundreds of ratings of the personality terms. What emerged eventually was Cattell's well-known list of 16 source traits. But other people who factor-analyzed data based on Cattell's clusters came up with different results. The first of these was Donald Fiske (1949), who worked with 22 of Cattell's rating scales and, after a year of calculating, concluded that *five basic traits* accounted for most of the intercorrelations. Similar studies yielding very similar results were done in later years, most notably by Tupes and Christal (1961) and Norman (1963).

By the mid-1960s, therefore, a handful of well-designed and painstakingly analyzed studies suggested that ratings of personality traits could be grouped into approximately five basic categories. Yet not until the 1980s did the significance of this finding begin to be realized more widely. During the 1980s and 1990s, a growing number of researchers began to reach a consensus about what has come to be called the **Five-Factor Model** of personality traits or, more simply, the Big Five (Angleitner & Ostendorf, 1994; Goldberg, 1993; John, 1989; McCrae & Costa, 1995). Among the most important contributors to this development have been John Digman (1990; Digman & Takemoto-Chock, 1981), Lewis Goldberg (1990), Robert McCrae and Paul Costa (Costa & McCrae, 1985; McCrae & Costa, 1987, 1990, 1995), and Jerry Wiggins (1996). Different researchers have suggested different names and slightly different conceptualizations for the five factors, but most agree that two of the factors are quite similar to what Eysenck called (a) extraversion–introversion and (b) neuroticism. Adopting Costa and McCrae's well-known labels, the other three factors of the Big Five may be called agreeableness, conscientiousness, and openness to experience. In chapter 5, we will examine each of these five trait clusters in detail.

Lewis Goldberg was one of the first personality psychologists to propose that the many different personality traits that can be attributed to people may be grouped into five basic clusters, called the Big Five. Goldberg's work stems from the "lexical hypothesis," which asserts that the most important individual differences in human behavior and experience are encoded in a society's language, or lexicon.

MEASURING TRAITS

CONSTRUCTING A TRAIT MEASURE

Most personality psychologists who study traits assume that people are able to make trait judgments with some degree of accuracy (Funder, 1995). The methods used to assess traits, therefore, tend to be relatively straightforward and simple. The most popular methods are self-report questionnaires and rating scales. These objective measures of personality ask the person to report directly on his or her own behavior, typically by answering a series of questions with "yes" or "no" answers or by making a rating—for instance, on a 1–7 scale—concerning the extent to which the person "agrees with" or "disagrees with" a particular item.

Although a paper-and-pencil test designed to measure a personality trait may appear simple and straightforward from the standpoint of the person filling out the scale, constructing a reliable and valid trait measure is not easy. Psychologists have developed and evaluated a number of approaches to test construction (Burisch, 1984; ; Wiggins, 1973), but there is no single approach that everybody agrees is the best for all testing situations. Nevertheless, most personality psychologists generally endorse a *construct approach* to test construction (Jackson, 1971; Jackson & Paunonen, 1980; Loevinger, 1957; Wiggins, 1973).

The construct approach begins with a clear conceptual definition of the trait of interest, usually embedded in a larger personality theory. Take, for instance, the trait of "conscientiousness." If we were to design a personality questionnaire to assess individual differences in conscientiousness, we might begin with the definition of and theory for this trait provided by Cattell (1965). One of Cattell's 16 basic "source traits" in human personality, conscientiousness is defined as a general disposition "governing conscientious, persevering, unselfish behavior and impelling the individual to duty as conceived by his [or her] culture" (p. 374). A highly conscientious person is "honest; knows what is right and generally does it, even if no one is watching him [her]; does not tell lies or attempt to deceive others; respects others' property." A highly unconscientious person is "somewhat unscrupulous; not too careful about standards of right and wrong where personal desires are concerned; tells lies and is given to little deceits; does not respect others' property" (p. 63). Most people fall somewhere between the two extremes. Cattell emphasizes that conscientiousness is "not just a rational politeness or conformity but a somewhat fierce 'categorical imperative' (to use Kant's description) of the kind exemplified by the biblical saints" (p. 94).

After defining our trait, we would begin writing *items,* which are the test questions or statements. Here are three items that Cattell wrote for his scale for conscientiousness (1965, p. 94):

> Do you usually keep emotions under control?
>
> Are you a person who is scrupulously correct in manners and social obligations and likes others to be the same?
>
> Are you cautious and considerate that you do not hurt people's feelings by unconsidered conversational remarks?

For each of these items, the respondent would answer "yes" or "no." In the case of these three items, "yes" answers indicate conscientiousness and "no" answers suggest unconscientiousness. Each item relates to the others in an additive way. Thus, a subject might receive one point for each "yes" answer on the scale. Adding up all the points would produce the total trait score for conscientiousness. Because some people, however, may answer "yes" to virtually any question ("yea-sayers") and others "no" to almost any question ("nay-sayers") regardless of content, we would do well to include items for which a "no" answer suggests conscientiousness and a "yes" answer suggests unconscientiousness (Jackson, 1971). Therefore, we might add such "reversed" items as these:

> Do you frequently find that you must "cut corners" and "bend the rules" in order to achieve your goals?

Do other people rarely describe you as a dutiful and highly responsible person?

In writing test items, our goal would be to generate an item pool that completely covers the content domain of conscientiousness. Therefore, we should aim to include a large number of items initially so that we might tap into the various manifestations of conscientiousness that our theory suggests might exist. In fact, it is a good idea, argue some test theorists, to include items that are hypothesized *not* to tap into the trait of interest—in other words, items that seem to have nothing to do with the trait of conscientiousness, such as these:

Do other people regard you as a dominant person?

Do you enjoy parties and other opportunities to get together with large groups of people?

In covering a content domain that is larger than that envisioned for our trait, we decrease the chances of excluding unexpectedly relevant items while increasing the chances of learning precisely where the boundaries of our trait lie—that is, finding what content the particular trait does and does not include (Loevinger, 1957; Wiggins, 1973).

In the next step of test construction, we would administer the item pool to a large number of individuals and examine the results to determine which items should be retained in the final version. There are many statistical procedures available for examining the empirical results at this stage. For instance, we would probably perform an **item analysis,** through which we would determine the contribution that each item makes to the scale by correlating the scores on each item with the total score. Those items that make a negligible contribution (that is, those that produce low correlations) to the total would then be dropped. Presumably a number of the conceptually irrelevant items that we included by design would be dropped at this stage, though those correlating highly with the overall score would be retained. Further, a number of items that we initially thought were tapping the trait well might be deleted for lack of correlation with the total.

We might also perform a factor analysis on the data, through which each item is correlated with every other item to determine empirical clusterings. Let us imagine that our final scale has 30 items. We might administer the scale to 500 persons and then perform a factor analysis to determine which items "hang together" in clusters. The factor analysis might yield two relatively independent clusters of items—*factors*—that appear to tap into two somewhat different facets of conscientiousness. Perhaps 10 of our items appearing to tap into moral concerns hang together as a first factor, and another 12 items having more to do with conscientiousness in work hang together to form a second, independent factor. We might conclude that the overall scale in fact assesses two separate, though related, ideas, two facets of the trait "conscientiousness"—"moral conscientiousness" and "task conscientiousness." Alternatively, we might decide that the two facets are in fact two separate traits, each having little to do with the other.

In the final step of test construction, we would examine the extent to which the trait measure predicts behavior. For instance, we might design a study in which people who fill out our conscientiousness measure participate in a laboratory experiment in which they are given various opportunities to choose between either responsible, conscientious behavior or competing, nonconscientious behavior. Or we might examine the relationship between conscientiousness scores on our test and behaviors thought to be conscientious in daily life, such as church attendance, contributions to charities, and community involvement. Or we might correlate people's scores on our measure of conscientiousness and ratings of the same people made by their friends and acquaintances, our prediction being that those individuals scoring high on our measure would be rated by their friends and acquaintances as significantly more responsible and dutiful than low-scoring individuals.

As a trait measure develops, researchers learn not only what the particular scale measures but also what it does *not* measure. Therefore, we would expect scores on our measure of conscientiousness would correlate positively with scores on *other* measures of conscientiousness. Evidence for positive associations between different measures of the same trait constitute **convergent validity:** the two measures are said to "converge" on the same trait (Campbell & Fiske, 1959). Further, scores on our measure of conscientiousness should not correlate with scores on measures of apparently unrelated traits. For instance, our theory of conscientiousness suggests that this trait should have little to do with such traits as "dominance," "extraversion," "intelligence," "friendliness," and so on. In other words, highly conscientious people should not be consistently high (or low) on dominance or on any other independent trait. If conscientiousness scores *were* highly positively (or negatively) correlated with dominance scores, we should suspect that our measure is in fact assessing something different from, or in addition to, "pure" conscientiousness. Evidence, therefore, that our trait measure does not correlate with measures of other, conceptually distinct, traits would support the **discriminant validity** of our measure (Campbell & Fiske, 1959).

CRITERIA OF A GOOD MEASURE

The construct approach to devising a personality trait measure follows logically from a crucial idea in personality psychology as a whole—the idea of **construct validity.** In its most general sense, construct validity simply refers to the extent to which a test measures what it says it measures. But more importantly, construct validity is a scientific *process.* Construct validity is the process of simultaneously validating a test and the construct that the test is measuring. Cronbach and Meehl (1955) introduced the concept of construct validity in order to address a common and vexing problem in personality psychology: How do you know whether a measure designed to assess something that you cannot observe directly is a good measure? Although we may be able to observe friendly behavior, we cannot directly observe "friendliness" per se. The trait of friendliness is an abstraction that cannot be directly seen, heard, touched, smelled, or tasted. The same could be said for all personality traits and, indeed, many other concepts in psychology overall, such as intelligence, prejudice, religious values, identity. These ineffable abstractions are termed *constructs.* Trait scales measure such constructs.

The process of construct validity begins with the construct itself, which is typically embedded in a larger theory of personality functioning. With an eye toward the theoretical meaning of the construct, the psychologist carefully designs a measure of the construct and then observes the extent to which the measure itself produces empirical results—observable behaviors—that conform to the theory. For instance, I might conduct a study to test my prediction that persons scoring high on my new measure of "friendliness" will spend more time smiling in a friendly laboratory interview than persons scoring low on the measure, under the theoretical assumption that smiling is generally an index of friendly sentiment. Should my prediction be confirmed in my study, I will have obtained some small evidence for the construct validity of the new measure of friendliness. Should my prediction not be supported by the data, I might begin to question the adequacy of my measure, the adequacy of my construct "friendliness," or perhaps the adequacy of the particular study I conducted to test the hypothesis linking friendliness to smiling.

Each new empirical finding with a particular personality test contributes to the **nomological network** for the construct that the test measures. The nomological network is the *interlocking system of empirically supported propositions that constitute the theory of a given* *construct.* The propositions specify how test performance should be related to particular nontest behaviors that can be directly assessed. Results from studies employing a particular trait measure feed back to change the nomological network, making for new propositions about the particular trait, thus redefining it and ultimately changing the theory in which it is embedded. There are numerous examples of this sort of thing in personality research—cases in which a particular trait assessed in a particular way starts out with one definition and theory, but over time (typically many years), and with extensive study, new empirical results change the trait's meaning and theory. For instance, early definitions of extraversion characterized it as a general tendency to be sociable and people-oriented, but subsequent research employing self-report scales to measure extraversion provided new evidence to suggest that the trait's meaning is also tied closely to positive emotionality and reward sensitivity. Therefore, over the many years psychologists conducted construct-validation research on extraversion, the meaning of the trait extraversion began to change.

Construct validity, therefore, refers to the extent to which empirical support has been gathered for the propositions contained in the construct's nomological network. Constructs and their measures that have generated a large amount of empirical support for a rich variety of propositions in the nomological network can be said to have the greatest degree of construct validity. However, construct validity is never carved in stone: Each new study employing a particular construct and its measure ultimately ties into the nomological network and thus contributes some kind of evidence—supportive or nonsupportive—for construct validity. A number of other forms of validity fall in the general category of construct validity (Table 4.4).

In addition to construct (and other forms of) validity, **reliability** is a cardinal criterion of a trait measure's worth. Reliability refers to the consistency of a particular personality measure. For self-report trait tests, two forms of reliability are especially important. In **test–retest reliability,** psychologists assess a test's *consistency over time.* Persons who score high on a particular trait upon first taking the test should score high again on the same test a second time, say, a few months later. Similarly, those who score low at Time 1 should score low again at Time 2. Test–retest reliability is usually calculated by correlating the subjects' scores on a measure at Time 1 with their corresponding scores at Time 2. The most reliable trait measures exhibit test–retest correlation coefficients of +.80 and higher over relatively short periods of time (such as a few months). In **split-half reliability,** a test's *internal consistency* is assessed by correlating subjects' scores on one half of a particular test with their corresponding scores on the other half. If a test is internally consistent, each part of the test yields comparable results; indeed, each test item can be seen as contributing to a homogenous pool of information about a given trait.

Beyond validity and reliability, personality psychologists have identified a number of other criteria of a test's worth. *Utility* is a criterion frequently raised—a test that provides practical information that can be used for specific purposes is preferred over one that cannot. Burisch (1984) suggests that *economy* and *communicability* should routinely be considered—all other things being equal, a short test is better than a long one (economy), and a test with results that are easily interpreted and communicated to others should be preferred to one with results that are more ambiguous. In addition, a number of personality psychologists argue that trait measures should be as free as possible of **social desirability** bias (Edwards, 1957; Jackson & Messick, 1958). This means that a good trait measure should not be influenced greatly by a person's desire to present a favorable or socially desirable facade. One common method of determining the extent to which social desirability plays into a particular trait measure is to correlate scores on the given measure with scores on a standardized

TABLE 4.4	FORMS OF VALIDITY IN PERSONALITY TESTING
Construct	The extent to which a test measures the construct that it is theoretically intended to measure. Construct validity increases as empirical support is garnered for the various propositions contained in the construct's nomological net. Construct validity is the most basic and encompassing form of validity, and other forms of validity can be seen as derivatives from it.
Content	The degree to which the items of a test cover the entire content domain of a construct and are not confounded with other content.
Convergent	The extent to which different measures of the same construct relate to one another.
Criterion	The extent to which a test is associated with external behaviors that it is designed to predict. When a test seeks to predict criterion behaviors that will occur in the future, we speak of "predictive validity." When the criterion behaviors are obtained at the current time, we speak of "concurrent validity."
Discriminant	The extent to which different measures of different constructs do *not* relate to one another.
Face	The extent to which test items seem, in the eyes of the respondent, to measure what they are supposed to measure. Face validity refers to the degree to which a respondent views the test as fair and appropriate under the given conditions of administration

SOURCE: From "Personality Structure and Assessment," by D. N. Jackson & S. V. Paunonen, 1980. In M. R. Rosenzweig and L. W. Porter (Eds.), *Annual Review of Psychology: Vol. 31* (pp. 503–552), Palo Alto, CA: Annual Reviews, Inc.

social desirability scale. Low, nonsignificant correlations between this and another trait measure suggest that the latter is relatively free of social desirability bias. In truth, however, many trait scales contain some social desirability bias, mainly because many traits have an implicit evaluative dimension. Therefore, personality psychologists have basically learned to live with this bias in self-report scales.

TRAIT INVENTORIES

It is often useful in personality research and in clinical work to assess many different traits at once. To do so, psychologists sometimes call upon omnibus **personality inventories,** which contain numerous trait scales, each scale comprising a subset of items contained in the large item pool for the inventory.

The **Minnesota Multiphasic Personality Inventory (MMPI)** has been the most widely used and thoroughly researched personality measure in the past 60 years. Developed by a psychologist, Starke Hathaway, and a psychiatrist, J. C. McKinley, in the 1930s, the MMPI condenses questions that might be asked in a lengthy psychiatric interview into an efficient paper-and-pencil form. The original test contains 550 statements such as "I have nightmares every few nights," "At times I feel like smashing things," "I would like to be a florist," and "I am sure I am being talked about." For each item, the respondent simply answers "true" or "false." The items are grouped into 10 different scales—hypochondriasis, depression, hysteria, psychopathic-deviancy, masculinity–femininity, paranoia, psychasthenia, schizophrenia, hypomania, and social introversion. The inventory also contains scales designed to assess the extent to which the subject is lying, faking, or responding in a careless fashion.

The MMPI was originally designed to be a *clinical* diagnostic instrument. Scores on the various scales were designed to assist the psychologist or psychiatrist in distinguishing various

FEATURE 4.A

NARCISSISM: THE TRAIT OF EXCESSIVE SELF-LOVE

In the ancient Greek legend, the beautiful boy Narcissus falls so completely in love with the reflection of himself in a pool that he plunges into the pool and drowns. If we are to believe a number of contemporary journalists, psychologists, and social critics, something very much like the fate of Narcissus is happening all around us today. American society is a "culture of narcissism," wrote Christopher Lasch (1979) more than two decades ago. The ethic of the "me generation" encouraged us all to love ourselves first and foremost, to seek, develop, perfect, and master *the self*. As a result, many of us are incapable of mature love for and commitment to others and are unwilling to devote ourselves to pursuits that transcend our own selfish concerns, to social institutions and communities that have traditionally integrated individuals within society (Bellah, Madsen, Sullivan, Swidler, & Tipton, 1985). In the eyes of the popular press, the narcissistic young person or middle-aged American adult today is obsessed with perfecting his body at the health club, desperately trying to "be all that she can be," "born to buy" and to accumulate both high-priced possessions and exotic personal experiences.

A number of prominent psychoanalysts consider **narcissism** to be the prototypical pathology of our time, rendering the "narcissistic personality disorder" one of the most popular and talked-about clinical syndromes of the past 20 years. But narcissism may also be viewed as a personality trait upon which relatively normal people who do not suffer from a clinical syndrome nonetheless differ. Raskin and Hall (1979, 1981) constructed a self-report questionnaire designed to measure the trait of narcissism. The Narcissistic Personality Inventory (NPI) includes 54 pairs of items. For each pair, the subject chooses the one item that he or she agrees with more. Here are some examples of the items that indicate narcissism:

- I really like to be the center of attention.
- I have a natural talent for influencing people.

- I like to look at my body.
- I think I am a special person.
- Everybody likes to hear my stories.
- I insist on the respect that is due to me.
- I will never be satisfied until I get all that I deserve.

The NPI taps four dimensions of narcissism: exploitiveness/entitlement, superiority, leadership, and self-absorption. The first of these four factors—exploitiveness/entitlement—is believed to be associated with psychological maladjustment, including anxiety, depression, and lack of empathy for others (Emmons, 1984; Watson, Grisham, Trotter, & Biderman, 1984). In general, males score significantly higher on all four dimensions of narcissism than do females.

Raskin and Shaw (1988) found that students scoring high on narcissism tended to use significantly more first-person singular pronouns *(I, me, my)* in spontaneous speech. Emmons (1984) found that narcissism is positively associated with other measures of dominance, exhibitionism, and self-esteem, and negatively associated with deference toward others. Some research suggests that college students scoring high in narcissism express more hostility and are more likely to behave aggressively when they are insulted compared with students lower in narcissism (Bushman & Baumeister, 1998; Rhodewalt & Morf, 1995, 1998). Narcissism has also been linked to extreme mood swings and intensity of emotional experience in daily life (Emmons, 1987). With respect to this last finding, it is believed that the narcissist's superficial smugness masks a deeper insecurity and narcissistic vulnerability (Kernberg, 1980). Narcissists may be more sensitive to both success and failure experiences than are most other people, experiencing intense joy when the self is uplifted with success but devastating depression and anger in the wake of even minor setbacks.

Wink (1991, 1992a, 1992b) has distinguished among three types of narcissism observable in

(CONTINUES)

FEATURE 4.A *(CONTINUED)*

women studied over time. The *hypersensitive* narcissists display a "covert" quality of narcissism that is linked to feelings of vulnerability, hostility, and depression. In Wink's longitudinal study, women who had high scores on hypersensitivity at age 43 were characterized by a downward spiral in their fortunes and resources during their 20s and 30s and by a lack of success either in a career or as a homemaker. The *willful* narcissists, by contrast, exhibit an "overt" quality of narcissism. From college days through midlife, they were consistently described as self-assured, grandiose, and exhibitionistic. Finally, the *autonomous* narcissists express a healthy form of narcissism. They were described at age 43 as creative, empathic, achievement-oriented, and individualistic. Following conflict in their 20s, the autonomous women experienced substantial personality growth into midlife. Hypersensitivity

and willfulness, but not autonomy, were associated with evidence of troubled childhood relations with parents, particularly with mothers. In addition, willfulness was associated with early identification with a willful father.

Finally, a recent Internet survey of more than 3,000 individuals shows that narcissism tends to be higher in men than women, tends to decline in older adults, and is exhibited at higher average levels in individualistic societies, such as the United States and Canada, than in more collectivist societies in Asia and the Middle East (Foster, Campbell, & Twenge, 2003). The cross-cultural findings support the hunch of many cultural critics who maintain that the ethos of individualism running through many Western societies, especially the United States, tends to foster narcissistic tendencies.

---

psychopathologies. Indeed, the MMPI was constructed by administering various items to different diagnostic groups—such as schizophrenics, manic-depressives, anxiety neurotics—and determining which items they repeatedly endorsed. This general method of construction, called the **criterion-key method,** assumes that a valid scale for, say, the "trait" of "depression" will consist of items that people whom clinicians have diagnosed as "depressives" frequently endorse, regardless of the content of those items and regardless of the theory of depression with which one is working. Therefore, if known depressives repeatedly answer "true" to the item "I am a Chicago Cubs fan," then this item becomes part of the scale for diagnosing depression, even though one is hard-pressed to come up with a cogent theoretical reason for its inclusion. The criterion-key method contrasts markedly with the theory-oriented construct method of test construction outlined earlier in this chapter.

Despite the fact that the MMPI scales were designed to assess *abnormality,* the test has been used to assess individual differences among normal people as well, though with limited success (Kunce & Anderson, 1984). Even as a tool for clinical diagnosis, the MMPI has been resoundingly criticized for weak reliability and validity with respect to many of the scales, and for the fact that many of the test items seem out of date. In response to some of these critiques, psychologists developed a revised and updated version of the test, the MMPI-2. Containing 567 items, the MMPI-2 is widely used today in clinical assessment.

The **California Psychological Inventory (CPI)** was designed to assess a broad range of traits applicable to normal populations. Developed by Harrison Gough in the 1950s, the CPI was originally administered to thousands of normal individuals, resulting in a pool of 462 true/false items. The items are grouped into 20 scales, measuring such traits as dominance, sense of acceptance, self-control, and achievement via independence (Table 4.5). Compared with the MMPI, the individual scales on the CPI show relatively high reliabilities. Evidence for validity comes from many sources, including correlations between subjects' trait scores and ratings of the subjects made by friends and acquaintances. One major

TABLE 4.5	SCALES ON THE CALIFORNIA PSYCHOLOGICAL INVENTORY

	Scale	Brief Description of a High Scorer
1.	Dominance	Confident, assertive, dominant, task-oriented
2.	Capacity for status	Ambitious, wants to be a success, independent
3.	Sociability	Sociable, likes to be with people, friendly
4.	Social presence	Self-assured, spontaneous; a good talker; not easily embarrassed
5.	Self-acceptance	Has good opinion of self, sees self as talented and as personally attractive
6.	Independence	Self-sufficient, resourceful, detached
7.	Empathy	Comfortable with self and well-accepted by others; understands the feelings of others
8.	Responsibility	Responsible, reasonable, takes duties seriously
9.	Socialization	Comfortably accepts ordinary rules and regulations; finds it easy to conform
10.	Self-control	Tries to control emotions and temper; takes pride in being self-disciplined
11.	Good impression	Wants to make a good impression; tries to do what will please others
12.	Communality	Fits in easily; sees self as a quite average person
13.	Well-being	Feels in good physical and emotional health; optimistic about the future
14.	Tolerance	Is tolerant of others' beliefs and values, even when different from or counter to own beliefs
15.	Achievement via conformance	Has strong drive to do well; likes to work in settings where tasks and expectations are clearly defined
16.	Achievement via independence	Has strong drive to do well; likes to work in settings that encourage freedom and individual initiative
17.	Intellectual efficiency	Efficient in use of intellectual abilities; can keep on at a task where others might get bored or discouraged
18.	Psychological mindedness	More interested in why people do what they do than in what they do; good judge of how people feel and what they think about things
19.	Flexibility	Flexible; likes change and variety; easily bored by routine life and everyday experience; may be impatient, and even erratic
20.	Femininity/Masculinity	On this scale, a person scoring in the femininity direction is seen as sympathetic, helpful, sensitive to criticism, and tending to interpret events from a personal point of view. A person scoring in the masculinity direction is seen as decisive, action-oriented, not easily subdued, and rather unsentimental.

SOURCE: Adapted from *California Psychological Inventory: Administrator's Guide* (pp. 6–7), by H. G. Gough, 1987, Palo Alto, CA: Consulting Psychologists Press.

criticism of the CPI, however, is that the different scales tend to overlap, showing correlations with each other of .50 and higher. Apparently, each scale does not assess an independent and unique trait (Thorndike, 1959). Nonetheless, many experts agree that the CPI is one of the best personality inventories in use today.

Gough argues that the CPI's scales tap into common **folk concepts** of personality. Folk concepts are categories of personality that arise naturally out of human interactions in most, if not all, societies. For example, most cultures signify a concept of social responsibility—a tendency to act in accord with the good of the group rather than out of pure self-interest. Within each culture, individuals vary widely in the extent to which they and their

Harrison Gough developed the California Psychological Inventory (CPI), an omnibus self-report questionnaire that assesses individual differences in 20 traits assumed to be instrumental in effective psychological functioning. Gough views CPI traits as "folk concepts" of personality that people routinely use, even if implicitly, to make sense of social interaction.

behavior implicitly endorse this folk concept. The two CPI scales of "socialization" and "responsibility" aim to assess this important individual difference. A substantial body of research supports the construct validity of these scales. For example, Gough and Bradley (1992) administered the CPI to hundreds of delinquent and criminal men and women as well as a comparable group of control subjects. Delinquent and criminal adults scored significantly lower than control subjects on a number of different CPI scales (such as empathy and achievement via conformance), but the two scales that showed the strongest difference were socialization and responsibility.

Recent work with the CPI has revealed three *vectors* or general dimensions that underlie the more specific folk-concept scales. Vector 1 pertains to an interpersonal orientation, which ranges from an involved, participatory approach to life on one end to a detached, privacy-seeking orientation on the other. Vector 2 pertains to norms and values, ranging from a norm-accepting to a norm-rejecting pole. Vector 3 pertains to what Gough calls "ego integration," which extends from self-defeating and interpersonally unacceptable behavior on one end to self-realization and superior ego functioning on the other.

The first two vectors may be crossed to produce four distinct lifestyles, or ways of living. *Alphas* are high on Vectors 1 and 2; they are interpersonally involved and rule respecting. *Betas* are more detached and internalized (low on Vector 1) but still rule accepting. *Gammas* tend to enter into the interpersonal arena but remain dubious about its norms and conventions. They are interpersonally engaged but rebellious or dismissive of rules and regulations. Finally, *deltas* seek escape from the interpersonal world and reject its norms and values. Research in career assessment suggests that alphas do best in leadership and managerial roles, betas function well in subordinate support positions, gammas look for and are adept at creating change, and deltas work best alone in fields such as art, literature, and (depending on their abilities) mathematics (Gough, 1995). Ego integration from Vector 3 may be seen as modifying all four types. For example, alphas who are high in ego integration may show impressive leadership skill, but alphas low in ego integration may prove to be authoritarian and invasive. Deltas who are high in ego integration may be visionary and prescient in very personal ways, as in artistic or musical accomplishment. Deltas with low ego integration, however, may experience disintegrative conflict and may react with explosive violence or with disabling psychological disorders.

Another well-regarded trait inventory is the **Personality Research Form (PRF),** developed by Douglas Jackson in the 1960s. This instrument incorporates a number of advances in test construction and format that were not available to the authors of the MMPI and CPI. In constructing and validating the PRF, Jackson closely followed the construct approach outlined earlier in this chapter. The resulting test contains 320 true/false items, making up 20 independent scales. Each of the scales purports to measure a basic personality "need," taken from a list delineated by Murray (1938). This list includes the needs for dominance, affiliation, achievement, aggression, and nurturance. The different PRF scales show much less overlap than occurs in the CPI, and a substantial body of research supports the validity of many of the scales in predicting attitudes, values, and behavior. In addition, Paunonen, Jackson, and Keinonen (1990) have developed a nonverbal, pictorial version of the PRF in which each item is represented by a line drawing of a figure performing a need-relevant behavior. (See Figure 4.2.) For each item, the subject is asked to indicate the likelihood that he or she might engage in the behavior represented in the drawing. The nonverbal PRF looks to be a promising research tool for cross-cultural personality research and for use with populations who are not linguistically adept.

Paul Costa and Robert McCrae (1985, 1992) have developed self-report inventories to assess the Big Five traits. The **NEO-PI-R** (Neuroticism-Extraversion-Openness Personality Inventory Revised) consists of 240 items assessing the Big Five traits of neuroticism, extraversion–introversion, openness to experience, agreeableness, and conscientiousness. For each item, the respondent indicates the extent to which he or she agrees or disagrees on a five-point rating scale. Costa and McCrae have divided each of the Big Five traits into six subtraits, called *facets*. For example, the six facets making up extraversion–introversion are *activity level, assertiveness, excitement seeking, positive emotions, gregariousness,* and *warmth*. Each item is keyed to a particular facet. Items such as "When I do things, I do them vigorously" and "My life is fast-paced" contribute to the activity

Paul T. Costa, Jr. (left) and Robert R. McCrae (right) developed a highly influential inventory (the NEO-PI-R) to assess individual differences in the five-factor model of personality traits, or the Big Five. They label the five trait categories as extraversion, neuroticism, agreeableness, conscientiousness, and openness to experience.

FIGURE 4.2	TWO NONVERBAL TRAIT ITEMS

On the Nonverbal Personality Questionnaire, Item A depicts aggressive behavior while Item B shows thrill seeking.

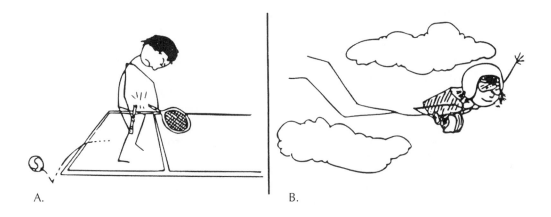

A.   B.

SOURCE: From "The Structured Nonverbal Assessment of Personality," by S. V. Paunonen, D. N. Jackson, & M. Keinonen, 1990, *Journal of Personality, 58,* p. 485.

level facet of extraversion. Therefore, each person receives a score on each of six facets for each of five traits, resulting in an individual profile of 30 scores.

The trait and facet scales of the NEO-PI-R show good test–retest and split-half reliability. Significant correlations with other measures of the Big Five traits contribute to the construct validity for this measure and for the Big Five taxonomy in general. Costa and McCrae have also developed peer-report versions of the NEO-PI-R. In several studies, they have compared self-reports on Big Five traits with the ratings made by spouses and other peers. McCrae and Costa (1990) report substantial agreement of self-ratings with peer and spouse ratings on all five factors. Agreement between self and spouse tends to be higher than between self and other peers, probably because spouses tend to know each other better than do other peers.

THE CONTROVERSY OVER TRAITS

Even as he constructed the entire field of personality psychology around the central concept of the trait, Gordon Allport (1937) was aware of the controversy over traits. The behaviorists who dominated American psychology in the 1930s saw no reason to acknowledge the importance, even the existence, of traits. After all, traits were hypothesized to exist within the person rather than in the observable public sphere. Unlike behavior, traits could not be directly observed. Furthermore, the behaviorists' commitment to environmentalism made them skeptical about the idea that individual-difference variables within the organism—rather than differences in the environment—might account for individual differences in behavior. And why would anybody want to study individual differences between persons anyway? Research psychologists of the 1930s focused their energies on basic processes, such as perception and learning—processes that were assumed to play themselves out in similar ways from one organism to the next. The differences between organisms that might be detected represented unimportant and doubtlessly random variability. This variability should be of no interest to serious research psychologists.

While trait advocates like Allport, Cattell, and Eysenck pressed on, skepticism about the utility of trait concepts persisted over the decades. In the 1950s, researchers became especially concerned about test-taking styles in trait assessment (Christie & Lindauer, 1963; Edwards, 1957; Jackson & Messick, 1958). Do trait scales really measure the traits they claim to measure, or do they instead merely assess a person's general style of responding to personality scales? Some people try to make themselves look good; a few try to make themselves look bad; some people will say "yes" or "agree" to almost anything; others will persistently say "no." It doesn't matter what particular trait the scale is designed to measure, some skeptics argued, because what the score on the test gives you is a measure of response style rather than the trait itself. The controversy eventually led to refinements in test construction to minimize the bias of response sets, as well as the realization that some response styles are themselves important aspects of personality.

A favorite criticism of traits is that they are labels designed to stereotype and even discriminate against people. Influenced by labeling theory in sociology and social psychology, some writers in the 1960s argued against the use of diagnostic categories such as "schizophrenic" and "obsessive-compulsive disorder" in the assessment of psychological functioning. Such labels were seen to be discriminatory against those unfortunate people whose problems in living were deemed "mental illness" by an oppressive society. Labels served to control people, to keep them in their place (Goffman, 1961). While personality traits are not psychiatric labels, trait theories suffered by guilt through association. Saying that somebody is relatively "low on the trait of agreeableness" is also a label that reifies, or makes overly concrete, what some people consider to be a dubious way of talking about people. Traits are sugar-coated stereotypes. Rather than celebrating human diversity, traits simply lump people into groups. While very strong arguments against these positions have been repeatedly spelled out (e.g., Block, 1981; Hogan, DeSoto, & Solano, 1977; Johnson, 1997; McCrae & Costa, 1995; Wiggins, 1973), this kind of criticism of personality traits can still be heard, especially outside the field of psychology.

The most significant critique ever levied against traits, however, came from a book with the innocuous title *Personality and Assessment,* written in 1968 by the personality psychologist Walter Mischel. Mischel revived a problem in trait assessment that was identified by Allport back in 1937. It is what Allport called the problem of "generality versus specificity." Ideally, traits refer to relatively general tendencies in behavior. A critical assumption of trait theories is that people do indeed show some general consistency in their behavior across situations and over time. If, by contrast, behavior is more specific to the situation, rather than cross-situationally general, then the entire concept of trait comes into question. Mischel (1968, 1973, 1977) called trait concepts into serious question. Because behavior is more situationally specific than cross-situationally general, Mischel maintained, personality trait measures are not particularly useful in the prediction of behavior. And if they can't predict behavior, then what good are they?

MISCHEL'S CRITIQUE

The concept of trait implies that behavior is, to a certain extent, cross-situationally consistent: An extraverted person, for instance, is supposed to act in an extraverted, outgoing manner in many different settings, as a general trend across various situations. Mischel argued instead that human behavior is much more situationally specific than the concept of trait would suggest. In the traditions of behaviorism and modern social-learning theory (chapter 3), Mischel maintained that behavior is shaped largely by the exigencies of a given situation. That people act in consistent ways across different situations, reflecting an underlying consistency of personality traits, is a myth.

Mischel's argument was not new. Behaviorists had made many of the same points, though usually in a different context, since the early days of John Watson (1924). Mischel's thesis, however, was extremely powerful because of the wealth of empirical data he presented. Reviewing scientific literature on such personality variables as honesty, dependency, aggression, rigidity, and attitudes toward authority, Mischel showed that the correlations between (a) personality-trait scores, as determined by personality tests and rating procedures and (b) actual behavior in a particular situation were generally low, rarely exceeding the modest level of +.30. Furthermore, the correlation between indices of the same kind of behavior (such as "honest behavior," "friendly behavior," or "aggressive behavior") emitted by the same persons across different situations was also low.

For example, a classic study of moral behavior in more than 8,000 school children (Hartshorne & May, 1928) found that copying from the answer key on one classroom test showed only the modest correlation of +.29 with another form of cheating whereby students inflated their own scores on a different test. The major lesson from this study, argued Mischel, is that individual differences in moral behavior are not consistent across different situations: Children who cheat on one particular test don't necessarily cheat on another. If one wishes to predict the extent to which different children will actually cheat in a particular situation, it makes little sense to invoke a general trait of "honesty" upon which children can be said to differ. As Skinner might have put it in *Walden Two,* there is no such thing as an "honest" or a "dishonest" child, only honest or dishonest behavior displayed in a given situation.

Mischel (1968, 1973) suggested the disturbing possibility that personality traits exist nowhere but in the mind of the observer. The same argument has been forcefully made by social psychologists such as Jones and Nisbett (1972) and Ross (1977), who speak of the **fundamental attribution error**—a general tendency for people to overemphasize traits and underemphasize situations when explaining the causes for *other* people's behaviors. According to this view, when people are asked to explain why another person does what he or she does, they are likely to invoke a general *personality* trait: "Randy punched another basketball player because Randy is an aggressive person" or "Martha got 100% on the mathematics exam because she is brilliant." When asked to explain their own behavior, on the other hand, people are more likely to invoke the specific *situation:* "I punched another basketball player because I was provoked to do so" or "I scored 100% on the mathematics exam because I studied hard." The implication here is that trait psychologists, in attempting to predict and explain the behavior of other people, repeatedly commit the same fundamental attribution error. Personality traits, therefore, are no more than convenient but misleading labels about other people. They exist in the mind of the observing psychologist, not in the personality of the person being observed.

If personality traits exist in the minds of observers rather than in the behavior of those they observe, then traits may tell us more about how people think about other people's behavior than they tell us about behavior itself. In one of the more acerbic critiques of trait conceptualizations, Shweder (1975) insisted that when trait researchers do indeed demonstrate empirical correlations among different traits (e.g., between, say, "dominance" and "aggressiveness"), their findings simply reflect the semantic similarity of the constructs involved. For example, Passini and Norman (1966) asked students to rate people *whom they had never met* on a number of personality scales. The raters were instructed to base these ratings on what they imagined these people might be like. Factor analysis of the ratings yielded a structure of correlations among the different scales that was almost identical to those structures obtained in other studies employing the same scales— studies in which the raters *were* acquainted with the subjects they were to rate or in which they directly observed subjects' behavior.

Shweder interpreted results like these to suggest that our ratings of personality traits are probably based more on our knowledge of how words (trait descriptors) go together than on our observation of real behavioral associations. If the traits of dominance and aggressiveness, for instance, seem to be similar in meaning, then we assume that behavioral manifestations of these traits are similarly correlated. In this view, people develop a set of assumptions about how certain trait words go together and then they apply these assumptions uncritically in judging the behavior of others. Each person, therefore, develops his or her own *implicit personality theory* (Bruner & Tagiuri, 1954)—a set of associations in the person's mind. Some have suggested that once people have formed an initial impression about where another person stands on a given trait continuum, then they use their implicit personality theories to infer the person's relative standing on other

With the publication of his book, *Personality and Assessment* (1968), Walter Mischel ignited a firestorm of controversy in the 1970s and early 1980s regarding the validity of self-report trait scales and the very viability of the concept of the personality trait. While most personality psychologists today believe that traits are indispensable for a healthy psychology of personality, Mischel's critique raised awareness in the field regarding the situated nature of human conduct and the limits of personality theories built solely on dispositional traits.

traits as well (Berman & Kenny, 1976). Thus, traits are convenient categories for our perceptions rather than real characteristics of the persons we perceive.

Mischel's critique of personality traits and other highly critical reviews of personality psychology as a whole (for example, Fiske, 1974) launched what has been termed the *person–situation debate* in personality psychology. Defenders of traits (such as Alker, 1972; Block, 1977; Hogan, DeSoto, & Solano, 1977) argued that Mischel had (a) misrepresented many trait theories and trait theorists, (b) selectively reviewed the empirical literature in an unfair way, and (c) overlooked many methodologically sophisticated studies that supported cross-situational consistency of behavior and the inner coherence of personality. Supporters of the Mischel position (such as Argyle & Little, 1972; Shweder, 1975) marshaled more data to buttress their "situationist" claims, often invoking findings from social psychology documenting the influence of situations on behavior.

Throughout the 1970s, a doctrine of **situationism** seemed to threaten the viability of the trait concept in particular and, according to some views, the very enterprise of personality psychology *in toto*. The doctrine may be summarized in four points:

1. Behavior is highly situation-specific, not cross-situationally consistent.
2. Individual differences within a situation are attributed primarily to measurement error rather than broad internal dispositions.
3. Observed response patterns can be causally linked to the stimuli present in the situation.
4. The experiment is the most appropriate method for discovering such stimulus–response links. (Krahe, 1992, p. 29)

In other words, situations rather than traits drive and shape human behavior, a fact that is clearest under the well-controlled conditions of a laboratory experiment. Observed behavioral differences among persons in the same situation are small, unimportant, or the result of errors or biases on the part of observers and/or methods of measurement. With its conceptual emphasis on the external environment (situation) and methodological preference for controlled laboratory experimentation, situationism came to be associated with certain aspects of the behaviorist legacy—that is, with social-learning theories such as Bandura's and Rotter's (chapter 3) and with the kind of research conducted by experimental social psychologists.

The person–situation debate seemed to die down in the mid 1980s (Krahe, 1992; Maddi, 1984; West, 1983), as most advocates appeared to settle on something they claimed they were advocating all along: a compromise position of **interactionism.** As the eminent psychologist Kurt Lewin said more than 60 years ago, behavior is a function of the person (and his or her traits) in interaction with the environment (Lewin, 1935). Yet this seemingly simple, even obvious, statement is more complex than might first be evident, and there still exists considerable controversy as to how it is to be interpreted. There are many ways to conceive of and study the interaction of the person and the environment in the prediction of human behavior. Mischel's critique and the subsequent person–situation debate stimulated considerable thought and research in the field of personality psychology and shaped the thinking of a generation of personality psychologists.

AGGREGATING BEHAVIORS

According to Mischel, traits do not work well in the prediction of behavior because behavior itself is not very consistent from one situation to the next. The lack of such cross-situational consistency in behavior poses a formidable problem for trait theories. However,

In response to Mischel's critique of traits, Seymour Epstein showed that well-designed self-report trait scales can be strong predictors of behavioral trends when behavior is aggregated across different situations. Trait scores are generally better at predicting cross-situational trends than they are at predicting exactly what a person will do in a single, particular situation.

personality psychologist Seymour Epstein suggested a solution to the problem that is quite old and familiar, making that perennial observation that "sometimes the obvious escapes us." For Epstein and a number of personality psychologists, the answer to the problem of cross-situational consistency in human behavior is **aggregation** (Epstein, 1979, 1986).

To understand Epstein's argument, we have to recall how a psychologist might construct a questionnaire designed to measure a particular personality trait. That procedure involves generating a large pool of "items," which is then reduced through a number of different methods to an economical scale with maximum reliability and validity. Each item on the test is seen as contributing something to the test as a whole: Each item zeroes in on the trait from a slightly different angle. Such zeroing in is necessary because a trait is a complex construct that might be manifested in a large number of ways, and no single item can successfully capture all the complexity. Therefore, psychologists get as close as they can to a "pure" measure of a trait, minimizing measurement error by constructing tests with multiple items—that is by *aggregating* test items. Even the simplest trait test, therefore, requires more than 1 or 2 items if it is to be considered reliable. Within reason and all other things being equal, the more items a test has, the more reliable it will be.

With this in mind, then, consider a typical personality study in which an investigator administers a questionnaire containing many items designed to assess a particular trait and correlates scores on that measure with a single instance of behavior, perhaps emitted under laboratory conditions, shown by the respondent. While the trait measure itself may be highly reliable by virtue of aggregation of test items, the single measure of behavior is likely to be highly unreliable, unrepresentative, and saturated with error. It is no wonder, stated Epstein, that Mischel's review of the personality literature found so much inconsistency between trait measures and behavior. According to Epstein, Mischel clearly identified a problem, but he misinterpreted its primary cause. *Overall, the trait measures are sound; it is the single measures of behavior that are at fault.* Substantial consistency between trait scores and behavior across different situations should appear, Epstein maintained, when single instances of behavior are aggregated across many different situations. Trait scores, therefore, should predict consistent trends in behavior across different situations and over time.

A growing body of research suggests that Epstein was right. Figure 4.3 presents data from Epstein (1979) that show that the reliability of a number of different measures—ranging from headaches and stomachaches to social behavior—increases as the number of occasions upon which the measures are taken increases. Therefore, if we wish to obtain a reliable estimate of a person's blood pressure, positive mood, verbal eloquence, food consumption, smile frequency, or whatever, we will do better to sample the phenomenon in question on numerous occasions. As Figure 4.3 shows, the greater the degree of aggregation over time, the higher the reliability of the measure and the closer we get to a pure, stable, and representative estimate of behavior.

In an impressive review, Rushton, Brainerd, and Presley (1983) illustrated the usefulness of aggregation in 12 different areas of psychological research. Especially interesting was their discussion of the famous Hartshorne and May (1928) study of moral behavior—a study that Mischel (1968) cited forcefully as an example of failure to find cross-situational consistency in behavior. Suggesting that the findings in this study have perennially been

| **FIGURE 4.3** | **RELIABILITY AND AGGREGATION** |

For a number of different measures, reliability (measured as correlations between scores on even days and odd days) increases as the researchers collect and aggregate more data over longer periods of time. (The correlations were obtained by correlating the mean of odd days with the mean of an equal number of even days. The values plotted are the means of the correlations for the variables in a category.)

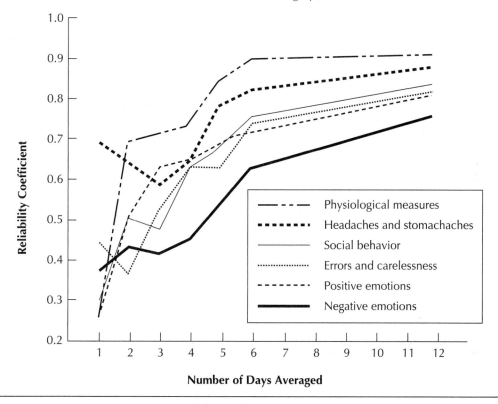

SOURCE: From "The Stability of Behavior: 1. On Predicting Most of the People Much of the Time," by S. Epstein, 1979, *Journal of Personality and Social Psychology, 37,* 1097–1126.

misinterpreted, Rushton argued that children's moral behavior manifested considerable consistency when appropriate behaviors were aggregated across different tests and situations. Although any single behavioral test of "honesty" correlated, on the average, only .20 with any other single test of honesty, much higher relationships were found when the measures were aggregated into meaningful groups and correlated with other combined behavioral measures, with teachers' ratings of the children, or with children's moral-knowledge scores. Often these correlations were on the order of .50 or .60. For example, a battery of tests measuring cheating by copying correlated +.52 with another battery of tests measuring other types of classroom cheating. Contrary to Mischel's conclusion, aggregation reveals that the children in the Hartshorne and May (1928) study showed consistent individual differences in cheating behavior. Thus, some children may indeed be consistently more honest than others.

Like any good research procedure, aggregation can be used wisely or foolishly (Epstein, 1986). For instance, merely lumping together different instances of behavior will not necessarily increase reliability in measurement. Aggregated items must "hang together" conceptually and/or empirically. In determining how to aggregate data, the psychologist must keep clearly in mind what he or she wishes to learn from a particular study. Therefore, if a child's aggressive behavior toward her sister is a topic of interest, the researcher should not aggregate aggression across different targets (such as aggression toward father, mother, brother, or pets) but should nevertheless aggregate across occasions with the sister. Similarly, if a researcher wishes to know how three different situations differentially influence altruistic behavior in college students, it would be useless to aggregate data across the different situations. In this case, the data should be aggregated across students—the researcher would seek to cancel out individual differences in students in order to see more clearly the situational effects for all students in general.

Critics of aggregation argue that it bypasses rather than resolves the problem of cross-situational consistency in behavior (Mischel & Peake, 1982). When researchers aggregate behaviors across many different situations, they fail to show how a particular trait score predicts particular behavior in a particular situation. In settling for predicting general trends across a wide variety of situations, they sacrifice a great deal of precision with respect to any particular situation—precision that may come from a careful analysis of the exigencies in the situation itself. Recent research, however, has examined more precisely the extent to which different kinds of situations and different traits can be successfully examined through aggregation. The results of these studies suggest that aggregation works better across certain kinds of situations than across others.

For example, Moskowitz (1990) examined behavioral manifestations of dominance and friendliness in six different laboratory situations—two involving a same-sex friend, two involving a male stranger, and two involving a female stranger. Friendly and dominant behaviors were rated by observers and by the subjects themselves. As in other studies of aggregation, behavioral self- and observer ratings pooled across the six situations were more strongly correlated with each other than were ratings made within any particular situation itself. But cross-situational consistency was stronger across certain situations than across others. In particular, the greatest degree of convergence between self-ratings and observer ratings on dominance and friendliness occurred *in the two situations with friends.* Less consistency was revealed across the four situations with strangers. Moskowitz concludes that "validity varies as a function of the situation" (p. 1105). Aggregating across different situations in which one is interacting with close friends reveals especially strong levels of cross-situational consistency in behavior. Aggregating across different situations in which one is interacting with strangers reveals less consistency. In the former case, behavior appears to be more strongly shaped by traits. In the latter, situational influences appear to be stronger.

MODERN INTERACTIONISM

In the aftermath of Mischel's critique of traits and the subsequent person–situation debate, many personality psychologists today endorse some variation of what Krahe (1992) calls the doctrine of *modern interactionism.* The core of the modern interactionist approach is captured in four basic postulates:

1. Actual behavior is a function of a continuous process of multidirectional interaction or feedback between the individual and the situation he or she encounters.

2. The individual is an intentional, active agent in this interactional process.

3. On the person side of the interaction, cognitive and motivational factors are essential determinants of behavior.

4. On the situation side, the psychological meaning of situations for the individual is the important determining factor. (pp. 70–71)

Persons Versus Situations Versus Interactions

There are many different ways of thinking about interactionism (Ozer, 1986). One approach, termed **mechanistic interactionism** (Endler, 1983), derives from the concept of an interaction effect as it appears in certain statistical procedures. In mechanistic interactionism, a person's trait constitutes one independent predictor, the situation constitutes a second independent predictor, and the interaction between trait and situation constitutes a third predictor. The dependent variable, or outcome to be predicted, is some form of measurable behavior. In such a study, a significant effect for the trait–situation interaction indicates (a) that there exists a statistical tendency for the trait to be associated with the behavior *when a particular level of the situation* is involved, or similarly, (b) that there exists a tendency for the situation to be associated with the behavior *when a particular level of the trait* is involved.

Many studies in personality and social psychology draw implicitly upon a mechanistic model of interactionism. A good example of this approach is a study of altruism by Romer, Gruder, and Lizzadro (1986). The researchers administered questionnaires designed to identify two types of college students, enrolled in a psychology class, likely to show helping behavior. One type, scoring high on the need for nurturance (need to care for others) but low on the need for succorance (need to be cared for by others), was called "altruist." The other type, scoring high on both needs for nurturance and succorance, was called "receptive–giving." Helping behavior was operationalized as the student's volunteering to help a distressed experimenter complete a research project by participating in a psychological experiment. The experimenter appealed for the student's help over the phone. In one scenario (the "no-compensation" situation), the student was told that his or her help was desperately needed but that the experimenter could not offer any course credit for the help. The "compensation situation" involved the same plea but in this situation the student was promised that course credit would be received as compensation.

The researchers believed that helping behavior was likely to be a function of the interaction of personality and situation. Specifically, they predicted that altruists would show high levels of helping behavior in situations in which they were *not likely to be compensated* given that their need for succorance was low. Receptive–giving persons, on the other hand, should show high levels of helping behavior in situations in which they *were likely to be compensated,* since their need for succorance was high. As Figure 4.4 shows, the percentage of students agreeing to help is well predicted as an interaction of person and environment supporting the interactional hypothesis. Altruists helped more in the no-compensation condition than they did in the compensation condition. Receptive–giving students showed the reverse pattern, exhibiting higher levels of helping when compensated.

Reciprocal Interactionism

While mechanistic interactionism partitions the variance in behavior into that accounted for by persons, situations, and their interactions, **reciprocal interactionism** conceives of a more fluid and complex pattern in which person, situation, and behavior continually and reciprocally influence one another (Endler, 1983).

It is probably some form of reciprocal interactionism that is regularly implied by most personality psychologists when they say that behavior is a function of the interaction of person and environment. It has, however, proven extremely difficult to design studies that can measure dynamic, reciprocal interactions in a meaningful way (Ozer, 1986). One successful effort however, is the work of Emmons, Diener, and Larsen (1986) and Emmons and Diener (1986b), who have offered two alternative models of reciprocal interactionism. The "choice of situations" model suggests that people select situations and avoid others on the basis of certain personality traits and needs. The "affect congruence" model suggests that people experience greater positive affect and less negative affect in situations congruent with their personality characteristics. Research in support of congruence can be found in many places (Ickes, Snyder, & Garcia, 1997). There are several lines of evidence to support the proposition that people choose to enter and spend time in situations that promote the expression of their own trait-relevant behavior, and that they often enjoy doing so. A long tradition of research in career psychology shows that people flourish in their work environments when there is a good fit between their personality traits and the characteristics of the environment

---

FIGURE 4.4   PERSONALITY, COMPENSATION, AND HELPING BEHAVIOR

The percentage of individuals who helped is a function of (a) personality type (altruistic versus receptive–giving) and (b) the situational condition (compensation versus no compensation).

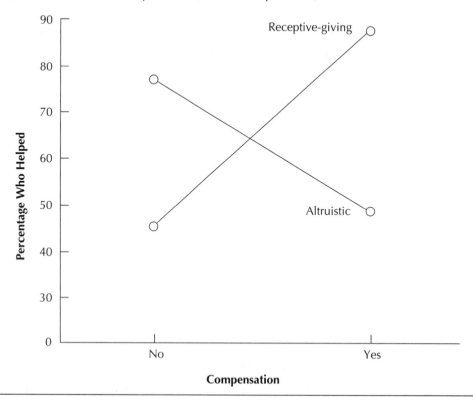

SOURCE: From "A Person–Situation Approach to Altruistic Behavior," by D. Romer, C. L. Gruder, & T. Lizzadro, 1986, *Journal of Personality and Social Psychology, 51,* p. 1006.

(Holland, 1996). Lack of congruence between traits and work situations, by contrast, leads to dissatisfaction, unstable career paths, and lowered performance levels.

Traits as Conditional Statements

Throughout the years of the person–situation debate and up to the present time, Walter Mischel has continued to offer astute observations and critiques of trait psychology. His recent theorizing appears to leave more room for the working of broad dispositional traits than was the case when he offered his first important critique in 1968. Nonetheless, he has continued to underscore the issue of variability in responding across situations (Mischel & Shoda, 1995, 1998). How do we put together the fact that people act in very different ways from one situation to the next with the fact that broad personality traits appear to account for trends in behavior across situations? As Mischel and Shoda (1998, p. 229) put it, how do we "reconcile dynamics and dispositions"?

Like many personality psychologists today, Mischel ascribes to an interactionist approach for understanding human behavior. But Mischel has articulated the nature of the interaction in more detail than is usually the case. While conceding that aggregation studies support the general idea that traits predict a modicum of behavioral consistency across different situations, Mischel has turned his attention to a second kind of consistency—consistency in variation. People change their behaviors from one situation to the next in consistent ways, Mischel asserts. And people differ from one another in their characteristic ways of doing so. Let us take a simple example. Matthew and Julie are both relatively easygoing people, but both of them can become very irritated in certain situations. When a teacher or parent offers advice to Matthew, he tends to be gracious and accepting, but he becomes very irritated when his friends or siblings tell him what to do. By contrast, Julie finds her mother's and her teacher's suggestions for how she should improve her life extremely annoying, but she is quite willing to take the same kind of advice from her friends. In an overall sense, Matthew and Julie don't seem to differ in their level of irritability, but each of them becomes irritable in a different situation. For Matthew, *if* peers give him advice, *then* he becomes irritated, but *if* authority figures offer advice, *then* he is gracious. For Julie, *if* authority figures give her advice, *then* she becomes irritated, but *if* peers offer advice, *then* she is gracious. Matthew and Julie each show a different consistency in *if … then* relations.

An *if … then* relation is a *conditional statement*. *If* certain conditions are satisfied, *then* a particular result will occur. In the cases of Matthew and Julie, *if* a particular situation occurs (*if* peer offers advice, *if* authority offers advice), *then* a particular behavioral response is expressed (*then* person is irritated, *then* person is gracious). Mischel and his colleagues have conducted studies to document consistencies in *if … then* relations, arguing that this kind of conditional and interactional consistency is an extremely important and underrated aspect of personality functioning. In one study, the researchers collected behavioral observations of 84 children (the average age was 10 years old) attending a 6-week summer camp. The children's behavior was painstakingly documented. Specifically, within each hour of camp activity, observers recorded the frequency with which five different types of situations occurred: (1) peer teased, provoked, or threatened the child; (2) adult warned the child; (3) adult punished the child by giving him or her "time out"; (4) peer initiated positive social contact; and (5) adult praised the child verbally. Within each situation, the observers recorded the frequency of five different kinds of behavior on the part of the child: (1) verbal aggression, (2) physical aggression, (3) whined or displayed babyish behavior, (4) complied or gave in, and (5) talked prosocially. Crossing the five situations with the five behavioral responses results in 25 different conditional patterns. For example, one pattern would be *if* adult warned the child, *then* the child whined. Another would be *if* a peer initiated positive social contact, *then* the child engaged in verbal aggression. And so on. The design of this study enabled the researchers, therefore, to examine in detail 25 different kinds of interactions, each conceived as an *if … then* relation.

The most interesting results from the camp study were the *intraindividual profiles* that the observers obtained. For each individual child, the researchers were able to calculate a number of different profiles exhibiting consistency in behavioral variability. Figure 4.5 gives examples from four different children. The solid line for each profile charts the relative occurrence of the behavior verbal aggression in each of five different situations during one time period (Time 1) in the study. The broken line charts the relative occurrence of the same kind of behavior across the same five situations at a second time period (Time 2). As you can see, for three of the four children, the profile at Time 1 matches closely the profile at Time 2. For example, in both time periods, Child 17 shows low levels of verbal aggression in situations of peer approach and peer teasing, moderate levels in situations of adult praise and adult warn, and very high levels of verbal aggression in the situation of adult punishment. By contrast, at both Time 1 and Time 2, Child 9 shows high levels of verbal aggression in the peer approach situation and generally moderate levels in the other four. The two lines for Child 17 match more closely than do the two corresponding lines for Child 9, indicating somewhat greater stability or consistency in behavioral variability for Child 17. The one child who shows low consistency in variability is Child 48, whose verbal aggression appears to be moderate across all five situations at Time 1 but high in situations of peer tease and adult praise at Time 2.

In the camp study, the researchers documented considerable consistency in *if … then* relations for most of the children. Combining the results of all 84 children, they also found that intraindividual profiles were, on the average, highest for the behaviors of verbal aggression and compliance and lowest for prosocial talk. This means that children tended to be most consistent from Time 1 to Time 2 in the patterning of their verbal aggression and compliance behaviors across the five different situations, while they tended to be somewhat less consistent from Time 1 to Time 2 in the patterning of their prosocial talk across the five situations. Yet even for prosocial talk, the intraindividual profiles showed significantly more than a chance amount of consistency in behavioral variability.

The camp study is one of the best examples anywhere of research inspired by an interactionist view of personality. Mischel and his colleagues have reconceptualized individual differences dimensions in such a way as to reconcile dispositions and dynamics. The "traits" that these researchers focus on are consistent individual differences in the variability that people show across different situations for the same kind of behavior. Individual differences in behavioral variability offer a new way to think about traits and about the ways in which people differ from one another in consistent ways. Furthermore, Mischel's work reflects growing interest in personality, social, and developmental psychology in lawful and predictable variability in responding across situations and over time (Fleeson, 2001). As one example of this interest, Brown and Moskowitz (1998) have recently shown that variations in dominant, submissive, agreeable, and quarrelsome behaviors follow predictable cycles from one week to the next. In the overall, these four classes of behavior tend to rise over the course of the week, reaching a peak on Wednesday or Thursday, and then drop rather precipitously by the weekend. Some individuals, furthermore, show predictable daily cycles in behavioral fluctuation, Brown and Moskowitz reveal. In particular, highly extraverted

| FIGURE 4.5 | **PROFILES OF BEHAVIORAL VARIABILITY** |

Variability in verbal aggression across five different conditions differs for four different children.

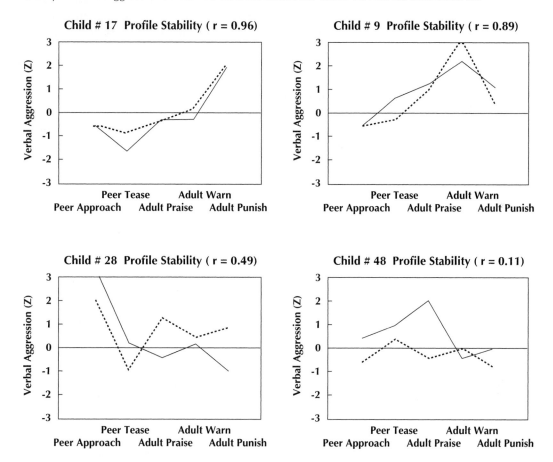

NOTE: The two lines indicate the profiles based on two different samples of occasions in which each child encountered each type of psychological situation, shown as Time 1 (solid) and Time 2 (broken).

SOURCE: From "Intra-individual stability in the organization and patterning of behavior: Incorporating psychological situations into the idiographic analysis of personality," by Y. Shoda, W. Mischel, and J. C. Wright, 1994, *Journal of Personality and Social Psychology, 65*, p. 678.

individuals tend to engage in increasingly more social behaviors as the day wears on, exhibiting an especially wide range of social activities with a large number of people in the evening.

CONCLUSION

Mischel's (1968) critique of traits launched a 20-year debate in personality psychology about the extent to which differences in internal personality dispositions versus external situational variables should be taken into consideration in the prediction of behavior. Initially, Mischel (1968) mounted a forceful attack against traits and strongly urged personality psychologists to refocus their attention on external situational variables. This argument spawned the position of situationism, which seemed to hold sway for most of the 1970s. The proponents of trait approaches launched a series of intellectual counterattacks in the late 1970s and 1980s. Some of their best ammunition came from aggregation studies, which showed that individual differences in well-measured personality traits were indeed predictive of general behavioral trends when those trends were observed across many different situations and over time. Still, when it comes to predicting behavior in any particular situation, a single personality trait is likely to account for only a modest amount of variance. Focusing research attention on each of several different kinds of situations, Mischel and his colleagues have recently documented strikingly consistent individual differences in response variability. Thirty years after his original critique of traits, Mischel has come around to an interesting kind of trait idea—the idea that major, traitlike, individual differences in people's behavior can be observed at the level of *if ... then* relations.

The person–situation debate helped to refine psychologists' thinking about traits and situations (Funder & Colvin, 1991; Kenrick & Funder, 1988). Personality research today would appear to be much more interactional in spirit and design than it was 30 years ago. Psychologists appear to have a much better appreciation of the extent to which personality dispositions and situational exigencies interact in the making of behavior. At the same time, the general concept of a personality trait has emerged from the controversy stronger than ever before. As we will see in the next two chapters, personality psychologists have utilized trait measures and trait theories in new and powerful ways in the past 20 years. As studies employing aggregation designs made a stronger case for the predictive efficacy of personality traits, psychologists in the 1980s were also examining the longitudinal stability of traits over the life course, the origins of traits in genetic differences and environmental effects, the psychobiological underpinnings of traits, and the extent to which a viable taxonomy of traits could be developed. It is to these issues that we will turn in the next two chapters.

SUMMARY

1. Personality traits are broad individual differences between people in characteristic thoughts, feelings, and behaviors. Psychologists typically conceive of traits as bipolar linear dimensions that capture general, global, and stable dispositions of personality. People can be compared and contrasted with respect to their traits. Psychologists have traditionally disagreed about the technical nature of traits, with opinions ranging from those who argue that traits are neuropsychic structures that exert a causal influence on an actor's behavior to those who suggest that traits are mere cognitive categories used by observers to make sense of social life.

2. Characterizations of personality traits can be found in ancient texts. A pupil of Aristotle,

Theophrastus generated one of the earliest known trait lists through his semihumorous character sketches. Later, the Greek physician Galen codified the humoral theory of traits, delineating four basic personality types that were each linked to characteristic bodily fluids. The sanguine, phlegmatic, melancholic, and choleric types were later depicted by the philosopher Kant and have been recaptured in Eysenck's modern theory of personality traits. Scientific research on traits began in the late 19th century and was greatly promoted by advances in statistics, such as the invention of the correlation coefficient and factor analysis.

3. Two highly influential trait theorists of the 20th century were Gordon Allport and Raymond B.

Cattell. Allport centered the entire discipline of personality psychology on the concept of trait, which he defined as a neuropsychic structure responsible for consistencies in behavior over time and across situations. Allport distinguished between common traits, upon which many people could be compared, and personal dispositions, which were characteristics that were unique to a given person. While Allport's approach to traits tended toward the literary, Cattell developed a rigorously quantitative program for trait research. Combining life record (L) data, questionnaire (Q) data, and laboratory test (T) data, Cattell distinguished between surface and source traits. Through extensive factor analysis, he derived 16 basic source traits (measured on Cattell's 16PF inventory) that, he believed, accounted for the lion's share of variance in personality. In Cattell's characteristic approach to research, scores on source traits, states, social roles, and situational factors were combined into a weighted specification equation to predict a person's behavior.

4. Another pioneer in trait psychology, Hans Eysenck used factor analysis to develop a highly influential theory that accounted for human individuality through three basic traits—extraversion–introversion, neuroticism, and psychoticism. Eysenck argued that each of the three traits is linked to individual differences in neurophysiology.

5. Building on the work of Allport and Cattell and employing some of Eysenck's concepts as well, many personality psychologists today believe that the entire universe of trait concepts can be divided into five general trait domains or clusters, called the Big Five. According to one widely cited description, the five basic factors of personality traits can be labeled extraversion, neuroticism, openness to experience, agreeableness, and conscientiousness.

6. Most personality traits can be measured through self-report scales. The construction of self-report trait measures typically follows a systematic approach of item generation, item analysis, evaluation of the item pool, and efforts to predict external behavior from the items that make up the final scale. A trait scale should show high test–retest reliability and internal consistency (split-half reliability). Ultimately, a scale's worth is understood in terms of construct validity. Construct validation is the process of simultaneously validating a scale and the construct it is designed to measure, and it involves the gradual articulation of a nomological network of research findings. Beyond reliability and construct validity, other indices of the worth of a trait scale include utility, economy, and communicability.

7. Personality psychologists have developed a number of omnibus personality inventories that measure individual differences in many traits at the same time. The oldest of these is the clinically oriented Minnesota Multiphasic Personality Inventory (MMPI). Popular and well-designed inventories used in contemporary trait research include the California Psychological Inventory (CPI), the Personality Research Form (PRF), and the NEO-PI-R (the Neuroticism-Extraversion-Openness Personality Inventory Revised). The NEO-PI-R measures individual differences in each of the Big Five traits and provides for each trait six individual facet scores.

8. Since the time of Allport, the concept of a personality trait has been controversial. The most important critique of the concept was levied by Walter Mischel in the late 1960s. While the concept of trait assumes some degree of cross-situational consistency in behavior, Mischel argued that behavior is much more situationally specific than cross-situationally consistent. He also suggested that trait labels exist more in the minds of observers than in the actual personality of the person being observed. Mischel's review of the literature suggested that trait scores fail to predict what a person will do in particular situations. Mischel's critique launched the person–situation debate in personality psychology, which ran through the 1970s and 1980s and eventually shaped a good deal of thinking in personality psychology today.

9. In response to the Mischel critique, researchers began to employ the method of aggregation in trait research. By pooling or aggregating

behavioral scores across many different situations and over time, researchers obtained more reliable assessments of the behavior to be predicted by trait scores. Aggregation studies have shown that trait scores often account for substantial variance in behavioral trends across situations and over time.

10. Many psychologists have endeavored to tease apart the interaction of traits and situations in the prediction of behavior. Mechanistic interactionism divides up the variance in dependent behaviors into that accounted for by the trait, that accounted for by the situation, and that accounted for by the interaction of trait and situation. Reciprocal interactionism conceives of a more fluid and complex pattern in which person, situation, and behavior continually and reciprocally influence one another. A third approach to interactionism focuses on individual differences in behavioral variability across situations. According to this approach, each person shows a relatively consistent pattern of changing behavior from one situation to the next. Individual differences in these patterns of behavioral change may be understood as characteristic differences in *if … then* relations. As the person–situation debate has died down and researchers have come to endorse different forms of interactionism, psychologists have developed a clearer understanding of the relations between traits and situations in the prediction of behavior. In addition, the concept of the personality trait itself would seem to have emerged from the debate as a more powerful and useful concept than perhaps it has ever been before.

Five Basic Traits

Ernest Tupes and Raymond Christal worked at the Lackland Air Force Base in the mid-1950s. As research psychologists, Tupes and Christal were given the job of developing personality scales to evaluate U.S. Air Force Academy cadets. Borrowing scales devised by the famous trait psychologist Raymond B. Cattell (1947), the researchers administered a series of questionnaires to the cadets and statistically analyzed the results. Their analysis led them to conclude that the many different traits that might account for broad and socially consequential differences in human individuality could be boiled down to five basic dimensions or factors. They named the five factors (1) "surgency/extraversion," (2) "emotional stability," (3) "culture," (4) "agreeableness," and (5) "conscientiousness." Tupes and Christal (1958, 1961) communicated their findings in an obscure technical report published by the Air Force. No newspapers picked up the story, and only a handful of people read the original report.

One person who apparently did read the report, however, was personality psychologist Warren Norman, who conducted his own factor-analytic study of trait ratings and arrived at a very similar five-factor solution. Norman (1963) suggested that the five dimensions might represent "an adequate taxonomy of personality attributes" (p. 582). Although Norman eventually changed his mind and decided that the richness of human individuality could never be reduced to five basic factors, a small group of researchers suspected that he was on to something good. Among them was Lewis Goldberg, who borrowed an old idea from Sir Francis Galton (1884) that we know today as the **lexical hypothesis.** Put simply, personality description can be found in the lexicon, that is, in the words that make up a language. If you look at the words that people use to describe people, you will find all the traits that you need to describe human individuality, Galton suggested. During the 1960s and 70s, when many psychologists questioned the value of the very concept of "personality trait" (e.g., Mischel, 1968), Goldberg and his intrepid colleagues worked quietly and steadily, collecting gazillions of adjectival ratings made by people who were given the less-than-exciting task of reading through long lists and rating themselves or others they knew on each adjective listed. After conducting countless factor analyses, Goldberg (1990; Saucier & Goldberg, 1996) eventually concluded that a five-factor structure best accounted for the interrelations among trait ratings, whether those ratings were of the self or ratings of others. Other researchers working with the lexical hypothesis came to the same conclusion (Angleitner, Ostendorf, & John, 1990; DeRaad, Mulder, Kloosterman, & Hofstee, 1988; Digman & Takemoto-Chock, 1981; Sneed, McCrae, & Funder, 1997).

In the 1980s and 90s, personality psychology rediscovered the original insights of the Tupes and Christal report. Researchers factor-analyzed all sorts of personality scales and adjective ratings to find roughly the same five factors that Tupes and Christal saw in the ratings of Air Force cadets. Comparable five-factor schemes have been proposed by German and Dutch psychologists, and studies have identified similar, though not always identical, factor structures in trait inventories written in Japanese, Chinese, Tagalog (Filipino), modern Hebrew, Estonian, Hungarian, and languages in India, among others (Allick & Realo, 1997; Church, 2000; Church & Katigbak, 1989; Church, Reyes, Katigbak, & Grimm, 1997; DeRaad & Szirmak, 1994; John & Srivastava, 1999; McCrae & Costa, 1997b; Narayanan, Mensa, & Levine, 1995). Of course, not all of these studies show exactly the same thing. For example, a study of trait ratings among Filipino high-school and college students found dimensions that strongly paralleled four of the five dimensions found in English, but a fifth dimension referring to emotional stability (neuroticism) did not find a clear match in the Filipino students' language (Church et al., 1989). Another set of studies examining traits in seven languages argues for a six-factor model (Ashton et al., 2004). Some researchers object to using the statistical procedure of factor analysis to derive fundamental personality traits (Block, 1995).

Others believe that the five-trait structure leaves out or overlooks other important dispositional dimensions (Paunonen & Jackson, 2000). Within the growing community of researchers who employ the five-factor framework, furthermore, there is still considerable disagreement on what the factors should be called and how each should be defined. One of the factors, for example, has been variously labeled as "culture" (Norman, 1963), "intellectance" (Hogan, 1986), and "openness to experience" (McCrae & Costa, 1985b).

Despite the diversity of views, nonetheless, there appears to be a general consensus in the field today that the thousands of traits that might be imagined for human personality can be reduced to a very manageable set of five or so basic groups, clusters, or dimensions. To label those dimensions, I will borrow Costa and McCrae's influential and easy-to-remember framework. I will refer in this chapter to the five factors of extraversion *(E)*, neuroticism *(N)*, openness to experience *(O)*, agreeableness *(A)*, and conscientiousness *(C)*. Each of the areas can be further subdivided into six *facets*, or subordinate traits, Costa and McCrae suggest. The six facets of neuroticism, for example, are anxiety, angry hostility, depression, self-consciousness, impulsiveness, and vulnerability. While not all researchers accept Costa and McCrae's view of facets, I will refer to them again and again in this chapter, because I think the facets help to convey the many meanings and possible components of each of the five large factors. In this chapter, I will examine research and theory that fall roughly within each of the Big Five trait domains. Table 5.1 lists Costa and McCrae's version of the Big Five factors with the corresponding labels for facets.

E: EXTRAVERSION

When I began teaching at Northwestern University, my office was located in a building that also housed the graduate school of business and management. Offices and seminar rooms for my department were on one side of the building, and the business school occupied the other side. The business school ran a small cafeteria that also served as a study lounge, and

---

TABLE 5.1	THE BIG FIVE TRAITS AND THEIR FACETS AS MEASURED ON THE NEO-PI-R

E: Extraversion	*O:* Openness to Experience	*C:* Conscientiousness
Warmth	Fantasy	Competence
Gregariousness	Aesthetics	Order
Assertiveness	Feelings	Dutifulness
Activity	Actions	Achievement striving
Excitement seeking	Ideas	Self-discipline
Positive emotions	Values	Deliberation
N: Neuroticism	*A:* Agreeableness	
Anxiety	Trust	
Angry hostility	Straightforwardness	
Depression	Altruism	
Self-consciousness	Compliance	
Impulsiveness	Modesty	
Vulnerability	Tender-mindedness	

I would occasionally walk over there to grab lunch or a mid-afternoon snack. The place was a beehive of activity—students talking, laughing, working in groups, everything very busy and upbeat. Every time I went there, I was struck by how different this place was from comparable settings I had come to know as a graduate student myself and as a faculty member. The students looked and acted differently. For starters, they wore beautiful and presumably expensive clothes. The women wore nicely tailored suits; the men often sported ties. I almost never saw blue jeans or T-shirts in this cafeteria. Second, the students were so much more lively and outgoing than those I have typically known. I am not suggesting that most graduate students in psychology and related fields are depressive people who do not know how to have fun. But these business and management students seemed different. So much talk and laughter, so much earnest activity, always in groups. And so much smiling! I thought if I smiled that much my face would hurt. I found the place very refreshing and energizing at first, but after a while I began to feel as if I were drowning in a sea of extraversion. Eventually, I quit going. I have to admit that I like the library better.

My little anecdote proves nothing, is completely unscientific, and can be interpreted in many different ways. My impression was that the graduate students in business and management were much more outgoing, lively, and sociable than most other graduate students I have known. But I have to concede that I have never observed a setting of graduate students exactly comparable to the study lounge I described. Maybe if you put 100 psychology graduate students into a study lounge situation exactly like this one, they would show the same patterns of outgoing behavior, group activity, lively discussion, and seemingly incessant smiling and laughter. I think not, but I could be wrong. Surely, this kind of social setting pulls for and encourages the kind of behavior I repeatedly observed. As we saw in chapter 3 and in the context of the person–situation debate of the 1970s and 1980s, a strong case must be made for the idea that behavior patterns are always a function of situational opportunities and constraints. We must understand behavior in its social context. Contexts that encourage and support extraverted behavior are likely to produce extraverted behavior.

For the sake of argument, however, let us say that I am right at a behavioral level in surmising that those business students I encountered behaved in more outgoing and lively ways than a comparable group of psychology graduate students might behave, even in the same social setting. The reasons for such a difference, should it exist, could be couched in terms of the socialization of graduate students. Northwestern's business school emphasizes the methods of case analysis and group projects. Business school students are taught to work on case problems together in "teams" or groups. This is part of their socialization as graduate students. By contrast, graduate training in psychology is somewhat more individualistic. Students do work in groups, but a great deal of study involves working alone, as in reading texts and articles and writing papers. There is more emphasis on students' developing their own unique perspectives, typically expressed most fully in students' Ph.D. dissertations. On the topic of clothing, this line of reasoning seems especially valid. The business students were better dressed because the norms of the business world typically require this. They "looked the part" of young managers and business professionals. In addition, they probably had more money than psychology graduate students I have known, which they could use to purchase fine clothing. (Indeed, some of the business students had come back to school after enjoying some financial success in the business world.)

The behavioral differences I observed can be accounted for by considering the environmental, contextual, and socialization differences between the business and the psychology graduate students I encountered. But such an accounting cannot rule out another very simple and plausible possibility—a possibility that is not inconsistent with these other explanations but that instead can complement them. Put simply, maybe their traits are a little different. Maybe business students are a bit more extraverted than other graduate students I have known. On the average, maybe business graduate students score slightly more in the direction of the extraversion pole on a general trait continuum and psychology graduate students score slightly more in the direction of the introversion pole. It would not need to be a big difference—just a tendency, a slight difference in the mean or average tendencies of each of the two groups. This possibility fits many people's intuitive sense that individuals who are drawn to the worlds of business, management, and marketing are and need to be rather outgoing in their behavior and very comfortable working with other people. By contrast, people expect that research scientists and academics, the professions to which many psychology graduate students are headed, are likely to be somewhat more introverted. These intuitions, of course, could be wrong, and if they are taken too seriously or interpreted too rigidly, they can lead to stereotypic thinking. But research in career psychology provides some support for the hunch, suggesting that extraversion is associated with participation and success in the business world (Eysenck, 1973; Holland, 1996). People who are especially outgoing, lively, energetic, enthusiastic, warm, gregarious, and sociable may gravitate toward activities and roles that capitalize on these characteristics.

As a mildly introverted person myself, I ended up avoiding the study lounge and seeking out settings that were quieter and more conducive to individual reading and study, as the research suggests I should (Eysenck, 1973). Sure, I enjoy being with people; I have a good time at parties (usually). But I do not think I would enjoy a job that required the high levels of teamwork and intense social interaction that many people enjoy as business managers and in other more "people-oriented" professions. I just can't summon up the necessary extraversion.

SOCIAL BEHAVIOR AND COGNITIVE PERFORMANCE

As we saw in chapter 2, human beings evolved to live in groups. We are, by human nature, social beings. Therefore, individual differences regarding our sociality should prove very important to us. We notice broad differences between people in the way they orient themselves to each other, and as a consequence, perhaps we have many words in our language to describe those differences. Whereas we may describe some people as "outgoing" and "sociable," we use words such as "shy," "inhibited," "withdrawn," "taciturn," and "quiet" to describe others. The one trait domain that captures many of these words and characterizations is **extraversion** (*E*).

The first modern theorists of *E* emphasized its social meanings. The psychoanalytic clinician Carl Jung (1936/1971) wrote that extraverts direct their psychological energy outward to the social world, whereas introverts direct it inward toward private thought and fantasy. Although he rejected Jung's clinical speculation in favor of rigorous laboratory research, Hans Eysenck (1952, 1967) made the same distinction. For Eysenck, the extravert is outgoing, sociable, and enthusiastic, but also somewhat impulsive and heedless. The introvert, by contrast, is more quiet and withdrawn, but also more contemplative, deliberate, and less likely to take bad risks. Extraverts are more *socially dominant* than introverts. They exhibit considerable energy and enthusiasm in social situations. Therefore, we would expect that extraverts might have more friends than introverts. But introverts might have deeper friendships with a few people. Eysenck also suggested that most people lie somewhere in the middle of the *E* continuum, half-way between the extraversion and the introversion poles. Most people, therefore, are *ambiverts*.

Eysenck developed and validated the first self-report scales to assess individual differences in E. A large body of research shows that differences in E as assessed on questionnaires such as those developed by Eysenck are meaningfully related to corresponding differences in social behavior. For instance, extraverts talk more and sooner when they meet someone than do introverts (Carment, Miles, & Cervin, 1965) and engage in more eye contact when interacting with another (Rutter, Morley, & Graham, 1972). Extraverts even show firmer handshakes than introverts (Chaplin, Phillips, Brown, Clanton, & Stein, 2000). Among college students, extraverts study in places that afford opportunities for social interaction (like the business school study lounge I described) whereas introverts seek out more secluded spots (Campbell & Hawley, 1982). Introverts are somewhat more likely to live alone (Diener, Sandvik, Pavot, & Fujita, 1992). Extraverts do more gambling (Wilson, 1978). Extraverts also tend to be more sexually active than introverts (Giese & Schmidt, 1968). Wilson and Nias (1975) have shown that extraverts are more permissive in their sexual attitudes than introverts, confess to higher levels of sex drive, and are less prone to nervousness and inhibition in sexual relations. In the occupational realm, extraverts are drawn to and excel in occupations that involve dealing directly with other people, such as sales, marketing, personnel work, and teaching (Diener et al., 1992; Wilson, 1978). By contrast, introverts tend to prefer more solitary pursuits, sharing many interests with artists, research scientists, mathematicians, and engineers (Bendig, 1963).

Laboratory research has also examined relations between E and various forms of cognitive performance. It appears that extraverts and introverts show different cognitive strengths and weaknesses with respect to certain tasks and under certain conditions. For example, extraverts tend to show superior performance to introverts on tasks requiring divided attention, resistance to distraction, and resistance to interference (Eysenck, 1982; Lieberman & Rosenthal, 2001). Relative to introverts, extraverted locomotive drivers show better detection of railway signal stimuli (Singh, 1989), extraverted post office trainees tend to perform better on a demanding speeded mail-coding task (Matthews, Jones, & Chamberlain, 1992), and extraverted TV viewers show better short-term recall of television news broadcasts (Gunter & Furnham, 1986).

Conversely, introverts tend to perform better on tasks requiring vigilance and careful attention to details (Harkins & Geen, 1975). Some evidence suggests that introverts show better long-term memory for words (Howarth & Eysenck, 1968) and superior performance under conditions of very low arousal, as when deprived of sleep for long periods of time (Matthews, 1992). To the extent differences are found in learning styles, extraverts tend to show a preference for speed over accuracy, whereas introverts focus more on accuracy over speed. Accordingly, Brebner and Cooper (1985) characterize extraverts as "geared to respond" and introverts as "geared to inspect."

FEELING GOOD

A significant body of research has found that E is positively associated with reports of feeling good about life. In other words, extraverts report greater levels of *positive affect* in everyday life than do introverts. Costa and McCrae (1980a, 1984) have conducted a number of studies in which they administered self-report measures of E and subjective well-being to large samples of adults. Measures of subjective well-being tap into two independent features: positive affect (reports of good feelings) and negative affect (reports of bad feelings). Costa and McCrae have consistently found that, for both men and women, E is positively associated with reports of good feelings but unrelated to reports of bad feelings. In other words, extraverts report more positive affect than introverts, but they do not necessarily report less negative affect. Similar results have been obtained by other researchers (e.g., Emmons & Diener, 1986a; Watson, Clark, McIntyre, & Hamaker, 1992).

Why do extraverts report more positive feelings than introverts? One explanation is that extraverts may be less responsive to punishment than introverts. Introverts appear to dwell on the negative and punitive features of certain social situations (Graziano, Feldesman, & Rahe, 1985). Researchers report that introverts recall less positive information and rate others less positively in social situations (Lishman, 1972), report interpersonal disagreements as being more aversive (Norman & Watson, 1976), and anticipate more disagreements between themselves and others than do extraverts (Cooper & Scalise, 1974).

Extraverts are more likely than introverts to continue responding in the face of punishment and frustration. Pearce-McCall and Newman (1986) exposed each of 50 introverted and 50 extraverted college men to one of two "pretreatment conditions" in a problem-solving experiment: either a "reward condition" in which the student received $2.50 for good performance or a "punishment condition" in which the student was told that his earnings had dwindled from $5.00 to $2.50 because of poor performance. (In reality, the students had been randomly assigned to the groups, and actual performance thus had nothing to do with whether they received rewards or punishments.) After the pretreatment, the students made bets on how well they might perform on a subsequent problem-solving task. In comparison with those introverts who had received pretreatment punishment, extraverts who had been punished placed larger wagers on their ability to succeed, reported higher levels of expecting to succeed, and expressed greater confidence that they could "control" the situation in the future. As Figure 5.1 shows, extraverts and introverts did *not* differ in their betting behavior following the reward pretreatment but *did* differ markedly following punishment, with extraverts making significantly higher wagers.

In another problem-solving experiment, Patterson, Kosson, and Newman (1987) showed that extraverts typically fail to pause following punishment, pushing ahead to the next trial before they can learn from their mistakes. Impulsively seeking out rewards, extraverts may actually be motivated by punishment to work even faster and more impulsively, failing to reflect on the reasons for punishment. In some situations, therefore, extraverts may show an overly impulsive approach to problem solving, continuing to produce errors even after they are punished for doing so (Nichols & Newman, 1986).

Research suggests yet other explanations for the relationship between E and positive affect. Barrett (1997) asked 56 students to complete a self-report measure of E and then report on their emotional states three times a day—in the morning, afternoon, and evening—for 90 consecutive days. As in prior research, he found that E was positively associated with the momentary reports of positive moods. However, at the end of the 90 days, Barrett also asked the students to rate what their mood states *had been* over the course of the 90 days. Barrett found that the retrospective ratings of what moods the students remembered experiencing did not match exactly the reports of the mood states made at the time they were experienced. But the mismatches were not random. When thinking back over the 90 days, extraverts tended to recall even more positive moods than they in fact reported during the 90-day period. In other words, extraversion is associated both with reporting greater positive affect and remembering even greater positive affect later than what was reported at the time. In a similar vein, Mayo (1990) found that extraversion was associated with the tendency to remember a greater number of happy scenes from the past. The tendency to recall the past in more positive terms than it was experienced at the time may contribute to the generally positive and upbeat emotional life that extraverts tend to experience.

FIGURE 5.1   **BETTING BEHAVIOR AND INTROVERSION/EXTROVERSION**

Introverts and extraverts bet the same amount of money after receiving a reward, but follow-ing a punishment, extraverts show higher levels of betting and introverts show lower levels.

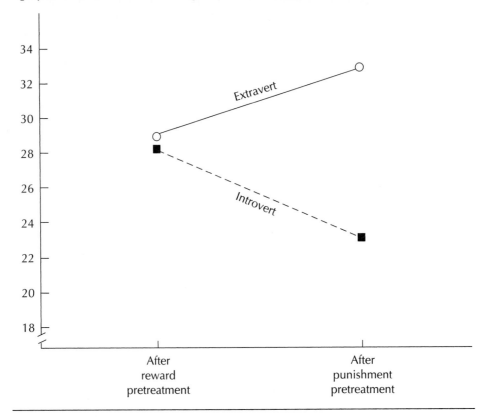

SOURCE: From "Expectation of Success Following Noncontingent Punishment in Introverts and Extraverts," by D. Pearce-McCall & J. P. Newman, 1986, *Journal of Personality and Social Psychology, 50*, p. 442.

To what extent is the positive association between extraversion and positive affect a function of the greater levels of participation in social activities that extraverts show? Brandstatter (1994) argues that extraverts are more assertive in social situations, which gives them more social competence and effectiveness. Their positive emotional states may be a direct function of this kind of social skill. Argyle and Lu (1990) tested a similar idea by con-ducting what is called a *path analysis* with different psychological measures. A path analysis enables the researcher to sort out both direct and indirect effects of variables on one another. As Figure 5.2 illustrates, Argyle and Lu found a positive and significant association between extraversion and social competence (path coefficient = .49) and then a positive and signifi-cant association between social competence and happiness (path coefficient = .36). This means that there is a significant direct effect of extraversion on social competence and signif-icant and direct effect of social competence on happiness. Extraversion, therefore, exerts an indirect effect on happiness by virtue of the path that runs through social competence. When you statistically remove that pathway, however, you are still left with a positive direct association between extraversion and happiness (path coefficient = .28). Putting this in simple English, Figure 5.2 tells you that the association between extraversion and happiness in this study happens in two different ways. First, highly extraverted people tend to have more social skills and competence, which tends to produce or lead to more happiness. Second, even after you account for this first relationship, there is still some leftover direct effect of extraversion on happiness itself. Social skills explain some of the story, but not all of it.

Just how strong and consistent is the relation between E and positive emotions? Psychologists differ on this issue. One camp argues that the relation between E and positive emotions is so consistent that E itself should be renamed "Positive Emotionality" or "Positive Affectivity" (Tellegen, 1985; Watson & Tellegen, 1985). According to this view, positive affect constitutes the emotional core of what has traditionally been called extraversion (Lucas, Diener, Grob, Suh, & Shao, 2000; Watson & Clark, 1997). Independent measures of E and positive affects correlate in the range of +.20 to +.50 across different studies, and the two sets of measures tend to predict some of the same sorts of things. For example, measures of positive affectivity predict high levels of social activity, such as frequency of dating and attending parties and socializing over dinner or drinks (Watson & Clark, 1997).

Evidence supporting the idea that positive emotion is central to the trait of extraversion comes from a clever study done by Lucas and Diener (2001). The researchers administered a self-report scale of E to 87 college undergraduates and then asked them to rate how happy they would be if they were to engage in each of 247 different situations and activities. The situations were taken from a previous study in which students listed common *social* and *nonsocial* events in their daily lives and then rated them as *pleasant, moderately*

FIGURE 5.2   EXTRAVERSION'S EFFECT ON HAPPINESS

In this path model, the findings show that the positive effect of extraversion on happiness is due partly to a direct correlation between two variables and partly to extraversion's positive association with social competence, which itself predicts happiness.

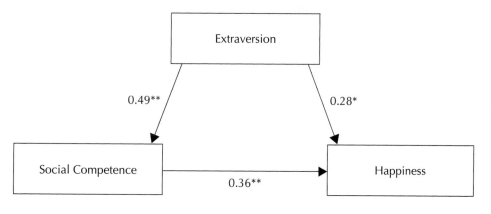

NOTES: *$p < .05$, **$p < .01$

SOURCE: Adapted from "Happiness and Social Skills," by. M. Argyle & L. Lu, 1990, *Personality and Individual Differences, 11,* p. 1260.

pleasant, moderately unpleasant, or *unpleasant.* For example, a *pleasant social* activity might be "I'm talking with my best friend on the phone"; an *unpleasant social* activity might be "I'm in a heated argument with my boyfriend or girlfriend"; a *pleasant nonsocial* event might be "I am by myself reading an interesting book"; an *unpleasant nonsocial* event might be "I am alone and cleaning up at work." Table 5.2 shows the main results of the study. As expected, extraversion was positively associated with ratings of *pleasant* and *moderately pleasant social* events. In other words, extraverts reported greater happiness than did introverts when engaging in positive experiences with other people. However, Table 5.2 also shows that extraversion predicted higher levels of happiness in *pleasant nonsocial* events, too. In other words, extraverts reported more positive feelings in pleasant situations of all kinds—both social and nonsocial. Such findings suggest that extraverts may be more sensitive to rewarding experiences of many kinds in daily life, even those positive experiences that have nothing to do with social interaction.

Other researchers interpret the literature on extraversion and affect as suggesting that while positive affect and extraversion are indeed correlated, they are by no means the same thing. Accordingly, Costa and McCrae (1992) view positive emotions as but one of six facets of *E.* Yet other researchers are more skeptical about the association between the trait of extraversion and positive emotion states (Matthews & Deary, 1998). Some studies show rather low correlations (in the range of +.20) between *E* and measures of positive affectivity. Furthermore, high *E* can be associated with lower positive affect in some situations. As an example of the latter point, Brandstatter (1994) found that *E* was associated with positive affect when mood ratings were collected in social situations, but extraverts reported significantly lower levels of positive emotion, compared with introverts, when they were alone. Brandstatter's findings remind us that traits must be viewed in interactional terms. While *E* may generally be associated with positive emotions over time and across different settings, there may be certain situations in life in which extraversion makes you feel worse rather than better.

TABLE 5.2	**CORRELATIONS BETWEEN EXTRAVERSION SCORES AND RATINGS OF EXPECTED HAPPINESS IN SOCIAL AND NONSOCIAL EVENTS VARYING ON PLEASANTNESS**

Social Events	
Pleasant	.34**
Moderately pleasant	.24*
Moderately unpleasant	.03
Unpleasant	−.18
Nonsocial Events	
Pleasant	.31**
Moderately pleasant	.19
Moderately unpleasant	.01
Unpleasant	−.10

NOTES: *$p < .05$, **$p < .01$

SOURCE: Adapted from "Understanding Extraverts' Enjoyment of Social Situations: The Importance of Pleasantness," by R. E. Lucas & E. Diener, 2001, *Journal of Personality and Social Psychology, 81,* p. 347.

EXTRAVERSION AND THE BRAIN

Eysenck believed that individual differences in *E* stemmed ultimately from inborn differences in the brain's *reticular activating system* (*RAS*). A network of nerve fibers ascending from the spinal cord to the thalamus, the RAS is implicated in physiological *arousal*. Eysenck argued that the RAS is set or tuned differently for extraverts and introverts. In extraverts, the RAS is set at a relatively low level; therefore, extraverts are generally less aroused than introverts. In order to achieve an optimal level of arousal, extraverts must seek out stimulation, especially rewarding social stimulation. By contrast, the RAS of the typical introvert is set at a relatively high level. The introvert is more aroused to begin with, and more easily aroused to reach a level of stimulation that is so high as to be aversive. In order to achieve an optimal level of arousal, the introvert must often avoid social stimulation. Put simply, extraverts crave social stimulation because they are chronically underaroused while introverts often avoid the same social stimulation in order to avoid becoming over-aroused (Eysenck, 1967, 1973).

Eysenck's biologically based theory of extraversion has stimulated hundreds of scientific studies (Geen, 1997; Matthews & Deary, 1998; Stelmach, 1990). A number of studies do suggest that extraverts often crave more stimulation than do introverts. At low-to-moderate levels of stimulation, furthermore, introverts appear to be more physiologically reactive to sensory input, compared to extraverts. But support for Eysenck's fundamental idea—that extraverts and introverts differ in their characteristic levels of arousal—has not been forthcoming. Researchers have used many different measures to assess overall arousal, including the brain's electroencephalogram (EEG) patterns, electrodermal activity (e.g., how much the skin sweats), heart rate, and functional brain scanning techniques. The results of the many studies have been inconsistent. Many researchers, in fact, reject out of hand the concept of general arousal (Geen, 1997; Zuckerman, 1998). The core argument against the concept comes from many studies that suggest that various indices of what might be general arousal—brain wave activity, heart rate, skin conductance, and so on—are themselves not highly correlated. There would appear to be many different kinds of arousal and different indices of these different kinds. Furthermore, when one part of the brain is aroused and active, other parts may be inhibited and quiet. Eysenck viewed the RAS as a general arousal system that would turn neural stimulation on and off like a faucet. However, it appears that the brain is more complex than Eysenck's original proposals suggested.

Recent research on the biological underpinnings of extraversion has focused on neurotransmitters and cortical processes that may be implicated in *reward-seeking*. Neurotransmitters are chemicals in the nerve cell that are responsible for transmitting a nerve impulse across the synapse (the small gap between nerve cells), moving the impulse from one cell to the next. One particular neurotransmitter that appears to be associated with reward and pleasure is **dopamine.** Studies have shown that animals will work hard to obtain doses of dopamine, even harder than they might work to obtain food. Cocaine and certain other drugs of abuse mimic dopamine in the nervous system, which accounts for the pleasure associated with taking them. (At the same time, cocaine ends up depleting the natural levels of dopamine in a person's system, leading to insatiable cravings for more of the drug.) In that dopamine is involved in rewards and pleasure and given that extraversion seems to be centrally concerned with reward-seeking and sensitivity to rewards, a number of personality psychologists have begun to suspect that dopamine may be linked to extraversion, albeit in very complex ways. One view suggests that extraversion, dopamine, and reward-seeking may be linked within a single system in the brain.

Jeffrey Gray (1982, 1987) coined the term **behavioral approach system,** or **BAS,** to refer to a hypothesized system in the brain that is responsible for motivating behavior aimed at achieving goals and obtaining positive emotional rewards. Gray proposes that the BAS is made up of various pathways and structures in the brain that are implicated in the release of the neurotransmitter dopamine and involved in the working of certain regions that make up the brain's limbic system. Studies with rats have indicated that reward in the brain is associated with the release of dopamine in the mesolimbic system running through the medial forebrain bundle to centers in the brain's frontal lobes (Zuckerman, 1995). On the human level, individual differences in mesolimbic dopaminergic pathways and related structures are hypothesized to support differences that people exhibit in reward-seeking behaviors. While some people characteristically approach positive incentives and reap the rewards of good feelings when their goals are achieved, other people are less eager to approach, more cautious, and thereby less likely to experience the positive emotional rewards that may come from successful goal achievement.

From Gray's perspective, the BAS links up with the trait of *impulsivity.* Impulsive behavior is uninhibited and forward looking; the impulsive person moves rapidly and sometimes thoughtlessly toward potentially rewarding stimuli. In Eysenck's original formulation, extraverts were thought to be impulsive, as well. Some conceptions of extraversion have suggested that impulsivity is a component of *E.* For example, Sutton and Davidson (1997) write that "individuals with a relatively strong BAS (more sensitive and responsive to incentives) are more likely to be extraverted and impulsive" (p. 204). Zuckerman (1995) writes that the BAS "probably subsumes several basic traits, including extraversion, impulsivity, and sensation seeking" (p. 329). In a similar line of thinking, Tellegen (1985) has proposed that *E* be renamed "positive affectivity" and that behavior related to this trait is likely to be directed by the working of the BAS. According to Tellegen, extraversion (positive affectivity) represents individual differences in sensitivity to pleasurable, reward-producing incentives. Different theorists have proposed, therefore, that *E* may be linked to the activity of a hypothesized brain system called the BAS. The link between *E* and the BAS, then, comes by virtue of its association with impulsivity (Gray), with positive affect states (Tellegen), or with both.

Scientists have not yet put together a clear story about how *E* may be related to the BAS at the level of brain functioning. But two lines of recent research are suggestive. In the first line of research, investigators have tried to find direct links between dopaminergic activity and *E* in humans. Depue, Luciana, Arbisi, Collins, and Leon (1994) selected individuals who scored high and low on self-report measures of *E* and gave each of them a substance that induces dopamine activity in the brain. They found that the substance stimulated higher levels of dopaminergic activity among extraverts compared with introverts. In other words, extraverts and introverts differed with respect to the reactivity of the mesolimbic dopaminergic system. The results are generally consistent with the idea that the characteristic good cheer and approach behavior in the face of incentives seen in extraverts may be linked to enhanced activity of the neurotransmitter dopamine in certain parts of the brain. But much more research is needed to clarify the specifics of such a relationship.

The second line of research involves the brain's electrical activity. Studies employing EEG measurements show that positive affect, as expressed by smiling, is associated with activation of the left-frontal and anterior portions of the brain (Davidson, 1992). In laboratory studies, researchers have induced positive emotions and approach behavior by showing film clips (Davidson, Ekman, Saron, Senulis, & Friesen, 1990) and providing monetary rewards (Sobotka, Davidson, & Senulis, 1992) to adults, and by providing human infants with pleasant-tasting foods (Fox & Davidson, 1986), as they monitored the brain's electrical activity from multiple scalp sites. These manipulations systematically influenced the asymmetry of electrical activity in anterior (front) but not posterior (back) regions of the brain. Pleasant film clips, pleasant tastes, and monetary incentives all increased left-sided anterior activity, whereas unpleasant film clips, unpleasant tastes, and threat of monetary loss increased brain activity in the anterior right regions. The findings are consistent with a recent study showing that greater left than right superior frontal activation is associated with self-report measures of psychological well-being (Urry et al., 2004). Furthermore, clinical and laboratory observations suggest that the left prefrontal cortex may be a biological substrate of approach behavior and positive affect. Clinical reports have shown that patients with damage to portions of the brain located in or near the left prefrontal cortex are more likely than patients with damage to other brain regions to exhibit depressive symptomatology. Lesions of these brain regions may result in a deficit of approach behavior, which when combined with negative life events, culminates in depression (Davidson, 1993).

In sum, a small but growing body of research suggests that individual differences in *E* may be linked to a hypothesized behavioral approach system (BAS) in the brain. Scientists have not pinned down just what this system is composed of or how it works. Some studies suggest that dopaminergic pathways in the brain are implicated in the BAS. Others point to the electrical activity of the left anterior regions of the cortex. The story is likely to become increasingly complex as more research is conducted. For example, a recent study challenges the idea that left anterior activity is exclusively associated with positive affect. Harmon-Jones and Allen (1998) provide data showing that individuals predisposed toward *anger* exhibit the same kind of EEG asymmetries associated with the BAS. Harmon-Jones and Allen suggest that anger motivates approach behavior in the face of incentives, even though it is a negatively valenced emotion. From their perspective, the BAS is more about active approach in human behavior rather than positive affect per se. Other investigators suggest that systems and factors beyond dopaminergic activity and EEG asymmetry are likely to be implicated in the BAS (Zuckerman, 1998). Included in these other factors may be hormones such as testosterone and cortisol and enzymes such as monoamine oxidase (MAO). Remarking on the complexity of all of this, Zuckerman (1995) writes:

> We do not inherit personality traits or even behavior mechanisms as such. What is inherited are chemical templates that produce and regulate proteins involved in building the structure of nervous systems and the neurotransmitters, enzymes, and hormones that regulate them. We are not born as extraverts, neurotics, impulsive sensation seekers, or antisocial personalities, but we are born with differences in reactivities of brain structures and levels of regulators like MAO. How do these differences in biological traits shape our choices in life from the manifold possibilities provided by environments? (pp. 331–332)

We do not know the answer to Zuckerman's last question. But researchers have begun to collect some intriguing clues.

N: NEUROTICISM

You would be hard-pressed to find a character who is not neurotic in Fyodor Dostoyevsky's greatest novel *The Brothers Karamazov.* Dostoyevsky (1881/1933) fills his story with all manner of zealots and buffoons, hysterical women and raving men whose fears, obsessions, and insecurities torment them from the first page to the last. Neuroticism can be the stuff of

FEATURE 5.A

EXTREME SPORTS AND THE
SENSATION SEEKING TRAIT

When I was growing up, there were only two things that my father insisted upon. The first was that I absolutely had to be a Chicago Cubs fan. As a consequence, I have borne the cross of rooting for a loser ever since 1962. The second thing was that I was absolutely never to ride on a motorcycle. I think a good friend of my father's was killed in a biking accident, but I am not sure. Now, many boys and young men, and probably many women as well, would find my father's second commandment to be harsh and unreasonable. But if truth be told, I have *never* had a desire to ride on a motorcycle (even though I did it a couple of times in high school under peer pressure). I also don't care for snowboarding, I hate amusement park rides, and I would never jump out of a plane with a parachute. Okay, call me a baby. It is true that some of these things scare me (skydiving, for example). But I also just don't get the thrill that I think other people get from these kinds of activities. All of these ads on TV for extreme sports and dangerous adventures—I just don't get it. Why would anybody want to do these things? Thankfully, personality psychologist Marvin Zuckerman (1978, 1998) has identified and named a trait for my "problem." Zuckerman would say that I am very low on the trait of sensation seeking.

Sensation seeking is the "need for varied, novel, and complex sensations and experiences and the willingness to take physical and social risks for the sake of such experiences" (Zuckerman, 1979, p. 10). Sensation seeking incorporates four related factors: (a) thrill and adventure seeking (interest in activities involving physical risk), (b) experience seeking (desire for new experiences through music, art, travel, meeting unusual people, mood-altering drugs), (c) disinhibition (pursuit of pleasure through parties, social drinking, sex with various partners, gambling), and (d) boredom susceptibility (restlessness in unchanging environments and dislike of dull people). A substantial body of research supports the construct validity of the sensation seeking trait

For some people, rock climbing may be a good way to express the sensation-seeking trait. People who score high on measures of sensation seeking show a strong inclination toward varied, novel, and complex sensations and experiences, and they are willing to take physical and social risks to enjoy these things. Research suggests that sensation seekers tend to have relatively low levels of monoamine oxidase (MAO) in their bloodstream – an enzyme that may exert an inhibitory effect on the central nervous system.

(Roberti, 2003). For example, people scoring high on Zuckerman's sensation seeking scale tend to engage in more activities involving physical risk, show greater use of recreational drugs, gamble more and make larger bets, manifest a greater variety of sexual experiences with a greater number of partners, prefer complex artistic forms to simpler ones, and are more likely to break social conventions and laws in order to have exciting experiences, compared to individuals who score low in sensation seeking.

(CONTINUES)

FEATURE 5.A *(CONTINUED)*

Zuckerman has explored many different biological markers of sensation seeking (Zuckerman & Kuhlman, 2000). Among the most important appears to be the enzyme monoamine oxidase (MAO). MAO helps to regulate the level of neurotransmitters in the body by breaking down the neurotransmitter in the synapse between two cells after it has allowed a nerve impulse to pass from one cell to the next. The efficient operation of the nervous system relies on this process of chemical breakdown. MAO essentially works as a block or brake on the nervous system, decomposing neurotransmitters and inhibiting neurotransmission.

Research suggests that individuals high in sensation seeking tend to have *lower* levels of MAO in their bloodsteams. As a result, Zuckerman reasons, high sensation seekers may regularly experience higher levels of neurotransmitters (especially dopamine) in the nervous system. With low MAO levels, sensation seekers experience less inhibition in the nervous system and, therefore, may show less control over their behavior, thoughts, and emotions. While people like me who are low in sensation seeking may often feel the need to inhibit risky impulses, sensation seekers plunge ahead to enjoy the thrill, even in the face of danger.

great fiction, as we see especially in the character of Dmitri, the oldest son of Fyodor Karamazov. His mother dead and his father drunk, the 3-year-old Dmitri is raised by the faithful family servant, Grigory. Grigory is selflessly devoted to the boy, but Dmitri grows to be an unruly young man with violent passions. He drops out of the Russian equivalent of high school, enlists in the military, does a tour of duty in the Caucasus mountains, is promoted but then demoted after he fights a duel, leads a wild life, and gets into debt. Upon his return to civilian life, Dmitri becomes obsessed with obtaining from his dissolute father the extensive property and fortune that he, mistakenly it turns out, believes his father owes him. When his father is murdered, Dmitri becomes the prime suspect.

By his own admission, Dmitri suffers from the curse of the Karamazovs. Psychologically speaking, the curse manifests itself as a proclivity for obsessing over the tiniest trifles, as well as the big contradictions, in human life and the complete inability to control one's emotions in response to those trifles and conflicts. Emotional life is a roller coaster careening out of control. At five o'clock Dmitri leaps for joy, but by 5:05 he has fallen into the pit of despair. He is tormented by these emotional contradictions and by a sense that humankind is fated to suffer incessantly and to wallow in that suffering. "Everything in the world is a riddle," Dmitri laments.

> But I cannot solve the riddle. I will never be able to solve it. Never! For I'm a Karamazov. For when I do leap into the abyss I pitch in head foremost and heels up, and am positively pleased to be falling in that degrading attitude, and pride myself upon it. And in the very depths of that degradation I suddenly begin a hymn. Let me be accursed. Let me be vile and base, but let me, too, kiss the hem of the garment in which my God is clothed. Though I may be following the devil, I am Thy son, O Lord, and I love Thee, and I feel the joy without which the world cannot exist and have its being. … What a terrible lot of mysteries there are! Too many riddles weigh men down on earth. We must solve them as best we can, and try to keep a dry skin in the water. Beauty! I can't endure the thought that a man of lofty mind and heart begins with the ideal of the Madonna and ends with the ideal of Sodom. What's still more dreadful is that a man with the ideal of Sodom in his soul does not renounce the ideal of the Madonna, and his heart is on fire with that ideal, genuinely on fire, just as in the days of his youth and innocence. Yes, man is broad, too broad, indeed. I'd have him narrower. (pp. 79–80)

Dmitri wishes that human beings were drawn more narrowly. He wishes that they did not experience such a broad and confusing range of emotional states. He wishes they did not harbor such contradictory passions of the soul. As a devout Christian who finds his own sensual lust to be overwhelming, Dmitri cannot understand why God would design man to desire both "Sodom" and "the Madonna." In other words, how can a man or a woman want desperately to be evil and good at the same time? Human beings are contradictions—they want opposite things. While many people seem to know this at some level and seem more-or-less able to cope with it, as we might say today, Dostoyevsky's characters do not cope very well. For all their passion and their wholehearted engagement of the world, people like Dmitri spend a great deal of time in life being miserable. And not just people like Dmitri. Neuroticism casts a wide net in literature and life. There are many, many ways to be miserable—many styles of human unhappiness. But almost by definition, they all have in common the experience of negative emotions such as fear, anxiety, sadness, shame, guilt, and despair. The problem of neuroticism is the problem of negative emotionality. How bad do we feel? And how able are we to regulate, modulate, control, and cope with the bad feelings that will inevitably befall us?

THE MANY WAYS TO FEEL BAD

The second of the Big Five trait clusters is known by many names, but the most common label is **neuroticism.** Measures of chronic anxiety, depression, excessive emotionality, nervousness, moodiness, hostility, vulnerability, self-consciousness, and hypochondriasis all converge in this general factor, which is most generally described as a continuum from emotional instability to emotional stability. Watson and Clark (1984) point out that this general personality dimension is concerned with individual differences among people in their experience of negative emotions, such as sadness, anger, fear, anxiety, guilt, and the like. Consequently, they label the dimension "negative affectivity" (Watson & Tellegen, 1985). People who score high on this general trait have a tendency to be distressed and upset in many realms of their lives. They are chronically worried, nervous, and insecure, and they hold a low opinion of themselves. People who score low on *N*, on the other hand, are generally calm, relaxed, hardy, secure, self-satisfied, and rather unemotional.

A considerable body of research suggests that individual differences in neuroticism are linked to differences in the experience of negative emotional states. In these studies, researchers typically employ self-report measures of *N* containing items such as those presented in Table 5.3. *N* is consistently associated with reports of unpleasant moods, higher tension levels, and a preponderance of negative emotional experiences (Emmons & Diener, 1986a; Matthews, Jones, & Chamberlain, 1989; Thayer, 1989; Watson & Clark, 1992). People high in neuroticism are lonelier (Stokes, 1985) and less satisfied with interpersonal relationships in their lives (Atkinson & Violato, 1994) than are people low in neuroticism. Clinical patients suffering from affective disorders such as depression and generalized anxiety show elevated levels of *N* (Eysenck & Eysenck, 1985) and of similar traits related to negative affect (Clark, Watson, & Mineka, 1994). College students high in *N* report more stress symptoms and higher levels of homesickness (Matthews & Deary, 1998). These results concerning *N* contrast with those from research on extraversion, suggesting that *E* is associated with positive affect states. As we have already seen, extraverts tend to report greater levels of good feeling about themselves than do introverts. But extraverts and introverts do *not* differ with respect to bad feelings. Persons scoring high on *N*, by contrast, report more bad feelings than do persons scoring low on *N*, but they do not necessarily

TABLE 5.3	QUESTIONNAIRE ITEMS ASSESSING NEUROTICISM (N)

1. Do you sometimes feel happy, sometimes depressed, without any apparent reason?
2. Does your mind often wander while you are trying to concentrate?
3. Are you inclined to be moody?
4. Are you frequently "lost in thought" even when you are supposed to be taking part in a conversation?
5. Are you sometimes bubbling over with energy and sometimes very sluggish?
6. Are your feelings rather easily hurt?
7. Do you get attacks of shaking or trembling?
8. Are you an irritable person?
9. Are you troubled with feelings of inferiority?
10. Do you suffer from sleeplessness?

SOURCE: From *Eysenck on Extraversion* (pp. 33, 43–45), by H. J. Eysenck, 1973, New York: John Wiley & Sons.

report fewer good feelings. Rather than being opposites, good feelings and bad feelings seem to be rather independent. Thus, to oversimplify somewhat, extraverts report high levels of good feelings, introverts report low levels of good feelings, persons high in neuroticism report high levels of bad feelings, and persons low in neuroticism report low levels of bad feelings (Costa & McCrae, 1980a, 1984; Emmons & Diener, 1985; Meyer & Shack, 1989; Watson & Clark, 1984).

Individual differences in *N* have been shown to predict a number of important behavioral and attitudinal trends. For example, *N* has been associated with complaints about poor health among men (Costa & McCrae, 1980b). In a study following the daily life of 43 undergraduate students over the course of a semester, Larsen and Kasimatis (1991) found that students high in *N* tended to report a greater number of illnesses. Ormel and Wohlfarth (1991) found that high levels of *N* were a significantly stronger predictor of psychological distress than were environmental factors, such as negative changes in one's life situation. Individuals high in *N* are likely to see the problems of middle age as a "crisis" according to Costa and McCrae (1978). Among older adults, high levels of neuroticism combined with high levels of daily stress are especially predictive of poor quality of life (Mroczek & Almeida, 2004). In a 50-year longitudinal study of 300 married couples, neuroticism scores of both husbands and wives were a major predictor of divorce (Kelly & Conley, 1987).

Why is *N* so strongly associated with so many bad things? Bolger and Schilling (1991) conducted a study of daily stressors that provides insight into this question. The researchers recruited 339 adults who provided daily reports of minor stressful events and mood for 42 consecutive days. Each day the respondents indicated how strongly they had felt each of 18 emotions over the previous 24 hours. Emotion items included indices of anxiety, depression, and hostility, such as "nervous," "tense," "irritable," "worthless," and "angry." In addition, each respondent indicated whether or not he or she experienced any of nine different kinds of stressors during the day, including "overload at work," "argument with spouse," "argument with child," and "transportation problem." Scores on *N* were determined from an 11-item neuroticism scale that was administered before the daily reporting began.

The results indicated that on average, high-*N* adults were more distressed than low-*N* adults over the six-week period, as indexed by the daily mood reports. The sources of their distress were three. First, high-*N* adults tended to report a greater number of daily stressors than did low-*N* adults. Now one could argue that this is because high-*N* individuals complain more; perhaps they are overly sensitive and tend to report minor events that most other people would overlook. The results show, however, that the difference was *not* due to over-sensitivity on the part of high-*N* adults, for reports from their spouses tended to support the accuracy of their own accounts of stressful events. In essence, then, high neuroticism appears to *expose* individuals to a greater number of stressful daily events. Especially significant in this regard were stressful events having to do with interpersonal conflict. Of the nine stressor categories, "argument with spouse" and "argument with other" were the two areas that showed the largest distinction between high-*N* and low-*N* adults.

A second source of distress was the respondents' *reactivity* to stressful events. Not only did the high-*N* subjects report a greater number of stressful events, but their negative emotional reactions to stressful events were significantly stronger than the negative emotional reactions to stressful events shown by low-*N* respondents. In fact, reactivity to stressful events was *twice as important* as exposure to stressful events as an explanation for the link between *N* and distress. The authors argue that this reactivity in high-*N* adults is a result of ineffective coping strategies such as self-blame and wishful thinking. Rather than taking constructive steps to deal with stressful situations, high-*N* individuals rely on self-defeating strategies that do not relieve their anxiety, depression, and hostility in the face of daily setbacks.

A third source of distress among high-*N* individuals was *unrelated to stressful events*. The authors show that as much as 60% of the relationship between neuroticism and distress had nothing to do with either the bad things that happened to the high-*N* individuals or their overly negative reactions to these bad things. In addition to a greater exposure to stressful situations and a greater negative reaction to such stressors when they occur, it appears that there is a general negativity about life among high-*N* adults that cannot be explained by what happens on a daily basis. Even when bad things aren't happening, neuroticism brings with it bad feelings.

Other studies suggest that *N* is associated with inappropriate and awkward behavior in a number of different social situations. In one experiment, college men scoring either high or low on *N* were randomly assigned to one of two experimental conditions: a "low-intimacy" or a "high-intimacy" condition (Chaikin, Derlega, Bayma, & Shaw, 1975). In the low-intimacy condition, the participant spoke over the phone with a stranger who was a fellow student and who had been previously trained to talk about topics that were superficial and nonintimate, such as his house or apartment, how his family got together, and so on. In the high-intimacy condition, the person spoke over the phone with a fellow student who had been previously trained to talk about topics that were highly intimate, such as the birth-control methods he would prefer to use in marriage, the number of times he had cried as an adult, the frequency of his sexual behavior, and how he had felt when he saw his father hit his mother. The subjects were each given a list of topics to discuss over the phone. The topics varied with respect to their intimacy level, and thus the study's dependent variable was the amount of intimacy content that the participant introduced into the conversation.

Figure 5.3 presents the major finding of the study—subjects scoring low in *N* adjusted their level of intimacy to correspond to the level introduced by the experimental condition. In other words, when the fellow student disclosed intimate information (the high-intimacy condition) the participant reciprocated, offering intimate information about himself. Similarly, when the fellow student kept the conversation light and nonintimate, the participant reciprocated with less intimate information about himself. Men high in *N*, on the other hand, did *not* adjust their intimacy disclosure to the condition, disclosing at moderate levels of intimacy regardless of what the fellow student said. The results suggest that persons high in *N* find it difficult to adjust their social behavior to meet situational

---

FIGURE 5.3 INTIMACY AND NEUROTICISM

Under low intimacy conditions, individuals high and low on neuroticism show equivalent levels of intimate behavior, but when the conditions call for higher levels of intimacy, individuals with low neuroticism show higher (and appropriate) levels compared with individuals high in neuroticism.

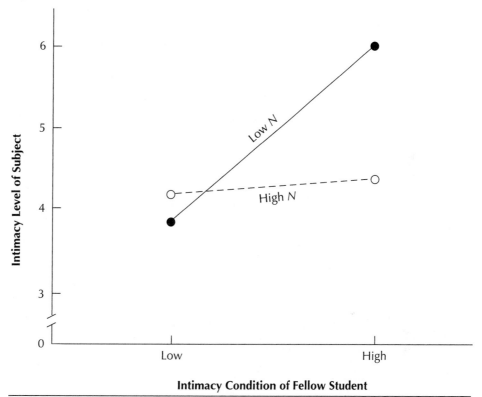

Intimacy Condition of Fellow Student

SOURCE: Adapted from "Neuroticism and Disclosure Reciprocity," A. L. Chaikin, V. J. Derlega, B. Bayma, & J. Shaw, 1975, *Journal of Consulting and Clinical Psychology, 43,* p. 16.

demands. Neurotic individuals appear to be oblivious to social cues, perhaps too self-preoccupied to note what their environments are saying to them.

STRESS AND COPING

N is the trait that is most strongly and consistently related to stress symptoms of various kinds. We have already seen that *N* is linked to negative emotional states and problems in interpersonal relationships. High levels of *N* are also associated with self-reports of illnesses and various somatic symptoms, though *N* does not itself appear to be a risk factor for serious diseases (Wiebe & Smith, 1997). The relation between *N* and stress-proneness is evident in other aspects of everyday functioning as well. For example, individuals high in *N* report that they are more prone to carelessness and everyday errors in thinking (Matthews, Coyle, & Craig, 1990). Automobile drivers high in *N* are more prone to stress in the form of anger, irritation, anxiety, and lack of confidence (Matthews, Dorn, & Glendon, 1991). Another cor-

FEATURE 5.B

ARE WE LIVING IN THE AGE OF ANXIETY?

It has become almost a cliché in modern Western society to say that life is more hectic and complex today than it used to be. Many middle-class Americans long for "the good old days" when life was simpler and when people seemed to enjoy life more. It is not altogether clear, however, exactly when the good old days were! Many Americans romanticize the 1950s, when television shows such as *Ozzie and Harriet* and *The Andy Griffith Show* celebrated traditional family values, small-town life, and the domestic bliss of American suburban life. Others contend that the 1950s, situated before the Women's Movement and the Civil Rights gains of the next two decades, may have only been good for a small group of white males. In the eyes of some social critics (e.g., Myers, 2000; Putnam, 2000) and many common folk, Americans were less anxious 50 years ago than they are today. Is this true?

Personality psychologist Jean M. Twenge thinks that it is. Twenge (2000) examined children's and college students' neuroticism scores on personality trait scales collected between the years of 1952 and 1993. In an impressive analysis, Twenge gathered the mean scores on scales measuring traits that fall under the general rubric of neuroticism in 170 studies of American college students and 99 samples of American grade-school and high-school students appearing in the published psychological literature in the 1950s, 60s, 70s, 80s, and early 90s. Twenge found that scores on neuroticism-based scales increased steadily over the time frame she sampled.

College students who completed anxiety scales in the 1950s tended to score lower than students who completed the same or similar scales in the 1960s, and they were lower than the 1970s, and so on. The highest average scores appeared in the 1980s and 1990s. Twenge's results are very robust. Consider this: The *average* American child in the 1980s reported *more* anxiety than child psychiatric patients in the 1950s! The data suggest that American young people today report much higher levels of anxiety than did young people 30 or 40 years ago.

What are we to make of these findings? Some skeptics argue that the trend Twenge found results from a greater willingness to report anxiety today compared to years ago. People may have been just as anxious in the good old days, but reporting these kinds of problems may have been considered socially inappropriate at the time. Others accept Twenge's findings as an indictment on contemporary life in the United States. Twenge herself argues that rising scores on neuroticism and related traits may signal the breakdown of family and community ties over the past 40 years and the perception among Americans of increased threat. Interestingly, economic indicators appear to have little to do with the trend. Twenge's data show no effects of economic downturns or periods of prosperity. In the overall, Americans today are much wealthier than they were in the 1950s. But we may also feel more hassled, more worried, and less secure about our lives.

relate of *N* is self-reported sexual problems such as nervousness, guilt, and inhibition (Eysenck, 1976). Neuroticism tends to be high in certain types of criminals, such as those who feel that they are socially inadequate (Eysenck, Rust, & Eysenck, 1977), and in alcoholics and drug abusers (Furnham, 1992). Another study showed that individuals high in *N* tend to drink more alcoholic beverages, and to drink alone, on days when they experience negative interpersonal interactions (Mohr, Armeli, Tennen, Carney, Affleck, & Hromi, 2001).

These correlational results, however, do not directly answer a fundamental question: Does neuroticism *cause* stress, or does stress cause neuroticism? Both possibilities seem reasonable. It is possible that being high on *N* to begin with predisposes a person to stress experiences. But the reverse possibility also seems plausible: High levels of stress may make us more neurotic. Researchers who have tried to tease out these causal relations have obtained evidence for both possibilities, but it would seem that the first of the two has recently garnered more support. For example, Ormel and Wohlfarth (1991) report a longitudinal study of 296 Dutch adults who were given measures of N at the beginning of the study (Time 0) and then asked about stressful life events and psychological distress 6 (Time 1) and 7 (Time 2) years later. Stressful events were broken down into endogenous and exogenous events. Endogenous events are those that are strongly influenced by the person's own behavior, such as serious marital discord, whereas exogenous events are those that are more likely to originate in outside sources, such as accidents and illnesses. The researchers found that both endogenous and exogenous events at Time 1 had an impact on psychological distress at Time 1 and Time 2. In other words, high reports of stresses such as illness and marital problems were associated with high levels of overall distress at that time (6 years after the beginning of the study: Time 1) and one year later (Time 2). However, a much stronger predictor of distress at Times 1 and 2 was the person's score on N at Time 0. Neuroticism scores strongly predicted levels of psychological distress 6 and 7 years later. N also predicted endogenous life events. Individuals high in neuroticism at Time 0 experienced more self-generated stressful events 6 years later, which in turn predicted psychological distress.

Magnus, Diener, Fujita, and Pavot (1993) conducted a similar study, administering measures on two occasions 4 years apart. They found that high levels of N predisposed a person to experience a greater number of stressful events in the next 4 years. However, the number of stressful events experienced during the 4-year period did not predict the neuroticism score at the end of the period, after statistically accounting for the original N score. In simple terms, the data suggest that N tends to cause stressful events, not the reverse. The researchers offer two reasons for this association. They argue that people high in N tend to react to a wider variety of events in negative ways. The very same event—say, finding yourself stuck for a semester with an obnoxious roommate—might represent a minor hassle for a person low in N but a major stressor for a person high in N. Second, they suggest that people high in N "bring it on themselves" sometimes. Their difficulties in social interaction may actually initiate negative events in their lives such as job loss, divorce, and other setbacks and failures.

Longitudinal studies have examined the causal relations between the trait of N and clinical depression. Here the research provides equivocal results, in part because a tendency toward depression is one aspect of N itself. Some reviews have suggested that heightened N may be seen as a symptom or result of clinical depression (Barnett & Gotlib, 1988). An acute bout of depression can leave lasting emotional scars, and among those scars may be the heightened levels of anxiety and distress associated with N. However, recent studies also suggest that being high on N to begin with may predispose some people to major depressive episodes (Bagby, Joffe, Parker, Kalemba, & Harkness, 1995). In a 12-year longitudinal study of depression, Surtees and Wainwright (1996) showed that, out of many clinical, demographic, and social measures taken at the beginning of the study, one of the strongest predictors of poor outcome in treatment for depression was the trait of neuroticism.

When stressful events do occur, how do people high in neuroticism cope with them? The simple answer is "not very well." Research suggests that individuals high in N go into a stressful situation with a negative view of things to begin with. They tend to appraise what is already a negative situation in even more negative terms. They tend to see themselves as having relatively few resources and relatively weak support systems to help them cope with the problem (Stokes & McKirnan, 1989). Rather than adopting an action plan for coping with the stressful situation, individuals high in N may adopt "emotion-focused" or avoidant coping strategies (Endler & Parker, 1990). Instead of tackling the problem that is causing the stress, they may focus their efforts on soothing their fears and calming their nervousness, or they may simply seek to escape the whole problem through drinking, drug use, or even just staying in bed.

Bolger (1990) studied how medical students coped with the stress of the Medical College Admission Test (MCAT), a grueling day-long ordeal that weighs heavily in medical school admission decisions. Bolger followed 50 pre-medical students during the three-week period before they took the MCAT. Students high in *N* tended to cope with the stress of the impending exam by daydreaming, engaging in fantasies of escape, or wallowing in self-blame for not studying more. As a result, over the course of the three-week period their levels of anxiety continued to increase. By contrast, students low in *N* either tried to prepare for the exam, sought support from friends, or simply reassured themselves that the whole situation was not as bad as it initially seemed. Consequently, their anxiety levels did not increase as much over the three-week period. We see, then, that different levels of *N* are associated with different strategies for coping with stress. Some coping strategies, furthermore, are more effective in dampening stress than are others. The low-*N* students managed their stress better than did high-*N* students. But, you may ask, how did the students perform on the exam? Here you may be surprised. The results of the MCAT exams showed that the two groups did *not* differ. Neuroticism itself was not associated with performance levels on the MCAT. While the students high in *N* suffered more stress and coped badly with the stress over the three-week period, they did just as well on the exam as did their low-*N* counterparts.

NEUROTICISM AND THE BRAIN

Eysenck (1967) argued that the biological roots of neuroticism lay in the workings of the brain's *limbic system*. One of the oldest parts of the brain (in terms of human evolution), the limbic system was once considered to be the seat of all emotional experience. Current research on and thinking about the brain, however, contends that the many parts of the limbic system—the amygdala, septum, hippocampus, and prefrontal cortex—are involved in many different functions, including memory and other cognitive processes. Furthermore, emotional responses appear to be mediated also by other parts of the brain outside the limbic system. Nonetheless, one region that was originally viewed to be a part of the limbic system does appear to be implicated in the experience and regulation of one particular emotional response. That region is the tiny **amygdala,** and the emotion with which it seems to be associated is *fear*.

In Latin, the word *amygdala* means almond. Early anatomists named a small, almond-shaped region in the forebrain the amygdala. Brain researchers now believe that certain parts of the amygdala activate behavioral, autonomic, and endocrine responses to the presence or perception of *danger* (LeDoux, 1996). When the amygdala receives a stimulus indicating that the organism senses (or even imagines) a dangerous threat, this almond-shaped agent mobilizes a number of different systems designed to defend the organism against whatever may be threatening it. The amygdala may set into motion systems that ultimately stimulate stress hormones and heightened blood pressure and may invoke startle responses and sudden freezing in the presence of a threat. The amygdala is centrally involved in the conditioning of fear. LeDoux (1996) writes that "research by several laboratories has shown that lesions of the central nucleus [of the amygdala] interfere with essentially every measure of conditioned fear, including freezing behavior, autonomic responses, suppression of pain, stress hormone release, and reflex potentiation" (p. 158). Animals and humans who suffer damage to certain

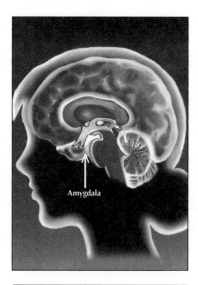

Individual differences in neuroticism may signal subtle differences in the functioning of the brain's Behavioral Inhibition System (BIS). Recent research suggests that parts of the brain's amygdala—a small, almond shaped structure in the forebrain—may play an important role in the BIS and may be implicated in fear conditioning and other negative-affect experiences that are typically associated with neuroticism.

parts of the amygdala may be unable to experience normal fear responses and may consequently be unable to learn what to fear in the world.

Several psychologists have proposed that the amygdala is part of a **behavioral inhibition system (BIS)** in humans and related animals (e.g., Davis, 1986; LeDoux, 1996). The behavioral inhibition system mediates responses to threat and signs of danger, punishment, and extreme novelty. Once activated, the BIS may stimulate intense vigilance and attention in the wake of threat, and it may ultimately help to produce responses that lead to defensive withdrawal from a threatening situation. The behavioral inhibition system (BIS), therefore, stands in sharp conceptual contrast to the behavioral approach system (BAS). While the BAS arouses a person to move toward desired incentives that promise positive emotional reward, the BIS causes a person to draw back from goals in the anticipation of a negative emotional punishment. My BAS may motivate me to walk confidently into a room of good friends to enjoy the night's party, but my BIS may keep me standing on the perimeter should I find myself in a very different sort of gathering at which, say, I know very few people, and they all look intimidating. In the first situation, I act spontaneously and on *impulse;* I am comfortable and ready for fun. In the second situation, I feel *anxious* and vigilant; I scan the room warily; I look for opportunities to escape.

The emotional quality of BIS-induced responding, therefore, is likely to be fear and anxiety. Gray (1987) proposes that while individual differences in impulsivity may be linked to variations in the BAS, individual differences in the trait of anxiety correspond to variations in the BIS. Under all conceptions of the terms, anxiety is viewed to be a major component of neuroticism, which itself is sometimes called "negative affectivity" (Watson & Tellegen, 1985). Consequently, some researchers argue that the biological bases for individual differences in *N* reside in the behavioral inhibition system. Put in simple terms, people high in neuroticism have developed, for whatever reasons, a dominant and readily activated BIS, compared with individuals low in neuroticism. Like the BAS, the BIS is a hypothesized functional system, rather than a clearly defined location in the brain. The amygdala may play an important role in the BIS, but it is one role among many different roles played by many different neuronal and hormonal agents and networks. Table 5.4 summarizes hypothesized connections between the BAS and BIS on the one hand and personality traits on the other.

You may recall that recent research employing EEG patterns suggests that the behavioral approach system may be indexed by activation of the left anterior regions of the cortex. In a parallel fashion, researchers have suggested that the BIS may be linked to activation of the *right* anterior regions of the cortex. Sutton and Davidson (1997) administered self-report measures of behaviors likely to be associated with BAS and BIS activity among 46 students, employing a questionnaire procedure developed by Carver and White (1994). BAS-linked behaviors included responses that are typically associated with extraversion and positive affectivity, while BIS-linked behaviors included those that are associated with neuroticism and negative affectivity. The researchers calculated a simple BIS/BAS index by subtracting the BIS score from the BAS score. This index, then, assessed the relative strength of BIS-linked versus BAS-linked behaviors. They then took various EEG readings of all of

TABLE 5.4	HYPOTHESIZED LINKAGES BETWEEN PERSONALITY TRAITS AND BRAIN SYSTEMS	
	Extraversion	**Neuroticism**
Alternative trait name (Tellegen)	Positive affectivity	Negative affectivity
Gray's trait dimension*	Impulsivity	Anxiety
Eysenck's proposed biological substrate	Reticular activating system	Limbic system
Purpose of brain system	Response to incentives, positive approach, positive emotions	Response to punishments, withdrawal or vigilance in the face of theat or novelty, negative emotions (especially fear)
Associated brain pathways and structures	Dopaminergic pathways	Amygdala
Associated EEG activity	Left anterior cortex	Right anterior cortex

* Jeffrey Gray's (1982, 1987) theory of personality traits positions the dimensions of impulsivity and anxiety within a two-dimensional coordinate space that is tilted 45 degrees from the dimensions of *E* and *N*. Thus, in Gray's terms the extravert is high on impulsivity and low on anxiety, the introvert is low on impulsivity and high on anxiety, the highly neurotic individual is high on impulsivity and high on anxiety, and the emotionally stable (low neuroticism) individual is low in impulsivity and low on anxiety.

the students on two different occasions. The results of their study showed that prefrontal EEG asymmetry was strongly associated with the BIS/BAS behavioral score. Those students who showed relatively more EEG activity in the right anterior region, compared with the left, tended to score toward the BIS end of the BIS/BAS scale, whereas those who showed relatively more left anterior activity scored toward the BAS end of the behavioral scale. EEG measures from other parts of the cortex were unrelated to the behavioral scores.

Recent research supports the idea that individual differences in *N* or in traits related to *N* may be linked to individual differences in a behavioral inhibition system. The BIS is as yet a loosely configured construct, but it would appear to implicate the functioning of parts of the brain's amygdala and be indexed by heightened activity in the right anterior regions of the brain. Future research promises to give us a clearer and more articulated picture of the biological underpinnings of the human tendency to experience anxiety, fear, and other negative emotional states.

O: OPENNESS TO EXPERIENCE

The third of the Big Five traits is something of a curiosity. In his original formulation of 16 basic source traits, Cattell (1943) included a dimension of "intelligence." On the "intelligence" scale of the 16PF trait inventory, a person responds to a series of self-report items that essentially ask him or her to rate the extent of his or her own intelligence. These self-ratings, however, are only modestly correlated with intelligence scores obtained on IQ tests. To nobody's surprise, including Cattell's, how intelligent a person rates him- or herself is not the same thing as how intelligent a person turns out to be as measured on a test of intellectual *ability*. Nonetheless, while many personality psychologists may view intelligence, as measured on cognitive tests, to lie somewhat outside the central domain of personality per se, the extent to which a person thinks that he or she is intelligent would appear to be an interesting self-ascribed personality trait. Early factor-analytic studies of English-language traits showed that self-ratings of intelligence tended to cluster with ratings on other trait dimensions, such as measures of reflectiveness, imagination, tender-mindedness, aesthetic sensitivity, and preference for complexity in life. In his early five-factor model, Norman (1963) identified a dimension of "culture" as including traits having to do with how reflective, imaginative, artistic, and refined a person is. High scorers were thought to be intellectually rounded, broad and insightful; low scorers were narrow, unimaginative, and even crude and boorish. Reflecting its association with intelligence and intellectual interests, other researchers have labeled this trait domain "inquiring intellect" (Fiske, 1949) and "intellectance" (Digman, 1990). In this chapter we will use the label popularized by Costa and McCrae: **openness to experience** (or simply, **O**).

Whether we call it culture, intellectance, or openness to experience, this trait would seem, on first blush, to be a very good thing. Many classical models of personality development and growth describe the mature individual as being reflective and imaginative, as having insight and a broad perspective on life (e.g., Erikson, 1963; Fromm, 1973; Loevinger, 1976; Rogers, 1951; Vaillant, 1977; White, 1975). Pioneers in the sciences, arts, and religion are often highly imaginative and innovative people whose insights can have a dramatic impact on their respective fields. For example, Gardner (1993) focuses on the development of creative genius in the lives of Freud, Picasso, Einstein, Gandhi, Martha Graham (dance), Igor Stravinsky (music), and T. S. Eliot (literature). Not only are all seven of Gardner's protagonists readily described as high in *O*, but a great deal of their development as creators and as people can be viewed as a progressive enrichment, over time, of their experiential openness.

A similar conclusion can be drawn from biographies of political revolutionaries and some individuals who dedicate their lives to social change (Andrews, 1991; Colby & Damon, 1992). For example, Colby and Damon trace the intellectual and political development of Andrei Sakharov, a physicist and political activist in the former Soviet Union. Sakharov headed the Soviet efforts in the 1940s and 1950s to develop the hydrogen bomb. But over time, Sakharov became increasingly disenchanted with life in the Soviet Union. Furthermore, he began to question the wisdom of developing weapons that were ultimately aimed at destroying human civilization on earth. Sakharov was a bold and innovative scientist whose intellectual daring began in early adulthood to generalize to the domains of political and social life. As he read and learned more and interacted with a progressively wider array of colleagues and associates, Sakharov began to carve out for himself the role of social critic and dissident in an authoritarian society. As he matured through middle age, Sakharov became more and more open to new experiences, expressing what Colby and Damon (1992) describe as a "striking openness to moral change" and an "active receptiveness" to important social influences in his world (p. 13). Sakharov gained more and more confidence in his radical ideals and expanded his revolutionary vision for a freer and more just society. Eventually, he became the most prominent dissident in the entire Soviet Union. A tireless advocate for democracy and human rights, Sakharov came to symbolize the revolutionary intellectual whose transformative vision for a better society inspired not only Russians but people from around the globe. In the case of Sakharov, openness to experience helped to catalyze a heroic struggle against authoritarian oppression.

But Sakharov's life story does not inspire everybody. The leaders of the former Soviet Union, for example, and the many Russian citizens who were deeply committed to the communist regime saw Sakharov as a dangerous threat and a malcontent rather than a hero. In a less comfortable example that is closer to home, Fidel Castro led a revolution in Cuba in the 1950s. As he began to translate his radical ideas into the reality of a socialist state, Castro was vilified in the United States and cast in the role of enemy. Described as daring, imaginative, unconventional, and intellectually insightful as a young man, Castro has never been a hero for most Americans. While we may be able to come up with good reasons to distinguish Castro from, say, Sakharov or Stravinsky, my example illustrates a basic curiosity about O. Put simply, O invokes a great deal of ambivalence for many people. What seems on first blush to be a trait that is linked to such good things as creativity and psychological maturity may also invoke more negative associations.

Our ambivalence about O is especially evident in the realm of politics. One of the most popular U.S. presidents in recent memory was Ronald Reagan. Yet even President Reagan's greatest admirers would *not* describe him as high in openness to experience. Indeed, it was partly Reagan's unquestioning embrace of a small number of simple principles in life and politics that made him so admirable to many Americans. Yet President Reagan's detractors viewed the same characteristics in decidedly negative terms, describing him as rigid, simple-minded, and out of touch with the complexities of life. By contrast, President Bill Clinton was generally viewed, even by his detractors, as creative, imaginative, complex, curious, and having very broad interests. But his high openness to experience seemed to come with a cost, according to many of his critics. From his time as governor of Arkansas through his two-term presidency, Clinton was repeatedly criticized for being too "slick" and lacking a moral and political center of conviction. In politics and in life more generally, one person's "intellectual daring" is another person's "intellectual recklessness"; one person's "broad-mindedness" is another person's "lack of conviction"; one person's "independence of mind" is another person's "disregard for the viewpoints of others." Unlike *N,* it is hard to decide whether O is really a good or a bad thing. Your evaluation of the concept may indeed partly depend on where you stand on this personality dimension.

CORRELATES OF O

McCrae and Costa (1997a) describe O as fundamentally "a matter of inner experience and mental phenomena related to the scope of [a person's] awareness and the intensity of [his or her] consciousness" (p. 835). Openness to experience is manifested in the depth, breadth, and permeability of a person's conscious experience and in the desire or drive to expand that experience to encompass a richer array of sensations, perceptions, thoughts, and feelings. Openness may be expressed in many different domains. On the NEO-PI-R, McCrae and Costa identify six different facets of openness: fantasy, aesthetics, feelings, actions, ideas, and values. Therefore, the person high in O may reveal a rich and elaborate fantasy life, may be especially sensitive to the aesthetic dimensions of life, may experience a greater range of personal feelings, may seek out a wider range of activities in life, may hold many different and even contradictory ideas, and may express a complex and highly differentiated value system. In the overall, persons high in O are described by themselves and by others who know them as especially original, imaginative, creative, complex, curious, daring, independent, analytical, untraditional, artistic, liberal, and having broad interests. Persons low in O are described as conventional, down-to-earth, uncreative, simple, incurious, nonadventurous, conforming, nonanalytical, unartistic, traditional, conservative, and having narrow interests. Sample items from a self-report measure of O are presented in Table 5.5.

TABLE 5.5	**QUESTIONNAIRE ITEMS ASSESSING OPENNESS TO EXPERIENCE (O)**

1. I enjoy concentrating on a fantasy or daydream and exploring all its possibilities, letting it grow and develop.
2. I am sometimes completely absorbed in music I am listening to.
3. Without strong emotions, life would be uninteresting.
4. I enjoy trying new and foreign foods.
5. I find philosophical arguments boring. (reversed)
6. The different ideas of right and wrong that people in other societies have may be valid for them.

SOURCE: These items come from the NEO Openness Scales. From "Openness to Experience," by R. R. McCrae and P. T. Costa, Jr., in R. Hogan and W. H. Jones (Eds.), *Perspectives in Personality* (Vol. 1, pp. 145–172), 1985, Greenwich, CT: JAI Press.

In one of the earliest investigations of *O,* McCrae and Costa (1980) administered a number of trait scales and a sentence-completion exercise to 240 adults between the ages of 35 and 80 years. On the sentence-completion exercise, the participants were presented with sentence fragments such as "A good father/" and "Rules are/" and were asked to complete the sentences in any way they wished. Table 5.6 provides examples of how persons high and low on *O* responded to this task. Persons scoring high on *O* on the trait scales provided richer and more complex responses on the sentence-completion test, compared with persons scoring low in *O.* Their responses reveal a more differentiated fantasy life, more psychological insight, and a greater variety of experience. Whereas persons low in *O* held to rather rigid and traditional views of authority and society (Rules are/ "there to obey"), persons high in *O* tended to reject, or at least question, these stereotypical attitudes, revealing more flexible and personalized understandings of rules, authority, the family, and sex roles (Rules are/ "necessary, but civil disobedience is one way to change them for 'progress'"). The study suggests that openness to experience is associated with a more complex, nonconforming, and individualized understanding of the world.

Persons high in *O* are thought to have broad intellectual and aesthetic interests. This does not mean, however, that these people are necessarily highly intelligent. McCrae and Costa (1985a) argue that intelligence and *O* are very different constructs. To support this claim of the discriminant validity of trait scales assessing *O,* McCrae and Costa report a correlation of +.32 between vocabulary scores on a standard adult intelligence (IQ) test and openness to experience in a sample of 253 men. Remember that, to show discriminant validity, one must prove that a particular trait scale does *not* measure the same thing that scales of *other* traits measure. In this case, the correlation of +.32 suggests a statistically significant but rather modest relationship between intelligence and *O,* meaning that the two measures—intelligence (via vocabulary) and openness to experience—seem to be measuring somewhat different dimensions of human functioning. Education level is also positively associated with *O.* In a nationwide sample of nearly 10,000 adults older than age 35, researchers found a positive correlation between number of years of education and scores on a short scale measuring openness to experience (McCrae & Costa, 1997a). The label of "culture" for this personality dimension suggests that such an association is not surprising. The Western tradition of a liberal arts education aims to expose the student to a wide range of intellectual experiences and to encourage a critical attitude toward accepted values and assumptions. Therefore, there is reason to believe that a strong liberal arts education should promote openness to experience. At the same time, it may be true that people with high levels

TABLE 5.6	SENTENCE-COMPLETION RESPONSES OF MEN SCORING HIGH AND LOW ON OPENNESS TO EXPERIENCE (O)

LOW

Sentence Stem	Response
Rules are	there to obey.
	laws to be governed by for the best interests of all concerned.
My main problem	is financial.
When they avoided me	I wondered why.
If my mother	gave a command, it was done.
A husband has a right to	come home and find his wife looking nice.

HIGH

Sentence Stem	Response
Rules are	things that should be flexible enough to fit the real world.
	necessary, but civil disobedience is one way to change them for "progress."
My main problem	is I am too emotional or sensitive sometimes.
When I am criticized	I try to remain open-minded and not get defensive. It doesn't always work, however.
A good father	remembers the anxieties of childhood.
The worst thing about being a man	is the false image built for us by society.

SOURCE: From "Openness to experience," by R. R. McCrae and P. T. Costa, Jr., *Journal of Personality and Social Psychology, 39,* p. 1186.

U.S. Presidents Ronald Reagan (1981–88) and Bill Clinton (1993–2000) are often portrayed as opposite ends of the trait continuum for openness to experience, with Reagan being seen as low and Clinton as high. Research has shown that low openness is sometimes associated with both cognitive rigidity and clear values while high openness is sometimes associated with intellectual flexibility and tolerance but also some degree of ambivalence regarding basic values and beliefs. The same distinction was clearly drawn in the 2004 Presidential election between George W. Bush and John Kerry.

of openness to experience to begin with might be more likely to obtain such an education or more likely to find such an educational experience to be especially broadening.

People high in O appear to welcome challenge and change. For example, in one study of career changes in adults younger than age 55, 64% of the men and 71% of the women who changed jobs over a particular time period scored above the midpoint on O (McCrae & Costa, 1985b). Whitbourne (1986) interviewed 34 women and 23 men (average age 41 years) about anticipated work and family changes. Such changes might include seeking different work, finding employment outside the house, adding another child to the family, or retiring. Openness to experience, assessed via a questionnaire, was positively associated with anticipated change in life, as was age. In other words, older adults and adults scoring high in O anticipated more changes in their lives in the future. (In a 12-month follow-up of the same adults, however, O was not significantly associated with the number of *actual* changes that had occurred.)

Within the general domain of O resides an interesting trait that goes by the name of *absorption.* Absorption is formally defined as a predisposition to "experience emotional and cognitive alterations across a variety of situations" (Roche & McConkey, 1990, p. 92). The concept of absorption has its origins in Auke Tellegen's research into why some people seem especially susceptible to hypnotism and some do not. Tellegen and Atkinson (1974) found that hypnotizable individuals were more open to and more likely to have subjective experiences in which their attention was fully engaged by some object or event, resulting in an altered sense of reality. To assess individual differences in a predisposition to show such experience, they designed the Tellegen Absorption Scale (TAS), which later became part of Tellegen's (1982) Multidimensional Personality Questionnaire (MPQ).

Absorption is associated with an intense and vivid fantasy life. Persons who score high on absorption may become so immersed in their imaginative experiences that they lose all track of time, place, and identity (Pekala, Wenger, & Levine, 1985). Research shows that absorption is positively related to reports of parapsychological phenomena, such as out-of-body experiences, as well as reports of naturally occurring altered states of consciousness. According to a factor-analytic study, absorption connects closely to those aspects of O that invoke aesthetic sensitivity, unusual perceptions and associations, fantasy and dreams, unconventional views of reality, and awareness of inner feelings. It is perhaps due to the presence of the trait of absorption within the broader trait domain of O that researchers have found O to be positively associated with mild forms of magical and bizarre thinking (West, Widiger, & Costa, 1993). Individuals high in O are also more likely to believe in "esoteric and dubious phenomena, such as astrology and the existence of ghosts" (Epstein & Meier, 1989, p. 351).

Dollinger and Clancy (1993) conducted an interesting study examining how personality traits relate to artistic self-expression. Each of the 201 college students completed questionnaire measures of O and other traits and was then instructed to obtain photographs that expressed his or her individual identity. The researchers provided these instructions:

> We want you to describe how you see yourself. To do this, we would like you to take or have someone take 12 photographs that tell who you are. These photographs can be of anything just as long as they tell something about who you are. You should not be interested in your skill as a photographer. Keep in mind that the photographs should describe who you are as you see yourself. When you finish you will have a book about yourself that is made up of only 12 photographs. (Dollinger & Clancy, 1993, p. 1066)

The researchers collected all the photograph books and proceeded to rate the students' work on a number of different artistic and psychological dimensions. People high in *O* tended to receive significantly higher ratings on the artistic *richness* of their photographic essays. Richness referred to the extent to which the photographic arrangement expressed abstract, self-reflective, and aesthetically compelling qualities. Students high in *O* produced work that showed a creative and imaginative interpretation of the photography task, evidence of an aesthetic or artistic sensibility, and illumination of a wide range of self-expressive themes. By contrast, the photographic essays produced by students low in *O* tended to be rated as especially concrete, commonplace, prosaic, unimaginative, and dull. With respect to other traits, the researchers found that low *E* and high *N* among *women* also predicted richness. In other words, introverted and relatively anxious (neurotic) women tended to construct photographic essays that were more imaginative and self-expressive compared with extraverted and emotionally stable women. These relationships between *E* and *N* on the one hand and richness on the other were not found, however, among men. Finally, the researchers also found that extraverted students (men and women) were more likely than introverted students to illustrate interpersonal themes in their photographs.

Folk beliefs suggest that a vivid imagination and high levels of creativity may come with a price. The ancient Greeks spoke of the "divine madness" of creative genius, and in modern times many accounts have been written suggesting that especially creative people may be plagued by self-doubts and suffer from periods of severe depression. At least one study has examined the relation between depression and openness to experience. Wolfenstein and Trull (1997) administered self-report measures of *O* and depression to 143 college students. The students were chosen to comprise three groups—those who were currently suffering from depression, those who reported severe bouts of depression in the past, and those who reported that they had never experienced a bout of severe depression. The researchers found that those students who were currently depressed and/or who reported high levels of depressive symptoms on the self-report measures tended to score high on two of the facets of *O:* aesthetics and feelings. In other words, those students who showed a strong appreciation for art and beauty (aesthetics facet of *O*) and especially vivid and intense emotions (feelings facet of *O*) were more likely to be depressed than those students who scored low on the *O* facets of aesthetics and feelings. Although the results from only one study do not establish a well-documented finding, the study nonetheless reinforces the more general view that being high in *O* may bring with it both positive and negative characteristics and outcomes.

How do people differing on *O* cope with the inevitable stresses and the setbacks of everyday life? McCrae and Costa (1997a) report that *O* is positively associated with using intellectualization as a defense mechanism and negatively associated with using denial. People high in *O* are more likely to try to explain away their problems and to translate deeply personal issues into more abstract and depersonalized rationalizations. By contrast, people low in *O* are more likely to deny the existence of the problems in the first place or to distract themselves from paying concerted attention to the sources of stress.

McCrae and Costa (1986) examined the relations between the traits of *O, E,* and *N* on the one hand and coping with stress on the other in two large adult samples. Men and women who had reported a recent stressful life event participated in the study. Stressful events included losses (such as the death of a parent), threats (such as an illness in the family), and challenges (such as marriage). The participants completed a questionnaire that asked them to recall the particular stressful event and to indicate which of a series of 27 coping strategies they had ever used in dealing with it.

Table 5.7 shows that *E*, *N*, and *O* were significantly associated with use of particular coping strategies. Neuroticism, for example, was correlated with the coping strategies of hostile reaction, escapist fantasy, self-blame, sedation, withdrawal, wishful thinking, passivity, and indecisiveness. Virtually all of these coping strategies were rated by the participants as extremely *in*effective in dealing with stress. Extraversion and openness to experience, on the other hand, were associated with a number of effective coping strategies. *E* was correlated with rational action, positive thinking, substitution, and restraint. Adults high in *O* were more likely to use humor in dealing with stress; those low in *O* relied heavily on faith. McCrae and Costa argue that basic personality traits manifest themselves in times of stress by predisposing people to adopt certain corresponding coping strategies. While the choice of a coping strategy is likely partly determined by the nature of the stressful event and other situational factors, stable and internal personality traits such as *E*, *N*, and *O* also play an important determining role.

THE AUTHORITARIAN PERSONALITY

Among the Big Five traits, *O* appears to be the one that relates directly to certain political beliefs and attitudes. Within Western societies, high levels of *O* tend to be associated with moderate-to-liberal political viewpoints, while low levels of *O* tend to be associated with moderate-to-conservative points of view (McCrae & Costa, 1987, 1997a). To the extent that political liberalism may challenge traditional authority and argue for significant social change, its appeal to people high in openness might be expected. Similarly, conservative

TABLE 5.7	COPING STRATEGIES ASSOCIATED WITH E, N, AND O
Extraversion *(E)*	
Positive thinking:	thought about the good side, the positive aspects of the situation.
Rational action:	took some direct action to change the circumstances that were giving you a problem.
Restraint:	resisted making snap judgments or hasty decisions.
Substitution:	found satisfaction somewhere else in life.
Neuroticism *(N)*	
Escapist fantasy:	spent time daydreaming to forget your troubles.
Hostile reaction:	became irritable and took it out on others.
Indecisiveness:	thought about the problem over and over without really reaching a decision.
Passivity:	procrastinated and delayed while others were waiting for you.
Sedation:	used tranquilizers, alcohol, meditation, or relaxation exercises to calm yourself down.
Self-blame:	blamed yourself, felt guilty, or became apologetic.
Wishful thinking:	just wished that the problem would be gone or that help would come.
Withdrawal:	withdrew from others and attempted to cope with the problem by yourself.
Openness to Experience *(O)*	
Faith *(negatively correlated with O):*	just put your faith in God, or other people, or institutions.
Humor:	saw humor in the situation.

SOURCE: "Personality, Coping, and Coping Effectiveness in an Adult Sample," by R. R. McCrae & P. T. Costa, Jr., 1986, *Journal of Personality, 54,* pp. 393, 404–405.

positions in many contemporary Western democracies tend to underscore traditional social conventions and authoritative systems, which are likely to appeal to people low in *O*. Among Chinese high school students in Hong Kong, high levels of *O* are associated with the desire to adopt the political norms of Western democracy whereas low scores on *O* are associated with skepticism about social change and a preference for traditional Chinese ways (Yik & Bond, 1993). The way in which *O* relates to political views, therefore, is a function of the sociopolitical context and the traditions of the society within which the person lives. What might be viewed as "conservative" in one setting can be seen as "liberal" in another. Nonetheless, it would appear that high levels of *O* tend to correlate with political and social beliefs that underscore progressive change, skepticism toward traditional authority, and tolerance for competing viewpoints. By contrast, low levels of *O* tend to fit more congenially with political and social beliefs that emphasize stability over change, obedience toward traditional authority, and preference for a uniform or unifying point of view.

When it comes to the relation between personality traits and political viewpoints, what is arguably the most influential idea ever developed in personality psychology is the concept of the **authoritarian personality.** Deeply troubled by the rise of Nazi fascism in Germany during the 1930s and 1940s, the psychoanalyst and social critic Erich Fromm (1941) identified an authoritarian character type prevalent among Western Europeans of the day, especially among the lower-middle classes in Germany. Authoritarian men and women sought desperately to *escape from the freedom* that modern capitalist societies afforded them, by striving to idealize authority and by yearning to pledge unqualified allegiance to those in power above *and* to receive the same allegiance from those below. Fromm believed that the authoritarian character structure was partly responsible for Hitler's fateful domination of German politics. Historical and economic conditions had conspired to create in the minds of the German people a readiness and a willingness to be dominated by powerful authority. This partly explains, argued Fromm, how an otherwise intelligent and sensible German populace could rally around such a ruthless tyrant and passively acquiesce to the Nazi programs of persecution, enslavement, and genocide.

Following up on some of Fromm's ideas, a group of eminent social scientists launched an ambitious study of authoritarianism among Americans, resulting in the publication of a landmark book, *The Authoritarian Personality* (Adorno, Frenkel-Brunswik, Levinson, & Sanford, 1950). Conducting extensive interviews of groups of American adults who indicated that they were highly prejudiced against Jews and other ethnic and religious minorities, the researchers developed a questionnaire, the California F [for "Fascism"] Scale, to measure authoritarianism. Authoritarianism was identified as a cluster of nine attitudes and traits, each tapped by certain items on the F Scale. The nine characteristics made up a coherent personality syndrome or type:

1. *Conventionalism:* Rigid adherence to conventional, middle-class values
2. *Authoritarian submission:* Uncritical attitude toward authority
3. *Authoritarian aggression:* Tendency to be on the lookout for and to condemn or punish people who violate conventional values
4. *Anti-intraception:* Opposition to imaginative and subjective aspects of life, to such things as art, literature, and psychology
5. *Superstition and stereotypy:* The belief in mystical determinants of the individual's fate, and the tendency to think in rigid categories
6. *Power and toughness:* Preoccupation with dominance and strength

7. *Destructiveness and cynicism:* Generalized hostility toward people

8. *Projectivity:* The disposition to believe that wild and dangerous things go on in the world; the projection outward of unconscious emotional impulses

9. *Sex:* Exaggerated concern with sexual "goings on"

Heavily influenced by psychoanalytic theory, the authors of *The Authoritarian Personality* argued that authoritarianism had its roots in a complex web of family dynamics. In essence, a highly repressive family environment sows the seeds for the development of authoritarianism. The child represses strong biological impulses because of an overly punitive environment, ultimately projecting those impulses onto others in a defensive way. Parents who are emotionally distant and highly punitive fail to provide appropriate models for healthy identification, stunting ego development in the child and keeping the superego (or conscience) from being fully integrated into the personality. A pervasive sense of personal weakness and dependency on others, and perhaps a latent homosexuality in men, may further underlie the authoritarian syndrome.

Hundreds of empirical studies have been done on the authoritarian personality, employing the original F-test and subsequent scales that have incorporated many improvements in psychometric design (Altemeyer, 1981, 1988; Dillehay, 1978; Winter, 1996). A substantial body of research suggests positive relations between authoritarianism and a number of attitudinal variables such as extremely conservative political values, anti-Semitism, distrust of outsiders, and highly punitive attitudes toward those deemed to be "deviant" in a society. Duncan, Peterson, and Winter (1994) found that authoritarian women and men espouse traditional sex-role attitudes and are hostile toward feminism and the women's movement. Peterson, Doty, and Winter (1993) found that authoritarians hold hostile and punitive attitudes toward people with AIDS, drug users, and the homeless. Among Dutch students, authoritarianism strongly predicted ethnocentric prejudice, as evidenced in strong support among authoritarians for a Dutch political party that advocated the expulsion of immigrant workers (Meloen, Hagendoorn, Raaijmakers, & Visser, 1988). Authoritarianism is associated with support for the caste system among citizens of India (Hassan & Sarkar, 1975) and with nostalgia for the old Soviet regime and distrust of democratic reforms among citizens of Russia (McFarland, Ageyev, & Abalakina-Paap, 1992).

Authoritarians tend to cherish the traditions of their own group but are highly distrustful of the traditions of other groups. Among North American college students, authoritarianism is associated with support for pro-Christian religious instruction in the public schools (Altemeyer, 1993). The same study, however, shows that authoritarian North American students are *opposed* to pro-Muslim religious instruction in public schools of Muslim countries! Authoritarians tend to be highly respectful of traditional authority in their own society, and they find the questioning of authority to be highly distasteful. They have relatively little tolerance for those who disobey authority or whose lifestyle and viewpoints contradict or call into question the legitimacy of traditional authority. Authoritarians will advocate a strong defense of traditional authority, especially when they perceive that authority is being threatened (Doty, Peterson, & Winter, 1991; Sales, 1973). It is perhaps no surprise, therefore, that authoritarianism among American citizens was positively associated with strong support for U.S. involvement in the Vietnam war in the 1960s and 1970s (Izzett, 1971) and in the Persian Gulf war of 1990–91 (Winter, 1996). Shortly before the onset of the Persian Gulf war, American students high in authoritarianism advocated stronger U.S. responses, including even the use of nuclear weapons.

After the war was over, these students took greater pride in the American victory and were less likely to express any regrets about the loss of Iraqi lives caused by the war.

The authoritarian personality is one manifestation of the low end of the trait continuum for openness to experience. For sure, not all people who score low on *O* would be classified as authoritarian. But authoritarianism tends to be highly negatively associated with *O*, meaning that there is a strong tendency for low scores on *O* to be associated with high scores on measures of authoritarianism. Trapnell (1994) reported a correlation of -.57 between *O* and Altemeyer's (1981) measure of right-wing authoritarianism in a sample of 722 individuals. This is a very robust correlation in a sample so large. While low *O* and authoritarianism are by no means the same thing, they would appear to covary and to share many similarities. Like authoritarians, people low in *O* are expected to value conventional norms and rules and to be suspicious of complex, imaginative, and nonconforming expressions of the human spirit—expressions that may threaten the security of the status quo. At the heart of the overlap between low *O* and authoritarianism, moreover, may be an intolerance of ambiguity. Winter (1996) suggests that "the key component of authoritarianism is actually a cognitive style—intolerance of ambiguity or rigidity" (p. 218). The person low in *O* prefers simple solutions and clear answers to life's problems. Too much abstraction, too much complexity, too many different points of view get in the way of *the truth.* Consistent with this interpretation are the findings of Peterson and Lane (2001) who show that authoritarianism in students is negatively correlated with grades in liberal arts courses, though not in courses geared toward technical knowledge. The authors suggest that authoritarian students find it difficult to deal with the cognitive ambiguity that often prevails in a liberal arts curriculum, the mix of conflicting views and theories, and the disquieting demand to make sense of difficult intellectual and human problems in the absence of a clear-cut system of absolute truth.

The authoritarian personality, therefore, would appear to share some basic features with low levels of the trait openness to experience. Not only do empirical findings show a strong association between low *O* and authoritarianism, but the two constructs are defined in somewhat similar ways. Perhaps the most important commonality between the two is an intolerance for ambiguity. At the same time, there would seem to be features of authoritarianism that have little to do with *O*. For example, the classic definition of the authoritarian personality includes such characteristics as "authoritarian aggression," "power and toughness," and "destructiveness and cynicism" (Adorno et al., 1950). These characteristics seem to relate to other trait domains in the Big Five taxonomy. Authoritarianism may be something of a blend—combining low levels of *O* with trait constructs that are found in one or more of the other four trait clusters. The obvious candidate for inclusion in this regard is the Big Five trait domain of agreeableness *(A)*. The low pole of *A* includes such descriptors as "aggressive," "cruel," and "tough-minded." At minimum, the authoritarian personality may represent a trait combination of low *O* and low *A*.

C AND *A:* CONSCIENTIOUSNESS AND AGREEABLENESS

It has been claimed that when Sigmund Freud was once asked what makes for psychological health and maturity in the adult years he answered simply, in German: *Lieben und Arbeiten.* To love and to work. Virtually any trait can have some influence on our closest personal relationships and the important work we do. But the Big Five traits of conscientiousness (*C*) and agreeableness (*A*) seem thematically to be especially close to the worlds of work and love, respectively. C and A speak directly to those instrumental roles we associate with work, from schoolwork to job performance, and with love, from friendships, to romance, to parenting.

The Big Five trait domain of **conscientiousness** (**C**) encompasses a great many characteristics of personality that center on how hard-working, self-disciplined, responsible, reliable, dutiful, well-organized, and persevering a person is. At the high end of the C continuum, people may be described as well-organized, efficient, and dependable (Goldberg, 1990). They approach tasks in a systematic and orderly fashion. They analyze problems logically. They provide concise answers to questions and perform according to exacting standards in their work and their play. You can depend on conscientious people. Self-disciplined and duty-bound, they are reliable and responsible in their dealings with other people. They are rarely late for meetings; they don't miss class. Conscientious people plan their lives carefully, according to principles and goals. While they may seem overly cautious at times, they are, nonetheless, able to make hard decisions and stick by them when things get rough. They are persistent, steady, predictable, conventional, and thrifty. At the other end of the continuum, people low on the C dimension tend to be disorganized, haphazard, inefficient, careless, negligent, and undependable. It is difficult to predict what they will do from one situation to the next, so erratic and inconsistent is their behavior. Life lacks plan and purpose. Low-C people may be lazy and slothful, indecisive and wishy-washy, extravagant and impractical. Unconscientious people have little regard for serious standards of work or morality. While their spontaneity may seem like a breath of fresh air in the face of stale social conventions, their irresponsibility and utter inability to stand *by others* or stand *for anything* in the long run make them very poor risks in friendship and in love.

People high in **agreeableness** (**A**) are nice men and women. But they are more than nice. Agreeableness incorporates the expressive qualities of love and empathy, friendliness, cooperation, and care. Indeed, the term *agreeableness* may be a bit too meek for the A domain in traits, a domain that includes such concepts as altruism, affection, and many of the most admirably humane aspects of human personality (Digman, 1990; John & Srivastava, 1990). Individuals at the high end of the A continuum are described as interpersonally warm, cooperative, accommodating, helpful, patient, cordial, empathic, kind, understanding, courteous, natural, and sincere (Goldberg, 1990). They are also described as especially honest, ethical, and selfless—peace-loving humanists, committed to their friends and their family, and to the social good. Their counterparts on the other end of the A continuum, however, get some of the worst press in the entire Big Five lexicon. They are antagonistic, belligerent, harsh, unsympathetic, manipulative, disingenuous, scornful, crude, and cruel. While the low-Cs may be unreliable, the low-As are untrustworthy and malicious. They operate with wanton disregard of other's feelings. They get in fights. They hurt people.

WORK

The trait domain of C would appear to have extensive relevance for the world of work. Hogan and Ones (1997) identify the three central themes of C as control, orderliness, and hard work. McCrae and Costa (1997b) divide the C domain into the six facets of competence, order, dutifulness, achievement striving, self-discipline, and deliberation. People who score high on measures of C are described as hard-working, responsible, well-organized, and productive. These would appear to be characteristics of personality that would promote success in the world of work. Of course, there are many factors, both within the person and in the environment, that can predict occupational success. But one is hard pressed to imagine a work situation in which being high in C would *not* be an asset.

Results from applied research in work settings underscore the importance of conscientiousness (Hogan, Hogan, & Roberts, 1996; Hogan & Ones, 1997). Barrick and Mount (1991) reviewed a large number of studies examining how the various trait scales that can be subsumed within the Big Five framework have been used to predict occupational success in a wide range of work settings. Of the Big Five traits, *C* was the one that consistently predicted success across different organizations, jobs, and situations. Examining professional positions, police work, business managers, salespersons, and skilled and semiskilled jobs, Barrick and Mount found that employees scoring high on measures subsumed under *C* were rated more highly by supervisors on such dimensions as job proficiency and training proficiency. The correlations between *C* and job ratings are typically in the +.25 range. While these are not extremely robust correlations, they are typically statistically significant, and they indicate that measures of *C* have practical utility in predicting important occupational outcomes. Furthermore, *C* proves to be an even stronger predictor as the level of occupational autonomy increases. Barrick and Mount (1993) showed that as the level of autonomy and responsibility for a given job goes up, individual differences in conscientiousness become even more powerful predictors of job performance. Longitudinal studies indicate that high levels of *C* predict job success many years in the future. In a study of graduates of an elite women's college, Roberts (1994) found that measures of *C*-related traits taken in college predicted successful participation in the paid labor force 20 years later.

Why is *C* so consistently related to job performance? There are probably many reasons. First, people high in *C* work very hard to begin with. They may put in longer hours and put forth greater effort to achieve the goals of their job. Second, they may be better organized and efficient. Among the many different features of conscientiousness is the tendency to exert an organizing control over one's environment, to be able to prioritize tasks and schedule events in ways that maximize productivity. Third, people high in *C* tend to play by the rules. They believe in and behave in accord with the norms, values, and standards set forth by society in general and by various socializing institutions in particular—institutions such as one's school, church, or company. They see themselves as being dutiful, principled, and honest. Hogan and Ones (1997) identify conformity and impulse control to be important ingredients in the mix of traits that make up *C*. Industrial-organizational psychology has developed a number of *integrity tests* to assess these important qualities in employees. Integrity tests are typically filled with items that fit under the Big Five domains of conscientiousness and (low) neuroticism. Reviewing the research in this area, one study estimates the average correlation between integrity tests and ratings of job performance in a variety of settings to be +.41, suggesting a very robust relationship between the two (Ones, Viswesvaran, & Schmidt, 1993).

The fact that people high in *C* tend to be relatively more rule-abiding than those scoring low in *C* has been documented in many ways. For example, Roberts and Bogg (2004) showed that young women scoring high on dimensions of *C* were less likely than those scoring lower to abuse alcohol and drugs during their early- and middle-adult years. One of the most useful measures of *C* is the Socialization scale of the California Psychological Inventory (CPI; see chapter 4), which was originally developed to distinguish between delinquents and nondelinquents. In developing the Socialization scale, Gough (1960) proposed that people are normally distributed along a continuum of socialization from those who are unusually scrupulous and conscientious on one end to those who are hostile to society's rules and conventions on the other. In the middle of the continuum are most citizens, who are generally compliant and tend to obey many, if not most, of society's rules. Decades of research on the CPI scale for Socialization show that it is a very valuable predictor of behaviors that are relevant to rule compliance. Relatedly, scales that measure personal *reliability* (another component of C) are negatively associated with irresponsible behaviors in the workplace. People who score *low* on these scales tend to miss work more often, tend to be recommended for counseling because of problems on the job, and tend to be fired more often from jobs. By contrast, those scoring high on personal reliability receive more commendations from their supervisors (Hogan & Ones, 1997). Low scores on personal reliability are also positively associated with blood alcohol levels of persons arrested for drunk driving (Hogan & Ones, 1997). In a study of almost 500 young adults, Arthur and Graziano (1996) found that overall levels of C were negatively associated with automobile accidents. In other words, drivers who described themselves as self-disciplined, responsible, reliable, and dependable were less likely to be involved in car accidents than those drivers who rated themselves lower on these characteristics of C.

Even before we learn to drive, it appears that conscientiousness can confer important benefits. The best predictor of educational achievement may be a person's overall intellectual aptitude, as assessed on intelligence tests and other aptitude measures. Beyond these, however, C may play an important role. Renaming C the "will to achieve," Digman (1989) reviews many studies to suggest that this dimension of personality can account for a good deal of the variance in achievement left unexplained by aptitude measures. In other words, intelligence is not the only thing that matters when it comes to predicting school grades (Gray & Watson, 2002). Conscientiousness is also very important. In a similar vein, Graziano and Ward (1992) examined adjustment to junior high school in a sample of 91 adolescents. Classroom teacher ratings of how well the students had adjusted to the challenges of school were positively associated with students' self-ratings of C.

Beyond conscientiousness, other personality traits have been shown to predict occupational success for particular occupations or under particular conditions. As I described a few pages back, extraversion has been linked to success in certain arenas of business, such as sales and management. One study indicates that agreeableness is associated with career stability (Laursen, Pulkkinen, & Adams, 2002). Agreeableness is also a good predictor of job success in some situations. Along with low levels of N, high levels of A are strongly associated with positive ratings of employees working in customer service jobs (Hogan, Hogan, & Roberts, 1996). When exchanging merchandise or making inquiries about products, customers prefer to deal with emotionally stable and friendly service providers. Employees high in A also appear to work very well in teams (Barrick & Mount, 1993). They cooperate well with other employees and they work hard to reach group consensus. By contrast, however, high A is negatively associated with ratings of creativity and autonomy among managers. Agreeableness can sometimes get in the way of innovation. Individuals who are especially kind, considerate, and cooperative may have a somewhat more difficult time formulating bold initiatives and carrying out independent courses of action. For these efforts it may sometimes help to be at least moderately disagreeable.

LOVE

Agreeable people are easier to love than disagreeable people. They may also be better lovers, or at least better friends, collegial colleagues, caring caregivers. Part of their value in the realm of love is their sincere commitment to other people and their willingness to conform to the norms of interpersonal communion. Like people high in C, they play by the rules, but in this case it is the rules of intimacy, love, and personal commitment. You can trust them. They will not betray you. Nor will they go out of their way to disagree with you. Digman and

Takemoto-Chock (1981) suggest the label "friendly compliance" (versus "hostile noncompliance") for this trait domain. Hogan (1982) calls it "social likability." McCrae and Costa (1997b) list trust, straightforwardness, altruism, compliance, modesty, and tender mindedness as the six facets of *A*. As we saw in chapter 2, human beings evolved to live in small groups in which interpersonal cooperation likely proved crucial for individual and group survival. Agreeableness, then, would appear to have profound evolutionary significance:

> If we recognize that 99% of human evolution occurred when humans lived in hunting/gathering bands consisting of approximately 30 individuals and if we recognize that cooperation is seen as an essential attribute in such groups, then it is plausible that an individual's agreeableness might be a dimension receiving special attention. It is not implausible that dispositional disagreeableness and selfishness could lead to exclusion from social groups. (Graziano & Eisenberg, 1997, p. 798)

An important component of *A* is what Graziano and Eisenberg (1997) call "prosocial tendencies." Prosocial behavior is typically defined as voluntary behavior intended to benefit others. People who engage in high levels of prosocial behavior are typically described with trait words that fit well into the *A* domain, such as sympathetic, generous, kind, helpful, and considerate. A considerable body of research in developmental psychology examines the family conditions and learning experiences under which prosocial behavior is nurtured and encouraged. Cross-cultural research shows that children who are routinely expected to assist in caring for other family members are more prosocial than children from cultures in which such expectations are not stressed (Whiting & Whiting, 1975). Moreover, children are more likely to engage in prosocial actions when they have been exposed to altruistic models or when they have been instructed in the virtues of putting others' welfare on a par with their own. An important body of research has sought to articulate the main features and determinants of the "altruistic personality" in adulthood. Strong predictors of altruistic behavior among adults are measures of sympathy, social responsibility, mature perspective taking, and high moral standards (Bierhoff, Klein, & Kramp, 1991; Carlo, Eisenberg, Troyer, Switzer, & Speer, 1991; Krueger, Hicks, & McGue, 2001; Oliner & Oliner, 1988).

In the realm of direct caregiving, we would expect that mothers and fathers who are dispositionally high in *A* might be more effective in their parenting roles than parents low in *A*. Belsky, Crnic, and Woodworth (1995) administered trait measures to mothers and fathers when their children were 10 months of age and then observed the parents as they interacted with their children in their own homes when the children were 15 and 21 months old. They also obtained measures of transient mood states and daily hassles reported by the parents just before the 15-month and 21-month assessments. Their results indicated that being an agreeable parent (high *A*) contributes to high levels of positive mood and thereby to high levels of cognitive stimulation and low levels of neglect and detachment in interactions with children. *A* was an especially strong predictor of quality of parenting in mothers. The trait of neuroticism was also implicated. High levels of *N* contributed to negative moods and to experiencing daily hassles, which were associated with insensitivity in interactions with children. The researchers concluded that "from a child's perspective, it would appear that one is better off—in terms of the pleasure of everyday interactions with mother—having a parent who is agreeable and not neurotic" (p. 926).

In the realm of friendship, research suggests that agreeableness is associated with interpersonal sensitivity and conflict resolution. Young adolescents high in *A* manage to avoid fights and conflicts with others and are much less likely to be bullies or targets of bullies, compared to those low in agreeableness (Jensen-Campbell, Adams, Perry, Workman, Furdella, & Egan, 2002). When faced with conflict situations, those high in *A* exhibit behavioral strategies aimed at defusing the conflict and maintaining warm and friendly relations with others (Jensen-Campbell & Graziano, 2002). Agreeableness is also associated with efforts to moderate one's own strong emotions in order to keep relationships running smoothly (Tobin, Graziano, Vanman, & Tassinary, 2000).

In the realm of love, Shaver and Brennan (1992) examined the relations between Big Five trait ratings and adult attachment styles. As we saw in chapter 2, Bowlby and Ainsworth's theory of caregiver–infant attachment has been expanded to incorporate individual differences in adult attachment styles. Adults with a secure attachment style find it relatively easy to get close to others. They seem especially comfortable with intimacy, friendship, and love. Adults with an anxious-ambivalent style, by contrast, desire closeness but either draw back from others or feel that they drive others away when they attempt to establish intimate relationships. Adults with an "avoidant" attachment style feel that they cannot trust other people and therefore withdraw from close relationships.

Shaver and Brennan administered a measure of attachment styles and standard questionnaire for assessing the Big Five Traits to 242 college students. Figure 5.4 shows the mean trait scores for the three groups of attachment styles. Students showing the secure attachment style scored significantly higher on agreeableness compared with those with the avoidant styles. Anxious-ambivalent students scored in between—not significantly higher nor lower than the other two groups. Extraversion and neuroticism also showed significant differences. Students with secure attachment scored significantly higher on *E* and lower on *N* than avoidant and anxious-ambivalent students. Conscientiousness and openness were unrelated to attachment. The results suggest that a secure attachment style in early adulthood is linked with traits denoting energy and positive affect *(E)*, interpersonal warmth *(A)*, and low levels of negative affectivity or neuroticism *(N)*. Correlational studies such as this one cannot tell us about the causal relations between traits and attachment styles—whether, that is, trait levels precede or lead to certain attachment styles, attachment styles lead to traits, or the two are caused by some third factor, such as early caregiving experiences or genetic effects. But the research is still instructive as to how traits and relational styles line up with each other. And it is further noteworthy for its attempt to bring together two lines of personality theory and research—attachment and traits—that are usually thought to be quite separate.

A longitudinal study by Asendorpf and Wilpers (1998) was designed to examine the causal effects of personality traits on the quality of social relationships. The researchers tracked the social relationships of 132 German students over the course of 18 months, beginning when the students entered the university as freshmen. On six different occasions over the 18-month period, the students completed extensive questionnaires describing the status of the most important relationships in their lives. The questionnaires examined romantic relationships, friendships, and family relationships. Among the most important features of these relationships assessed on the questionnaires were amount of contact spent with other people, amount of available social support, conflict in relationships, and falling in love. In addition, the students participated in a 21-day intensive diary exercise. During the 21-day period, they recorded all social interactions they participated in by filling out a set of standard forms at the end of each day. To assess individual differences in traits, self-report measures of the Big Five factors were administered to the students every six months.

FIGURE 5.4	MEAN SCORES ON THE BIG FIVE TRAITS AS A FUNCTION OF ADULT ATTACHMENT STYLE

Students showing secure attachment styles tend to score higher on traits of extraversion and agreeableness and lower on neuroticism compared to students with insecure (anxious and avoidant) attachment styles.

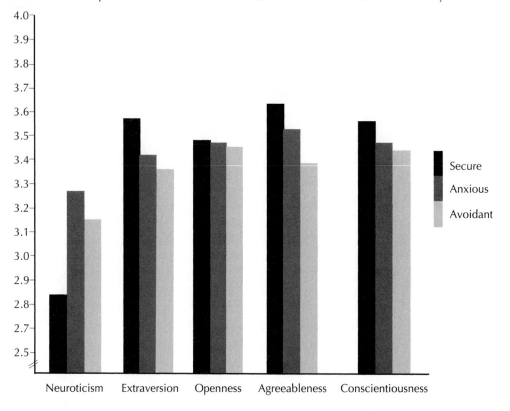

NOTE: Items were answered on a 1–5 continuum with higher scores indicating higher ratings on the given trait dimension. A total of 226 subjects participated in the study.

SOURCE: "Attachment Styles and the "Big Five" Personality Traits: Their Connections With Each Other and With Romantic Relationship Outcomes," by P. R. Shaver & K. A. Brennan, 1992, *Personality and Social Psychology Bulletin, 18,* p. 539.

Because they obtained multiple measures of traits and social relationships over an extended period of time, Asendorpf and Wilpers were able to determine the extent to which traits predict relationships and relationships predict traits. The results showed that whereas students' traits remained relatively stable over time, their relationships changed in many significant ways. In general, individual differences in personality traits influenced social relationships, but not vice versa. The traits of extraversion, conscientiousness, and agreeableness influenced the number and quality of the students' social relationships, whereas strong changes in these relationships had no effect on any of the Big Five personality scales. Being high in extraversion led to developing relatively large social networks, spending more time in social interactions, and feeling that one has more social support from friends. In addition, extraverts were more likely to fall in love over the 18-month period than were introverts. Conscientiousness predicted higher levels of contact with family members. The authors speculated that the more conscientious students may have felt stronger bonds and more obligations to their home families than students low in *C*. Agreeableness predicted levels of conflict. Students high in *A* were less likely than those low in *A* to experience conflict in their relationships with members of the opposite sex. Agreeable people are predisposed to turn the other cheek in times of interpersonal stress and avoid serious conflicts with those they love. They do not antagonize their lovers, and they are not readily antagonized. In the tumultuous world of love, people high in agreeableness are able to maintain relative harmony and peace.

LIFE

The benefits of conscientiousness and agreeableness may go beyond the worlds of work and love. Recent research suggests that high levels of *C* and *A* may enhance overall quality of life and even promote longevity. McCrae and Costa (1991) showed that self-report measures of *C* and *A* are positively correlated with psychological well-being. In a sample of 429 adults, both conscientiousness and agreeableness were positively related to reports of positive affect, negatively related to reports of negative affect, and positively related to total well-being. McCrae and Costa suggest that high levels of conscientiousness and agreeableness create life conditions that promote well-being. They write:

> Although personality traits may directly affect the tendencies to experience positive or negative emotions, they may also have indirect effects on well-being: Certain traits may be instrumental in creating conditions that promote happiness or unhappiness. In particular, the dimensions of *A* and *C* might be hypothesized to have instrumental effects on well-being. Agreeable individuals are warm, generous, and loving; conscientious people are efficient, competent, and hard-working. The interpersonal bonds that *A* fosters and the achievements and accomplishments that *C* promotes may contribute to greater quality of life and higher life satisfaction. This is perhaps what Freud meant when he suggested that *Liebe und Arbeit*, love and work, were the keys to psychological health and happiness. (McCrae and Costa, 1991, p. 228)

The role of personality traits in determining how long a person may actually live has been examined in an impressive longitudinal study of intellectually gifted men and women. In 1921, Lewis Terman and his associates launched what has become the most famous longitudinal study in the history of psychology. Terman chose more than 1,500 children (mean age 11 years) living in California who all scored at very high levels on standard tests of intellectual aptitude. These extremely bright boys and girls—later dubbed the "Termites"—were administered various psychological measures and followed up at 5- to 10-year intervals for the rest of their lives. Indeed, the survivors are still being followed. Many of the Termites grew up to be very successful people. Included in the sample are many businesspeople, physicians, lawyers, teachers, writers, and scientists. Nonetheless, a wide range of lifestyles and occupational groups are represented.

By the year 1986, about two-thirds of the participants in the original Terman sample were still alive. All of the survivors were at least 70 years old by this time. A group of researchers culled through the massive data sets available for the Termites to obtain measures of childhood personality traits, family stresses, parental divorce during childhood, adult adjustment,

FEATURE 5.C

EYSENCK'S PSYCHOTICISM: LOW A, LOW C, AND SOME OTHER BAD THINGS

Hans Eysenck proposed that the entire gamut of personality characteristics can be divided neatly into three super traits: extraversion–introversion, neuroticism, and psychoticism. The first two of Eysenck's Big Three correspond well to the dimensions of E and N in the Big Five framework. But what about psychoticism? Eysenck (1952) proposed that a susceptibility to psychosis represented an important dimension of personality. Even in the 19th century, the founders of modern psychiatry observed that the biological relatives of schizophrenics and other psychotics often showed signs of abnormality themselves, such as bizarre ideas. Might there not be an underlying susceptibility to psychosis that, in mild form, is present in the general population? Eysenck believed there was, and he developed questionnaires to assess individual differences among people in the extent to which they expressed characteristics that, in stronger forms, are typically associated with the severe mental illnesses that are grouped under the label of psychosis.

Questionnaire measures of psychoticism ask questions about such things as liking practical jokes that harm others, indifference to the suffering of animals and children, experiencing bizarre thoughts and feelings, preferring unusual or antisocial activities, and a host of other behavioral and attitudinal characteristics. People who score high on psychoticism are described as highly impulsive, aloof, nonconforming, aggressive, inhumane, and lacking in responsibility. They have disregard for the law, for danger, and for the feelings of others. They have a taste for the bizarre and even the macabre. They tend to hold dogmatic and extreme attitudes about social issues—standing on the extreme right or left wing of political issues. By contrast, people low in psychoticism are described as cooperative, empathic, tender-minded, and conventional. Consistent with these generalizations, research has shown that people high on psychoticism

tend to have unsatisfactory marriages, poor work records and low levels of occupational satisfaction, higher incidence of infidelity, a greater willingness to engage in high-risk behaviors of many kinds, and favorable attitudes about the use of violence (Corr, 2000). A strong antisocial theme runs through the psychoticism literature, suggesting that this dimension may tap into tendencies toward both psychosis and psychopathy.

The susceptibility to psychosis-psychopathy is evident from an early age (Corr, 2000). Children who score high on the child version of Eysenck's psychoticism scale are more prone to learning and behavioral difficulties and antisocial behaviors. They also tend to be disliked by teachers, who see their behavior as spiteful and disruptive. Experimental research indicates that people high in psychoticism may have deficits in stimulus processing, as seen in their inability to inhibit unimportant and irrelevant stimuli. The same problem of stimulus inhibition is characteristic of some schizophrenics, such as those who report recurrent hallucinations. In addition, defective stimulus processing may result in impaired learning of society's rules, which may account for the poor socialization that is so characteristic of psychoticism. This inability to inhibit irrelevant input, however, can also have a positive side to it. Some individuals high in psychoticism produce especially rich and fluid cognitive associations, which may actually enhance their creativity.

Where does psychoticism fit into the Big Five scheme? A great deal of the content in Eysenck's conceptualization of psychoticism can be found on the low poles of agreeableness and conscientiousness. Like people who score low on both C and A, individuals high in psychoticism are irresponsible, nonconforming, cruel, and aggressive. Those scoring low in psychoticism, by contrast would appear to be relatively agreeable and conscientious. Beyond A and C, there would appear to be some

(CONTINUES)

FEATURE 5.C (CONTINUED)

other elements in Eysenck's conception. The strong impulsivity component can be found in some characterizations of extraversion and neuroticism. The rigid and extreme ideological beliefs may reflect low openness to experience. The most bizarre and psychotic-like traces of psychoticism, however, are difficult to place within the Big Five space. Personality and clinical psychologists have not reached a consensus on the extent to which the Big Five dimensions can capture the vicissitudes of abnormal psychology. Some argue that the characteristics of different psychopathologies are qualitatively different from those that define the realm of normal personality. Others argue that psychopathologies are not different in kind but simply amount, that the behavioral patterns we associate with psychopathological types are the product of extreme scores on the same dimensions of personality that can be used to assess individual differences in the "normal" range of human functioning. This controversy is not going to be resolved in the near future. As for the trait of psychoticism, however, it makes good sense to say that what Eysenck saw as a susceptibility to psychosis and psychopathy looks a lot like very low *A* and very low *C*, with a few other very bad things thrown in.

and health behaviors (Friedman, Tucker, Schwartz, Tomlinson-Keasy, Martin, Wingard, & Criqui, 1995; Friedman, Tucker, Tomlinson-Keasy, Schwartz, Wingard, & Criqui, 1993). Their goal was to use psychological and social factors present in childhood and adulthood to predict longevity. In one analysis, the authors compared data from those Termites who had died before the age of 70 and those who lived beyond 70. In another procedure commonly used in epidemiological studies, they employed what is called a statistical *survival analysis.* A survival analysis estimates the effects of a series of predictors on the probability of people living to advanced ages.

One of the strongest predictors of longevity in human beings is gender. As has been documented time and again, the researchers working with the Terman sample found that the female subjects tend to live longer than the male subjects. A history of family stresses was also significantly associated with longevity—the greater the stress, the lower the longevity. Among the strongest predictors, however, was also childhood personality. In particular, childhood ratings of personality traits subsumed under the general umbrella of *conscientiousness predicted how long the men and women in the Terman study were likely to live.* Conscientious and socially responsible children in the Terman study are statistically more likely to live into old age than their less conscientious peers. The results of the survival analysis for *C* are shown in Figure 5.5. The four curves show the survival probability for high-*C* females, low-*C* females, high-*C* males, and low-*C* males as a function of age. Consider females first. Terman women who in childhood scored high on conscientiousness traits have about an 82% probability of living to be at least 70 years of age while women who in childhood scored low in conscientiousness show about a 77% probability of living to be age 70. Among the Terman men, the probabilities of living to at least age 70 for high-*C* versus low-*O* groups are approximately 73% and 67%, respectively. While these may not sound like large differences, they are rather striking for studies of this sort. The authors point out that the effects of childhood *C* on longevity are about as statistically strong as the biological risk factors of high blood pressure and serum cholesterol. In other words, the negative effect of high blood pressure on longevity is about as strong as the negative effect of low conscientiousness on longevity. Other childhood personality traits measured in this study—sociability (an aspect of *E*), self-esteem, emotional stability *(N)*, and energy level—did not predict longevity.

FIGURE 5.5	SURVIVAL AND CONSCIENTIOUSNESS

The probability of a 20-year-old's surviving to advanced ages is a function of gender (females live longer) and the trait of conscientiousness (high conscientiousness is associated with greater longevity). Note: High = scoring in the top 25% of the distribution on C in childhood. Low = scoring in the bottom 25% of the distribution on C in childhood.

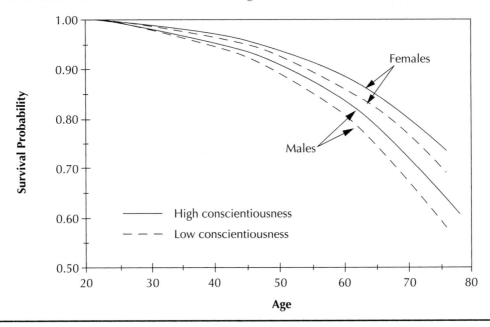

We do not know why children who are highly conscientious grow up to live longer than children who are low on conscientiousness. Are high-C children more likely to adopt a healthful lifestyle when they grow up? Are they more careful and less likely to take risks? Do they live longer because they develop successful careers and avocations that keep them busy and satisfied with life? The authors of the Terman study point out that tracing the mechanisms that link C to longevity is a very difficult task. They also remind us that these results, as provocative as they are, come from only one study, and like any study, it has limitations. All of the participants in the study were white and intellectually gifted. Most grew up to be members of the middle and upper-middle classes, and they all lived in American society during the middle of the 20th century. The contours of their lives were doubtlessly shaped by a myriad of cultural, historical, and personal factors. The Terman study is the first to document a significant link between childhood personality traits and longevity across seven decades of life. The results suggest that the Big Five domain of conscientiousness may have important implications not only for the quality of life but for how long people actually live. More research is needed, however, to tease apart this relationship and to examine, in more detail, the ways in which personality traits may impact the long course of adult life.

SUMMARY

1. How might you ever organize the many different personality traits that could be invoked to account for human individuality? In the 1980s, an answer to this question began to emerge as the result of decades of research employing statistical analysis of responses to trait questionnaires and rating scales. A growing number of personality psychologists today believe that traits can be organized into five basic trait clusters—called the Big Five. While considerable disagreement still exists with respect to the exact meanings of each of the Big Five traits, one well-established taxonomy labels the five: extraversion–introversion *(E)*, neuroticism *(N)*, openness to experience *(O)*, conscientiousness *(C)*, and agreeableness *(A)*. Cross-cultural studies of trait ratings suggest that factors resembling most, if not all, of these five dimensions can be found in many different languages and cultures.

2. Introduced to modern psychology by Carl Jung and Hans Eysenck, extraversion– introversion *(E)* encompasses such qualities of human personality as gregariousness, assertiveness, excitement seeking, and positive affectivity. Highly extraverted people are described as generally outgoing, sociable, and energetic; highly introverted people (low in *E*) are seen as generally withdrawn, quiet, and introspective. Arguably the most well-researched trait in all of personality psychology, extraversion has been empirically linked to individual differences in social behavior, occupational choice, learning, and emotional life. Recent studies on *E* show that highly extraverted people tend to experience more positive emotional events in their lives and report higher levels of happiness and life satisfaction compared with introverted people. Possible reasons for this relationship include enhanced social skills, confidence and assertiveness in social relations, and a tendency to ignore or gloss over social punishments on the part of extraverts. Empirical support for the connection

between *E* and positive emotions is so consistent that some psychologists have argued that *E* should be renamed "positive affectivity."

3. Eysenck argued that individual differences in *E* were the product of innate differences in the organization of the central nervous system. More specifically, he suggested that by virtue of differences in the functioning of the brain's reticular activating system, people differ with respect to characteristic levels of arousal and arousability. Extraverts operate at a generally lower level of arousal, he reasoned, and therefore seek out more stimulation to raise arousal to an optimal level. By contrast, introverts operate at a generally higher level of arousal, and therefore they reach an optimal level more quickly, after which they are likely to withdraw from social stimulation. Empirical support for Eysenck's biologically based ideas has been mixed, in part because psychologists today question the validity of the concept of general cortical arousal. A newer line of research has suggested, however, that individual differences in *E*, or positive affectivity, may be linked to a behavioral approach system (BAS) in the brain. The BAS is hypothesized to govern positive approach behaviors in response to incentives. Important components of the BAS may be dopamine pathways and electrical activity in the left anterior portion of the brain.

4. Eysenck also pioneered theory and research on the second of the Big Five traits: neuroticism *(N)*. Measures of chronic anxiety, depression, excessive emotionality, nervousness, moodiness, hostility, vulnerability, self-consciousness, and hypochondriasis all converge in this general factor, which is most generally described as a continuum from emotional instability (high *N*) to emotional stability (low *N*). Individual differences in *N* have been linked to a wide range of behavioral outcomes, from interpersonal communication patterns

to reports of health problems. Research shows that individuals high in N experience more negative emotional events, compared with individuals low in N. The connections between N and negative affect are so consistent that some psychologists argue that N should be renamed "negative affectivity." People high in N experience more stress in their lives, and they tend to employ relatively ineffective and nonproductive coping strategies for dealing with the stress.

5. While Eysenck believed that individual differences in N were biologically rooted in differences in the brain's limbic system, more recent approaches have implicated what has been called a behavioral inhibition system (BIS). The BIS is hypothesized to mediate responses to threat and signs of danger, punishment, and extreme novelty. One key component in the BIS may be a tiny, almond-shaped region in the forebrain called the amygdala, which appears to be implicated in the production and control of fear. In addition, electrical activity in the right anterior regions of the brain have also been linked to experiences of negative affectivity.

6. Variously called "culture," "intellectance," and "inquiring intellect," the trait cluster of openness to experience (O) encompasses many dimensions of personality that relate to cognitive functioning. While intelligence itself is generally not viewed to be part of O per se, people high in O have many intellectual interests; they are also described as imaginative, curious, broad-minded, creative, intellectually daring, nontraditional, and complex. By contrast, those scoring low in O are usually viewed to be unimaginative, pragmatic, down-to-earth, having narrow interests, and relatively simple. O is positively associated with level of education. While O has been empirically linked to such things as having a rich and complex emotional life and displaying flexibility in response to life challenges, it has also been linked to less positive outcomes such as beliefs in esoteric and dubious phenomena and to mild forms of magical and bizarre thinking. The only Big Five trait to be directly associated with political attitudes, people high in O tend to be somewhat more liberal in their sociopolitical outlooks (underscoring progressive change, skepticism toward traditional authority, and tolerance for competing viewpoints) while people low in O tend to be more conservative (underscoring stability over change, obedience toward authority, and preference for a uniform or unifying point of view).

7. One interesting personality constellation that is associated with extremely *low* scores on O is the authoritarian personality. Authoritarianism combines rigid adherence to conventional values, uncritical attitudes toward authority, opposition to the imaginative and subjective aspects of life, power and toughness, cynicism, and a tendency to condemn those who do not fit into the traditional frameworks of society and religion. Research has shown that authoritarians tend to express higher levels of overt prejudice toward outgroups and stronger support for aggressive actions in response to threat. Although low O and authoritarianism are not the same thing, they have much in common. At the heart of their commonality is an intolerance for ambiguity.

8. Conscientiousness (C) encompasses a great many trait terms that center on how hard-working, self-disciplined, responsible, reliable, dutiful, well-organized, and persevering a person is. Individual differences in C are consistent predictors of instrumental effectiveness in work. Across many different types of occupational groups, employees who are high in C are rated by their supervisors and co-workers as more competent and proficient. Low C, by contrast, is associated with job absenteeism and being fired from jobs. In general, people high in C are more rule-abiding than those low in C, a finding that is reflected in the fact that low C is correlated with alcohol abuse, criminality, and even poor driving. A seven-decade longitudinal study of intellectually gifted women and men shows that ratings of conscientiousness-related traits in childhood are predictive of longevity. Adults who were rated as high in conscientiousness as children were statistically more likely to live to

an older age compared with adults who were rated as children to be low in *C*.

9. Variously labeled "friendly compliance" and "social likability," agreeableness *(A)* incorporates the expressive qualities of love and empathy, friendliness, cooperation, care, altruism, and affection. The negative pole of *A* denotes qualities of antagonism and aggressiveness. Research has shown that highly agreeable mothers provide their infants with more warmth and cognitive stimulation, compared with mothers scoring low on *A*. Research has also connected *A* to attachment styles and the quality of romantic love. College students high in *A* tend to have fewer disagreements and conflicts with members of the opposite sex.

10. Eysenck's concept of psychoticism refers to a tendency toward psychopathy and psychosis. This trait seems to incorporate very low levels of agreeableness and conscientiousness as well as a host of other troubling characteristics, such as bizarre and illogical thinking patterns. In general, the Big Five trait scheme, and most research on personality traits, mainly concerns individual differences within relatively normal samples. Psychoticism, therefore, has not received extensive research attention within personality psychology. Psychologists disagree about the extent to which severe psychopathology can be conceived in terms of the same categories that apply to normal personality trait dimensions.

You may not be old enough to have gone to your first high school reunion. I have only been to one. In 1982 I went back to Gary, Indiana, for my 10-year reunion (class of '72, Gary Lew Wallace High School). As I remember it, probably 200 people showed up for the reunion, out of a graduating class of almost 500. So many things change in your life between your 18th and 28th birthdays, especially if you move away from home after graduation. Returning to the scene of so much adolescent anxiety, I was now a young adult, married, employed, well-educated, and more confident in life than I had been 10 years before. I felt I had changed, and I am sure that many of my former classmates in the crowd felt that they had changed significantly, too. After all, we had all grown up now; many of us had gone on to earn college degrees; some had joined the military; many had traveled; most of us were working; many had started families; a few were embarking on a second (or even third) marriage. Certainly, our life circumstances had changed.

But had *we* changed? Were we really different, as people, than we were before? For some of us, the answer surely seemed to be yes. Take, for example, Mary Anne Cromwell (I've changed the names). I hardly recognized her. I remembered Mary Anne Cromwell as a shy and painfully thin adolescent girl, poorly dressed, not very popular. I know she was the butt of jokes. I am ashamed to admit that as a junior I spread rumors that an ex-friend of mine was in love with Mary Anne; I wanted to get back at him for some insult he had hurled my way (I don't remember what it was). Mary Anne sat next to me in junior-year trigonometry, and I don't believe we ever exchanged words. Well, the 10-year reunion could be labeled "Mary Anne's revenge." Mary Anne had grown up to be a beautiful woman, attracting a crowd of men at the reunion who seemed not even to know that she existed 10 years before. Mary Anne had gone on to get an M.B.A., and she had already enjoyed considerable success in business. What struck me most, though, was her increased poise and her assertiveness. Gone was the timidity and the awkwardness I remembered. Now, you may say that I just didn't know her very well in high school, and that certainly is true. Maybe she always had this poise, and I never saw it. But not too many other people saw it either, it seemed, for everybody I spoke with at the reunion seemed astounded by how much Mary Anne Cromwell had changed.

But let's look at a counter-example—Robert Amundson. Robert is the guy about whom I spread the rumors concerning Mary Anne Cromwell back in our junior year. After my prank, Robert had the good sense to dump me as a friend and move on to more exalted social circles. Actually, Robert was always a social climber, which was one of the reasons our friendship was stormy and short-lived. In high school, I remember him as socially dominant, outgoing, spontaneous, and not especially conscientious. His social dominance was clearly in evidence the night of the reunion. Just like old times, Robert was the center of attention. It seemed to me that he boasted just as much as he always had. He dominated conversations, as he always had. People seemed to accord his opinions an especially high status, just as they always had. The only difference I could see with respect to Robert Amundson was his newfound eagerness to talk with Mary Anne Cromwell.

While Mary Anne Cromwell seemed to have changed significantly, my overall impression from the high school reunion was that Robert Amundson was more the norm. The evidence for continuity in personality seemed very powerful to me that night. I could not help but be struck by how most people seemed so much the same as they had been ten years before. Ten years had passed and yet almost everybody was so recognizable in their characteristic social mannerisms, their modes of relating to others, the way they spoke, even the things they spoke about. Michael still had the best sense of humor. Roberta was still nonconventional and rebellious. Kevin was still obsessed with sports. Barbara still danced in a provocative way. Keith still seemed depressed.

My observations about Mary Anne's "poise," Robert's "social dominance," and Keith's "depressiveness" were attributions about the personality *traits* these people seemed to display, as seen in high school and 10 years later. Do people's dispositional traits change over time? Or do traits remain stable? Can we expect that Robert Amundson will still be socially dominant when I see him, God willing, at my 40-year high-school reunion? Will Mary Anne Cromwell go through new changes over time? What can we expect from Michael or Barbara 40 years after graduating from high school? The issue of stability and change in personality traits leads naturally to a related question: *Where do personality traits come from, anyway?* They don't just emerge out of thin air. Traits must develop, in some sense, over time. Is their development driven by our genes? By our environments? These are surely some of the most interesting questions in all of personality psychology. Some of the answers that are beginning to emerge from personality research may fit your expectations. But I bet some will surprise you.

THE CONTINUITY OF TRAITS

In everyday talk, attributing a trait to a person presupposes a certain degree of continuity over time. If I tell you, for example, that my nephew is a very "agreeable" person, I am implying that his high level of agreeableness has some staying power over time. Despite momentary fluctuations, I am suggesting that he *tends to be* agreeable. Just how long-term that staying power might be, however, is not clear from my attribution. Do I mean that he is likely still to be an agreeable person a week from now? Yes, I do mean to suggest that. What about next year? Probably. Twenty years from now? I don't know. Am I suggesting that he will continue to be a relatively agreeable person for the rest of his life? No, I am not necessarily saying that.

When people use trait terms in everyday talk, they seem to be operating from an implicit assumption that certain features of human individuality are more-or-less stable "for a while." My nephew is a highly agreeable person, and I expect that he will remain highly agreeable for a while. It is not clear how long "for a while" is. But it is long enough in time to allow me to attribute a trait. For this reason, psychologists expect personality trait scales to show high test–retest reliability in the short run (chapter 4). Traits are not supposed to change dramatically from, say, one day to the next. If they did, then they wouldn't be "traits." Therefore, a trait scale that gives wildly different scores for a given individual from one day or week to the next is thought to lack test–retest reliability, and such a scale is likely to be rejected by the scientific community. But what about a given trait for a given person over the long haul? Beyond the "for a while," how much continuity can we expect in traits from one year to the next? From young adulthood to middle adulthood? From childhood through old age?

TWO KINDS OF CONTINUITY

Before we can begin to answer these questions, we need to distinguish between two very different meanings of continuity in personality traits.

The first meaning is **absolute continuity.** Caspi (1998) defines absolute continuity as "constancy in the quantity or amount of an attribute over time" (p. 346). In absolute terms, "how much" social dominance did Robert Amundson have in 1972 and in 1982? Let us say that we administered a well-validated scale of this trait to Robert in 1972, and at that time he scored 27. On the exact same scale in 1982, he again scored 27. In this case, we could say that Robert showed absolute continuity on the trait of social dominance over a 10-year span. But the concept of absolute continuity is virtually never applied to the single individual. Instead, absolute continuity is usually understood in terms of group averages on a given trait (Caspi, 1998). As an example, we might compare the average social dominance score for the graduates of Gary Lew Wallace High School obtained in 1972, when they were 18 years of age, with the average score obtained from the same group of people 10 years later, when they were 28. Such a study would help us answer this question: How much absolute continuity do we observe on social dominance across a 10-year period in the lifespan? If the average scores for age 18 and 28 are highly similar, then we might conclude that the *group,* as a whole, exhibited continuity on this trait. People were no more or less socially dominant, on the average, at age 28 compared with age 18.

The issue of absolute continuity comes into important play when personality psychologists consider certain hypotheses and expectations about human *development.* For example, some developmental theories suggest that adolescence is a time of confusion and anxiety for many people, but that things settle down a bit as individuals move into adulthood (e.g., Blos, 1979). With respect to my reunion experience, then, we might expect that the group average scores on measures of "anxiety" or "insecurity" or even "rebelliousness" might have been higher among my peers in 1972, when we were high school students, than in 1982, when we were young adults. Our expectations would suggest that absolute continuity would *not* occur across this developmental time period, that people in general would change, and that these changes would be captured in changing average scores over time. I did not have the foresight to administer personality tests to my classmates in 1972 and 1982. But my overall gut impressions suggested to me that while there may have been absolute continuity on many traits, a few things did seem to have changed *for the group as a*

Individual differences in personality traits tend to show substantial differential continuity over time. In the same way that this woman is recognizable at three different points in her life, so too may certain personality dispositions— e.g., extraversion, agreeableness, neuroticism—be recognizable over time.

whole. My nonscientific sense was that as 28-year-olds we were generally more comfortable with our lives and our identities in the overall than we had been in high school. Had someone done the study, I would have expected a slight drop in social anxiety from age 18 to age 28 for the group as a whole, and perhaps a slight increase in friendliness, too. But we will, of course, never know.

Differential continuity refers to "the consistency of individual differences within a sample of individuals over time, to the retention of an individual's relative placement in a group" (Caspi, 1998, p. 345). When I suggest that Robert Amundson seemed to be as socially dominant at age 28 as he was at age 18, I am making a statement about differential continuity. I am suggesting that, *relative to his peers,* Robert tends to be pretty high on the social dominance dimension. Differential continuity is always a matter of individuals' relative standing to one another on a given dimension. In the case of Robert's social dominance, I might suggest that in a random sample of, say, 100 of my classmates from Gary Lew Wallace, Robert was probably about the second or third most socially dominant person in 1972. My observations 10 years later suggested to me that he remained toward the top on this dimension, compared again with his peers. But the extent to which the trait social dominance shows differential continuity in my example is a product of not only Robert's placement on the social dominance dimension, but everybody else's placement, too. For there to be high levels of differential continuity for this trait, not only would Robert need to continue to score toward the top of the distribution over time, but other people would also need to hold their relative positions on this trait over time. In other words, if social dominance shows high differential continuity over a 10-year span, then Robert would need to continue to score very high (let's say a "10" on a 10-point scale), Barbara (who, let us say, scored an "8" in 1972) would need to continue to score moderately high, I would need to continue to score in the medium range (let's figure I was around a "5"), and Keith (who scored "2" in 1972) would need to continue to score in the low range. In simple terms, Robert, Barbara, Dan, and Keith would "stay the same" over the 10-year period relative to one another on this trait. They would each continue to hold their positions in the distribution.

The extent to which individuals continue to hold their relative positions on a trait dimension over time is typically calculated with a correlation coefficient (chapter 1). The correlation is calculated between the same individuals' scores on the same trait at Time 1 (in this case, 1972, at age 18) and Time 2 (1982, age 28). High correlation coefficients (those approaching the value of +1.0) suggest high differential continuity. If, for example, we actually had obtained social dominance scores from 100 of my classmates in 1972 and again (the same 100 classmates) in 1982, then we could calculate the correlation between those two sets of scores. Had we done so and had we obtained, let us say, a correlation value of +.80, we would have evidence for very strong differential continuity on this trait. The high value of the correlation coefficient (+.80) would tell us that people tended to hold their relative positions on the given trait over the 10-year span. Thus, a person's score on the trait in 1972 would be a good predictor of the same person's score on the same trait assessed 10 years later. By contrast, had we obtained, let us say, the modest correlation value of +.10 in this study, then we would have to conclude that social dominance, as measured by our scale, does not show strong differential continuity. Low differential continuity means that people's relative positions on the given dimension change unpredictably over time. Thus, if there were low differential continuity on the trait, it would be very difficult to predict a person's social dominance score at age 28 from his or her score at age 18, because individuals' relative positions to one another on this trait would appear to vary markedly over time. In the case of low differential continuity, Keith may have been "low" in social dominance at age 18, but there's no telling where he might score 10 years later. Low differential continuity suggests that people change relative to one another over time on a given dimension. Low differential continuity does not, however, tell us in what direction people change. It simply says that their scores are likely to fluctuate unpredictably.

It is important to note that absolute continuity and differential continuity are completely unrelated to each other. Absolute continuity typically refers to the consistency of the average score on a given trait over time, while differential continuity refers to the stability of individual differences in scores. Because these two metrics are independent of each other, information about one of these forms of continuity tells you little, if anything, about the other. Therefore, just because you have high absolute continuity on a given trait does not mean that you necessarily have high differential continuity. Let me take you, then, through four simple hypotheticals.

In the first hypothetical, we have *high* absolute continuity and *high* differential continuity. Let us imagine that this was the case for social dominance in my reunion example. We would say that the group average score on social dominance at age 18 was very similar to the group average score at age 28 (high absolute continuity), and the relative positions of individuals on the dimension of social dominance did not change much from age 18 to age 28 (high differential continuity). For the second hypothetical, let us consider *low* absolute continuity but *high* differential continuity. Let us imagine that this was the case for the dimension of social anxiety in the reunion example. As a group, the social anxiety average decreased significantly, let us say, from age 18 to age 28, but individuals' relative positions vis-à-vis one another were stable. In this example, the entire group became less anxious over time, perhaps suggesting greater maturity and social poise. But the people who were the most anxious at age 18 still tended to be the most anxious at age 28, even though their absolute scores went down. Keith scored a "10" in 1972 on social anxiety, but his score "improved" dramatically to a "7" in 1982. Given that almost everybody's scores improved (decreased), however, Keith is still toward the high social anxiety end. In the case, then, of low absolute continuity combined with high differential continuity, the entire distribution of scores may shift in one direction or another, but individuals' relative positions in the distribution might not change much. As we will see, this pattern is pretty common for some traits.

In the third hypothetical, *high* absolute continuity is combined with *low* differential continuity. This is a bit harder to imagine, but it is still quite possible in principle. What you would have is a trait or feature for which the group average is stable over time but for which the distribution of individual differences is unstable. Let us imagine this scenario for the idea of "warm feelings for my parents." Let us imagine that in 1972 and again in 1982 we asked my classmates to report on a 1–10 scale how warm their feelings were for their parents. The class averages in 1972 and 1982 were highly similar—let us say, around 7.0. In both years, furthermore, people showed a broad distribution of scores. Some people felt very warm feelings for their parents, and some reported feeling cold and angry toward them. But the people who had the warmest feelings toward parents in 1972 were *not necessarily the same people* who had the warmest feelings toward their parents in 1982. Robert identified strongly with his parents in 1972, but since they divorced in the interim his feelings toward both of them have cooled markedly. By contrast, Barbara felt a medium level of warmth in 1972, but over time she has warmed up considerably. Keith felt low levels of warmth in both years. Mary Anne felt very warm in 1972 but now reports less warmth for her parents. And so on. In simple terms, you cannot predict the individual scores on this dimension in 1982 based on the individual scores in 1972. The overall group mean hasn't changed much, but people's individual positions in the distribution have changed rather randomly.

Our fourth hypothetical is one in which *both* absolute and differential continuity are *low*. For this example, I need to move out of the personality realm and consider the variable of "personal income." As a group, the 28-year-olds were making considerably more money in 1982 than they were as 18-year-olds in 1972. Thus, absolute continuity on personal income would be very low. But differential continuity might also be low. The people who were making the most money at age 18 (let us say through part-time and summer jobs) were not necessarily the same ones making the most money at age 28, after people had moved differentially into careers. Mary Anne was never employed in high school, so her personal income was zero. But at age 28, she was making considerably more money than most of the other people in the class, by virtue of her successful business. Keith had a lucrative summer job, so his annual personal income was toward the top of the distribution in 1972. But he dropped out of college and has held a series of low-paying jobs ever since, so in 1982 he was making considerably less than Mary Anne and most other people in the class. An examination of other individual cases in my hypothetical example might show that personal income at age 18 was a poor predictor of personal income at age 28. Thus, while the entire distribution of scores shifted markedly to the higher end of the income spectrum from 1972 to 1982 (low absolute continuity), individuals did not hold onto their initial relative positions in the distribution (low differential continuity).

DIFFERENTIAL CONTINUITY IN THE ADULT YEARS

People are especially interested in knowing whether individual differences in various psychological qualities are consistent over time. The most informative research on this topic has examined differential continuity in personality traits in the adult years. Psychologists have conducted a number of longitudinal studies to examine this issue. In a longitudinal study, the researchers follow the same group of individuals over time to chart continuity and change in psychological variables. Differential continuity in personality traits is typically assessed by correlating trait scores at Time 1 with trait scores obtained later at Time 2 (and again at subsequent follow-ups). By their very nature, longitudinal studies require a great deal of time to complete. Studies begun decades ago finally began to yield important results on differential continuity of traits in the 1980s and 1990s (e.g., Conley, 1985a, 1985b; Costa, McCrae, & Arenberg, 1980; Finn, 1986; McCrae & Costa, 1990; Helson & Moane, 1987; Schuerger, Zarrella, & Hotz, 1989). To date, results have been collected from studies that examine intervals of as much as 50 years over the adult life course. What do these studies show?

Longitudinal studies show *remarkable differential continuity in personality traits over the adult lifespan.* For example, Conley (1985b) analyzed data from a 50-year longitudinal study of several hundred adults. All newlyweds at the beginning of the study, the participants rated themselves and were rated by their spouses on a series of personality trait dimensions in 1935–1938, 1954–1955, and 1980–1981. Supporting the inter-rater reliability of trait dimensions, Conley found that spouse ratings tended to agree with self-ratings on many personality traits. For example, a husband who saw himself as highly conscientious was likely to be viewed as highly conscientious by his wife as well. With respect to differential continuity, both self-ratings and spouse-ratings showed considerable consistency over time. Ratings that make up the Big Five dimensions of extraversion and neuroticism showed particularly strong longitudinal consistency. Further support for differential continuity was evidenced by the fact that self-ratings on a given trait at Time 1 tended to predict spouse-ratings of a given trait at Time 2, and so on. In other words, differential continuity in trait ratings was displayed when examining (a) self-ratings over time, (b) spouse ratings over time, and (c) the ability of one kind of rating to predict another kind of rating of the same trait over time.

Costa, McCrae, and Arenberg (1980) assessed a number of different traits at two different times for 460 male volunteers in the Baltimore Longitudinal Study of Aging. At the time of the first testing, the participants ranged in age from 17 to 85 years. Correlations between extraversion scores at Time 1 and Time 2, separated by a 6- to 12-year period, were generally above +.70, indicating substantial differential continuity. The researchers likewise found high stability coefficients for ratings making up the trait of neuroticism. Results from longitudinal studies have also examined the Big Five traits of openness to experience, agreeableness, and conscientiousness. Table 6.1 displays results from some of these studies. In general, substantial differential continuity has been shown for all five of these large trait clusters across intervals of time ranging from 3 to 30 years. Correlations between Time 1 and Time 2 assessments are different for different studies, different time intervals, and different measures. Looking across the studies, however, the observer notices that many correlation coefficients are around +.65. This is a very high correlation, especially when you consider the fact that personality trait scales are not perfectly reliable measures anyway. Because a scale is not likely to give exactly the same score for a person from one day to the next (test–retest reliabilities are typically around +.85 or so), documenting longitudinal consistency over many years at the magnitude of a +.65 correlation coefficient is especially impressive. Costa and McCrae (1994) point out that if such scales were perfectly reliable, then the correlations over long periods of time would be even higher.

Is the evidence for differential continuity in personality traits so strong as to suggest that personality traits are set in stone by the time we reach our adult years? The general answer is no. Despite the evidence for impressive stability over time, trait scores are not perfectly stable. As we have already suggested, one reason for instability is the error of the measures themselves. But going beyond error, there still appears to be some room for change and fluctuation in traits. Differential continuity is substantial but not all-powerful. The wide range of longitudinal stability coefficients displayed in Table 6.1 suggests that there is still change that occurs over time. People's positions in the distribution can and do change from one assessment to another. Robert Amundson will not necessarily score at the top of the pack on social dominance 20 years from now, though of course he may, and it is highly unlikely (though not impossible) that he would score toward the bottom. Personality trait scores at Time 1 in adulthood are good but not perfect predictors of scores on those same traits at Time 2.

One of the factors that influences the strength of differential continuity is the length of the time interval between testing. The longer the time interval, the lower the differential continuity. This makes intuitive sense. We would expect that people would show less stability in trait scores over a 20-year period as compared with a 5-year period. One group of researchers (Schuerger, Zarrella & Hotz, 1989) reviewed 89 longitudinal studies of personality traits, focusing especially on the Big Five dimensions of extraversion and neuroticism (anxiety). They found that test–retest correlations on traits tended to decline as the time interval increased. Figure 6.1 summarizes their results. As you can see, differential continuity tends to be higher (around +.70) for short time intervals (e.g., 1 year), and it tends to decrease gradually as the time interval lengthens, reaching a level of about +.50 for very long time intervals (e.g., more than 10 years). The researchers also found that extraversion

| TABLE 6.1 | STABILITY COEFFICIENTS FOR SELECTED TRAIT SCALES IN ADULT SAMPLES |

Factor/Scale	Source	Time Interval	r
Neuroticism			
NEO-PI	Costa & McCrae, 1988a	6 years	.83
16PF: Tense	Costa & McCrae, 1978	10 years	.67
ACL: Adaptability	Helson & Moane, 1987	16 years	.66
Neuroticism	Conley, 1985b	18 years	.46
MMPI factor	Finn, 1986	30 years	.56
Extraversion			
NEO-PI	Costa & McCrae, 1988a	6 years	.82
ACL: Self-confidence	Helson & Moane, 1987	16 years	.60
Social extraversion	Conley, 1985b	18 years	.57
Sociability	Costa & McCrae, 1992	24 years	.68
MMPI factor	Finn, 1986	30 years	.56
Openness to Experience			
NEO-PI	Costa & McCrae, 1988a	6 years	.83
16PF: Tender minded	Costa & McCrae, 1978	10 years	.54
Thoughtfulness	Costa & McCrae, 1992	24 years	.66
Intellectual interests	Finn, 1986	30 years	.62
Agreeableness			
NEO-PI	Costa & McCrae, 1988a	3 years	.63
Agreeableness	Conley, 1985b	18 years	.46
Friendliness	Costa & McCrae, 1992	24 years	.65
Low cynicism	Finn, 1986	30 years	.65
Conscientiousness			
NEO-PI	Costa & McCrae, 1988a	3 years	.79
16PF: Conscientiousness	Costa & McCrae, 1978	10 years	.48
ACL: Endurance	Helson & Moane, 1987	16 years	.67
Impulse control	Conley, 1985b	18 years	.46

SCALE NAMES:

NEO-PI is the Neuroticism-Extraversion-Openness Personality Inventory

16PF is the Sixteen Personality Factor Scale

ACL is the Adjective Checklist

MMPI is the Minnesota Multiphasic Personality Inventory

SOURCE: From "Set Like Plaster? Evidence for the Stability of Adult Personality," by P. T. Costa, Jr., and R. R. McCrae, in Can Personality Change? (pp. 32), by T. F. Heatherton and J. L. Weinberger (Eds.), 1994, Washington, DC: APA Press.

tends to show slightly higher differential continuity than the trait of neuroticism (anxiety) and higher continuity than the overall average of other traits as well.

Another factor that influences differential continuity is the age of the participants in the study. A common belief is that as people age they change less and less, relative to one another. Given comparable time intervals, are older people more likely to show higher differential continuity than younger people? For example, would we expect to find that the test–retest correlations on traits over a 5-year span would be lower for, say, young adults (tested first at

FIGURE 6.1	TRAIT CONTINUITY WITH INCREASING TIME INTERVALS

As the time between trait assessments increases, the test–retest correlations on the trait decreases, suggesting less differential consistency over time. Nonetheless, at 198 months (an interval of 16.5 years) differential continuity for traits overall is rather high (between +.55 and +.60).

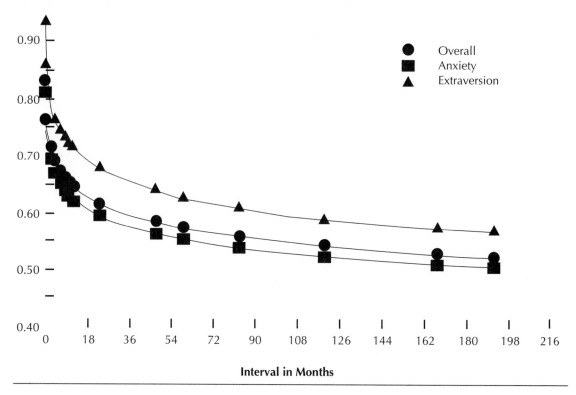

SOURCE: Adapted from "Factors That Influence the Temporal Stability of Personality by Questionnaire," by J. M. Schuerger, K. L. Zarrella, & A. S. Hotz, 1989, *Journal of Personality and Social Psychology, 56,* 781.

age 20 and then at age 25) than for middle-aged adults (tested first at age 40 and then at age 45)? Roberts and DelVecchio (2000) investigated this question in a comprehensive review of studies reporting data on longitudinal consistency of personality traits. In keeping with general expectations, they found that stability coefficients were lowest in studies of children's traits (averaging around +.41), rose to higher levels among young adults (averaging around +.55), and then reached a plateau for adults between the ages of 50 and 70 (averaging around +.70). The results suggest that we should expect greater and greater differential continuity in personality traits as people age up through late mid-life. Early in the lifespan, there is considerable movement in the distribution of scores, and individuals do not hold onto their places in the distribution as firmly over time. But as people move into adulthood and eventually into late middle-age, stability coefficients increase and the distributions of trait scores show less internal fluctuation and more interindividual continuity.

The study by Robert and DelVecchio raises the issue of personality traits *in children.* The results of their review suggest that trait ratings in children show less differential continuity than do trait ratings in adulthood. Because children seem to be developing at a more rapid pace and in a more fluid manner than adults, however, many psychologists have historically been reluctant to view children's traits in the same kinds of terms for studying adult traits. Indeed, most research on personality traits per se has focused on adults. But what is the relation between aspects of children's personality and adult personality traits? Do adult traits develop out of comparable, though perhaps less stable, dimensions in children? To address these questions we must consider the phenomenon of *temperament* as it is observed and measured in the early years of life, even in infancy.

CHILDHOOD PRECURSORS: FROM TEMPERAMENT TO TRAITS

I had a professor once who remarked that all parents are environmentalists until they have their second child. Before the second child, the parents may believe that the development of their firstborn is mainly a product of the kinds of environments they provide for their child—say, the warmth of the family environment, the quality of daycare, and so on. It is not until parents see just how different the second child is, compared with the first, and indeed how different the second one is *from the very beginning*—from the first weeks of life onward—that parents may begin to appreciate the power of inborn differences among children. My professor was being facetious, but not completely. The point he was making is that the possibility of inborn differences in personality functioning becomes rather apparent when we observe how different children seem to be from one another, even at birth. Differences in basic behavioral style, often observed early in life and presumed to be under significant and rather direct biological control, are often viewed as indications of **temperament** (Caspi, 1998; Kagan, 2000). According to Gordon Allport (1961):

> Temperament refers to the characteristic phenomena of an individual's nature, including his susceptibility to emotional stimulation, his customary strength and speed of response, the quality of his prevailing mood, and all the peculiarities of fluctuation and intensity of mood, these being phenomena regarded as dependent on constitutional make-up, and therefore largely hereditary in origin. (p. 34)

Developmental psychologists have devised a number of methods for measuring temperament and a number of conceptual schemes for understanding what they measure. The simplest and best-known scheme was delineated by Thomas, Chess, and Birch (1970), based on their interviews of mothers of babies. They distinguished among three different types of temperament patterns. **Easy babies** show consistently positive mood, low-to-moderate intensity of emotional reactions, and regular sleeping and eating cycles. **Difficult babies** show consistently negative moods, intense emotional reactions, and irregular sleeping and eating cycles. **Slow-to-warm-up babies** reveal a combination of the previous two forms, with relatively negative moods, low intensity of emotional reactions, and the tendency to withdraw from new events at first but then approach them later. Other researchers have adopted more fine-grained schemes for categorizing temperament. For instance, Rothbart (1986) enumerates six temperament dimensions reliably observed in infants in the first year of life: activity level, smiling and laughter, fearfulness, distress to limitations, "soothability," and vocal activity.

One temperament dimension that has received a great deal of attention is what Jerome Kagan (1989) calls *behavioral inhibition.* Extremely inhibited young children show great timidity in the face of new events and people. Kagan has shown that about 15% of Caucasian children in the second year of life are consistently shy and emotionally subdued in unfamiliar situations ("inhibited children") whereas another 15% are consistently sociable and affectively spontaneous ("uninhibited children"). As 2-year-olds, inhibited children may be especially reluctant to play with an unfamiliar toy. Later, in kindergarten they may shy away from new activities and people, showing a kind of stagefright in new situations. Compared with uninhibited children, inhibited children show intense physiological responses, such as more dilated pupils and higher heart rates, when confronted with mildly stressful social situations. In addition, inhibited children show higher levels of morning cortisol in the blood (indicating heightened arousal) compared with uninhibited children, a difference that is also apparent when comparing shy, inhibited rhesus monkeys with their more sociable peers. Kagan argues that extremely shy and extremely sociable children constitute two separable genetic types whose striking behavioral differences are partly a function of different thresholds of reactivity in the brain's limbic system. Inhibited children have a lower threshold of reactivity. They are more easily aroused in social situations and respond by withdrawing.

Kagan's physiological portrait of temperamental inhibition is reminiscent of Eysenck's (chapter 5) account of the trait introversion. Eysenck argued that introverts are overly aroused in general and that their withdrawal behavior is an effort to decrease arousal levels. In addition, recent research suggests that behaviorally inhibited children are more likely to show neural activation of the right frontal lobe while uninhibited children are more likely to show activation of the brain's left frontal lobe (Kagan, 1994). As we saw in chapter 5, right frontal activity is associated with negative affectivity (including emotions of fear and depression) and the behavioral inhibition system, whereas left frontal activity has been linked to positive affectivity (including emotions of joy and happiness) and the behavioral approach system. Will Kagan's excessively inhibited children grow up to be introverted and anxious adults? Will uninhibited children become extraverted adults? Kagan believes that the link between inhibition and some combination of introversion and neuroticism in adulthood will eventually be shown. Out of every 100 Caucasian newborns, Kagan maintains, approximately 20 will show extreme irritability and excitability shortly after birth. By the age of 2 years, 75% of these (say, 15 or so) will be very shy, timid, and fearful when they meet unfamiliar people, are put in unfamiliar rooms, or encounter unfamiliar objects. By adolescence, 10 will still be very shy, and by adulthood you are likely to find that 6 or 7 of the original 20 are extremely introverted in their behavior. The two-thirds who lost their excessive shyness by adulthood may have been strongly influenced by environmental experiences encouraging them to be more outgoing. Indeed, American society tends to favor outgoing and sociable people. Like the 6 or 7 resultant introverts, however, the former inhibited children who grew up to be somewhat less introverted than we might have originally expected retain what Kagan believes to be a "shyness physiology." Further research is needed to assess the validity of Kagan's interpretation.

To date, few longitudinal studies have examined the relationship between early childhood temperament variables on the one hand and adult personality traits on the other. Furthermore, the methods and conceptual systems used by researchers studying infant and child temperament on the one hand and adult personality on the other have historically been very different. For example, many temperament scales rely on maternal reports or behavioral observations of infants and children. By contrast, research on personality traits has tended to favor self-report rating scales. Temperament theorists have proposed a number of different taxonomies for organizing such temperament dimensions as irritability, positive affect, activity level, rhythmicity, adaptability, sensory threshold, soothability, intensity of mood, and a host of other dimensions that seem especially applicable to children (Caspi, 1998; Rowe, 1997). Trait researchers have also proposed many different systems, as we saw in chapter 4, but in recent years the Big Five taxonomy has won considerable support as a comprehensive framework for adult personality traits. Some researchers have recently argued that the Big Five framework could be used to classify dimensions of childhood functioning, too, including variables that have traditionally been viewed as part of temperament (Kohnstamm, Halverson, Mervielde, & Havill, 1998). But others are skeptical that such an easy conceptual match can be found (Kagan, 2000).

One recent study, however, does shed some light on the relationship between childhood temperament and adult personality (Caspi et al., 2003). For many years, personality psychologist Avshalom Caspi and his colleagues have worked on the Dunedin Study, a longitudinal investigation of approximately 1,000 individuals born between April 1972 and March 1973 in the town of Dunedin, New Zealand. Participants have been tested at ages 3, 5, 7, 9, 11, 13, 15, 18, 21, and 26 years. At age 3, each child in the study participated in a 90-minute developmental testing session, from which psychologists rated the children on 22 behavioral characteristics. The ratings were statistically grouped to produce five different temperament types. The *well-adjusted* children (*n* = 405) showed appropriate levels of self-control when it was demanded of them, expressed adequate self-confidence, and did not become unduly upset when confronting novel situations. The *undercontrolled* children (*n* = 106, 62% of whom were boys) were impulsive, restless, negativistic, and distractible, and they showed strong and volatile emotional reactions. The *confident* children (*n* = 281) adjusted to the testing situation quickly and showed the characteristics of friendliness, impulsivity, and enthusiasm. The *inhibited* type (*n* = 80, 60% of whom were girls) included children who were socially reticent, fearful, and easily upset by the examiner. Finally, the

Temperament refers to basic differences in behavioral style that are assumed to be part of a person's genetic endowment. While some babies tend to smile a lot, others may tend to show a more difficult temperament.

reserved children ($n = 151$) were timid and somewhat uncomfortable in the testing session, but they showed less shyness and caution than did the inhibited children.

What were these girls and boys like at age 26? The researchers administered self-report personality scales to all of the participants at age 26, and they collected trait ratings of the same individuals from their friends and acquaintances. The researchers documented modest, though impressive, continuity in certain personality dimensions. The children who were most predictable turned out to be the undercontrolled and inhibited types. Over a 23-year span, the undercontrolled children grew up to score highest on trait measures of negative emotionality. Compared to others in the group, they were easily upset, likely to overreact to minor events, and reported feeling mistreated, deceived, and betrayed by others. They were also described by others as antagonistic, unreliable, tense, and narrow-minded. In terms of the Big Five dimensions, it appears that the undercontrolled pattern of childhood temperament predicts high levels of neuroticism and low levels of agreeableness and conscientiousness in young adulthood. The inhibited children grew up to show an overcontrolled and nonassertive personality style, showing high scores on traits measuring constraint and low scores on traits related to positive emotionality. In terms of the Big Five, the inhibited temperament pattern appears to predict low levels of extraversion (high introversion) in young adults. The three remaining temperament types did not show clear-cut personality profiles in adulthood, but some continuity was still observed. For example, confident children tended to become somewhat extraverted adults and reserved children tended toward introversion and low openness to experience at age 26.

Caspi (1998) views temperament as the psychobiological core around which personality is structured. Through a process of **developmental elaboration,** temperament dimensions gradually develop into more fully articulated personality traits. Developmental elaboration is a complex interplay through which inborn tendencies shape and are shaped by environmental inputs over a long period of time. Table 6.2 spells out six mechanisms of

TABLE 6.2	SIX MECHANISMS OF DEVELOPMENTAL ELABORATION: HOW TEMPERAMENT DIMENSIONS DEVELOP INTO PERSONALITY TRAITS
Learning processes	Temperamental differences impact what children learn and how they learn it, which contributes to the formation of personality traits.
Environmental elicitation	Temperamental differences elicit different reactions from the environment, which may reinforce the initial differences.
Environmental construal	Temperamental differences influence how children understand and process information about their environments, shaping their experiences of the environments.
Social and temporal comparisons	Temperamental differences impact how children compare themselves with others and with themselves over time, which shapes their developing self-concepts.
Environmental selection	Temperamental differences influence how children choose environments, which in turn influences the development of personality traits. Children may choose environments that are consistent with their temperaments to begin with, reinforcing dispositions that are already present.
Environmental manipulation	Once children's self-concepts are firmly established, they will alter, modify, or manipulate their environments to match, confirm, or elaborate the temperamental dispositions they already have.

developmental elaboration. Inborn temperament differences influence (a) how children learn, (b) how they construe their environments, (c) how other people in the environment respond to them, (d) how they compare themselves to other children, (e) what kinds of environments they choose, and (f) how they manipulate environments once they choose them. The physical and social environments that they construe, choose, and manipulate, in turn, feed back to influence their development further. Initial dispositions appearing even in infancy may gradually gain strength and scope and become more cognitively and socially elaborated over time. Over a long and complex developmental trajectory, certain inborn temperament dispositions, then, get strengthened and articulated to become full-fledged personality traits, Caspi argues. The results from the Dunedin Study show that certain predictable trajectories can indeed be documented. But the results also show a considerable amount of unpredictability and discontinuity over the long haul. Inborn temperamental tendencies may lay down a rough template for the development of adult personality traits. But the template appears to be quite flexible and subject to substantial alteration by virtue of environmental inputs.

THE ORIGINS OF TRAITS: GENES AND ENVIRONMENTS

It is a common observation that genetically identical twins—that is, *monozygotic* (MZ) twins—tend to be remarkably similar. Not only do they look very much alike, but it seems that their interests, tastes, styles, and behavior patterns are often strikingly concordant. By contrast, *dizygotic* (DZ), or fraternal twins, tend to look no more similar to each other than any other set of biological siblings, and their behaviors often seem to be equally discordant as well. In that they developed out of the same zygote, monozygotic twins have the same genetic makeup; dizygotic twins have only about half of their genes in common. In the 1980s, a group of researchers at the University of Minnesota undertook a large study of about 350 sets of MZ and DZ twins, a number of whom, from infancy onward, *had been raised apart* (Bouchard, Lykken, McGue, Segal, & Tellegen, 1990). In most of these cases, the twins had been given up for adoption, and each of the two members of the twin pair was adopted by a different family. Thus, each grew up not knowing his or her twin. Bringing the twin pairs back together for the study, the researchers were struck by some of the amazing similarities in personality revealed in the MZA (monozygotic, raised apart) twin pairs:

> While videotaping an interview with one [MZA] twin, we discovered he was an accomplished raconteur with a fund of amusing anecdotes, so, while interviewing the co-twin, we asked him if he knew any funny stories. "Why sure," he said, leaning back with a practiced air. "I'll tell you a story" and proceeded to demonstrate his concordance. A pair of British MZAs, who had met for the first time as adults just a month previously, both firmly refused in their separate interviews to express opinions on controversial topics; since long before they discovered each other's existence, each had resolutely avoided controversy. Another pair were both habitual gigglers, although each had been raised by adoptive parents whom they described as undemonstrative and dour, and neither had known anyone who laughed as freely as she did until finally she met her twin. Both members of another pair independently reported that they refrained from voting in political elections on the principle that they did not feel themselves well enough informed to make wise choices. A pair of male MZAs, at their first adult reunion, discovered that they both use Vadmecum toothpaste, Canoe shaving lotion, Vitalis hair tonic, and Lucky Strike cigarettes. After that meeting, they exchanged birthday presents in the mail that proved to be identical choices, made independently in separate cities.

There were two "dog people" among the MZA individuals; one showed her dogs, and the other taught obedience classes—they were an MZA pair. Only two of the more than 200 individual twins reared apart were afraid to enter the acoustically shielded chamber used in our psychophysiology laboratory, but both separately agreed to continue if the door was wired open—they were a pair of MZA twins. When at the beach, both women had always insisted on entering the water backwards and then only up to their knees; they were thus concordant, not only in their phobic tendencies, but also in the specific manifestations of their timidity. There were two gunsmith hobbyists among the group of twins; two women who habitually wore seven rings; two men who offered a (correct) diagnosis of a faulty wheel bearing on Bouchard's [one of the researcher's] car; two who obsessively counted things; two who had been married five times; two captains of volunteer fire departments; two fashion designers; two who left little love notes around the house for their wives . . . in each case, an MZA pair. (Lykken, McGue, Tellegen, Bouchard, 1992, pp. 1565–1566)

Are these examples just coincidences? The authors of the account concede that a few of the many incredible similarities they observed among MZA pairs could have been flukes, due to chance. But the sheer number and detail of the similarities observed suggest that there is more than just coincidence going on here. How can it be that MZ siblings who have never lived a day in the same household, who have been raised in different families and grown up in different neighborhoods, who have attended different schools and made different sets of friends, who have indeed never even met each other—how can it be that they should turn out to be so much alike? We should, perhaps, not be surprised that they would look alike. Most of us accept the idea that our appearance is strongly driven by our genetic endowment. But personality traits seem different.

Up to this point in this chapter, we have learned that individual differences in personality traits are fairly stable over the adult lifespan, showing substantial differential continuity from early adulthood onward. We have learned that temperamental differences in infancy and childhood, assumed to reflect a psychobiological substrate for human individuality, are often striking and readily recognized by parents, teachers, and other socializing agents. We have speculated that temperament dimensions in early childhood may eventually become elaborated through a long and complex series of person environment interactions into full-fledged personality traits in the adult years. Implicit in our discussion has been the idea that personality traits develop out of some combination of genetic and environmental effects. But we have not been specific about this. The anecdotal examples from the University of Minnesota study of identical twins raised apart strongly hint that a person's genetic makeup is a major factor in determining his or her standing on personality trait dimensions. Should we believe the anecdotes? Is "nature" stronger than "nurture" when it comes to determining personality traits? How can we separate genetic from environmental effects on personality traits? Where do personality traits *ultimately* come from?

THE LOGIC OF TWIN AND ADOPTION STUDIES

Let us begin with a simple truth: You cannot have personality, you cannot have behavior, you cannot have life without *both* genes and environments. In a fundamental sense, your personality traits and mine are products of the interaction of our genes and our environments, for indeed genes cannot have any impact on behavior if there is no environment within which the person can act, and environments can have no impact on behavior if there are no genes out of which to make the person in the first place. In that genes fundamentally depend on environments and environments fundamentally depend on genes in the making of a person, nature and nurture are tightly intertwined in a given human life. Each of us is a complex and evolving product of the interaction between nature and nurture.

Having said that, we must now encounter a second, less simple truth: It does make scientific sense to examine the relative influences of genetic differences and environmental differences on the variability we perceive in a given sample or population of organisms. Let me give an example. Full-grown (adult) human beings differ noticeably with respect to height. Some people are taller than other people. Does it make sense to try to understand the reasons for these differences among people by appealing to genes and environments? You bet it does. We can sensibly ask what the relative contributions are of genetic and environmental variance in determining differences between people in height. Note how I have framed this statement. I am not talking here about why any particular individual is tall or short. I am instead talking about variability in height *in a group of individuals*—why it is that people differ on height. Research suggests that in the United States about 90% of the variability in height is associated with genetic differences among people, while only about 10% is associated with such environmental differences as nutritional levels and social class (Rowe, 1999). People who tend to have genetic endowments that produce relative tallness (people who are most likely tall themselves) tend to have taller children than people whose genetic endowments code for shortness. Nutritional differences among people account for a tiny part of the difference—the main factor is the genes. Americans can eat and eat and eat; they can do stretching exercises; they can try to improve their posture—but all of this will probably not make them much taller than they would have been anyway had they not gone to these extreme measures.

Now you need to realize two very important implications of the scientific finding concerning height. The first implication is that our figure of 90% refers to differences in the group; it does not apply to any particular person. It would be silly to say that 90% of a person's height comes from his genes and 10% of his height comes from his environment. For a 6-foot-tall man, that would mean that 7.2 inches of his height came from his environment. This kind of statement makes no sense. Instead, we have to remember that we are accounting here for *differences or variability* among people, not for any particular person's height. In accounting for the wide range of variability in height among Americans, we can say that 90% of the variability is due to genetic variability: People have different genes, and different genes produce different heights. The second implication of our statement about height is that the percentages of "variability accounted for" that we identified (90% for genetic differences, 10% for environmental differences) depend dramatically on characteristics of the population to begin with. It is definitely true that severe malnutrition *can* dramatically stunt people's growth, proving that a certain kind of environment *can* have a major impact. But the incidence of severe malnutrition and starvation is thankfully very low in most modern societies, so few people in the group are faced with these circumstances. But in a society where many people were on the brink of starvation while many others had plenty to eat, environmental differences could certainly play a larger role in determining height. In such a context, we would expect the relative contribution of genetic differences to be lower than 90% and the relative contribution of environmental differences to be higher than 10% in determining differences among people in height. These sorts of group estimates depend critically on the characteristics of the population from which the group is drawn.

With my example of height, I am introducing you to one of the most misunderstood concepts in all of psychology—the idea of the **heritability quotient.** A *heritability quotient estimates the proportion of variability in a given characteristic that can be attributed to genetic* *differences between people.* In the case of height among American adults, the heritability quotient is estimated to be 90%. This group statistic tells us how much of the observed variation in height is associated with genetic variation among people in the group. The example of height is noncontroversial, since most of us realize that height seems to "run in families." The example is also noncontroversial for another reason. While scientists have never found a particular gene that codes exclusively for height, we do not have a hard time believing that genes strongly influence height. Genes are merely segments of DNA. In these segments, biochemically active molecules are arranged in a sequence analogous to letters in a word. These "letters"—which essentially comprise the four biochemical bases of thymine, adenine, cytosine, and guanine—make up the genetic code, with different combinations of three letters in sequence coding for each of the 22 amino acids that make up the building blocks of proteins. Genes are directly implicated, then, in the making of proteins and other basic biochemical events. A phenomenon as complex as people's height is determined by the working of many different genes.

We move now from the relatively noncontroversial topic of heritability in height to heritability as it applies to personality traits. We have already acknowledged that an individual's particular personality traits are a complex product of genes interacting with environments. But as we did with height, we can consider the extent to which genetic differences and environmental differences account for variability in traits across many people. As with height, we must remember that heritability refers not to the individual but to accounting for variance in groups. We must remember that variance in groups is due to many factors within a group. We must remember that genetic influences on traits, should we find them, are indirect and complex. Just as there is no single gene that determines a person's height, so, too, is there no single gene that matches cleanly to a particular personality trait. Finally, we must understand that discussion of genetic difference among people must always be understood against a backdrop of tremendous genetic similarity across our species. Humans are highly similar to one another genetically. Many human genes—about 90% of them—are identical from one individual to another. In discussing heritability we are focusing exclusively on the 10% of the human genome that does vary.

The two main methods through which behavioral scientists have sought to make heritability estimates for personality traits are studies of twins and studies of adopted children. In the case of twin studies, the usual design is to obtain a sample of monozygotic (MZ) twins and a sample of dizygotic (DZ) twins, to administer measures of traits or other variables to the participants, to compute correlations between the trait scores for respective members of twin pairs, and finally to compare the magnitude of the correlations obtained for the MZ twins and the DZ twins. Let us make up an example. Say that we administered a measure of the trait "punctuality" to a sample of 50 MZ twin pairs and 50 DZ twin pairs—200 participants in all. In the DZ subsample, we obtained a correlation coefficient of +.30 between punctuality scores of respective twins. This means that there was a modest positive association between punctuality scores of the twins—when one member of the twin pair scored high on punctuality, there was a slight tendency for the other member of the twin pair to score high, and so on. Among the MZ twins, we obtained a correlation coefficient of +.50, indicating a much stronger positive association. While DZ twins seem to be moderately similar to each other on this trait, MZ twins appear to be rather more similar to each other, as indicated by the stronger magnitude of the correlation coefficient. Why should that be? MZ twins and DZ twins share environments, but while MZ twins also share all their genes, DZ twins share only half their genes on the average. In simple terms, the big difference between the MZ and DZ pairs is in genetic similarity. If the MZs are more similar to each other on punctuality than the DZs, then the difference may be due to their greater genetic similarity. Punctuality would appear to be heritable.

How heritable might punctuality be in our hypothetical example? Researchers have developed a simple formula for estimating heritability in twin studies. The formula makes certain assumptions that are not necessarily true in all studies, but for our purposes here the formula works well to illustrate the concept. To provide a rough estimate of heritability in twin studies, one may simply subtract the DZ correlation from the MZ correlation and then multiply by 2. In other words:

$$h^2 = 2(r_{mz} - r_{dz})$$

where h^2 is the heritability quotient, r_{mz} is the correlation between respective trait scores for MZ twins, and r_{dz} is the correlation between respective trait scores for DZ twins. Plugging in our numbers for the punctuality example, we find that

$$h^2 = 2(.50 - .30)$$

Our rough estimate for heritability is .40. According to the logic of this make-believe study, approximately 40% of the variability in the trait of punctuality in this population can be attributed to genetic differences among people. Approximately 60% of the variance in punctuality, therefore, remains at this point unexplained.

Adoption studies follow a similar logic. In this case, researchers typically examine the extent to which adoptive children share similar traits with members of their adoptive families, typically with siblings. Like DZ twins, biologically related siblings share about 50% of common genetic endowment. By contrast, adopted children are biologically unrelated to the members of their adoptive family, and therefore have 0% common genetic endowment. As in twin studies, researchers may wish to compare correlations between trait scores of two different groups: pairs of biological siblings (50% common genetic endowment) and pairs of nonbiologically related (e.g., adoptive) siblings (0% common genetic endowment). Evidence for heritability can be obtained when correlations between trait scores of biologically related siblings significantly exceed correlations between trait scores of nonbiologically related (e.g., adoptive) siblings.

Adoption studies shed light on nature and nurture in other ways, too. Say, for example, that a researcher is able to locate the biologically related parents or siblings of adoptive children and administer trait measures to them. In this case, any significant positive correlations that a researcher would obtain between trait scores of adopted children and biologically related relatives would have to be due to genetic effects, since these individuals did not share environments. In a similar way, any significant positive correlations obtained between trait scores of adopted children and their (nonbiologically related) siblings would have to indicate common environmental effects. Remember that adoptive siblings share no common genetic endowment with their siblings in the adoptive family. Consequently, if we were to find a significant positive correlation between punctuality scores of adoptive siblings, then we would have to conclude that growing up in the same family had some effect in making these siblings somewhat similar to each other on this trait.

Twin and adoption studies are natural experiments through which researchers are able to estimate the relative power of genetic and environmental differences in accounting for trait variation within a sample of people. The logic of twin and adoption studies undergirds research in the growing field of **behavior genetics.** Behavior genetics is a scientific

Identical twins not only typically look alike, but they may also show similar personality traits. Studies examining traits in identical and fraternal twins typically show heritability estimates of around 50%, suggesting that approximately half of the variation in trait scores can be attributed to genetic differences between people.

SOURCE: Rebecca R. Pallmeyer.

discipline—with roots in psychology, genetics, biology, and related fields—that explores the empirical evidence concerning the relative influences of genetic and environmental factors in accounting for variability in human behavior (Rowe, 1997, 1999). Increasingly in recent years, research in behavioral genetics has employed complex statistical modeling procedures in which data from different family constellations and types are combined to test hypotheses about nature and nurture. Still, twin and adoption studies form the basis for many of the field's central findings about heritability of personality traits. Now that we have covered the basics, we must ask: What does the research show?

HERITABILITY ESTIMATES OF TRAITS

The research shows that *virtually all personality traits that can be reliably measured are at least moderately heritable.* The evidence is especially compelling from twin studies. A huge study of about 13,000 adult twins in Sweden obtained heritability estimates of slightly more than 50% for both extraversion and neuroticism traits (Floderus-Myrhed, Pedersen, & Rasmuson, 1980). Other twin studies have yielded moderately high heritability quotients (between .30 and .60) for a range of personality traits measured on a number of scales and personality inventories (Loehlin & Nichols, 1976; Rushton, Fulker, Neale, Nias, & Eysenck, 1986). In the University of Minnesota study, broad heritability estimates (greater than 40%) were obtained for the traits of leadership/mastery, traditionalism (tendency to follow rules and respect authority), stress reaction (similar to neuroticism), absorption (the tendency to become engrossed in sensory experiences), alienation, well-being, avoidance of harm, and aggressiveness (Tellegen et al., 1988).

In an authoritative review of behavioral genetic studies in personality, Robert Plomin and colleagues (1990) conclude that

> genetic influence on self-report measures of personality is nearly ubiquitous. Much of this evidence relies on comparisons between correlations for identical, or monozygotic (MZ), and fraternal, or dizygotic (DZ), twins. On average, across diverse personality dimensions, MZ correlations are about .50 and DZ correlations are about .30. These twin correlations suggest that genetic influence on personality is not only significant but substantial. Doubling the difference between the two correlations results in an estimate that heritability, the proportion of phenotypic variance explained by genetic variance, is 40%. (Plomin, Chipuer, & Loehlin, 1990. p. 226)

Studies conducted in the 1990s directly examining the Big Five traits add further support for the conclusions of this review. Table 6.3 shows intraclass correlations on self-report measures of the Big Five traits for a sample of 123 MZ and 127 DZ twin pairs (Jang, Livesley, & Vernon, 1996). As you can see, the correlations for MZ pairs range from +.37 for conscientiousness to

+.58 for openness to experience, while the correlations for DZ pairs range from +.18 for neuroticism to +.27 for conscientiousness. For the traits of neuroticism, extraversion, and openness, the MZ correlations are more than twice as large in magnitude as the DZ correlations. Based on these correlations and other statistical procedures, the authors of the study concluded that heritabilities for the Big Five traits were mainly in the 40% to 50% range, with the strongest heritability in this study shown for openness to experience.

Other studies have shown similar heritability estimates for self-report measures of the Big Five traits. Loehlin, McCrae, and Costa (1998) used sophisticated statistical procedures that attempt to fit data to various theoretical models in a re-analysis of self-report trait ratings made by 490 MZ and 317 DZ twin pairs in 1962, when all the participants were high school students. The authors obtained heritability estimates ranging from 51% to 58% for the Big Five traits. They concluded that the Big Five trait dimensions are substantially and about equally heritable. Jang, McCrae, Angleitner, Riemann, and Livesley (1998) analyzed twin data from Canada and Germany and found that not only do the Big Five dimensions show substantial heritability but that many of the smaller traits or facets that make up each of the Big Five summary dimensions also appear to be substantially heritable.

Conservatively speaking, then, twin studies consistently suggest that personality traits are at least moderately heritable and in some cases substantially so. Heritability estimates are typically in the 40% to 50% range, though some studies show even greater values (e.g., Loehlin, Neiderhiser, & Reiss, 2003). This simple story, however, gets a bit more complicated when you consider two puzzling findings that continue to emerge. The first is that some studies show MZ correlations that are *more than twice as high as* DZ correlations. Indeed, the data in Table 6.3 reveal this to be true for openness, extraversion, and neuroticism. As another example, in four large twin studies of extraversion and neuroticism totaling more than 23,000 pairs of twins, the weighted average MZ and DZ correlations were about .51 and .18, respectively. For neuroticism, the corresponding MZ and DZ correlations were .48 and .20, respectively (Loehlin, 1989). The conventional wisdom on twin studies is that, because MZ twins share 100% common genes and DZ twins share 50% common genes, MZ twins should be no more than twice as similar to one another as DZ twins. In other words, genetic variance should be *additive*. A second puzzling finding is that studies of adoption yield *significantly lower heritability estimates*. If heredity is a major factor in determining traits, then we would expect that biological siblings (50% common genes) should be significantly more similar to each other than adoptive siblings (0% common genes). But this does not seem to be the case. A number of adoption studies suggest

TABLE 6.3	TWIN CORRELATIONS FOR THE BIG FIVE TRAITS	
	MZ Twins	**DZ Twins**
Neuroticism	.41	.18
Extraversion	.55	.23
Openness	.58	.21
Agreeableness	.41	.26
Conscientiousness	.37	.27

SOURCE: Adapted from "Heritability of the Big Five Personality Dimensions: A Twin Study," by K. L. Jang, W. J. Livesley, & P. A. Vernon, 1996, *Journal of Personality, 64*, 584.

surprisingly small differences between correlations, yielding heritability estimates around 20% (Loehlin, Willerman, & Horn, 1987; Scarr, Webber, Weinberg, & Wittig, 1981).

Let us put these two puzzling findings in the simplest possible language: First, for some traits (such as extraversion) *identical twins seem to be even more similar to each other* (more than twice as similar to each other as fraternal twins) than expected. Second, adoption studies suggest that *biological siblings are less similar to each other* (only barely more similar to each other than are adoptive siblings) than expected. Your relative standing on personality traits bears only modest similarity to that of your biological siblings (including fraternal twins), your parents, your cousins, or anybody else to whom you are biologically related, unless, of course, you have an identical twin, in which case the two of you are likely to be remarkably similar (Dunn & Plomin, 1990). When it comes to personality traits measured on self-report questionnaires, why are you likely to be so remarkably similar to an identical twin and so remarkably dissimilar to anybody else with whom you share common genes?

One possible explanation is **nonadditive genetic variance.** Genes may not influence traits in a linear, additive way, but rather combine and interact in a "configural" pattern in which all components are essential and "the absence of, or a change in any one (i.e., any gene) can produce qualitative or a large quantitative change in the result" (Lykken et al., 1992). Thus, if two individuals (DZ twins or any biological siblings) share only 50% common genes, they may be *less than half* as similar to each other as are two individuals (MZ twins) who share 100% common genes: Because genes influence traits in a nonadditive fashion, 100% is, in a sense, *more than twice* as large as 50%. I am not likely to be concordant with my brother (we are not MZ twins) on, say, extraversion because the nonadditive genetic configurations that may be required to give us a similar extraversion makeup cannot occur (unless we share 100% of our genes). There is a threshold in trait genetics. Either your genotype is the same as another person's (MZ twins) or it isn't (everybody else). If it is the first, then your trait ratings are likely to be very similar to those of your MZ twin, the data suggest. If it is the second, you are probably not especially similar (in traits) to anybody in your family, although there is likely to be some modest similarity. Merely sharing 50% common genes with another (a sibling) does not make much of a bang in making the two of you all that similar. In this sense, 50% *is not much more than* 0%. Thus, biological siblings (non-MZs) are not very much more similar to each other than are adoptive siblings. This may be one of the answers, write Dunn and Plomin (1990), to the question of "why siblings are so different."

The possibility of nonadditive genetic effects on personality traits is an example of what some psychologists call **emergenesis.** Emergenesis is "an emergent property of a configuration of genes or perhaps a configuration of more basic traits that are themselves genetic in origin" (Lykken et al., 1992, p. 1569). What this means in English is that certain patterns of genes may give rise to particular behavioral tendencies that would not themselves be produced, even in a weaker or more attenuated form, by the pieces that make up the pattern. The behavioral tendency is an emergent property of the pattern. A simple analogy for this comes from playing poker. Think of your biological mother and father as each holding a hand of six cards, which represent their genes. The cards all come from the same deck, so your mother's and father's cards are different from each other—that is, they are genetically dissimilar. Your mother has an ace, two kings, a seven, a five, and a four. Your father has a king, a jack, a ten, a seven, and two sixes. To make you, they each randomly contribute (copies of) three cards (half their genes) to make a new hand. You (the new hand) get both of your mother's kings, her seven, your father's king, his seven, and his four. What do you have? You have a "full house"—three kings and two sevens (and a four). A full house is a pretty good poker hand, and (more importantly) it is very different from the hands your parents have. They each have "two of a kind." The point I am making (besides showing that you have beaten your parents in poker) is that the value of your poker hand is determined by its unique configuration of cards. The cards came from two other hands that did not have this unique configuration. The full house is an emergent property of the new configuration. So, too, may certain behavioral tendencies be emergent properties that come from particular configurations of genes. Genotypes are like poker hands with millions and millions of cards. The cards combine in complex ways to produce a wondrous variety of patterns. With the exception of MZ twins, every person is dealt a unique hand.

SHARED ENVIRONMENT

What about the environment? If heritabilities for personality traits are in the 40% to 50% range, that still leaves more than 50% of the variance in trait scores unaccounted for. That must mean half or more of the variance in personality traits can be explained by environmental effects, such as child-rearing styles, family patterns, schools, neighborhoods, and the like. Right? Not exactly. The issue of environmental effects on traits turns out to be much more complicated than you might expect and, for many people, quite surprising.

Let us begin with data from the University of Minnesota study that examined twins reared together and apart (Tellegen et al., 1988). Table 6.4 provides intraclass correlations for a number of self-report personality trait scales for MZ twins only. In the first column you find correlations for 217 MZ twin pairs who each grew up in the same family. In the second column, you find correlations for 44 MZ twin pairs reared apart. Each of these 44 cases involves adoption. One member of the MZ pair, therefore, grew up in one particular family and the other member of the MZ twin pair grew up in another family. In most cases, the twins had no contact with each other in childhood and were reunited (in some cases for the first time) by the University of Minnesota study. Therefore, the first group of MZ twins were reared together, sharing a common childhood environment. The second group was reared apart.

TABLE 6.4	TWIN CORRELATIONS FOR MONOZYGOTIC TWINS REARED TOGETHER AND APART	
Trait	**MZ Together**	**MZ Apart**
Well-being	.58	.48
Social potency	.65	.56
Achievement	.51	.36
Social closeness	.57	.29
Stress reaction	.52	.61
Alienation	.55	.48
Aggression	.43	.46
Control	.41	.50
Harm avoidance	.55	.49
Traditionalism	.50	.53
Absorption	.49	.61
Mean correlation	**.52**	**.49**

SOURCE: Adapted from "Personality Similarity in Twins Reared Apart and Together," by A. Tellegen, D. J. Lykken, T. J. Bouchard, Jr., K. J. Wilcox, N. L. Segal, & S. Rich, 1988, *Journal of Personality and Social Psychology, 54*, 1035.

What do you make of the correlations in Table 6.4? First, we see that the correlational values for the MZ twins reared together on such traits as "social potency" and "stress reaction" are in line with what we have come to expect in studies that have examined other and similar traits. The correlations range from +.41 to +.65 for the 11 traits listed, with an average value of +.52. This is old news; these correlations are very similar, for example, to those displayed for MZ twins in Table 6.3 for the Big Five traits. The second thing we should note in Table 6.4, however, is that the correlational values for the twins reared apart are, in many cases, almost identical to those of the MZ twins reared together. The average value is +.49. What does this mean? It essentially means that MZ twins reared apart are just about as similar to each other as MZ twins reared together. But shouldn't the common environments experienced by the MZ twins reared together be worth something? Given the substantial heritability of personality traits, we should not be surprised that MZ twins reared apart would have similar traits. But shouldn't MZ twins *reared together* be even *more* similar to each other? Looking over Table 6.4, the only trait that seems to show an expectable pattern like this is social closeness, for which the MZ-together correlation (+.57) is markedly larger than the MZ-apart correlation (+.29). Otherwise, the evidence for the effects of common environment is sparse.

In general, twin studies and adoption studies have shown that *growing up in the same family seems to have little impact on personality traits.* There are a few exceptions to this rule (e.g., Borkenau, Riemann, Angleitner, & Spinath, 2001). For example, there is some evidence that certain traits having to do with intimacy and love for others, such as the "social closeness" trait tapped in the Minnesota study, may show family environment effects (Plomin, Chipuer, & Loehlin, 1990; Waller & Shaver, 1994). Juvenile delinquency, furthermore, appears to show considerable influence of family environment, although adult criminality does not (Miles & Carey, 1997). Another exception involves severe maltreatment. Child abuse and extraordinary neglect do appear to have deleterious effects on psychological development, which show up clearly in personality traits. But these sometimes tragic situations are still relatively rare, at least in modern societies. The vast majority of children grow up in families that, while imperfect, offer expectable rudimentary care (Scarr, 1997). It is, therefore, within this broad spectrum of average expectable environments that research has repeatedly failed to show measurable effects of family environments on personality traits.

For example, it appears that most of the modest positive association (correlation) found between siblings (including DZ twins) on personality traits is a function of the fact that siblings share about half of their genes in common. Once you take into consideration the trait similarity that is due to genetic similarity, there is virtually no trait similarity left over to attribute to the fact that the siblings grew up in the same environments. Adoption studies offer even clearer evidence. Typically, adoptive children show virtually no predictable similarity on traits to the members of the families who adopt them, even after they have lived in the family for many years. Eaves, Eysenck, and Martin (1989), for example, found that the correlation between adopted children and their *biological* mothers (whom they had never met) on extraversion was +.21, while the correlation between these same children and their adoptive mothers (who raised them) was essentially zero (-.02).

If you find nothing counterintuitive in these results, then you are not reading carefully enough. These studies are saying that the kind of family environment people experience growing up has little or no effect on their personality traits. How caring and loving your parents were, the level of conflict in your family, the quality of the schools you attended, the kind of neighborhood you lived in, the church your family went to, how much your parents emphasized discipline and hard work growing up, the degree of wealth or poverty you experienced—none of this mattered. Nor will it matter with respect to your own children's traits, the research suggests. In teaching personality psychology for almost 25 years, my experience has been that students (and many colleagues) simply do not believe these results. How can it be that family doesn't matter? Such a claim flies in the face of some of our most cherished beliefs.

There is no easy way to get around these findings. The data are clear: Approximately half of the variance in personality traits can be attributed to genetics; with a few exceptions, very little of the variance can be attributed to family environment. This still leaves, however, about half of the variance in personality traits. What accounts for the large amount of variation that cannot be accounted for by genetic and family effects? There are two answers. First, trait measures contain error, which adds unexplainable variation. Even the most reliable index of extraversion does not give you exactly the same score for the same person from one day to the next. Test–retest reliabilities of good trait measures may be between +.80 and +.90—really good, but not perfect. These scales are not as accurate and reliable as thermometers. Therefore, it is likely that some of that unexplained variance in traits is simply a function of error in the measures. Psychologists have estimated that as much as 10% to 20% of the variance in scores for trait measures in any given sample is simply due to the inherent imperfections in the measurement devices used. Nonetheless, this still leaves a lot of variance unexplained.

The second answer involves making a key distinction between two different kinds of environmental effects. Up until now, when I have been talking about environmental effects on traits, I have been implicitly referring to what behavior geneticists call **shared environment** effects. Shared environment effects are those *environmental influences that operate to make family members alike.* These would include various kinds of conditions and experiences that different members of a family might share and that might, therefore, work to increase similarity among family members. Most of what we think of when we think of family environments fits into the concept of shared environment—such things as amount of family conflict, warmth, discipline, and so on. Also included would be social class, parents' education, and other social structural variables that impact the family as a whole. As we have already noted, shared family environment effects on personality traits appear to be surprisingly small. By contrast, **nonshared environment** effects are *environmental influences that operate to make family members unalike.* Many researchers now believe that nonshared environmental effects must account for the rest of the variance in personality traits. But what is a nonshared environment, and how would these effects work?

NONSHARED ENVIRONMENT

If you talked to my wife and her brother, you would never think that the two grew up in the same family. While my wife recalls many happy family scenes and lively interactions among her siblings, her brother remembers a lot more tension and conflict. Their accounts of what are supposedly the very same scenes from the past—a family vacation in the Canadian Rockies, for example—have virtually nothing in common. It makes you wonder about social reality—does it even exist or is it all in the minds of the beholders? Their discordant accounts also, however, begin to make clear the concept of nonshared environments. Just because people grow up in the same family, it does not follow that they experience the family in the same way. Indeed, there are many factors within family environments that vary significantly across family members. A good example is birth order. Firstborn and laterborn children occupy very different positions in the family system. A major part of the firstborn's

BIRTH ORDER: A NONSHARED ENVIRONMENTAL EFFECT

In his popular book, *Born to Rebel: Birth Order, Family Dynamics, and Creative Lives,* Frank Sulloway (1996) makes a very strong case for the power of birth order as a nonshared environmental influence in personality. Adopting a Darwinian perspective on family dynamics, Sulloway argues that children compete for parental investment in any family setting. Blessed with a natural advantage by virtue of being first on the scene, oldest children are likely to identify strongly with the parents and to adopt the traditional viewpoints of authority writ large. By contrast, later-borns must define themselves over and against the dominant firstborns so that they can carve out a niche that will bring them parental resources. Consequently, later-borns are more likely to adopt a rebellious and contrarian attitude toward authority. One interesting result of this development is that later-borns should be more open to innovation and change. In simple trait terms, firstborns should be more dominant (an aspect of extraversion in the Big Five) and perhaps conscientious while later-borns should be more open to experience.

Sulloway finds rather extraordinary support for his hypotheses by examining historical records. In one of his studies, he surveyed the published responses of 19th-century scientists to the introduction of Darwin's theory of evolution. Darwin (himself a later-born) launched a scientific revolution that defied the authority of the church as well as many accepted scientific canons of the day. Following the publication of his landmark *Origin of the Species* in 1859, the historical record shows that later-born scientists were 4.4 times more likely to support Darwin's revolutionary views than were firstborn scientists. During the hundred years or so before the publication of Darwin's theory but during which time evolutionary ideas were being debated in the scientific community, later-born scientists were 9.1 times more likely to support evolutionary perspectives than were firstborns. Sulloway finds similar results for initial reactions of scientists to the

discoveries of Copernicus, Newton, and Freud. Eager to embrace perspectives that challenge the status quo, later-borns are more open to innovation and more willing to accept radical theoretical change, Sulloway contends. More conservative and invested in the norms of authority, firstborns resist these innovations at first, though if the innovation begins to bear fruit, firstborns will eventually catch on. Once they do catch on, firstborns will strive to attain dominant positions in the new status quo.

Sulloway's predictions are not new. The same kinds of hypotheses were put forth by the psychoanalytic theorist Alfred Adler (chapter 11 in this book) in the early years of the 20th century. Adler predicted that firstborns should be relatively conservative and power-oriented while second-borns should be rebellious, competitive, and skeptical of authority. Despite Adler's theorizing and Sulloway's compelling historical examples, empirical research on personality traits and birth order has not produced many clear-cut findings (Falbo, 1997; Forer, 1977; Sampson, 1962; Schooler, 1972). These studies tend to correlate birth order with trait measures in samples of unrelated individuals. However, a recent study examining individuals *within the same families* provided corroborating evidence for Sulloway's claims. First-borns tended to score higher on achievement and conscientiousness scales compared to their younger siblings, and the younger siblings showed higher levels of rebelliousness and agreeableness (Paulhus, Trapnell, & Chen, 1999).

Birth order may exert some measurable effect on personality, but the effect is mediated by such demographic factors as sex, social class, and ethnicity, and by a host of other variables that are more difficult to assess. Without intensive study of each family, it is difficult to know what a particular ordinal position means in a particular family constellation. A firstborn son in a large intact Catholic family living in a working-class section of Boston is likely to have a very different experience of family life than a firstborn

(CONTINUES)

FEATURE 6.A *(CONTINUED)*

daughter of a small but wealthy Florida family where the parents are divorced and in which neither parent claims a religious affiliation, both parents travel extensively, and the daughter spends the weekdays with Mom and the weekends with Dad.

Nonetheless, Sulloway's historical presentation has rekindled interest among psychologists in birth order, and new research may be in the offing. Many

laypersons are convinced that their own ordinal position in the family profoundly shaped who they are. Parents often explain differences in their children in terms of birth order. Indeed, I have found myself doing it. By the age of 10, my older daughter seemed to have "bought the system," as a friend of mine says. My younger one—she was born to rebel.

---

nonshared environment may be the exalted status of being the oldest, biggest, strongest, and smartest. The second-born may need to scramble to find a comfortable niche in the family system, making for a very different experience of family life. As you will see in Feature 6.A, psychologists and laypersons alike have expressed considerable interest in the issue of birth order effects as one kind of nonshared environmental influence on personality traits.

Rowe (1999) lists six categories of nonshared family effects. *Perinatal trauma* are injuries or damage sustained by the fetus before birth. Trauma of this sort differentiate the child from all other family members from the beginning. *Accidental events* run the gamut from physical injuries to winning the raffle prize at the state fair. Chance happenings and lucky breaks may have an impact on personality, serving to differentiate a child further from other family members. *Family constellation* is Rowe's third category, and it includes birth order and birth spacing between siblings. A fourth category is *sibling mutual interaction*. Children in a family interact with one another in complex ways over time, forming alliances of various sorts, competing and cooperating, adopting a wide range of social roles. The third daughter in a family of five children may develop an especially close relationship with the youngest daughter, who goes to her for help and counsel. The second daughter is left out of this relationship and establishes a closer bond instead with the oldest child in the family, who is the only son. It is possible that such nonshared family patterns might have some differential impact on the development of personality traits. Fifth is *unequal parental treatment*—a favorite in many families. Mom always liked you the most! Dad played sports with the sons but ignored the daughters. And so on. Finally, there are *influences outside the family*, such as teachers and peers. Though we lived in the same home and went to the same school, my brother and I had very different friends and different teachers. Such differential experience may have some impact on the development of personality traits.

To date, ideas are many but good data are few when it comes to understanding the workings of nonshared environment effects. While proposals about such nonshared influences as differential parental treatment (within the family) and peer group effects (outside the family) seem reasonable (e.g., Harris, 1995), there is not yet much research to support the claims directly. The entire arena of nonshared environment influences on personality traits remains wide open for future research.

As portrayed in Figure 6.2, Dunn and Plomin (1990) estimate that nonshared environment effects account for as much as 35% of the variance in personality traits. They attribute 40% to genetic effects, 20% to measurement error, and only 5% to the effects of shared environments. Given what we know to date, their estimates make good sense. However, it is important to note that the 35% figure for nonshared environments comes by way of a

FIGURE 6.2   **COMPONENTS OF VARIANCE IN PERSONALITY TRAITS**

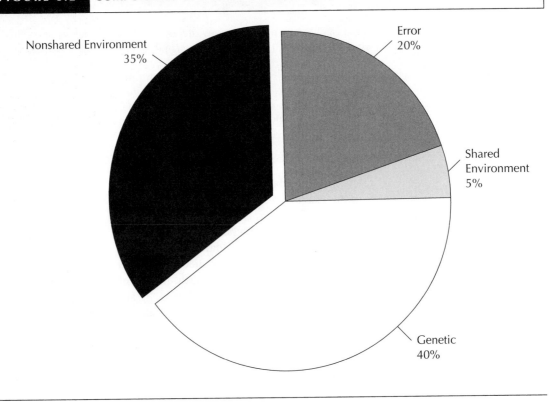

SOURCE: From *Separate Lives: Why Siblings Are So Different* (p. 50), by J. Dunn & R. Plomin, 1990, New York: Basic Books.

process of elimination. The logic is this: We have strong evidence for heritabilities of at least 40% for almost all personality traits; we have little evidence to support a figure any higher than about 5% for shared environment effects, and it may indeed be even lower; we have good reason to believe that error accounts for at least 10% to 20% of the variance, so we'll round up. That leaves us with 35% unexplained variance. The 35% must be attributable to nonshared environment effects *because there is nothing left to attribute it to!* Therefore, while it makes good sense to contend that personality traits may be influenced by nonshared environments, we do not as yet know exactly what those environments are or how they work.

HOW GENES SHAPE ENVIRONMENTS

When we attempt to account for variation in personality traits by appealing to genetic and environmental effects, we typically assume that genes and environments are two different things. In a literal sense, this is true. Genes are segments of DNA; environments are things like families, neighborhoods, and social classes. But, in another sense, the separation between the two is misleading, for the effects of genes and environments often get mixed up in the making of behavior. Rather than exerting independent effects on behavior, genes and environments seem to work together. However, this collaboration between the two is not fully reciprocal. Environments cannot readily influence a person's genes. No matter how many soothing experiences a temperamentally irritable infant enjoys, the genes that are (partially) responsible for that irritable temperament will not be altered. The behavior may change; the infant may even become a much less irritable person; but the genes, they stay the same. By contrast, genes themselves do seem to influence environments. Genes alter and shape how people experience their environments, and genes shape what environments people will choose to experience.

As a striking indication of just how mixed up genes can be in the determination of environments, recent studies in behavior genetics suggest that *environments themselves are heritable.* For example, MZ twins reared together report their environments to be more highly similar than do DZ twins reared together. Plomin and Bergman (1991) reviewed many different measures of socialization environments and concluded that these measures are likely to be confounded with genetic variation. We typically see the environments as "out there," independent of the observer. And, of course, environments themselves literally have no DNA. But researchers typically measure "out there" environments through the reports of people who are experiencing them. To find out how warm and responsive an adolescent's parents are, a researcher may ask the adolescent. The adolescent's report of her environment, however, is influenced by her own genotype. People may be predisposed to see their environments in a certain way. "What appear to be stable and enduring features of the environment," writes Caspi (1998, p. 352), "may be a reflection of stable, enduring, and partially heritable individual differences" in personality traits.

Researchers have found that the influence of genetic differences on perceptions of environments seems to increase with age. Elkins, McGue, and Iacono (1997) examined how MZ and DZ twins in two different age groups—11-year-old boys and 17-year-old boys—described their family environments. All of the twins in this study were males. MZ twins were more similar than DZ twins in their reports of parent–son conflict, parental involvement, and overall support from parents. This finding suggests that these dimensions of the family environment, as measured through the perceptions of the male adolescents in this study, are partially heritable. In addition, the 17-year-olds showed significantly higher heritabilities on family dimensions than did the 11-year-olds, especially in the realm of the father–son relationship. The researchers argued that as adolescents get older, their own partially heritable personality tendencies take on more and more power in shaping their perceptions of their environments. In addition, older adolescents may have more control over their respective environments, shaping their worlds to fit more closely their own genotypes. As children grow up and assume greater responsibility for their own lives, their environments may come under greater and greater genetic control.

But the influence of genes on environments can be traced back even to the first few months of life. Genetic influences manifest themselves through the creation of environments. By virtue of their genetic endowments, infants shape their environments in subtle ways, and those environments, in turn, shape the development of personality, which further shapes environments in an endless cycle of mutual influence. Scarr and McCartney (1983) distinguish among three different ways in which one's genetic endowment, or genotype, may shape the environments that ultimately shape the development of personality traits.

The first way is *evocative influence:* people respond to a child according to his or her genotype. Easy babies may evoke different patterns of caregiving than difficult babies. Smiling and active babies are likely to receive more attention, at least in many middle-class

American families, than somber and irritable ones. Even at the level of infant temperament, therefore, the genotype subtly influences the social environment, which in turn influences the development of the baby.

The second form of genotype-environment influence is *passive influence.* The child's biological parents provide an environment for the child that is compatible with *their own* genotypes, which are similar to the genotypes of their biological children. For example, parents who are genetically inclined to read well and enjoy reading are likely to buy more books for their children and to read to them. Their children are likely, then, to enjoy books and to read well. Twin studies of cognitive abilities suggest that reading ability and interest in reading are influenced by heredity. Thus, by virtue of sharing genetic similarities with the biological parents, a child is likely to be exposed to environments that are relatively consonant with his or her own genotype, since it is the parental genotypes that partially determine those environments.

Finally, *active influence* manifests itself in the direct selection of and search for environments that fit one's genotype. Active niche choosing and niche creating are well documented in research and everyday experience. A gregarious boy will seek out friends in his neighborhood and thereby partially create the environments that will have an influence on his development. An athletic girl will join the softball team. To the extent that gregariousness and athletic ability are determined by one's genotype, these examples suggest how genotypes may exert an impetus in niche choosing. While evocative and passive influences are likely to predominate in childhood and early adolescence, Scarr and McCartney suggest that the process of active influence of genotype on environment may intensify as the person moves into and through adulthood.

CHANGE AND COMPLEXITY

The very concept of a personality "trait" is biased in favor of continuity over change and simplicity over complexity. Traits are by definition more-or-less stable over time, at least stable enough to warrant the label of "trait" rather than the more fleeting notions of "state," "mood," "momentary feeling," and so on. I have reviewed evidence in this chapter suggestive of substantial differential continuity in trait scores across the adult years. The evidence for heritability of traits, furthermore, implicitly supports a continuity view. We know our genes don't change; therefore, if personality traits are partially determined by genes, then it should not be surprising that over long durations traits do not change very much either. Ideally, traits are simple. By "simple," I mean that they convey clear, straightforward, and nonconditional behavioral tendencies in people. What determines any given behavior in any given situation is likely to be a complex blend of many factors, including many different traits. But in trait psychology, we can single out one discrete personality dimension and examine its manifestations across a range of situations. Over many different situations and over time, highly extraverted people *tend to* engage in more conversations, meet more people, and attend more social events than do highly introverted people. Straightforward and simple. (And generally true.)

If traits were *not* relatively stable over time and if traits did *not* predict simple and broad behavioral tendencies across situations and over time, then it would be very difficult, I would submit, to build a credible science of personality psychology. Our common understanding of human nature purports that people differ from one another in recognizable ways, that at least some of these differences can be communicated in simple words and ideas, and that these differences have some staying power over time. Personality research supports all these claims. But there is more to it. In what remains of this chapter, I seek to emphasize the countervailing notions of change and complexity as they apply to personality traits. I will make three general points:

1. Despite the strong evidence for differential continuity, personality traits can be shown to change over time.

2. Traits are organized in different patterns, and different patterns change in different ways over time.

3. Those aspects of human individuality that appear *most* likely to change dramatically over time may not be traits at all.

DIFFERENT MEANINGS OF CHANGE

We have already seen that the idea of "continuity" in personality traits has different meanings. So, too, does the idea of change. Some of these meanings parallel the meanings I have already identified for continuity. Recall that *absolute* continuity in traits is typically measured via group averages. If the average score on the trait "exhibitionism" in a group of college seniors is close to the average score this same group showed three years earlier as freshmen, then we can say that exhibitionism in this sample shows absolute continuity over a three-year span. But if the seniors score significantly lower (or higher) as a group than they did as freshmen, then we have evidence for personality change. As a group, these students have moved in a particular direction with respect to this particular trait. This is a common way to think about personality change. By contrast, recall that *differential* continuity refers to the stability of individual differences in trait scores. We have seen that evidence for differential continuity of traits in adulthood is impressive. Nonetheless, even here some change can be seen, for not everybody maintains his or her relative standing in a given trait distribution over time. In an 8-year longitudinal study, for example, Roberts, Caspi, and Moffitt (2001) demonstrated that even when test–retest correlations on traits are relatively high for the sample, most people show substantial change in at least *one in five traits* over that time frame. Sandy may increase in extraversion; Jennifer may decrease in conscientiousness; Sam may stay about the same in all traits. In other words, some people change in some traits more than other people do.

The idea of personality change conjures up other associations as well. Although change can be for the better or for the worse, people typically strive to change for the better over time. Psychotherapists and counselors are in the business of promoting personality change under the banners of "adjustment," "adaptation," "increased mental health," "better coping," "recovery," and so on. These terms for change suggest processes of healing and solving life problems. Change becomes the cure or solution. A set of related ideas comes from our understandings of personality *development,* and such associated notions as "maturation," "fulfillment," and "self-actualization." Here we are talking about change in a particular direction and toward something that is usually seen as bigger, better, higher, further along, or more "age appropriate." Change as growth. Ever optimistic about the possibilities of personality growth, Gordon Allport (1961) argued that personality development should ideally move in the direction of five criteria for maturity:

1. emotional security and the regulation of behavior by social rules designed to reduce interpersonal friction and obtain social rewards;

2. the capacity for investing the self in significant life projects and endeavors rather than being preoccupied with immediate needs;

3. the capacity for compassionate and intimate relations with others;

4. a realistic appraisal of self and others; and

5. the establishment of a personally derived philosophy of life.

As we will see in chapter 9, other developmental theorists have offered their own visions of what personality change *should* look like as people move across the lifespan. Lifespan personality change has been studied by many different researchers, including sociologists and anthropologists. Researchers have tended to adopt variations on two basic research designs. In **cross-sectional studies,** researchers typically compare data from individuals in two or more discrete age groups. For example, a cross-sectional study might compare mean (average) scores on the trait openness to experience among 20-year-old, 30-year-old, and 40-year-old American adults, all sampled in the year 2000. In **longitudinal studies,** by contrast, researchers typically follow a single sample of individuals over time, comparing scores at different age points. Thus, a longitudinal study begun in the year 2000 might obtain openness to experience scores from a sample of 20-year-old American adults and then obtain scores again from the same sample when they turned 30 (2010) and 40 (2020) years of age.

Cross-sectional and longitudinal studies have different strengths and weaknesses. For our purposes, it is worth noting one important limitation of cross-sectional studies. Because cross-sectional studies examine differences among age groups at a given point in time, they do not really examine change and development directly. In our example above, if 40-year-olds score lower in openness to experience than 20-year-olds, we cannot conclude for sure that this is a developmental change. It may instead be an example of a **cohort effect.** In the cross-sectional study, the 20-year-olds and the 40-year-olds are from different birth cohorts. The 20-year-olds were born in 1980; the 40-year-olds in 1960. The two groups are different in age, for sure, but as cohorts they also experienced different historical events and represent different historical generations. Should we find that the 40-year-olds are lower on openness, we would have to entertain the possibility that the difference between the two groups might be due to different historical experiences of the two cohorts rather than to developmental change per se. It may not be the case that as you get older, you become less open. Instead, perhaps the advent of the Internet in the 1990s profoundly shaped the young minds of the now 20-year-old cohort, making them more open to innovation and change than they would have been had they all grown up in the 1970s. This is not to suggest that cross-sectional studies are not useful in determining personality change. But findings from cross-sectional studies typically need to be supplemented by findings from longitudinal studies before researchers can come to clear conclusions about lifespan change in personality.

TRAIT CHANGE IN THE ADULT YEARS

In general, cross-sectional and longitudinal studies do *not* show *dramatic* shifts in personality over the course of the adult lifespan. But evidence for *gradual* and systematic changes in all of the Big Five trait domains *can* nonetheless be found. Overall, studies suggest that traits related to extraversion *(E)*, neuroticism *(N)*, and openness to experience *(O)* may decline gradually from early through middle adulthood while traits related to agreeableness *(A)* and conscientiousness *(C)* may rise gradually during that period. For example, college students typically score higher on measures of *E, N,* and *O* than do middle-aged adults, while their scores on *A* and *C* tend to be lower (Costa & McCrae, 1994). A large cross-sectional study conducted among German, Portuguese, Italian, Croatian, and South Korean adults showed a similar pattern: higher levels of *E, N,* and *O* and lower levels of *A* and *C* among college-aged adults compared with middle-aged adults (McCrae et al., 1999). Figure 6.3 shows the data for conscientiousness and openness to experience. As you can see, mean levels for *C* tend to increase gradually and for *O* to decrease as you move from the age 18–21 group through ages 22–29, 30–49, and 50+. An even larger cross-sectional study collected Big Five trait scores from personality scales posted on the Internet. A total of 135,515 adults between the ages of 21 and 60 participated in the Internet study (Srivastava, John, Gosling, & Potter, 2003). The results showed that scores on *A* and *C* increased through early and middle adulthood while scores on *N* for women (but not men) decreased across the same span.

Longitudinal studies show age changes that parallel these cross-sectional findings. In longitudinal follow-ups of college students, Watson and Walker (1996) reported declines in negative affect (related to *N*), and Mortimer, Finch, and Kumka (1982) reported declines in sociability (related to *E*) as the participants in their study moved toward middle adulthood. Jessor (1983) found longitudinal increases in achievement (related to *C*). McGue, Bacon, and Lykken (1993) followed 127 pairs of twins over a 10-year span. The average age of the twins at the beginning of the study was about 20 years old. Although the researchers did not find the expected decrease in extraversion scores over that 10-year period, they did report declines in stress reaction (related to *N*), absorption (related to *O*), and aggression (indicating an increase in *A*), and they found increases in achievement and control (both related to *C*). Helson and Klohnen (1998) found decreases in negative emotionality *(N)* and increases in constraint (*C*) in a sample of 80 women traced from age 27 to 43. Helson and Klohnen also found increases in positive affect. Reviewing research findings such as these, Aldwin and Levensen (1994) conclude that "there appears to be a decrease in levels of neuroticism and increases in those personality traits [e.g., aspects of *C* and *A*] reflecting competence from early adulthood to midlife" (p. 194).

The development toward greater levels of competence, autonomy, and responsibility with increasing maturity in adulthood is a common theme in longitudinal studies of adult development conducted in the United States (Cartwright & Wink, 1994; Stewart & Vandewater, 1993; Vaillant, 1977). Two especially influential studies in this regard are the AT&T Study (Howard & Bray, 1988) and the Mills College Longitudinal Study (Helson, 1967; Helson & Wink, 1992).

The AT&T Study followed a sample of 266 male managerial candidates at AT&T over 20 years, from the late 1950s, when the men were in their 20s, to the late 1970s, when they were in their 40s. The men were studied in assessment centers, where they were put through behavioral simulations, interviewed, and administered a variety of cognitive, personality, attitudinal, and biographical measures. A major focus of the study was to explore career and personal development among managers in corporate America. One interesting finding in the study was a strong drop in measures of ambition over the 20-year span. At the beginnings of their managerial careers, the young men showed strong levels of ambition and somewhat unrealistic expectations of how far they might climb in the company structure. After only 8 years in the company, however, their ambition scores dropped sharply and they expressed more realistic views of the possibilities of promotion. Still, the managers maintained strong interest in their jobs and strong motivation to do their jobs well. Substantial increases were noted over the 20-year period in measures of autonomy. The men showed increasing levels of independence and focus on productive work as they moved from their

FIGURE 6.3	CONSCIENTIOUSNESS AND OPENNESS TO EXPERIENCE RELATED TO AGE IN FIVE NATIONS

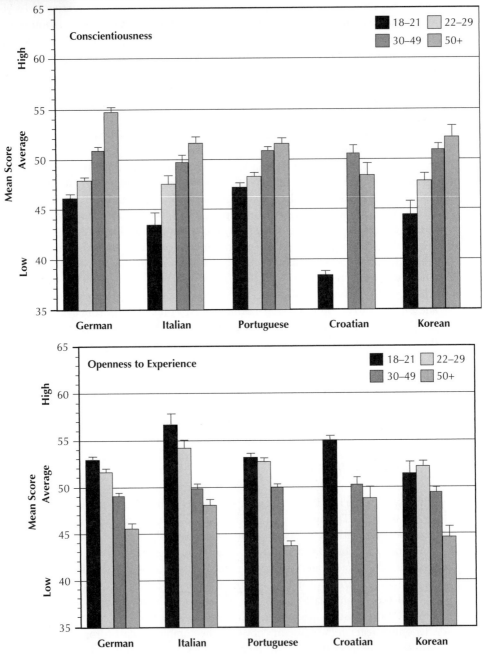

SOURCE: Adapted from "Age Differences in Personality Across the Adult Lifespan: Parallels in Five Cultures," by R. R. McCrae, P. T. Costa, Jr., M. P. de Lima, A. Simoes, F. Ostendorf, A. Angleitner, I. Marusic, et al., 1999, *Developmental Psychology, 35,* 474 (top), 472 (bottom).

mid-20s to their mid-40s. Increasing autonomy, however, may have exacted something of an interpersonal cost for this cohort of men. Over time, the men showed decreases in measures of friendliness and empathy for others. The authors of the study suggest that a move away from brash ambition and toward productive autonomy may characterize many men as they mature from their early years in the work world toward their middle years, during which they typically assume greater and greater levels of responsibility.

The Mills Longitudinal Study began with 140 women who graduated in 1958 or 1960 from Mills College, a small and elite West Coast college for women. As college seniors, the women completed a number of standard personality measures. They were recontacted by mail at ages 27, 43, and 52. The Mills cohort is an especially interesting one because of the significant historical events these women experienced in young and middle adulthood. At the time of their college graduation, American society generally expected these women to forego careers in favor of marriage and family life. But the Women's Movement of the 1960s and early 1970s galvanized the ambitions of many of these women and strongly impacted how they thought about the relationship between work and family life. A significant number of the women went on to achieve considerable success in their careers, in some cases breaking into male-dominated professions. Researchers have traced both personality change and continuity in the Mills cohort, and they have supplemented their findings on the women with measures of personality obtained from a subset of the women's husbands as well (Helson & Stewart, 1994).

Examining the period from college graduation to age 43, Helson and Moane (1987) documented increases in overall scores on responsibility, self-control, and responsiveness to others among the Mills women. Between the ages of 43 and 52, furthermore, significant changes were noted on a number of other traits. As they moved through their 40s and into their early 50s, the women became increasingly *less* dependent and self-critical and increasingly *more* confident and decisive. Over this time period, significant increases were also noted on the variables of coping through intellectuality, logical analysis, and tolerance for ambiguity. Evidence from this study indicated that the women became increasingly more comfortable with their self-conceptions over time and came to believe more strongly that their accomplishments and commitments reflected well their basic needs and aspirations (Helson & Wink, 1992).

Some theorists have suggested that men and women show different developmental trajectories with respect to personality traits in young adulthood and midlife. For example, Gutmann (1987) has proposed that young parents (say, in their 20s) are likely to show traditional sex-role patterns, with men scoring higher than women on agentic dimensions such as dominance and competence, and women higher on communal dimensions such as nurturance. But once men and women move out of the direct parenting roles (say, in their late 40s), women may become increasingly agentic and men increasingly communal. The Mills Study provides some data to support part of Gutmann's claim. Wink and Helson (1993) compared the Mills women and their husbands in the early parental (age 27) and postparental (age 52) periods of life. Figure 6.4 shows the results for a cluster of self-report adjectives indicative of instrumental "competence." High scorers

A pioneering researcher in the area of adult personality development, Ravenna Helson has reported many important findings from the Mills College Longitudinal Study. Women who graduated from Mills in the late 1950s showed increasing levels of confidence, decisiveness, independence, and tolerance for ambiguity as they moved through their midlife years.

FIGURE 6.4 **COMPETENCE RATINGS AND ADULT DEVELOPMENT**

The average scores on competence, measured via the Adjective Check List, increase from early parental to postparental years for wives, more so than for husbands. The figure also shows competence scores for wives' parents in their postparental period, suggesting that as wives age their competence levels come to match their fathers' (relatively high) competence levels, rather than their mothers' (relatively low) levels.

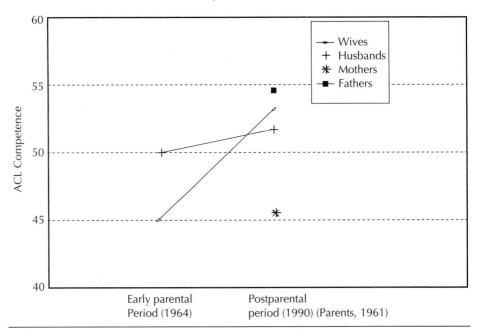

SOURCE: Adapted from "Personality Change in Adulthood," by R. Helson & A. J. Stewart, in *Can Personality Change?* (p. 214), by T. F. Heatherton & J. L. Weinberer (Eds.), 1994, Washington, DC: APA Press.

---

on competence described themselves as goal-oriented, organized, thorough, practical, efficient, clear-thinking, realistic, precise, and confident. As you can see in the figure, women at age 27 scored lower than their husbands on this dimension, but at age 52 they scored about the same. Figure 6.4 also shows the mean scores for a subsample of the *parents* of the women, contacted in 1961 (shortly after the women had graduated from Mills). As you can see, the women's then-midlife fathers scored much higher on competence than did their wives (the women's mothers). The findings point to the effect of changing gender roles and historical events on personality traits. At age 27, the Mills women looked much like their mothers with respect to competence scores. But by age 52, they looked much more like their fathers had looked when they were of comparable age. The increased societal acceptance of women's agency and the movement out of direct parental roles may have combined to bolster the self-confidence of these women in midlife and pull them in the direction of a more agentic and goal-oriented approach to life.

Overall, longitudinal studies of adult development support a case for significant change in personality traits, at least through midlife. (Studies of traits in later adulthood, however, are scarce.) The available data suggest that against the backdrop of considerable stability in individual differences in traits over the adult life course, developmental trends in overall levels can still be observed. As men and women move from early to middle adulthood, they tend to become gradually more comfortable with themselves, showing decreasing levels of self-criticism, negative affect, and other indices of neuroticism. Indices of positive affect appear to rise, even when extraversion scores tend gradually to drop. At the same time, adults appear to increase in responsibility, self-confidence, autonomy, and certain other indices of conscientiousness. Increases in self-confidence are especially apparent in well-educated women. Though the data are not completely consistent, there is some evidence of a "warming up" in personality from early to middle-adulthood, as people may become somewhat more agreeable and nurturant over time. People tend to feel somewhat better about themselves as they grow older, at least into middle age, and somewhat better about other people, too.

PATTERNS OF TRAITS OVER TIME

Many years ago, Jack Block (1971, 1981, 1993) and his colleagues devised a procedure for personality research that has shed considerable light on the issue of personality continuity and change over the human lifespan. While most trait research employs self-report scales that assess individual traits, Block has advocated the use of expert observers who evaluate overall patterns of traits in people's lives. Block pioneered the use of the **California Q-sort** in personality assessment. The Q-sort consists of 100 statements about personality (such as "Is a genuinely dependable and responsible person," "Has a wide range of interests," "Is skeptical, not easily impressed") that a rater sorts into nine different piles, ranging from those statements deemed by the rater to be most characteristic of the individual being rated to those being least characteristic.

One reason the Q-sort is an appealing method is that each of the 100 items is grouped into one of the nine stacks with other items that are relatively equally characteristic of the same individual. Such a procedure enables the researcher to examine *patterns* of personality traits within the person. Furthermore, comparing Q-sorts of the same individual over time allows the researcher to examine the longitudinal coherence of these patterns.

In one study, Block trained 36 psychologists to compose Q-sorts for 70 men and 76 women at four different points in the participants' lives. For the four different points in time, Block assembled four separate files, one each for information obtained about the participant when he or she was in early adolescence (age 13–14), late adolescence (15–17), his or her 30s, and his or her 40s. For each of the files, then, a trained psychologist composed a Q-sort for each participant, arranging the 100 personality descriptors into nine groups based on the wide variety of information on the person contained in the file.

One of the most influential personality psychologists in the second half of the 20th century, Jack Block used the California Q-sort and other measures to chart developmental patterns in adult lives. Block highlighted the importance of two broad constructs of human individuality – ego control and ego resilience.

Block (1981) identified clusters of individuals manifesting similar patterns of traits over time. Each cluster represented a personality type, specified in terms of an individual's displaying a particular pattern of traits that evolve in a particular fashion over time. For example, men who are "belated adjusters" appear rebellious and belligerent in adolescence, but they develop in the direction of conscientiousness and prosocial behavior as adults. As another example, women categorized as "cognitive copers" start out as overly sensitive and insecure in their junior-high years, but they mature over time to emerge as warm, introspective, and independent adults. Other types for men include what Block called "unsettled undercontrollers" and "vulnerable over controllers" and for women what he labelled as "hyperfeminine repressives" and "vulnerable undercontrollers."

Underlying the personality types identified by Block are two central dimensions of personality that organize many different aspects of human functioning. The first is what Block calls **ego control** (Block & Block, 1980). Ego control is the extent to which a person typically modifies the expression of impulses. At one extreme of the ego control continuum are undercontrolled people who cannot inhibit their desires and impulses, cannot delay gratification for longer-term rewards. Such people may become enthusiastic about many different things in their lives, but their involvements are fleeting and frustrating. They are distractible and exploratory and seem to live a relatively impromptu rather than planned life. At the other extreme are overcontrolled people who are especially conforming and restrained. Their lives may be well scripted, but their inhibitions sometimes keep them from spontaneous joy and creativity. In general, it would seem that a rating somewhere in the middle of the ego control continuum is one that best fits contemporary American views concerning appropriate adaptation to life and mental health.

The second major dimension underlying Block's types is **ego resiliency.** This is the capacity to *modify* one's typical level of ego control—in either direction—to adapt to the demands of a given situation. In contrast to ego control, ego resiliency would appear to be a characteristic for which "more is better." People who are high on ego resiliency are resourceful and flexible and able to adapt to a wide range of life challenges. In a study of the extent to which adolescents are able to delay immediate gratification to obtain longer-term benefits, Funder and Block (1989) found that ego resiliency, ego control, and intelligence all contributed to the significant prediction of delay behavior. Teenagers who scored high on Q-sort ratings suggestive of high ego resiliency and strong (less impulsive) ego control, as well as those who scored high on measures of IQ, tended to reveal the highest levels of adaptive delay behavior.

Taking a somewhat different tack, Norma Haan (1981) has analyzed longitudinal data obtained from 136 adults, some of whom were included in Block's (1981) analysis, for developmental trends in six basic personality factors: *cognitively invested* (verbally fluent, intellectual, philosophically inclined, achievement-oriented), *emotionally under/overcontrolled* (highly volatile and dramatic *versus* calm and restricted), *open/closed self* (self-aware and insightful *versus* conventional and repressive), *nurturant/hostile* (warm and responsive *versus* cold and suspicious), *under/overcontrolled heterosexual* (uninhibited *versus* inhibited in the realm of sexual expression), and *self-confident.* Haan's statistical analyses showed that Q-sort scores on these six dimensions were relatively stable for both men and women over time but more stable for women. Men were more likely than women to show significant change on these dimensions, especially between late adolescence and adulthood. Over time, both men and women, furthermore, appeared to become more cognitively invested, more open to self, more nurturant, and more self-confident. Sexual expressiveness, on the other hand, appeared to reach high levels in late adolescence, drop to lower levels when the subjects were in their 30s, and then rise again to surprisingly strong levels when the participants reached their 40s.

Integrating the work of Block and Haan with a number of other approaches to personality structure, including the Big Five personality traits, York and John (1992) developed a new typology of women's personality at midlife—what they call "the four faces of Eve." York and John argue that personality types should be defined as prototypes rather than discrete categories of traits. As such, types lack clear boundaries but rather shade into each other. While some persons exemplify the central features of a given type, other people appear to reside on the fuzzy boundaries between types, as mixtures or blends that are especially difficult to characterize in a clear-cut fashion.

York and John analyzed longitudinal data on 103 graduates (from the years 1958 and 1960) of Mills College. Included in the data were follow-up questionnaires administered in 1981, when the women were in their early-to-mid-40s. York and John employed a statistical procedure called "inverse factor analysis," whereby individuals rather than variables are intercorrelated across a wide range of personality characteristics. In the current study, the procedure provided a numerical estimate of the extent to which each of the 103 women was well represented on each of four "person factors": *Individuated, Traditional, Conflicted,* and *Assured*. In this person-centered rather than variable-centered approach, therefore, each woman in the study could be viewed in terms of "how much" of her personality was well captured by each of the four factors. Some women proved to be "exemplars" of particular factors—"pure" Individuated, Traditional, Conflicted, or Assured types. Other women, by contrast, expressed characteristics that were spread across a number of factors. For example, one woman might appear on the border between Individuated and Traditional; another might show equal elements of three types.

Exemplars of the Individuated type combined strong ambitions in life with interpersonal warmth and sensitivity. They tended to manifest the highest levels of ego resiliency of all four types and relatively low levels of ego control, suggesting that they were spontaneous and uninhibited in their expression of impulses but that they knew well when to hold themselves back and when to let go. Of all the types, they were the most flexible and adaptive in the expression of their feelings, needs, and desires. With respect to the Big Five traits, they tended to score high on measures of extraversion *(E)*, agreeableness *(A)*, and openness to experience *(O)*. By contrast, the women who exemplified best the Traditional person factor expressed characteristics indicative of high levels of ego control, as well as high scores on the Big Five trait conscientiousness *(C)*. Like the Individuated women, the Traditionals were rated as especially agreeable *(A)*, but unlike the Individuated women they expressed very conservative values about the proper role of women in contemporary society. While they were described as especially giving and sympathetic, the Traditionals were also more prone to feelings of guilt than were women exemplifying the other types.

Exemplars of the Conflicted person factor consistently showed the lowest levels of ego resiliency and highest levels of neuroticism *(N)*. They appeared less satisfied with themselves than the other types; they were described as anxious, hostile, and aloof. Finally, the Assured women appeared to be the most emotionally stable of the four groups, though their stability hinted at narcissism and an interpersonally detached approach to life. They were the most confident, rational, productive, and skeptical women in the group. They showed relatively high levels of ego resiliency and conscientiousness *(C)* and the lowest levels of neuroticism *(N)*. They were the least likely to suffer from guilt and doubt. But they were also the least likely of all the types to engage in fantasy and introspection.

In sum, personality typologies organize groups of trait dimensions into patterns that show both continuity and change over time. Typologies are popular with some personality psychologists because, it is sometimes argued, they provide a more holistic, person-centered

FEATURE 6.B

HAPPINESS OVER THE HUMAN LIFESPAN

For many of us, happiness is the bottom line in life. We try to do things that make us happy and avoid things that make us unhappy. When we evaluate how our lives are going, one of the first things we may ask ourselves is this: Am I really happy? Most people report that they are at least moderately happy with their lives. But who are the happiest people? Who are the most unhappy? What causes happiness? And does happiness change over time?

Happiness proves to be an interesting window through which to view continuity and change in personality. Psychologists often use the term "well-being" to refer to what most laypeople mean when they talk of happiness. Well-being is made up of different components, but three main parts of it appear to be positive affect, negative affect, and life satisfaction (Diener, 1984; Myers & Diener, 1995). Although well-being itself may not qualify as a personality trait (there is debate about that idea), some of the conclusions we have drawn in this chapter about traits can be loosely applied to the area of well-being. As with traits, for example, there is evidence for both continuity and change in well-being over the human lifespan.

Virtually everybody knows that well-being can fluctuate from one moment to the next. When you receive that unexpected high grade on a tough assignment, you are likely to feel good, and your well-being shoots way up. A person you are in love with tells you that he or she never wants to see you again, and you find your well-being plummeting to the ocean floor. Some psychologists argue that well-being fluctuates around a *set point* for every individual. Different people have different set points; some people may be predisposed to be happier than others, this argument goes. Evidence for the set point idea comes from studies showing that despite fluctuations, individual differences in well-being show considerable differential continuity over time (Costa, McCrae, & Zonderman, 1987; Watson & Walker, 1996). There is also surprising evidence to suggest that well-being itself may be

heritable. In a study of more than 2,000 twins, Lykken and Tellegen (1996) report that MZ pairs were substantially more similar to each other on a self-report measure of well-being than were DZ pairs. Retesting their participants over a 10-year span, the authors tried to estimate a set point value for each participant, which they determined to be "the stable component of subjective well-being" (p. 186). They concluded that the heritability of this stable component could be as high as 80%.

If individual differences in well-being are strongly driven by genetic differences, do environmental effects have much influence on how happy we are? The answer appears to be that they do in the short run, but perhaps their influence in the long run is less. Day-to-day changes in well-being parallel shifting successes and failures in our lives, but each of us tends eventually to return to our own set point, research suggests. Macrosocial variables such as race, sex, and social class have surprisingly little impact on overall well-being (Myers & Diener, 1995). In the United States, men and women, blacks and whites, show comparable mean levels of well-being. Income and education are only mildly and positively associated with happiness, accounting for less than 2% of the variance in well-being in Lykken and Tellegen's study (1996). Other predictors of well-being include being married and having strong religious convictions, but again these variables show surprisingly small associations with how happy people are. Lykken and Tellegen (1996) offer the disquieting conclusion that happiness is mainly the luck of the draw, a matter of heritability and chance external events:

> If the transitory variations of well-being are largely due to fortune's favors, whereas the midpoint of these variations is determined by the great genetic lottery that occurs at conception, then we are led to conclude that individual differences in human happiness—how one feels at the moment and also how happy one feels on average over time—are primarily a matter of chance. (p. 189)

(CONTINUES)

FEATURE 6.B (CONTINUED)

Do overall levels of happiness change over the lifespan? We have seen that while individual differences in traits can be highly stable, changes in overall levels of trait scores can still be observed over the lifespan. For the variable of subjective well-being, different theories of adult development propose different variations on this same theme. One view has it that since people encounter greater physical limitations and health problems as they get older and because they must endure an increasing number of losses, older adults should show lower levels of well-being than younger adults. By contrast, some theories argue that older adults are better able than the young to regulate their emotional lives by exerting selective control over their interpersonal worlds, which may lead to increases in well-being with age (Baltes & Baltes, 1990; Carstensen, 1995). Findings from different studies provide something of a mixed picture on this question. In a unique cross-sectional examination, for example, Ingelhart (1990) compared single-item self-report happiness ratings made by young, midlife, and elderly adults in 16 countries. He found that some nations showed decreases in happiness among their oldest cohorts (e.g., France, Japan), some showed increases (e.g., Britain, Ireland), some showed a dip in happiness in midlife (e.g., The Netherlands, Canada), and others showed no difference across the age cohorts (e.g., the United States, Greece).

Mroczek and Kolarz (1998) completed an especially comprehensive study of positive and negative affect in 2,727 Americans ranging in age from 25 to 74 years. Controlling for a host of sociodemographic, personality, and contextual factors, the authors documented systematic relations between age and well-being. Overall, Mroczek and Kolarz found that positive affect tends to go up and negative affect tends to go down across the age span they studied. However, a more detailed analysis revealed different variations on this general pattern for men and women. With respect to positive affect, both men and women showed an increase with age, but men who also scored *high on the trait of extraversion* reported high levels of positive affect *at all ages*. With respect to negative affect, scores went down for men over the lifespan, but women did not show an age-related decrease. Furthermore, among the men marital status had a moderating effect. It was mainly for *married men* that an inverse relation between age and negative affect was found. Older married men showed especially low levels of negative affect. Marriage may increasingly help men, as they get older, to regulate their own emotional states and select the kinds of social and instrumental experiences that minimize feelings of sadness, anger, and despair.

The full answer to the question of how much happiness changes and remains the same over the human lifespan has not yet been spelled out. But Mroczek and Kolarz's careful study shows that the ultimate answer, if one ever arises, will be a complicated one and dependent on many factors.

---

understanding of human behavior and experience than is possible through the examination of single, independent traits (Mumford, Stokes & Owens, 1990; Ozer & Gjerde, 1989; Wink, 1996; Zeldow & Bennett, 1997). Furthermore, the kind of typological research inspired by Jack Block's work underscores complexity and change in personality over time, while also providing strong support for the continuity and coherence of adult personality.

WHAT ELSE MIGHT CHANGE?

It has always been easier to document continuity in personality traits than meaningful and systematic change (Heatherton & Weinberger, 1994). In this chapter, we have seen that evidence for differential continuity in traits, at least across much of the adult lifespan, is very impressive. Of course, the continuity is not perfect, and over many decades of time the retest correlations on personality traits drop somewhat. Still, individual differences in traits show remarkable longitudinal stability. The stability is surely due in part to the significant heritabilities of traits and to the ways in which genotypes contribute to the selection of environments that are consistent with those genotypes themselves. We have also seen that changes in trait levels do indeed occur, as documented in longitudinal studies of individual traits themselves and of constellations or patterns of traits. For example, neuroticism scores seem to drop slowly and conscientiousness scores to increase gradually over the adult lifespan. Developmental movements toward greater levels of autonomy, warmth, and social responsibility have been documented in studies following young adults into their midlife years.

Nonetheless, many adults feel that they have changed in many *other* ways over time (Levinson, 1978; McAdams, 1993; Roberts & Newton, 1987). People often report dramatic turning points in their lives, episodes of quantum change (Miller & C'deBaca, 1994) through which they feel personally transformed. People speak of religious conversions, life-changing events, personal awakenings, recovery and revitalization, changing priorities and goals, identity crises, and the like. People often feel that they have developed through "stages," embarked on personal journeys, and undertaken personal projects designed to fulfill, improve, or even remake the self. Furthermore, psychotherapists and counselors devote themselves to helping people change their lives for the better. An entire industry of self-help guides—from 12-step programs to spiritual advisors—has grown up in North America and other modern societies over the past 40 years, premised on the deeply held belief that people can and do change. Given the widespread belief in personality change and the sustained efforts of so many mental health professionals to promote change in personality over time, might we not expect to see *more* and perhaps more dramatic evidence for personality change than we have seen in this chapter?

One response to my question is this: No, we should not expect to see more change, once we realize just how hard it is to change. The massive scientific literature on the effects of psychotherapy and psychoeducational efforts to induce change is littered with hundreds of failed efforts to change people's lives and thousands of studies showing that even when change occurs, it is hard-won and halting. People may feel that significant events in their lives have major impacts on changing their personalities, but these beliefs may be mistaken, argue some experts. Caspi and Moffitt (1993) argue that, if anything, major life changes sometimes accentuate or consolidate the trait tendencies that people have to begin with. Facing a new challenge or encountering a major life transition, an extravert may end up coping with the life change by displaying the same outgoing and sociable tendencies that he or she has been predisposed to display all along, maybe even more so. Consistent individual differences among people sometimes appear most glaring in times of transition, Caspi and Moffitt argue. Events that might be thought to change people may have the paradoxical effect of affirming who they were and how they behaved in the first place.

A second answer to my question goes like this: Sure, people change, but not so much their traits. Significant personality change may occur, but that change may not be captured in a person's trait scores (McAdams, 1992b, 1994). As I suggested earlier in this chapter, the concept of the trait is better designed to express the way in which personality is continuous over time rather than the way in which personality changes. The assumption of some degree of longitudinal consistency is built into the very definition of a trait. Dispositional trait measures speak to a level of personality functioning where we expect to see considerable stability and continuity over time. But there may be other levels, other manifestations of human individuality that more readily express how it is that people believe they change over time—and indeed how it is that they really *do* change over time, if not with respect to their traits. Psychotherapists and counselors do not usually aim their interventions directly at personality traits. More often, they tackle specific problems, some of which may have implications for traits. Similarly, when people think of significant personality changes in their own lives, they do not always couch those changes in terms of basic dispositional traits. Their language may suggest instead something more particular than a trait, something that must be understood in the full context of their own lives.

Beyond traits, what other aspects of personality might change over time? A short list might include characteristic desires and wants, goals and motives, life plans and projects, values and beliefs, coping strategies and defense mechanisms, patterns of interests, developmental concerns, conscious preoccupations, hopes, wishes, fears, aversions, expectations for intimate relationships, confidence in one's identity, vision for the future, understanding of the past. All of these things are features of a person's unique adaptation to the world at any given point in time. All of these features go into the making of human individuality, and yet none of them is well expressed as a trait. Personality psychology seeks to give a scientific account of human individuality. Dispositional traits such as extraversion and conscientiousness provide indispensable information about human individuality. It is hard to imagine a science of personality *without* traits. But there is more to personality than traits, as we will see in the chapters to come.

SUMMARY

1. Over the human lifespan, to what extent do our personality traits change and to what extent do they remain the same? There are many different meanings of personality continuity and change. With respect to continuity, two different meanings can be distinguished: absolute continuity, or consistency in the amount of trait shown, typically assessed by examining group averages at different points in time; and differential continuity, or stability in individual differences in trait scores over time.

2. Longitudinal studies show remarkable differential continuity in personality traits over much of the adult lifespan. Even for periods of 30 years, individual differences in personality traits show considerable stability, especially with respect to the Big Five dimensions of extraversion, neuroticism, and openness to experience. Stability appears to increase with age, such that differential continuity over, say, a 5-year period among middle-aged adults is higher than differential

continuity over a 5-year period for adolescents and younger adults.

3. Although few studies have examined directly the longitudinal relation between childhood and adult personality characteristics, many psychologists believe that childhood temperament dimensions may provide a core around which adult traits eventually develop. Temperament refers to differences in basic behavioral style, observed early in life and presumed to be under significant and rather direct biological control. Aspects of temperament that have received the greatest research attention include behavioral inhibition, intensity of mood, soothability, irritability, activity level, positive affect, and persistence.

4. Caspi has proposed that through a process of developmental elaboration, temperament dimensions in childhood gradually develop into more fully articulated personality traits in adulthood. He has identified six mechanisms that make this process work: learning processes, environmental

elicitation, environmental construal, social and temporal comparisons, environmental selection, and environmental manipulation.

5. In a fundamental sense, personality traits are a product of a complex interaction between people's genetic endowments and their environmental opportunities and constraints. But genetic and environmental effects on variance in trait scores of groups of individuals can be separated out and estimated from studies of twins—MZ (identical) and DZ (fraternal) pairs—and from adoption studies in which children are brought up in families with whom they do not share a genetic lineage. Twin and adoption studies show that the impressive differential continuity exhibited for personality traits may be partly due to heritability. The research provides strong evidence that at least 40% to 50% of the variance in personality trait scores in a given group can be accounted for by genetic differences among people in the group. Moderate to substantial heritabilities have been shown for virtually all personality traits measured, including all of the Big Five factors.

6. While genetic influences appear to account for around half the variance in trait scores, the influence of shared environments—such as child-rearing styles, social class, and other common experiences that siblings share—is surprisingly small, bordering on zero in many studies. Researchers in behavior genetics now believe that, along with genetic differences, *non*shared environmental effects may account for a significant portion of variance in personality traits. Whereas shared environment effects are environmental influences that operate to make family members alike, nonshared environmental effects are environmental influences that operate to make family members different. Nonshared environmental influences might include perinatal trauma, accidental events, family constellation patterns (e.g., birth order), patterns of interaction among siblings, differential parental treatment, and influences outside the family such as peer groups and teachers.

7. Although studies can separate the relative effects of genetics and environments in accounting for trait variability, genetic differences may themselves influence environments. Recent studies in behavior genetics suggest that self-reports of environments themselves are heritable. Genetic differences may shape how people experience their environments and what environments they choose to experience. Genotypes can shape environments in at least three ways: through evocative influence, whereby a person's genetically driven tendencies evoke responses from the environment that reinforce those tendencies; through passive influence, whereby a person grows up in environments that are created by individuals (e.g., biological parents) who have similar genotypes, such that the environments one experiences from the beginning are likely to have some correspondence to one's own genotype; and active influence, through which a person's genotype influences how an individual acts upon, manipulates, and transforms the environments that he or she chooses to experience. Whereas evocative and passive influences may predominate in childhood, active genotype-environment influences are more likely to characterize adult behavior.

8. Against the backdrop of substantial differential continuity in traits, research has also documented gradual and systematic changes in absolute values of personality dimensions. Both cross-sectional and longitudinal studies suggest that from adolescence and early adulthood through late middle-adulthood, traits related to the Big Five factors of extraversion, neuroticism, and openness to experience may decline somewhat, and traits related to agreeableness and conscientiousness may increase. A handful of longitudinal studies document movements toward increasing responsibility, autonomy, and self-confidence as people move from early to middle adulthood, especially among well-educated women. People tend to feel somewhat better about themselves as they grow older, at least into middle age, and somewhat better about other people, too.

9. Patterns of both continuity and change over time have been documented in the longitudinal studies conducted by Jack Block and his colleagues, employing the ipsative measure called the California Q-Sort. Block's research has generated a taxonomy of personality types, each of which exists as a constellation of different traits developing over time. Underlying these constellations are the personality dimensions of ego control and ego resiliency. Recent studies employing the Q-Sort with women have generated four different personality types: individuated, traditional, conflicted, and assured.

10. The concept of a personality trait is somewhat better suited for displaying continuity in person-ality over time, rather than change. Significant change in personality may occur outside the realm of personality traits, as in changing patterns of life goals, tasks, projects, values, coping strategies, interest patterns, visions for the future, and reconstructions of the past. Personality traits provide an indispensable starting point for the understanding of human individuality. But a full and detailed account requires a consideration of personality features that are not necessarily well expressed as traits. We may view dispositional traits as occupying the first level of personality. In the chapters that follow, we will move to the second and third levels—characteristic adaptations and integrative life stories.

Filling in the Details: Characteristic Adaptations to Life Tasks

CHAPTER 7

Motives and Goals: What Do We Want in Life?

When my younger daughter was about 5 years old, she asked me what my job was. I told her I was a professor of psychology.

"What is that?" Amanda asked.

"Well, I teach students about psychology," I replied.

"What is psychology?" she wanted to know.

"It's about human behavior," I explained. "I study why people do what they do."

"Oh." She rolled her eyes. "Well, why *do they* do what they do?"

"I really don't know, sweetheart. I guess that's why I study it."

"I know why people do what they do."

"Oh?"

Looking at me with a mixture of pity and disgust, Amanda proclaimed: "Because *they want to,* that's why."

She marched out of the room, no doubt wondering how her father could be so stupid. It is a basic fact of life: People do what they want to do. Even at age 5, Amanda knew something very important about human behavior. With no graduate training in psychology, she had developed her own implicit theory of human **motivation.** People have inside of them wants, desires, aims, intentions. People act upon these wants, producing behavior. At its root, the word motivation refers to "movement." What gets people moving? What *energizes* and *directs* human behavior? Like Amanda, theorists of human motivation going back more than 2,000 years have suggested that people want things, that they are motivated to get what they want (and to avoid what they don't want), that they develop goals to obtain those things they want, and that they act upon those goals. Furthermore, many have suggested that what we want is often derived directly from what we *need* (Lewin, 1935; Murray, 1938). Motivational psychologist Eric Klinger (1987) expands Amanda's theory of human motivation and gives it a Darwinian spin so that it even applies to animals:

> We animals have our drastic differences, but almost all of us—from amoebas to humans—have at least one behavioral imperative in common: We almost all have to go out and get the things we need in order to survive and procreate. We have to identify them, reach out or ambulate toward them, and bring them to those of our organs that can make use of them. Our morphology, our physiology, and our behavioral organization are all arranged so as to satisfy this imperative. This means that, from the beginning, animals have necessarily been constructed to pursue necessary goals, which means in turn that they have been shaped by the requirements of goal pursuit. Goal-striving, and therefore motivation in the larger sense, are integral facets of life as an animal. (Klinger, 1987, p. 337)

With its focus on motives and goals, this chapter takes us beyond the important individual differences in behavior typically associated with personality traits to a second level of personality description. In chapters 4 through 6, I showed that dispositional traits (Level 1 in personality) help to provide an initial sketch of human individuality. It is now time, however, to fill in some of the details in that sketch. To begin filling in the details, we need to move beyond dispositional traits and consider the various kinds of characteristic adaptations that define a particular human life. Characteristic adaptations are more specific and particular aspects of human individuality that are contextualized in time, place, or social role. Characteristic adaptations make up Level 2 of personality. *Motives and goals are one class of characteristic adaptations.* They are those aspects of personality that speak directly to what Amanda considers to be a basic fact of human behavior—that people *want* things and they *act* upon those wants.

But what do people want?

THE PSYCHOANALYTIC VIEW

The most influential psychologist of the 20th century was Sigmund Freud (1856–1939). Freud was the prime inventor of a particular kind of psychology—usually called **psychoanalysis.** Drawing on extensive case studies of therapy patients seen in medical settings, Freud and his followers developed psychoanalysis outside the mainstream of scientific psychology. But psychoanalysis has had a substantial impact on personality psychology proper, to say nothing of its pervasive cultural influence in the 20th-century West. Anthropology, political science, literature, literary criticism, art, and the cinema all acknowledge certain Freudian underpinnings and influences. Psychoanalytic theories, valid or not, have even crept into our everyday parlance, as we speak knowingly today of inhibitions, repressed memories, the Oedipus complex, and Freudian slips.

At the heart of the psychoanalytic view of personality is Freud's theory of motivation. The theory can be boiled down to four basic propositions. I call them the principles of (a) determinism, (b) drive, (c) conflict, and (d) the unconscious. First, forces over which we have little control *determine* all human behavior and experience. We are not the masters of our fate. We are more like pawns in life's chess game. Somebody else is making the moves. Second, these powerful forces exist within us, for the most part, and they can typically be traced back to primitive drives or instincts. Most important are our drives for sexuality and aggression. What do people want? We want sexual satisfaction and suitable outlets for our aggression. Third, the forces that determine all our behavior and experience are in perpetual *conflict* with one another, which causes us anxiety. There is no avoiding conflict and anxiety in life—conflict between our primitive urges and societal constraints certainly, but also conflicts deep within our selves. We want too much that we can never have; we are destined, therefore, to be miserable. Fourth (and arguably worst), we do not even know what those forces that determine our behavior and those conflicts that precipitate our anxiety are—in other words, the most important determinants of and conflicts in our lives are outside of our consciousness. They are *unconscious* to us. We are unconscious to them. We have virtually no control over our lives. We are conflicted and anxious. And we do not know why.

For Freud, sexuality and aggression are the ultimate wellsprings of human motivation. They provide the motive force, the drive, the thrust for all of our behavior. Quite literally, as Freud saw it, sexuality and aggression serve as the primal energy sources for psychological life. Influenced by 19th-century models of energy mechanisms, Freud conceived of the human mind as a machine that uses energy, and he believed that this psychic energy was drawn from biological instincts. Freud eventually settled on the idea that there exist two sets of instincts or drives: (a) sexuality and all other **life instincts** (this group of instincts is sometimes termed "**Eros**") and (b) aggression and all other **death instincts** (sometimes grouped under the name of "Thanatos") (Freud, 1920/1955). Life and death instincts are usually expressed in indirect and complex ways. Even 17-year-old boys do not spend *all* of their time fantasizing about sex and conquest and running around looking for opportunities for direct instinctual gratification. There are too many constraints in the real world, too many tasks to attend to in everyday life, and too much complexity and restraint built into the human mind to permit the direct translation of drive into behavior. Instead, our instincts get played out in fantasies and dreams, and they get expressed in very subtle and sublimated ways in everyday behavior. So subtle, in fact, that we are likely not even to notice. But, of course, that is precisely the psychoanalytic point.

THE UNCONSCIOUS

In *Notes from Underground,* the Russian novelist Fyodor Dostoyevsky wrote:

> Every man has some reminiscences which he would not tell to everyone, but only to his
> friends. He has others which he would not reveal even to his friends, but only to himself,
> and that in secret. But finally there are others which a man is even afraid to tell himself,
> and every decent man has a considerable number of such things stored away. (1864/1960)

Those fearsome things that Dostoyevsky said were "stored away" by every "decent
man" (or woman) constitute what Freud called the **unconscious.** A fundamental proposition of every psychoanalytic approach to personality is that much of what we know and
feel is outside our conscious awareness. Our lives are driven by intrapsychic mysteries that
transpire at an unconscious level, buried deep beneath the manifest surface of everyday
waking consciousness. We do not, and typically cannot, know what the "real" reasons are
for what we do because the prime determinants of human behavior are split off from what
we typically can grasp in conscious everyday experience. Freud's earliest clinical cases convinced him that the neurotic symptoms from which his patients suffered stemmed from
personal conflicts and fantasies, often sexual and aggressive in nature, that had been
actively pushed out of consciousness (Breuer & Freud, 1895). For example, an intensely

This painting, by Salvador Dali (1938), evokes images of primary
process thought and the Freudian unconscious. Freud imagined the
unconscious realm of human thought to be a vast and mysterious storehouse of instinctual urges, repressed images, and long-forgotten memories, devoid of rationality and crying out for immediate gratification.

negative experience from the past may no longer be consciously remembered, but the event lives on in the unconscious and plays itself out in conscious experience through debilitating symptoms, anxiety, and dread. The patient is clueless about the causes of his or her suffering, for the original event can no longer be recalled. In Freud's view, conscious experience is but the tip of the iceberg in human life. Most of the iceberg is underwater—that is, most of what is really important in human life lies beneath the surface of consciousness.

The idea that much of who we are is outside of our awareness, residing in a shadowy unconscious realm, is not original with Freud. The notion that behavior is shaped by unconscious determinants was clearly in evidence some 100 years prior to Freud's theorizing (Ellenberger, 1970). For instance, the philosophies of Arthur Schopenhauer (1788–1860) and Friedrich Nietzsche (1844–1900) emphasized aspects of human functioning that are outside of consciousness, typically emotional and irrational urges that are antagonistic to conscious reason.

Nineteenth-century Romantics, such as the poets William Wordsworth and John Keats, generally placed the person's heroic and creative powers in an unconscious, though sometimes accessible, realm. Hypnotism was used to gain access to the unconscious mind as early as 1784, and one of Freud's teachers, Jean Martin Charcot, employed the method with legendary effectiveness. Baumeister (1986) and Gay (1986) argue that middle-class adults in 19th-century Europe accepted the general idea of an inner world unknowable to the conscious self. Baumeister even asserts that Victorian men and women were preoccupied with the involuntary revelation of this inner self to others. While you might not be able to attain conscious insight into the deep secrets of your own mind, the Victorians believed there was always the danger of inadvertently disclosing the nature of your own unconscious to others, who as objective outside observers might even come to know you better than you know yourself!

In his **topographical model** of human functioning, Freud distinguished among conscious, preconscious, and unconscious regions of the mind. The conscious region contains what a person is currently aware of. People typically can verbalize their conscious experience and can think about it in a logical way. The preconscious region contains material about which the person is not currently aware but which *could readily enter awareness* should the person decide to retrieve the material. Therefore, the preconscious region may be seen as corresponding to what most of us think of as ordinary memory. I may not currently be aware of the color of my daughter's bicycle but I can easily remember what the color is if I decide to move my thinking in that direction, thereby bringing up material from the preconscious to the conscious region. The preconscious contains a vast storehouse of important as well as trivial information that is reliably at our disposal.

By contrast, material residing in the unconscious region of the mind cannot be readily retrieved. Rather the unconscious contains elements of experience that have been actively *repressed*. In part, the unconscious is a repository for ideas, images, urges, and feelings that are associated with conflict, pain, fear, guilt, and so on. Therefore, unconscious material is unconscious *for a reason*. The mind is topographically organized such that material that is incompatible with the dominant self-protective mask of consciousness is cast into an unconscious abyss. We cannot bear to know certain things about ourselves. Therefore, we do not (consciously) know them. Yet what resides in the unconscious profoundly affects our behavior and experience, even though we do not know we are being affected. Repressed unconscious material is expressed in disguised or symbolic form, as in neurotic symptoms or when unconscious instinctual urges are indirectly satisfied in dreams, fantasy, play, art, work, or virtually any other arena of meaningful human intercourse.

FEATURE 7.A

SIGMUND FREUD AND THE BIRTH OF PSYCHOANALYSIS

Sigmund Freud came of age in a world very different from ours. It was a world of kings and queens and empires—a 19th-century European "old world" that was still highly aristocratic and, by our standards today, extremely oppressive. It was a world yet to experience a major global war or the threat of nuclear annihilation. It was a world that would have found unthinkable our contemporary belief that, for instance, women should be allowed to vote or that the child of a poor black mother might someday become a great leader, writer, or scientist. The first-born son in a struggling Jewish family, Freud dreamed of being a great scientist from the age of 5 onward. As Napoleon conquered lands and peoples, young Sigmund dreamed of conquering the mind, exploring new territories of knowledge and becoming their lord and master. Referring to his own childhood and his unalloyed love for his mother, Freud later wrote: "A man who has been the indisputable favorite of his mother keeps for life the feeling of a conqueror, the confidence of success that often induces real success" (in Jones, 1961, p. 6).

The heroes of Freud's youth were the great Romantics of the early 19th century, such as Napoleon, the conqueror, and Goethe, the German writer and philosopher. Flourishing between approximately 1790 and 1850, **Romanticism** was a European intellectual movement that rejected classical teachings emphasizing reason, order, and the common good and celebrated instead the vigorous and passionate life of the individual (Cantor, 1971; Russell, 1945). As an adult, Freud fashioned a revolutionary theory of the mind that reflected his Romantic heritage. From Romanticism he adopted the idea that the individual person and society are destined to live in constant conflict. Romantics like Goethe and the poets William Blake and Lord Byron saw society as inherently oppressive in that it demands conformity to ensure social order. The Romantic self rebels against oppression to seek

Sigmund Freud and his daughter, Anna. Arguably the most influential psychologist of the 20th century, Freud (1856–1939) was the founder of the broad intellectual, therapeutic, and cultural movement that goes by the name of "psychoanalysis." Freud argued that human behavior is motivated by unconscious drives associated with aggression and sexuality.

freedom and transcendence, often through the passionate pursuit of art or love. Romanticism taught Freud to focus on the uniqueness of the inner self and its development over time. For the Romantics, the development of the inner self was virtually a moral duty (Jay, 1984; Langbaum, 1982). In the famous Romantic drama, Goethe's Faust seeks self-fulfillment at all costs, going so far as to sell his soul to the devil to guarantee the full experiencing of his inner, unique being. Of psychoanalysis and the devil, one scholar writes, "to experience Freud is to partake a second time of the forbidden fruit" (Brown, 1959, pp. xi–xii). The Romantics glorified

(CONTINUES)

FEATURE 7.A *(CONTINUED)*

the emotional and irrational aspects of human nature. Freud, too, came to see human beings as irrational by nature, but unlike his Romantic heroes, Freud was never able to celebrate that irrationality. Freud eventually taught that unconscious and irrational wishes concerning sexuality and aggression are the most basic motivators of the person's behavior, but that these wishes must be channeled into indirect and disguised expressions within an orderly society if the human being is to adapt to society and to survive. Despite his Romantic heritage, Freud was too much the rational scientist himself, and an upstanding member of conservative middle-class society, to endorse the free reign of sex and passion.

In 1873, Freud enrolled in the University of Vienna to study natural science. There he met the eminent physiologist Ernst Brücke. Working under Brücke's tutelage for three years, Freud learned that all natural phenomena must be explained in physical and chemical terms. From the standpoint of science, no spiritual or otherworldly forces could be invoked to account for the real world. Scientists of the day were fascinated with the power of machines and used machines as metaphors for their theories. A machine is a complex mechanical system that uses energy through work. The psychoanalytic theory that Freud would eventually bring forth viewed the mind as a psychic machine that uses energy. The energy is derived from biologically rooted instincts, such as sex and aggression. The system works according to the 19th-century laws of conservation of energy. The mind transforms a fixed amount of energy derived from instincts into useful work, Freud eventually argued, transforming a fixed amount of raw sensual and aggressive energy into various forms and expressions of human thought, feeling, desire, and behavior. From another teacher, Jean Martin Charcot, Freud learned that the mind's energy could work in strange ways. In 1885, Freud traveled to Paris to attend Charcot's lectures and demonstrations on hypnosis. Charcot investigated the symptoms and causes of **hysteria,** a common psychological disturbance of the 19th century in which patients suffered from bizarre bodily symptoms, such as paralysis of the limbs and visual disorders, that had no apparent *physical* cause. Charcot was fabulously successful in

removing hysteric symptoms through hypnosis, suggesting to Freud that hysteria resulted from the patient's peculiar *ideas,* which themselves were manifestations of the mind's energy.

As a physician in Vienna, Freud worked with Joseph Breuer in the treatment of the hysterical symptoms exhibited by their neurotic patients, employing hypnosis and other psychological techniques. Breuer and Freud came to recognize that while hysterical symptoms may appear to be random and bizarre, they are in fact meaningfully organized according to an intricate emotional logic that guides the neurotic's life. The symptoms symbolize an unresolved conflict or problem that may be traced back to intensely negative childhood experiences. Though no longer consciously remembered, an emotionally abrasive experience from childhood presses for release and goads the patient to find symptomatic expression of the discomfort within. In the famous case of Anna O., Breuer discovered that hysterical symptoms could be removed through a "talking cure," through which the patient talked through daytime hallucinations, fantasies, symptoms, and so on. The talking unstrangled the archaic emotions that were producing the neurotic symptoms, releasing the trapped emotional energy and temporarily freeing the patient from debilitating symptoms and distress.

The psychoanalytic tradition was launched when Breuer and Freud collaborated to investigate the psychological underpinnings of hysteria. Their work culminated in the publication of *Studies in Hysteria* (1893–1895/1955), wherein they wrote that "hysterics suffer mainly from reminiscences" (p. 7). In other words, the bodily symptoms of hysteria are caused by problems in the memory of emotionally charged events. Freud was almost 40 years old when he and Breuer published their discoveries. But the two physician/scientists had a major falling out over the interpretation of their clinical cases, with Breuer objecting to Freud's insistence that hysterical symptoms typically have sexual meanings. They parted, bitter enemies, and Freud entered a very difficult but ultimately productive period in his life, a time he later romanticized as that "glorious heroic age" of "splendid isolation" (Freud, 1914/1957, p. 22). During this

(CONTINUES)

FEATURE 7.A *(CONTINUED)*

time, Freud began a self-analysis wherein he subjected his own thoughts, fantasies, feelings, and dreams to an intensive scrutiny and from which, he later argued, he derived his greatest psychological insights. The next 10 years (between 1895 and 1905) were to witness the maturation of Freud's most important ideas concerning the interpretation of dreams, the psychopathology of everyday life, the role of the sexual instinct in human development, and the workings of the unconscious.

From about 1905 until his death in 1939, Freud established himself as the father of the psychoanalytic movement. A gifted writer who won the coveted Goethe Prize for literature in 1930, Freud filled 24 volumes on psychoanalysis, including wide-ranging essays and monographs on theory and clinical practice as well as special papers addressing religious,

cultural, and artistic questions. Table 7.1 lists a few of his most important writings with capsule summaries of their contents. Attracting a large number of intellectual followers, Freud founded the Vienna Psychoanalytic Society. The group held regular meetings and published a journal. In 1909, American psychologist G. Stanley Hall invited Freud to Clark University, in Worcester, Massachusetts, where he delivered a famous series of lectures. Freud's writings were eventually translated into English and other languages as psychoanalysis became an international movement. By the time of his death, on the eve of World War II, Sigmund Freud was easily the most venerated psychologist in the world, but also the most maligned, for his ideas have always been viewed as extremely controversial.

REPRESSION AND REPRESSORS

Research in cognitive science has shown conclusively that a great deal of everyday mental life is outside of conscious awareness. People perceive, learn, and remember many things without being consciously aware of doing so (Kihlstrom, 1990; Schacter, 1996). These kinds of nonconscious cognitive operations are manifestations of *implicit* information processing in human beings. Furthermore, much of what we feel and think about people and social situations appears to be driven by nonconscious, automatic mental processes (Bargh, 1997). The mind has evolved to take in highly familiar and routine information in an effortless and automatic fashion in order to free up conscious and explicit mental processes to focus on the immediate problems at hand. In a sense, then, scientific evidence documenting the many ways in which the human mind operates in an implicit, automatic, and nonconscious manner supports Freud's general view that mental life is largely outside conscious awareness (Westen, 1998).

But Freud was mainly concerned with thoughts, feelings, desires, and memories that may be stored away in an inaccessible, unconscious realm *because they threaten the person's well-being*. These thoughts, feelings, desires, and memories are actively rejected or repressed. In the psychoanalytic view, **repression** is an inescapable fact of daily life. "The essence of repression lies simply in the function of rejecting and keeping something out of consciousness," Freud wrote (1915/1957, p. 105). To protect themselves from psychological harm, human beings repress certain mental processes and the threatening content associated with them. Everybody represses. But do some people repress more than others?

Some psychoanalytically oriented researchers argue that individual differences in repressiveness constitute an important feature of personality. Weinberger, Schwartz, and Davidson (1979) describe **repressors** as persons who experience little anxiety on a conscious level and who adopt a highly defensive approach to life. The researchers were able to classify certain individuals as exhibiting an especially repressive coping style by virtue of

| TABLE 7.1 | SELECTED WRITINGS OF SIGMUND FREUD |

Date	Title	Thesis
1895	Studies in Hysteria (with J. Breuer)	Neurotic symptoms are the result of "reminiscences" and can be relived through a psychological talking cure. Neurotic disturbances are creative solutions to unconscious conflicts, usually concerning sexuality.
1900	The Interpretation of Dreams	Dreams are compromises in wish fulfillments and must be understood a s creative products of unconscious processes such as condensation, displacement, and symbolism. All dreams can be interpreted by employing free association to trace the latent undercurrents of manifest content.
1901	The Psychopathology of Everyday Life	Like neurotic symptoms and dreams, many accidents and mistakes we make in daily life have important psychological meaning and can be traced back to unconscious conflicts and instinctual urges.
1905	Three Essays on the Theory of Sexuality	The sexual instinct develops through childhood stages designated as oral, anal, and phallic, before reaching maturity in adolescence. Children are overtly sexual beings whose pregenital manifestations of sex are similar to what polite society calls "perversions" in adults.
1913	Totem and Taboo	The Oedipus complex in children involves unconscious desires to make love to the parent of the opposite sex while killing the parent of the same sex. Freud speculates that social institutions such as government and religion have their historical origins in a prehistoric real-life enactment of the Oedipal complex, whereby the patriarch of a primal horde was overthrown by younger men and killed and eaten. The new younger leaders then prescribed laws and rules to inhibit sex and aggression and assuage their guilt.
1920	Beyond the Pleasure Principle	Two basic instinctual urges are the underlying motivators of all behavior and experience: life instincts, expressed directly in sexuality; and death instincts, expressed in aggression.
1923	The Ego and the Id	The human mind is structured into three compartments: the id, wherein reside unconscious impulses and thoughts; the ego, which serves the id by channeling the id's energy into realistic pursuits; and the superego, which is an internal representation of the parents exerting a moral force. The id operates according to the pleasure principle, and the ego operates according to the reality principle.
1930	Civilization and Its Discontents	Human beings and societies are in constant conflict. Whereas the individual is motivated by unconscious sexual and aggressive impulses, society is built on the repression of sex and aggression. As a result, humans are generally anxious, miserable, and often neurotic.

NOTE: There is no substitute for reading Freud in the original. Indeed, part of his power as a theorist is the beauty of his writing, captured wonderfully in James Strachey's authoritative English translations of the original German. Unfortunately, many secondary sources on Freud are rather dry and technical compared with the rich original work. An exception is C. Monte's *Beneath the Mask: An Introduction to Theories of Personality* (Fort Worth, TX: Harcourt Brace, 1995), which has two long and splendid chapters on the evolution of Freud's thinking.

their scores on two self-report, paper-and-pencil questionnaires—one measuring anxiety (the Manifest Anxiety Scale; Taylor, 1953) and the other defensiveness, or "social desirability" (Crowne & Marlowe, 1964), which indicates the extent to which a person will describe the self in socially acceptable and overly "nice" ways. In an experiment in which people were exposed to verbal phrases containing sexual and aggressive content, repressors reported very low levels of subjective distress compared with "low-anxious" (low anxiety, low defensiveness) and "defensive–high-anxious" (high anxiety, high defensiveness) individuals. At the same time, however, physiological measures indicated that the repressors experienced significantly higher levels of internal arousal than did the low-anxious and defensive–high-anxious subjects. In other words, whereas the repressors claimed that the sexual and aggressive content did not make them anxious, their bodily processes suggested otherwise. From a psychoanalytic perspective, the repressors did not *consciously* perceive the drive-related stimuli as threatening. Their heightened physiological arousal, however, indicated that the threat may have instead been perceived at an *unconscious* level.

Penelope Davis has conducted a series of interesting studies examining how repressors recall emotional experiences in their lives. In one study, female college students were asked to recall six kinds of personal experiences from childhood—general memories, experiences of happiness, sadness, anger, fear, and wonder (Davis & Schwartz, 1987). As Figure 7.1 shows, repressors (low anxiety, high defensiveness) recalled significantly fewer negative memories than did low-anxious (low anxiety, low defensiveness) and high-anxious (high anxiety, low defensiveness) individuals. The results are consistent with the psychoanalytic hypothesis that repression involves inaccessibility to negative memories. However, the results also indicate, as can be seen in Figure 7.1, that repressors tended to report somewhat fewer *positive* memories as well, suggesting that repression may also involve a more general failure to retrieve emotional memories of various kinds.

In a second study, Davis (1987) found that repressors recalled fewer childhood experiences in which they felt happy, sad, angry, fearful, guilty, and self-conscious compared with other individuals. The inhibition was especially pronounced for fear and self-consciousness experiences. But she also showed that when recalling memories in which *someone else* felt happy, sad, angry, or fearful, repressors actually reported substantially *more* experiences. The findings suggest that repression is not simply a general memory deficit. Repressors actually report a greater number of memories involving emotional experiences of other people. But when it comes to recalling events in which the strong emotions experienced *are their own,* and especially when those emotions entail painful states of fear and self-consciousness, repressors seem to have difficulty summoning such memories into awareness. Fear and self-consciousness occur in situations in which attention is focused on the self in an evaluative and especially threatening way. What may make these kinds of experiences the most suitable grist for the repression mill is that they directly threaten the self with a negative evaluation, more so even than experiences of sadness, anger, and other negative emotions. Repression may operate most powerfully in the domain of self-evaluation. We may be most prone to repress those experiences in which the self is judged in a negative manner.

Why is it that some people have such a difficult time recalling and articulating negative emotional memories? What makes repressors different from other people? Hansen and Hansen (1988) explored what they called "the architecture of repression," described as the mechanisms whereby emotionally tagged memories, especially unpleasant memories, are left inaccessible. They argue that repressors have an "associative network" for negative emotional experiences that is substantially less complex and more discrete than that found for negative memories experienced by other people. For repressors, negative recollections have a characteristically simple structure, and these memories are split off from other memories, isolated outside the main network of interrelated autobiographical recollections. Repressors and nonrepressors organize their episodic memories in different ways. Repressors simplify negative memories to emphasize a single dominant feeling, as a way of

| FIGURE 7.1 | AVERAGE NUMBER OF MEMORIES RECALLED |

Repressors show significantly fewer memories of sadness, anger, and fear compared with high-anxious and low-anxious individuals.

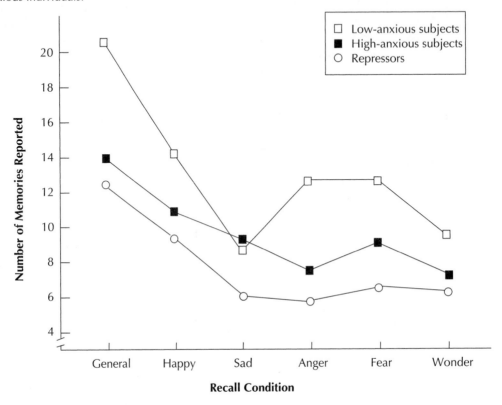

SOURCE: "Repression and the Inaccessibility of Affective Memories," by P. J. Davis and G. E. Schwartz, 1987, *Journal of Personality and Social Psychology, 52,* p. 158.

keeping these memories from connecting in their minds to other autobiographical memories containing other feelings. By contrast, nonrepressors tend to describe their negative memories in more complex terms, emphasizing a number of different emotional states in the same memory and integrating the negative memory with the main lines of their autobiographical self.

Hansen and Hansen (1988) obtained evidence for their interpretation in a study of 433 undergraduate women and men, each of whom was assigned to recall, describe, and evaluate either an angering, embarrassing, sad, or fearful event from the past. For the particular event to be recalled, the participants were told to picture the situation in their minds and to remember as vividly as they could how it felt (to be angry, embarrassed, sad, or fearful) at that particular moment. After writing a description of the experience on a sheet of paper, the participants were asked to rate how they felt in the situation according to 10 different emotion dimensions—angry, embarrassed, sad, fearful, anxious, disgusted, ashamed, depressed, surprised, and happy. The results showed that each negative memory elicits a montage of different emotional reactions. For example, when subjects were asked to recall memories of sadness, they rated their feelings in these memories as very sad, but they also tended to rate highly feelings of depression, anger, and fear. By contrast, sad memories did not tend to elicit feelings of shame or embarrassment. For sad memories, then, the researchers determined that sadness was the dominant emotion but that other nondominant emotions of depression, anger, and fear could also be identified. Similarly, embarrassing memories showed the dominant emotion of embarrassment but were also tagged with the nondominant emotion of shame. Each category of emotional memory (angering, embarrassing, sad, and fearful), therefore, specified a corresponding dominant emotion and a set of nondominant emotions.

Differences between repressors and other individuals were revealed in the nondominant emotions, but not in the dominant ones. For any given negative event, repressors and nonrepressors reported comparable levels of dominant emotion intensity. For example, embarrassing memories were rated just as emotionally embarrassing by repressors as by nonrepressors. But repressors tended to rate the nondominant emotions associated with the given memory at less intense levels. Embarrassing memories, therefore, produced less shame for repressors than for nonrepressors. Sad memories produced less depression, anger, and fear for repressors than for nonrepressors. And so on. In purifying their particular memories to underscore a dominant emotional reaction rather than a host of related but nondominant emotions, repressors cordon off the negativity associated with any given memory, keeping it from spreading to other recollections of the past. Write Hansen and Hansen (1988), "repression is fundamentally a phenomenon of the relatively impoverished structure of the repressor's memory linked to the less elaborate, more discrete emotional tags with which the repressor's memorial representations are associated" (p. 816). To protect the self from threat, repression works to keep negative memories from connecting to each other, rendering each a simple monad unto itself.

Moving on to more recent studies of repression, Myers and Brewin (1994) showed that while repressors report fewer negative memories from childhood, they nonetheless tend to recall their parents as being especially indifferent or neglecting. In other words, repressors may keep out of awareness especially negative emotional experiences, but negativity in general manages to seep into their accounts of their lives, couched in more general, abstract, and less threatening terms. Cutler, Larsen, and Bunce (1996) examined daily diaries to find that repressors not only recall fewer memories of unpleasant emotions, but they also appear to experience less intense negative emotion in daily life. Bonanno, Davis, Singer, and Schwartz (1991) showed that repressors are especially skilled at shifting their attention away from material that they wish to ignore. But the attentional shift may come with a price. Having a repressive coping style has also been associated with a variety of health problems, including asthma, cancer, hypertension, and suppressed immune function (Schwartz, 1990; Weinberger, 1990).

In sum, research on repressors has identified an important individual difference variable that appears to capture some of Freud's fundamental concept of repression. Some people do seem to employ repression as a coping strategy more so than do others, and this difference in people is associated with measurable outcomes with respect to everyday information processing, autobiographical memory, and even physical health. However, the research leaves open the question of just how common and important repression is for everybody. While Freud argued that repression is a universal fact of psychic life, research on repressors suggests that people differ rather substantially with respect to how extensively they employ repression as a way of dealing with anxiety.

THE EGO'S DEFENSES

In one of his last theoretical innovations, Freud (1923–1961) proposed an integrative model of how the mind is organized. Figure 7.2 presents a picture of the model. Freud concluded that the mind can be broken down into three independent structures: id, ego, and superego. Each of the three exists for a different purpose. The major conflicts that produce anxiety in adults' lives are often the result of disagreements among these three different agents of the mind. Resolving conflicts, therefore, involves forging creative agreements that enable the three to coexist with one another and with the outside world in relative, if short-lived, tranquility.

The most primitive structure is the **id** (German: *das Es,* or "the it"). Completely submerged in the unconscious, the id is the home of the instinctual impulses of sex and aggression and their derivative wishes, fantasies, and inclinations. The id is a chaotic, seething cauldron that provides all the instinctual energy for mental life. The id knows no inhibitions; it obeys no logical or moral constraints; it is completely out of touch with the outside world of reality, and will remain so always. The activity of the id is dictated solely by the **pleasure principle:** Pleasure derives from the reduction of tension in the immediate gratification of impulses. The id, furthermore, is the driving force behind **primary process**

FIGURE 7.2	FREUD'S MODEL OF THE PSYCHE

The id, ego, and superego are the three main regions in Freud's model of the human mind.

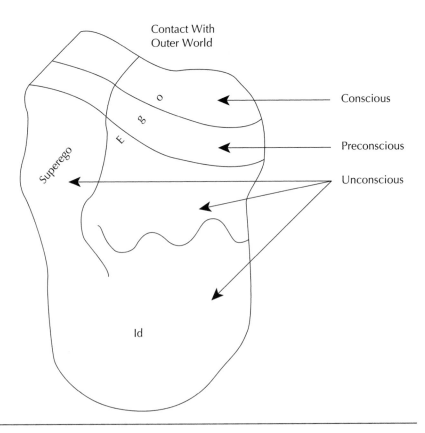

thinking—the loose, fluid, and irrational kind of thinking that we associate with dreaming. Primary process thought is motivated by the sexual and aggressive instincts.

If the mind remained "all id," the human being would quickly encounter very serious trouble. Though the id finds satisfaction in hallucinatory wish fulfillment, the organism cannot function for long on wish and fantasy alone. Beginning in infancy, therefore, a second structure of the mind emerges out of the id. This is the **ego** (German: *das Ich,* or "the I"). Borrowing its energy from the id instincts, the ego exists as the "handmaiden" to the id, working tirelessly to mediate between the blind demands of its master and the constraints imposed by logic and the external world. The ego thus helps ensure the safety and self-preservation of the organism by adopting the **reality principle** in conducting its affairs and by relying on the power of rational thought. The reality principle enables the individual to suspend immediate instinctual gratification until either an appropriate object or environmental condition arises that will satisfy the instinct. The ego is able to weigh the demands of the outside world and balance them with the needs and impulses expressed by the id, so to produce behaviors and modes of experience that best use the id's raw energy. In order to accomplish this task, the ego is manifested as **secondary process** thinking, which is conscious, deliberate, and geared toward solving problems in a rational and realistic manner.

While the id is completely submerged within the unconscious, the ego manifests itself partly in certain conscious ways. When a person functions as a rational and self-reflective decision maker in the face of life's many challenges, he or she is displaying the ego's conscious powers. But significant aspects of the ego are unconscious, as well. A good deal of coping with the inevitable conflicts that arise in daily life is carried out unconsciously by the ego through **defense mechanisms.** A defense mechanism is *an unconscious strategy of the ego that distorts reality in order to lessen anxiety.* In the defense mechanism of *projection,* for instance, the person unconsciously attributes to other people certain of his or her own characteristics the existence of which within the self provoke unacceptable levels of anxiety. Therefore, a man who harbors strong unconscious uncertainties about his own masculinity may be more likely than most people to accuse other men of being homosexual. This is not a conscious deceit but rather a subtle and unconscious strategy of the ego to ward off anxiety by distorting, to a certain extent, objective reality. Table 7.2 describes some other defense mechanisms commonly employed by the ego.

Emerging later in childhood, the **superego** (German: *das überich,* or "the over-I") is a primitive internalized representation of the norms and values of society as acquired through identification with the parents. As such, the superego is akin to an internalized authority that repeatedly tells the person what he or she should and should not be doing, as if the parents had been consumed and become personified inside the self. The superego is typically a strict and inflexible agent who insists on the renunciation or repression of the id's instinctual demands. Whereas the id yells out, "Yes! Go for it—now!" the superego sternly replies, "No! Not in a million years!" Despite the opposing points of view, however, the id and superego share a number of characteristics. Both, for instance, are demanding and inflexible, both are blind to the constraints and demands of the outside world. Only the ego engages in secondary-process thinking and operates according to the reality principle.

With the establishment of the superego, the ego now faces a third taskmaster and powerful source of conflict. The first, the reality of the outside world, poses objective dangers that produce *realistic anxiety;* the second, the id, threatens the ego with *neurotic anxiety* about the ever-present possibility of an uncontrollable release of instinctual energy; now the third source of conflict, the superego, adds the problem of *moral anxiety,* which may take the form of feelings of guilt over moral transgressions or regret in failing to live up to

TABLE 7.2	SOME DEFENSE MECHANISMS OF THE EGO	
Mechanism	**Definition**	**Simple Example**
Repression	A dangerous impulse is actively and totally excluded from consciousness.	An aging father fails to recognize his own feelings of hostility toward his strong, athletic son.
Projection	Attributing one's own unacceptable and disturbing thoughts and impulses to someone else.	A man preoccupied with doubts about his own heterosexuality frequently accuses others of being homosexual.
Reaction formation	Warding off an unacceptable impulse by overemphasizing its opposite in thought and behavior.	A man threatened by his desire to dominate others and to be aggressive thinks of himself as a passive sort of person and acts accordingly.
Rationalization	Devising an extremely "reasonable" explanation or excuse for an event or behavior that threatens the person's esteem.	A wife explains her husband's repeated infidelity as a product of his unfortunate upbringing or an overly seductive environment.
Regression	Retreating to an earlier and more primitive stage or mode of behavior in order to avoid pain, threat, or anxiety.	A mother lapses into diversionary "baby talk" with her daughter whenever she confronts a tough decision or threatening situation.
Displacement	Shifting an impulse from a threatening to a nonthreatening object.	Angry at his boss because of a demotion, the businessman goes home and argues with his wife.
Sublimation	Channeling socially unacceptable impulses into acceptable, even admirable, behavior.	The surgeon channels aggressive energy into constructive medical work; the artist employs the libido to produce a masterpiece.

perfect ideals. The ego is a lonely agent of reasonableness amidst a host of uncompromising and relentless forces and factors. Dependent on the id for its energy, beholden to the superego as the lowly child to an omnipotent parent, and faced with almost impossible demands from the real world, the ego is perennially beleaguered, and occasionally it may even break down, resulting in neurotic symptoms. No wonder that Freud was pessimistic about the possibilities of human happiness.

But many psychoanalytically oriented theorists who followed Freud—beginning with Anna Freud (1946) and including Heinz Hartmann (1939), Erik Erikson (1950), and Robert White (1959, 1963a)—were much more optimistic about the potential of the ego. According to these **ego psychologists,** the ego promotes healthy adaptation to life through the functions of learning, memory, perception, and synthesis. More than a hapless defender, the ego is a master integrator. It organizes experience so that the organism can become an effective and competent member of society. Furthermore, in its efforts to cope with anxiety the ego has at its disposal a formidable arsenal of weapons, including a wide range of defense mechanisms (Cramer, 1991, 2002; A. Freud, 1946; Schafer, 1968; Vaillant, 1977). The working of defense mechanisms is a topic that has attracted a considerable body of empirical research in personality (Paulhus, Fridhandler, & Hayes, 1997) and social psychology (Baumeister, Dale, & Sommer, 1998). The research suggests that people do consistently employ effective defensive strategies in dealing with anxiety and stress.

There is considerable consensus among psychoanalysts that some defense mechanisms are relatively primitive and immature (such as denial) while others are more complex and mature (such as sublimation) (Anthony, 1970; A. Freud, 1946). The most significant empirical research on the development of defense mechanisms has been conducted by Phebe Cramer (1991, 2002; Cramer & Brilliant, 2001). Cramer has tested the hypothesis that immature defense mechanisms should arise early in life and then taper off, while mature mechanisms should develop somewhat later. She has focused on three defense mechanisms. The most primitive of the three is **denial,** in which the person baldly refuses to acknowledge an anxiety-provoking event. For instance, a young child visiting the doctor may insist that he is not afraid of a shot, or a recently widowed woman may claim she feels no grief. Denial may be employed by people of all ages, argue psychoanalysts, but it tends to be most common among the very young. Adults tend to use denial only in the most upsetting and threatening situations. More mature than denial is **projection,** in which the person attributes unacceptable internal states and qualities to external others. For instance, an adolescent girl who doubts her own religious values may accuse others of being "sinful," or a businessman insecure about his own marriage may suspect that many of his colleagues are having extramarital affairs. Projection requires that standards of "good" and "bad" be internalized such that the "bad" can be projected outward. Therefore, the use of projection should await the development of conscience (Freud's superego) in middle childhood. The most mature defense mechanism studied by Cramer is **identification,** whereby the person forms an enduring mental representation of significant others. The person replicates the behavioral traits of others as a way of coping. Requiring the clear differentiation of self and others and a complex understanding of differences among various people, identification becomes an effective defense in adolescence and should remain so throughout life (Blos, 1979).

In one study Cramer analyzed the creative stories told or written by 320 children representing four age groups: young children (ages 4–7), intermediate (ages 8–11), early adolescent (9th and 10th grades), and late adolescent (11th and 12th grades). Each child was asked to look at two specially chosen pictures and make up an imaginative story about each. The stories were analyzed for examples of defense mechanisms. As Figure 7.3 shows, the stories told by the youngest children contained a preponderance of denial themes, whereas those written or told by the children in the older three groups showed little denial. Projection and identification, on the other hand, were relatively low among the young children and increased markedly thereafter. The findings support the psychoanalytic hypothesis that these three defense mechanisms differ in relative maturity, with denial most prominent in the youngest children and projection and identification more evident in older children and adolescents.

The power of defense mechanisms is most apparent during times of great stress. Dollinger and Cramer (1990) described an unusual study of the use of ego defenses among children who witnessed a traumatic event. Preadolescent boys from two rural Illinois towns were playing a league soccer game when a thunderstorm necessitated a delay in the action. The children retreated to their parents' cars to wait out the storm. Shortly after the game resumed, a lightning bolt struck the field and knocked down all participants and most of the children and adults on the sidelines. One boy was hit directly by the bolt. Never regaining consciousness, he died one week after the incident.

Clinical psychologists and counselors met regularly with the children who witnessed the tragedy and with their families. As part of their counseling efforts, the professionals took a number of measures of psychological variables during the course of the treatment.

FIGURE 7.3	DEFENSE MECHANISMS IN FOUR AGE GROUPS

From primary school age (Pri), through intermediate school age (Int) and early adolescence (EA), into late adolescence (LA), scores on the primitive defense mechanisms of denial decrease while scores on more mature defense mechanisms (projection and identification) increase.

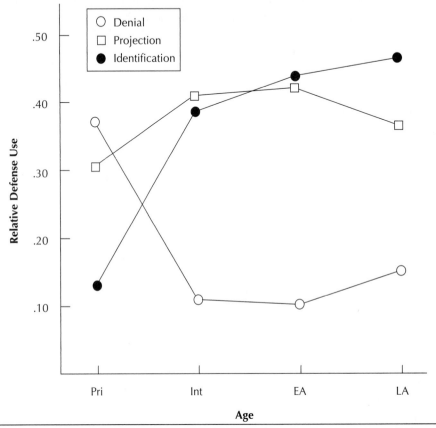

SOURCE: From "The Development of Defense Mechanisms," by P. Cramer, 1987, *Journal of Personality, 55,* 607.

An especially useful index was an *upset rating* made by psychologists to gauge the overall level of emotional distress experienced by each child. The upset rating proved to be strongly related to parents' reports of children's sleep disturbances and somatic complaints after the event and to children's reports of fears (e.g., fears of storms, of dying, of bodily penetration, and of separation anxiety). In addition, children who scored high on emotional upset tended to avoid soccer in the subsequent two-year interval.

Children's imaginative stories told in response to pictures were also obtained. The pictures depicted scenes with lightning present. Examining the stories written by 27 10-to-13-year-old boys, Dollinger and Cramer found that denial was used as a defense at significantly higher levels in this sample than is typical in children of this age, probably because of the severity of the trauma. Psychoanalytic theory suggests that primitive defenses are more likely to appear during the most stressful points of a person's life. In addition, younger boys used significantly more denial than older boys, in keeping with previous research. Most interesting, however, was the relation between defense mechanisms and emotional upset. The stories written by those boys who showed the lowest levels of emotional upset tended to display the highest levels of *projection*. The authors point out that in boys of this age, projection is the most age-appropriate defense; denial is somewhat too primitive and identification too mature. It would appear that projection served these preadolescent boys quite well in their attempts to cope with the anxiety, fear, and sadness they experienced in the wake of the lightning incident. Those boys who showed low levels of projection exhibited high levels of emotional upset. For the most part, denial and identification were not effective defenses for coping with the upset. Only projection was negatively associated with upset. It would be expected, however, that denial would have been most effective among children at much younger ages than those in this sample and that identification would have proven most effective for adults. The lightning study underscores the psychoanalytic-developmental hypothesis that age-appropriate defense mechanisms may be most effective in warding off anxiety and helping people cope.

Like children, adults differ markedly with respect to the kinds of defense mechanisms they regularly employ. While some adults, like children, consistently use relatively immature mechanisms such as denial, others regularly adopt the more mature and complex strategies for dealing with anxiety and stress, such as identification, sublimation, and humor. George Vaillant (1971, 1977) has investigated the relationship between these characteristic defensive styles and overall adult adjustment. In a small sample of well-educated men studied over a 25-year period, Vaillant found that men's consistent use of mature defenses was positively associated with an overall index of adjustment, including physical health, career advancement, and marital enjoyment. Similarly, Vaillant and Drake (1985) found that the use of mature defenses predicted greater levels of interpersonal intimacy and meaningful and productive work in a large sample of working-class men. In a sample of 91 young adults, Cramer (2002) found that use of more primitive defense mechanisms was associated with higher levels of anxiety. Young adults who relied on denial showed multiple signs of behavioral immaturity. Among men, furthermore, projection was associated with a suspicious and hyperalert style of interacting with other people.

To sum up, the psychoanalytic view of human motivation suggests that our behavior, thought, and feelings are energized and directed by unconscious desires that ultimately stem from sexual and aggressive instincts. The many desires we have conflict with each other, with our internalized moral standards, and with the constraints of the outside world. Such conflict leads to anxiety. From the psychoanalytic perspective, characteristic adaptations in personality refer to specific ways in which individuals express sexual and aggressive drives and cope with motivational conflicts. Repressors deflect away stimuli that might lead to excessive anxiety, and they subsequently recall fewer emotionally negative events. Different defense mechanisms specify characteristic ways in which people cope with anxiety and intrapsychic conflict. Empirical research suggests that children and adults regularly use defense mechanisms to ward off anxiety and cope with stress. In keeping with hypotheses derived from Freud and the ego psychologists, defense mechanisms may be arranged in a developmental hierarchy, ranging from primitive defenses employed by young children to mature mechanisms shown by adults. Older children use more mature defenses than younger children, and defenses that are especially age-appropriate may be the most effective in dealing with stress. Among adults, the use of mature defense mechanisms is associated with greater social adjustment and occupational achievement.

THE HUMANISTIC VIEW

In the middle years of the 20th century, psychoanalysis vied with behaviorism for preeminence among American psychologists. Indeed, the two most famous names in 20th-century psychology were probably Freud and Skinner. For all their differences, psychoanalytic and behaviorist theories had one thing in common. Both believed that human behavior is motivated by forces over which the individual has little control. While Freud argued that human beings act in response to unconscious drives for sexuality and aggression, different behaviorist accounts identified biological drives such as hunger and thirst (Hull, 1943) and/or environmental contingencies of reinforcement (Skinner, 1938) as the fundamental motivators for behavior. Neither tradition put much stock in conscious thought and reason or in the higher and nobler aspirations of men and women. In response to the mechanistic and deterministic theories offered in psychoanalytic and behaviorist circles, therefore, a group of psychologists developed what eventually came to be seen as a third wave in American psychology. In the 1950s, 60s, and 70s, **humanistic** theorists offered a more optimistic and self-determining vision for American psychology. Humanistic theorists like Carl Rogers and Abraham Maslow argued that human beings are motivated by higher purposes that distinguish them from the rest of the animal kingdom. From the humanistic perspective, the supreme motivator is the *striving to actualize and perfect the self.*

CARL ROGERS'S THEORY

Born in Oak Park, Illinois, in 1902, Carl Rogers grew up in a deeply religious and financially secure family. After receiving a degree in history and attending the Union Theological Seminary in New York, Rogers moved to clinical psychology and earned a Ph.D. in 1931. He worked as a staff psychologist in a child-guidance center before moving to Ohio State University and then the University of Chicago, where he directed the Counseling Center. It was at Chicago in the 1950s that his point of view became a major force in psychological theory and practice, following the publication of his major work, *Client-Centered Therapy: Its Current Practice, Implications, and Theory* (Rogers, 1951). Rogers's developing humanistic perspective contrasted markedly with the prevalent psychoanalytic approaches to therapy and with popular behavioral approaches, such as behavior modification. Many of the hallmarks of Rogers's **client-centered therapy**—his emphasis on the therapist's warmth and sincerity, empathy, acceptance, role playing, and the dignity of the client—have become mainstays of a wide variety of therapeutic and educational approaches employed by clinicians, social workers, teachers, child-care workers, and other helping professionals today. It is difficult to overestimate Rogers's profound influence on clinical practice and education.

Carl Rogers (1902–1987) was a leading humanistic psychologist from the middle years of the 20th century. He developed client-centered psychotherapy and articulated a theory of human motivation that emphasized positive growth and self-actualization.

Rogers offered a simple and elegant theory of personality and motivation. In Rogers's view, the person must be understood from the perspective of his or her **phenomenal field.** The phenomenal field is the entire panorama of a person's experience, the person's subjective apprehension of reality. It is the individual's overall frame of reference. To learn about another person's phenomenal field, the psychologist must listen carefully to the person's subjective report of experience, thereby achieving empathy with the other. The roots of behavior are in the phenomenal field, Rogers claimed. Unconscious conflicts, biological needs, environmental influences, and all other forces impinging on the experiencing person are rendered meaningful or irrelevant through—and only through—the phenomenal field.

Human behavior and experience are guided by one basic striving in life. Writes Rogers, "The organism has one basic tendency and striving—to actualize, maintain, and enhance the experiencing organism" (1951, p. 487). There is "an inherent tendency of the organism to develop all its capacities in ways which serve to maintain or enhance the person" (1959, p. 196). All urges, desires, wants, goals, values, and motives may be subsumed under the general umbrella of *organismic enhancement.* Each person's fundamental mandate in life is to become all that he or she can become, to fulfill one's inner potential. In so doing, the person advances toward greater differentiation, independence, and social responsibility over the lifespan. People change through conscious, goal-directed choices. Choices must be clearly perceived if the person is to continue *becoming,* to continue moving toward full actualization of inner potential.

The person who is able to fulfill his or her potential is described as the **fully functioning person.** For the fully functioning person, the self has expanded to encompass the lion's share of the phenomenal field. The person is, therefore, consciously aware of the many different facets of his or her life, is able to integrate seemingly inconsistent aspects of experience into a coherent whole. Such a person leads a life that is rich in emotional experience and self-discovery. He or she is reflective, spontaneous, flexible, adaptable, confident, trusting, creative, and self-reliant. The fully functioning person operates according to the **organismic valuing process.** This means that those experiences in accord with the basic organismic-actualizing tendency are viewed as satisfying and therefore are approached and maintained. Those that are contrary to actualization—those experiences that do not promote growth and fulfillment—are avoided or minimized. All people experience a need for *positive regard,* or the desire to be loved and accepted by others. The fully functioning person is likely to have experienced a great deal of **unconditional positive regard.** This means that he or she has been loved and accepted by others in an uncritical and noncontingent manner. People need to be loved for their very existence as persons, through the kind of unconditional love that the ancient Greeks and the Christian church have called *agape.* Regard from others promotes basic *self-regard.* Every person needs to be regarded positively both by others and by him- or herself.

But love and acceptance are often conditional: We are praised, rewarded, liked, admired, and blessed for particular things that we do, say, think, and feel. Such conditional positive regard from others leads to the apprehension of **conditions of worth.** We come to believe that certain aspects of our experience are worthy and others are not worthy. A young boy who is repeatedly praised for good school performance may introject this condition of worth and make it a positive part of the self-structure. The person builds a self-image commensurate with what other important people, who provide the person with positive regard, urge him or her to adopt.

Those aspects of self that are viewed by others as not worthy may ultimately be denied or distorted, for they engender no positive regard and may, instead, be the harbingers of punishment. For instance, a young girl who enjoys vigorous sports may be criticized by her parents or peers for playing basketball with the boys. Their regard for her becomes conditional:

dependent on her adherence to appropriate feminine roles. As a result, she may revise her self-image to deny that she enjoys playing vigorous sports. Her conscious denial hides an inner truth, which results in inner conflict and distress.

Like Freud, Rogers believed that people suffer from important conflicts, many of which involve unconscious issues in their lives. But the conflicts derive from conflicts between the self and apprehended conditions of worth rather than between instinctual forces and superego demands. Rogers was much more optimistic than Freud about the possibility of living without conflict, of transcending conditions of worth to accept the self unconditionally. If we attain the fully functioning status, Rogers argued, we no longer impose conditions of worth on our experience but accept our entire organismic experience as good and fulfilling.

ABRAHAM MASLOW'S PSYCHOLOGY OF BEING

Abraham Maslow was born in Brooklyn, New York, in 1908, the son of Jewish parents who had emigrated from Russia. In contrast to Rogers, Maslow grew up isolated and very unhappy in a socially and economically deprived family. He earned his Ph.D. in psychology from the University of Wisconsin in 1934 under the tutelage of Harry Harlow, completing a dissertation on the sexual behavior of monkeys. At first an ardent behaviorist, Maslow's firsthand experience with his own children convinced him that this mechanistic approach to the person was not for him. Sometime around the beginning of World War II, Maslow experienced a profound personal conversion that eventually led to his formulation of a humanistic alternative in psychology. According to his own reports, he witnessed a pathetic and beggarly civilian parade designed to drum up support for the war, shortly after the bombing of Pearl Harbor. In Maslow's eyes, the parade only underscored the futility and

Abraham Maslow (1908–1970) developed a humanistic theory of motivation that delineated a hierarchy of needs, ranging from basic physiological needs up through the drive for self-actualization.

tragic waste of war. With tears streaming down his face, he made a firm vow: to prove that human beings were capable of achievements grander than hate and destructiveness, and to do so by studying the people in the world who seemed to be the psychologically *healthiest* (Hall, 1968). In 1951, Maslow became a professor at Brandeis University where he gained international fame as the foremost spokesman for humanistic personality theory.

Maslow shared Rogers's view that human beings strive to actualize their inner potential. His term for this fundamental human striving is **self-actualization.** But Maslow (1954, 1968) suggested that the need for self-actualization is undergirded by at least four other kinds of needs, forming a **need hierarchy** (Figure 7.4). At the base of the hierarchy are *physiological* needs, such as the needs for food, water, and sleep. Above them are *safety* needs: the needs for structure, security, order, avoidance of pain, and protection. *Belongingness and love* needs are the third level. People desire to be accepted and loved by others and to form affiliative, loving, and intimate unions. Next are the *esteem* needs, which refer to needs for self-respect and esteem from others, the desire to be seen by others and by the self as a competent and effective organism. Finally, there are the needs for *self-actualization,* which motivate the person to fulfill his or her own potential above and beyond the lower needs.

FIGURE 7.4   MASLOW'S NEED HIERARCHY

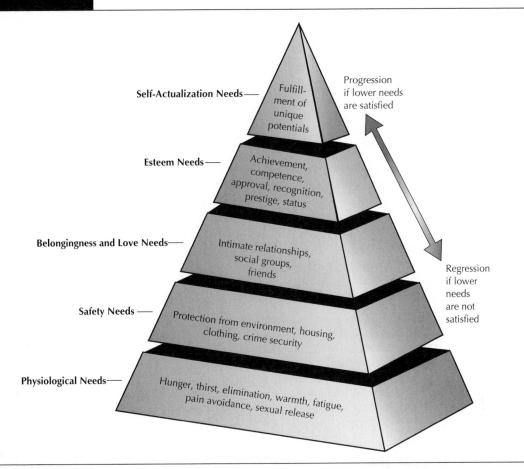

The key notion in Maslow's need hierarchy is that higher needs cannot generally be addressed until the lower needs are satisfied. For instance, a starving man will not act in accord with his needs for belongingness until he has secured food (physiological needs) and a safe position in life (security needs). A lonely woman will not be able to fulfill her needs for esteem until she finds belongingness and love. Self-actualization sits at the pinnacle of the hierarchy. We cannot expect people to fulfill their innate potential, says Maslow, until they have taken care of business at the lower and more basic levels of the hierarchy.

While many theories of personality derive from clinicians' work with neurotics and other people suffering psychological pain, Maslow is especially refreshing for his opposite point of view. Though he was a clinician, Maslow's theory of motivation was most heavily influenced by his understanding of the healthiest people, the most mature and actualized people among us. From interviewing friends and clients, reading biographies, and conducting structured research, Maslow sketched a personological portrait of the "self-actualizing" person, or "self-actualizer" (SA). Table 7.3 lists some of the characteristics Maslow identified as common in SAs.

An important characteristic of the SA is his or her proclivity for **peak experiences.** Peak experiences are just what they sound like: wonderful moments of happiness, ecstasy, transcendence. Put simply, SAs have more of these than do the rest of humankind. Yet virtually anyone can have a peak experience. Maslow sampled peak experiences among his friends and some of his college students by asking them to respond to this request:

> I would like you to think of the most wonderful experience or experiences in your life; happiest moments, ecstatic moments, moments of rapture, perhaps from being in love, or from listening to music or suddenly "being hit" by a book or a painting, or from some great creative moment. First list these. And then try to tell me how you feel in such acute moments, how you feel *differently* from the way you feel at other times, how you are at the moment a different person in some ways. (Maslow, 1968, p. 71)

Maslow's admittedly impressionistic analysis of the responses to his request suggested that in peak experiences people perceive and understand their world from the standpoint of **being cognition (B-cognition).** In B-cognition, the "experience or the object tends to be seen as a whole, as a complete unit, detached from relations from possible usefulness, from expediency and from purpose" (Maslow, 1968, p. 74). The "percept is exclusively and fully attended to" (p. 74), and "perception can be relatively ego-transcending, self-forgetful, egoless" (p. 79). There may even be a "disorientation in time and space" (p. 80), through which the person loses the subjective sense of time passing or of existing in a particular place. Most of all, though, B-cognition makes for a *unity* of consciousness:

> In some reports, particularly of the mystic experience or the religious experience or philosophical experience, the whole of the world is seen as unity, as a single rich live entity. In other of the peak experiences, most particularly the love experience and the aesthetic experience, one small part of the world is perceived as if it were for the moment all of the world. In both cases the perception is of unity. Probably the fact that the B-cognition of a painting or a person or a theory retains all the attributes of the whole of Being, i.e., the B-values, derives from this fact of perceiving it as if it were all that existed at the moment. (Maslow, 1968, p. 88)

TABLE 7.3   **SOME CHARACTERISTICS OF SELF-ACTUALIZING PERSONS**
Superior perception of reality
Increased acceptance of self, of others, and of nature
Increased spontaneity
Increased detachment and desire for privacy
Greater freshness of appreciation and richness of emotional reaction
Increased autonomy and resistance to conformity
Higher frequency of peak experiences
Increased identification with the human species
Improved interpersonal relationships
More democratic character structure
High levels of creativity

SOURCE: Modified from *Toward a Psychology of Being* (2nd ed., p. 26), by A. H. Maslow, 1968, New York: D. Van Nostrand.

INTRINSIC MOTIVATION AND SELF-DETERMINATION THEORY

We value peak experiences for the intensely positive feelings they provide and for their ability to involve us so fully in the best that life has to offer. These kinds of experiences are so good that they almost render the question of motivation meaningless. What I mean is that you don't typically have to explain to people *why* you would like to feel ecstasy, excitement, vitality, or any of the B-cognitions that Maslow suggests may accompany the most wonderful moments in our lives. It is patently obvious that virtually anybody would want to feel these things. I, for one, can't think of anybody I've ever met who would say that he or she is not interested in feeling utter joy. In other words, peak experiences seem to be *self-reinforcing* experiences. We are likely to value them in and of themselves—not because they lead to any other goal but because the good feelings that accompany them are themselves the "goal." Put differently, especially positive experiences in our lives may be *intrinsically motivating*. No outside motivation or incentive is needed. Indeed, providing a reward might have the paradoxical effect, some would say, of robbing the experience of its value and worth.

Research on **intrinsic motivation** suggests that providing rewards and incentives for intrinsically enjoyable behaviors may work not to reinforce but rather to undermine these behaviors. Research on intrinsic motivation began in the early 1970s with the observation that in certain situations material rewards produce surprising *decreases* in human performance (Deci, 1975; Lepper & Greene, 1978). While traditional theories of reinforcement, such as Skinner's behaviorism (chapter 3), tell us that people learn and perform best when they are rewarded for what they do, numerous studies show that receiving an extrinsic reward has its *costs* in certain situations. Extrinsic rewards may undermine the intrinsic value of certain behaviors and reduce the person's perceived freedom to do what he or she wants to do.

Consider these simple experiments conducted by Deci (1971). College students were typically asked to solve a series of interesting mechanical puzzles. In the experimental condition, the students were told that they would be paid $1 for each puzzle solved during a specified period of time. In the control condition, the students were given no information about monetary rewards. After the time period had elapsed, the students were given an opportunity to choose from a number of different activities available to them. Their behavior during this free-choice period was observed through a one-way mirror. Deci found that those students who had been promised payment for their puzzle performance (the experimental group) spent significantly less time playing with the puzzle during the free-choice period than did the students who were not promised payment (control group). Furthermore, the students who were paid for their performance reported that they enjoyed the puzzle task less and found it less interesting than did the students who were not paid.

What do these differences mean? Deci concluded that the students who received an extrinsic reward for their performance experienced a decrease in intrinsic motivation. The reward undermined their interest in the puzzles. Now that they were no longer being paid for their performance, they saw little reason to continue playing with the puzzles. Similar studies have produced parallel results. For instance, Lepper, Greene, and Nisbett (1973) found a decrease in children's intrinsic motivation when they were rewarded for their artwork. Children who had received rewards for using certain highly desirable materials in their artwork were less motivated to use those same art materials days later than were those children whose use of the materials had not been rewarded before. College students working on interesting word games became less intrinsically motivated when external deadlines were imposed than when none were applied (Amabile, DeJong, & Lepper, 1976). The external contingency of a deadline, like an external reward, shifts the person's perceived reason for undertaking a task from the intrinsic qualities of the task itself to extrinsic factors. The person loses interest in the task when he or she comes to see the motivation for doing the task as prompted from the outside.

Rewards, however, do not always undermine intrinsic motivation (Eisenberger & Cameron, 1996; Rawsthorne & Elliot, 1999). First, a task must be intrinsically interesting if the costs of reward are to be seen. In boring routine tasks, the introduction of a reward may increase a person's interest in the task and improve performance (Calder & Staw, 1975). Second, not all rewards in all situations are equal. While money, grades, and other more or less material rewards that are clearly contingent on performance may undermine intrinsic motivation in certain situations, such social reinforcers as verbal praise and encouragement are likely to increase intrinsic motivation. Furthermore, it depends on exactly what aspect of behavior is being rewarded. Rewards for *effort* (trying hard) are perceived differently from rewards for *ability* (doing well).

In an important theoretical development, Edward Deci and Richard Ryan have integrated research on intrinsic motivation into the broader framework of what they call **self-determination theory** (Deci & Ryan, 1980, 1985, 1991; Ryan, 1991, 1995). According to their view, intrinsic motivation is "the energizing basis for natural organismic activity" (Deci & Ryan, 1991, p. 244). Human beings are endowed with a natural tendency to encounter new challenges that will promote their self-development. Intrinsically motivated behaviors are experienced with "a full sense of choice, with the experience of doing what one wants, and without the feeling of coercion or compulsion" (Deci & Ryan, 1991, p. 253), such that the person spontaneously engages in activity that appears inherently interesting and enjoyable. Such activity "emanates from oneself, and is thus *self*-determined" (p. 253).

Intrinsically motivated behavior, therefore, is self-determined. By contrast, behavior that is not self-determined may be perceived by the actor as *controlled* or *amotivated.* Controlled behavior occurs when a person acts to meet the demands of some internal or external force; even though controlled behaviors may be "intentional," they feel as if they are things that the person does not truly want to do. Amotivated behaviors are unintentional and often disorganized because the person cannot regulate his or her own actions. For example, under the stress of an imminent writing deadline, a newspaper reporter may wander around her office in a daze. She cannot bring herself to do what she wants to do. She feels that she cannot possibly complete her project in the short time period allotted, so her behavior becomes random and amotivated.

Self-determination begins at birth. Deci and Ryan write:

> According to our perspective, a central feature of human nature is an active agency and a synthetic tendency that we ascribe to the self. From the time of birth, human beings are oriented toward the active exercise of their capacities and interests. They seek out optimal challenges, and they attempt to master and integrate new experiences. In other words, they are engaged in a developmental process that is intrinsic to their nature and is characterized by the tendency toward a more elaborate and extensive organization. (1991, pp. 238–239)

The infant is endowed with a nascent self—a vital core of personality that contains the potential for tremendous expansion. As Deci and Ryan (1991) put it, "the nature of life is to overtake itself" (p. 239). The self seeks to overtake its initial boundaries and limitations, to grow, to master its surroundings, to appropriate things, people, ideas, and environments, to make that which is nonself part of the self. As the infant masters and synthesizes

Ed Deci (left) and Richard Ryan (right) developed self-determination theory, an influential framework for human motivation that shares some similarities with humanistic theories. Deci and Ryan argue that intrinsically rewarding and self-determined behavior is motivated by organismic needs for autonomy, competence, and relatedness.

new experiences, the self becomes more encompassing (it takes in more things) and more integrated (it organizes its contents into meaningful systems). Over time, self-determined behavior enhances the development of self, and as the self develops, more and more of the person's behavior may become self-determined. An expanded self makes for a greater degree of *self-involvement* in behavior. The person's experience of life becomes akin to that of the "author" or "owner" of his or her own behavior. Behavior becomes less controlled and amotivated. Action becomes incorporated within and guided by the self.

Deci and Ryan argue that self-determined behavior stems from three basic psychological needs (see also Sheldon, Elliot, Kim, & Kasser, 2001). First, the need for *competence* encompasses the person's strivings to control the outcomes of events and to experience a sense of mastery and effectiveness in dealing with the environment. Second, the need for *autonomy* involves the desire to feel that one is independent of external pressures and able to relate to the world as an origin rather than a pawn. Third, the need for *relatedness* encompasses a person's strivings to care for others, to feel that others are relating to the self in authentic and mutually supportive ways, and to feel a satisfying and coherent involvement with the social world more generally. The three needs generate self-determined behavior, and self-determined behavior promotes development, or what Deci and Ryan call *organismic integration*. Organismic integration has two facets—unity of the self and integration into the social order. Over time, self-determined behavior helps the person experience his or her inner life in a more cohesive and unified manner, and it helps involve the person in coherent and meaningful interactions with other people.

Sheldon and Kasser (1995) distinguish between the self-determination theory concept of organismic integration on the one hand and the more common notion of personality congruence on the other. Personality congruence refers to the extent to which a person's goals are consistent with one another and, therefore, work well together. For example, a successful entrepreneur's goals of (a) becoming rich and (b) traveling around the world may be consistent with each other in that his success in making money will enable him to pay for expensive vacations. These two goals suggest some personality congruence. However, these goals do not make a strong case for organismic integration. Organismic integration concerns the extent to which a person's goals are self-determined and consistent with organismic needs. In the case of the entrepreneur, getting rich is viewed as an extrinsic rather than intrinsic goal. Extrinsic goals include such things as financial success, social recognition, and physical attractiveness. When goals are linked to needs for autonomy, competence, or interpersonal relatedness, organismic integration is enhanced. In two research studies, Sheldon and Kasser show that students scoring high on measures of organismic integration tend to report more positive daily moods, heightened vitality, and engagement in meaningful daily activities. Other studies have shown that as people make significant progress in the attainment of goals that contribute to the needs for autonomy, competence, and interpersonal relatedness, they experience higher levels of mental health and adjustment, self-actualization, and psychological well-being (Reis, Sheldon, Gable, Roscoe, & Ryan, 2000; Sheldon & Elliot, 1999; Sheldon & Kasser, 1998).

Not only should developing goals that meet organismic needs be associated with positive feelings and behaviors, but self-determination theory suggests that pursuing extrinsic goals that do not promote organismic integration should be associated with lower levels of psychological well-being. Kasser and Ryan (1996) argue that the classic "American dream" is a story of financial success and material well-being. Yet, these extrinsic goals may do little to promote feelings of autonomy, competence, and interpersonal relatedness. In samples of both college students and adults, Kasser and Ryan found that the relative importance and efficacy of extrinsic aspirations for financial success, an appealing appearance, and social recognition were associated with *lower* vitality and self-actualization and more physical symptoms. Conversely, the relative importance and efficacy of intrinsic aspirations for self-acceptance, affiliation, community feeling, and physical health were associated with higher well-being and less distress. According to Kasser and Ryan, there is a dark side to the classic American dream. American society's obsession with material wealth may undermine the pursuit of intrinsic goals that promote organismic integration. As they get richer and live yet more comfortable lives, Americans may be losing sight of the goals in life most able to give them a sense of deep happiness and meaning.

The development of the self is a product of an intricate dialectic between the person and the social world. Deci and Ryan view the social world in terms of the opportunities and constraints it may provide for self-determined behavior. Three social dimensions are particularly important. First, the social environment may offer *autonomy support*. In other words, it may be encouraging of choice and innovation in behavior. Environments that discourage choice function to control a person's behavior. Second, the social environment may provide *structure* for behavior. Highly structured environments provide clear guidelines about what kinds of behaviors lead to what kinds of outcomes, and they give the actor explicit feedback concerning how "well" he or she is doing in the environment. Third, the social environment may offer interpersonal *involvement*. Involvement describes the degree to which significant others (e.g., parents, teachers, friends, spouse) are interested in and devote time and energy to a relationship. All in all, social contexts that provide high levels of autonomy support, *moderate* structure, and that contain involved others are optimal for encouraging self-determined behavior and organismic integration.

In sum, intrinsically motivated behavior is inherently interesting and enjoyable, involves optimally challenging tasks and activities, and is often performed in the absence of external rewards. Such behavior is self-determined. Self-determined behavior serves the basic needs of competence, autonomy, and relatedness. Self-determined behavior flourishes in environments that support autonomy, provide moderate structure, and involve people who care about the person and are invested in the person's life. Self-determined behavior makes for organismic integration, by promoting unity of one's inner life and integration into a social order. In keeping with the humanistic views of Rogers and Maslow, Deci and Ryan argue that self-determination ultimately enables the person to experience the "true self," so that he or she may lead an "authentic" life.

THE DIVERSITY VIEW

The psychoanalytic view suggests that basic drives for sexuality and aggression are the well-springs of human behavior. The humanistic view contends that all people strive to become self-determining and self-actualized organisms. Yet another view of motivation argues that *human beings are motivated by many different things.* Some people are motivated by certain classes of goals and incentives; other people are motivated by other goals and incentives. John may be strongly motivated by achievement needs; Sara has devoted her life to helping others; Brian wants to get into graduate school in anthropology; Maria is strongly driven by contrasting motives for intimacy and power, and the conflict makes her anxious; Maria's brother, Miguel, has never known this conflict, for his main drive in life is to make money. The diversity view rejects the idea that human behavior and experience can be reduced to a small set of basic drives or needs. Instead, it puts forth the common-sense proposition that when it comes to motive and goals, everybody is different.

HENRY MURRAY'S THEORY OF NEEDS

The most well-known representative of the diversity tradition in the study of human motivation is Henry Murray's theory of needs. Murray was a monumental figure in the history of personality psychology whose contributions to the biographical study of lives will be examined in chapter 12 of this textbook. For now, what is important is Murray's (1938) conception of needs. Murray argued that human lives must always be understood in the context of time. People live both in response to the past and in anticipation of the future. As we move through our daily lives, we bind together our remembrances of things past and our expectations about what is to come:

> What he [the human being] does is related not only to the settled past but also to shadowy preconceptions of what lies ahead. Years in advance he makes preparations to observe an eclipse of the sun from a distant island in the South Pacific and, lo, when the moment comes, he is there to record the event. With the same confidence another man prepares to meet his god. Man lives in an inner world of expected press (pessimistic or optimistic), and the psychologist must take cognizance of them if he wishes to understand his conduct or his moods, his buoyancies, disappointments, resignations. Time-binding makes for continuity of purpose. (Murray, 1938, p. 49)

The directedness of human lives becomes apparent over time. A given momentary behavior may seem meaningless in light of the current situation in which it is displayed. But with respect to the person's life over time, the behavior may be seen as part of a purposeful sequence of actions. Time-binding provides lives with their characteristic direction and purpose. But what forces direct and select the ways in which human beings organize their lives and bind their time? Such forces, according to Murray, reside both within the organism and in the organism's environment. Within the organism are located the basic physiological and psychological **needs.** In the environment are located the various situational constraints and opportunities for need expression, or what Murray called **press** (plural = press). When a particular need repeatedly interacts with a particular press over an extended period of time, you have what Murray called a **thema.** Therefore, human motivation must be understood in terms of the interaction of needs and press to produce themas.

Murray defined a need as a

construct (convenient fiction or hypothetical concept) which stands for a force (the physico-chemical nature of which is unknown) in the brain region, a force which organizes perception, apperception, [interpreting perceptions], intellection [thinking], conation [striving], and action in such a way as to transform in a certain direction an existing unsatisfying situation. (Murray, 1938, pp. 123–124)

Therefore, a need is the representation of a brain force that energizes, directs, selects, and organizes human perceiving, thinking, feeling, and striving. It operates to transform an unsatisfying situation into a more satisfying one. In this last regard, Murray's view of needs is similar to Freud's in that both held to the doctrine of *tension-reduction*. The tension for a particular need builds up over time and then is released through need-satisfying thought or behavior. However, Murray departed from Freud dramatically with respect to the kinds of human needs he identified. *Viscerogenic* needs are physiological wants and desires such as the need for air, water, and sentience (sleep). More relevant for personality, however, are the *psychogenic* needs, such as the needs for autonomy, achievement, affiliation, dominance, play, order, and so on. Murray proposed 20 basic psychogenic needs, each of which exerts important effects on human behavior. Table 7.4 defines selected psychogenic needs from Murray's influential taxonomy.

At any given point in time, human behavior may be organized by a number of different viscerogenic and psychogenic needs operating simultaneously. But some needs are likely to be stronger or "prepotent" relative to others at a given time. Stronger or more urgent needs sometimes override weaker ones, as when a person's strong craving for dominance moves him to act in Machiavellian ways that violate his need for affiliation. In other instances, different needs may fuse, thereby working together to attain the same behavioral end. Playing softball with one's friends may, for example, satisfy the needs for affiliation, dominance, and play. Another important kind of relation among needs is *subsidiation*. A subsidiary need is one that operates in service of another. For example, a person may act in an aggressive way (revealing a strong aggressive need) in order to avoid pain (the need for harm avoidance). In this instance, the aggressive need serves the more encompassing need to avoid pain. The only reason the person desires to be aggressive is in order to remain safe.

Needs also interact with dispositional traits. In general, the way in which a person achieves a goal may be partly determined by traits, such as extraversion–introversion. But the nature of the goal itself is more likely determined by needs. Traits and needs, therefore, fulfill different functions in the personality: needs establish goals; traits describe behavioral means whereby goals are met (McClelland, 1981; Winter, John, Stewart, Klohnen, & Duncan, 1998). In a sense, needs tell us *why* a person does what he does; traits tell us *how*.

Just as the concept of "need" represents the significant determinants of behavior within the person so the concept of "press" represents the effective or significant determinants of behavior in the environmental situation. A press is a tendency in the environment to facilitate or obstruct the expression of a need. Wrote Murray, "the *press* of an object is what it can *do to the subject or for the subject*—the power that it has to affect the well-being of the subject in one way or another" (1938, p. 121). Such an "object" may indeed be a person or some feature of an interpersonal situation. Murray distinguished between *alpha* and *beta* press. An alpha press is made up of characteristics in the environment as they exist in reality or as objective inquiry discloses them. By contrast, a beta press is the person's subjective impression of those characteristics in the environment. Beta press, therefore, is always a matter of interpretation.

TABLE 7.4	SELECTED PSYCHOGENIC NEEDS FROM MURRAY (1938)
Need	**Brief Definition**
Achievement	To accomplish something difficult. To master, manipulate, or organize physical objects, human beings, or ideas. To do this as rapidly and as independently as possible. To overcome obstacles and attain a high standard. To excel oneself. To rival and surpass others. To increase self-regard by the successful exercise of talent.
Affiliation	To draw near and enjoyably cooperate or reciprocate with an allied other (an other who resembles the subject or who likes the subject). To please and win affection of a cathected object. To adhere and remain loyal to a friend.
Aggression	To overcome opposition forcefully. To fight. To revenge an injury. To attack, injure, or kill another. To oppose forcefully or punish another.
Autonomy	To get free, shake off restraint, break out of confinement. To resist coercion and restriction. To avoid or quit activities prescribed by domineering authorities. To be independent and free to act according to impulse. To be unattached, irresponsible. To defy convention.
Dominance	To control one's human environment. To influence or direct the behavior of others by suggestion, seduction, persuasion, or command. To dissuade, restrain, or prohibit.
Exhibition	To make an impression. To be seen and heard. To excite, amaze, fascinate, entertain, shock, intrigue, amuse, or entice others.
Harm avoidance	To avoid pain, physical injury, illness, and death. To escape from a dangerous situation. To take precautionary measures.
Nurturance	To give sympathy to and gratify the needs of a helpless object: an infant or any object that is weak, disabled, tired, inexperienced, infirm, defeated, humiliated, lonely, dejected, sick, mentally confused. To assist an object in danger. To feed, help, support, console, protect, comfort, nurse, heal.
Order	To put things in order. To achieve cleanliness, arrangement, balance, neatness, tidiness, and precision.
Play	To act for "fun" without further purpose. To like to laugh and make jokes. To seek enjoyable relaxation of stress. To participate in games, sports, dancing, drinking, cards.
Sentience	To seek and enjoy sensuous impressions.
Sex	To form and further an erotic relationship. To have sexual intercourse.
Succorance	To have one's needs gratified by the sympathetic aid of an allied object. To be nursed, supported, sustained, surrounded, protected, loved, advised, guided, forgiven, consoled. To remain close to a devoted protector. To always have a supporter.
Understanding	To ask or answer general questions. To be interested in theory. To speculate, formulate, and alyze, and generalize.

SOURCE: From *Explorations in Personality* (pp. 152–226), by H. A. Murray, 1938, New York: Oxford University Press.

The full dynamics of human behavior are revealed in the interaction of needs and press, producing a thema. Imagine this example. A college student's strong need for order cannot be well expressed in her ceramics class, in which she is forced to work with materials that are sloppy and difficult to control. A thema develops whereby her inability to act in an orderly fashion initially produces a great deal of anxiety, which quickly gives way to an attitude of "don't worry about it, you don't have to be neat." The thema is the entire pattern of need/press interaction. In these kinds of unruly experiences (press), she experiences anxiety because her need for order cannot be expressed. But the anxiety eventually gives way to relaxation. Indeed, the relaxation response may be a function of the arousal of her need for play. Themas sometimes involve multiple needs and press.

THE THEMATIC APPERCEPTION TEST

Murray (1938) developed many methods for the study of personality, but the most popular and influential has probably been the Thematic Apperception Test, or TAT (Morgan & Murray, 1935; Murray, 1943). In the TAT, a person is presented with a series of ambiguous picture cues and is asked to compose, either verbally or in writing, a story in response to each. The TAT is considered a "projective test," in that the person assumedly projects his or her own needs, wishes, conflicts, and so forth onto the ambiguous picture cue. The ambiguous picture cue is merely a stimulus designed to put into motion the process of constructing an imaginative narrative response (Lindzey, 1959). In Murray's view, such narrative responding reveals partially hidden themes of the personality, especially those concerning basic needs, conflicts, and complexes.

Murray (1943) provided rough guidelines for interpreting the stories told in response to TAT pictures. He believed that the psychologist should first identify the *hero* in the story—usually the main character or the character who most resembles the storywriter. Second, the psychologist should consider the hero's *motives, trends, and feelings.* Careful attention should be paid to story content that indicates psychogenic needs: a story in which the main character is trying to succeed in a difficult task would indicate a strong *n* Achievement; another story in which the character seeks friendship with others would suggest the affiliation motive. Third, the psychologist should note the *forces in the hero's environment* that impinge upon or provide opportunities for need-expression. Murray believed that a TAT story may reveal as much about how a person perceives the world as it does about internal needs. Fourth, the *outcomes* of stories may indicate the extent to which the storyteller believes that his or her own needs can be fulfilled in daily life. In this regard, Murray suggested that the psychologist keep track of the ratio of happy to unhappy story endings. Fifth, the psychologist should document the recurrent combinations of particular needs and particular environmental situations (what Murray termed *press*) across the stories. A need/press combination constitutes a simple *thema*. Sixth, *interests and sentiments* may appear in the story content. The psychologist may be able to obtain information on the storyteller's feelings about particular kinds of people (for example, authority figures, older women, children) or about particular aspects of the environment (such as politics, religion, the natural world). Regardless of how the psychologist interprets the TAT, Murray emphasized that "the conclusions that are reached by an analysis of TAT stories must be regarded as good 'leads' or working hypotheses to be verified by other methods, rather than as proved facts" (1943, p. 14).

The most profitable use of the TAT is to view it as an indicator of psychogenic needs, or **motives.** Three such motives have been studied in great detail: achievement, power, and intimacy. In considering each of these three motives, we will focus on the research tradition fathered by personality psychologist David C. McClelland. Reconceptualizing Murray's notion of "need," McClelland defined a motive as a recurrent preference or readiness for a particular quality of experience, which energizes, directs, and selects behavior in certain situations. The achievement motive, therefore, refers to the quality of human experience entailed in *doing better;* the power motive refers to *having impact;* and the intimacy motive denotes *feeling close.* McClelland (1980) argued that motives lie outside a person's conscious awareness and cannot, therefore, be accurately assessed through conscious self-report. By sampling the everyday stream of imaginative thought, the TAT enables the researcher to find central themes that may indicate unconscious motives.

ACHIEVEMENT MOTIVATION

David McClelland and John Atkinson pioneered the use of the TAT to assess individual differences in achievement motivation (Atkinson, 1958; Atkinson & Birch, 1978; McClelland, Atkinson, Clark, & Lowell, 1953). The most important innovation of their approach was the derivation and validation of an objective, reliable, and quantitative system to score TAT stories for achievement motivation. In their original derivation studies, McClelland and Atkinson asked college students to write short TAT stories under various laboratory conditions. In one condition, the students were first administered a series of cognitive tasks (such as unscrambling words) and then were told that their performance on the tasks would be an indication of their general intelligence and leadership ability. It was assumed that such instructions would temporarily *arouse* achievement thoughts and feelings in these subjects, and that these thoughts and feelings would be projected onto the stories written on the TAT, administered immediately following the task. In another (neutral) condition, students were administered the same tasks but were told that the tasks were newly developed and not likely to be valid measures of much of anything. It was assumed that these subjects would be less aroused with respect to achievement strivings than the subjects in the first group.

McClelland and his colleagues detected a number of consistent content differences between the groups. Students in the arousal group tended to write more stories involving characters striving to do better, compared with students in the neutral group. Subsequent comparisons from different studies and various refinements produced a content scoring system for the TAT. The system is made up of the particular content themes that consistently differentiated between stories written under achievement arousal and under neutral conditions. The themes involve the story characters' behaviors, attitudes, and feelings about task performance.

Although the achievement-motive scoring system was derived by examining group differences in narrative content, the system has proven extremely sensitive and valuable as an index of *individual differences* within groups. In a typical individual-differences study, a large number of people are administered the TAT under standardized *neutral* conditions. The subjects' TAT stories are then scored by trained coders according to the standard system developed by McClelland and Atkinson. Motive scores fall into a distribution, ranging from high to low. It is assumed that each person's "natural" level of achievement motivation will be expressed in TAT stories written under such neutral, nonarousing conditions.

Substantial empirical literature suggests that people who score high on TAT achievement motivation behave in different ways than people who score low, supporting the construct validity of the TAT measure. For instance, people high in achievement motivation tend to prefer and show high performance in tasks of moderate challenge

David McClelland (1917–1998) pioneered research employing the Thematic Apperception Test (TAT) to assess individual differences in motives for achievement, power, and intimacy/affiliation. In his most famous book, *The Achieving Society* (1961), McClelland treated cultural texts, such as children's readers, as if they were TAT stories, coding them for achievement imagery and showing how the relative density of achievement themes in these texts predicted a society's economic growth.

that provide immediate feedback concerning success and failure; they tend to be persistent and highly efficient in many kinds of performance, sometimes cutting corners or cheating in order to maximize productivity; they tend to exhibit high self-control and a future time perspective; they thrive on personal challenge; and they tend to be restless, innovative, and drawn toward change and movement (Atkinson, 1957: Atkinson & Raynor, 1978; Crockett, 1962; Feather, 1961; Heckhausen, 1967; McClelland, 1961, 1985; Mischel, 1961; Mischel & Gilligan, 1964; Spangler, 1992; Winter & Carlson, 1988; Zurbriggen & Sturman, 2002). Some of the best-established findings in this regard are summarized in Table 7.5.

Young adults who are high in achievement motivation tend to be drawn to careers in business. In one study, for example, men with high achievement motivation in college tended to become employed in small businesses years later (McClelland, 1965). Research also suggests that high achievement motivation is associated with certain indices of success in the business world (Andrews, 1967; Jenkins, 1987; McClelland & Boyatzis, 1982; McClelland & Franz, 1992; Tekiner, 1980). McClelland argued that business is a good match for the achievement motive, because business requires that people take moderate risks, assume personal responsibility for their own performance, pay close attention to feedback in terms of costs and profits, and find innovative ways to make products or provide services. These hallmarks of **entrepreneurship** precisely characterize the behavior and attitudes of people high in achievement motivation (McClelland, 1985).

One of the more intriguing applications of McClelland's approach to achievement motivation is the analysis of *societal and historical differences.* McClelland (1961) argued that entire societies and historical epochs differ in overall achievement motivation. While some societies actively promote achievement values and entrepreneurship, others appear less motivated to do so; in addition, a particular society's preoccupation with achievement may wax and wane over time. Such societal and historical differences should correspond to economic growth and ultimately to the rise and decline of entire states, regions, or peoples.

TABLE 7.5	SELECTED CORRELATES OF HIGH ACHIEVEMENT MOTIVATION

High aspirations but moderate risk taking

Preference for situations in which personal responsibility can affect results

Tendency to take personal credit for success but blame others or the situation for failures

Cheating and/or bending the rules in order to reach a desired goal in an efficient and expeditious manner

Penchant for travel

Self-control, inhibition, and delay of gratification

Preference for somber colors and formal fashion

Extended future time perspective

Upward social mobility and higher educational attainment

Entrepreneurial activity and innovation

Success in business

Being reared in a family in which parents set high standards for performance

Scheduled feeding during infancy and relatively stringent toilet training

NOTE: Much of the research on achievement motivation has focused exclusively on men. While the relatively few studies investigating correlates of achievement motivation in women are generally consistent with results for men, there are some areas (such as entrepreneurship and risk taking) in which virtually no data on women have been obtained (Stewart & Chester, 1982).

How might a personality psychologist measure societal differences in achievement motivation? McClelland argued that the procedure is virtually identical to that used with individuals: imaginative stories should be coded for achievement themes. Selected passages from a society's representative folktales, myths, textbooks, or even its popular literature can be coded as if they were discrete TAT stories in order to provide a rough estimate of overall achievement motivation in a society at a particular time in history. McClelland assumed that these narrative expressions reflect pervasive cultural assumptions and values.

In *The Achieving Society,* McClelland (1961) reported a study in which he collected second- and fourth-grade readers (elementary school textbooks) published from 1920 to 1929 from 23 different countries and scored selected passages for achievement themes. McClelland found that achievement motive themes in children's readers in the 1920s were positively correlated with his index of economic growth, even when other societal factors, such as differences in natural resources, were taken into consideration. In other words, economic growth between 1929 and 1950 was much more pronounced in those countries showing a strong emphasis on achievement in children's readers in the 1920s (such as Turkey, Israel, and India) than in countries whose children's readers showed relatively few achievement themes (such as Italy, Belgium, and Algeria). A society's books for children mirror prevalent cultural values that are inculcated in children through various socialization processes, such as schooling and child training. Socialization for achievement encourages children to be masterful and independent, to plan for the future, to take moderate risks, and to value efficiency and gradual improvement or growth. McClelland argued that such training likely increases the achievement motivation of young boys and girls, who eventually develop a preference and proclivity for entrepreneurship as adults, which ultimately makes for greater economic growth.

Another index of a society's economic vitality is the proliferation of inventions and innovations. Figure 7.5 presents the rather striking findings from a study of the relationship between achievement motivation expressed in children's readers and the number of patents per capita issued to inventors over a period of 140 years in the United States (de Charms & Moeller, 1962). The rise and decline in the number of U.S. patents issued between the years 1810 and 1950 neatly parallels the rise and decline of achievement imagery in American children's readers. A similar relationship was discovered between achievement imagery in English popular literature and the amount of coal imported by England during the years 1550 to 1800. Again, changes in collective achievement motivation predicted economic growth. A positive relation between achievement motivation and economic growth can be seen in non-Western, preliterate societies, as well. Among 39 preliterate tribes, 75% of those with high achievement content in their folktales were characterized as having at least some full-time entrepreneurs, as contrasted with only 38% of the tribes with less amounts of achievement imagery in their folktales.

POWER MOTIVATION

The **power motive** is a recurrent preference for having an impact on other people. People high in power motivation strive to wield power and to feel stronger, more masterful, more influential than others. Like the achievement motive, this recurrent desire for power energizes, selects, and directs human behavior in predictable ways. Also like achievement motivation, individual differences in the power motive are assessed through objective content analysis of TAT stories.

FIGURE 7.5	ACHIEVEMENT IMAGERY IN CHILDREN'S READERS AND SOCIETAL PRODUCTIVITY

As achievement imagery in children's school reading books increases over time, the number of patents issued in the United States also increases; as the achievement imagery decreases, patent numbers follow suit. The data are from the United States between the years 1810 and 1950.

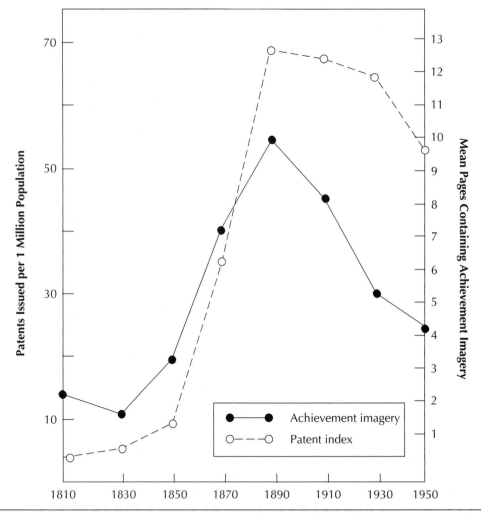

SOURCE: From "Values Expressed in American Children's Readers: 1800–1950," by R. de Charms & G. H. Moeller, 1962, *Journal of Abnormal and Social Psychology, 64,* 139.

Following procedures developed by McClelland and others (Uleman, 1966; Veroff, 1957), David Winter (1973) derived the coding system for power motivation through comparing stories written by people under power-arousal and neutral conditions. Power themes in TAT stories typically involve story characters' efforts to have a strong impact on each other, through both positive (e.g., persuasion) and negative (e.g., aggression) means. People who characteristically write TAT stories containing many of these themes are deemed to be high in power motivation. Many studies attest to the construct validity of the TAT coding system for power motivation. Interestingly, empirical findings paint two very different pictures of people high in power motivation. On the one hand, power motivation is sometimes associated with aggression, exploitative interpersonal relationships, and (among men) profligate sexuality (Schultheiss, Dargel, & Rohde, 2002; Winter, 1973; Zurbriggen, 2000). On the other hand, power motivation has also been linked to membership in voluntary organizations, efforts to make positive contributions to groups and society, and creative problem solving (Fodor, 1990; Fodor & Greenier, 1995). It appears that power motivation can manifest itself in both destructive/immature and constructive/mature ways (McClelland, 1975).

Because people high in power motivation desire to have an impact on others, a number of researchers have explored the ways in which such impact is accomplished. Fodor and Smith (1982) investigated how students high in power motivation direct the behaviors of others in group decision making. Forty groups containing five students each met to discuss a business case study that concerned whether a company should market a new microwave oven. In each group, a leader was appointed. Based on a prior administration of the TAT, half the leaders scored extremely high on the power motive and half scored extremely low. In addition, half the groups were given the opportunity to win a group reward for superior performance (in order to build "high group cohesiveness") and half were offered no reward ("low group cohesiveness"). Each group member was given a fact sheet containing information that could be shared with the group during discussion.

Three major dependent variables were assessed in Fodor and Smith's study: (a) the number of *facts* from the sheet that each person shared with the group during discussion, (b) the number of alternative *proposals* for marketing the microwave considered by the group, and (c) the level of *moral concern* evidenced by the group, which was determined by

a rating of the extent to which the group discussed such issues as the possible harmful effects of microwave radiation on people's health and the ethical propriety of various marketing strategies. Those groups in which the leader was high in power motivation tended to offer fewer facts and proposals and to show less moral concern, compared with groups headed by a low-power leader (Table 7.7). The level of group cohesiveness, on the other hand, did not influence the results. The authors interpreted these findings to mean that leaders high in power motivation encourage what social psychologists call *group-think*—a form of hasty decision making characterized by diffusion of responsibility, failure to consider long-term ramifications, and the domination by a single strong leader whose opinion generally goes unchallenged. In a related vein, a study of real-life and hypothetical negotiation scenarios showed that individuals high in power motivation were much less likely than those low to offer concessions and compromises (Langner & Winter, 2001).

David Winter is a leading expert on power motivation and a pioneer in the area of political psychology. Among Winter's most intriguing studies are those in which he has correlated motivational imagery in the inaugural addresses given by U.S. Presidents with their subsequent performance in office.

A large number of studies have shown that people who perennially adopt strong leadership roles and/or rise to positions of high influence tend to score relatively high in power motivation (McAdams, Rothman, & Lichter, 1982; McClelland & Boyatzis, 1982; McClelland & Burnham, 1976; Winter, 1973). The most intriguing line of research in this regard is probably Winter's (1987, 1996; Donley & Winter, 1970) studies of American presidents. Winter has

TABLE 7.6	**SELECTED CORRELATES OF HIGH POWER MOTIVATION**

Holding elected offices

Preference for careers in which one directs the behavior of individuals in accordance with preconceived plans and with the use of positive and negative sanctions (careers such as executive, teacher, and psychologist)

Career success among women in power-related occupations but not in careers emphasizing interpersonal relationships

Active, forceful, and influential in small groups

Effective organizational leader

Accumulation of prestige possessions, such as luxury cars and major credit cards

Taking large risks in order to gain visibility

Agentic, assertive style of friendship that emphasizes self-display and helping the other

Getting into arguments

Writing letters to the newspaper

Somewhat negative self-image

Prone to impulsive and aggressive behavior (men only)

Precocious and exploitative sexual activity (men only)

Instability in romantic relationships (men only)

Being reared in a family in which parents were relatively permissive concerning sexual behavior and aggression

analyzed the published inaugural addresses of virtually all the American presidents, going back to George Washington, for achievement, power, and intimacy motivation. Winter has argued that, despite the help of speech-writers and the influences of various socio-historical forces and events, the motivational imagery contained in these major speeches partially reflects the president's own personality. Presidents scoring particularly high in power motivation include Franklin D. Roosevelt, Harry Truman, John Kennedy, and Ronald Reagan. Winter (1987) correlated motive scores with various ratings of the presidents made by historians and political scientists. Power motivation was positively associated with ratings of "presidential greatness" ($r = +.40$) and number of historically significant decisions made

TABLE 7.7	**AVERAGE NUMBER OF FACTS AND PROPOSALS AND MEAN MORAL CONCERN RATINGS OF DISCUSSION GROUPS**					
	LEVEL OF GROUP COHESIVENESS					
	LOW			**HIGH**		
Level of N Power in President	**Facts**	**Proposals**	**Moral Concern**	**Facts**	**Proposals**	**Moral Concern**
Low	17.5	4.8	1.7	16.3	1.4	1.4
High	14.2	4.0	0.9	14.8	3.2	1.1

SOURCE: From "The Power Motive as an Influence on Group Decision Making," by E. M. Fodor & T. Smith, 1982, *Journal of Personality and Social Psychology, 42,* 183.

($r = +.51$). In other words, those presidents who have been rated as especially forceful and influential by political scholars tend to be the same ones whose inaugural addresses indicated especially high levels of power motivation. In addition, presidents high in power motivation were also more likely to lead the United States into war ($r = +.52$).

What about the personal lives of people high in power motivation? Some research suggests that *men* high in the need for power experience numerous difficulties in romantic relationships with women (e.g., Stewart & Rubin, 1976). At the same time, well-educated *women* high in power motivation tend to marry successful men (Winter, McClelland, & Stewart, 1981). Further, Veroff (1982) reports that power motivation in women is positively associated with marital *satisfaction*. While high-power women tend to report happy marriages, men high in power motivation show a higher divorce rate (McClelland, Davis, Kalin, & Wanner, 1972) and a greater degree of marital *dissatisfaction* (Veroff & Feld, 1970). At the root of the high-power man's apparent dissatisfaction with and instability in romantic heterosexual relations may be a latent fear of women and the control they may exert. Slavin (1972) has shown that men high in power motivation express more themes of "feminine evil" in their fantasies than do men lower on the motive. These themes include females harming men through physical contact, females exploiting men, females rejecting men, females proving unfaithful in relationships, and females triumphing over men. In this regard, Winter and Stewart (1978) report that men high in power motivation, when asked to draw pictures of women, produce sometimes frightening and bizarre sketches with exaggerated sexual characteristics.

In the area of health, studies by McClelland and his colleagues suggest a possible association between power motivation and susceptibility to disease (McClelland, 1979; McClelland, Alexander, & Marks, 1982; McClelland, Davidson, Floor, & Saron, 1980; McClelland & Jemmott, 1980; McClelland, Ross, & Patel, 1985). However, the association seems fairly complex. McClelland (1979) has argued that a strong need for power increases a person's vulnerability to illnesses of various sorts *if* the person's need for power is inhibited, challenged, or blocked. Especially vulnerable are individuals who show *all* of the following characteristics: (a) high power motivation, (b) low intimacy motivation, (c) high self-control (sometimes called "activity inhibition" and suggesting a tendency to "block" or "inhibit" one's own expression of power), and (d) high levels of power-related stresses (Jemmott, 1987).

Some evidence suggests that people high in power motivation are predisposed to show heightened activation of the sympathetic nervous system when faced with obstacles to or frustrations in the experience of having impact and feeling strong (Fodor, 1984, 1985). If power motivation is associated with heightened sympathetic activity, then one might expect it also to be associated with elevated blood pressure. In three different samples of German and American men, McClelland (1979) documented just such an association. In one sample followed longitudinally, 61% of the men scoring above average on a TAT index of power + self-control (taken when they were in their 30s) showed elevated diastolic blood pressure 20 years later, compared with only 23% of the men scoring below average on this index.

There is empirical evidence, albeit scattered, to suggest that high power motivation may be modestly associated with small deficits in the body's immune system. If this is true, one might expect high power motivation to be implicated indirectly in the breakdown of the body's defenses to sickness and disease. McClelland and Jemmot (1980) administered the TAT to 95 students and obtained self-report measures of health problems and life stresses. They classified each life stress identified by a participant as either a power/achievement event, an affiliation/intimacy event, or "other." Examples of power/achievement events included troubles with an employer, a substantial academic disappointment, and participating in a major sports event. The results of the study indicated that the students with (a) relatively high power motivation, (b) relatively high activity inhibition (self-control), and (c) an above-average number of power/achievement stresses over the past year reported more physical illnesses in the previous 6 months than did other students. In addition, the illnesses they reported were more severe. Thus, the highly controlled and highly power-oriented person may "bottle-up" his or her frustrations in such a way as to tax an internal physiological equilibrium. The result may be a greater number of colds, bouts of flu, and other maladies, especially during times of excessive power stress.

INTIMACY MOTIVATION

While our desires for achievement and power may motivate us to assert ourselves in effective and influential ways and to control, even master, our environments, our longings for close and warm relationships with other human beings pull us in a different direction, to the private life of intimate interpersonal communion (Bakan, 1966). Indeed, for some of us, the desire for intimacy is even grander and more compelling than our wishes for success, fame, and transcendence. As the novelist E. M. Forster wrote, "It is the private life that holds out the mirror to infinity; personal intercourse, and that alone, that ever hints at a personality beyond our daily vision" (1910, p. 78).

While all people doubtlessly desire to engage in close, warm, and communicative interaction with other people, some seem consistently more preoccupied with such intimate experience than others. **Intimacy motivation** is a recurrent preference for experiences of warm, close, and communicative interaction with others (McAdams, 1980, 1982a). Like the achievement and power motives, individual differences in intimacy motivation are assessed through content analysis of TAT stories. The coding system was originally derived by comparing stories written by individuals involved in activities and events designed to elicit friendly and caring behavior to stories written by individuals in neutral conditions (McAdams, 1980).

Research supports the construct validity of the intimacy motive as assessed on the TAT. People who are characteristically high in intimacy motivation spend more time, over the course of a normal day, thinking about relationships with others than do people scoring lower in intimacy motivation (McAdams & Constantian, 1983). People high in intimacy motivation partake in a greater number of friendly conversations over the course of a normal day, and they laugh, smile, and make more eye contact when conversing, compared with people low in intimacy motivation (McAdams & Constantian, 1983; McAdams, Jackson, & Kirshnit, 1984). The high-intimacy person is likely to value close, one-on-one exchanges over boisterous group activities. When confronted with a large group, he or she is likely to promote group harmony and cohesiveness, viewing group activities as opportunities for everybody to get involved rather than for one or two people to dominate the action (McAdams & Powers, 1981). Partly for this reason, people high in intimacy motivation are rated by their friends and acquaintances as especially "sincere," "natural," "loving," "not dominant," and "not self-centered" (McAdams, 1980).

McAdams, Healy, and Krause (1984) investigated the relation between intimacy and power motivation on the one hand and patterns of friendship on the other. In this study, 105 college students wrote TAT stories, subsequently scored for intimacy and power motivation, and then described in some detail 10 friendship episodes that had occurred in their lives in the previous 2 weeks. A friendship episode was defined as any interaction with a friend that lasted at least 15 to 20 minutes. For each episode, the student provided information on how many friends were involved in the episode, what activity was undertaken, what the friends talked about, what role the person played in the episode, and what emotions were experienced.

Table 7.8 shows the main results of the study. Students high in intimacy motivation tended to report friendship episodes involving one-on-one interaction with a single other friend ("dyads") rather than "large-group" interactions (friendship episodes involving 5 or more people) and to describe conversations in which the participants in the episode disclosed personal information about themselves ("self-disclosure"). Therefore, when they got together with their friends, high-intimacy students were more likely than low-intimacy students to talk about, and listen to their friends talk about, their own fears, hopes, feelings, fantasies, and other highly intimate topics. Power motivation, on the other hand, was associated with large-group interactions and assertive friendship activities, such as making plans, initiating conversations, and helping others. In general, intimacy motivation is associated with a *communal* friendship style that places prime importance on *being* together and *sharing* secrets with others, while power motivation is associated with an *agentic* friendship style that emphasizes *doing* things and *helping* others (McAdams, 1984a, 1988a).

In another study, students high in intimacy motivation engaged in a greater number of dyadic interactions over a one-week period of time, reported higher levels of self-disclosure with close friends, and experienced more positive emotion in their relationships, compared with students low in intimacy motivation (Craig, Koestner, & Zuroff, 1994). High intimacy motivation appears to sensitize people to opportunities for caring and empathic behavior. Not surprisingly, therefore, people who express callousness and contempt for others tend to score extremely low on intimacy motivation (Smith, 1985).

Because so many psychologists, novelists, and poets have told us that loving relationships with others are the key to happiness and well-being, we are certainly justified in asking whether high intimacy motivation leads to health, happiness, and overall life satisfaction. A few studies have examined the question directly. In one, McAdams and Vaillant (1982) found that high intimacy motivation at age 30 among male graduates of Harvard College significantly predicted overall psychosocial adjustment 17 years later,

TABLE 7.8	CORRELATIONS BETWEEN MOTIVES AND FRIENDSHIP PATTERNS IN COLLEGE STUDENTS	

| | MOTIVE | |
Friendship Measure[a]	Intimacy	Power
Dyads (2 friends)	.20*	−.23*
Large groups (5 or more)	−.10	.21*
Listening role	.43***	−.15
Assertive role	−.04	.43***
Self-disclosure	.49***	−.16

NOTE: Total number of subjects was 105 (70 female and 35 male).

[a]These measures were based on students' descriptions of 10 friendship episodes that occurred in their lives in the previous 2 weeks.

*$p < .05$, ***$p < .001$

SOURCE: Adapted from "Social Motives and Patterns of Friendship," by D. P. McAdams, S. Healy, & S. Krause, 1984, *Journal of Personality and Social Psychology, 47,* 834.

when the men were in their mid-40s. Men high in intimacy motivation in early adulthood reported greater marital satisfaction, job satisfaction, and even a marginally higher income at midlife compared with men scoring low in intimacy motivation.

In a second study, McAdams and Bryant (1987) drew upon a nationwide sample of more than 1,200 U.S. adults who were administered the TAT and a structured interview (Veroff, Douvan, & Kulka, 1981). The researchers found that, though intimacy motivation appears to bring certain benefits for both men and women, the benefits do not seem to be exactly the same for both sexes. High-intimacy women are relatively happy and satisfied, compared with low-intimacy women. On the other hand, high-intimacy men are *not* necessarily happier and more satisfied than low-intimacy men, but they do report less strain in life and less uncertainty.

Zeldow, Daugherty, and McAdams (1988) examined the relation between social motives assessed on the TAT and students' adjustment to medical school. Students high in intimacy motivation and low in power motivation showed the highest levels of well-being. However, those high in intimacy motivation and *high* in power motivation were more depressed, neurotic, fatalistic, and self-doubting in their first years of medical school, a relationship that was significant for both males and females. The authors suggested that the rigors of medical school make it extremely difficult for students with strong needs to feel close to others *and* to feel powerful and agentic to find satisfaction for their competing desires. By the time the students had finished their first two years and entered their clerkships, however, the negative effects of the high-intimacy/high-power pattern were no longer evident. A later study of this same cohort showed that those medical students high in intimacy motivation were more likely to choose pediatrics as a medical specialty than were students scoring low in intimacy motivation (Zeldow & Daugherty, 1991).

A major sex difference has been found in research on intimacy motivation. Analysis of thousands of TAT stories, written mostly by college undergraduates in the United States, suggests that women tend to score higher than men on intimacy motivation (McAdams, Lester, Brand, McNamara, & Lensky, 1988; Smith, 1985). The difference is small but relatively consistent, and it is in keeping with the generally accepted view in American society that women tend to be more concerned with interpersonal relationships than are men (Bakan, 1966; Gilligan, 1982; Lewis, 1985). Even among fourth and sixth graders, girls score higher on intimacy motivation than boys (McAdams & Losoff, 1984). Interestingly, consistent sex differences in overall levels of achievement and power motivation have *not* been observed (Stewart & Chester, 1982).

A motive that bears resemblance to intimacy motivation and that is also assessed via the TAT is the **affiliation motive** (Atkinson, Heyns, & Veroff, 1954; Boyatzis, 1973). Drawn from Murray's (1938) original list of psychogenic needs, affiliation motivation is the desire to establish, maintain, or restore positive-affect relations with others. TAT stories in which characters actively strive to improve or restore their relationships with others tend to score high on affiliation themes. McClelland (1975) has combined affiliation-motive scores with scores on achievement and power to yield interesting motivational profiles linked to behavior and attitudes. In general, however, the evidence for the construct validity of the affiliation motive is rather weak (Boyatzis, 1973), with many empirical studies yielding insignificant or contradictory results. Affiliation motivation tends to be positively correlated with intimacy motivation. To the extent that the two motive systems differ, the intimacy motive appears to emphasize the qualities of *being* in a warm and close relationship, whereas the affiliation motive emphasizes *doing*, or striving to achieve relationships.

IMPLICIT AND SELF-ATTRIBUTED MOTIVES

The research employing the TAT to assess individual differences in motives of achievement, power, and intimacy rests on one crucial assumption, an assumption that Murray and McClelland share with Freud: *People are not consciously aware of their motives.* If motives were directly accessible to consciousness, psychologists would not need to use a projective measure like the TAT to tap motivational themes in narrative. Instead, people could simply report the strength of their motives on self-report questionnaires, like those used to assess dispositional traits (chapter 4). Indeed, numerous self-report questionnaires have been developed to assess such constructs as achievement motivation (for example, Jackson, 1974). But these self-report questionnaires provide scores that rarely correlate significantly with TAT scores of purportedly the same motive. For example, questionnaire measures of achievement motivation are typically uncorrelated with McClelland's TAT measure of achievement motivation (Entwisle, 1972; Klinger, 1966; Niitamo, 1999). A similar lack of convergence has been demonstrated for power and intimacy motivation (King, 1995; McClelland, 1985; Schultheiss & Brunstein, 2001). But how can this be? If the two measures are assessing the same thing—say, two measures of achievement motivation—shouldn't they be highly correlated?

McClelland and his colleagues argue that the two measures are *not* assessing the same thing (Koestner, Weinberger, & McClelland, 1991; McClelland, 1980; McClelland, Koestner, & Weinberger, 1989; Schultheiss & Brunstein, 1999). Achievement motivation measured via a self-report questionnaire is different from achievement motivation measured via the TAT. Questionnaire measures of achievement tendencies are *respondent* measures in which the subject is limited in what kinds of responses he or she can make. For example, on a self-report assessment, the subject is asked to mark "true" or "false" for each item, or to rate an item on a Likert-type scale. By contrast, the TAT is what McClelland called an *operant* measure. In an operant measure, the subject is able to generate his or her own unique response. The ambiguous picture cues for the TAT provide stimuli for virtually any kind of open-ended, narrative-like response the subject wishes to reveal.

Consequently, respondent questionnaire measures tap into people's conscious evaluations of their own achievement tendencies, or what McClelland called *self-attributed motives.* By contrast, the operant TAT measure samples people's spontaneous narrative thought, revealing less-than-conscious *implicit motives.* Explicit, self-attributed motives are really personality traits. Assessed via respondent questionnaires, a person's conscious evaluation of the overall extent to which he or she values, say, achievement goals is functionally an aspect of what the Big Five theorists describe as conscientiousness (*C:* chapter 5 in this book). Similarly, self-report measures of intimacy tendencies are likely to be aspects of Big Five agreeableness *(A).* Like other traits, these measures are expected to predict general trends in behavior. But McClelland and his colleagues have argued that the trends they predict are rather different from those associated with individual differences in implicit motives. Because respondent measures of self-attributed motives tap into a person's conscious image of him- or herself, these self-report questionnaires should predict what people do in situations that explicitly demand behavior that is in accord with the motive. For example, people high in self-attributed achievement should perform well in highly structured social situations in which they are expected to perform well, behaving in accord with a conscious, cognitively elaborated self-image of a high-achieving person. By contrast, operant measures of implicit motives tap into naturally occurring trends in spontaneous thought, which themselves indicate people's deeper and less-consciously elaborated longings. Therefore, people

high in TAT-based achievement motivation are likely to show long-term trends of spontaneous achievement activity. Put simply, people high on self-attributed achievement motivation seek out the *social* incentives of being seen (by others) as an achievement-oriented
person whereas people high on implicit (TAT-based) achievement motivation seek out *activity* incentives because they enjoy achievement (that is, doing well) for achievement's sake. Put
yet another way, self-attributed motives connect to extrinsic rewards ("I value achievement
because I am reinforced by others for doing so") whereas implicit motives are intrinsically
motivating ("I value achievement because of the enjoyment of achievement itself")
(Koestner & McClelland, 1990). Table 7.9 reviews these distinctions.

Recent reviews of research provide some support for McClelland's distinction between
self-attributed and implicit motives (Spangler, 1992; Winter, John, Stewart, Klohnen, &
Duncan, 1998). For example, Spangler (1992) reviewed 105 research articles on achievement motivation. He found that across all the studies, TAT-based (implicit) achievement
motivation was, at best, a modest predictor of achievement behaviors. However, when
Spangler divided up the studies into those assessing situations containing social incentives
and those assessing situations with activity incentives, McClelland's predictions were born
out. In studies in which the dependent variable was achievement behavior in social situations that put pressure on the subject to do well, the TAT-based achievement motivation
was not a strong predictor of performance, whereas self-attributed achievement motivation was. By contrast, in studies in which the dependent variable was naturally occurring
achievement behavior (under conditions with few social incentives but strong activity
incentives), TAT-based achievement motivation proved to be a very strong and significant
predictor of performance, whereas self-attributed achievement motivation was not.

A related controversy concerning TAT-based measures of implicit motives concerns
the reliability of the TAT itself. In chapter 4, I introduced the issues of test–retest reliability

TABLE 7.9	SELF-ATTRIBUTED MOTIVES VERSUS IMPLICIT MOTIVES	
	Self-Attributed Motives	**Implicit Motives**
Definition	Conscious, cognitively elaborated image of self as oriented toward partic-ular goal states	Recurrent, nonconscious desires for particular goal states
Measures	Respondent: questionnaires, rating scales, and other measures in which the participant responds in a forced-choice format to a circumscribed stim-ulus situation	Operant: TAT and other methods in which the participant provides a spontaneous response to an open-ended, ambiguous stimulus, such as a TAT picture
Incentives	Social: The motive is related to behav-ior that is in keeping with social norms and expectations of a given situation	Activity: The motive is related to naturally occurring behavior that is valued for its own sake
Personality level	Level 1: Self-attributed motives are sim-ilar to dispositional traits, such as those comprising the Big Five clusters (chap-ters 4–6 in this book)	Level 2: Implicit motives are less like traits and more like the charac-teristic adaptations in personality, more contextualized, contingent, and less stable over time than traits (chapters 7–9 in this book)

and internal consistency in the measurement of traits. The same kinds of psychometric standards have been applied to TAT-based measures, though defenders of the TAT have sometimes argued that the application is not altogether appropriate (Atkinson, Bongort, & Price, 1977; Reuman, Alwin, & Veroff, 1984). Critics of the TAT maintain that the test shows low test–retest reliability and internal consistency. Although the details of these controversies are beyond the scope of this book, there are two important points to make about the limitations of TAT assessments of human motives. First, despite its potential for revealing rich narrative data for personality, the TAT is a somewhat less reliable measure than a typical well-constructed personality questionnaire, all other things being equal. Under the best conditions, test–retest correlations for TAT motives are still lower (around $r = +.55$) than those for the best-established self-report traits (around $r = +.85$) (Lundy, 1985; Winter & Stewart, 1977). Ironically, this limitation stems directly from a cardinal TAT strength—the measure's exceptional *sensitivity*. Because the TAT is more sensitive to factors and influences in the person and in the situation than are most questionnaires assessing personality traits, a TAT assessment of motivation will naturally "reflect" a lot of extraneous and irrelevant material, like the subject's mood at the time of testing. There is no way to rid the TAT of this problem without undermining its essential sensitivity.

Second, the motives of achievement, power, and intimacy assessed on the TAT are probably less stable over time than are personality traits, such as extraversion and neuroticism, which are generally assessed on questionnaires. As we saw in chapter 6, certain basic personality traits show marked longitudinal consistency. For instance, a highly extraverted person at age 16 is likely to be relatively extraverted at age 60. Part of the reason for this stability in certain traits over time may reside in their presumed biological or genetic basis, as in the case of extraversion. Although comparable TAT data do not exist, motives do not appear to be as stable over time as certain basic traits. Further, there is no evidence at present to suggest a clear genetic basis for motives.

The possibility that motives may change over time to a greater extent than basic traits reflects a fundamental distinction between motives (as characteristic adaptations, Level 2 in personality) and dispositional traits (Level 1): *Motives deal with goals and desires; traits refer to basic behavioral style.* Whereas it seems plausible to assume that a basic personality style is established early in life, perhaps partly as a function of biological temperament, and carried forward into adulthood as a stable set of dispositional traits (Level 1), it appears equally reasonable to suggest that desires and goals (Level 2) may change markedly over the human life course. Motive scores indicate the major goal areas with which a person is concerned at a particular time in his or her life. For example, a person may experience high needs for intimacy and achievement in college, but these needs may subside somewhat in later years—in his or her 30s or 40s—to be "replaced" by high levels of power motivation. Less stable than traits but more enduring than temporary moods and states, motives appear to reflect major thematic goals, desires, and preoccupations during *a given period* of a particular person's life.

PERSONALIZED GOALS

All motivational concepts are contextualized *in time.* Motives are defined in terms of desired or anticipated goal states, and these goal states exist *in the future.* If we say that you are high in power motivation, we are saying that you recurrently desire to have impact on your world, that you want power, that you will articulate more specific goals for the future through which you hope to be able to experience power. By matter of contrast, if we say that you are high on the trait of extraversion, we have said nothing about what you recurrently desire, what you want, or what your goals for the future are. Extraversion is not in and of itself a motivational concept. You do not need to talk about goals and future time to understand the meaning of extraversion. I am not saying that power motivation is a more important concept than extraversion; I am simply saying that it is different—different in kind. Both concepts are equally important in understanding personality. But they are important for different reasons. Dispositional traits (like extraversion) sketch out the broad outline of human individuality, which is what Level 1 of personality is all about. In focusing on the goal-directed nature of human behavior *in time,* by contrast, motives move us to Level 2 in personality, the level of characteristic adaptations.

Motives for achievement, power, and intimacy go beyond dispositional traits to fill in some of the details of human individuality, but even more detail and specificity can be observed when psychologists examine the personalized goals that people formulate and pursue in daily life and the ways in which those goals translate into behavior. Like motives, personalized goals speak to what people want in life. But personalized goals are more specific. Maria may want power in general, showing a high level of implicit power motivation. But her power motivation is likely to be expressed through some goals and not others. Among her current goals in life are (a) to be accepted into law school and (b) to win the election for senior class president. By contrast, she sets forth no goals concerning the experience of power in, say, her personal relationships or in the area of sports. If we know Maria has high power motivation, we certainly know something very important about her. But to know more of the details, we need to explore the various concerns, strivings, projects, and tasks she is currently working on—the personalized goals that speak to why Maria does what she does.

Personality psychologists have proposed a number of different terms to refer to personal goals (Cantor & Zirkel, 1990; Freund & Baltes, 2000). For example, Robert Emmons (1986, 1992) defines **personal strivings** as "characteristic, recurring goals that a person is trying to accomplish" (1992, p. 292). Personal strivings are typically daily concerns and goals around which people organize their behavior. They can range from such concrete goals as "I'm trying to lose weight" to abstract aims like "I'm trying to figure out the meaning of my life." Emmons (1999) reports that fewer than half of the personal strivings typically reported in his research fit neatly under the big three motive categories of achievement, power, and intimacy. Other common categories include strivings for personal growth and health, self-presentation, independence, avoidance, spirituality, and generativity (helping the next generation). Emmons (1999) has found that intimacy strivings and generativity strivings are associated with independent ratings of psychological well-being. In other words, people who describe a greater number of strivings having to do with warm and close relationships (intimacy) and with making positive contributions to society and the future (generativity) are happier and more satisfied with their lives, compared with individuals who have fewer intimacy and generativity strivings. By contrast, power strivings and avoidance strivings tend to be associated with lower levels of psychological well-being and greater levels of anxiety. Spiritual strivings tend to be associated with low levels of conflict among life goals and what Emmons terms the overall integration of the personality. Emmons maintains that spiritual strivings are especially powerful carriers of life meaning for many people.

Like personal strivings, **personal projects** also provide a rich picture of the psychosocial ecology of everyday life. Brian Little (1989, 1998, 1999) conceives of the personal project as a series of activities coordinated to achieve a specific personal goal. Like Emmons, Little emphasizes the wide range of projects that people propose, from trivial pursuits to magnificent obsessions. Dispositional traits may have an impact on project pursuits. Research has shown that people high on the trait of openness to experience (*O:* chapter 5) tend to propose a wider diversity of projects, compared with those scoring low on *O* (Little, Lecci, & Watkinson, 1992). High levels of neuroticism (*N:* chapter 5), furthermore, are associated with experiencing high levels of stress in the pursuit of projects (Little, 1999). Neuroticism is also associated with pursuing projects and goals that involve avoidance (Elliot, Sheldon, & Church, 1997). In other words, people high in *N* are more likely than those scoring low in *N* to pursue such projects as "avoiding dealing with my mother," "staying away from obnoxious men," and "escaping stress." Rather than pursuing positive end states, they seek to avoid negative ones. Avoidance goals, furthermore, appear to be more common among certain cultural groups than others. For example, Elliot, Chirkov, Kim, and Sheldon (2001) found that Asian-Americans adopted more avoidance goals than non–Asian-Americans, and persons from South Korea and Russia adopted more avoidance goals than those in the United States.

When you think about how well or badly your life is going or how happy or unhappy you are with the present state of your life, you are likely to make some kind of explicit or implicit assessment of the status of your goals. Are you satisfied with the goals you have set? Are you making progress toward achieving important goals? Do your goals conflict with one another? Psychologists who study goal concepts such as personal strivings and personal projects have focused a great deal of attention on the relationships between goals and psychological well-being (e.g., Pomerantz, Saxon, & Oishi, 2000). They have found that goal-directed, purposive behavior is intimately tied up with the overall assessments people make of the quality of their lives. For example, considerable research suggests that when people feel they are making substantial progress in meeting the most important goals in their lives, they report higher levels of life satisfaction and emotional well-being (Pervin, 1989, 1996). As another example, Palys and Little (1983) found that individuals who reported involvement in enjoyable and moderately difficult projects oriented toward short-term goals tended to be happier and more satisfied with their lives. Adults with less enjoyable and highly difficult projects oriented to the long term tended to score low on happiness and life satisfaction. In addition, relatively happy participants reported that they shared involvement in their goals with a supportive network of friends, family, and acquaintances.

In examining the relations between personal projects and well-being, Little routinely asks research participants to evaluate each of their personal projects on five dimensions: (a) *meaningfulness* (how worthwhile the project is, how enjoyable I find the project to be, how much the project contributes to my sense of identity), (b) *manageability* (how easy the project is, how much control I have over the project, how much time I have to do the project well), (c) *support* (to what extent other people support the project, how visible my project is for other people), (d) *efficacy* (how well my project is progressing, how capable I am of achieving the project), and (e) *stress* (how anxious or depressed the project makes me, how much I worry about the project). In constructing and living out our personal projects, Little finds, we need to strike a balance between "meaning" and "manageability." In some cases such long-term and abstract projects as "making myself into a better human being" may prove highly meaningful but too hard to manage effectively. On the other hand, short-term and concrete projects such as "cooking delicious dinners for my spouse" may be fairly manageable but may not provide a satisfactory level of meaning in one's life. The challenge is to organize one's purposive behavior according to personal projects that are grand enough and humble enough to be both meaningful and manageable. The organization of purposive behavior is always accomplished in an interpersonal context. Personal projects are constantly negotiated and renegotiated with important people in one's life and within the opportunities and constraints offered by one's family, community, profession, and society at large. Within a complex social context, it is essential that people find effective ways to *communicate* their personal projects to others. Other people need to know clearly what goals you have in mind for your life if they are to facilitate the accomplishment of those goals and find creative ways to integrate their goals with yours.

Emmons has examined what happens when different personal strivings conflict with one another. For instance, your striving to "improve my relationship with my mother" may conflict with your striving to "gain independence." Emmons (1986) administered various personal strivings measures to 40 undergraduate students who then reported their daily moods and thoughts for three weeks. Positive emotional experiences during that period were positively associated with reports of strivings that were highly valued and for which the person had experienced success in the past. Negative emotional experiences were associated with striving ambivalence and with greater levels of conflict between different strivings. In a similar study, Emmons and King (1988) found that conflict and ambivalence in strivings were associated with higher levels of negative affect, depression, neuroticism, and psychosomatic complaints, and with a greater number of illnesses and visits to the campus health center. In examining the connections between strivings and behavior, the researchers also found that when people reported conflicting strivings they often were unable to act upon those strivings but instead spent an inordinate amount of time thinking about the conflict itself. To sum up, high levels of conflict among strivings lead to poor health, low levels of happiness, high levels of depression and anxiety, and a tendency to ponder obsessively about conflictual strivings rather than acting upon them.

Finally, research by Brunstein, Schultheiss, and Grassmann (1998) returns us to the more general motives assessed on the TAT and relates the motives to personal goals and psychological well-being. In an initial testing session, the researchers administered the TAT to a group of German college students and then asked them to list two agentic (achievement- or power-oriented) goals and two communal (intimacy- or affiliation-related) goals. For each goal, the students also evaluated how much progress they had recently made in accomplishing the goal. Over the following two weeks, the students each completed a series of mood checklists at regular intervals, to assess overall psychological well-being. The researchers scored the TAT stories for the standard motives developed by McClelland and his associates, classifying achievement and power motivation as "agentic" (self-oriented) motives and intimacy and affiliation motivation as "communal" (other-oriented) motives. To arrive at a single agency-communion motivational score, they simply subtracted the TAT communion score (intimacy + affiliation motives) from the TAT agency score (achievement + power motives). Consequently, the higher the overall score, the more agentic (achievement and power oriented) was a person's overall motivational stance, whereas the lower the score the more communal (intimacy and affiliation oriented).

The results of the study showed an interaction between motivational scores and goal progress in the prediction of well-being. In a nutshell, students with highly agentic motivational profiles (high power and achievement motivation relative to affiliation and intimacy motivation on the TAT) reported greater levels of psychological well-being (as determined by the mood checklists) *when they were making progress on agentic goals,* relative to other students. Similarly, students with communal motivational profiles (high affiliation and intimacy motivation relative to power and achievement motivation on the TAT) reported greater levels of well-being *when they were making progress on communal goals.* The key thing to know here is that well-being is a function of progress and success in the pursuit of *motive-congruent goals.* When you are making good progress and receiving good support on daily goals that are congruent with your more general motivational tendencies, you are likely to be experiencing positive emotions and satisfaction. In general, making progress toward goals is a good thing for everybody. But some goals are more important for well-being than others. Of most importance are those most valued goals that encapsulate experiences that are congruent with what an individual most deeply wants out of life.

In conclusion, many personality psychologists and laypeople find personal goals to be such an important aspect of human individuality because of both their links to psychological well-being and the general belief that goals, unlike perhaps traits and more general tendencies in personality, may be relatively easy to change or work on. Personal strivings and projects are subject to change, modification, growth, and the influence of the environment. Psychotherapists and counselors of many different persuasions often spend a great deal of time working on people's goals, helping their clients to refashion goals into more realistic terms, helping people find ways to get support from their environment for their goals, moving people in the direction of new goals that are both meaningful and manageable, helping people make their goals more congruent with their general motivational tendencies, their personality traits, and the constraints and opportunities they face in the environment. And when people work on their own lives, when they try to make changes for the better, they often begin by re-evaluating their own personal goals.

SUMMARY

1. If dispositional traits make up a first level of personality, motives and goals are important characteristic adaptations at the second level. Motivational concepts concern the internal forces and factors that energize and direct human behavior, including those most important and recurrent human wants, needs, and desires.

2. Introduced by Sigmund Freud more than 100 years ago, the psychoanalytic view of human motivation suggests that behavior is ultimately determined by unconscious sexual and aggressive drives and by the complex intrapsychic conflicts that arise in daily life. Unconscious processes work to repress threatening impulses, thoughts, and feelings. While repression is universal, research suggests that some individuals may use repression more than do others. Repressors report little anxiety on a conscious level, but they adopt a highly defensive approach to life. Research suggests that repressors report fewer negative memories from their past and are able to keep emotionally negative scenes separated from one another in memory.

3. Freud's structural model divides the psyche into id, ego, and superego. The id obeys the pleasure principle; the ego operates according to the reality principle; and the superego works as a primitive moral voice, representing the internalized rules of authority. Caught in the middle of the impulsive id, harsh superego, and demanding outside world, the ego seeks to resolve motivational conflicts and reduce anxiety. Defense mechanisms are unconscious strategies that the ego employs to reduce anxiety while distorting reality in the process. Considerable research on defense mechanisms supports the psychoanalytic view that defenses can be arranged on a developmental continuum from least to most mature. Among children, age-appropriate defenses are associated with more effective coping; among adults, more mature defenses are associated with psychosocial adaptation.

4. The humanistic view of motivation prioritizes conscious experience and self-actualizing tendencies. Carl Rogers developed a highly influential humanistic theory of personality and psychotherapy that posited one, all-encompassing motivational force—the motive to actualize or fulfill the self. Rogers's approach urges the psychologist to explore the person's phenomenal field of

conscious experience through empathy and, ideally, unconditional positive regard. Like Rogers, Abraham Maslow developed a humanistic theory of personality that underscored the motive for self-actualization. Maslow argued that self-actualizing tendencies are built on more basic needs for physiological equilibrium, safety and security, belonging and love, and self-esteem. Highly self-actualized individuals espouse humanistic virtues and have a greater number of peak experiences in life.

5. A central idea in humanistic psychology is that intrinsically motivated behavior is valued for its own sake rather than for the rewards that may follow it. Research on intrinsic motivation suggests that material rewards can sometimes undermine people's interest in the activities for which they are rewarded. Growing out of research on intrinsic motivation, Deci and Ryan's self-determination theory proposes that human beings are endowed with a natural motivation to encounter new challenges that will promote organismic integration. Self-determined, intrinsically motivated behavior often meets basic human needs for autonomy, competence, and interpersonal relatedness. Self-determination theory has stimulated research on how self-determined behaviors that stem from needs for autonomy, competence, and interpersonal relatedness enhance growth and well-being whereas behaviors in the service of material wealth, seeking prestige, and other extrinsic rewards tend to undermine morale and stifle organismic growth.

6. The diversity view of human motivation posits a large number of different motives or needs. Murray's influential motivational theory proposes a taxonomy of approximately 20 psychogenic needs that energize and direct behavior in concert with environmental forces or press. As one assessment device for the measurement of individual differences in psychogenic needs or motives, Murray developed the Thematic Apperception Test (TAT). On the TAT, participants tell or write imaginative stories in response to picture cues. The stories are coded for various content themes indicative of implicit (unconscious) motivational tendencies. Motivational research with the TAT has focused on the needs for achievement, power, and intimacy.

7. The achievement motive is a recurrent preference or readiness for experiences of doing well and being successful. People high on TAT-measured achievement motivation tend to be highly efficient in their goal-directed activity, show high achievement aspirations but moderate risk taking, show high levels of self-control and delay of gratification, and show a range of behaviors and attitudes that promote successful entrepreneurship. The extent to which a society encourages achievement motivation can be estimated by scoring folk tales, children's readers, and popular literature for achievement themes, as if these documents were TAT stories. David McClelland has shown that a society's achievement motivation is associated with economic growth.

8. The power motive is a recurrent preference or readiness for experiences of having an impact and feeling strong. People high on TAT-measured power motivation show a mixture of characteristics associated with both aggression and leadership. They tend to be active and forceful in small groups, to accumulate prestige possessions, and to be drawn to public office and professions that involve directing the behavior of others. Among men, power motivation is associated with instability in romantic relationships. With respect to physical health, some research suggests that individuals with strong but inhibited power motivation may be susceptible to disease, especially when they experience high levels of power stress.

9. The intimacy motive is a recurrent preference for experiences of warm, close, and communicative interaction with others. People high on TAT-based intimacy motivation tend to be seen by others as especially loving and sensitive, exhibit more eye contact and smiling in friendly interactions, are more self-disclosing and intimate with their friends, and engage in a wide range of behaviors suggestive of an especially communal approach to life. Intimacy motivation is also positively associated with psychological well-being. Whereas consistent gender differences have not

been shown for achievement and power motivation, women score consistently and significantly higher than men on the intimacy motive.

10. Whereas research on implicit motives for achievement, power, and intimacy examines general goal states, another line of recent research has focused on more specific personal goals themselves—variously labeled as personal strivings or personal projects. Research suggests that personal goals are intimately involved in people's psychological well-being. People are happiest when they are making progress in pursuing their personal goals, especially when those goals are consistent with more general motivational trends in their personality. Goals for intimacy and for making positive contributions to other people tend to be associated with positive emotion whereas goals concerning avoidance and personal power are associated with negative emotions. Goal conflict and ambivalence may undermine life satisfaction. Goal-directed activity often involves a meaning/manageability tradeoff. Sometimes the most meaningful and involving goals are the most difficult to attain, so the challenge is to organize purposive behavior according to goals that are grand enough and yet humble enough to be both meaningful and manageable.

CHAPTER 8

Self and Other: Social-Cognitive Aspects of Personality

We live in an information age, dominated by computers. Just a few years ago, computers were huge, scary-looking machines housed only in universities, military and government centers, and major research institutions. Today, many American families own more than one personal computer, and computers can be found in your car's engine, your kitchen's appliances, and your little sister's toys. Psychologists use computers to collect and analyze data in their research. But one of the computer's biggest impacts in psychology—and arguably in society as well—is the *metaphor* it gives us for human life. Not only do we all use computers. We are all *like* computers in many ways. And we were like them even before they—the computers, that is—were invented.

Like computers, we take in, process, store, and retrieve information from the environment. Information comes to us through our sense organs, but like any good computer we do not simply receive that input in a passive manner. We work on it. We perform operations on the information, manipulating it and using it according to the complex software of the human mind. The ultimate output of this activity is human behavior. Human beings process information in order to act. Our perceptions, impressions, inferences, judgments, and memories eventually influence what we do.

Social-cognitive approaches to personality psychology begin with the assumption that human beings are complex information processing systems that operate in social environments (Cervone, Shadel, & Jencius, 2001; Kihlstrom & Hastie, 1997). Among the most important inputs in human life are our perceptions and impressions of others, which shape and are shaped by our perceptions and impressions of ourselves. Social-cognitive approaches to personality focus on how people make and use *mental representations* of themselves, of others, and of their social worlds and how those representations are implicated in social behavior. People formulate images, concepts, beliefs, values, plans, and expectations that govern what they do, and what they do comes to influence the nature of these mental representations. Put simply, cognition influences social behavior, and social behavior influences cognition.

People differ from one another with respect to the kinds of self-representations and social construals they characteristically formulate and act upon. Consequently, an essential domain of human individuality is the social-cognitive representations that people create. Like motives and goals (chapter 7), social-cognitive adaptations in personality take us beyond broad dispositional traits to spell out the contextualized and contingent nature of human lives (Bandura, 1999; Cervone & Shoda, 1999a, 1999b; Mischel, 1999). If traits provide a rough sketch of human individuality, then the characteristic mental representations of self and social behavior that people construct—their characteristic self-conceptions, beliefs, values, and so on—help to fill in many of the details.

In this chapter, I examine characteristic adaptations in personality described in social-cognitive approaches to studying persons. I begin with George Kelly's (1955) theory of personal constructs, which is arguably the first social-cognitive theory of personality ever developed. Although Kelly's theory predates the computer age, his view of the person as an active interpreter of the social world presaged the many social-cognitive conceptions that have followed. I then consider cognitive styles in personality, which speak to individual differences in the ways people process information in the world. Finally, I describe a number of contemporary social-cognitive ideas in personality psychology, including social intelligence, self-schemas, explanatory style, and the cognitive regulation of social behavior.

THE PSYCHOLOGY OF PERSONAL CONSTRUCTS

George A. Kelly (1905–1966) labored in relative obscurity as a school teacher, aeronautical engineer, and clinical psychologist until he wrote and published his two-volume *The Psychology of Personal Constructs* in 1955. The book took the field of personality psychology by storm. It presented a boldly original theory of the person that seemed to bear little if any resemblance to the classic personality theories of the day, such as those proposed by Freud, Jung, Rogers, Maslow, Murray, Allport, Eysenck, Cattel, and the behaviorists. The unusual terms Kelly proposed became part of the standard lexicon of personality psychology—terms such as *personal construct, range of convenience, fixed-role therapy,* and *Rep Test.* Indeed, Kelly became something of an overnight celebrity in the field of personality psychology. Unfortunately, however, his one major book is the only comprehensive statement of the theory ever produced. An early death prevented his developing and refining the theory further. Nonetheless, what Kelly left us with was a provocative view of human nature and a set of stimulating ideas about human individuality, grounded in the image of the person as an inquisitive *scientist* seeking to predict, control, and explain the social world.

GEORGE KELLY'S THEORY

As we saw in chapter 7, many personality theories have traditionally assigned a central role to human motivation. Why do people do what they do? What gets behavior going? What internal motives, needs, drives, desires, and so on energize and select human action? In a

striking departure from common practice in personality psychology, Kelly (1955) asserted that the "problem" of human motivation is not a problem at all. The search for underlying principles to explain *why* people do what they do is futile, he asserted. We need not posit behavior approach and inhibition systems (chapter 5), sexual and aggressive instincts (Freud), principles of reinforcement (behaviorists), needs and motives (Murray, McClelland), or goals, strivings, or the urge toward self-actualization (Rogers, Maslow) to explain what motivates people to act. People are alive. They act by virtue of being alive. It's really quite simple.

Well, not that simple. Kelly's radical dismissal of the concept of motivation is really only partial, for his theory implies a fundamental principle of motivation itself (Hogan, 1976; Shotter, 1970): *A person is motivated to predict or anticipate what will happen to him or her.* What moves people to act is their desire to know what the world has in store for them. Fundamentally, the person is like a scientist, seeking to predict and control events:

George A. Kelly (1905–1966) developed a highly influential theory of personality that described human beings as lay scientists who seek to organize, predict, and control their world. Kelly's psychology of personal constructs places human cognition at the center of personality.

> Mankind, whose progress in search of prediction and control of surrounding events stands out so clearly in light of the centuries, comprises the men we see around us every day. The aspirations of the scientist are essentially the aspirations of all men. (Kelly, 1955, p. 43)

Table 8.1 summarizes the main points of Kelly's theory in terms of the postulates and corollaries he presented in *The Psychology of Personal Constructs.* Kelly's model for human life is a common sense brand of science. As we saw in chapter 1, the first step of scientific inquiry is the classification of experience. Science begins when the observer seeks to make initial sense of the

TABLE 8.1	**KELLY'S FUNDAMENTAL POSTULATE AND ELEVEN COROLLARIES**

Fundamental Postulate: A person's processes are psychologically channelized by the ways in which he or she anticipates events.

Construction Corollary: A person anticipates events by construing their replications.

Individuality Corollary: Persons differ from one another in their construction of events.

Organization Corollary: Each person characteristically evolves, for his or her convenience in anticipating events, a construction system embracing ordinal relationships between constructs.

Dichotomy Corollary: A person's construction system is composed of a finite number of dichotomous constructs.

Choice Corollary: A person chooses for himself or herself that alternative in a dichotomized construct through which he or she anticipates the greater possibility for extension and definition of his or her system.

Range Corollary: A construct is convenient for the anticipation of a finite range of events only.

Experience Corollary: A person's construction system varies as he or she successively construes the replications of events.

Modulation Corollary: The variation in a person's construction system is limited by the permeability of the constructs within whose range of convenience the variants lie.

Fragmentation Corollary: A person may successively employ a variety of construction subsystems which are inferentially incompatible with each other.

Communality Corollary: To the extent that one person employs a construction of experience which is similar to that employed by another, his or her psychological processes are similar to those of the other person.

Sociality Corollary: To the extent that one person construes the construction process of another, he or she plays a role in a social process involving the other person.

SOURCE: Modified from *The Psychology of Personal Constructs,* by G. Kelly, 1955, New York: W.W. Norton.

world by imposing some kind of organization upon it. What William James called the "blooming, buzzing confusion" of subjective human experience must be ordered, classified, and divided into categories if the scientist is to know anything at all. From these initial classifications are built synthesizing theories, from which are subsequently deduced discrete hypotheses to be tested through experimentation and other systematic procedures.

According to Kelly, each of us classifies his or her world by developing **personal constructs,** which are characteristic ways of construing how some things are alike and some things are different from one another. Every construct is *bipolar* (the "dichotomy corollary" in Table 8.1), specifying how two things are similar to each other (lying on the same pole) and different from a third thing (lying at the opposite pole). For example, I may routinely classify my friends in terms of the personal construct "serious/funny." Grant and Jack are relatively serious; Dean differs from them both in that he is relatively funny. All three friends are, in fact, similar to and different from one another in a great many ways. Despite the blooming, buzzing complexity of my experiences with these friends, I nevertheless anticipate my interactions with them, in part, by virtue of the construct "serious/funny." The construct helps me predict and control my interpersonal world. I know from past experiences with these friends (the "experience corollary") that when I am with Jack or Grant we will usually talk seriously about professional issues or current events; getting Dean to talk seriously about anything at all, on the other hand, requires a lot of extra effort.

People are best understood in terms of their own construct systems. Each person develops his or her own construct system that contains a number of constructs organized into a hierarchy ("organization corollary"). This means that within any construct system certain constructs are *superordinal* (encompassing many other constructs) and others are *subordinal* (being encompassed by larger constructs). Thus, the subordinal construct of "helpful/unhelpful" may be encompassed by the more general superordinal construct of "friendly/unfriendly." Every person's construct system is unique ("individuality corollary"), which means that everybody divides up subjective experience in a slightly different way. To know another person's construct system is to see the world through his or her eyes ("sociality corollary").

Within a given person's construct system, particular constructs differ from one another with respect to their **range of convenience** ("range corollary"). Thus, the construct "friendly/unfriendly" may have a wide range of convenience: It is likely to guide the person's anticipations of events in a large number of situations. By contrast, the construct "liberal/conservative" is likely to have a narrower range of convenience for most people. For most people, "friendly/unfriendly" is a more salient and determining dimension in their interactions with other people than is "liberal/conservative." Of course, there are marked individual differences across persons with respect to range. For instance, a politically astute woman who is especially sensitive to political issues may utilize the construct "liberal/conservative" in a wide range of situations. She may be tuned in to information in her environment suggestive of political meaning. Therefore, one of the first dimensions upon which she judges people may be their perceived political persuasion. At a cocktail party, she is introduced to a middle-aged man who looks like a banker, dressed in a three-piece suit. His hair is impeccably groomed; his wristwatch, expensive. She immediately says to herself, "I think this guy is a political conservative; I bet he usually votes Republican." Of course, she may be wrong. She may learn that he is an activist lawyer for the American Civil Liberties Union and that he always votes for liberal candidates. The woman need not be wedded to her initial hunch; constructs are more like hypotheses to be tested than like assumed facts. But the hunch provides her with an important starting point in her interaction, a way of anticipating what may or may not happen next. Anticipations guide behavior and experience. In the words of Kelly's "fundamental postulate," "a person's processes are psychologically channelized by the ways in which he [or she] anticipates events" (Kelly, 1955, p. 46).

Constructs differ in other ways, too. Some constructs are highly *permeable* whereas others are not ("modulation corollary"). A permeable construct is open to modification and the introduction of new elements. A person with an especially permeable construct system is likely to be seen by others as very open-minded. By contrast, a person who is unable to modify his or her constructs in light of new information and expanding experiences is likely to be viewed by others as relatively rigid and inflexible. Complete permeability, however, is not altogether good. If a construct is so permeable that it changes with virtually every relevant happening, it does not function well as an aid in anticipating events. Another problem can arise when different constructs within a person contradict each other. When a person's constructs are mutually incompatible and contradictory ("fragmented"), then he or she is likely to have a difficult time making consistent sense of the world and anticipating events in an adaptive way ("fragmentation corollary").

Kelly's personal-construct theory provides an interesting perspective from which to view a number of traditional concepts in personality psychology. Take, for instance, the concept of "the unconscious." Kelly sees no need to posit a mysterious unconscious domain to which have been consigned repressed wishes and conflicts. In Kelly's cognitive view, "the unconscious" is merely those constructs that are nonverbal, submerged, or suspended. For certain constructs, we are unable to assign a verbal name; thus, we may not be aware of them. Other constructs are submerged beneath other constructs or suspended from the construct system because they do not seem to fit. A highly fragmented construct system, therefore, is likely to contain submerged or suspended constructs of which the person is not aware. Yet these unconscious constructs continue to "channelize" behavior and experience.

Kelly views "anxiety" as "the recognition that the events with which one is confronted lie outside the range of convenience of one's construct system" (Kelly, 1955, p. 482). In other words, when we confront inexplicable events in the world for which our construct system does not seem to be prepared, we experience anxiety. Ultimately, then, anxiety is a fear of the unknown—the fear that the blooming, buzzing confusion cannot be understood. "Guilt" is a "perception of one's apparent dislodgment from his core role structure" (Kelly, 1955, p. 502). "Core role structure" is the construction a person has of who he or she is in relation to significant people, such as parents. It is embedded within the person's general construct system. In essence, then, guilt follows the perception that one is no longer living according to an especially valued aspect of one's personal-construct system.

EXPLORING PERSONAL CONSTRUCTS: THE REP TEST

Despite the formal postulates and corollaries, Kelly's theory of personal constructs has an appealing common sense quality that fits well with most people's daily experience. One of the best ways to get a feel for Kelly's approach is to participate in the **Role Construct Repertory Test (Rep Test)**, a personality assessment procedure designed by Kelly to explore personal constructs in people's lives. The Rep Test is a very flexible procedure that can be used in clinical work and in research. It is also easy to administer to yourself, and it is fun to take.

One version of the Rep Test asks you to make a series of comparisons among those people who play important roles in your life. Kelly defined a role as an understanding or expectation of what particular people in a person's life do. The role of "mother," therefore, consists of a person's understanding of how mothers behave in various situations. The first step in the Rep Test is to compile a Role Title List. Let us consider 15 different roles in your life. For each of the 15 roles listed in Table 8.2, write the name of the person who fits the description presented. Do not repeat names. If any role title appears to call for a duplicate name, substitute the name of another person whom the second role suggests to you.

When you have listed 15 people who play important roles in your life, compare and contrast them in a way to discern some of the important personal constructs you employ to make sense of your interactions with these people. Table 8.3 lists 15 sets of numbers. Each set contains three numbers, referring to the role titles you have listed above. Thus, the number "14" refers to "the most successful person whom you know personally." For each set of three numbers, think of how the people corresponding to the *first two* numbers are *similar* to each other and at the same time *different from* the person corresponding to the *third* number. Write a word or phrase in the blank under "Similar" to denote how the two are similar and then a contrasting word under "Contrast" to denote how the two people differ from the third. For example, the first set presents the numbers "9, 11, 14" (corresponding to "Boss," "Sought Person," and "Successful Person," respectively). Imagine that the Boss you have in mind is similar to your Sought Person in that they are both "easygoing" and that they both differ from the Successful Person who seems, by contrast, "hard-driving." You would write "easygoing" in the "Similar" blank and "hard-driving" under "Contrast."

Each of the 15 pairings of "Similar" and "Contrast" represents a single construct. At this point, the analysis of your responses can take many different paths. You may wish to look carefully at the ways in which you characterize certain critical contrasts in your life,

TABLE 8.2	**ROLE TITLE LIST**

1. Your mother or the person who has played the part of mother in your life   _____

2. Your father or the person who has played the part of father in your life   _____

3. Your brother nearest your age; if you have no brother, the person who is most like one   _____

4. Your sister nearest your age; if you have no sister, the person who is most like one   _____

5. A teacher you liked or the teacher of a subject you liked   _____

6. A teacher you disliked or the teacher of a subject you disliked   _____

7. Your closest girl (boy) friend immediately before you started going with your wife (husband) or present closest girl (boy) friend [Ex-Flame]   _____

8. Your wife (husband) or closest present girl (boy) friend   _____

9. An employer, supervisor, or officer under whom you served during a period of great stress [Boss]   _____

10. A person with whom you have been closely associated who, for some unexplainable reason, appears to dislike you [Rejecting Person]   _____

11. The person whom you have met within the past six months whom you would most like to know better [Sought Person]   _____

12. The person whom you would most like to be of help to, or the one whom you feel most sorry for [Pitied Person]   _____

13. The most intelligent person whom you know personally   _____

14. The most successful person whom you know personally   _____

15. The most interesting person whom you know personally   _____

such as those between Ex-Flame and current Boy (Girl) Friend. Or you may wish to look at the overall pattern of constructs you have delineated. How do the various constructs relate to one another? Are some constructs subordinal or superordinal to other constructs? Do you use many different constructs? Do you tend to use certain constructs again and again? If you tend to view many of the similar–contrast characterizations in terms of, say, the construct "honest/dishonest," or some variation on this idea, then you may conclude that this is an especially robust and meaningful construct in your life.

Procedures have been developed for quantifying results from the Rep Test for personality research. One line of research examined individual differences in *cognitive complexity* as revealed by the Rep Test (Crockett, 1965). People who use many different kinds of constructs are said to manifest higher levels of cognitive complexity. They tend to view the world in a highly differentiated manner. People who use few different kinds of constructs are viewed as having a simpler, more global construct system.

Another line of research examined *construct similarity* among friends and acquaintances (Duck, 1973, 1979). Researchers have administered various forms of the Rep Test to college students and then examined their patterns of peer interaction and friendship formation. In general, those students who have similar construct systems tend to become close friends and to remain friends for longer periods of time. For example, Duck and Spencer (1972) obtained personal-construct measures for female college freshmen at the beginning of the

TABLE 8.3	PERSONAL CONSTRUCTS, REPRESENTED BY "SIMILAR" AND "CONTRAST" PARINGS		
		Similar	**Contrast**
1.	9, 11, 14	_____	_____
2.	10, 12, 13	_____	_____
3.	2, 5, 12	_____	_____
4.	1, 4, 8	_____	_____
5.	7, 8, 12	_____	_____
6.	3, 13, 6	_____	_____
7.	1, 2, 9	_____	_____
8.	3, 4, 10	_____	_____
9.	6, 7, 10	_____	_____
10.	5, 11, 14	_____	_____
11.	1, 7, 8	_____	_____
12.	2, 7, 8	_____	_____
13.	3, 6, 9	_____	_____
14.	4, 5, 10	_____	_____
15.	11, 13, 14	_____	_____

SOURCE: Adapted from *The Psychology of Personal Constructs*, by G. Kelly, 1955, New York: W.W. Norton.

school year. The women in the study had all been assigned to the same residence hall. Though they were unacquainted at the beginning of the study, those women who shared similar constructs were most likely to become friends over the course of the school year. In another study, similarity of constructs was a more significant predictor of friendship formation than was similarity on self-report measures of traits (Duck & Craig, 1978). In other words, friends may be drawn together not so much by a perception that they behave in the same kinds of ways (that they are both extraverted or achievement-oriented, for instance) but rather by the perception that they see the world in the same way. People look to match their subjective experience with that of others. People look for affirmation of their own conscious meanings in the meanings of others. In relating to fellow men and women, *sharing meanings* may be more important than *doing* the same thing.

COGNITIVE STYLES AND PERSONALITY

Kelly viewed the person to be like a scientist, continually categorizing experience and testing out hypotheses as he or she anticipates and reacts to events in the world. In more contemporary terms, people are constantly processing information about the world in order to anticipate and adapt to the challenges of social life. Kelly's individuality corollary stressed that people differ from one another in the manner in which they construe events. Indeed, individual differences in styles of processing information have been recognized for centuries. Suedfeld (2000) writes that the recognition that people think differently from one another goes back to the myths of antiquity—for example, Homer's epic tales show how the subtle and occasionally convoluted thought patterns of Odysseus contrast markedly with the straightforward, simple cognitions of Achilles. **Cognitive styles** are people's "characteristic and typically preferred modes of processing information" (Sternberg & Grigorenko, 1997, p. 700). In principle, cognitive styles are not the same thing as cognitive *abilities*, like verbal, numeric, and spatial abilities measured on intelligence tests. While cognitive abilities assess *how well* a person performs on cognitive tasks, cognitive styles tap instead into a person's characteristic *way* or *manner* of processing information. As such, cognitive styles exist on the borderline between what has traditionally been associated with personality and what has traditionally been associated with intelligence and cognition.

Psychologists have studied many different kinds of cognitive styles, and they have studied them for many different reasons. In recent years, educational psychologists have been especially interested in identifying different styles of learning among students in order to improve teaching in the schools (Sternberg & Grigorenko, 1997). Cognitive style is partly captured in the Big Five trait taxonomy, via the trait cluster of openness to experience (*O*: chapter 5). People high in *O* tend to process information in a more nuanced, differentiated, and abstract manner, research suggests, while those low in *O* see fewer distinctions and adhere to concrete and clearly defined categories. Indeed, many personality constructs relate to information processing in one way or another, and psychologists have been very interested in studying the relations between individual differences in, for example, traits and motives on the one hand and ways of perceiving and thinking on the other. Still, certain constructs stand out for their explicit focus on characteristic styles of information processing and for the systematic research that psychologists have conducted on them. In what follows, I consider two dimensions of cognitive style that have received a great deal of attention from personality psychologists. They are (a) field independence–dependence and (b) integrative complexity.

FIELD INDEPENDENCE–DEPENDENCE

In the 1940s, Solomon Asch and Herman A. Witkin began studying how people decide whether an object is perpendicular to the ground or tilted to some degree. They asked people sitting in tilted chairs placed in custom-built tilted rooms to adjust their chairs until they felt that they were in an upright position—objectively perpendicular to the ground (Witkin, 1949). The task is tricky because the tilted room provides visual information that conflicts with the body's inner cues concerning what is upright. Some people tilt their chairs to become perpendicular to the (tilted) room; others ignore the tilt of the room and adjust their chairs according to inner cues. The people who use the room as the reference for their adjustment exhibit a **field-dependent** style for solving the problem. Their perception and judgment of perpendicularity depend on the "field," or environment. The people who bypass the field and make their perception and judgment according to inner cues show a **field-independent** style.

For more than 50 years Witkin and his colleagues have come to understand field independence–dependence as a broad and pervasive cognitive style that underlies many important personality differences (Bertini, Pizzamiglio, & Wapner, 1986; Goodenough, 1978; Lewis, 1985; Witkin, Goodenough, & Oltmann, 1979). The dimension has two poles. At one extreme, highly field-independent people process information in an especially analytical and differentiated style. They rely on internal frames of reference that enable them to act upon information in a highly autonomous fashion. At the other extreme, highly field-dependent people employ external frames of reference available in the field. They tend to base their perceptions on the external context within which they occur. Each pole has certain benefits and liabilities, depending on specific conditions. Therefore, neither end of the continuum is "better" than the other. Most people fall somewhere in the middle of the field independence–dependence continuum.

Field-independent people are adept at pulling information out of an embedding context. A good example of this is identifying camouflaged figures, as assessed on the **Embedded Figures Test** (Witkin, 1950). In Figure 8.1, the problem is to locate a square, like the one shown in A, that is hidden in the picture of the coffeepot shown in B. (The solution is shaded in C.) As you may discover for yourself, the several parts of the square in B are difficult to imagine as belonging to the same (square) figure. Instead, the right half of the square is immediately seen as part of the coffeepot while the left is seen as part of the background. To find the camouflaged square, it is necessary to *restructure the perceptual field.* People who are field-independent restructure the perceptual field so that they perform quite well in camouflage tasks.

In general, field independence is associated with greater levels of perceptual and cognitive restructuring. Field-independent people tend to reshape information from the environment according to internalized plans, rules, and goals to a greater extent than do people who are field dependent. They tend to view information in the nonsocial world in a highly differentiated manner. In one study, 32 field-dependent and 32 field-independent college women solved a series of anagrams (scrambled words) under various conditions (Frank & Noble, 1985). The results showed that field-independent students solved the anagrams more quickly and found the task easier than did field-dependent students. The field-independent students found it easier to provide a disorganized field with organization. Field-independence predicts the ability to block out irrelevant information and focus attention on central tasks and stimuli in complex learning situations (Messick, 1994; Richardson &

FIGURE 8.1   AN EMBEDDED SQUARE

Find the square shown in A camouflaged in the coffeepot shown in B. (The solution is shaded in C.)

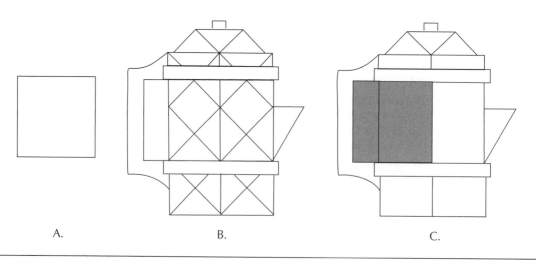

A.   B.   C.

SOURCE: From "Field Dependence," by D. R. Goodenough, in H. London and J.E. Exner (Eds.), *Dimensions of Personality* (p. 175), 1978, New York: John Wiley & Sons.

Turner, 2000). For example, field-independent eighth-graders learn more effectively than their field-dependent peers in complex computer environments that provide hyper-media based instruction (Weller, Repman, Lan, & Rooze, 1995). Field-independent police officers make more accurate judgments under high-stimulation crime conditions, compared to field-dependent officers. In simulated crime scenarios, the field-independent officers were better able to ignore distracting sights and sounds and were more accurate in deciding when to shoot their guns (Vrij, van der Steen, & Koppelaar, 1995).

Like Kelly's model of the scientist, the field-independent person approaches the world as a hypothesis-tester, systematically differentiating causes and effects and analyzing the world in terms of its separate parts. Not surprisingly, people who are field-independent are drawn to careers that require cognitive restructuring and objective analysis of information, such as careers in science, mathematics, management, and mechanics. By contrast, field-dependent people are more global and intuitive in processing information about the world. They tend to engage in less cognitive restructuring, accepting information from the environment in its own contextual terms, rather than employing internal plans and guidelines for information processing. Interestingly, field-dependent people tend to be more interested in humanitarian and social-welfare professions, such as careers in the ministry, social work, teaching young children, the social sciences, and selling and advertising (Goodenough, 1978).

Cognitive style appears to have significant influences on interpersonal functioning. Numerous studies suggest that the field-dependent person is more sensitive to social context than the field-independent person. Field-dependent people pay closer attention to interpersonal cues and social information. They tend to spend more time looking at people than at inanimate objects and to make more sustained eye contact when talking with others. Field-dependent people prefer being physically closer to others than do field-independent persons. In one study, for example, participants were required to give prepared talks on several topics to the experimenter, and the physical distance between the speaker and the experimenter was measured during the presentations (Justice, 1969). Field-dependent speakers chose to stand closer to their listeners than did field-independent speakers. In another study of interpersonal distance, field-dependent people showed more speech disturbances when seated 5 feet away from their conversational partners than when seated only 2 feet away. In contrast, the interpersonal distance had less of an effect on field-independent speakers (Greene, 1973).

In general, women score toward the field-dependent end of the continuum, whereas men score toward the field-independent end. This gender difference is not huge, but it is relatively consistent across studies. From childhood to adulthood, people develop in the direction of field independence. Thus, children are generally more field dependent than adults. Nonetheless, individual differences in elementary school are predictive of adult differences. Thus, a boy who is relatively field independent compared with his male peers at age 10 is likely to remain somewhat more field independent than his peers 20 years later. Certain socialization practices have been associated with differences in cognitive style. In

Field-dependence may be adaptive in predominantly agrarian societies, such as in rural China, wherein people need to pay careful attention to the concrete particulars of their physical and social environments.

TABLE 8.4	SELECTED RESEARCH FINDINGS ON FIELD INDEPENDENCE—DEPENDENCE

Correlates of Field Independence

Greater accuracy in estimating what confused or distorted images "should" look like

Better problem solving in tasks requiring unconventional use of common objects and tools

Hypothesis-testing approach to complex problems

Experiences of guilt rather than shame

Tendency to describe other people in negative terms

Preference for solitary games in childhood

Careers in mathematics and science, such as physics, architecture, and engineering; in health professions such as medicine and dentistry; and in certain practical occupations such as carpentry, farming, and mechanics

Socialization patterns emphasizing independence and autonomy

Predominant in hunting societies

Unrelated to overall academic achievement

Correlates of Field Dependence

Tendency to rely on other people for guidance

Greater sensitivity to nuances of interpersonal relationships

Higher levels of eye contact

Better memory for names and faces

Knowing more people and being known by more people

Greater levels of self-disclosure with other people

Experiences of shame rather than guilt

Tendency to describe other people in relatively positive terms

Preference for social play in childhood

Careers in helping humanitarian occupations such as social worker, minister, and rehabilitation counselor; in certain teaching areas such as elementary school and social sciences; and in certain business occupations such as selling, advertising, and personnel

Socialization patterns emphasizing conformity and dependence on authority

Predominant in agricultural societies

SOURCE: Adapted from Goodenough (1978), Singer (1984), Witkin et al. (1979).

general, evidence supports the common sense conclusion that development proceeds toward greater field independence when socialization encourages separation from parental control. A more tightly organized and controlling milieu, on the other hand, is likely to encourage field dependence. In general, field-independent people report that their parents were relatively permissive, whereas field-dependent persons often report an emphasis on parental authority in their families.

Some of the most interesting findings on field independence–dependence come from cross-cultural studies. Witkin and Berry (1975) provide evidence that migratory hunting-and-gathering tribes tend to be field independent, whereas societies organized around sub-sistence-level agriculture tend to be more field dependent. Hunting-and-gathering societies are constantly on the move from one geographical setting to the next. Field-independence would appear to be an adaptive cognitive style for this migratory and predatory lifestyle. Witkin and Berry (1975) write:

> The ecological demands placed upon persons pursuing a hunting and gathering subsistence economic life style require the ability to extract key information from the surrounding context for the location of game and the ability to integrate these bits of information into a continuously fluctuating awareness of the hunter's location in space for the eventual safe return home. (p. 16)

On the other hand, agrarian societies are much more sedentary. Because agrarian societies stay put for long periods of time, their members build up elaborate systems of social interaction. Adherence to group norms may become more valuable to group survival than autonomous individual functioning.

INTEGRATIVE COMPLEXITY

Whereas individual differences in field-independence/dependence refer to styles of *perceiving* the world, certain other cognitive styles studied by personality psychologists focus on differences in *reasoning* about or interpreting the world. **Integrative complexity** is the extent to which a person reasons about issues in a sophisticated and integrative manner (Suedfeld, Tetlock, & Streufert, 1992). People high in integrative complexity make many conceptual distinctions and see many interconnections when interpreting and making sense of intellectual and social issues. People low in integrative complexity, by contrast, see fewer distinctions and tend to reason about the world in a holistic and simplistic manner.

Individual differences in integrative complexity are assessed through content analysis of written material (Baker-Brown et al., 1992). For example, a person's account of a particular experience, a speech or diary entry, an essay, an argument, or a letter written to a friend can all be scored for integrative complexity. The researcher rates particular passages in the text with respect to the degree of differentiation and integration shown. Passages that rely on simplistic explanations and isolated single judgments receive relatively low scores. Those that bring in many different perspectives and that balance different explanations and considerations receive relatively high scores for integrative complexity. While people differ with respect to their characteristic levels of integrative complexity, each person may also exhibit many different levels, depending on the situation. For example, when a college student writes a love letter to her boyfriend, she may show a rather low level of integrative complexity. But in composing a history essay to explain economic changes in Europe during the 1800s, her expressed integrative complexity may be higher.

Some of the most creative research on integrative complexity has been conducted by Philip Tetlock on political reasoning and by Peter Suedfeld on literary correspondence. In one especially provocative study, Tetlock (1981a) analyzed selected speeches of 20th-century American presidents before and after their elections to office. He found that integrative complexity was generally low while the man was campaigning for the presidency but rose markedly after he was elected. Tetlock interpreted the finding to mean that presidential candidates tend to present issues in simplistic black-and-white terms in order to get elected but, once elected, adopt more complex reasoning patterns. Interestingly, when incumbent presidents begin campaigning for a second term, the integrative complexity levels of their rhetoric drop again, as they again seek to sway the voters by simplifying the issues.

Coding Supreme Court decisions (Tetlock, Bernzweig, & Gallant, 1985) and the political rhetoric of American senators (Tetlock, 1981b; Tetlock, Hannum, & Micheletti, 1984) and of members of the British House of Commons (Tetlock, 1984), Tetlock has made a compelling case for a connection between political ideology and integrative complexity. Politicians with relatively liberal voting records (for the most part, liberal Democrats in the United States Senate and moderate socialists in the British House of Commons) tend to exhibit higher levels of integrative complexity in their speeches than do those with relatively conservative voting records. Also low in integrative complexity are politicians with extremely liberal (such as extreme socialists in the Britain) or extremely conservative views. The data for the British House of Commons are displayed in Figure 8.2.

Tetlock explains his findings in terms of *value plurality*. He argues that *freedom* and *equality* are the two fundamental values upon which Western political rhetoric is often evaluated. Conservatives tend to value freedom over equality. Extreme liberals (socialists, communists) value equality over freedom. Moderate liberals, however, value both. Therefore, a moderate liberal is likely to fashion a more complex political ideology in order to accommodate his or her allegiance to both freedom and equality—two values that often conflict. While a traditionally conservative politician in Great Britain or the United States is likely to oppose increases in taxes for welfare spending because of the belief that citizens should be free to spend their hard-earned money on what they want, the liberal may find the issue more difficult in that he or she places a premium on equality as well as freedom. According to the value of equality, tax dollars should support those who are less well-off.

FIGURE 8.2   **INTEGRATIVE COMPLEXITY AND POLITICAL AFFILIATION**

In the British House of Commons, politicians with moderate to moderately liberal affiliations tend to show the highest levels of integrative complexity as determined from political speeches.

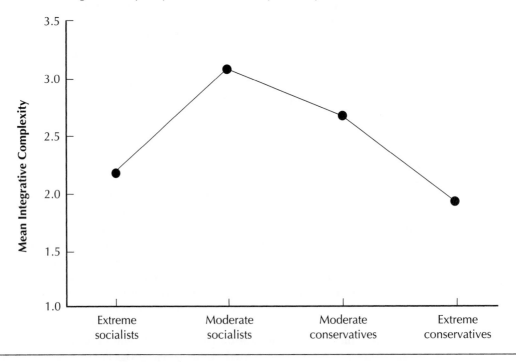

SOURCE: From "Cognitive Style and Political Belief Systems in the British House of Commons," by P. E. Tetlock, 1984, *Journal of Personality and Social Psychology, 46,* 370.

Yet, freedom dictates low taxes and laissez faire capitalism. As a result, the liberal is likely to bring in more considerations and find more shades of grey in political rhetoric about such issues as taxation and social programs. In Tetlock's view, the liberal is more complex and conflicted. From the standpoint of the conservative, on the other hand, the liberal may seem "wishy-washy" or "afraid to take a stand."

A very different approach to integrative complexity is apparent in the research of Suedfeld on the relation between social events and literary correspondence (Porter & Suedfeld, 1981; Suedfeld, 1985). Porter and Suedfeld (1981) analyzed the personal correspondence of five eminent British novelists of the 19th and 20th centuries: Charles Dickens, George Eliot, George Meredith, Arnold Bennett, and Virginia Woolf. Each novelist's life was divided into 5-year periods and the investigators randomly sampled between 10 and 20 paragraphs from the novelist's personal correspondence for each period. Each paragraph was scored on a 7-point scale, ranging from very low to very high integrative complexity. Table 8.5 provides an example of a verbatim paragraph scoring relatively low and another scoring relatively high in integrative complexity.

Porter and Suedfeld correlated integrative complexity scores with various historical events and personal changes in the novelists' lives. They found that integrative complexity scores *decreased* during times of war but *increased* during periods of civil unrest. War appeared to exert a simplifying effect on literary correspondence. During periods in which their countries were involved in international combat, the novelists tended to present issues in relatively undifferentiated terms, failing to take into consideration multiple and complex points of view. Porter and Suedfeld speculate that war has the general effect of restricting the "information flow" in the environment. By contrast, civil unrest (such as major political changes) appeared to evoke a more flexible and integrative outlook, perhaps by stimulating new ideas and possibilities in the environment's information flow.

With respect to personal changes, Porter and Suedfeld found that integrative complexity decreased during times of illness, was unrelated to other stressful events, increased with age, and decreased shortly before death. The last finding is especially intriguing in that research on life-span developmental psychology has suggested that just before people die they experience a marked decrease in cognitive functioning, called a *terminal drop*. In another study, Suedfeld and Piedrahita (1984) examined the correspondence of 18 eminent individuals during the last 10 years of their lives. Supporting the hypothesis of terminal drop, they found that integrative complexity scores fell markedly in the last 5 years before death for those who died of a protracted illness and during the year immediately prior to death for those who died suddenly.

In general, research suggests that high levels of integrative complexity are associated with making more informed and well-balanced decisions, with open-mindedness and tolerance for ambiguity in confronting complex issues, and with cognitive self-direction. Nonetheless, high integrative complexity can sometimes come with a cost. High scorers sometimes find it difficult to make a clear-cut decision based on firm moral principles. For example, during the debate on slavery before the American Civil War, moderate leaders and politicians who sought compromise on this issue tended to score high on integrative complexity, based on coding of their public speeches. By contrast, the abolitionists—who argued strongly that slavery should be abolished—tended to score low, as did the leaders and politicians who defended slavery. We see here that what virtually everybody today would view as the morally right choice—to abolish slavery—was most strongly pushed and clearly articulated by leaders whose speeches scored relatively *low* for integrative complexity. (Interestingly, their arch-opponents—leaders arguing in favor of keeping the slavery system in place—also scored low.) By contrast, those

TABLE 8.5	VERBATIM PASSAGES FROM THE CORRESPONDENCE OF EMINENT NOVELISTS SCORED FOR INTEGRATIVE COMPLEXITY

Low on integrative complexity (score = 2)

Tonight I finished First Principles. I suppose that I can never have again the same thrills of admiration as this book has given me. If any book could be called the greatest book in the world, I suppose this can. I have never read anything a tenth part so comprehensive. And it makes its effects by sheer honest argumentative force. There are no ornaments of brilliance, wit, ingenuity, or even eloquence. Yet the closing pages of Part I, and the closing pages of Part II, are equally overwhelming in their effect. Faults there, of course, are in it but it is surely the greatest achievement of any human mind. This I do think. And Spencer has not yet come into his own, in England. As a philosopher, in the real sense—not as a discoverer, or a man of science—but as a philosopher, he is supreme in the history of intelligence. I say this, not because I have read all the other great ones, but because I cannot imagine the possibility of anyone having produced anything else as great as First Principles. [Note that in this passage the author elaborates on an absolute rule or declaration. There is little by way of alternative perspectives discussed.]

High on integrative complexity (score = 6)

The professor says you do not consort with Germans at all. I am grieved at this. I am sure you do not altogether underrate the fine qualities of German youth; but perhaps your immediate sympathies, and a somewhat exaggerated sensitiveness, stand in your way. It will be a pity, if this is so, and for more reasons than one. If you do not cultivate the people you are living amongst in your youth, you will fail in having pleasant places to look back at—landmarks of your young days. And besides, the Germans are your hosts, and you owe them at least a guest's thankfulness. I esteem them deeply for their fine moral qualities. Just now they are abusing us roundly, but that will pass away. I know they have the capacity for friendship, and that as a rule English friendships are not so lasting. Look around you, and try to be accessible to your German associates. Consider whether you are not yielding to luxurious pre-dispositions in your marked preference for English ones. You will see enough of the latter when you return here. [This passage shows simultaneous operation of alternatives and consideration of the functional relations between them.]

SOURCE: From "Integrative Complexity in the Correspondence of Literary Figures: Effects of Personal and Societal Stress," by C. A. Porter & P. Suedfeld, 1981, *Journal of Personality and Social Psychology, 40,* 325–326.

leaders adopting more complex and integrative arguments took intermediate, and morally compromised, positions in the debate—for example, they argued that slavery might still be tolerated in the South but prevented from spreading to the new territories of the United States. In this interesting and troubling historical case, high levels of integrative complexity seem to have clouded people's moral vision (Tetlock, Armor, & Peterson, 1994).

In another study suggesting costs for high integrative complexity, researchers studied interactions among graduate business management students (Tetlock, Peterson, & Berry, 1993). The students showing high levels of integrative complexity were rated by their peers as more creative, as might be expected, but also as more disagreeable, narcissistic, and lacking in conscientiousness. The students low in integrative complexity were viewed as simple, acquiescent, and conforming, but they were also seen as being warm, giving, and more self-controlled, compared with the students high in integrative complexity. In some situations, then, there would appear to be an interpersonal downside for high integrative complexity.

SOCIAL-COGNITIVE THEORY AND THE PERSON

Contemporary social-cognitive approaches in personality psychology view the person as a more-or-less rational and planful knower who actively seeks information in the social

RELIGION, RELIGIOUS VALUES, AND PERSONALITY

The United States is one of the most religious societies in the Western industrialized world (Sherkat & Ellison, 1999). For many Americans, religious values exert an important influence on their self-conceptions and their views of the world. As such, religious values and beliefs are good examples of characteristic adaptations in personality—individual-difference variables that (like motives, goals, and social-cognitive aspects of personality) are more specific and contextualized features of human individuality than are dispositional traits.

For most of the 20th century, psychologists either ignored or dismissed the role of religion in personality and mental health. In the last 10 to 15 years, however, many researchers have finally turned their attention to religion and religious values. They have conducted medical, psychological, and sociological studies and surveys that measure many different aspects of religious experience, such as religious affiliation, church attendance and participation, religious behaviors (e.g., prayer, meditation), and religious methods for coping with adversity and stress. The bottom line finding is that, at least among Americans, *religious beliefs and participation in religious activities tend to be positively associated with many features of physical and mental health* (Dillon & Wink, 2004; Emmons & Paloutzian, 2003; George, Ellison, & Larson, 2002; Seybold & Hill, 2001).

Religious involvement is positively associated with many indices of physical health and wellness. Those who attend religious services on a regular basis, for example, tend to live longer than those who are not involved in religious organizations, and they tend to lead healthier lifestyles. They are less likely to use tobacco and illegal drugs, and they show lower levels of alcohol abuse. Their blood pressure and cholesterol levels tend to be lower. Religious involvement is associated with lower levels of heart disease, cirrhosis, emphysema, stroke, kidney failure, and cancer mortality. Following major surgery, highly religious adults

tend to show fewer health complications and lower levels of stress compared to less religious adults. With respect to mental health, religious involvement is positively associated with self-esteem, life satisfaction, and overall psychological functioning. Religious involvement predicts lower levels of depression, delinquency, criminal behavior, and even divorce. A strong predictor of marital happiness is a couple's mutual involvement in religious activities. The positive effects of religion appear to be especially powerful among African Americans and among socially marginalized groups in American society.

The benefits of religion may stem from many sources. In the United States, churches, synagogues, and mosques provide members with close-knit communities where people share values and goals and care for each other during difficult times. People develop close friendships in religious organizations; they join informal support groups of various kinds; they come to associate with a broad range of individuals who may be of help to them in many different ways. Ministers, priests, rabbis, and other religious leaders may provide counseling or offer advice as to how a troubled member may obtain help from social-service agencies and other community-based resources. Religious involvement enhances social support and raises a person's *social capital*—the network of social relations upon which a person may draw to meet the many different challenges of life (Putnam, 2000). Higher levels of social support and social capital are themselves good predictors of health and well-being.

Strong religious values provide some people with answers to deep questions about life, providing a sense of security and hope in the face of adversity. Some researchers have speculated that the kind of security and optimism that some especially religious people enjoy may exert a calming physiological effect. Chronic activation of the body's sympathetic nervous system—associated with heightened levels of fear and anxiety—has been linked to illness and

(CONTINUES)

FEATURE 8.A (CONTINUED)

reduced longevity. Religious involvement may help to lower chronic stress and reduce the wear and tear on the body's vital organs that come from repeated over-activation of the sympathetic nervous system.

The positive effects of religion are especially evident when people express what psychologist Kenneth Pargament (2002) calls *intrinsic* religious values and *positive religious coping*. Intrinsic religious values come from within; they reflect religious choices that people have made freely and thoughtfully. By contrast, *extrinsic* religiosity may feel forced or coerced and is motivated by guilt, fear of rejection, or social conformity. Intrinsically religious people show higher levels of well-being, sociability, and intellectual flexibility, and lower levels of depression, anxiety, and social dysfunction, compared to extrinsically religious people. When facing difficult periods in life, intrinsically motivated people often use such positive coping strategies as praying to God for assistance, seeking support from clergy and congregation members, and looking for positive blessings amidst adversity.

Pargament also suggests that certain especially severe and rigid forms of religion—such as Christian fundamentalism—appear to show both negative and positive correlates. Research has consistently shown that adherents to strict, fundamentalist religious viewpoints tend to be more narrow-minded, authoritarian, and prejudiced. Among Christians, Jews, Muslims, and Hindus, strict fundamentalism is associated with distrust of people who hold other points of view and prejudice against such out-groups as homosexuals. At the same time, Christian fundamentalism in the United States has been associated with such positive features as optimism, religious and spiritual well-being, and marital satisfaction. Pargament writes: "Strict systems of religious belief and practice provide individuals with an unambiguous sense of right and wrong, clear rules for living, closeness with like-minded believers, a distinctive identity, and, most important, the faith that their lives are sanctioned and supported by God. These are strong advantages" (2002, p. 172). At the same time, these advantages may exact social costs such as intolerance for those who do not share the same beliefs.

world and draws upon a rich storehouse of social knowledge in order to regulate his or her own behavior and enact plans and goals in a wide range of social environments (Cantor & Kihlstrom, 1989; Cantor & Zirkel, 1990; Cervone & Shoda, 1999b; Higgins, 1999; Kihlstrom & Hastie, 1997; Markus & Wurf, 1987; Shoda, 1999). Like Kelly, these approaches suggest that people are especially adept at construing and anticipating social situations in ways that enhance their ability to predict and control the social world. Within the rich storehouse of social information upon which people routinely draw are their most salient personal constructs for categorizing social experience. In their emphasis on human agency and their portrait of an active and self-organizing knower, social-cognitive theories also underscore themes that are at the heart of some humanistic approaches to personality, including especially Deci and Ryan's (chapter 7) self-determination theory. These theories provide an optimist take on human nature: As human beings, we are potentially rational and effective; we are intelligent and planful in our social interactions; we are flexible in the strategies we employ to obtain our goals; our behavior is responsive to situational demands, but it is also coherent and self-organized.

SOCIAL INTELLIGENCE

Nancy Cantor and John Kihlstrom argue that the key to understanding personality coherence is **social intelligence** (Cantor & Kihlstrom, 1985, 1987, 1989). Each person brings a set of skills, abilities, and knowledge to every social situation. Such "lawful intraindividual variability, especially across situations, is precisely the characteristic we ascribe to intelligence" (Cantor & Kihlstrom, 1985, p. 16). They write, "intelligent action, as contrasted with the instinctual or the reflexive, is flexible rather than rigidly stereotyped, discriminative rather than indiscriminate, and optional rather than obligatory" (p. 16). The implication is that people differ in social intelligence. Some people appear to have more than others. More important, however, people use their social intelligence in different ways to interpret and solve current tasks and problems in life.

In Cantor and Kihlstrom's view, social interaction involves problem solving. The social world confronts each of us with a series of mundane and momentous problems that call for socially intelligent behavior. We must interpret each problem we encounter and devise a strategy for mastering it, or at least for coping with it. For each social situation, the person asks such questions as "What do I want here?" "What are the likely consequences of my actions?" "How can I get what I want?" In working through the various facets of a social problem (situation), the person draws extensively on a repertoire of social intelligence, which "is stored in memory as organized knowledge" and which "forms the structural basis for personality" (p. 18).

Social intelligence consists of three different kinds of organized knowledge: *concepts, episodes,* and *rules.* Concepts and episodes may be grouped together as aspects of *declarative* knowledge. Think of them as "things" that are contained in the information storehouse. Concepts are the abstract and categorical things contained in the storehouse, such as concepts of who you are and what you typically expect to happen in social life. Concepts are aspects of what Cantor and Kihlstrom call **declarative-semantic knowledge.** Episodes are more concrete and particular kinds of things contained in the storehouse, such as memories of particular scenes in your life. These make up **declarative-episodic knowledge.** The distinction between the two forms of declarative knowledge—concepts (declarative-semantic knowledge) and episodes (declarative-episodic knowledge)—is a fundamental distinction in cognitive psychology. Many cognitive psychologists believe that the brain processes these two kinds of declarative knowledge very differently. Consequently, your conception of yourself as, say, "an honest person" (declarative-semantic) involves different brain processes and is itself a very different piece of knowledge compared with your memory of one particular episode in your life (declarative-episodic) in which you acted in an especially honest fashion. In contrast to both concepts and episodes, rules are aspects of what Cantor and Kihlstrom identify as **procedural knowledge.** Whereas concepts and episodes are like things contained in the mind's storehouse, rules are not things but rather procedures or processes that determine how things are used.

Among the most important concepts that make up declarative-semantic knowledge are your concepts of self, others, and social interaction—all of which you have accumulated over the many social experiences that make up your life. Every person has accumulated a very large store of concepts about who he or she is, what other people are like, and what a person should expect to happen in social interaction. Concepts of *self* are perhaps the most salient components of declarative-semantic knowledge, and I will have much more to say about them later in this chapter when I consider the topics of self-schemas, self-complexity, possible selves, and self-guides. Among the different concepts of *other* people contained in declarative-semantic knowledge are what Mark Baldwin (1992) calls **relational schemas.** Relational schemas are mental representations of especially important interpersonal relationships that a person has experienced. Baldwin's idea is very similar to

Nancy Cantor and John Kilhlstrom developed the concept of social intelligence. Their approach to personality emphasizes the different ways that people think about, remember, and reason through social situations in life.

what you may recall from chapter 2 as the notion of "working models" of attachment relationships. Over the course of social life, we each come to expect certain kinds of interactions with certain people. Therefore, your relational schema (working model) of your relationship with your mother may involve her tending to reprimand you when you are not especially conscientious whereas your relational schema for your interactions with your best friend may involve having lots of fun and staying up late at night talking about your problems. Our relational schemas guide and shape our expectations and reactions in social relationships, and as social relationships unfold they may also come to influence our relational schemas. As important aspects of declarative-semantic knowledge and, more generally, social intelligence, relational schemas serve as "cognitive maps in navigating the social world" (Fehr, Baldwin, Collins, Patterson, & Benditt, 1999, p. 301).

Our declarative-semantic knowledge about self and other may also encode our expectations about the extent to which certain human attributes may or may not change over time. Take, for example, the attributes of "intelligence" and "honesty." Rachel may take it for granted that these attributes are more-or-less fixed for any given person. In other words, Rachel believes that the "amount" of intelligence or honesty that a person "has" does not (and cannot) change much over time. A smart person will remain smart; a person who is not very smart is not likely to get much smarter over time. By contrast, Katie believes that these attributes develop over time. People can become smarter over time, with experience and training. People who are not very honest may become more honest over time with the right kind of social experiences, she believes. Rachel and Katie show contrasting implicit theories about the nature of human attributes. According to Carol Dweck (1996; Dweck, Chiu, & Hong, 1995), Rachel holds implicitly to an **entity theory** of human attributes—attributes are fixed entities that do not change over time. By contrast, Katie appears to believe in an **incremental theory**—attributes are malleable and can change incrementally over time. Dweck's research shows that people who hold entity-based theories tend to interpret their own and other people's actions in terms of fixed traits ("I failed the test because I am dumb"; "He stole the bread because he is dishonest") whereas those holding incremental theories focus less on broad traits and more on the situational and temporary forces that influence action ("I failed the test because I used the wrong strategy in studying for it"; "He stole the bread because he was desperate"). Dweck maintains that entity-based theories can undermine a person's efforts, especially when the person faces failure. People with entity-based implicit theories tend to feel helpless when they meet failures, because they believe that they cannot change the fixed traits that are responsible for their failures. By contrast, incrementalists, like Katie, respond in a more proactive manner to setbacks and are more likely to work hard to master the challenges they face. Their motivation to do so is grounded in an implicit belief that people (including themselves) *can* change, develop, and grow.

Procedural knowledge consists of various competencies, strategies, and rules "that enable us to form impressions of others, make causal attributions, encode and retrieve social memories, and predict social behaviors" (Cantor & Kihlstrom, 1985, p. 20). People operate according to a great many rules and strategies when engaging in socially intelligent behavior, and many of these rules are outside conscious awareness. Of special interest are **causal attributions**—how people understand the causes of events. Bernard Weiner (1979, 1990) developed a well-known scheme for understanding causal attributions, especially as they apply to outcomes of success and failure. To explain why a person succeeded or failed in a given task, we often resort to one or more of four basic attributions: ability, effort, task difficulty, and luck. Why, for example, did Maria receive a low grade on her term paper for American Literature 101? Her failure to do well on this assignment might be explained in terms of ability: Maria is simply not a very good writer. Or it may be explained in terms of effort: Maria did not put much time into the paper; she didn't try hard enough. Both ability and effort are *internal* attributions. They suggest that the cause of Maria's failure lies in factors within Maria—her poor ability or her weak effort. By contrast, we may explain Maria's failure in terms of task difficulty: The assignment was too hard, too ambiguous; perhaps, the professor expected too much or failed to give the students enough time to write a good paper. Or we may say that Maria was just plain unlucky on this assignment. During the same week that her paper was due, Maria's boyfriend broke up with her and her mother called to say that she did not have enough money to pay the recent tuition bill. Because of her bad luck, Maria was distracted and failed to write the kind of paper she would normally write. Task difficulty and luck are *external* attributions: The causes of her failure are in the environment, not in Maria herself. The four attributions may also be organized along the lines of *stability*. Ability and task difficulty refer to stable factors; effort and luck are unstable. Maria's luck may change or she may try harder next time.

In general, people tend to make internal and stable attributions when accounting for successes in their lives. Had Maria received an "A" on the assignment, she might attribute her good fortune to her strong writing ability. By contrast, people tend to make unstable attributions when accounting for failure—not trying hard enough, or bad luck. In the wake of a failure, an unstable attribution has the advantage of suggesting that things are likely to change in the future. It would seem, therefore, that explaining failure in terms of momentary causes such as effort or luck helps protect one's self-esteem. Things will be better next time. I'm still okay. Nonetheless, people differ markedly in their characteristic attributional patterns. As we will see later in this chapter, some empirical evidence suggests that chronically depressed people tend to make causal sense of their successes and failures in ways that go against the norms. They may tend to explain their own successes in terms of unstable factors (e.g., "I got lucky") but their failures in terms of causes that are internal and stable (e.g., "I failed because I'm stupid").

SELF-SCHEMAS

A central concept in social-cognitive approaches to personality is the **schema.** A schema is any abstract knowledge structure. Fiske and Taylor (1984) write that a schema is a "cognitive structure that represents one's general knowledge about a given concept or concept domain" (p. 13). There are many ways to think about schemas. You may view them as "filters" or "templates" that we use to perceive, organize, and understand information, much like Kelly's concept of a "personal construct." Neisser (1976) writes that a schema is like a "format" in a computer-programming language. Formats specify that information must be of a certain sort if it is to be interpreted coherently. The format allows the program to deal effectively with a particular kind of information while ignoring or downplaying the rest. A person's schemas go beyond the information given by (a) simplifying information when there is too much for the person to handle efficiently and (b) filling in gaps when information is missing.

Every person employs a large set of schemas to make sense of the world. Social-cognitive approaches to personality contend that human adaptation is accomplished through the schematic processing of social information. Furthermore, schemas are applied to the self. Each person builds up a view of the self, a **self-schema** or series of self-schemas that structure the processing of self-relevant information and guide behavior. A self-schema is like all other schemas in that it simplifies incoming information and fills in gaps when information is missing. For example, if an important part of a young man's self-schema is the idea that he is especially attractive to women, he is likely to pick up information from the social environment that confirms his view and ignore or fail to process information that seems irrelevant. Seeing the puzzled facial expression of a woman sitting next to him in class, he may assume that she is thinking of him and wondering if he might ask her out. But self-schemas differ from other schemas, too. Self-schemas are generally (a) larger and more complex than other schemas, (b) richer in their network of associations and relationships among components, (c) more frequently activated in daily information processing, and (d) loaded with emotion (Markus & Sentis, 1982). One's own self-schema contains a vast and complex array of emotionally laden information. For each of us, it is probably our most popular, most frequently used schema.

The self-schema does not contain all information about the person. Rather, it emphasizes personally significant information about the self. We tend to place at the center of the self-schema those self-defining properties such as our name, representative aspects of physical appearance, significant personal relationships, and perceived traits, motives, values, and goals that we view as most representative of who we are. Figure 8.3 illustrates a small portion of a hypothetical person's self-schema. Many concepts may be linked with the self-schema, because we experience most things with reference to the self. In Figure 8.3, the self is linked to food and graduate school. Other concepts in memory that are not self-relevant, such as "ladders" and "gorillas," are not shown as connected to the self. Repeated associations of the self with other concepts and structures will lead to stronger and more certain links. Eventually, there may be some overlap between the self and another concept, as when a person takes up jogging and comes to see himself or herself as possessing many of the characteristics of other joggers.

A major finding in research on self-schemas is that people process information that is especially relevant to their self-schemas in highly efficient ways (Lewicki, 1984; Markus, 1977, 1983; Markus & Smith, 1981). In a classic study, Hazel Markus (1977) investigated the dimension of "independence–dependence" in self-schemas. Depending on how college students presented themselves in an initial phase of her research, Markus classified each as

FIGURE 8.3	PORTION OF A HYPOTHETICAL SELF-SCHEMA

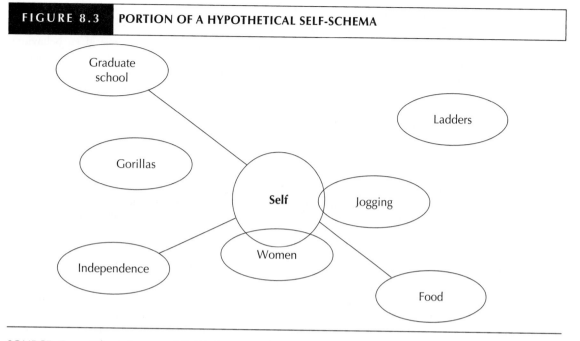

SOURCE: From "The Influence of Self-Schema on the Perception of Others," by H. Markus & J. Smith, in N. Cantor and J. F. Kihlstrom (Eds.), *Personality, Cognition, and Social Interaction* (pp. 244), 1981, Hillsdale, NJ: Lawrence Erlbaum.

having a strong independence schema, a strong dependence schema, or as aschematic (having neither). Three to four weeks later, the students participated in an experiment in which adjectives were presented on a screen one at a time. The adjectives were either *schema-relevant* (related to independence or dependence) or *schema-irrelevant* (related to the dimension of "creativity"). The student's task was to press one of two buttons, labeled either ME or NOT ME, to indicate whether the adjective described him or her.

Those students whose self-schemas underscored dependence showed faster reaction times in response to dependent adjectives than they did to schema-inconsistent (independent) adjectives and schema-irrelevant adjectives. Markus concluded that the dependent schematics were accustomed to thinking of themselves as "conforming," "obliging," and so on and could, therefore, make these judgments more quickly. The independent schematics showed a similar pattern of results, with faster reaction times to independent adjectives. The aschematics, on the other hand, did not differ at all in their processing times for dependent and independent words. Aschematics appeared not to have defined themselves with respect to independence and to be equally at ease labeling their behavior in these terms. They apparently did not have a structure for independence–dependence to guide their processing of information about the self.

Studies similar to Markus's have shown that people with self-schemas emphasizing particular areas are readily able to (a) evaluate new information with respect to its relevance for the particular area, (b) make judgments and decisions in the domain with relative ease and certainty, (c) retrieve episodes and other behavioral evidence from their past that illustrates the particular area, (d) predict future behavior in the area, and (e) resist information that is counter to the prevailing schema (Markus & Smith, 1981).

Markus (1983) hypothesizes that a self-schema emerges as a person begins to experience feelings of personal responsibility in a particular domain of behavior. "Acquiring a self-schema becomes equivalent to staking out a personal claim in a given behavioral arena," writes Markus (1983, p. 561). "It is as if one is saying 'I have control over my actions here' (or 'I would like to have control over my actions here' or 'I am both the cause and the consequence of actions in this domain')." As a self-schema develops, the person becomes more concerned with his or her own behavior in the particular domain and seeks to exert control over the causes and consequences of that behavior.

Individuals differ from one another in regard to the kinds of self-schemas they develop. Differences in the *content* of self-schemas—the self-relevant material contained within a schema—are virtually infinite in that no two people see themselves in identical ways. Differences in the *structure* of self-schemas can also be observed. For instance, some people present highly articulated and complex self-schemas, whereas other people see themselves in simpler terms (Linville, 1987), a personality difference that is called **self-complexity.** Some people have many different self-aspects, which are kept relatively separate from one another. Each aspect of their self-schema may be connected to a particular role they play in life, but the different roles may be relatively unconnected. Therefore, should they experience failure or trouble with respect to one area in their self-schema, other areas may remain relatively unscathed. In a sense, these people with high levels of self-complexity manage to compartmentalize the many different aspects of the self-schema, such that what happens in one aspect has little effect on the others. By contrast, people low in self-complexity present a less differentiated self-schema. For people low in self-complexity, feelings associated with a bad event in one aspect of life tend to spill over into other aspects as well. In the wake of failure in one domain, misery may spread quickly across the entire self-schema (Dixon & Baumeister, 1991; Linville, 1987; Rafaeli-Mor & Steinberg, 2002).

POSSIBLE SELVES

A significant portion of our behavior may be guided as much by who we *might* be as by who we are. A young man trains for years to become an Olympic swimmer. A struggling author labors over what she hopes will become "the great American novel." A married couple save all their extra money so that they will never sink into poverty. In each of these cases, the person strives to become something, or to avoid becoming something, that he or she is (currently) not. In these and countless other instances, people behave according to what Markus and Nurius (1986) call **possible selves.** Possible selves "represent individuals' ideas of what they might become, what they would like to become, and what they are afraid of becoming." They are "the cognitive components of hopes, fears, goals, and threats and they give the specific self-relevant form, meaning, organization, and direction to these dynamics" (Markus & Nurius, 1986, p. 954).

In the view of Markus and Nurius, the self-schema contains multiple generalizations about the current and past self as well as prominent possible selves that link the self to the future. The possible selves that we wish to become in the future might be "the successful self, the creative self, the rich self, the thin self, or the loved and admired self." On the other hand, "the dreaded possible selves could be the alone self, the depressed self, the incompetent self, alcoholic self, the unemployed self, or the bag lady self" (Markus & Nurius, 1986, p. 954).

Each possible self is a *personalized* construction that has been articulated in rich detail. Therefore, if one of my dreaded possible selves is "the unemployed self," then I am likely to have developed a painfully clear picture of what this self would be like. I might imagine

GENDER, SEX, AND SCHEMA

With the strong impact of the women's movement in the United States in the 1970s, many American psychologists conducted research on the extent to which men and women identify with sex-role stereotypes. According to common social lore, men are supposed to be strong, assertive, independent, and instrumental—that is, masculine. And women are supposed to be gentle, caring, dependent, and expressive—in other words, feminine. Psychologists developed a number of self-report measures of *sex-role orientation* to assess the extent to which people saw themselves as relatively masculine or relatively feminine. Arguing that masculinity and femininity were not opposite but rather independent dimensions, many researchers showed that scoring high on both of these dimensions—that is, showing **psychological androgyny**—might be a preferred orientation in contemporary American society (Bem, 1981). In recent years, individual differences in self-ascribed masculine and feminine traits have been reconceptualized in social-cognitive terms. In her **gender schema theory,** Sandra Bem (1981, 1987) suggests that people differ in the extent to which they understand their lives and contexts in gender-related terms. Some people repeatedly process social information along the lines of gender, showing strong gender schemata. Other people are relatively "aschematic" with respect to gender, less inclined to interpret social life in terms of masculinity and femininity.

Bem argues that individual differences in sex-role orientations are best understood in terms of different gender schemas. A man who scores high on masculinity or a woman who scores high on femininity exhibits a strong gender schema, or generalized tendency to process information on the basis of sex-linked associations. These people should be especially sensitive to gender differences in daily information processing. Androgynous and undifferentiated men and women show weaker gender schemas. They are less likely to see and interpret the world in terms of gender.

In a famous experiment that has been repeated many times, Bem (1981) administered a sex-role inventory (the BSRI) to college students and then engaged the students in a memory task. She first presented a list of 61 words in random order consisting of proper names (such as *Henry, Deborah*), animal names, *(gorilla, butterfly),* verbs *(hurling, blushing),* and articles of clothing *(trousers, bikini).* Within each of the four categories, some of the words were masculine oriented *(Henry, gorilla, hurling, trousers)* and some were feminine oriented *(Deborah, butterfly, blushing, bikini).*

After the words were presented, the students were given 8 minutes to write down as many of the words that they could remember in any order. The important finding in the study concerns the *order* in which words were remembered. College students with strong gender schemas (masculine men and feminine women) tended to show higher levels of *clustering* in their recall of words. This means that they tended to string together words of the same gender designation. For instance, if the first word they remembered and wrote down was *Henry* (a masculine word), their second word remembered was likely to be masculine as well (for example, *hurling*). Thus, sex-typed men and women (those with strong gender schemas) tended to group together masculine and feminine words in recall. In Bem's words, they "spontaneously imposed a gender-based classification system on the stimulus array" (1987, p. 267). Non–sex-typed men and women—those with presumably weaker gender schemas—showed lower levels of clustering. These students tended not to use gender as an organizing principle for recalling the words.

MacKenzie-Mohr and Zanna (1990) examined the role of men's gender schemas and their tendency to treat women as sexual objects in a nonsexual or professional setting. Gender-schematic (high on masculinity, low on femininity) and gender-aschematic college males watched either a pornographic or neutral video and were then interviewed by a female research assistant. The researchers reasoned that viewing a pornographic video would likely "prime" or make salient thoughts about heterosexual relations among the

FEATURE 8.B *(CONTINUED)*

men. As a result, gender-schematic men would be more likely than gender-aschematic men to adopt a "heterosexuality schema" in subsequent interaction with a woman in a professional setting, thinking and acting in a relatively sexist manner. The results of the experiment supported the researchers' prediction. Even though she did not know anything about the men she interviewed, the female research assistant experienced her interaction with the gender-schematic men who had viewed the pornographic video as more sexually provocative than interaction with subjects in the other three conditions (schematic/neutral, aschematic/pornography, aschematic/neutral). For example, she reported that gender-schematic men who had viewed the pornographic video were more likely than the other men to look at her body while she was interviewing them. In addition, these men tended to sit closer to her than men in the other conditions. Finally, all the men were asked to describe their interaction with the female assistant immediately after the interview. In the first minute

of this free-recall task, 72% of the information recalled by the gender-schematic men who had viewed the pornographic video centered on the interviewer's physical characteristics, compared with 49% of the information recalled by men in the other three conditions. Summing up their results, the authors write:

> For gender-schematic males, exposure to nonviolent pornography seems to influence the way they view and act toward a woman in a task-oriented (or "professional") situation. These males were seen by the female experimenter as more sexually motivated, they positioned themselves closer to her, and they had faster reaction times and greater recall for information about her physical appearance. Importantly, these males also recalled less about the survey the female experimenter was conducting. These variables all triangulate on the conclusion that this group of males treated our female experimenter, who was interacting with them in a professional setting, in a manner that was both cognitively and behaviorally sexist. (MacKenzie-Mohr & Zanna, 1990, p. 305)

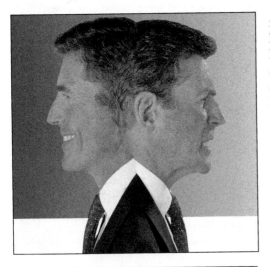

Research on possible selves and on self-guides suggests that people tend to formulate multiple self-conceptions. We may feel that we assume one kind of self in certain areas of our lives and another (perhaps contrasting) kind of self in certain other areas.

myself losing confidence in my ability to support my family, having to sell the house, struggling to get by on food stamps, living in an overpriced and undersized apartment in a "bad section" of the city, spending long hours with nothing to do, applying for menial jobs for which I feel overqualified, being humiliated in the presence of my parents, resenting my peers who have profitable jobs, gradually sinking into despair and hopelessness. Although many people may fear unemployment, my unemployed self is personally crafted to be unique to my personality. If this is an important possible self within my general self-concept, then I am likely to go to great lengths to avoid its realization.

Markus and Nurius view possible selves as the crucial link between motivation and cognition in self-understanding. Markus and Nurius contend that people are motivated by strong internal needs, desires, and inclinations. But these motivational dynamics are not activated in personality functioning until they are transformed into self-relevant form. Therefore, my fear of being unemployed may be a personalized translation of a strong "power motive" (chapter 7) combined with certain fears rooted in my past history. Motives, fears, desires, hopes, and dreams are given expression through possible selves. In this sense, then, possible selves function first as *incentives* for future behavior—they are selves to be approached or avoided.

A second function of possible selves is *self-evaluation.* Possible selves provide frameworks by which the person can evaluate how well or poorly his or her life is going. Possible selves are therefore powerful structures for determining the meaning of personal events. For example, a junior in college who desires to become a physician will evaluate her current standing with regard to that possible self in very negative terms should she be carrying an extremely low grade-point average. Her boyfriend, whose most cherished possible self involves his future career as a professional athlete, will feel good about his prospects after being drafted for a professional team. His equally low grade-point average has less impact on his self-evaluation in that it is not linked to a dominant possible self.

In sum, the concept of possible selves leads to two interesting implications. First, the self may be viewed as a complex schema or knowledge structure within which is contained a finite number of personified characters. Each possible self personifies specific and highly personal information connected to the person's basic needs, wants, and fears. Second, an important aspect of the self is information about who the person *might be* in the future. Markus and Nurius view the self-schema as encompassing not only what "is me" now but also what "might be me" in the future, whether I like it or not.

SELF-GUIDES

E. Tory Higgins (1987) suggests that self-knowledge encompasses three major domains: the *actual self,* the *ideal self,* and the *ought self.* The actual self consists of your representation of the attributes that someone (yourself or another) believes you actually possess. The ideal self consists of your representation of the attributes that someone (yourself or another) would like you, ideally, to possess—that is, a representation of hopes, aspirations, or wishes. The ought self consists of your representation of the attributes that someone (yourself or another) believes you should or ought to possess—that is, a representation of duties, obligations, or responsibilities. Each of the three domains, furthermore, may be seen from either the person's *own* standpoint or the standpoint of a significant *other* in the person's life, such as a parent, spouse, or friend. Therefore, the "actual/own self" consists of the characteristics that the person believes he or she actually possesses. The "actual/other self" consists of the characteristics that the person believes that a significant other believes he or she (the person) actually possesses. Similarly, Higgins distinguishes between "ideal/own self" and "ideal/other self" and between "ought/own self" and "ought/other self."

According to Higgins's (1987) **self-discrepancy theory,** problems occur when various selves in different domains or from different standpoints are inconsistent, or discrepant, with one another. Two kinds of discrepancies are especially salient, and each leads to a corresponding emotional reaction. Discrepancies between the *actual/own* self and *ideal* (either own or other) selves leads to the experience of *dejection-related emotions,* such as sadness, disappointment, and shame. In these cases, the person believes that he or she has been unable to attain hopes, dreams, or aspirations that either the person him- or herself or a significant other has set for him or her. When my own baseball performance failed to live up to my father's (and my own) hopes and dreams, I felt dejected and downcast. A huge discrepancy between actual and ideal was revealed. On the other hand, discrepancies between the *actual/own* self and *ought* (either own or other) self leads to the experience of *agitation-related emotions,* such as fear, anxiety, guilt. In these cases, the person believes he or she has failed to live up to standards (established by self or other) for good, dutiful, or responsible behavior. The agitated emotions stem from the experience of feeling that one is being punished (by self or other) for not doing what one ought to do.

A number of research studies support Higgins's characterization of the linkages between self-discrepancies and negative emotional experiences (Higgins, 1987). In most of these studies, college students list traits or attributes that describe the various selves that Higgins has identified. The researchers code matches and mismatches in traits across the various self domains. For instance, a person might describe his actual/own self as "ambitious," "honest," "sincere," "friendly," and "hot-tempered" and his ought/own self as "honest," "friendly," "easygoing," "forgiving," and "helpful." In this example, we can identify two clear matches—both lists contain "honest" and "friendly"—and one clear mismatch—"hot-tempered" and "easygoing" seem to be discrepant. The greater the number of mismatches, the greater the discrepancy and corresponding negative emotional reaction. The link between discrepancy and negative emotion is strongest, Higgins maintains, for self domains that the person judges to be the most relevant in his or her life.

In one study, Higgins administered these kinds of self-description measures and (1 month later) various assessments of *depression* (involving dejection-related emotions) and *anxiety* (involving agitation-related emotions) to undergraduate students. Figure 8.4 displays the results. As predicted, actual/ought discrepancies predicted anxiety (but not depression) whereas actual/ideal discrepancies predicted depression (but not anxiety). Students who felt that they were not living up to their ideal selves reported high levels of sadness and depression. Those who felt they were not living up to their ought selves reported high levels of fear and anxiety.

Ideal selves and ought selves may be called **self-guides** in that they offer standards and goals to which a person may aspire and against which a person may compare his or her current life situation. Higgins (1997) argues that these two self-guides represent two very different motivational foci in social behavior. A *promotion* focus is associated with strong ideal self-guides, sensitivity toward positive outcomes, and approach strategies in social behavior. A *prevention* focus is associated with strong ought self-guides, a sensitivity toward negative outcomes, and avoidance strategies in social behavior. Higgins's distinction between promotion and prevention focus is highly reminiscent of the distinction between the behavioral approach system (BAS) and the behavioral inhibition system (BIS) for personality traits, as I described it in chapter 5, and parallels distinctions between approach and avoidance goals that have been made by motivational and learning psychologists for many years (e.g., Lewin, 1935; Maslow, 1954; Miller & Dollard, 1941).

Research conducted by Daniel Ogilvie (1987) has examined a different kind of discrepancy in self-conceptions. Whereas Higgins focuses on the extent to which the actual self *differs* from other positive selves (ideal and ought), Ogilvie turns things around to discern the extent to which the actual self is *similar* to *undesired* selves. Undesired selves contain attributes that the person fears, dreads, hates, and actively seeks to exclude from experience. Ogilvie suggests that we may be in closer touch with our undesired selves than with our ideal and ought selves. Our undesired selves are likely to be rooted in concrete past experiences in which we felt humiliation, despair, fear, anger, and so on. Our ideal and ought selves, on the other hand, are more hypothetical. They are abstractions toward which we strive but which we rarely attain.

Ogilvie (1987) obtained students' characterizations of their actual, ideal, and undesired selves and measured the "distance" between each student's selves through a complicated statistical procedure that positions selves in a hypothetical space. Questionnaire

FIGURE 8.4	SELF-GUIDES AND NEGATIVE EMOTION

Discrepancies between actual and ought self-guides are associated with anxiety while discrepancies between actual and ideal self-guides are associated with depression.

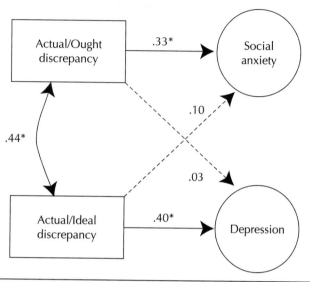

NOTE: The numbers on the arrows are akin to correlation coefficients: the higher their values, the stronger the association.

*$p < .01$.

measures of life satisfaction were also obtained. The results showed that the distance between a person's ideal and actual selves was negatively associated with life satisfaction. In other words, the greater the discrepancy between ideal and actual, the lower the life satisfaction. The distance between a person's undesired and actual self was positively associated with life satisfaction. People whose actual selves were "far away from" their undesired selves were happier with their lives. Most important, however, the second result was much stronger than the first. This is to say that the distance between undesired and actual selves was a much stronger predictor of life satisfaction than was the distance between ideal and actual selves. The implication of Ogilvie's findings is straightforward and intriguing: If we want to be happy, we will do better to avoid being the way we dread being rather than striving to be the way we wish to be.

SCHEMAS, ATTRIBUTIONS, AND EXPLANATORY STYLE: THE CASE OF DEPRESSION

Social-cognitive approaches to personality have proven especially valuable in efforts to understand the phenomenon of depression. In the past 25 years, there has been a veritable explosion of scientific research on the ways in which people who are chronically depressed process information in daily life. Scores of books and hundreds of scientific articles have addressed the topic. A number of major theories have been developed. While these theories differ from one another in important ways and while scientific research does not consistently

The emotional experience of depression is associated with particularly negative through patterns, such as negative schemata and an explanatory style that attributes negative events to internal, stable, and global causes.

support all of their tenets, a general theme cuts across all cognitive approaches to human depression: *Depressed people perceive, understand, and interpret their worlds and themselves in a peculiar and dysfunctional way.* Cognitive theories of depression do not deny that other noncognitive factors may be implicated in the experience of depression, especially biological factors that may predispose some people to chronic depression. But they do assert that at the center of the depressive experience are depressive cognitions—depressive thoughts, beliefs, values, attributions, schemas. Some theories suggest that these cognitions *cause* the emotional feelings of sadness and despair; others suggest that the depressive cognitions are a *result* of depression.

Psychotherapist Aaron Beck was one of the first to offer a cognitive theory of depression (Beck, 1967, 1976). Beck observed that depressed people typically hold a negative view of themselves, are pessimistic about the future, and have a tendency to interpret ongoing experience in a negative manner. These negative interpretations lead to feelings of sadness and despair. During an episode of depression, the depressed person is caught in a downward spiral, as bad thoughts lead to bad feelings, which lead to more bad thoughts and more bad feelings. Therefore, depressed people tend to see the world through **depressive schemas.** Depressive schemas *distort* reality by casting information in a negative light. For instance, depressives tend to recall more negative and unpleasant adjectives (such as *bleak, dismal, helpless*) in memory tasks than do nondepressed people (Derry & Kuiper, 1981; McDowall, 1984). They tend to have a difficult time recalling positive themes from stories (Breslow, Kocis, & Belkin, 1981). Depressives tend to recall unpleasant memories more rapidly than pleasant ones (Lloyd & Lishman, 1975). They tend to remember failures and forget successes (Johnson, Petzel, Hartney, & Morgan, 1983). In describing various positive and negative autobiographical memories, depressed college students tend to recall more *different kinds* of negative episodes from their pasts and fewer different kinds of positive episodes than do nondepressed students (McAdams, Lensky, Daple, & Allen, 1988).

Inspired by Beck's schema theory, a good deal of the cognitive research on depression has assumed that depressives *negatively distort* reality. Ingram (1984) has argued that depressed people have a difficult time summoning up positive self-schemas, even in the wake of positive events in their lives. In one laboratory experiment, depressed and nondepressed college students were provided with either positive ("success" condition) or negative ("failure" condition) feedback concerning their performance on a multiple-choice test (Ingram, Smith, & Brehm, 1983). (The bogus feedback was not related to their actual performance on the test, though the students thought that it was at the time.) The students then listened to a prerecorded set of 48 adjectives. After each adjective was presented, the student answered either "yes" or "no" to one of four different questions about the adjective:

1. Was the adjective read by a male? (structural question)
2. Does the adjective rhyme with _____? (phonemic)
3. Does the adjective mean the same as _____? (semantic)
4. Does the word describe you? (self-referent)

According to Ingram, the four different questions call for four different levels of information processing. At the "deepest" level of processing is the self-referent question, for it asks the student to make a very personal judgment about the applicability of the adjective to his or her personality. At the most superficial levels are the structural and phonemic questions, which simply ask the student to make a judgment about the acoustical sound of the adjective as it was heard on the tape.

Following the tape and associated questions, each student was asked to recall as many of the adjectives as possible. The results are shown in Table 8.6. Nondepressed students tended to recall more positive self-references in the success condition (5.13) than in the failure condition (3.06). Depressed students, on the other hand, recalled about the same number of positive self-referents in both conditions (3.04 vs. 3.33). The authors argued that the success feedback preceding the recall task activated a positive self-schema for the nondepressed students sensitizing them to positive adjectives about themselves. Therefore, they recalled a large number of positive adjectives about themselves in the success condition. By contrast, the success feedback was *not* effective in activating a positive self-schema in the minds of the depressed students, who remembered about the same low number of positive self-referent adjectives in both conditions.

An influential cognitive approach to depression is Seligman and Abramson's **reformulated learned-helplessness theory.** In his early research with animals, Martin Seligman (1975; Seligman & Maier, 1967) discovered that dogs subjected to uncontrollable aversive stimulation, like random electric shocks, eventually become helpless and do not act to avoid the shocks even when they have a clear opportunity to do so. Analogously, Seligman reasoned, human beings subjected to uncontrollable negative events in life will eventually learn to be helpless and will become chronically depressed. In their reformulated interpretation of learned helplessness, Seligman and Abramson (Abramson, Seligman, & Teasdale, 1978; Peterson & Seligman, 1984) link helplessness and depression to cognitive attributions, or what they have most recently called an **explanatory style.** They argue that depressed people experience the world in a helpless fashion by virtue of their characteristic patterns of assigning causality and explaining events.

According to the reformulated learned-helplessness model, depressives tend to explain *negative* events in their lives as stemming from *internal, global,* and *stable* causes. For example, they may attribute their low grade on an examination to their own general "stupidity"—"I am generally stupid" (stupidity is *internal* to the person, rather than a feature of the external situation); "I am stupid in many things" *(global);* and "I will always be stupid" *(stable).* On the other hand, depressives tend to explain *positive* events in their lives as stemming from *external, specific,* and *unstable* causes. Therefore, they may view a high grade on an examination as a lucky break. The high grade might be due to an easy test

TABLE 8.6	SELF-REFERENCE SCORES FOR RECALLED WORDS	
	Success	**Failure**
Depressed	3.04	3.33
Nondepressed	5.13	3.06

SOURCE: From "Depression and Information Processing: Self-schemata and the Encoding of Self-Referent Information," by R. E. Ingram, T. W. Smith, & S. S. Brehm, 1983, *Journal of Personality and Social Psychology, 45,* 417.

(external) in a particular area *(specific)* that is not likely to occur again in the future *(unstable)*. In essence, the depressive person's explanatory style accentuates the importance of negative events by suggesting that they are due to broad and uncontrollable forces. At the same time, it minimizes the importance of positive events by suggesting that they are specific flukes that are not likely to recur.

Seligman's attributional approach to learned helplessness has stimulated a great deal of empirical research. Overall, the findings provide modest support for the model, though there are many inconsistencies in the research literature (Coyne & Gotlib, 1983; Peterson & Seligman, 1984; Peterson, Villanova, & Raps, 1985; Robins, 1988). A number of studies have shown that depressed people tend to attribute failures to internal, global, and stable factors, though the obtained relationships between these attributional patterns and depression are sometimes weak (Robins, 1988). Further, other sorts of nonattributional dimensions of information processing, such as the person's expectations about the extent to which particular negative events are "intended" or "likely to happen again," appear to be associated with depression, too (Gong-Guy & Hammen, 1980; Hammen & Cochran, 1981). In addition, many researchers appear to be skeptical about Seligman's claim that attributional patterns precede or cause depression. Teasing out such a causal relation requires a longitudinal study in which cognitions and depressive symptomology are monitored over time. Data from an intensive longitudinal case study collected by Peterson, Luborsky, and Seligman (1983) offer interesting support for the causal role of attributions. Other studies, however, are less supportive. For instance, Cochran and Hammen (1995) undertook a 2-month longitudinal study of college students and depressed outpatients and concluded that "in terms of the direction of causality, the data were more consistent in indicating that depression causes cognitions than in indicating the reverse" (p. 1562).

A person's characteristic explanatory style is a very important feature of the procedural knowledge that composes an individual's social intelligence. It should not be surprising, therefore, to learn that explanatory style is associated with a range of behavioral outcomes that go well beyond the phenomenon of depression. Researchers have examined the role of explanatory style in school achievement, job performance, success in sports, physical health, and longevity.

Nolen-Hoeksema, Girgus, and Seligman (1986) assessed explanatory style among school children. The children showed wide variation in characteristic styles, with some children exhibiting the kind of pessimistic style characteristic of depression. The children showing a pessimistic explanatory style (internal, stable, and global explanations for bad outcomes) were rated by teachers as showing more helpless behaviors and fewer mastery behaviors in school. They also scored lower in standardized achievement tests and, as has been shown with adults, scored higher on measures of depressive symptoms.

Seligman and Schulman (1986) studied life insurance sales agents over the course of one year. At the beginning of the year, the researchers measured the agents' explanatory style. Agents showing the pessimistic explanatory style at the beginning of the year sold less insurance during the year than did the agents with an optimistic style. The agents with the pessimistic style were also more likely to quit the company. Seligman, Nolen-Hoeksema, Thornton, and Thornton (1990) used a similar methodology to study women's and men's college swimming teams. They found that pessimistic explanatory style measured at the beginning of the season predicted relatively poor swimming performance during the season.

Peterson, Seligman, and Vaillant (1988) reported results from a 50-year longitudinal study of men who graduated from Harvard College in 1938 and 1940. In 1946, when they were in their late 20s, 99 of the men who had served in World War II responded to open-ended questions about their difficult war experiences. The researchers scored these narrative accounts for explanatory style and then related the scores to the men's subsequent physical health as assessed in periodic medical checkups. Explanatory style was a significant predictor of health over a 40-year span. Those men whose essays (written in their late 20s) showed an optimistic explanatory style exhibited significantly better health in their medical checkups in their 40s, 50s, and 60s, compared with the men whose essays showed a pessimistic explanatory style.

Another longitudinal investigation suggests that explanatory style may even predict how long people live! Peterson, Seligman, Yurko, Martin, and Friedman (1998) coded open-ended questionnaires written in 1936 and 1940 by participants in the Terman longitudinal study of the intellectually gifted (chapter 5) for explanatory style. The open-ended questions asked the participants to account for disappointments, failures, and negative relationships they had experienced in their lives and to describe their most serious personal flaws. The globality aspect of explanatory style—attributing negative events to global causes—predicted mortality as of 1991. In other words, those individuals who tended to explain negative events in terms of global causes in their early to middle adult years tended to die earlier than individuals who used a more optimistic explanatory style. Explanatory style was especially predictive of untimely death among men, and it predicted especially well accidental and violent deaths. According to the authors of the study, attributing global causes to negative events is a form of cognitive *catastrophizing*. Globality taps a pervasive style of catastrophizing about bad events, expecting them to occur across diverse situations and thereby magnifying even small misfortunes into potential catastrophes. This kind of explanatory style is hazardous, they maintain, because it tends to be associated with poor problem solving, social estrangement, and risky decision making. If you believe that every bad event is indicative of a potential catastrophe, you may come to see the world as a frighteningly untrustworthy place—a place wherein it does not pay to be prudent and rational because all your good efforts may be swept away in a moment by large and uncontrollable forces. If you hold the belief that catastrophes will inevitably occur, you may even adopt a "who cares" or "what the hell" attitude about life. "It doesn't matter what I do."

THE REGULATION OF SOCIAL BEHAVIOR

The ultimate purpose of social intelligence is to guide social behavior. The concepts, episodes, and rules that people draw on to process information about the self and social life prove their worth in the crucible of everyday interpersonal action. Social-cognitive perspectives in personality psychology portray people as planful and more-or-less effective actors who move across a wide range of demanding social situations virtually every day. Therefore, the social-cognitive adaptations we have sampled in this chapter—personal constructs, cognitive styles, self-schemas, possible selves, explanatory styles, and the like—all contribute to the implementation of intelligent social behavior—that is, behavior aimed at solving the many problems in social living that individuals face.

As we saw in chapter 7, such behavior is typically goal directed in some manner, motivated by the anticipation of accomplishing particular goals or ends in social life. Social-cognitive theories of personality view human beings as purposive social actors, processing social information in ways that promote the accomplishment of personal goals, strivings, projects, tasks, and the like (Bandura, 1999; Cantor & Kihlstrom, 1989; Dweck, 1996; Cervone & Shoda, 1999b; Markus & Nurius, 1986). Social-cognitive adaptations *regulate* social behavior in the service of personal goals. These goals may be nested in a *hierarchy*

FEATURE 8.C

WHAT OR WHO CONTROLS MY BEHAVIOR? RESEARCH ON LOCUS OF CONTROL

Among the intellectual forerunners to social-cognitive approaches in personality psychology are George Kelly's personal construct theory and the social learning theories developed by Rotter and Bandura in the 1950s and 1960s. A key concept in Rotter's theory (chapter 3) is *expectancy,* which he defined as the subjectively held probability that a particular reinforcement will occur as the outcome of specific behavior. **Locus of control** refers to individual differences in expectancy. People with an *internal* locus of control expect reinforcements (rewards) to follow their own actions. In other words, they believe that their own behavior controls the consequences that subsequently follow—subsequent reinforcing events are contingent on the person's behavior. The person with an *external* locus of control expects that his or her behavior will not lead to predictable reinforcement. Rather, reinforcements are dispensed by external sources of control, such as powerful others, chance, luck, and so forth. Reinforcing events do not appear to be contingent on his or her behavior.

You may notice that locus of control bears some resemblance to explanatory style. For both concepts, the focus is on what a person believes to be the ultimate cause of social behavior. But locus of control is a more general concept than explanatory style and it is more oriented toward the reinforcing consequences that may follow a person's behavior. In research on explanatory style, people are asked to attribute cause in specific social scenarios. For example, I may be confronted with a particular bad event in my life and asked what the causes were of that event. For locus of control, by contrast, people are asked more general questions about their overall beliefs concerning personal agency and the power of the external environment. For example, I might be asked which of the following two statements I most agree with: "What happens to me is my own doing" or "Sometimes I feel that I don't have enough control over the direction my life is taking" (Rotter, 1966). The first option suggests

an internal locus of control whereas the second suggests an external locus of control.

Many self-report scales have been developed to measure locus of control (Phares, 1978). The most well-known measure is the **I-E Scale** (Rotter, 1966), which contains 29 forced-choice items like the example I have given above. Rotter's scale assumes that locus of control is a broad, generalized factor that cuts across many different domains in which expectancies might reveal themselves. In the past 20 years, however, psychologists have developed a number of specialized scales designed to assess beliefs about control in specific domains. These include scales to assess locus of control as it pertains to one's understanding of marriage (Miller, Lefcourt, Holmes, Ware, & Saleh, 1986), affiliation situations (Lefcourt, Martin, Fick, & Saleh, 1985), intellectual functioning (Lachman, 1986), and health (Wallston & Wallston, 1981).

The I-E Scale has been used in literally thousands of research studies, and the massive literature suggests that locus of control is an extremely important social-cognitive variable in personality. The research suggests that, in general, *internal* locus of control is associated with many positive outcomes in life, from better academic achievement to better interpersonal relationships. For example, people with an internal locus of control tend to show less compliance and conformity, greater perceived competence and independence, greater efforts to acquire information from the environment, greater knowledge about their own health and sicknesses, more positive attitudes about physical exercise, lower levels of cigarette smoking, lessened susceptibility to hypertension and heart attack, and greater levels of overall psychological adjustment, compared with people who have an external locus of control (Lachman, 1986; Phares, 1978,). People with an internal locus of control tend to be healthy and independent information seekers who adapt well to many of life's

FEATURE 8.C (CONTINUED)

challenges. However, internal locus of control is not always an asset. In *nonresponsive* environments, wherein efforts to exert personal control are repeatedly thwarted, the person with an internal locus of control may encounter many difficulties and report lower levels of satisfaction, compared with people who have an external locus of control (Janoff-Bulman & Brickman, 1980; Rotter, 1975). Believing that reinforcements will come from your own efforts can work against you when you find yourself in an environment that does not value personal agency and individual effort.

such that concrete and simple goals are contained within more abstract and complex goals (Carver & Scheier, 1988; Hyland, 1988; Vallacher & Wegner, 1987). According to some social-cognitive perspectives, there exists for every person a hierarchy of levels of behavioral control, with various levels of standards or goals arranged from the most concrete and narrow to the most abstract and broad organizing principles. The lower levels indicate how the action is to be carried out, whereas the higher levels provide information on the purposes or implications of the action. Goals or standards can be characterized at different levels within this hierarchy, and people may be said to differ as to the level at which they characterize their goals within the hierarchy.

Charles Carver and Michael Scheier have developed a representative hierarchical model of how cognition regulates purposive behavior (Carver & Scheier, 1981, 1988, 1992; Scheier & Carver, 1981). The model draws heavily on the concept of **feedback.** In a feedback loop, a system regulates itself around a set point, as in a thermostat. Deviations from the set point stimulate adjustment activities, which are terminated when the set point is once again achieved. In the case of a thermostat, the set point might be 65 degrees Fahrenheit. When the temperature in the room dips below 65 degrees, the thermostat turns on the furnace, which will shut off when the air temperature reaches or exceeds the set point. In the case of human behavior, the set point might be any goal, standard, or reference value against which behavior is compared. These comparison points for behavior, however, come in almost an infinitude of forms, and include such things as values, self-schemas, situational expectancies, and conscious intentions.

Figure 8.5 illustrates the feedback relation between comparison points and behavior. According to the model, a person is constantly monitoring his or her own behavior and the behavior of others. Sometimes people literally watch what they are doing (as in weight-lifting rooms with mirrored walls), but, more often, "monitoring your behavior is a matter of sensing in a vague, general way the qualities you've been displaying in your actions" (Carver & Scheier, 1988, p. 476). When the perception of your behavior matches well the goal or standard to which you are comparing the perception, then you do not alter your behavior. This is analogous to the thermostat's sensing that the air temperature is still above 65 degrees—the furnace is not switched on. However, when the person perceives a *discrepancy* between the current behavior and some goal, standard, or value to which the behavior is compared, he or she changes behaviors in order to move closer to the comparison point. Therefore, if in the middle of a conversation in which you desire to be friendly, you feel that you are beginning to offend the person to whom you are speaking, you will probably change your behavior in some way. You may begin to compliment the person, or you may change the topic to something lighter and friendlier in order to move the interaction toward the goal. Once the goal is achieved, you may change goals and alter your

FIGURE 8.5   A SIMPLE SELF-REGULATION SYSTEM

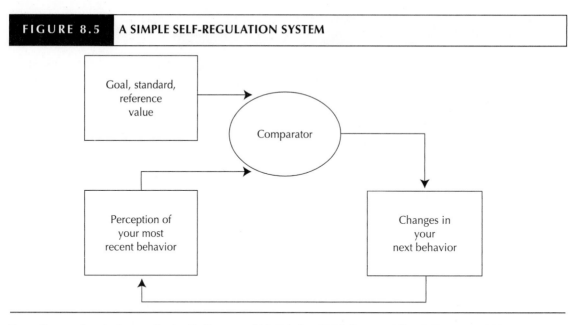

From *Perspectives in Personality,* by C. Carver and M. Scheier, 1988, Boston, Allyn & Bacon, p. 476.

behavior accordingly. According to Carver and Scheier (1988), "behavior is inherently purposive (even if the purposes underlying some acts are pretty trivial)." As they put it, "human life is viewed as a continual process of establishing goals and intentions, and adjusting current patterns of behavior so as to match them more closely, using informational feedback as a guide to progress" (Carver & Scheier, 1988, p. 476).

The goals and intentions that regulate human behavior are dynamic; they shift from one situation to the next and over time. Thus, the process of self-regulation is continuous and neverending. Every change in output (behavior) creates a change in the perceived present condition. This new input, then, must be checked against the reference value, which itself will change over time. There is a continuous interplay between making adjustments to action and evaluating the effects of those adjustments. Better regulation, furthermore, is accomplished by closer self-scrutiny. Therefore, any environmental condition that promotes a person's self-examination is likely to promote the smooth and effective regulation of behavior, as numerous experimental studies have shown.

In these studies, a person's self-focus is accentuated in some way, as when the person must observe his or her own behavior in a mirror (Wicklund & Duvall, 1971). The result of the self-focus is increased goal matching in behavior. In one study, Carver (1975) chose students who either opposed or favored the use of punishment in teaching. Several weeks after the students' attitudes on punishment were assessed, they participated in a laboratory task in which they administered punishments for errors committed by a person they thought (erroneously) was another subject in the study. In the self-focus condition, the students observed their own administration of punishments in a mirror. In the control condition, no mirror was present. As Figure 8.6 shows, the students in the self-focus condition tended to act in close accord with their values. Those who said they opposed punishment delivered only low levels of punishment; those in favor of punishment administered

FIGURE 8.6	SELF-FOCUS AND THE LINK BETWEEN BEHAVIOR AND VALUES

Individuals who are in a self-focus condition tend to deliver punishments that are in accord with their personal views on punishment, whereas individuals not focused on the self show behavior less clearly connected to their values.

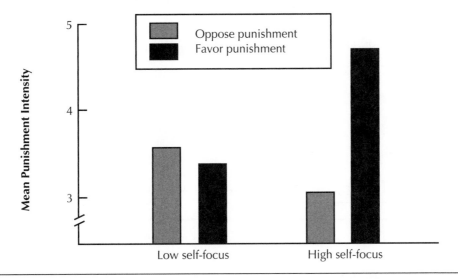

SOURCE: From *Perspectives in personality,* by C. Carver and M. Scheier, 1988, Boston, Allyn & Bacon, p. 480.

high levels. In the low self-focus (control) condition, however, the students did not differ on the punishments they administered as a function of their values. In other words, when they were not explicitly monitoring their own behavior, they tended not to regulate what they were doing in accord with their stated beliefs about punishment.

The feedback loops that regulate human behavior are much more complex than the simple illustration portrayed in Figure 8.5. To deal with this complexity, Carver and Scheier propose a **feedback hierarchy** made up of subordinate and superordinate goals. According to this view, illustrated in Figure 8.7, the output of one feedback loop becomes the reference value for the feedback loop subordinate to it (Powers, 1973). Higher-order or superordinate levels in the hierarchy provide reference values for lower levels. There are many possible levels, but the three highest ones in the hierarchy are *program, principles,* and *system concept.*

At the program level, behavior is guided by expected scripts or general guidelines for courses of action. Many of our daily intentions operate at the program level, from taking out the garbage to preparing for an examination. At the principles level, behavior is regulated by overriding qualities that might be realized through various scripts or programs. For example, a woman may see herself as a generally "friendly" person. This self-ascription serves as a principle for behavior, providing the reference value of "being as friendly as I can be" for various scripts or programs she may enact. Finally, her principle of friendliness may itself be regulated and organized by the highest level in the hierarchy, the level of system concept. Here reside the highest abstractions for behavioral analysis, such as the "generalized

FIGURE 8.7 **A THREE-TIERED HIERARCHY OF FEEDBACK SYSTEMS**

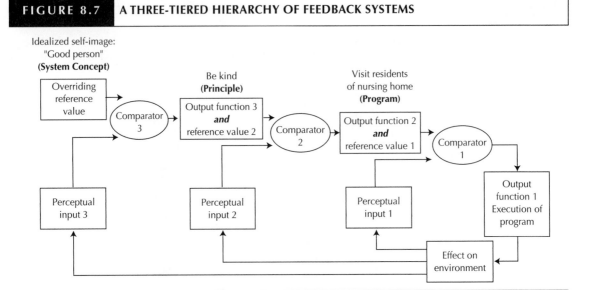

SOURCE: From *Perspectives in personality*, by C. Carver and M. Scheier, 1988, Boston, Allyn & Bacon, p. 482.

sense of self that people try to maintain over time and place" (Carver & Scheier, 1988, p. 483). One's general sense of self, sometimes called *identity*, is an overarching regulator for behavior. It provides reference values for the principles level in the hierarchy, which in turn provides reference values for the program level, and so on.

A similar point of view is expressed in Vallacher and Wegner's (1987) **action identification theory**. According to Vallacher and Wegner, an action can be identified in a wide variety of ways, ranging from the most concrete to the most abstract. For example, the same behavior can be identified as "moving wooden pieces on a board," "playing a game of chess," or "improving my mind through intellectual stimulation." Lower-order identifications frame action in simple behavioral terms: Writing a term paper is reduced to "making marks on a sheet of paper." Higher-order identifications frame action in broad conceptual terms: Writing a term paper may be elevated to "striving for excellence in academics." Research on action identifications suggests that when both a low-level and high-level identification are available, people tend to adopt the higher one, as long as they can do so comfortably. In other words, people tend to view (and regulate) their activities *in as abstract a way as they can without difficulty.* When faced with difficulty, however, they will retreat from higher-order to lower-order identifications. Such a move may make it easier to master the challenges of a given act. Once the problem is resolved, movement toward a higher-level identification may ensue.

A fascinating application of this point of view may be found in Roy Baumeister's (1990) theory of suicide as an "escape from self." Baumeister suggests that suicide may result from a relentless cognitive movement from higher-order to lower-order identifications in response to tremendous pain and suffering. According to this view, a person first experiences a series of painful setbacks in a number of different life domains, such as romantic involvements and work life. These failures are attributed to the self. The person may come to believe that he is at fault for the bad things that have happened, or he may believe that he is a helpless victim of forces he cannot control. In either case, what results is a painful state of self-awareness.

To escape this excruciating self-awareness, the person launches into a process that Baumeister calls **cognitive deconstruction**. Cognitive deconstruction involves a dramatic slide from relatively adaptive, higher-order thinking into a narrowly focused and concrete frame of mind that blocks out emotion and erases concerns for meaning. The person comes to adopt a narrower and narrower time perspective, as concerns for the future give way to an obsessive focus on the here-and-now. The person comes to focus on progressively more concrete events, as well. For example, eating a meal may be cognitively reduced to moving the food from plate to mouth. The person obsessively focuses on the molecular action of moving the knife and fork in order to blot out any awareness of the larger contexts for action, for those larger contexts are painful. To think of the act as "eating" might lead to thoughts about "having meals," which might remind the person of the people with whom he has shared meals in the past, who indeed may be the sources of his current pain. Better, then, to focus consciousness on the fork.

As life becomes reduced in time and space, the person abandons higher-level meanings (as in "What is my life about?") for the relatively meaningless minutiae of simple acts (as in "Will I move the food to my mouth again?"). This intense focus on only the most immediate, concrete, and meaningless things works to divest life of its characteristic emotional tone. Operating at the lowest possible level of action identification, the person has retreated from time, thought, feeling, and significance. The retreat has not enabled him, however, to master the challenges of a simpler order of life. There is still too much pain and suffering awaiting him, should he seek to reverse the tide of deconstruction. Thus, the suicide act may follow as a final retreat from the complexity of life to the simplicity of death, a tragic result of a progressively more nihilistic narrowing of one's cognitive focus, the ultimate escape from self.

In conclusion, Baumeister's conception illustrates that even a human action as portentous as suicide can be understood in terms of social-cognitive processes—the mental representations that a person forms to construe the self and social behavior. Social-cognitive processes are involved in virtually every behavior we exhibit in daily life. In that persons differ from one another with respect to their characteristic personal constructs, self-schemas, explanatory styles, and other social-cognitive adaptations, social-cognitive processes constitute an essential aspect of human individuality. Like motives and goals (chapter 7), social-cognitive adaptations specify many of the particulars of human personality. Social-cognitive adaptations tell us how people perceive and interpret the social world. It is indeed impossible to understand people if we do not have some sense of how they understand who they are and what constitutes the world in which they live.

SUMMARY

1. Social-cognitive approaches to personality psychology focus on the mental representations that people form to process information about the self, other people, and social behavior. Social-cognitive adaptations are the characteristic personal constructs, cognitive styles, beliefs, expectancies, attributions, self-conceptions, and the like that people draw upon in their efforts to meet the many demands of social life. Along with personal goals, social-cognitive adaptations help to regulate social behavior. Like motives and goals, furthermore, social-cognitive adaptations go beyond general personality traits to specify some of the contingent and contextualized details of human individuality.

2. Developed in the 1950s, George Kelly's theory of personal constructs foreshadowed many of the central themes of contemporary social-cognitive theory. Kelly viewed the person as akin to a scientist, seeking to categorize and make sense of his or her environment in order to predict and control it. According to Kelly, people develop personal constructs based on their perceptions of social events, and these constructs help to guide subsequent social behavior. A personal construct is a characteristic way of construing how some things are alike and some things are different from one another. Constructs differ from one another in terms of such dimensions as permeability and range of convenience. People differ from one another with respect to the content and organization of their construct systems.

3. Cognitive styles refer to individual differences in people's characteristic and typically preferred modes of processing information. One of the most well-researched cognitive styles is field independence–dependence. Highly field-independent people process perceptual information in an especially analytical and differentiated style, whereas highly field-dependent people process perceptual information in a more global and contextual style. Individual differences in field independence–dependence have been linked to a wide range of cognitive, social, and behavioral outcomes.

4. A second well-researched cognitive style is integrative complexity. Whereas field independence–dependence concerns differences in perception of stimuli, integrative complexity refers to styles of reasoning. Integratively complex individuals reason about issues in a highly differentiated manner, construing many distinctions and nuances and taking into consideration multiple points of view. By contrast, integratively less complex or simple individuals see fewer distinctions and nuances and tend to rely instead on a handful of broad principles or categories. Integrative complexity appears to wax and wane as a function of age and situations. Nonetheless, individual differences in overall integrative complexity can be assessed. People high in integrative complexity tend to make more well-informed and well-balanced evaluations of complex issues, are more open-minded and tolerant, and show considerable cognitive self-direction, but they also may sometimes encounter more difficulty in making clear-cut decisions based on moral principles, compared with individuals low in integrative complexity.

5. Social-cognitive perspectives on personality view the person as a planful and more-or-less effective agent in the social world who is able to respond in flexible ways to a wide range of social situations. The person's social effectiveness is largely determined by what Cantor and Kihlstrom call social intelligence. Social intelligence consists of the characteristic concepts, episodes, and rules that a person draws on to solve social problems in everyday life.

6. Perhaps the most salient components of declarative-semantic social knowledge are self-schemas, or knowledge structures about the self. Each person builds up conceptions of the self—self-schemas—that structure the processing of self-relevant information and guide behavior. People process information that is relevant to their self-schemas in highly efficient ways. Contemporary social-cognitive views tend to emphasize the multiplicity of self-schemas. People may have many different images of themselves, including possible selves. Possible selves represent an individual's ideas of what he or she might become or what he or she fears becoming. Possible selves are cognitive vehicles for carrying a person's most important motives, desires, hopes, dreams, and fears.

7. Self-knowledge can be further broken down into actual, ideal, and ought selves. Ideal selves incorporate attributes that a person strongly desires to possess whereas ought selves contain attributes that a person believes he or she should possess. Ideal selves connect to a promotion focus in life, sensitivity toward positive outcomes, and approach strategies in social interaction. Ought selves connect to a prevention focus, sensitivity toward negative outcomes, and avoidance strategies in social behavior. People often experience discrepancies

between different selves. Large discrepancies between actual and ideal selves have been associated with depression whereas large discrepancies between a person's actual and ought selves have been linked to anxiety.

8. Social-cognitive theories have proven especially useful in understanding depression. While some approaches have focused on depressive schemata, others have examined the attributional or explanatory style that depressed people employ to make sense of good and bad events in life. Research suggests that depression is associated with a pessimistic explanatory style, through which people attribute the causes of negative events to internal, stable, and global factors. This style of explaining negative social events may lead to self-blame and feelings of hopelessness and helplessness. Pessimistic explanatory styles are also associated with poor school performance, poor work performance, poor performance in athletics, poor health, and even untimely death.

9. Gender schema theory suggests that people differ in the extent to which they understand their lives and contexts in gender-related terms. People with strong gender schemas tend to process social information along the lines of traditional gender stereotypes.

10. The ultimate purpose of social intelligence is to guide social behavior. Social-cognitive adaptations such as personal constructs, cognitive styles, self-schemata, possible selves, and explanatory styles help to regulate social behavior in the service of personal goals. Self-regulatory goals and standards may be nested in a hierarchy from simple and concrete action goals to more complex and abstract organizing principles. Intelligent social behavior, therefore, may be regulated by informational feedback systems, organized hierarchically, whereby such things as personal constructs and self-schemata serve as reference points against which current behavior is compared. Deviations from the reference point stimulate change in behavior, as the system seeks to accomplish social goals that are consistent with a person's mental representations of the self and the social world.

CHAPTER 9

Developmental Stages and Tasks

Martin Luther was a Catholic monk in his early 20s when he suddenly fell raving to the ground one day and began roaring like a bull. According to three of Luther's contemporaries who witnessed the event, young Martin began screaming like one possessed by a demon after reading a passage in the New Testament about Christ's cure of a man who could not speak (Mark 9:17–27). In the midst of his fit, Martin was heard to exclaim *"Ich bin nit! Ich bin nit!"* ("I am not! I am not!"). Occurring during a period of profound religious doubt in Luther's life, his exclamation was a desperate cry of negation: "I am *not* this; I am *nothing;* I do *not* know who I am!"

Luther's emotional outburst took place some time around the year 1507 in the monastery choir, located in the German town of Erfurt. In psychological terms, the basic problem in young Luther's life at this time was that of *ego identity* (Erikson, 1958, 1959; McAdams, 1985a). In essence, young Luther was unable to formulate a coherent and convincing answer to the two fundamental questions of identity: "Who am I?" and "How do I fit into the adult world?" However, Luther soon made substantial headway in resolving his identity problem. By 1512, he had worked out an ideological solution. By 1517, he was translating the solution into radical public action. And by 1522, he had achieved the status of a religious and political celebrity destined to become one of the most influential men in the history of Western civilization. How did Luther do this? And what does his struggle tell us about personality today?

MARTIN LUTHER'S IDENTITY CRISIS

Martin Luther (1483–1546) is credited with starting the massive religious and cultural movement termed the Protestant Reformation, through which many Europeans severed their ties with the Roman Catholic Church and ultimately formed the various Protestant denominations of Christianity, such as the Lutherans, Methodists, Presbyterians, and Baptists. He is also credited with bringing the sacred writings of Christianity to the common people by providing the first authoritative translation of the Bible into German. He was a voluminous writer and a great preacher, and he wrote some of the most inspiring hymns in the Christian musical tradition. Outside the immediate domain of the church, Luther has been viewed as a monumental *political* figure in German history—one of the fathers of German nationalism and a hero for some revolutionaries. Of course, all of this would have been impossible to predict that day in the choir when young Martin fell raving to the ground. In 1507, Martin Luther was living out a rather conventional life story of the "good monk"—devoted to the Catholic Church and properly respectful of the authority of the Roman pope. The story changed radically, however, as Luther came to fashion a new kind of identity that provided his life with a sense of purpose.

One of the most provocative applications of personality theory to the life course of a single adult is Erik Erikson's (1958) psychobiographical analysis of Luther's identity formation, entitled *Young Man Luther.* Erikson began his analysis with the "fit in the choir." In this critical life event, Luther expresses the utter terror and confusion of a young man who has come to deny the very assumptions upon which he has built his own sense of who he is and how he fits into the adult world. The fit in the choir symbolizes the low point of Luther's identity struggle—the point in his own life where he felt cut off from all that had previously provided his life with meaning. In Luther's biography, this incident is sandwiched between two other key events.

Martin Luther (1483–1546) was the subject of Erik Erikson's famous case study of identity, *Young Man Luther.* Erikson (1958) showed how the leader of the Protestant Reformation struggled over many years to develop a sense of an adult self that provided his life with some measure of unity and purpose. According to Erikson, identity versus role confusion marks the key developmental task of young adulthood.

The first event took place in the summer of 1505. At this point, Luther was following the career path sketched out for him by his father, a middle-class copper miner and early capitalist named Hans Luder. Hans wanted his son to be a lawyer. Entering the University of Erfurt in 1501, Martin appeared destined to fulfill his father's wishes. On one fateful summer evening, however, Martin was returning to the university by foot in a fierce thunderstorm when a bolt of lightning struck the ground near him, hurling him to the earth and sending him into what some biographers have claimed was a convulsion. Before he knew what was happening, the 18-year-old Martin screamed out, "Help me St. Anne . . . I want to be a monk!" On his safe return to Erfurt, he entered the monastery, telling his friends and eventually his father that his experience in the thunderstorm affirmed a commitment to the Catholic church.

This would-be-lawyer-turned-monk was no ordinary religious novice. He prayed more than the other monks. He tortured his body and his mind by denying himself even the simplest earthly comforts and ruminating obsessively, day and night, over the meaning of the tiniest nuances of scripture. Erikson suggests that Martin's initial love affair with the Catholic church and with the idea of being the most devout monk the church had ever seen was too intense, too passionate, and it provided a thin disguise for a deeper doubt and ambivalence:

> It makes psychiatric sense that under such conditions a young man with Martin's smoldering problems, but also with an honest desire to avoid rebellion against an environment which took care of so many of his needs, would subdue his rebellious nature by gradually developing compulsive-obsessive states characterized by high ambivalence. His self-doubt thus would take the form of intensified self-observation in exaggerated obedience to the demands of the order; his doubt of authority would take the form of an intellectualized scrutiny of the authoritative books. This activity would, for a while longer, keep the devil in his place. (Erikson, 1958, p. 137)

But who was the Devil? And where was his "place"? As 21st-century readers, it is difficult for most of us to understand how literal a force Luther believed the Devil to be in his life. In the monastery at Erfurt, Luther struggled daily with the Devil, seeing him, fleeing him, fighting him, debating him, hating him, fearing him as a real person with superhuman power. Though many people of Luther's day believed, like Luther, that the Devil could be seen and tangibly experienced in daily life as if he were a flesh-and-blood person, few were as completely obsessed with the Devil's doings as was the troubled monk. In Luther's words, the Devil was "the old evil foe." In every human's raging war with the Devil, faith in God served as "the mighty fortress" and "sword and shield victorious." The battle cry was set to music in Luther's most famous hymn:

> *A mighty fortress is our God,*
>
> *A sword and shield victorious;*
>
> *He breaks the cruel oppressor's rod*
>
> *And wins salvation glorious.*
>
> *The old satanic foe*
>
> *Has sworn to work us woe!*

With craft and dreadful might

He arms himself to fight.

On earth he has no equal.

More significant from a psychological standpoint, however, was Luther's *projection* of the Devil onto others. Throughout his life, Luther cast his enemies in the guise of the Devil, responding to them in the same way he daily responded to the old evil foe. The best example is the Catholic pope (and the church establishment he represented) who became for Luther and his life story the prototype of the Devil incarnate.

The seeds of Luther's discontent with the pope and the church were sown in the Erfurt monastery as he witnessed the enactment of corrupt church policies. Chief among these was the practice of selling indulgences, through which a Christian could pay money to the church to purchase salvation for his or her dead relatives. The selling of indulgences was to become a rallying point for the entire Protestant Reformation as it came to represent both corruption in the church and the Catholic view of salvation as a commodity to be bought and sold.

By the time of his fit in the choir, then, Luther was renouncing his old identity as an obedient monk, identifying the Roman church as the enemy rather than the savior, and groping furiously for an alternative image of self with which to build a new identity. According to Luther's own account, his spiritual questioning and reformulation culminated in 1512 in a revelation of truth that took place in the Wittenberg tower. There, Luther was struck with a new insight into the meaning of the last sentence of Romans 1:17: "The just shall live by faith."

In the tower, Luther envisioned a new image of God more directly accessible to the common person than the distant God of the Catholic orthodoxy. According to Luther's radically new reading of this old passage, salvation was to be achieved by faith, not through good works or the sale of indulgences. God was not to be viewed as a distant force who waits for the day of judgment to decide if each man's and woman's earthly deeds merit entrance into the kingdom of heaven. Rather, men and women encounter God in the here and now—personally, rather than through the institutions of the church—through God's son Jesus; men and women need only accept Jesus—have faith that Jesus is the son of God—in order to be redeemed. For Luther, this religious insight consolidated his new identity.

The course Luther's life followed after the revelation in the tower of Wittenberg is summarized in Table 9.1. These public events and developments marked the rise of Luther as a religious leader in Europe and the spread of his influence in the Protestant Reformation. Over the course of his adult years, Luther continued to "work on" his identity. He continued to change and develop with respect to his understanding of who he was and how he fit into the world. But many of the key incidents that spoke to his identity concerns occurred in his late adolescent and early adult years. It is during this critical period in the human lifespan, Erikson argued, that many of us *first* confront the problem of identity. By contrast, children in grade school are not generally worried about who they are and how they fit into the adult world. And people in their 60s and 70s may not typically be as concerned about identity, either. Erikson's concept of identity is, therefore, a characteristic *developmental* adaptation. It is an aspect of personality that involves the resolution of important *life tasks* during a particular *stage* of development.

Some of the most illuminating features of human individuality cannot be understood outside of a developmental context. Erikson's concept of identity is one of those features. In accounting for Martin Luther's individuality, we might talk about his high conscientiousness and neuroticism. At the level of dispositional traits (chapters 4 through 6),

TABLE 9.1	MAJOR EVENTS IN THE LIFE OF MARTIN LUTHER
1483	Born into a strict and pious mining family in Eisleben in eastern Germany
1501	Became a student at Erfurt, then the best university in Germany
1505	January: graduated from Erfurt; May: to please father, Luther took up law; July: the thunderstorm incident, in which he vowed to St. Anne to become a monk; he entered the Augustinian cloister at Erfurt without telling his family
1507	Became a priest and celebrated his first mass at age of 23; then fell into severe doubts, which may have precipitated the "fit in the choir"
1512	Became doctor of theology at age 28 and gave his first lectures on the Psalms at the University of Wittenberg, where he experienced the revelation "in the tower"; formulated the essential Protestant doctrine that human beings are saved by faith, not by good works; despite having developed a revolutionary viewpoint, Luther still considered himself orthodox at this point
1517	Emerged as a practical reformer by preaching against the system of indulgences; On October 31st, he nailed to the door of Wittenberg Castle Church his 95 theses "For Elucidation of the Virtues of Indulgences"; This event has traditionally been seen as the starting point of the Protestant Reformation
1518	Luther was accused by many of heresy; he wrote to the pope in defense of his views
1520	The pope publicly condemned Luther and his followers and gave him 60 days to retract his heretical views; Luther publicly burned the document of condemnation; wrote major treatises on church reform
1521	The pope moved to have Luther excommunicated (expelled) from the church; Luther went into hiding
1522	Due to growing public support, Luther came out of hiding and resumed activity at Wittenberg; published German translation of the New Testament and continued controversial writing; composed hymns, including "A Mighty Fortress Is Our God"; Luther's activities began to motivate radical evangelists and political movements in Germany
1525	After expressing initial sympathy for the peasants' demands that serfdom be abolished, Luther sided instead with the lords and princes and called for the extermination of the "murdering hordes" of peasants; Luther married an ex-nun
1526	First son, Hans, born; Hans was followed by two more sons and two daughters
1526–1546	In these years, Luther was always active; he composed hymns, translated the Old Testament, issued many pamphlets, engaged in controversies with other reformers, and traveled extensively; he became the authoritarian father of the movement he had started
1546	Died in Eisleben

SOURCE: From *Luther,* by J. Osborne, 1961, New York: Criterion Books.

Martin Luther was consistently hard-working and strong-willed, he was subject to intense emotional mood swings, he could be stubborn and obsessive, and he seemed to oscillate between the two poles of openness to experience—that is, at times he was open-minded and advocated change, while at other times he was authoritarian and wedded to the orthodoxy. At the level of motives (chapter 7), Martin Luther seemed to move from high achievement motivation in his youth and early adulthood to high power motivation in midlife. In terms of social-cognitive adaptations, he had a relatively simple construct system (Kelly) that was dominated by the bipolarity of God versus the Devil. Indeed, the Devil may have represented one of Luther's possible selves (chapter 8), though the most undesired one. His explanatory style emphasized *external*, stable, and global forces: He believed that God and the Devil were the ultimate causes of earthly events. We can learn much about Martin Luther by invoking the concepts of personality from previous chapters of this book. But what Erikson believed to be the most important part of Luther's personality portrait—Luther's struggle to construct an identity—is left out until we begin to see his life in its full developmental context.

This chapter presents what I believe to be the two most integrative and influential theories of *development* to be found in personality psychology today. Erik Erikson's theory of psychosocial development lays out eight stages of life through which individuals progress, from birth to death. Each stage sets forth an agenda for human individuality by specifying the central psychosocial concerns an individual faces during that period in his or her life. Especially significant for students of personality psychology are the early-adult stage of identity, as illustrated in Martin Luther's case, and the two stages following it—intimacy and generativity. These three stages comprise the bulk of the human lifespan—from early adulthood up to old age. The ways in which people meet the challenges of identity, intimacy, and generativity are among the most interesting and socially significant aspects of human individuality to be found. Jane Loevinger offers a second influential developmental model—a theory of the development of the ego. For Loevinger, the ego is a person's characteristic manner of making sense of experience. While Erikson focuses more on the emotional and social aspects of the developing person, Loevinger's theory emphasizes cognition and knowing. Like the perspectives on personality covered in chapter 8, Loevinger examines how people make sense of themselves and the world in which they live. But unlike the approaches in chapter 8, Loevinger spells out the development of this sense making, from infancy into adulthood.

Human lives are set in time. At any given time point, certain developmental issues and developmentally anchored ways of knowing the world can take center stage in a person's life, as identity did when Martin Luther was a young man. Erikson and Loevinger provide us with two powerful frameworks for identifying these developmental adaptations.

ERIK ERIKSON'S THEORY OF PSYCHOSOCIAL DEVELOPMENT

Erik Homburger Erikson was born of Danish parents, in 1902, in Frankfurt, Germany. His father, a Protestant, abandoned the family prior to Erik's birth, and his Jewish mother subsequently married Dr. Theodor Homburger, a Jewish pediatrician. Growing up as Erik Homburger, the boy was a tall, fair-haired, and blue-eyed Jew of Scandinavian descent. To his Jewish peers, he did not look like a Jew. But he was not fully accepted by his non-Jewish peers, either. Thus, from an early age, Erikson cultivated an image of self as *outsider,* forced to define clearly how he was different from as well as similar to others in his environment (Friedman, 1999).

An unexceptional student, Erik Homburger never earned a university degree of any kind. Dashing his adoptive father's hopes that he become a physician, he wandered around Europe in his early 20s, studying briefly at art schools and painting children's portraits. "I was an artist then," he later wrote, "which can be a European euphemism for a young man with some talent, but nowhere to go" (Erikson, 1964, p. 20). During this very difficult period, Homburger experienced a crisis in identity that brought with it excessive anxiety and even occasional panic. A major problem was the young artist's inability to work with discipline and regularity (Erikson, 1975). In 1927, he moved to Vienna and accepted a teaching position at a small school established for children of Freud's patients and friends. He was received warmly by a group of psychoanalysts who included Dorothy Burlingham and Anna Freud, and he eventually undertook training in psychoanalysis with and was

Erik H. Erikson (1902–1994) articulated a highly influential theory of psychosocial development that divided the human life cycle into eight stages. Each stage poses a key challenge for the developing person and for the social world within which the person develops.

psychoanalyzed by Anna Freud. In 1933, Homburger emigrated to the United States and settled in Boston, where he worked as a psychoanalyst for children and associated temporarily with Henry Murray at the Harvard Psychological Clinic. In 1939, he became a naturalized American citizen and officially adopted the surname of Erikson, a highly symbolic event that marked the maturation of his own identity.

DEVELOPMENTAL STAGES IN CHILDHOOD

The strongest intellectual influence on Erik Erikson was Sigmund Freud. As we saw in chapter 7, Freud argued that the ultimate forces behind human behavior and experience are unconscious sexual and aggressive drives. Freud (1905/1953) proposed a model of human development that traced the evolution of sexual drives from birth to puberty. Freud used the word **libido** to refer to the energy that he believed was derived from sexual drives. He set forth five stages of the libido's development. In each stage, the libido expresses itself through a particular zone of the body, called an **erogenous zone.** In the first stage of development, for example, the libido is expressed through the mouth. The infant experiences sensual pleasure in sucking at the mother's breast and other oral activities. In Freud's view, the infant's sucking held more significance than the mere taking in of bodily nutrients. Sucking held psychological significance as well, establishing a bond between the caregiver and the infant and providing a model for later relationships in life.

Erikson's major innovation was to take Freud's *psychosexual* stages of the libido and transform them into a developmental model of *psychosocial* tasks. Erikson (1959, 1963, 1968, 1982) identified eight stages of human development and their corresponding psychosocial tasks. The first five stages, which run through adolescence, roughly parallel Freud's five psychosexual stages. The last three of Erikson's stages extend development through middle age and the later years. For all 8 stages, Erikson underscored the interpersonal-social-cultural-historical context within which the developmental tasks are given their various meanings.

For Erikson, each stage is defined by a polarity in which a positive feature of the stage is pitted against a negative feature. The polarity sets up a psychosocial conflict. At each of Erikson's eight stages, changes within the individual and within the individual's social world combine to create a central conflict that defines the stage. The conflict must be addressed, though not necessarily resolved, within the given stage, says Erikson, before the individual may move to the next stage. In a sense, the individual's experiences give rise to a unique question at each stage, which is typically "asked" and eventually "answered" through the individual's behavior. Though this question may not be consciously posed by the individual, the overall pattern of the individual's behavior within a given stage is structured as if the individual were asking a particular question. I outline the stages, their corresponding questions, and other associated features in Table 9.2.

For Freud, psychosexual development begins with sucking:

> Sucking at the mother's breast is the starting-point of the whole of sexual life, the unmatched prototype of every later sexual satisfaction, to which phantasy often enough returns in times of need. This sucking involves making the mother's breast the first object of the sexual instinct. I can give you no idea of the important bearing of this first object upon the choice of every later object, of the profound effects it has in its

	TABLE 9.2	**ERICKSON'S EIGHT STAGES OF LIFE**			
	Age	Psychosexual Stage (Freud)	Psychosocial Issue	Central Question	Associated Virtue
1.	Infancy	Oral	Trust vs. mistrust	How can I be secure?	Hope
2.	Early childhood	Anal	Autonomy vs. shame and doubt	How can I be independent?	Will
3.	Childhood (play age)	Phallic	Initiative vs. guilt	How can I be powerful?	Purpose
4.	Childhood (school age)	Latency	Industry vs. inferiority	How can I be good?	Competence
5.	Adolescence and young adulthood	Genital	Identity vs. role confusion	How do I fit into the adult world? Who am I?	Fidelity
6.	Young adulthood		Intimacy vs. isolation	How can I love?	Love
7.	Mature adulthood		Generativity vs. stagnation (or self-absorption)	How can I fashion a "gift"?	Care
8.	Old age		Ego integrity vs. despair	How can I receive a "gift"? (the "gift of life")	Wisdom

transformations and substitutions in even the remotest regions of our sexual lives. (Freud, 1916/1961, p. 314)

We see in this marvelous quotation Freud's idealization of the mother–infant bond. In the first year of life, the baby obtains both nourishment and pleasure from sucking at the breast (or bottle). Sucking reduces the tension caused by the hunger drive, and the reduction of tension feels good. The mother is generally the source of these good feelings, the provider of food and pleasure. She becomes the infant's first human love object. From this oral expression of the libido develops a lasting image of an ideal sensual experience, a legacy of pleasure that we, as adults, are fortunate enough to reexperience only in the most rewarding of our intimate relationships.

The infant in the **oral stage** is completely dependent on caregivers for the satisfaction of basic bodily needs. When the tensions produced by needs are consistently and regularly satisfied (reduced), the infant comes to perceive the environment as a relatively predictable and soothing milieu, laying the groundwork for healthy psychosexual development. Erikson agreed with Freud that for the first year or so of life the libido is centered in the oral zone as sucking at the mother's breast or bottle becomes the starting point of sexual life. However, the expression of the libido through oral activity is only a part of a larger, multidimensional development of a series of interpersonal relationships in the first year of life. These relationships determine the extent to which the infant will experience basic **trust** or security on the one hand and basic **mistrust** or insecurity on the other. Most important, sucking forms a bond of love between the mother and the infant. More than anything else, this bond of love has the potential to provide the infant with a sense of trust and security in the first year, a feeling or understanding that the world is safe, the environment is predictable, and life is trustworthy. Experiences of mistrust or insecurity will inevitably arise in the first year of life. The infant must and will experience both trust and mistrust: Healthy development is a function of the balance between the two.

In Freud's psychosexual model, the next stop for the libido is the **anal stage.** During the second and third years of life, the toddler's sensual energy is expressed mainly in "holding in" and "letting go" of feces. Retention and elimination involve regular cycles of tension buildup and release, again providing the experience of bodily, sensual pleasure. As the child's sphincter muscles mature, he or she becomes better able to determine when and where the "letting go" will occur. Successful toilet training, therefore, signals a certain degree of mastery over the sexual instinct in that the libido comes under the control of socially prescribed schedules. Being able to control one's bowels is indeed one of the first great accomplishments of the self, suggesting a sense of autonomy and self-mastery that may be reexperienced in subsequent episodes of personal success.

Erikson reinterpreted this second stage as centered on **autonomy *versus* shame and doubt.** Again, Erikson agreed with Freud that, as far as psychosexuality in the toddler is concerned, the libido expresses itself through anal activity, as in the holding in and letting go of feces. For Erikson, however, the centerpiece of the 2- or 3-year-old's psychosocial experience is the struggle to attain a certain degree of autonomy, freedom, independence, and mastery of the self, and to avoid humiliation, shame, doubt, and other experiences in which the child's budding sense of self-sufficiency is threatened. Therefore, toilet training is important not so much as an expression of the libido but as an achievement of self-mastery and control. Major advances in locomotion, language, and exploratory play in the second and third years of life provide unprecedented opportunities for attaining a certain degree of independence in the world. The child's environment must support his or her fledgling efforts to master the self and obtain a modicum of independence. As Erikson put it, the "environment must back him [the child] up in his wish to 'stand on his own feet' lest he be overcome by that sense of having exposed himself prematurely and foolishly which we call shame, or that secondary mistrust, that looking back which we call doubt" (1963, p. 85). The overlapping psychosocial themes of the second chapter of life, therefore, are independence, self-mastery, self-control, and the avoidance of humiliation.

Simply being autonomous and independent, however, is not enough for the average 4-year-old. Between the ages of 3 and 5, Freud argued, the child enters the third stage of psychosexual development, the **phallic stage.** At this time, the libido is centered in the genital region. Children become fascinated with their own sex organs and become overtly curious about sexual practices among adults. During the phallic stage, children may begin masturbating. These manifest expressions of the libido's latest adventures are mirrored by unconscious wishes regarding sexuality and aggression aimed at the parents. Because children may unconsciously experience sexual feelings toward one parent and aggressive feelings toward another at this time (Freud believed), Freud named this dynamic the *Oedipus complex*, after the ancient Greek story of the young man who unwittingly killed his father and slept with his mother. (As we will see in chapter 11, the story of Oedipus is central to the Freudian approach to interpreting life stories.)

Unconsciously preoccupied with Freud's Oedipus complex, and confronting numerous challenges to efforts to move forward and to expand influence in the world, the naturally egocentric child in Erikson's third stage of the life cycle is preoccupied with questions of *power*. **Initiative *versus* guilt** is the basic psychosocial issue for the preschool boy or girl. At this time in the life cycle, children begin to take initiative in their daily lives—striving to master, divide, and conquer their worlds. They experience guilt when their aggressive attempts to make the world their own run afoul and as they, often unwittingly, threaten to hurt or damage others and their environment.

Erikson observed major sex differences in this third developmental chapter in the ways children carry out initiative and seek power. Boys tend to adopt a more **intrusive mode** of operation, which includes "the intrusion into other bodies by physical attack; the intrusion into other people's ears and minds by aggressive talking; the intrusion into space by vigorous locomotion; the intrusion into the unknown by consuming curiosity" (Erikson, 1963, p. 87). Girls tend to adopt a more **inclusive mode** of operation that can be "teasing, demanding, and grasping" (p. 88). Both boys and girls, however, are "on the make," to use Erikson's felicitous term. Though their styles may differ, both boys and girls at this stage in development strongly desire to make the world their own—to be king or queen, all-powerful and all-important, the center of everything.

In the grade-school years, the child enters the fourth stage, called **latency.** Freud suggested that during latency the libido is rarely expressed in an overt manner. Rather, children channel instinctual energy into play, schoolwork, and peer relations. The elementary-school years are a time of expanding socialization as children come to internalize the values, norms, rules, and skills offered by society. For Erikson, the elementary-school child has begun a very important phase in which he or she will repeatedly face the challenges of **industry *versus* inferiority.** While internal changes such as the resolution of the Oedipus complex may help usher in this period, society overtly marks the transition with the virtually universal custom of beginning systematic instruction—schooling—of children at this time in their lives.

Beginning at age 6 or 7, children in most cultures undergo some form of systematic instruction outside the family. This schooling is designed to render the young boy or girl proficient in using the *tools* and assuming the *roles* of adulthood (Erikson, 1963). Tools include the basic implements of daily life in the society, ranging from bows and arrows to computers, which extend the powers of the human body and mind to promote the economic, technological, political, educational, and religious systems. Roles include those particular structured activities that adults perform with more or less skill as working members of society, such as the roles of teacher, parent, hunter, priest, and healer. Though children have been exposed to these tools and roles in previous stages, it is now time to learn about them in a systematic and societally scripted way.

The protagonist of the fourth stage in Erikson's scheme, therefore, is the industrious schoolchild immersed in the "reading-'riting-'rithmetic" of his or her culture. The child learns the rudimentary skills required to become a productive member of society, as well as the proper modes and manners of conduct expected outside the workplace. Erikson (1963) writes, "It is at this point that wider society becomes significant in its ways of admitting the child to an understanding of meaningful roles in its technology and economy" (p. 260). The elementary school child is learning how to be a good worker, a good citizen, and a good member of society.

Because this learning applies to matters that are both material and moral, economic and ethical, we may characterize the central psychosocial question of this stage as "How can I be good?" It is during this highly formative developmental period that churches and schools deliver their most influential lessons on how to be a good boy or girl. And though we may be able to distinguish from an early age the subtle differences between being "good" by getting an "A" on a spelling test and being "good" by telling the truth (Nucci, 1981), both involve *being good* and thus converge on the central theme of experience for the schoolchild living Erikson's fourth stage.

EARLY OBJECT RELATIONS

In his highly influential model of personality development, Erik Erikson broadened Freud's original conception of psychosexual stages to encompass the social and cultural world of the developing person. For Freud, the infant's sucking at the breast provides oral gratification of the libido; for Erikson, the sucking helps to establish a long-term attachment bond and an unconscious sense that the social world can be trusted. Like Erikson (1963), other psychoanalytically oriented theorists of the 1950s, 60s, and 70s proposed models of development that departed substantially from Freud's original views (Fairbairn, 1952; Guntrip, 1971; Kohut, 1971; Mahler, Pine, & Bergman, 1975; Winnicott, 1965). But whereas Erikson moved psychoanalytical thinking outward to society and culture, many of these theorists looked further inward to the intrapsychic arena of **object relations** in the first three years of life.

In the psychoanalytic tradition, the term "object relations" means interpersonal relationships. This odd usage comes from Freud's original idea that other people become the "targets" or "objects" of our sexual desires/drives. If I say, then, that my wife is the object of my libido, that means that I direct my sexual/sensual energies toward her. More generally, it means that I have a strong emotional relationship with her. Object relations theorists focus on these relationships, but they are especially interested in how these deep involvements with others are played out in unconscious fantasy, and especially in the unconscious fantasy life of infants and very young children. Like the attachment theorists we studied in chapter 2 of this book, object relations theorists argue that we internalize models of close relationships in the first few years of life, and these internalized object relations exert a critical influence on long-term personality development.

Margaret Mahler (1968; Mahler et al., 1975) developed an influential theory of object relations that focuses on the process of **separation-individuation.** According to Mahler, the infant begins life in a self-contained and oblivious state, begins to feel a sense of merger or symbiosis with others (objects) around the age of 3 months, and then gradually differentiates the self from that symbiotic union. The process of differentiating a separate self from the primitive sense of symbiosis or oneness with objects—the very process of separation-individuation—begins, then, around 5 or 6 months of age. In the first phase of separation-individuation (5–9 months of age), *differentiation of body image* occurs. The infant begins to understand that its body is separate from the objects of its desires. As the infant begins to move and maneuver, it may check back with its primary object (e.g., mother, caregivers), making eye contact with her or exchanging sounds for assurance that, while she is no longer in perfect unity with the infant, she is still there.

In the second phase, called *practicing* (10–14 months), the infant's expanded locomotor abilities enable it to explore the inanimate environment with much greater ease. The physical presence of the mother and other preferred caregivers promotes the infant's explorations, and when the mother is absent the infant may display low-keyed behavior, inhibiting exploration while focusing on an internalized, imagined maternal object (an image of the mother in the child's mind). Finally, in the third *rapprochement* phase of separation-individuation (14–24 months), the child develops an increased awareness of the mother's separateness and may undergo a crisis wherein the conflict between the urge to reunite with her and the urge to separate completely becomes intense. Eventually, though, the child moves through this difficult period and establishes a stable sense of self and other, achieving what Mahler called *emotional object constancy.*

Heinz Kohut's (1971, 1977, 1984; Wolf, 1982) influential version of object-relations theory is often called **self psychology.** At the center of personality, argued Kohut, is the **bipolar self.** Its two poles are (a) ambitions for power and success and (b) idealized goals and values. Linking the two poles in what Kohut described as a "tension arc" are the person's basic talents and skills. In a sense, a person is driven by ambitions and guided by idealized goals and values in accord with talents and skills. The bipolar self is structured in the early years of life as the child interacts with important

(CONTINUES)

FEATURE 9.A (CONTINUED)

self-objects in the environment. Self-objects are people so central to our lives that we feel that they are, in a sense, parts of us. The bipolar self evolves through relationships with self-objects.

In most cases, the most salient self-object in the first year or two of life is the mother. The mother is what Kohut calls the original *mirroring self-object*. With respect to the development of the self, one of the mother's main roles is to *mirror* the child's grandiosity. This means that she must confirm and admire the child's strength, vigor, health, and specialness. She must reflect and celebrate the child's budding agency and power. The mirroring relationship establishes, consolidates, and affirms the ambition pole of the bipolar self. Somewhat later in development, the mother or the father may serve as the *idealizing self-object*. The child admires and

identifies with idealizing self-objects as sources of strength, care, and calmness. The idealizing relationship establishes and affirms the second pole of the bipolar self, wherein are located the idealized goals and values.

Healthy mirroring and idealizing in early object relations paves the way for the development of a healthy and autonomous bipolar self. But mirroring and idealizing often go awry, Kohut maintains, resulting in the development of numerous pathologies of selfhood. Most common is probably the problem of pathological *narcissism*. In Kohut's view, extreme narcissists display an excess of pathological self-love and a disregard for others because early object relations in their lives never succeeded in providing them with the deep sense that they are special, worthy, and good.

THE PROBLEM OF IDENTITY

For Erikson, the early stages are but a prelude to the main act of late adolescence and young adulthood. As we saw in the life of Luther, it is at this time in the life course that the person seriously addresses the question of *identity:* Who am I? The four stages of childhood leave the person with a unique pool of resources and handicaps, strengths and weaknesses that will be called upon in the making of an identity. In this sense, the past (the early stages) partly determines the future (the later stages). But to a certain extent, the reverse is also true. The adolescent or young adult looks back upon childhood now and comes to *decide what childhood meant.* In that this decision is made after childhood actually happened, in some sense, the late (that which follows childhood) partly determines the early (childhood itself). We cannot literally change what has happened already, but we can change its meaning. This new meaning thus becomes another part of and influence upon the making of identity. In addressing the issue of identity, we look back to the past in order to arrive at a plausible explanation that tells us how we came to be and where we may be going in the future. In *Young Man Luther*, Erikson wrote:

> To be adult means among other things to see one's own life in continuous perspective, both in retrospect and prospect. By accepting some definition as to who he is, usually on the basis of a function in an economy, a place in the sequence of generations, and a status in the structure of society, the adult is able to selectively reconstruct his past in such a way that, step for step, it seems to have planned him, or better he seems to have planned it. In this sense, psychologically we *do* choose our parents, our family history, and the history of our kings, heroes, and gods. By making them our own, we maneuver ourselves into the inner position of proprietors, of creators. (Erikson, 1958, pp. 111–112)

Adolescence and Young Adulthood

In Freud's theory of psychosexual development, puberty marks the beginning of the libido's last stage—the **genital stage**—and the end of development. The physiological changes of puberty—such as the enlargement of the penis and testicles for boys, menstruation and the development of breasts for girls, changes in the distribution of body hair, changes in voice, the adolescent growth spurt—and the associated awakening of overt sexual longing in the teenage years signal the end of the libido's transformations. Erikson, too, viewed puberty as an ending and a transformation. It marks the end of childhood, thus closing the chapters of trust, autonomy, initiative, and industry. And it denotes the movement to a new stage that has momentous psychosocial consequences. For Erikson, physiological puberty combined with a number of other developments in the teenage years to usher in the psychosocial stage of **identity** *versus* **role confusion.**

Why do we confront the identity issue first in adolescence? There are many answers to this question, but they can be generally grouped into three categories: body, cognition, and society. First, as adolescents we find ourselves the unwitting inhabitants of new adultlike bodies—both wonderful and frightening—that seem qualitatively different from what we have known before. As you probably remember from your own experience, attaining physiological puberty is not simply a matter of getting bigger, as was the bodily transition from, say, age 6 to age 7. The emergence of primary and secondary sexual characteristics and the eruption of overt sexual longings at puberty tell us that, with respect to our bodies and our biologies, we are now truly different from what we used to be. Puberty, thus, may mark a turning point in the adolescent's perceived developmental course, as childhood comes to represent, in the adolescent's mind, a bygone era. In other words, the physical changes of puberty may help jog us into this sort of realization: "Hey, I'm not what I used to be: I'm not a kid anymore; I'm different from what I was before, but I am not sure what I am now."

Second, cognitive development may play a major role in launching the identity chapter of Erikson's generic life story. The developmental psychologist Jean Piaget (Inhelder & Piaget, 1958) argued that in adolescence many people enter the cognitive stage of **formal operations.** According to Piaget, at this time in the life cycle we are first able to think about

Adolescence ushers in a period of identity exploration. In their late teens and early 20s, young people living in modern societies face the challenge of finding a place for themselves in the complex adult world and developing an understanding of themselves that provides their life with meaning, unity, and purpose.

the world and about ourselves in highly abstract terms. In formal operations, one is able to reason about what is and what might be in terms of verbally stated and logically deduced hypotheses. Before adolescence, argues Piaget, we simply cannot do this. Therefore, the 10-year-old skillfully classifies and categorizes the world with wonderful accuracy and aplomb but is cognitively bound to the concrete world of *what is* rather than the abstract world of *what might be.* Ask a smart American 10-year-old to recite the capitals of the 50 states of the United States and you should not be surprised if he or she rattles them off with 100% precision. However, if you ask that same prodigy to speculate as to what the capitals of the United States might be if there were only 10 states, he or she is likely to have more trouble. First, the child may argue that the proposition is inherently ridiculous because the United

States *is* in fact made up of 50 states. Second, he or she may find it extremely difficult to devise a systematic plan for determining what the criteria of a capital should be in this hypothetical scenario. The 10-year-old is a slave to concrete facts: Reality is everything. For the adolescent or adult blessed with formal operations, on the other hand, reality is understood as a *subset* of what might be. The real is one manifestation of the hypothetical, and viable and internally consistent alternative realities can also be imagined.

The serious questioning of the self—asking "Who am I?" and "How do I fit into the adult world?"—is catalyzed by the cognitive emergence of formal operations. The adolescent may look at the realities of the present and the past and contrast them with hypothetical possibilities concerning what might have been (in the past) and what might be (in the present and in the future). This introspective and abstract orientation to self and world may result in the formulation of hypothetical ideals: the ideal family, religion, society, life (Elkind, 1981). Adolescents begin to take seriously the possibilities of alternative lives and systems of living, motivating them in some cases to explore new and previously unthinkable ways of experiencing the world and to question those things learned in childhood that now seem "old." Furthermore, the adolescent may observe his or her own behavior and thought and come to question what the basic links are among the various different and conflicting ways in which he or she approaches the world: "Is there a real *me* behind all the different roles I play?" Such a cognitive problem is not likely to occur in the mind of the 10-year-old:

> During the early years, the child has different selves and is not bothered by inconsistencies between them, by his lack of unity or wholeness. He may be one person with his parents, another with his friends, and still another in his dreams. The limitations of [childhood thinking] permit such shifting about and contradictions. ... The idea of a unitary or whole self in which past memories of who one was, present experiences of who one is, and future expectations of who one will be, is the sort of abstraction that the child simply does not think about. ... With the emergence of formal operations in adolescence, wholeness, unity, and integration become introspectively real problems. Central to the idealism of adolescence is concern with an ideal self. Holden Caulfield's preoccupation with phoniness is a striking example of this concern. [Holden Caulfield is the teenaged hero of J. D. Salinger's well-known novel *The Catcher in the Rye*.] He, and many young people like him, become critical of those who only play at roles, who are one moment this and another moment that. This critical stance is taken toward themselves as well. Wholeness is, thus, an *ideal* conceived in late adolescence; a goal which may be pursued thereafter. (Breger, 1974, pp. 330–331)

But the physiological and cognitive changes of adolescence do not tell the whole story of identity's emergence at this time as the central psychosocial issue in the individual's life. A third factor is society. Paralleling the changes taking place within the individual are shifts in society's expectations about what the individual, who was a child but who is now almost an adult, should be doing, thinking, and feeling. Erikson (1959) wrote, "It is of great relevance to the young individual's identity formation that he be responded to, and be given function and status as a person whose gradual growth and transformation make sense to those who begin to make sense to him" (p. 111). In general, Western societies expect their adolescents and young adults to examine the occupational, ideological, and interpersonal opportunities around them and to begin to make some decisions about what their lives as adults are to be about. This is to say that both society and the young person are ready for the young person's identity experiments and explorations by the time that he or she has, in fact, become a young person. As Erikson described it:

The period can be viewed as a psychosocial moratorium during which the individual through free role experimentation may find a niche in some section of his society, a niche which is firmly defined and yet seems to be uniquely made for him. In finding it the young adult gains an assured sense of inner continuity and social sameness which will bridge what he was as a child and what he is about to become, and will reconcile his conception of himself and his community's recognition of him. (1959, p. 111)

There is, however, a tension in all of this. It is the tension between the niche carved out by society and the individual's desire to carve out his or her own niche. In constructing an identity that "fits" into society's roles and expectations, the young person should not blindly conform to what the family in particular or society in general wants him or her to do. In a sense, this is what Luther first did, in his initial decision to become a monk. But as we saw later, Luther eventually went beyond the niche carved out for him in the monastery to create a new and unique identity within his expanding and evolving world. Yet Luther did not—indeed could not—separate completely from society and its expectations. Even in the most revolutionary lives, Erikson maintains, *the individual and society create identity together.* The adolescent or adult should be neither victim nor master of his or her socio-historical environment. Rather, the relationship between the self and society in the development of healthy identity is best characterized as one of dynamic tension.

Identity Statuses

One way to view identity is to focus on the *process* of formulating answers to the questions "Who am I?" and "How do I fit into the adult world?" during adolescence and young adulthood. According to this approach, the formation of identity in the adolescent and early adult years involves two related steps. In the first step, the young person breaks away from childhood beliefs and views, questions assumptions about the self and the world, and begins to investigate alternatives. During this first step of exploration, the person may challenge many of the viewpoints presented by parents, schools, churches, and other figures and institutions of authority. He or she may also come to question the past, wondering what might have been had things occurred differently in the earlier chapters of life—how life might be different now, for instance, if the person had been born into a different family, a different social class, a different ethnic group, a different society, a different period in history. Moving from what was and is to what might have been and what might be, the formal-operational thinker may begin to sample alternative beliefs, values, ideologies, behaviors, and lifestyles, searching for that overall approach to life that seems to "fit." The exploration ends in the second step of identity formation in which the young person makes commitments to various roles and outlooks that define how the young person sees him- or herself fitting into the adult world. In the second step, the questions and doubts of the exploration phase are resolved, and identity ceases to be a pressing psychosocial concern.

James Marcia (1966, 1980; Marcia, Waterman, Matteson, Archer, & Orlofsky, 1993) employs a semistructured interview to ask questions about exploration and commitment as they apply to the two areas of life that Erikson repeatedly suggested were at the heart of identity: (a) *occupation,* or what work role in society the person will occupy; and (b) *ideology,* or what the person's fundamental beliefs and values are, especially in the areas of religion and politics. Based on the responses to the interview, psychologists are able to classify young persons into one of four different **identity statuses,** displayed in Table 9.3. Each status may be viewed as a particular developmental position with respect to identity that the person holds at the current period in his or her life. Over time, people may move from one

TABLE 9.3	FOUR IDENTITY STATUSES	
	PROCESS	
Status	**Exploration, Crisis, Questioning**	**Commitment, Resolution**
Identity achievement	Yes	Yes
Moratorium	Yes	No
Foreclosure	No	Yes
Identity diffusion	No	No

status to another, as identity is negotiated and reworked in different ways (Bourne, 1978; Waterman, 1982). Marcia's methodology and classification scheme have stimulated a large body of research over the past 30 years. Most of these studies have been done with college students, who as late adolescents and young adults are likely to be dealing, in one form or another, with the issue of identity *versus* role confusion.

In terms of Erikson's theory, the most developmentally advanced of the four identity statuses is **identity achievement.** Identity achievers have gone through a period of exploration and have come out of it having made commitments to well-articulated occupational and ideological goals and positions. They have successfully met the challenge of Erikson's fifth psychosocial stage and are now ready to begin the sixth. Identity achievers strive for internalized goals and rely on their own skills and capacities in meeting daily challenges. Less concerned with winning their parents' love than are young persons in some of the other identity statuses, identity achievers may perceive their parents in balanced though somewhat ambivalent terms (Jordan, 1971; Josselson, 1973).

Several studies indicate that identity achievers are more academically inclined than persons in the other statuses. Cross and Allen (1970) showed that identity achievers received higher grades in college courses. Marcia and Friedman (1970) found that, among women, identity achievers chose more difficult college majors. Orlofsky (1978) found that identity achievers scored very high on the TAT measure of achievement motivation (chapter 8). Other studies suggest that identity achievers make decisions, especially moral decisions, in an autonomous and principled fashion. They tend not to conform to peer pressure and social norms (Adams, Ryan, Hoffman, Dobson, & Nielson, 1984; Toder & Marcia, 1973). And they tend to base their moral decisions on abstract principles of justice and social contract rather than the conventional laws of societies and the egocentric needs of individuals (Podd, 1972).

The second identity status identified by Marcia is **moratorium.** People in moratorium are currently exploring identity issues but have not yet made commitments. You might say that these people do not know yet who they are and they know that they do not know. Uncertainty about the present and future may launch, as we saw with Luther in the monastery, a full-blown identity crisis. But the moratoriums of the present should become the identity achievers of the near future as they pass from the sometimes anxiety-provoking period of exploration to stable commitment. Consequently, like identity achievers, moratoriums in college are usually viewed as relatively "mature" in Marcia's scheme, and many of the empirical findings for identity achievers also apply to individuals classified as moratorium. For example, both identity achievers and moratoriums create richer and more individualistic conceptions of themselves, compared with individuals in other identity statuses (Dollinger & Dollinger, 1997).

Marked *ambivalence* is probably the best term to describe the characteristic relationship between the young person in moratorium and his or her parents. In moratorium, the individual may seek greater psychological distance from the family, rejecting old identifications and ingrained values and beliefs and setting up the parents or other authority figures as temporary **negative identities** (Erikson, 1959). These negative identities come to represent everything the young person does *not* want to be. Therefore, parents may be cast into the unenviable role of "the enemy" in the adolescent's battle to discover what to believe and how to live as an adult. It is not surprising, then, that adolescents and young adults in moratorium often report stormy and contradictory feelings about their parents (Josselson, 1973; Marcia, 1980) as well as relatively high levels of general anxiety (Marcia, 1967; Oshman & Manosevitz, 1974). On the other hand, young adults in moratorium are often described as extremely friendly, likable, sensitive, and insightful (Josselson, 1973; Marcia, 1980).

In Erikson's terms, the person in the third status of **foreclosure** has failed to meet the identity challenge. In foreclosure, the young person fails to explore, but makes commitments to unquestioned positions taken from childhood. Rather than risk the uncertainty that might accompany a serious questioning of the past and of authority, the young person in foreclosure has opted for the security of childhood roles, beliefs, and expectations. With respect to occupation, the foreclosed individual "chooses" to do exactly what important authority persons have suggested, or perhaps insisted, he or she do. With respect to ideology, beliefs and values from childhood are transported into early adulthood intact and unsullied—rarely questioned and never reformulated. Not surprisingly, foreclosures report that they are very close to their parents, especially sons to fathers. They tend to describe their homes as loving and affectionate (Donovan, 1975).

Foreclosures appear the "best behaved" of the statuses (Marcia, 1980). College students in this status tend to study diligently, keep regular hours, and appear happy. The good behavior may be grounded in relatively traditional and conventional values adopted wholesale from authorities such as parents and the church. Indeed, a number of studies suggest that foreclosures adopt a more *authoritarian* outlook on the world than people in the other statuses (Marcia, 1966, 1967; Marcia & Friedman, 1970; Schenkel & Marcia, 1972). As we saw in chapter 5, authoritarianism is a constellation of traits and attitudes centered on submission to and reverence for strong authority, conventional societal values, and rigid standards of right and wrong. Foreclosures tend to show rigid, authoritarian responses to moral dilemmas and tend to obey the dictates of powerful authority, even when the authority asks them to do things that seem wrong (Podd, 1972). With respect to other personality variables, foreclosures score extremely low on autonomy and anxiety, and they tend to show unrealistically high levels of aspiration (Marcia, 1966, 1967; Orlofsky, Marcia, & Lesser, 1973).

Marcia's fourth identity status, **identity diffusion,** is the most enigmatic. Like foreclosures, individuals in the diffusion status have yet to enter exploration, but, unlike foreclosures, they have yet to make commitments. With few strong allegiances to the past and few explicit commitments to a particular future, these young men and women appear to be afloat in a sea of ambiguity. The few studies that have obtained clear findings on diffusions suggest that they may be best characterized by the word *withdrawal.* Donovan (1975) found that diffusions tended to feel out of place and socially isolated. They saw their parents as distant and misunderstanding, and they approached new relationships with extreme caution. Josselson (1973) points to fantasy and withdrawal as favorite coping strategies for women of diffusion status. Summarizing the little available evidence, Marcia (1980) concludes that diffusions "seemed to sense little past to integrate, little future for which to plan; they were only what they felt in the present" (p. 176).

Ruthellen Josselson (1996) conducted an intensive longitudinal study of 30 women who were categorized as college seniors into Marcia's identity statuses based on interviews conducted in 1972. Josselson found evidence for both continuity and change in identity from the college years into midlife. Describing them as *pathmakers,* Josselson (1996) shows that the women who were identity achievers in college moved ahead into their 30s and 40s with "a sense of conviction in the basic meaningfulness of their lives and choices" (p. 101). For pathmakers, "self-doubt was present but not disabling—they were aware that they might have made other choices, that some of their choices had led to pain or dead ends, but these women had the capacity to rally themselves and choose again, hoping to do so with better understanding and insight" (p. 101). The women who held the moratorium status in college continued to act as *searchers* in their 30s and 40s. Compared with pathmakers, they experienced more self-doubt and self-criticism and reported more vivid emotions and strong spirituality. Nonetheless, most of the searchers did, sooner or later, "find themselves," as Josselson puts it, and made the kinds of occupational, ideological, and interpersonal commitments so characteristic of pathmakers.

Ruthellen Josselson has conducted influential research on the development of women's identity from adolescence into midlife. Her in-depth narrative studies illustrate how some women who show identity achievement in college develop the life pattern of pathmakers in their midlife years. Other identity patterns identified by Josselson include searchers, guardians, and drifters.

Significant growth and development were also apparent among college foreclosures (Josselson's *guardians*) and those classified as identity diffuse in college *(drifters).* Though they remained more rigid and moralistic than other groups, guardians used their firm principles as a foundation upon which to build new and interesting self-conceptions. By midlife, many of the guardians had discovered "inner aspects [of themselves] they had long ago buried. What was silenced was given voice as they learned to live on their own authority" (Josselson, 1996, p. 70). Finally, the college drifters showed life paths that were "checkered and complex" (p. 168), but most of them had made considerable progress by midlife in organizing their lives around commitments and goals. Drifters reported the greatest number of regrets about their past, perhaps because of missed opportunities to seize the identity issue when it first appeared to them in their college years. Nonetheless, the drifters were actively exploring their options and revising their lives into their 30s and 40s. Josselson concludes that the central theme of their lives was "growing into greater consciousness and control" (p. 168). Making up for lost time, the women who drifted through identity diffusion as college students were now facing head-on the challenges of identity formation in their midlife years.

Identity and Intimacy

Erikson's stage model suggests that once an adult has arrived at some tentative answers to the question of "Who am I?" he or she is then psychosocially ready to begin the sixth stage of life, **intimacy *versus* isolation.** The relationship between these two stages, however, can be very complex. Many people seem to define themselves (identity) through intimate relationships with others. The proper sequence for the stages may indeed be reversed in many lives. Intimacy issues may arise before identity issues in many cases. Some have

Erikson identified intimacy versus isolation as a prime developmental task in young adulthood. According to Erikson, people who address identity issues before they embark on commitments in intimacy are better prepared, psychosocially speaking, for the difficult challenges of adult love and commitment.

suggested that women's lives in American society have traditionally exemplified a merging of intimacy and identity issues, such that a woman's identity is intricately connected to her intimate relationships. The establishment of the adult self and the development of intimate relationships may be difficult to separate from each other. Nonetheless, Erikson favored an idealized sequential scheme, suggesting that a person may be unable to be "truly" intimate with others until he or she has first made considerable progress in addressing the identity issue.

Most of the personality research that has addressed intimacy from an explicitly Eriksonian perspective has examined the relation between the resolution of identity and the quality of intimacy. Following Marcia's concept of identity status, Orlofsky, Marcia, and Lesser (1973) developed the parallel idea of **intimacy status.** These researchers devised a semistructured interview designed to determine the quality of intimacy in a person's life. Based on the respondent's answers to questions about dating, friendships, and interpersonal commitments, he or she may be classified as showing one of four intimacy statuses. Ranging from most intimate to least intimate, these are "intimate," "preintimate," "stereotyped relationships," and "isolate" (Table 9.4).

The small body of research employing identity and intimacy status constructs shows a modest but significantly positive correlation between the two measures. Orlofsky, Marcia, and Lesser (1973) found that male college students who showed the relatively mature identity statuses of identity achievement and moratorium tended also to exhibit the more mature intimacy statuses of intimate and preintimate. Tesch and Whitbourne (1982) examined the relation between identity and intimacy in 48 men and 44 women in their mid-20s. The subjects were administered the standard identity-status and intimacy-status interviews. The authors added a fifth intimacy status, termed "merger," which designated relationships in which one partner dominated the other. Some of the results of the study are displayed in Table 9.5. Men and women who had successfully resolved identity questions (identity achievement) tended to show relatively high levels of intimacy (intimate status). Those showing the lowest levels of identity resolution (identity diffusion) tended also to score at low levels of intimacy (preintimate, stereotyped, isolate).

Kahn, Zimmerman, Csikszentmihalyi, and Getzels (1985) examined the relation between the extent to which a young adult resolves identity problems on the one hand, and the quality of married life—assessed 18 years later—on the other. They found that the degree of identity resolution in young adulthood predicted the establishment (for men) and the stability (for women) of marital relationships at midlife. Young men with high levels of identity resolution were more likely to marry, whereas those with low levels of identity tended to remain bachelors. Young women with high levels of identity were less likely to experience divorce and separation in their marriages compared with young women scoring low on identity.

TABLE 9.4	FOUR INTIMACY STATUSES IN STUDIES OF COLLEGE STUDENTS

Intimate	The person works at developing mutual personal relationships and has several close friends with whom he or she discusses personal matters. He or she is involved in a committed love relationship. This sexual relationship is mutually satisfactory. The person is able to express both angry and affectionate feelings in the relationship. The person is generally interested in others.
Preintimate	The person has dated but is not involved in a committed love relationship. He or she is aware of the possibilities of relating intimately with another. The person has close friendships. The person has respect for the integrity of others, openness, responsibility, and mutuality. He or she feels conflicted about commitment, and love relationships may tend to be ambivalent.
Stereotyped	The person ranges from the moderately constricted and immature type of individual who has yet to go beyond superficial dating relationships to the playboy/playgirl type. Generally he or she has several friends; however, these relationships lack significant depth. He or she may date regularly but generally does not get involved.
Isolate	The isolated person lacks enduring personal relationships. Though he or she may have a few peer acquaintances seen infrequently, he or she rarely initiates social contact and rarely dates. The anxiety accompanying close personal contact forces the person to withdraw into isolation. The person tends to be anxious and immature and generally lacking in assertiveness and social skills. The isolated individual may present him- or herself as bitter and mistrustful or smug and self-satisfied.

SOURCE: From "Ego Identity Status and the Intimacy Versus Isolation Crisis of Young Adulthood," by J. L.Orlofsky, J. E. Marcia, & I. M. Lesser, 1973, *Journal of Personality and Social Psychology, 27,* 211–219.

TABLE 9.5	RELATIONSHIP BETWEEN IDENTITY STATUS AND INTIMACY STATUS IN A STUDY OF YOUNG ADULTS

	IDENTITY			
Intimacy	**Achievement**	**Foreclosure**	**Moratorium**	**Diffusion**
	Males			
Intimate	8	2	0	2
Merger	2	3	0	0
Preintimate	4	1	0	4
Stereotyped	0	2	0	1
Isolate	0	0	0	3
	Females			
Intimate	7	4	0	1
Merger	0	2	0	1
Preintimate	3	1	3	1
Stereotyped	1	0	0	3
Isolate	0	0	0	0

SOURCE: Numbers represent number of subjects (frequencies). From "Intimacy and Identity Status in Young Adults," by S. A. Tesch & S. K. Whitbourne, 1982, *Journal of Personality and Social Psychology, 43,* 1049.

GENERATIVITY AND ADULT DEVELOPMENT

The last two stages in Erikson's eight-stage model of psychosocial development correspond roughly to middle and later adulthood. Middle adulthood focuses on caring for and leaving a legacy to benefit the next generation. In later adulthood, the person is concerned with looking back upon his or her own life and coming to accept life as something that has been good.

Generativity *versus* stagnation is the seventh stage in Erikson's scheme, generally identified with that long period in the life course that follows early adulthood but comes before "old age." The prototype for generativity is raising children. By being good and caring parents, Erikson argued, many adults fulfill their basic "need to be needed" (Erikson, 1963) and directly promote the next generation. Yet there are many other ways to be generative, especially in one's occupational life, in creative activity, and through community involvements such as Girl Scouts, Little League, charitable contribution, church activities, and the like. In all of these endeavors, the generative adult acts on "the desire to invest one's substance in forms of life and work that will *outlive the self*" (Kotre, 1984, p. 10). The generative adult commits him or herself to some activity that is larger than his or her own life, investing significant time and creative energy into an endeavor that will "live on." Kotre (1984) identifies four different ways in which adults may be generative: through biological, parental, technical, and cultural generativity (Table 9.6). Connecting all four are *acts of caring*. In his psychobiographical study of the life of Mahatma Gandhi, Erikson (1969) wrote:

> A mature man of middle age has not only made up his mind as to what, in the various compartments of his life, he does and does not *care for*, he is also firm in his vision of what he *will* and *can* take *care of*. He takes as his baseline what he irreducibly is and reaches out for what only he can, and therefore, must *do*. (p. 255)

A Model of Generativity

Beyond Erikson, a number of theorists have written about the role of generativity in the adult life course (e.g., Browning, 1975; Cohler, Hostetler, & Boxer, 1998; Gutmann, 1987; Kotre, 1984, 1999; Neugarten, 1968; Peterson & Stewart, 1990; Snarey, 1993; Stewart & Vandewater, 1998; Vaillant & Milofsky, 1980). Generativity has been variously described as a biological drive to reproduce oneself, an instinctual need to care for and be needed by

TABLE 9.6	**FOUR TYPES OF GENERATIVITY**
Type	**Description**
Biological	Begetting, bearing, and nursing offspring *Generative object:* the infant
Parental	Nurturing and disciplining offspring, initiating them into a family's traditions *Generative object:* the child
Technical	Teaching skills—the "body" of a culture—to successors, implicitly passing on the symbol system in which the skills are embedded *Generative objects:* the apprentice, the skill
Cultural	Creating, renovating, and conserving a symbol system—the "mind" of a culture—explicitly passing it on to successor *Generative objects:* the disciple, the culture

SOURCE: From *Outliving the Self: Generativity and the Interpretation of Lives.* (p. 12), by J. Kotre, 1984, Baltimore, MD: Johns Hopkins University Press.

others, a philosophical urge for transcendence and symbolic immortality, a developmental sign of maturity and mental health in adulthood, and a social demand to create a productive niche in society. It has been identified with behavior (such as raising children), with motives and values (concern for preserving what is good and making other things better), and with a general attitude about the world (having a broad perspective and understanding one's place in the sequence of generations).

In order to create an integrative framework to guide research on generativity, my colleagues and I developed a model of generativity that brings together some of the best ideas on the concept and suggests specific ways to measure different dimensions of generativity (McAdams, 2001b; McAdams & de St. Aubin, 1992; McAdams, Hart, & Maruna, 1998; McAdams & Logan, 2004). The model suggests that generativity is a *configuration of seven psychosocial features,* all of which center on the personal and societal goal of *providing for the next generation.* To understand this model, you should think of generativity as something that exists both within the person and in the person's world. It is as much a quality of environments as it is a quality of people. In that generativity links the person and the social world, generativity can "happen" only in a psychosocial context, when certain variables within the person and in the person's world come together to provide for the next generation.

The model of generativity is presented in Figure 9.1. Starting on the far left, Boxes 1 and 2 in the model identify ultimate motivational sources for generativity. The first of these is (1) *cultural demand.* All human cultures demand that adults provide for the next generation. These demands are implicitly encoded in the societal expectations for age-appropriate behavior. In American society, we do not expect 10-year-old children to provide primary care for the next generation. We generally do not expect them to be thinking about the legacy they will leave after they die. But as people move into young- and middle-adulthood, we come to expect an increasing awareness of and commitment to their roles as providers. One of the reasons generativity emerges as a psychosocial issue in the adult years is that society comes to demand that adults take responsibility for the next generation, in their roles as parents, teachers, mentors, leaders, organizers, "creative ritualizers" (Browning, 1975), and "keepers of the meaning" (Vaillant & Milofsky, 1980). As adults move through their 30s and 40s, those who are unable or unwilling to contribute to and assume responsibility for the next generation, usually through family or work, are considered "off time" and at odds with the expected "social clock" (Neugarten & Hagestad, 1976; Rossi, 2001).

But generativity doesn't happen only because society wants it to. Many theorists suggest that generativity springs as much from deeply rooted (2) *inner desire* as it does from cultural demand. Two sharply contrasting desires have typically been identified. The first is a desire for symbolic immortality. As Kotre (1984) and Becker (1973) suggest, adults desire to defy death in symbolic ways by constructing legacies that live on. In generativity, the adult creates, promotes, nurtures, or generates something or someone in "one's own image"—as an extension of the self. One's generative legacy can be as humble as a wise piece of advice offered to a coworker. It can be as grand as raising a large family, building a business, composing a song, painting a picture, leading a community, making a discovery, or even building a nation. Ideally, the product of one's generative efforts outlives the self, such that mature adults ultimately come to define themselves in terms of what they leave behind. In middle adulthood and beyond, writes Erikson, "I am what survives me" (1968, p. 141). The second desire is what Erikson terms the "need to be needed," the desire to nurture others, to be of use to those who are in need. While the desire for immortality suggests power and self-expansion, the need to be needed reveals generativity's soft and loving side.

FIGURE 9.1	SEVEN FEATURES OF GENERATIVITY

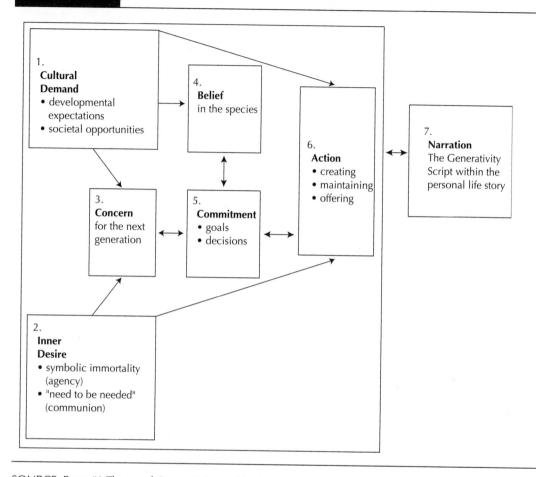

SOURCE: From "A Theory of Generativity and Its Assessment Through Self-report, Behavioral Acts, and Narrative Themes in Autobiography," by D. P. McAdams & E. de St. Aubin, 1992, *Journal of Personality and Social Psychology, 62,* 1005.

One of the most fascinating aspects of generativity is its conflictual essence—it celebrates the infinite expansion of the self and the surrender of the self at the same time. To be especially generative is to want to live forever and to want to give oneself up completely for the good of others, at the same paradoxical time.

Cultural demand and inner desire combine to promote in adulthood a conscious (3) *concern* for the next generation. Thus, developmental expectations about making a contribution to the next generation and inner desires for agentic immortality and communal nurturance come together in adulthood to promote the extent to which the person cares for and about the development of the next generation. Along with concern, an adult may develop what Erikson (1963, p. 267) calls a (4) *"belief* in the species" (Van de Water & McAdams, 1989). This is a basic and general belief in the fundamental goodness and worthwhileness of human life, specifically as envisioned for the future. To believe in the (human) species is to place hope in the advancement and betterment of human life in succeeding generations, even in the face of strong evidence of human destructiveness and deprivation. A strong belief in the species can help an adult translate his or her concern for the next generation into (5) generative *commitment*, taking responsibility for the next generation and making decisions to establish goals and strivings for generative behavior. When such a belief is lacking, however, the adult may find it difficult to make a strong generative commitment, because it may appear that a generative effort may not be very useful, anyway. Why commit yourself to promoting the next generation, some might say, if you think that the world is headed for disaster anyway and there is little you can do about it?

Guided by commitment, which itself is a product of demand, desire, concern, and belief, a person may act, may actually do something to provide for the next generation. Generative (6) *action* may be expressed in any of three loosely related guises: (a) creating, (b) maintaining, or (c) offering. First, generative action may involve giving birth to people, things, and outcomes—making, creating, generating, formulating, or discovering that which may be seen as "good." Second, generative action may involve passing on good things—preserving, conserving, maintaining, fostering, cultivating, nurturing that which is deemed worthy of such behavior—as in raising children, preserving good traditions, protecting the environment, and enacting rituals (in the school, home, or church) that link generations and assure continuity over time (Browning, 1975; Erikson, 1982). Third, generative action may involve the seemingly selfless offering up of that which has been created or maintained—passing something or someone on to the next generation as a gift, granting the gift its own autonomy and freedom (Becker, 1973; McAdams, 1985a). For example, the truly generative father is both a self-aggrandizing creator and a self-sacrificing giver. Biologically and socially, he creates a child in his own image, working hard and long to promote the development of the child and to nurture all that is good and desirable in the child. But he must eventually grant the child his or her own autonomy, letting go when the time is right, letting the child develop his or her own identity, make his or her own decisions and commitments, and ultimately create those offerings of generativity that will distinguish that child as someone who was "given birth to" in order to "give birth to."

Recent research has examined the relations among generative action, commitment, and concern and their relative salience at different points in the adult life course. In order to assess individual differences in an adult's conscious *concern* for the next generation, McAdams and de St. Aubin (1992) developed and validated the Loyola Generativity Scale (LGS), a 20-item self-report questionnaire. To assess *action,* they employed a behavior checklist that asks a person to endorse the number of times in the preceding two months that he or she had engaged in a number of different behavioral acts, many of which suggest generativity. Examples of possible generative acts are "taught somebody a skill," "served as a role model for a young person," and "performed a community service." Generative *commitments* were assessed by asking persons to describe 10 "personal strivings" (Emmons, 1986; chapter 7 in this book) or current goals that they were involved in, and then coding the responses for themes of generativity (McAdams, de St. Aubin, & Logan, 1993). Studies show that generative concern and generative actions are significantly positively correlated. In other words, people who express a greater concern for the next generation on the LGS also tend to report a greater number of generative behaviors over the preceding two months. Concern and action are also positively associated with number of generative commitments.

McAdams, de St. Aubin, and Logan (1993) administered measures of generativity to a community sample of 152 adults, divided into 3 age groups: young adults (ages 22–27), midlife adults (ages 37–42), and older adults (ages 67–72). Controlling for educational and income differences among the 3 groups, the researchers found a significant effect of age/cohort on generativity. Overall, midlife adults tended to score higher than younger and older adults, as can be seen in Table 9.7. In keeping with Erikson's idea that generativity is an especially salient issue of middle adulthood, the researchers found that generative concern and action were higher among adults between the ages of 37 and 42 than they were among younger adults in their mid 20s and older adults around the age of 70. (Other studies have also documented a rise in generativity scores through midlife; refer to Rossi, 2001.)

Not all measures of generativity show the same age-related patterns. For example, older adults in Table 9.7 tended to score just as high as midlife adults on generative *commitments*. By contrast, young adults showed remarkably low scores on generative commitments. Adults between the ages of 22 and 27 years rarely reported that the things they were trying to do everyday (their personal strivings) involved such generative goals as becoming involved with younger people, caring for others, or making creative contributions to others. By way of illustration, consider the daily commitments reported by three women in the study—ages 26, 40, and 68 years, respectively. The young woman reports she is typically trying to "make my job more interesting than it really is," "be more open to others," "figure out what I want to do with my life," "be a good person," "enjoy life," "avoid uncomfortable situations," "keep up with current events," "be well-liked," "make my life more interesting and exciting," and "make others believe I am completely confident and secure." Her strivings appear to revolve around social acceptance and the maintenance of daily well-being. There is no generative content, though she wishes to "be a good person." By contrast, the midlife woman describes 4 of her 10 strivings in generative terms. She is trying to "be a positive role model for young people," "explain teenage experiences to my son and help him work through difficult situations," "provide for my mother to the best of my ability," and "be helpful to those who are in need of help." Similarly, the 68-year-old woman writes that she is trying to "counsel another who was recently let go from job due to cutbacks," "help another daughter with her sick child," "help as a volunteer at a nonprofit organization," "assist a candidate running for election," and "offer financial aid to someone close (friend or relative) if needed."

The final feature of the model of generativity is (7) generative *narration*. Adults make sense of cultural demand, inner desire, concern for the next generation, belief in the species, generative commitment, and their own actions of creating, maintaining, and offering up in terms of their own narrative understanding of their lives, evolving over time. Adults, therefore, consciously and unconsciously narrate for themselves and others

TABLE 9.7	MEAN SCORES ON THREE FEATURES OF GENERATIVITY BY AGE/COHORT		
	Ages 22–27	**Ages 37–42**	**Ages 67–72**
Generative concern	40.14 (7.28)	41.82 (6.95)	38.26 (9.59)
Generative commitments	1.62 (1.43)	3.28 (1.78)	3.39 (2.19)
Generative action	26.63 (8.64)	31.55 (10.25)	28.16 (11.74)

NOTE: Numbers in parentheses are standard deviations.

SOURCE: From "Generativity among young, midlife, and older adults," by D. P. McAdams, E. de St. Aubin, & R. L. Logan, 1993, *Psychology and Aging, 8,* 225.

Generativity, the centerpiece of Erikson's midlife stage of development, is about making a positive difference for the next generation. As illustrated in these photographs, adults can be generative by raising and caring for children, doing community work, engaging in political activity, and in a wide range of other behaviors designed to leave a positive legacy of the self for future generations.

a *generativity script.* This is an inner story of the adult's own awareness of where efforts to be generative fit into his or her own personal history, into contemporary society and the social world he or she inhabits, and, in some extraordinary cases, into society's own encompassing history. In the context of a person's self-defining life story (a concept that I will explore in greater detail in chapter 10), the generativity script provides the adult with an envisioned ending. As adults envision how their own life stories will end, they give birth to new people (children), new ideas, and new creations that ultimately "outlive the self." Although generativity is likely to be a major concern from early adulthood onward, it may assume special prominence at midlife as the social clock suggests that the person begin the process of constructing endings, of figuring out how the story will eventually end. Of course, the literal end to life is a long way off for most midlife adults. But their apprehension that they are now at the midway point orients them to endings, motivating them to make sense again of the past and present in terms of an envisioned future ending.

Individual Differences in Generativity

In the 1990s, a number of researchers began to measure individual differences in various aspects of generativity and to relate these differences to a range of behaviors and outcomes. As I have already mentioned, my colleagues and I developed a series of paper-and-pencil measures for assessing generative concerns, commitments, and actions. Examples of items from the Loyola Generativity Scale and the Generative Behavior Checklist appear in Table 9.8. Other researchers have used clinical ratings of case data (Snarey, 1993; Vaillant & Milofsky, 1980), classifications of semistructured interview responses (Bradley & Marcia, 1998), self-ratings of generative attributes (Ochse & Plug, 1986; Ryff & Heincke, 1983; Whitbourne, Zuschlag, Elliot, & Waterman, 1992), Q-sort personality profiles (Himsel, Hart, Diamond, & McAdams, 1997; Peterson & Klohnen, 1995), content analysis of TAT stories (Peterson & Stewart, 1996), ratings of life goals (McAdams, Ruetzel, & Foley, 1986), and content analysis of diaries and other autobiographical texts (Epsin, Stewart, & Gomez, 1990; Peterson &

TABLE 9.8	SELECTED ITEMS FROM TWO GENERATIVITY MEASURES

The Loyola Generativity Scale: **Generative Concern**

For each item, mark "0" if the statement *never* applies to you, "1," if the statement *sometimes* applies to you, "2" if the statement *often* applies to you, or "3" if the statement *always* applies to you.

1. I try to pass along knowledge I have gained through my experiences.
2. I have made and created things that have had an impact on other people.
3. I have important skills that I try to teach others.
4. If I were unable to have children of my own, I would like to adopt children.
5. I have a responsibility to improve the neighborhood in which I live.
6. I feel as though my contributions will exist after I die.

The Generative Behavior Checklist: **Generative Acts**

Consider how often you have performed each of the behaviors listed below *during the past two months*. For each item, mark a "0" if you have not performed the behavior, mark a "1" if you have performed the behavior one time, or mark a "2" if you have performed the behavior more than once during the two-month period.

1. Read a story to a child
2. Taught somebody a skill
3. Donated blood
4. Attended a neighborhood or community meeting
5. Produced a piece of art or craft
6. Gave money to a charity
7. Assumed a leadership position in a group

SOURCE: From "A Theory of Generativity and Its Assessment Through Self-report, Behavioral Acts, and Narrative Themes in Autobiography," by D. P. McAdams & E. de St. Aubin, 1992, *Journal of Personality and Social Psychology, 62,* 1003–1015.

Stewart, 1990). The research employing these measures suggests that individual differences in generativity are significantly implicated in parenting behavior, social involvements, and psychological well-being.

An adult does not need to be a parent to be highly generative (Erikson, 1963, 1969). But highly generative adults exhibit different approaches to parenting compared with less-generative adults. Peterson and Klohnen (1995) found that highly generative women who were also mothers invested considerably more energy and commitment in parenting and showed an "expanded radius of care" (p. 20) compared with less-generative mothers. In two other studies, researchers have found that generativity in adults is associated with an *authoritative* approach to parenting (Peterson, Smirles, & Wentworth, 1997; Pratt, Danso, Arnold, Norris, & Filyer, 2001). As you may recall from chapter 3 in this book, authoritative parenting combines an emphasis on high standards and discipline with a child-centered and caring approach to raising children. Authoritative parents provide their children with a good deal of structure and guidance, but they also give their children a strong voice in making family decisions. In studies done primarily in the United States, authoritative patterns of parenting have been consistently associated with a number of positive outcomes in children, including higher levels of moral development and greater self-esteem.

In a large-scale study of children enrolled in public and private elementary schools, Nakagawa (1991) found that parents scoring high on the Loyola Generativity Scale tended to help their children with their homework more, show higher levels of attendance at school functions, and evidence greater knowledge about what their children were learning in school, compared with parents scoring lower in generativity. In a sample of both African-American and white parents, another team of researchers found that high levels of generativity were associated with valuing trust and communication with one's children and viewing parenting as an opportunity to pass on values and wisdom to the next generation (Hart, McAdams, Hirsch, & Bauer, 2001).

If parenting within the family is seen as the most private and local realm of generative expression, social involvements among one's peers, in churches, in the community, and through political action offer opportunities for a more public expression of generativity. It would be expected, therefore, that highly generative adults should show especially strong involvements in civic and/or religious affairs. In their study of African-American and white adults ranging in age from 35 to 65 years, Hart et al. (2001) found that high levels of generativity were associated with more extensive networks of friends and social support in the community and greater levels of satisfaction with social relationships. In addition, generativity was positively associated with church attendance and with involvement in church activities (also Dillon & Wink, 2004; Rossi, 2001). Furthermore, adults scoring high in generativity were more likely than those scoring lower to have voted in the last U.S. presidential election, to have worked for a political party or campaigned for a candidate, and to have called or written to a public official about a social concern or problem. Cole and Stewart (1996) found that generative concern among both African-American and white women in midlife correlated highly with measures of sense of community and political efficacy, suggesting that adults with strong generative concerns also tend to express strong feelings of attachment and belongingness in their communities and tend to view themselves as effective agents in the political process. Peterson et al. (1997) showed that generativity is positively associated with interest in political issues. And Peterson and Klohnen (1995) found that highly generative women showed more prosocial personality characteristics. Finally, in a nationwide sample of more than 3,000 midlife adults, generativity was the strongest psychological predictor of caring and doing for others at work, in the family, and in the community, even after controlling statistically for the effects of age and other demographic factors (Rossi, 2001).

Erikson believed that generativity was good for society and for the individual, too. The benefits of generativity should be seen in the strengthening of social institutions and the linking of individuals to both benevolent cultural traditions and progressive social change. At the same time, generativity should benefit the generative adult him- or herself. Erikson viewed generativity to be a sign of both psychosocial maturity and psychological health in the adult years. But what do the data show?

The data show that Erikson was probably right. Longitudinal investigations by Vaillant (1977) and Snarey (1993) have shown that ratings of generativity are positively associated with the use of mature coping strategies during times of stress and with clinically derived overall ratings of psychosocial adaptation. Studies employing the Loyola Generativity Scale and the Generative Behavior Checklist have consistently shown that these measures correlate moderately positively with self-reports of life satisfaction, happiness, self-esteem, and sense of coherence in life and negatively with depression (de St. Aubin & McAdams, 1995; McAdams, Hart, & Maruna, 1998). Similarly, Ackerman, Zuroff, and Moscowitz (2000) showed that generativity was positively associated with positive emotions, satisfaction with life, and work satisfaction among midlife adults. Among younger adults, generativity was associated with positive feelings about home life. Among midlife adults, self-report generative concern is negatively correlated with the Big Five trait of neuroticism (de St. Aubin & McAdams, 1995; Peterson et al., 1997). In a longitudinal study of women graduates from Radcliffe College and the University of Michigan, Stewart and Ostrove (1998) reported that, among a host of variables, quality of midlife roles and generativity were the only significant predictors of later midlife well-being.

Finally, in a nationwide study of American adults, Keyes and Ryff (1998) provided the most extensive documentation of generativity's relation to psychological well-being. The researchers found that nearly all their measures of generativity significantly predicted a composite measure of psychological and social well-being. Providing emotional support to younger people, feeling more obligated to society, having more concern for the next generation, seeing oneself as a generative resource, and possessing more generative personal qualities were all associated with higher levels of psychological and social well-being. As the authors conclude, "generative behavior, generative social obligations, and generative self-definitions are key ingredients in the recipe for psychological wellness" in adulthood (Keyes & Ryff, 1998, p. 249).

Integrity

The last stage of the life cycle, according to Erikson, is centered on the psychosocial issue of **ego integrity *versus* despair.** In old age, says Erikson, generativity fades as a major concern, and the adult becomes preoccupied with looking back and either accepting or rejecting one's own life as it was. In order to have integrity, the person must accept graciously his or her own life story as something that, for all its faults and foibles, "had to be and that, by necessity, permitted no substitutions" (Erikson, 1963, p. 268).

Erikson described integrity as a postnarcissistic approach to life through which a person looks back, reviews, and critiques the one life story that has been produced. Butler (1975) agrees, suggesting that many elderly people undertake a **life review,** through which they reflect upon the past in order to "settle accounts." Ego integrity seems to involve attaining a certain distance from one's own life. The elderly person who looks for integrity in life steps out of the life he or she has been making and remaking since adolescence— steps away from identity, in a postnarcissistic fashion. Now it is time to look back at the life as it was—not as something to be revised yet again, but as something to accept, enjoy, even savor (McAdams, 1993). With this acceptance comes a new wisdom, writes Erikson, which exists as the final virtue of the human life cycle. On the other hand, when the person is unable to accept his or her life as a gift, he or she experiences bitter despair.

Ego integrity and despair are probably the least examined of all of Erikson's ideas, the two most shrouded in conceptual mystery. One of the great mysteries concerns exactly *when* people encounter this final challenge of the lifespan. "Old age" is a very imprecise term. Many Americans who have been employed retire around the age of 65 or 70. The years of retirement may be seen as a postgenerative period in some, if not many, lives. Though many adults in their 70s and 80s continue to be generative by being grandparents and making other contributions to the next generation, others (finances and health willing) disengage themselves from virtually all generative pursuits and devote themselves to relaxation, fun, and golf. Does the concept of ego integrity aptly capture what is going on at this time? How do we make psychological sense of this kind of postgenerative period of the lifespan? Should it be seen as a kind of return to childhood? A reward for hard work? An escape? How does the older person make sense of this chapter in his or her life story in terms of those preceding it?

These are difficult questions that have generally not been addressed in personality theory and research. The healthy, postgenerative years that some American adults enjoy probably function in accord with a great many psychosocial demands that we do not yet clearly understand. To the extent that these years have anything to do with the urge to find ego integrity, they may be viewed as a movement away from seeing one's own life as a narrative in time. For some older adults, the "on-time" transition may, ironically, be a *transcendence* of time and the making sense of their life in time. In other words, the postgenerative years of healthy retirement may be the right time for loosening time's grip on the self. Certain Eastern religions and mystical traditions speak of the "eternal moment" that people experience when they have attained true wisdom and enlightenment. The enlightened person no longer struggles to make sense of beginnings, middles, and endings—time's great demarcations—in terms of unifying conceptions of the self and the world. The person simply exists in the moment, embracing all time in the present twinkling of an eye. Perhaps this is part of Erikson's message on ego integrity and why its attainment in the human life cycle must necessarily await the end.

JANE LOEVINGER'S THEORY OF EGO DEVELOPMENT

The highly influential theory of ego development proposed by Jane Loevinger (1976) is a neat complement to Erikson's theory of psychosocial development. Like Erikson, Loevinger proposed a broad theory that has implications for understanding the entire lifespan (Loevinger, 2002; Manners & Durkin, 2001; Westenberg, Blasi, & Cohn, 1998). Like Erikson, Loevinger utilized concepts that can be found in the psychoanalytic tradition. For example, Erikson is often viewed to be an "ego psychologist," and one of his central concepts is "ego identity." Similarly, Loevinger focused on the development of "ego." The two theories differ with respect to what aspects of human experience they seek to explain. By specifying a series of developmental tasks that confront all people as they move from birth to death, Erikson's model set forth an agenda for the *content* of human life. Erikson focused on *what* we do at certain stages in the lifespan—for example, in infancy we "do" trust versus mistrust; in late adolescence we begin to do identity. By contrast, Loevinger's theory focuses mainly on *structure* as opposed to content. Structure refers to *how* something is organized or designed. Loevinger is interested in how we make sense of and synthesize our experience as we move across the human lifespan. In simple terms, Erikson tells us what life contains, and Loevinger tells us how we organize (in our mind) those contents.

STAGES OF THE EGO

In Loevinger's (1976) view, the ego is "the striving to master, to integrate, to makes sense of experience" (p. 5). It is the general process by which each of us synthesizes or puts together our experience as our own. This fundamental process of selfhood—this sense of the ego or "I" as an active interpreter of experience—changes in significant ways over the course of human life. Loevinger's model of ego development charts those changes over time.

Loevinger's model is theoretically grounded in what she terms the *cognitive developmental paradigm* in personality psychology (Loevinger, 1987). Epitomized in the monumental work of Jean Piaget on cognitive development, this broad approach to psychology views the individual as an active knower who structures experience in ever more adequate and complex ways. Development is viewed as progression through hierarchical stages.

Jane Loevinger pioneered the empirical study of ego development in personality psychology. Each of the stages in Loevinger's model specifies a particular way in which a person makes sense of self and the world. Higher stages of ego development show greater complexity, tolerance, and sophistication in meaning making.

Earlier stages must be mastered before subsequent stages can be approached. Each stage builds on its predecessor and ultimately encompasses all that comes before it. Movement from one stage to the next is a complex product of both internal maturation and external forces, which are in constant reciprocal interaction. Higher stages of development are "better" than lower ones, providing interpretive structures for the world that are more differentiated, integrated, and adequate. These and other basic tenets of cognitive developmentalism are spelled out in great detail in the huge corpus of Piaget's work (for example, Piaget, 1970; Inhelder & Piaget, 1958); in the influential writings of Kohlberg (1969, 1981) on moral development; in Perry (1970) on intellectual and ethical development; in Selman (1980) on interpersonal understanding; and in Baldwin (1897), Werner (1957), and many college textbooks on developmental psychology.

Loevinger's stages of ego development are summarized in Table 9.9. Each stage is designated by a name (for example, the "impulsive" stage) and an "I" label (for example, "I-2"). Each stage provides an overall framework of meaning that the person employs to make sense of the world. The framework of meaning can be understood in many specific areas. Table 9.9 specifies three areas: impulse control, interpersonal mode, and conscious preoccupations. In general, as one moves from lower to higher stages, the ego becomes less the slave of immediate impulses and more a flexible agent that operates according to internalized standards of conduct. Interpersonally, the person moves from egocentrism through conformity to relative autonomy and mutual interdependence. With increased maturity, the issues that preoccupy the person's consciousness become less concerned with body and appearance and more centered on the internal life of feelings

TABLE 9.9	LOEVINGER'S STAGES OF EGO DEVELOPMENT			
STAGE		**TYPICAL MANIFESTATIONS**		
Label	**Name**	**Impulse Control**	**Interpersonal Mode**	**Conscious Preoccupations**
I-2	Impulsive	Impulsive	Egocentric, dependent	Bodily feelings
Delta	Self-protective	Opportunistic	Manipulative, wary	"Trouble," control
I-3	Conformist	Respect for rules	Cooperative, loyal	Appearances, behavior
I-3/4	Conscientious-Conformist	Exceptions allowable	Helpful, self-aware	Feelings, problems, adjustment
I-4	Conscientious	Self-evaluated standards, self-critical	Intense, responsible	Motives, traits, achievements
I-4/5	Individualistic	Tolerant	Mutual	Individuality, development, roles
I-5	Autonomous	Coping with conflict	Interdependent	Self-fulfillment, psychological causation
I-6	Integrated		Cherishing individuality	Identity

NOTE: The first stage (I-1) is hypothesized to be nonverbal and therefore not readily measurable.
SOURCE: From *Paradigms of Personality* (p. 226), by J. Loevinger, 1987, New York: W.H. Freeman.

and fantasies as well as internalized goals and plans. With development, the person becomes more cognitively complex, adopting more sophisticated frames of reference for understanding the world. Simplistic black-and-white thinking gives way to more subtle analyses and, ultimately, to a tolerance for ambiguity and paradox.

Loevinger's model of the ego is a developmental typology. While people are expected to progress through the stages in the order in which they appear, people differ with respect to their terminal level of development. In other words, people reach a particular stage and then quit moving upward, and different people quit at different stages. Individual differences in a given group are understood in terms of stages. An adult who is at the "conformist" stage of ego development (I-3) is a different "type" of person than an adult who is at the higher "autonomous" stage (I-5). Given that ego development seems to taper off after early adulthood (Lee & Snarey, 1988), it is not likely that the conformist adult will ever "catch up" with peers scoring at the autonomous level. This is a different understanding of "stage" than we see in Erikson, who assumed that normal human development involves the movement through *all* stages of psychosocial development.

The Infant

As we will see later, Loevinger measures a person's ego development through a sentence-completion test. Because this test requires verbal ability, infants and very young children cannot take it. Consequently, Loevinger's method of assessment does not enable her to measure the development of the ego in the earliest years. The first stage of ego development is a preverbal stage, Loevinger maintains, but her theory does not explicitly address what this stage is all about. A number of other theorists, however, have focused their attention on the first few years of human life, and some of their ideas help to put Loevinger's stage scheme into context.

Most theories of self assume that an infant is born without a sense of self-as-subject—without a sense of the "I." For example, Allport (1955) suggested that an early sense of self develops out of basic bodily experiences in the first year of life. In his interpersonal theory of psychiatry, Harry Stack Sullivan (1953) argued that a basic self-system emerges in the first few years of life to cope with the anxiety experienced in the presence of caregivers. In Freud's view (chapter 7), the ego emerges out of the id in order to meet the demands of the outside world. In addition, the infant comes to understand its separateness from mother with the realization that mother does not meet its every need. According to Mahler (Feature 9.A), the self emerges out of interpersonal relationships via a gradual process of separation-individuation. In general, various theories affirm the view of developmental psychologist Susan Harter (1983), who writes:

> The infant's first task is the development of a sense of self as subject. Thus, the infant must come to appreciate that he or she exists as an active causal agent, a source and controller of actions, separate from other persons and objects in the world. Once this "existential" self . . . has been differentiated from others, the infant must learn to recognize those particular features, characteristics, and categories that define the self as object. A representation of self that the infant can identify must be developed. (p. 279)

The precise sequence whereby the infant first develops a sense of the I as an active causal agent and then begins to formulate a self-concept has been outlined by developmental researchers such as Michael Lewis and Jeanne Brooks-Gunn in their studies of visual **self-recognition** (Amsterdam, 1972; Bertenthal & Fischer, 1978; Lewis, 1990; Lewis & Brooks-Gunn, 1979). In these studies, infants are observed as they behave in front of mirrors or as they watch themselves on videotape or in photographs. Lewis and Brooks-Gunn

Ego development begins with self-recognition. Research suggests that children begin to recognize themselves in mirrors and to develop a basic sense of self in the second year of life.

(1979) studied infants between the ages of 5 and 24 months, employing a wide variety of measures such as attention, emotional displays, play, use of the mirror to locate objects, pointing at the self, and labeling the self.

Studies show that between 5 and 8 months, infants show a wide variety of self-directed behaviors in front of mirrors. For example, they smile at their images and watch their bodies intently. However, they do not recognize distinctive features of their own bodies, and they do not appear to differentiate themselves from others. There is no evidence that they understand that what they see in the mirror is a reflection of themselves. Between 9 and 12 months, infants begin to understand the reflecting quality of mirrors. They will use mirrors to reach for actual objects attached to their bodies. Between 12 and 15 months, infants consolidate an initial sense of self as an independent causal agent. They will now use the mirror to locate other people and objects in space. When a person or object is spotted in the mirror, the infants will reach toward the actual person or object rather than toward the mirror. On videotape, infants are able to distinguish between their own movements and the movements of others.

Now that the basic sense of I is established, an infant is ready to build an initial conception of the self. This can be seen in mirror studies using infants between the ages of 15 and 18 months. In one version of this research, the mother applies rouge to the nose of her baby, leaving a large red spot that the baby can readily see when placed in front of the mirror. Infants younger than about 15 months of age will see the spots but not recognize them as alterations of their own faces. They may point at the spots in the mirror, but they are not likely to point directly at their own noses. After 15 to 18 months of age, most infants will touch their own noses when they see the rouge, showing that they have internalized an image of what their own faces should look like, that they recognize the image in the mirror as their own, and that they understand that the mark on the nose observed in the mirror signals that their own faces have been altered. The self continues to develop with the advent of language and the infant's increasingly sophisticated self-recognition behavior between the ages of 18 and 24 months.

The Child

A major theme in many theories about the childhood self is the progressive movement from egocentric *impulsivity* to sociocentric *conventionality*. The synthesizing framework of meaning whereby the younger child makes sense of the world is generally viewed to be simple, concrete, one-dimensional, and rather "selfish." By the time the child has reached the age of 9 or 10 years, however, the ego has become a more sophisticated and socialized structure for interpreting the world.

Loevinger (1976) argues that the self of early childhood is locked in an *impulsive* (I-2) stage. The child acts on impulse as a way of expressing the self. In general, the orientation of the impulsive stage is egocentric. The world is seen as a concrete setting for the satisfaction of personal wants and needs. The child is demanding and dependent in interpersonal relationships. Morality is primitive—what Kohlberg (1969) viewed as "preconventional morality," wherein the child understands good behavior to be simply and only that which is rewarded and bad to be that which is punished.

The impulsive stage as a general frame of reference is structurally quite simple. The child's classification of people into general categories of good *versus* bad is a global value judgment rather than an articulated moral judgment per se. Good and bad may be confounded with "nice to me" and "mean to me" or with "clean" and "dirty." Though emotional experiences may be intense during this time, the child's verbal descriptions of these experiences are relatively crude and global. The impulsive individual's orientation is primarily toward the present rather than toward the past or future. Loevinger states that the child who remains too long at this stage may be seen by others as "uncontrollable" or "incorrigible" (1976, p. 16).

Gradually the impulsive stage gives way to what Loevinger calls the *self-protective (delta) stage* of ego development. In Loevinger's view, self-protective individuals have "an appreciation of the world's rules, however wide their world may be, and know that it is to their advantage to play by the rules most of the time, (1987, p. 227). The self is a short-term hedonist at this stage, striving for the fulfillment of needs. The good life is the easy, happy life. Friendships may be viewed as nice things, to be collected, much like money: An older child or adult who stagnates at this stage may become opportunistic and deceptive in relations with others. As Loevinger (1976) puts it, "for such a person, life is a zero-sum game; what one person gains, someone else has to lose" (p. 17).

In late childhood and early adolescence, many people move from an egocentric frame of reference to an identification of one's own welfare with that of a group. This marks the developmental leap into what Loevinger calls the *conformist* (I-3) stage. Morality becomes what Kohlberg (1969) termed "conventional," defined strictly by the rules and norms of social groups or even society as a whole. People, as well, are essentially defined according to their group allegiances. The conformist values cooperation, niceness, and loyalty to the group.

According to Sullivan (1953), the conformist child or early adolescent is pressed by the emerging need for interpersonal intimacy to move beyond the safe maneuvers of the self-system and connect with others in collaborative and intimate ways. Interpersonal harmony, closeness, sharing, and identification with the other become the self's most cherished goals. The person seeks to find a special friend, or *chum*, who is as much like the self as possible. The welfare of the chum becomes a prime consideration, as important as one's own welfare. Through intimacy experienced with the chum, the self is able to affirm its fundamental *sameness* with another human being.

The Adolescent

If the ego of late childhood and early adolescence develops in the direction of conformity and celebrates its sameness with other selves, the self's movement through adolescence and into young adulthood is generally believed to be in the opposite direction. Many theories of self and identity suggest that the teenage years are marked by a search for individuality and uniqueness (Blos, 1979; Erikson, 1968). In Loevinger's model, conformity gives way to higher stages that emphasize how the person is no longer bound to social convention. From many different perspectives, adolescence in Western societies is often viewed as an extended *rite of passage* through which the person transforms him- or herself into an individuated adult (Conger & Petersen, 1984; Lapsley & Rice, 1988). In seeking individuality, the adolescent strives to integrate the various aspects of the self. Damon and Hart (1982) write:

> Virtually all researchers have found that, with development, adolescent self-understanding shows an increasing use of psychological and social relational concepts for describing the "Me," more prominent belief in the "I's" agency and volitional power, and a tendency

toward integration of the disparate aspects of the self into an internally consistent construct system. (p. 855)

As we have already seen, "the integration of the disparate aspects of the self" is Erikson's concept of identity. In formulating an identity, the adolescent and young adult must fashion satisfying answers to the questions "Who am I?" and "How do I fit into the adult world?" The search for identity is the search for unity and purpose in life. To experience unity and purpose, a person must construct a new image of self—a new Me— that incorporates the self into the world of work and love while providing opportunities for expressing unique talents, dispositions, and inclinations. The ego of adolescence and early adulthood, therefore, is an ever-discerning identity maker.

Many societies mark a person's passage from a child self to a young-adult self with a ceremony, such as the Jewish Bas Mitzvah.

According to Loevinger's theory, adolescence may usher in the transitional *conscientious/ conformist* (I-3/4) stage, as the young person realizes that it is impossible to live up to all of the standards of his or her self-defining group. The break with the group and conventional thinking begins slowly with an increasing self-awareness and an appreciation for a situation's multiple possibilities. The person becomes increasingly aware of his or her inner life. In the subsequent *conscientious* (I-4) stage of ego development, the adolescent or adult has moved considerably away from conventional standards and has substituted internalized personal standards. The major elements of adult conscience are now present: long-term, self-evaluated goals and ideals; differentiated self-criticism; and a sense of responsibility. Human behavior is understood in terms of internal determinants, such as traits and motives. The person experiences a rich and differentiated inner life.

The Adult

In realizing its full potential, the adult ego can become a prodigiously complex and sophisticated framework for making sense of the world. Loevinger's highest stages of ego development celebrate the synthesizing power of the adult ego. Nonetheless, Loevinger maintains that most adults fall well short of the self's highest levels. Research employing Loevinger's model of ego development suggests that most American adults score around the conscientious/conformist transition stage. Very few reach the highest echelons of her ego hierarchy. Writings on the adult self consistently reveal that many people are unable, due to a host of internal and external circumstances, to realize the full potential of selfhood. Somewhere along the line, the knower stagnates, and the process of synthesizing experience—the ego itself—settles into a routine that may be adequate for daily functioning but that is less than inspiring for further growth.

Let us, however, follow the ideal and unencumbered scenario as set forth in Loevinger's scheme. At the *individualistic* (I-4/5) stage of ego development, the ego develops a greater tolerance for the individuality of others and a greater awareness of the conflict between heightened individuality and increased emotional dependence. Though the realization that conflict is an inherent part of the human condition has not yet emerged, the person at the individualistic stage manifests an increased ability to tolerate paradox and contradiction—a sign of greater cognitive complexity. Distinctions are made between inner reality and outward appearances; between psychological and physiological responses; between process and outcome. Psychological causality and psychological development, "which are notions that do not occur spontaneously below the Conscientious Stage, are natural modes of thought" to people at the individualistic level (Loevinger, 1976, p. 23).

The *autonomous* (I-5) stage of ego development emerges with the capacity to cope adequately with the conflicts of the individualistic level. The individual at this level reveals tolerance for ambiguity and high cognitive complexity. He or she has acquired a respect for the autonomy of others while realizing that emotional interdependence is inevitable. Self-fulfillment partly replaces personal achievement as a central preoccupation in consciousness. The person at this stage expresses feelings vividly and convincingly, including sensual experiences, poignant sorrows, and existential humor intrinsic to the paradoxes of life. He or she formulates broad and abstract social ideals and makes decisions accordingly (Kohlberg's "post-conventional" morality). This developmental position is rare among adolescents and adults.

Rarer still is the fully *integrated* (I-6) individual. This is the most difficult stage to achieve. In general, most of what is true for the autonomous stage is also true at this level with the added elements of "cherishing individuality" and the full "consolidation of identity" (Loevinger, 1976, p. 26). At the two highest stages of ego development, the person transcends the polarities of earlier stages, seeing reality as complex and multifaceted. Opposites, from the vantage points of earlier stages, may be reconciled at the highest levels of ego development. Some of Maslow's "self-actualized" individuals (chapter 7) may be examples of people who have attained the integrated stage of ego development.

Most Western formulations of the self's maturation in adulthood may be critiqued for their overemphasis on themes of independence, autonomy, and self-sufficiency (Broughton & Zahaykevich, 1988; Josselson, 1988). Yet themes of inclusion, connection, and interdependence can be seen in Loevinger's and many other recent formulations of self-development, as well as in Erikson's conceptions of intimacy, generativity, and integrity in adulthood. Harter (1983) suggests that the highest level of the adult self may involve "the coordination of one's own identities over a lifetime, with those of others and with cultural values, so as to form a meaningful whole" (p. 317).

In a somewhat similar vein, certain Eastern conceptions as well as humanistic theories such as those of Maslow (chapter 7) suggest that ultimate selfhood entails *transcendence* of the individual ego and a *unity* with the cosmos. Such an "egoless" state is characterized by a total loss of self-consciousness and self-observation. Certain forms of Buddhism urge the adult to destroy the "illusion" of a separate I or ego. Enlightenment awaits the renunciation of self and the realization that one is subsumed by a larger whole. The same idea is expressed in other religious traditions. For example, the Christian concept of *grace* flies in the face of Western notions of the ego as an active and intentional agent. According to this theological view, Christian salvation cannot be willed. Instead, the person must surrender the self to the power of Christ's gift of love and redemption.

MEASURING EGO DEVELOPMENT

Loevinger's model of ego development has been especially influential in personality psychology because the ego stages can be measured via a standardized sentence-completion test, the **Washington University Sentence Completion Test for Ego Development (WUSCTED)** (Loevinger & Wessler, 1970). The WUSCTED is composed of a series of sentence stems, such as "The thing I like about myself is ..." and "At times she worried about ..." For each stem, the person writes an ending to the sentence. Each response is classified into one of Loevinger's stages, ranging from impulsive (I-2) to integrated (I-6), according to carefully designed scoring manuals (Hy & Loevinger, 1996; Loevinger, Wessler, & Redmore, 1970; Redmore, Loevinger, & Tamashiro, 1978). The scores are then tabulated and a final ego-stage score is derived according to a numerical formula. The WUSCTED is an especially useful instrument for examining individual difference in ego development among adolescents or adults. Because the test relies solely on verbal expression, all subjects must be able to read and write.

Table 9.10 presents sample responses scored for ego development to the especially self-relevant sentence stem of "I am ..." Loevinger's measure of ego development tends to be moderately correlated with intelligence test scores, with correlations between the two averaging between .20 and .35 (Cohn & Westenberg, 2004). Ego development is not synonymous

TABLE 9.10	SAMPLE RESPONSES OF WOMEN TO THE SENTENCE STEM "I AM..."
Stage	**Sample Responses**
(I-2) Impulsive	a good girl.
	always good and respectful.
	a very pretty child when I want to be; I am *(age deleted)* and have been told to be good, so I try.
(Delta) Self-protective	easily hurt, ugly, nosy and not very tactful.
	crazy and in love.
	completely frustrated with selfish people.
(I-3) Conformist	a student.
	lucky to have such a wonderful husband.
	happy, and in a good mood, so please forgive my foolishness.
(I-3/4) Conscientious/Conformist	content most of the time.
	worried about my love affair.
	hoping for a successful future.
(I-4) Conscientious	lucky, because I love life.
	no better than anybody else.
	sorry for causing mother to worry about me.
(I-4/5) Individualistic	a rather complex person—as we all are, I think.
	a woman, a wife, a student, an individual person.
	hopeful that the state of man will become universally better.
(I-5) Autonomous	an introvert, shy, with a desire to be friendly and outgoing.
	too much in love with everything, and, I imagine, too unrealistic!
	woman living and creating life.
(I-6) Integrated	aware of human frailty and weakness, yet I believe that man can, through his own efforts, improve his own lot.

SOURCE: Excerpted from *Measuring Ego Development 2. Scoring Manual for Women and Girls* (pp. 275–286), by J. Loevinger, R. Wessler, & C. Redmore, 1970, San Francisco: Jossey-Bass.

with intellectual ability. The WUSCTED appears to have adequate test–retest reliability and internal consistency (Redmore & Waldman, 1975). Scorers trained with Loevinger's extensive scoring manuals show very high reliability in their scoring of sentence stems.

A growing body of research attests to the construct validity of Loevinger's model of ego development and its measurement via the WUSCTED (Hauser, 1976; Lee & Snarey, 1988; Loevinger, 1979, 1983, 1984, 1987; Manners & Durkin, 2001; Westenberg et al., 1998). Cross-sectional studies of people from different age groups show that, in general, adults score slightly higher than adolescents and that older adolescents score higher than younger adolescents, supporting the developmental assumptions of Loevinger's measure (Loevinger, 1984). In junior high and high school, girls tend to score slightly higher than boys, but boys may catch up in college (Loevinger, Cohn, Bonneville, Redmore, Streich, & Sargent, 1985). In adulthood, men and women show comparable overall levels of ego development (Cohn, 1991). Overall, the most common (modal) stage score for American young people between the ages of 16 and 26 is I-3/4, the conscientious/conformist transition stage (Holt, 1980).

Ego development is positively associated with moral development as assessed according to Kohlberg's stage model (Lee & Snarey, 1988). With respect to personality traits, McCrae and Costa (1980) found no relationship between ego level and objective measures of extraversion and neuroticism. However, openness to experience (chapter 5) was strongly associated with ego development. People at higher (post-conformist) stages of ego development tend to score relatively high on openness to experience, reflecting an openness toward and tolerance for alternative points of view and strong aesthetic and intellectual interests. In another study pertaining to the Big Five traits, ego development among *women* was most strongly associated with openness to experience, but among *men* the strongest relation was between ego development and conscientiousness (Einstein & Lanning, 1998). Rootes, Moras, and Gordon (1980) investigated sociometrically evaluated maturity in 60 college women. After completing the WUSCTED, each woman evaluated all the others with respect to their potential for mature functioning in four adult social roles: career, marriage, parenthood, and community involvement. Ego development was positively related to peer ratings of maturity in careers and community involvement. However, it was unrelated to maturity in the two more interpersonally oriented social roles—marriage and parenthood.

Ego development is negatively associated with indices of deviance on the MMPI among adolescents (Gold, 1980) and measures of delinquency among inner-city girls (Frank & Quinlain, 1976). In general, however, ego development is *not* consistently associated with mental health and well-being. People at high stages are generally no more nor less likely to suffer from mental illness compared with people at lower stages. But mental illness may take different forms at different stages. For example, Noam (1998) has suggested that higher-stage individuals may suffer more *internalizing* forms of mental illness (e.g., depression) whereas lower-stage individuals may express mental illness in *externalizing* ways (e.g., antisocial behavior).

As you might expect, social conformity tends to peak at the middle conformist and conscientious/conformist levels of ego development and to decrease thereafter (Hoppe, 1972). Rosznafszky (1981) looked at ego development and individual differences in personality traits theoretically associated with particular ego stages. Employing the Q-sort personality ratings (chapter 6) of 91 hospitalized male veterans made by nurses, therapists, and the patients. Rosznafszky found strong connections between stages and ratings. Impulsive (I-2) veterans manifested significantly higher levels of confused thinking, poor socialization, and limited self-awareness. Conformist (I-3) and conscientious/conformist (I-3/4) veterans placed great value on rules, accepted social conventions, material possessions, and physical appearance, and they appeared highly stable. Veterans at higher levels (I-4 and I-4/5) revealed greater insight into their own personality traits and motivations behind behavior, and expressed concern about interpersonal communication.

Oliver John and his colleagues at the University of California, Berkeley, have recently argued that Loevinger's stages of ego development map nicely onto a tripartite typology of personality characteristics (John, Pals, & Westenberg, 1998; Pals & John, 1998). In chapter 6, I described personality typologies, such as those developed by Jack Block (1971), which attempt to account for human individuality in terms of coherent *patterns* of traits. York and John (1992) used Q-sort ratings and inverse factor analysis to derive four different personality types among the midlife women they studied. Three of those types are the *Conflicted, Traditional,* and *Individuated* types. In terms of traits, Conflicted types showed high levels of neuroticism and low levels of ego resiliency, described by raters as generally anxious, hostile, and aloof. Traditional women were high in conscientiousness and ego control, tended to hold very traditional values, and suffered from relatively high levels of guilt. The Individuated women were rated as especially high in ego resilience and openness to experience, and they showed strong levels of individual ambition and personal warmth. John et al. (1998) argue that personality characteristics of Conflicted types map onto those associated with relatively low levels of ego development, Traditional types map onto middle levels, and Individuated types share characteristics with high levels of ego development.

John et al. (1998) tested their hypothesis in a sample of women who graduated from Mills College in 1958 and 1960, the same sample used in York and John's (1992) study and in a number of longitudinal reports described in chapter 6 of this book. When the women were 43 years of age, the researchers classified each into one of the personality types outlined by York and John, based on a wide set of personality descriptors. In addition, each woman at age 43 completed the Washington University Sentence Completion Test, which was scored for stages of ego development. In this highly educated sample, the ego scores tended to be higher than those commonly found among American adults. Nonetheless, scores from across the ego range—from impulsive (I-2) to integrated (I-6)—were found. The researchers grouped the ego scores into three "regions." The low region consisted of impulsive (I-2) and self-protective (delta) scores; the middle region consisted of conformist (I-3), conscientious/conformist, and conscientious (I-4) scores; the high region included individualistic (I-4/5), autonomous (I-5), and Integrated (I-6) stages. The researchers predicted that Conflicted women would score in the low region for ego development, Traditional women in the middle region, and Individuated women in the high region.

Figure 9.2 shows the results of the study. As you can see, the findings support the researchers' hypothesis. For example, all of the women scoring in the impulsive (I-2) and self-protective stages of ego development were classified as Conflicted based on independent personality ratings. The middle region contains women of all three types, but the Traditionals predominate. Indeed, all of the women in the conformist (I-3) stage were rated as Traditional. The highest region of ego development has the highest percentages of Individuated women, although a few Conflicted women score at even the highest stages. In conclusion, the study by John et al. (1998) documents interesting linkages between ego development stages and independent ratings of personality characteristics comprising typologies. Women scoring at the highest levels of ego development tend to be classified by psychologists as Individuated and thereby rated as highly open-minded, introspective, and

FIGURE 9.2	PERSONALITY PROTOTYPES AND EGO DEVELOPMENT

The chart shows the distribution of three different personality prototypes—conflicted, traditional, and individuated—at each of six different levels of ego development. Conflicted types are overrepresented in the lowest stage, traditionals in the middle stages, and individuated at the highest stages.

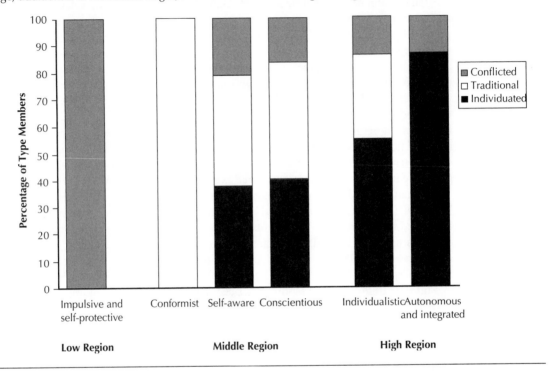

SOURCE: From "Personality Prototypes and Ego Development: Conceptual Similarities and Relations in Adult Women," by O. P. John, J. L. Pals, & P. M. Westenberg, 1998, *Journal of Personality and Social Psychology, 74,* 1102.

resilient under stress. Women in the middle regions of ego development tend to adopt conventional cultural norms and are seen as generally Traditional and dutiful. At the lowest levels of ego development, women are viewed as Conflicted, showing defensiveness, ambivalence, and high levels of dissatisfaction with self.

CONCLUSION

The two main theories of personality development that I have described in this chapter provide different but complementary views of how human individuality evolves across the human lifespan. Jane Loevinger's model of ego development charts the evolving sense of subjective selfhood—the ego—as it develops from a primitive and egocentric stance in childhood through stages of social conformity in the middle regions of ego development to the higher stages of autonomy and integration. Loevinger's theory focuses on systematic change over time in *how* people make sense of their subjective experience, the *structure of* their meaning-making efforts. Erik Erikson's theory of psychosocial development focuses less on the how and more on the *what*—that is, what kinds of psychosocial tasks and challenges a person faces as he or she moves across the lifespan, from birth to death. Each of Erikson's stages is defined by the *content* of a psychosocial dilemma, couched as a contrast between, for example, trust versus mistrust (infancy) or generativity versus stagnation (middle adulthood). If a person lives into old age, Erikson maintains, he or she will move through all eight of the psychosocial stages. By contrast, Loevinger's model suggests that most people will not reach the highest stages of ego development. Like Maslow's hierarchy of needs (chapter 7), Loevinger's model is hierarchical; the highest stages are built upon the lower ones, and most of us are unable to climb all the way to the top. Erikson's stages build on one another only in a very loose sense, in that successes in early stages can help promote development through later ones. But the later stages are not really "higher" in a hierarchical sense; they are simply "later" in time. You don't "climb up" Erikson's stage model; instead, you move across it, over time.

Both Loevinger and Erikson alert us to the fact that critical aspects of human individuality are contextualized in developmental time. If we are to understand a person fully, we must tap into those constructs of individuality that are anchored in development. Concepts such as "generativity" and "the conformist stage of ego development" cannot be understood outside the context of developmental time. Unlike dispositional traits (chapters 4-6), these kinds of concepts require a developmental framework to flesh out their meaning. Among other things, developmental adaptations suggest that people at different stages of development are to be understood with respect to different theoretical concepts. For example, a personality portrait of a 45-year-old woman would be very incomplete if it did not address the characteristic ways in which she has met the challenges of generativity versus stagnation. A personality portrait of a 21-year-old man, by comparison, may leave blank the concept of generativity but will instead focus on issues of identity and, perhaps, intimacy. In this sense, developmental constructs are contingent and contextualized. In sharp contrast, it makes perfect sense to speak of personality traits, such as extraversion and neuroticism, as they apply to both the 45-year-old woman and the 21-year-old man. Less contingent and contextualized than characteristic adaptations, personality traits offer generalizations about behavior that may be applicable across many different life contexts. A full account of human individuality, therefore, requires both kinds of perspectives. Traits (chapters 4-6) provide an initial sketch of human individuality; characteristic adaptations such as motives and goals (chapter 7), cognitive representations of self and other (chapter 8), and developmental tasks and stages (chapter 9) help to fill in the details.

SUMMARY

1. Erik Erikson's psychobiography of Martin Luther, the 16th-century church reformer, sets the stage for a consideration of developmental adaptations in the study of human individuality. Erikson documents the protracted identity crisis that Luther experienced as a young adult, beginning in 1505 when he decided to become a monk and culminating in 1517 when he nailed to the castle door in Wittenberg the 95 theses that instigated the Protestant Reformation in Europe. Erikson's concept of "identity" is a classic developmental adaptation, in that it specifies a particular psychosocial issue that lies at the heart of human individuality during a particular period in the lifespan. Like motives and goals (chapter 7) and like social-cognitive adaptations (chapter 8), developmental tasks and stages go beyond dispositional personality traits (chapters 4–6) to flesh out the details of human individuality.

2. Erikson articulated a highly influential theory of psychosocial development. The theory sets forth eight stages of development, each defined by a critical psychosocial dilemma. Erikson's stages build on Freud's model of psychosexual development, but they go well beyond Freud in emphasizing social context and interpersonal relations and in extending developmental change across the entire human lifespan, from birth to death. Erikson argued that at each stage a person's life must be understood on three different but interrelated levels—body, ego, and family and culture.

3. The first four stages in Erikson's scheme mark the childhood years. In the first stage of trust versus mistrust, the infant forms attachment bonds with caregivers and establishes a sense of security in the world. In autonomy versus shame and doubt, the toddler begins to develop a sense of an autonomous self. The stage of initiative versus guilt parallels Freud's phallic stage, within which the young child struggles with the dynamics of power and sexuality. Children in the third stage are "on the make," as Erikson puts it, as they vigorously seek to make the world conform to their own, sometimes egocentric, wants and viewpoints. The fourth stage of industry versus inferiority marks the child's movement into a broader world of socialization, as represented in schooling. Of central significance during this fourth stage are the developing use of tools and the emergence of important social roles.

4. Adolescence ushers in Erikson's fifth stage— identity versus role confusion. With the emergence of genital sexuality, advent of formal operational thinking, and rising cultural expectations concerning this period in the lifespan, adolescents first confront the psychosocial questions of "Who am I?" and "How do I fit into the adult world?" The problem of identity is the problem of finding unity and purpose amidst the diversity and contradictions of modern adult life. In order to consolidate an identity, a young person must develop an occupational niche and formulate a personal ideology. Research on identity has identified four different identity statuses among young people: identity achievement (the person has explored identity options and subsequently made identity commitments), moratorium (the person is currently exploring identity options but has not yet made commitments), foreclosure (the person did not explore options but made commitments to childhood or conventional modes of being), and diffusion (the person has not explored options and has not yet made commitments).

5. In Erikson's model, the person is best able to confront the sixth stage of intimacy versus isolation after successfully consolidating an identity at Stage 5. In intimacy versus isolation, the young adult seeks to form long-term bonds with others, epitomized in marriage or long-term romantic commitments. With the resolution of intimacy, the person is then psychosocially ready to address the issue of generativity versus stagnation (the seventh stage). To be generative is to generate a legacy of the self for the good of future generations. The prototype of generativity is giving birth to and raising children, but generativity can also be experienced and expressed in mentoring, teaching, volunteer work, community involvements, and a wide range of other behaviors.

6. Recent theoretical and empirical work on generativity has distinguished among many different features of the concept. According to one model, generativity begins with desires for both symbolic immortality (agency) and nurturance (communion) which are reinforced and augmented by cultural demands and expectations concerning how men and women should behave as they move into and through midlife. Desire and demand give rise to a concern for the next generation, which may lead to generative commitments and goals designed to translate concern into action. Generative actions may take the form of creating or giving birth to new things (and people), maintaining that which is deemed to be of good use for the future generation, and offering up those things that have been created or maintained to others. What Erikson identified as a belief in the species, or a faith in the worthwhileness of the human enterprise, helps

to enhance and vitalize generative efforts. Recent research has focused on individual differences in generativity, with studies showing that adults who score high on paper-and-pencil measures of generativity tend to combine warmth and discipline in effective ways as parents, tend to be highly involved in community and religious activities, and tend to show higher levels of psychological well-being. Following generativity versus stagnation, the last stage in Erikson's scheme is ego integrity versus despair, associated with old age and the challenge to accept graciously the life that one has been given.

7. While Erikson's theory focuses on the content of developmental tasks, Jane Loevinger's theory of ego development focuses on the structure of the self, or ego, as it develops over time. The ego is the master synthesizing "I" that adapts to the world and makes sense of it. The ego develops through stages, moving from primitive and ego-centric ways of knowing to more complex, differentiated, and integrated perspectives.

8. Although the newborn may not have a sense of subjective self, the ego emerges in development during the first two years of life. Studies of self-recognition behavior show that human infants develop a sense of self-as-subject—an active, causal ego—by the time they are about 18 months of age. During this time, the ego is in a preverbal stage. Loevinger's stage model begins once this initial stage has been consolidated. Thus, the first measurable stage of ego development in her scheme is the impulsive (I-2) stage.

9. Through childhood, adolescence, and adulthood, the sense of self moves through the impulsive stage to more socialized stages of conformity and conventionality. In the conformist (I-3) stage of ego development, the self interprets the world from the standpoint of "fitting in" to groups, seeking social acceptance and approval. The self begins to emancipate itself from convention in the conscientious/conformist and conscientious (I-4) stages of ego development, wherein self-evaluated standards replace concrete rules and group norms as guides for behavior. At the higher stages of ego development—the autonomous (I-5) and integrated (I-6) stages—the subjective self becomes highly differentiated and nuanced in its interpretation of experience. Higher stages are marked by concerns for self-fulfillment and actualization and the resolution of conflicts that emerge when individuality collides with interdependence.

10. Individual differences in stages of ego development are assessed through a sentence-completion test, developed by Loevinger and her colleagues. The test has generated a considerable amount of research. Studies show, for example, that while females score higher than males on ego development in adolescence, gender differences disappear by adulthood.

Making a Life:
The Stories We Live By

A year or two before he was assassinated, the Reverend Martin Luther King, Jr., came to a small city in the Midwestern part of the United States to speak to civic and religious leaders and to rally citizens, black and white, for civil rights. Jerome Johnson was assigned to be King's bodyguard. Johnson was a black policeman in his early 30s, an ambitious man who had been a football star in high school and who completed a tour of duty with the U.S. Air Force. Johnson dreamed of becoming a police chief. But he was frustrated. No black man had ever even been promoted to sergeant in that city, let alone been seriously considered for chief. Johnson's fellow officers counseled against taking the promotional exam. His friends told him that he should be satisfied with what he had. Johnson was beginning to lose hope in his dream. He was seriously considering quitting the force.

And then Martin Luther King, Jr., came to town, and this event turned Jerome Johnson's life around. In a life-story interview conducted more than 30 years later, Johnson described what happened:

> [The turning point in my life] was back during the time I had mentioned earlier [in the interview] about my thoughts and feelings about not taking the promotional exam the department had. Even thinking about leaving the police force because I felt it was a hopeless thing that a black could ever be a police chief. I mentioned before about quitting the basketball team [in college] and I have to say I had given strong thoughts to leaving the police force because of what I saw was happening to minorities there, you know, about [bad] assignments and all that stuff that happened. And then it was at the time I was assigned to be the bodyguard for Dr. Martin Luther King. And he was here, I think maybe two, three days. And so I spent some time with him. ... [On the last day] he was getting ready to leave, and he was standing in front of the hotel and waiting for transportation to take him to the airport. And we started talking, and I told him how frustrated I was about the fact that no black had ever been promoted. Maybe it's time to move on [I told him] because I didn't see there was anything that was gonna change at all. And he just said a couple of things, just very briefly he said, you know, he said, "Never give up." And that was basically the end of the conversation, and I thought about that before, but when he said it to me, and the way he said, "Keep the faith," you know, and "Never give up," you know, and "Never stop dreaming the dream," you know. And I held on to that, and I went on, and things changed. ... He turned me around from walkin' out the door. (McAdams & Bowman, 2001, pp. 3–4)

Jerome Johnson eventually took the exam and was promoted to sergeant. In the years following, he continued to rise through the ranks in the police department. He eventually realized his dream and became the first African-American police chief in that Midwestern town. After serving as chief, he took an early retirement. Today, Johnson spends more time with his wife and adult children. He plans to write a book about his experiences on the force. He hopes to be a grandfather soon. He invests a great deal of energy in volunteer community work with black youth.

Notice the structure of Jerome Johnson's turning point scene. The scene begins in hopelessness, but the situation is transformed rather dramatically by a fortuitous meeting with Martin Luther King, Jr. In simple terms, there is a movement in the scene from a negative situation to a positive outcome. Johnson's life story, as he tells it in retirement, is filled with similar redemptive scenes, in which bad events turn good. He begins the account of his life in this way. He was born during the Great Depression of the 1930s: "I was a Depression baby," Johnson begins, "so we went through some very difficult times, when there was, you know, no food and there was no money available. I do remember the struggles and things we had to overcome, and I really remember the hungry stomach and I remember the Christmases when there was nothing under the tree" (McAdams & Bowman, 2001, p. 6). But these difficult times eventually got better, and amidst the suffering Johnson recalls scenes of tremendous kindness and care. People were hungry, yes, but people also helped each other:

> I think about how growing up that things were like a real community. I mean, even though we were young and we were struggling and people all around you were all struggling, we all, people contributed to each other, you know. If we didn't have enough food, someone would bring us something. Vice versa, my dad would bring something in, and we'd be able to share that with somebody else, and just kind of a community of responsibility that was there and I think has always made an impact upon me, that people reached out and helped each other then. (McAdams & Bowman, 2001, pp. 6–7)

Jerome Johnson was an above-average student in school and a first-rate athlete. In a large and overwhelmingly white high school in the early 1950s, he excelled in football and basketball. In his senior year, he was voted captain of the football team. Johnson made many friends among the white students. He remembers fondly the many good teachers he had, and the football coach who worked hard to bring more black students onto the team. But like all his black peers, he was also victimized by racial prejudice. In one scene, his mother runs home in tears after attending a basketball game during which the opposing team taunted Jerome by calling him a "nigger." In another scene, school administrators refuse to permit Johnson, as football captain, to walk out on stage with the homecoming queen to lead the traditional homecoming pep rally before the school's biggest game of the year. He is black, and the homecoming queen is white. The image of a beautiful white woman and a strong black man standing together on stage and jointly whipping the crowd into a frenzy was just too jarring for some white teachers, students, and parents in this small American city in the early 1950s. Forty years later, Johnson says that he still feels pain when he recalls the homecoming scene.

But Johnson persevered, and prospered. Repeatedly, bad events turned into good outcomes. The high school "environment was very difficult to deal with," he concedes, but "I think the things I faced there helped me to be stronger in my lifetime" (McAdams & Bowman, 2001, p. 8). Through college and the Air Force, Johnson suffered his fair share of disappointments and setbacks, but he continued to grow in confidence and hope. Returning home after his military service, Johnson took on a series of jobs but made no progress until he joined the police force. In his mid 20s, he began to make long-term plans for his life. He will marry and have a family. He will rise through the ranks and eventually become police chief. He will do volunteer work in his community. He will build up a reputation as a good family man, solid citizen, and upstanding representative of the black middle class. He will be a leader. When asked to describe the high point in his life story, Johnson gives a detailed account of how he planned assiduously and worked so hard to become police chief, the strategic relationships he cultivated along the path, the vision he articulated for the future of the force. Throughout Johnson's story, he is the ever-hopeful protagonist who works hard to overcome obstacles and accomplish his goals. In his spare time, Johnson reads books about slave life and the history of blacks, "What they went through and overcame." "I guess I'm kind of one-dimensional on this," Johnson admits (McAdams & Bowman, 2001, p. 9). His favorite stories from childhood were his grandfather's tales of overcoming adversity.

What might we say about Jerome Johnson's personality? Given the proper research instruments, we could certainly evaluate his dispositional traits. Indeed, the questionnaires

Johnson completed suggest that he scores high in conscientiousness and agreeableness, in the moderate range on openness to experience and extraversion–introversion, and low in neuroticism. As we saw in chapters 4 through 6, trait attributions such as these provide an invaluable outline of a person's dispositional signature. To fill in some of the details, we might move to a second level of personality description, to specify the characteristic adaptations in Jerome Johnson's life (chapters 7 through 9). He would appear to be a man with strong achievement motivation and clear goals to be a grandfather and to continue his work as a community volunteer in the future (chapter 7). In terms of Kelly's cognitive theory, Johnson has developed strong personal constructs around the polarity of "hard work versus laziness" and "helping others versus self-indulgence"; his self-schemata likely capture these important social-cognitive distinctions that he repeatedly makes (chapter 8). With respect to developmental adaptations, Johnson appears to be in Erikson's seventh stage of "generativity versus stagnation"—indeed he appears to be a highly generative man—and his sentence-completion responses place him roughly in the Conscientious/Conformist stage (I-3/4) in Loevinger's developmental scheme (chapter 9). The Conscientious/Conformist stage is the most common ego stage among American adults.

Dispositional traits and characteristic adaptations do a good job of outlining and fleshing out some of the most important features of Jerome Johnson's individuality. But when we hear Johnson describe his encounter with Martin Luther King, Jr., and his account of growing up poor in the Depression and rising in society to become a chief of police, we may feel that the trait attributions and the analysis of motivational, social-cognitive, and developmental adaptations leave something out. We may feel that while we have a good understanding of behavioral consistencies in Johnson's life (via traits) and a good understanding of what his central motives and goals are, how he characteristically construes self and social behavior, and what developmental tasks he currently faces, we may nonetheless feel that something is missing from the picture. That something is *what Jerome Johnson's life means in the overall to Jerome Johnson.* In modern society, many men and women expect that their own lives and the lives of others should be endowed with some central meaning, some overall unity and purpose (Taylor, 1989). As we saw in chapter 3, cultural modernity has raised people's awareness of the extent to which they are responsible for constructing a self or identity that provides their own lives with some sense of overall meaning. While traits, motives, values, stages, and so on may hint at important meanings that people develop in their lives, none of the constructs that personality psychologists study at what I have identified in this book as Levels 1 and 2 have the breadth and scope to provide a full account of overall meaning and purpose in life. None of these concepts is integrative enough; none is able to put together the many different aspects of a human life into some kind of meaningful whole.

In the modern world, what gives human lives meaning and purpose? Many scholars have recently argued that modern lives are meaningful to the extent that they conform to or express culturally meaningful *stories* (Bruner, 1990; Cohler, 1982; Josselson, 1995; MacIntyre, 1984; McAdams, 1985b, 1990; Polkinghorne, 1988). In the modern world, writes Anthony Giddens (1991), "a person's identity is not to be found in behavior, nor—important though this is—in the reactions of others, but in the capacity *to keep a particular narrative going*" (p. 54). Jerome Johnson tells a life story in which negative events are repeatedly redeemed by positive outcomes. Beginning in the Great Depression and running into the late 1990s, it is a story of steady progress in the face of many obstacles, especially those obstacles related to race and class. The key event in the story is a transformative encounter with a famous historical person. Jerome Johnson's life story is unique to Jerome Johnson, but like most any life story constructed by an American adult, it is filled with some of the classic features of Western narrative: a setting, main characters (including heroes and villains), plots and subplots (stimulated by problems or conflicts), key scenes (high points, low points, turning points), and an envisioned ending (imagined for the future). Like you and me, Jerome Johnson "has" and is "working on" a life story. In order to provide a detailed account of Jerome Johnson's individuality, we must have some understanding of that story.

In this chapter, we will focus on people's life stories. We will see that a life story is not simply an objective account of "what really happened" in the past. Though life stories are (and should be) grounded in reality, they are nonetheless *imaginative and creative productions that each of us constructs and reconstructs as we move through our adult years.* Put differently, *we make a life by making a story,* and the stories we make become parts of who we are (Habermas & Bluck, 2000). A person's internalized and evolving life story—what we call a person's *narrative identity*—is just as much a part of his or her personality as are his or her dispositional traits and characteristic adaptations (McAdams, 1995, 1996a; Singer, 2004). While life stories are no less or more important for understanding a person than are traits and adaptations, they do provide a different kind of information about human individuality. Put simply, traits (Level 1) provide a dispositional outline concerning cross-situational trends in behavior; characteristic adaptations (Level 2) fill in the details by specifying motivational, social-cognitive, and developmental issues and concerns; life stories (Level 3) tell us how a person sees his or her life in the overall and over time and what the *overall meaning and purpose of that life* might be. All three levels of personality are important. In order to obtain as full an account as possible of human individuality, the personality psychologist needs to examine the person's patterning of dispositional traits, characteristic adaptations, and integrative life stories.

THE MEANING OF STORIES

THE NARRATING MIND

Human beings are storytellers by nature. In its many guises as folk tale, legend, myth, epic, history, pantomime, motion pictures, and even the evening news, that form of expression we call "the story" appears in every known human culture (Mink, 1978; Sarbin, 1986). The story is a natural package for organizing many different kinds of information. Storytelling appears to be a fundamental way of expressing ourselves and our worlds to others (Coles, 1989; Howard, 1989; Linde, 1990; Vitz, 1990). Think of the last time you tried to explain something really important about yourself to another person. The chances are good that you accomplished this task by telling a story. Or think of an especially intimate conversation from your past. I suspect that what made the conversation good was the kind of stories that were told and the manner in which the stories were received. Indeed, much of what passes for everyday conversation between people is storytelling of one form or another. We are born to tell stories, some scholars suggest. This is part of what makes us so different from both the beasts and the computers.

Imagine our ancient ancestors, at day's end, in that ambiguous interlude between the victories and defeats of the daylight and the deep sleep of the dark. Home from the hunt, or resting at the end of a day's foraging for food, providing for the young, or defending the tribe, our primordial forebears sit down together and take stock. Before night falls, they tell stories of the day. They pass the time by making sense of past time. They tell of their experiences to entertain and enlighten each other, and perhaps, on occasion, just to stay awake. E. M. Forster (1954), the novelist and essayist, once wrote: "[Primordial] man listened to stories, if one may judge by the shape of his skull. The primitive audience was an audience of shock-heads, gaping round the campfire, fatigued with contending against the mammoth or the whooly rhinoceros, and only kept awake by suspense. What would happen next?"

The stories told at day's end created a shared history of people, linking them in time and event, as actors, tellers, and audience in an unfolding drama of life that was made more in the telling than in the actual events to be told. Stories are not like the secretary's minutes of the last meeting, written to report exactly what transpired at the meeting and at what time. Stories do not work to replay a videotaped past that can be objectively known and reviewed. Stories are less about facts and more about meanings. In the subjective and embellished telling of the past, the past is constructed—history is made. The history is judged to be true or false not solely with respect to its adherence to empirical fact. Rather h*istory* is judged with respect to such narrative criteria as "believability" and "coherence." There is a *narrative truth* in life that seems quite removed from logic, science, and empirical demonstration (Spence, 1982). It is the truth of a "good story." In the words of one writer, this is a form of truth with which our ancient ancestors were intimately familiar:

> No one in the world knew what truth was till someone had told a story. It was not there in the moment of lightning or the cry of the beast, but in the story of those things afterwards, making them part of human life. Our distant savage ancestor gloried as he told—or acted out or danced—the story of the great kill in the dark forest, and that story entered the life of the tribe and by it the tribe came to know itself. On such a day against the beast we fought and won, and here we live to tell the tale. A tale much embellished but truthful even so, for truth is not simply what happened but how we felt about it when it was happening, and how we feel about it now. (Rouse, 1978, p. 99)

A !Kung bushman enthralls his audience with a story. People tell stories in all human cultures. Stories function to entertain and instruct, and they are used to explain and integrate human lives.

Contemporary research in cognitive neuroscience suggests that the human brain is designed to construe experience in narrative terms. Damasio (1999, p. 30) writes that "consciousness begins when brains acquire the power, the simple power I must add, of telling a story without words, the story that there is life ticking away in an organism." What Damasio is saying here is that human consciousness is a matter of mentally taking on the position of a *narrator*. Consciousness involves the continuous narration or telling of lived experience, a kind of stream of online narration that flows through the minds of most sentient human beings. The telling does not, at first, require words, but the eventual development of language certainly influences the quality of our consciousness. While the brain may contain many different modules each designed to perform a specific function, integration amidst the multiplicity is nonetheless achieved by virtue of the brain's power to construct and interpret personal experience through stories. In an article entitled "Automatic Brains, Interpretive Minds," Roser and Gazzaniga (2004, p. 56) write: "At the highest levels of consciousness, a *personal narrative* is constructed. This narrative makes sense of the brain's own behavior and may underlie the sense of a unitary self."

Jerome Bruner (1986, 1990) suggests that human beings evolved to interpret personal experience in terms of stories. He argues that human beings understand the world in two very different ways. The first is what Bruner terms the **paradigmatic mode** of thought. In the paradigmatic mode, we seek to comprehend our experience in terms of tightly reasoned analyses, logical proof, and empirical observation. We seek to order our world in terms of logical theories that explain events and help us predict and control reality. In the paradigmatic mode, we look for cause-and-effect relationships. When we understand how our car's engine works or how a water molecule is formed from the joining of two hydrogen atoms and one oxygen atom, then we are employing successfully our gifts of logical, causal reasoning. Much of our educational training reinforces the paradigmatic mode. Good logicians and scientists are especially well-trained in this general way of thinking.

By contrast, the **narrative mode** of thought concerns itself with stories, which themselves are about "the vicissitudes of human intention" organized in time (Bruner, 1986). In stories, events are not explained in terms of physical or logical causes. The narrative mode

does not generally operate in the realm of automobile engines or molecular chemistry. Instead, it deals with human wants, needs, and goals. In the narrative mode, events are explained in terms of *human actors striving to do things over time.* If I am to tell a good story about anything, then I must present a believable narrative concerning the motivated actions and meaningful ends of human behavior, rendered in time, with beginning, middle, and end. Therefore, I may wish to explain a friend's unusual behavior this weekend in terms of my understanding of what the friend wants in life and why he has never been able to get it, going back in my account to frustrations he experienced three years ago with his wife. To understand him and his behavior, I say, you must know the story I am to tell. Similarly, to understand what drives Jerome Johnson to defy the demographic odds and become the first African-American police chief in his city, you must understand *his* story as he understands it, from the Depression years to his meeting with Martin Luther King, Jr., to his current vision for his retirement years. We must comprehend his storied account of his intentions organized in time.

One of the pioneers in narrative psychology, Jerome Bruner distinguishes between two different modes of human thought and expression. In the paradigmatic mode, people use logic, empirical observation, and causal analysis to explain how the world works. In the narrative mode, by contrast, people construct stories to convey how people translate their wants and intentions into behavior extended over time.

Good novelists and poets are masters of the narrative mode. These storywriters are especially effective when they, in Bruner's words, "mean more than they can say" (Cordes, 1986). In other words, a good story will generate many different meanings, functioning to trigger presuppositions in the reader. We have all had the experience of comparing what we "got out" of a good story—say, a movie, play, or novel—to the view of a friend, only to learn that the two of us have read or understood the same story in very different ways. This is part of the reason that stories are fun and valuable, for they give us many different ideas and opinions around which we can have friendly, and sometimes not-so-friendly, conversations and arguments. Good stories seem to *give birth* to many different meanings, generating "children" of meaning in their own image.

Stories are almost everywhere: A scene from the popular television show "Friends."

By contrast, masters of the paradigmatic mode try to "say no more than they mean" (Bruner, in Cordes, 1986). A good scientist or logician works for clarity and precision. Scientific and logical explanations are constructed in such a way as to block the triggering of presuppositions. These explanations do not create other explanations in their own image. They do not encourage differences of opinion. If they did, they would be accused of being vague or ambiguous, of generating too many different and competing interpretations for what demands a single objective truth. For all its power and precision, the paradigmatic mode is a strangely humbler form of thought than story making. While it seeks to untangle cause and effect and to explain the workings of the world in the clearest and most rational manner possible, it is not generally able to make much sense of human desire, goal, and social conduct.

HEALING AND INTEGRATION

We are drawn to stories for many reasons. Stories entertain us, making us laugh and cry, keeping us in suspense until we learn how it is all going to turn out. Stories instruct. We learn how to act and live through stories; we learn about different people, settings, and ideas (Coles, 1989). Stories may teach us moral lessons, too. Aesop's fables and the parables of Jesus suggest lessons—some simple and some profound—about good and bad behavior, moral and immoral ways of conducting our lives, dilemmas concerning what is right and what is wrong. Beyond entertaining and edifying us, stories may also function to integrate aspects of our lives and to heal that which is sick or broken. Some scholars and scientists have suggested that *integration* and *healing* are two primary psychological functions of stories and storytelling. Stories may bring our lives together when we feel shattered, mend us when we are broken, heal us when we are sick, help us cope in times of stress, and even move us toward psychological fulfillment and maturity.

The psychoanalyst Bruno Bettelheim (1977) wrote eloquently about the psychological power of children's fairytales. Bettelheim believed that such stories as "Jack and the Beanstalk" and "Cinderella" help children work through internal conflicts and crises. When a 4-year-old listens to the story of Cinderella, Bettelheim suggests, she may unconsciously identify with the heroine and vicariously experience Cinderella's frustration and sadness and her eventual triumph. Similarly, children may identify with such male heroes as Jack, who faces the menacing giant but eventually outwits him and escapes much the richer and wiser. The protagonists of these stories are unassuming children, like the listeners, and their deeply felt fears and concerns match closely the unconscious fears lurking in the hearts of children. In Bettelheim's view, the fairytale speaks softly and subtly to the child, gently but steadily promoting psychological growth and adaptation. The fairytale encourages the child to face the world with confidence and hope. Cinderella and Jack live happily ever after. Wicked stepsisters and ogres are punished in the end. Things have a way of working out, even when they look really scary.

As adults, we too may identify strongly with the protagonist of a story, experiencing vicariously what the character experiences and emerging from the narrative encounter happier, better adjusted, more enlightened, or improved in some way. In *When Bad Things Happen to Good People*, Rabbi Harold Kushner (1981) tells many true stories of pain and heartbreak from the lives of people he has known and, in some cases, loved. The book has been a great comfort to many people. Good friends whose baby was stillborn have told me that Kushner's book helped them deal with their grief. In this case, they identified strongly with the author himself, who was motivated to write the book after his own son died at an early age. By hearing a story with which they could relate intimately, my friends worked through an emotionally wrenching period in their own lives. Kushner reports that the stories helped *him*, too. By collecting and considering the tales of grief and suffering he had encountered in his years as a rabbi, Kushner reports, he was able to piece together parts of his own shattered life.

Simply writing or performing a story about oneself can prove to be an experience of healing and growth, as many who have written their own autobiographies will attest. A good autobiography puts life into story form, complete with setting, characters, recurrent themes and images, and the self-conscious reconstruction of human time through narrative. One of the first and most famous autobiographies in Western history was written by the Christian Saint Augustine (354–430 A.D.). His *Confessions* is a retrospective self-analysis written to regroup and recover from what he described as a "shattered" and "disordered" state of mind. By composing the story, Augustine was able to construct a unified view of himself and his place in God's creation and to orient to the envisioned future with direction and purpose (Jay, 1984).

Many men and women have tried to do what Augustine did, with varying degrees of success. There are many reasons to write an autobiography, but one commonly expressed is the desire to find some kind of personal integration—to put the pieces together into a meaningful whole. The writer may feel that the time in life has finally come to undertake this kind of synthesizing project. It may seem a natural time to look back. Or, like Augustine, the writer may feel a great deal more urgency, looking to the story as a salvation for or solution to an impending crisis in life.

In his brief autobiography entitled *The Facts*, the novelist Philip Roth (1988) writes that he is seeking to "depathologize" his own life, to set things right after years of confusion and trouble. In Roth's case, the process of composing a life story involves distilling from his own complex past the stark truisms—"the facts"—concerning how he came to be a writer. Roth describes this process as a clearing away of the many layers of stories that he has created as a prolific novelist in order to arrive at a core of truth—shredding through the layers of superficial narrative in order to get at a single and simple tale to believe. The task is tricky and perhaps not well advised, as Roth seems to admit at the beginning and the end of the book when he engages in an imaginary conversation with Nathan Zuckerman, who is the fictional hero of a series of Roth's novels. Zuckerman tells Roth that he is a fool to strip away the stories in his fiction, for those are as much a part of Roth as anything else. Zuckerman seems to imply that he, Zuckerman, is more a part of Roth than is Roth himself—than is the Roth, that is, who functions as the central character in *The Facts*. Without me, Zuckerman seems to be saying, you (Roth) are a pretty boring and superficial fellow. "This is what you get in practically any artist without his imagination," Zuckerman says.

"Your medium for the really merciless, self-evisceration, your medium for genuine self-confrontation, is me" (pp. 184–185).

Perhaps Roth actually agrees with Zuckerman, at least to a point. How else might you explain his choice of the most clichéd kind of chapter titles you could imagine for an autobiography? He gives his chapters such titles as "Joe College," "Girl of My Dreams," and "All in the Family." Is Roth telling the reader that, when you strip away "the Roth" that he has projected onto his own fictional characters, such as Zuckerman, all you are left with is cliché? Is he saying that without our imaginations, our lives reduce to simplistic platitudes and worn-out expressions? Is he saying that "the facts" are not enough? In Roth's case, autobiography turns ironic and self-mocking, as the storywriter comes to doubt the validity of the story he has composed. Yet the whole process seems to be enlightening, as well as entertaining. The reader feels that he or she *does* learn something important about Roth. And the reader may feel, too, that Roth has discovered something about himself, that he has made progress toward the goal of "depathologizing" his own life.

The healing power of story arises as a major theme in certain forms of psychotherapy, wherein the explicit goal of treatment is the depathologizing of life. For instance, some psychoanalysts maintain that the development of a coherent life story is a major goal in therapy. According to this view, psychoanalysis involves the coordination of successive narrations whereby the analyst and the client come to construct more adequate and vitalizing stories about the self (Schafer, 1981). Writes Marcus (1974), "human life is, ideally, a connected and coherent story, with all the details in explanatory place, and with everything (or as close to everything as is practically possible) accounted for, in its proper causal or other sequence." Similarly, "illness amounts at least in part to suffering from an incoherent story or an inadequate narrative account of oneself." The therapist and the client work together to produce a healing narrative of the self (Borden, 1992). Some psychological problems and a great deal of emotional suffering stem from our failures in making sense of our lives through story. Therapists help us rewrite and revise our stories of self (White & Epston, 1990). The process may produce a triumphant transformation, like that in the case of Saint Augustine. Or progress may be slower and less obvious, in therapeutic fits and starts, as Roth cautions in his own explorations in healing the self.

Researchers have explored the extent to which life-storytelling can have positive effects on coping and mental health. Most notably, James Pennebaker (1988, 1989b, 1992, 1997; Pennebaker, Mehl, & Niederhoffer, 2003) and his colleagues have conducted a series of studies on the salutary effects of disclosing narrative accounts of personal traumas. Volunteer participants in Pennebaker's studies receive instructions such as these:

James Pennebaker has conducted many studies showing that personal disclosure of negative life events leads to positive health outcomes and mental well-being. Translating difficult life experiences into a coherent story appears to enhance life and promote self-understanding.

Once you are seated in the experimental cubicle and the door is closed, I want you to write continuously about the most upsetting or traumatic experience of your entire life. Don't worry about the grammar, spelling, or sentence structure. In your writing I want you to discuss your deepest thoughts and feelings about the experience. You can write about anything you want, but whatever you choose, it should be something that has affected you very deeply. Ideally, it should be about something you have not talked with others about in detail. It is critical, however, that you let yourself go and touch those deepest emotions and thoughts that you have. I should warn you that many people find this study quite upsetting. Many people cry during the study and feel somewhat sad or depressed during and after it. (Pennebaker, 1989b, p. 215)

Many of the respondents in these studies are college students. Following are some representative sketches:

> A female who has lived in fear for several weeks because of the physical and psychological harassment of a jealous woman who has apparently hired two thugs.
>
> A male who, in his high school years, was repeatedly beaten by his stepfather. After attempting suicide with his stepfather's gun, the stepfather humiliated the subject by laughing at his failed attempt.
>
> A female who, in a fit of rage at her father, accused him of marital infidelity in front of her mother. The accusation, which apparently was true and unknown to the mother, led to the separation and divorce of the parents and overwhelming guilt on the part of the daughter.
>
> A female who, at the age of 10, was asked to clean up her room because of her grandmother who was to visit the home that evening. The girl did not do so. That night, the grandmother slipped on one of the girl's toys and broke her hip. The grandmother died a week later during a hip operation.
>
> A man who, at age 9, was calmly told by his father that he was divorcing the boy's mother because their home life had been disrupted ever since the boy had been born. (Pennebaker, 1989b, p. 218)

As many as one quarter of the participants in these studies cry during their disclosures, and many feel depressed for a time after the telling. Yet the respondents tend to rate the experience of disclosing the traumatic event to be especially valuable, and 98% of them say that they would do the experiment again. More important, the narrative act of translating personal trauma into words appears to have long-term health benefits. For example, Pennebaker and Beall (1986) required 46 healthy undergraduates to write about either the most traumatic and stressful experience of their lives or about a trivial assigned topic *for four consecutive days.* Of those assigned to write about traumatic events, one experimental group wrote about the facts surrounding the trauma but not their feelings about the trauma (trauma-factual condition), another about their feelings concerning the trauma but not the facts (trauma-emotion), and a third about both their feelings and the facts concerning the trauma (trauma-combination group). A six-month followup questionnaire revealed that the participants who disclosed information about both the facts and their feelings in the traumatic event had better health during those six subsequent months than did the participants in the other three groups. As Figure 10.1 shows, the trauma-combination group showed the lowest number of visits to the student health center during that period. The authors argued that the opportunity to tell the *full story* of a stressful experience from the past—providing both the facts and one's feelings about the facts—works to enhance one's health.

These findings are consistent with studies showing how personal confession and disclosure of negative events can improve health and minimize unwanted thoughts about traumas. Pennebaker and O'Heeron (1984) surveyed people whose spouses had died in automobile accidents or suicides. They found that individuals who ruminated obsessively about the death of their spouse had more health problems during the year following the death. But those who talked with others about their spouses' deaths reported (a) fewer problems with unwanted ruminations and obsessive thoughts and (b) fewer health problems during the following year. Greenberg and Stone (1992) found a drop in physician visits for students who wrote about deeply traumatic events compared with students who

FIGURE 10.1	SELF-DISCLOSURE STORIES OF HEALTH

Students who wrote stories about both the facts and the feelings they experienced during a personal trauma had fewer health care visits (and presumably fewer illnesses) compared with other students who wrote only about the feelings or the facts of a personal trauma or who wrote stories about nonpersonal topics.

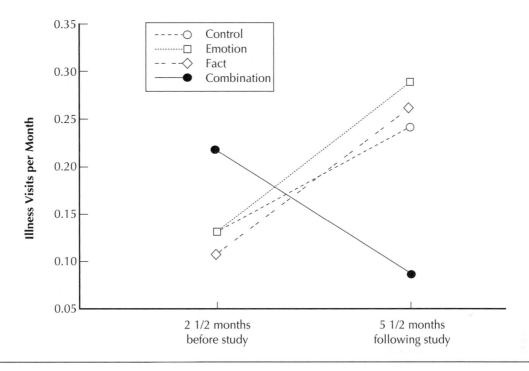

SOURCE: From "Confronting a Traumatic Event: Toward an Understanding of Inhibition and Disease," by J. W. Pennebaker & S. K. Beall, 1986, *Journal of Abnormal Psychology, 95*, 274–281.

either wrote about mild traumas or those who wrote about superficial topics. Francis and Pennebaker (1992) found that those who wrote about traumas once a week for four consecutive weeks had fewer absentee days and improved liver enzyme function in the two months after writing, compared with controls. Obtaining a series of blood samples on each participant, Pennebaker, Kiecolt-Glaser, and Glaser (1988) found that students who wrote about traumas over four consecutive days showed improved immune-system functioning by the fourth day, compared with those who wrote about trivial events.

Why does disclosure of traumatic events improve health? Pennebaker (1988) argues that the process of actively inhibiting feelings and thoughts about negative events requires excessive physiological work, as in higher heart rate, skin conductance, and blood pressure. Over the long haul, the effects of physiological arousal accumulate, leading to such stress-related illnesses as infections, ulcers, and so on. Furthermore, the more that a person tries to inhibit thoughts and emotions, the more he or she is likely to think about that which is being inhibited, leading to heightened anxiety and arousal (Wegner, Schneider, Carter, & White, 1987). But confiding and consciously confronting the perceptions and feelings associated with a traumatic event allow for the integration or cognitive reorganization of the event. The narrative disclosure of the event enables the person to "put it behind" him or her, to "close the book" on the problem. This leads to a reduction in physiological arousal, and it negates the need for further obsessing and inhibiting.

But what is it about disclosure itself that makes for the reduction in physiological arousal and obsessive thought? Research by Pennebaker (1992) suggests two important factors: (a) the degree of negative emotion expressed and (b) the extent to which a traumatic event is reconstructed as a *well-formed story.* Employing a computer content coding scheme to analyze accounts of traumatic events, Pennebaker discovered that people whose health improved the most following disclosure used significantly more negative emotion words and fewer positive emotion words compared to other people. In addition, individuals whose health improved evidenced overall higher levels of story organization and increasing degrees of acceptance and optimism compared with those who failed to improve. Indeed, those who did not improve evidenced a gradual deterioration in their stories. They started their writing sessions with a clear story that, over time, fell apart. Pennebaker concludes that "both the disclosure of negative emotion and the building of a clear cognitive story are important components in healthy writing" (1992, p. 5). The movement over time toward a well-constructed story, then, is a desired outcome in writing and in some forms of therapy, and it appears to bring with it benefits for health.

FEELING AND STORY: TOMKINS'S SCRIPT THEORY

Silvan Tomkins (1911–1991) was the first psychologist to develop a broad theory of personality centered on life stories. Tomkins argued that people organize emotionally-charged life experiences into self-defining scripts. Among the important life scripts he identified were commitment scripts and nuclear scripts.

The central role of story and storytelling in human lives is one defining feature of the broad perspective on personality offered by Silvan Tomkins (1911–1991). A drama student who wrote plays as a college undergraduate, Tomkins came to psychology as a storywriter. It was through dramatic narrative that Tomkins first wrestled with the question that ultimately drove his life's work: "What do human beings really want?" (Tomkins, 1981, p. 306). In search of an answer, Tomkins entered graduate school in psychology in 1930 but left a year later, disappointed with what he saw as psychology's failure to address adequately the question of motivation, or what people want. He then turned to philosophy to study logic and the theory of value, receiving a Ph.D. Tomkins eventually returned to psychology to work with Henry Murray at the Harvard Psychological Clinic. Tomkins's early work reflected the influence of Murray, as he published a book on the TAT (Tomkins, 1947) and devised a new projective test called the Tomkins–Horn Picture Arrangement Test (Tomkins & Miner, 1957).

Though Tomkins initially accepted Murray's belief that psychogenic needs were the main factors in human motivation (chapter 7 in this book), he soon departed from this view in favor of a theory emphasizing **affect,** or human emotion. As Tomkins tells it, two personal discoveries led directly to his own conviction that affects, not drives (Freud) or needs (Murray), are the primary motivators of human behavior.

The first discovery occurred in the late 1940s when Tomkins was struck by the sudden insight that such affects as excitement, joy, and anger are independent of drives, such as hunger and sexuality, but *amplify* drives by providing them with motivational power. In Tomkins's view, for instance, the sex drive in and of itself is *not* generally a strong motivator of behavior. Rather, sex moves the person to act in a sexual manner when amplified (strengthened) by the affect of excitement. Tomkins's second discovery occurred when he became a father:

> The second critical discovery occurred when my son was born in 1955 while I was on sabbatical leave. Beginning shortly after his birth, I observed him daily, for hours on end. I was struck with the massiveness of the crying response. It included not only very loud vocalization and facial muscular responses, but also large changes in blood flow to the face and engagement of all the striate musculature of the body. It was a massive total bodily response which, however, seemed to center on the face. Freud had suggested that the birth cry was the prototype of anxiety, but my son didn't seem anxious. What, then, was the facial response? I labeled it distress. Next, I was to observe intense excitement on his face when he labored after the first few months of his life to shape his mouth to try to imitate the speech he heard. He would struggle minutes on end and then give up, apparently exhausted and discouraged. I noted the intensity of the smiling response to his mother and to me, and again I became aware that nothing in psychoanalytic theory (and any other personality theory at that time) paid any attention to the specificity of enjoyment as contrasted with excitement. (Tomkins, 1981, p. 309)

In collaboration with psychologists Carroll Izard and Paul Ekman, Tomkins has articulated a broad theory of human emotion that proposes the existence of some 10 primary affects, each rooted in human biology and evolution (Ekman, 1972; Izard, 1977; Tomkins, 1962, 1963; Tomkins & Izard, 1965). Each affect is linked to characteristic movements of the muscles in the face. Thus, the face may be considered the organ of emotion. Later, Tomkins expanded his theory to encompass the concepts of *scene* and *script*, providing a dramaturgical and narrative approach to personality that is reminiscent of his entry into psychology, more than 70 years ago, as a writer of plays (Carlson, 1981; Tomkins, 1979, 1987).

AFFECTS

When I worked in the steel mills in Gary, Indiana, I became friends with a man called "Tiny." I was a college student working summers; he was about 40 years old, married with three children, and he had never finished the sixth grade. Tiny's dream was to be a coal miner; by contrast, I could think of nothing more gruesome. I hated the steel mills; Tiny didn't mind the work, and he often tried to cheer me up when I was particularly fed up and discouraged. I don't understand why we liked each other when we had so little in common. But I remember that we talked a lot, and I especially remember one conversation we had— I think the original topic was women and marriage—when Tiny cryptically observed, "Emotion is everything." In his own way, Tiny seemed to hit on the central point of human living in Tomkins's theory of personality. As Tomkins puts it:

> The primary function of affect is urgency via analogic and profile amplification to make one care by feeling. … Without affect amplification nothing else matters, and with its amplification anything can matter. (1981, p. 322)

According to Tomkins, natural selection has operated on humans to favor the evolution of a highly differentiated and specialized system of emotions. Therefore,

> the human being is equipped with innate affective responses which bias him to want to remain alive and to resist death, to want sexual experiences, to want to experience novelty

and to resist boredom, to want to communicate, to be close to and in contact with others of his species and to resist the experience of head and face lowered in shame.
(Tomkins, 1962, p. 27)

Those emotions most often identified as primary by Tomkins include interest/excite-
ment, enjoyment, surprise, distress, anger, disgust, fear/anxiety, sadness, shame, and guilt.
The first two are positive emotions; surprise can be positive, negative, or neither: and the
last seven are negative emotions. In general, people seek to maximize experiences of positive emotions and minimize experiences of negative ones.

Each of the primary emotions can be distinguished on a number of different levels.
First, each *feels* qualitatively different from all the others. For example, the phenomenology
of surprise—the sudden increase in arousal in the wake of an unexpected event—is very
different from the phenomenology of shame, joy, or sadness. Second, each emotion is
innately linked to a specific *facial response.* As Darwin (1872/1965) believed more than 100
years ago, human beings have evolved with particular facial expressions for showing particular emotions: enjoyment by the smile; surprise and interest/excitement by raised eyes and
a focused, head-forward stance; sadness by a drooping mouth and slackening jaw muscles;
disgust by tightened muscles beneath the nose and wrinkling of the nose; anger by
clenched and exposed teeth and a flushed complexion; and fear by widened eyes. Each of
these facial expressions sends sensory feedback from the face to the brain, and some psychologists believe that this feedback is instrumental in the experience of the emotion itself,
especially in infancy. In one sense, then, the experience of joy is the result of the sensory
information sent to the brain by the smiling face. In addition, facial expressions send social
information to other persons who may observe the individual's smiles, frowns, or sneers.

Particular facial expressions, therefore, are thought to be natural manifestations of
primary emotions. Evidence for this proposition comes from many sources. Cross-cultural
research suggests that people from very different societies tend to agree on what facial
responses "go with" what emotions. For instance, research by Izard (1971, 1977) and
Ekman, Friesen, and Ellsworth (1972) showed that when people from 12 different countries
were shown photographs selected to represent fundamental emotions, the percentage of
agreement was very high. Mexicans, Brazilians, Germans, Japanese, Americans, and members of certain preliterate tribes tend to agree about the meaning of different facial expressions. Even when there is no obvious change in facial expression, the occurrence of certain
emotions can be shown by measuring electrical activity in the face and brain. In one study,
individuals were asked to imagine pleasant and unpleasant scenes while changes in the
electrical muscular impulses in their faces were monitored (Schwartz, Fair, Greenberg,
Freedman, & Klerman, 1974). The results indicated that electrical activity in the face
matches the muscular movements that have been documented for various emotions. For
example, during happy thoughts, the same facial muscles that produce a smile show
increased electrical activity even though the facial expression appears blank.

While primary emotions appear to be biologically linked to specific facial expressions, different cultures establish different **display rules** that determine the appropriateness of expressing certain emotions through facial behavior in certain situations (Ekman, 1972, 1992). In
American society, for example, it is generally considered more appropriate for women than
men to cry when experiencing the emotion of sadness. While some societies sanction the full
expression of many different affects in a wide variety of situations, other societies are more cir-
cumspect and may strongly discourage the public display of strong emotions.

A last way in which different emotions can be distinguished is in terms of their developmental course. As Izard (1978) has asserted, "emotions emerge as they become adaptive

According to Tomkins, the face is the organ of emotion. Basic emotions like fear, joy, anger, sadness, excitement, and disgust form the core of life scenes, which form the core components of scripts.

in the life of the infant" (p. 390). The cry of the newborn is generally a sign of *distress*, an extremely rudimentary emotion that signals that something is not quite right in the world. The distress cry motivates caregivers to attend to the infant and address the source of distress. The origins of *enjoyment* may reside in the early social smile and face-to-face interaction with the caregiver that is usually displayed by infants by 2 months of age. Out of early joyful interactions develop the caregiver–infant attachment bond and the first love relationship in the baby's life, as we saw in chapter 2.

Interest/excitement can be traced back to at least the third and fourth months of life, when infants are engaged in what the developmental psychologist Jean Piaget (1970) viewed as attempts to "make interesting events last." The function of interest/excitement is to focus and maintain attention and to motivate exploratory activity. Interest is activated by novelty and change and serves as the basis for the infant's first self-initiated interactions with the world of objects. *Fear* and *sadness* may appear in the second half of the first year of life, especially in response to novelty, separation, and loss. It is quite common for 8-month-old infants to fear strangers and to cry when separated from their mothers and fathers. Finally, the emergence of *shame* and (later) *guilt* generally awaits the development of self-consciousness in the second year, following the child's consolidation of an initial sense of self (chapter 9).

Tomkins also suggested that certain affects line up with certain beliefs and values. A person's philosophical, political, and religious values may be built upon an emotional foundation. In his research on *personal ideologies*, Ed de St. Aubin (1996, 2000) tested hypotheses drawn from Tomkins's writings. Tomkins identified two different ideological approaches to life: *normativism* and *humanism.* Politically conservative in nature, normativism asserts that human beings are inherently flawed or evil and, therefore, need to be held in check by strong rules and clearly defined contingencies. More liberal in orientation, humanism sees human beings as good or capable of goodness, and it tends to affirm self-expression and love as basic human values. Tomkins suggested that normativists are more likely than humanists to emphasize the affects of excitement and anger in their personal experiences whereas humanists are more likely to emphasize affects of joy and fear. Coding narrative accounts of autobiographical memories for discrete affects, de St. Aubin found support for part of Tomkins's claim. Adults scoring high on a normativism scale tended to recall negative memories associated with anger while those high in humanism recalled negative memories associated with fear and distress. Although many people believe that their belief systems are perfectly rational and objective, Tomkins's theory and the research by de St. Aubin suggest that what we believe to be good and true about the world may be partly driven by what we tend to *feel.*

SCENES AND SCRIPTS

Basic Concepts

If affect is the supreme motivator in life, scenes and scripts are the great organizers. Tomkins views the person as a playwright who fashions his or her own personal drama from the earliest weeks of life. The basic component of the drama is the **scene,** the memory of a specific happening or event in one's life that contains at least one affect and one object of that affect. Each scene is an "organized whole that includes persons, place, time, actions, and feelings" (Carlson, 1981, p. 502). We may each view our own lives, therefore, as a series of scenes, one after the other, extending from birth to the present. But certain kinds of scenes appear again and again, and certain typical groupings or families of scenes can be discerned. **Scripts** enable us to make sense of the relations among various scenes. A script is a set of rules for interpreting, creating, enhancing, or defending against a family of related scenes (Carlson, 1988). Each of us organizes the many scenes in our lives according to our own idiosyncratic scripts.

The *short-term* importance of any particular scene in a person's life is likely to be a function of the quality of the affect in the scene. In thinking back over yesterday's events, therefore, you may recall a particular happening that stands out because of the intense emotion you experienced during it. For instance, the lunchtime volleyball game you played with friends may have elicited strong feelings of joy, an argument with your mother may have brought forward feelings of anger, or the conversation you had with an attractive man or women may have elicited excitement—each of these scenes could conceivably stand out as special or important, for that given day. The *long-term* importance of a scene in the context of a person's entire life drama or narrative is likely to be a function of **psychological magnification,** which is the process of connecting related scenes into a meaningful pattern. To connect scenes into meaningful patterns, we must recognize basic similarities and differences among various scenes. For instance, an argument with your mother may remind you of a similar disagreement you had with a professor. In both cases, say, what began as a friendly exchange deteriorated into shouting over a petty difference of opinion. The two arguments appear to be *analogs* of each other. Psychological magnification often works by constructing such analogs—the detection of similarities in different experiences. When construing analogs in your life, you are likely to get that feeling of "here we go again," replaying the same scenario over and over. According to Tomkins, *negative*-affect scenes are often psychologically magnified through the formation of analogs. Therefore, in making sense of the many scenes of fear or sadness in your life, you are likely to discern the ways in which these scenes are essentially similar.

When, by contrast, you focus on *differences* in organizing various life scenes, you are employing psychological magnification to construct *variants.* You are most likely to do this, argues Tomkins, in the magnification of *positive*-affect scenes. Therefore, in construing the many experiences of joy in your past, you are likely to focus on the ways in which the various scenes differ around a stable core. Consider joyful family gatherings. Last summer's family reunion, Thanksgiving dinner two years ago, and the day your mother brought your baby sister home from the hospital may all stand out in your life narrative as joyful scenes. While the various scenes are similar in some ways, you are likely to magnify them such that differences are accentuated. Therefore, the family reunion may stand out as "special" for the great conversation you had with your uncle who works for the FBI; the highlight of the Thanksgiving dinner may have been your sister's announcement that she and her boyfriend were planning to get married; and the day you saw your baby sister for the first time may stand out for the overwhelming feelings of tenderness and affection you felt.

Types of Scripts

While psychologists have been able to identify a finite number of basic human affects, the number of possible scenes and scripts in human life appears to be much larger. Therefore, no definitive list of scenes and scripts has been developed. However, Tomkins has identified at least two types of scripts that seem especially significant in human life and that help organize in powerful ways people's life narratives. These are commitment scripts and nuclear scripts (Carlson, 1988; Tomkins, 1987).

In a **commitment script,** the person binds him- or herself to a life program or goal that promises the reward of intense positive affect. A commitment script involves a long-term investment in "improving things." The person may have a vision of the ideal life or the ideal society and dedicate his or her life to realizing or accomplishing this vision. According to Tomkins, commitment scripts begin with an intensely positive early scene or series of scenes from childhood. This scene of enjoyment or excitement comes to represent an optimistic ideal of what might be—a Garden of Eden from the past that holds out the hope of a paradise in the future, the pursuit of which becomes one's life task.

In a commitment script, the person organizes scenes around a clearly defined and undisputed goal (Table 10.1). Therefore, commitment scripts are *not* likely to entail significant conflict between competing goals or troubling ambivalence about any single goal. The person whose life is organized around a strong commitment script strives, instead, to accomplish his or her desired paradise with singleness of purpose and steadfast dedication, much like Jerome Johnson as he pursued his dream to be a police chief. Even in the face of great obstacles and repeated negative-affect experiences, such a person focuses steadily on the object of commitment, laboring under the conviction that "bad things can be overcome" (Carlson, 1988).

In sharp contrast to commitment scripts are **nuclear scripts,** which are generally marked by ambivalence and confusion about one's life goals. A nuclear script always involves

TABLE 10.1	COMMITMENT SCRIPTS VERSUS NUCLEAR SCRIPTS	
	TYPE OF SCRIPT	
Script Feature	**Commitment**	**Nuclear**
Ratio of positive to negative affect	Positive greater than negative	Negative greater than positive
Affect socialization	Intense, rewarding	Intense, ambivalent
Clarity of ideal scene	Clear, monistic	Confusing, pluralistic
Magnification of scenes via	Variants	Analogs
Sequences	"Bad things can be overcome"	"Good things turn bad"

SOURCE: Adapted from "Exemplary Lives: The Uses of Psychobiography for Theory Development," by R. Carlson, 1988, *Journal of Personality, 56,* 111.

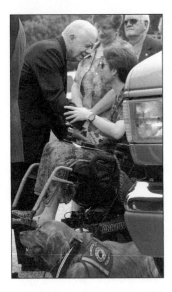

In his efforts to promote human rights and world peace, former U.S. President Jimmy Carter exhibits many of the characteristics that Tomkins identified for the commitment script.

complex approach–avoidance conflicts. The person is irresistibly drawn toward and repelled by particularly conflictual scenes in his or her life narrative. The result is a life narrative that resembles the literary form of tragedy.

A nuclear script begins with a **nuclear scene,** which is a positive childhood scene that eventually turns bad. As a good scene, it may involve the experience of enjoyment or excitement in the presence of others, especially those others who may provide the person with "stimulation, guidance, mutuality, support, comfort and/or reassurance." The scene turns bad with the appearance of "an intimidation, or a contamination, or a confusion, or any combination of these which jeopardize the good scene" (Tomkins, 1987, p. 199). What begins, therefore, as joyful or exciting turns frightening, disgusting, contemptuous, shameful, or sad. A nuclear script is initially formed as an attempt to reverse the nuclear scene, to turn the bad scene into a good scene again. The attempt is only partially successful, however, as the person ultimately appears fated to repeat the nuclear scene continually through subsequent analog scenes.

Carlson (1981) describes a nuclear scene from the early childhood of one Jane W., a 37-year-old college professor:

Four-year-old Janie is playing when she hears her mother cry for help. Running into the hall, she finds her mother lying on the floor in a heap of boxes, having fallen from a makeshift ladder to the attic. Mother asks Janie to call her father. Father arrives, helps mother to her feet, and supports her as they walk to the living room with Janie hovering nearby. Janie hears her father say "Sit here, honey" and promptly perches on the designated couch. Father angrily yells, "Get out of here!" and pushes Janie away so that her mother may lie down. Janie retreats in confusion, feeling deeply ashamed. (p. 504)

It turns out that Jane's mother was pregnant at the time of the fall and that this event probably caused her subsequent miscarriage. Further, when Jane's father said, "Sit here, honey," he was probably speaking to her mother, though of course the 4-year-old Janie assumed he was addressing her.

Carlson identifies five key features in this scene: (a) good things turn bad, (b) seduction and betrayal, (c) disorientation in space, (d) affects of shame and anger, and (e) withdrawal and inhibition. Each of these features was replayed in subsequent scenes in Jane's life, attesting to the power of the nuclear scene as the precipitating event in a nuclear script. Evidence for the psychological magnification of this scene through the formation of many analogs is evident in Jane's memories of her past, and in her dreams, fantasies, and interpersonal relationships. For example, she experienced many instances in her adult life in which she felt disoriented in space, in the same way she was disoriented in the nuclear scene when her father pushed her off the couch to make room for her mother. Further, each of her 30 dream reports was characterized by repeated shifts in location. Shame, which was the dominant affect in the original scene, was abundantly evident as a recurrent emotional experience in both dreams and daily life. Inhibition and withdrawal were evident in autobiographical data suggesting that, despite her competence in many realms of life, Jane was often "frozen" at critical moments, especially when a difficult decision was to be made. Jane's inhibition was also evident in her repeated difficulties in mastering realms of physical activity, especially athletics and games.

Carlson suggests that at least two other scenes from Jane's childhood might be considered nuclear scenes, giving birth to nuclear scripts. The point of the analysis of the case of

Jane, however, is not to show how any of these scenes actually *caused* subsequent events. Carlson does not contend that Jane is inhibited today *because* of the scene on the couch. Rather, the couch scene is a nuclear scene because it *organizes* the narrative of her life, giving meaning to many different experiences and serving as a template or pattern for other scenes in the story. As dramatists and storytellers of the self, human beings seek to discern a narrative order in their lives so that they may cast the many discordant events of the past into a meaningful and coherent life story. A major undercurrent in Jane's life story is a nuclear script about how good things can lead to disorientation, withdrawal, and shame.

NARRATIVE IDENTITY

In chapter 9, I introduced Erik Erikson's concept of *identity.* According to Erikson, beginning in adolescence and young adulthood modern people are faced with the psychosocial challenge of constructing a self that provides their lives with unity, purpose, and meaning. For the first time in the life course, these questions become problematic, and interesting: "Who am I?" "How do I fit into the adult world?" As we address these questions, Erikson maintained, we begin to construct what he called a *configuration,* which includes "constitutional givens, idiosyncratic libidinal needs, significant identifications, effective defenses, successful sublimations, and consistent roles" (Erikson, 1959, p. 116). The identity configuration works to integrate "all identifications with the vicissitudes of the libido, with the aptitudes developed out of endowment, and with the opportunities offered in social roles." The formulation of an identity configuration brings with it "the accrued confidence that the inner sameness and continuity prepared in the past are matched by the sameness and continuity of one's meaning for others" (Erikson, 1963, p. 261). Therefore, the identity configuration serves to *integrate,* or bring into a meaningful pattern, many different things. It brings together skills, values, goals, and roles into a coherent whole. It brings together what the person can and wants to do with what opportunities and constraints for action exist in the social environment. It brings together aspects of the remembered past with the experienced present and the anticipated future.

What might this unique "configuration" of identity look like? In my own theoretical writing, I have argued that the identity configuration of which Erikson speaks should be seen first and foremost as an integrative *life story* that a person begins to construct in late adolescence and young adulthood (McAdams, 1984b, 1985a, 1985b, 1987, 1993, 1997b, 2001a). A growing number of personality, social, cognitive, developmental, and clinical psychologists today describe identity in terms of a narrative or story that people construct in a social world (Angus & McLeod, 2004; Conway & Holmes, 2004; Fivush & Haden, 2003; Pratt & Friese, 2004; Schachter, 2004; Singer, 2004). Following Singer (2004) and others, we will use the term **narrative identity** to refer to the internalized and evolving story of the self that a person consciously and unconsciously constructs to bind together many different aspects of the self. Narrative identity provides a person's life with some degree of unity, purpose, and meaning.

It is in adolescence that we first come to recognize that, living in a modern society, our lives *need* some form of purpose and meaning. Unlike children, adolescents have the cognitive ability and the psychosocial motivation to see their lives as evolving narratives that they are able to "work on" over time. In Piaget's (1970) terms, adolescents are able to think in an abstract, formal-operational manner. The abstract problem of unity and purpose in life now poses itself as a meaningful conundrum. Able to entertain hypothetical realities through formal operational thought and motivated to re-evaluate personal history and to

FEATURE 10.A

TIME AND STORY IN BALI

The philosopher Paul Ricoeur (1984) writes that "time becomes human time to the extent it is organized after the manner of narrative; narrative in turn is meaningful to the extent it portrays the features of temporal existence" (p. 3). What Ricoeur means is that human beings tend to comprehend time in terms of story. Therefore, stories work well when they make good sense of time. When we comprehend our actions over time, we see what we do in terms of story. We see actions leading to reactions, goals attained, obstacles confronted, intentions realized and frustrated over time, tension building to climax, climax giving way to denouement, tension building again as we continue to move and change, moving forward from yesterday to today to tomorrow.

Imagine a society, however, in which human conduct is *not* situated in time as we understand it. The anthropologist Clifford Geertz (1973) describes just such a society among the people of Bali. Bali is an Indonesian island just east of Java. Its native inhabitants live within a culture that is radically different from ours in many ways. Three intriguing differences stand out in Geertz's account—differences in time, conduct, and identity.

First, Balinese life follows a complex and irregular calendar that seems neither to move forward nor represent regular cycles. Time is classified by holidays. In Bali, today's "date" refers to how much time has elapsed since the last holiday and how much is left until the next one. Holidays fall irregularly on dates determined by overlapping cycles. As Geertz (1973) puts it, "the cycles and supercycles are endless, unanchored, unaccountable, and, as their internal order has no significance, without climax. They do not accumulate, they do not build, and they are not consumed. They don't tell you what time it is; they tell you what kind of time it is" (p. 393). For the Balinese, time is "punctual" rather than "durational." To know today's date is not to know time as we think of it; rather it is simply to know what kind of day today is. This is like calling today "Heavenday" and tomorrow "Baseball." In exactly a "week" from today (a "week" by our standards; the Balinese do

not speak of weeks), we may have the day "Marshmallow." We do not know when the day "Heavenday" or "Marshmallow" will happen again, though of course each *will* happen again, some time. In this system, each day is punctuated like a discrete moment. It is not related to other days in a sequence of time.

Second, human conduct itself also seems to be punctual rather than durational. It is as if the Balinese act and interact with one another in ways that themselves are outside of time, Geertz maintains. Each moment is discrete. Actions do not seem to build to climax and resolution the way we might expect they should. "Absence of climax," Geertz (1973) writes, is a remarkable quality of Balinese social behavior:

> It amounts to the fact that social activities do not build, or are not permitted to build, toward definitive consummations. Quarrels appear and disappear, on occasion they even persist, but they hardly ever come to a head. Issues are not sharpened for decision, they are blunted and softened in the hope that the mere evolution of circumstances will resolve them, or better yet, that they will simply evaporate. Daily life consists of self-contained, monadic encounters in which something either happens or does not, intention is realized or it is not, a task is accomplished or not. (p. 403)

Geertz is suggesting that, in Bali, social life does not seem to be construed in storied terms. Each moment is a discrete performance, standing alone outside of time, rather than a connected episode in a time-organized plot. Social activities follow one another, but they do not march to some destination, gather toward some denouement. Both time and life are punctual, unstoried.

Third, as it goes for time and conduct in Bali, so it goes for a person's identity. Geertz observes that the Balinese go to great lengths to "depersonalize" each other so that everybody may be seen as a "stereotyped contemporary." This can be seen even in the giving of names. An adult in Bali does not

(CONTINUES)

have a distinct name that differentiates him or her from everybody else. Instead, he or she is named according to offspring. Thus, I might be called "Father of Ruth." Were Ruth to grow up and have a child named Paul, she would no longer be called "Ruth" but rather "Mother of Paul." At that time, my name would become "Grandfather of Paul" (which might also be the name of Ruth's father-in-law). And so on. The naming pulls one to the present moment and out of any kind of meaningful time duration. Ruth and I are now linked in identity by virtue of our joint cooperation in the production of Paul. Paul is like the present moment; in a sense, he is all that matters, and he defines who I and my daughter are. The implicit aim, says Geertz, is to create a society that collapses time to the discrete present and blurs distinctions between people.

We are all more or less the same in Bali. Even though things change, reality remains the same. No climaxes. No resolution of tension. No denouement. Balinese life does not conform to the kinds of stories we, as Westerners, know and tell. Indeed, it seems to defy our sense of what story is all about.

Geertz's fascinating account should remind us that ours is not the only way to see time and story. In its sharp contrast, however, Geertz's portrait also brings into bold relief the extent to which most of us think about time as story, and story in terms of time. I suspect that few of us wish to exchange permanent places with one of the Balinese. Coming from a culture that stresses individual identity and the linear nature of time, we are not likely to feel comfortable in a society that seems to lie outside of time and personal identity. We may concede that their culture works for the Balinese, that perhaps it works so well as to make them quite happy and fulfilled. Geertz does not compare them to us on these points. But the reasons the Balinese seem so strange to us is that we, unlike them, appear to live according to narrative assumptions about time and lives. And we, unlike them, appear to value strongly the individuality of our own life course. Take our stories of the past away from us and each of us would be forced to live as stereotyped contemporaries, out of time and out of self.

explore new possibilities for the future, we begin to operate as both historians of the past and prophets for the future, seeking to cast our time-driven lives into narratives that work. Our first attempts to do this may seem naive and fantastical. Examining diaries and personal correspondence of adolescents, Elkind (1981) finds evidence for the construction of *personal fables*—fantastical stories about the self, underscoring the teenager's sense that he or she is unique in the world, destined for great goodness or badness, and forever misunderstood by others. For some adolescents, the personal fable may serve as a "rough first draft" of an evolving identity narrative, a story that will become more realistic and plausible in the years to come. Moving into young adulthood, Hankiss (1981) identifies *ontological strategies* that people adopt to explain how they came to be. For example, in a "dynastic" ontological strategy, a young adult fashions a story about how a very positive past life has now given birth to a very positive current life. By contrast, a "compensatory" strategy involves a story of how a bad past has given birth to a good present, as in the proverbial "rags to riches" life story celebrated by many Americans throughout our nation's history. (See Table 10.2.)

Habermas and Bluck (2000) argue that it is not until adolescence that people can effectively use *life story schemas* to organize their lives. The life story schema is a mental structure or pattern for putting a life into story form, for making a narrative identity out of a human life. Habermas and Bluck suggest that people have to be able to exercise at least four different mental skills in order to construct a coherent life story, as summarized in Table 10.3. First and most basic, they must be able to construct little, goal-directed stories

TABLE 10.2	VIEWS FROM SIX DIFFERENT SCHOLARS ON THE RELATION BETWEEN STORIES AND HUMAN LIVES	

Source	Concept	Description
Northrop Frye, literary scholar (1957)	Mythic archetypes	There exist four fundamental story forms, which reflect four stages of human existence and the four seasons. *Comedy* highlights birth and spring; *romance* depicts the passion and adventure of youth and early adulthood, and the season of summer; *tragedy* suggests deterioration and eventual dying in later adulthood, and the season for autumn; *irony* depicts death and winter.
Lawrence Elsbree, literary scholar (1982)	Generic plots	There exist five basic plots in stories, each reflecting a fundamental human striving: (a) establishing a home; (b) fighting a battle; (c) taking a journey; (d) enduring suffering; and (e) pursuing consummation or completion.
Jean-Paul Sartre, philosopher (1964)	True novels	The essential form of the self is a retrospective story, or "true novel," that creates order out of the chaos of experience. Because contemporary religion and social institutions no longer provide people with sacred myths with which to identify, modern men and women are faced with seeking truth and meaning through creating their own myths about themselves. Ideally, a person's own true novel should reflect a central truth or dilemma about his or her historical epoch.
Alasdair MacIntyre, philosopher (1984)	Moral virtues	The "good" in human life must be understood in the context of narrative. What is good for a single person is what contributes to the completion of his or her life story. What is good for humankind must be derived from an analysis of the features that are common to all life stories.
David Elkind, developmental psychologist (1982)	Personal fable	In early adolescence, a person may construct a fantastical story about the self, underscoring the teenager's sense that he or she is unique in the world, destined for great goodness or badness, and forever misunderstood by others. Elkind sees personal fable as a relatively normal phenomenon that is partly a result of the beginning of formal operational thinking. In terms of narrative theory of identity, personal fable may be a "rough draft" of an evolving narrative identity that will mature and become more realistic in later years.
Agnes Hankiss, sociologist (1981)	Ontological strategy	In early adulthood, people attempt to explain how they "came to be" (ontology) by "mythologically rearranging" the past and evaluating the present according to one of four different strategies: (a) dynastic (good past, good present), (b) antithetical (good past, bad present), (c) compensatory (bad past, good present), or (d) self-absolutory (bad past, bad present).

about single episodes in their lives. Habermas and Bluck call this *temporal coherence* because it shows that a person can narrate a sequence of actions that happen over time. Most children can do this by the time they enter kindergarten, and they get better at it as they grow older. Second, people must be able to conform their autobiographical understanding to

TABLE 10.3	FOUR FORMS OF COHERENCE IN THE LIFE STORY
Temporal coherence	Accounting for a goal-directed life episode by telling a story about it
Biographical coherence	Knowing the cultural expectations regarding the nature and timing of life episodes and events across the life course
Causal coherence	Linking multiple life episodes into a meaningful sequence that provides a causal explanation
Thematic coherence	Deriving an integrative theme or principle about the self from a narrated sequence of episodes

SOURCE: From "Getting a Life: The Emergence of the Life Story in Adolescence," by T. Habermas & S. Bluck, 2000, *Psychological Bulletin, 126,* 748–769.

society's expectations of the life course, what Habermas and Bluck call *biographical coherence.* By early adolescence, most people have a pretty good sense of society's expectations regarding the life course—for example, that people go to school when they are young, that they eventually leave home and often get married, that having and raising children may follow, that people may retire in their 60s or 70s, that people rarely live beyond age 90, and so on. Third, *causal coherence* begins to emerge in mid-adolescence as people become able to connect multiple events in their lives into a single causal narrative. For example, a 15-year-old may explain how she reached her current level of disappointment regarding a boyfriend by telling the story of how the relationship began, developed, and then suddenly deteriorated. By connecting a series of events into a causal sequence, she is able to explain in narrative the reasons for her current despair. Finally, people become increasingly effective with respect to *thematic coherence* as they move into and through late adolescence. In thematic coherence, a person is able to derive a general theme or principle about themselves based on a narrated sequence of personal events. A life story schema, then, involves an implicit understanding of temporal, biographical, causal, and thematic coherence as each applies to a single life. Once people have this understanding, they are able to use it to develop their own narrative identities.

Therefore, we begin to construct narrative identities—that is, self-defining life stories—in adolescence and young adulthood. But we do not begin our stories from scratch. And we do not quit working on our stories as we move beyond our early adult years. The origins of life stories can be traced back to infancy, and the process of life storymaking continues well into midlife and beyond (Cohler, 1982; McAdams, 1990, 1993). In infancy and childhood, we are implicitly "gathering material" for the story we will someday compose. The kind of material we gather—the many experiences we have, people we meet, and challenges we face—may ultimately influence the nature of the story we someday construct. For example, secure attachments in childhood may increase the chances that the stories we construct later in life will have a trusting and optimistic *narrative tone* (McAdams, 1993). When we arrive in adolescence ready to make sense of who we are, we are already bestowed with a wealth of experience that constitutes some of the most important "stuff" out of which our identities will be made. These are the biographical resources for our life stories. There is much that we can do with these resources, many possibilities that we can create. But in identity, as in life, we can never fully transcend our resources.

A person's life story is a *psychosocial construction* (McAdams, 1996a). This means that although the story is constructed by the person whose story it is, the possibilities for story construction—narrative identity formation—are determined by culture. Indeed, there is a sense in which the person co-authors identity with culture. Different kinds of stories make sense in different kinds of cultures. For example, Martin Luther's narrations (chapter 9) about physical encounters with devils made sense in 16th-century Germany, but they strike the modern ear as quite odd (Erikson, 1958). A member of a rural Indian village may account for his feelings of tranquility this morning as resulting from the "cool and dispassionate" food he ate last night (Shweder & Much, 1987). His story will make sense to his peers in the village, but it will not fit expectations for life-narrative accounts in contemporary Boston. Furthermore, within modern societies like the contemporary United States, different groups are given different narrative opportunities and face different narrative constraints. Especially relevant here are gender, race, and class divisions in modern society (chapter 3). Feminist author Carolyn Heilbrun (1988) remarks that many women have traditionally "been deprived of the narratives, or the texts, plots, or examples, by which they might assume power over—take control of—their own lives" (p. 17). The historical and contemporary life experiences of many African Americans do not coalesce nicely into the kind of life-narrative forms most valued by the white majority in the United States (Boyd-Franklin, 1989). Life stories, therefore, reflect gender and class divisions and the patterns of economic, political, and cultural power that prevail in society, within which individual lives are embedded (Franz & Stewart, 1994; Rosenwald & Ochberg, 1992).

As psychosocial constructions, life stories are based on empirical facts, but they also go beyond facts. For example, take this fact from my own life: I was born on February 7, 1954. This fact can be documented through my birth certificate. My own life story, therefore, includes this simple fact concerning the date of my birth. Another fact about my birth was that I was a premature infant—weighing 3 pounds and 13 ounces at birth. Now, here is where it gets murky. My father always told me growing up that the doctors said I had a 50/50 chance to live because I was so premature. Looking back on what I have learned about my father over the past 45 years, I now think he made up that "fact." But maybe he didn't. In any case, that conversation with the doctor has always been part of my life story, even though it may never have happened. This is to say that growing up, I always considered myself to be an especially lucky person—the 50/50 coin flip at birth came up heads, and I lived. More importantly, I think that an early knowledge that I might have died has always sensitized me to the possibility of my own death, the death of others whom I love, and the overall fragility of human life. I also believe this knowledge about my past has made me a relatively cautious person, unwilling to take big risks in life—or perhaps I merely rationalize my caution in this way. In recent years, the doctor's conversation has come to play itself out in my growing realization that since I may have been lucky to survive, I need to be very careful that I do something worthwhile with my life, as a kind of payback for getting the lucky break early on. Now, you realize that I consciously suspect that the conversation with the doctor never took place. But part of my life story has been constructed around the possibility that the conversation did happen. I have imaginatively appropriated certain "facts" and possibilities in my own unique way, to make a story that makes sense to me. Consequently, life stories are not purely factual, but neither are they purely fiction. They lie somewhere in between.

Let us go back to Jerome Johnson, the African-American police chief who had a fateful encounter with the Reverend Martin Luther King, Jr. Did Johnson's meeting with King "really" convince him to stay the course and take the police department promotional exam? How can we ever know? Perhaps Johnson would still have taken the exam had he never met King. Perhaps he would have become police chief anyway. And while I am pretty confident that Jerome Johnson did not completely fabricate the King story, how do we know the conversation occurred exactly as he said it did? Did King really say, "Never stop dreaming the dream"? Does it matter? What does matter is that Johnson sees this event today, as he has reconstructed it, as the most important turning point in his life story. The reconstructed scene is a central element of Jerome Johnson's self-defining narrative. If you are to understand who Jerome Johnson is and how he makes sense of his own life, you must know his account of his brief meeting, sometime in the mid-1960s, with Dr. Martin Luther King, Jr.

STORY THEMES AND EPISODES

How might a psychologist obtain information concerning a person's life story? Typically, life-story accounts are obtained through structured interviews or open-ended written questionnaires (McAdams, 1999). Table 10.4 outlines a standard life-story interview that I have employed in my own research. This is the interview protocol that Jerome Johnson followed. In this interview, the participant is first asked to think of his or her life as if it were a book with chapters and to identify each chapter and outline each chapter's contents. Next, the participant describes eight key scenes or episodes that stand out in the story as especially important or self-determining events. These include a high-point event, a low-point event,

TABLE 10.4	A LIFE STORY INTERVIEW
1. Life chapters	Participant divides life into its main chapters and provides a plot summary for each
2. Eight key episodes	For each of eight scenes, participant describes what happened, who was involved, what he or she was thinking and feeling in the scene, and what he or she thinks the scene says about who he or she was, is, or might be. The eight episodes are: a. High point b. Low point c. Turning point d. Earliest memory e. Important childhood episode f. Important adolescent episode g. Important adult episode h. One other important episode
3. Life challenge	Participant identifies and describes the biggest challenge or problem he or she has faced in life, how the challenge developed, and what he or she has done to meet the challenge
4. Main characters	Participant identifies and describes in detail the one character with the most positive influence in the story and the one with the most negative influence
5. Future plot	Participant provides an account of where the story is going, what will happen next, what the future chapters will look like, including main goals, dreams, and fears for the future
6. Personal ideology	A series of questions on fundamental values, religious and political beliefs, and so on, including how those values have developed over time
7. Life theme	Participant identifies a single integrative theme in the life story

SOURCE: From *The Stories We Live By: Personal Myths and the Making of the Self,* by D. P. McAdams, 1993, New York: William Morrow.

and a life-story turning point. For each episode, the respondent should describe in detail exactly what happened, who was involved, what he or she was thinking and feeling during the event, and what the event may say about his or her life story overall. In subsequent questions, the participant is asked to describe the main life challenge he or she has faced, important positive and negative characters in the story, the future chapters of the story (including goals and dreams for the future), and an account of his or her fundamental religious, ethical, and political values and how they were formed. At the end of the interview, the participant is asked to look back over the story and identify a central theme or message. The interview takes about 2 hours to complete. Typically, the interview is tape-recorded and transcribed into a typed copy, which is then subjected to various kinds of analyses.

There are many ways to analyze a life-story account. In recent years, researchers have been especially interested in identifying the central *thematic lines* in life stories. Thematic lines refer to what the characters in the story recurrently want or desire (McAdams, 1985a). In many stories, characters are often trying to get some form of power or love, or both. More generally, thematic lines often reflect what Bakan (1966) has called *agency* and *communion*. As we saw in chapters 3, Bakan identified agency and communion as two fundamental modalities in all living forms. Agency refers to the individual's efforts to expand, assert, perfect, and protect the self, to separate the self from others, and to master the environment within which the self resides. With respect to personality traits (chapters 4 through 6), agency is captured in concepts such as dominance and extraversion and is reflected as well in achievement and power motivation (chapter 7). Communion refers to the individual's efforts to merge with other individuals, to join together with others in bonds of love, intimacy, friendship, and community. With respect to traits, communion is captured in concepts such as agreeableness and nurturance, and it is also reflected in intimacy and affiliation motivation. Life stories may be compared and contrasted with respect to the strength and salience of agentic and communal thematic lines. In an agentic life story, characters strive for power, achievement, independence, mastery, and so on. In a life story dominated by communal themes, characters strive for friendship, love, intimacy, community, and so on. Some life stories contain high levels of both agentic and communal themes. And some life stories are low on both agency and communion.

Researchers have coded life stories for agency and communion themes in various ways. My colleagues and I developed and validated a system that breaks down agency and communion into four main subthemes each (McAdams, Hoffman, Mansfield, & Day, 1996). Each of these subthemes can be reliably coded in narrative accounts of key episodes in a life story, such as accounts of life story high points and turning points. Table 10.5 lists the subthemes. For agency, life-story episodes can be reliably coded for subthemes of self-mastery, status/victory, achievement/responsibility, and empowerment. For communion, life-story episodes can be reliably coded for subthemes of friendship/love, dialogue, care/help, and unity/togetherness.

Research suggests that themes of agency and communion in life stories are consistently related to people's motivational tendencies. For example, my colleagues and I have consistently found that people who tell life stories filled with the agency subthemes, like those listed in Table 10.5, tend to score relatively high on TAT achievement and power motivation and tend to list personal strivings concerning being successful and feeling strong (McAdams, 1982b, 1984a; McAdams, Hoffman, Mansfield, & Day, 1996). People who tell life stories high on communion subthemes tend to score relatively high on TAT intimacy motivation and to list personal strivings concerning establishing warm and close relationships

TABLE 10.5	**THEMES OF AGENCY AND COMMUNION IN SIGNIFICANT AUTOBIOGRAPHICAL EPISODES**

Agency

Self-mastery	The protagonist strives to successfully master, control, enlarge, or perfect the self. Through forceful and effective action, the protagonist is able to strengthen the self, to become a larger, wiser, or more powerful agent in the world.
Status/victory	The protagonist attains a heightened status or prestige among peers through receiving a special recognition or winning a contest or competition.
Achievement/ responsibility	The protagonist attains success in the achievement of tasks, jobs, or instrumental goals or in the assumption of important responsibilities.
Empowerment	The protagonist is enlarged, enhanced, empowered, ennobled, built up, or made better through an association with something larger or more powerful than the self.

Communion

Love/friendship	The protagonist experiences an enhancement of erotic love or friendship toward another person.
Dialogue	The protagonist experiences a reciprocal and noninstrumental form of communication or dialogue with another person or group of others.
Caring/help	The protagonist provides care, assistance, nurturance, help, aid, support, or therapy for another, promoting physical, material, social, or emotional welfare or well-being for another person.
Unity/togetherness	The protagonist experiences a sense of oneness, unity, harmony, synchrony, togetherness, belongingness, allegiance, or solidarity with a group of people, a community, or even all of humankind.

SOURCE: From "Themes of Agency and Communion in Significant Autobiographical Scenes," by D. P. McAdams, B. J. Hoffman, E. D. Mansfield, & R. Day, 1996, *Journal of Personality, 64,* 339–377.

with others. Barbara Woike (1995; Woike, Gershkovich, Piorkowski, & Polo, 1999) has conducted a number of studies showing links between agentic and communal themes on the one hand and TAT motives on the other. In asking individuals to describe their most memorable life experiences, Woike has shown that agentic stories line up with power and achievement motivation while communal stories tend to link to the intimacy motive. In addition, Woike has demonstrated that motives (Level 2 in personality) link not only to the content of life stories (Level 3) but also to the cognitive style that the storyteller displays when describing a most memorable experience. People with strong power and/or achievement motivation tend to employ an analytical and differentiated style when describing agentic events, perceiving more differences, separations, and oppositions in their life stories. By contrast, people with strong intimacy motivation, as assessed on the TAT, tend to employ a synthetic and integrated style when describing communal events, detecting similarities, connections, and congruence among different elements in their life stories.

Whereas agency and communion refer to content themes in autobiographical recollections, the concepts of differentiation and integration refer more to the structure or style of the narrative. With respect to structure, life stories vary widely in terms of narrative complexity. Highly complex stories contain many different ideas and plots and articulate many different connections among these elements. By contrast, simpler stories contain fewer plots and develop fewer interconnections among elements. Complex stories are not better or worse than simpler stories; they are just different. For example, contrast the multiple characters and complex subplots contained in a typical novel by Charles Dickens (e.g., *David Copperfield*) or Fyodor Dostoyevsky (e.g., *The Brothers Karamazov*) to the spare elegance of F. Scott Fitzgerald's *The Great Gatsby* or Ernest Hemingway's *The Old Man and the Sea*. All four of these novels are classics; the fact that two of them are structurally more complex than the other two seems irrelevant in determining their overall worth as literary products.

Certain personality variables at Levels 1 (traits) and 2 (characteristic adaptations) may be associated with narrative complexity in life stories. For example, a recent study of life-narrative accounts written by students and by midlife adults shows that individuals high in the trait of openness to experience (*O*: chapter 5) tend to recall and construct more complex autobiographical memories (McAdams, Anyidoho, Brown, Huang, Kaplan, & Machado, 2004). Research suggests that Loevinger's concept of ego development (chapter 9) is also correlated with the complexity of people's life stories. In a study of 50 life stories, I found that adults high in ego development tended to include more different kinds of plots in their stories than did adults low in ego development (McAdams, 1985a). Helson and Roberts (1994) found that midlife women high in ego development were more likely than those scoring low to narrate negative life scenes in such a way as to suggest that they had changed considerably through the adversity. More complex stories may involve greater levels of change in the characters. In a study of how college students narrate their own religious development, my colleagues and I found that students high in ego development (conscientious, or I-4 and above in Loevinger's scheme) were more likely to articulate a story of *transformation and growth,* suggesting that they had gone through significant religious doubts and uncertainties and were developing toward a new and more personalized religious perspective (McAdams, Booth, & Selvik, 1981). By contrast, students relatively low in ego development (mainly in the conformist, or I-3, stage) tended to deny that they had ever gone through a crisis in faith or described a period of questioning in their life that was then abandoned as they returned to their original beliefs. The low-ego development students, therefore, tended to construct a narrative of *stability and consistency.* Furthermore, they tended to accentuate the role of group standards and the beliefs of others, showing the conformist mindset associated with Loevinger's low-middle stages. Below are two verbatim accounts of religious crises. The first example is from a woman high in ego development. The second is from a man in the low-middle range of ego development (Loevinger's conformist, or I-3, stage). What differences do you see between these two accounts?

> A college student high (autonomous stage, I-5) in ego development: I think most of the serious questions evolved out of ethical problems—friends aborting fetuses, shady practices at my place of work, etc. Right and wrong were no longer clear—if they ever had been. These single issues were maybe resolved one by one, but greater ones arose. I guess one's appreciation (in the pure sense) of evil increases proportionate to age and experience. [On a trip to Germany] I stood at the ovens of Dachau [the World War II concentration camp] and asked how my Sunday-school class God could have let it happen. The questioning has not yet been resolved, but nor has it been abandoned. I rejoice in the opportunity to rail like Job against my God. (McAdams, 1985a, p. 221)

> A college student low (conformist stage, I-3) in ego development: I search for what is real. At college my previous assumptions concerning the Bible, the nature of God, and my personal beliefs and experiences were questioned and, as I perceived it, threatened. The Bible was said to be nonauthoritative, only a book. God was more of a concept and

ideal and not a friend. My personal experience of conversion and of sensing God was considered to be a subjective emotional experience. I prayed and prayed and read a variety of books presenting a variety of ways of looking at God. My search was led by a sense inside me that said that Jesus was real, God is alive, and the Bible is his Word. Looking at people's lives was the main reason for *re-accepting my first views.* I looked at people and watched their lives to see who was different in a good sense—who really cared and loved others. Then I looked at what they believed and listened to them. They also confirmed my inner yearnings. The academic look at God lacked life and life-giving potential. It was interesting and logical, but it didn't have what I was looking for in my life. (McAdams, 1985a, pp. 222–223)

Researchers sometimes focus on narrative accounts of one or two key episodes in a person's life rather than the entire life story per se (Thorne, Cutting, & Skaw, 1998). Pillemer (1998) has focused on people's recollections of momentous events in their lives. These personal event memories depict a single scene or moment in life that stands out for its rich sensory imagery and the great detail that the person remembers. Pillemer underscores the importance of four kinds of events that are vividly recalled: (a) *originating* events, marking the beginning of a plot line in the story; (b) *turning points,* marking a significant change from one plot line to another; (c) *anchoring* events, representing the stability or continuity of a given plot line; and (d) *analogous* events, displaying a pattern of activity that is very similar to what can be seen in a family of other events in the life story.

Jefferson Singer (1995; Singer & Salovey, 1993) has coined the term **self-defining memories** to denote recollections of events in one's life that the person believes to have been especially influential in shaping who he or she is. A self-defining memory is "vivid, affectively charged, repetitive, linked to other similar memories, and related to an important unresolved theme or enduring concern in an individual's life" (Singer & Salovey, 1993, p. 13). Moffitt and Singer (1994) collected narrative accounts of self-defining memories and reports of personal strivings or goals (chapter 7) from college students. They found that students who recalled more self-defining memories relevant to the attainment of their strivings expressed greater levels of positive affect about their memories. In addition, participants who reported a high number of strivings involving avoiding undesirable outcomes also recalled fewer self-defining memories with positive emotional themes. Blagov and Singer (2004) found that well-adjusted students with moderate to high levels of self-restraint expressed self-defining memories that were richer in meaning and personal significance. In the same study, more repressed or defensive students described memories that were overly general and lacking in emotional detail. Singer (1997) has also documented the role of self-defining memories in the life stories of men addicted to alcohol and drugs. These memories are typically devoid of positive agency and communion themes. Recovery from addiction involves recrafting a life story that affirms agency and communion, argues Singer, and establishes new self-defining memories that sustain hope and commitment.

McLean and Thorne (2003) coded self-defining memories written by college students for themes of separation, closeness, and conflict and for the extent to which the memories illustrated learning lessons and gaining insight. The memory accounts were also divided between those involving parents and those involving peers. McLean and Thorne found that college students tended to relate self-defining memories with their parents that contained many themes of both separation and closeness. Divorce served as a powerful catalyst for many students' stories, illustrating separation when the parents split up and closeness when the subjects themselves provided comfort for their grieving parents. Conflict appeared more often in self-defining memories with parents than with peers. But conflict memories were often also the same memories that were seen as promoting growth and insight. Other studies have shown that accounts of self-defining memories exhibiting growth and insight are associated with psychological well-being and higher levels of psychosocial maturity (Bauer & McAdams, 2004).

Life-narrative researchers also study the interpersonal and social conditions under which self-defining memories and other autobiographical scenes are formulated and communicated. In an interesting set of studies, Pasupathi (2001) arranged interviews between best friends in which one friend told the other an important event from his or her life. The experimenter randomly assigned each listener to one of two conditions. In one condition, the listener was told by the experimenter to listen attentively to the personal account that his or her friend was to tell. In the other, the listener was asked to focus his or her mind on a particular distracting task while trying to listen to the friend's account. (The task was to keep track in one's head of how many times the friend said any word that begins with "th.") The listeners were also told *not* to tell their friends about their instructions but simply to play out one of the two very different listening roles. The results showed that tellers find it a bit annoying and even depressing when their friends seem to be distracted in the conversation. Those tellers whose friends listened attentively rated the conversation as more pleasant and rewarding than did those tellers whose friends were secretly counting "th" words. More interesting was what happened weeks later, when the tellers came back to the laboratory and were asked to recall the conversations they originally had. Those tellers whose friends had been distracted had a much more difficult time remembering the personal accounts they shared, compared to those whose friends were listening to them attentively. The quality of the conversation impacted subsequent autobiographical memory. The bottom-line conclusion is that when audiences do not focus on our personal stories of meaningful events in our lives, we tend to dismiss or even forget those stories.

Fortunately for many of us, people do often listen attentively, especially when we are sharing stories we consider to be especially significant in our lives. Avril Thorne (2000; Thorne & McLean, 2003) has studied the extent to which people find attentive listeners for memories of trauma and other highly emotional events. Her research shows that a surprisingly large number of people tell stories of highly personal experiences, including self-defining memories, soon after the experiences occur. The practice of sharing stories with intimate others is so common that Thorne uses the term *intimate memories* to refer to the most salient and self-defining episodes in a person's life. Audiences serve many purposes in life storytelling. Like therapists and counselors, good listeners can provide empathy and encouragement for the teller of a sad or traumatic tale. Sharing stories also builds warmth and intimacy between friends. In addition, Thorne argues that people articulate and clarify the meanings and the nature of their self-defining memories with each new telling. Audiences help us figure out what our stories mean, and they subtly work to shape and change our stories over time.

TYPES OF STORIES

Since the time of Aristotle, scholars have speculated about the extent to which the world of stories might be reduced to a finite number of types. Aristotle identified four mythic archetypes, or basic story forms: comedy, tragedy, romance, and irony. Some researchers have provided case data to suggest that life stories may contain elements of each of these four mythic archetypes (Crewe, 1997; McAdams, 1985a; K. Murray, 1989). Focusing on the protagonist's developmental movement, Gergen and Gergen (1986) distinguish among stability, progressive, and regressive life narratives. In stability narratives, the main character does not develop or change very much; in progressive narratives, the main character grows and expands over the course of time; in regressive narratives, the main character goes backward or loses developmental ground over the course of the story. Along with many other authors, Gergen and Gergen (1986) identify what Joseph Campbell (1949) labeled as the *myth of the hero* to be a common narrative form for the establishment of identity in Western cultures, especially among men. Appearing in countless tales and stories from a wide range of cultures, the hero myth is a story of separation, initiation, and return. The general form goes like this: "A hero ventures forth from the world of common day into a region of supernatural wonder; fabulous forces are there encountered and decisive victory is won; the hero comes back from this mysterious adventure with the power to bestow boons [gifts, advantages] on his fellow man" (Campbell, 1949, p. 30).

Campbell's hero myth is an especially linear narrative; the protagonist moves forward over time and continues to grow, expand, and progress. Gergen and Gergen (1993) suggest that such a linear structure may work well for mapping the lives of some men but that women's life stories are rather less linear. Instead, women may construct stories with more multiple and contradictory plot lines, with recursive or cyclical movements and ambivalent emotional states. Furthermore, Gergen and Gergen suggest, women's life stories may be more *embodied* than men's, more intimately linked to their understanding of and experiences with their own bodies. Other authors have suggested that the structures of women's stories, as well as those of economically and culturally disadvantaged groups, remain largely a mystery to psychologists, in that these stories have often been silenced or trivialized in patriarchal societies (Heilbrun, 1988; Stewart, 1994).

While some authors have tried to develop general taxonomies of story types, others have worked from the bottom up by identifying patterns they observe in particular studies of, say, "work" stories (Mishler, 1992; Ochberg, 1988) or "parenting" stories (Pratt, Danso, Arnold, Norris, & Filyer, 2001). For example, Modell (1992) identified common themes and narrative strategies in the stories that birth parents tell about why they gave up their children for adoption. Walkover (1992) found that married couples on the edge of parenthood crafted stories about their imagined future in which they romanticized and idealized the children they were about to have, suggesting an implicit (but irrational) belief in the perfectibility of childhood. Linn (1997) identified common narrative types among Israeli soldiers who refused to engage in what they believed to be immoral acts of aggression. Gregg (1996) identified a hybrid narrative form that mixes themes of modernity and traditional Islamic faith among contemporary young Moroccans. In her study of life stories constructed by American adults, Linde (1990) found that many of her participants routinely borrowed stock images and themes from popular psychology to make narrative sense of their own lives. In a study of published autobiographies of ex-criminals, Maruna (1997, 2001) identified a common life-narrative form that most of the authors seemed to draw on to explain how they got into crime and how they eventually got out of it. In this standard *reform narrative,* early scenes of passive victimization lead to a delinquent quest and repeated scenes of "bottoming out." The negative cycle is not broken until the protagonist experiences a second chance for agency and/or communion, often through the intervention of a good friend or potential lover. The final life-story chapters consolidate reform through the protagonist's generative efforts to "give something back" to the world as he endeavors to help other actual and would-be criminals develop their own reform stories.

In an intensive interview study, my colleagues and I compared the life stories of 40 midlife adults who had distinguished themselves for high levels of what Erikson called generativity (chapter 9) to the stories constructed by 30 less-generative adults, both groups matched for demographic characteristics (McAdams, Diamond, de St. Aubin, & Mansfield, 1997). The 40 highly generative adults were chosen for their generative efforts in paid work or volunteer activities and for their high scores on self-report measures of generativity. The 30 less-generative adults scored low on our generativity scales and evidenced only modest concern for the next generation through their paid work and volunteer activities. The highly generative adults were much more likely than their less-generative peers to formulate life stories that approximated what we termed a *commitment story*, similar to Tomkins's (1987) concept of a commitment script. Table 10.6 summarizes the five main themes of the commitment story: (a) early advantage, (b) suffering of others, (c) moral steadfastness, (d) redemption sequences, and (e) prosocial goals for the future. Although every person's life story was unique, the highly generative adults, as a whole, showed statistically significantly higher levels of these five themes in their life stories compared with those of the less-generative adults.

Overall, the prototypical commitment story constructed by the highly generative adults in McAdams, Diamond, de St. Aubin, and Mansfield (1997) was a story in which the protagonist comes to believe early on that he or she has a special advantage or blessing that contrasts markedly to the pain and misfortunes suffered by others. From an early age onward, then, the protagonist feels special in a positive way. Maybe I am my mother's favorite child; maybe I am blessed with a special talent; maybe my family was poor, but the people in our

TABLE 10.6	**THE COMMITMENT STORY: FIVE THEMES CHARACTERIZING LIFE STORIES CONSTRUCTED BY HIGHLY GENERATIVE ADULTS**
1. Early advantage	As a young child, the story's protagonist enjoys a special advantage or blessing that singles him or her out in the family or vis-à-vis peers. From an early age onward, the protagonist feels that he or she is special in a positive way.
2. Suffering of others	Early in the story, the protagonist witnesses the suffering or misfortune of other people and feels sympathy or empathy for them. Objects of the protagonist's concern might include the sick, dying, disabled, mentally ill, economically disadvantaged, or any of a number of other groups or individuals that might require special care or help.
3. Moral steadfastness	By adolescence, the protagonist has established a clear and coherent belief system that governs his or her life. The belief system, often rooted in religion, remains relatively stable and steadfast over time. Once the belief system is established, the protagonist does *not* experience profound ideological doubt, uncertainty, or crisis.
4. Redemption sequences	Bad or affectively negative life events are immediately followed by good or affectively positive outcomes. The bad scene is redeemed, salvaged, made better by what follows.
5. Prosocial future	In looking to the future chapters of the life story, the protagonist sets goals that aim to benefit society in general or its institutions.

SOURCE: From "Stories of Commitment: The Psychosocial Construction of Generative Lives," by D. P. McAdams, A. Diamond, E. de St. Aubin, & E. Mansfield, 1997, *Journal of Personality and Social Psychology, 72,* 678–694.

neighborhood were especially friendly and they helped one another out, as Jerome Johnson, the black police chief, related in his life story. While I am fortunate, others suffer. Highly generative adults were much more likely than nongenerative adults to recall early experiences in which they witnessed the suffering of others and felt empathy for those other people. Experiencing the world as a place where people need to care for others (because some are blessed and some suffer), the protagonist commits the self, typically in adolescence or even earlier, to living in accord with a set of clear and enduring values and personal beliefs that continue to guide behavior across the course of the story (moral steadfastness). Moving ahead with the confidence of early blessing and steadfast belief, the protagonist encounters his or her fair share of personal misfortune, disappointment, and even tragedy in life, but these bad events often become transformed or "redeemed" into good outcomes, sometimes because of the protagonist's own efforts and sometimes by chance or external design. Jerome Johnson's chance meeting with Martin Luther King, Jr., is a good example of just such a redemption sequence. Thus, bad things happen, but they often turn good. Looking to the future with an expanded radius of care, the protagonist sets goals that aim to benefit others, especially those of the next generation, and to contribute to the progressive development of society as a whole and of its more worthy institutions.

While our original study of commitment stories focused mainly on white, middle-class adults, a second qualitative study examined the life stories of 35 midlife African-American adults, approximately half of whom scored extremely high on our measures of generativity and half of whom scored extremely low (McAdams & Bowman, 2001). The analysis confirmed the differences we observed in the first study. Highly generative African-American adults, such as Jerome Johnson, were more likely than less-generative African-American adults to construct commitment stories to make sense of their lives. In addition, the life stories of black adults revealed other themes that were not generally observed among whites. For example, the narrative accounts of the African-American participants, both highly generative and less-generative, were noteworthy for the early emergence of danger and threat in the story, the clear identification of a (bad) antagonist against whom the (good) protagonist struggled, and the powerful and beneficent role of religion and extended kin networks in coping with the dangers and the antagonists that life presents. In both studies with white and black adults, nonetheless, the commitment story appears to be an especially powerful identity format for modern adults who are committed to doing good work for the next generation. This kind of story provides a way of talking about and thinking about one's life that sustains and supports a caring, compassionate, and responsible approach to social life. While doubtlessly many kinds of life stories might be associated with strong generativity, the commitment story would appear to qualify as one story type that, in contemporary American society, may be worth emulating (McAdams, 2005).

One of the most appealing features of the commitment story is the **redemption sequence.** In a redemption sequence, a bad or emotionally negative scene turns suddenly good or emotionally positive. The bad episode is redeemed by the good that follows it. The theme of redemption is found in myths and folklore worldwide, and it is an especially powerful idea in all of the world's major religions (James, 1902/1958; Miller & C'deBaca, 1994; von Franz, 1980). Redemption sequences capture the hope that experiences of fear, loss, sadness, guilt, and the like can lead to outcomes that affirm joy, excitement, and other positive emotional states. In sharp contrast, a **contamination sequence** is the move in narrative from an emotionally positive or good scene to an emotionally negative or bad outcome. In a contamination sequence, the initial good scene is spoiled, ruined, contaminated, or undermined by what follows it. Contamination sequences suggest that good events cannot be trusted to last, that bad outcomes will inevitably follow even the best moments in life. Therefore, while redemption sequences sustain hope and commitment in narrative, contamination sequences suggest despair, hopelessness, and the endless repetition of a negative past. Redemption and contamination sequences come in many varieties. Table 10.7 provides some condensed examples gleaned from recent life-narrative studies.

We have already seen that redemption sequences in life narratives are related to individual differences in adults' generativity. But do redemption and contamination sequences connect to other aspects of psychological functioning? We might expect, for example, that people who construct life narratives with a preponderance of redemption sequences should also report higher life satisfaction and better overall mental health compared with individuals with fewer redemption sequences. By contrast, we might expect that contamination sequences should be negatively associated with mental well-being. To test these hypotheses, my colleagues and I collected life-narrative data and self-report measures of

---

TABLE 10.7	**CONDENSED EXAMPLES OF REDEMPTION AND CONTAMINATION SEQUENCES**

Redemption Sequences

Father dies ➔ the family becomes emotionally closer

Loneliness of childhood ➔ protagonist becomes a resilient adult

Severe depression ➔ protagonist recovers and feels euphoric

Pain of delivery ➔ birth of a beautiful baby

Divorce ➔ protagonist develops better relationship with her son

Protagonist is fired from job ➔ comes to see himself as a whole person

Drugs, dereliction ➔ protagonist moves to a new place, changes name, gets life organized

A very bad teaching experience ➔ protagonist moves to a new school and experiences success

Severe criticism from a co-worker ➔ protagonist becomes a better employee

Traffic accident ➔ all of a sudden "it became a cool experience"

Contamination Sequences

Marriage is wonderful ➔ spouse says she wants a divorce

Protagonist is proud at graduation ➔ father comments on how fat she looked onstage

Joy at birth of first son ➔ protagonist learns child has a serious disorder

Protagonist marries the man she loves ➔ he starts to have extramarital affairs

Protagonist gets a desired promotion ➔ the new job brings frustrations and hassles

Protagonist builds model airplane, is proud, takes it to school ➔ class bully breaks the plane

Looking forward to class trip ➔ protagonist is horrified by poverty she sees on the trip

New house is a joy ➔ repairs and bills become a nightmare

Sex is great before marriage ➔ after they marry, wife is no longer interested

Playing happily in a park ➔ young protagonist is injured and cannot find parents

Protagonist receives a gift ➔ gift is stolen

NOTE: The designation of " ➔ " connects the first scene to the outcome and thus means "leads to," "is followed by," or "results in."

SOURCE: Adapted from "Narrating Life's Turning Points: Redemption and Contamination," by D. P. McAdams & P. J. Bowman, in *Turns in the Road: Narrative Studies of Lives in Transition* (pp. 3–34), by D. P. McAdams, R. Josselson, and A. Lieblich (Eds.), 2001, Washington, DC: APA Books.

psychological well-being from two different samples of participants (McAdams, Reynolds, Lewis, Patten, & Bowman, 2001). The first sample consisted of 74 adults between the ages of 35 and 65 years. In life-story interviews, each adult described eight key life episodes, including a life-story high point, low point, and turning point. The second sample consisted of 125 college students, each of whom completed a lengthy, open-ended questionnaire asking the participant to describe in full 10 key life episodes, again including a life-story high point, low point, and turning point. We coded all the episodes for redemption sequences; however, since the students related very few contamination sequences in their written accounts, we coded for contamination sequences only the scenes described by the adults. We then correlated the redemption and contamination scores with self-report measures of psychological well-being.

Table 10.8 presents some of the results from the adult sample in this study. As you can see, redemption scores in life stories were significantly and positively associated with life satisfaction, self-esteem, and sense of life coherence and negatively associated with self-reported depression. By contrast, contamination sequences were highly and negatively associated with the three indices of well-being and positively associated with depression. The data from the student sample replicated the results for redemption sequences. Overall, then, people who construct life stories in which bad events are redeemed by good outcomes tend to be more satisfied with their lives, report higher self-esteem and life coherence, and show lower levels of depression compared with people who have fewer redemption sequences in their life stories. By contrast, people who construct life stories with relatively more contamination sequences, wherein good events are suddenly spoiled or ruined, tend to be highly depressed and report especially low levels of satisfaction, self-esteem, and life coherence compared with individuals whose life stories show few contamination sequences.

Why do redemption sequences in life stories predict well-being and contamination sequences predict depression? The reasons are at least twofold. First, it is probably true that redemption and contamination sequences reflect objective realities from the past. Therefore, happier people may be happier because they have enjoyed many events in the past in which good outcomes did, indeed, follow bad events. These sequences are reflected in their life stories. However, a second reason surely relates to the selective power of memory and the constructive nature of life narratives. Redemption and contamination sequences reflect implicit *choices* that people make in how they understand and narrate

TABLE 10.8	CORRELATIONS BETWEEN REDEMPTION AND CONTAMINATION SEQUENCES ON THE ONE HAND, AND SELF-REPORT INDICES OF WELL-BEING ON THE OTHER, IN 74 MIDLIFE ADULTS	
Well-Being	**Redemption**	**Contamination**
Life satisfaction	.37**	−.40***
Self-esteem	.28*	−.56***
Life coherence	.33**	−.46***
Depression	−.32**	.49***

NOTE: *$p < .05$; **$p < .01$; ***$p < .001$.

SOURCE: From "When Bad Things Turn Good and Good Things Turn Bad: Sequences of Redemption and Contamination in Life Narrative, and Their Relation to Psychosocial Adaptation in Midlife Adults and in Students," by D. P. McAdams, J. Reynolds, M. Lewis, A. Patten, & P. J. Bowman, 2001, *Personality and Social Psychology Bulletin, 27,* 208–230.

their autobiographical past. Choice is implicated not only in the selection of what particular scene to narrate but also in how to narrate the scene, how to frame its antecedents and consequences, and what conclusions to draw from it. In a redemption sequence, the individual narrates a sequence in which a very bad scene eventually results in some kind of positive outcome. In many instances, there are likely to be multiple outcomes for any particular event in a person's life. Yet the person telling the story in a redemptive manner manages, as Jerome Johnson did repeatedly in his life story, to elaborate on a particularly positive outcome. By contrast, the person who tells a contamination sequence manages to find the negative consequence of a particularly positive scene, and some people may be especially wont to reconstruct their lives in this manner. In both cases, the consequences may have really occurred, but there are likely to have been other consequences as well, some of which the individual has chosen not to narrate.

Therefore, it is likely that individual differences in the ways in which people narrate self-defining memories reflect both differences in the objective past and differences in the styles and manners in which people choose to make narrative sense of life. Furthermore, the individual styles employed are likely to be both the causes and the consequences of different levels of psychosocial adaptation. Thus, depressed and nongenerative people may be especially prone to narrating life in contamination terms, and the tendency to narrate life via contamination sequences may exacerbate depression itself and undermine the person's efforts to make positive contributions to the next generation. Similarly, people who feel relatively satisfied with their lives and feel that they are making important contributions to others may be especially prone to narrating their lives in redemptive terms, which in turn may further enhance their generative efforts and their sense of well-being.

WHAT IS A GOOD STORY?

People are working on their life stories, consciously and unconsciously, throughout most of their adult years. At times the work is fast and furious, as during phases of exploration and moratorium. Periods of major identity change may follow significant life changes, such as getting married or divorced, having one's first child, changing jobs, changing residences, losing one's parents or one's spouse, menopause, or retirement. They may also correspond to symbolic watersheds in the life course, such as hitting one's 40th birthday, the marriage of one's last child, the death of one's parents, retirement, or even getting those first gray hairs. During these periods, adults may call into question some of the assumptions they have lived by. They may recast their life stories to embody new plots and characters and to emphasize different scenes from the past and different expectations for the future. They may set new life goals. The sense of the story's ending may change substantially, and as the envisioned ending changes, the entire narrative may become oriented in a very different way. At other times, however, adults experience relative stability in identity. During these more tranquil periods, the story evolves slowly and in a very small way. Adults may refine slightly their life themes or tinker in minor ways with the sense of an ending. During these periods, major identity change may not seem to occur.

We see, therefore, that it is misleading to characterize the development of the life story in adulthood as either a smooth and continuous affair or a rollercoaster process of repeated change and growth. Rather, the development is both smooth and sudden, tranquil and tumultuous. Times of dramatic change and reformulation may be followed by long periods in which very little storymaking seems to occur. Every life is different in this regard, and every life story follows a unique course of development.

WHEN DID IDENTITY BECOME A PROBLEM?

The problem of narrative identity may be a modern problem, most characteristic of middle-class Westerners living in industrial societies. In more agrarian and traditional societies and at earlier points in history, the problem of contructing a self-defining life story may not have been as crucial. In societies in which sons are expected to grow up to do what their fathers do and daughters are expected to follow directly in the footsteps of their mothers, identity is *conferred* upon the young person by a social structure. In such a context, ideology and occupation are received from established authorities, exploration of alternatives is minimal, and commitment to the status quo is a fait accompli.

Even among the intellectuals of Western societies, however, the notion that a person should find or create a unique self may be a relatively recent idea. In his book *Identity: Cultural Change and the Struggle for Self*, psychologist Roy Baumeister (1986) asks at what point in the history of Western civilization identity became a central concern. When did Westerners begin to report that they were experiencing identity "crises" in their own lives? As Baumeister views it, evidence of identity exploration and crisis may be gleaned from reports of two different kinds of problems in human living. The first is the problem of *continuity over time*. In this case, identity poses itself as a problem when the person begins to wonder or worry about the extent to which he or she is essentially the same kind of person over time: "Am I the same today as I was 3 years ago?" "Will I be the same 10 years from now?" The second is the problem of *differentiation*. In this case, identity confronts the person with the task of determining how he or she is different from other people—others who, on the surface at least, seem quite similar to the self. In Baumeister's view, then, the person in the throes of an identity crisis is preoccupied with how he or she is essentially the same over time and how he or she is essentially different from other people.

Baumeister concludes that identity was not a major problem in Western societies before 1800, although many trends emerged before this time to

prepare the way for it to become a problem. Medieval society in Europe operated on the basis of lineage, gender, home, and social class. A person's identity was assigned to him or her according to these external criteria. Even during the medieval era, however, certain strains of individualism emerged, including Christianity's emphasis on individual judgment and on individual participation in the church ritual. The Protestant Reformation split the ideological consensus of Europe and made religious belief a serious identity problem for many educated people. The rise of capitalism opened up economic opportunities and created an upwardly mobile middle class. Many people of the 17th and 18th centuries, therefore, confronted significant choices in their religious beliefs—whether to follow Rome or the Protestants, for instance—and enjoyed the prospect of enhancing one's material well-being in life through entrepreneurial activity in the marketplace. Other developments before 1800 that paved the way for identity's emergence as a central problem in human lives include a general rise in individualistic attitudes, increased desires for privacy, and the growing recognition that one's private self may be quite different from one's public self.

As Europe entered what has been termed the Romantic era in the last decade of the 1700s, the two great institutions of church and state were undergoing major transformation. While the Christian church's power and influence were waning rapidly, Europeans were also questioning the legitimacy of long-established political systems, as happened in the French Revolution. Men and women of the Romantic era substituted creativity, passion, and cultivation of the inner self for Christianity as new models for identity formation. If the self were not determined by God, then its construction was left to the individual. The Romantics also became increasingly dissatisfied with the relationship of the individual to society. This dissatisfaction was expressed as a concern with individual freedom, and it eventually gave birth to various Utopian movements as well as the rise of anarchism in the 19th century. In general, Europeans

(CONTINUES)

after 1800 believed that society's consensus about basic truths and ultimate values had been lost. The person was now to fashion a personal ideology as a foundation for identity.

In the 20th century, the concern for identity grew stronger as Westerners witnessed a great proliferation of occupational and ideological choices. In addition, many social critics lamented a growing alienation among contemporary adults who, more than ever before, felt cut off from and had lost faith in authoritative institutions (Lasch, 1979; Lifton, 1979; Sartre, 1965). In the Romantic literature of the 19th century, individual heroes struggled valiantly against societal constraints. In much of 20th-century literature, on the other hand, the individual feels overwhelmed, even helpless, and more concerned than ever with finding continuity over time and establishing differentiation vis-à-vis other people.

Who am I? How do I fit into the adult world? In the wake of the industrial revolution, widespread urbanization, the decline of traditional religion, the rise of capitalism, the growing alienation of workers from their work, the demystification of life by science, the discovery of the unconscious, two world wars, and the atom bomb, these two questions appear more vexing today than ever before. As the literary critic Robert Langbaum (1982) puts it, identity may now be "*the* spiritual problem of our time" (p. 352).

Nonetheless, certain developmental trends in storymaking may be observed as people move into and through midlife. There is a sense in which the development of identity in the midlife years should ideally move in the direction of *increasingly good narrative form* (McAdams, 1993; 1996b; Rosenwald & Ochberg, 1992; White & Epston, 1990). Six standards of good life-story form may be identified: (a) coherence, (b) openness, (c) credibility, (d) differentiation, (e) reconciliation, and (f) generative integration. The prototype of "the good story" in human identity—the life narrative that suggests considerable maturity in the search for unity and purpose in life—is one that receives high marks on these six narrative standards.

Coherence refers to the extent to which a given story makes sense on its own terms. Do the characters do things that make sense in the context of the story? Do the motivations for their behavior make sense in terms of what we know about how human beings generally act? Do events follow events in a causal manner? Do parts of the story contradict other parts? A story that lacks coherence is one that leaves the reader scratching his or her head, wondering why things turned out in such an inexplicable, puzzling way. Some stories, however, are almost too coherent. They hang together so neatly that they seem too consistent to be true. A life story need not make everything fit together in a person's life. We do not need perfect consistency in order to find unity and purpose in life. Indeed, a good life story is one that also shows considerable *openness* to change and tolerance for ambiguity. Such a story propels the person into the future by holding open a number of different alternatives for future action and thought. Life stories need to be flexible and resilient. They need to be able to change, grow, and develop as we ourselves change. Openness is, nonetheless, a difficult criterion to judge in life narrative, for there is always the danger that too much openness reflects lack of commitment and resolve.

A third standard is *credibility*. The good, mature, and adaptive life story cannot be based on gross distortions. Identity is not a fantasy. People create their identities, for sure. But they do not create them out of thin air, as one might a poem or a story of pure fiction. In identity, the good story should be accountable to the facts that can be known or found out. While identity is a creative work of the imagination, it is still grounded in the real world in which we all must live.

The good story is rich in characterization, plot, and theme. The reader is drawn into an intricately textured world in which full-bodied characters develop in intriguing ways over time, and their actions and interactions define compelling plots and subplots, as tension builds to climax and then resolution. In other words, good story tends to be richly *differentiated.* Similarly, a life story should develop in the direction of increasing differentiation. As the adult matures and gathers new experiences, his or her narrative identity takes on more and more facets and characterizations. It becomes richer, deeper, and more complex. As differentiation increases, however, the adult may seek *reconciliation* between and among conflicting forces in the story, harmony and resolution amidst the multiplicity of self. The good story raises tough issues and dynamic contradictions. And the good story provides narrative solutions that affirm the harmony and integrity of the self. Reconciliation is one of the most challenging tasks in the making of life stories, especially in midlife and beyond.

The sixth standard for good story in identity is what might be called *generative integration.* To understand well this last criterion, we must again remember that a life story is about a human life. It is not simply a story that one might read in *The New Yorker* magazine. It is a mythic rendering of a particular life of a real person living in a particular society at a particular point in history. The life story seeks coherence, credibility, and reconciliation to a greater extent than might some very good stories that are purely fiction. Similarly, the human life exists in a social and ethical context that does not generally apply, or apply in the same way, to other kinds of stories (Booth, 1988). In mature identity, the adult is able to function as a productive and contributing member of society. He or she is able to take on adult roles in the spheres of work and family. He or she is able and willing to promote, nurture, and guide the next generation, to contribute in some small or large way to the survival, enhancement, or progressive development of the human enterprise. Mature identity in adulthood requires a creative involvement in a social world that is larger and more enduring than the self. It is to that world, as well as to the self, that the story is to be oriented. Ideally, the storymaker's search for unity and purpose in life should benefit both the person fashioning the story and the society within which the story is fashioned.

SUMMARY

1. While personality traits provide an initial sketch and characteristic adaptations fill in the details of human individuality, narrative approaches to personality address directly the question of what a life means, in particular what it means to the person who is living it. More than traits, motives, stages, and so on, life stories convey the overall meaning and purpose of a human life. In order to provide a full account of human individuality, therefore, the personality psychologist must examine people's self-defining life narratives.

2. Human beings are storytellers by nature, and stories appear in every known human culture. The narrative mode of human knowing emphasizes the realization of human intention organized in time whereas the paradigmatic mode of human knowing explains natural events in terms of material cause-and-effect relationships. Stories have certain recognizable structures and features, such as settings, characters, and temporally organized action sequences.

3. While stories entertain and inform, they also serve to integrate and heal. One prime psychological function of autobiographical writing is to bind together disparate aspects of a person's life in order to construct a narrative that confers unity and purpose on life. Many forms of psychotherapy implicitly or explicitly urge the client to re-story his or her life. Research also suggests that narrating personal events can

enhance health and well-being. Studies by Pennebaker show that disclosing narrative accounts of personal trauma can facilitate coping with trauma and can help prevent sickness and promote good physical health.

4. Tomkins's script theory of personality puts the role of narratives at the center of human individuality. The theory begins by positing the motivational primacy of discrete human affects, such as joy, excitement, sadness, and anger. Affects energize and direct human behavior, which over time becomes organized into scenes and scripts.

5. Tomkins views the person as a playwright who fashions a self-defining drama by linking affectively charged scenes together into life scripts, a process that he terms psychological magnification. Positive-affect scenes are magnified through variants, as the mind accentuates differences among them as variations on a theme. Negative-affect scenes are magnified through analogs, as the mind accentuates similarities and repetitions among different negative events. Scenes can be organized into many kinds of scripts. Two important scripts identified by Tomkins are commitment scripts, which involve clear ideal scenes and the striving to overcome obstacles, and nuclear scripts, which involve ambivalent and confusing scenes and the repetition of sequences in which good things turn bad.

6. McAdams's narrative approach focuses on Erikson's concept of identity. According to this view, identity is itself a life story that the person begins constructing in late adolescence and young adulthood. As an internalized and evolving narrative of the self, the life story integrates disparate roles and brings together the reconstructed past, perceived present, and anticipated future in order to provide a person with a purposeful identity in modern life. Culture provides the narrative resources for identity, and life stories are strongly shaped by gender, social structure, and the material and ideological givens of a particular society.

7. Research has examined life-story scenes or episodes for the central themes of agency and communion. Studies have shown that self-defining episodes, such as life-story high points and turning points, reflect thematic tendencies that can be predicted from personality variables outside the story itself, such as social motives and ego development. People scoring high on power and achievement motivation, therefore, tend to construct (and remember) life episodes emphasizing agency while people high in intimacy motivation tend to construct (and remember) more communal life episodes. High stages of ego development have been associated with greater levels of complexity and change in accounts of important life-narrative scenes.

8. Self-defining memories are vivid, emotionally charged, and repetitive memories that are related to an unresolved theme or issue in a person's life story. Research suggests that self-defining memories and other important autobiographical scenes are often rehearsed and modified in repeated telling with friends. The quality of these interpersonal exchanges also influences how the original scene is recalled and told again.

9. Recent research has sought to delineate different types of life stories. One general type that has been identified in studies of midlife adults is the commitment story, similar to Tomkins's commitment script. In the commitment story, the protagonist (a) enjoys an early family blessing or advantage, (b) is sensitized to the suffering of others at an early age, (c) is guided by a clear and compelling personal ideology that remains relatively stable over time, (d) transforms or redeems bad scenes into good outcomes, and (e) sets goals for the future to benefit society and its institutions. Variations on the commitment life story appear to be relatively common among highly generative midlife adults—that is, adults committed to promoting the well-being of youth and the next generation. For both midlife adults and students, the tendency to construct life stories in which bad events are ultimately redeemed into good outcomes is associated with greater psychological well-being.

10. Some life stories may be better or more adaptive than others. Over the human lifespan and with maturity, people's life stories should ideally move in the direction of greater coherence, openness, credibility, differentiation, reconciliation, and generative integration.

Interpreting People's Stories: From Freud to Feminism

People often tell stories about their lives. But how are those stories to be interpreted? Your best friend tells you a terrible secret about her family. Your mother tells you that her life was miserable until the day you were born. Your barber or hair stylist, knowing that you are taking a class in personality psychology, tells you about a dream she had a few nights ago. She was flying over Mt. Everest on a pair of scissors. "What does it mean?" she asks. In a job interview, you say, "I have been interested in this area of work since I was a little child. It all began . . ." Later, you wonder why you told it that way. What did you mean?

In life-narrative research, in clinical work, and in other applied settings, psychologists often hear or read stories about people's lives. Occasionally, they encounter full-blown life-narrative accounts, as in a life-story interview or written autobiography. More often, they hear bits and pieces—a dream here, an early memory there, an episode with mom or dad or the disenchanted spouse, a narrative account of the important things that have happened lately, and so on. Like everybody else, psychologists find that they have to make sense of these stories in some way or another. Often they fall back on common sense or implicit assumptions about what kinds of stories can be told in what sorts of situations, based on past experience and training. Sometimes psychological researchers employ objective content-analysis systems to codify and quantify narrative accounts, as we saw in chapter 10. Most of these methods of interpretation—be they (usually) informal or (occasionally) codified—assume that meanings can be drawn from the texts of people's lives in a more-or-less straightforward manner. People say what they mean, for the most part. If we listen hard, show empathy, employ a modicum of discipline and objectivity in our interpretation, we should be able to figure something out. We should be able to understand something about a person from the stories a person tells.

But interpretation is not always so easy. People's stories sometimes conceal as many meanings as they reveal. Not only do people sometimes lie to others when they tell stories, but they sometimes lie to themselves. Self-deception is a common feature of daily life, perhaps an adaptive one. And even when no deception is involved, do we ever really know what we mean—what we fully mean—when we tell a story? And can we ever know what other people mean, especially if they don't really know themselves?

This chapter is about the tricky business of interpreting the stories people tell. Going back more than 100 years to Sigmund Freud's (1900/1953) *The Interpretation of Dreams*, psychologists have puzzled over the question of interpretation. Freud believed that many stories in life—dreams among them—are designed to trick the listener. If you think you know what they mean, you are fooling yourself. Carl Jung and Alfred Adler, two early followers of Freud who broke from the master to develop their own influential theories of personality, developed their own characteristic approaches to interpretation. Jung believed that stories were filled with symbols and myths; Adler focused on the beginnings and the endings of narrative accounts, where the key ideas in a person's style of life were to be found. In the last few decades of the 20th century, a number of other theorists offered intriguing insights into the interpretation of life stories. In particular postmodernist and feminist approaches looked to culture, social structure, and other complex forces and factors within the social environment to find the keys to good interpretation.

In this chapter, I survey different ways that personality psychologists have devised to interpret the stories people tell about their lives. My emphasis is on those approaches that underscore the complexities and the contradictions of interpretation. Like the great works of poetry and fiction, people's life stories are subject to a wide range of different interpretations. People's stories are indeed literary products, in a sense, and the interpretation of these stories is something of a literary effort, as Freud knew and as contemporary postmodern theorists also know. I will survey a number of different approaches in this chapter, but they all have one thing in common. From Freud to contemporary feminists, all agree that *people's stories are not what they seem.* This is why interpretation is so hard, and so interesting.

FREUDIAN INTERPRETATION

Like everything else that is important in psychology, Sigmund Freud argued, the meanings of our lives and the stories about our lives lie hidden in the unconscious. Freud believed that human behavior and experience are determined by forces over which we have very little control and about which we are generally unaware. Of prime importance in this regard are unconscious urges regarding sexuality and aggression (chapter 7 in this book). The ways in which sexuality and aggression play themselves out in human lives are infinite. Yet certain common patterns may be discerned. From the psychoanalytic standpoint, the most common pattern is revealed in the fantasy lives of young children, wherein they may feel unconscious sexual feelings toward one parent and highly aggressive, even murderous, feelings toward another. This is, of course, the **Oedipus complex.** But the Oedipus complex is more than an unconscious problem facing preschoolers. More importantly, it is *the fundamental story* for making sense of any life from a Freudian standpoint. It is (almost literally) the mother (and father) of all (life) stories, Freud believed. To understand how Freud made sense of stories, then, you have to know and appreciate the story of Oedipus.

THE STORY OF OEDIPUS

One of the most famous tragic dramas in Western culture, Sophocles' *Oedipus Rex* was first performed in Athens between 430 and 426 B.C.E. The protagonist of the story is King Oedipus, a brilliant and courageous man in the prime of life who, at the outset of the play, has ruled the city of Thebes for many years. In the opening scene, a group of citizens, in despair over the recent famine and pestilence that have plagued Thebes, has gathered in front of the palace to ask the king for help. They have faith in the abilities of Oedipus to work wonders, for long ago he solved a great riddle and delivered the Thebans from the curse of the Sphinx. A monster with a woman's head and breasts and the body of a lion, the Sphinx had once sat on a rock outside Thebes and killed all travelers who could not answer her riddle: What animal walks on four feet in the morning, two at noon, and three at night? The clever Oedipus was the first to come up with the correct response: *man* (who crawls on fours when a child, walks erect in adulthood, and hobbles on a cane when he is old). Upon hearing the correct answer, the Sphinx killed herself. The Thebans, in gratitude, married the young Oedipus to their recently widowed queen, Jocasta, making him king of Thebes.

Freud believed that the stories people tell about their lives – via dreams, symptoms, and everyday rationalizations – conceal deeper meanings in the unconscious. Psychoanalytic interpretation involves making manifest and clear what is latent, hidden, and implicit in human lives.

Oedipus learns that the city now faces a greater curse brought on by the evil deeds of one of its citizens. He pledges to find the villain and free Thebes a second time. A blind prophet, Tiresias, tells Oedipus the truth about the villain: that it is he, the king. But there is more. The nature of his villainy is an unspeakable horror: Oedipus has unknowingly killed his father (the former king of Thebes, Laius) and made love to his mother (the queen, his wife, Jocasta). Patricide and incest are his unforgivable and yet unwitting crimes, and for these Thebes now pays the price of the gods' curse. Incredulous and enraged, Oedipus listens as the blind Tiresias reveals the long-hidden truth that only he can see:

> *And I tell you again:*
>
> *The man you have been looking for all this time,*
>
> *The damned man, the murderer of Laios,*
>
> *That man is in Thebes. To your mind he is foreign-born,*
>
> *But it will soon show that he is a Theban,*
>
> *A revelation that will fail to please.*
>
> *A blind man,*
>
> *Who has his eyes now; a penniless man, who is rich now;*
>
> *And he will go tapping the strange earth with his staff*
>
> *To the children with whom he lives now he will be*
>
> *Brother and father—the very same; to her*
>
> *Who bore him, son and husband—the very same*
>
> *Who came to his father's bed, wet with his father's blood.*

(O'Brien & Dukore, 1969, p. 21)

Oedipus, Jocasta, and all of Thebes eventually come to realize that Tiresias' vision is clear and true. Because of an oracle predicting that their son would kill his father and sleep with his mother, the king and queen of Thebes—Laius and Jocasta—long ago pierced the ankles of their newborn boy and left him to die on a lonely mountainside. A shepherd took pity on the boy, giving him to another shepherd, who gave him to the king and queen of another town, who named the boy "Oedipus" (meaning "swollen foot") and raised him as their own son, never telling him about his true origin. As a youth, Oedipus went to Delphi and learned of the oracle that he should grow up to murder his father and sleep with his mother. So that he could not fulfill what the gods had destined to be his fate, Oedipus fled, eventually happening upon the Sphinx, solving the riddle, and becoming the triumphant king of Thebes. As an impetuous man of the sword, he killed his share of men along the way. One of these was Laius, slaughtered in a forgettable skirmish at the intersection of three roads.

The price of Oedipus' crime is enormous. When she finally realizes that her husband is in fact her son, Jocasta hangs herself. Oedipus rips the golden brooches from his dead mother's gown and plunges them deep into his eyes. Blinded now like Tiresias, he finally sees the truth. At the end of the play, Oedipus banishes himself to a distant land. In later dramas (*Antigone, Oedipus at Colonnus*), he returns as something of a wise sage whose advice is greatly valued. In summary, then, *Oedipus Rex* is the story of a strong and clever young man who becomes an all-powerful king but eventually falls from glory and is maimed because of an unspeakable crime. The fall from power brings with it a kind of wisdom, in that Oedipus now knows "the truth" and eventually achieves a status, like that of Tiresias, of the blind sage. The crimes he commits are outside of Oedipus' own awareness. He kills his father and sleeps with his mother without knowing that he has done either—in other words, *unconsciously.*

So it goes with the young boy—and maybe the young girl. At an unconscious level, the young boy in the phallic stage of psychosexual development (approximately ages 3 through

In this production of *Oedipus Rex,* Jocasta comforts Oedipus, who is both her lover and her son. Freud believed that the ancient story of Oedipus provides a narrative model for the psychological dynamics of power and love, especially as they play themselves out in the unconscious lives of boys and men.

5) desires to have his mother as Oedipus had Jocasta. The desire to have the other in a powerful and sensual manner means investing the libido in that person—the process of *object choice.* In a vague, unspeakable, and mysterious way, claimed Freud, young boys seek to possess—to conquer in a powerful and an erotic manner—a primal feminine love object that exists in their fantasies and may correspond in reality to their own mothers. Equally vague and unspeakable is an unconsciously perceived threat—that from a powerful masculine force that stands in the way of the boy's conquests, represented by the father who threatens to castrate the boy. What Freud termed **castration anxiety** literally means the fear that one's penis will be cut off, but more profoundly it may symbolize the child's fear that he will, like Oedipus, lose his power (and his love object as well). Thus, the boy harbors an unconscious wish to kill the father, as Freud indeed discovered in the analysis of his own unconscious life.

The normal resolution of the Oedipus complex follows the ancient myth. The young boy eventually comes to identify with the aggressor of his fantasies, seeking to be like the father so to have the mother in a vicarious manner. The unconscious shift from object choice to identification marks both a major defeat and a victory for the boy. Like Oedipus, he can no longer be "king." On an unconscious level, the young boy at the close of the Oedipal period understands that he is weaker, smaller, and more mortal than he (unconsciously) ever imagined. The loss of power is a kind of castration, symbolized in the Greek myth when Oedipus blinds himself. Omnipotence is replaced by a definite but painful sense of limitations. Yet, from the standpoint of healthy personality development, the Oedipal defeat is ultimately a good thing. Like the blind Oedipus who knows the truth, the young boy who suffers the Oedipal defeat eventually attains the rudiments of a certain kind of wisdom and maturity. Identification with the father (and to a lesser extent with the mother as well) at the end of the Oedipus complex leaves the boy with a basic moral attitude about life, encapsulated in what Freud termed the *superego.* Without the superego, the child would become a ruthless, though perhaps clever, tyrant—able to solve riddles, surely, but woefully deficient in the more challenging task of living in a moral society.

The little boy's resolution of the Oedipus complex is the prototype for the general tendency of all of civilized humankind to repress certain instinctual urges and establish in their place great institutions of social organization, such as government and religion. Freud's most powerful and controversial rendition of this argument is *Totem and Taboo* (1913/1958)—a wildly speculative account of human prehistory that can be interpreted in literal terms or as a Freudian allegory (Hogan, 1976). In *Totem and Taboo,* Freud followed Darwin in claiming that, long ago in the history of the human species, people lived in primal hordes, each ruled by an autocratic father. Acting on his unfettered instinctual urges, the patriarchal leader kept the women of the horde for his own sexual delight and prohibited the younger men (his sons) from sharing in the bounty. This form of social organization ended, speculated Freud, when young men rose up collectively to kill the ruthless father, subsequently devouring his flesh in a totem meal. The young men symbolically accomplished an identification with the father by eating him. Collectively assuming his authority, the new rulers established fraternal social clans with strict taboos on free sexual expression, especially incest. From this first socially organized restriction of the sexual instinct evolved more elaborate restricting structures, such as bodies of laws and norms designed to quell the wild instinctual impulses of men.

But what about women? Freud attempted to adapt his Oedipal theorizing to the unconscious lives of girls and women, but even he was forced to admit that his efforts were far from satisfactory. The young girl's unconscious dilemma begins with a positive attraction toward the mother, a mixture of object choice and identification. However, the fantasized mother figure disappoints the girl when the daughter realizes that both she and the mother lack a penis, which may symbolize a lack of power. The little girl may blame the mother for the perceived deficiency, resulting in what Freud termed **penis envy.** As a result, the girl shifts some of her unconscious affections to a "stronger" father figure. The girl eventually resolves her Oedipus complex by repressing her attraction to the father and completing an identification with the mother.

Whereas the boy resolves the Oedipus complex by identifying with the father who threatens him with castration, the little girl is, in a sense, already "castrated," suggested Freud, in that she has no penis. Therefore, she cannot fear castration. Because she lacks the fear, the little girl may feel less urgency to resolve the complex via identification. For many girls, Freud suggested, the Oedipus complex may last a very long time, and for some it is only partially resolved (Freud, 1933/1964). In addition, because the superego is the heir to the Oedipus complex, many women develop superegos that are weaker and less independent than those developed by men. This may be interpreted to suggest that women have less moral sensibility than men. Another interpretation is to suggest that the woman's superego is less dogmatic and harsh, perhaps freeing her up to make moral decisions in a more flexible manner. It is probably fair to say, however, that Freud's inclinations—steeped as they were in the patriarchal world in which he lived—tended in the direction of the first interpretation.

Freud's views on the Oedipus complex in women were very controversial, even at the time of their publication. Many felt it unwise to apply a male-dominated model of sexuality to women, arguing that the little girl's Oedipal attachment develops out of her intrinsic femininity undergoing its own maturation processes. Clara Thompson, an influential analyst writing around the time of Freud's death, took issue with the claim that women literally envy the male penis. Rather, women wish to be men's equals; if such a desire for the penis exists, it is in fact a symbolic desire for power and privilege, qualities typically bestowed upon men in male-dominated societies (Thompson, 1942). Other analysts, such as Karen Horney (1939), argued that the Oedipus complex is a product of culture rather than instinct, and that its development for both men and women is strongly shaped by societal expectations, opportunities, and institutions.

I have presented a simplified rendition of the Oedipus complex in both sexes. Freud suggested complicated variations on the standard script. For instance, early object choice of both boys and girls may be directed toward *both* mother and father. Similarly, identifications that resolve the complex may incorporate both father and mother (Freud, 1923/1961). A given family's particular dynamics and constellation surely shape the Oedipal scenario, but Freud also emphasized that the complex unfolds along certain biologically mandated lines. Exactly how it is played out in the unconscious, therefore, is a complex product of the interaction of biology and experience.

With respect, furthermore, to this chapter's focus on *interpretation* let me add one more point. Freud was probably wrong in claiming that *all* children go through something like an Oedipus complex in their preschool years. Indeed, scientific research has never been able to find support for that claim. What seems more likely is that Freud hit upon a general narrative script that can be applied to many different lives, though by no means all, and one whose dynamics may be found at almost any age. In a metaphorical but deeply profound sense, the Oedipus story is about how characters struggle to live out their strong desires regarding love and power, how they are often disappointed in this quest, how they must often give up what they want most in order to live together in harmony, how an individual may feel both love and hatred toward the same person, how men compete with each other for the favor of a woman, how the young rise up to rebel against authority, and how the rebels eventually become the authorities themselves. These are universal themes.

A CASE OF OEDIPAL DYNAMICS: THE DEATH OF YUKIO MISHIMA

Freud's concept of the Oedipus complex is one of the richest sources of interpretation in the psychoanalytic tradition. While Freud's claims regarding the universality of the Oedipus complex in the lives of children is surely wrong, there is little doubt that dramatic instances of Oedipal dynamics can be observed in *some* people's lives. Let me give you one example. As a college student, I became fascinated with the writings and the life of Yukio Mishima, a Japanese novelist who committed suicide in 1970. I wanted to figure out why this tremendously successful man would, at age 46, plunge a dagger into his stomach. I believe Freud's theory of the Oedipus complex sheds some light on the mystery.

The Japanese novelist, Yukio Mishima (1925–1970), admires a sword of the type he eventually used to kill himself. One interpretation of Mishima's death and life suggest that he struggled with a very complicated Oedipus complex for most of his life, involving a confusion of object choice and identification aimed both at men he loved and at himself.

The morning he killed himself, Yukio Mishima rose early, shaved slowly and carefully, showered, and put on a fresh white cotton loincloth and a military uniform. On a table in the hall, he left the final installment of his last novel. The envelope was addressed to his publishers, who were to send a representative for it later that day. At the front gate of his home, Mishima met with four students, and the five of them drove to a Tokyo army base. According to a plan rehearsed for weeks, Mishima and the four fought off a group of army personnel with their swords, took hostage one General Mashita, and forced a temporary truce whereby a thousand men of the 32nd Infantry Regiment were to gather in front of the headquarters at noon to hear Mishima deliver a patriotic speech. Constant heckling cut the speech short. Mishima and the four then retreated to a back room and, as planned for weeks, performed the Japanese ceremonial rite of *seppuku*, in which he shouted a last salute to the Emperor of Japan and then plunged a samurai dagger deep into his stomach, forcing the cutting edge across his abdomen from left to right. One of the four students then chopped off his head. For years, Mishima had rehearsed this gory suicide in numerous plays and stories he wrote, and in his private fantasies.

Yukio Mishima was in the prime of his life when he enacted the suicide on November 25, 1970. He was healthy, successful, famous, rich, and, according to most who knew him, relatively happy. With more than 100 full-length books to his credit, he was considered by many the single greatest novelist of modern Japan. And he was much more than a novelist. He was a playwright, a sportsman, a film actor, the founder of a private army, a family man, and a world traveler. Indeed, one biographer characterized Mishima as the "Leonardo da Vinci of modern Japan" (Scott-Stokes, 1974).

From the many notable elements in Mishima's life history, let us briefly examine seven, drawn from Mishima's autobiographical writings (Mishima, 1958, 1970) and the English biographies written by Scott-Stokes (1974) and Nathan (1974).

1. On Mishima's 50th day of life (in 1925), his paternal grandmother took the infant away from his mother and moved him, crib and all, into her dark sickroom downstairs, where Mishima lived until he was 12. In the first few years, Mishima's mother was able to see her son only during times of feeding. Later in childhood, Mishima would meet her on an occasional secret rendezvous. For the most part Mishima's grandmother strictly controlled the environment of his early years. Because of her neuralgia, she could tolerate little noise. Mishima was allowed to play quietly with three carefully chosen cousins, all girls. As a young boy, Mishima spent many of his waking hours nursing his sick grandmother, sponging her brow, massaging her back and hip, bringing her medicine, and leading her to the toilet.

2. From the age of 4, Mishima was obsessed with bizarre fantasies of heroism that presaged his eventual suicide—fantasies "tormenting and frightening me all my life" (Mishima, 1958, p. 8). One of these fantasies was formed in response to seeing a handsome young laborer bearing buckets of animal excrement. The 4-year-old Mishima was fascinated with the figure of the "night-soil man," experiencing a confusing mixture of excitement, longing, and sadness in his presence. The night-soil man became, in Mishima's fantasy life, a model for the tragic hero whose body is in constant communion with death. As decaying matter, the feces symbolize death.

3. Mishima's fantasies of heroism were suffused with homosexual longing. His feelings for the night-soil man were replayed again and again in subsequent fantasies in which he felt a powerful sexual attraction to muscular young men. One of the students who accompanied Mishima on the day of his death is thought to have been his homosexual lover.

4. Though little solid information is available, Mishima's marriage of 13 years to Yoko Sugiyama appeared to most people to have been a happy one. In their many public appearances, Mishima and Yoko seemed to enjoy each other. Mishima often brought Yoko into his conversations with others, soliciting her opinions and apparently valuing her responses to a degree that was unusual for other male Japanese writers. The couple raised two children.

5. In the late 1950s, Mishima began to express dissatisfaction with the process of writing fiction. Despite the critical acclaim of his work, he began to see writing as a cowardly escape from reality. He began to contrast the *word* and the *act,* arguing that words were "corrosive" and that heroism in life could be attained only by the pure action of a strong and beautiful body.

6. In order to make his own body strong and beautiful, Mishima began, at the age of 30, a rigorous weight-lifting program that he followed religiously to the week he died. A

frail and sickly boy and youth, Mishima transformed himself in his 30s into the musclebound hero of his fantasies. In strange ways, weight lifting was connected to death in Mishima's mind. Attacking the barbell involved "ceaseless motion, ceaseless violent deaths, ceaseless escape from cold objectivity—by now, I could no longer live without such mysteries" (Mishima, 1970, p. 76). The "ceaseless violent deaths" of weight training prepared him for the glorious final death that would make him a tragic hero:

> I cherished a romantic impulse toward death, yet at the same time I required a strictly classical body as its vehicle. ... A powerful, tragic frame and sculpturesque muscles are indispensible in a romantically noble death. Any confrontation between weak, flabby flesh and death seemed to me absurdly inappropriate. (Mishima, 1970, pp. 27–28)

7. In the 1960s, Mishima created a private army, called the Shield Society. The army was dedicated to the revival of patriotism in modern Japan and to the ultimate defense of the Japanese emperor. Mishima said he wished to save Japan from both communism and Western capitalism. The army was composed of college students, for the most part, including the four who witnessed the *seppuku* on that November day in 1970.

What was the psychological meaning of Mishima's suicide? I believe that part of the meaning derives from a fundamental and fatal confusion in Mishima's life between "having" and "being" (McAdams, 1985c). In Freud's terms, it is an Oedipal confusion between **object choice** and **identification**. According to Freud, the person tends, on an unconscious level, to relate to important other people in his or her life in one or both of two very primitive ways. The person seeks either to *have the other in a powerful/sensual way* (object choice) or to *be the other* (identification). In object choice, the person unconsciously desires the other as an object of affection. He or she feels, unconsciously, a strong need to "own" the other person, to hold on to the other as the exclusive object of his or her sensual longings. This is, argued Freud, the basic unconscious way that preschool boys relate to their mothers (and/or mother figures in their environment) and preschool girls to their father (and/or father figures) in the Oedipus complex. Identification, on the other hand, involves the desire to be like the other, to take in all of the other's qualities and, quite literally at the unconscious level, to become the other. The desire to be the other is sometimes commingled with a strong fear of or hatred for the same other, as in the case of what psychoanalysts have termed *identification with the aggressor*. Identification is, argued Freud, the basic unconscious way that preschool boys relate to their fathers (and/or father figures) and preschool girls to their mothers (and/or mother figures) in the Oedipus complex.

Object choice and identification appear to be related to each other in an extremely interesting way. Freud suggests that, in some sense, *object choice is generally preferred at the unconscious level* and that *identification arises often when object choice is thwarted,* as is the case most commonly in the Oedipus complex. In other words, we seek first to *have* the other, but when we cannot have the other we seek to *be* the other. This is why, said Freud (1917/1957), people often take on the personal characteristics of loved ones after those loved ones have died. With the death of the other, object choice is no longer a possibility, and the person thus comes to identify with the lost object. A symbol for the identification with the other in dreams, fantasy, and mythology is *eating* the other—the literal "taking in" of the lost object.

Because of a complex host of factors, including his 12-year stay in his grandmother's sickroom, Mishima was never able to sort out, on the unconscious level, object choice and identification. Rather than developing a typical sensual orientation to his mother and coming to identify with a father figure in the Oedipus complex, Mishima came to project both object choice and identification onto the same alternative object: the tragic hero ini-tially identified as the night-soil man. Mishima's life story can thus be understood in terms of transformations over time in the tragic hero, whom he longed both *to have* and *to be*. In *Confessions of a Mask,* Mishima (1958) traces how the tragic hero was transformed in his childhood and adolescent fantasies from the night-soil man to a picture of Joan of Arc, then to the figure of the Christian martyr Saint Sebastian, and finally to his first real-life love object—a strapping teenaged boy named Omi.

At the age of 14, Mishima fell in love with a boy whom he also wished to become. Omi was the real-life personification of the tragic oedipal hero that Mishima had first identified as the night-soil man. In addition, Omi was everything that, in reality, Mishima was not. Whereas the teenaged Mishima was weak and sickly, Omi was strong and robust—the adored best athlete in class. Whereas Mishima was constantly absorbed in thought and fantasy, Omi seemed to be an unselfconscious youth devoted to the pure action of the body. Whereas Mishima was sheltered and naive, Omi seemed, in Mishima's perception, to exude real-world confidence, maturity, and an intimate acquaintance with sex, death, and heroism.

Mishima's homosexual love for Omi, however, came to a grinding halt one day on the playground when he felt pangs of jealousy while observing Omi's flawless performance on the parallel bars. In this moment, Mishima realized that he wished to be like Omi as much as he wished to have Omi in a sensual way. The fact that he was too weak and sickly to be like his lover infuriated Mishima, forcing him to abandon his object choice and, as Freud would have it, to accelerate his mission to *become* Omi, the tragic hero. Remember that eating the object may symbolize, in fantasy, identification with the object. The loss of Omi and subsequent identification with him are symbolized in a startling dream that Mishima had shortly after the playground scene in which he literally ate a naked young boy served to him on a platter.

In adulthood, Mishima struggled to become Omi through his rigorous weight-training program. By changing weak and flabby flesh into muscle, Mishima fashioned himself into the tragic hero that he had loved from the age of 4. No longer was his oedipal love object con-fined to internal fantasy or the external world. By becoming Omi and the night-soil man, *he came unconsciously to be his own lover.* Therefore, if he was to become Omi (identification), he *must have himself* (object choice). One result of this unconscious dynamic may have been the intensified narcissism of his later years: His egotistical manner suggested that he had quite literally fallen in love with himself. Another result, I would argue, was his suicide.

For Mishima, the Japanese rite of *seppuku* had always had a profoundly sexual signifi-cance. Since the age of 4, Mishima had romanticized death, and his novels and stories are filled with erotic images of death and killing. *Seppuku* was, for Mishima, a macabre sexual union with himself. It enabled him to consummate symbolically both his desire to be and to have Omi. In thrusting the dagger into his own stomach, Mishima became both the lover and the beloved—symbolically, both the male phallus and the female vagina. At the moment of death, he was able, therefore, to become the tragic hero of his Oedipal dreams and to have that same tragic hero simultaneously, in a deadly sexual union.

THE CASE OF DORA

In general, people have little insight into the meanings of their lives, Freud argued. But occa-sionally they may be able to catch a glimpse of the unconscious, sometimes through dreams. Yet even then, they are not likely to know how to make sense of the glimpses they do get unless they are schooled in the psychoanalytic method of interpretation. Illustrated mainly in the clinical case studies he published (see Table 11.1), Freud developed a psychoanalytic

TABLE 11.1	FOUR FAMOUS CASE STUDIES IN THE HISTORY OF PSYCHOANALYSIS
1. Anna O.	From 1880 to 1882, Josef Breuer treated this young hysteric, whose symptoms included paralysis of limbs, disturbed vision, and dual personality. The symptoms worsened with the death of her father in 1881. Breuer and Anna O. discovered the "talking cure," through which Anna O. experienced relief from the symptoms by talking about her daytime hallucinations and fantasies associated with the symptoms. The talking "unstrangled" the emotions that were producing neurotic symptoms. The therapy ended badly, however, after Anna O. experienced "phantom pregnancy" and "hysterical childbirth," unconsciously believing that Breuer had fathered a child within her.
2. Frau Emmy von N.	In 1889, Freud began treating Frau Emmy von N., employing the cathartic "talking cure" pioneered by Breuer. The patient suffered from facial ticks and speech disturbances. Freud attempted to trace each of her symptoms to its root by asking her under hypnosis to explain its meaning. Though the method met with some success early on, the patient's problems eventually escalated to include the refusal to eat. Freud came to realize that each of her symptoms was highly overdetermined: Each overt symptom represented many emotional threads woven into a single pattern. For example, refusing to eat was the manifest culmination of many latent associations centered on the arousal of disgust for the act of eating, disgust over cold meat and fat, fear of contracting a disease by eating with shared implements, and revulsion at the act of spitting into a spittoon at dinner.
3. Little Hans	Little Hans was a 5-year-old boy who suffered from an intense fear of horses. Though Freud saw the boy only once, he was able to offer a psychoanalytic interpretation of his symptoms based largely on letters written to him by the father of Little Hans. Freud suggested that Little Hans was experiencing an especially severe Oedipus complex. Little Hans was fascinated with his own penis, calling it his "widdler." He liked to touch his penis and desired that his mother touch it, too. She warned him not to do this and even threatened to have it cut off. Little Hans's fear of horses was a manifestation of castration anxiety. Horses, with their large "widdlers," represented his father, whom Little Hans both loved and feared as the source of castration.
4. The Rat Man	This 29-year-old man suffered from severe obsession neurosis. He was tormented in his mind by a fantasy of rats nibbling at the backside of his girlfriend. He also had similar thoughts of rats feeding on his father's anus. Early childhood experiences relating to toilet training and erotic feelings were partial sources of the rat image. As a child, the patient had seen a rat near his father's grave and fantasized that it had been nibbling at the corpse. The neurosis was precipitated shortly after the man's army captain told him about an Asiatic punishment involving live burial of a prisoner who was then attacked from behind by rats. Freud was able to show that the symptoms provided a temporary escape from conflict by preventing him from finishing his education, marrying a socially acceptable woman, and thereby ending his current relationship with his beloved mistress.

SOURCE: From *Studies on hysteria,* by J. Breuer & S. Freud, in Vol. 2 of T*he standard edition of the complete psychological works of Sigmund Freud,* by J. Strachey (Ed.), 1893–1898, London: Hogarth; "Analysis of a Phobia in a Five-Year-Old Boy," by S. Freud, in Vol. 10 of *The standard edition,* 1909/1955, London: Hogarth; "Notes Upon a Case of Obsessional Neurosis," by S. Freud, in *Three case histories* (pp. 15–102), by S. Freud, 1909/1963, New York: Collier Books

mode of investigation and interpretation that relies on decoding hidden and disguised meanings. From a psychoanalytic standpoint, interpretation is always a matter of going beneath the surface, beyond the obvious, to explore a mysterious realm of private imagery. Psychoanalytic interpretations seek to uncover secrets, solve mysteries, and decode disguised

AN ALTERNATIVE TAKE ON OEDIPUS: CHODOROW'S GENDER THEORY

Psychoanalyst Nancy Chodorow (1978) reinterprets the Oedipus complex from a feminist standpoint in order to explain gender differences in personality and the role of mothering in contemporary Western societies. Chodorow begins her argument with a stark, cross-cultural fact: *Women mother.* Biologically speaking, women bear children; sociologically speaking, women, in virtually all human societies, "take primary responsibility for infant care, spend more time with infants and children than do men, and sustain primary emotional ties with infants" (p. 3). Although the percentage of adult women employed in paid work outside the home has increased dramatically over the course of the 20th century in the United States and western Europe, mothering is still the province of women. Indeed, most babysitters, nannies, daycare workers, and nursery school teachers are women, and most boys and girls spend most of their early childhood in the company of women. Even in those two-career households in which fathers endeavor to engage in greater levels of childcare than the traditional masculine role has typically allowed, mothers still tend to do the lion's share of caregiving, especially with very young children, as empirical research has decisively shown (e.g., Biernat & Wortman, 1991).

Chodorow (1978) focuses on the different experiences of little girls and boys as they grow up in "a male dominant but father-absent family where women mother" (p. 40). She argues that by age 3 or 4, children have developed a basic sense of themselves as either female or male as a result, in part, of the different ways in which mothers relate to girls and boys. Even before the onset of the Oedipus complex, mothers tend to relate to girls with a greater sense of "openness and continuity" (p. 109). They identify more with their daughters than they do with their sons. Mothers and daughters experience greater levels of intimacy, merger, and a sense of oneness with each other. The relationship between mother and daughter becomes emotionally richer and more complex over time, a relationship of dependence,

attachment, and symbiosis. By contrast, "mothers experience their sons as a male opposite" (p. 110). Sons are viewed as differentiated from their mothers, and maternal behavior is geared toward enabling sons to attain independence and autonomy. While mothers may cherish their sons and love them intensely, their attitude toward sons will always be one of opposition: He is male; he is not like me; he will grow up to be different, separate.

Over the course of his career, Freud became increasingly aware of the different experiences of girls and boys in the preoedipal period. Freud observed that the girl's preoedipal attachment to her mother tends to last longer than the boy's attachment to mother and that the relationship between mother and daughter can be much more dramatically intense and ambivalent than that between mother and son. Nevertheless Freud felt compelled to describe the female Oedipus complex in terms that were parallel to the experience of boys. According to the orthodox Freudian position, the Oedipal girl shifts her affection from mother to father when she realizes that father possesses the coveted penis. Chodorow concedes that the little girl may become disappointed in her mother, or see her as a rival, and the little girl may indeed form a new attachment to her father. But the relationship between father and daughter is rarely strong enough to erase the enduring mother/daughter bond:

> For a girl ... there is no single oedipal mode or quick oedipal resolution, and there is no absolute "change of object." Psychoanalytic accounts make clear that a girl's libidinal turning to her father is not at the expense of, or a substitute for, her attachment to her mother. Nor does a girl give up the internal relationship to her mother which is a product of her earlier development. Instead, a girl develops important oedipal attachments to her mother *as well as* to her father. These attachments, and the way they are internalized, are built upon, and do not replace, her intense and exclusive preoedipal attachment to her mother. (Chodorow, 1978, p. 127)

(CONTINUES)

FEATURE 11.A *(CONTINUED)*

A girl's Oedipal situation, therefore, is multilayered and complex, and it affords no simple resolution. As a result, the girl's basic gender identity is developed in the context of an ongoing and richly nuanced relationship with mother. The feminine self is defined *in relation*. For little boys, however, gender identity is a greater puzzle, a mysterious problem to be solved. Even though the boy may identify with the father, he is not likely to acquire the intimate familiarity with the father's traditional roles—as the man who works outside the house in order to bring home money and support the family—that little girls naturally develop with their mothers. In a sense, the boy must figure out how to be a man on his own, *through opposition*. According to Chodorow, the little boy experiences his own masculinity in opposition to the world of women. He knows that men are different from women, but he doesn't know exactly how. The little boy identifies with a disembodied "position" in the world—he renders a guess about what the position of men might be, and then he patterns himself after the guess. The masculine self is defined through separation and guesswork. By contrast, the feminine self develops from the connectedness of human relations.

What are the results of these two very different experiences of the Oedipal period? Chodorow (1978) suggests that girls emerge from early childhood "with a stronger basis for experiencing another's needs and feelings as one's own." Girls come to experience themselves as "less differentiated than boys, as more continuous with and related to" other people (p. 167). Consciously and unconsciously, the girl experiences herself as continuous with her environment, connected in a web of intimacy (Gilligan, 1982). The boy, by contrast, must work to separate himself from the web, to identify the essential nature of maleness through separation, opposition, and individuation.

In addition, their differential experiences in the family prepare girls and boys for society's gender roles. Out of the mother/daughter bond emerge daughters with mothering capacities and the desire to mother, making for what Chodorow calls "the reproduction of mothering" from one generation to the next. By contrast, mothers (and fathers as nonmothers) produce sons whose nurturant capacities and needs are systematically curtailed and repressed, preparing the way for men's primary participation in the impersonal, nonfamily world of work and public life.

messages. The interpretive motto within the psychoanalytic tradition is this: Don't trust what you see; the surface is deceptive; the real truth lies between the lines and beyond the obvious. Let us examine in more detail Freud's peculiar method of making sense of stories by looking closely at one of his most famous case studies.

On October 14, 1900, Freud announced to his good friend, Wilhelm Fliess, that he was working on a case worth recording for history. "It has been a lively time," he wrote, "and I have a new patient, a girl of eighteen: the case has opened smoothly to my collection of picklocks" (Freud, 1954, p. 325). Three months later, the case was over. The "girl of eighteen" broke off therapy, putting an abrupt end to Freud's attempt to unlock the coffered treasures of her mind. Before the vaults were shut, however, Freud managed to escape with a few precious jewels. In January of the following year, Freud wrote the account of his short but exhilarating expedition: "Fragment of an Analysis of a Case of Hysteria" (1905/1963). He gave to the girl of 18 the name *Dora*.

Attractive, intelligent, articulate, and economically well-off, Dora was rarely happy with her life. She suffered from a number of symptoms that, Freud believed, were manifestations of the psychological disturbance termed *hysteria*. These included periodic difficulties in breathing, recurrent headaches; fainting spells, and violent attacks of nervous coughing often accompanied by a loss of voice. Though these symptoms took a physical form, they did not appear to have a physical cause. In addition, Dora was frequently depressed and irritable, argued incessantly with both her mother and her father, and had, on one recent occasion, hinted at suicide, leaving a note that said she could no longer endure life. Alarmed by her deteriorating condition, Dora's father insisted that she see his friend, Dr. Sigmund Freud, for therapy. Dora had seen many doctors during her troubled adolescent years, and she was very skeptical about Freud's ability to help her. During her regular visits with Freud over the next three months of therapy, Dora repeatedly disputed his interpretations and recommendations. At times the willful patient and her equally stubborn analyst seemed to spar like gladiators in a deadly game. When Freud felt he was on the brink of understanding more clearly the source of her problems, Dora suddenly quit therapy and deprived him of the interpretive victory he sought. Freud (1905/1963) was shocked and hurt: "Her breaking off unexpectedly, just when my hopes of a successful termination of the treatment were at their highest and her thus bringing those hopes to nothing—this was an unmistakable act of vengeance on her part" (p. 131).

Dora had good reason to take vengeance on the older generation, of which Freud was certainly a part. She had unwittingly become entangled in a web of deceit and infidelity that involved her father, mother, and a married couple who were their contemporaries— Herr and Frau K. Dora's father was a wealthy industrialist who had carried on a sexual affair with Frau K for many years. There is good reason to believe that Herr K knew of the affair and considered his friend's daughter—the teenaged Dora—to be a fair exchange for his wife, tacitly "handed over" to him as compensation for his tolerating the relationship between his wife and Dora's father. Herr K was extremely friendly to Dora, sending her frequent gifts and taking long walks with her. While Frau K nursed Dora's father back to health during his many illnesses, Dora worked as a babysitter for the K children and became a very good friend of her father's lover, discussing with Frau K a number of intimate topics, including sexuality. Unhappy in her marriage and repeatedly frustrated with her daughter, Dora's mother, on the other hand, spent most of her day cleaning house. All four adults attempted to conceal from Dora the truth about their tangled and pathetic lives. Dora, however, was well aware of the affair between her father and Frau K and suspected that her father, whom she claimed to love dearly, condoned Herr K's romantic interest in her. She may also have suspected that part of her father's reason for insisting on therapy was the hope that Freud would be able to convince Dora that no illicit affair was taking place. When he realized that Freud was more concerned about discerning the truth than lying to Dora, Dora's father lost interest in the therapy and apparently did not protest when his daughter terminated her sessions with Freud at the end of the year.

Two Traumatic Events

In her discussions with Freud, Dora revealed two incidents from her past in which Herr K had made sexual advances. Two years before, as they walked back to a vacation house from a visit to an Alpine lake, Herr K had proposed his love to Dora and, doubtlessly, intimated that the 16-year-old girl make love to him. Dora responded by slapping his face. Frightened and insulted, she told her mother of Herr K's proposition; her mother told her father, her father confronted Herr K about the report; and Herr K denied that any such event ever transpired and added that Dora was obsessed with sexual matters anyway—his wife had told him this—and doubtlessly fantasized the whole incident. Her father took Herr K's word over his daughter's. Two years before the incident, when Dora was 14, Herr K had suddenly embraced and kissed her at his place of business. Experiencing a "violent feeling of disgust" (Freud, 1905/1963, p. 43), Dora broke loose from Herr K and ran into the street. Though neither of them ever mentioned this first incident (until Dora reported it to Freud in therapy), Dora continued to be friendly to Herr K afterward, meeting him for regular walks, accepting his gifts, and babysitting for the children. It was not until the scene at the lake, two years later, that she began to express extreme dislike for Herr K.

Freud saw these two incidents as the traumatic kernels around which Dora formed her hysterical symptoms. Freud believed that all neurotic symptoms have meaning. In content and form, *neurotic symptoms are symbolic manifestations of unconscious fears, desires, conflicts, and mysteries.* Trying to connect Dora's symptoms to the two incidents with Herr K, Freud asked Dora to engage in **free association** in response to her memories of the events. A standard procedure in psychoanalysis, free association involves the patient letting his or her mind wander in response to a stimulus and reporting all thoughts (associations) aloud to the therapist as they occur. Freud believed that unconscious currents rise to the surface in free association and that the perceptive therapist can interpret the associations in order to make psychological sense of the case.

Based on Dora's associations to the two traumatic incidents, Freud arrived at a tentative and partial explanation for some of her symptoms, especially her troublesome bouts of coughing. Herr K was a handsome man toward whom the young Dora had obviously been attracted. Freud reasoned that the disgust Dora felt in response to Herr K's first kiss disguised her sexual interest. Her disgust took the place of excitement by the neurotic process of *reversal of affect*—a pleasurable emotion that is in some sense threatening (sexual excitement) is replaced by an unpleasurable one that is less threatening (disgust). In addition, Freud (1905/1963) believed, disgust is a common, though neurotic, "means of affective expression in the sphere of sexual life" (p. 47), especially on the part of women in response to the male sexual organ because it supposedly serves as a reminder of urination (and, relatedly, defecation). Furthermore, *displacement* of sensation transferred the positive sensation of sexual arousal from the lower region of the body (Dora's genitals) to the upper region (her thorax and mouth). Since the incident, Dora had occasionally been troubled by a sensory hallucination in which she could feel the pressure of Herr K's embrace on the *upper* part of her body. Freud speculated that when Herr K embraced her on that first fateful day, he was highly sensually aroused and that Dora felt in the *lower* part of her body, through the layers of clothing they both wore, the pressure of his erect penis:

> In accordance with certain rules of symptom-formation which I have come to know, and at the same time taking into account certain other of the patient's peculiarities, which were otherwise inexplicable—such as her unwillingness to walk past any man whom she saw engaged in eager or affectionate conversation with a lady—I have formed in my own mind the following reconstruction of the scene. I believe that during the man's passionate embrace she felt not merely his kiss upon her lips but also the pressure of his erect member against her body. The perception was revolting to her; it was dismissed from memory, repressed, and replaced by the innocent sensation of pressure upon her thorax, which in turn derived an excessive intensity from its repressed source. Once more, therefore, we find a displacement from the lower part of the body to the upper. On the other hand, the obsession which she exhibited in her behaviour was formed as though it were derived from the undistorted recollection of the scene. She did not like walking past any man who she thought was in a state of sexual excitement, because she wanted to avoid seeing for a second time the somatic sign which accompanies it. (Freud, 1905/1963, pp. 45–46)

As I described it in chapter 9, Freud believed that the mouth was the first erogenous zone. For the infant, the libido is centered in the oral zone, and sucking at the mother's breast is therefore the "starting point of the whole of sexual life, the unmatched prototype of every later sexual satisfaction," to which fantasy recurs in times of need (Freud, 1916/1961, p. 341). For Dora, the mouth retained an extraordinary sensual significance as she grew older. Compared with most other people, Freud argued, Dora had probably experienced excessive oral stimulation in childhood. She had been a thumbsucker for many years, continuing to derive sensual pleasure from sucking as she developed through her early and middle child years. A key childhood memory for Dora involved her sitting contentedly on the floor, sucking her thumb as she tugged at her brother's ear. Overlying this oral sensitivity was Dora's unconscious and highly charged personal symbolism for sucking. Again based on Dora's associations, Freud speculated that she unconsciously fantasized sexual relations between her father and Frau K in oral terms. Indeed, Dora consciously believed that her father was frequently impotent and that he therefore often obtained sexual satisfaction and experienced orgasm with Frau K through oral stimulation. (She had read about such sexual practices while babysitting for the K children.) Dora's sexual fantasy about her father and Frau K, combined with other images and experiences centered on orality, produced an oral symptom of hysteria: her persistent cough. A short time after Dora "tacitly accepted" Freud's interpretation (Freud, 1905/1963, p. 65), the cough disappeared.

The Dream of the Jewel-Case

During the course of therapy, Dora reported to Freud that she had again had a dream that she had dreamed in exactly the same way on a number of prior occasions. As one "royal road to the unconscious," a recurrent nighttime dream was a particularly rich piece of psychological data, in Freud's view, so he devoted a good deal of time and energy to interpreting it. Here is the dream as related by Dora:

> A house was on fire. My father was standing beside my bed and woke me up. I dressed myself quickly. Mother wanted to stop and save her jewel-case; but father said: "I refuse to let myself and my two children be burnt for the sake of your jewel-case." We hurried downstairs, and as soon as I was outside I woke up. (Freud, 1905/1963, p. 81)

Dora reported that she had first had this dream two years ago, on the three successive nights at the lake immediately following Herr K's proposition. Now it had come back, in the wake of her recollection of the same incident. What was the meaning of the dream? To find out, Freud asked Dora to associate freely to each part of the dream, letting her mind wander in response to each element and symbol and reporting aloud the stream of thought and affect as it spontaneously flowed. Freud tied the rich web of her dream associations together with the facts and conjectures of the case, attempting to make sense of both the dream and Dora's symptoms as alternative expressions of the same unconscious dynamics (see Figure 11.1).

Dora's first association is to a recent argument between her father and mother. For some reason that she does not understand, the dream reminds her of a parental dispute about locking her brother's bedroom door. Recently, Dora's mother wanted to lock the door at night, but her father objected, claiming that "something might happen in the night so that it might be necessary to leave the room" (Freud, 1905/1963, p. 82). Something like a *fire*, Freud conjectures, and Dora agrees. Dora then remembers that, two years ago at the lake, her father had worried about a fire. The family and the K's were staying during this time at a small wooden house that her father feared might easily burn down. This was precisely the

FIGURE 11.1	SOME ASSOCIATIONS FROM DORA'S DREAM OF THE JEWEL CASE

The many connections among these dream images, behavioral symptoms, and other elements in the Dora case are explained in the text and in Freud (1905/1963). Lines between boxes show associations; arrows show oppositions.

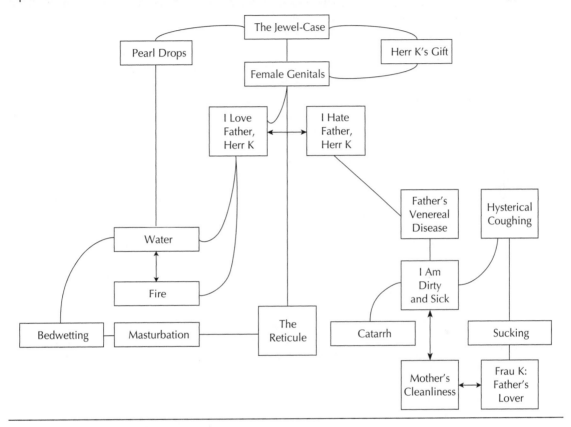

time that the dream first occurred and, of course, the time of Herr K's proposition. The fire in the dream is a natural outgrowth of these events.

Dora remembers that she returned from a walk with Herr K to the wooden house at noon and decided to take a nap on a sofa in one of the bedrooms. Shortly after lying down, she awoke, startled, to see Herr K standing beside her (as her father had awakened her and stood at the foot of her bed in the dream). She protested sharply, but Herr K responded that he was "not going to be prevented from coming into his own bedroom when he wanted" (Freud, 1905/1963, p. 84). Determined to stay clear of Herr K for the rest of their time on the lake, Dora secured a key for the bedroom, but Herr K subsequently stole the key! After that, she always *dressed quickly* in the bedroom, as she did in the dream, in fear that Herr K would break in on her at any time. On one level, then, the dream brings to resolution Dora's problem with Herr K. In the dream, her father *saved* her from the fire by whisking her through the unlocked door of her bedroom so that she could escape. In so doing, her father symbolically saved her from the "fiery" sexual advances of Herr K.

The significance of sexuality in the dream is best seen, argues Freud, in the image of the *jewel-case*. Dora's associations to this particular element in the dream bring to mind an argument between her father and mother about jewelry. Mother had wanted pearl *drop* earrings, but father insisted instead on buying her a bracelet. Dora is also reminded that Herr K had once bought her a jewel-case—one of his many gifts to her. Freud points out that the word "jewel-case" (*Schmuckkstchen* in German) is a common slang word for a virgin girl's *genitals.* Dora quickly retorts, "I knew you would say that" (Freud, 1905/1963, p. 87), a response that Freud remarks is "a very common way of putting aside a piece of knowledge that emerges from the repressed" (p. 87).

The dream concerns Herr K's attempt to make Dora's jewel-case his own—that is, to have sexual intercourse with her—and Dora's contradictory wishes (a) to escape his attempt and (b) to give in and thereby offer her jewel-case—her virginity, her genitals, her love—to him as a "gift." While her father functioned as a savior in the dream, he also represented, argues Freud, the object of Dora's own romantic/sexual longings, in accord with a young woman's Oedipus complex. The image of her father in the dream represents, argues Freud, both her father and Herr K—both of whom Dora loves, fears, and occasionally resents. The image of her mother represents both her mother and Frau K—both of whom she also resents and yet wishes, on some level, to be. Though her mother spurned her father's gifts, Dora would be happy to accept the bracelet from her father (symbolically accepting her father's love) and would be happy to return the favor with the gift of her jewel-case to him. *All of this is deeply unconscious.* On a conscious level, however, Dora knows that her mother offers her father no sexual satisfaction; similarly, Frau K offers none to her husband. Unconsciously, Dora believes that she would prove a better wife to either of these men.

At this point in the interpretation, Dora's dream appears to be a cleverly disguised rendition of the standard Oedipus complex in young women. It is complicated somewhat by actual events in her life involving Herr K, making two older men, rather than just one, the objects of her unconscious sexual longing. Things become much more complicated, however, with Freud's further interpretations of the dream, revealing a number of highly peculiar meanings that link the dream content to Dora's neurotic symptomatology. Dora's associations to *fire* run in the opposite direction to *water,* hinted at in her mother's pearl *drops.* Freud reminds Dora of an old folk belief that children who play with matches (fire) tend to wet their beds (water). (Dora claims she is not familiar with the belief.) The father's fear that "something might happen in the night so that it might be necessary to leave the room" (in Dora's first association to the dream) may suggest both fire and bedwetting. Dora reports that both her brother and she had problems with bedwetting well into childhood. In her case, the problem was most serious when she was age 7 and 8, so serious that her parents brought in a doctor. As in the dream, her father may have occasionally woken her up in the middle of the night to take her to the toilet, so that she would not wet her bed. The problem of bedwetting subsided shortly before Dora developed her first neurotic symptom: periodic difficulties in breathing, described as "nervous asthma" (Freud, 1905/1963, p. 90).

Bedwetting is an important association in the dream because of Freud's belief that bedwetting is intimately associated with *masturbation.*[1] Freud is never able to extract a conscious confession of childhood masturbation from Dora, although he believes that he has incontrovertible unconscious evidence one day in therapy when, after discussing at length the topic of masturbation in their previous session, Dora shows up wearing at her

---

1. Modern medical science has documented no link between childhood masturbation and enuresis. In 1901, however, many members of the medical establishment still held to the notion that masturbation was at the root of a number of personal illnesses and problems. Freud appears to have adhered to this view (Sulloway, 1979) and apparently believed that chronic bedwetting problems extending well into the elementary-school years were often by-products of excessive masturbation in children.

waist a small *reticule* (a small, purselike bag) that "she kept playing with, … opening it, putting a finger into it, shutting it again, and so on" (Freud, 1905/1963, p. 94). This innocent behavior, argues Freud, in fact symbolizes masturbation, the reticule serving as a substitute for the female genitals.

Based on these circumstances, Freud surmises that Dora masturbated frequently as a child of age 7 and 8; that she was, at the same time, an inveterate bedwetter, and that she experienced a great deal of guilt about both behaviors. Dora came to see both of them as *dirty* actions associated with sexuality. Indeed, all sexuality acquired a dirty connotation after Dora learned, at an early age, that her father had contracted a *venereal disease* by leading a sexually loose life before his marriage. In Dora's mind, Freud conjectures, her mother's obsession with *cleanliness* is a reaction to being dirtied by her husband's venereal disease. Freud is surprised that Dora is consciously aware of her father's disease, though Freud himself and many other people apparently were also aware of it. Dora's associations lead Freud to the conclusion that she blames her father for her illnesses—she believes he has passed on his venereal disease to her. She unconsciously believes, asserts Freud, that she has a sexually transmitted disease simply by being born of a father afflicted with one. There was no medical evidence for Dora's hypothesis, Freud points out, but Dora nonetheless believes the infectious connection to be true and cites as evidence her recurrent *catarrh*— an infectious secretion, manifested in periodic vaginal discharges, about which Dora felt great shame and disgust. On an unconscious level, the catarrh is one of Dora's psychological "proofs" that her many problems in life are her father's fault. Not only had he "handed her over" to Herr K, but he had also given her a dirty disease. The disease is a sexual disease. All sexual phenomena are dirty and bring about feelings of disgust, in Dora's private system of meaning. This is why, in part, Dora felt disgust, not sexual excitement, when Herr K kissed her in his office when she was 14 years old.

Many of Dora's symptoms affirm her unconscious convictions that (a) she is her father's daughter, (b) she, like him, is sick and dirty, and (c) this is because of sex. Though she is still drawn to sexuality and wishes unconsciously to consummate her love for her father and Herr K in typical oedipal fashion, venereal disease becomes her unconscious symbolic embodiment of sexual relations, and her neurotic symptoms all take on a sexual meaning. We have already seen how, for Freud, the cough symbolized oral sexuality and Dora's incestuous wishes concerning her father. Her difficulties in breathing, according to Freud, also express a sexual dynamic. Dora's father suffered from periodic shortness of breath, and doctors warned him that he should not exert himself too much. Thus, Dora's analogous symptom is another way of proving that she is her father's daughter and that her problems are due to his transgressions, not hers. Further, Freud submits that the difficulties in breathing may have stemmed from Dora's having heard, as a child of perhaps 7 or 8, her parents' heavy breathing while engaged in sexual intercourse. Her first asthmatic attacks occurred during a trip with her father to the mountains. Subsequently, Dora experienced difficulties in breathing when her father left home on trips. Thus, according to Freud, Dora was able to identify with her lost lover—her father—by acting in a way reminiscent of him. The dynamics behind her sympathetic imitation of her father's illnesses were, of course, completely unconscious.

Dora Revisited

Dora returned to Freud's office 15 months after terminating treatment to tell him that she had confronted Frau K and her father about their affair and Herr K about his inappropriate conduct. This brief interaction did not result in any further therapy, though Dora appeared to suffer still from hysterical symptoms. A year later she married and sometime afterwards bore her only child—a son. In an odd turn of events, Dora—whose real name was Ida—visited another psychoanalyst—Dr. Felix Deutsch—in 1922 for treatment of a hysterical symptom, announcing that she indeed was the famous patient of Freud's Dora case. According to Deutsch (1957), Dora never recovered from her neurosis. Her cough and asthma still plagued her 20 years after her last meeting with Freud. As an adult, she repeatedly accused others—her husband, her son, her few acquaintances—of persecuting and betraying her. In Deutsch's view, her husband was "slighted and tortured by her almost paranoid behavior" (p. 57). Indeed, one of Deutsch's acquaintances claimed that Dora was "one of the most repulsive hysterics" he had ever met. From what we can tell, Dora lived an extremely unhappy life, and she managed to make those around her almost equally unhappy (Deutsch, 1957; Rogow, 1978). She died of colon cancer in New York City in 1945, at the age of 63.

Even in 1901, Freud realized that his case of Dora was both a great success and a great failure. From the standpoint of psychotherapy, Freud was unable to effect a satisfactory solution or cure for Dora's deeply ingrained neurotic symptoms. This failure was due in part to Dora's resistance to Freud's interpretations. Just when Freud felt he was gaining insights into the nature of her neurosis, Dora broke off the therapy relationship. Furthermore, Freud admitted that certain key realizations about Dora came to him too late in the course of her therapy. For example, Freud seems to have underestimated the problems of **transference** and **countertransference** in the case (Muslin & Gill, 1978). Belatedly, Freud came to see that Dora was unconsciously transferring dynamics from her interactions with Herr K and her father onto the therapeutic relationship, unconsciously relating to Freud as father/lover/enemy. Moreover, Freud may have been unwittingly doing something very similar—countertransferring some of his own unconscious feelings about young neurotic women onto Dora.

Consistent with the patriarchal gender roles of his time, Freud seems to have behaved toward Dora in a very domineering manner (Kahane, 1985; Moi, 1981). He was too quick to dismiss her protestations of innocence and betrayal, and he showed shockingly little sympathy for Dora's plight as a young girl trapped in an intrigue that she did little to bring about (Blos, 1972; Rieff, 1959). Too young to be jaded and worn like her pathetic parents and the Ks, Dora could not blithely accept their betrayal of her and of each other. More than for childish revenge, more than even for love and acceptance, Dora may have been searching for what Erikson (1964) called *fidelity*—for honesty and truth in relationships, for sincere commitment to others as a way of defining the self.

While the Dora case, therefore, may reveal shortcomings in therapeutic technique and significant gender biases ingrained in Victorian society, Freud's analysis may also be considered a "success" with respect to its ability to illustrate psychoanalytic interpretation. From the standpoint of literature, the case has been hailed as a harbinger of a new genre of modern writing (Marcus, 1977; Rieff, 1959; Steele, 1982). Organized along multiple analytic perspectives rather than in chronological sequence and employing a number of modernist literary devices, the Dora case has been compared to the 20th century novels of Marcel Proust, Henry James, and James Joyce, and to the plays of Henrik Ibsen. In his account of Dora, Freud moves effortlessly among a number of different kinds of writing—chronological reports, theoretical asides, dramatic flashbacks, warnings to the reader—as the narrative spontaneously follows an inner logic, often looping back to convey multiple meanings at multiple levels.

PRINCIPLES OF INTERPRETATION
Text and Treaty

In thinking about psychoanalytic interpretation, it is helpful to focus on the metaphor of the *text*. For Freud, human behavior is like a text. The great texts in our literary traditions are rich enough in *text*ure to be interpreted on many different levels. A great poem or novel suggests a multitude of meanings, some of which may even be outside the awareness of the poet or novelist who produced the text. Thus, a masterpiece such as Herman Melville's *Moby-Dick* or James Joyce's *Ulysses* captures many meanings, and indeed literary critics make it their livelihood to discover and critique these various "truths." You may have done the same thing yourself, perhaps in a class on English literature. When writing your analysis of, say, Nathaniel Hawthorne's *The Scarlet Letter,* you may have come to the realization that, while your particular interpretation may have been valid, no single interpretation could possibly be complete. And so it is with every aspect of human behavior and experience, suggests Freud. *There is no single complete interpretation* of anything, no single answer. Rather, human behavior has multiple meanings, and like a text it can be interpreted on multiple levels. In Dora's dream, the jewel-case does not simply signify the female genitals. This may be one meaning—perhaps a particularly important one, in Freud's view—but it is not the only one, nor is this meaning necessarily better than alternative meanings. In much of our behavior and experience, suggests Freud, we are each like the master novelist, unconsciously constructing literary masterpieces—such as our dreams, our symptoms, and our relationships with others—that can be interpreted on more than a single level. Psychoanalysts, therefore, should be skilled in the interpretation of multivalent texts (Bakan, 1958).

A second useful metaphor is that of the political *treaty.* A treaty is a compromise among conflicting forces. Two countries at war decide to end hostilities, and so they draw up a treaty that is designed to keep the peace. In a good treaty, all conflicting sides make peace by forging compromises. And so it is again with our behavior and experience, says Freud. Much of what we do, say, and experience is a product of compromise among internal conflicting forces. These internal forces assume an infinitude of forms—from deeply repressed wishes concerning sexuality and aggression to conscious interests and aversions. At any given moment, a thousand and one voices are clamoring within us—most of them unconscious—and making conflicting demands. *We behave and experience in such a way as to appease as many of these voices as we can,* and we do this, for the most part, unconsciously. Dora loved her father dearly, and yet she hated him for having made her sick and dirty. While overtly displacing her hatred for her father onto Herr K, she could continue to claim, consciously, that she loved her father while continuing to hate him through K. Of course, she had good reason to hate Herr K, too. Therefore, slapping Herr K and openly expressing her disgust with his behavior enabled Dora to kill many birds of the unconscious with the same behavioral stone, forging a tentative peace treaty among the wishes and desires at war within her.

Manifest and Latent

Psychoanalysts distinguish between the *manifest* level of behavior and experience, which is consciously known and seen, and the *latent* level, which is hidden in the unconscious and must be discovered. In reality, the latent comprises *many* levels, in that behavior is complexly determined, like a text. In the dream of the jewel-case, the manifest level is the actual dream as Dora remembered it and as Freud reproduced it for us in print. The manifest level of any behavior and experience is relatively straightforward and concise. Dora's dream seems, on the surface, simple enough, a short, clear scenario about a fire and a jewel-case. The latent levels of the dream, however, consist of the hidden forces, conflicts, impulses, wishes, and other determinants that went into the making of the dream. These are the unconscious building blocks of the dream. Whereas the manifest content of the dream is a simple, five-sentence story, the latent content could fill a volume, Freud suggests. *There is always much more material in the latent arena than in the manifest,* and much of what is hidden as latent never comes to be known consciously. In Freud's terminology, the manifest content of the dream is **overdetermined** by the latent content. What Dora remembers as the manifest content of the dream is but the tip of a large, mostly submerged, iceberg.

Figure 11.2 illustrates the relationship between manifest and latent content in dreams. The process of moving from the manifest to the latent content is what Freud (1900/1953) termed *dream analysis.* The movement involves, as we saw in Dora's dream, the dreamer's associating freely to the various dream elements. The psychoanalyst listens carefully to the spontaneous associations in order to discern patterns and recurrent themes. Dora's first association to her dream was to a seemingly unrelated argument her parents had recently

FIGURE 11.2 MANIFEST AND LATENT DREAM CONTENT

Dream analysis involves the movement from manifest to latent content in the dream. The reverse movement, from latent to manifest, is what the dreamer does when he or she dreams, a process called dream work.

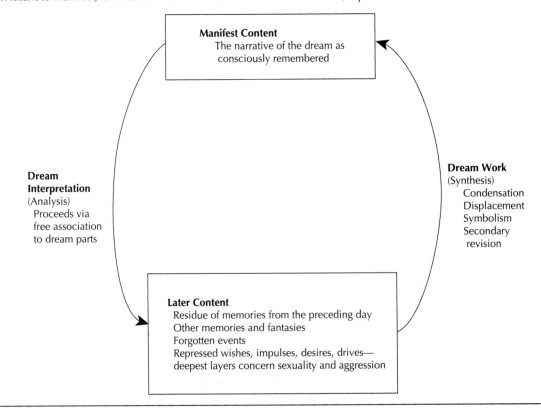

had about her brother's bedroom door. This association eventually led to a host of latent images and meanings, having to do with fire, water, masturbation, jewelry, and sexuality. In dream analysis, the dreamer and the therapist break the dream apart and attempt to discover its hidden mechanisms.

The reverse process, of moving from the latent to the manifest, is what the dreamer has already done by dreaming. This spontaneous and unconscious process of synthesizing, rather than analyzing, is what Freud termed **dream work.** Freud suggests that each dreamer draws upon the various determinants that reside in the latent arena and fashions a full-blown manifest dream out of them. We synthesize our dreams, unconsciously, out of the latent material at hand. Dreaming is, therefore, a highly creative act, and each dreamer is like a poet who makes artful verse from a vast storehouse of images, ideas, experiences, and words. Writes Ricoeur (1970), "dreams attest that we constantly mean something other than what we say, in dreams the manifest endlessly refers to hidden meaning; that is what makes every dreamer a poet" (p. 15).

Dream work operates by "cunning distortion" (Ricoeur, 1970). In its attempt to construct a satisfactory compromise among all the warring factions in the personality, dream work disguises, cajoles, and cuts deals, thereby transforming an unwieldy bulk of latent material into a tidy manifest story. The text is written, the treaty is forged, the dream is made—all unconsciously. What emerges as the manifest story, therefore, is a masterpiece of deceit, for the dream is indeed not what it seems to be. Dora's innocent dream about a fire masks an unconscious story about sexual love, bitter hatred, sickness and filth, betrayal, and childhood bedwetting. We need not accept Freud's particular interpretations of Dora's dream to appreciate the psychoanalytic assumption that dreams mean much more than we might initially think and that these meanings are disguised.

What methods does dream work employ to disguise the meanings of dreams? Freud suggests that there are many, but he describes in some detail four dream-work strategies that are frequently used. In **condensation,** the dreamer compresses various latent elements into a single manifest image or theme. In Dora's dream, the manifest father standing at her bedside is a condensation of her real father, Herr K, and perhaps a few other authority figures in her life whom she both loves and resents. It is largely through condensation that a dream can say so much with so little. **Displacement** involves a shift of emphasis in a dream from an important but potentially threatening source to a trivial but safer one, as when one displaces a powerful emotion from its intended object to a substitute. Thus, Dora displaces hatred for her diseased and dishonest father onto Herr K, experiencing overwhelming disgust and resentment in his presence rather than in the presence of her father.

Symbolism is the third method of dream work. Through symbolism, the dreamer conjures up concrete images and actions that convey hidden but common meanings. According to Freud, hollow, boxlike objects into which things can be inserted—such as Dora's reticule and her mother's jewel-case—may symbolize, at the latent level, the female genitals. Though Freud tended to see symbolism as less important than condensation and displacement in the dream work (Freud, 1900/1953), psychoanalysts have catalogued many different kinds of Freudian symbols that can be discerned in dreams, myth, legends, and literature (Grinstein, 1983; Hall, 1953). Many, though not all, of these concern various aspects of human sexuality. Finally, through a fourth method of dream work termed **secondary revision,** the dreamer unconsciously smooths over the dream's rough spots, fills in gaps, clears up ambiguities, and edits the dream experience into a more-or-less coherent story with a setting, characters, and plot. It is this smooth narrative form that is recalled as the manifest content of the dream.

Symptoms and Everyday Life

The interpretation of dreams is the model for all psychoanalytic intervention. Neurotic symptoms, artistic expressions, and certain everyday slips and mistakes are, like dreams, analogous to texts and treaties, with manifest and latent levels of meaning. To understand these phenomena, the psychoanalyst must piece together associations to manifest content as Freud pieced together Dora's associations to her dream. Similarly, symptom formation, artistic expression, and the "construction" of a mistake (a "Freudian slip") parallel dream work: All involve the creation of text-like and treaty-like products through condensation, displacement, symbolism, and other unconscious methods that disguise the true meanings of the behaviors they create. Figure 11.3 shows how the psychoanalyst's interpretation of each of these phenomena (moving from manifest to latent) mirrors dream interpretation, while the person's construction of each phenomenon (moving from latent to manifest) mirrors dream work.

FIGURE 11.3 | **SYMPTOMS AND EVERYDAY MISTAKES**

Like dreams, Freud maintained that psychological symptoms and everyday mistakes can be understood in terms of manifest and latent content.

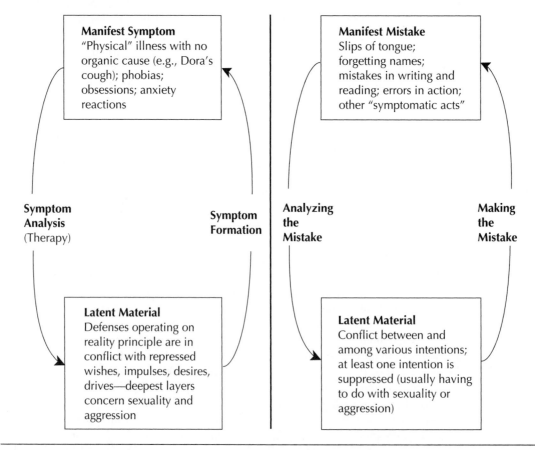

Dora's neurotic symptoms were ingenious products of complex unconscious dynamics, whereby internal conflicts were translated into physical infirmities. A good example is her hysterical coughing. Freud describes how Dora's most famous symptom was highly overdetermined and indicative of many different meanings at many different levels:

> We will now attempt to put together the various determinants that we have found for Dora's attacks of coughing and hoarseness. In the lowest stratum we must assume the presence of a real and organically determined irritation of the throat, which acted like the grain of sand around which an oyster forms its pearl. This irritation was susceptible to fixation, because it concerned a part of the body which in Dora had to a high degree retained its significance as an erotogenic zone. And the irritation was consequently well fitted to give expression to excited states of the libido. It was brought to fixation by what was probably its first psychological wrapping—her sympathetic imitation of her father—and by her subsequent self-reproaches on account of her "catarrh." The same group of symptoms, moreover, showed itself capable of representing her relations with Herr K; it could express her regret at his absence and her wish to make him a better wife. After a part of her libido had once more turned towards her father, the symptom obtained what was perhaps its last meaning; it came to represent sexual intercourse with her father by means of Dora's identifying herself with Frau K. I can guarantee that this series is by no means complete. (Freud, 1905/1963, pp. 101–102)

All neurotic symptoms—phobias, obsessions, compulsions, anxiety reactions, and so on—can be interpreted as overdetermined texts or treaties with disguised meanings at several levels. Neurotic patients such as Dora, therefore, are creative masters of symptom formation, though the profound meanings of their masterpieces are generally outside their own awareness. But such creativity is not limited to neurotics. All of us do much the same thing, argues Freud, in much of our everyday behavior and experience. We continuously create texts and forge compromises, and we display these masterpieces of overdetermination in the most unexpected and seemingly trivial ways. In *The Psychopathology of Everyday Life* (1901/1960), Freud gives many examples of slips of the tongue, forgetting names, mistakes in reading and writing, and everyday errors in simple actions that, like dreams and symptoms, can be interpreted as indicators of unconscious conflicts. Some of Freud's best examples, such as his forgetting a famous artist's name during a conversation on a train, are from his own life. In the case of Dora, her "symptomatic act" with the reticule is likewise an overdetermined example of the psychopathology of everyday life. A surprising amount of common behavior can be interpreted from a psychoanalytic framework, argues Freud, as each of us unconsciously betrays the secrets of the mind:

> He that has eyes to see and ears to hear may convince himself that no mortal can keep a secret. If his lips are silent, he chatters with his finger-tips; betrayal oozes out of him at every pore. And thus the task of making conscious the most hidden recesses of the mind is one which it is quite possible to accomplish. (Freud, 1905/1963, p. 96)

In what other ways do we forge unconscious treaties and compose overdetermined texts? In countless ways, suggests Freud: in our jokes (Freud, 1905/1960), our art (Freud, 1910/1957), our religious beliefs (Freud, 1927/1961), and our relationships with others (Freud, 1921/1955), to name a few. The psychoanalytic vision of human life is a profoundly radical portrait of *creative deceit*. Virtually all of our behavior is meaningful, but we unconsciously deceive ourselves and others so that we and they do not know what the behavior means. Our deceptions are the complex treaties and texts that we unconsciously and ingeniously weave. Psychoanalytic interpretation attempts to unravel our deceits and expose the truths that lie behind the creative cover-ups of everyday life.

THE JUNGIAN APPROACH: MYTH AND SYMBOL

A COLLECTIVE UNCONSCIOUS

For Freud, the secrets of each person's soul are buried in the person's unconscious. Those secrets are likely tied to sexual and aggressive themes for all of us. But because my experiences in life have been different from yours, my unconscious and your unconscious are different from each other. By contrast, a strong line of thinking in the psychoanalytic tradition has tended to emphasize the ways in which we all share certain features of our unconscious lives. Carl Jung was an early follower of Freud who eventually established a rival theoretical perspective that differed from Freud's in many ways. With respect to the issue of human motivation, for example, Jung broke with Freud's exclusive focus on sexual and aggressive instincts and argued instead that human beings are motivated by a spectacular pantheon of unconscious forces and factors—internal urges and images about unity, death, androgyny, wisdom, innocence, and yes, sex and aggression—all of which are the result, Jung believed, of our common evolutionary heritage (Stevens, 1983). The wellspring for these many-splendored sources of our everyday behavior is what Jung called the **collective unconscious.** The collective unconscious is a storehouse of archaic remnants from humankind's evolutionary past. It is our inherited racial memory, what all of us know by virtue of our membership in the human race, in the deepest and most inaccessible layer of the psyche. The collective unconscious is what human nature really is, in Jung's view. A result of our evolution as a species, it is the richly textured unconscious that each of us is born with and that each of us takes with us as we move across the human life cycle:

> The archetypal endowment with which each of us is born presupposes the natural life cycle of our species—being mothered, exploring the environment, playing in the peer group, adolescence, being initiated, establishing a place in the social hierarchy, courting, marrying, child-rearing, hunting, gathering, fighting, participating in religious rituals, assuming social responsibilities of advanced maturity, and preparation for death. (Stevens, 1983, p. 40)

Originally a disciple of Freud, Carl Jung (1875–1961) developed a rival approach to personality and psychotherapy that he called analytical psychology. Jung believed that Freud's interpretations of life stories focused too much on sex, aggression, and the personal unconscious. Jung's method of interpretation emphasizes archetypes and universal patterns and human beings' search for balance and wholeness.

The major structural components of the collective unconscious are **archetypes.** Archetypes are universal patterns or predispositions that structure how all humans consciously and unconsciously adapt to their world. As the major components of human nature, archetypes are inherited, but somewhat flexible, templates for human experience. They are not images or behaviors as such but rather are *predispositions* to develop universal images and to enact universal behavioral sequences (Jung, 1936/1969).

Table 11.2 describes some well-known Jungian archetypes, including the mother, the child, the wise old man, the trickster, and the hero. Evidence for the existence of each of these, Jung argued, is pervasive in ancient myths, dreams, and universal symbols. For instance, the image of *mother* is a universal thought-form coded in stories, legends, art, ritual, customs, and fantasy around the world. Throughout history, mothers have behaved in certain

TABLE 11.2	SELECTED JUNGIAN ARCHETYPES	
Archetype	**Description**	**Projected Symbols (Ancient and Modern)**
Mother	The embodiment of caregiving and fertility, which may be elicited in response to real mothers, grandmothers, spouses, and other nurturant figures; incorporates positive warm, supportive) and negative (rejecting, threatening) characteristics.	Earth Mother in ancient mythologies, Virgin Mary, Alma Mater, the Church, fairy godmothers, witches, dragons
Child-God	The embodiment of both innocence and future experience, representing "futurity" and potential for growth; often has divine or mystical powers.	Christ child, elves, dwarfs, the young Mozart, the child prodigy
Hero	The protagonist of the classic and universal hero myth: miraculous but humble birth followed by early proof of superhuman power, rapid rise to prominence, triumphant struggle with evil, fallibility to the "sin" of pride, and eventual fall through betrayal or heroic sacrifice.	Christ, Oedipus, King Arthur, Achilles, Abraham Lincoln, Martin Luther King, Jr.
Trickster	An early form of the hero archetype, fond of sly jokes, malicious pranks; possesses magical powers.	Hermes, Biblical demons, Harry Houdini
Wise Old Man	Embodiment of maturity and wisdom, able to foretell the future.	Oedipus in his later years, Tiresias, certain renditions of God-the-Father, prophets, Mahatma Gandhi
Anima	The hidden feminine side of man.	Various idealized images of women worshipped by men, such as Cleopatra, Helen of Troy, Virgin Mary, Mona Lisa; woman as temptress, mother, friend, mediator; woman as witch and bitch; cars, ships
Animus	The hidden masculine side of woman.	Various idealized images of men worshipped by women, such as Odysseus, Don Juan, Christ; man as seducer, hunter, statesman, mentor; man as pirate, rapist, outlaw
Shadow	The embodiment of unacceptable, animalistic desires and impulses; the "dark half" of personality.	Satan, devils, aliens, enemies, wild beasts, Hitler, Mussolini
Persona	The socially acceptable mask or front the person presents to the world. The persona is not a true archetypal form residing in the collective un-conscious but rather an individual and highly conscious creation. Nonetheless, the individual's persona is built upon unconscious patterns concerning how a good "actor" presents an appropriate mask and plays an appropriate role for the world. The persona generally hides or disguises the true potential of the self.	Actors and actresses

instinctually bounded ways such that a template or pattern of who mothers are and what they do has come to exist as an archetype in the human collective unconscious. Thus, the human infant has within him or her an unconscious prototype of what mother is—a genetic predisposition to react to her and understand her in certain ways. The infant's perception of mother will, of course, be influenced by real-life experiences with her, but the internal and unconscious mother archetype will set limits on those experiences and help structure how they are understood. The mother archetype may be "released" and expressed in thought and image in response to one's real mother, mother-in-law, grandmother, stepmother, or any other person, place, or thing associated with maternity.

Three particularly prominent archetypes in the collective unconscious are the **anima, animus,** and **shadow.** Within all males exists an unconscious template of femininity, called the anima. Based on men's collective experiences with women throughout time, the anima resides deep within all men as a hidden feminine side of their personalities. Similarly, within all women exists an unconscious masculine aspect, called the animus. The anima and the animus constrain actual interactions between the sexes, each sex apprehending the nature of the other through an unconscious filter. The shadow archetype consists of a variety of unacceptable and socially reprehensible desires and impulses, inherited by virtue of our evolution from lower forms of life. The animalistic shadow is the "dark half" of our personality that most of us would prefer not to recognize. It is expressed in mythology via demons, devils, and evil ones, and it is partially responsible, argued Jung, for the Judeo-Christian belief in original sin.

Like the Oedipus story for Freud, the archetypes provided Jung with models for life stories. Each archetype is like a character in a life story. Jungian interpretation centrally involves identifying archetypal patterns in the many different themes and images running through a person's life story. But whereas Freud's fascination with Oedipus may have predisposed him to search for tragedy in life narratives, Jung was taken with the narrative possibilities of adventure and the heroic quest.

INDIVIDUATION AND THE HEROIC QUEST

For Freud, the story of human life begins with the earliest stage of interpersonal dependency, what Freud viewed as the oral stage, and moves to stages of increasing independence and autonomy as the self builds strength and expands. The high point of early development is the unconscious drama of the Oedipus complex, the resolution of which marks the most significant socialization experience in the life cycle. The child who has passed through the Oedipal drama now has an unconscious sense of his or her own limitations as well as the moral sensibility that one needs for effective and cooperative social life. The later childhood years bring with them many important socialization experiences before full-fledged sexuality erupts in adolescence and ushers in the genital stage. The well-functioning personality of adolescence and adulthood is able to employ the ego's powers of defense and adaptation to cope with anxiety and resolve the conflicts that may arise when id, superego, and real-world forces inevitably collide. The mature adult copes more-or-less effectively with the anxiety of everyday life and manages to love others and to work productively in society.

For some readers, this story of development may be fine as far as it goes, but it may not go far enough. What about personality development in the adult years? Are there interesting changes and growth opportunities awaiting us after we move into the genital stage? Most psychoanalytic theorists have ignored this possibility, assuming that the most important determinants of personality are set down in the childhood years. But Carl Jung took a

A male archetype.

A female archetype.

very different view. In the same way that Jung expanded Freud's notion of the unconscious to encompass a collective unconscious filled with archetypes, so did Jung expand the general psychoanalytic view of personality development to chart significant changes in the adult years. In sharp contrast to Freud, Jung viewed personality development as a lifelong enterprise. Whereas a person's unique constellation of characteristics is established early in childhood for Freud, Jung saw possibilities for dramatic personality transformation across the human lifespan. During childhood, Jung argued, various components of the personality become established as separate entities. Psychic energy is expended on learning how to walk, how to talk, and other skills necessary for survival. Sexuality is not a prominent theme in the early years but becomes a significant force with the arrival of puberty and adolescence. In young adulthood, the person directs psychic energy toward learning a vocation, getting married, raising children, and becoming integrated into community life. Ideally, the young adult should be energetic, outgoing, and passionate in his or her active engagement of social reality.

Around the age of 40, however, a profound shift may be experienced, as the individual begins to move away from a passionate engagement of the world to an inner and more philosophical exploration of the self. Jung viewed midlife as the most important developmental period in the lifespan. Midlife is highlighted by a shift from materialism, sexuality, and propagation to more spiritual and cultural values. In addition, the adult may experience significant shifts in values, ideals, and interpersonal relationships at this time. Religion may become especially salient in the second half of the human life cycle, as the adult strives to find spiritual harmony, balance, and the full expression of the self. The goal of human development is the full development and flowering of the self, Jung argued. Jung used the term **individuation** to refer to the process of self-development. Individuation is a dynamic, complex, and lifelong balancing act whereby the person seeks to synthesize the

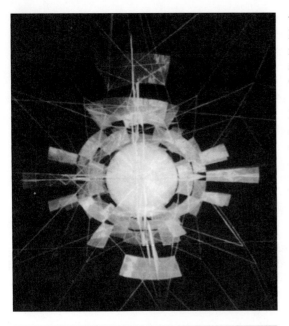

The Sun, a sculpture by Robert Lippold, is a modern-day mandala. For Jung, the mandala was a symbol of the unity of self.

various opposites in personality to become whole. Individuation, therefore, involves the full development of all aspects of the personality, both conscious and unconscious, and their ultimate integration within a grand unity.

Much of what may appeal to us in Jung stems from his characterization of human individuation. The development of the self is a heroic quest that each of us can and should undertake, an adventure in self-discovery of truly mythic proportions. Like the Greek Odysseus exploring unknown lands, battling ferocious beasts, and communicating daily with the gods, each of us is challenged to do battle with and to explore all that hides and rages in the distant lands within us. In the later years of one's life, individuation brings wholeness and completion. The mature self reconciles all opposites within a psychological circle of unity. The ancient symbol of this unity is the **mandala.** (*Mandala* is a Sanskrit word meaning "circle.") In various mythologies, religious rituals, and dreams and fantasies, Jung observed an array of mandala-like figures. According to Jung, the mandala is the perfect symbol of the self's unity and integrity achieved through the lifelong adventure of individuation.

INTERPRETING A DREAM SERIES

From its origins in Jung's break with Freud before the onset of World War I, Jungian psychology has shared with other strains in the psychoanalytic tradition a fascination with unconscious processes and the intrapsychic mysteries of the human soul. But in its emphasis on spirituality over sexuality and its portrayal of human development in terms of individuation across the life cycle, the Jungian alternative departs from Freud in a number of critical ways. Like Freud, Jung viewed dreams and symptoms as overdetermined manifest products replete with latent meanings. But whereas Freud viewed dreams as wish fulfillments originating in conflicts concerning sexual and aggressive urges, Jung portrayed dreams as *symbols* of the striving for *balance* in personality, as expressions of *universal myths,* and *anticipations* of life problems for the *future.*

What makes the human species so fascinating and so unique, according to Jung, is its use of symbols. A symbol is "a term, a name, or even a picture that may be familiar in daily life yet that possesses specific connotations in addition to its conventional and obvious meaning. It implies something vague, unknown, or hidden from us" (Jung, von Franz, Henderson, Jacobi, & Jaffe, 1964, p. 20). Symbols are especially useful in the apprehension of concepts and phenomena that we cannot fully define or comprehend. This is one reason that all religions employ symbolic language or images. Individuals produce symbols consciously and spontaneously, in the form of dreams. The psychologist who seeks to interpret the symbols of dreams should be careful not to get led astray by the dreamer's free associations. Whereas Freud distrusted the manifest content of dreams and sought to find meanings in the dreamer's far-flung associations, Jung argued that one should pay closer attention to the form and content of the manifest dream itself. Associations to the dream itself are also important, but the interpretation should repeatedly come back to the dream itself, Jung maintained, for it is in the dream proper that the symbols reside.

Whereas Freud argued that dreams fulfill hidden wishes, Jung saw dreams as seeking to restore balance and harmony in the self. For example, one of Jung's male patients reported a dream in which his gentle and attractive wife appeared as a drunken and disheveled hag. Jung's interpretation of the dream rejected the possibility that the man was in fact dreaming about his wife per se and entertained instead the hypothesis that the vulgar woman symbolized the feminine side of his own personality—the anima. Whereas he behaved in a gentlemanly fashion in public, the man's inner anima was harsh and repulsive. Interestingly, Jung concluded that the dream should *not* be seen as urging the man to "change" or "make better" this inner reality. Instead the dream urges the man simply to see, to acknowledge, and to integrate what already exists, so that the self may be apprehended in more balanced and holistic terms:

> In the Middle Ages, long before the physiologists demonstrated that by reason of our glandular structure there were both male and female elements in all of us, it was said that "every man carries a woman within himself." It is this female element in every male that I have called the "anima." [In this particular man's case] this "feminine" aspect is essentially a certain inferior kind of relatedness to the surroundings, and particularly to women, which is kept carefully concealed from others as well as from oneself. In other words, though an individual's visible personality may seem quite normal, he may well be concealing from others—or even from himself—the deplorable condition of "the woman within."
>
> That was the case with this particular patient: His female side was not nice. His dream was actually saying to him: "You are in some respects behaving like a degenerate female," and thus gave him an appropriate shock. (An example of this kind, of course, must not be taken as evidence that the unconscious is concerned with "moral" injunctions. The dream was not telling the patient to "behave better," but was simply trying to balance the lopsided nature of his conscious mind, which was maintaining the fiction that he was a perfect gentleman throughout.) (Jung et al., 1964, p. 31)

In the case of Dora, we see that Freud traced dream associations back to conflicts and issues rooted in Dora's adolescent and childhood past. The dream of the jewel-case connected to the masturbation and bedwetting of her early years and to her unconscious longings and fears about men, rooted in her early experiences with her father. By contrast, Jung's dream analyses sometimes focus on events yet to happen—on the future. Jung believed that "dreams may sometimes announce certain situations long before they actually happen" because they bring to consciousness a step-by-step movement toward danger of which the individual may not be previously aware (Jung et al., 1964, p. 50). For example, a man who had "developed almost a morbid passion for mountain climbing" (as a way of compensating, Jung argues, for his dissolute private life) began to dream of stepping off mountains into empty space (Jung et al., 1964, p. 50). The dream was a warning, in Jung's view, that the man was headed for disaster and that he should get his private life in order and cut back on his dangerous mountain ventures. The man did not heed the warning. Six months later he jumped off of a mountain and died.

The identification of archetypal themes and universal myths may be the most characteristic feature of Jungian dream analysis. This mode of interpretation is dramatically illustrated in Jung's interpretation of a series of dreams from the young daughter of a psychiatrist (Jung et al., 1964, pp. 69–82). At age 8, the girl recorded a series of her dreams in a notebook. Each dream account was fashioned like a fairy tale, beginning with the words, "Once upon a time …" While the dreams were very childlike, they contained uncanny images that were totally incomprehensible to her father. Puzzled and troubled, he brought the notebook to Jung. Jung describes 12 of the dreams:

1. "The evil animal," a snakelike monster with many horns, kills and devours all other animals. But God comes from the four corners, being in fact four separate gods, and gives rebirth to all the dead animals.

2. An ascent into heaven, where pagan dances are being celebrated; and a descent into hell, where angels are doing good deeds.

3. A horde of small animals frightens the dreamer. The animals increase to a tremendous size, and one of them devours the little girl.

4. A small mouse is penetrated by worms, snakes, fishes, and human beings. Thus the mouse becomes human. This portrays the four stages of the origin of mankind.

5. A drop of water is seen, as it appears when looked at through a microscope. The girl sees the drop is full of tree branches. This portrays the origin of the world.

6. A bad boy has a clod of earth and throws bits of it at everyone who passes. In this way, all the passers-by become bad.

7. A drunken woman falls into the water and comes out renewed and sober.

8. The scene is in America, where many people are rolling on an ant heap, attacked by the ants. The dreamer, in a panic, falls into a river.

9. There is a desert on the moon where the dreamer sinks so deeply into the ground that she reaches hell.

10. In this dream the girl has a vision of a luminous ball. She touches it. Vapors emanate from it. A man comes and kills her.

11. The girl dreams she is dangerously ill. Suddenly birds come out of her skin and cover her completely.

12. Swarms of gnats obscure the sun, the moon, and all the stars, except one. That one star falls upon the dreamer. (Jung et al., 1964, p. 70)

The remarkable series of dream accounts contains startling similarities to certain classical myths and stories from ancient texts and other arcane sources with which the little girl could surely have had no familiarity. Some of the dreams play out motifs and images from sacred Jewish and Christian writings, Jung argued. For example, the first dream recalls the early Greek fathers of the Christian church who argued that at the end of time everything would be restored by a redeemer to its original and perfect state. Yet the little girl apparently had no religious instruction whatsoever, and her father was not familiar with the particular religious stories to which her dreams seemed to refer. Some of the other dreams seem to connect to primitive myths that predate Christianity, as in archetypal stories of creation, the flood, and the quest of the hero. The element of fourness—as in the four corners of the first dream—plays a great role in many religions and philosophies and was familiar to students of Hermetic philosophy in the 18th century. The horned serpent appears in 16th-century Latin alchemy as the *quadricornutus serpens* (four-horned serpent), a symbol of Mercury and an antagonist of the Christian trinity. Needless to say, this is an extraordinarily obscure reference.

Jung was familiar with many ancient and esoteric myths and writings, but the little girl simply could not have consciously known about these sources, he maintained. The dream images, he argued, arose from a *collective* unconscious, wherein are stored archaic images and symbols whose meanings have been elaborated by humankind since the dawn of human history. Rather than instinctual urges concerning sex and aggression, the girls dreams were driven and shaped by the same archetypal patterns that shaped ancient myth and folklore—symbols of creation, death, rebirth, and so on. But why should this particular girl dream these particular dreams? Why, for instance, should the dreams be so preoccupied with death and destruction? A year later the girl died of an infectious illness. Could her strange dreams have foreshadowed this turn of events? It may seem unlikely, but Jung entertains the possibility, in light of his belief that dreams may sometimes predict future happenings by projecting into the future from current unconscious trends. Although he comes to no firm conclusion on this issue for this particular case, Jung writes:

> These dreams open up a new and rather terrifying aspect of life and death. One would expect to find such images in an aging person who looks back upon life, rather than to be given them by a child who would normally be looking forward. Their atmosphere recalls the old Roman saying, "Life is a short dream," rather than the joy and exuberance of springtime. For this child's life was like a *ver sacrum vovendum* (vow of vernal sacrifice), as the Roman poet puts it. Experience shows that the unknown approach of death casts an *adumbratio* (an anticipatory shadow) over the life and dreams of the victim. Even the altar in Christian churches represents, on the one hand, a tomb and, on the other, a place of resurrection—the transformation of death into eternal life. (Jung et al., 1964, p. 75)

Like Jung, Alfred Adler (1870–1937) was originally a follower of Freud, but he, too, broke off from the psychoanalytic orthodoxy to establish his own rival approach, called individual psychology. Compared to both Freud and Jung, Adler developed a more straight-forward approach to interpreting life stories, suggesting that early memories often hold the key themes for a person's overall style of life.

ADLER: BEGINNINGS AND ENDINGS

Interpreting the story of a person's life was a central, though implicit, goal for one of the most well-known and most misunderstood theorists in the history of personality psychology. I am speaking here of Alfred Adler (1870–1937). Long before the study of narrative and life stories became fashionable in psychology and the social sciences, Adler had a keen appreciation for the way in which the human life course may assume the form of a story. Adler is usually lumped together with Freud and the psychoanalysts because he was an early follower of Freud. But this grouping is misleading, for Adler's approach to personality, which he labeled **individual psychology,** actually bears little similarity to Freud or the tradition Freud launched. Adler made little use, for example, of the notion of unconscious processes, and he did not see human life as driven by erotic instincts. Furthermore, his theory has little to say about the kind of psychic conflict that is so important to most psychoanalytic approaches. Adler presented instead a very eclectic and original theory of the person that reveals an astute understanding of the role of psychosocially constructed narrative in human lives organized in time.

INDIVIDUAL PSYCHOLOGY

Alfred Adler was born in Vienna in 1870 of a middle-class Jewish family. He was a second son, who, throughout his childhood, found himself continually trying to match the high achievements of his older brother. His family constellation included an envious younger brother and three other siblings. Sibling position and rivalry in the family are major themes of Adler's theory of personality development, as he maintained that the second-born child often needed to rebel against authority in order to obtain power vis-à-vis the more conventional first-born. (I discussed this idea briefly in chapter 1 to illustrate the correlational method in personality research and considered it again in chapter 6 when we explored birth order as an environmental influence on personality.) Adler received a degree in medicine from the University of Vienna in 1895 and began a private practice shortly thereafter. In 1897, he married Raissa Epstein, an ardent socialist whom he met at a political convention. Though he was not a militant activist, Adler espoused a decidedly socialist political philosophy throughout his life. Unlike Freud and Jung, Adler identified strongly with the working classes, giving many lectures to workers' groups in Europe and the United States in the 1920s and 1930s.

In 1902, Adler met Freud and immediately became active in psychoanalytic circles. He became the first president of the Viennese Psychoanalytic Society in 1910, but he cut his ties with Freud only a year later after a series of bitter disputes. As early as 1908, Adler had taken issue with Freud's insistence that sexuality was at the center of human instinctual life. Adler argued instead for a basic motive of aggression, an idea that Freud, ironically, accepted some 12 years later in his reformulation of human motivation to include both life and death instincts. At the time of Adler's proposal, however, such a departure from orthodox psychoanalytic theory was not welcomed. Adler formed his own group under the auspices of individual psychology, and he eventually attracted followers from all over the world. During World War I, Adler served as a physician in the Austrian army, and after the war he established the first child-guidance clinics in Vienna. Foreseeing the imminent Nazi menace, he left Europe in the early 1930s and settled in New York, where he continued his practice as a psychiatrist and his extensive lecturing and writing on individual psychology.

In contrast to Freud and Jung, Adler represents a more straightforward theory of the person. It is premised on a view of humankind that emphasizes conscious thought and the social determinants of personality. Like the social-learning theorists of chapter 3, Adler suggests that personality is shaped by learning in a social environment. Like the cognitive approaches in chapter 8, individual psychology argues that people are generally conscious of the reasons for their behavior and are capable of making rational life decisions with regard to conscious life goals and plans. Like the humanistic theories of Rogers and Maslow (chapter 7), individual psychology paints a relatively optimistic picture of a developing and enhancing human organism, mastering the environment and creating the self over the human life course.

THE EARLIEST MEMORY

Human beings are fascinated with beginnings. We want to know "how it all started," "where things come from," what the "origins" of a particular event or phenomenon are. We tend to believe that we can understand something fully only when we know its beginnings. Witness our fascination with creation myths, the theory of evolution, and scientists' speculations about the "Big Bang." Indeed, the very first verse of the first chapter of the Bible—the book of Genesis, whose name itself means "beginnings"—reads: "In the beginning God created the heaven and the earth." For Christians and Jews, this verse has traditionally served as the ultimate explanatory utterance.

When it comes to explaining our own lives and the lives of others, we are just as strongly drawn to beginnings. From childhood onward, we want to know "where we came from" and what our "roots" might be. In this vein, Adler accorded a great deal of significance to the person's earliest memory. What a person can consciously remember from the earliest years holds clues about that person's present and future identity (Adler, 1927, 1931). In Adler's view, the earliest memory reveals major themes in a person's **style of life,** that is, the person's unique mode of adjustment to life, most notably including the person's self-selected goals and means of achieving them. Adler believed that each life was patterned according to a unique style, the central features of which are outlined through early relationships in the person's family.

Adler viewed the earliest memory as something like a personal creation myth or scene that implicitly foreshadows and symbolizes the overall tone of the person's subsequent life story. A number of his own examples are illuminating in this regard (Adler, 1927, 1931). Adler describes the case of a man whose first memory was that of being held in his mother's arms, only to be summarily deposited on the ground so that she could pick up his younger brother. His adult life involved persistent fears that others would be preferred to him, including extreme mistrust of his fiancée. Another man whose style of life emphasized fear and discouragement recalled falling out of his baby carriage. A woman who distrusted most people and feared that they would hold her back in her pursuits recalled that her parents prevented her from attending school until her younger sister was old enough to accompany her. And a young man who was being treated for severe attacks of anxiety recalled an early scene in which he sat at a window and watched workmen build a house, while his mother knitted stockings. To Adler, this recollection indicated that the young man was probably pampered as a child and that he preferred to be a spectator who watches things happen rather than a participant who makes things happen. Adler believed that this interpretation was supported by the man's current situation, in that he perennially became anxious whenever he tried to take up a new vocation. In an effective piece of vocational counseling, Adler suggested to this patient that he find an occupation that involves looking and observing. He took Adler's advice and became a successful art dealer.

Although psychologists outside Alderian circles have been slow to investigate the role of early memories in personality, a small flurry of research supports Adler's general insight that such memories illuminate current personality trends and strivings (Kihlstrom & Harackiewicz, 1982). Tying together early memories and Marcia's identity statuses (described in chapter 9), Orlofsky and Frank (1986) found that college students in identity achievement and moratorium expressed more mature developmental themes in their early memories compared with students in foreclosure and identity diffusion.

Bruhn and Schiffman (1982) analyzed early memories provided by more than 200 college students. Each student recalled earliest memories and filled out a questionnaire designed to assess the extent to which the student believed that he or she exerted effective control in the world. The early memories were analyzed from the standpoint of (a) mastery, (b) punishment, and (c) interpersonal difficulties. Bruhn and Schiffman found that those students who felt they had control over their worlds described early memories in which (a) they actively mastered the environment, (b) punishment was contingent on their own behavior, and (c) they caused their own interpersonal difficulties. Those students whose questionnaire responses indicated that they felt little control over their worlds expressed opposite themes. They tended to describe early memories in which (a) they were passive rather than active, (b) punishment was unrelated to their behavior, and (c) they were victims rather than causes of interpersonal difficulties. Some examples of these responses can be seen in Table 11.3. In this study, we see that early memories reveal the beginnings of a general orientation toward life. For those students who believed they could control and master the world, early memories emphasized how they had exerted control in the past. For

TABLE 11.3	EARLY MEMORIES ACCORDING TO FEELINGS OF CONTROL OVER THE WORLD	
Category of Memory	Example From Student High on Control	Example From Student Low on Control
Achievement mastery	I was playing with my dolls. I was teaching them spelling. Since I couldn't spell, I would write down random combinations of letters and take them to my mother. After many trials and errors I spelled "home"—the first word I ever wrote.	I remember sitting on the floor near my mother's feet and watching her iron. She was ironing a favorite outfit of mine. I remember stroking the skirt once or twice.
Punishment	When I wanted to put ketchup on my potatoes, my father said I would have to eat it even if I didn't like it. I poured a bottle of ketchup on the potatoes and was made to sit there until I ate every bite.	I wanted to prove that I was a "big boy" by going to the store alone. When I got home, my parents punished me for "running away from home."
Interpersonal difficulty	One day a carpenter came to fix the bathroom. I locked him and my mother in the bathroom. Finally after an hour a neighbor let them out.	I was wrestling with an older boy. He pinned me down and sat on me for more than 10 minutes. It hurt like hell.

NOTE: Feelings of control were assessed through a self-report questionnaire.

SOURCE: Adapted from "Predictors of locus of control stance from the earliest childhood memory," by A. R. Bruhn & H. Schiffman, 1982, *Journal of Personality Assessment, 46,*389-390.

the other students, however, early memories hint at a very different kind of story: a story premised on the assumption that the world controls them, that they cannot control it.

FICTIONAL FINALISM

In Adler's earliest theorizing, he argued that a prime motive for human behavior was striving to be aggressive. Later he replaced this motivational idea with a more general **will to power.** Adler believed that human beings want to feel strong and powerful in their interactions with the world and that they seek to avoid experiences in which they feel weak or inferior. Yet many children encounter repeated experiences of weakness and helplessness in the face of physical deficits and anomalies. Adler termed such deficits **organ inferiorities.** While these inferiorities can exert a debilitating effect on personality development, many people compensate for their own perceived inferiorities by working extra hard to strengthen what is weak. For example, a child who stutters may train him- or herself to be an exceptional speaker in adulthood. Or a child who is weak and sickly may undergo rigorous training to become a physical stalwart as an adult, as we saw in the case of Yukio Mishima.

Adler eventually abandoned his concept of will to power in favor of an even more general motivational tendency termed **striving for superiority.** He described this universal, innate tendency as the "great upward drive" of human behavior and experience:

> I began to see clearly in every psychological phenomenon the striving for superiority. It runs parallel to physical growth and is an intrinsic necessity of life itself. It lies at the root of all solutions to life's problems and is manifested in the way in which we meet

these problems. All our functions follow its direction. They strive for conquest, security, increase, either in the right or in the wrong direction. The impetus from minus to plus never ends. The urge from below to above never ceases. Whatever premises all our philosophers and psychologists dream of—self-preservation, pleasure principle, equalization—all these are but vague representations, attempts to express the great upward drive. (Adler, 1930, p. 398)

We see in this wonderful quotation that Adler meant something quite general and encompassing when he posited a universal striving for superiority. The striving aims toward superiority over the environment as well as perfection, completion, and wholeness. In the context of this general life force, Adler reconceptualized organ inferiority to refer more generally to any feeling of weakness that arises from a sense of incompletion or imperfection in any sphere of life. He also blended with his great upward drive the concept of **social interest,** or the person's innate sense of kinship with all humanity. According to Adler, the well-adjusted person strives for superiority and wholeness in his or her environment while expressing a true love for and communion with other people. An important individual difference in personality, therefore, is the prominence of social interest in the lives of different persons. In an attempt to operationalize this concept for research, Crandall (1980, 1984) developed a short social-interest questionnaire. Supporting Adler's theoretical claims, Crandall found that people with strong social interest score higher on various measures of psychological adjustment and report fewer negative results of stress in their lives, compared with people who are low in social interest.

Though all persons strive for completion and wholeness in their lives, each person strives in a different way and toward a different end. In the motivational terms of chapter 7, behavior is energized by the great upward drive of superiority but it is given direction and guidance by the person's thoughts about the future. A major theme in Adlerian psychology is that people are more oriented to the subjectively expected and hoped-for future than they are bound to the objective past:

> Individual Psychology insists absolutely on the indispensability of finalism for the understanding of all psychological phenomena. Causes, powers, instincts, impulses, and the like cannot serve as explanatory principles. The final goal alone can explain man's behavior. Experiences, traumata, sexual development mechanisms cannot yield an explanation, but the perspective in which these are regarded, the individual way of seeing them, which subordinates all life to the final goal, can do so. (Adler, 1930, p. 400)

According to Adler, persons understand their lives in terms of *final goals,* and they organize their behavior and experience accordingly. Early experiences, traumata, and so on are not in and of themselves the determinants of behavior. Rather, like Erikson, Adler argues that early events are subjectively reorganized in light of the (later) final goals. The final goals envisioned by each person are subjective expectations about what might happen in the future. They are products of the imagination, not empirical or logical facts. Envisioned final goals are fictions, with respect to which we act *as if* they were true. According to Adler, then, human behavior and experience is guided, for better or worse, by **fictional finalism.** What each of us perceives to be the final goal of our lives is a fiction that we create to give our lives direction and purpose. Though some fictions may be impossible to realize, they nonetheless function in our lives as supreme organizers for our strivings and ultimate explanations for our conduct. Adler was quick to point out that a widely unrealistic fictional finalism may be the root cause of a neurotic's misery. Yet, all people create fictions about the future of one sort or another. The most adaptive fictional finalism incorporates realistic expectations into an imaginative narrative about the future, capable of sustaining and stimulating the person's strivings for superiority, wholeness, and completion.

Adler present us with a theory of the person that assumes that the individual's life is a patterned psychosocial narrative that integrates past, present, and future, with beginnings, middles, and endings. People strive for narrative unity and purpose as their lives evolve over time.

LIVES AS TEXTS

Long before there were psychologists, human beings created and told stories about the problems and the possibilities in their lives. Poets, novelists, and film makers have continued to provide insights into life meanings through the stories they create, just as all of us—even as children—seek and find truths about ourselves and each other through making, hearing, and telling stories. Freud, Jung, and Adler believed that the interpretation of the stories people tell yield the deepest secrets about human personality. These three famous personality psychologists from the first half of the 20th century offered three very different perspectives on interpretation. Yet what all three had in common was a deep appreciation for ways in which lives are like stories and a commitment to sorting through the many different and complex meanings that those stories may reveal and conceal.

In the past 20 years, psychologists seem to have rediscovered the story (McAdams, 1999). A growing number of developmental psychologists are now examining children's astute appreciation for stories and the ways in which they use stories in discourse (e.g., Fivush & Haden, 2003; Lucariello, 1990; Pellegrini & Galda, 1990). Psychologists interested in education now stress the powerful role of stories in teaching and learning, especially in education for values, and in moral development (Tappan, 1990; Tappan & Brown, 1989; Vitz, 1990). Social and personality psychologists now explore the different kinds of narrative *accounts* that adults devise to cope with personal problems and to explain puzzling or problematic life events (e.g., Baumeister, Stillwell, & Wotman, 1990; Harvey, Weber, Galvin, Huszti, & Garnick, 1986; Leith & Baumeister, 1998). Lifespan theorists argue for the primacy of narrative in the understanding of adult lives. According to theorists such as Cohler (1982, 1990) and Whitbourne (1985), the adult life course should *not* be viewed as an orderly progression of developmental stages, nor as a predictable expression of stable personality traits, but rather as an evolving narrative, situated in culture and history.

Three influential spokespersons for *narrative psychology* are Theodore Sarbin (1986), Donald Polkinghorne (1988), and Jerome Bruner (1986, 1990). Sarbin (1986) argues that the narrative can serve as a **root metaphor** for contemporary psychology. According to Pepper (1942), a root metaphor is a basic analogy for understanding the world. The dominant root metaphor in Western civilization is *mechanism*, the basic analogy of the machine. "The kind of machine employed to provide imagery may be a clock, a dynamo, a computer, an internal combustion engine," or any other mechanism to which the workings of the human mind, human behavior, and human affairs may be compared (Sarbin, 1986, p. 6). Sarbin views the narrative as a liberating metaphor for psychology because narrative reveals part of what is distinctively human about human beings—humans, unlike machines, are by nature storytellers—and it provides for a nuanced understanding of how human lives are situated in social and historical context. Polkinghorne (1988) agrees. He argues that at the heart of the *human sciences*—the sciences concerned with human conduct—is *narrative knowing:*

Our lives are ceaselessly intertwined with narrative, with the stories that we tell and hear told, with the stories that we dream or imagine or would like to tell. All these stories are reworked in the story of our own lives which we narrate to ourselves in an episodic, sometimes semiconscious, virtually uninterrupted monologue. We live immersed in narrative, recounting and reassessing the meanings of our past actions, anticipating the outcomes of our future projects, situating ourselves at the intersection of several stories not yet completed. We explain our actions in terms of plots, and often no other form of explanation can produce sensible statements. (p. 160)

As we saw in chapter 10, Bruner (1986, 1990) suggests that the narrative mode of human thought is especially amenable to the analysis of human intention and action, whereas the paradigmatic mode better addresses the demands for physical cause-and-effect explanations, like those required in the physical sciences. Bruner (1990) also points out that within the human sciences stories are especially useful in providing explanations for events that do not fit socially expectable patterns. He writes, "the function of the story is to find an intentional state that mitigates or at least makes comprehensible a deviation from a canonical cultural pattern" (1990, pp. 49–50). Similarly, Chafe (1990) writes that people devise stories when a particular event or phenomenon is "difficult to account for" (p. 83). If I wake up in the morning, brush my teeth, read the paper, and then get in my car to drive to work, as I do most days, I will not be very motivated to create a story to explain what I did. Nothing really needs to be accounted for, in that my morning routine fits what Bruner calls a canonical cultural pattern. But if I wake up to find a baby lying in a basket on my doorstep, where the newspaper usually is, then there are stories to be learned and told, for events have transpired in a way that deviates from the expectable pattern. Where did this baby come from? Who abandoned her on my doorstep? What do I do now? As I rush the baby into the house, yell upstairs to my wife, and telephone the police, I am already creating narrations to explain what at the moment seems inexplicable.

If we extend this point to the field of personality psychology *in toto,* then we might suggest that each individual human life is analogous to an event or phenomenon that must be accounted for because each individual life, in one way or another, deviates from what Bruner calls the canonical cultural pattern. To put it another way, each person is unique. The uniqueness must be explained. It can best be explained through story. But stories themselves need to be explained, for their meanings are not always clear. In particular, stories often suggest many different things about the storyteller, as if the storyteller were speaking in different voices.

HERMANS'S DIALOGICAL SELF

In his dialogical theory of personality, Hubert Hermans (1988, 1991, 1992a, 1996; Hermans, Kempen, & van Loon, 1992) envisions the person as a multivoiced storyteller whose identity is expressed through dialogue. Different parts of the self speak to and about different aspects of personality that are especially valued. Because life is full of so many important things, a person's life story must employ many different voices to convey fully the richness of personal experience.

Hermans begins with the concept of **valuation.** A valuation is "anything that a person finds to be of importance when thinking about his or her life situation" (Hermans, 1988, p. 792). Valuations can include beloved persons in one's life as well as those whom one dislikes, disturbing dreams, difficult problems, cherished opportunities, memories of particularly

Hubert Hermans has developed a new and influential theory of personality that centers on the dialogical self. According to Hermans, the self is an ongoing story that is told (voiced) from many different perspectives. Photo courtesy of Vincent Hevern.

important events from the past, plans or goals for the future, and so on. Each valuation is a unit of meaning in the person's life. Each valuation has either a positive, negative, or mixed (ambivalent) emotional quality. Through self-reflection, people organize their valuations into narratives that situate them in time and space.

Hermans suggests that different persons' valuations can be interpreted in terms of two primary motivational systems. Adapting Bakan's (1966) concepts of agency and communion, Hermans distinguishes between agentic *S-motives* and communal *O-motives*. S-motives concern *self*-strivings for superiority, expansion, power, control, and so on. O-motives are *other*-oriented, longing for contact, union, and intimacy with others. These two motives give direction and organization to the wide variety of valuations in an individual's life story. A second dichotomy for organizing valuations is that between *positive* and *negative* affectivity. Different people may be compared and contrasted, then, with respect to the extent to which their valuation systems exhibit relatively high-to-low levels of S-motives, O-motives, positive affect, and negative affect.

Hermans has developed a *self-confrontation method* for collecting and assessing valuations. It is a method through which the research subject serves as a "co-investigator" rather than purely an object of investigation (Hermans & Bonarius, 1991). In other words, Hermans and his colleagues view the research enterprise as a matter of mutual cooperation between participants and researchers. Data are obtained through dialogue, or conversation, between the researcher and the research participant. The philosophy of this approach assumes that participants themselves are the "experts" when it comes to understanding their own lives. The researcher provides a series of questions to guide the conversation and to obtain a listing of the subject's most important valuations. Some of those questions are presented in Table 11.4.

The self-confrontation method typically yields between 20 and 40 discrete valuations for each participant. In the second phase of the research, the person goes back to each valuation and rates it, on 6-point scales, for each of 16 different emotion terms. Four of the terms refer to S-motives ("self-esteem," "strength," "self-confidence," and "pride"); four refer to O-motives ("caring," "love," "tenderness," and "intimacy"); four refer to positive affect only ("joy," "happiness," "enjoyment," and "inner calm"); and four refer to negative affect only ("worry," unhappiness," "despondency," and "disappointment"). For each valuation, the researcher then calculates an S index by summing ratings on the four corresponding S-motive affects and comparable indexes for O (O-motives), P (positive affect), and N (negative affect). Other important indices include the "S minus O" score, to determine whether self or other motive ratings are stronger for a given valuation, and the "P minus N" score to determine the relative strength of positive versus negative affect.

In terms of nomothetic research, Hermans has explored how certain patterns of valuations characterize certain groups of people. For example, Hermans (1992b) identified an interesting group of psychotherapy clients whose valuations manifested "unhappy self-esteem." Whereas a considerable body of research suggests that ratings of happiness and self-esteem are positively correlated, certain people go against the grain, revealing valuations that score high on both S and N. Compared to other psychotherapy clients, these individuals have developed narratives of the self in which especially meaningful events and persons elicit in them a paradoxical mix of self-respect and strength on the one hand and unhappiness on the

TABLE 11.4	**QUESTIONS USED TO ELICIT VALUATIONS IN THE SELF-CONFRONTATION METHOD**

Set 1: The Past

— Was there something in your past that has been of major importance or significance for your life and which still plays an important part today?

— Was there, in the past, a person, an experience, or circumstances that greatly influenced your life and still appreciably affects your present existence?

You are free to go back into the past as far as you like.

Set 2: The Present

— Is there in your present life something that is of major importance for, or exerts a great influence on, your existence?

— Is there in your present life a person or circumstance which exerts a significant influence on you?

Set 3: The Future

— Do you foresee something that will be of great importance for, or of major influence on, your future life?

— Do you feel that a certain person or circumstance will exert a great influence on your future life?

— Is there a goal or object that you expect to play an important role in your future life?

You are free to look as far ahead as you wish.

SOURCE: From "The Person as Co-investigator in Self-Research: Valuation Theory," by H. J. M. Hermans, 1991, *European Journal of Personality, 5,* 222.

other. Hermans and van Gilst (1991) identified another group of psychotherapy clients whose valuations resembled the affective ratings made by 10 students of the ancient story of Narcissus (Feature 4.A in this book). When we think of "narcissism" and the story of Narcissus, we usually think of a person who is self-centered—high "S" in Hermans's scheme. However, the pattern of ratings that best captured the meaning of the Narcissus myth was *low* S, *high* O, low P, and high N. Therefore, the psychotherapy clients whose valuations most closely resembled the Narcissus myth seemed to be suffering more from a frustrated longing for union with others, rather than an overabundance of self-striving.

Hermans suggests that the examination of valuations is a window into each person's uniquely positioned **dialogical self** (Hermans, Kempen, & van Loon, 1992). The subjective self—the "I"—is storyteller, but the storyteller moves from one I position to the next, making for multiple authors, multiple I's, for the same life story. Most views of the self with which we, as Westerners, are familiar are individualistic and rationalistic, viewing the I as a potentially rational and self-contained "thinker" or "knower." In Descartes' famous expression, "I think; therefore, I am." But Hermans rejects this prevailing view in favor of a dialogical self that is *multiple and embedded in dialogue.* As an author of its own life story, the I moves from one I position to another, adopting different perspectives from which to understand the self. The different I positions are in dialogue with each other. Hermans, Kempen, and van Loon (1992) write:

> We conceptualize the self in terms of a dynamic multiplicity of relatively autonomous *I* positions in an imaginal landscape. In its most concise form this conception can be formulated as follows. The *I* has the possibility to move, as in a space, from one position to the other in accordance with changes in situation and time. The *I* fluctuates

among different and even opposed positions. The *I* has the capacity to imaginatively endow each position with a voice so that dialogical relations between positions can be established. The voices function like interacting characters in a story. Once a character is set in motion in a story, the character takes on a life of its own and thus assumes a certain narrative necessity. Each character has a story to tell about experiences from its own stance. As different voices, these characters exchange information about their respective *Mes* and their worlds, resulting in a complex, narratively structured self. (pp. 28–29)

This is a difficult idea to comprehend at first. We take for granted that the self is singular in some sense, that *I* create *my* life story. We may concede that the story may have many characters, but it is a single *I* who creates them. From Hermans's point of view, however, the I is really a host of storytellers; there is no single perspective for an author, but rather many different positions from which the story is told. Each I position can establish itself as a more-or-less autonomous "voice." Drawing from the Russian literary critic M. M. Bakhtin (1973), Hermans conceives of the self as a *polyphonic novel*—a complex story with many voices. Each voice presents its own unified world, as in the great novels of Fyodor Dostoyevsky wherein different characters develop their own ideologies and world views, which in turn play off against each other:

> In Dostoyevsky's novels there is not one single author, Dostoyevsky himself, but several authors or thinkers (e.g., the characters Raskolnikov, Myshkin, Stavrogin, Ivan Karamazov, and the Grand Inquisitor). Each of these heroes has his own voice ventilating his own view, and each hero is authoritative and independent. A hero is not simply the object of Dostoyevsky's finalizing artistic vision but comes across as the author of its own ideology. According to Bakhtin, there is not a multitude of characters within a unified objective world, illuminated by Dostoyevsky's individual vision, but a plurality of perspectives and worlds: a polyphony of voices. As in a polyphonic composition, the several voices or instruments have different spatial positions and accompany and oppose each other in a dialogical relation. (Hermans, Kempen, & van Loon, 1992, p. 27)

In summary, Hermans offers a provocative theory of the self in which persons provide their lives with meaning by organizing their valuations into life narratives. Rather than seeing the narrative as the product of a single author—a single storymaking "I"—Hermans argues that the I moves in imagination from one authorial position to another, as if it were a single *body* moving over a variegated landscape offering many different scenic views. Certain positions, or viewpoints, become especially important over time, and these are the positions from which the I develops a distinctive voice. Ultimately, a life story is the product of many different authors—many different I positions. The different authors may contradict one another, as different characters in a polyphonic novel offer their own unique and discordant world views. Instead of an individual, rational self, the person is endowed with multiple storytelling selves, each in dialogue with the others.

MUSIC AND STORY: GREGG'S APPROACH

Another perspective on narrative that emphasizes the multiplicity of the self is offered by Gary Gregg (1991, 1995). Like Hermans, Gregg argues that the self is expressed through many different voices. For any given person, the different voices may seem to create a confusing cacophony; it may seem that there is little pattern, order, or organization to the different selves a person shows. However, closer examination of individual life stories convinces Gregg that beneath the phenotypic noise of clashing voices lies a genotypic piece

of music, complexly patterned and meaningful, expressing endless variatic
number of themes, like a fugue.

Music is the driving metaphor for Gregg's approach. Life stories reveal a mu_
ture of the self. The two primary axes of music are harmony (vertical) and melody (hoi.
zontal). Harmony is expressed in chords, as the musician plays different notes
simultaneously to create an instantaneous blend. Melody is expressed as a sequence of
notes, played over time. Harmony and melody are made possible by the structure of scales,
such as the familiar diatonic scale of whole and half notes within an octave. (If you are having trouble following this, just sing "do, re, mi, fa, so, la, ti, do" to remind yourself of what a
scale is. The range from the first "do" to the second "do" is called an octave.) How each note
is heard in a musical piece is determined by the musical structures of the scales employed.
For Gregg, personality is like a fugue, a musical form in which several voices play variations
on a single theme. Typically, one voice introduces the theme (melody), and others answer it
with variations, producing a dialogical form, a kind of musical conversation among the
voices. In each voice, the theme can be expressed in a wide variety of ways. One voice may
express the theme twice as quickly as another; another voice may change the rhythm of the
theme; a third may invert the theme; and so on. Each voice is, therefore, both *the same as*
and *different from* every other voice, in that each voice expresses the theme but is likely to
express it in a very different way. And so it is in personality, argues Gregg. Among the many
different voices of the self, one may discern an underlying "identity-in-difference" (p. 52).

Like Hermans and McAdams (chapter 10), Gregg suggests that the major themes of
human identity concern power and love, or what Bakan (1966) calls agency and communion. People often invest the meanings associated with these themes into concrete images and
objects in their worlds. For example, Gregg describes the case of "Sharon," a young woman
whose major life themes are captured in the images of "tofu" and "junk food." When Gregg
interviewed her in 1979, Sharon was one of two partners who had built a successful business
that manufactures and distributes tofu and other health foods in the Midwestern United
States. For Sharon, tofu was more than just health food. It rather symbolized *for her* an
entire "New Age" ideology celebrating diet, nutrition, exercise, good health, the simple life,
and social renewal—a personal ideology that provided her life with a great deal of coherence. As an entrepreneur running a cooperative business, she could be an autonomous,
healthy, and effective woman involved in improving the lives of those who worked in her
company and those who consumed her products. Tofu also symbolized a number of personal habits and commitments connected with her New Age ideology. In addition to keeping a nondairy vegetarian diet, she studied T'ai Chi, practiced Yoga meditation, attended
various self-fulfillment workshops, experimented with herbal medicines, campaigned
against nuclear energy, and worked to sustain egalitarian community institutions.

By contrast, junk food symbolizes Sharon's past, growing up in Wisconsin, in a large
family with an overweight mother, eating meat, dairy products, candy, and junk food. It
was a "warm, cozy, still-in-the-womb type of existence," but it eventually proved too sti-
fling and too indicative of what Sharon now views as an exceptionally unhealthy American
lifestyle—eat lots of junk, get fat, have lots of kids, drive lots of cars, keep consuming, get
lazier and lazier, die young. Junk food, therefore, symbolizes a way of living—a theme in
her narrative identity—that Sharon finds disgusting and wasteful. She never wants to be
fat. She believes she is not ready to start a family. Yet, recently, she has felt a craving to have
a baby. Pregnancy would make her "fat." The craving frightens her now, for it threatens to
undermine the healthy, New Age existence she has created for herself. In a sense, junk food
opposes tofu. In another sense, junk food and tofu are the same:

> To come to the theoretical point: Sharon craves love and nurturance in the form of dairylike foods. She differentiates this craving by symbolically differentiating its objects into natural and healthy foods, on the one hand, and chemicalized junk foods, on the other. Tofu and junk food thus stand in an essentially octave relation to each other: tofu is ice cream "raised" an octave, ice cream is tofu "lowered" an octave. The "raised" and "lowered" have moral, existential, and political meanings that are the essentials of "sublimation" and "regression," respectively. That is, tofu and ice cream encode the imperative she emphasizes in outlining her biography: to strive for autonomous self-nurturance against the recurrent beckoning of passive indulgence. They "work" by virtue of their "identity-in-difference." They are identical in some properties (their appearance, texture, and taste similarities make them interchangeable) and in the meanings these properties represent to her (nurturance, safety, and love). But at the same time they possess other properties that are different (origin, manufacturing, packaging, and preparation in particular) and so can represent antithetical meanings (natural versus artificial; healthy versus poisonous; industry versus lethargy). Logically represented: B = A and C = A, yet B does not equal C. The structural ambiguity of these symbols enables Sharon to establish an "octave" craving for nurturance via food into adult and autonomous versus infantile and dependent forms. (Gregg, 1991, p. 89)

What ultimately links and differentiates junk food and tofu, then, is their relation to each other as ends of an "octave." Each is like the "do" on the scale you sang to yourself a moment ago. But *tofu is the higher "do,"* the one an octave up. What makes it higher is its *moral significance.* Tofu connects to a New Age ideology within which Sharon finds a great deal that is good, right, and true. Tofu is the way people *should* live if the world is to be a better, happier, and healthier place. Junk food is lower because it connects to a slothful and wasteful lifestyle; it is bad, wrong, and false, in this sense. And yet there is another sense in which both tofu and junk food are good, in that both connote love and nurturance. Junk food is the easy love of her mother, cozy and warm. Tofu is a New Age kind of adult love, love for one's fellow woman or man, love between equals.

Tofu and junk food receive their moral significance from the culture in which Sharon lives. Her personal meanings for these symbols come ultimately from her experiences growing up in the 1950s and 60s in small-town Wisconsin and coming of age in the 1970s as a student at the University of Wisconsin. At the university, she was exposed to a wide variety of alternative lifestyles, out of which she developed her current New Age viewpoints. An essential point in Gregg's approach to lives is his insistence that personal meanings derive ultimately from social, political, economic, and cultural realities. Following the sociologist Emile Durkheim, Gregg argues that social organization provides general categories of thought to the members of any particular society. Social organizations are not necessarily kind and gentle, and encouraging of healthy development, self-actualization, and the like. Rather, social organizations embody stratification and oppression, as revealed in class, ethnic, and gender inequalities. The life narratives that people create to provide their lives with the "identity-in-difference" that we find in the musical fugue reflect and even reinforce the social order in many cases. Gregg writes:

> I have insisted that a reality exists outside of the narratives: a reality of social/political inequality into which each individual is "thrown" and in which each individual constructs a self as an ideological tool with which to struggle for power and a semblance of personal dignity—typically denying equality and dignity to groups of Others in the process. I have argued that this reality is to be found not only outside the narrative as its

efficient cause, but at its core, in the semantic/syntactic kernel that generates it: in [for example] Sharon's spiritual-dietary struggle for "New Age" self-sufficiency ... (p. 199)

In conclusion, Gregg's approach to the self as both music and text underscores the multiplicity of voices with which the self speaks (or sings). It views the self as an orchestration of voices, each a variation on one of a small number of themes, that are similar to and different from each other by virtue of their formal relations within the music. The voices express a great deal of tension and conflict within the music, as well as peace and resolution. Voices and themes are often symbolized in complexly determined and emotionally charged images or objects, as we see in Sharon's appropriation of the images of tofu and junk food. Voices and themes express both personal and cultural meanings. Personal meanings are typically couched in cultural terms, reflecting the macrosocial order of the world within which the self is made.

THE POSTMODERN SELF

The 1980s and 1990s brought a good deal of discussion among some social scientists about the unique problems of making sense of the self in a *postmodern* world (e.g., Davies & Harre, 1990; Denzin, 1989; Gergen, 1991; Holstein & Gubrium, 2000; Sampson, 1985, 1988, 1989a, 1989b; Shotter & Gergen, 1989). The term **postmodern** is used in many different ways to refer to an assortment of perceived trends in art, architecture, literature, the media, social organization, and human consciousness that seem to have come to the fore in Western thinking since the 1970s. It is difficult to characterize the idea of postmodernity in a few sentences, in part because it means different things in different arenas. At its heart, however, is a skeptical and playfully ironic attitude about grand systems, universal truths, and conventional ways of doing things (Harvey, 1990). In general, the postmodern attitude is to embrace, or at least "deal with," the ambiguity and multiplicity that follow a rejection of all universal claims. In a postmodern world, there ultimately are no large truths. Instead, there are various versions, accounts, narratives, and so on—"texts," all of them—each subjectively construed from a particular point of view. Texts change from one moment to the next. Nothing stays the same. "Postmodernism swims, even wallows, in the fragmentary and the chaotic currents of change as if that is all there is" (Harvey, 1990, p. 44). In general, we may celebrate postmodernity for its openness, tolerance, and dynamism. Yet at the same time, we may find the postmodern refusal to believe in anything for the long run, to count anything as holding intrinsic truth and goodness and value, to be discouraging and even frightening, especially since human beings seem always to have demanded that there be something enduring "to believe in."

The concept of narrative is especially appealing in considering the problems of the postmodern self. Lives are like texts, narratives that continue to be written and rewritten over time. But what are texts? They are nothing but patterns of words, pictures, signs, and other sorts of representations. There is nothing substantially "real" about them; nor is there any sense in which a text can be said to be really "true" or "good." In some ways, postmodernity dovetails with the influential literary movement of the 1970s and 1980s called *deconstructionism* (Derrida, 1972). Among the many claims of deconstructionism is the idea that literary texts have no inherent and stable meanings. Language is indeterminate. Every word is ambiguous in and of itself, and its particular meaning in a particular moment is dependent on its relation to other equally ambiguous words with which it is spoken or written.

If lives are like texts, then lives, too, have no inherent meanings (Denzin, 1989). People may think that they understand who they are, that their lives "stand for something" or "express something true." But they are mistaken, just as readers are mistaken when they think they have found a single meaning in a given novel or short story. The mistakes are to be expected, because "stories and texts are written 'as if' they do have centers. Thus, writers and readers presume and 'read into' texts real authors, real intentions, and real meanings" (Denzin, 1989, p. 45). From the standpoint of deconstructionism, however, these readings are fallacies. A valid deconstructionist reading of a text, by contrast, exposes the many *inconsistencies* and *contradictions* in the text, and even reveals how authors of texts who think they are saying something true, or making a particular point, subtly "turn on themselves," proving themselves wrong in the texts themselves even when they don't realize it! Exhibiting a postmodern theme, a deconstructionist interpretation of a text may be "playfully ironic" in its revelation of texts as merely "language games" (Harre, 1989).

If lives are like texts, people construct selves in and through the sharing of texts in *discourse*. In other words, identities are made through talk, by uttering words and putting forth symbols in a social context. Shotter and Gergen (1989) write, "The primary medium within which identities are created and have their currency is not just linguistic but textual; persons are largely ascribed identities according to the manner of their embedding within a discourse—in their own or in the discourses of others" (p. ix). In a sense, each moment of discourse brings with it a new expression of the self. Over time, expressions are collected and patched together, much like a montage or collage.

The central problem of the postmodern self, then, is that of *unity*. Because all texts are indeterminate, no single life can really mean a single thing, no organizing pattern or identity can be validly discerned in any single human life. In his provocative book, *The Saturated Self,* Kenneth Gergen (1991) makes this point quite forcefully:

> The postmodern condition more generally is marked by a plurality of voices vying for the right to reality—to be accepted as legitimate expressions of the true and the good. As the voices expand in power and presence, all that seemed proper, right-minded, and well understood is subverted. In the postmodern world we become increasingly aware that the objects about which we speak are not so much "in the world" as they are products of perspective. Thus, processes such as emotion and reason cease to be real and significant essences of persons; rather, in the light of pluralism we perceive them to be impostors, the outcomes of our ways of conceptualizing them. Under postmodern conditions, persons exist in a state of continuous construction and reconstruction; it is a world where anything goes that can be negotiated. Each reality of self gives way to a reflexive questioning, irony, and ultimately the playful probing of yet another reality. The center fails to hold. (p. 7)

Drawing on deconstructionism and other postmodern themes, Edward Sampson (1989a, 1989b) has argued that psychology needs to develop a new understanding of the person. Because postmodern life is so indeterminate and because technology and the global economy now link people together from all over the world, it no longer makes sense to think of persons as individuals. Indeed, thinking of persons as individuals has never made sense in many cultures. Geertz (1979) writes: "The Western conception of the person as a bounded, unique, more or less integrated motivational and cognitive universe, a dynamic center of awareness, emotion, judgment, and action, organized into a distinctive whole and set contrastively against other such wholes and against a social and natural background is, however incorrigible it may seem to us, a rather peculiar idea within the context of the world's cultures" (p. 229). The Western view of the person as a self-contained individual reached its zenith in the "modern" period of Western history, suggests Sampson, beginning in the 16th century and running into the 20th.

In Sampson's view, the person is a "location" of intersecting forces and interacting voices situated within a particular social community and linked in the postmodern era to many other communities around the globe. It is difficult to know just how literally to interpret Sampson's argument, however. He surely is not suggesting that biologically distinct organisms are not in fact individual organisms. My body is not your body. Psychologically, however, what I consider to be "my" self—that which is mine, that which I have authored—may not really be mine, Sampson suggests. "Persons become the *guardians of* particular assets, not their owners," Sampson writes (1989a, p. 919). Selves are "constitutive." "Persons are creatures whose very identities are constituted by their social locations" (Sampson, 1989a, p. 918). The stories of self are not inside the person, waiting to be told. Instead, the person seems to reside amidst the stories, which surround and define him or her. The self is as much "out there," in the swirl and confusion of the postmodern world, as it is in the mind of the person.

Although postmodernist theorists are skeptical about the ability of an interpreter to make good sense of any particular person's life story, postmodern approaches to selfhood nonetheless share with the other perspectives in this chapter a strong and abiding belief in the power of human narratives. Human life is storied, conceived in terms of settings, scenes, characters, plots, and themes. Stories are ideally suited to capture how a human actor, endowed with consciousness and motivated by intention, enacts desires and strives for goals over time and in social context (Barresi & Juckes, 1997). Life stories are psychosocial texts that are jointly crafted by the individual him- or herself and the culture within which the individual's life has meaning. Our stories reflect who we are, but they also reflect the world in which we live.

FEMINIST PERSPECTIVES

In recent years, scholars of life narrative have become especially interested in the possibilities and the problems in writing women's lives. Western biographers have mainly focused on white men whose political, military, scientific, artistic, athletic, religious, or entrepreneurial achievements have made them famous. Theirs have been the life stories that our society has traditionally valued most, the stories deemed most appropriate for telling and interpreting. In the last few decades of the 20th century, however, scholars, popular writers, film-makers, and others have turned their attention toward women, people of color, and members of disadvantaged groups in an effort to explore and present those life stories that have traditionally been marginalized and dismissed (Bateson, 1990; Franz & Stewart, 1994; Josselson & Lieblich, 1993; Josselson, Lieblich, & McAdams, 2003; Rosenwald & Ochberg, 1992). Through this process, personality psychologists are learning that approaches and frameworks traditionally used to make sense of middle-class white men's lives do not always work well when applied to other people.

Many psychologists today speak of **feminist** perspectives for studying behavior and interpreting human lives. All feminist perspectives place gender at the center of the interpretive process, paying special attention to women's behavior and women's lives. Still, there are many different kinds of feminist approaches in psychology (Riger, 1992, 2000). For example, some feminist perspectives hold that women and men know and experience the world in very different ways and that women's unique ways of knowing need to be better incorporated into psychological research and theory. Other feminist approaches reject the idea that men and women are fundamentally different but argue that societal and cultural factors—

especially those related to power and status—impact men and women in very different ways. By virtue of their traditionally subordinate status in public life, many feminist scholars argue, women have developed different strategies for adaptation and different models for making a life, compared to men. Still other feminist approaches underscore the similarities between men and women and argue forcefully that the differences people say they observe are as much a matter of gender stereotyping and/or discrimination as anything else.

One thing is certain, however. Psychologists who study the stories people tell about their lives today are much more sensitive than they were in the days of Freud, Jung, and Adler to issues of gender, power, and social structure. Interpreting women's lives offers challenges that are doubtlessly similar to and different from those that psychologists face when interpreting the lives of men. Personality psychologist Abigail Stewart (1994) argues that interpreting the stories of women's lives requires a set of strategies that are sometimes difficult to employ. She outlines seven "feminist strategies" that she has found especially useful in her own life-narrative work.

The first strategy is to keep an eye open for *what's been left out.* Traditional categories such as work and family may not always capture a woman's experience. Certain areas of women's experience, such as close same-sex friendships and the politics of the family, have rarely been explored by biographers and psychologists, and yet these uncharted domains may be central to understanding a woman's life. Stewart (1994) remarks, "Feminist theory would lead us to expect that the things that will be missing will be things that those who are not women are not likely to be able to know and things that those who have a stake in the status quo are unlikely to want to know" (p. 18).

A leading personality researcher and theorist, Abigail Stewart has outlined seven strategies for making narrative sense of women's lives. Feminist perspectives on life-story interpretation place gender at the center of the psychological analysis. Photo credit —Joanne Leonard.

Second, a psychologist should always analyze his or her *own role or position as it affects understanding and the research process.* While science may be seen as glorifying objective observation, life-narrative studies, for men or women, are inherently subjective and dialogical. By virtue of the researcher's gender, social position, and historical experiences, he or she stands in an implicit relationship to the subject of the study. That relationship will surely have an impact on what kind of interpretation the researcher makes.

Third, Stewart urges the psychologist to *identify women's agency in the midst of social constraint.* While we are all products of our cultural milieu, some biographers and psychologists are too quick to explain women's lives completely in terms of social forces and constraints. These kinds of explanations feed the stereotype of the woman as passive victim. Yet even under the most oppressive circumstances, human agency is a strong force to be reckoned with. Stewart writes that "within the context of relative powerlessness, women—like all people in a subordinate status—make choices and resist oppression" (p. 21).

Fourth, Stewart asserts that the psychologist interpreting the lives of women (and men) should use *gender as an analytic tool.* Beyond sex roles and stereotypes, the very concept of what it means to be a man or a woman varies across cultures and over historical time. Therefore, "in studying a woman's life we must always inquire into her understanding of gender, as well as the consistencies and inconsistencies between her understandings and those of the people closest to her and in the wider culture affecting her at the time" (p. 24). Relatedly and fifth, the psychologist must be sensitive to the precise ways in which *gender defines power relationships and in which power relationships are gendered.* Some feminist theorists emphasize that while gender seems to be related to people's bodies (men and women are anatomically different, by virtue of differences regarding sexuality and reproduction), gender is just as much about social power as it is about sex and reproduction. Characteristics and experiences that have been traditionally associated with being a woman or being a man may sometimes be better understood as the consequences of social power. "Many aspects of women's experience that are 'gendered'— that is, associated with maleness or femaleness—are also experiences of subordination and can be understood better in those terms" (p. 26).

Stewart's sixth strategy is to identify other significant aspects of an *individual's social position* and explore the implications of that position. Stewart points out that many middle-class, white women of the 1960s and 1970s assumed that their experience of the women's liberation movement was identical to that experienced by black women at the time. But they were wrong, many black scholars have since argued. While occupational and social opportunities opened up for white women, black women still faced obstacles connected less to their gender and more to issues of race and class. By failing to take into consideration the profound influences of social class and race/ethnicity on the experience of gender, researchers fail to comprehend the full meanings of women's experience.

Finally, Stewart warns researchers to be suspicious of psychological prescriptions that stem ultimately from the experiences of the male elite. In particular, she suggests that biographers of women should *avoid the search for a neatly unified and coherent self or voice.* The idea that people do or should strive to have a perfectly unified and consistent sense of self, grounded in fundamental life principles and coherent ideological stance, may come from observations of privileged men who, to put it simply, have the socioeconomic luxury to create these kinds of life stories. Stewart urges researchers to leave open the possibility that women's life stories are often more contingent and contextually nuanced than men's. While she does not wish to conclude that such a difference is itself a clear psychological fact, she believes it is most wise to avoid projecting onto women, and onto people of color, a cultural ideal that seems to characterize better the life experiences of middle- and upper-middle-class Euro-American men living in the last half of the 20th century.

Stewart's last theme reflects the post-modern emphasis on *multiplicity* in life narratives. People construct and tell stories to make sense of their lives in time. These stories help people to find some degree of unity and purpose in life. But the stories also express variability, multiplicity, and flux. Any good interpretation, therefore, must strike a balance between coherence and complexity. Human lives are neither neat nor random. A life story will present certain unifying and integrating features of human individuality, providing a clear window into how some things fit together nicely, into a coherent pattern. But a life story will also present ideas that do not fit into any simple form, suggesting multiplicity, flux, contradiction, and even confusion. From Freud to contemporary feminism, the interpretation of life's stories poses challenges that are among the most difficult and fascinating in all of psychology. What do our life stories mean? We will probably never have a complete answer to that question. But there is still much that we can learn and know. The unexamined life story may still be worth living, but it is poorer for the lack of an effort. Like the rest of us, personality psychologists do and should find the challenge of making sense of life's stories difficult to resist.

SUMMARY

1. How should we interpret the stories people tell and live by? Over the past 100 years, personality psychologists have struggled with this question. This chapter describes approaches to interpreting people's stories that come from psychodynamic theorists in the first half of the 20th century and more contemporary approaches that fall under the categories of the dialogical self, the postmodern self, and feminism. Despite their differences, what these approaches all have in common is their assertion that the stories people tell are not what they initially seem to be.

2. The paradigmatic story form in Freud's psychoanalytic theorizing is the myth of Oedipus. Beginning around age 4, Freud argued, children experience an unconscious drama concerning sexuality and power, called the Oedipus complex. In the Oedipus complex, the child shifts from a libidinal object choice to identification with respect to the parents, paving the way for the establishment of the superego. The Oedipus complex is the great socializing event of childhood, Freud thought, for it curbs the child's power and consolidates the moral sensibility necessary for living in human groups. Although Freud was surely wrong in contending that all children experience an Oedipus complex, clinicians and biographers have found the Oedipus complex to be a powerful explanatory narrative in some lives, as can be seen in the case of Yukio Mishima.

3. It has always been difficult to apply the concept of the Oedipus complex to little girls and women. Critics have taken issue with many of Freud's ideas in this regard, especially his explication of penis envy in girls. Nancy Chodorow has reinterpreted the Oedipus complex in terms of the sociology of gender. Her influential theory argues that during and after the Oedipal period little girls establish identity in relation to and little boys in opposition to their mothers, producing divergent developmental pathways for women and men respectively, which are reproduced in subsequent generations by virtue of the fact that the prime caregivers for both girls and boys are almost always women.

4. In general, the Freudian method of interpreting lives and life stories involves searching for hidden meanings in the manifest content of everyday life. Freud showed how dreams, slips of the tongue, symptoms, and indeed all aspects of human behavior and experience can be viewed as overdetermined treaties and texts. Like treaties, they exist as compromises among conflicting forces (for dreams: wish fulfillments); like texts, they must be interpreted on many different levels, with no ultimate and final meaning ever to be found. In the case of Dora, Freud illustrates the psychoanalytic interpretation of both symptoms (Dora's cough) and dreams (the dream of the jewel-case). Symptoms, dreams, and ultimately all of human experience are constructed according to the same principles—such as condensation and displacement—through which a multitude of unconscious forces, factors, and components are synthesized into a manifest expression whose ultimate identity is always disguised.

5. An early follower of Freud, Carl Jung eventually developed a rival psychoanalytic approach to interpretation that underscored the significance of a collective unconscious. According to Jung, the collective unconscious is a storehouse of archaic remnants from humankind's evolutionary past. The collective unconscious is inhabited by archetypes, which are universal patterns of experience that structure how people approach life. Common Jungian archetypes include the anima (a man's unconscious femininity), the animus (a woman's unconscious masculinity), and the shadow (reprehensible, bestial tendencies in all humans). Each archetype provides a model for a particular kind of character in the life story. Applied mainly to dreams and fantasies, Jung's method of interpretation emphasizes universal themes and the heroic quest for psychological individuation. Jung portrayed dreams as symbols of the striving for balance in personality, as

expressions of universal myths, and as anticipations of life problems for the future.

6. Alfred Adler developed a system for personality studies that emphasized the temporal nature of human lives. Adler's theory shows a keen appreciation for the way in which the human life course may assume the form of a story. According to Adler's individual psychology, the earliest memory serves as an origin myth for life, setting the stage for the development of a person's unique style of life. While the earliest memory sets up the story's beginning, the person's fictional finalism, or imagined goals for the future, provides the life story with direction and purpose and orients it toward an envisioned narrative ending. Main themes in the story relate to the agentic striving for superiority and the communal tendency toward social interest.

7. In the 1980s and 90s, personality psychologist Hubert Hermans developed a narrative theory of the dialogical self. The basic units of life stories are valuations, which may be classified in terms of positive and negative affect and in terms of agentic S-motives and communal O-motives. Valuations are organized into narratives through a dialogical process, or a conversation within the self among different voices. There is no single, overarching storyteller, but rather a collection of voices that produce a polyphonic novel, which is itself the self.

8. In another contemporary approach, Gary Gregg offers a narrative-based approach to understanding human lives which, like that of Hermans, emphasizes multiplicity and the self's involvement in dialogue. The driving metaphor in Gregg's theory, however, is music. Personality is akin to a musical fugue, with different voices expressing different melodies and motifs.

Especially noteworthy are examples in life narratives of emotionally charged images that reflect personal tendencies that are both opposite to each other and fundamentally similar, as different musical notes in an octave relation.

9. In recent years, a number of writers have employed the idea of narrative in considering the problems and possibilities of the postmodern self. According to some, the contemporary self is deconstructed into a swirl of fleeting stories and postures, expressed in the ever-changing discourse of contemporary life and in the particular cultural contexts within which selves are constituted. Postmodern theories of selfhood are skeptical of any integrative or unifying forces within the person. Nonetheless, these approaches share the view that human lives are storied and that life stories reflect both who the person is and what kind of world the person lives in.

10. In recent years, psychologists and biographers have turned their attention to the life stories of women, people of color, and members of other traditionally marginalized groups. Feminist approaches to interpreting life stories place gender at the center of the interpretive process. Abigail Stewart has argued that interpreting a woman's life story offers unique challenges for the psychologist. She outlines seven feminist strategies for the narrative study of women's lives: (a) pay attention to what has been left out, (b) analyze your own role and position vis-à-vis the subject of study, (c) identify women's agency in the midst of social constraint, (d) use gender as an analytic tool, (e) be aware of how gender defines power relationships, (f) identify other aspects of the subject's social position such as class and ethnicity, and (g) be skeptical of the search for a neatly unified and coherent self or voice.

CHAPTER 12

Writing Stories of Lives: Biography and Life Course

If you met Grope, you would be unimpressed. Picture a short, dark-haired, slightly disheveled young man, enrolled at Harvard College in the 1930s. Aside from his association with a prestigious university, he seems a rather unremarkable undergraduate—quiet, apathetic, uninvolved, and uninspired. By his own account, he is a "small frog in a big puddle," a "pretty nice guy." He is shy, and he speaks softly and rarely. He is a member of no extracurricular clubs or organizations. He dates no women and spends very little time studying. His withdrawal from so many instrumental and interpersonal activities enables him to "devote the maximum amount of time to sleep, relaxation, daydreaming, and playing bridge with a small clique" of buddies (Murray, 1955/1981, p. 544). Though you might call him lazy, there is nothing grossly wrong with Grope: He is not psychotic; he is not a psychopath; he has never committed a crime. We might be surprised to learn, therefore, that in his dreams, fantasies, and through the *story of his own life,* Grope longs to fly.

Icarus: An Ancient Story

In the ancient story of Icarus, a young boy fashions wings and flies toward the sun. As he soars higher and higher, the heat from the sun melts the wax in his wings, sending him plummeting to the sea below. The Icarus legend is a story about hot sun and cold sea, about fiery ambition ultimately quenched by watery defeat, about rising and falling. In a profound sense, the story of Icarus is the story of Grope's life. In a famous case study, Henry A. Murray (1955/1981) interpreted the life and the personality of this unassuming college student in terms of an ancient Greek story about a young boy who rises and then falls. According to Murray, Grope revealed a pervasive **Icarus complex.**

Grope was one of a number of students who volunteered to participate as subjects in a series of interviews, tests, and experiments conducted by Murray and his associates at the Harvard Psychological Clinic in the 1930s and 1940s (Murray, 1938). As a subject, Grope wrote a detailed autobiography that laid the groundwork for three subsequent 1-hour interviews. In addition, Grope was administered a series of questionnaires and rating scales and certain open-ended exercises, such as the Thematic Apperception Test (TAT) in which a person is asked to create imaginative stories in response to pictures.

Some highlights from Grope's autobiography: Grope was the first of three children born to a college-educated couple. Grope's earliest memory was dumping his supper on the floor in a fit of revenge aimed at his mother. Grope wet his bed and his pants regularly until about the age of 11. By sixth grade, he had established himself as the premier student and athlete in his class. By seventh, he had started his self-described "fall" from supremacy after losing weight, failing to grow even an inch in the course of a year, and suffering repeated colds and bouts of sluggishness. Grope seemed to rebound slightly in high school, as he was elected treasurer of his sophomore class, chosen to serve on the student council and yearbook staff, and applauded as "Biggest Joker" in the senior class upon graduation. Attending Harvard, however, marked another fall into the mediocrity of the small frog in the big puddle. At the time of his first interview, Grope viewed himself as entering a behavioral and emotional limbo: "I am just biding my time and waiting for the day when my 'soul' will *ignite* and this inner *fire* will send me hurtling (two rungs at a time) *up* the ladder of success" (Murray, 1955/1981, p. 543). Once his soul "ignited" and he began his ascent, Grope would be able to achieve what he saw as the ultimate values in life: "money, power, glory, and fame."

Murray tells us of a few of the stories Grope most liked to tell himself:

His major recurrent fantasy was one of landing on a desert island in the Pacific with a band of followers, discovering an inexhaustible spring of fresh water and an abundant food supply, and then founding a new civilization with himself as king and lawgiver. He often dreamed and daydreamed of self-propelled flights and of jumping off a high place and floating gracefully and gently to the ground. But he was almost equally hospitable to less extravagant fantasies: he considered becoming a prize fighter, an actor, an army general, a millionaire, an inventor, a psychiatrist, and a teacher. "It would be a lot of fun working with kids, teaching them with a sense of humor, and having them think you are a 'good guy.'" He has imagined himself a famous tap dancer, a singer, and a movie comedian. He is attracted by the stage and has a tentative plan of enrolling in some school of drama. His more immediate intention, however, is to enlist in the Air Corps and become a pilot. Although in his opinion world wars are preventable evils, he expects another one within fifteen years, which will destroy much or most of civilization. The two worst things that might happen to him are (a) to be maimed in the war and (b) to lose his self-confidence. Finally, he writes: "If I could remodel the world to my heart's content, I would establish a sound World Government and would like to be the dictator, a good dictator." He would be "most proud" of having his name "go down in history as a leader, or as an artist, or as a discoverer or inventor." (Murray, 1955/1981, pp. 542–543)

The story of Icarus was reflected in Grope's images of who he was and who he had been, Grope's fantastical scripts foreshadowing who he might be and what he might do in the future, the critical scenes in Grope's past that stood out as turning points in his own life story, and the ideological underpinnings of the story that celebrated money, fame, and glory as the ultimate life values. Drawing mainly from Grope's autobiography, dreams, fantasies, and narrative responses on the TAT, Murray delineated a number of recurrent themes in Grope's life, summarized in Table 12.1, that converged to form the Icarus complex.

The first theme in the Icarus complex is *urethral erotism,* which means the thematic association of "hot" sexuality and "wet" urination. Images of urethral erotism concern the "cathection of fire, 'burning' ambition, exhibitionism, and voyeurism" (Murray, 1955/1981, p. 548). Murray points to Grope's reported childhood belief that babies are made by urinating into a woman's rectum, the high incidence of fire imagery in Grope's imagination, a lifelong fascination with fire ("fire is a yellow-orange gas from outer space," Grope proclaimed as a precocious 6-year-old), and the persistent problem of enuresis (bed-wetting).

Murray argued that urethral erotism was fused, in the case of Grope, with a second theme of *ascensionism,* or sudden rising. Ascensionism assumed a variety of guises for Grope as he imagined himself riding through the air perched upon the buttocks of his childhood nurse (a significant night dream), shooting through space and landing on the planet Mars, hurtling up the ladder of success, and reaching dizzying heights of prestige and influence. Witness the merger of urethral erotism and ascensionism in this remarkable story Grope told in response to a TAT picture of a barn surrounded by snow and a winged horse flying across the sky:

> An old hermit went out into the woods and built himself a farm. After thirty years of living all by himself on the crops he produced, he got pretty tired of this humdrum existence, so he decided that he wanted to re-enter the competitive world, and try to sell, was planning on selling his crops, planning to build some sort of fortune. So he worked for a few years, couldn't seem to get very large crops, really good crops. They wouldn't grow. What he needed was more fertilizer, but he couldn't afford fertilizer in any quantity, so he was practically at his wit's end, and one night he decided to turn to religion; and as miracles will happen, the very next day Pegasus flew over and fertilized all his plants

TABLE 12.1	THE ICARUS COMPLEX IN THE CASE OF GROPE

Urethral Erotism

In short, sex was apperceived in urinary terms. Also he manifested, in high degree, every other concomitant of urethral erotism, as defined by Freud and his followers: cathection of fire, "burning" ambition, exhibitionism, and voyeurism. Remember Grope's bright saying: "Fire is a yellow-orange gas from outer space." Even today he "gets a thrill" by lighting wastepaper in his tin scrap basket and seeing it flare up. There is a high incidence of pertinent fire imagery in his projective protocols. Finally, there is the association of persistent enuresis and urethral erotism (dreams of urination accompanied by ejaculation) which we and others have found in a number of personalities. (p. 548)

Ascensionism

This is the name I have given to the wish to overcome gravity, to stand erect, to grow tall, to dance on tiptoe, to walk on water, to leap or swing in the air, to climb, to rise, to fly, or to float down gradually from on high and land without injury, not to speak of rising from the dead and ascending into heaven. There are also emotional and ideational forms of ascensionism—passionate enthusiasm, rapid elevations of confidence, flights of the imagination, exultation, inflation of spirits, ecstatic mystical up-reachings, poetical and religious—which are likely to be expressed in the imagery of physical ascensionism. (p. 548)

Cynosural Narcissism

This strikes me as a suitable term (more embracing than exhibitionism) to denote a craving for unsolicited attention and admiration, a desire to attract and enchant all eyes, like a star in the firmament. (p. 549)

Falling/Precipitation

"Falling" denotes an undesired or accidental descension of something (usually a human body or the status [reputation] of a person, but it may be feces, urine, or any cathected object). "Precipitation," on the other hand, means a consciously or subconsciously desired calamitous descension: the S allows himself to fall or leaps from a height (precipitative suicide), or he pushes another person over a cliff, throws something down, or purposely urinates or defecates on the floor. (p. 551)

Craving for Immortality

No doubt the narcissistic core in every man yearns for perpetual existence; but of all our subjects Grope is unexampled in giving Everlasting Life ("I might settle for 500 years") as one of his seven wishes for himself. (p. 553)

Depreciation and Enthrallment of Women, Bisexuality

Grope spoke contemptuously of his mother, and cynically of women generally. Love was never a felt experience. But, as his projective protocols made plain, women were nonetheless important, if not indispensable, to him as glorifying agents: a female was (a) someone to be "swept off her feet," to be driven "sex-mad" by the mere sight of him; (b) someone to applaud his exploits; (c) someone of "wide hips" to bear him sons; and (d) someone to mourn his death. As one might expect in such a person, there were abundant evidences of a suffusing feminine component coupled with some degree of homosexuality. This is best illustrated by a story he told in the Tri-Dimensional Test. A king announces he will give half his kingdom to the person who creates the most beautiful thing in the world. The last contestant (hero of the story) comes forward and says, "I have created a replica of myself." Whereupon the king says, "*That* is the most beautiful thing in the world, therefore *you* are the most beautiful thing in the world. Will you be my queen?" The king takes the hero as his male queen and gives his androgynous beauty half his kingdom. (p. 554)

SOURCE: From "American Icarus," by H. A. Murray, in E.S. Shneidman (Ed.), *Endeavors in Psychology: Selections from the Personology of Henry A. Murray* (pp. 535–556), 1955/1981, New York: Harper & Row.

[assumedly by urinating on them]. Not only that, but the cow in the barn bore him a daughter [impregnated by Pegasus?!—urethral erotism]; something he had always wanted. In the picture here, he is squinting in his happiness; feeling that life has really been rewarding. So the picture is the spirit of happiness. (Murray, 1955/1981, p. 549)

The third theme of the Icarus complex is *cynosural narcissism,* which denotes a craving for unsolicited attention and admiration. Grope's fantasies about who he might be in the future were populated by heroic images of self as the benevolent dictator, actor, prize fighter, inventor—all superstars acclaimed and venerated by millions. Murray commented on the significance of Grope's drawings for the Draw-A-Family Test in which he drew his own portrait twice the size of his father's and mother's, as well as his narrative response to a blank TAT card upon which he projected the image of a virtually naked, gigantic man surrounded by an adoring crowd. The man is the "most perfect physical specimen in all of Greece … a sensation … a wonderful box-office draw" (Murray, 1955/1981, p. 550).

Finally, the fourth theme of *falling/precipitation* is linked to the first three themes in a series of ascension–descension cycles that Murray perceived at a number of different levels. In Grope's early memories, dreams, and TAT responses, as well as in his reconstruction of his own "falls" from prominence in seventh grade and upon entering Harvard, what goes up always comes down, and with a crash. (Indeed, Grope's supper falls crashing to the floor in his earliest memory.) In one grizzly story Grope told in response to a TAT picture, six people eventually die, four by falling into water. The "cold sea" quenched the flaming ambition of both the ancient Icarus and his modern counterpart. The images of fire and water, sun and sea, recall the first theme of urethral erotism.

Why did Henry Murray decide to relate the fantasies and feelings of an unremarkable college undergraduate to the ancient story of Icarus? What is the point of saying that Grope has an Icarus complex? One might imagine that Murray could have used the Grope case as an entry into the more general topic of flying fantasies. Indeed, just such an exploration is the point of a fascinating recent book by Dan Ogilvie (2004). In *Fantasies of Flight,* Ogilvie examines the psychological dynamics behind dreams and stories about flying as illustrated in the lives of many different people, including Sir James Barre, who created the character of Peter Pan. But in the case study of Grope, Murray seems more focused on one particular story about flying and falling (the legend of Icarus) as it applies to one particular case (Grope). I believe that Murray settled on the Icarus story because only a story could account for so many different aspects of Grope's life as a whole. As we saw in chapter 10, stories serve to integrate lives. We construct and live according to our own internalized and evolving narratives of self—the integrative life stories that constitute our very identities. In the case of Grope, however, it is Murray, as much as Grope, who is looking to articulate a story. The Icarus legend gives Murray the story he needs to make sense of Grope's life. The Icarus legend provides Murray with an elegant and provocative narrative for making sense of some of Grope's fantasies and dreams, his imaginative responses to TAT pictures, his values and aspirations, his memories of the past, and the current malaise he is experiencing as an undirected college student without an identity. In short, the Icarus complex is *Murray's story about Grope.* In order to convey key aspects of Grope's individuality, Murray finds he must tell a story.

Lament for Icarus. In the ancient Greek myth, the young Icarus flew higher and higher until the heat of the sun melted the wax in his wings, sending him plummeting to the earth below. Henry A. Murray conceived of the Icarus Complex as a particular kind of life-story type to be found in those human lives that seem to soar and then to fall.

We typically do not (and should not) think of personality psychologists as storytellers. Like other behavioral scientists, personality psychologists typically work within what we identified in chapter 10 as the *paradigmatic mode* of knowing (Bruner, 1990). This means that personality psychologists collect reliable and valid data, test hypotheses, perform precise measurements, and attempt to uncover lawful cause-and-effect relations concerning human individuality. Every chapter in this textbook has illustrated different scientific methods and theories employed in paradigmatic personality research. Even psychologists who work with life stories, as we saw in chapters 10 and 11, typically use those stories in a paradigmatic, scientific manner, attempting, for example, to classify, systematize, and measure aspects of life narratives and to use those assessments in a paradigmatic way. Having said this, it is nonetheless also true that certain forms of personality study do involve the psychologist's operating in what Bruner (1990) has called the *narrative mode* of knowing. This does not mean that personality psychologists occasionally write novels and short stories (though there is no law that says they cannot). Instead, I am referring here to psychologically informed efforts to conduct *biographical studies* of individual cases (Elms, 1994). Because stories are so effective in conveying the meaning of a human life in time, personality psychologists sometimes try to account for individual lives by discovering, relating, or constructing integrative interpretive stories. In the case of Grope, Murray relied on the ancient story of Icarus to convey aspects of his individuality that he could not effectively convey in any other way.

In this last chapter in the text, I explore different ways in which personality psychologists employ integrative stories to make sense of human lives. Whereas in chapters 10 and 11 our focus was on the stories that people construct to make sense of their own lives, our focus in the current chapter is on the stories that psychologists employ to make sense of the lives of their research subjects. In a sense, the life stories we considered in chapters 10 and 11 may be seen as *first-person accounts*—the stories people construct to make sense of who they are. In this chapter, we will consider stories as *third-person accounts*—storied interpretations that *psychologists* construct to make sense of who other people are. These third-person interpretations may indeed draw upon the first-person accounts. For example, in order to develop his Icarus interpretation (third-person), Murray used as data stories that Grope told about his own life (first-person). In describing the uses of stories in personality research, Barresi and Juckes (1997) write, "Researchers use first-person narratives as source material and third-person narratives in describing and interpreting lives because the temporal nature of experience makes it difficult for human beings not to attribute order, direction, and purpose to experience. It is because lives are structured through experience in a story-like manner that their study takes the narrative form" (p. 693).

I begin the exploration by following Murray through his seminal work at the Harvard Psychological Clinic in the 1930s, where he launched what has come to be known as the "personological tradition" in personality psychology. The personological tradition has emphasized biography, myth, narrative, and the intensive investigation of the single case. The role of case studies in personality psychology was as controversial in Murray's day as it is today. I will examine the controversy and comment on the appropriate use of case studies in personality psychology. I then consider the related, and also controversial, topic of psychobiography, which usually refers to especially ambitious efforts to interpret the course of a single (and usually famous) individual's life in terms of broad personality theory. Psychologically oriented biographies have been used to develop theories of the adult life course, as in Daniel Levinson's research on the "seasons" of adult life. Finally, I reconsider social context and the vagaries of social training in adult lives by touching on the life course perspective as it applies to the stories people tell to make sense of human lives. The life course perspective brings us back to the issue of human agency and individuality, which is why personality psychology exists in the first place.

PERSONOLOGY AND THE STUDY OF LIVES

MURRAY AND THE HARVARD PSYCHOLOGICAL CLINIC

In 1927 Harvard University hired a little-known physician with a Ph.D. in biochemistry to serve as an assistant to Morton Prince, a prominent psychologist at the Harvard Psychological Clinic. Although the 34-year-old Henry Murray had begun to distinguish himself in medical research, he was virtually untrained in psychology proper, having taken (and not enjoyed) only one undergraduate course in the subject 15 years before. Born of a wealthy family in New York City in 1893, Murray had traveled and studied widely in his 20s and 30s. He had been unable to find a fulfilling intellectual project for himself until he read, in 1923, Carl Jung's *Psychological Types* and, shortly thereafter, spent a vacation with Jung. Murray later wrote, Jung "provided [me] with an exemplar of genius that settled the question of [my] identity to come" (1967, p. 291). "We talked for hours, sailing down the lake and smoking before the hearth of his Faustian retreat. … Within a month a score of bi-horned problems were resolved, and I went off decided on depth psychology" (Murray, 1940, p. 153). At about the same time in Murray's life, a number of other influences appeared to work together to nudge him in the direction of psychology, including his reading of romantic authors such as Dostoyevsky and Melville and his growing professional and personal relationship with Christiana Morgan, who shared Murray's strong interest in human personality (Anderson, 1988; Murray, 1940, 1967; Robinson, 1992). Two years after Murray signed on at the Harvard clinic, Morton Prince died. Murray succeeded him as the director.

Henry A. Murray (1893–1988) was one of the great pioneers in American personality psychology. He advocated a broad and interdisciplinary approach to studying human lives, and he put special emphasis on the interpretation of fantasy stories and autobiographical narratives.

Prince had started the clinic as a place where undergraduates might be taught abnormal psychology with the aid of clinical demonstrations (Robinson, 1992; White, 1981). Known for his work on hysteria, multiple personality, and unconscious mental processes, Prince was able to draw upon his own intriguing case accounts to make abnormal psychology vivid for the students. Indeed, he was even able to bring patients into the classroom so that they could display firsthand their often bizarre symptoms and strange abilities. While the method might sound like good pedagogy to us today, the Psychology Department at Harvard was not enthusiastic about Prince's showmanship, and they looked askance upon his enthusiasm for such unscientific-sounding phenomena. Thus, it was agreed that the clinic would be housed in a location far removed from the proper psychology laboratories, lest people get the wrong idea about what respectable psychology was supposed to be about. When Murray moved in to help, Prince's operation was moving along rather nicely. Classes were being taught and experiments were being undertaken in the domains of hypnotism and hysteria. A student at the clinic during this time, Robert White (1981) suggests in retrospect that if Prince had lived longer the clinic might have won some marginal respectability as a center for specialized research into rather peripheral human phenomena. Everything changed, however, when Murray took over:

I was present as a graduate student during the year before and the year after Prince's death, then absent for the next three years in a teaching position. When I returned, it was to a wholly different world. Everyone was talking about needs, variables, and a mysterious process called thematic apperception. Strange people were wandering in and out, neither staff, patients, nor students, but simply personalities undergoing study. The ship had radically changed its course.

When I recovered from my initial confusion I learned that certain important decisions had been made during the time I was away. First, because it was hard to interpret the results of an experiment when one knew nothing else about the subjects, the scheme had been adopted that all experimenters should use the same pool of subjects. Each worker could thus see his or her own findings in light of what the others had discovered. Second, the interpretations could be further enriched if one knew still more about the subjects, so it was decided to study them as individuals by means of interviews and tests. The third decision was the big one. If a lot of different workers were going to use each other's findings, there had to be a common language, a common scheme of variables, adequate to account for what was significant in personality. To accomplish such a purpose it was necessary to decide what really was significant, then work out a taxonomy to bring observation under orderly control. (White, 1981, p. 5)

Murray put the person at the center of inquiry. If the person is the center, then the investigator must become familiar with the person in many different contexts. Each person would be interviewed in depth and subjected to a wide assortment of data-gathering procedures. Different investigators should approach the person from different angles. The investigators should meet regularly to compare notes and synthesize their results on particular persons. Different investigators, therefore, made up what Murray called a *Diagnostic Council.* The diagnostic council entertained and synthesized information on the same person (subject) obtained from many different vantage points. So that different investigators would be able to communicate with one another, Murray devised an elaborate new nomenclature for personality processes. His comprehensive system provides a language for describing personality that remains highly influential today.

During the 1930s Murray headed a remarkable intellectual collaboration at the Harvard Psychological Clinic, bringing together scholars from academic psychology, psychoanalysis, anthropology, biology, and other disciplines to focus on personality study. Among the most noteworthy scholars who passed through the clinic in the years shortly before and after World War II were Robert White (this chapter), Donald MacKinnon, Jerome Frank, Saul Rosenzweig, R. Nevitt Sanford, Samuel Beck, M. Brewster Smith, Erik Erikson (chapter 9), Daniel Levinson (this chapter), Jerome Bruner (chapter 10), and Silvan Tomkins (chapter 10). The clinic became the setting for intensive, interdisciplinary, longitudinal studies of relatively normal college men. The overall aim of the research was to arrive at a complex understanding of the whole person. Murray's enterprise was especially remarkable in light of American psychology's commitment in the 1930s to the most rigorous and reductionistic methods and models of behavioral science. While American psychology glorified laboratory investigations of rats and pigeons, Murray sought to study real people in their natural habitats. While American psychology focused on the elementary laws of simple learning, Murray was fascinated with human motivation, especially as it functioned in complex and unconscious ways. While American psychology was decidedly suspicious of psychoanalysis, Jungian psychology, and anything smacking of nonorthodoxy, Murray invited scholars of all stripes, even some from the humanities, to partake in the heady intellectual discussions and analyses occurring at the clinic.

Murray himself looked to literature and mythology for inspiration in understanding human personality. He developed an abiding passion for the novels and short stories of Herman Melville, publishing in 1951 an influential analysis of Melville's *Moby-Dick* (Murray, 1951a). Drawing on Freud, Murray argues for an id/superego conflict between Captain Ahab and the mighty white whale. For Murray, Ahab represents the Devil and his forces of evil, psychologically transformed into the primitive forces of the id. And Moby-Dick himself, the great white sperm whale, is an incarnation of the Protestant God, a mighty superego projected outward.

The early work at the Harvard Psychological Clinic culminated in the publication of *Explorations in Personality* (Murray, 1938). In this landmark volume reporting the results of intensive studies of 50 college men, Murray and his colleagues envisioned a new agenda for what Murray came to call "personology." Murray conceived of personology as an interdisciplinary exploration of the psychology of persons, with particular emphasis on incorporating myth, folklore, biography, and investigations of the human imagination. Whereas psychologists of other persuasions studied discrete processes and functions of the human organism, the personologist was to operate on a more molar and synthetic level, casting his or her empirical eye upon the overall pattern of an individual's unique adaptation to the world. The personologist was to search for recurrent thematic constellations that characterized the individual as a whole. The molar approach to inquiry sacrifices a certain degree of precision and predictive power at the molecular level of particular behaviors and situations to achieve theoretical coherence at the level of the person.

A personological system must begin with a view of the person. What do you see when you see a person? Murray (1940) described what he saw:

> Instead of seeing merely a groomed American in a business suit, travelling to and from his office like a rat in a maze, a predatory ambulating apparatus of reflexes, habits, stereotypes, and slogans, a bundle of consistencies, conformities and allegiances to this or that institution—a robot in other words—I visualize (just as I visualize the activity of his internal organs) a flow of powerful subjective life, conscious and unconscious; a whispering gallery in which voices echo from the distant past; a gulf stream of fantasies with floating memories of past events, currents of contending complexes, plots and counterplots, hopeful intimations and ideals. To a neurologist such perspectives are absurd, archaic, tenderminded; but in truth they are much closer to the actualities of inner life than are his own neat diagrams of reflex arcs and nerve anastomoses. A personality is a full Congress of orators and pressure groups, of children, demagogues, communists, isolationists, war-mongers, mugwumps, grafters, log-rollers, lobbyists, Caesars and Christs, Machiavellis and Judases, Tories and Promethean revolutionists. And a psychologist who does not know this in himself, whose mind is locked against the flux of images and feelings, should be encouraged to make friends, by being psychoanalyzed, with the various members of his household. (pp. 160–161)

Murray was fascinated with the life and work of Herman Melville, the author of *Moby-Dick*. Here Gregory Peck is Captain Ahab in the movie version of Melville's classic. Murray saw the great white whale as an embodiment of the superego and Ahab as the id-like devil who is obsessed with destroying all moral authority.

There are many metaphors in this passage. Particularly powerful, however, is the metaphor of the personality as a "household" or "congress"—a collection of very different and often competing personages, like various *characters* in a narrative drama. To "know thyself," suggests Murray, is to become acquainted with the characters within oneself, to discern their disparate identities and the ways in which they interact with each other to produce the narrative of life. Thus, in Grope's life story a main character is Icarus. But there are doubtlessly many other characters in Grope's story, given that personality is extraordinarily complex and multifaceted. In the view of Elms (1987), Murray envisioned personality as a "fluid conglomerate" that is "constantly shifting, lacking a single stable core"; "individual combinations of components reign briefly and are then dethroned by new rulers" (Elms, 1987, pp. 3, 4). In other words, internal characters in the life story interact over time; certain protagonists capture center stage for a while, only to be replaced, eventually, by new heroes.

A key idea in Murray's system is that *human lives are set in time.* The human being is a "time-binding organism," Murray wrote. Not merely a creature of the moment, the person can look beyond immediate stimuli in the environment and immediate urges within to act in accord with one's own view of the past or future. Time is a defining feature of the person. Murray wrote that the "organism consists of an infinitely complex series of temporally related activities extending from birth to death" (1938, p. 39). The life course of the individual should, therefore, be the long unit of analysis for personology. While it is feasible to examine a person's life at a particular moment in time, one must never forget that such a venture represents an arbitrary selection of a part from the whole. One must never forget, therefore, that "the *history* of the organism *is* the organism" (p. 39). But what is a history? And how can an organism be a history? A history is a narrative reconstruction of how the past gave birth to the present, in light of an anticipated future. A history is a consensual interpretation of the past in light of what followed. It is a *story* about how events and changes *led up to* a subsequent state of affairs. Time, story, the person. Human beings are time-binding, story-telling creatures, whose lives themselves are situated in time, as time-binding narratives—past, present, future—to be interpreted by the personologist.

The smallest meaningful unit of time in human behavior is what Murray called the *proceeding*. A proceeding is a single episode of behavior abstracted from the temporal complexity of ongoing life. We may see it as a single instance of interaction between a person and his or her environment, an interaction long enough to initiate and complete "a dynamically significant pattern of behavior" (Murray, 1951b, p. 269). In that people may do more than one thing at a time, it is possible that at any given moment a person may be involved in more than one proceeding – what we commonly call today multi-tasking. For example, I may be talking to my mother on the phone while I am also flipping through a series of cards in my rolodex, searching for an address of one of my colleagues. I am involved in two proceedings at once. Murray argues that each proceeding is unique, and that a person's own uniqueness is a result in part of the cumulative effect of proceedings over time:

> Every proceeding leaves behind it some trace of its occurrence—a new fact, the germ of an idea, a re-evaluation of something, a more affectionate attachment to some person, a slight improvement of a skill, a renewal of hope, another reason for despondency. Thus, slowly, by scarcely perceptible graduations—though sometimes suddenly by a leap forward or a slide backward—the person changes from day to day. Since his familiar associates also change, it can be said that every time he meets with one of them, both are different. In short, every proceeding is in some respects unique. (Murray & Kluckhohn, 1953, p. 10)

When you take all of the overlapping proceedings during a given period of time you have what Murray called a *durance*. Durances range from short scenes in a person's life (a visit to grandmother's house) to longer periods that may be viewed as "chapters" in one's evolving life story (living with grandmother between the ages of 3 and 5). A 30-year-old stockbroker, for example, may divide his life into four long durances: childhood, college years, early 20s while working at first job and living alone, and last four years while working for a large company and living with his wife. In this case, the transition to a new job and the marriage occurred around the same time in the man's life, marking a transition from the third to the fourth long durance or life chapter. A long durance may also be made up of what Murray called *serials*. A serial is a relatively long and directionally organized series of proceedings involving a particular life domain. Examples of serials are particular friend-ships, marriages, careers, etc. Each serial, therefore, organizes a sequence of life events hav-ing to do with a particular important area of personal investment. Serials may interact, such that the problems in, say, one's marriage may influence how well things go in one's career.

Remember that human beings are time-binding organisms. We act and interact in the present with views of the past and future in mind. As we survey the various serials in our lives, we evaluate our well-being and progress in each with respect to goals and aims for the future. Where is this relationship with my girlfriend going? Should I be taking more politi-cal science courses to prepare for law school? Do I need to lose some weight before I take that trip to Florida? We often develop particular programs for given serial domains in order to meet future goals. Murray called these *serial programs*. A serial program is an orderly arrangement of subgoals stretching into the future for months or years such that achievement of the subgoals will assure progress toward some desired end state. Serial pro-grams provide our strivings with direction and purpose. And they often connect up with fundamental psychological needs.

If the directional nature of human lives is to be known, then human behavior must be viewed in terms of proceedings, durances, serials, and serial programs organized in time. As we saw in chapter 7, Murray argued that psychological needs help to organize human lives in time. Needs interact with environmental press to produce characteristic behavior patterns. Recurrent need—press interactions are called themes. Some lives are so domi-nated by a characteristic patterning of need, press, and theme that they may be said to exemplify a *unity-thema*. A unity-thema is a well-organized pattern of related needs and press that provides meaning to a large portion of the individual's life. Ultimately derived from infantile experience, a unity-thema may be viewed as the central, organizing motif of a person's life story. Grope's Icarus complex may qualify as one unity thema, though Murray preferred to call it a "complex." A unity-thema links the distant past with the pres-ent and anticipated future:

> A *unity-thema* is a compound of interrelated—collaborating or conflicting—dominant needs that are linked to press to which the individual was exposed on one or more par-ticular occasions, gratifying or traumatic, in early childhood. The theme may stand for a primary infantile experience or a subsequent reaction formation to that experience. But, whatever its nature and genesis, it repeats itself in many forms during later life. (Murray, 1938, pp. 604–605).

THE PERSONOLOGICAL TRADITION

World War II interrupted the program of research and theorizing at the Harvard Psychological Clinic as many researchers, including Murray himself, became involved in the war effort. Murray directed personality assessment programs for the Office of Strategic Services (OSS) a forerunner to the CIA. In order to choose the right men for sensitive positions in foreign espionage, Murray's staff designed a series of tests and assessment activities measuring a wide variety of abilities, competencies, traits, interests, opinions, and other personal characteristics assumed to predict human performance under oftentimes dangerous conditions. Reported in Murray's and the OSS Assessment Staff's (1948) *Assessment of Men,* the OSS assessment regimen was partly built on the principles of personology that Murray developed at the Harvard Psychological Clinic:

> Assessment was "multiform," which is to say that the "whole person" was scrutinized in numerous and various settings. There were standardized tests of intelligence and mechanical comprehension; personal history forms and interviews; group problem-solving sessions, some of them "leaderless"; various measures of physical strength and endurance; stress tests, debating tests, even an indirect assessment of the candidates' need and tolerance for alcohol. Using a six-point rating scale, the staff rated the candidates on eleven variables (motivation for assignment, energy and zest, practical intelligence, emotional stability, and so on). Brief personality profiles were prepared for a culminating staff meeting at which final recommendations were hammered out. It was the [Harvard Psychological] Clinic in a nutshell, complete with ingenious procedures, an informal social setting, heavy staff involvement, an expanded Diagnostic Council, and a modified version of the concluding biographical narrative. (Robinson, 1992, p. 282)

After the war, Murray's brand of personology continued to stimulate an interdisciplinary tradition of inquiry in the social sciences that is sometimes called *the study of lives.* The most prolific spokesman for this tradition has been Robert White (1948, 1952, 1963a, 1972, 1981, 1987). In books such as *The Study of Lives, Lives in Progress,* and *The Enterprise of Living,* White illustrated the value of Murray's program of personology by analyzing and bringing together intensive case studies of normal adults studied over time. Another important contributor to the study of lives was Donald MacKinnon (1962, 1963, 1965), who headed the Institute for Personality Assessment and Research (IPAR) at the University of California, Berkeley, and launched an influential series of studies of especially creative individuals.

Like Murray's original formulations for personology in the 1930s, the study of lives moved against the dominant tides in American academic psychology during the 1950s, 1960s, and 1970s. The study of lives requires a "generalist" approach to psychology whereby the investigator is able to draw from many different domains in order to construct a synthetic portrait of the human life in context. Yet American academic psychology became increasingly specialized after World War II and fewer and fewer psychologists cultivated a generalist perspective. Similarly, personality psychologists focused much of their energy after the war on the development and refinement of particular measures of carefully defined and specific constructs, such as particular personality traits. Psychology departments and research funding agencies tended to favor quantitative, construct-driven research over the more qualitative, person-driven approaches advocated by Murray, White, and other proponents of the study of lives. In the past 20 years, however, a number of trends in personality psychology and adjacent fields have come together to suggest that the study of lives is enjoying something of a renaissance. One small indication of this is the establishment of the Henry A. Murray Research Center for the Study of Lives, at Radcliffe College in 1979. Another is the founding of the Society for Personology in the early 1980s, a small organization dedicated to the principles of Murray's personology.

What are those principles? In organizing a collection of Murray's writings, Edwin Shneidman (1981) sets forth six general propositions that characterize Murray's personological approach and the tradition of studying lives that he and his followers developed.

1. *Personology (as well as the personologist) is shaped by numerous and various forces.* While many approaches to personality try to rule out competing explanations in order to arrive at the simplest and most consistent interpretation of an individual's behavior, Murray tended to welcome alternative formulations, suggesting that lives are shaped by a panoply of conflicting and inconsistent forces and factors. Recall his metaphor of the person as a "congress of orators and pressure groups." More than most other approaches, Murray challenges the psychologist to consider the person from many different standpoints, to consider forces existing in biology, society, culture, and history. This inclusive approach to inquiry is well illustrated in White's (1952, 1966, 1975) scrupulous analyses of the lives of three American adults—Hartley Hale, Joseph Kidd, and Joyce Kingsley. In each of these "lives in progress," White painstakingly documents the influence of biologically based drives and instincts, social motivations, constitutional endowments, learning patterns, psychosexual and psychosocial stages, values and beliefs, family dynamics, social structures, religion, and culture. Furthermore, both Murray and White leave room for the extraordinary influence of random events and luck on the course of human life. In Murray's own life, a chance meeting with a fellow passenger on a ship directed Murray's attention to the writings of Melville, which piqued his curiosity about psychology and ultimately led him to personology. With so many forces to consider, it should not be surprising to learn that lives are difficult to understand and that behavior is sometimes impossible to predict.

2. *Personology is a complex, lifelong, never-ending enterprise.* As we have seen, a cardinal feature of Murray's approach is the emphasis on human lives situated *in time.* The history of the organism is the organism. In the terms of White (1952, 1972), lives are always "in progress"; living is a constantly evolving "enterprise." The personologist is likely to be frustrated in his or her attempts to get a final read on any given life in progress, in that personality continues to be constructed and reconstructed across the lifespan. Any approach that attempts to fix the person in time—say, by focusing too closely on unchanging traits—fails to convey the dynamic quality of lives, in Murray's view.

3. *Personology focuses on the close examination of mental life—conscious and unconscious processes, including creativity.* Here Murray and the study of lives share affinities with psychoanalysis (chapters 7 and 11) and the cognitive movement in psychology (chapter 8). Like Freud and Jung, Murray wished to explore the deep gulf streams of the human unconscious. But like Kelly, he found human consciousness to be equally worthy of the psychologist's attention. For Murray, human lives are inherently creative, as people partially create themselves amidst the many forces and factors that shape that creation. But certain people are *more* creative than others. Either through the personalities they work to create or via their more tangible creative outpourings, individuals like Herman Melville reveal special gifts for transforming things and ideas into especially novel and useful combinations. In extraordinary creativity, boundaries between the conscious and unconscious are sometimes blurred. In some cases, a creative solution or configuration seems to spring forth spontaneously, like sea water shooting upward from the great whale's spout. One cannot fully control the creative urge. "The psyche is a *region* where creations may or may not flourish," but we cannot make them flourish, nor readily stop them from flourishing should they "wish" to flourish (Murray, 1959/1981, p. 322). One follows one's creative urges, even if this means that, like Melville, one sacrifices happiness and well-being along the way (Murray, 1959/1981; Robinson, 1992).

4. *Personology requires a multidisciplinary approach, as well as special strategies and techniques of investigation.* From the early days of the Harvard Psychological Clinic, through the OSS programs on assessing men, to the present-day interest among personologists in biography and narrative methods of analysis, psychologists who have followed Murray's agenda have tended to distrust the conventional methods of assessing personality dispositions, such as self-report questionnaires and rating scales. They have argued that personality must be examined instead from the standpoints of widely diverse methodologies, especially those that allow the participant to create imaginative responses. Murray's (1938) *Explorations* describes more than 20 innovative methods of assessing personality, including the well-known Thematic Apperception Test (TAT), and measures of musical reverie, imaginal productivity, reactions to frustration, memories for failures, and autobiography. White's analyses of lives in progress employ interviews, autobiographical accounts, story responses to the TAT, intelligence tests, personality questionnaires, and many more. Murray suggested that a Diagnostic Council should synthesize the many different kinds of data on a single personality. Multiple researchers, therefore, might arrive at a coherent interpretation of a single case by pouring over a wide assortment of data and then discussing their different points of view.

5. *Personology studies living, historical, fictional, and mythological figures as well as special human "complexes."* As we saw in the case of Grope, Murray was not reluctant to borrow from ancient mythology to shed light on the shadowy workings of a contemporary life in progress. The "Icarus Complex" is one of a number of different portraits, inspired by literature and mythology, that have been composed by personologists in the Murray tradition. Murray (1962) himself described a malignantly narcissistic personality syndrome by detailing "The Personality and Career of Satan." David McClelland (1963) delineated a "Harlequin Complex," to suggest that some women have historically held a strange fascination with death—death viewed as a seducer. Drawing inspiration from the character of Ishmael in Melville's *Moby Dick,* Kenneth Keniston (1963) painted a prophetic personological portrait of youthful alienation in the early 1960s. He wrote of a "prototypically alienated young man, separated partly by his own volition from the people, institutions, and beliefs which sustain most young men at his age in America; rejecting the forms by which most American men and women live; and condemned, like the Biblical Ishmael by his past and like Melville's Ishmael by his own temper, to live on the outskirts of society" (p. 42). Todd Schultz (1996) described an "Orpheus Complex" in the lives of some creative writers who, like the ancient Greek character Orpheus, are compelled to work through experiences of profound loss by writing about them. For Murray, McClelland, Keniston, Schultz, and others in this tradition, clues into the meanings of human lives may be found almost anywhere. Some of the richest sources are indeed outside science per se, in the great works of religion, mythology, and literature.

6. *Personology encompasses a wide range of concerns, from specific practical issues to human values and urgent global problems.* Murray held strong views on a wide range of issues inside and outside of psychology, and he translated some of those views into print. After World War II, he became increasingly convinced that the survival of humankind in a nuclear age depended on the establishment of a world democratic government and the universal adoption of an enlightened humanistic philosophy to augment impersonal science and replace authoritarian religious systems (Murray, 1960/1981). Although others who have followed in the tradition Murray began have been somewhat

less vocal in their pronouncements about social policy, the study of lives has always endeavored to situate personality within the complex social and cultural forces of the day, implicitly examining how human lives are impacted by the social opportunities and constraints produced by national and international events and by social policies.

Murray's humanistic inclinations are also reflected in the metaphors and models for human growth and development that have come out of case research in the study of lives. For example, White (1975) describes five general growth trends in human personality, observable across different case studies of American men and women. In White's view, healthy personality development involves:

1. *The stabilization of ego identity.* Over time, people should develop a clearer and more coherent understanding of who they are and how they fit into the adult world.

2. *The freeing of personal relationships.* Traumatic and conflictual experiences from childhood may exert negative influences on relationships later on, but healthy development involves a freeing of the self from the negativities of the past and the positive engagement of others in mutual, collaborative, intimate interpersonal relationships.

3. *The deepening of interests.* Children and adolescents form short-term and superficial interest in many different areas, but as one moves into adulthood one should begin to focus interests and develop competence in those arenas of living that are deemed central to the self.

4. *The humanizing of values.* The direction of moral development is away from simple, authoritarian, and egocentric perspectives toward greater complexity in moral reasoning and greater tolerance for other points of view.

5. *The expansion of caring.* As people mature, their emotional investments in other people deepen considerably and they cultivate relationships of care and commitment for children, friends, lovers, spouses, and even casual acquaintances and fellow citizens of the world.

SCIENCE AND THE SINGLE CASE

Since the time of Murray's *Explorations,* the study of lives has always been controversial because of its unswerving commitment to the psychology of the single case. While many personality psychologists would submit that "the whole person" is ideally the appropriate unit of analysis for personality studies, very few have taken this idea as literally as have Murray, White, and those other advocates of the study of lives who argue for "exploring personality the long way" (White, 1981, p. 3). To explore personality the long way, they maintain, one must focus inquiry on the single human life, examined over time through the *case study.* As we saw in chapter 1, a case study is a "systematic presentation of information about the life of a single unit" (Runyan, 1982, p. 127). In personality psychology, the single unit is the individual life. But the case-study method has been used profitably, though sparingly, in many branches of psychology, from neuroscience to social psychology. Outside of psychology proper, case studies have been extensively employed in anthropology, sociology, and political science. The "single unit" of analysis in an anthropological case study may be a particular culture or subculture; the sociologist may focus on a specific demographic group or organization; the political scientist may investigate a single political institution or event. In all of these instances, the scientist investigates in depth a single, specific phenomenon within its real-life context, synthesizing many different kinds of data drawn from multiple sources.

Going back to Freud, personality psychologists have used case studies in a number of different ways (McAdams & West, 1997). In his famous clinical cases, such as the analysis of Dora (chapter 11), Freud portrayed the complex workings of psychic conflict and neurosis in the single life. For the most part, Freud's cases served to *exemplify* and showcase his own theory. As we saw in his analysis of Dora, Freud found much in her case to confirm his theoretical views of oral fixations and the Oedipus complex. Allport (1942) criticized Freud and the psychoanalysts for ignoring individuality in their efforts to confirm general theories. By paying closer attention to those aspects of the case that were unusual or even unique, Allport suggested, the psychologist might *discover* new things about personality and develop new theories. Yet another use of case studies is *comparison*. Psychologists can compare different constructs with one another—say, extraversion (chapter 5) and intimacy motivation (chapter 7)—by illustrating how they play out in a single case study. Different personality theories can also be compared with respect to their applicability to the single case. For many years now, a common assignment in college classes on personality has been to take two of the grand theories of personality—say, Freud and Rogers—and compare how they would each approach a particular case study. White's (1952) case studies of lives in progress have been used for this purpose on countless occasions. In an intensive case study of an extraordinary man who sailed around the globe in a small boat, Nasby and Read (1997) drew upon psychological tests and personal documents to compare and contrast the uses of the Big Five trait model (chapter 5 in this book) and the life-story model of identity (chapter 10) in the analysis of a single life.

Critics of the case study method have argued that such efforts are too subjective and too focused on the idiosyncrasies of a single life to be of much scientific use. After all, science is supposed to aim at generating common laws and theories that should apply to many different lives, not just a single case. More specifically, criticism of case studies has focused on five important issues: (a) reliability, (b) internal coherence, (c) interpretive truth, (d) external validity, and (e) the problem of discovery versus justification in the study of lives. Let us consider each of these issues in turn.

First, critics have argued that the analysis of the single case is inherently unreliable. You cannot count on the results obtained, suggest many critics. A different observer of the case data could readily come up with a very different interpretation. The problem is particularly serious in psychoanalytic case studies, such as that of Dora (chapter 11), because of the many leaps in inference typically involved. Psychologists employing case studies often must analyze complex *qualitative data*—data that are not readily quantified. The case-study researcher faces the triple task of (a) arriving at a high-level inference or interpretation about a critical aspect of the whole person's functioning by making sense of (b) an overabundance of unwieldy, qualitative data (c) in the absence of explicit rules for quantifying the data. The result, therefore, may be a highly *subjective* interpretation of the case with which another researcher, analyzing the same data in his or her own equally subjective way, may not agree.

The problem of low interjudge reliability in personality research is not limited to case studies, however. Scoring reliability tends to be a problem with qualitative data in general, such as interview conversations, reports of dreams, stories, and other open-ended response formats that are not readily quantified. In principle, a case study need not rely on qualitative data (Runyan, 1982) but can employ a wide range of data-gathering and data-interpreting methods, from the most quantifiable and reliable questionnaires and rating scales to the most qualitative and unreliable dream reports and interviews. Murray advocated a judicious blending of qualitative and quantitative measures, synthesized by a Diagnostic Council. Qualitative data, furthermore, may be translated into quantitative form through rigorous scoring rules and content-analysis systems (e.g., Smith, 1992). Interviews may be videotaped and later subjected to objective content analysis to increase scoring reliability. To the extent that specific scoring rules for carefully recorded qualitative data are delineated and objectively employed, interjudge reliability will increase, and the personologist will be better able to count on the results and interpretations that are made. However, quantified scoring of qualitative data usually exacts a price, too. Important information can be lost because it cannot readily be translated into numbers.

A major criterion for judging the adequacy of a case study is the degree to which the psychologist's interpretation makes sense given the facts of the case. Does the analysis hang together? Is it consistent with what is known about the individual being studied? Is it *internally coherent*? A major problem with the criterion of internal coherence in evaluating case studies, however, is that many different explanations of a given case could conceivably be offered, each one equally internally coherent. As D. T. Campbell (1975) and others have pointed out, the human mind has an uncanny ability to make internal sense out of just about anything, even if that thing seems senseless at first. Thus, a given psychologist may have little trouble coming up with a coherent explanation for the facts in virtually any case study, after those facts have become known. Campbell warns that social scientists should be aware of these *post hoc* explanations. He adds, however, that there is probably no way to get around them completely. Indeed, Campbell suggests that for certain questions about human behavior and experience, the case study may be "the only route to knowledge—noisy, fallible, and biased though it may be" (1975, p. 179). Therefore, personologists should evaluate carefully and critically their own interpretations of intensive case studies.

The personologist who seeks to formulate an internally coherent interpretation of an individual case usually proceeds according to an implicit **pattern-matching plan** (Bromley, 1986; D. T. Campbell, 1975; Runyan, 1982). Approaching the case data openly but with certain theoretical expectations that help orient his or her approach, the personologist looks for a *conceptual pattern* in the data that makes logical and psychological sense—the Icarus pattern, for example. The conceptual pattern that emerges gives rise to theoretical implications, which then function as a minitheory from which predictions can be generated and evaluated by looking at additional data in the case. Ideally, the personologist should function as a devil's advocate for his or her own interpretation, objectively testing the implications of that interpretation against the data of the case. The personologist should, in fact, invite alternative explanations of the same case from other investigators, and the scientific community should be able to evaluate rival interpretations of the same case against each other, in the way a judge or jury evaluates the cases made by opposing lawyers, to determine which one seems to be the best (Bromley, 1986; D. T. Campbell, 1975).

What is a *true* interpretation in the study of the single life? While many people would say that truth means correspondence to the objective "facts" of the case, some investigators of human lives argue that, in addition to factual truth, case studies should be evaluated according to standards of *narrative truth* (Habermas, 1971; Schafer, 1981; Spence, 1982). Writes one scholar,

> Narrative truth can be defined as the criterion we use to decide when a certain experience has been captured to our satisfaction; it depends on continuity and closure and the extent to which the fit of the pieces takes on an aesthetic finality. Narrative truth is what we have in mind when we say that such and such is a good story, that a given

explanation carries conviction, that *one* solution to a mystery must be true. Once a given construction has acquired narrative truth, it becomes just as real as any other kind of truth. (Spence, 1982, p. 31)

According to this view, the psychologist who seeks the true meaning of the single case must engage in **hermeneutics**—the art and science of interpreting texts (Ricoeur, 1970; Schafer, 1981; Steele, 1982). For centuries, hermeneutics was confined to sacred texts, such as the holy books of Christianity, Judaism, and Islam. In the past 150 years, however, certain social scientists such as Dilthey (1900/1976) and Stern (in Allport, 1968) have brought hermeneutics into psychology and sociology, arguing that human lives and human societies are analogous to holy scriptures that hold within them many meanings. For Dilthey, hermeneutics involves a *dialogue* between investigator and text—be the "text" a holy book or another person—designed to decipher the many signs and symbols conveyed by the text. Through this highly subjective dialogue with the text emerge meaning and truth.

Interpreters of texts and single cases, therefore, often aim for narrative truth, argue Schafer and Spence. They evaluate their own interpretations according to the standards of "good story." A good story (a) is internally coherent, (b) makes for a continuous plot line in which early events "cause" or logically lead to later events, (c) embodies closure or a sense of things fitting into a final form, and (d) is aesthetically pleasing (Spence, 1982). Yet, narrative truth is at best but one criterion of a "good" interpretation of a human life. Indeed, the interpretation of the single case can be profitably compared with the construction of scientific theories, as described in chapter 1 of this book. Like a theory, an interpretation of a case study consists of a set of propositions designed to explain events. Scientists agree that, in principle, some theories are better than others, though they may disagree as to exactly which ones are better and worse. Scientists judge theories according to the criteria of (a) comprehensiveness, (b) parsimony, (c) coherence, (d) testability, (e) empirical validity, (f) usefulness, and (g) generativity (see chapter 1). Similarly, in determining the "goodness" (rather than truth) of interpretations of the single case, the best that we can do may be to follow these same criteria. A good interpretation of the single case, therefore, may be one that (a) takes into consideration a comprehensive body of case information, (b) is simple and straightforward, (c) is internally coherent and consistent in the same way, perhaps, that a good story is, (d) provides hypotheses about human behavior that can be tested empirically, (e) is in accord with what empirical studies have documented to be valid, (f) is useful, and (g) generates new ideas.

But even if a personologist formulates an exceptionally illuminating interpretation of a single life in progress, what can the single case tell us about people in general? How can a single case be representative of any sample or population beyond itself? This is the problem of *external validity,* and because of this problem some psychologists dismiss case studies out of hand. They argue that experiments and large-scale correlation studies are more powerful research strategies because they allow the scientists to sample many different subjects drawn from a large population. These approaches also allow the researcher to compare and contrast different individuals, and "comparison is essential to science" (Carlsmith, Ellsworth, & Aronson, 1976, p. 39). The answer to poor external validity in the single case study, according to this view, is to sample many different individuals whose behavior and experience are studied in a more limited fashion, the general assumption being that many individuals together are more representative of a large population than is one.

In response to this criticism of case studies, some psychologists suggest that investigators collect multiple cases that can be compared and contrasted, gradually building up representative samples in given areas of investigation. Bromley (1986) maintains that personologists should eventually attempt to group and classify multiple cases, identifying key features of cases that distinguish them one from the other. In this way, certain exemplary cases could be chosen as prototypes that exhibit several distinguishing features of a given phenomenon. Other cases could then be compared and contrasted to the prototypes to determine the extent to which their features match those exhibited in the "ideal" or "pure" case.

Other proponents of the intensive study of the single case concede that single case studies can never be representative of large populations, but they counter that such cases need not be representative anyway. First of all, very few single experiments or correlation studies in personality psychology can truly claim to obtain fully representative samples. As we saw in chapter 1, the scientist should strive to obtain the sample most appropriate for the given question to be addressed. The assumption that his or her sample is fully representative of a particularly robust population, however, may be based on the misguided belief that a single empirical study can establish truth once and for all, and for all time (Gergen, 1973).

Second, external validity refers to sampling of not only *subjects* but *situations* and *topics,* too (Brunswik, 1956; Dukes, 1965). Although a case study samples only one subject, it samples many different situations and topic areas in that participant's life. Conversely, an experiment or correlational study that samples many participants probably samples only a few situations and a few areas of human functioning.

Third, generalization from a single case should be assessed in light of the soundness of the given analysis of that case rather than a prior notion about how "typical" a given case is. When a scientist makes a good interpretation of a case, he or she is justified in asserting that the analysis should hold for *comparable cases,* that is, cases of that sort (Mitchell, 1983). In case-study research, then, "the cases themselves come to define the population" (Bromley, 1986, p. 288). Grope, for example, might be an exemplar for the Icarus complex—a unity-thema to which a small number of other lives might also be assimilated. The extent to which Grope is a "prototypical" case against which psychologists could compare others may be determined by analyzing the entire family of cases within that genre.

Whatever one concludes about the external validity of any particular case study, certain general advantages of case studies over other research approaches that employ larger subject samples should be acknowledged. Unlike most other methods, "a case study allows an investigation to retain the holistic and meaningful characteristics of real-life events" (Yin, 1984, p. 14). A good case study may provide insight into a person's experience, clarifying what at first may have seemed incomprehensible; a good case study may effectively portray the person's social and historical milieu; and a good case study may deepen the reader's sympathy and empathy for the individual, while being vivid, evocative, and emotionally compelling to read (Runyan, 1982). (See Table 12.2.)

Finally, in chapter 1 I made an important distinction between two different ways of doing science. In the *context of discovery,* the scientist derives ideas, builds theories, and comes up with various hypotheses about a given phenomenon. In the *context of justification,* on the other hand, the scientist tests the validity of ideas, theories, and hypotheses that have already been derived. These two approaches to science build on each other as ideas are formulated, tested, and reformulated over time in a given area of scientific investigation. For which of these two contexts, then, is the single case appropriate? Should we derive (discover) theories through cases? Should we test (justify) theories through cases? Should we do neither? Should we do both?

TABLE 12.2	SIX RULES FOR PREPARING A PSYCHOLOGICAL CASE STUDY

1. The investigator must report truthfully on the person's life and circumstances and must be accurate in matters of detail.

2. The aims and objectives of the case study must be stated explicitly.

3. The case study should include an evaluation of the extent to which the stated aims and objectives have been achieved.

4. If the inquiry deals with material of deep emotional significance for the subject, then it must be carried out by someone trained and equipped to establish and manage a close, fairly long, and possibly difficult personal relationship.

5. The subject must be understood in the context of the specific historical, social, and symbolic world in which he or she lives.

6. The case report should be written in good plain English in a direct and objective way without, however, losing its human interest as a story. This can be done with sympathy and imagination and with due regard for high standards of evidence and argument.

SOURCE: From *The Case-Study Method in Psychology and Related Disciplines* (24–25), by D. B. Bromley, 1986, New York: John Wiley & Sons.

A case study may be utilized to *disprove* a particular hypothesis that asserts that a given phenomenon is always true (Dukes, 1965). For instance, if scientists claim that event B always follows event A, then a single case in which B does not follow A would disprove the hypothesis. Unfortunately, there are very few such universal claims in personality psychology, and therefore this particular context-of-justification use of the case study is rare.

The prevailing view, then, is that cases are rarely useful in the context of justification, at least with respect to testing general propositions. Especially when it comes to justifying general cause-and-effect relationships, case studies are vastly inferior to experiments. As vehicles for discovery, however, case studies may be extremely useful, indeed much more useful than experiments, correlational designs, and any other imaginable mode of investigation. As emphasized in chapter 1, the context of discovery is a freewheeling realm in scientific inquiry. Ideas, hypotheses, and theories may be discovered in a multitude of ways, and among the most fruitful ways, as far as the personality psychologist is concerned, is the intensive study of the single case. Studies of lives in the tradition of Murray and White are goldmines for the derivation of ideas, hypotheses, and theories, which may then be put to the test via conventional scientific methodologies of justification.

BIOGRAPHY, NARRATIVE, AND LIVES

How do we come to understand fully the life course of a single person? What is the most effective medium through which we may view the single life evolving over time so that we may discover what that whole life is all about? Along with Erik Erikson (chapter 9), Murray, White, and those personologists dedicated to the "study of lives" suggested that a psychologically informed *biography* is probably the best means for capturing a human life situated in time. Erikson is particularly well known in this regard for his psychobiographies of Martin Luther (1958), Mahatma Gandhi (1969), and George Bernard Shaw (1959).

Yet, most personality psychologists have *not* historically viewed themselves as biographers (Elms, 1988). Despite the intuitively appealing claim that people may be best understood in

STUDYING FAMOUS PEOPLE IN HISTORY

In the vast majority of the research studies conducted by psychologists and social scientists, the participants are relatively normal people similar to you and me. For example, a researcher might wish to study the relation between a particular personality trait—say, conscientiousness (chapter 5)—and involvement in extracurricular activities in a sample of, say, 100 college students. For research purposes, the assumption is that the subjects, or participants in the study, are essentially interchangeable. Of course, we realize that each person is unique in many ways. But for the nomothetic and statistical purposes of the study, we can treat each individual as if he or she were the same, in order to examine trends or relations in the sample as a whole. But sometimes psychologists study individuals who are chosen because they are indeed so different from everybody else. Sometimes the subjects in the study are Beethoven, Catherine the Great, Elvis Presley, Shakespeare, and the like. These are individuals who have to some degree "made a name for themselves" in history. As research subjects, they stand out from the crowd.

Psychologist Dean Keith Simonton (1976, 1994) has devoted his career to studying what he calls "significant samples." Rather than college undergraduates or middle-aged businesspersons, Simonton recruits the likes of classical composers, Nobel laureates, U.S. presidents, and even famous psychologists as subjects for his studies. Of course, most of these people are dead. But as we saw in Erik Erikson's analysis of Martin Luther (chapter 9), we can learn much about personality from the study of eminent historical figures. Although we may not be able to interview them or give them standard psychological tests, eminent figures often leave behind diaries, memoirs, creative works, and other artifacts that may prove to be valuable data for the personality psychologist. As we saw in chapter 7, for example, David Winter was able to analyze the inaugural addresses of U.S. presidents in order to measure achievement, power, and intimacy motivation. In chapter 11, I described how I studied the novels and autobiographical writings of

Yukio Mishima in order to generate a psychoanalytic interpretation of his suicide. Furthermore, the accomplishments (and failures) of eminent individuals are part of the public record, and the evaluation of those accounts by historians and other experts can also inform psychological research.

Simonton identifies four different traditions in the study of eminent individuals. The first and oldest is what he calls *historiometric* research. In these studies, researchers extract quantitative and indirect assessments from historical data. An early example is a study called *Early Mental Traits of Three Hundred Geniuses* (Cox, 1926), in which the researcher made estimates of intellectual abilities and personality tendencies based on the archival records for 300 historical figures deemed to be especially intelligent. Historiometric studies can be used to test hypotheses. For example, Simonton (1989) evaluated the compositions of 172 classical composers for melodic originality and other musical attributes. He found that the musical pieces composed toward the very end of a composer's career tend to be somewhat less original and complex than his or her earlier compositions, but also especially moving and popular. These "swan songs" seem to make a powerful and elegant musical statement. They are the composer's last and culminating work, and as such they prove to be especially memorable and well-received in the long run.

A second tradition of research with significant samples is the *psychometric* approach. In these studies, researchers administer direct measurements, such as surveys and interviews, to eminent individuals while they are still alive. Developing methods pioneered by Henry Murray in his work during World War II, researchers at the University of California's Institute for Personality Assessment and Research (IPAR) conducted psychometric studies of eminent architects, writers, and scientists. In these studies, the researchers identified men and women whose artistic or scientific contributions to their fields were already well-recognized for excellence. The researchers were mainly interested in exploring the development of creativity over the

(CONTINUES)

FEATURE 12.A *(CONTINUED)*

lifespan and the relationship of creative genius to other aspects of personality (e.g., Barron, 1969; Dudek & Hall, 1984).

Psychobiographical research is Simonton's third tradition. As we see later in this chapter, psychobiographical studies were launched by Sigmund Freud's seminal study of Leonardo da Vinci. Psychobiographical studies are radically different from historiometric and psychometric investigations (Elms, 1994). While historiometric and psychometric studies are typically quantitative and nomothetic, psychobiography involves qualitative investigations of the single, idiographic case, studied over time. Furthermore, a psychobiography usually involves the application of a broad theoretical framework, typically a Freudian or psychodynamic approach. Especially popular have been psychobiographies of political figures, such as the numerous analyses of Adolf Hitler, Woodrow Wilson, and Richard M. Nixon.

Finally, the *comparative* tradition shares with psychobiography an emphasis on qualitative and indirect assessments of eminent individuals, but it tends to incorporate multiple cases that are compared and contrasted to one another. An excellent example is Howard Gardner's (1993) *Creating Minds,* in which he examined the lives and works

of seven especially creative men and women who lived in the first half of the 20th century. Gardner chose the seven carefully to represent seven different "fields" and seven different and corresponding types of creativity: Sigmund Freud in psychology, Albert Einstein in physics, T. S. Eliot for literature, Pablo Picasso for the visual arts, Igor Stravinsky for music, Martha Graham for dance, and Mahatma Gandhi for creative social leadership. Across the seven cases, Gardner observed interesting commonalities in the development of a creative career, such as the requirement of a 10-year apprenticeship period in which each mastered the conventions of the discipline and the need to downplay interpersonal relationships in order to devote the self unswervingly to creative work. Gardner also illuminated differences among the seven, reflective both of personality variables and of mental and structural differences in the kinds of creative enterprises with which they were involved.

The world's libraries and archives are filled with fascinating data for personological investigations. Studies of eminent individuals can shed light on principles of personality that are common to all of us. And they can illuminate startling differences and unique patterns of individuality as well.

Personological studies of eminent individuals can illuminate interesting patterns of human individuality. Left: Albert Einstein, physicist. Right: Jennifer Lopez (J-Lo), actress and singer.

their biographical contexts, biographical approaches to the person have traditionally occupied a controversial and ambiguous status in personality psychology (Anderson, 1981; Runyan, 1982, 1990). Critics have asserted that biographical methods of investigation, such as case studies, are generally too unwieldy and subjective for clear and rigorous scientific study and that biographical examinations of the single case lack reliability and external validity, as discussed above. Biography's defenders counter that these critics hold an overly narrow view of science, that good biographical studies are highly illuminating, and that personologists are essentially shirking their intellectual responsibility to study the whole person if they dismiss biography out of hand. Nonetheless, the past 20 years have witnessed an upsurge of interest in and a growing acceptance of biographical and autobiographical approaches and frameworks among personality psychologists and other social scientists (Bertaux, 1981; McAdams, 1999; McAdams & Ochberg, 1988; Moraitis & Pollack, 1987; Runyan, 1990; Schultz, 2005; Wiggins, 2003).

PSYCHOBIOGRAPHY

Before the 20th century, literary biographers rarely employed psychological concepts to interpret the lives of their subjects. During the Roman Empire, Plutarch (A.D. 46–120) wrote the *Lives of the Noble Greeks and Romans,* taking as subjects such famous men as Pericles (the Athenian statesman) and Julius Caesar. Essentially, Plutarch composed moral vignettes from history to illustrate exemplary character traits such as honesty and courage. In the Middle Ages, Christian scholars wrote **hagiographies** to venerate the saints. These biographical accounts of the lives of great Christians were written mainly to glorify God and to teach the reader about faith. Many followed a standard form, culminating in the saint's trial before a court of "unbelievers" and his or her sentencing and execution—mirroring the story of Christ's trial and crucifixion. These religious tales, however, were not penetrating explorations in personality. Instead, they functioned as moral and spiritual lessons.

In the 17th century, biography began to assume a more sophisticated form when biographers such as Izaak Walton, who wrote about the lives of high churchmen, and John

The hagiography and art of the early Christian period depicted the lives of saints to teach people about being faithful. Hagiographies were an early form of biography in the West. The life stories typically depicted the saint's suffering, martyrdom, and ultimate veneration, mirroring the Christian story of Jesus.

Aubrey, who focused on more common folk, began to think of themselves as literary artists (Gittings, 1978). As artists, therefore, they sought to create narratives that were entertaining and artistically satisfying. The most artful and illuminating early biography—indeed, the most famous biography in Western literature—was published by James Boswell in 1791. In *The Life of Samuel Johnson,* Boswell wrote about Dr. Johnson (1709–1784), the prominent English author, critic, and lexicographer who traveled in the elite circles of European intellectual society. In striking contrast to his eminent subject, the younger Boswell was a loud-mouthed gossip and a heavy drinker, initially known more for his womanizing than his literary talents. At the age of 22, Boswell befriended Johnson (then age 54), and for years after they traveled together.

Boswell's study was a flesh-and-blood portrait that explored many facets of Johnson's life, from Johnson's sparkling conversations with the great men of the day to his persistent depression. Though Boswell clearly admired his subject, the central aim of his analysis was not to eulogize. Rather, he sought to explore the many dimensions of Johnson's character so as to illustrate the sweep and grandeur of one particular life. Boswell's biography was one of the first to entertain the problem of the biographer's own relationship to the subject of the study. Indeed, Johnson was something of a father-figure and a best friend for the younger Boswell. Yet their relationship was ambivalent and multilayered. As he moved in his text from one passage to the next, Boswell played the various roles of critic, fan, observer analyst, and participant in relation to Johnson's life.

In 1910, Freud wrote *Leonardo da Vinci and a Memory of his Childhood,* considered to be the first **psychobiography.** Much of Freud's interpretation rested on his analysis of a fantasy from Leonardo's childhood in which, "when I was still in the cradle, a vulture came down to me, opened my mouth with his tail and struck me many times with his tail against my lips" (Freud, 1916/1947, pp. 33–34). In a much-disputed line of reasoning, Freud speculated that this particular fantasy symbolizes themes of homosexuality and infantile dependency. On one level, the vulture's tail is a phallic symbol, suggesting a male homosexual

Joseph Boswell (left) and the subject of his classic, 18th-century biography, Samuel Johnson (right).

fantasy about fellatio. On another level, the vulture represents mother, an association for which Freud found some indirect evidence in Egyptian mythology. In this case, the tail is the breast, and the fantasy an expression of Leonardo's longing to regress to the secure maternal world of oral dependency.

In order to preserve his mother as the sole love object in his life, Leonardo subsequently turned away from all gross sensual activities and dedicated himself to the life of the mind. The small portion of libido not exhausted in his relentless scientific and artistic work was transformed into an ideal love of boys, for boys offered no viable threat to his consuming love for mother. Thus, homosexuality served to protect his love of mother. During his early adult years, Leonardo's severe sexual inhibition carried over into his creative life, too. Despite his genius, Leonardo repeatedly failed to complete his artistic projects, producing many "unfinished masterpieces" with which he was never thoroughly satisfied. Around the age of 50, however, he was rejuvenated, Freud maintained, by reexperiencing the love of his mother through meeting and eventually painting the woman who has become known as the Mona Lisa.

Psychobiography may be defined as "the systematic use of psychological (especially personality) theory to transform a life into a coherent and illuminating story" (McAdams, 1988b, p. 2, italics omitted). In psychobiography, the life to be transformed is usually that of a famous, enigmatic, or paradigmatic figure. Most psychobiographies are more comprehensive than Freud's brief sketch of Leonardo. Many psychobiographical studies take the entire life, from birth to death, as their subject of study, aiming to discern, discover, or formulate the central story of the entire life, a story structured according to psychological theory.

Leonardo da Vinci's self-portrait from a sketch in his notebooks. Sigmund Freud's effort to interpret aspects of Leonardo's creativity and sexuality is generally considered to be the first psychobiography.

In the case of Leonardo, Freud's theory of choice was, of course, psychoanalysis. Yet psychobiography need not employ a strictly psychoanalytic framework (Runyan, 1982). Many psychobiographies have drawn on the theories of Jung, Erikson, and the object-relations approaches to personality (e.g., de St. Aubin, 1998). Psychobiographies have also been written from the theoretical standpoints of social-learning theory (Mountjoy & Sundberg, 1981), humanistic psychology (Rogers, 1980), existential psychology (Sartre, 1981), McClelland's theory of motives (Winter & Carlson, 1988), and Tomkins's theory of scripts (Carlson, 1988). Furthermore, many contemporary biographies, written by nonpsychologists, draw liberally from personality theory. While some of these use theory naively or inappropriately, others have been celebrated as masterful and illuminating, such as Leon Edel's monumental study of the American author Henry James (Edel, 1985).

Since Freud's *Leonardo*, many psychobiographies have been written, and advances in understanding particular lives have been made (Elms, 1994; Schultz, 2005). Still it is very difficult to write a *good* psychobiography. The best-intentioned psychobiographers face major constraints and obstacles that usually do not confront other kinds of researchers. For instance, the subjects of their studies are often dead and thus cannot be interviewed, tested, or directly observed. The data for the analysis come in a troubling variety of forms—from unsubstantiated hearsay about the person being studied, to personal correspondence and other writings, to publicly documented facts about the person's life. The most reliable data (such as birthdate or number of siblings) may be the least illuminating. The most intriguing data (such as personal fantasies, reflections, or dreams) may be the least reliable and the most difficult to interpret in an intellectually responsible way. Indeed, one of the problems facing some psychobiographers is the sheer amount of biographical data they face. How does one choose which data to interpret?

Irving Alexander (1988) provides nine helpful guidelines by which the psychobiographer may reduce huge amounts of data to manageable quantities, by identifying which data are worthy of further consideration and which may be tossed aside for the time being. Alexander argues that the data may be evaluated in terms of primacy, frequency, uniqueness, negation, emphasis, omission, error, isolation, and incompletion (Table 12.4). Each

TABLE 12.3	COMMON CRITICISMS OF PSYCHOBIOGRAPHY
Critical-period fallacy	Some psychobiographers overemphasize the influence of one early "critical period," such as the first year of life or the Oedipal period, while neglecting formative influences at later stages.
Eventism	Attempting to explain major trends in a human life solely in terms of one or two key or "traumatic" events is poor practice. While some events are obviously more important than others, the entire life must be viewed as a complex and multiply determined whole.
Inadequate evidence	Some psychobiographical interpretations rest on limited or erroneous evidence. The psychobiographer must synthesize many different kinds of data from multiple sources that converge on a particular interpretation. He or she must check and doublecheck historical and biographical sources.
Neglect of social and historical factors	Too many psychobiographies do not take into careful consideration the complex social and historical context within which the individual's life is or was embedded. A person's life is strongly shaped by culture. The biographer cannot understand the life if he or she does not attempt to understand the culture.
Originology	Many biographers attempt to trace everything about a person to its origins in childhood. Given that the issue of continuity and consistency in personality from childhood to adulthood is a controversial one in personality and development psychology, the biographer runs the risk of placing too much emphasis on childhood events as determinants of adult outcomes.
Overpathologizing	A good psychobiography should not aim to reduce an entire life to a particular psychiatric syndrome or neurotic tendency. A life must be evaluated in terms of both its weaknesses and strengths.
Reconstruction	The psychoanalytically oriented biographer may reconstruct unknown or unsubstantiated childhood events from known adult outcomes. For instance, a biographer may assume that an anally retentive and compulsive adult experienced severe toilet training as a toddler. In the absence of evidence from childhood, these kinds of reconstructions are usually unwarranted.

SOURCE: From "Psychobiographical Methodology: The Case of William James," by J. W. Anderson, in L. Wheeler (Ed.), *Review of Personality and Social Psychology* (Vol. 2, pp. 245–272), 1981, Beverly Hills, CA: Sage; *Uncovering Lives: The Uneasy Alliance of Biography and Psychology,* by A. C. Elms, 1994, New York: Oxford University Press; and *Life Histories and Psychobiography: Explorations in Theory and Method,* by W. M. Runyan, 1982, New York: Oxford University Press.

TABLE 12.4	NINE GUIDELINES FOR EXTRACTING PSYCHOBIOGRAPHY DATA
Primacy	That which comes *first;* "The association of 'first' with importance has a long-standing history in folklore and in human customs and mores. Certainly in psychology the idea is upheld in the importance assigned to early experience in the development of personality by both Freud and Adler and countless successors. The first as the 'foundation stone' upon which structures are built is also a common metaphor in language."
Frequency	That which appears *often;* "For the most part, we are tuned to frequency or repetition as increasing signs of certainty and of importance. The kind of importance a frequent message has, however, may be complex in terms of its value for the discovery of dynamic sequence. In many instances, frequency may be an expression of powerful conscious value schemas."
Uniqueness	That which is *singular,* odd; "A powerful example of this occurred in the autobiographical sketch of a paid student volunteer intensively studied in a graduate personality assessment course. The student recalled an incident from his first year in elementary school: At the end of a school day he returned home to find his mother hanging from a rope in her bedroom, a description that he followed only with a statement that he was sent off to a private school shortly afterward. Uniqueness in this instance is signaled not only by the event itself but by the kind of response to the event reported by the subject."
Negation	That which is denied, or turned into its *opposite;* "Imagine, for example, a therapeutic interview in which a dream about the father is mentioned, followed by the statement, 'Let's move on to something else. *It's not* that I think talking about father would drive me crazy, it usually leads to a feeling of helplessness.'"
Emphasis	That which is *underscored* or stressed; The biographer should be aware of that which seems either overemphasized or underemphasized. "Overemphasis can usually be detected when the hearer or reader begins to wonder why so much attention is focused on something considered to be so commonplace. 'I just could not get over the fact that this person, a native of the country, for whom I as a tourist had inquired about directions, took such pains to make sure I understood how to find my way. From that moment on I adored my visit to _____.' would be an example chosen by the criterion of overemphasis for retention in the reduced data pool. Its ultimate transformation might be, unexpected attention (kindness) when in distress ➔ euphoria. This may be an analogue of the expectation that when one is in trouble, no help is expected."

(CONTINUES)

may be viewed as a rule for storymaking employed by the biographer who seeks to discern or create the central story of a life. Each gives the biographer a clue about what may be important in narrative. Thus, the guideline of *primacy* suggests that what comes first in stories is especially significant; *uniqueness* suggests that what stands out as odd and intriguing in a story may be of special consequence; *omission* suggests that what seems to be missing in the story may be revealing; *distortion* and *isolation* suggest that when something in the story does not follow logically, the biographer should seek to straighten it out; and *incompletion* suggests that when stories do not end properly, the biographer should seek to understand why. The psychobiographer must be sensitive to the clues in the data suggesting how the story of a person's life is to be discovered, created, and told (Edel, 1984; McAdams, 1988b).

While Alexander's nine guidelines may assist the biographer in identifying the important data in a particular life, he or she is still faced with the task of using psychological theory

TABLE 12.4	NINE GUIDELINES FOR EXTRACTING PSYCHOBIOGRAPHY DATA *(CONTINUED)*
Omission	That which is *missing;* "An illustrative example might be one in which the subject describes a memory of being punished by his mother after she had accused him of hostile behavior toward a sibling. The retelling goes on to include the subject's feelings as a results of the mother's actions but speaks not at all to whether he had in fact treated the other child in the manner suggested. What is omitted is attention to the subject's role in a sequence with a negative outcome which must be investigated for its possible repetitive properties."
Error, or Distortion	That which is a *mistake;* "In written exposition this is sometimes indicated by obvious undetected error by the subject in an otherwise error free or minimally error-prone sample. An example might be the statement, 'I came from a family of tall people, my father is 6'5", my brother is 6'4", my mother is 9'5", and I am the runt at 5'8".' This not only calls attention to the possible importance of the size dimensions in the life of the subject but highlights (error signaled by incredibility) the overvaluing of mother on whatever dimension the size variable symbolizes, and by contrast the undervaluing of the writer who is described uniquely as a runt. Underlying these pointers there most likely exists a dynamic set of conditioned sequences constituting the subject's view of the family drama."
Isolation	That which is alone, or *doesn't fit;* "I remember how we saved a touchdown by our opponents in a high school football game by something we learned from observing their game films. Oh! Did I remember to bank the fire in the fireplace before I left the house to come here? The films showed that the quarterback … "
Incompletion	That which is *not finished;* "'All through college I dated John. It started as a casual friendship, but within a short period of time we found that we enjoyed the same interests and people. By the time we reached senior year we were making plans for a future together. Marriage, while not an immediate prospect, was our ultimate goal. Three years later I married Fred Perkins, whom I had recently met, and moved to Pittsburgh where we have lived ever since.' This illustrates an uncompleted fragment or portion of a descriptive segment about courtship and marriage which in itself has an aura of completion."

SOURCE: From "Personality, Psychological Assessment, and Psychobiography," by I. E. Alexander, 1988, *Journal of Personality, 56,* 269–278.

to organize the data into an illuminating and coherent narrative. Psychological theory must be applied with flexibility and grace. Too many psychobiographers force life-history data into rigid theoretical categories, as if to prove that all aspects of a particular life fit perfectly in an existing theoretical scheme. Others apply theory in the most desultory and trite ways, relentlessly dragging a human life, say, through each of Erikson's eight psychosocial stages or Murray's 20 psychogenic needs. Still others fail to understand the single life within its particular social, cultural, and historical matrix, reducing complex behavior and experiences, for instance, to early problems in toilet training or single traumatic events. These kinds of psychobiographies are boring. Worse, they make straightjackets out of theories and caricatures out of lives. In a sophisticated psychobiography, the data and the theory relate to each other as equals, as if they were two speakers in a lively conversation. Each influences and is influenced by the other, and each respects the other's integrity. Therefore, the skilled psychobiographer uses theory in a subtle and nuanced manner, making sense out of what can be made sensible, struggling with complexity and contradiction, knowing when to back off from lofty theories and let the concrete, unique human life speak for itself.

WHY DID VAN GOGH CUT OFF HIS EAR?

On the evening of December 23, 1888, Vincent van Gogh, then 35 years old, cut off the lower half of his left ear and took it to a brothel, where he requested to see a prostitute named Rachel. He handed her the ear and asked that she "keep this object carefully."

Van Gogh (1853–1890) is famous today for the many brilliant expressionist masterpieces he painted during his short and very troubled life. The Dutch artist developed a unique style of painting— using rough strokes and bold colors to portray scenes that are often haunting and ominous—a style that even the most untutored art observers immediately recognize. While millions of art lovers have enjoyed his paintings, psychologists and biographers have puzzled over his life. The incident with the ear stands out as the most memorable of all van Gogh's odd behaviors. We can't help but wonder, over and over: Why did van Gogh cut off his ear?

Psychologist William McKinley Runyan (1981, 1982) has surveyed the psychobiographical literature on van Gogh and identified at least 13 different psychological explanations for this bizarre incident in the artist's life. Here are a few of the more interesting ones:

1. He was frustrated by the failure to establish a working and friendly relationship with his fellow artist Paul Gauguin and turned his resultant aggressive feelings toward himself.

2. He felt conflict over his homosexual feelings toward Gauguin. The ear was a phallic symbol (the Dutch slang word for penis, *lul,* resembled the Dutch word for ear, *lel*), and the act was a symbolic self-castration.

3. He was imitating the actions of bullfighters with whom he had been especially impressed in his visits to Arles. In such events, the matador receives the ear of the bull as an award, displays his prize to the crowd, and then gives the ear to the lady of his choice.

4. He was influenced by a number of newspaper reports concerning Jack the Ripper, who mutilated the bodies of prostitutes, sometimes cutting off their ears. Adopting the masochistic over the sadistic approach, van Gogh turned on himself.

5. He was reenacting a scene from the New Testament in which Simon Peter cuts off the ear of Malchus, a servant of the high priest, who had come to seize Christ. Van Gogh had been thinking about this event recently and had tried to paint it.

6. He was experiencing auditory hallucinations and during a psychotic episode cut off his ear to silence the disturbing sounds.

What do we make of these different, competing interpretations? Are they all right, or wrong (in one way or another)? Are some better interpretations than others?

Runyan argues that competing psychobiographical interpretations can be reasonably compared and contrasted and evaluated according to clear standards. Different explanations may be judged according to standards such as

(1) their logical soundness, (2) their comprehensiveness in accounting for a number of puzzling aspects of the events in question, (3) their survival of tests of attempted falsification, such as tests of derived predictions or retrodictions, (4) their consistency with the full range of available relevant evidence, (5) their support from above, or their consistency with more general knowledge about human functioning or about the person in question, and (6) their credibility relative to other explanatory hypotheses. (Runyan, 1982, p. 47)

Runyan maintains that there is room for more than one good explanation for any given biographical event. Indeed, events are highly overdetermined, and influences from many different levels may come to bear in producing a particular behavior in a particular situation.

Carefully weighing the various explanations for van Gogh's behavior, Runyan favors those interpretations that emphasize the role of the artist's brother, Theo. The ear-cutting incident and two later mental

(CONTINUES)

FEATURE 12.B *(CONTINUED)*

breakdowns coincide with Vincent's learning that Theo is to be married, Theo's wedding, and the birth of Theo's first child. Each of these events may have reinforced Vincent's fear that he was losing his brother's care and his financial support. In the past, van Gogh had exhibited masochistic responses to rejection. In 1881, he had visited the parents of Kee Voss, a woman whom he loved. When he learned that Kee had left the house to avoid seeing him, he thrust his hand into the flame of a lamp and vowed to keep it there until she returned. On one level at least, Vincent may have cut off his ear in response to the perceived loss of and rejection by his brother.

But, then, why did he mutilate himself in this way? Why the ear? And why did he give it to this

particular prostitute? The Jack-the-Ripper explanation seems farfetched, for there is no evidence that van Gogh was familiar with or impressed by the exploits of this criminal. Runyan also finds little support for explanations emphasizing symbolic castration. Van Gogh had been impressed, however, by the bullfights. And he had pondered over the scene in the Garden of Gethsemane when Peter cut off Malchus's ear. Perhaps these latter two interpretations hold a grain of truth. Perhaps not. Without more definitive evidence from the life of the artist, at least a few plausible but competing interpretations will invariably remain.

THE SEASONS OF ADULT LIFE

Around the time that Henry Murray was launching the personological tradition in psychology, sociologists and other social scientists became especially interested in collecting *life histories* from many different walks of life in order to expose and explain societal problems such as delinquency and crime (e.g., Shaw, 1930). Sociologist John Dollard (1935) argued that life histories should provide biographical accounts that mirror society and the cultural milieu. The spirit and method of their efforts motivated Charlotte Bühler (1933) and Else Frenkel (1936) to collect and analyze autobiographical accounts written by almost 400 European men and women in the 1930s, representing various nationalities, social classes, and vocations. Whenever possible, the written accounts were supplemented by letters, diaries, and other personal documents produced by the subjects. The content analysis of all the data "revealed rather sharply demarcated phases through which every person passed in the course of his life" (Frenkel, 1936, p. 2). Over sixty years ago, Bühler and Frenkel proposed a surprisingly contemporary and detailed model of adult development complete with five well-articulated stages and numerous references to a kind of "midlife crisis" around the age of 40. More concerned with general principles in all lives than with the uniqueness of any single life, these researchers focused on three dimensions of the adult biography: (a) significant external events (such as economic and political changes, war), (b) internal reactions to these events (such as thoughts, feelings, wishes), and (c) specific accomplishments and creative contributions to life. Following are a few of their more interesting findings:

1. During the first half of life, a person's subjective experience appears strongly influenced by bodily needs and short-term wishes, but the latter half is marked by a preoccupation with internalized duties that one "has set himself, or which have been set for him by society, or which have come from some code of values such as religion or science" (Frenkel, 1936, p. 15). Deviations from this general pattern were observed only in subjects who had been diagnosed by psychiatrists as neurotic.

2. Lives in which the pursuit of sexual gratification takes precedence over work and child rearing suffer "an unquestionable subjective decline in the second half" (p. 20).

3. Experiences of loneliness and daydreaming peak in late adolescence and again in the midforties. The latter period is also occasioned by a transitory reexamination of one's past and, in many cases, a heightened interest in literature.

4. The search for a "meaning in life" begins in late adolescence.

The life-history studies conducted by Bühler and Frenkel in the 1930s presaged narrative studies of adult life stages which became very popular in the 1970s and 80s. In both instances, psychologists collected first-person narrative accounts in order to generate their own third-person narratives about the developmental course of adult life. Bühler and Frenkel began to articulate a general narrative about adult life stages in which the protagonist begins to search for the meaning of his or her life in adolescence (as Erikson was later to suggest) and later experiences a second chapter of self-examination and questioning in the 40s—what we might now call a midlife crisis.

It is now commonplace in American society to talk about adult development in terms of predictable stages, phases, seasons, and the continual evolution of the self. This way of narrating the adult life course is apparent in Erikson (chapter 9) and Jung (chapter 11), but it was given an especially strong stimulus in the 1970s and 80s by theorists such as Gould (1980), Levinson (1978), and Vaillant (1977), and by popular books such as Gail Sheehy's (1976) *Passages.*

Daniel Levinson (1978, 1981) formulated a detailed and influential model of the "seasons of man's life," based in part on biographical interviews of 40 American men. Levinson and his colleagues interviewed men between the ages of 35 and 45 years who were employed in one of four occupational groups: biology professors, novelists, business executives, and hourly workers in industry. Each man was interviewed 6 to 10 times, each interview lasting between 1 and 2 hours. Participants were asked to tell their life stories, concentrating mainly on the years from adolescence onward. Although the interviewers did not follow a standardized format of questions and answers, they were guided by a number of general considerations for the investigations, such as these:

1. We have to cover various "areas of living" such as family of origin, education, occupation, love relationships, marriage and family of procreation, leisure, bodily health and illness, ethnicity, religion, politics, and relation to self.

2. Within each area, it is essential to trace the sequence over the adult years, being alert to major events, choices, and turning points, as well as to the character of relatively stable periods.

3. We must learn about the "interpretation" of the areas. Occupational and family life, for example, are often closely intertwined.

4. As a series of interviews progresses, the interviewer gets a sense of different "chapters" in the life story: three years in military service; four to five years of relatively transient living; the years of starting a family and getting settled in a new city and job. It is important to comprehend the overall character of life within each of these chapters, as well as the kinds of changes that occurred within it. Here the emphasis is on the patterning among the many areas of living—the forms of integration as well as the contradictions, gaps, and fragments.

5. In the lives of many persons, there are occasional periods, lasting a few months to a few years, that constitute dramatic "high points" or "rock bottom" periods. These times often mark the end of one life phase and the beginning of another. They must be examined from many vantage points.

6. We are interested in the participant's view of his life as a whole, and of the interrelations among various parts and times within it. ... [The past is] part of the present, and the biographer must so represent it. Likewise, the person's defined plans and more shadowy imaginings of the future shape and are shaped by the present. The future, too, forms a part of the present that the biographer must explore. (Levinson, 1981, pp. 61–62)

The central concept in Levinson's model is the individual **life structure,** which "refers to the patterning or design of the individual life at a given time" (Levinson, 1978, p. 99). One of the more encompassing concepts in personality theory, the individual life structure includes the individual's sociocultural world (class, religion, family, political systems, historical era), his participation in this world (relationships and roles with respect to significant people and institutions in his life), and various "aspects of the self," which may remain stable or may be transformed over time. Levinson views adult development as the evolution of the life structure. From adolescence through middle age, the life structure evolves through periods (seasons) of relative calm and periods of significant transition.

The first period in Levinson's scheme, Early Adult Transition (ages 17–22), roughly corresponds to the late-adolescent and early-adult period in which Erikson (1959) places the psychosocial crisis of identity *versus* role confusion (see Figure 12.1). The young man leaves home for college, the military, first employment, or some other living situation in which he begins to assume financial independence from his parents and achieves greater levels of autonomy. During the next phase, Entering the Adult World (ages 22–28), many young men explore adult roles and responsibilities and make provisional occupational commitments that link them to the wider society. In the late 20s, the man is likely to formulate a *dream* for the future. According to Levinson, the dream may include visions of occupational success and enhanced prestige, the development of a fulfilling family life, the establishment of certain kinds of relationships with friends and peers, and many other hopes and goals for the self, family, and significant others. Another significant aspect of development in the twenties, according to Levinson, is the establishment of a relationship with a *mentor*. The mentor is a man or woman who is usually somewhat older and more experienced than the young adult and therefore well positioned to shepherd the young adult through some of the difficult and challenging periods of the twenties. Mentors would appear to be most valuable and most common in the professional workplace. For example, a graduate student or junior professor heading for a career in college academia may find a mentor in his advisor. Through actions and advice, the adviser can teach the younger man how to make his way in the world of higher education, how to teach effectively, do good research, obtain governmental grants, get along with colleagues, and so on.

Around the age of 30, some men may encounter a significant transition period in which they feel the need to consolidate or rethink their tentative commitments from the 20s. The "Age 30 Transition" is followed by a period of Settling Down (early 30s). During Settling Down, the man is trying to carve a niche in the world and establish a timetable for advancement in his occupation, while simultaneously putting down roots in the sphere of his family. According to Levinson, the man in his early 30s is preoccupied both with "making it" and "building a nest," and he invests himself dearly in issues of order, stability, security, and control. By this time he has often generated a dream for the future, which will serve as a motivating vision of what he would like to accomplish and become.

With its emphasis on order and control, the Settling Down period of the 30s is oddly reminiscent of Erikson's second stage of psychosocial development: the toddler's period of autonomy *versus* shame and doubt. Like the toddler, the man in his early 30s seeks to control self and environment as an independent and autonomous agent. For the toddler, the

FIGURE 12.1   **LEVINSON'S SEASONS OF A MAN'S LIFE**

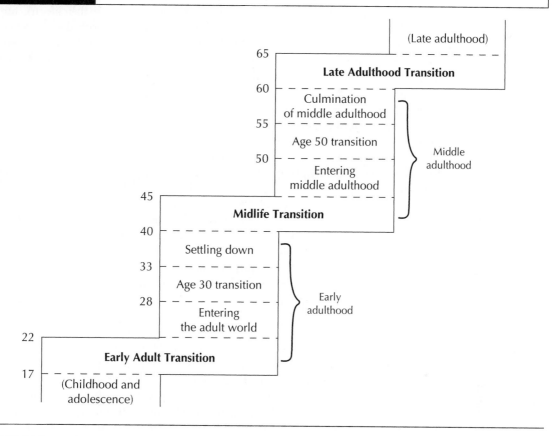

SOURCE: From *The Seasons of a Man's Life* (p. 57), by D. J. Levinson, 1978, New York: Alfred A. Knopf.

next phase is Oedipal: Freud's universal ontogenetic tragedy of becoming the conquering king and then falling from power, captured in Erikson's third stage of initiative *versus* guilt. Levinson's next phase of the life structure—Becoming One's Own Man, or BOOM—likewise has a certain Oedipal ring to it:

> BOOM tends to occur in the middle to late 30s, typically in our sample around 35–39. It represents the high point of early adulthood and the beginning of what lies beyond. A key element in this period is the man's feeling that, no matter what he has accomplished to date, he is not sufficiently his own man. He feels overly dependent upon and constrained by persons or groups who have authority over him or who, for various reasons, exert great influence upon him. The writer comes to recognize that he is unduly intimidated by his publisher or too vulnerable to the evaluation of certain critics. The man who has successfully risen through the managerial ranks with the support and encouragement of his superiors now finds that they control too much and delegate too little, and he impatiently awaits the time when he will have the authority to make his own decisions and to get the enterprise really going. The untenured faculty member imagines that once he had tenure he will be free of all the restraints and demands he's been acquiescing to since graduate school days. (The illusions die hard!) (Levinson, Darrow, Klein, Levinson, & McKee, 1974, pp. 250–251.)

BOOM sets the stage for the Midlife Transition. During this period (ages 40–45 years), 80% of the men Levinson interviewed encountered serious doubts concerning the directions of their lives. Taking stock of the various areas of commitment making up their life structures, many came to question the validity and worth of their hitherto most cherished goals and their plans for attaining them. For many, the Midlife Transition represented the bust following BOOM. Marital satisfaction, job performance, and enjoyment of outside pursuits declined. Confusion and despair became common as the sense of having established a home and a niche in the adult world, consolidated during Settling Down, gradually disintegrated, replaced by the nagging apprehension that one's life had been directed by and for the sake of illusions.

The Midlife Transition may be a very painful period in a man's life. Some of the men in Levinson's sample emerged from this period "cynical, estranged, unable to believe in anything" (Levinson, 1978, p. 108). Many others, however, benefited from the searching reevaluation of life structure precipitated by the transition. Those who benefited fashioned new life structures that opened up new opportunities and outlets for fulfillment in family, work, and friendships. Thus, the Midlife Transition may eventuate in a rejuvenated life structure in the second half of life—a restabilization around new plans and goals designed to maximize the individual's potential for fulfillment in many realms of life, especially the realms of intimacy and generativity.

Roberts and Newton (1987) describe four studies examining the life course of women, each of which employed Levinson's approach. Across the four studies, biographies from 39 contemporary women (ranging in age from 31 to 53, most middle-class and employed outside the home) were analyzed for the relevance and meaning of such Levinsonian concepts as (a) the dream, (b) the mentor, (c) the Age 30 Transition, and (d) the Midlife Transition. The authors conclude that these women passed through the same developmental seasons that Levinson sketched out for men. But a number of important differences were also noted. For example, women's dreams tended to be more complex and conflictual than men's, incorporating competing demands and hopes for family life and career success. Second, the women were much less likely than Levinson's men to report the existence of a satisfying mentoring relationship. Third, the women tended to place less emphasis than did Levinson's men on the importance of a Midlife Transition. However, they were more likely than the men to underscore the Age 30 transition as a period of accelerated and often dramatic personality change. This seemed to be especially true for women who by age 30 had not yet married or started a family. Some of these women began to feel a sense of urgency at this time. Soon it might be "too late" to become pregnant and bear children, some worried. Some of the women also began to question seriously the commitments they made in their 20s, and began to formulate a new life structure and a new dream to move them more rewardingly into their 30s. It would appear, therefore, that the Age 30 Transition *in women* could be somewhat analogous to the Midlife Transition *in men*. Both periods are described as having the potential for an urgent reexamination of the life structure because of the feeling that, in some sense or another, "time is running out."

The general idea that the adult life course may be viewed in terms of a sequence of periods or seasons is a controversial one today. Outside of in-depth biographical explorations such as Levinson's, researchers have not found a great deal of support for a dramatic Midlife Transition in adult lives. For example, Costa and McCrae (1980a) developed a Midlife Crisis Scale to reflect the stresses of this portion of life identified by Levinson. No age differences were found on this scale in a large sample of men aged 33 to 70. Rossi

(1980) and others have argued that the whole concept of an orderly life course in adulthood, complete with a progression of stages or seasons, does not accommodate well the lives of working-class adults and the lives of women. Levinson's stages may be descriptive of the lives of white, upper-middle class, professional men in America who entered midlife in the 1960s and 70s, but they may not generalize well to other samples.

On the other side of the coin, Helson and Wink (1992) found empirical support for some of Levinson's ideas in a longitudinal study of 101 women, followed between their early 40s and early 50s. The researchers document the existence of noteworthy developmental change around the age of 40, akin to a midlife transition, followed by increasing security, confidence, and decisiveness. Mercer, Nichols, and Doyle (1989) report data on women's lives that is both consistent with and different from Levinson's scheme. Overall, women in their study "tended to experience developmental periods at later ages and in sequences that were much more irregular" than those reported by Levinson (p. 180). However, something akin to a Midlife Transition manifested itself around the age of 40. The authors describe the age-40 time as a "Liberating Period" in many women's lives:

> For many women, the age-40 liberating period was the time of formulating a life dream. If they had rushed or were pushed into earlier choices such as marriage or had taken on a foreclosure identity, this was the time they focused on themselves. Earlier, their intense relationships with their husbands and children had had priority. (p. 182)

For many of the women in this study, therefore, the Midlife Transition signaled "A time to be yourself" (p. 182).

THE LIFE COURSE

Like Murray, Levinson sought to capture the time-binding nature of human life. Using first-person narrative accounts (autobiographical interviews), he constructed a third-person developmental story about how certain men living in the United States in the 1960s and 70s described their own development from late adolescence through midlife. The plot entails periods (chapters) of relative calm (e.g., Settling Down), which eventually give way to periods of transformation and tumult (e.g., the midlife transition). The setting is post–World War II corporate America; the protagonist is the middle-class, well-educated white man; heroes include the mentor and the special woman who inspires the man's progress; the high point is BOOM; the low point is the advent of the midlife transition; the plot moves forward according to the development of the dream; the theme is meeting the challenges of change.

The most interesting plot turn in this story is the midlife transition. In contemporary American society, midlife or middle age is considered to last from roughly age 40 to age 65. Certain biological changes play a role in demarcating this period of life, such as the end of the childbearing years. But for the most part, midlife is *socially* defined, based on the assumptions that most Americans have about the course of human life (Cohler, 1982; Lachman, 2001). Midlife is situated in the temporal course of the human lifespan according to what Neugarten (1968) called the **social clock.** The social clock is a set of expectations about age-appropriate transitions, setting the standards against which individuals evaluate the extent to which their lives are "on time" (Cohler & Boxer, 1984). Graduating from college in one's early 20s, raising a family in one's 20s and 30s, seeing the children leave home in one's 40s, witnessing parents' deaths in one's 50s and 60s, retiring at age 65 or 70—these are a few transitions in the lifespan that, in contemporary middle-class American society, are considered "on time." Many Americans expect to live well into their 70s and 80s. The midlife chunk of time is seen as comprising that period following early adulthood and preceding the retirement years.

As the adult enters midlife, he or she comes to realize that the life course is likely to be about half over and that there is now less time ahead in the future than behind in the past. Such a realization may lead to an increased concern with one's own mortality (Marshall, 1975; Sill, 1980), or what Neugarten and Datan (1974) call the "personalization of death." Experiences of loss become more salient—loss of others through death of parents and friends and through separation from children who have moved away, loss of vitality through changes in athletic and reproductive capacities, and loss of hopes and aspirations through the inevitable disappointments—both on-time and off-time—that accompany adult life (Jacques, 1965; Kernberg, 1980; Levinson, 1981).

Psychologists have observed a number of behavioral and attitudinal trends in midlife that may, on one level or another, be viewed as responses to one's growing, on-time concern about mortality. The middle years may bring an increase in the use of reminiscences in daily life (Livson & Peskin, 1980; Lowenthal, Thurnher, Chiriboga, & Associates, 1975), an enhanced appreciation for the internal world of thoughts and feelings, and somewhat less interest in establishing new interpersonal and instrumental engagements (Neugarten, 1979). According to Jung (1961), it is not until midlife that men are finally able to accept and integrate their suppressed femininity (the *anima*) and that women are able to express an inner masculinity (the *animus*), as we saw in chapter 11. With the end of active parenting at midlife, Gutmann (1987) argues, women are likely to become more instrumental and executive in their approach to life, eschewing the dependent and self-effacing ways of their youth. Midlife men, on the other hand, are more likely to abandon the vigorous and aggressive manner of young adulthood in favor of more passive and contemplative roles.

At the age of 29, Spanish painter Francisco Jose de Goya y Lucientes displayed the idealism and optimism of a romantic.

In a famous paper, Jacques (1965) suggested that midlife may mark significant changes in the adult's efforts to be creative. Jacques examined biographical information and artistic productions for 310 painters, composers, poets, writers, and sculptors "of undoubted greatness or of genius" (p. 502). Included in his list were Mozart, Michelangelo, Bach, Gauguin, Raphael, and Shakespeare. Jacques found that before midlife the artists were more likely to produce masterpieces in a rapid and passionate fashion, as "hot-from-the-fire" productions. Their work tended to be highly optimistic and idealistic, laden with themes of pure desire and romance. After the age of about 40, however, the artists appeared to work in a more deliberate fashion, creating more refined and "sculpted" masterpieces. With the increasing concern over mortality at midlife, youthful idealism gave way to a more contemplative pessimism and a "recognition and acceptance that inherent goodness is accompanied by hate and destructive forces within" (Jacques, 1965, p. 505). Creative products speak a more philosophical and sober language during and after midlife—a result, says Jacques, of the artist's own confrontation with the prospect of death.

Though men and women may be at the prime of their lives in their middle years, the social clock suggests that the end of life is closer to the present than is the beginning of life. It is likely, therefore, that midlife men and women should be especially concerned with *endings.* In their 40s and 50s, men and women in contemporary Western societies begin to consider in more detail and with greater urgency the problem of construing appropriate imagined endings for their self-defining life narratives. Even though the literal end of life is likely to be far off in the future, thoughts about endings become more and more salient as people move through their middle-adult years, deeply influencing the stories that people continue to construct to make sense of their lives.

Most lifespan developmental psychologists agree that important changes occur during the midlife years. But they disagree when it comes to saying that such changes occur at a particular time (e.g., the early 40s) and as part of a cleanly demarcated midlife crisis or

By age 69, Goya's work had lost the idealism of youth. Instead, his paintings depicted the realities of life, including pain and suffering, as in *The Execution of Madrilenos* on the Third of May, 1808.

transition. Levinson's attempt to write a generic story of men's lives in time has been highly influential, but it is but one kind of story about adult development. The study of human individuality should leave room for more stories. Consequently, theorists and researchers who adopt what has been called a **life course** perspective tend to see more diversity and unpredictability in the interpretive stories social scientists might invoke to account for adult lives over time. Cohler, Hostetler, and Boxer (1998) describe this view:

> The course of development is much less clearly ordered than stage theories would predict and cannot be understood apart from either larger social and historical trends or unique events within particular lives. Certain sequentially negotiated tasks across the adult life course, related to work, intimate partnership, providing for the next generation, and dealing with the finitude of life, appear to be ubiquitous within contemporary society, yet no simple checklist can capture the full range of variation in developmental pathways or the ways in which certain tasks and prescribed social roles are experienced. (p. 266)

A life course perspective on writing stories of lives offers an especially nuanced and situated approach to adult development. In the spirit of chapter 3 in this textbook, individual lives are viewed in their full social, cultural, and historical contexts, allowing for tremendous variety in developmental pathways that is observed across many different lives, across cultures, and across historical epochs (Bronfenbrenner, 1994; Dannefer, 1984; Elder, 1995). Life stories are shaped by economic conditions, cultural norms, social change, historical events, and chance happenings. At the same time, individuals exert their own agentic influence on the course of development, actively co-constructing their lives in a complex and evolving social context. A life-course perspective, therefore, brings to the fore (a) social time and timing, (b) social roles and relationships, and (c) the role of human agency and individual variability in psychosocial development in the adult years.

Social timing "refers to the incidence, duration, and sequence of roles and to related age expectations and beliefs" concerning the course of human life as understood in a given society or social context (Elder, 1995, p. 14). Thus, the extent to which a given social event or role is "on-time" or "off-time" is of prime importance for social life and individual well-being. Cohler and Boxer (1984) have argued that the experience of positive morale, or life satisfaction, is significantly determined by the sense of being on-time for expectable role transitions or life changes. Adults who move through role changes in a timely manner, line up their own life narratives with the stories that society holds up as the models for good development. Being off-time, therefore, brings with it a special challenge in life storytelling.

Social timing concerns the sequencing and patterning of *social roles.* Roles strongly influence the ways in which developmental tasks are met. For example, MacDermid, Franz, and DeReus (1998) have argued that Erikson's concept of generativity should not be viewed as a stage or chapter in a generic narrative of life but rather as a dynamic arrangement of roles, each carrying its own story line. Generativity is spread out unevenly across work, marital, parental, civic, and religious roles, and the strength or quality of generativity in one role is no predictor of the strength or quality of generativity in another. Within any given life, furthermore, generativity may move around from one role to another, according to the dictates of the social clock, on-time and off-time events, and a host of other factors. Over the adult life course, generativity ebbs and flows and spreads itself across different roles and life domains, sometimes in an unpredictable manner. Furthermore, particular love and family relationships, friendships, and other unpredictable interpersonal bonds strongly impact how generativity plays itself out. Life course theorists speak of *linked lives* (Elder, 1995) and *social convoys* (Kahn & Antonucci, 1981) to underscore the many senses in which individual development is thoroughly interdependent. People's lives and the stories they construct to make sense of them are linked to the lives and stories of those with whom they share significant involvements. Over time, people move through life with a group of family, friends, and colleagues—like a convoy traveling across a storied landscape, from one chapter to the next.

Social timing, social roles, and social relationships shape life stories, but people are not passive recipients of these shaping influences. Adults actively construct their lives within social contexts, as interpretive *agents* who appropriate life experience and make it their own. Indeed, adults often defy social clocks and fly in the face of conventional social norms and roles. They make meaning out of life on their own terms. Most amazingly, everybody does this is a different way.

This is why human individuality is so utterly fascinating. We are all so fundamentally the same, so rooted in human nature and evolution. We are all so thoroughly determined by cultural context, so tightly linked to family, society, history. And yet we are all so completely different, and so self-determining in the stories we tell to convey just how different we are. It is mainly because people are so different from one another, so different in the ways they begin life and the developmental pathways they follow over life's course, that psychologists have bothered to study this thing called "personality." It is because people are so complexly different, so different from one another in so many different ways, that we must think about human individuality in terms of this textbook's multiple levels of dispositional traits, characteristic adaptations, and life stories. You can't reduce these differences to a simple attribution or two; you can't sum it all up in four simple types or five different traits. There is simply too much variability, too much diversity to account for. And this is why, in my view, personality psychology is just about the most interesting thing in the world.

SUMMARY

1. The ancient story of Icarus—the boy who flew so close to the sun that it melted his wings and sent him plummeting to the sea below—provided the theoretical model for a famous case study written by Henry Murray about an unassuming college undergraduate. Combining themes of rising, falling, urethral eroticism, narcissism, and craving for immortality, the Icarus complex was Murray's storied interpretation of the student's life, based in part on the student's stories. Murray's interpretation is an example of psychologists' efforts to construct third-person narratives to interpret person's lives in time, often relying on those individuals' own first-person narrative accounts.

2. In the 1930s, Murray launched the personological traditional in the social sciences, assembling an interdisciplinary team of researchers at the Harvard Psychological Clinic. The personological tradition emphasized biography, myth, narrative, and the intensive exploration of the single case in the study of human lives.

3. A key feature of Murray's personological viewpoint was that human beings are time-binding organisms. The history of the organism is the organism, Murray suggested, which mandated the use of biographical methods of inquiry. In decomposing a life in time, the personologists can begin by focusing on the single proceeding or life episode and work up to durances (strings of overlapping proceedings), serials (long-term sequences within a given life domain), and serial programs (sequences that extend in a goal-directed manner into the future). Lives are given direction by internal needs and environmental press, which interact to form life themes. A self-defining patterning of needs, press, and theme constitutes a unity theme, which is the central, organizing motif of a person's life story.

4. A major figure in the personological tradition was Robert White, who championed the intensive study of the single case. White's case studies illustrate important growth trends in personality over time. With healthy personality development over the adult life course, White argued, five growth trends are revealed: (a) the stabilization of ego identity, (b) the freeing of personal relationships, (c) the deepening of interests, (d) the humanizing of values, and (e) the expansion of caring.

5. Even before the time of Murray, case studies were used to exemplify personality theories, to provide new data for theory development, and to compare the contrast different constructs and theories as they might apply to the single life set in time. Yet case studies have always been controversial. Critics of case study methodology have argued that cases are inherently too subjective, unreliable, and unwieldy to be of good scientific use. In evaluating the appropriateness of case study research, one needs to pay close attention to issues of reliability, internal coherence, interpretive truth, external validity, and the fundamental distinction in science between discovery and justification. A reasoned consideration of the strengths and limitations of case studies suggests a number of appropriate venues in which they can be scientifically valuable, including especially the derivation of new ideas, hypotheses, and theoretical insights.

6. Psychobiography is the systematic use of psychological theory to transform a life into a coherent and illuminating story. Beginning with Freud's famous study of Leonardo da Vinci, psychobiographies have typically employed psychodynamic theories to construct broad theoretical interpretations of the lives of relatively famous people. While many criticisms have been levied against psychobiography, advances in method and theory have been observed in recent years, and scholars have developed informal standards for the evaluation of different psychobiographical efforts.

7. To help organize the voluminous data that a psychological biographer might gather, Alexander has delineated nine guidelines for determining which data might prove most useful for the narrative interpretation. He suggests that the data need to be evaluated with respect to primacy, frequency, uniqueness, negation, emphasis, omission, error, isolation, and incompletion.

8. Daniel Levinson and other life-stage theorists have articulated a generic story of adulthood around the metaphor of "seasons of life." Basing his conception on intensive interviews of mainly middle-class, middle-aged American men, Levinson formulated a model of the evolution of a man's life structure from adolescence through middle age. The life structure is the overall design of a man's life. Especially important in the evolution of the structure are the man's articulation of a life dream and the influence of a mentor. An especially dramatic chapter in Levinson's third-person story of adult life is the midlife transition, which typically entails a thoroughgoing re-evaluation of one's life commitments and priorities. While many lifespan researchers agree that important changes in life structure may occur sometime in the midlife years, they disagree on the prevalence of a dramatic and circumscribed midlife crisis. Some efforts have been made to extend Levinson's model to the lives of women, with mixed success.

9. In partial reaction to stage models of adult life, the life course perspective tends to emphasize social timing, social roles and relationships, and the power of human agency and individuality. The life course perspective sees adult development as more historically and culturally determined and socially contingent than is apparent in life-stage theories. According to the life course perspective, life stories are shaped by economic conditions, cultural norms, social change, historical events, and chance happenings. At the same time, individuals exert their own agentic influence on the course of development, co-authoring their lives in a complex and evolving social context.

10. In underscoring human agency and individuality, the life course perspective reminds us of the importance of personality psychology in general and the efforts of personality psychologists to formulate scientifically credible accounts of human individuality.

Glossary

A

A-babies insecurely attached infants who manifest a good deal of avoidant behavior in the presence of the caregiver. Contrast with *B-babies* and *C-babies*.

absolute continuity the extent to which a personality attribute exists in the same amount over time. Absolute continuity usually refers to group averages on personality characteristics assessed at two or more points in time. Contrast to *differential continuity*.

achievement motivation a recurrent preference or desire for experiences of doing well and being successful; also called the "need for achievement." Individual differences in achievement motivation may be assessed through the TAT.

act frequency Buss and Craik's approach to personality study whereby the researcher views personality dispositions as summary categories containing discrete and representative behavioral acts.

action-identification theory a theory suggesting that people may identify the same behavior at many different levels of abstraction, ranging from the most concrete identifications (pushing a finger to hit a computer key) to the most abstract (typing an explanation for why the stock market crashed in 1929). People tend to identify behaviors at the most abstract level at which they feel comfortable.

Adult Attachment Interview an interview for adults developed by Mary Main and colleagues, focused on the person's recollections of his or her own childhood attachments to parents. The interview yields four types of attachment: secure/autonomous, dismissing, preoccupied, and unresolved.

affect a term usually designating emotion.

affiliation motivation a recurrent preference or desire for establishing, maintaining, or restoring positive affective relationships; also called the "need for affiliation." Individual differences in affiliation motivation may be assessed through the TAT.

agency Bakan's general concept for the tendency to separate self from others, to master, dominate, and control the self and the environment. Contrast with *communion*.

agreeableness one of the Big Five traits, agreeableness encompasses personality descriptors having to do with interpersonal warmth, altruism, affection, empathy, cooperation, and other communal facets of personality.

aggregation the principle in psychological measurement that urges an investigator to collect many different samples of the same behavior across many different situations and/or over time in order to obtain a reliable estimate of personality and behavioral trends.

amygdala a small, almond shaped region in the forebrain linked to the experience of fear and responses to danger. Certain parts of the amygdala are hypothesized to be implicated in the working of the behavioral inhibition system (BIS) and, by extension, individual differences in traits associated with negative affectivity, or neuroticism.

anal stage the second stage of psychosexual development, according to Freud, wherein libidinal expression is concentrated in the anus, manifested in bowel movement, and shaped by toilet training.

analytical psychology Carl Jung's theory of personality.

anima the unconscious archetype of femininity in men (Jung).

animus the unconscious archetype of masculinity in women (Jung).

archetypes Jung's structural elements of the collective unconscious, referring to universal patterns or predispositions that influence how all humans consciously and unconsciously adapt to their world. Common archetypes include "the mother," "the child," "the hero," "the anima," "the animus," and "the shadow."

associationism the doctrine that various objects and ideas that are contiguous in time or space come to be connected, or associated, with each other into meaningful units.

attachment a bond of love formed between two people, especially infant and caregiver, in which various behaviors are organized into an evolutionarily adaptive system designed to ensure close physical proximity of the two.

attachment behaviors in infancy, these include sucking, clinging, following, vocalizing, and smiling.

attachment styles three styles of approaching romantic relationships developed from research on adult romantic love. The three styles parallel Ainsworth's attachment types for infants: secure, avoidant, and resistant (anxious/ambivalent).

authoritarian personality a pattern of attitudes and traits suggesting an overly conventional, rigid, aggressive, hostile, and power-oriented kind of person.

autonomy *versus* shame and doubt the second stage in Erikson's scheme of psychosocial development, during which the toddler seeks to establish him- or herself as an independent and competent agent in the environment.

B

B-babies securely attached infants, who use the caregiver as a secure base from which to explore the world. Contrast with *A-babies* and *C-babies*.

behavioral approach system (BAS) in Gray's trait theory, one of two brain systems dealing with human emotionality. As the biological grounding for the trait "impulsivity," the BAS mediates positive affect and arouses a person to seek rewards. The BAS and impulsivity may be contrasted to the BIS (behavioral inhibition system) and anxiety. Other investigators have suggested that the BAS may be related to extraversion.

behavioral inhibition system (BIS) in Gray's trait theory, one of two brain systems dealing with human emotion-

ality. As the biological grounding for the trait "anxiety," the BIS mediates negative affect and motivates a person to inhibit goal-based behavior in order to avoid punishment. The BIS and anxiety may be contrasted to the BAS and impulsivity.

behavior genetics a scientific field, with roots in genetics, biology, psychology, and related fields, that explores the empirical evidence concerning the relative influences of genetic and environmental factors in accounting for variability in human behavior.

behaviorism an intellectual tradition in psychology emphasizing the rigorous and objective study of observable behavior shaped by learning and the environment.

being cognition Maslow's term for perceiving and understanding objects and events in terms of their wholeness.

belief in the species Erikson's term for the adult's hope for and faith in humankind, enabling him or her to be generative.

Big Five five broad personality traits assumed by some researchers to subsume the entire domain of possible traits. According to one formulation, the Big Five are extraversion–introversion, neuroticism, openness to experience, conscientiousness, and agreeableness. See *Five-Factor Model.*

bipolar self Kohut's term for the center of personality, made up of the opposite poles of ambitions and goals, which are connected via a tension arc of talents and skills.

C

California Psychological Inventory (CPI) a popular personality inventory for normal samples providing scores on 20 trait scales.

California Q-sort a standard assessment procedure in which psychologists

sort 100 statements about personality into a normal distribution designed to explain many different facets of a single person.

case study an in-depth investigation of a single individual, sometimes conducted over a substantial period of time.

castration anxiety in Freudian theory, the Oedipal boy's unconscious fear that his penis will be cut off, symbolizing a loss of power.

causal attributions the perceived causes of events.

C-babies insecurely attached infants who manifest a good deal of resistance and ambivalence in the presence of the caregiver. Contrast with *A-babies* and *B-babies*.

character structure in Hogan's socioanalytic theory, the person's characteristic ways of displaying the self to family members, especially parents. Contrast with *role structure.*

characteristic adaptation a motivational, cognitive, or developmental concern the meaning of which comes in part from the particular temporal, situational, or social role–oriented context within which it is embedded. Characteristic adaptations—such as goals, motives, plans, schemas, and stages—comprise Level 2 of personality, as set forth in this textbook. Level 1 is made up of dispositional traits and Level 3 is made up of integrative life stories.

classical conditioning a form of simple learning whereby an unconditioned stimulus is repeatedly paired with a conditioned stimulus such that the conditioned stimulus, originally not likely to evoke a response, comes to be associated with the unconditioned stimulus so that it eventually does evoke a conditioned response.

client-centered therapy Rogers's brand of psychotherapy, emphasizing empathy, sincerity, warmth, acceptance, role playing, and respect for the dignity of the client.

cognitive deconstruction
Baumeister's characterization of the dramatic slide from higher-order and abstract thinking to a narrowly focused and concrete frame of mind that may accompany periods of severe distress, even leading up to suicide.

cognitive niche   the particular position that human beings have evolved to occupy in the evolutionary landscape, whereby their main adaptive advantages center on the computational powers of the human mind. The human mind has evolved to enable human beings to adapt to the many threats and challenges faced in the environment through mental manipulations of situations, innovative strategies for attaining goals, analysis, reasoning, language, and so on.

cognitive/social-learning/person variables   Mischel's characteristic styles or strategies for approaching situations. Mischel lists five types of cognitive/social learning/person variables: competencies, encoding strategies, expectancies, subjective values, and self-regulatory systems and plans.

cognitive styles   characteristic and typically preferred modes of processing information, such as field independence–dependence and integrative complexity.

cohort effect   a finding with respect to a particular psychological phenomenon that is a function of the particular historical cohort being studied, rather than, say, due to developmental factors. In cross-sectional studies, it is difficult to disentangle cohort and developmental effects because different age cohorts are examined at the same time.

collective unconscious   Jung's concept for an inherited storehouse of human potential that is a result of the evolution of the species, containing unconscious patterns and images called *archetypes*.

collectivism   as a cultural construct, a meaning system emphasizing the priority of the collective or in-group over and against the individual self. Many Asian societies are considered to be relatively collectivist. Contrast to *individualism*.

commitment script   one kind of script identified by Tomkins, in which a person binds him- or herself to a life program or goal that promises the reward of intense positive affect.

common trait   Allport's term for any trait that can be viewed as a disposition upon which many people differ. From the standpoint of nomothetic research, psychologists often study common traits, comparing and contrasting people's trait scores. Contrast to *personal disposition*.

communion   Bakan's general concept for the tendency to merge or unite with others, to surrender the self as part of a larger whole. Contrast with *agency*.

complex   in Jung's theory, a clustering of emotionally charged ideas through which the psyche expresses itself.

condensation   an aspect of Freud's concept of dream work whereby different latent elements are fused into a single manifest element.

conditioned generalized reinforcers in operant conditioning, reinforcers that acquire their power because of their associations with a large variety of other reinforcers.

conditions of worth   in Rogers's theory, the belief that some aspects of one's experience are good or worthy and others are not worthy.

conscientiousness   one of the Big Five traits, conscientiousness encompasses personality descriptors denoting self-control, dependability, responsibility, persistence, and an achievement-oriented approach to life.

conservation of energy   the 19th-century idea, adopted by Freud in his

libido theory, that a system runs on a fixed amount of energy that cannot be created or destroyed.

construct validity   the extent to which a test measures the construct that it is theoretically intended to measure. Construct validity increases as empirical support is garnered for the various propositions contained in the construct's nomological net. Construct validity is the most basic and encompassing form of validity, and other forms of validity can be seen as derivatives of it.

contamination sequence   a movement in a life story from an affectively positive to an affectively negative scene. Contrast with *redemption sequence*.

content validity   the degree to which the items of a test cover the entire content domain of a construct and are not confounded with other domains.

context of discovery   the process of discovering new ideas and building theories in science. Contrast with *context of justification*.

context of justification   the process of testing ideas derived from theory in science. Contrast with *context of discovery*.

continuous reinforcement   reinforcement of a particular response after every occurrence. Contrast with *partial reinforcement*.

convergent validity   the extent to which different measures of the same construct relate to each other. Contrast with *discriminant validity*.

coping strategies   patterns of thought and behavior aimed at relieving anxiety and stress.

correlational design   a methodology for research whereby the scientist examines the extent to which variables covary or relate to each other. Contrast with *experimental design*.

countertransference   a term used in psychoanalytic therapy to refer to the therapist's tendency to relate to the patient in a way that unconsciously repeats or plays out his or her (the therapist's) own relationships with personally important people. Contrast with *transference*.

criterion-key method of test construction a method of test construction employed with the MMPI, in which items are chosen solely for their differential endorsement by subjects in different criterion groups.

criterion validity the extent to which a test is associated with external behaviors that it is designed to predict.

cross-sectional study a research design in which different age cohorts are compared to each other at a given point in time. Contrast to *longitudinal study*.

culture a tradition of rules and mores embraced by a particular society of people.

D

D-babies a recent classification category in attachment research, the D-baby suffers from disorganized or disoriented attachment patterns with the caregiver, appearing dazed and confused in the presence of the attachment object. This pattern is found among some victims of child abuse.

death instincts Freud's concept for a group of instinctual drives assumed to motivate the person toward behavior and experience promoting one's own death and destruction or aggression toward others. Contrast with *Eros* and *life instincts*.

declarative-episodic knowledge knowledge of experiences, thoughts, and actions of other people (person memory) and one's personal autobiographical record (autobiographical memory).

declarative-semantic knowledge abstract and categorical information that the person gleans over time concerning various phenomena.

deduction reasoning from the abstract and general to the concrete and particular. Contrast with *induction*.

defense mechanisms unconscious strategies of the ego (Freud) designed to distort reality in order to lessen anxiety.

denial a primitive defense mechanism in which the person baldly refuses to acknowledge an anxiety-provoking event.

depressive schemas the overly negativistic frameworks for interpreting reality that depressed people often employ.

developmental elaboration the process through which childhood temperament dimensions may gradually develop into full-fledged personality traits in adulthood. Caspi has identified six mechanisms of developmental elaboration: learning processes, environmental elicitation, environmental construal, social and temporal comparisons, environmental selection, and environmental manipulation.

dialectical humanism Fromm's view that the person's behavior is the complex and overdetermined product of internal needs manifesting themselves within the external social arrangements prescribed by a society at a particular moment in history.

dialogical self Hermans's concept of the self as a multiple narrator of experience. The dialogical self is a dynamic multiplicity of relatively autonomous I positions in an imagined landscape. Each I position develops its own voice, or point of view.

differential continuity the longitudinal consistency of individual differences. Differential continuity assesses the extent to which people maintain their relative positions within a particular distribution with respect to a particular personality characteristic over time. Contrast to *absolute continuity*.

difficult babies one of three temperament types identified by Thomas, Chess, and Birch, referring to babies with consistently negative moods, intense emotional reactions, and irregular sleeping and eating cycles. Contrast with *easy babies* and *slow-to-warm-up babies*.

discriminant validity the extent to which different measures of different constructs do *not* relate to each other.

displacement an aspect of Freud's concept of dream work whereby the dreamer unconsciously shifts the emphasis in a dream from an important but threatening source to a trivial but safer one, as when one displaces a powerful emotion from its intended object to a substitute.

display rules societal norms for the expression of different emotions.

dopamine a neurotransmitter implicated in reward-seeking behavior and the experience of pleasure.

dream work Freud's term for the processes utilized unconsciously by the dreamer as he or she creates a manifest dream from latent unconscious material. Aspects of dream work include condensation, displacement, symbolism, and secondary revision.

E

easy babies one of three temperament types identified by Thomas, Chess, and Birch, referring to babies with consistently positive mood, low-to-moderate intensity of emotional reactions, and regular sleeping and eating cycles. Contrast with *difficult babies* and *slow-to-warm-up babies*.

ego one of three divisions in Freud's structural model of the mind, serving as the mediator among the id, super-ego, and external reality, and operating according to the reality principle. According to Loevinger, a person's overall framework of meaning, the master synthesizing I.

ego control the extent to which a person is able to reign in impulses ranging from extreme undercontrol to overcontrol. One of two basic dimensions of personality in Jack Block's approach to personality typologies. See also *ego resiliency.*

ego integrity *versus* despair the eighth and last stage of psychosocial development in Erikson's scheme, associated with old age and the acceptance or rejection of one's own life as something that was.

ego psychology a modern derivative of Freudian theory emphasizing the adaptive and integrating power of the ego over and against the id and superego.

ego resiliency the capacity to modify one's typical level of ego control—toward either more control or less control of impulses—to adapt to demands of the situation. One of the two basic dimensions of personality in Jack Block's approach to personality typologies. See also *ego control.*

Embedded Figures Test a test of field-independence/field-dependence in which a person attempts to find forms hidden in an embedding field.

emergenesis an emergent property of a configuration of genes. Some personality characteristics may be a product of emergenesis whereby a unique combination of genes produces an effect that would not be produced, in even an attenuated form, by the parts that make up the configuration. See also *nonadditive genetic variance.*

entity theory a person's implicit belief that human attributes are fixed entities. Contrast with *incremental theory.*

entrepreneurship a collection of behavioral and attitudinal characteristics associated with high achievement motivation, including moderate risk taking, personal responsibility for performance, striving for productivity and innovative change, and careful attention to costs and profits.

environment of evolutionary adaptedness (EEA) the hypothesized world of the Pleistocene Epoch during which human beings evolved and human nature was forged. It is believed that humans evolved over a 2 to 4 million

year span as hunters and gatherers living in small, migratory groups.

erogenous zones bodily sites for libidinal expression, including the mouth, anus, and genitals.

Eros Freud's *life instincts.*

expectancy in Rotter's and Mischel's social-learning theories, a subjectively held probability that a particular reinforcement will occur as the outcome of a specific behavior.

experience sampling method method of collecting samples of daily behavior, thought, and affect through the use of electronic pagers and other such devices.

experimental design a methodology for research whereby the scientist manipulates or alters one variable of interest (the independent variable) to observe its effect on another variable of interest (the dependent variable).

explanatory style the characteristic way in which a person attributes cause in explaining social events. A debilitating explanatory style is implicated in depression. Depressed people tend to explain negative events in their lives as due to internal, stable, and global causes.

exploitative type Fromm's characterization of the aggressive and self-centered person, who exploits other people and the environment.

extraversion–introversion a broad personality trait identified in many theories (including Eysenck's and Jung's) denoting a tendency to be outgoing, sociable, and impulsive on the one hand (extraversion) versus a tendency to be inwardly oriented, withdrawn, and deliberate on the other (introversion).

F

face validity the extent to which test items seem, in the eyes of the respondent, to measure what they are supposed to measure.

factor analysis a statistical procedure through which various items (as

on a self-report questionnaire) are correlated with each other to determine the empirical clustering of the items.

feedback the self-regulation of a system through the repeated accumulation of information concerning the system's deviation from a particular set point or goal.

feedback hierarchy a system in which the output of one feedback loop becomes the reference value for the feedback loop that is subordinate to it.

feminist (approaches to interpretation) approaches to the interpretation of life stories that place gender at the center of the inquiry and tend to emphasize the effects of social and cultural factors on the similar and different ways in which men and women make lives.

fictional finalism Adler's concept for an envisioned end or goal with respect to which the person orients his or her strivings. The goal is fictional in that it has not been realized and indeed may likely not be fully realized, but it still serves to energize and direct behavior.

field-independence/field-dependence a general dimension of cognitive style ranging from highly analytical and differentiated processing of information (field-independence) to highly contextual and global processing (field-dependence).

Five Factor Model a conception of personality traits that has become increasingly accepted in recent years, indicating that traits can be grouped into five basic categories. See *Big Five.*

folk concepts on the California Psychological Inventory (CPI), the name employed for the various trait scales to denote categories of personality that arise naturally out of human interactions in most, if not all, societies. Examples of the folk-concept scales include "responsibility," "socialization," and "flexibility."

foreclosure one of Marcia's four identity statuses, referring to the person who has not explored identity options but has rather made commitments to identity goals and outcomes that arose from childhood and remained unquestioned.

formal operations Piaget's term for abstract, hypothetico-deductive thinking, generally evidenced in adolescence and adulthood.

free association a procedure used in psychoanalytic therapy in which the patient lets his or her mind wander in response to a stimulus or event and reports all thoughts (associations) aloud to the therapist, spontaneous and uncensored.

fully functioning person in Rogers's theory, the person who has attained maturity and actualization and is therefore consciously aware of the many different facets of his or her life and able to symbolize many seeming inconsistent aspects of experience and integrate them into a coherent whole.

fundamental attribution error a general tendency for people to overemphasize traits and underemphasize situations in explaining the causes of other people's behavior.

G

gender schema theory Sandra Bem's theory concerning the ways in which people differ with respect to their tendency to understand their life and the world in gender-related terms.

generation those people born at the same point in historical time and who thereby develop a shared understanding of the world, common beliefs and aims, and a shared generational style.

generativity *versus* stagnation the seventh stage of psychosocial development in Erikson's scheme, in which the adult seeks to guide the next generation and generate a legacy of the self.

genital stage Freud's fifth and last stage of psychosexual development,

attained at puberty with full sexual maturation.

H

hagiographies biographical accounts of the lives of Christian saints written in the Middle Ages to venerate the Christian life.

heritability quotient a numerical estimate of the proportion of variability in a given characteristic that can be attributed to genetic differences between people.

hermeneutics the art and science of interpreting texts.

higher-order conditioning the formation of complex associations in classical conditioning through which conditioned stimuli, which have obtained their eliciting power through associations with unconditioned stimuli, come to be associated with other neutral stimuli, which themselves become conditioned stimuli by virtue of the association.

hoarding type Fromm's characterization of the person who strives to accumulate possessions, power, and love, and to hold on to all that is accumulated.

humanistic psychology a general orientation in psychology that rose to prominence in the 1960s, emphasizing the creative, optimistic, and self-actualizing tendencies of human beings.

hysteria a form of psychopathology in which a person suffers from bodily symptoms, such as blindness or paralysis, that have no physical or biological cause.

I

Icarus complex Murray's concept for a cluster of themes in personality functioning, including urethral erotism, ascensionism, cynosural narcism, falling, craving for immortality,

and depreciation and enthrallment of women—all modeled after the ancient Greek story of Icarus.

id one of three main divisions in Freud's structural model of the mind, serving as the home for instinctual impulses of sex and aggression and their unconscious derivative wishes, fantasies, and inclinations.

identification Freud's concept for the unconscious desire to "be" or to "be like" the other person. Contrast with *object choice.*

identity achievement one of Marcia's four identity statuses, referring to the person who has explored various identity options and successfully made commitments to realistic identity goals.

identity diffusion one of Marcia's four identity statuses, referring to the person who has not yet explored identity options and who has not made commitments.

identity status Marcia's concept referring to the extent to which a young person has explored and made commitments to different identity options, especially in the realms of occupation and ideology. The four statuses are identity achievement, moratorium, foreclosure, and identity diffusion.

identity *versus* role confusion the fifth stage in Erikson's scheme of psychosocial development, during which the adolescent strives to answer the questions "Who am I?" and "How do I fit into the adult world?"

ideological setting in the life-story model of identity, the background of a person's fundamental beliefs and values which provide the life story with a taken-for-granted setting.

idiographic Allport's term for an approach to personality study that focuses on the uniqueness of the individual case. Also called morphogenic. Contrast with *nomothetic.*

I–E Scale a popular self-report measure of locus of control, developed by Rotter.

inclusive fitness an organism's overall (total, inclusive) ability to maximize the replication of the genes that were operative in its design. Natural selection has designed organisms to act in ways that maximize inclusive fitness. In human beings, behavioral systems and mechanisms that work, directly or indirectly, to promote the reproduction of one's own genes (and those same genes one shares with biological relatives) enhance inclusive fitness.

inclusive mode Erikson's concept for the young girl's characteristic approach to the world, involving "teasing, demanding, and grasping" in an attempt to "snare" others.

incremental theory a person's implicit belief that human attributes are changeable characteristics that may be improved with effort. Contrast to *entity theory.*

individual differences characteristics of persons that can be said to differ with respect to amount or degree from one person to the next. Such concepts as personality "traits," "motives," "schemas," and "stages" are typically understood as aspects of individual differences in personality. These may be contrasted to *species-typical characteristics,* which are assumed to be more-or-less universal features of persons, that is, most all members of the human species.

individual psychology a term used to designate the personality theory developed by Alfred Adler.

individuation the full development of the self in Jungian theory, understood as a dynamic, complex, and life-long process whereby the person seeks to synthesize the various opposites in personality in order to become whole (Jung).

individualism as a cultural construct, a meaning system emphasizing the autonomy and independence of the individual over and against the collective. The United States, Canada, Australia, and the democracies of northern and western Europe are considered to be relatively individualist cultures. Contrast to *collectivism.*

induction reasoning from the concrete and the particular to the abstract and general. Contrast with *deduction.*

industry *versus* inferiority the fourth stage in Erikson's scheme of psychosocial development, during which the schoolboy or schoolgirl receives systematic instruction from social institutions and begins to learn how to use the tools and adopt the characteristic roles of society.

initiative *versus* guilt the third stage in Erikson's scheme of psychosocial development, during which the young child experiences the Oedipus complex and becomes increasingly concerned with issues of power and taking initiative.

instinct for Freud, a mental representation of a physical or bodily need. Instincts are the ultimate motivators of behavior, providing the energy whereby action is driven and guided. In modern ethology, instincts are biologically rooted and adaptive motivational tendencies giving rise to particular urges, emotions, and behavioral plans that can be influenced, within limits, by the environment.

instrumental conditioning learning influenced by reinforcement and punishment. See *operant conditioning.*

integrative complexity the extent to which a person sees and interprets events in differentiated and integrated ways.

interactionism the general view that behavior is a function of the interaction of the person and the environment.

internalized objects internal representations of others with whom one has been involved in emotionally charged relationships, as discussed in object-relations theories.

interview a method of collecting data whereby the interviewer asks questions and engages the subject in a conversation with a purpose.

intimacy motivation a recurrent preference or desire for experiences of warm, close, and communicative interaction with others. Individual differences in intimacy motivation may be assessed through the TAT.

intimacy status parallel to Marcia's concept of *identity status,* referring to the characteristic quality of a person's interpersonal relationships and commitments at a given point in time. At least four statuses have been identified: intimate, preintimate, stereotyped relationships, and isolate.

intimacy *versus* isolation the sixth stage of psychosocial development in Erikson's scheme, in which the young adult seeks to establish long-term affiliations with spouse, co-workers, friends, and so on.

intrinsic motivation motivation from within, rather than from external reinforcers and rewards.

intrusive mode Erikson's concept for the young boy's characteristically phallic and aggressive approach to the world.

item analysis a procedure in test construction whereby the investigator determines the relative contribution of each item to the total score on the test.

K

kin selection one evolutionary principle used to explain altruism, whereby an organism will engage in a helping or even self-sacrificial behavior that promotes the survival or reproductive success of kin.

L

latency Freud's fourth stage of psychosexual development, associated with elementary-school years, wherein the libido is rarely expressed in an overt manner.

L-data one of three data sources for Cattell; information pertaining to a person's real-life behavior, such as ratings of the person's behavior made by peers or spouse. Contrast to *Q-data* and *T-data*.

lexical hypothesis the idea that the most important individual differences in personality functioning are encoded in language. Many researchers working with the lexical hypothesis have argued for a five-factor model of personality traits.

libido Freud's concept for the sensual energy of sexual or life instincts.

life course the span of human life. The "life course perspective" in psychology today tends to emphasize the influence of social context, history, timing, social roles, and human agency on the multiple developmental pathways that people follow over time.

life instincts Freud's concept for a group of instincts serving sexual reproduction and survival. Contrast with *death instincts.*

life review the process of taking stock of one's entire life, often evidenced in old age.

life-story model of identity the view that identity may be seen as a dynamic life story integrating a person's reconstructed past, present, and anticipated future into a coherent narrative whole that provides life with unity and purpose.

life story an internalized and evolving narrative of the self that integrates the reconstructed past, perceived present, and anticipated future. Beginning in late adolescence and young adulthood, many persons in modern societies construct life stories to provide their lives with some semblance of unity, purpose, and meaning. Life stories confer upon personality the quality of "identity." Life stories comprise

Level 3 of personality. Level 1 is made up of dispositional traits, and Level 2 is made up of characteristic adaptations.

life structure Levinson's concept referring to the overall patterning or design of an individual's life at a given time.

locus of control a personality dimension referring to individual differences in the extent to which a person believes that reinforcements are contingent on his or her behavior. A person who believes that behavior will lead to predictable reinforcements is said to have an *internal* locus of control; the person who believes that behavior and reinforcements tend to be unrelated—thus, assuming that external forces such as luck, fate, or powerful others determine reinforcement—is said to have an *external* locus of control.

longitudinal study a study in which researchers follow the same group of individuals over time to assess continuity and change in personality characteristics. Contrast to *cross-sectional study.*

M

macrocontext the most encompassing and distal contexts for behavior, including social class, gender, race, culture, and the historical context.

mandala the ancient symbol of unity, representing individuation in Jungian psychology.

marketing type Fromm's characterization of the person who seeks to market him- or herself as a commodity to be bought and sold in the societal and interpersonal marketplace.

mechanistic interactionism the procedure of partitioning the variance in behavior into that accounted for by the person, by the situation, and by the person-situation interaction. Contrast with *reciprocal interactionism.*

metatrait the trait of having or not having a particular trait, which is con-

ceptually independent of one's score on a trait scale. For a given trait, the behavior of "traited" people (those who "have" the trait) should be more predictable from trait scores than the behavior of "untraited" people (those who do not have the trait).

microcontext the more immediate and short-term environmental contexts for behavior, such as the particular social situation within which a person's behavior is displayed.

midlife crisis a period of profound personal questioning and reformulations reported by some men and women during their late 30s, 40s, or early 50s.

Minnesota Multiphasic Personality Inventory (MMPI) A very widely used personality inventory, containing 550 true-false statements and 10 different clinical scales.

modernity a cultural concept referring to the economic, political, and cultural systems spawned by the Industrial Revolution and related developments in the 19th and 20th centuries. Modernity ushered in a new way of thinking about the self—the self as a reflexive project that a person works on. Given that the modern self has considerable depth and dynamism, a major psychological challenge for modern people is to integrate the self into a unifying and purposeful whole.

monoamine oxidase (MAO) an enzyme responsible for breaking down neurotransmitters in the synapses between nerve cells. Individuals high in the sensation seeking trait tend to have lower levels of MAO in their bloodstreams.

moratorium one of Marcia's four identity statuses, referring to the person who is currently exploring various identity options but has not yet made commitments.

morphogenic see *idiographic.*

motivation a term used to denote the forces and factors, usually viewed as residing within the person, that energize and direct behavior. Common motivational ideas in personality psychology include wants, desires, needs, goals, strivings, projects, and tasks.

motive a term sometimes used synonymously with Murray's *need*. McClelland defines a motive as a recurrent preference or readiness for a particular quality of experience, which energizes, directs, and selects behavior in certain situations.

N

narcissism a preoccupation with the self, manifested in an apparent excess of self-love, grandiose sense of self-importance, and the need for constant attention and praise.

narrative identity a term used to refer to the integrative life story that people begin to construct in late adolescence in order to provide their lives with meaning and purpose. See also *life story*.

narrative mode one of two general modes of human thought, according to Jerome Bruner, referring to the human tendency to make sense of experience through stories. Stories are centrally concerned with the vicissitudes of human intention organized in time. Contrast to *paradigmatic mode*.

natural selection the process whereby those characteristics of organisms that promote survival and reproductive success come to predominate over less-adaptive characteristics in the course of evolution.

need in Murray's theory, a construct that stands for a force in the brain region that organizes perception, apperception, intellection, conation, and action in such a way as to transform in a certain direction an existing unsatisfying situation.

need hierarchy Maslow's ladder of needs, in which physiological needs provide a foundation for the succes-sive emergence and satisfaction of safety needs, belongingness and love needs, esteem needs, and actualizing needs, respectively.

negative identities Erikson's term for representations, often embodied in other people, of everything that a person does *not* want to become.

NEO-PI-R the Neuroticism-Extraversion-Openness Personality Inventory Revised, developed by Costa and McCraw. The NEO-PI-R is a 240-item self-report inventory designed to measure the Big Five traits of neuroticism, extraversion, openness to experience, agreeableness, and conscientiousness. For each of the five traits, there are six sub-scales assessing individual facets of that trait.

neuroticism a broad personality trait, identified primarily with the theory of Eysenck, denoting a tendency to experience chronic anxiety, depression, emotional lability, nervousness, moodiness, hostility, vulnerability, self-consciousness, and hypochondriasis.

nomological network the interlocking system of propositions that constitute the theory of a given construct and the empirical findings that support or fail to support those propositions.

nomothetic Allport's term for an approach to personality study that seeks to discover general laws for all persons. Contrast with *idiographic*.

nonadditive genetic variance the configural or interactive influence of genes on traits. Nonadditive genetic variance has been invoked to explain why the ratio of trait concordance for MZ twins and DZ twins is sometimes greater than 2.0, as in the case of recent studies on extraversion.

nonshared environment a term referring to the effects on personality characteristics that come from environments that family members do not share. Nonshared environmental effects are environmental influences that operate to make family members different from each other. Contrast with *shared environment*.

nuclear episode in the life-story model of identity, a particular scene that stands out in the story as especially important, often a high point, low point, or turning point in the story.

nuclear scene in Tomkins' script theory, a very good childhood scene that eventually turns very bad.

nuclear script one kind of script identified by Tomkins, marked by ambivalence and confusion about one's life goals.

O

object choice Freud's concept for the unconscious desire to "have" the other (another person) in a powerful and sensual way. In object choice, the person seeks to invest his or her libido, or sexual energy, in another. Contrast with *identification*.

object-relations theories a group of theories, owing varying intellectual debts to Freud, which center around the person's emotionally charged relationships with other people and the resultant development of representations of those people in the unconscious realms of the mind.

observational learning learning through observing an event and then imitating what is observed.

Oedipus complex Freud's concept denoting an unconscious struggle of power and sensuality experienced by boys and girls in the phallic stage of psychosexual development. In short, the child unconsciously desires to have the parent of the opposite sex in a powerful and sensual way but ultimately is forced to renounce that desire and settle for an unconscious identification with the same-sex parent.

openness to experience a broad personality trait, assessed by Costa and McCrae among others, designating a cluster of characteristics having to do with how reflective, imaginative, artistic, and refined a person is.

operant conditioning learning influenced by reinforcement and punishment through which behavior is modified by its consequences. In operant conditioning, freely emitted behaviors will increase when followed by positive consequences (reinforcement) or decrease when followed by negative consequences (punishment).

oral stage the first stage of psychosexual development, according to Freud, wherein the libido is expressed mainly through oral activities.

organ inferiorities Adler's concept for deficits and anomalies in the person with respect to which the person strives to compensate.

organismic valuing process in Rogers' theory, the fully functioning person's ability to view events and developments from the standpoint of his or her own growth and maturation.

overdetermination Freud's idea that the manifest content of dreams, symptoms, and certain other forms of behavior and experience are determined or caused by a vast amount of latent material, including unconscious wishes, impulses, and conflicts.

P

paradigmatic mode (of thought) one of two general modes of human thought, identified by Jerome Bruner, referring to the human ability to understand reality through tightly reasoned analyses, propositional logic, and cause-and-effect relationships in the physico-chemical world. Contrast to *narrative mode*.

partial reinforcement intermittent reinforcement of a particular response. Contrast with *continuous reinforcement*.

pattern-matching plan a procedure whereby an investigator seeks to find conceptual coherence in a case study according to certain preconceived theoretical assumptions or hypotheses.

peak experiences episodes in one's life filled with joy, excitement, wonder, and so on; emphasized as signs of self-actualization in Maslow's humanistic theory.

penis envy in Freudian theory, the Oedipal girl's unconscious disappointment concerning her lack of a penis, symbolizing a lack of power.

personal construct Kelly's concept of a characteristic way of construing how some things are alike and some things are different from each other.

personal disposition Allport's term for any trait that is especially characteristic of a particular individual. From the standpoint of the idiographic examination of the single case, the psychologist may search for a handful of personal dispositions that express the particular person's uniqueness. Contrast to *common trait*.

personality inventories self-report questionnaires containing many personality-trait scales.

Personality Research Form (PRF) a personality inventory assessing individual differences in 20 of Murray's psychogenic needs.

personal projects activities with which a person is currently involved that are designed to achieve personal goals.

personal strivings characteristic goals that individuals try to achieve through their daily behavior.

phallic stage the third stage of psychosexual development, according to Freud, wherein the libido is expressed through the genital region. The phallic stage is associated with ages 3–5 years and centers around the *Oedipus complex*.

phenomenal field Rogers' term for the entire panorama of a person's experience, and subjective apprehension of reality.

pleasure principle in Freudian theory, the principle whereby the id operates, dictating that the individual seek immediate gratification of instinctual impulses and wishes. Contrast with *reality principle*.

positive reinforcement the presentation of a stimulus that increases the probability of the behavior it follows, commonly viewed as a reward.

possible selves a person's representations of what he or she would like to become, might become, or would be afraid to become.

postmodern referring to a diverse set of trends perceived in Western culture since the 1970s and emphasizing a skeptical and ironically playful attitude toward grand systems, universal truths, and authoritative conventions of virtually every kind.

power motivation a recurrent preference or desire for experiences of having an impact on others and on one's own environment; also called the "need for power." Individual differences in power motivation may be assessed through the TAT.

press in Murray's theory, a term denoting a determinant of behavior in the environment. A press can be seen as a situational opportunity or obstacle to the expression of a need in behavior.

primary process a very loose and irrational form of thinking driven by instinctual demands and associated with Freud's *id*. Contrast with *secondary process*.

procedural knowledge various competencies, strategies, and rules that enable the person to form impressions of others, make attributions, encode and retrieve memories, and predict social behaviors.

productive type Fromm's characterization of the most mature personality type, manifested in the person who fulfills his or her inner potential to become a creative worker and lover within a well-defined social identity.

projection a common defense mechanism in which the person attributes unacceptable internal states and qualities to external others.

proprium Allport's concept for the self, or all aspects of personality that make for inward unity.

psychoanalysis a general term for the approach to psychology pioneered by Freud and others who tend to focus on the unconscious determinants of behavior, intrapsychic conflict, and instinctual drives concerning sexuality and aggression. The term also denotes the process of engaging in psychotherapy from a psychoanalytic standpoint.

psychobiography the systematic use of psychological (especially personality) theory to transform a life into a coherent and illuminating story.

psychological androgyny the combination of masculine and feminine characteristics. A person who is highly androgynous sees him- or herself as possessing traits highly characteristic of both masculine and feminine sex-role stereotypes.

psychological magnification in Tomkins's script theory, the process of connecting related scenes into a meaningful pattern. Positive affect scenes are often magnified through the production of variants, or variations around a stable core. Negative affect scenes are often magnified through the production of analogs, or the detection of similarities in different scenes.

Q

Q-data one of three data sources for Cattell; self-report data on questionnaires, such as self-ratings and scores on self-report personality questionnaires. Contrast to *L-data* and *T-data*.

R

range of convenience Kelly's concept of the extent to which a given personal construct is likely to guide a person's interpretation of events and the behavior he or she is likely to show.

reality principle in Freudian theory, the principle whereby the ego operates, pushing the individual toward behavior aimed at coping with conflicting demands, rationally weighing choices, and defending against various threats to the well-being of the person. Contrast with *pleasure principle*.

receptive type Fromm's characterization of the person who fulfills his or her needs by adopting a passive and dependent orientation in life, manifesting traits of cowardice, submissiveness, and sentimentality.

reciprocal altruism one evolutionary principle used to explain altruism, whereby an organism will aid another organism when such behavior is likely to result in reciprocation of the aid by the other organism at a later time.

reciprocal interactionism the viewpoint suggesting that behavior, the person, and the environment influence each other through repeated and mutual transactions. Contrast with *mechanistic interactionism*.

redemption sequence a movement in a life story from an affectively negative to an affectively positive scene. Contrast with *contamination sequence*.

reformulated learned-helplessness theory an attributional interpretation of depressive cognition, emphasizing the depressed person's tendency to explain negative events in his or her life as caused by internal, stable, and global factors.

reinforcement value in Rotter's social-learning theory, the subjective attractiveness of a particular reinforcement.

relational schema a cognitive structure representing regularities in patterns of interpersonal relationships. As an important aspect of declarative-semantic knowledge in social intelligence, relational schemas encode important information about what to expect when interacting with certain people and, therefore, serve as cognitive maps in navigating the social world.

reliability the consistency of a particular measure. Three forms of reliability are test–retest, split-half, and interscorer.

repression Freud's concept for the process of casting thoughts, memories, feelings, and conflicts out of consciousness, rendering them unremembered.

repressors as operationalized in recent research, individuals who show low levels of anxiety but high levels of defensiveness. Research suggests that repressors have less access than do other people to negative emotional memories about the self.

Role Construct Repertory (Rep) Test Kelly's test designed to explore personal constructs in people's lives.

role structure in Hogan's socioanalytic theory, the person's characteristic ways of displaying self to one's colleagues, friends, peers, and children, and even to society at large.

Romanticism an intellectual movement in Western civilization (circa 1790–1850) rejecting classical teachings of reason, order, and the common good in favor of the celebration of the vigorous and passionate life of the individual.

root metaphor a basic analogy for understanding the world. Pepper has identified the following root metaphors: animism, mysticism, formism, mechanism, organicism, and contextualism.

S

scene a concept in Tomkins's script theory referring to a specific happening or event in one's life that contains at least one affect and one object of the affect.

schema an abstract knowledge structure.

script according to Tomkins, a set of rules for interpreting, creating, enhancing, or defending against a family of related scenes. According to Abelson, encoded knowledge of stereotypic event sequences.

secondary process rational cognitive activity associated with the functioning of the ego (Freud). Contrast with *primary process.*

secondary revision an aspect of Freud's concept of dream work whereby the dreamer unconsciously smoothes over the dream's rough spots, fills in gaps, clears up ambiguities, and edits the dream experience into a more-or-less coherent account.

self-actualization a term from humanistic psychology referring to the fundamental human striving toward fulfilling one's entire potential.

self-complexity the degree to which a person's system of self-schemas is differentiated and compartmentalized. Individuals high in self-complexity have many different and separate self-schemas; individuals low in self-complexity have fewer self-schemas.

self-defining memories recollections of events in one's life that the person believes to have been especially influential in shaping the self. According to Singer, self-defining memories are vivid, affectively charged, repetitive, linked to other similar memories, and related to an important theme of enduring concern in the person's life story.

Self-determination theory Deci and Ryan's theory of how rewards interact with intrinsic motivation to shape purposive and intrinsically rewarding behavior. This kind of self-determined behavior often connects to basic needs for autonomy, relatedness, and competence.

self-discrepancy theory a theory put forth by Higgins focusing on the emotional outcomes of various discrepancies among actual, ideal, and ought selves.

self-efficacy Bandura's concept referring to a person's belief that he or she can successfully carry out courses of action required to deal with various challenging situations.

self-esteem a person's subjective, affective evaluation of the self.

self-guides In Higgins' self-discrepancy theory, self-guides are the ideal selves and ought selves against which the person compares the actual self.

self-objects in Kohut's theory, people who are so central to an individual's life that he or she feels that they are part of him or her.

self psychology a contemporary derivative of psychoanalytic theory, championed by Heinz Kohut, which is concerned with how people find unity and cohesiveness in life.

self-recognition the ability to recognize the self, especially in a mirror reflection as in studies with babies and toddlers.

self-schema an abstract knowledge structure about the self.

sensation seeking the need for varied, novel, and complex sensations and experiences and the willingness to take physical and social risks for the sake of such experiences, measured on a scale developed by Zuckerman.

separation-individuation Mahler's term for the process of gaining independence from early symbiotic unions with caregivers and establishing a coherent sense of self and of others.

shadow the unconscious archetype representing a variety of socially unacceptable, even bestial, desires and impulses, inherited by virtue of humankind's evolution from lower forms (Jung).

shared environment a term referring to the effects on personality characteristics that come from environments that family members have in common. Shared environment effects are environmental influences that operate to make family members alike. Twin and adoption studies suggest that shared environments have very little effect on most personality traits. Contrast to *nonshared environment.*

situational prototypes an abstract set of features about a given class of situations.

situationism a general point of view, linked to social learning theory and the impact of experimental social psychology, that behavior is best explained and predicted by reference to the situation within which behavior occurs. The person-situation debate of the 1970s and early 1980s pitted situationism against trait perspectives in personality psychology.

Sixteen Personality Factor Questionnaire (16PF) Cattell's self-report inventory designed to measure individual differences in 16 source traits.

slow-to-warm-up babies one of three temperament types identified by Thomas, Chess, and Birch, referring to babies with relatively negative moods, low intensity of emotional reactions, and the tendency to withdraw from new events at first but approach them later. Contrast with *easy babies* and *difficult babies.*

social clock a set of expectations about age-appropriate transitions, setting the standards against which individuals evaluate the extent to which their lives are "on time."

social-cognitive approaches to personality theories and conceptions of personality that emphasize the extent to which human beings are information processing systems who use schemas, beliefs, values, expectancies, and other cognitive constructs to guide their behavior in the social world.

social desirability a term denoting the person's desire to present a favorable impression in responding to test items.

social ecology the many different environmental contexts that situate a person's behavior. The social ecology includes the proximal contexts of the immediate situation (microcontexts) as well as the progressively more encompassing and distal contexts of family, community, society, culture, and history.

social intelligence each person's set of skills, abilities, and knowledge about social situations.

social interest Adler's concept for the person's innate sense of kinship with all humanity.

social-learning theories theories, such as those proposed by Rotter, Mischel, and Bandura, that adopt certain emphases of behaviorism but blend these with a greater emphasis on cognitive variables and social relationships.

social structure the conditions of society that differentiate people along the lines of power and status. The most common lens through which to view social structure is social class. Research indicates that social class has a profound effect on how people see themselves and the world.

socioanalytic theory Hogan's theory of personality, emphasizing the evolutionary adaptiveness and ritualized social quality of patterns of human behavior.

sociosexuality the extent to which an individual will (restricted sociosexuality) or will not (unrestricted sociosexuality) insist on closeness and commitment in an interpersonal relationship before engaging in sexual intercourse with the partner. Recent thinking in evolutionary personality psychology suggests that both restricted and unrestricted sociosexuality patterns may have proven adaptive (for both men and women) throughout evolution, in conjunction with various environmental constraints and selection pressures.

source traits Cattell's 16 basic factors underlying the many different surface traits that might be identified.

specification equation Cattell's approach to behavioral prediction whereby different trait scores for an individual are plugged into an equa-tion and given differential weights according to the extent to which each is deemed to be relevant to the particular situation in which behavior is to occur.

split-half reliability the extent to which a test's results are consistent across different parts of the test, that is, the extent of internal consistency in the test.

stimulus generalization the expansion of a conditioned response so that it is evoked in response to a wide variety of stimuli that resemble the conditioned stimulus in some way.

Strange Situation an experimental procedure used to assess individual differences in the quality of caregiver–infant attachment, by subjecting the infant to brief separations from the caregiver and novel events.

striving for superiority Adler's concept for the "great upward drive" of human behavior, leading to perfection, completion, and wholeness.

style of life Adler's term for a person's unique mode of adjustment to life, most notably including the person's self-selected goals and means of achieving them.

superego one of the three main divisions in Freud's structural model of the mind, serving as a primitive internalized representation of the norms and values of society as acquired through identification with the parents at the resolution of the Oedipus complex.

surface traits Cattell's term for the many readily observable traits that can be found as clusterings of related behaviors. Underlying the many surface traits are a smaller number of source traits.

symbolism an aspect of Freud's concept of dream work whereby the dreamer conjures up concrete images and actions that convey hidden but common meanings.

T

TAT see *Thematic Apperception Test.*

T-data one of three data sources for Cattell; observations of behavior under controlled conditions, as in the laboratory. Contrast to *L-data* and *Q-data.*

temperament individual differences in basic behavioral style assumed to be present at birth in some form and, thus, largely biologically determined.

test–retest reliability the extent to which a test's results are consistent over time.

thema in Murray's theory, a particular behavioral unit represented as a need/press interaction.

Thematic Apperception Test (TAT) an assessment procedure, devised by Murray and Morgan, in which the subject writes or tells stories in response to a set of ambiguous picture cues.

theory a set of interrelated statements proposed to explain certain observations about reality.

topographical model Freud's model of the mind, which distinguishes among the conscious, preconscious, and unconscious regions. The conscious corresponds to everyday awareness; the preconscious contains the contents of ordinary memory, to which awareness may be directed at any time; and the unconscious contains wishes, feelings, memories, and so on that have been repressed because they threaten the well-being of the conscious self.

trait a general term in personality psychology referring to an individual-difference variable assumed to reflect an underlying, internal, and stable personality disposition. Traits are generally viewed to be linear and bipolar in nature, additive and independent, and suggestive of relatively broad individual differences in social and/or emotional functioning. Dispositional traits comprise Level 1 of personality, as set forth in this book. Level 2 is made up of characteristic adaptations, and Level 3 is made up of integrative life stories.

transference a term used in psychoanalytic therapy to refer to the patient's tendency to relate to the therapist in a way that unconsciously repeats or plays out his or her relationships with other personally important people. Contrast with *countertransference.*

trust *versus* mistrust the first stage in Erikson's scheme of psychosocial development, in which the infant seeks to establish a hopeful and trusting relation with the environment.

U

unconditional positive regard in Rogers' theory, love and acceptance provided in an uncritical and noncontingent manner.

unconscious the state of being outside of awareness. For Freud, the unconscious is a shadowy realm of the mind wherein reside repressed thoughts, feelings, memories, conflicts, and the like.

utilitarianism intellectual movement of the 18th and 19th centuries, associated with Bentham and Mill, arguing that the general good is defined in terms of the greatest good for the greatest number of people.

V

valuation in Hermans' theory of the self, anything that a person deems important in his or her life situation. Valuations are units of meaning in the life narrative. Each valuation is positive, negative, or ambivalent in emotional tone.

W

Washington University Sentence Completion Test for Ego Development (WUSCTED) Loevinger's standardized assessment device for assessing stages of ego development: impulsive, self-protective, conformist, conformist/conscientious, conscientious, individualistic, autonomous, and integrated.

will to power in Adler's theory, the striving to feel strong and powerful in interactions with the world, later generalized by Adler to become a "striving for superiority."

working model in Bowlby's theory of attachment, a representation of the caregiver built up in the mind of the infant. A working model of the attachment object is an unconscious set of expectations about the caregiver's behavior and one's relation to the caregiver and serves as the earliest template for human love.

References

A

Abramson, L.Y., Seligman, M.E.P., & Teasdale, J.P. (1978). Learned helplessness in humans: Critique and reformulation. *Journal of Abnormal Psychology, 87,* 49–74.

Ackerman, S., Zuroff, D., & Moscowitz, D.S. (2000). Generativity in midlife and young adults: Links to agency, communion, and well-being. *International Journal of Aging and Human Development, 50,* 17–41.

Adams, G.R., Ryan, J.H., Hoffman, J.J., Dobson, W.R., & Nielson, E.C. (1984). Ego identity status, conformity behavior, and personality in later adolescence. *Journal of Personality and Social Psychology, 47,* 1091–1104.

Adler, A. (1927). *The practice and theory of individual psychology.* New York: Harcourt Brace World.

Adler, A. (1930). Individual psychology. In C. Murchison (Ed.), *Psychologies of 1930.* Worcester, MA: Clark University Press.

Adler, A. (1931). *What life should mean to you.* Boston: Little Brown.

Adorno, T.W., Frenkel-Brunswik, E., Levinson, D.J., & Sanford, R.N. (1950). *The authoritarian personality.* New York: Harper & Brothers.

Ainsworth, M.D.S. (1967). *Infancy in Uganda: Infant care and the growth of love.* Baltimore, MD: Johns Hopkins University Press.

Ainsworth, M.D.S. (1969). Object relations, dependency, and attachment: A theoretical review of the infant–mother relationship. *Child Development, 40,* 969–1025.

Ainsworth, M.D.S. (1989). Attachments beyond infancy. *American Psychologist, 44,* 709–716.

Ainsworth, M.D.S., Blehar, M.C., Waters, E., & Wall, T. (1978). *Patterns of attachment.* Hillsdale, NJ: Lawrence Erlbaum.

Ainsworth, M.D.S., & Bowlby, J. (1991). An ethological approach to personality development. *American Psychologist, 46,* 333–341.

Akbar, N. (1991). The evolution of human psychology for African Americans. In R.L. Jones (Ed.), *Black psychology* (3rd ed., pp. 99–124). Berkeley, CA: Cobb & Henry.

Alexander, I.E. (1988). Personality, psychological assessment, and psychobiography. *Journal of Personality, 56,* 265–294.

Aldwin, C.M., & Levensen, M.R. (1994). Aging and personality assessment. In P.M. Lawton and J.A. Teresi (Eds.), *Annual review of gerontology and geriatrics* (Vol. 14, pp. 182–209). New York: Springer.

Alker, H.A. (1972). Is personality situationally specific or intrapsychically consistent? *Journal of Personality, 40,* 1–16.

Allick, J., & Realo, A. (1997). Emotional experience and its relation to the Five-factor model in Estonian. *Journal of Personality, 65,* 625–647.

Allport, G.W. (1937). *Personality: A psychological interpretation.* New York: Holt, Rinehart & Winston.

Allport, G.W. (1942). *The use of personal documents in psychological science.* New York: Social Science Research Council.

Allport, G.W. (1950). *The individual and his religion.* New York: Macmillan.

Allport, G.W. (1954). *The nature of prejudice.* Cambridge, MA: Addison-Wesley.

Allport, G.W. (1955). *Becoming: Basic considerations for a psychology of personality.* New Haven, CT: Yale University Press.

Allport, G.W. (1961). *Pattern and growth in personality.* New York: Holt, Rinehart & Winston.

Allport, G.W. (1965). *Letters from Jenny.* New York: Harcourt, Brace & World.

Allport, G.W. (1968). *The person in psychology: Selected essays.* Boston: Beacon Press.

Allport, G.W., Bruner, J.S., & Jandorf, E.M. (1941). Personality under social catastrophe: Ninety-five life histories of the Nazi revolution. *Character and Personality, 10,* 1–22.

Allport, G.W., & Odbert, H.S. (1936). Trait-names, a psychological study. *Psychological Monographs, 47*(1, Whole No. 211).

Allport, G.W., & Vernon, P.E. (1933). *Studies in expressive movement.* New York: Macmillan.

Altemeyer, B. (1981). *Right-wing authoritarianism.* Winnepeg: University of Manitoba Press.

Altemeyer, B. (1988). *Enemies of freedom: Understanding right-wing authoritarianism.* San Francisco: Jossey-Bass.

Altemeyer, B. (1993). *Authoritarianism in American legislators.* Address at the annual meeting of the International Society of Political Psychology, Cambridge, MA.

Amabile, T.M., DeJong, W., & Lepper, M.R. (1976). Effects of externally imposed deadlines on subsequent intrinsic motivation. *Journal of Personality and Social Psychology, 34,* 92–98.

Amsterdam, B.K. (1972). Mirror self-image reactions before age two. *Developmental Psychology, 5,* 297–305.

Anderson, C.A., & Bushman, B.J. (2002). The effects of media violence on society. *Science, 295,* 2377–2378.

Anderson, C.A., Carnagey, N.L., & Eubanks, J. (2003). Exposure to violent media: The effects of songs with violent lyrics on aggressive thoughts and feelings. *Journal of Personality and Social Psychology, 84,* 960–971.

Anderson, J.W. (1981). Psychobiographical methodology: The case of William James. In L. Wheeler (Ed.), *Review of personality and social psychology* (Vol. 2, pp. 245–272). Beverly Hills, CA: Sage.

Anderson, J.W. (1988). Henry A. Murray's early career: A psychobiographical exploration. *Journal of Personality, 56,* 139–171.

Anderson, L.R., & Blanchard, P.N. (1982). Sex differences in task and social-emotional behavior. *Basic and Applied Social Psychology, 3,* 109–139.

Anderson, W. (1970). *Theophrastus: The character sketches.* Kent, OH: Kent State University Press.

Andrews, J.D.W. (1967). The achievement motive in two types of organizations. *Journal of Personality and Social Psychology, 6,* 163–168.

Andrews, M. (1991). *Lifetimes of commitment: Aging, politics, psychology.* Cambridge: Cambridge University Press.

Angelou, M. (1970). *I know why the caged bird sings.* New York: Random House.

Angleitner, A., & Ostendorf, F. (1994). Temperament and the big five factors of personality. In C.F. Halverson, Jr., G.A. Kohnstamm, and R.P. Martin (Eds.), *The developing structure of temperament and personality from infancy to adulthood* (pp. 69–90). Hillsdale, NJ: Lawrence Elbaum.

Angleitner, A., Ostendorf, F., & John, O.P. (1990). Toward a taxonomy of personality descriptors in German: A psycho-lexical study. *European Journal of Personality, 4,* 89-118.

Angus, L.E., & McLeod, J. (2004). (Eds.). *Handbook of narrative and psychotherapy.* London: Sage.

Anthony, E.J. (1970). The behavior disorders of childhood. In P.H. Mussen (Ed.), *Carmichael's handbook of child psychology* (Vol. 1, pp. 667–764). New York: John Wiley & Sons.

Archer, J. (1988). The sociobiology of bereavement: A reply to Littlefield and Rushton. *Journal of Personality and Social Psychology, 55,* 272–278.

Arend, R., Gove, F.L., & Sroufe, L.A. (1979). Continuity of individual adaptation from infancy to kindergarten: A predictive study of ego-resiliency and curiosity in preschoolers. *Child Development, 50,* 950–959.

Argyle, M., & Little, B.R. (1972). Do personality traits apply to social behavior? *Journal for the Theory of Social Behavior, 2,* 1–35.

Argyle, M., & Lu, L. (1990). Happiness and social skills. *Personality and Individual Differences, 11,* 1255–1262.

Arthur, W., Jr., & Graziano, W.G. (1996). The five-factor model, conscientiousness, and driving accident involvement. *Journal of Personality, 64,* 593–618.

Asendorpf, J.B., & Wilpers, S. (1998). Personality effects on social relationships. *Journal of Personality and Social Psychology, 74,* 1531–1544.

Ashton, M.C., Lee, K., Perguini, M., Szarota, P., de Vries, R.E., Di Blas, L., Boies, K., de Raad, B. (2004). A six-factor structure of personality-descriptive adjectives: Solutions from psycholexical studies in seven languages. *Journal of Personality and Social Psychology, 86,* 356–366.

Atkinson, J.W. (1957). Motivational determinants of risk-taking behavior. *Psychological Review, 64,* 359–372.

Atkinson, J.W. (Ed.). (1958). *Motives in fantasy, action, and society.* Princeton, NJ: D. Van Nostrand.

Atkinson, J.W., & Birch, D. (1978). *An Introduction to motivation* (2nd ed.). New York: D. Van Nostrand.

Atkinson, J.W., Bongort, K., & Price, L.H. (1977). Explorations using computer simulation to comprehend TAT measurement of motivation. *Motivation and Emotion, 1,* 1–27.

Atkinson, J.W., Heyns, R.W., & Veroff, J. (1954). The effect of experimental arousal of the affiliation motive on thematic apperception. *Journal of Abnormal and Social Psychology, 49,* 405–410.

Atkinson, J.W., & Raynor, J.O. (Eds.). (1978). *Motivation and achievement* (2nd ed.). Washington, DC: Winston.

Atkinson, M., & Violato, C. (1994). Neuroticism and coping with anger: The transituational consistency of coping responses. *Personality and Individual Differences, 17,* 769–782.

B

Bagby, R.M., Joffe, R.T., Parker, J.D.A., Kalemba, V., & Harkness, K.L. (1995). Major depression and the five-factor model of personality. *Journal of Personality Disorders, 9,* 224–234.

Bailey, J.M., Gaulin, S., Agyei, Y., & Gladue, B.A. (1994). Effects of gender and sexual orientation on evolutionarily relevant aspects of human mating psychology. *Journal of Personality and Social Psychology, 66,* 1081–1093.

Bakan, D. (1958). *Sigmund Freud and the Jewish mystical tradition.* New York: D. Van Nostrand.

Bakan, D. (1966). *The duality of human existence: Isolation and communion in Western man.* Boston: Beacon Press.

Bakan, D. (1971). *Slaughter of the innocents.* Boston: Beacon Press.

Baker-Brown, G., Ballard, E.J., Bluck, S., de Vries, B., Suedfeld, P., & Tetlock, P.E. (1992). The conceptual/integrative complexity scoring manual. In C.P. Smith (Ed.), *Motivation and personality: Handbook of thematic content analysis* (pp. 401–418). New York: Cambridge University Press.

Bakhtin, M.M. (1973). *Problems of Dostoyevsky's poetics.* Ann Arbor, MI: Ardis. (Transl. By R.W. Rotsel). (Original work published 1929).

Baldwin, J.M. (1897). *Mental development in the child and the race.* New York: Macmillan.

Baldwin, M.W. (1992). Relational schemas and the processing of social information. *Psychological Bulletin, 112,* 461–484.

Ball, D.W. (1972). The definition of situation: Some theoretical and mythological consequences of taking W.I. Thomas seriously. *Journal for the Theory of Social Behaviour, 2,* 61–82.

Baltes, P.B., & Baltes, M.M. (1990). Psychological perspectives on successful aging: The model of selective optimization with compensation. In P.B. Baltes and M.M. Baltes (Eds.), *Successful aging: Perspectives from the behavioral sciences* (pp. 1–34). Cambridge, England: Cambridge University Press.

Bandura, A. (1965). Influence of models' reinforcement contingencies on the acquisitions of imitative responses. *Journal of Personality and social Psychology, 1,* 589–595.

Bandura, A. (1971). *Social learning theory.* Morristown, NJ: General Learning Press.

Bandura, A. (1977). *Social learning theory* (2nd ed.). Englewood Cliffs, NJ: Prentice-Hall.

Bandura, A. (1989). Human agency in social cognitive theory. *American Psychologist, 44,* 1175–1184.

Bandura, A. (1999). Social cognitive theory of personality. In L. Pervin and O. John (Eds.), *Handbook of personality: Theory and research* (2nd ed., pp. 154–196). New York: Guilford Press.

Bandura, A., Ross, D., & Ross, S.A. (1961). Transmission of aggression through imitation of aggressive models. *Journal of Abnormal and Social Psychology, 63,* 575–582.

Bandura, A., Ross, D., & Ross, S.A. (1963). Imitation of film-mediated aggressive models. *Journal of Abnormal and Social Psychology, 66,* 3–11.

Bandura, A., & Schunk, D.H. (1981). Cultivating competence, self-efficacy, and intrinsic interest through proximal self-motivation. *Journal of Personality and Social Psychology, 41,* 586–598.

Barenbaum, N.B. (1997). The case(s) of Gordon Allport. *Journal of Personality, 65,* 743–755.

Barenbaum, N.B., & Winter, D.G. (2003). Personality. In I.B. Weiner (Ed.), *Handbook of psychology: Vol. 1. History of psychology* (pp. 177–203). New York: Wiley.

Barnett, P.A., & Gotlib, I.H. (1988). Psychosocial functioning and depression: Distinguishing among antecedent, concomitant, and consequences. *Psychological Bulletin, 104,* 97–126.

Barresi, J., & Juckes, T.J. (1997). Personology and the narrative interpretation of lives. *Journal of Personality, 65,* 693–719.

Barrett, L.F. (1997). The relationships among momentary emotion experiences, personality descriptions, and retrospective ratings of emotion. *Personality and Social Psychology Bulletin, 23,* 1100–1110.

Barrick, M.R., & Mount, M.K. (1991). The Big Five personality dimensions and job performance: A meta-analysis. *Personnel Psychology, 44,* 1–26.

Barrick, M.R., & Mount, M.K. (1993). Autonomy as a moderator of the relationship between the Big Five personality dimensions and job performance. *Journal of Applied Psychology, 78,* 111–118.

Barron, F. (1969). *Creative person and creative process.* New York: Holt, Rinehart & Winston.

Bateson, M.C. (1990). *Composing a life.* New York: Plume.

Bauer, J.J., & McAdams, D.P. (2004). Personal growth in adults' stories of life transitions. *Journal of Personality, 72,* 573–602.

Baumeister, R.F. (1986). *Identity: Cultural change and the struggle for self.* New York: Oxford University Press.

Baumeister, R.F. (1990). Suicide as escape from self. *Psychological Review, 97,* 90–113.

Baumeister, R.F., Dale, K., & Sommer, K.L. (1998). Freudian defense mechanisms and empirical findings in modern social psychology: Reaction formation, projection, displacement, undoing, isolation, sublimation, and denial. *Journal of Personality, 66,* 1081–1124.

Baumeister, R.F., Stillwell, A., & Wotman, S.R. (1990). Victim and perpetrator accounts of interpersonal conflict: Autobiographical narratives about anger. *Journal of Personality and Social Psychology, 59,* 994–1005.

Baumgarten, F. (1933). Die Charaktereigenschaften. [The character traits.] In *Beitrge zur Charakter und Persnlichkeitsforschung* (Whole No. 1). Bern: A Francke.

Baumrind, D. (1971). Current patterns of parental authority. *Developmental Psychology Monograph, 4*(1, Pt. 2).

Beck, A.T. (1967). *Depression: Clinical, experimental, and theoretical aspects.* New York: Hoeber.

Beck, A.T. (1976). *Cognitive therapy and the emotional disorders.* New York: International Universities Press.

Becker, E. (1973). *The denial of death.* New York: The Free Press.

Becker, S.W., & Eagly, A.H. (2004). The heroism of women and men. *American Psychologist, 59,* 163–178.

Bellah, R.N., Madsen, K., Sullivan, W.M., Sandler, A., & Tipton, S.M. (1985). *Habits of the Heart.* Berkeley, CA: University of California Press.

Bellah, R.N., Madsen, R., Sullivan, W.M., Swidler, A., & Tipton, S.M. (1991). *The good society.* New York: Knopf.

Belsky, J., Crnic, K., & Woodworth, S. (1995). Personality and parenting: Exploring the mediating role of transient mood and daily hassles. *Journal of Personality, 63,* 905–929.

Bem, S.L. (1981). Gender schema theory: A cognitive account of sex typing. *Psychological Review, 88,* 354–364.

Bem, S.L. (1987). Gender schema theory and the romantic tradition. In P. Shaver and C. Hendrick (Eds.), *Sex and gender: Review of personality and social psychology* (Vol. 7, pp. 251–271). Beverly Hills, CA: Sage.

Bendig, A.W. (1963). The relation of temperament traits of social extraversion and emotionality to vocational interests. *Journal of General Psychology, 69,* 311–318.

Benedict, R. (1934). *Patterns of culture.* Boston: Houghton Miflin.

Berkowitz, J., & Powers, P.C. (1979). Effects of timing and justification of witnessing aggression on the observer's punitiveness. *Journal of Research in Personality, 13,* 71–80.

Berman, J.S., & Kenny, D.A. (1976). Correlational bias in observer ratings. *Journal of Personality and Social Psychology, 34,* 263–273.

Bernstein, B.A. (1970). A sociolinguistic approach to socialization: With some reference to educability. In F. Williams (Ed.), *Language and poverty: Perspectives on a theme .* Chicago: Markham.

Bertaux, D. (Ed.). (1981). *Biography and society: The life history approach in the social sciences.* Beverly Hills, CA: Sage.

Bertenthal, B.I., & Fischer, K.W. (1978). Development of self-recognition in the infant. *Developmental Psychology, 14,* 44–50.

Bertini, M., Pizzamiglio, L., & Wapner, S. (Eds.). (1986). *Field dependence in psychological theory, research, and application.* Hillsdale, NJ: Lawrence Erlbaum.

Bettelheim, B. (1977). *The uses of enchantment: The meaning and importance of fairy tales.* New York: Vintage Books.

Bierhoff, H.W., Klein, R., & Kramp, P. (1991). Evidence for the altruistic personality from data on accident research. *Journal of Personality, 59,* 263–280.

Biernat, M., & Wortman, C.B. (1991). Sharing of home responsibilities between professionally employed women and their husbands. *Journal of Personality and Social Psychology, 60,* 844–860.

Blagov, P.S., & Singer, J.A. (2004). Four dimensions of self-defining memories (specificity, meaning, content, and affect) and their relationships to self-restraint, distress, and repressive defensiveness. *Journal of Personality, 72,* 481–511.

Block, J. (1965). *The challenge of response sets: Unconfounding meaning, acquiescence, and social desirability in the MMPI.* New York: Appleton-Century-Crofts.

Block, J. (1971). *Lives through time.* Berkeley, CA: Bancroft Books.

Block, J. (1977). Advancing the psychology of personality: Paradigmatic shift or improving the quality of research? In D. Magnusson and N.S. Endler (Eds.), *Personality at the crossroads: Current issues in interactional psychology.* Hillsdale, NJ: Lawrence Erlbaum.

Block, J. (1981). Some enduring and consequential structures of personality. In A.I. Rabin, J. Arnoff, A.M. Barclay, and R.A. Zucker

(Eds.), *Further explorations in personality* (pp. 27–43). New York: John Wiley & Sons.

Block J. (1993). Studying personality the long way. In D.C. Funder, R.D. Parke, C. Tomlinson-Keasey, and K. Widaman (Eds.), *Studying lives through time: Personality and development* (pp. 9–41). Washington, DC: American Psychological Association Press.

Block, J. (1995). A contrarian view of the five-factor approach to personality description. *Psychological Bulletin, 117,* 187–215.

Block, J.H., & Block, J. (1980). The role of ego control and ego resiliency in the organization of behavior. In W.A. Collins (Ed.), *Development of cognition, affect, and social relations* (pp. 39–101). Hillsdale, NJ: Lawrence Erlbaum.

Bloom, A. (1987). *The closing of the American mind: How education has failed democracy and impoverished the souls of today's students.* New York: Simon & Schuster.

Blos, P. (1972). The epigenesis of the adult neurosis. In *The psychoanalytic study of the child* (Vol. 27). New York: Quadrangle.

Bolger, N. (1990). Coping as a personality process: A prospective study. *Journal of Personality and Social Psychology, 59,* 525–537.

Bolger, N., & Schilling, E.A. (1991). Personality and the problems of everyday life: The role of neuroticism in exposure and reactivity to daily stressors. *Journal of Personality, 59,* 355–386.

Bonanno, G.A., Davis, P.J., Singer, J.L., & Schwartz, G.E. (1991). The repressor personality and avoidant information processing: A dichotic listening study. *Journal of Research in Personality, 25,* 386–401.

Booth, W.C. (1988). *The company we keep: An ethics of fiction.* Berkeley, CA: University of California Press.

Borden, W. (1992). Narrative perspectives in psychosocial intervention following adverse life events. *Social Work, 37*(2), 135–141.

Borkenau, P., Riemann, R., Angleitner, A., & Spinath, F.M. (2001). Genetic and environmental influences on observed personality: Evidence from the German Observational Study of Adult Twins. *Journal of Personality and Social Psychology, 80,* 655–668.

Bouchard, T.J., Jr., Lykken, D.T., McGue, M., Segal, N.L. & Tellegen, A. (1990). Sources of human psychological differences: The Minnesota Study of Twins Reared Apart. *Science, 250,* 223–228.

Bourne, E. (1978). The state of research on ego identity: A review and appraisal (Part 1). *Journal of Youth and Adolescence, 7,* 223–255.

Bowlby, J. (1969). *Attachment and loss. Vol. 1: Attachment.* New York: Basic Books.

Bowlby, J. (1973). *Attachment and loss. Vol. 2: Separation.* New York: Basic Books.

Bowlby, J. (1980). *Attachment and loss. Vol. 3: Loss.* New York: Basic Books.

Bowlby, J. (1988). *A secure base.* New York: Basic Books.

Bowman, P.J. (1989). Research perspectives on black men: Role strain and adaptation across the adult life cycle. In R.L. Jones (Ed.), *Black adult development and aging* (pp. 117–150). Berkeley, CA: Cobb & Henry.

Bowman, P.J. (1990). Coping with provider role strain: Adaptive cultural resources among black husband-fathers. *Journal of Black Psychology, 16,* 1–21.

Boyatzis, R.E. (1973). Affiliation motivation. In D.C. McClelland and R.S. Steele (Eds.), *Human motivation: A book of readings* (pp. 252–276). Morristown, NJ: General Learning Press.

Boyd-Franklin, N. (1989). *Black families in therapy: A multisystems approach.* New York: Guilford Press.

Bradley, C.L., & Marcia, J.E. (1998). Generativity-stagnation: A five-category model. *Journal of Personality, 66,* 39–64.

Brandstatter, H. (1994). Well-being and motivated person-environment fit: A time-sampling study of emotions. *European Journal of Personality, 8,* 75–94.

Brebner, J., & Cooper C. (1985). A proposed unified model of extraversion. In J.T. Spence and C.E. Izard (Eds.), *Motivation, emotion, and personality.* Amsterdam: North-Holland.

Breger, L. (1974). *From instinct to identity: The development of personality.* Englewood Cliffs, NJ: Prentice-Hall.

Breslow, R., Kocis, J., & Belkin, B. (1981). Contribution of the depressive perspective to memory function in depression. *American Journal of Psychiatry, 183,* 227–230.

Breuer, J., & Freud, S. (1893–1898). *Studies on hysteria.* In Vol. 2 of J. Strachey (Ed.), *The standard edition of the complete psychological works of Sigmund Freud.* London: Hogarth.

Brewer, M.B., & Caporael, L.R. (1990). Selfish genes versus selfish people: Sociobiology as origin myth. *Motivation and Emotion, 14,* 237–243.

Brody, L. (1999). *Gender, emotion, and the family.* Cambridge, MA: Harvard University Press.

Bromley, D.B. (1986). *The case-study method in psychology and related disciplines.* New York: John Wiley & Sons.

Bronfenbrenner, U. (1979). *The ecology of human development.* Cambridge, MA: Harvard University Press.

Bronfenbrenner, U. (1994). Ecological models of human development. In

T. Husten and T.N. Postlewaite (Eds.), *International encyclopedia of education* (2nd Ed.). New York: Elsevier Science.

Broughton, J.M. & Zahaykevich, M.K. (1988). Ego and ideology: A critical review of Loevinger's theory. In D.K. Lapsley and F.C. Power (Eds.), *Self, ego, and identity: Integrative approaches* (pp. 179–208). New York: Springer-Verlag.

Brown, K.W., & Moskowitz, D.S. (1998). Dynamic stability of behavior: The rhythms of our interpersonal lives. *Journal of Personality, 66*, 105–134.

Brown, N.O. (1959). *Life against death.* New York: Random House.

Browning, D.S. (1975). *Generative man: Psychoanalytic perspectives.* New York: Dell.

Bruhn, A.R. & Schiffman, H. (1982). Prediction of locus of control from the earliest childhood memory. *Journal of Personality Assessment, 46*, 380-390.

Bruner, J.S. (1986). *Actual minds, possible worlds.* Cambridge, MA: Harvard University Press.

Bruner, J.S. (1990). *Acts of meaning.* Cambridge, MA: Harvard University Press.

Bruner, J.S., & Tagiuri, R. (1954). The perception of people. In G. Lindzey (Ed.), *Handbook of social psychology* (Vol. 2). Reading, MA: Addison-Wesley.

Brunstein, J.C., Schultheiss, O.C., & Grassmann, R. (1998). Personal goals and emotional well-being: The moderating role of motive dispositions. *Journal of Personality and Social Psychology, 75*, 494–508.

Brunswik, E. (1956). *Perception and the representative design of psychological experiments.* Berkeley, CA: University of California Press.

Bühler, C. (1933). *Der menschliche lebenslauf als psychologisches problem.* Leipzig: S. Hirzel Verlag.

Burisch, M. (1984). Approaches to personality inventory construction: A comparison of merits. *American Psychologist, 39*, 214–227.

Bushman, B.J., & Baumeister, R.F. (1998). Threatened egotism, narcissism, self-esteem, and direct and displaced aggression: Does self-love or self-hate lead to violence. *Journal of Personality and Social Psychology, 75*, 219–229.

Buss, A.H. (1986). Social rewards and personality. *Journal of Personality and Social Psychology, 44*, 553–563.

Buss, D.M. (1988). The evolution of human intrasexual competition: Tactics of mate attraction. *Journal of Personality and Social Psychology, 54*, 616–628.

Buss, D.M. (1989a). Sex differences in human mate preference: Evolutionary hypotheses tested in 37 cultures. *Brain and Behavior Sciences, 12*, 1–49.

Buss, D.M. (1989b). Conflict between the sexes: Strategic interference and the evocation of anger and upset. *Journal of Personality and Social Psychology, 56*, 735–747.

Buss, D.M. (1991a). Evolutionary personality psychology. In M.R. Rosenzweig and L.W. Porter (Eds.), *Annual review of psychology* (pp. 459–491). Palo Alto, CA: Annual Reviews, Inc.

Buss, D.M. (1991b). Conflict in married couples: Personality predictors of anger and upset. *Journal of Personality, 59*, 663–688.

Buss, D.M. (1995). Evolutionary psychology: A new paradigm for psychological science. *Psychological Inquiry, 6*, 1–30.

Buss, D.M. (1997). Evolutionary foundations of personality. In R.

Hogan, J. Johnson, and S. Briggs (Eds.), *Handbook of personality psychology* (pp. 317–344). San Diego, CA: Academic Press.

Buss, D.M., & Barnes, M. (1986). Preferences in human mate selection. *Journal of Personality and Social Psychology, 50*, 559–570.

Buss, D.M., & Cantor, N. (1989). Introduction. In D.M. Buss and N. Cantor (Eds.), *Personality psychology: Recent trends and emerging directions* (pp. 1–12). New York: Springer-Verlag.

Buss, D.M., & Craik, K.H. (1983). Act prediction and the conceptual analysis of personality scales: Indices of act density, bipolarity, and extensity. *Journal of Personality and Social Psychology, 45*, 1081–1095.

Buss, D.M., & Craik, K.H. (1984). Acts, dispositions, and personality. In B.A. Maher and W.B. Maher (Eds.), *Progress in experimental personality research* (Vol. 13, pp. 241–301). Orlando, FL: Academic Press.

Butler, R.N. (1975). *Why survive? Being old in America.* New York: Harper & Row.

Byrne, D., & Kelly, K. (1981). *An introduction to personality* (3rd Ed.). Englewood Cliffs, NJ: Prentice-Hall.

C

Calder, B.J., & Staw, B.M. (1975). The interaction of intrinsic and extrinsic motivation: Some methodological notes. *Journal of Personality and Social Psychology, 31*, 76–80.

Campbell, D.T. (1975). "Degrees of freedom" and the case study. *Comparative Political Studies, 8*, 178–193.

Campbell, D.T., & Fiske, D.W. (1959). Convergent and discriminant validity by the multitrait-multi-method matrix. *Psychological Bulletin, 56,* 81–105.

Campbell, J. (1949). *The hero with a thousand faces.* New York: Bollingen Foundation, Inc.

Campbell, J.B., & Hawley, C.W. (1982). Study habits and Eysenck's theory of introversion-extraversion. *Journal of Research in Personality, 16,* 139–146.

Cantor, N., & Kihlstrom, J.F. (1985). Social intelligence: The cognitive basis of personality. In P. Shaver (Ed.), *Self, situations, and social behavior* (pp. 15–34). Beverly Hills, CA: Sage.

Cantor, N., & Kihlstrom, J.F. (1987). *Personality and social intelligence.* Englewood Cliffs, NJ: Prentice-Hall.

Cantor, N., & Kihlstrom, J.F. (1989). Social intelligence and cognitive assessments of personality. In R.S. Wyer, Jr., and T.K. Srull (Eds.), *Advances in social cognition: Vol. II. Social intelligence and cognitive assessments of personality* (pp. 1–59). Hillsdale, NJ: Lawrence Erlbaum.

Cantor, N., Mischel, W., & Schwartz, J.C. (1982). A prototype analysis of psychological situations. *Cognitive Psychology, 14,* 45–77.

Cantor, N., & Zirkel, S. (1990). Personality, cognition, and purposive behavior. In L. Pervin (Ed.), *Handbook of personality theory and research* (pp. 135–164). New York: Guilford Press.

Cantor, N.F. (1971). *Western civilization, its genesis and destiny: The modern heritage. From 1500 to the present.* Glenview, IL: Scott, Foresman and Company.

Carlo, G., Eisenberg, N., Troyer, D., Switzer, G., & Speer, A.L. (1991). The altruistic personality: In what contexts is it apparent? *Journal of Personality and Social Psychology, 61,* 450–458.

Carlsmith, J.M., Ellsworth, P.C. & Aronson, E. (1976). *Methods of research in social psychology.* Reading, MA: Addison-Wesley.

Carlson, R. (1971). Where is the person in personality research? *Psychological Bulletin, 75,* 203–219.

Carlson, R. (1981). Studies in script theory: I. Adult analogs of a childhood nuclear scene. *Journal of Personality and Social Psychology, 40,* 501–510.

Carlson, R. (1984). What's social about social psychology? Where's the person in personality research? *Journal of Personality and Social Psychology, 47,* 1304–1309.

Carlson, R. (1988). Exemplary lives: The uses of psychobiography for theory development. *Journal of Personality, 56,* 105–138.

Carlson V., Cicchetti, D., Barnett, D., & Braunwald, K. (1989), Disorganized/disoriented attachment behaviors in maltreated infants. *Developmental Psychology, 25,* 525–531.

Carment, D.W., Miles, G.D., & Cervin, V.B. (1965). Persuasiveness and persuasability as related to intelligence and extraversion. *British Journal of Social and Clinical Psychology, 4,* 1–7.

Carstensen, L.L. (1995). Evidence for a life-span theory of socioemotional selectivity. *Current Directions in Psychological Science, 4,* 151–155.

Cartwright, L.K., & Wink, P. (1994). Personality change in women physicians from medical student years to mid-40s. *Psychology of Women Quarterly, 18,* 291–308.

Carver, C.S. (1975). Physical aggression as a function of objective self-awareness and attitudes towards punishment. *Journal of Experimental Social Psychology, 11,* 510–519.

Carver, C.S., & White, T.L. (1994). Behavioral inhibition, behavioral activation, and affective responses to impending reward and punishment: The BIS/BAS scales. *Journal of Personality and Social Psychology, 67,* 319–333.

Carver, C.S., & Scheier, M.F. (1981). A control systems approach to behavioral self-regulation. In L. Wheeler (Ed.), *Review of personality and social psychology* (Vol. 2, pp. 107–140). Beverly Hills, CA: Sage.

Carver, C.S., & Scheier, M.F. (1988). *Perspectives on personality.* Boston, MA: Allyn & Bacon.

Carver, C.S. & Scheier, M.F. (1992). *Perspectives on personality* (2nd ed.). Boston, MA: Allyn & Bacon.

Caspi, A. (1998). Personality development across the life course. In W. Damon (Ed.), *Handbook of child psychology* (5th Ed.). *Vol. 3. Social, emotional, and personality development* (pp. 311–388). New York: John Wiley & Sons.

Caspi, A., Harrington, H.L., Milne, B., Amell, J.W., Theodore, R.F., & Moffitt, T.E. (2003). Children's behavioral styles at age 3 are linked to their adult personality traits at age 26. *Journal of Personality, 71,* 495–513.

Caspi, A., & Moffitt, T.E. (1993). When do individual differences matter? A paradoxical theory of personality coherence. *Psychological Inquiry, 4,* 247–271.

Cattell, R.B. (1943). The description of personality: Basic traits resolved into clusters. *Journal of Abnormal and Social Psychology, 38,* 476–506.

Cattell, R.B. (1947). Confirmation and clarification of the primary personality factors. *Psychometrika, 12,* 197–220.

Cattell, R.B. (1950). *Personality: A systematic, theoretical, and factual study.* New York: McGraw-Hill.

Cattell, R.B. (1957). *Personality and motivation structure and measurement.* Yonkers-on-Hudson, NY: World Book.

Cattell, R.B. (1965). *The scientific analysis of personality.* Baltimore, MD: Penguin.

Cattell, R.B. (1990). Advances in Cattellian personality theory. In L.A. Pervin (Ed.), *Handbook of personality theory and research* (pp. 101–110). New York: Guilford Press.

Cervone, D., Shadel, W.G., & Jencius, S. (2001). Social-cognitive theory of personality assessment. *Personality and Social Psychology Review, 5,* 33–51.

Cervone, D., & Shoda, Y. (1999a). Beyond traits in the study of personality coherence. *Current Directions in Psychological Science, 8,* 27–32.

Cervone, D., & Shoda, Y. (1999b). Social-cognitive theories and the coherence of personality. In D. Cervone and Y. Shoda (Eds.), *The coherence of personality: Social-cognitive bases of consistency, variability, and organization* (pp. 3–33). New York: Guilford Press.

Chafe, W. (1990). Some things that narratives tell us about the mind. In B.K. Britton and A.D. Pellegrini (Eds.), *Narrative thought and narrative language* (pp. 79–98). Hillsdale, NJ: Lawrence Erlbaum.

Chaikin, A.L., Derlega, V.J., Bayma, B., & Shaw, J. (1975). Neuroticism and disclosure reciprocity. *Journal of Clinical and Consulting Psychology, 43,* 13–19.

Chaplin, W.F., Phillips, J.B., Brown, J.D., Clanton, N.R., & Stein, J.L. (2000). Handshaking, gender, personality, and first impressions. *Journal of Personality and Social Psychology, 79,* 110–117.

Charme, S.T. (1984). *Meaning and myth in the study of lives: A Sartrean perspective.* Philadelphia: University of Pennsylvania Press.

Chodorow, N. (1978). *The reproduction of mothering: Psychoanalysis and the sociology of gender.* Berkeley, CA: University of California Press.

Christie, R., & Lindauer, F. (1963). Personality structure. In *Annual review of psychology* (Vol. 14, pp. 201–230). Palo Alto, CA: Annual Reviews, Inc.

Church, A.T. (2000). Culture and personality: Toward an integrated cultural trait psychology. *Journal of Personality, 68,* 651–703.

Church, A.T., & Katigbak, M.S. (1989). Internal, external, and self-report structure of personality in a non-Western culture: An investigation of cross-language and cross-cultural generalizability. *Journal of Personality and Social Psychology, 57,* 857–872.

Church, A.T., Reyes, J.A.S., Katigbak, M.S., & Grimm, S.D. (1997). Filipino personality structure and the Big Five model: A lexical approach. *Journal of Personality, 65,* 477–528.

Clark, L.A., Watson, D., & Mineka, S. (1994). Temperament, personality, and the mood and anxiety disorders. *Journal of Abnormal Psychology, 103,* 103–116.

Cloninger, C.R. (1987). A systematic method for clinical description and classification of personality variants. *Archives of General Psychiatry, 44,* 573–588.

Cochran, S.D., & Hammen, C.L. (1985). Perceptions of stressful life events and depression: A test of attributional models. *Journal of Personality and Social Psychology, 48,* 1562–1571.

Cohler, B.J. (1982). Personal narrative and the life course. In P. Baltes & O.G. Brim, Jr. (Eds.), *Life span development and behavior* (Vol. 4, pp. 205–241). New York: Academic Press.

Cohler, B.J. (1990). The life-story and the study of resilience and response to adversity. New England Symposium on Narrative Studies, Clark University.

Cohler, B.J., & Boxer, A.M. (1984). Personal adjustment, well-being, and life events. In C.Z. Malatesta and C.E. Izard (Eds.), *Emotion in adult development* (pp. 85–100). Beverly Hills, CA: Sage.

Cohler, B.J., Hostetler, A.J., & Boxer, A. (1998). Generativity, social context, and lived experience: Narratives of gay men in middle adulthood. In D.P. McAdams and E. de St. Aubin (Eds.), *Generativity and adult development: How and why we care for the next generation* (pp. 265–309). Washington, DC: APA Press.

Cohn, L.D. (1991). Sex differences in the course of personality development: A meta-analysis. *Psychological Bulletin, 109,* 252–266.

Cohn, L.D., & Westenberg, P.M. (2004). Intelligence and maturity: Meta-analytic evidence for the incremental and discriminant validity of Loevinger's measure of ego development. *Journal of Personality and Social Psychology, 86,* 760-772–

Colby, A., & Damon, W. (1992). *Some do care: Contemporary lives of moral commitment.* New York: The Free Press.

Cole, E.R., & Stewart, A.J. (1996). Meanings of political participation among black and white women: Political identity and social responsibility. *Journal of Personality and Social Psychology, 71,* 130–140.

Coles, R. (1989). *The call of stories: Teaching and the moral imagination.* Boston: Houghton Mifflin.

Comer, R.J. (1995). *Abnormal psychology* (5th ed.). New York: W.H. Freeman.

Conger, J.J., & Petersen, A.C. (1984). *Adolescence and youth: Psychological development in a changing world* (3rd ed.). New York: Harper & Row.

Conley, J.J. (1985a). A personality theory of adulthood and aging. In R. Hogan and W.H. Jones (Eds.), *Perspectives in personality* (Vol. 1, pp. 81–116). Greenwich, CT: JAI Press.

Conley, J.J. (1985b). Longitudinal stability of personality traits: A multitrait-multimethod-multioccasion analysis. *Journal of Personality and Social Psychology, 49,* 1266–1282.

Conway, M.A., & Holmes, A. (2004). Psychosocial stages and the accessibility of autobiographical memories across the life cycle. *Journal of Personality, 72,* 461–480.

Cooper, J., & Scalise, C.J. (1974). Dissonance produced by deviations from life-styles: The interaction of Jungian typology and conformity. *Journal of Personality and Social Psychology, 29,* 566–571.

Cordes, C. (1986). Narrative thought neglected. Interview with Jerome Bruner in the *APA Monitor* (monthly newspaper of the American Psychological Association).

Costa, P.T., Jr., & McCrae, R.R. (1978). Objective personality assessments. In M. Storandt, I.C. Siegler, and M.F. Elias (Eds.), *The clinical psychology of aging* (pp. 119-143). New York: Plenum.

Costa, P.T., Jr., & McCrae, R.R. (1980a). Influence of extraversion and neuroticism on subjective well-being: Happy and unhappy people. *Journal of Personality and Social Psychology, 38,* 668–678.

Costa, P.T., Jr., & McCrae, R.R. (1980b). Somatic complaints in males as a function of age and neuroticism: A longitudinal analysis. *Journal of Behavioral Medicine, 3,* 245–257.

Costa, P.T., Jr., & McCrae, R.R. (1984). Personality as a lifelong determinant of well-being. In C.Z. Malatesta and C.E. Izard (Eds.), *Emotion in adult development* (pp. 141–158). Beverly Hills, CA: Sage.

Costa, P.T., Jr., & McCrae, R.R. (1985). *The NEO Personality Inventory.* Odessa, FL: Psychological Assessment Resources.

Costa, P.T., Jr., & McCrae, R.R. (1988a). Personality in adulthood: A six-year longitudinal study of self-reports and spouse ratings on the NEO Personality Inventory. *Journal of Personality and Social Psychology, 54,* 853–863.

Costa, P.T., Jr., & McCrae, R.R. (1988b). From catalog to classification: Murray's needs and the five-factor model. *Journal of Personality and Social Psychology, 55,* 258–265.

Costa, P.T., Jr., & McCrae, R.R. (1992). *The NEO-PI-R: Professional manual.* Odessa, FL: Psychological Assessment Resources.

Costa, P.T., Jr., & McCrae, R.R. (1994). Set like plaster? Evidence for the stability of adult personality. In T.F. Heatherton and J.L. Weinberger (Eds.), *Can personality change?* (pp. 21–40). Washington, DC: APA Press.

Costa, P.T., McCrae, R.R. & Arenberg, P. (1980). Enduring dispositions in adult males. *Journal of Personality and Social Psychology, 38,* 793–800.

Costa, P.T., Jr., McCrae, R.R., & Zonderman, A.B. (1987). Environmental and dispositional influences on well-being: Longitudinal followup of an American national sample. *British Journal of Psychology, 78,* 299–306.

Costa, P.T., Jr., McCrae, R.R., Zonderman, A.B., Barbano, H.E., Lebowitz, B., & Larson, D.M. (1986). Cross-sectional studies of personality in a national sample: 2. Stability in neuroticism, extraversion, and openness. *Psychology and Aging, 1.* 144–149.

Cox, C. (1926). *The early mental traits of three hundred geniuses.* Stanford, CA: Stanford University Press.

Coyne, J.C., & Gotlib, I.H. (1983). The role of cognition in depression: A critical appraisal. *Psychological Bulletin, 94,* 472–505.

Craig, J-A., Koestner, R., & Zuroff, D.C. (1994). Implicit and self-attributed intimacy motivation. *Journal of Social and Personal Relationships, 11,* 491–507.

Craik, K. (1986). Personality research methods: An historical perspective. *Journal of Personality, 54,* 18-51.

Cramer, P. (1991). *The development of defense mechanisms.* New York: Springer-Verlag.

Cramer, P. (2002). Defense mechanisms, behavior, and affect in young adulthood. *Journal of Personality, 70,* 103–126.

Cramer, P., & Brilliant, M.A. (2001). Defense use and defense understanding in children. *Journal of Personality, 69,* 297–322.

Crandall, J.E. (1980). Adler's concept of social interest: Theory, measurement and implications for adjustment. *Journal of Personality and Social Psychology, 39,* 481–495.

Crandall, J.E. (1984). Social interest as a moderator of life stress. *Journal of Personality and Social Psychology, 47,* 164–174.

Crewe, N.M. (1997). Life stories of people with long-term spinal cord injury. *Rehabilitation Counseling Bulletin, 41,* 26–42.

Crockett, H.J., Jr. (1962). The achievement motive and differential occupational mobility in the United States. *American Sociological Review, 27,* 191–204.

Crockett, W.H. (1965). Cognitive complexity and impression formation. In B.A. Maher (Ed.), *Progress in experimental personality research* (Vol. 1, pp. 47–90). New York: Academic Press.

Cronbach, L.J., & Meehl, P.E. (1955). Construct validity in psychological tests. *Psychological Bulletin, 52,* 281–302.

Cross, H., & Allen, J. (1970). Ego identity status, adjustment, and academic achievement. *Journal of Consulting and Clinical Psychology, 34,* 288.

Crowne, D.P., & Marlowe, D. (1964). *The approval motive: Studies in evaluative dependence.* New York: Wiley.

Cunningham, M.R. (1981). Sociobiology as a supplementary paradigm for social psychological research. In L. Wheeler (Ed.), *Review of personality and social psychology* (Vol. 2, pp. 69–106). Beverly Hills, CA: Sage.

Cushman, P. (1990). Why the self is empty: Toward a historically situated psychology. *American Psychologist, 45,* 599–611.

Cutler, S.S., Larsen, R.J., & Bunce, S.C. (1996). Repressive coping style and the experience and recall of emotion: A naturalistic study of daily affect. *Journal of Personality, 65,* 379–405.

D

Damasio, A. (1999). *The feeling of what happens: Body and emotion in the making of consciousness.* Orlando, FL: Harcourt.

Damon, W., & Hart, D. (1982). The development of self-understanding from infancy through adolescence. *Child Development, 53,* 841–864.

Dannefer, D. (1984). Adult development and social theory: A paradigmatic reappraisal. *American Sociological Review, 49,* 100–116.

Darwin, C. (1859). *On the origin of the species by means of natural selection.* New York: Appleton.

Darwin, C. (1872/1965). *The expression of the emotions in man and animals.* Chicago: University of Chicago Press.

Davidson, R.J. (1992). Emotion and affective style: Hemispheric substrates. *Psychological Science, 3,* 39–43.

Davidson, R.J. (1993). Cerebral asymmetry and emotion: Conceptual and methodological conundrums. *Cognition and Emotion, 7,* 115–138.

Davidson, R.J., Ekman, P., Saron, C.D., Senulis, J.A., Friesen, W.V. (1990). Approach-withdrawal and cerebral asymmetry: Emotional expression and brain physiology. *Journal of Personality and Social Psychology, 58,* 330–341.

Davilla, J., & Sargent, E. (2003). The meaning of life (events) predicts changes in attachment security. *Personality and Social Psychology Bulletin, 29,* 1383–1395.

Davis, M. (1986). Pharmacological and anatomical analysis of fear conditioning using the fear-potentiated startle paradigm. *Behavioral Neuroscience, 100,* 814–824.

Davis, P.J. (1987). Repression and the inaccessibility of affective memories. *Journal of Personality and Social Psychology, 53,* 585–593.

Davis, P.J., & Schwartz, G.E. (1987). Repression and the inaccessibility of affective memories. *Journal of Personality and Social Psychology, 52,* 155–162.

Dawkins, R. (1976). *The selfish gene.* New York: Oxford University Press.

De Charms, R., & Moeller, G.H. (1962). Values expressed in American children's readers: 1800–1950. *Journal of Abnormal and Social Psychology, 64,* 136–142.

Deci, E.L. (1971). Effects of externally mediated rewards on intrinsic motivation. *Journal of Personality and Social Psychology, 18,* 105–115.

Deci, E.L., & Ryan, R.M. (1980). The empirical exploration of intrinsic motivational processes. In L. Berkowitz (Ed.), *Advances in experimental social psychology* (Vol. 13, pp. 39–80). New York: Academic Press.

Deci, E.L., & Ryan, R.M. (1985). *Intrinsic motivation and self-determination in human behavior.* New York: Plenum.

Deci, E.L., & Ryan, R.M. (1991). A motivational approach to self: Integration in personality. In R. Diestbier and R.M. Ryan (Eds.), *Nebraska symposium on motivation: 1990* (pp. 237–288). Lincoln, NE: University of Nebraska Press.

Dentan, R.N. (1968). *The Semai: A non-violent people of Malaysia.* New York: Holt, Reinhart & Winston.

Denzin, N.K. (1989). *Interpretive biography.* Newbury Park, CA: Sage.

Depue, R.A., Luciana, M., Arbisi, P., Collins, P., & Leon, A. (1994). Dopamine and the structure of personality: Relationship of agonist-induced dopamine activity to positive emotionality. *Journal of Personality and Social Psychology, 67,* 485–498.

deRaad, B., Mulder, E., Kloosterman, K., & Hofstee, W.K. (1988). Personality-descriptive verbs. *European Journal of Personality, 2,* 81–96.

Derrida, J. (1972). *Positions.* Chicago: University of Chicago Press.

Derry, P.A., & Kuiper, N.A. (1981). Schematic processing and self-reference in clinical depression. *Journal of Abnormal Psychology, 90,* 286–297.

de St. Aubin, E. (1996). Personal ideology polarity: Its emotional foundation and its manifestation in individual value systems, religiosity, political orientation, and assumptions concerning human nature. *Journal of Personality and Social Psychology, 71,* 152–165.

de St. Aubin, E. (1998). Truth against the world: A psychobiographical exploration of generativity in the life of Frank Lloyd Wright. In D.P. McAdams and E. de St. Aubin (Eds.), *Generativity and adult development: How and why we care for the next generation* (pp. 391–428). Washington, DC: APA Press.

de St. Aubin, E. (1999). Personal ideology: The intersection of personality and religious beliefs. *Journal of Personality, 67,* 1105–1139.

de St. Aubin, E., & McAdams, D.P. (1995). The relations of generative concern and generative action to personality traits, satisfaction/happiness with life, and ego development. *Journal of Adult Development, 2,* 99–112.

Deutsch, F.A. (1957). A footnote to Freud's "Fragment of an analysis of a case of hysteria." *Psychoanalytic Quarterly, 26,* 155–162.

deWaal, F. (1996). *Good natured: The origins of right and wrong in humans and other animals.* Cambridge, MA: Harvard University Press.

Diener, E. (1984). Subjective well-being. *Psychological Bulletin, 95,* 542–575.

Diener, E., Sandvik, E., Pavot, W., & Fujita, F. (1992). Extraversion and subjective well-being in a U.S.

probability sample. *Journal of Research in Personality, 26,* 205–215.

Digman, J.M. (1989). Five robust trait dimensions: Development, stability, and utility. *Journal of Personality, 57,* 195–214.

Digman, J.M. (1990). Personality structure: Emergence of the five-factor model. In M.R. Rosenzweig and L.W. Porter (Eds.), *Annual review of psychology* (Vol. 41, pp. 417–440). Palo Alto, CA: Annual Reviews, Inc.

Digman, J.M., & Takemoto-Chock, N.K. (1981). Factors in the natural language of personality: Reanalysis, comparison, and interpretation of six major studies. *Multivariate Behavioral Research, 16,* 149–170.

Dillehay, R.C. (1978). Authoritarianism. In H. London and J.E. Exner (Eds.), *Dimensions of personality* (pp. 85–128). New York: John Wiley & Sons.

Dillon, M., & Wink, P. (2004). American religion, generativity, and the therapeutic culture. In E. de St. Aubin, D.P. McAdams, and T.C. Kim (Eds.), *The generative society* (pp. 153–174). Washington, DC: APA Books.

Dilthey, W. (1900/1976). The development of hermeneutics. In H.P. Rickman (Ed.), *W. Dilthey: Selected writings.* Cambridge: Cambridge University Press.

Dixon, T.M., & Baumeister, R.F. (1991). Escaping the self: The moderating effect of self-complexity. *Personality and Social Psychology Bulletin, 17,* 363–368.

Dixon, V.J. (1976). World views and research methodology. In L. King, V.J. Dixon, and W. Nobles (Eds.), *African philosophy: Assumptions and paradigms for research on black*

persons. Los Angeles: Fanon Center Publication.

Doi, L.T. (1962). Amae: A key concept for understanding Japanese personality structure. In R.J. Smith and R.K. Beardsley (Eds.), *Japanese culture: Its development and characteristics* (pp. 132–139). Chicago: Aldine.

Dollard, J. (1935). *Criteria for the life history.* New Haven: Yale University Press.

Dollinger, S.J., & Clancy, S.M. (1993). Identity, self, and personality: II. Glimpses through the autophotographic eye. *Journal of Personality and Social Psychology, 64,* 1064–1071.

Dollinger, S.J., & Cramer, P. (1990). Children's defensive responses and emotional upset following a disaster: A projective assessment. *Journal of Personality Assessment, 54,* 116–127.

Dollinger, S.J., & Dollinger, S.M.C. (1997). Individuality and identity exploration: An autophotographic study. *Journal of Research in Personality, 31,* 337–354.

Donley, R.E., & Winter, D.G. (1970). Measuring the motives of public officials at a distance: An exploratory study of American presidents. *Behavioral Science, 15,* 227–236.

Donovan, J.M. (1975). Identity status and interpersonal style. *Journal of Youth and Adolescence, 4,* 37–55.

Dostoyevsky, F. (1881/1933). *The brothers Karamazov.* New York: The Heritage Press.

Dostoyevsky, F. (1864/1960). *Notes from underground* and *The grand inquisitor.* New York: Dutton (Transl. by Ralph E. Matlaw).

Doty, R.M., Peterson, B.E., & Winter, D.G. (1991). Threat and authoritarianism in the United States, 1978–1987. *Journal of Personality and Social Psychology, 61,* 629–640.

Duck, S.W. (1973). *Personal relationships and personal constructs: A study of friendship formation.* London: John Wiley & Sons.

Duck, S.W. (1979). The personal and interpersonal in construct theory: Social and individual aspects of relationships. In P. Stringer and D. Bannister (Eds.), *Constructs of sociality and individuality* (pp. 279–297). London: Academic Press.

Duck, S.W., & Craig, G. (1978). Personality similarity and the development of friendship: A longitudinal study. *British Journal of Social and Clinical Psychology, 17,* 237–242.

Duck, S.W., & Spencer, C. (1972). Personal constructs, and friendship formation. *Journal of Personality and Social Psychology, 23,* 40–45.

Dudek, S.Z., & Hall, W.B. (1984). Some test correlates of high level creativity in architects. *Journal of Personality Assessment, 48,* 351–359.

Duke, M.P. (1986). Personality science: A proposal. *Journal of Personality and Social Psychology, 50,* 382–385.

Dukes, W.F. (1965). *N* =1. *Psychological Bulletin, 64,* 74–79.

Duncan, L.E., & Agronick, G.S. (1995). The intersection of life stage and social events: Personality and life outcomes. *Journal of Personality and Social Psychology, 69,* 558–568.

Duncan, L.E., Peterson, B.E., & Winter, D.G. (1994). *Authoritarianism and gender roles: Toward a psychological analysis of hegemonic relationships.* Unpublished manuscript, University of Michigan.

Dunn, J., & Plomin, R. (1990). *Separate lives: Why siblings are so different.* New York: Basic Books.

Dweck, C.S. (1996). Capturing the dynamic nature of personality. *Journal of Research in Personality, 30,*348-362.

Dweck, C.S., Chiu, C., & Hong, Y. (1995). Implicit theories and their role in judgments and reactions: A world from two perspectives. *Psychological Inquiry, 6,* 267–285.

Dworkin, R.H. & Goldfinger, S.H. (1985). Processing bias: Individual differences in the cognition of situations. *Journal of Personality, 53,* 480–501.

E

Eagly, A.H. (1987). *Sex differences in social behavior: A social role interpretation.* Hillsdale, NJ: Erlbaum.

Eagly, A.H., & Crowley, M. (1986). Gender and helping behavior: A meta-analytic review of the social psychological literature. *Psychological Bulletin, 100,* 283–308.

Eagly, A.H., & Johnson, B.T. (1990). Gender and leadership style: A meta-analysis. *Psychological Bulletin, 108,* 233–256.

Eagly, A.H., & Steffen, V.J. (1986). Gender and aggressive behavior: A meta-analytic review of the social psychological literature. *Psychological Bulletin, 100,* 309–330.

Eagly, A.H., & Wood, W. (1991). Explaining sex differences in social behavior: A meta-analytic perspective. *Personality and Social Psychology Bulletin, 17,* 306–315.

Eagly, A.H., & Wood, W. (1999). The origins of sex differences in human behavior: Evolved mechanisms versus social roles. *American Psychologist, 54,* 408–423.

Eaves, L.J., Eysenck, H.J., & Martin, N.J. (1989). *Genes, culture, and personality.* London: Academic Press.

Edel, L. (1984). *Writing lives: Principia biographica.* New York: W.W. Norton.

Edel, L. (1985). *Henry James: A life.* New York: Harper & Row.

Edwards, A.L. (1957). *The Edwards Personal Preference Schedule.* New York: The Psychological Corporation.

Egeland, B., & Farber, E.A. (1984). Infant–mother attachment: Factors related to its development and change over time. *Child Development, 57,* 753–771.

Egeland, B., & Sroufe, L.A. (1981). Attachment and early maltreatment. *Child Development, 52,* 44–52.

Einstein, D., & Lanning, K. (1998). Shame, guilt, ego development, and the five-factor model of personality. *Journal of Personality, 66,* 555–582.

Eisenberg, N., & Lennon, R. (1983). Sex differences in empathy and related capacities. *Psychological Bulletin, 94,* 100–131.

Eisenberger, R., & Cameron, J. (1996). Detrimental effects of reward: Reality or myth? *American Psychologist, 51,* 1153–1166.

Ekman, P. (1972). Universal and cultural differences in facial expression of emotion. In J.R. Cole (Ed.), *Nebraska symposium on motivation* (Vol. 26). Lincoln, NE: University of Nebraska Press.

Ekman, P. (1992). Facial expressions of emotion: New findings, new questions. *Psychological Science, 3,* 34–38.

Ekman, P., Friesen, W.V., & Ellsworth, P.C. (1972). *Emotion in the human face: Guidelines for research and an integration of findings.* New York: Pergamon.

Elder, G.H., Jr. (1995). The life course paradigm: Social change and individual development. In P. Moen, G.H. Elder, Jr., and K. Luscher (Eds.), *Examining lives in context: Perspectives on the ecology of human development* (pp. 101–139).

Washington, DC: American Psychological Association Press.

Elkind, D. (1981). *Children and adolescents* (3rd ed.). New York: Oxford University Press.

Elkins, I.J., McGue, M., & Iacono, W. (1997). Genetic and environmental influences on parent–son relationships: Evidence for increasing genetic influence during adolescence. *Developmental Psychology, 33,* 351–363.

Ellenberger, H. (1970). *The discovery of the unconscious.* New York: Basic Books.

Elliot, A.J., Chirkov, V.I., Kim, Y., & Sheldon, K.M. (2001). A cross-cultural analysis of avoidance (relative to approach) personal goals. *Psychological Science, 12,* 505–510.

Elliot, A.J., Sheldon, K.M., & Church, M.A. (1997). Avoidance personal goals and subjective well-being. *Personality and Social Psychology Bulletin, 23,* 915–927.

Elms, A.C. (1987). The personalities of Henry A. Murray. In R. Hogan and W.H. Jones (Eds.), *Perspectives in personality* (Vol. 2, pp. 1–14). Greenwich, CT: JAI Press.

Elms, A.C. (1988). Freud as Leonardo: Why the first psychobiography went wrong. *Journal of Personality, 56,* 19–40.

Elms, A.C. (1994). *Uncovering lives: The uneasy alliance of biography and psychology.* New York: Oxford University Press.

Elsbree, L. (1982). *The rituals of life: Patterns in narratives.* Port Washington, NY: Kennikat Press.

Emmons, R.A. (1984). Factor analysis and construct validity of the Narcissistic Personality Inventory. *Journal of Personality Assessment, 48,* 291–300.

Emmons, R.A. (1986). Personal strivings: An approach to personality and subjective well-being. *Journal of Personality and Social Psychology, 51,* 1058–1068.

Emmons, R.A. (1987). Narcissism: Theory and measurement. *Journal of Personality and Social Psychology, 52,* 11–17.

Emmons, R.A. (1999). *The psychology of ultimate concerns: Motivation and spirituality in personality.* New York: Guilford Press.

Emmons, R.A., & Diener, E. (1985). Personality correlates of subjective well-being. *Personality and Social Psychology Bulletin, 11,* 89–97.

Emmons, R.A., & Diener, E. (1986a). Influence of impulsivity and sociability on subjective well-being. *Journal of Personality and Social Psychology, 50,* 1211–1215.

Emmons, R.A., & Diener, E. (1986b). An interactional approach to the study of personality and emotion. *Journal of Personality, 54,* 371–384.

Emmons, R.A., Diener, E., & Larsen, R.J. (1986). Choice and avoidance of everyday situations and affect congruence: Two models of reciprocal interactionism. *Journal of Personality and Social Psychology, 51,* 815–826.

Emmons, R.A., & King, L.A. (1988). Conflict among personal strivings: Immediate and long-term implications for psychological and physical well-being. *Journal of Personality and Social Psychology, 54,* 1040–1048.

Emmons, R.A., & Paloutzian, R.F. (2003). The psychology of religion. *Annual Review of Psychology, 54,* 377–402.

Endler, N., & Parker, J. (1990). Multidimensional assessment of coping: A critical review. *Journal of Personality and Social Psychology, 58,* 844–854.

Entwisle, D.R. (1972). To dispel fantasies about fantasy-based measures of achievement motivation. *Psychological Bulletin, 77,* 377–391.

Epsin, O., Stewart, A.J., & Gomez, C.A. (1990). Letters from V: Adolescent personality development in sociohistorical context. *Journal of Personality, 58,* 347–364.

Epstein, S. (1973). The self-concept revisited: Or a theory of a theory. *American Psychologist, 28,* 404-416.

Epstein, S. (1979). The stability of behavior: 1. On predicting most of the people much of the time. *Journal of Personality and Social Psychology, 37,* 1097–1126.

Epstein, S. (1986). Does aggregation produce spuriously high estimates of behavior stability? *Journal of Personality and Social Psychology, 50,* 1199–1210.

Epstein, S., & Meier, P. (1989). Constructive thinking: A broad coping variable with specific components. *Journal of Personality and Social Psychology, 57,* 332–350.

Erikson, E.H. (1950). *Childhood and society.* New York: Norton.

Erikson, E.H. (1958). *Young man Luther: A study in psychoanalysis and history.* New York: W.W. Norton.

Erikson, E.H. (1959). Identity and the life cycle: Selected paper. *Psychological Issues, 1*(1), 5–165.

Erikson, E.H. (1963). *Childhood and society* (2nd ed.). New York: W.W. Norton.

Erikson, E.H. (1964). *Insight and responsibility.* New York: W.W. Norton.

Erikson, E.H. (1968). *Identity: Youth and crisis.* New York: W.W. Norton.

Erikson, E.H. (1969). *Gandhi's truth: On the origins of militant nonviolence.* New York: W.W. Norton.

Erikson, E.H. (1975). *Life history and the historical moment.* New York: W.W. Norton.

Erikson, E.H. (1982). *The life cycle completed: A review.* New York: W.W. Norton.

Eron, L.D. (1982). Parent–child interaction, television, violence, and aggression of children. *American Psychologist, 37,* 197–211.

Eron, L.D. (1987). The development of aggressive behavior from the perspective of a developing behaviorism. *American Psychologist, 42,* 435–442.

Evans, G.W. (2004). The environment of childhood poverty. *American Psychologist, 59,* 77–92.

Eysenck, H.J. (1952). *The scientific study of personality.* London: Routledge & Kegan Paul.

Eysenck, H.J. (1967). *The biological basis of personality.* Springfield, IL: Thomas.

Eysenck, H.J. (1973). *Eysenck on extraversion.* New York: John Wiley & Sons.

Eysenck, H.J. (1976). *Sex and personality.* London: Open Books.

Eysenck, H.J., & Eysenck, S.B.G. (1964). *Manual of the Eysenck Personality Inventory.* London: University of London Press.

Eysenck, H.J., & Eysenck, M.W. (1985). *Personality and individual differences: A natural science approach.* New York: Plenum Press.

Eysenck, H.J., & Wilson, G.D. (1976). *Know your personality.* New York: Penguin.

Eysenck, M.W. (1982). *Attention and arousal: Cognition and performance.* New York: Springer.

Eysenck, S.B.G., Rust, J., & Eysenck, H.J. (1977). Personality and the classification of adult offenders. *British Journal of Criminology, 17,* 169–179.

F

Fagles, R. (Trans.). (1990). Homer's *The Iliad.* New York: Penguin.

Fairbairn, W.R.D. (1952). *Psychoanalytic studies of the personality: The object relation theory of personality.* London: Routledge & Kegan Paul.

Falbo, T. (1997). To rebel or not to rebel? Is this the birth order question? *Contemporary Psychology, 42,* 938–939.

Feather, N.T. (1961). The relationship of persistence at a task to expectation of success and achievement-related motives. *Journal of Abnormal and Social Psychology, 63,* 552–561.

Feeney, J.A., & Noller, P. (1990). Attachment style as a predictor of adult romantic relationships. *Journal of Personality and Social Psychology, 58,* 281–291.

Fehr, B., Baldwin, M., Collins, L., Patterson, S, & Benditt, R. (1999). Anger in close relationships: An interpersonal script analysis. *Personality and Social Psychology Bulletin, 25,* 299–312.

Finn, S.E. (1986). Stability of personality self-ratings over 30 years: Evidence for an age/cohort interaction. *Journal of Personality and Social Psychology, 50,* 813–818.

Fiske, D.W. (1949). Consistency of the factorial structures of personality ratings from different sources. *Journal of Abnormal and Social Psychology, 44,* 329–344.

Fiske, D.W. (1974). The limits of the conventional science of personality. *Journal of Personality, 42,* 1–11.

Fiske, S.T., & Taylor, S.E. (1984). *Social cognition.* Reading, MA: Addison-Wesley.

Fivush, R., & Haden, C. (Eds.). (2003). *Autobiographical memory and the construction of a narrative self: Developmental and cultural perspectives.* Mahwah, NJ: Lawrence Erlbaum.

Fleeson, W. (2001). Toward a structure- and process-integrated view of personality: Traits as density distributions of states. *Journal of Personality and Social Psychology, 80,* 1011–1027.

Floderus-Myrhed, B., Pedersen, N., & Rasmuson, I. (1980). Assessment of heritability for personality, based on a short form of the Eysenck Personality Inventory: A study of 12,898 twin pairs. *Behavior Genetics, 10,* 153–162.

Fodor, E.M. (1984). The power motive and reactivity to power stresses. *Journal of Personality and Social Psychology, 47,* 853–859.

Fodor, E.M. (1985). The power motive, group conflict, and physiological arousal. *Journal of Personality and Social Psychology, 49,* 1408–1415.

Fodor, E.M. (1990). The power motive and creativity of solutions to an engineering problem. *Journal of Research in Personality, 24,* 338–354.

Fodor, E.M., & Greenier, K.D. (1995). The power motive, self-affect, and creativity. *Journal of Research in Personality, 29,* 242–252.

Fodor, E.M., & Smith, T. (1982). The power motive as an influence on group decision making. *Journal of Personality and Social Psychology, 42,* 178–185.

Fodor, J. (1983). *The modularity of mind.* Cambridge, MA: MIT Press.

Fonagy, P., Steele, H., & Steele, M. (1991). Maternal representations of attachment during pregnancy predict the organization of infant–mother attachment at one year of age. *Child Development, 62,* 891–905.

Forer, L.K. (1977). Bibliography of birth order literature in the '70s. *Journal of Individual Psychology, 33,* 122–141.

Forgas, J.P. (1978). Social episodes and social structure in an academic setting: The social environment of an intact group. *Journal of Experimental Social Psychology, 14,* 434–448.

Forgas, J.P. (1983). Episode cognition and personality: A multidimensional analysis. *Journal of Personality, 51,* 34–48.

Forster, E.M. (1910). *Howards end.* Hammondsworth, Middlesex: Penguin.

Forster, E.M. (1954). *Aspects of the novel.* San Diego, CA: Harcourt Brace Jovanovich.

Foster, J.D., Campbell, W.K., & Twenge, J.M. (2003). Individual differences in narcissism: Inflated self-views across the lifespan and around the world. *Journal of Research in Personality, 37,* 469–485.

Fox, N.A., & Davidson, R.J. (1986). Taste-elicited changes in facial signs of emotion and asymmetry of brain electrical activity in human newborns. *Neuropsychologia, 24,* 417–422.

Fraley, R.C. (2002). Attachment stability from infancy to adulthood: Meta-analysis and dynamic modeling of developmental mechanisms. *Personality and Social Psychology Review, 6,* 123–151.

Francis, M.E., & Pennebaker, J.W. (1992). Putting stress into words: The impact of writing on physiological, absentee, and self-reported emotional well-being measures. *American Journal of Health Promotion, 6,* 280–287.

Frank, B.M., & Noble, J.P. (1985). Field independence-dependence and cognitive restructuring. *Journal of Personality and Social Psychology, 47,* 1129–1135.

Frank, S., & Quinlain, D. (1976). Ego developmental aspects of female delinquency. *Journal of Abnormal Psychology, 85,* 505–510.

Franz, C., & Stewart, A. (Eds.). (1994). *Women creating lives: Identities, resilience, and resistance.* Boulder, CO: Westview Press.

Frenkel, E. (1936). Studies in biographical psychology. *Character and Personality, 5,* 1–35.

Freud, S. (1900/1953). The interpretation of dreams. In Vols. 4 and 5 of *The standard edition of the complete psychological works of Sigmund Freud.* London: Hogarth.

Freud, S. (1901/1960). The psychopathology of everyday life. In Vol. 6 of *The standard edition.* London: Hogarth.

Freud, S. (1905/1953). Three essays on the theory of sexuality. In Vol. 7 of *The standard edition.* London: Hogarth.

Freud, S. (1905/1960). Jokes and their relation to the unconscious. In Vol. 8 of *The standard edition.* London: Hogarth.

Freud, S. (1905/1963). *Dora: An analysis of a case of hysteria.* (With an Introduction by P. Rieff). New York: Macmillan.

Freud, S. (1909/1955). Analysis of a phobia in a five-year-old boy. In Vol. 10 of *The standard edition.* London: Hogarth.

Freud, S. (1909/1963). Notes upon a case of obsessional neurosis. In S. Freud, *Three case histories* (pp. 15–102). New York: Collier Books.

Freud, S. (1910/1957). Five lectures on psychoanalysis. In Vol. 11 of *The standard edition.* London: Hogarth.

Freud, S. (1913/1958). Totem and taboo. In Vol. 13 of *The standard edition.* London: Hogarth.

Freud, S. (1914/1957). On narcissism: An introduction. In Vol. 14 of *The standard edition.* London: Hogarth.

Freud, S. (1915/1957). Repression. In Vol. 14 of *The standard edition.* London: Hogarth.

Freud, S. (1916/1947). Leonardo da Vinci: A study in psychosexuality. New York: Vintage Books. (Tranls. By A.A. Brill).

Freud, S. (1916/1961). Introductory lectures on psychoanalysis. In Vols. 15 and 16 of *The standard edition.* London: Hogarth.

Freud, S. (1917/1957). Mourning and melancholia. In Vol. 14 of *The standard edition.* London: Hogarth.

Freud, S. (1920/1955). Beyond the pleasure principle. In Vol. 18 of *The standard edition.* London: Hogarth.

Freud, S. (1921/1955). Group psychology and the analysis of the ego. In Vol. 18 of *The standard edition.* London: Hogarth.

Freud, S. (1923/1961). The ego and the id. In Vol. 19 of *The standard edition.* London: Hogarth.

Freud, S. (1927/1961). *The future of an illusion.* In Vol. 22 of *The standard edition.* London: Hogarth.

Freud, S. (1930/1961). *Civilization and its discontents.* In Vol. 21 of *The standard edition.* London: Hogarth.

Freud, S. (1933/1964). New introductory lectures. In Vol. 21 of *The standard edition.* London: Hogarth.

Freud, S. (1954). *The origins of psychoanalysis: Letters to Wilhelm Fliess, drafts and notes, 1897–1902.* M. Bonaparte, A Freud, and E. Kris (Eds.). New York: Basic Books.

Freund, A.M., & Baltes, P.B. (2000). The orchestration of selection, optimization, and compensation: An action-theoretical conceptualization of a theory of developmental regulation. In W.J. Perrig and A. Grob (Eds.), *Control of human behavior, mental processes, and consciousness* (pp. 35–58). Mahwah, NJ: Erlbaum.

Friedman, H.S., Tucker, J.S., Schwartz, J.E., Tomlinson-Keasy, C., Martin, L.R., Wingard, D.L., & Criqui, M.H. (1995). Psychosocial and behavioral predictors of longevity: The aging and death of the "Termites." *American Psychologist, 50,* 69–78.

Friedman, H.S., Tucker, J.S., Tomlinson-Keasy, C., Schwartz, J.E., Wingard, D.L., & Criqui, M.H. (1993). Does childhood personality predict longevity? *Journal of Personality and Social Psychology, 65,* 176–185.

Friedman, L. (1999). *Identity's architect: A biography of Erik H. Erikson.* New York: Pantheon.

Fromm, E. (1941). *Escape from freedom.* New York: Farrar & Rinehart.

Fromm, E. (1973). *The anatomy of human destructiveness.* New York: Holt, Rinehart and Winston.

Funder, D.C. (1995). On the accuracy of personality judgment: A realistic approach. *Psychological Review, 102,* 652–670.

Funder, D.C., & Block, J. (1989). The role of ego-control, ego-resiliency, and IQ in delay of gratification in adolescence. *Journal of Personality and Social Psychology, 57,* 1041–1050.

Funder, D.C., & Colvin, C.R. (1991). Explorations in behavioral consistency: Properties of persons, situations, and behaviors. *Journal of Personality and Social Psychology, 60,* 773–794.

Furnham, A. (1992). *Personality at work: The role of individual differences in the workplace.* London: Routledge.

G

Galton, F. (1894). Measurement of character. *Fortnightly Review, 36,* 179-185.

Gangestad, S.W. (1989). The evolutionary history of genetic variation: An emerging issue in the behavioral genetic study of personality. In D.M. Buss and N. Cantor (Eds.), *Personality psychology: Recent trends and emerging directions* (pp. 320–332). New York: Springer-Verlag.

Gangestad, S.W., & Simpson, J.A. (1990). Toward an evolutionary history of female sociosexual variation. *Journal of Personality, 58,* 69–96.

Gangestad, S.W., Simpson, J.A., DiGeronimo, K., & Biek, M. (1992). Differential accuracy in person perception across traits: Examination of a functional hypothesis. *Journal of Personality and Social Psychology, 62,* 688–698.

Gardner, H. (1993). *Creating minds.* New York: Basic Books.

Garnett, A.C. (1928). *Instinct and personality.* New York: Dodd, Mead & Company.

Gay, P. (1984). *The bourgeois experience: Victoria to Freud: Vol. 1. The education of the senses.* New York: Oxford University Press.

Gay. P. (1986). *The bourgeois experience: Victoria to Freud: Vol. 2. The tender passion.* New York: Oxford University Press.

Green, R.C. (1981). Behavioral and physiological reactions to observed violence: Effects of prior exposure to aggressive stimuli. *Journal of Personality and Social Psychology, 40,* 868–875.

Geen, R.C. (1997). Psychophysiological approaches to personality. In R. Hogan, J.A. Johnson, and S. Briggs (Eds.), *Handbook of personality psychology* (pp. 387–414). San Diego, CA: Academic Press.

Geertz, C. (1973). *The interpretation of cultures.* New York: Basic Books.

Geertz, C. (1979). From the native's point of view: On the nature of anthropological understanding. In P. Rabinow and W.M. Sullivan (Eds.), *Interpretive social science* (pp. 225–241). Berkeley, CA: University of California Press.

George, C., Kaplan, N., & Main, M. (1985). An adult attachment interview: Interview protocol. Unpublished manuscript, University of California at Berkeley.

George, L.K., Ellison, C.G., & Larson, D.B. (2002). Explaining the relationships between religious involvement and health. *Psychological Inquiry, 13,* 190–200.

Gergen, K.J. (1973). Social psychology as history. *Journal of Personality and Social Psychology, 20,* 209–320.

Gergen, K.J. (1982). *Toward transformation in social knowledge.* New York: Springer-Verlag.

Gergen, K.J. (1991). *The saturated self: Dilemmas of identity in contemporary life.* New York: Basic Books.

Gergen, K.J., & Gergen, M.M. (1986). Narrative form and the construction of psychological science. In T.R. Sarbin (Ed.), *Narrative psychology* (pp. 22–44). New York: Praeger.

Gergen, M.M., & Gergen, K.J. (1993). Narratives of the gendered body in popular autobiography. In R. Josselson and A. Lieblich (Eds.), *The narrative study of lives* (Vol. 1, pp. 191–218). Thousand Oaks, CA: Sage.

Giddens, A. (1991). *Modernity and self-identity: Self and society in the late modern age.* Stanford, CA: Stanford University Press.

Giese, H., & Schmidt, S. (1968). *Student sexuality.* Hamburg: Rowohlt.

Gilligan, C.A. (1982). *In a different voice: Psychological theory and women's development.* Cambridge, MA: Harvard University Press.

Gittings, R. (1978). *The nature of biography.* Seattle, WA: University of Washington Press.

Gjerde, P. (2004). Culture, power, and experience: Toward a person-centered cultural psychology. *Human Development, 47,* 138–157.

Glaser, B.G., & Strauss, A.L. (1967). *The discovery of grounded theory.* Chicago: Aldine.

Goffman, E. (1959). *The presentation of self in everyday life.* Garden City, NY: Doubleday.

Goffman, E. (1961). *Asylums: Essays on the social situation of mental patients and other inmates.* Chicago: Aldine.

Gold, S.N. (1980). Relations between level of ego development and adjustment patterns in adolescents. *Journal of Personality Assessment, 44,* 630–638.

Goldberg, L.R. (1990). An alternative "description of personality": The Big-Five factor structure. *Journal of Personality and Social Psychology, 59,* 1216–1229.

Goldberg, L.R. (1993). The structure of phenotypic personality traits. *American Psychologist, 48,* 26–34.

Gong-Guy, E., & Hammen, C.L. (1980). Causal perceptions of stressful live events in depressed and nondepressed outpatients. *Journal of Abnormal Psychology, 89,* 662–669.

Goodenough, D.R. (1978). Field dependence. In H. London and J.E. Exner (Eds.), *Dimensions of personality* (pp. 165–216). New York: John Wiley & Sons.

Gough, H.G. (1960). Theory and measurement of socialization. *Journal of Consulting Psychology, 24,* 23–30.

Gough, H.G. (1987). *California Psychological Inventory: Administrator's guide.* Palo Alto, CA: Consulting Psychologists Press.

Gough, H.G. (1995). Career assessment and the California Psychological Inventory. *Journal of Career Assessment, 3,* 101–122.

Gough, H.G., & Bradley, P. (1992). Delinquent and criminal behavior as assessed by the revised California Psychological Inventory. *Journal of Clinical Psychology, 48,* 298–308.

Gould, R.L. (1980). Transformations during early and middle adult years. In N.J. Smelser and E.H. Erikson (Eds.), *Themes of work and love in adulthood* (pp. 213–237). Cambridge, MA: Harvard University Press.

Gray, E.K., & Watson, D. (2002). General and specific traits of personality and their relation to sleep and academic performance. *Journal of Personality, 70,* 177–206.

Gray, J.A. (1982). *The neuropsychology of anxiety: An enquiry into the functions of the septo-hippocampal system.* New York: Oxford University Press.

Gray, J.A. (1987). Perspectives on anxiety and impulsivity: A commentary. *Journal of Research in Personality, 21,* 493–509.

Graziano, W.G., & Eisenberg, N. (1997). Agreeableness: A dimension of personality. In R. Hogan, J.A. Johnson, and S. Briggs (Eds.), *Handbook of personality psychology* (pp. 795–824). San Diego, CA: Academic Press.

Graziano, W.G., Feldesman, A.B., & Rahe, D.F. (1985). Extraversion, social cognition, and the salience of aversiveness in social encounters. *Journal of Personality and Social Psychology, 49,* 971–980.

Graziano, W.G., & Ward, D. (1992). Probing the Big Five in adolescence: Personality and adjustment during a developmental transition. *Journal of Personality, 60,* 425–439.

Greenberg, M.A., & Stone, A.A. (1992). Writing about disclosed versus undisclosed traumas: Immediate and long-term effects on mood and health. *Journal of Personality and Social Psychology, 63,* 75–84.

Greene, L.R. (1973). *Effects of field independence, physical proximity, and evaluative feedback on affective reactions and compliance in a dyadic interaction.* Unpublished doctoral dissertation, Yale University.

Greenfield, P.M., Keller, H., Fuligni, A., & Maynard, A. (2003). Cultural pathways through universal development. In S.T. Fiske, D.L. Schacter, and C. Zahn-Waxler (Eds.), *Annual Review of Psychology, 54,* 461–490. Palo Alto, CA: Annual Reviews, Inc.

Gregg, G.S. (1991). *Self-representation: Life narrative studies in identity and ideology.* New York: Greenwood Press.

Gregg. G. (1995). Multiple identities and the integration of personality. *Journal of Personality, 63,* 617–641.

Gregg. G. (1996). Themes of authority in life-histories of young Moroccans. In S. Miller and R. Bourgia (Eds.), *Representations of power in Morocco.* Cambridge, MA: Harvard University Press.

Grinstein, A. (1983). *Freud's rules of dream interpretation.* New York: International Universities Press.

Guilford, J.P., (1959). *Personality.* New York: McGraw-Hill.

Gunter, B., & Furnham, A. (1986). Sex and personality differences in recall of violent and non-violent shows from three presentation modalities. *Personality and Individual Differences, 6,* 829–838.

Guntrip, H. (1971). *Psychoanalytic theory, therapy, and the self.* New York: Basic Books.

Gutmann, D. (1987). *Reclaimed powers: Toward a new psychology of men and women in later life.* New York: Basic Books.

H

Haan, N. (1981). Common dimensions of personality development: Early adolescence to middle life. In D.H. Eichorn, J.A. Clausen, N. Haan, M.P. Honzik, and P.H. Mussen (Eds.), *Present and past in middle life* (pp. 117-151). New York: Academic Press.

Habermas, J. (1971). *Knowledge and human interests.* Boston: Beacon.

Habermas, T., & Bluck, S. (2000). Getting a life: The emergence of the life story in adolescence. *Psychological Bulletin, 126,* 748–769.

Hall, C.S. (1953). *The meaning of dreams.* New York: Harper & Row.

Hall, C.S., & Lindzey, G. (1957). *Theories of personality.* New York: John Wiley & Sons.

Hall, J.A. (1984). *Nonverbal sex differences: Communication accuracy and expressive style.* Baltimore, MD: John Hopkins University Press.

Hall, M.H. (1968). A conversation with Abraham H. Maslow. *Psychology Today, 2*(92), 35–37, 54–57.

Hamilton, W.D. (1964). The genetical evolution of social behaviour. *Journal of Theoretical Biology, 7,* 1–52.

Hammen, C., & Cochran, S. (1981). Cognitive correlates of life stress and depression in college students. *Journal of Abnormal Psychology, 90,* 23–27.

Hampson, S.E. (1988). *The construction of personality* (2nd ed.). London: Routledge.

Hankiss, A. (1981). On the mythological rearranging of one's life history. In D. Bertaux (Ed.), *Biography and society: The life history approach in the social sciences* (pp. 203–209). Beverly Hills, CA: Sage.

Hansen, R.D., & Hansen, C.H. (1988). Repression of emotionally tagged memories: The architecture of less complex emotions. *Journal of Personality and Social Psychology, 55,* 811–818.

Hanson, N.R. (1972). *Patterns of discovery: An inquiry into the conceptual foundations of science.* Cambridge: Cambridge University Press.

Harkins, S.G., & Geen, R.G. (1975). Discriminability and criterion differences between extraverts and introverts during vigilance. *Journal of Research in Personality, 9,* 335–340.

Harmon-Jones, E., & Allen, J.J.B. (1998). Anger and frontal brain activity: EEG asymmetry consistent with approach motivation despite negative affective valence. *Journal of Personality and Social Psychology, 74,* 1310–1316.

Harre, R. (1989). Language games and the texts of identity. In J. Shotter and K.J. Gergen (Eds.), *Texts of identity* (pp. 20–35). London: Sage.

Harre, R., & Gillett, G. (1994). *The discursive mind.* London: Sage.

Harris, J.R. (1995). Where is the child's environment? A group socialization theory of development. *Psychological Bulletin, 102,* 458–489.

Hart, H.M., McAdams, D.P., Hirsch, B.J., & Bauer, J. (2001). Generativity and social involvement among African Americans and white adults. *Journal of Research in Personality, 35,* 208–230.

Harter, S. (1983). Developmental perspectives on the self-system. In P.H. Mussen (Ed.), *Handbook of child psychology (4th ed.): Vol. 4. Socialization, personality, and social development* (pp. 275–386). New York: John Wiley & Sons.

Hartmann, H. (1939). *Ego psychology and the problem of adaptation.* New York: International Universities Press.

Hartshorne, H., & May, M.A. (1928). *Studies in the nature of character: Vol. 1. Studies in deceit.* New York: Macmillan.

Harvey, D. (1990). *The condition of postmodernity: An enquiry into the origins of cultural change.* Cambridge: Basil Blackwell.

Harvey, J.H., Weber, A.L., Galvin, K.S., Huszti, H.C., & Garnick, N.N. (1986). Attribution in the termination of close relationships: A special focus on the account. In R. Gilmour and S. Duck (Eds.), *The*

emerging field of personal relationships (pp. 189–201). Hillsdale, NJ: Lawrence Erlbaum.

Hassan, M.K., & Sarkar, S.N. (1975). Attitudes toward caste system as related to certain personality and sociological factors. *Indian Journal of Psychology, 50,* 313–319.

Hauser, S.T. (1976). Loevinger's model and measure of ego development: A critical review. *Psychological Bulletin, 80,* 928–955.

Hazan, C., & Shaver, P. (1987). Romantic love conceptualized as an attachment process. *Journal of Personality and Social Psychology, 52,* 511–524.

Hazan, C., & Shaver, P. (1990). Love and work: An attachment-theoretical perspective. *Journal of Personality and Social Psychology, 59,* 270–280.

Hazen, N.L., & Durrett, M.E. (1982). Relationship of security of attachment to exploration and cognitive mapping abilities in 2-year-olds. *Development Psychology, 18,* 751–759.

Heatherton, T.F., & Weinberger, J.L. (Eds.). (1994). *Can personality change?* Washington, DC: APA Press.

Heckhausen, H. (1967). *The anatomy of achievement motivation.* New York: Academic Press.

Heilbrun, C.G. (1988). *Writing a woman's life.* New York: Norton.

Helson, R. (1967). Personality characteristics and developmental history of creative college women. *Genetic Psychology Monographs, 76,* 205–256.

Helson, R., & Klohnen, E.C. (1998). Affective coloring of personality from young adulthood to midlife. *Personality and Social Psychology Bulletin, 24,* 241–252.

Helson, R., & Moane, G. (1987). Personality change in women from college to midlife. *Journal of Personality and Social Psychology, 53,* 176–186.

Helson, R., & Roberts, B.W. (1994). Ego development and personality change in adulthood. *Journal of Personality and Social Psychology, 66,* 911–920.

Helson, R., & Stewart, A.J. (1994). Personality change in adulthood. In T.F. Heatherton and J.L. Weinberer (Eds.), *Can personality change?* (pp. 201–225). Washington, DC: APA Press.

Helson, R., & Wink, P. (1992). Personality change in women from early 40s to the early 50s. *Psychology and Aging, 7,* 46–55.

Hermans, H.J.M. (1988). On the integration of nomothetic and idiographic research methods in the study of personal meaning. *Journal of Personality, 56,* 785–812.

Hermans, H.J.M. (1991). The person as co-investigator in self-research: Valuation theory. *European Journal of Personality, 5,* 217–234.

Hermans, H.J.M. (1992a). Telling and retelling one's self-narrative: A contextual approach to life-span development. *Human Development, 35,* 361–375.

Hermans, H.J.M. (1992b). Unhappy self-esteem: A meaningful exception to the rule. *Journal of Psychology, 126,* 555–570.

Hermans, H.J.M. (1996). Voicing the self: From information processing to dialogical interchange. *Psychological Bulletin, 119,* 31–50.

Hermans, H.J.M., & Bonarius, H. (1991). The person as co-investigator in personality research. *European Journal of Personality, 5,* 199–216.

Hermans, H.J.M., & Hermans-Jansen, E. (1995). *Self-narratives: The construction of meaning in psychotherapy.* New York: Guilford Press.

Hermans, H.J.M., Kempen, H.J.G., & van Loon, R.J.P. (1992). The dialogical self: Beyond individualism and rationalism. *American Psychologist, 47,* 23–33.

Hermans, H.J.M., & van Gilst, W. (1991). Self-narrative and collective myth: An analysis of the Narcissus story. *Canadian Journal of Behavioural Science, 23,* 423–440.

Hess, R.D., & Shipman, V.C. (1965). Early experience and the socialization of cognitive modes in children. *Child Development, 34,* 869–886.

Higgins, E.T. (1987). Self-discrepancy: A theory relating self and affect. *Psychological Review, 94,* 319–340.

Higgins, E.T. (1997). Beyond pleasure and pain. *American Psychologist, 52,* 1280–1300.

Higgins, E.T. (1999). Persons and situations: Unique explanatory principles or variability in general principles? In D. Cervone and Y. Shoda (Eds.), *The coherence of personality: Social-cognitive bases of consistency, variability, and organization* (pp. 61–93). New York: Guilford Press.

Himsel, A.J., Hart, H.M., Diamond, A., & McAdams, D.P. (1997). Personality characteristics of highly generative adults as assessed in Q-Sort ratings of life stories. *Journal of Adult Development, 4,* 149–161.

Hoffman, M.L. (1981). Is altruism part of human nature? *Journal of Personality and Social Psychology, 40,* 121–137.

Hogan, R. (1976). *Personality theory: The personological tradition.* Englewood Cliffs, NJ: Prentice-Hall.

Hogan, R. (1982). A socioanalytic theory of personality. In M. Page (Ed.), *Nebraska symposium on motivation* (pp. 55–89). Lincoln, NE: University of Nebraska Press.

Hogan, R. (1986). *Hogan Personality Inventory manual.* Minneapolis, MN: National Computer Systems.

Hogan, R. (1987). Personality psychology: Back to basics. In J. Aronoff, A.I. Rabin, and R.A. Zucker (Eds.), *The emergence of personality* (pp. 79–104). New York: Springer.

Hogan, R., DeSoto, C.B., & Solano, C. (1977). Traits, tests, and personality research. *American Psychologist, 32,* 255–264.

Hogan, R., Jones, W.H., & Cheek, J.M. (1985). Socioanalytic theory: An alternative to armadillo psychology. In B.R. Schlenker (Ed.), *The self and social life* (pp. 175–198). New York: McGraw-hill.

Hogan, J., & Ones, D.S. (1997). Conscientiousness and integrity at work. In R. Hogan, J.A. Johnson, and S. Briggs (Eds.), *Handbook of personality psychology* (pp. 849–870). San Diego, CA: Academic Press.

Hogan, R., Johnson, J., & Briggs, S. (Eds.). (1997). *Handbook of personality psychology.* San Diego, CA: Academic Press.

Holland, D. (1997). Selves as cultured: As told by an anthropologist who lacks a soul. In R.D. Ashmore and L. Jussim (Eds.), *Self and identity: Fundamental issues* (pp. 160–190). New York: Oxford University Press.

Holland, J.L. (1996). Exploring careers with a typology: What we have learned and some new directions. *American Psychologist, 51,* 397–406.

Holt, R.R. (1962). Individuality and generalization in the psychology of personality: An evaluation. *Journal of Personality, 30,* 377–402.

Holt, R.R. (1980). Loevinger's measure of ego development: Reliability and national norms for male and female short forms. *Journal of Personality and Social Psychology, 39,* 909–920.

Hoppe, C. (1972). *Ego development and conformity behavior.* Unpublished doctoral dissertation, Washington University in St. Louis.

Horney, K. (1939). *New ways in psychoanalysis.* New York: Norton.

Howard, G.S. (1989). *A tale of two stories: Excursions into a narrative psychology.* Notre Dame, IN: University of Notre Dame Press.

Howard, A., & Bray, D. (1988). *Managerial lives in transition: Advancing age and changing times.* New York: Guilford Press.

Howarth, E., & Eysenck, H.J. (1968). Extraversion, arousal, and paired-associate recall. *Journal of Experimental Research in Personality, 3,* 114–116.

Huesmann, L.R., & Miller, L.S. (1994). Long-term effects of repeated exposure to media violence in childhood. In L.R. Huesmann (Ed.), *Aggressive behavior: Current perspectives* (pp. 153–186). New York: Plenum Press.

Hull, C. (1943). *Principles of behavior.* New York: Appleton-Century-Crofts.

Hy, L.X., & Loevinger, J. (1996). *Measuring ego development* (2nd ed.). Mahwah, NJ: Erlbaum.

Hyland, M.E. (1988). Motivational control theory: An integrative framework. *Journal of Personality and Social Psychology, 55,* 642–651.

I

Ickes, W., Snyder, M., & Garcia, S. (1997). Personality influences on the choice of situations. In R. Hogan, J.A. Johnson, and S. Briggs (Eds.), *Handbook of personality psychology* (pp. 165–195). San Diego, CA: Academic Press.

Ingelhart, R. (1990). *Cultural shift in advanced industrial societies.* Princeton, NJ: Princeton University Press.

Ingram, R.E. (1984). Toward an information-processing analysis of depression. *Cognitive Therapy and Research, 8,* 443–478.

Ingram, R.E., Smith, T.W., & Brehm, S.S. (1983). Depression and information processing: Self-schemata and the encoding of self-referent information. *Journal of Personality and Social Psychology, 45,* 412–420.

Inhelder, B., & Piaget, J. (1958). *The growth of logical thinking from childhood to adolescence.* New York: Basic Books.

Inkeles, A. (1960). Industrial man: The relation of status to experience, perception, and value. *American Journal of Sociology, 66,* 1–31.

Inkeles, A., & Smith, D. (1974). *Becoming modern: Individual change in six developing countries.* Cambridge, MA: Harvard University Press.

Irons, W. (2001). Religion as a hard-to-fake sign of commitment. In R.M. Nesse (Ed.), *Evolution and the capacity for commitment* (pp. 292–309). New York: Russell Sage Foundation.

Izard, C.E. (1971). *The face of emotion.* New York: Appleton-Century-Crofts.

Izard, C.E. (1977). *Human emotions.* New York: Plenum.

Izard, C.E. (1978). On the ontogenesis of emotions and emotion—cognition relationships in infancy. In M. Lewis and L.A. Rosenblum (Eds.), *The development of affect* (pp. 389–413). New York: Plenum.

Izzett, R.R. (1971). Authoritarianism and attitudes toward the Vietnam war as reflected in behavioral and self-report measures. *Journal of Personality and Social Psychology, 17,* 145–148.

J

Jackson, D.N. (1971). The dynamics of structured personality tasks. *Psychological Review, 78,* 229–248.

Jackson, D.N. (1974). *The Personality Research Form.* Port Huron, MI: Research Psychologists Press.

Jackson, D.N., & Messick, S. (1958). Content and style in personality assessment. *Psychological Bulletin, 55,* 243–252.

Jackson, D.N., & Paunonen, S.V. (1980). Personality structure and assessment. In M.R. Rosenzweig and L.W. Porter (Eds.), *Annual review of psychology: Vol. 31* (pp. 503–552). Palo Alto, CA: Annual Reviews, Inc.

Jacques, E. (1965). Death and the midlife crisis. *International Journal of Psychoanalysis, 46,* 502–514.

James, W. (1892/1963). *Psychology.* Greenwich, CT: Fawcett.

James, W. (1902/1958). *The varieties of religious experience.* New York: New American Library of World Literature.

Jang, K.L., Livesley, W.J., & Vernon, P.A. (1996). Heritability of the Big Five personality dimensions: A twin study. *Journal of Personality, 64,* 577–591.

Jang, K.L., McCrae, R.R., Angleitner, A., Riemann, R., & Livesley, W.J. (1998). Heritability of facet-level traits in a cross-cultural twin sample: Support for a hierarchical model of personality. *Journal of Personality and Social Psychology, 74,* 1556–1565.

Janoff-Bulman, R., & Brickman, P. (1980). Expectations and what people learn from failure. In N.T. Feather (Ed.), *Expectancy, incentive, and failure* . Hillesdale, NJ: Lawrence Erlbaum.

Jay. P. (1984). *Being in the text: Self-representation from Wordworth to Roland Barthes.* Ithaca, NY: Cornell University Press.

Jemmott, J.B., III. (1987). Social motives and susceptibility to disease: Stalking individual differences in health risks. *Journal of Personality, 55,* 267–298.

Jenkins, S.R. (1987). Need for achievement and women's careers over 14 years: Evidence for occupational structure effects. *Journal of Personality and Social Psychology, 53,* 922–932.

Jenkins, S.R. (1994). Need for power and women's careers over 14 years: Structural power, job satisfaction, and motive change. *Journal of Personality and Social Psychology, 66,* 155–165.

Jensen-Campbell, L.A., Adams, R., Perry, D.G., Workman, K.A., Furdella, J.Q., & Egan, S.K. (2002). Agreeableness, extraversion, and peer relations in early adolescence: Winning friends and deflecting aggression. *Journal of Research in Personality, 36,* 224–251.

Jensen-Campbell, L.A., & Graziano, W.G. (2001). Agreeableness as a moderator of interpersonal conflict. *Journal of Personality, 69,* 323–362.

Jensen-Campbell, L.A., Graziano, W.G., & West, S.G. (1995). Dominance, prosocial orientation, and female preferences: Do nice guys really finish last? *Journal of Personality and Social Psychology, 68,* 427–440.

John, O.P., Pals, J.L., & Westenberg, P.M. (1998). Personality prototypes and ego development: Conceptual similarities and relations in adult women. *Journal of Personality and Social Psychology, 74,* 1093–1108.

John, O.P., & Srivastava, S. (1999). The Big Five trait taxonomy: History, measurement, and theoretical perspectives. In L. Pervin and O.P. John (Eds.), *Handbook of personality: Theory and research* (2nd ed., pp. 102–138). New York: Guilford Press.

Johnson, J.A. (1997). Units of analysis for the description and explanation of personality. In R. Hogan, J.A. Johnson, and S. Briggs (Eds.), *Handbook of personality psychology* (pp. 73–93). San Diego, CA: Academic Press.

Johnson, J.E., Petzel, T.P., Hartney, L.M., & Morgan, L.M. (1983). Recall and importance ratings of completed and uncompleted tasks as a function of depression. *Cognitive Therapy and Research, 7,* 51–56.

Jones, E. (1961). *The life and work of Sigmund Freud.* New York: Basic Books.

Jones, E.E., & Nisbett, R.E. (1972). The actor and the observer: Divergent perceptions of the causes of behavior. In E.E. Jones, D.E. Kanouse, H.H. Kelley, R.E. Nisbett, S. Valins, and B. Weiner (Eds.), *Attribution: Perceiving the causes of behavior* (pp. 79–94). Morristown, NJ: General Learning Press.

Jones, J.M. (1983). The concept of race in social psychology: From color to culture. In L. Wheeler and P. Shaver (Eds.), *Review of personality and social psychology* (Vol. 4, pp. 117–150). Beverly Hills, CA: Sage.

Jones, W.H., Couch, L., & Scott, S. (1997). Trust and betrayal: The psychology of getting along and getting ahead. In R. Hogan, J. Johnson, and S. Briggs (Eds.), *Handbook of personality psychology* (pp. 465–482). San Diego, CA: Academic Press.

Jordan, D. (1971). *Parental antecedents and personality characteristics of ego identity statuses.* Unpublished doctoral dissertation, State University of New York at Binghampton.

Josselson, R.L. (1973). Psychodynamic aspects of identity formation in college women. *Journal of Youth and Adolescence, 2,* 3–52.

Josselson, R.L. (1988). The embedded self: I and Thou revisited. In D.K. Lapsley and F.C. Power (Eds.), *Self, ego, and identity: Integrative approaches* (pp. 91–106). New York: Springer-Verlag.

Josselson, R. (1995). Narrative and psychological understanding. *Psychiatry, 58,* 330–343.

Josselson, R. (1996). *Revising herself: The story of women's identity from college to midlife.* New York: Oxford University Press.

Josselson, R., & Lieblich, A. (Eds.). (1993). *The narrative study of lives* (Vol. 1). Thousand Oaks, CA: Sage.

Josselson, R., Lieblich, A., & McAdams, D.P. (Eds.). (2003). *Up close and personal: The teaching and learning of narrative research.* Washington, DC: APA Books.

Judson, H.F. (1980). The rage to know. *Atlantic Monthly.*

Jung, C.G. (1936/1969). *The archetypes and the collective unconscious.* In Vol. 9 of *The collected works of C.G. Jung.* Princeton, NJ: Princeton University Press.

Jung, C.G. (1936/1971). Psychological typology. In H. Read and others (Eds.), *The collected works of C. G. Jung* (Vol. 6, pp. 542–555). Princeton, NJ: Princeton University Press.

Jung, C.G. (1961). *Memories, dreams, reflections.* New York: Vintage.

Jung, C.G., von Franz, M.-L., Henderson, J.L., Jacobi, J., & Jaffe, A. (1964). *Man and his symbols.* Garden City, NY: Doubleday.

Justice, M.T. (1969). *Field dependency, intimacy of topic and interpersonal distance.* Unpublished doctoral dissertation, University of Florida.

K

Kagan, J. (1984). *The nature of the child.* New York: Basic Books.

Kagan, J. (1989). Temperamental contributions to social behavior. *American Psychologist, 44,* 668–674.

Kagan, J. (1994). *Galen's prophecy.* New York: Basic Books.

Kagan, J. (2000). Temperament. In A. Kazdin (Ed.), *Encyclopedia of psychology.* New York: Oxford University Press.

Kahane, C. (1985). Introduction: Why Dora now? In C. Bernheimer and C. Kahane (Eds.), *In Dora's case: Freud–hysteria–feminism* (pp. 19–31). New York: Columbia University Press.

Kahn, S., Zimmerman, G., Csikszentmihalyi, M., & Getzels, J.W. (1985). Relations between identity in young adulthood and intimacy at midlife. *Journal of Personality and Social Psychology, 49,*1316–1322.

Kahn, R., & Antonucci, T. (1981). Convoys of social support: A life-course approach. In S. Kiesler, J. Morgan, and V. Oppenheimer (Eds.), *Aging: Social change* (pp. 383–405). New York: Academic Press.

Kashima, Y., Yumaguchi, S., Kim, U., Choi, S-C., Gelfand, M.J., & Yuki, M. (1995). Culture, gender, and self: A perspective from individualism-collectivism research. *Journal of Personality and Social Psychology, 69,* 925–937.

Kasser, T., & Ryan, R.M. (1996). Further examining the American dream: Differential correlates of intrinsic and extrinsic goals. *Personality and Social Psychology Bulletin, 22,* 280–287.

Kelly, E.L., & Conley, J.J. (1987). Personality and compatibility: A prospective analysis of marital stability and marital satisfaction. *Journal of Personality and Social Psychology, 52,* 27–40.

Kelly, G. (1955). *The psychology of personal constructs.* New York: W.W. Norton.

Keniston, K. (1963). Inburn: An American Ishmael. In R.W. White (Ed.), *The study of lives* (pp. 40–70). New York: Holt, Rinehart & Winston.

Kenrick, D.T. (1989). A biosocial perspective on mates and traits: Reuniting personality and social psychology. In D.M. Buss and N. Cantor (Eds.), *Personality psychology: Recent trends and emerging directions* (pp. 308–319). New York: Springer-Verlag.

Kenrick, D.T., & Funder, D.C. (1988). Profiting from controversy: Lessons from the person-situation debate. *American Psychologist, 43,* 23–34.

Kenrick, D.T., Keefe, R.C., Bryan, A., Barr, A., & Brown, S. (1995). Age preferences and mate choice among homosexuals and heterosexuals: A case for modular psychological mechanisms. *Journal of Personality and Social Psychology, 69,* 1166–1172.

Kernberg, O. (1980). *International world and external reality.* New York: Jason Aronson.

Keyes, C.L.M., & Ryff, C.D. (1998). Generativity in adult lives: Social structural contours and quality of life consequences. In D.P. McAdams and E. de St. Aubin (Eds.), *Generativity and adult development: How and why we care for the next generation* (pp. 227–263). Washington, DC: APA Press.

Kihlstrom, J.F. (1990). The psychological unconscious. In L. Pervin (Ed.), *Handbook of personality theory and research* (pp. 445–464). New York: Guilford Press.

Kihlstrom, J.F., & Harackiewicz, J.M. (1982). The earliest recollection: A new survey. *Journal of Personality, 50,* 134–148.

Kihlstrom, J.F., & Hastie, R. (1997). Mental representations of persons and personality. In R. Hogan, J. Johnson, and S. Briggs (Ed.), *Handbook of personality psychology* (pp. 711–735). San Diego, CA: Academic Press.

King, L.A. (1995). Wishes, motives, goals, and personal memories: Relation of measures of human motivation. *Journal of Personality, 63,* 985–1007.

Kirkpatrick, L.A. (1999). Toward an evolutionary psychology of religion and spirituality. *Journal of Personality, 67,* 921–952.

Klages, L. (1926/1932). *The science of character.* London: George Allen & Unwin.

Klinger, E. (1966). Fantasy need achievement as a motivational construct. *Psychological Bulletin, 66,* 291–308.

Klinger, E. (1987). Current concerns and disengagement from incentives. In F. Halisch and J. Kuhl (Eds.), *Motivation, intention, and volition* (pp. 337–347). Berlin: Springer-Verlag.

Kobak, R.R., & Hazan, C. (1991). Attachment in marriage: Effects of security and accuracy of working models. *Journal of Personality and Social Psychology, 60,* 861–869.

Koestner, R., & McClelland, D.C. (1990). Perspectives on competence motivation. In L. Pervin (Ed.), *Handbook of personality:*

Theory and research (pp. 527–548). New York: Guilford Press.

Koestner, R., Weinberger, J., & McClelland, D.C. (1991). Task-intrinsic and social-extrinsic sources of arousal for motives assessed in fantasy and self-report. *Journal of Personality, 59,* 57–82.

Kohlberg, L. (1969). Stage and sequence: The cognitive-developmental approach to socialization. In D.A. Goslin (Ed.), *Handbook of socialization theory and research* (pp. 347–480). Skokie, IL: Rand McNally.

Kohlberg, L. (1981). *The philosophy of moral development: Moral stages and the idea of justice* (Vol. 1). *Essays on moral development.* New York: Harper & Row.

Kohn, M.L. (1969). *Class and conformity: A study in values.* Homewood, IL: Dorsey Press.

Kohn, M.L., Naoi, A., Schoenbach, C., Schooler, C., & Slomczynski, K.M. (1990). Position in the class structure and psychological functioning in the United States, Japan, and Poland. *American Journal of Sociology, 95,* 964–1008.

Kohn, M.L., & Schooler, C. (1969). Class, occupation, and orientation. *American Sociological Review, 34,* 659–678.

Kohn, M.L., & Schooler, C. (1973). Occupational experience and psychological functioning: An assessment of reciprocal effects. *American Sociological Review, 38,* 97–118.

Kohnstamm, G.A., Halverson, C.F., Jr., Mervielde, I., & Havill, V.L. (1998). *Parental descriptions of child personality: Developmental antecedents of the Big Five?* Mahweh, NJ: Lawrence Erlbaum.

Kohut, H. (1971). *The analysis of the self.* New York: International Universities Press.

Kohut, H. (1977). *The restoration of the self.* New York: International Universities Press.

Kohut, H. (1984). *How does analysis cure?* Chicago: University of Chicago Press.

Konner, M. (1983). *The tangled wing: Biological constraints on the human spirit.* New York: Harper & Row.

Kotre, J. (1984). *Outliving the self: Generativity and the interpretation of lives.* Baltimore, MD: Johns Hopkins University Press.

Kotre, J. (1999). *Making it count: How to generate a legacy that gives meaning to your life.* New York: The Free Press.

Krahe, B. (1992). *Personality and social psychology: Toward a synthesis.* London: Sage.

Kretschmer, E. (1921). *Korperbau und charakter.* Berlin: Springer.

Krueger, R.G., Hicks, B.M., & McGue, M. (2001). Altruism and antisocial behavior: Independent tendencies, unique personality correlates, distinct etiologies. *Psychological Science, 12,* 397–402.

Kunce, J.T., & Anderson, W.P. (1984). Perspectives on uses of the MMPI in nonpsychiatric settings. In P. McReynolds and G.J. Chelune (Eds.), *Advances in psychological assessment* (Vol. 6, pp. 41–76). San Francisco: Jossey-Bass.

Kushner, H. (1981). *When bad things happen to good people.* New York: Avon.

L

Labov, W. (1972). *Language in the inner city.* Philadelphia: University of Pennsylvania Press.

Lachman, M.E. (1986). Locus of control in aging research: A case for multi-dimensional and domain-specific assessment. *Psychology and Aging, 1,* 34–40.

Lachman, M.E. (Ed.). (2001). *Handbook of midlife development.* New York: Wiley.

LaFreniere, P.J., & Sroufe, L.A. (1985). Profiles of peer competence in the preschool: Interrelations between measures, influence of social ecology, and relation to attachment history. *Developmental Psychology, 21,* 56–69.

Langbaum, R. (1982). *The mysteries of identity: A theme in modern literature.* Chicago: University of Chicago Press.

Langner, C.A., & Winter, D.G. (2001). The motivational basis of concessions and compromise: Archival and laboratory studies. *Journal of Personality and Social Psychology, 81,* 711–727.

Lapsley, D.K., & Rice, K. (1988). The "new look" at the imaginary audience and personal fable: Toward a general model of adolescent ego development. In D.K. Lapsley and F.C. Power (Eds.), *Self, ego, and identity: Integrative approaches* (pp. 109–129). New York: Springer-Verlag.

Larsen, R.J., & Kasimatis, M. (1991). Day-to-day symptoms: Individual differences in the occurrence, duration, and emotional concomitants of minor daily illness. *Journal of Personality, 59,* 387–423.

Lasch, C. (1979). *The culture of narcissism: American life in an age of diminishing expectations.* New York: W.W. Norton.

Laursen, B., Pulkkinen, L., & Adams, R. (2002). The antecedents and correlates of agreeableness in adulthood. *Developmental Psychology, 38,* 591–603.

Leary, T. (1957). *Interpersonal diagnosis of personality.* New York: Ronald Press.

LeDoux, J. (1996). *The emotional brain: The mysterious underpinnings of emotional life.* New York: Touchstone Books.

Leith, K.P., & Baumeister, R.F. (1998). Empathy, shame, guilt, and narratives of interpersonal conflicts: Guilt-prone people are better at perspective taking. *Journal of Personality, 66,* 1–37.

Lee, L., & Snarey, J. (1988). The relationship between ego and moral development: A theoretical review and empirical analysis. In D.K. Lapsley and F.C. Power (Eds.), *Self, ego, and identity: Integrative approaches* (pp. 151–178). New York: Springer-Verlag.

Lefcourt, H.M., Martin, R.A., Fick, C.M., & Saleh, W.E. (1985). Locus of control for affiliation and behavior in social interactions. *Journal of Personality and Social Psychology, 48,* 577–759.

Lepper, M.R., & Greene, D. (1978). *The hidden costs of reward: New perspectives on the psychology of human motivation.* New York: Halsted.

Lepper, M.R., Greene, D. & Nisbett, R.E. (1973). Undermining children's intrinsic interest with extrinsic rewards: A test of the "overjustification" hypothesis. *Journal of Personality and Social Psychology, 28,* 129–137.

LeVine, R.A. (1982). *Culture, behavior, and personality* (2nd ed.). New York: Aldine.

LeVine, R.A. (2001). Culture and personality studies, 1918–1960: Myth and history. *Journal of Personality, 69,* 803–818.

Levinson, D.J. (1978). *The seasons of a man's life.* New York: Alfred A. Knopf.

Levinson, D.J. (1981). Explorations in biography: Evolution of the individual life structure in adulthood. In A.I. Rabin, J. Aronoff, A.M. Bar-clay, and R.A. Zucker (Eds.). *Further explorations in personality* (pp. 44–79). New York: John Wiley & Sons.

Levinson, D.J., Darrow, C.M., Klein, E.B., Levinson, M.H., & McKee, B. (1974). The psychosocial development of men in early adulthood and the mid-life transition. In D. Ricks, A. Thomas, and M. Roff (Eds.), *Life history research in psychopathology* (Vol. 3). Minneapolis, MN: University of Minnesota Press.

Levy, K.N., Blatt, S.J., & Shaver, P.R. (1998). Attachment styles and parental representations. *Journal of Personality and Social Psychology, 74,* 407–419.

Lewicki, P. (1984). Self-schemata and social information processing. *Journal of Personality and Social Psychology, 47,* 1177–1190.

Lewin, K. (1935). *A dynamic theory of personality.* New York: McGraw-Hill.

Lewis, H.B. (1985). Depression vs. paranoia: Why are there sex differences in mental illness? *Journal of Personality, 53,* 150–178.

Lewis, M. (1990). Self-knowledge and social development in early life. In L. Pervin (Ed.), *Handbook of personality theory and research* (pp. 277–300). New York: Guilford Press.

Lewis, M., & Brooks-Gunn, J. (1979). *Social cognition and the acquisition of self.* New York: Plenum.

Lieberman, M.D., & Rosenthal, R. (2001). Why introverts can't always tell who likes them: Multitasking and nonverbal decoding. *Journal of Personality and Social Psychology, 80,* 294–310.

Lifton, R.J. (1979). *The broken connection: On death and the continuity of life.* New York: Simon & Schuster.

Linde, C. (1990). *Life-stories: The creation of coherence.* Palo Alto, CA: Institute for Research on Learning, Monograph No. IRL90–0001.

Lindzey, G. (1959). On the classification of projective techniques. *Psychological Bulletin, 56,* 158–168.

Linn, R. (1997). Soldiers' narratives of selective moral resistance: A separate position or the connected self? In A. Lieblich and R. Josselson (Eds.), *The narrative study of lives* (Vol. 5, pp. 94–112). Thousand Oaks, CA: Sage.

Linville, P.W. (1987). Self-complexity as a cognitive buffer against stress-related illness and depression. *Journal of Personality and Social Psychology, 52,* 663–676.

Lishman, W.A. (1972). Selective factors in memory. Part I: Age, sex, and personality attributes. *Psychological Medicine, 2,* 121–138.

Little, B.R. (1989). Personal projects analysis: Trivial pursuits, magnificent obsessions, and the search for coherence. In D.M. Buss and N. Cantor (Eds.), *Personality psychology: Recent trends and emerging directions* (pp. 15–31). New York: Springer-Verlag.

Little, B.R. (1998). Personal project pursuit: Dimensions and dynamics of personal meaning. In P.T.P. Wong and P.S. Fry (Eds.), *The human quest for meaning: Handbook for research and clinical applications* (pp. 193–212). Mahwah, NJ: Lawrence Erlbaum.

Little, B.R. (1999). Personality and motivation: Personal action and the conative evolution. In L.A. Pervin and O. John (Eds.), *Handbook of personality: Theory and research* (2nd ed., pp. 501–524). New York: Guilford Press.

Little, B.R., Lecci, L., & Watkinson, R. (1992). Personality and personal projects: Linking Big Five and PAC units of analysis. *Journal of Personality, 60,* 501–525.

Livson, N., & Peskin, H. (1980). Perspectives on adolescence from longitudinal research. In J. Adelson (Ed.), *Handbook of adolescent psychology* (pp. 47–98). New York: John Wiley & Sons.

Lloyd, G.G., & Lishman. W.A. (1975). Effect of depression on the speed of recall of pleasant and unpleasant experiences. *Psychological Medicine, 5,* 173–180.

Locke, J. (1690). *An essay concerning human understanding.* Excerpted in R.J. Herrnstein and E. G. Boring (Eds.). (1965). *A source book in the history of psychology* (pp. 584–586). Cambridge, MA: Harvard University Press.

Loehlin, J.C. (1989). Partitioning environmental and genetic contributions to behavioral develoment. *American Psychologist, 44,* 1285–1292.

Loehlin, J.C., McCrae, R.R., & Costa, P.T., Jr. (1998). Heritabilities of common and measure-specific components of the Big Five personality factors. *Journal of Research in Personality, 32,* 431–453.

Loehlin, J.C., Neiderhiser, J.M., & Reiss, D. (2003). The behavior genetics of personality and the NEAD Study. *Journal of Research in Personality, 37,* 373–387.

Loehlin, J.C., & Nichols. R.C. (1976). *Heredity, environment, and personality: A study of 850 sets of twins.* Austin, TX: Texas University Press.

Loehlin, J.C., Willerman, L., & Horn, J.M. (1987). Personality resemblance in adoptive families: A 10-year followup. *Journal of Personality and Social Psychology, 53,* 961–969.

Loevinger, J. (1957). Objective tests as instruments of psychological theory. *Psychological Reports, 3,* 635–694.

Loevinger, J. (1976). *Ego development.* San Francisco: Jossey-Bass.

Loevinger, J. (1979). Construct validity of the sentence-completion test of ego development. *Applied Psychological Measurement, 3,* 281–311.

Loevinger, J. (1983). On ego development and the structure of personality. *Developmental Review, 3,* 339–350.

Loevinger, J. (1984). On the self and predicting behavior. In R.A. Zucker, J. Aronoff, and A.I. Rabin (Eds.), *Personality and the prediction of behavior* (pp. 43–68). New York: Academic Press.

Loevinger, J. (1987). *Paradigms of personality.* New York: W.H. Freeman.

Loevinger, J. (2002). Confessions of an iconoclast: At home on the fringe. *Journal of Personality Assessment, 78,* 195–208.

Loevinger, J., Cohn, L.D., Bonneville, L.P., Redmore, C., Streich, D.D., & Sargent, M. (1985). Ego development in college. *Journal of Personality and Social Psychology, 48,* 947–962.

Loevinger, J., & Wessler, R. (1970). *Measuring ego development 1. Construction and use of a sentence-completion test.* San Francisco: Jossey-Bass.

Loevinger, J., Wessler, R., & Redmore, C. (1970). *Measuring ego development 2. Scoring manual for women and girls.* San Francisco: Jossey-Bass.

Lohr, J.M., & Staats, W.W. (1973). Attitude conditioning in Sino-Tibetan languages. *Journal of Personality and Social Psychology, 26,* 196–200.

Lorenz, K. (1969). *On aggression.* New York: Harcourt, Brace & World.

Lowenthal, M.F., Thurnher, M., Chiriboga, D., & Associates. (1975). *Four stages of life: A comparative study of men and women facing transitions.* San Francisco, CA: Jossey-Bass.

Lucariello, J. (1990). Canonicality and consciousness in child narrative. In B.K. Britton and A.D. Pellegrini (Eds.), *Narrative thought and narrative language* (pp. 131–150). Hillsdale, NJ: Lawrence Erlbaum.

Lucas, R.E., & Diener, E. (2001). Understanding extraverts' enjoyment of social situations: The importance of pleasantness. *Journal of Personality and Social Psychology, 81,* 343–356.

Lucas, R.E., Diener, E., Grob, A., Suh, E.M., & Shao, L. (2000). Cross-cultural evidence for the fundamental features of extraversion. *Journal of Personality and Social Psychology, 79,* 452–468.

Lundy, A. (1985). The reliability of the Thematic Apperception Test. *Journal of Personality Assessment, 49,* 141–145.

Lykken, D.T., McGue, M., Tellegen, A., & Bouchard, Jr., T.J. (1992). Emergenesis: Genetic traits that may not run in families. *American Psychologist, 47,* 1565–1577.

Lykken, D., & Tellegen, A. (1996). Happiness is a stochastic phenomenon. *Psychological Science, 7,* 186–189.

Lyons-Ruth, K. (1996). Attachment relationships among children with aggressive behavior problems: The role of disorganized early attachment patterns. *Journal of Consulting and Clinical Psychology, 64,* 64–73.

Lyons-Ruth, K., Connell, D.B., Zoll, D., & Stahl, J. (1987). Infants at social risk: Relations among infant maltreatment, maternal behavior, and infant attachment behavior. *Developmental Psychology, 23,* 223–232.

M

Maccoby, E.E., & Jacklin, C.N. (1974). *The psychology of sex differences.* Stanford, CA: Stanford University Press.

Maccoby, E.E., & Martin, J.A. (1983). Socialization in the context of the family: Parent–child interaction. In P.H. Mussen (Ed.), *Handbook of child psychology* (4th ed., Vol. 4, pp. 1–102). New York: John Wiley & Sons.

MacDermid, S.M., Franz, C.E., & DeReus, L.A. (1998). Generativity: At the crossroads of social roles and personality. In D.P. McAdams and E. de St. Aubin (Eds.), *Generativity and adult development: How and why we care for the next generation* (pp. 181–226). Washington, DC: APA Press.

MacIntyre, A. (1984). *After virtue.* Notre Dame, IN: University of Notre Dame Press.

Mackenzie-Mohr, D., & Zanna, M.P. (1990). Treating women as sexual objects: Look to the (gender schematic) male who has viewed pornography. *Personality and Social Psychology Bulletin, 16,* 296–308.

MacKinnon, D.W. (1962). The nature and nurture of creative talent. *American Psychologist, 17,* 484–495.

MacKinnon, D.W. (1963). Creativity and images of the self. In R.W. White (Ed.), *The study of lives* (pp. 250–279). New York: Prentice-Hall.

MacKinnon, D.W. (1965). Personality and the realization of creative potential. *American Psychologist, 20,* 273–281.

Maddi, S.R. (1984). Personology for the 1980s. In R.A. Zucker, J. Aronoff, and A.I. Rabin (Eds.), *Personality and the prediction of behavior* (pp. 7–41). New York: Academic Press.

Magnus, K., Diener, E., Fujita, F., & Pavot, W. (1993). Extraversion and neuroticism as predictors of object life events: A longitudinal analysis. *Journal of Personality and Social Psychology, 65,* 1046–1053.

Magnusson, D. (1971). An analysis of situational dimensions. *Perceptual and Motor Skills, 32,* 851-867.

Mahler, M.S. (1968). *On human symbiosis and the vicissitudes of individuation: Infantile psychosis.* New York: International Universities.

Mahler, M.S., Pine, F., & Bergman, A. (1975). *The psychological birth of the human infant.* New York: Basic Books.

Main, M. (1981). Avoidance in the service of attachment: A working paper. In K. Immelmann, G. Barlow, L. Petrinovich, and M. Main (Eds.), *Behavioral development: The Bielefeld interdisciplinary project*. New York: Cambridge University Press.

Main, M. (1983). Exploration, play, and cognitive functioning related to mother–infant attachment. *Infant Behavior and Development, 6,* 167–174.

Main, M. (1991). Metacognitive knowledge, metacognitive monitoring, and singular (coherent) vs. multiple (incoherent) model of attachment. In C.M. Parkes, J. Stevenson-Hinde, and P. Marris (Eds.), *Attachment across the life cycle* (pp. 127–159). London: Tavistock/Routledge.

Main, M., Kaplan, N., & Cassidy, J. (1985). Security in infancy, childhood, and adulthood: A move to the level of representation. *Monographs of the Society for Research in Child Development, 50*(1 & 2), 66–104.

Manners, J., & Durkin, K. (2001). A critical review of the validity of ego development theory and its measurement. *Journal of Personality Assessment, 77,* 541–567.

Mannheim, K. (1952). The problem of generations. In *Essays on the sociology of knowledge.* New York: Oxford University Press. (Originally published in 1928.).

Manning, M.M., & Wright, T.L. (1983). Self-efficacy expectancies and the persistence of pain control in childbirth. *Journal of Personality and Social Psychology, 45,* 421–431.

Marcia, J.E. (1966). Development and validation of ego identity status. *Journal of Personality and Social Psychology, 3,* 551–558.

Marcia, J.E. (1967). Ego identity status: Relationships to change in self-esteem, "general maladjustment," and authoritarianism. *Journal of Personality, 35,* 119–133.

Marcia, J.E. (1980). Identity in adolescence. In J. Adelson (Ed.), *Handbook of adolescent psychology* (pp. 159–187). New York: John Wiley & Sons.

Marcia, J.E., & Friedman, M.L. (1970). Ego identity status in college women. *Journal of Personality, 38,* 249–263.

Marcia, J.E., Waterman, A.S., Matteson, D.R., Archer, S.L., & Orlofsky, J.L. (1993). *Ego identity: A handbook for psychosocial research.* New York: Springer-Verlag.

Marcus, S. (1977). Freud and Dora: Story, history, case history. In T. Shapiro (Ed.), *Psychoanalysis and contemporary science* (pp. 389-442). New York: International Universities Press.

Markus, H. (1977). Self-schemata and processing information about the self. *Journal of Personality and Social Psychology, 35,* 63–78.

Markus, H. (1983). Self-knowledge: An expanded view. *Journal of Personality, 51,* 543–565.

Markus, H.R., & Kitayama, S. (1991). Culture and the self: Implications for cognition, emotion, and motivation. *Psychological Review, 98,* 224–253.

Markus, H.R., Kitayama, S., & Heiman, R.J. (1998). Culture and "basic" psychological principles. In E.T. Higgins and A.W. Kruglanski (Eds.), *Social psychology: Handbook of basic principles* (pp. 857–913). New York: Guilford Press.

Markus, H., & Nurius, P. (1986). Possible selves. *American Psychologist, 41,* 954–969.

Markus, H., & Sentis, K. (1982). The self in social information processing. In J. Suls (Ed.), *Psychological perspectives on the self* (Vol. 1, pp. 41–70). Hillsdale, NJ: Lawrence Erlbaum.

Markus, H., & Smith, J. (1981). The influence of self-schema on the perception of others. In N. Cantor and J.F. Kihlstrom (Eds.), *Personality, cognition, and social interaction* (pp. 233–262). Hillsdale, NJ: Lawrence Erlbaum.

Markus, H.R., & Wurf, E. (1987). The dynamic self-concept: A social psychological perspective. In M.R. Rosenzweig and L.W. Porter (Eds.), *Annual review of psychology* (Vol. 38, pp. 299–337). Palo Alto, CA: Annual Reviews, Inc.

Marshall, V. (1975). Age and awareness of finitude in developmental gerontology. *Omega, 6,* 113–129.

Martin, J.A. (1981). A longitudinal study of the consequence of early mother–infant interaction: A microanalytic approach. *Monographs of the Society for Research in Child Development, 46*(3, Serial No. 190).

Maruna, S. (1997). Going straight: Desistance from crime and life narratives of reform. In R. Josselson and A. Lieblich (Eds.), *The narrative study of lives* (Vol. 5, pp. 59–93). Thousand Oaks, CA: Sage.

Maruna, S. (2001). *Making good: How ex-convicts reform and rebuild their lives.* Washington, DC: APA Books.

Maslow, A.H. (1954). *Motivation and personality.* New York: Harper & Row.

Maslow, A.H. (1968). *Toward a psychology of being* (2nd ed.). New York: D. Van Nostrand.

Matas, L., Arend, R., & Sroufe, L.A. (1978). Continuity of adaptation in the second year: The relationship between quality of attachment and later competence. *Child Development, 49,* 547–556.

Matthews, G. (1992). Extraversion. In A.P. Smith and D.P. Jones (Eds.), *Handbook of human performance: Vol. 3. State and trait.* London: Academic Press.

Matthews, G., Coyle, K., & Craig, A. (1990). Multiple factors of cognitive failure and their relationships with stress vulnerability. *Journal of Psychopathology and Behavioral Assessment, 12,* 49–64.

Matthews, G., & Deary, I. (1998). *Personality traits.* Cambridge, England: Cambridge University Press.

Matthews, G., Dorn, L., & Glendon, A.I. (1991). Personality correlates of driver stress. *Personality and Individual Differences, 12,* 535–549.

Matthews, G., Jones, D.M., & Chamberlain, A.G. (1989). Interactive effects of extraversion and arousal on attention task performance: Multiple resources or encoding processes? *Journal of Personality and Social Psychology, 56,* 629–639.

Matthews, G., Jones, D.M., & Chamberlain, A.G. (1992). Predictors of individual differences in mail coding skills, and their variation with ability level. *Journal of Applied Psychology, 77,* 406–418.

Mayo, P.R. (1990). A further study of the personality-congruent recall effect. *Personality and Individual Differences, 10,* 247–252.

McAdams, D.P. (1980). A thematic coding system for the intimacy motive. *Journal of Research in Personality, 14,* 413–432.

McAdams, D.P. (1982a). Intimacy motivation. In A.J. Stewart (Ed.), *Motivation and Society* (pp. 133–171). San Francisco: Jossey-Bass.

McAdams, D.P. (1982b). Experiences of intimacy and power: Relationships between social motives and autobiographical memory. *Journal of Personality and Social Psychology, 42,* 292–302.

McAdams, D.P. (1984a). Human motives and personal relationships. In V. Derlega (Ed.), *Communication, intimacy, and close relationships* (pp. 41–70). New York: Academic Press.

McAdams, D.P. (1984b). Love, power, and images of the self. In C.Z. Malatesta and C.E. Izard (Eds.), *Emotion in adult development* (pp. 159–174). Beverly Hills, CA: Sage.

McAdams, D.P. (1985a). *Power, intimacy, and the life story: Personological inquiries into identity.* New York: The Guilford Press.

McAdams, D.P. (1985b). The "imago": A key narrative component of identity. In P. Shaver (Ed.), *Review of personality and social psychology* (Vol. 6, pp. 115–141). Beverly Hills, CA: Sage.

McAdams, D.P. (1985c). Fantasy and reality in the death of Yukio Mishima. *Biography: An Interdisciplinary Quarterly, 8,* 292–317.

McAdams, D.P. (1987). A life-story model of identity. In R. Hogan and W.H. Jones (Eds.), *Perspectives in personality* (Vol. 2, pp. 15–50). Greenwich, CT: JAI Press.

McAdams, D.P. (1988a). Personal needs and personal relationships. In S.W. Duck (Ed.), *Handbook of personal relationships* (pp. 7–22). London: John Wiley & Sons.

McAdams, D.P. (1988b). Biography, narrative, and lives: An introduction. *Journal of Personality, 56,* 1–18.

McAdams, D.P. (1992). How the I and the Me come to be: Attachment vs. intimacy. Invited address, Sixth International Conference of the Society for the Study of Personal Relationships, Orono, Maine.

McAdams, D.P. (1992b). The five-factor model in personality: A critical appraisal. *Journal of Personality, 60,* 329–361.

McAdams, D.P. (1993). *The stories we live by: Personal myths and the making of the self.* New York: William Morrow.

McAdams, D.P. (1994). Can personality change? Levels of stability and growth in personality across the life span. In T.F. Heatherton and J.L. Weinberger (Eds.), *Can personality change?* (pp. 229–314). Washington, DC: APA Press.

McAdams, D.P. (1995). What do we know when we know a person? *Journal of Personality, 63,* 365–396.

McAdams, D.P. (1996a). Personality, modernity, and the storied self: A contemporary framework for studying persons. *Psychological Inquiry, 7,* 295–321.

McAdams, D.P. (1996b). Narrating the self in adulthood. In J. Birren, G. Kenyon, J.E. Ruth, J.J.F. Shroots, and J. Svendson (Eds.), *Aging and biography: Explorations in adult development* (pp. 131–148). New York: Springer.

McAdams, D.P. (1997a). A conceptual history of personality psychology. In R. Hogan, J. Johnson, and S. Briggs (Eds.), *Handbook of personality psychology* (pp. 3–39). San Diego, CA: Academic Press.

McAdams, D.P. (1997b). The case for unity in the (post)modern self: A modest proposal. In R. Ashmore and L. Jussim (Eds.), *Self and identity: Fundamental issues* (pp. 46–78). New York: Oxford University Press.

McAdams, D.P. (1999). Personal narratives and the life story. In L. Pervin and O. John (Eds.), *Handbook of personality: Theory and research* (2nd ed., pp. 478–500). New York: Guilford Press.

McAdams, D.P. (2001a). The psychology of life stories. *Review of General Psychology, 5,* 100–122.

McAdams, D.P. (2001b). Generativity in midlife. In M.E. Lachman (Ed.), *Handbook of midlife development* (pp. 395–443). New York: Wiley.

McAdams, D.P. (2005). *The redemptive self: The stories Americans live by.* New York: Oxford University Press.

McAdams, D.P., Anyidoho, N.A., Brown, C., Huang, Y.T., Kaplan, B., & Machado, M.A. (2004). Traits and stories: Links between dispositional and narrative features of personality. *Journal of Personality, 72,* 761–784.

McAdams, D.P., Booth, L., & Selvik, R. (1981). Religious identity among students at a private college: Social motives, ego stage, and development. *Merrill-Palmer Quarterly, 27,* 219–239.

McAdams, D.P., & Bowman, P.J. (2001). Narrating life's turning points: Redemption and contamination. In D.P. McAdams, R. Josselson, and A. Lieblich (Eds.), *Turns in the road: Narrative studies of lives in transition* (pp. 3–34). Washington, DC: APA Books.

McAdams, D.P., & Bryant, F. (1987). Intimacy motivation and subjective mental health in a nationwide sample. *Journal of Personality, 55,* 395–413.

McAdams, D.P., & Constantian, C.A. (1983). Intimacy and affiliation motives in daily living: An experience sampling analysis. *Journal of Personality and Social Psychology, 45,* 851–861.

McAdams, D.P., Diamond, A., de St. Aubin, E., & Mansfield, E. (1997). Stories of commitment: The psychosocial construction of generative lives. *Journal of Personality and Social Psychology, 72,* 678–694.

McAdams, D.P., & de St. Aubin, E. (1992). A theory of generativity and its assessment through self-report, behavioral acts, and narrative themes in autobiography. *Journal of Personality and Social Psychology, 62,* 1003–1015.

McAdams, D.P., de St. Aubin, E., & Logan, R.L. (1993). Generativity among young, midlife, and older adults. *Psychology and Aging, 8,* 221–230.

McAdams, D.P., Healy, S., & Krause, S. (1984). Social motives and patterns of friendship. *Journal of Personality and Social Psychology, 47,* 828–838.

McAdams, D.P., Hart, H.M., & Maruna, S. (1998). The anatomy of generativity. In D.P. McAdams and E. de St. Aubin (Eds.), *Generativity and adult development: How and why we care for the next generation* (pp. 7–43). Washington, DC: APA Press.

McAdams, D.P., Hoffman, B.J., Mansfield, E.D., & Day, R. (1996). Themes of agency and communion in significant autobiographical scenes. *Journal of Personality, 64,* 339–377.

McAdams, D.P., Jackson, R.J., & Kirshnit, C. (1984). Looking, laughing, and smiling in dyads as a function of intimacy motivation and reciprocity. *Journal of Personality, 52,* 261–273.

McAdams, D.P., Lensky, D.B., Daple, S.A., & Allen, J. (1988). Depression and the organization of autobiographical memory. *Journal of Social and Clinical Psychology, 7,* 332–349.

McAdams, D.P., Lester, R., Brand, P., McNamara, W., & Lensky, D.B.

(1988). Sex and the TAT: Are women more intimate than men? Do men fear intimacy? *Journal of Personality Assessment, 52,* 397–409.

McAdams, D.P., & Logan, R.L. (2004). What is generativity? In E. de St. Aubin, D.P. McAdams, and T.C. Kim (Eds.), *The generative society* (pp. 15-31). Washington, DC: APA Books.

McAdams, D.P., & Losoff, M. (1984). Friendship motivation in fourth and sixth graders: A thematic analysis. *Journal of Social and Personal Relationships, 1,* 11–27.

McAdams, D.P., & Ochberg, R.L. (Eds.). (1988). *Psychobiography and life narratives.* Durham, NC: Duke University Press.

McAdams, D.P., & Powers, J. (1981). Themes of intimacy in behavior and thought. *Journal of Personality and Social Psychology, 40,* 573–587.

McAdams, D.P., Reynolds, J., Lewis, M., Patten, A., & Bowman, P.J. (2001). When bad things turn good and good things turn bad: Sequences of redemption and contamination in life narrative, and their relation to psychosocial adaptation in midlife adults and in students. *Personality and Social Psychology Bulletin, 27,* 208–230.

McAdams, D.P., Rothman, S., & Lichter, S.R. (1982). Motivational profiles: A study of former political radicals and politically moderate adults. *Personality and Social Psychology Bulletin, 8,* 593–603.

McAdams, D.P., Ruetzel, K., & Foley, J.M. (1986). Complexity and generativity at mid-life: Relations among social motives, ego development, and adults' plans for the future. *Journal of Personality and Social Psychology, 50,* 800–807.

McAdams, D.P., & Vaillant, G.E. (1982). Intimacy motivation and psychosocial adjustment: A longitudinal study. *Journal of Personality Assessment, 46,* 586–593.

McAdams, D.P., & West, S. (1997). Introduction: Personality psychology and the case study. *Journal of Personality, 65,* 757–783.

McAndrew, F.T. (2002). New evolutionary perspectives on altruism: Multilevel-selection and costly-signaling theories. *Current Directions in Psychological Science, 11,* 79–82.

McClelland, D.C. (1951). *Personality.* New York: Holt, Rinehart & Winston.

McClelland, D.C. (1961). *The achieving society.* New York: D. Van Nostrand.

McClelland, D.C. (1963). The Harlequin complex. In R.W. White (Ed.), *The study of lives* (pp. 94–119). New York: Holt, Rinehart & Winston.

McClelland, D.C. (1965). *N* achievement and entrepreneurship: A longitudinal study. *Journal of Personality and Social Psychology, 1,* 389–392.

McClelland, D.C. (1975). *Power: The inner experience.* New York: Irvington.

McClelland, D.C. (1979). Inhibited power motivation and high blood pressure in men. *Journal of Abnormal Psychology, 88,* 182–190.

McClelland, D.C. (1980). Motive dispositions: The merits of operant and respondent measures. In L. Wheeler (Ed.), *Review of personality and social psychology* (Vol. 1, pp. 10–41). Beverly Hills, CA: Sage.

McClelland, D.C. (1981). Is personality consistent? In A.I. Rabin, J. Aronoff, A.M. Barclay, & R.A. Zucker (Eds.), *Further explorations in personality* (pp. 87–113). New York: John Wiley & Sons.

McClelland, D.C. (1985). *Human motivation.* Glenview, IL: Scott, Foresman.

McClelland, D.C., Alexander, C., & Marks, E. (1982). The need for power, stress, immune function, and illness among male prisoners. *Journal of Abnormal Psychology, 91,* 61–70.

McClelland, D.C., Atkinson, J.W., Clark, R.A., & Lowell, E.L. (1953). *The achievement motive.* New York: Appleton-Century-Crofts.

McClelland, D.C., & Boyatzis, R.E. (1982). The leadership motive pattern and long term success in management. *Journal of Applied Psychology, 67,* 737–743.

McClelland, D.C., & Burnham, D.H. (1976). Power is the great motivator. *Harvard Business Review,* March-April, 100–110, 159–166.

McClelland, D.C., Davidson, R.J., Floor, E., & Saron, C. (1980). Stressed power motivation, sympathetic activation, immune function, and illness. *Journal of Human Stress, 6*(2), 11–19.

McClelland, D.C., Davis, W.N., Kalin, R., & Wanner, E. (1972). *The drinking man: Alcohol and human motivation.* New York: The Free Press.

McClelland, D.C., & Franz, C.E. (1992). Motivational and other sources of work accomplishments in midlife: A longitudinal study. *Journal of Personality, 60,* 679-707.

McClelland, D.C., & Jemmott, J.B., III. (1980). Power motivation, stress, and physical illness. *Journal of Human Stress, 6*(4), 6–15.

McClelland, D.C., Koestner, R., & Weinberger, J. (1989). How do self-attributed and implicit motives differ? *Psychological Review, 96,* 690–702.

McClelland, D.C., Ross, G., & Patel, V. (1985). The effect of an academic examination on salivary norepinephrine and immunoglobulin levels. *Journal of Human Stress, 11*(2), 52–59.

McCrae, R.R., & Costa, P.T., Jr. (1980). Openness to experience and ego level in Loevinger's Sentence Completion Test: Dispositional contributions to developmental models of personality. *Journal of Personality and Social Psychology, 39,* 1179–1190.

McCrae, R.R., & Costa, P.T., Jr. (1985a). Updating Norman's "adequate taxonomy": Intelligence and personality dimensions in natural language and in questionnaires. *Journal of Personality and Social Psychology, 49,* 710–721.

McCrae, R.R., & Costa, P.T. Jr. (1985b). Openness to experience. In R. Hogan and W.H. Jones (Ed.), *Perspectives in personality* (Vol. 1, pp. 145–172). Greenwich, CT: JAI Press.

McCrae, R.R., & Costa, P.T., Jr. (1986). Personality, coping, and coping effectiveness in an adult sample. *Journal of Personality, 54,* 385–405.

McCrae, R.R., & Costa, P.T., Jr. (1987). Validation of the five-factor model of personality across instruments and observers. *Journal of Personality and Social Psychology, 52,* 81–90.

McCrae, R.R., & Costa, P.T., Jr. (1989). The structure of interpersonal traits: Wiggins' circumplex and the five-factor model. *Journal of Personality and Social Psychology, 56,* 586–595.

McCrae, R.R., & Costa, P.T., Jr. (1990). *Personality in adulthood.* New York: Guilford Press.

McCrae, R.R., & Costa, P.T., Jr. (1991). Adding *Liebe und Arbeit:* The full five-factor model and well-being. *Personality and Social Psychology Bulletin, 17,* 227–232.

McCrae, R.R., & Costa, P.T., Jr. (1995). Trait explanations in personality psychology. *European Journal of Personality, 9,* 231–252.

McCrae, R.R., & Costa, P.T., Jr. (1996). Toward a new generation of personality theories: Theoretical contexts for the five-factor model. In J. Wiggins (Ed.), *The five-factor model of personality: Theoretical perspectives* (pp. 51–87). New York: Guilford Press.

McCrae, R.R., & Costa, P.T., Jr. (1997a). Conceptions and correlates of openness to experience. In R. Hogan, J. Johnson, and S. Briggs (Eds.), *Handbook of personality psychology* (pp. 825–847). San Diego, CA: Academic Press.

McCrae, R.R., & Costa, P.T., Jr. (1997b). Personality trait structure as a human universal. *American Psychologist, 52,* 509–516.

McCrae, R.R., Costa, P.T., Jr., de Lima, M.P., Simoes, A., Ostendorf, F., Angleitner, A., Marusic, I., et al. (1999). Age differences in personality across the adult lifespan: Parallels in five cultures. *Developmental Psychology, 35,* 466-477.

McDowall, J. (1984). Recall of pleasant and unpleasant words in depressed subjects. *Journal of Abnormal Psychology, 93,* 401–407.

McFarland, S.G., Ageyev, V.S., & Abalakina-Papp, M.A. (1992). Authoritarianism in the former Soviet Union. *Journal of Personality and Social Psychology, 63,* 1004–1010.

McGue, M., Bacon, S., & Lykken, D.T. (1993). Personality stability and change in early adulthood: A behavioral genetic analysis. *Developmental Psychology, 29,* 96–109.

McKenna, F.P. (1984). Measures of field dependence: Cognitive style or cognitive ability? *Journal of Personality and Social Psychology, 47,* 593–603.

McLean, K.C., & Thorne, A. (2003). Late adolescents' self-defining memories about relationships. *Developmental Psychology, 39,* 635–645.

Mead, G.H. (1934). *Mind, self, and society.* Chicago: University of Chicago Press.

Meehl, P.E. (1954). *Clinical versus statistical prediction: A theoretical analysis and a review of the evidence.* Minneapolis, MN: University of Minnesota Press.

Meloen, J.D., Hagendoorn, L., Raaijmakers, Q., & Visser, L. (1988). Authoritarianism and the revival of political racism: Reassessments in the Netherlands of the reliability and validity of the concept of authoritarianism by Adorno et al. *Political Psychology, 9,* 413–429.

Mercer, R.T., Nichols, E.G., & Doyle, G.C. (1989). *Transitions in a woman's life: Major life events in developmental context.* New York: Springer.

Messick, S. (1994). The matter of style: Manifestations of personality in cognition, learning, and teaching. *Educational Psychologist, 29,* 121–136.

Meyer, G.J., & Shack, J.R. (1989). Structural convergence of mood and personality: Evidence for old and new directions. *Journal of Personality and Social Psychology, 57,* 691–706.

Mikulincer, M. (1995). Attachment style and the mental representation of the self. *Journal of Personality and Social Psychology, 69,* 1203–1215.

Mikulincer, M. (1997). Adult attachment style and information processing: Individual differences in curiosity and cognitive closure. *Journal of Personality and Social Psychology, 72,* 1217–1230.

Mikulincer, M., Florian, V., & Weller, A. (1993). Attachment styles, coping strategies, and posttraumatic psychological distress: The impact of the Gulf War in Israel. *Journal of Personality and Social Psychology, 64,* 817–826.

Mikulincer, M., & Nachson, O. (1991). Attachment styles and patterns of self-disclosure. *Journal of Personality and Social Psychology, 61,* 321–331.

Miles, D.R., & Carey, G. (1997). Genetic and environmental architecture of human aggression. *Journal of Personality and Social Psychology, 72,* 207–217.

Miller, J.G. (1984). Culture and the development of everyday social explanation. *Journal of Personality and Social Psychology, 46,* 961–978.

Miller, N.E., & Dollard, J. (1941). *Social learning and imitation.* New Haven, CT: Yale University Press.

Miller, P.C., Lefcourt, H.M., Holmes, J.G., Ware, E.E., & Saleh, W.E. (1986). Marital locus of control and marital problem solving. *Journal of Personality and Social Psychology, 51,* 161–169.

Miller, W.R., & C'deBaca, J. (1994). Quantum change: Toward a psychology of transformation. In T.H. Heatherton and J.L. Weinberger (Eds.), *Can personality change?* (pp. 253–280). Washington, DC: APA Press.

Mills, C.W. (1959). *The sociological imagination.* New York: Oxford University Press.

Millon, T. (Ed.). (1973). *Theories of psychopathology and personality* (2nd ed.). Philadelphia: W.B. Saunders.

Mink, L.O. (1978). Narrative form as a cognitive instrument. In R.H. Canary and H. Kozicki (Eds.), *Literary form and historical understanding* (pp. 129–149). Madison, WI: University of Wisconsin Press.

Minuchin, S. (1974). *Families and family therapy.* Cambridge, MA: Harvard University Press.

Mischel, W. (1961). Delay of gratification, need for achievement, and acquiescence in another culture. *Journal of Abnormal and Social Psychology, 62,* 543–552.

Mischel, W. (1968). *Personality and assessment.* New York: John Wiley & Sons.

Mischel, W. (1973). Toward a cognitive social learning reconceptualization of personality. *Psychological Review, 80,* 252–283.

Mischel, W. (1977). On the future of personality measurement. *American Psychologist, 32,* 246–254.

Mischel, W. (1979). On the interface of cognition and personality: Beyond the person–situation debate. *American Psychologist, 34,* 740–754.

Mischel, W. (1986). *Introduction to personality* (4th Ed.). New York: Holt, Rinehart & Winston.

Mischel, W. (1999). Personality coherence and dispositions in a cognitive-affective personality system (CAPS) approach. In D. Cervone and Y. Shoda (Eds.), *The coherence of personality: Social-cognitive bases of consistency, variability, and organization* (pp. 61–93). New York: Guilford Press.

Mischel, W., & Gilligan, C. (1964). Delay of gratification, motivation for the prohibited gratification, and response to temptation. *Journal of Abnormal and Social Psychology, 69,* 411–417.

Mischel, W., & Peake, P.K. (1982). Beyond déjà vu in the search for cross-situational consistency. *Psychological Review, 89,* 730–755.

Mischel, W., & Shoda, Y. (1995). A cognitive-affective system theory of personality: Reconceptualizing situations, dispositions, dynamics, and invariance in personality structure. *Psychological Review, 102,* 246–268.

Mischel, W., & Shoda, Y. (1998). Reconciling processing dynamics and personality dispositions. In J.T. Spence, J.M. Darley, and D.J. Foss (Eds.), *Annual review of psychology* (pp. 229–258). Palo Alto, CA: Annual Reviews, Inc.

Mishima, Y. (1958). *Confessions of a mask.* New York: New Directions Books.

Mishima, Y. (1970). *Sun and steel.* New York: Grove Press.

Mishler, E. (1992). Work, identity, and narrative: An artist-craftsman's story. In G.C. Rosenwald and R.L. Ochberg (Eds.), *Storied lives: The cultural politics of self-understanding* (pp. 21–40). New Haven, CT: Yale University Press.

Mitchell, J.C. (1983). Case and situation analysis. *The Sociological Review, 31,* 187–211.

Modell, J. (1992). How do you introduce yourself as a childless mother? Birthparent interpretations of parenthood. In G.C. Rosenwald and R.L. Ochberg (Eds.), *Storied lives: The cultural politics of self-understanding* (pp. 76–94). New Haven, CT: Yale University Press.

Moen, P., Elder, G.H., Jr., & Luscher, K. (Eds.). (1995). *Examining lives in context: Perspectives on the ecology of human development.* Washington, D.C.: American Psychological Association Press.

Moffitt, K.H., & Singer, J.A. (1994). Continuity in the life story: Self-defining memories, affect, and approach/avoidance personal strivings. *Journal of Personality, 62,* 21–43.

Mohr, C.D., Armeli, S., Tennen, H., Carney, M.A., Affleck, G., & Hromi, A. (2001). Daily interpersonal experiences, context, and alcohol consumption: Crying in your beer and toasting good times. *Journal of Personality and Social Psychology, 80,* 489–500.

Moi, T. (1981). Representation of patriarchy: Sexuality and epistemology in Freud's Dora. *Feminist Review, 9*, 60–73.

Monte, C.F. (1995). *Beneath the mask: An introduction to theories of personality* (5th Ed.). Fort Worth, TX: Harcourt Brace.

Moos, R.H. (1973). Conceptualizations of human environments. *American Psychologist, 28*, 652–665.

Moos, R.H. (1974). Systems for the assessment and classifications of human environments: An overview. In R.H. Moos and P.M. Insel (Eds.), *Issues in social ecology* (pp. 5–28). Palo Alto, CA: National Press Books.

Moos, R.H. (1976). *The human context: Environmental determinants of behavior*. New York: John Wiley & Sons.

Moraitis, G., & Pollack, G.H. (Eds.). (1987). *Psychoanalytic studies of biography*. Madison, CT: International Universities Press.

Morgan, C.D., & Murray, H.A. (1935). A method for investigating fantasies: The Thematic Apperception Test. *Archives of Neurology and Psychiatry, 34*, 289-306.

Mortimer, J.T., Finch, M.D., & Kumka, D. (1982). Persistence and change in development: The multidimensional self-concept. In P.B. Baltes and O.G. Brim, Jr. (Eds.), *Life span development and behavior* (Vol. 4, pp. 264–315). New York: Academic Press.

Moskowitz, D.S. (1990). Convergence of self-reports and independent observers: Dominance and friendliness. *Journal of Personality and Social Psychology, 58*, 1096–1106.

Mountjoy, P.J., & Sundberg, M.L. (1981). Ben Franklin the protobehaviorist I: Self-management of behavior. *The Psychological Record, 31*, 13–24.

Mroczek, D.K., & Almeida, D.M. (2004). The effect of daily stress, personality, and age on daily negative affect. *Journal of Personality, 72*, 355–378.

Mroczek, D.K., & Kolarz, C.M. (1998). The effect of age on positive and negative affect: A developmental perspective on happiness. *Journal of Personality and Social Psychology, 75*, 1333–1349.

Mumford, M., Stokes, G.S., & Owens, W.A. (1990). *Patterns of life history: The ecology of human individuality*. Hillsdale, NJ: Lawrence Erlbaum.

Murray, H.A. (1938). *Explorations in personality*. New York: Oxford University Press.

Murray, H.A. (1940). What should psychologists do about psychoanalysis? *Journal of Abnormal and Social Psychology, 35*, 150–175.

Murray, H.A. (1943). *The Thematic Apperception Test: Manual*. Cambridge, MA: Harvard University Press.

Murray, H.A. (1951a). *In nomine diaboli*. *New England Quarterly, 24*, 435–452.

Murray, H.A. (1951b). Some basic psychological assumptions and conceptions. *Dialectica, 5*, 266–292.

Murray, H.A. (1955/1981). American Icarus. In E.S. Shneidman (Ed.), *Endeavors in psychology: Selections from the personology of Henry A. Murray* (pp. 535–556). New York: Harper & Row.

Murray, H.A. (1959/1981). Vicissitudes of creativity. In E.S. Schneidman (Ed.), *Endeavors in psychology: Selections from the personology of Henry A. Murray* (pp. 312–330). New York: Random House.

Murray, H.A. (1960/1981). Two versions of man. In E. Shneidman (Ed.), *Endeavors in psychology: Selections from the personology of*

Henry A. Murray (pp. 581–604). New York: Harper & Row.

Murray, H.A. (1962). The personality and career of Satan. *Journal of Social Issues, 28*, 36–54.

Murray, H.A. (1967). The case of Murr. In E.G. Boring and G. Lindzey (Eds.), *A history of psychology in autobiography* (Vol. 5, pp. 285–310). New York: Appleton-Century-Crofts.

Murray, H.A., & Kluckhohn, C. (1953). Outline of a conception of personality. In C. Kluckhohn, H.A. Murray, and D. Schneider (Eds.), *Personality in nature, society, and culture* (2nd ed., pp. 3–52). New York: Knopf.

Murray, H.A. with staff. (1948). *Assessment of men*. New York: Rinehart & Co.

Murray, K. (1989). The construction of identity in the narratives of romance and comedy. In J. Shotter & K.J. Gergen (Eds.), *Texts of identity* (pp. 176–205). London: Sage.

Muslin, H., & Gill, M. (1978). Transference in the Dora case. *Journal of the American Psychoanalytic Association, 26*, 311–328.

Myers, D. (2000). *The American paradox: Spiritual hunger in an age of plenty*. New Haven, CT: Yale University Press.

Myers, D.G., & Diener, E. (1995). Who is happy? *Psychological Science, 6*, 10–19.

Myers, L.B., & Brewin, C.R. (1994). Recall of early experience and the repressive coping style. *Journal of Abnormal Psychology, 103*, 288–292.

N

Nakagawa, K. (1991). *Explorations into the correlates of public school reform and parental involvement*. Unpublished doctoral dissertation, Human Development and Social

Policy, Northwestern University, Evanston, IL.

Narayanan, L., Mensa, S., & Levine, E.L. (1995). Personality structure: A culture-specific examination of the five-factor model. *Journal of Personality Assessment, 64,* 51–62.

Nasby, W., & Read, N. (1997). The life voyage of a solo circumnavigator: Integrating theoretical and methodological perspectives. Introduction. *Journal of Personality, 65,* 787-794.

Nathan, J. (1974). *Mishima: A biography.* Boston: Litle, Brown.

Neisser, U. (1976). *Cognition and reality: Principles and implications of cognitive psychology.* San Francisco, CA: W.H. Freeman.

Neugarten, B.L. (Ed.). (1968). *Middle age and aging.* Chicago: University of Chicago Press.

Neugarten, B.L. (1979). Time, age, and the life cycle. *American Journal of Psychiatry, 136,* 887–894.

Neugarten, B.L., & Datan, N. (1974). The middle years. In S. Arieti (Ed.), *American handbook of psychiatry* (Vol. 1). New York: Basic Books.

Neugarten, B.L., & Hagestad, G.O. (1976). Aging and the life course. In R.H. Binstock and E. Shanas (Eds.), *Handbook of aging and the social sciences* (pp. 35-57). New York: Van Nostrand Reinhold.

NICHD Early Child Care Research Network. (2001). Child-care and family predictors of preschool attachment and stability from infancy. *Developmental Psychology, 37,* 847–862.

Nichols, S.L., & Newman, J.P. (1986). Effects of punishment on response latency in extraverts. *Journal of Personality and Social Psychology, 50,* 624–630.

Nicholson, I. (2002). *Inventing personality: Gordon Allport and the science of selfhood.* Washington, DC: APA Books.

Niitamo, P. (1999). *"Surface" and "depth" in human personality: Relations between explicit and implicit motives.* Helsinki: Finnish Institute of Occupational Health.

Noam, G. (1998). Solving the ego development-mental health riddle. In P.M. Westenberg, A. Blasi, and L.D. Cohn (Eds.), *Personality development: Theoretical, empirical, and clinical investigations of Loevinger's conception of ego development* (pp. 271–295). Mahwah, NJ: Erlbaum.

Nolen-Hoeksema, S., Girgus, J.S., & Seligman, M.E.P. (1986). Learned helplessness in children: A longitudinal study of depression, achievement, and explanatory style. *Journal of Personality and Social Psychology, 51,* 435–442.

Norman, R.M.G., & Watson, L.D. (1976). Extraversion and reactions to cognitive inconsistency. *Journal of Research in Personality, 10,* 446–456.

Norman, W.T. (1963). Toward an adequate taxonomy of personality attributes: Replicated factor structure in peer nomination personality ratings. *Journal of Abnormal and Social Psychology, 66,* 574–583.

Nucci, L. (1981). Conceptions of personal issues: A domain distinct from moral or societal concepts. *Child Development, 52,* 114–121.

O

O'Brien, R., & Dukore, B.F. (1969). *Tragedy: Ten major plays* (Sophocles' *Oedipus Rex*). New York: Bantam Books.

Ochberg, R.L. (1988). Life stories and the psychosocial construction of careers. *Journal of Personality, 56,* 173–204.

Ochse, R., & Plug, C. (1986). Cross-cultural investigations of the validity of Erikson's theory of personality development. *Journal of Personality and Social Psychology, 50,* 1240–1252.

Ogilvie, D.M. (1987). The undesired self: A neglected variable in personality research. *Journal of Personality and Social Psychology, 52,* 379–385.

Ogilvie, D.M. (2004). *Fantasies of flight.* New York: Oxford University Press.

Oliner, S.P., & Oliner, P.M. (1988). *The altruistic personality: Rescuers of Jews in Nazi Europe.* New York: The Free Press.

Ones, D.S., Viswesvaran, C., & Schmidt, F.L. (1993). Comprehensive meta-analysis of integrity test validation: Findings and implications for personnel selection and theories of job performance. *Journal of Applied Psychology, 78,* 679–703.

Orlofsky, J.L. (1978). Identity formation, achievements, and fear of success in college men and women. *Journal of Youth and Adolescence, 7,* 49–62.

Orlofsky, J.L., & Frank, M. (1986). Personality structure as viewed through early memories and identity status in college men and women. *Journal of Personality and Social Psychology, 50,* 580–586.

Orlofsky, J.L., Marcia, J.E., & Lesser, I.M. (1973). Ego identity status and the intimacy versus isolation crisis of young adulthood. *Journal of Personality and Social Psychology, 27,* 211–219.

Ormel, J., & Wohlfarth, T. (1991). How neuroticism, long-term difficulties, and life situation changes influence psychological distress: A longitudinal model. *Journal of Personality and Social Psychology, 60,* 744–755.

Osborne, J. (1961). *Luther.* New York: Criterion Books.

Oshman, H., & Manosevitz, M. (1974). The impact of the identity crisis on the adjustment of late adolescent males. *Journal of Youth and Adolescence, 3,* 107–216.

Ozer, D.J. (1986). *Consistency in personality: A methodological framework.* New York: Springer-Verlag.

Ozer, D.J., & Gjerde, P.F. (1989). Patterns of personality consistency and change from childhood through adolescence. *Journal of Personality, 57,* 483–507.

Ozer, E.M., & Bandura, A. (1990). Mechanisms governing empowering effects: A self-efficacy analysis. *Journal of Personality and Social Psychology, 58,* 472–486.

P

Pals, J.L., & John, O.P. (1998). How are dimensions of adult personality related to ego development? An application of the typological approach. In P.M. Westenberg, A. Blasi, and L. Cohn (Eds.), *Personality development: Theoretical, empirical, and clinical investigations of Jane Loevinger's conception of ego development* (pp. 113–132). Hillsdale, NJ: Erlbaum.

Palys, T.S., & Little, B.R. (1983). Perceived life satisfaction and the organization of personal project systems. *Journal of Personality and Social Psychology, 44,* 1221–1230.

Pargament, K.I. (2002). The bitter and the sweet: An evaluation of the costs and benefits of religiousness. *Psychological Inquiry, 13,* 168–181.

Parke, R.D., & Walters, R.H. (1967). Some factors influencing the efficacy of punishment training for inducing response inhibitions. *Monographs of the Society for Research in Child Development, 32*(1, Serial No. 109).

Passini, F.T., & Norman, W.T. (1966). A universal conception of personality structure? *Journal of Personality and Social Psychology, 4,* 44–49.

Pasupathi, M. (2001). The social construction of the personal past and its implications for adult development. *Psychological Bulletin, 127,* 651–672.

Patterson, C.M., Kosson, D.J., & Newman, J.P. (1987). Reaction to punishment, reflectivity, and passive avoidance learning in extraverts. *Journal of Personality and Social Psychology, 52,* 565–575.

Paulhus, D.L., Fridhandler, B., & Hayes, S. (1997). Psychological defense: Contemporary theory and research. In R. Hogan, J. Johnson, and S. Briggs (Eds.), *Handbook of personality psychology* (pp. 543–579). San Diego, CA: Academic Press.

Paulhus, D.L., Trapnell, P.D., & Chen, D. (1999). Birth order effects on personality and achievement within families. *Psychological Science, 10,* 482–488.

Paunonen, S.V., & Jackson, D.N. (2000). What is beyond the Big Five? Plenty! *Journal of Personality, 68,* 821–835.

Paunonen, S.V., Jackson, D.N., & Keinonen, M. (1990). The structured nonverbal assessment of personality. *Journal of Personality, 58,* 481–502.

Pearce-McCall, D., & Newman, J.P. (1986). Expectation of success following noncontingent punishment in introverts and extraverts. *Journal of Personality and Social Psychology, 50,* 439–446.

Pederson, D.R., Moran, G., Sitko, C., Campbell, K., Ghesquire, K., & Acton, H. (1990). Maternal sensitivity and the security of infant–mother attachment: A Q-sort study. *Child Development, 61,* 1974–1983.

Pekala, R.J., Wenger, C.F., & Levine, R.L. (1985). Individual differences in phenomenological experience: States of consciousness as a function of absorption. *Journal of Personality and Social Psychology, 48,* 125–132.

Pellegrini, A.D., & Galda, L. (1990). The joint construction of stories by preschool children and an experimenter. In B.K. Britten and A.D. Pellegrini (Eds.), *Narrative thought and narrative language* (pp. 113–130). Hillsdale, NJ: Lawrence Erlbaum.

Pennebaker, J.W. (1988). Confiding traumatic experiences and health. In S. Fisher and J. Reason (Eds.), *Handbook of life stress, cognition, and health* (pp. 669–682). New York: Wiley.

Pennebaker, J.W. (1989a). Stream of consciousness and stress: Levels of thinking. In J.S. Uleman and J.A. Bargh (Eds.), *Unintended thought* (pp. 327–349). New York: Guilford Press.

Pennebaker, J.W. (1989b). Confession, inhibition, and disease. In L. Berkowitz (Ed.), *Advances in experimental social psychology* (Vol. 22, pp. 211–244). New York: Academic Press.

Pennebaker, J.W. (1992). Putting stress into words: Health, linguistic, and therapeutic implications. Paper presented at the American Psychological Association Convention, Washington, DC.

Pennebaker, J.W. (1997). Writing about emotional experiences as a therapeutic process. *Psychological Science, 8,* 162–166.

Pennebaker, J.W., & Beall, S.K. (1986). Confronting a traumatic event: Toward an understanding of inhibition and disease. *Journal of Abnormal Psychology, 95,* 274–281.

Pennebaker, J.W., Kiecolt-Glaser, J.K., & Glaser, R. (1988). Disclosure of traumas and immune function: Health implications for psychotherapy. *Journal of Consulting and Clinical Psychology, 56,* 239–245.

Pennebaker, J., Mehl, M.R., & Niederhoffer, K.G. (2003). Psychological aspects of natural language use: Our words, our selves. *Annual Review of Psychology, 54,* 547–577.

Pennebaker, J.W., & O'Heeron, R.C. (1984). Confiding in others and illness rate among spouses of suicide and accidental death victims. *Journal of Abnormal Psychology, 93,* 473–476.

Pepper, S. (1942). *World hypotheses.* Berkeley, CA: University of California Press.

Perry, W.C. (1970). *Forms of intellectual and ethical development in the college years.* New York: Holt, Rinehart & Winston.

Pervin, L.A. (Ed.). (1989). *Goal concepts in personality and social psychology.* Hillsdale, NJ: Lawrence Erlbaum.

Pervin. L. (Ed.). (1990). *Handbook of personality theory and research.* New York: Guilford Press.

Pervin, L. (1996). *The science of personality.* New York: Wiley.

Peterson, B.E., Doty, R.M., & Winter, D.G. (1993). Authoritarianism and attitudes toward contemporary social issues. *Personality and Social Psychology Bulletin, 19,* 174–184.

Peterson, B.E., & Klohnen, E.C. (1995). Realization of generativity in two samples of women at midlife. *Psychology and Aging, 10,* 20–29.

Peterson, B.E., & Lane, M.D. (2001). Implications of authoritarianism for young adulthood: Longitudinal analysis of college experiences and future goals. *Personality and Social Psychology Bulletin, 27,* 678–689.

Peterson, B.E., Smirles, K.A., & Wentworth, P.A. (1997). Generativity and authoritarianism: Implications for personality, political involvement, and parenting. *Journal of Personality and Social Psychology, 72,* 1202–1216.

Peterson, B.E., & Stewart, A.J. (1990). Using personal and fictional documents to assess psychosocial development: The case study of Vera Brittain's generativity. *Psychology and Aging, 5,* 400–411.

Peterson, B.E., & Stewart, A.J. (1996). Antecedents and contexts of generativity motivation at midlife. *Psychology and Aging, 11,* 21–33.

Peterson, C., Luborsky, L., & Seligman, M.E.P. (1983). Attributions and depressive mood shifts: A case study using the symptom–context method. *Journal of Abnormal Psychology, 92,* 96–103.

Peterson, C., & Seligman, M.E.P. (1984). Causal explanations as a risk factor for depression: Theory and evidence. *Psychological Review, 91,* 347–374.

Peterson, C., Seligman, M.E.P., & Vaillant, G.E. (1988). Pessimistic explanatory style is a risk factor for physical illness: A thirty-five year longitudinal study. *Journal of Personality and Social Psychology, 55,* 23–27.

Peterson, C., Seligman, M.E.P., Yurko, K.H., Martin, L.R., & Friedman, H.S. (1998). Catastrophizing and untimely death. *Psychological Science, 9,* 127–130.

Peterson, C., Villanova, P., & Raps, C.S. (1985). Depression and attributions: Factors responsible for inconsistent results in the published literature. *Journal of Abnormal Psychology, 94,* 165–168.

Pettigrew, T.F. (1997). Personality and social structure: Social psychological contributions. In R. Hogan, J. Johnson, and S. Briggs (Eds.), *Handbook of personality psychology* (pp. 417–438). San Diego, CA: Academic Press.

Petty, R.E., & Cacioppo, J.T. (1981). *Attitudes and persuasion: Classical and contemporary approaches.* Dubuque, IA: Wm. C. Brown.

Phares, E.J. (1957). Expectancy changes in skill and chance situations. *Journal of Abnormal and Social Psychology, 54,* 339–342.

Phares, E.J. (1978). Locus of control. In H. London and J.E. Exner, Jr. (Eds.), *Dimensions of personality* (pp. 263–304). New York: John Wiley & Sons.

Piaget, J. (1970). *Genetic epistemology.* New York: Columbia University Press.

Pillemer, D.B. (1998). *Momentous events, vivid memories.* Cambridge, MA: Harvard University Press.

Pinker, S. (1997). *How the mind works.* New York: Norton.

Plomin, R., & Bergman, C.S. (1991). The nature of nurture: Genetic influences on "environmental" measures. *Behavioral and Brain Sciences, 14,* 373–386.

Plomin, R., Chipuer, H.M., & Loehlin, J.C. (1990). Behavioral genetics and personality. In L. Pervin (Ed.), *Handbook of personality theory and research* (pp. 225–243). New York: Guilford Press.

Podd, M.H. (1972). Ego identity status and morality: The relationships between two developmental constructs. *Developmental Psychology, 6,* 497–507.

Polkinghorne, D. (1988). *Narrative knowing and the human sciences.* Albany, NY: State University of New York: Press.

Pomerantz, E.M., Saxon, J.L., & Oishi, S. (2000). The psychological trade-offs of goal investment. *Journal of Personality and Social Psychology, 79,* 617–630.

Popper, K. (1959). *The logic of scientific discovery.* New York: Basic Books.

Porter, C.A., & Suedfeld, P. (1981). Integrative complexity in the correspondence of literary figures: Effects of personal and societal stress. *Journal of Personality and Social Psychology, 40,* 321–330.

Powers, W.T. (1973). Feedback: Beyond behaviorism. *Science, 179,* 351–356.

Pratt, M.W., Danso, H.A., Arnold, M.L., Norris, J.E., & Filyer, R. (2001). Adult generativity and the socialization of adolescents: Relations to mothers' and fathers' parenting beliefs, styles, and practices. *Journal of Personality, 69,* 89–120.

Pratt, M.W., & Friese, B. (Eds.). (2004). *Family stories and the life course: Across time and generations.* Mahwah, NJ: Lawrence Erlbaum.

Putnam, R.D. (2000). *Bowling alone: The collapse and revival of American community.* New York: Simon & Schuster.

R

Rafaeli-Mor, E., & Steinberg, J. (2002). Self-complexity and well-being: A review and research synthesis. *Personality and Social Psychology Review, 6,* 31–58.

Raskin, R.N., & Hall, C.J. (1979). A narcissistic personality inventory. *Psychological Reports, 45,* 590.

Raskin, R.N., & Hall, C.J. (1981). The Narcissistic Personality Inventory: Alternate form reliability and further evidence of construct validity. *Journal of Personality Assessment, 45,* 159–162.

Raskin, R.N., & Shaw, R. (1988). Narcissism and the use of personal pronouns. *Journal of Personality, 56,* 393–404.

Rawsthorne, L.J., & Elliot, A.J. (1999). Achievement goals and intrinsic motivation: A meta-analytic review. *Personality and Social Psychology Review, 3,* 326–344.

Redmore, C., Loevinger, J., & Tamashiro, R. (1978). *Measuring ego development: Scoring manual for men and boys.* Unpublished manuscript.

Redmore, C., & Waldman, K. (1975). Reliability of a sentence completion measure of ego development. *Journal of Personality Assessment, 39,* 236–243.

Reichenbach, H. (1938). *Experience and prediction.* Chicago, IL: University of Chicago Press.

Reis, H.T., Sheldon, K.M., Gable, S.L., Roscoe, J., & Ryan, R.M. (2000). Daily well-being: The role of autonomy, competence, and relatedness. *Personality and Social Psychology, 26,* 419–435.

Rescorla, R.A. (1988). Pavlovian conditioning: It's not what you think it is. *American Psychologist, 43,* 151–160.

Reuman, D.A., Alwin, D.F., & Veroff, J. (1984). Assessing the validity of the achievement motive in the presence of random measurement error. *Journal of Personality and Social Psychology, 47,* 1347–1362.

Revelle, W. (1995). Personality processes. In L.W. Porter and M.R. Rosenzweig (Eds.), *Annual review of psychology* (Vol. 46, pp. 295–328). Palo Alto, CA: Annual Reviews, Inc.

Rhodewalt, F., & Morf, C.C. (1998). On self-aggrandizement and anger: A temporal analysis of narcissism and affective reactions to success and failure. *Journal of Personality and Social Psychology, 74,* 672–685.

Richardson, J.A., & Turner, T.E. (2000). Field dependence revisited I: Intelligence. *Educational Psychology, 20,* 255–270.

Ricoeur, P. (1970). *Freud and philosophy: An essay on interpretation.* New Haven, CT: Yale University Press.

Ricoeur, P. (1984). *Time and narrative* (Vol. 1). Chicago: University of Chicago Press. (Translated by Kathleen McGlaughlin and David Pellauer.)

Rieff, P. (1959). *Freud: The mind of a moralist.* Chicago: University of Chicago Press.

Riger, S. (1992). Epistemological debates, feminist voices: Science, social values, and the study of women. *American Psychologist, 47,* 730–740.

Riger, S. (2000). *Transforming psychology: Gender in theory and practice.* New York: Oxford University Press.

Roberti, J.W. (2003). A review of behavioral and biological correlates of sensation seeking. *Journal of Research in Personality, 38,* 256–279.

Roberts, B.W. (1994). *A longitudinal study of the reciprocal relation between women's personality and occupational experience.* Unpublished doctoral dissertation, University of California, Berkeley.

Roberts, B.W., & Bogg, T. (2004). A longitudinal study of the relationships between conscientousness and the social-environmental factors and substance-use behaviors that influence health. *Journal of Personality, 72,* 325–353.

Roberts, B.W., Caspi, A., & Moffitt, T. (2001). The kids are alright: Growth and stability in personality development from adolescence to adulthood. *Journal of Personality and Social Psychology, 81,* 670–683.

Roberts, B.W., & DelVecchio, W. (2000). The rank-order consistency of personality from childhood to old age: A quantitative review of longitudinal studies. *Psychological Bulletin, 126,* 3–25.

Roberts, J.E., Gotlib, I.H., & Kassel, J.D. (1996). Adult attachment security and symptoms of depression: The mediating role of dysfunctional attitudes and low self-esteem. *Journal of Personality and Social Psychology, 70,* 310–320.

Roberts, P., & Newton, P.M. (1987). Levinsonian studies of women's adult development. *Psychology and Aging, 2,* 154–163.

Robins, C.J. (1988). Attributions and depression: Why is the literature so inconsistent? *Journal of Personality and Social Psychology, 54,* 880–889.

Robinson, D.N. (1981). *An intellectual history of psychology.* New York: Macmillan.

Robinson, F.G. (1992). *Love's story told: A life of Henry A. Murray.* Cambridge, MA: Harvard University Press.

Roche, S.M., & McConkey, K.M. (1990). Absorption: Nature, assessment, and correlates. *Journal of Personality and Social Psychology, 59,* 91–101.

Rogers, C.R. (1942). *Counseling and psychotherapy: Newer concepts in practice.* Boston: Houghton.

Rogers, C.R. (1951). *Client-centered therapy.* Boston: Houghton-Mifflin.

Rogers, C.R. (1959). A theory of therapy, personality, and interpersonal relationships, as developed in the client-centered framework. In S. Koch (Ed.), *Psychology: A study of a science* (Vol. 3). New York: McGraw-Hill.

Rogers, C.R. (1980). Ellen West and loneliness. In C.R. Rogers, *A way of being.* Boston: Houghton-Mifflin.

Rogler, L.H. (2002). Historical generations and psychology: The case of the Great Depression and World War II. *American Psychologist, 57,* 1013–1023.

Rogow, A.A. (1978). A further footnote to Freud's "Fragment of an analysis of a case of hysteria." *Journal of the American Psychoanalytic Association, 28,* 331–356.

Romer, D., Gruder, C.L., & Lizzadro, T. (1986). A person–situation approach to altruistic behavior. *Journal of Personality and Social Psychology, 51,* 1001–1012.

Rootes, M.D., Moras, K., & Gordon, R. (1980). Ego development and sociometrically evaluated maturity: An investigation of the validity of the Washington University Sentence-Completion Test of Ego Development. *Journal of Personality Assessment, 44,* 613–620.

Rosenwald, G.C., & Ochberg, R.L. (Eds.). (1992). *Storied lives: The cultural politics of self-understanding.* New Haven, CT: Yale University Press.

Roser, M., & Gazzaniga, M.S. (2004). Automatic brains—interpretive minds. *Current Directions in Psychological Science, 13,* 56–59.

Ross, L.D. (1977). The intuitive psychologist and his shortcomings: Distortions in the attribution process. In L. Berkowitz (Ed.), *Advances in Experimental Social Psychology* (Vol. 10). New York: Academic Press.

Rossi, A.S. (1980). Life-span theories and women's lives. *Signs, 6*(1), 4–32.

Rossi, A.S. (Ed.). (2001). *Caring and doing for others.* Chicago: University of Chicago Press.

Rosznafszky, J. (1981). The relationship of level of ego development to Q-sort personality ratings. *Journal of Personality and Social Psychology, 41,* 99–120.

Roth, P. (1988). *The facts: A novelist's autobiography.* London: Penguin.

Rothbart, M.K. (1986). Longitudinal observation of infant temperament. *Developmental Psychology, 22,* 356–365.

Rotter, J.B. (1954). *Social learning and clinical psychology.* Englewood Cliffs, NJ: Prentice-Hall.

Rotter, J.B. (1966). Generalized expectancies for internal versus external control of reinforcement. *Psychological Monographs, 80*(1, Whole No. 609).

Rotter, J.B. (1972). *Applications of a social learning theory of personality.* New York: Holt.

Rotter, J.B. (1975). Some problems and misconceptions related to the construct of internal versus external reinforcement. *Journal of Consulting and Clinical Psychology, 43,* 56–67.

Rouse, J. (1978). *The completed gesture: Myth, character, and education.* NJ: Skyline Books.

Rowe, D.C. (1997). Genetics, temperament, and personality. In R. Hogan, J. Johnson, and S. Briggs (Eds.), *Handbook of personality psychology* (pp. 367–386). San Diego, CA: Academic Press.

Rowe, D.C. (1999). Heredity. In V.J. Derlega, B.A. Winstead, and W.H. Jones (Eds.), *Personality: Contemporary theory and research* (2nd ed., pp. 66–100). Chicago: Nelson-Hall.

Runyan, W.M. (1981). Why did Van Gogh cut off his ear? The problem of alternative explanations in psychobiography. *Journal of Personality and Social Psychology, 40,* 1070–1077.

Runyan, W.M. (1982). *Life histories and psychobiography: Explorations in theory and method.* New York: Oxford University Press.

Runyan, W.M. (1990). Individual lives and the structure of personality psychology. In A.I. Rabin, R.A. Zucker, R.A. Emmons, and Frank (Eds), *Studying persons and lives* (pp. 10–40). New York: Springer.

Rushton, J.P., Brainerd, C.J., & Presley, M. (1983). Behavioral development and construct validity: The principle of aggregation. *Psychological Bulletin, 94,* 18–38.

Rushton, J.P., Fulker, D.W., Neale, M.C., Nias, D.K., & Eysenck, H.J. (1986). Altruism and aggression: The heritability of individual differences. *Journal of Personality and Social Psychology, 50,* 1192–1198.

Russell, B. (1945). *A history of Western philosophy.* New York: Simon & Schuster.

Rutter, D.R., Morley, I.E., & Graham, J.C. (1972). Visual interaction in a group of introverts and extraverts. *European Journal of Social Psychology, 2,* 371–384.

Ryan, R.M. (1991). The nature of the self in autonomy and relatedness. In J. Strauss and G.R. Goethals (Eds.), *The self: Interdisciplinary approaches* (pp. 208–238). New York: Springer-Verlag.

Ryan, R.M. (1995). Psychological needs and the facilitation of integrative processes. *Journal of Personality, 63,* 397–427.

Ryff, C.D., & Heincke, S.G. (1983). Subjective organization of personality in adulthood and aging. *Journal of Personality and Social Psychology, 44,* 807–816.

S

Sales, S.M. (1973). Threat as a factor in authoritarianism: An analysis of archival data. *Journal of Personality and Social Psychology, 28,* 44–57.

Sampson, E.E. (1962). Birth order, need achievement, and conformity. *Journal of Abnormal and Social Psychology, 64,* 155–159.

Sampson, E.E. (1985). The decentralization of identity: Toward a revised concept of personal and social order. *American Psychologist, 40,* 1203–1211.

Sampson, E.E. (1988). The debate on individualism: Indigenous psychologies of the individual and their role in personal and societal functioning. *American Psychologist, 43,* 15–22.

Sampson, E.E. (1989a). The challenge of social change for psychology: Globalization and psychology's theory of the person. *American Psychologist, 44,* 914–921.

Sampson, E.E. (1989b). The deconstruction of the self. In J. Shotter and K.J. Gergen (Eds.), *Texts of identity* (pp. 1–19). London: Sage.

Sarbin, T.R. (1986). The narrative as a root metaphor for psychology. In T.R. Sarbin (Ed.), *Narrative psychology: The storied nature of human conduct* (pp. 3–21). New York: Praeger.

Sartre, J.-P. (1965). *Essays in existentialism.* Secaucus, NJ: The Citadel Press.

Sartre, J.-P. (1981). *The family idiot: Gustave Flaubert, 1821–1857* (Vol. 1). Chicago: University of Chicago Press (Transl. By C. Cosman.).

Saucier, G., & Goldberg, L.R. (1996). The language of personality: Lexical perspectives on the five-factor model. In J.S. Wiggins (Ed.), *The five-factor model of personality: Theoretical perspectives* (pp. 21–50). New York: Guilford Press.

Sawyer, J. (1966). Measurement and prediction, clinical *and* statistical. *Psychological Bulletin, 66,* 178–200.

Scarr, S. (1997). Why child care has little impact on most children's development. *New Direction in Psychological Science, 6,* 143–148.

Scarr, J., Webber, P.L., Weinberg, R.A., & Wittig, M.A. (1981). Personality resemblance among adolescents and their parents in biologically related and adoptive families. *Journal of Personality and Social Psychology, 40,* 885–898.

Scarr, S., & McCartney, K. (1983). How people make their own environments: A theory of genotype environment effects. *Child Development, 54,* 424–435.

Schachter, E. (2004). Identity configurations: A new perspective on identity formation in contemporary society. *Journal of Personality, 72,* 167–199.

Schacter, D. (1996). *Searching for memory.* New York: Basic Books.

Schafer, R. (1968). *Aspects of internalization.* New York: International Universities Press.

Schafer, R. (1981). Narration in the psychoanalytic dialogue. In W.J.J. Mitchell (Ed.), *On narrative* (pp. 25–49). Chicago: University of Chicago Press.

Scheier, M.F., & Carver, C.J. (1981). Private and public aspects of self. In L. Wheeler (Ed.), *Review of personality and social psychology* (Vol. 2, pp. 189–216). Beverly Hills, CA: Sage.

Schenkel, S., & Marcia, J.E. (1972). Attitudes toward premarital intercouse in determining ego identity status in college women. *Journal of Personality, 40,* 472–482.

Schneider, B.H., Atkinson, L., & Radif, C. (2001). Child–parent attachment and children's peer relations: A quantitative review. *Developmental Psychology, 37,* 86–100.

Schooler, C. (1972). Birth order effects: Not here, not now! *Psychological Bulletin, 78,* 161–175.

Schuerger, J.M., Zarrella, K.L., & Hotz, A.S. (1989). Factors that influence the temporal stability of personality by questionnaire. *Journal of Personality and Social Psychology, 56,* 777–783.

Schultheiss, O.C., & Brunstein, J.C. (1999). Goal imagery: Bridging the gap between implicit motives and explicit goals. *Journal of Personality, 67,* 1–37.

Schultheiss, O.C., & Brunstein, J.C. (2001). Assessment of implicit motives with a research version of the TAT: Picture profiles, gender differences, and relations to other personality measures. *Journal of Personality Assessment, 77,* 71–86.

Schultheiss, O.C., Dargel, A., & Rohde, W. (2002). Implicit motives and sexual motivation and behavior. *Journal of Research in Personality, 37,* 224–230.

Schultz, W.T. (1996). An "Orpheus Complex" in two writers-of-loss. *Biography: An Interdisciplinary Quarterly, 19,* 371–393.

Schultz, W.T. (Ed.). (2005). *The handbook of psychobiography.* New York: Oxford University Press.

Schutte, N.S., Kenrick, D.T., & Sadalla, E.K. (1985). The search for predictable settings: Situational prototypes, constraint, and behavioral variation. *Journal of Personality and Social Psychology, 49,* 121–128.

Schwartz, G.E. (1990). Psychobiology of repression and health: A systems approach. In J.L. Singer (Ed.), *Repression and dissociation: Implications for personality theory, psychopathology, and health* (pp. 405–434). Chicago: University of Chicago Press.

Schwartz, G.E., Fair, P.L., Greenberg, P.S., Freedman, M., & Klerman, J.L. (1974). Facial electromyography in the assessment of emotion. *Psychophysiology, 11,* 237.

Scott-Stokes, H. (1974). *The life and death of Yukio Mishima.* New York: Farrar, Straus & Giroux.

Seligman, M.E.P. (1975). *Helplessness: On depression, development, and death.* San Francisco: W.H. Freeman.

Seligman, M.E.P., & Maier, S.F. (1967). Failure to escape traumatic shock. *Journal of Experimental Psychology, 74,* 1–9.

Seligman, M.E.P., Nolen-Hoeksema, S., Thornton, N., & Thornton, K.M. (1990). Explanatory styles as a mechanism of disappointing athletic performance. *Psychological Science, 1,* 143–146.

Seligman, M.E.P., & Schulman, P. (1986). Explanatory style as a predictor of productivity and quitting among life insurance sales agents. *Journal of Personality and Social Psychology, 50,* 832–838.

Selman, R.L. (1980). *The growth of interpersonal understanding.* New York: Academic Press.

Frese and J. Sabini (Eds.), *Goal directed behavior: The concept of action in psychology* (pp. 503–549). Hillsdale, NJ: Lawrence Erlbaum.

Seybold, K.M., & Hill, P.C. (2001). The role of religion and spirituality in mental and physical health. *Current Directions in Psychological Science, 10,* 21–24.

Shaver, P.R., & Brennan, K.A. (1992). Attachment styles and the "Big Five" personality traits: Their connections with each other and with romantic relationship outcomes. *Personality and Social Psychology Bulletin, 18,* 536–545.

Shaver, P., & Rubenstein, C. (1980). Childhood attachment experience and adult loneliness. In L. Wheeler (Ed.), *Review of personality and social psychology* (Vol. 1, pp. 42–73). Beverly Hills, CA: Sage.

Shaw, C. (1930). *The jackroller: A delinquent boy's own story.* Chicago: Univrsity of Chicago Press.

Sheehy, G. (1976). *Passages: Predictable crises of adult life.* New York: E.P. Dutton.

Sheldon, K.M. (2004). *Optimal human being: An integrated multi-level perspective.* Mahwah, NJ: Lawrence Erlbaum.

Sheldon, K.M., & Elliot, A.J. (1999). Goal striving, need satisfaction, and longitudinal well-being: The self-concordance model. *Journal of Personality and Social Psychology, 76,* 482–497.

Sheldon, K.M., Elliot, A.J., Kim, Y., & Kasser, T. (2001). What is satisfying about satisfying events? Testing 10 candidate psychological needs. *Journal of Personality and Social Psychology, 80,* 325–339.

Sheldon, K.M., & Kasser, T. (1995). Coherence and congruence: Two aspects of personality integration. *Journal of Personality and Social Psychology, 68,* 531–543.

Sheldon, K.M., & Kasser, T. (1998). Pursuing personal goals: Skills enable progress, but not all progress is beneficial. *Personality and Social Psychology Bulletin, 24,* 1319–1331.

Sheldon, W.H. (1940). *The varieties of human physique: An introduction to constitutional psychology.* New York: Harper.

Sherkat, D.E., & Ellison, C.G. (1999). Recent developments and current controversies in the sociology of religion. *Annual Review of Sociology, 25,* 363–394.

Shneidman, E.S. (Ed.). (1981). *Endeavors in psychology: Selections from the personology of Henry A. Murray.* New York: Harper & Row.

Shoda, Y. (1999). Behavioral expressions of a personality system: Generation and perception of behavioral signatures. In D. Cervone and Y. Shoda (Eds.), *Personality coherence: Social-cognitive bases of consistency, variability, and organization* (pp. 155–181). New York: Guilford Press.

Shoda, Y., Mischel, W., & Wright, J.C. (1994). Intraindividual stability in the organization and patterning of behavior: Incorporating psychological situations into the idiographical analysis of personality. *Journal of Personality and Social Psychology, 65,* 674-687.

Shotter, J. (1970). Men, and man-makers: George Kelly and the psychology of personal constructs. In D. Bannister (Ed.), *Perspectives in personal construct theory.* New York: Academic Press.

Shotter, J., & Gergen, K.J. (1989). Preface and Introduction. In J. Shotter and K.J. Gergen (Eds.), *Texts of identity* (pp. ix–xi). London: Sage.

Shweder, R.A. (1975). How relevant is an individual difference theory of personality? *Journal of Personality, 43,* 455–484.

Shweder, R.A., & Sullivan, M.A. (1993). Cultural psychology: Who needs it? *Annual Review of Psychology, 44,* 497–523.

Shweder, R.A., & Much, N.C. (1987). Determinants of meaning: Discourse and moral socialization. In W.M. Kurtines and J.L. Gerwirtz (Eds.), *Moral development through social interaction* (pp. 197–244). New York: Wiley.

Sill, J. (1980). Disengagement reconsidered: Awareness of finitude. *Gerontologist, 20,* 457–462.

Simonton, D.K. (1976). Biographical determinants of achieved eminence: A multivariate approach to the Cox data. *Journal of Personality and Social Psychology, 33,* 218–226.

Simonton, D.K. (1989). The swansong phenomenon: Last-works effects for 172 classical composers. *Psychology and Aging, 4,* 42–47.

Simonton, D.K. (1994). *Greatness: Who makes history and why.* New York: Guilford Press.

Simpson, J.A. (1990). Influence of attachment styles on romantic relationships. *Journal of Personality and Social Psychology, 59,* 971–980.

Simpson, J.A., & Gangestad, S.W. (1991). Individual differences in sociosexuality: Evidence for convergent and discriminant validity. *Journal of Personality and Social Psychology, 60,* 870–883.

Simpson, J.A., & Gangestad, S.W. (1992). Sociosexuality and romantic partner choice. *Journal of Personality, 60,* 31–51.

Simpson, J.A., Gangestad, S.W., & Biek, M. (1993). Personality and nonverbal social behavior: An ethological perspective on relationship initiation. *Journal of Experimental Social Psychology, 29,* 434–461.

Simpson, J.A., Rholes, W.S., & Neligan, J.S. (1992). Support seeking and support giving within couples in an anxiety-provoking situation: The role of attachment styles. *Journal of Personality and Social Psychology, 62,* 434–446.

Simpson, J.A., Rholes, W.S., & Phillips, D. (1996). Conflict in close relationships: An attachment perspective. *Journal of Personality and Social Psychology, 71,* 899–914.

Singer, J.A. (1995). Seeing one's self: Locating narrative memory in a framework of personality. *Journal of Personality, 63,* 429–457.

Singer, J.A. (1997). *Message in a bottle: Stories of men and addiction.* New York: The Free Press.

Singer, J.A. (2004). Narrative identity and meaning-making across the adult lifespan: An introduction. *Journal of Personality, 72,* 437–459.

Singer, J.A., & Salovey, P. (1993). *The remembered self: Emotion and memory in personality.* New York: The Free Press.

Singer, J.L. (1984). *The human personality.* San Diego, CA: Harcourt Brace Jovanovich.

Singh, I.L. (1989). Personality correlates and perceptual detectability of loco-

motive drivers. *Personality and Individual Differences, 10,* 1049–1054.

Skinner, B.F. (1938). *Behavior of organisms.* New York: Appleton-Century-Crofts.

Skinner, B.F. (1948/1962). *Walden two.* New York: Macmillan.

Skinner, B.F. (1971). *Beyond freedom and dignity.* New York: Alfred A. Knopf.

Skinner, B.F. (1979). *The shaping of a behaviorist.* New York: Alfred A. Knopf.

Slade, A. (1987). Quality of attachment and early symbolic play. *Developmental Psychology, 23,* 78–85.

Slavin, M.O. (1972). *The theme of feminine evil: The image of women in male fantasy and its effects on attitudes and behavior.* Unpublished doctoral dissertation. Harvard University.

Smith, C.P. (Ed.). (1992). *Motivation and personality: Handbook of thematic content analysis.* New York: Cambridge University Press.

Smith, R.J. (1985). The concept and measurement of social psychopathy. *Journal of Research in Personality, 19,* 219–231.

Snarey, J. (1993). *How fathers care for the next generation: A four-decade study.* Cambridge, MA: Harvard University Press.

Sneed, C.D., McCrae, R.R., & Funder, D.C. (1997). Lay conceptions of the Five-factor model and its indicators. *Personality and Social Psychology Bulletin, 24,* 115–126.

Sobotka, S.S., Davidson, R.J., & Senulis, J.A. (1992). Anterior brain electrical asymmetries in response to reward and punishment. *Electroencephalography and Clinical Neurophysiology, 83,* 236–247.

Spangler, W.D. (1992). Validity of questionnaire and TAT measures of need for achievement: Two meta-analyses. *Psychological Bulletin, 112,* 140–154.

Spence, D.P. (1982). *Narrative truth and historical truth: Meaning and*

interpretation in psychoanalysis. New York: Norton.

Spence, J.T. (1985). Gender identity and its implications for concepts of masculinity and femininity. In T.B. Sonderegger (Ed.), *Nebraska symposium on motivation.* Lincoln, NE: University of Nebraska Press.

Sprecher, S., Sullivan, Q., & Hatfield, E. (1994). Mate selection preferences: Gender differences examined in a national sample. *Journal of Personality and Social Psychology, 66,* 1074–1080.

Srivastava, S., John, O.P., Gosling, S.D., & Potter, J. (2003). Development of personality in early and middle adulthood: Set like plaster or persistent change? *Developmental Psychology, 84,* 1041–1053.

Sroufe, L.A. (1983). Infant–caregiver attachment and patterns of adaptation in the preschool: The roots of maladaption and competence. In M. Perlmutter (Ed.), *Minnesota symposium on child psychology* (Vol. 16, pp. 41–83). Minneapolis, MN: University of Minnesota Press.

Sroufe, L.A. (1985). Attachment classification from the perspective of infant–caregiver relationships and infant temperament. *Child Development, 56,* 1–14.

Sroufe, L.A., & Waters, E. (1977). Attachment as an organizational construct. *Child Development, 48,* 1184–1199.

Steele, R.S. (1982). *Freud and Jung: Conflicts of interpretation.* London: Routledge & Kegan Paul.

Steinberg, L., Darling, N.E., & Fletcher, A.C. (1995). Authoritative parenting and adolescent adjustment: An ecological journey. In P. Moen, G.H. Elder, Jr., & K. Luscher (Eds.), *Examining lives in context: Perspectives on the ecology of human development* (pp. 423–466). Washington, D.C.: American Psychological Association Press.

Stelmach, R.M. (1990). Biological bases of extraversion: Psychophysiological evidence. *Journal of Personality, 58,* 293–311.

Stelmack, R.M., & Stalikas, A. (1991). Galen and the humour theory of temperament. *Personality and Individual Differences, 16,* 543–560.

Stern, D.N. (1985). *The interpersonal world of the infant: A view from psychoanalysis and developmental psychology.* New York: Basic Books.

Sternberg, R.J., & Grigorenko, E.L. (1997). Are cognitive styles still in style? *American Psychologist, 52,* 700–712.

Stevens, A. (1983). *Archetypes.* New York: Quill.

Stewart, A.J. (1994). Toward a feminist strategy for studying women's lives. In C. Franz and A.J. Stewart (Eds.), *Women creating lives: Identities, resilience, resistance* (pp. 11–35). Boulder, CO: Westview Press.

Stewart, A.J., & Chester, N.L. (1982). Sex differences in human social motives. In A.J. Stewart (Ed.), *Motivation and society* (pp. 172–218). San Francisco, CA: Jossey-Bass.

Stewart, A.J., & Healy, M.J., Jr. (1989). Linking individual development and social changes. *American Psychologist, 44,* 30–42.

Stewart, A.J., & Ostrove, J.M. (1998). Women's personality in middle age: Gender, history, and mid-course corrections. *American Psychologist, 53,* 1185–1194.

Stewart, A.J., & Rubin, Z. (1976). Power motivation in the dating couple. *Journal of Personality and Social Psychology, 34,* 305–309.

Stewart, A.J., & Vandewater, E.A. (1993). Career and family clocks in a transitional cohort: The Radcliffe class of 1964. In K. Hulbert and D. Schuster (Eds.), *Women's lives through time: Educated American women of the twentieth century* (pp. 235–258). San Francisco: Jossey-Bass.

Stewart, A.J., & Vandewater, E.A. (1998). The course of generativity. In D.P. McAdams and E. de St. Aubin (Eds.), *Generativity and adulthood: How and why we care for the next generation* (pp. 75–100). Washington, DC: APA Press.

Stier, D.S., & Hall, J.A. (1984). Gender differences in touch: An empirical and theoretical review. *Journal of Personality and Social Psychology, 47,* 440–459.

Stokes, J.P. (1985). The relation of social network and individual difference variables to loneliness. *Journal of Personality and Social Psychology, 48,* 981–990.

Stokes, J.P., & McKirnan, D.J. (1989). Affect and the social environment: The role of social support in depression and anxiety. In P.C. Kendall and D. Watson (Eds.), *Anxiety and depression: Distinctions and overlapping features* . New York: Academic Press.

Suedfeld, P. (1985). APA Presidential addresses: The relation of integrative complexity to historical, professional, and personal factors. *Journal of Personality and Social Psychology, 49,* 1643–1651.

Suedfeld, P., & Piedrahita, L.E. (1984). Intimations of mortality: Integrative simplification as a precursor of death. *Journal of Personality and Social Psychology, 47,* 848–852.

Suedfeld, P., Tetlock, P.E., & Streufert, S. (1992). Conceptual/integrative complexity. In C.P. Smith (Ed.), *Motivation and personality: Handbook of thematic content analysis* (pp. 376–382). New York: Cambridge University Press.

Sullivan, H.S. (1953). *The interpersonal theory of psychiatry.* New York: W.W. Norton.

Sulloway, F.J. (1979). *Freud: Biologist of the mind.* New York: Basic Books.

Sulloway, F.J. (1996). *Born to rebel: Birth order, family dynamics, and creative lives.* New York: Pantheon.

Surtees, P.G., & Wainwright, N.W.J. (1996). Fragile states of mind: Neuroticism, vulnerability and the long-term outcome of depression. *British Journal of Psychiatry, 169,* 338–347.

Sutton, S.K., & Davidson, R.J. (1997). Prefrontal brain asymmetry: A biological substrate of the behavioral approach and behavioral inhibition systems. *Psychological Science, 8,* 204–210.

T

Tappan, M. (1990). Hermeneutics and moral development: Implementing narrative representation of moral experience. *Developmental Review, 10,* 239–265.

Tappan, M., & Brown, L. (1989). Stories told and lessons learned: Toward a narrative approach to moral development and moral education. *Harvard Educational Review, 59,* 182–205.

Taylor, C. (1989). *Sources of the self: The making of the modern identity.* Cambridge, MA: Harvard University Press.

Taylor, J. (1953). A personality scale of manifest anxiety. *Journal of Abnormal and Social Psychology, 48,* 285–290.

Tekiner, A.C. (1980). Need achievement and international differences in income growth: 1950–1960. *Economic Development and Cultural Change,* 293–320.

Tellegen, A. (1982). *Brief manual for the Differential Personality Questionnaire.* Unpublished manuscript, University of Minnesota.

Tellegen, A. (1985). Structures of mood and personality and their relevance to assessing anxiety, with an emphasis on self-report. In A.H. Tuma and J.D. Masser (Eds.), *Anxiety and the anxiety disorders* (pp. 681–716). Hillsdale, NJ: Lawrence Erlbaum.

Tellegen, A., & Atkinson, G. (1974). Openness to absorbing and self-altering experiences ("absorption"), a trait related to hypnotic susceptibility. *Journal of Abnormal Psychology, 83,* 268–277.

Tellegen, A., Lykken, D.J., Bouchard, T.J., Jr., Wilcox, K.J., Segal, N.L., & Rich, S. (1988). Personality similarity in twins reared apart and together. *Journal of Personality and Social Psychology, 54,* 1031–1039.

Tesch, S.A., & Whitbourne, S.K. (1982). Intimacy and identity status in young adults. *Journal of Personality and Social Psychology, 43,* 1041–1051.

Tetlock, P.E. (1981a). Pre- to post-election shifts in presidential rhetoric: Impression management or cognitive adjustment? *Journal of Personality and Social Psychology, 41,* 207–212.

Tetlock, P.E. (1981b). Personality and isolationism: Content analysis of senatorial speeches. *Journal of Personality and Social Psychology, 41,* 737–743.

Tetlock, P.E. (1984). Cognitive style and political belief systems in the British House of Commons. *Journal of Personality and Social Psychology, 46,* 365–375.

Tetlock, P.E., Armor, D., & Peterson, R.S. (1994). The slavery debate in antebellum America: Cognitive style, value conflict, and the limits of compromise. *Journal of Personality and Social Psychology, 66,* 115–126.

Tetlock, P.E., Bernzweig, J., & Gallant, J.L. (1985). Supreme Court decision making: Cognitive style as a predictor of ideological consistency of voting. *Journal of Personality and Social Psychology, 48,* 1227–1239.

Tetlock, P.E., Hannum, K., & Micheletti, P. (1984). Stability and change in the complexity of senatorial rhetoric: Testing the cognitive versus rhetorical style hypotheses. *Journal of Personality and Social Psychology, 46,* 979–990.

Tetlock, P.E., Peterson, R.S., & Berry, J.M. (1993). Flattering and unflattering personality portraits of integratively simple and complex managers. *Journal of Personality and Social Psychology, 64,* 500–511.

Thayer, R.E. (1989). *The biopsychology of mood and arousal.* Oxford: Oxford University Press.

Thomas, A., Chess, S., & Birch, H.G. (1970). The origin of personality. *Scientific American, 223,* 102–109.

Thompson, C. (1942). Cultural pressures in the psychology of women. *Psychiatry, 5,* 311–339.

Thorne, A. (2000). Personal memory telling and personality development. *Personality and Social Psychology Review, 4,* 45–56.

Thorne, A., Cutting, L., & Skaw, D. (1998). Young adults' relationship memories and the life story: Examples or essential landmarks? *Narrative Inquiry, 8,* 1–32.

Thorne, A., & McLean, K.C. (2003). Telling traumatic events in adolescence: A study of master narrative positioning. In R. Fivush and C. Haden (Eds.), *Autobiographical memory and the construction of a narrative self* (pp. 169–185). Mahwah, NJ: Lawrence Erlbaum.

Thorndike, R.L. (1959). Review of the California Psychological Inventory. In O.K. Buros (Ed.), *Fifth mental measurements yearbook.* Highland Park, NJ: Gryphon Press.

Tidwell, M-C.O., Reis, H.T., & Shaver, P.R. (1996). Attachment, attractiveness, and social interaction: A dairy study. *Journal of Personality and Social Psychology, 71,* 729–745.

Tobin, R.M., Graziano, W.G., Vanman, E.J., & Tassinary, L.G. (2000). Personality, emotional experience, and efforts to control emotions. *Journal of Personality and Social Psychology, 79,* 656–669.

Toder, N., & Marcia, J.E. (1973). Ego identity status and response to conformity pressure in college

women. *Journal of Personality and Social Psychology, 26,* 287–294.

Tolman, E.C. (1948). Cognitive maps in rats and men. *Psychological Review, 55,* 189–208.

Tomkins, S.S. (1947). *The Thematic Apperception Test.* New York: Grune & Stratton.

Tomkins, S.S. (1962). *Affect, imagery, consciousness* (Vol. 1). New York: Springer.

Tomkins, S.S. (1963). *Affect, imagery, consciousness* (Vol. 2). New York: Springer.

Tomkins, S.S. (1979). Script theory. In H.E. Howe, Jr., and R.A. Dienstbier (Eds.), *Nebraska symposium on motivation* (Vol. 26, pp. 201–236). Lincoln, NE: University of Nebraska Press.

Tomkins, S.S. (1981). The quest for primary motives: Biography and autobiography of an idea. *Journal of Personality and Social Psychology, 41,* 306–329.

Tomkins, S.S. (1987). Script theory. In J. Aronoff, A.I. Rabin, and R.A. Zucker (Eds.), *The emergence of personality* (pp. 147–216). New York: Springer.

Tomkins, S.S., & Izard, C.E. (1965). *Affects, cognition, and personality.* New York: Springer.

Tomkins, S.S., & Miner, J.R. (1957). *The Tomkins—Horn picture arrangement test.* New York: Springer.

Tooby, J., & Cosmides, L. (1992). The psychological foundations of culture. In J.H. Barkow, L. Cosmides, and J. Tooby (Eds.), *The adapted mind: Evolutionary psychology and the generation of culture* (pp. 19–136). New York: Oxford University Press.

Trapnell, P.D. (1994). Openness versus intellect: A lexical left turn. *European Journal of Personality, 8,* 273–290.

Trapnell, P.D., & Wiggins, J.S. (1990). Extension of the Interpersonal Adjective Scales to include the Big

Five dimensions of personality. *Journal of Personality and Social Psychology, 59,* 781–790.

Triandis, H.C. (1997). Cross-cultural perspectives on personality. In R. Hogan, J. Johnson, and S. Briggs (Eds.), *Handbook of personality psychology* (pp. 439–464). San Diego, CA: Academic Press.

Triandis, H.C., & Gelfand, M.J. (1998). Converging measurement of horizontal and vertical individualism and collectivism. *Journal of Personality and Social Psychology, 74,* 118–128.

Triandis, H.C., & Suh, E.M. (2002). Cultural influences on personality. *Annual Review of Psychology, 53,* 133–160.

Trivers, R.L. (1971). The evolution of reciprocal altruism. *Quarterly Review of Biology, 46,* 35–57.

Tupes, E.C., & Christal, R. (1958). *Stability of personality trait rating factors obtained under diverse conditions* (USAF ASD Technical Note, No. 58–61). Lackland Air Force Base, TX: U.S. Air Force.

Tupes, E.C., & Christal, R. (1961). *Recurrent personality factors based on trait ratings* (Tech. Rep. No. ASD-TR-61-97). Lackland Air Force Base, TX: U.S. Air Force.

Twenge, J.M. (2000). The age of anxiety? Birth cohort changes in anxiety and neuroticism, 1952–1993. *Journal of Personality and Social Psychology, 79,* 1007–1021.

U

Uleman, J.S. (1966). *A new TAT measure of the need for power.* Unpublished doctoral dissertation, Harvard University.

Urry, H.L., Nitschke, J.B., Dolski, I., Jackson, D.C., Dalton, K.M., Mueller, C.J., Rosenkranz, M.A., Ryff, C.D., Singer, B.H., & Davidson, R.J. (2004). Making a life worth living: Neural correlates of well-being. *Psychological Science, 15,* 367–372.

V

Vaillant, G.E. (1971). Theoretical hierachy of adaptive ego mechanisms. *Archives of General Psychiatry, 24,* 107–118.

Vaillant, G.E. (1977). *Adaptation to life.* Boston: Little, Brown.

Vaillant, G.E., & Drake, R.E. (1985). Maturity of ego defense in relation to DSM III Axis II personality disorder. *Archives of General Psychiatry, 42,* 597–601.

Vaillant, G.E., & Milofsky, E. (1980). The natural history of male psychological health: IX. Empirical evidence for Erikson's model of the life cycle. *American Journal of Psychiatry, 137,* 1349–1359.

Vallacher, R.R., & Wegner, D.M. (1987). What do people think they're doing? Action identificaiton and human behavior. *Psychological Review, 94,* 3–15.

Van de Water, D., & McAdams, D.P. (1989). Generativity and Erikson's "belief in the species." *Journal of Research in Personality, 23,* 435–449.

vanIJzendoorn, M.H., & Bakermans-Kranenburg, M.J. (1996). Attachment representations in mothers, fathers, adolescents, and clinical groups: A meta-analytic search for normative data. *Journal of Consulting and Clinical Psychology, 64,* 8–21.

Veroff, J. (1957). Development and validation of a projective measure of power motivation. *Journal of Abnormal and Social Psychology, 54,* 1–8.

Veroff, J. (1982). Assertive motivation: Achievement versus power. In A.J. Stewart (Ed.), *Motivation and society* (pp. 99–132). San Francisco: Jossey-Bass.

Veroff, J., Douvan, E., & Kulka, R. (1981). *The inner American.* New York: Basic Books.

Veroff, J., & Feld, S.C. (1970). *Marriage and work in America.* New York: Van Nostrand Reinhold.

Vitz, P.C. (1990). The use of stories in moral development: New psychological reasons for an old education method. *American Psychologist, 45,* 709–720.

von Franz, M. (1980). *The psychological meaning of redemption motifs in fairy tales.* Toronto: Inner City Books.

Vrij, A., van der Steen, J., & Koppelaar, L. (1995). The effects of street noise and field independence on police officers' shooting behavior. *Journal of Applied Social Psychology, 25,* 1714–1725.

W

Walkover, B.C. (1992). The family as an overwrought object of desire. In G.C. Rosenwald and R.L. Ochberg (Eds.), *Storied lives: The cultural politics of self-understanding* (pp. 178–191). New Haven, CT: Yale University Press.

Waller, N.G., & Shaver, P.R. (1994). The importance of nongenetic influences on romantic love styles: A twin-family study. *Psychological Science, 5,* 268–274.

Wallston, K.A., & Wallston, B.S. (1981). Health locus of control scales. In H.M. Lefcourt (Ed.), *Research with the locus of control construct: Assessment methods* (Vol. 1, pp. 189–243). New York: Academic Press.

Waterman, A.S. (1982). Identity development from adolescence to adulthood: An extension of theory and a review of research. *Developmental Psychology, 18,* 341–358.

Watson, D., & Clark, L.A. (1984). Negative affectivity: The disposition to experience aversive emotional states. *Psychological Bulletin, 96,* 465–490.

Watson, D., & Clark, L.A. (1992). Affects separable and inseparable: On the hierarchical arrangement of the negative affects. *Journal of Personality and Social Psychology, 62,* 489–505.

Watson, D., & Clark, L.A. (1997). Extraversion and its positive emotional core. In R. Hogan, J. Johnson, and S. Briggs (Eds.), *Handbook of personality psychology* (pp. 767–793). San Diego, CA: Academic Press.

Watson, D., Clark, L.A., McIntyre, C.W., & Hamaker, S. (1992). Affect, personality, and social activity. *Journal of Personality and Social Psychology, 63,* 1011–1025.

Watson, D., & Tellegen, A. (1985). Toward a consensual structure of mood. *Psychological Bulletin, 98,* 219–235.

Watson, D., & Walker, L.M. (1996). The long-term stability and predictive validity of trait measures of affect. *Journal of Personality and Social Psychology, 70,* 567–577.

Watson, J.B. (1913). Psychology as the behaviorist views it. *Psychological Review, 20,* 158–177.

Watson, J.B. (1924). *Behaviorism.* Chicago: University of Chicago Press.

Watson, J.B., & Raynor, R. (1920). Conditional emotional reactions. *Journal of Experimental Psychology, 3,* 1–14.

Watson, P.J., Grisham, S.O., Trotter, M.V., & Biderman, M.D. (1984). Narcissism and empathy: Validity evidence for the Narcissistic Personality Inventory. *Journal of Personality Assessment, 48,* 301–305.

Wegner, D.M., Schneider, D.J., Carter, S.R., & White, T.L. (1987). Paradoxical effects of thought suppression. *Journal of Personality and Social Psychology, 53,* 5–13.

Weinberger, D.A. (1990). The construct validity of the repressive coping style. In J.L. Singer (Ed.), *Repression and dissociation: Implications for personality theory, psychopathology, and health* (pp.

337–386). Chicago: University of Chicago Press.

Weinberger, D.A., Schwartz, G.E., & Davidson, R.J. (1979). Low-anxious, high-anxious, and repressive coping styles: Psychometric patterns and behavioral and physiological responses to stress. *Journal of Abnormal Psychology, 88,* 369–380.

Weiner, B. (1979). A theory of motivation for some classroom experiences. *Journal of Educational Psychology, 71,* 3–25.

Weiner, B. (1990). Attribution in personality psychology. In L. Pervin (Ed.), *Handbook of personality theory and research* (pp. 465–485). New York: Guilford Press.

Weller, H.G., Repman, J., Lan, W., & Rooze, G. (1995). Improving the effectiveness of learning through hypermedia-based instruction: The importance of learner characteristics. *Computers in Human Behavior, 11,* 451–465.

Werner, H. (1957). The concept of development from a comparative and an organismic point of view. In D. Harris (Ed.), *The concept of development.* Minneapolis, MN: University of Minnesota Press.

West, K.Y., Widiger, T.A., & Costa, P.T., Jr. (1993). *The placement of cognitive and perceptual aberrations within the five-factor model of personality.* Unpublished manuscript. University of Kentucky, Lexington, KY.

West, S.G. (1983). Personality and prediction: An introduction. *Journal of Personality, 51,* 275–285.

Westen, D. (1995). A clinical-empirical model of personality: Life after the Mischelian ice age and the NEO-lithic era. *Journal of Personality, 63,* 495–524.

Westen, D. (1998). Unconscious thought, feeling, and motivation: The end of a century-long debate.

In R.F. Bornstein and J.F. Masling (Eds.), *Empirical perspectives on the psychoanalytic unconscious* (pp. 1–43). Washington, DC: APA Press.

Westenberg, P.M., Blasi, A., & Cohn, L.D. (Eds.). (1998). *Personality development: Theoretical, empirical, and clinical investigations of Loevinger's conception of ego development.* Mahwood, NJ: Erlbaum.

Whitbourne, S.K. (1985). The psychological construction of the life span. In J.E. Birren and K.W. Schaie (Eds.), *Handbook of the psychology of aging* (2nd ed., pp. 594–618). New York: Van Nostrand Reinhold.

Whitbourne, S.K. (1986). Openness to experience, identity flexibility, and life changes in adults. *Journal of Personality and Social Psychology, 50,* 163–168.

Whitbourne, S.K., Zuschlag, M.K., Elliot, L.B., & Waterman, A.S. (1992). Psychological development in adulthood: A 22-year sequential study. *Journal of Personality and Social Psychology, 63,* 260–271.

White, J.L., & Parham, T.A. (1990). *The psychology of blacks: An African-American perspective.* Englewood Cliffs, NJ: Prentice-Hall.

White, M., & Epston, D. (1990). *Narrative means to therapeutic ends.* New York: Norton.

White, R.W. (1948). *The abnormal personality.* New York: Ronald Press.

White, R.W. (1952). *Lives in progress* (1st ed.). New York: Holt, Rinehart & Winston.

White, R.W. (1959). Motivation reconsidered: The concept of competence. *Psychological Review, 66,* 297–333.

White, R.W. (1963a). Sense of interpersonal competence: Two case studies and some reflections on origins. In R.W. White (Ed.), *The study of lives* (pp. 72–93). New York: Prentice-Hall.

White, R.W. (Ed.). (1963b). *The study of lives: Essays on personality in honor of Henry A. Murray.* New York: Prentice-Hall.

White, R.W. (1966). *Lives in progress* (2nd ed.). New York: Holt, Rinehart & Winston.

White, R.W. (1972). *The enterprise of living: A view of personal growth.* New York: Holt, Rinehart & Winston.

White, R.W. (1975). *Lives in progress* (3rd ed.). New York: Holt, Rinehart & Winston.

White, R.W. (1981). Exploring personality the long way: The study of lives. In A.I. Rabin, J. Aronoff, A.M. Barclay, and R.A. Zucker (Eds.), *Further explorations in personality* (pp. 3–19). New York: John Wiley & Sons.

White, R.W. (1987). *Seeking the shape of personality: A memoir.* Marlborough, NH: The Homstead Press.

Whiting, B.B., & Whiting, J.W.M. (1975). *Children of six cultures.* Cambridge, MA: Harvard University Press.

Wicklund, R.A., & Duvall, J. (1971). Opinion change and performance facilitation as a result of objective self-awareness. *Journal of Experimental Social Psychology, 7,* 319–342.

Wiebe, D.J., & Smith, T.W. (1997). Personality and health: Progress and problems in psychosomatics. In R. Hogan, J.A. Johnson, and S. Briggs (Eds.), *Handbook of personality psychology* (pp. 891–918). San Diego, CA: Academic Press.

Wiedenfeld, S.A., O'Leary, A., Bandura, A., Brown, S., Levine, S., & Raska, K. (1990). Impact of perceived self-efficacy in coping with stressors on components of the immune system. *Journal of Personality and Social Psychology, 59,* 1082–1094.

Wiggins, J.S. (1973). *Personality and prediction: Principles of personality assessment.* Reading, MA: Addison-Wesley.

Wiggins, J.S. (1992). Have model, will travel. *Journal of Personality, 60,* 527–532.

Wiggins, J.S. (Ed.). (1996). *The five-factor model of personality: Theoretical perspectives.* New York: Guilford Press.

Wiggins, J.S. (2003). *Paradigms of personality assessment.* New York: Guilford.

Wiggins, J.S., & Trapnell, P.D. (1997). Personality structure: The return of the Big Five. In R. Hogan, J. Johnson, and S. Briggs (Eds.), *Handbook of personality psychology* (pp. 737–766). San Diego, CA: Academic Press.

Wilson, E.O. (1978). *On human nature.* Cambridge, MA: Harvard University Press.

Wilson, G.D. (1978). Introversion-extroversion. In H. London and J.E. Exner, Jr. (Eds.), *Dimensions of personality* (pp. 217–261). New York: John Wiley & Sons.

Wilson, G.D., & Nias, D.K.B. (1975). Sexual types. *New Behavior, 2,* 330–332.

Wink P. (1991). Two faces of narcissism. *Journal of Personality and Social Psychology, 61,* 590–597.

Wink, P. (1992a). Three types of narcissism in women from college to midlife. *Journal of Personality, 60,* 7–30.

Wink. P. (1992b). Three narcissism scales for the California Q-set. *Journal of Personality Assessment, 58,* 51–66.

Wink, P. (1996). Transition from the early 40s to the early 50s in self-directed women. *Journal of Personality, 64,* 49–69.

Wink, P., & Helson, R. (1993). Personality change in women and their partners. *Journal of Personality and Social Psychology, 65,* 597–605.

Winnicott, D.W. (1965). *The naturational processes and the facilitating environment.* New York: International Universities Press.

Winter, D.G. (1973). *The power motive.* New York: The Free Press.

Winter, D.G. (1987). Leader appeal, leader performance, and the motive profiles of leaders and followers: A study of American Presidents and elections. *Journal of Personality and Social Psychology, 52,* 196–202.

Winter, D.G. (1996). *Personality: Analysis and interpretation of lives.* New York: McGraw-Hill.

Winter, D.G., & Barenbaum, N.B. (1999). History of modern personality theory and research. In L.A. Pervin and O. John (Eds.), *Handbook of personality: Theory and research* (2nd Ed., pp. 3–27). New York: Guilford Press.

Winter, D.G., & Carlson, L.A. (1988). Using motive scores in the psychobiographical study of an individual: The case of Richard Nixon. *Journal of Personality, 56,* 75–103.

Winter, D.G., John, O.P., Stewart, A.J., Klohnen, E.C., & Duncan, L.E. (1998). Traits and motives: Toward an integration of two traditions in personality research. *Psychological Review, 105,* 230–250.

Winter, D.G., McClelland, D.C., & Stewart, A.J. (1981). *A new case for the liberal arts: Assessing institutional goals and student development.* San Francisco, CA: Jossey-Bass.

Winter, D.G., & Stewart, A.J. (1977). Power motive reliability as a function of retest instructions. *Journal of Consulting and Clinical Psychology, 45,* 436–440.

Winter, D.G., & Stewart, A.J. (1978). The power motive. In H. London and J.E. Exner (Eds.), *Dimensions of personality* (pp. 391–447). New York: John Wiley & Sons.

Witkin, H.A. (1950). Individual differences in ease of perception of embedded figures. *Journal of Personality, 19,* 1–15.

Witkin, H.A., & Berry, J. (1975). Psychological differentiation in cross-cultural perspective. *Journal of Cross-Cultural Psychology, 6,* 4–87.

Witkin, H.A., Goodenough, D.R., & Oltmann, P.K. (1979). Psychological differentiation: Current status. *Journal of Personality and Social Psychology, 37,* 1127–1145.

Woike, B.A. (1995). Most-memorable experiences: Evidence for a link between implicit and explicit motives and social cognitive processes in everyday life. *Journal of Personality and Social Psychology, 68,* 1081–1091.

Woike, B.A., Gershkovich, I., Piorkowski, R., & Polo, M. (1999). The role of motives in the content and structure of autobiographical memory. *Journal of Personality and Social Psychology, 76,* 600–612.

Wolf, E.S. (1982). Comments on Heinz Kohut's conceptualization of a bipolar self. In B. Lee (Ed.), *Psychosocial theories of the self* (pp. 23–42). New York: Plenum.

Wolfenstein, M., & Trull, T.J. (1997). Depression and openness to experience. *Journal of Personality Assessment, 69,* 614–632.

Wright, J.C., & Mishel, W. (1987). A conditional approach to dispositional constructs: The local predictability of social behavior. *Journal of Personality, 53,* 1159–1177.

Wright, R. (1994). *The moral animal.* New York: Pantheon.

Wynne-Edwards, V.C. (1963/1978). Intergroup selection in the evolution of social systems. In T.H. Clutton-Brock and P.H. Harvey (Eds.), *Readings in sociobiology* (pp. 10–19). San Francisco, CA: Freeman.

Y

Yik, M.S.M., & Bond, M.H. (1993). Exploring the dimensions of Chinese person perception with indigenous and imported constructs: Creating a culturally balanced scale. *International Journal of Psychology, 28,* 75–95.

Yin, R.K. (1984). *Case study research: Design and methods.* Beverly Hills, CA: Sage.

York, K.L., & John, O.P. (1992). The four faces of Eve: A typological analysis of women's personality at midlife. *Journal of Personality and Social Psychology, 63,* 494–508.

Z

Zeldow, P.B., & Bennett, E. (1997). Stability of a Q-sort model of optimal mental health. *Journal of Personality Assessment, 69,* 314–323.

Zeldow, P.B., & Daughterty, S.R. (1991). Personality profile and specialty choices of students from two medical school classes. *Academic Medicine, 66,* 283–287.

Zeldow, P.B., Daugherty, S.R., & McAdams, D.P. (1988). Intimacy, power, and psychological well-being in medical students. *The Journal of Nervous and Mental Disease, 176,* 182–187.

Zimbardo, P.G., & Leippe, M.R. (1991). *The psychology of attitude change and social influence.* New York: McGraw-Hill.

Zuckerman, M. (1978). Sensation seeking. In H. London and J.E. Exner (Eds.), *Dimensions of personality* (pp. 487–560). New York: John Wiley & Sons.

Zuckerman, M. (1979). *Sensation seeking: Beyond the optimal level of arousal.* Hillsdale, NJ: Lawrence Erlbaum.

Zuckerman, M. (1991). *Psychobiology of personality.* Cambridge, England: Cambridge University Press.

Zuckerman, M. (1995). Good and bad humours: Biochemical bases of personality and its disorders. *Psychological Science, 6,* 325–332.

Zuckerman, M. (1998). Psychobiological theories of personality. In D.F. Barone, M. Hersen, and V.B. Van Hasselt (Eds.), *Advanced personality* (pp. 123–154). New York: Plenum.

Zuckerman, M., & Kuhlman, D.M. (2000). Personality and risk-taking: Common biosocial factors. *Journal of Personality, 68,* 999–1029.

Zukav, G. (1979). *The dancing Wu Li masters: An overview of the new physics.* New York: William Morrow & Company.

Zurbriggen, E.L. (2000). Social motives and cognitive power-sex associations: Predictors of aggressive sexual behavior. *Journal of Personality and Social Psychology, 78,* 559–581.

Zurbriggen, E.L., & Sturman, T.S. (2002). Linking motives and emotions: A test of McClelland's hypotheses. *Personality and Social Psychology Bulletin, 28,* 521–535.

Zuroff, D.C. (1986). Was Gordon Allport a trait theorist? *Journal of Personality and Social Psychology, 51,* 993–1000.

Credits

PHOTOS

1: B. Schonborn / Photo Researchers, Inc. 14: © Rhoda Sidney / The Image Works. 16: Gjon Mili / Life Magazine © Time Inc. 28: Archives of the History of American Psychology, University of Akron. 39: Kenneth Murray/ Photo Researchers, Inc. 41 (top): © Charles & Josette Lenars / Corbis. 41 (bottom): © Annie Griffiths Belt / Corbis. 52: Courtesy of Robert Hogan. 54: Corbis Digital Stock. 56: © Ilyas Dean / The Image Works . 58: University of Virginiga Psychology Department. 59: B. Schonborn / Photo Researchers, Inc. 72: Courtesy of B. F. Skinner. 80: Photo by Chuck Painter, News Service, Stanford University. 84: © Photo Researchers, Inc. 90: PhotoDisc Inc. 95: (left) PhotoDisc, Inc. 95: (right) PictureQuest. 106: © Digital Vision Ltd. / SuperStock. 111: Courtesy of Rebecca R. Pallmeyer. 119: Courtesy of Historical Collections & Services, Claude Moore Health Sciences Library, University of Virginia. 122: Times Newspapers Ltd., London. 125: Courtesy of Hans J. Eysenck. 127: Courtesy of Professor Goldberg. 136: Courtesy of Harrison Gough. 137: (left) Courtesy of Paul Costa. 137: (right) Courtesy of Robert McCrae. 140: Courtesy of Walter Mischel. 142: Courtesy of Seymour Epstein. 166: Corbis Digital Stock. 175: © SuperStock, Inc. / SuperStock. 180: (far left) Dirck Halstead / Time & Life Pictures. 180: (mid-left) Evan Agostini / Getty Images Entertainment. 180: (mid-right) Pool / Getty Images News. 180: (far right) Alex Wong / Getty Images News. 204 (left): © PhotoEdit. 204 (middle): © PhotoEdit. 204 (right): © Phil Borden / PhotoEdit. 213 (left): © Laura Dwight / Corbis. 213 (right): © SuperStock, Inc. 220: Courtesy, Rebecca R. Pallmeyer. 235: Courtesy, Ravenna Helson. 237: Courtesy of Jack Block. 247: © Digital Vision Ltd. / SuperStock. 251: Courtesy of Wadsworth Athenaeum, Hartford. 253: © Hulton-Deutsch Collection / Corbis. 266: Courtesy of Carl Rogers. 268: AP / Wide World Photos. 273: Courtesy of Ed Deci. 273: Courtesy of Richard Ryan. 279: Courtesy of David McClelland. 283: Courtesy of Wesleyan University. 301: Courtesy of Brandeis University, Waltham, MA. 309: Dan Hardy / Anthro-Photo File. 318: Bob Kalmbach / Courtesy of University of Michigan. 318: Pat C. Helgseson / University of Arizona. 324: © Digital Vision Ltd. / SuperStock. 328: © Comstock Images / Getty Images. 343: Dirk v. Mallinckrodt / Alamy. 559: UPI / Bettmann / Corbis. 353: Carolyn A. McKeone / Photo Researchers, Inc. 358: Courtesy of Ruthellen Josselson. 359: Carolyn A. McKeone / Photo Researchers, Inc. 366: (top left) Getty Images. 366: (top right) David McNew / Getty Images News. 366: (bottom left) Getty Images. 366: (bottom right) Getty Images. 371: Courtesy of Washington University, St. Louis, MO. 373: George Zimbel / Monkmeyer Press. 375: Comstock Images / Getty Images. 385: "Woman in a Yellow Dress" Max Kurweil © Ali Meryer / Corbis. 391: Nat Farbman, Life Magazine, 1947, Time, Inc. 392: Courtesy of Jerome Bruner. 627: AP / Wide World Photos. 395: Courtesy of James Pennebaker. 398: Courtesty of Dan P. McAdams. 401 (left): © SuperStock. 401 (middle): © SuperStock. 401 (right): Courtesy of Paul Ekman. 404: Getty Images News. 429: Hulton Archive / Getty Images. 431: Courtesy of the Guthrie Theatre. 433: Elliot Erwit / Magnum Photos. 452: Hulton Archive / Getty Images. 455: (left) © SuperStock, Inc. 455: (right) "Woman in a Yellow Dress" Max Kurweil © Ali Meryer / Corbis. 456: The Metropolitan Museum of Art. 459: Brown Brothers. 466: Courtesy of Vincent Hevern. 474: Courtesy of Abigail Stewart. 483: "Lament for Icarus" by Herbert Draper, The Tate Gallery, London / Art Resource, NY. 485: Courtesy of Harvard University News Office. 487: © Superstock. 500 (left): © Bettmann / Corbis. 500 (right): Getty Images Entertainment. 501: Giraudon / Art Resource, NY. 502 (left): National Portrait Gallery, London. 502 (right):

National Portrait Gallery, London. **503:** Alinari / Art Resource, NewYork. **514:** Alinari / Art Resource, New York. **515:** UPI / Bettmann (BBC); Museo del Prado.

FIGURES

Figure 2.1, p. 64. "Peer Competence and Attachment History," based on P. J. LaFreniere & L. A. Sroufe, © 1985, Profiles of peer competence in the preschool: Interrelations between measures, influence of social ecology, and relation to attachment history, *Developmental Psychology, 21,* pp. 56-69, p. 63.

Figure 3.2, p. 81. "Four Steps of Observational Learning," based on A. Bandura, © 1977, *Social Learning Theory,* p. 23. Reprinted by permission of Prentice Hall, Englewood Cliffs, New Jersey.

Figure 3.A.1, p. 87. "A Two-Dimensional Classification of Parenting Patterns," based on E. F. Maccoby & J. A. Martin, © 1983, Socialization in the context of the family: Parent-child interaction, in P. H. Mussen (Ed.), *Handbook of Child Psychology,* 4th ed., Vol. 4, *Socialization, personality, and social development,* pp. 1-102, p. 39. Reprinted by permission of John Wiley & Sons, Inc., New York.

Figure 4.1, p. 126. "The Four Ancient Personality Types," based on H. J. Eysenck, © 1973, *Eysenck on extraversion,* New York: John Wiley & Sons, Inc., p. 18.

Figure 4.2, p. 137. "Two Nonverbal Trait Items," based on S. V. Paunonen, D. N. Jackson, & M. Keinonen, The structured nonverbal assessment of personality, *Journal of Personality, 55,* p. 485. © 1990 by Duke University Press. Reprinted by permission.

Figure 4.3, p. 143. "Reliability and Aggregation," based on APA, S. Epstein, © 1979, The stability of behavior: 1. On predicting most of the people much of the time, *JPSP, 37,* pp. 1087-1126.

Figure 4.4, p. 146. "Personality, Compensation, and Helping Behavior," based on D. Romer, C. L. Gruden, & T. Lizzardo, © 1986, A person-situation approach to altruistic behavior, *JPSP, 51,* pp. 1001-1012, p. 1006.

Figure 5.1, p. 160. "Betting Behavior and Introversion/Extraversion," based on APA, D. Pearce-McCall & J. P. Newman © 1987, Expectation of success following noncontingent punishment in introverts and extraverts, *JPSP, 50,* pp. 439-446, p. 442.

Figure 5.3, p. 171. "Intimacy and Neuroticism," based on APA, A. L. Chaiken, V. J. Derlega, B. Bayman, & J. Shaw, © 1975, Neuroticism and disclosure reciprocity, *Journal of Consulting and Clinical Psychology, 43,* pp. 13-19, p. 16.

Figure 5.4, p. 192. "Mean Scores on the Big Five Traits as a Function of Adult Attachment Style," reprinted by permission of Sage Publications from P. R. Shaver & K. A. Brennan in Attachment styles and the Big Five personality traits: Their connections with each other and with romantic relationship outcomes, *Personality and Social Psychology Bulletin, 18.* © 1992, p. 536-545.

Figure 6.2, p. 228. "Components of Variance in Personality Traits," based on pie chart from page 50 of *Separate Lives: Why Siblings Are So Different* by J. Dunn and R. Plomin. Copyright 1990 by Basic Books, Inc. Reprinted by permission of Basic Books, a division of HarperCollins Publishers, Inc.

Figure 8.1, p. 308. "An Embedded Square," based on D. R. Goodenough, "Field dependence," © 1978. In H. London and J. E. Exner, Jr., (Eds.), *Dimensions of Personality* (pp. 165-216. Reprinted by permission of John Wiley & Sons, Inc.

Figure 8.2, p. 312. "Integrative Complexity and Political Affiliation," based on P. E. Tetlock, "Cognitive style and political belief systems in the British House of Commons." *JPSP, 46,* © 1984, pp. 365-375, p. 370.

Figure 8.3, p. 321. "Portion of a Hypothetical Self-Schema," based on H. Markus and J. Smith, "The influence of self-schema on the perceptions of others." © 1981. In N. Cantor and J. F. Kihlstrom (Eds.), *Personality, Cognition, and Social Interaction* (pp. 233-262). Reprinted with permission from Erlbaum, p. 244.

Figure 8.4, p. 327. "Self-Guides and Negative Emotion," based on E. T. Higgins, "Self-discrepancy: A theory relating self and affect." *Psychological Review, 94,* © 1987, pp. 319-340.

Figure 8.5, p. 334. "A Simple Self-Regulation System," based on Charles S. Carver & Michael F. Scheir, *Perspectives on Personality.* Copyright © 1988 by Allyn and Bacon. Boston, MA. Reprinted by permission, p. 476.

Figure 8.6, p. 335. "Self-Focus and the Link Between Behavior and Values," based on Charles S. Carver & Michael F. Scheir, *Perspectives on Personality.* Copyright © 1988 by Allyn and Bacon. Boston, MA. Reprinted by permission, p. 480.

Figure 8.7, p. 336. "A Three-Tiered Hierarchy of Feedback Systems," based on Charles S. Carver & Michael F. Scheir, *Perspectives on Personality.* Copyright © 1988 by Allyn and Bacon. Boston, MA. Reprinted by permission, p. 482.

TEXT AND TABLES

Table 1.1, p. 6. "A Trait Questionnaire," from G. Wilson, Introversion/extraversion. In H. London & J. E. Exner, *Dimensions of Personality,* (pp. 217-261). 1978, p. 219.

Table 2.1, p. 47. "What Upsets Men and Women in Romantic Relationships?," from American Psychological Association, D. Buss, Conflict between the sexes: Strategic interference and the evocation of anger and upset, *JPSP, 56.* © 1989, pp. 735-747.

Chapter 2, p. 52. Lines from The Iliad by Homer, translated by Robert Fagles, copyright © 1990 by Robert Fagles. Introduction and Notes copyright © 1990 by Bernard Knox. Used by permission of Viking Penguin, a division of Penguin Putnam Inc.

Table 2.2, p. 57. "The Origins of Human Morality and Altruism," from C. Hazan & P. Shaver (1987) Romantic love conceptualized as an attachment process. *JPSP, 59,* p. 515. Used by permission of Cindy Hazan.

Table 3.4, p. 100. Key Differences Between Independent and Interdependent Construals of Self, from H. Markus & S. Kitayama (1991). Culture and the self: Implications for cognition, emotion, and motivation. *Psychological Review, 98,* p. 230. Used by permission of Hazel Markus.

Table 4.3, p. 124. "The Fifteen Source Traits of Personality Assessed by the 16PF," from G. Matthews & I. J. Deary, (1998) *Personality traits.* New York: Cambridge University Press, p. 22. Reprinted with the permission of Cambridge University Press.

Table 4.5, p. 135. "Scales on the California Psychological Inventory," modified and reproduced by special permission of the Publisher, Consulting Psychologists Press, Inc., Palo Also, CA 94303 from *California Psychological Inventory* by Harrison G. Gough, Ph.D. Copyright 1987 Consulting Psychologists Press, Inc., pp. 6-7. All rights reserved. Further reproduction is prohibited without the Publisher's written consent.

Table 7.7, p. 284. "Average Number of Facts and Proposals and Mean Moral Concern Ratings of Discussion Groups," from APA, for E. M. Fodor & T. Smith, The power motive as an influence on group decision making, *JPSP, 42.* © 1982, pp. 178-185, p. 183.

Table 8.5, p. 314. "Verbatim Passages From the Correspondence of Eminent Novelists Scored for Integrative Complexity," from APA, for C. A. Porter & P. Suedfeld, Integrative complexity in the correspondence of literary figures: Effects of personal and societal stress, *JPSP, 40.* © 1981, pp. 321-330, pp. 325-326.

Table 8.6, p. 329. "Self-Reference Scores for Recalled Words," from APA, for R. E. Ingram, T. W. Smith, & S. S. Brehm, Depression and information processing: Self schemata and the encoding of self-relevant information, *JPSP, 45.* © 1983, pp. 412-420, p. 417.

Chapter 11, p. 430. Lines from *Oedipus Rex* by Sophocles. Bantam Books in R. O'Brien & B. F. Dukore, *Tragedy: Ten Major Plays (Sophocles' Oedipus Rex).* © 1969, p. 21.

Name Index

Two indexes are provided for your use. The Subject Index presents all topics presented in this book. The Author index lists all authors cited in the text.

Subject Index

Two indexes are provided for your use. The Subject Index presents all topics presented in this book. The Author index lists all authors cited in the text.

An *f* after a page number indicates a figure. A *t* after a page number indicates a table.